Lecture Notes in Computer Sc

Commenced Publication in 1973
Founding and Former Series Editors:
Gerhard Goos, Juris Hartmanis, and Jan van Leeuwen

Andrea Fusiello   Vittorio Murino
Rita Cucchiara (Eds.)

Computer Vision – ECCV 2012

Workshops and Demonstrations

Florence, Italy, October 7-13, 2012
Proceedings, Part III

 Springer

Andrea Fusiello
Università degli Studi di Udine
Dipartimento di Ingegneria Elettrica,
Gestionale e Meccanica (DIEGM)
Via delle Scienze, 208, 33100 Udine, Italy
E-mail: andrea.fusiello@uniud.it

Vittorio Murino
IIT Istituto Italiano di Tecnologia
Via Morego 30, 16163 Genoa, Italy
E-mail: vittorio.murino@iit.it

Rita Cucchiara
Università degli Studi di Modena e Reggio Emilia
Strada Vignolege, 905, 41125 Modena, Italy
E-mail: rita.cucchiara@unimore.it

ISSN 0302-9743   e-ISSN 1611-3349
ISBN 978-3-642-33884-7   e-ISBN 978-3-642-33885-4
DOI 10.1007/978-3-642-33885-4
Springer Heidelberg Dordrecht London New York

Library of Congress Control Number: 2012948004

CR Subject Classification (1998): I.4, I.5, I.2.10, I.2, H.5, H.3

LNCS Sublibrary: SL 6 – Image Processing, Computer Vision, Pattern Recognition, and Graphics

Typesetting: Camera-ready by author, data conversion by Scientific Publishing Services, Chennai, India

Printed on acid-free paper

Springer is part of Springer Science+Business Media (www.springer.com)

Foreword

The European Conference on Computer Vision is one of the top conferences for researchers in this field and is held biennially in alternation with the International Conference on Computer Vision. It was first held in 1990 in Antibes (France) with subsequent conferences in Santa Margherita Ligure (Italy) in 1992, Stockholm (Sweden) in 1994, Cambridge (UK) in 1996, Freiburg (Germany) in 1998, Dublin (Ireland) in 2000, Copenhagen (Denmark) in 2002, Prague (Czech Republic) in 2004, Graz (Austria) in 2006, Marseille (France) in 2008, and Heraklion (Greece) in 2010. To our great delight, the 12th conference was held in Florence, Italy.

ECCV has an established tradition of very high scientific quality and an overall duration of one week. ECCV 2012 began with a keynote lecture from the honorary chair, Tomaso Poggio. The main conference followed over four days with 40 orals, 368 posters, 22 demos, and 12 industrial exhibits. There were also 9 tutorials and 21 workshops held before and after the main event. For this event we introduced some novelties. These included innovations in the review policy, the publication of a conference booklet with all paper abstracts and the full video recording of oral presentations.

This conference is the result of a great deal of hard work by many people, who have been working enthusiastically since our first meetings in 2008. We are particularly grateful to the Program Chairs, who handled the review of about 1500 submissions and co-ordinated the efforts of over 50 area chairs and about 1000 reviewers (see details of the process in their preface to the proceedings). We are also indebted to all the other chairs who, with the support of our research teams (names listed below), diligently helped us manage all aspects of the main conference, tutorials, workshops, exhibits, demos, proceedings, and web presence. Finally we thank our generous sponsors and Consulta Umbria for handling the registration of delegates and all financial aspects associated with the conference.

We hope you enjoyed ECCV 2012. Benvenuti a Firenze!

October 2012

Roberto Cipolla
Carlo Colombo
Alberto Del Bimbo

Preface

Welcome to the Workshops and Demonstrations proceedings of the 12th European Conference on Computer Vision, held during October 7–13, 2012 in Florence, Italy. We are delighted that the main ECCV 2012 was accompanied by 21 workshops and 22 demonstrations.

We received 38 workshop proposals on diverse computer vision topics. The evaluation process was not easy because of the high quality of the submissions, and the final 21 selected workshops complemented the main conference program. They were mostly one-day workshops, with a few limited to half day, and one workshop lasting one day and a half. In the end, the addressed workshop topics constituted a good mix between novel current trends and traditional issues, without forgetting to address the fundamentals of the computational vision area.

On Sunday, October 7, three workshops took place: the 5th Workshop on Non-Rigid Shape Analysis and Deformable Image Alignment (NORDIA), the First Workshop on Visual Analysis and Geo-Localization of Large-Scale Imagery, and the Workshop on Web-scale Vision and Social Media.

The majority of the workshops were held on Friday 12 and Saturday 13. On October 12 we had nine workshops: WebVision, the Workshop on Computer Vision for the Web, with only invited speakers, the traditional PASCAL Visual Object Classes Challenge 2012 (VOC2012) Workshop, the 4th International Workshop on Video Event Categorization, Tagging and Retrieval (VECTaR 2012), the First International Workshop on Re-Identification (Re-Id 2012), the Workshop on Biological and Computer Vision Interfaces, also with only invited speakers, VISART, "Where Computer Vision Meets Art" Workshop, the Second Workshop on Consumer Depth Cameras for Computer Vision (CDC4CV), the Workshop on Unsolved Problems in Optical Flow and Stereo Estimation, and the "What's in a Face?" Workshop.

On October 13, ten workshops were held: The remaining half day of the WebVision Workshop, the 4th Color and Photometry in Computer Vision Workshop, the Third Workshop on Computer Vision in Vehicle Technology: From Earth to Mars, the Second Workshop on Parts and Attributes, the Third IEEE International Workshop on Analysis and Retrieval of Tracked Events and Motion in Imagery Streams (ARTEMIS 2012), the First Workshop on Action Recognition and Pose Estimation in Still Images, the Workshop on Higher-Order Models and Global Constraints in Computer Vision, the Workshop on Information Fusion in Computer Vision for Concept Recognition, the QU3ST Workshop "2.5D Sensing Technologies in Motion: The Quest for 3D", and the Second International Workshop on Benchmarking Facial Image Analysis Technologies (BeFIT 2012).

We hope that participants enjoyed the workshops, together with the associated 179 papers included in these volumes.

Following the tradition of the major conferences in the field, ECCV 2012 was also proud to host live demonstrations given by companies and academic research groups. These were presented during the days of the main conference and are described in detail in the papers of the last volume.

Presenting a demo is one of the most concrete and exciting ways of demonstrating results of research and providing strong interaction between researchers, practitioners, and scholars in many topics, both theoretical and practical, of computer vision.

Among the proposed demos, submitted with a four-page summary together with slides, videos and rich supplementary material, after peer-review, we selected 22 demos on different subjects spanning topics such as biometry, content-based retrieval, classification and categorization, vision for computer graphics, 3D vision for interfaces, tracking and pose estimation, gesture analysis for human–computer interaction, text recognition, augmented reality, surveillance, and assisted driving.

Demos were presented by authors coming from different nations of Europe (Czech Republic, France, Germany, Italy, The Netherlands, Spain, Switzerland, and UK) and of the rest of the world (Australia, China, Japan, Taiwan, and USA).

The best demo was selected based on the scientific value and the technical presentation as well as the success in researcher interaction during the Demo Sessions.

We believe the scientific prototypes and the technical demonstrations presented at ECCV 2012 will contribute to strengthen the great success of computer vision technologies in industrial, entertainment, social, and everyday applications.

Finally, we would like to thank the individual chairs of each workshop (listed in the respective workshop programs) for soliciting and reviewing submissions, and the demo proposers, who made it possible to build such a rich supplementary program beside the main ECCV 2012 scientific plan.

October 2012

Andrea Fusiello
Vittorio Murino
Rita Cucchiara

Organization

General Chairs

Roberto Cipolla   University of Cambridge, UK
Carlo Colombo   University of Florence, Italy
Alberto Del Bimbo   University of Florence, Italy

Program Coordinator

Pietro Perona   California Institute of Technology, USA

Program Chairs

Andrew Fitzgibbon   Microsoft Research, Cambridge, UK
Svetlana Lazebnik   University of Illinois at Urbana-Champaign, USA
Yoichi Sato   The University of Tokyo, Japan
Cordelia Schmid   INRIA, Grenoble, France

Honorary Chair

Tomaso Poggio   Massachusetts Institute of Technology, USA

Tutorial Chairs

Emanuele Trucco   University of Dundee, UK
Alessandro Verri   University of Genoa, Italy

Workshop Chairs

Andrea Fusiello   University of Udine, Italy
Vittorio Murino   Istituto Italiano di Tecnologia, Genoa, Italy

Demonstration Chair

Rita Cucchiara   University of Modena and Reggio Emilia, Italy

Industrial Liaison Chair

Björn Stenger   Toshiba Research Europe, Cambridge, UK

Web Chair

Marco Bertini   University of Florence, Italy

Publicity Chairs

Terrance E. Boult   University of Colorado at Colorado Springs, USA
Tat Jen Cham   Nanyang Technological University, Singapore
Marcello Pelillo   University Ca' Foscari of Venice, Italy

Publication Chair

Massimo Tistarelli   University of Sassari, Italy

Video Processing Chairs

Sebastiano Battiato   University of Catania, Italy
Giovanni M. Farinella   University of Catania, Italy

Travel Grants Chair

Luigi Di Stefano   University of Bologna, Italy

Travel Visa Chair

Stefano Berretti   University of Florence, Italy

Local Committee Chair

Andrew Bagdanov   MICC, Florence, Italy

Local Committee

Lamberto Ballan   Giuseppe Lisanti
Laura Benassi   Iacopo Masi
Marco Fanfani   Fabio Pazzaglia
Andrea Ferracani   Federico Pernici
Claudio Guida   Lorenzo Seidenari
Lea Landucci   Giuseppe Serra

Workshops Organizers

5th Workshop on Non-Rigid Shape Analysis and Deformable Image Alignment (NORDIA)

Stefano Berretti	University of Florence, Italy
Alexander Bronstein	Tel Aviv University, Israel
Michael Bronstein	University of Lugano, Switzerland
Umberto Castellani	University of Verona, Italy

First Workshop on Visual Analysis and Geo-Localization of Large-Scale Imagery

Mubarak Shah	University of Central Florida, USA
Luc Van Gool	ETH Zurich, Switzerland
Asaad Hakeem	ObjectVideo, USA
Alexei Efros	Carnegie Mellon University, USA
Niels Haering	ObjectVideo, USA
James Hays	Brown University, USA
Hui Cheng	SRI International Sarnoff, USA

Workshop on Web-Scale Vision and Social Media

Lamberto Ballan	University of Florence, Italy
Alex C. Berg	Stony Brook University, USA
Marco Bertini	University of Florence, Italy
Cees G.M. Snoek	University of Amsterdam, The Netherlands

WebVision: The Workshop on Computer Vision for the Web

Manik Varma	Microsoft Research India
Samy Bengio	Google, USA

The PASCAL Visual Object Classes Challenge 2012 (VOC2012) Workshop

Chris Williams	University of Edinburgh, UK
John Winn	MSR Cambridge, UK
Luc Van Gool	ETH Zurich, Switzerland
Andrew Zisserman	University of Oxford, UK
Alex Berg	Stony Brook University, USA
Fei-Fei Li	University of Stanford, USA

4th International Workshop on Video Event Categorization, Tagging and Retrieval (VECTaR 2012)

Tieniu Tan	Chinese Academy of Sciences, China
Thomas S. Huang	University of Illinois at Urbana-Champaign, USA
Ling Shao	University of Sheffield, UK
Jianguo Zhang	University of Dundee, UK
Liang Wang	Chinese Academy of Sciences, China

First International Workshop on Re-Identification (Re-Id 2012)

Marco Cristani	University of Verona, Italy
Shaogang Gong	Queen Mary University London, UK
Yan Shuicheng	NUS, Singapore

Workshop on Biological and Computer Vision Interfaces

Olivier Faugeras	INRIA, France
Pierre Kornprobst	INRIA, France

VISART: "Where Computer Vision Meets Art" Workshop

João Paulo Costeira	IST Lisbon, Portugal
Gustavo Carneiro	University of Adelaide, Australia
Nuno Pinho da Silva	IST Lisbon, Portugal
Alessio Del Bue	Istituto Italiano di Tecnologia, Italy

Second Workshop on Consumer Depth Cameras for Computer Vision (CDC4CV)

Andrea Fossati	ETH Zurich, Switzerland
Jürgen Gall	Max-Planck-Institut für Informatik, Germany
Helmut Grabner	ETH Zurich, Switzerland
Xiaofeng Ren	Intel Labs, USA
Kurt Konolige	Industrial Perception, USA
Seungkyu Lee	Samsung, South Korea
Miles Hansard	Queen Mary University London, UK

Workshop on Unsolved Problems in Optical Flow and Stereo Estimation

Daniel Kondermann	University of Heidelberg, Germany
Bernd Jähne	University of Heidelberg, Germany
Daniel Scharstein	Middlebury College, USA

"What's in a Face?" Workshop

Arun Ross	West Virginia University, USA
Alice O'Toole	University of Texas, USA
Maja Pantic	Imperial College London, UK
Antitza Dantcheva	West Virginia University, USA
Stefanos Zafeiriou	Imperial College London, UK

4th Color and Photometry in Computer Vision Workshop

Theo Gevers	University of Amsterdam, The Netherlands
Raimondo Schettini	University of Milano Bicocca, Italy
Joost van de Weijer	Universitat Autònoma de Barcelona, Spain
Todd Zickler	Harvard University, USA
Javier Vazquez-Corral	Universitat Autònoma de Barcelona, Spain

Third Workshop on Computer Vision in Vehicle Technology: From Earth to Mars

Atsushi Imiya   IMIT, Japan
Antonio M. López   UAB/CVC, Spain

Second Workshop on Parts and Attributes

Christoph H. Lampert   IST, Austria
Rogerio S. Feris   IBM Research, USA

Third IEEE International Workshop on Analysis and Retrieval of Tracked Events and Motion in Imagery Streams (ARTEMIS 2012)

Anastasios Doulamis   TUC, Greece
Nikolaos D. Doulamis   NTUA, Greece
Jordi Gonzàlez   UAB/CVC, Spain
Thomas B. Moeslund   University of Aalborg, Denmark
Marco Bertini   University of Florence, Italy

First Workshop on Action Recognition and Pose Estimation in Still Images

Vittorio Ferrari   University of Edinburgh, UK
Ivan Laptev   INRIA/Ecole Normale Superieure, France
Josef Sivic   INRIA/Ecole Normale Superieure, France
Bangpeng Yao   Stanford University, USA

Workshop on Higher-Order Models and Global Constraints in Computer Vision

Karteek Alahari   INRIA-WILLOW/Ecole Normale Superieure, France
Dhruv Batra   TTI-Chicago, USA
Srikumar Ramalingam   MERL, USA
Nikos Paragios   Paristech, France
Rich Zemel   University of Toronto, Canada

Workshop on Information Fusion in Computer Vision for Concept Recognition

Jenny Benois-Pineau   LABRI, University of Bordeaux, France
Georges Quenot   LIG INPG, Grenoble, France
Tomas Piatrik   Queen Mary University London, UK
Bogdan Ionescu   LAPI, University Politehnica of Bucharest, Romania

QU3ST Workshop - 2.5D Sensing Technologies in Motion: The Quest for 3D

David Fofi   Université de Bourgogne, France
Adrien Bartoli   Université d'Auvergne, France

Second International Workshop on Benchmarking Facial Image Analysis Technologies (BeFIT 2012)

Hazim Kemal Ekenel   KIT, Germany/Istanbul Technical University, Turkey
Gang Hua   Stevens Institute of Technology/IBM Research, USA
Shiguang Shan   Chinese Academy of Sciences, China

Sponsoring Companies and Institutions

Gold Sponsors

Silver Sponsors

Bronze Sponsors

IBM Research

Institutional Sponsors

Table of Contents

Third Workshop on Computer Vision in Vehicle Technology: From Earth to Mars

Second Workshop on Parts and Attributes

Third IEEE International Workshop on Analysis and Retrieval of Tracked Events and Motion in Imagery Streams (ARTEMIS 2012)

2.5D Sensing Technologies in Motion: The Quest for 3D (QU3ST)

Second International Workshop on Benchmarking Facial Image Analysis Technologies (BeFIT 2012)

ECCV Demonstrations

Pixels, Stixels, and Objects

David Pfeiffer, Friedrich Erbs, and Uwe Franke

Daimler AG, Research & Development, Sindelfingen, Germany

Abstract. Dense stereo vision has evolved into a powerful foundation for
the next generation of intelligent vehicles. The high spatial and temporal
resolution allows for robust obstacle detection in complex inner city scenarios, including pedestrian recognition and detection of partially hidden
moving objects. Aiming at a vision architecture for efficiently solving an
increasing number of vision tasks, the medium-level representation named
Stixel World has been developed. This paper shows how this representation
forms the foundation for a very efficient, robust and comprehensive understanding of traffic scenes. A recently proposed Stixel computation scheme
allows the extraction of multiple objects per image column and generates
a segmentation of the input data. The motion of the Stixels is obtained by
applying the 6D-Vision principle to track Stixels over time. Subsequently,
this allows for an optimal Stixel grouping such that all dynamic objects
can be detected easily. Pose and motion of moving Stixel groups are used
to initialize more specific object trackers. Moreover, appearance-based object recognition highly benefits from the attention control offered by the
Stixel World, both in performance and efficiency.

Fig. 1. Dense disparity image and the corresponding Stixel World representing the
three-dimensional environment in front of the vehicle. The colors encode the distances,
with red = close, green = far away, and gray = freespace. The arrows show the motion
vector of the tracked objects. This medium-level representation achieves a reduction
of the input data from hundreds of thousands of single depth measurements to a few
hundred Stixels only.

1 Introduction

Driver assistance in complex urban environments is a challenging task requiring
comprehensive perception of static and moving objects. There is no doubt that
stereo vision will play a dominant role in in this context. However, there are two
main challenges:

A. Fusiello et al. (Eds.): ECCV 2012 Ws/Demos, Part III, LNCS 7585, pp. 1–10, 2012.

First, the growing number of necessary recognition tasks and their complexity ask for a proper vision architecture that replaces today's independent application-specific modules. This paper proposes such an architecture that bridges the gap between pixels, objects, and the complete representation of the dynamic scene.

Secondly, adverse weather and difficult lightning conditions ask for algorithms of extreme robustness. This can be achieved best if the information contained in the image sequence is optimally exploited. This means that research has to look for algorithms that maximize the probability to find the best solution. The algorithms presented in this paper are a step towards that goal.

Semi-global matching (SGM) [14] outperforms all known local disparity estimation schemes [26]. In [13], Gehrig showed how to run this powerful scheme on energy-efficient FPGA hardware allowing to compute dense high quality depth maps in real-time. On the downside, this high density leads to a large computational burden when the resulting data has to be processed and evaluated by a constantly increasing number of subsequent vision tasks.

In order to minimize the required bandwidth and the computational burden of subsequent vision tasks, we introduced the so called "Stixel World" [2,25], a versatile and extremely compact three-dimensional medium-level representation. As shown in Figure 1, the three-dimensional information is represented by a few hundreds of small rectangular sticks of certain width, height and velocity.

The paper is organized as follows: Section 2 summarizes related work, before the optimization scheme used to compute the (multi-layered) Stixel World is described in Section 3. Section 4 deals with the Stixel tracking for estimating the motion state of individual Stixels. In Section 5, the optimal segmentation of the Stixel World into stationary and moving objects is discussed, before we show in Section 6 that the Stixel World can act as a highly efficient attention control for object classification.

2   Related Work

The most popular method in robotics and driver assistance for representing 3D environments is to project depth information to occupancy grids [7,20] or digital elevation maps (DEM) [17,18]. These maps model the likelihood of the environment to be occupied. They are used to extract scene attributes such as freespace [1] and obstacle information [23], the location of curbs and sidewalks [22,27], and various other scene and application-relevant features.

However, in the light of the quality of today's stereo schemes, even a DEM only represents parts of the information contained in the disparity image. In order to represent 3D environments more accurately, we introduced the Stixel World that utilizes the fact that most man-made objects can be approximated by planar surfaces with approximately vertical orientation [2]. Position and height of Stixels limiting the free space are computed in a cascade of different algorithms (occupancy grid, freespace, height segmentation) using dynamic programming (DP) [4]. A related procedure has been recently adopted by [5].

By design, these schemes are limited to just extracting the first row of obstacles, this way forbidding the proper handling of partial occlusion, a quite central challenge in driver assistance. Besides that, given the vulnerability of such a cascade of independent processing steps, we have decided to rework the Stixel computation from scratch [25].

The key motivation for this was the work of Gallup et al. [12]. Their objective is to create 3D volumetric object models. Multiple depth maps from different LIDAR scans are accumulated in a single Cartesian histogram-based elevation map. Thereafter, each cell is split into alternating either *"empty"* or *"occupied"* box volumes. By relying on DP, the authors yield the optimal segmentation for every cell of the grid which we consider the major benefit of this procedure.

Felzenszwalb et al. have presented an inspiring scheme [10] as well. They use appearance cues to assign semantic information to image regions. Monocular images are segmented using a continuous upper and lower bound with ordering constraints. The resulting upper part is called *"background"*, the middle region is assigned to *"object"* (e.g. for infrastructure) and the bottom region to *"floor"*. Again, the authors rely on DP and thus guarantee to find the optimum segmentation. However, their approach is limited to a single object per column only.

Further, Liu et al. [19] use appearance cues to assign semantic information to images using a five parts model (top, left, right, bottom, and center, e.g. for segmenting rooms). Their model constraints are very strict and thus inflexible. They rely on a graph cut [6,16] based approach that approximates a 2D optimum.

In [15], Hoiem et al. presented a scheme to assign the labels of type planar (*"ground"*), vertical (*"object"*), and sky to super-pixels. For this purpose, the authors rely on a greedy algorithm while exploiting pairwise patch affinities. They use an appearance-based boosted decision-tree classifier on a trained data set to infer the probabilities for the class affiliation.

3   The Stixel World

Our man-made environments are dominated by either horizontal or vertical planar surfaces. While horizontal surfaces typically correspond to the ground, the vertical ones relate to objects, such as solid infrastructure, pedestrians, or cars.

This perception model is the basic idea of the Stixel World. In the sense of a super-pixel, each Stixel approximates a certain part of an upright oriented object together with its distance and height. In [25], we have presented a probabilistic approach to compute the Stixel World for a stereo image pair in a single global optimization scheme. The problem of Stixel extraction is derived as a classical maximum a-posteriori estimation problem, this way ensuring to obtain the best segmentation result for the current stereo disparity input. An example result for our method is shown in Figure 1.

Given the left camera image I of a stereo image pair and the corresponding disparity image D (all of size $w \times h \in \mathbb{N}^2$), a multi-layered Stixel World corresponds to a column-wise segmentation $L \in \mathbb{L}$ of I into the classes $C = \{o, g\}$ (*"object"* and *"ground/road"*) of the following form

$$L = \{L_u\}, \text{ with } 0 \leq u < w$$
$$L_u = \{s_n\}, \text{ with } 1 \leq n \leq N_u \leq h$$
$$s_n = \{v_n^b, v_n^t, c_n, f_n(v)\}, \text{ with } 0 \leq v_n^b \leq v_n^t < h, c_n \in C \qquad (1)$$

The total number of segments s_n for each column u is given by N_u, the image row coordinates v_n^b (base point) and v_n^t (top point) mark the beginning and end of each segment. The term $f_n(v)$ is an arbitrary function providing the depth of that segment at row position v (with $v_n^b \leq v \leq v_n^t$). All segments s_{n-1} and s_n are adjacent. This implicitly guarantees that every image point is assigned to exactly one label.

Modeling all segments as piecewise planar surfaces reduces the function set f_n to a set of linear functions. Object segments are assumed to have a constant disparity while ground segments follow the disparity gradient of the ground surface. The idea of relying on such basic functions is illustrated in Figure 2.

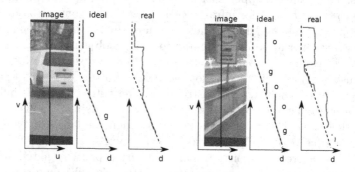

Fig. 2. Data model visualization. The blue line across the image marks the column for segmentation. Red and green denote the ideal segmentation into object and ground. The dashed line is the expected ground profile. The actual disparity measurement vector for the particular scenario is marked using purple.

The computation of the Stixel World is addressed as a MAP estimation problem. Consequently, we seek for the most probable labeling L^*, such that

$$L^* = \arg\max_{L \in \mathbb{L}} P(L \mid D). \qquad (2)$$

Applying Bayes' theorem allows to rewrite the posterior probability $P(L \mid D)$ as $P(L \mid D) \sim P(D \mid L) \cdot P(L)$. This way, we obtain the product of the conditional probability density of D given L and the prior probability density $P(L)$.

Here, $P(D \mid L)$ rates the probability of the input D given a certain labeling L and thus represents the data term for the optimization. The second term $P(L)$ embodies the overall probability for each individual labeling L and is the lever to incorporate our world model. In related work, this term is also referred to as the smoothness term. Hence, it allows to support the segmentation with a certain set of physically motivated world assumptions. For example, this includes the following:

- Bayesian information criterion: The number of objects captured along every column is small. Dispensable cuts should be avoided.
- Gravity constraint: Flying objects are unlikely. The ground-adjacent object segment usually stands on the ground surface.
- Ordering constraint: The upper of two adjacent object segments has a greater depth. Reconstructing otherwise (e.g. for traffic lights, signs or trees) is still possible if sufficiently supported by the input data.

To manage the complexity of this segmentation task, neighboring column labelings L_u are considered individually. Further, we treat all disparity measurements $d_{u,v} \in D$ as mutually independent which allows to generalize the disparity input to the vertical disparity vector $D_u \in D$. Additionally, the data input within D_u is stated as independent from all column labels $L_{\hat{u}}$ with $u \neq \hat{u}$. As a result we obtain

$$P(L \mid D) \sim \prod_{u=0}^{w-1} \underbrace{P(D_u \mid L_u)}_{\text{data term}} \cdot \underbrace{P(L_u)}_{\text{prior}}. \qquad (3)$$

Finally, dynamic programming [4] is used to infer L^* in real-time. Further details about this Stixel extraction scheme are described in [25].

4 Stixel Tracking

To estimate the motion state of Stixels, the so called "6D-Vision" scheme presented by Franke et al. [11] is used.

In the original form, pixels are tracked over time and image positions as well as disparities are measured at each time step. Assuming a constant motion of the tracked features and a known motion of the observer, a Kalman filter uses these measurements to simultaneously estimate 3D-position and 3D-motion for each tracked feature[1]. Figure 3 shows the obtained result if this algorithm is applied to a turning bicyclist. The arrows point to the expected positions 0.5 sec ahead.

Now, the same principle is applied to precisely estimate the motion state of Stixels [24]. Then, based on this motion information, it is straightforward to determine potential collisions with the ego vehicle (cf. [21]).

Given that in our applications objects of interest are expected to move earthbound, the estimated state vector can be reduced to 4D which is the position and velocity, i.e. $\underline{X} = (\underline{x}^T, \underline{v}^T)^T$. The dynamic Stixel results for the bicyclist scenario are illustrated in Figure 3 on the right side. As a byproduct of this simplification, the estimation puts fewer requirements on the ego-motion estimation. In practice, the vehicle's inertial sensors are sufficient to compensate for its own motion state. Interestingly, the motion vectors are highly parallel, although the estimation is done independently. This shows the low noise the 6D-Vision scheme achieves thanks to the temporal integration.

---

[1] For more information and illustrative material visit: www.6D-Vision.com

Fig. 3. A bicyclist taking a left turn in front of our vehicle. The left side shows the result when using 6D-Vision point features. The right side shows the corresponding Stixel result.

5 Stixel Motion Segmentation

Many applications in driver assistance require to know the class type and motion state of other objects. Therefore, in terms of establishing a well structured architecture for modern vision system, gaining this comprehension is an important part of the subsequent processing steps.

So far, Stixels are a compact representation of the local three-dimensional environment, but they do not provide any explicit knowledge about which Stixels belong together and which do not.

With this objective, we have presented an approach that moves towards the grouping of tracked Stixels into the motion classes *"right headed"*, *"left headed"*, *"with us"* and *"oncoming"* as well as *"static background"* [9]. This idea is illustrated in Figure 4 showing the motion segmentation result for the scenario depicted in Figure 1 as well as another exemplary scenario.

Fig. 4. The motion segmentation result obtained using graph cut based optimization. The coloring encodes the individual motion class. Static background is uncolored. The left side shows the result for the scenario depicted in Figure 1, the right shows another traffic situation.

Again, in the style of the described Stixel computation, this task is understood as a MAP estimation problem. Given the dynamic Stixel World, the goal is to find the particular labeling of Stixels into the previously mentioned motion classes that conforms best with our prior knowledge about the current local 3D environment.

Besides assuming rigid motion and striving for spatial smoothness of the segmentation, we use statistics obtained from annotated training data to express where in the scene which type of motion is likely to appear. For this purpose, we model this problem using a conditional Markov random field [6,16] with a maximum clique size of two, thus considering direct neighbor relationships. The most probable and therefore best class assignment is found by minimizing

$$E = \sum_{i=1}^{N} \Psi\left(l_i^t \mid Z^t, L^{t-1}\right) + \lambda \sum_{(i,j)\in N^2} \Phi\left(l_i^t, l_j^t \mid Z^t, L^{t-1}\right). \tag{4}$$

In this context, $Z^t = \{z_i^t\}$ denotes the Stixel measurement vector at time step t and $L^t = \{l_i^t\}$ are the correspondingly assigned labels. The term Ψ incorporates the unary terms and Φ considers mutual relations between neighboring Stixel labels, such that

$$\Psi\left(l_i^t \mid Z^t, L^{t-1}\right) = \underbrace{p\left(z_i^t \mid l_i^t\right)}_{\text{data term}} \cdot \underbrace{p\left(l_i^{t-1} \mid l_i^t\right)}_{\text{temporal expectation}} \cdot \underbrace{p\left(l_i^t\right)}_{\text{prior}}, \text{ and} \tag{5}$$

$$\Phi\left(l_i^t, l_j^t \mid Z^t, L^{t-1}\right) = \begin{cases} -\log\left(p_{\text{equal}}\left(\Delta_{\text{disp}}\right)\right) & , \text{ if } l_i^t = l_j^t \\ -\log\left(1 - p_{\text{equal}}\left(\Delta_{\text{disp}}\right)\right) & \text{otherwise.} \end{cases} \tag{6}$$

The smoothness term $\Phi\left(l_i^t, l_j^t \mid Z^t, L^{t-1}\right)$ is modeled as a Potts model. In doing so, we favor neighboring Stixels to belong to the same label type. The best labeling is extracted using the popular α-expansion graph cut [16]. All control input and algorithmic parameters (e.g. including the weighting factor λ) have been optimized using a large manually annotated sequence data base ($+30,000$ frames) of urban traffic. Further examples for inner city scenarios are illustrated in Figure 5 showing both the tracked Stixel World as well as the motion segmentation results.

6   Object Recognition

A major motivation for the development of the Stixel World was to allow for an efficient attention control of high-level vision tasks. While the easy detection of moving objects as presented in the last section is one example, the recognition of cars, pedestrians and bicyclists is another one which is usually solved by means of classification.

Naturally, the more one knows about the current environment, the less effort must be spent to extract the objects of interest. Accordingly, Enzweiler et al. [8] addressed the exemplary task of vehicle classification (cf. Figure 6) using Stixels and compared this approach against a monocular and a stereo-based attempt.

For the monocular approach there are no prior clues about the 3D environment to exploit. Thus, one is forced to test lots of hypotheses spread across the image covering all possible scales that the objects of interest might have. To obtain reasonable results, we used approximately $50,000$ hypotheses per image.

In case of using stereo, the depth data can be easily used to sort out potentially weak hypotheses in advance, e.g. by considering the correlation of depth and

Fig. 5. Results of the Stixel computation, the Kalman filter-based motion estimation, and the motion segmentation step. Arrows on the base points of the Stixels denote the estimated motion state. The right side shows the corresponding labeling result obtained by graph cut optimization. Furthermore, the color scheme encodes the different motion classes (right headed, left headed, with us, and oncoming). Uncolored regions are detected as static background.

scale. This strategy allowed to reduce the hypotheses set by another order of magnitude, such that about 5,000 remaining hypotheses had to be classified.

Now, using Stixels to control the attention made it possible to address this challenge quite elegantly. Since Stixels inherently encode where in the scene, at which distance, and at which scale objects are to be found, it is just straightforward to directly use this prior knowledge for the hypotheses generation step. This way, we were able to reduce the number of required hypotheses once again by a whole magnitude, such that we ended up at a total of 500 only.

In retrospect, the key conclusion from our experiments is not just that using Stixels allows to speed up the classification by almost a factor of 10 (vs. stereo).

Fig. 6. The goal is to classify front and rear views of other vehicles. Usually, this requires to spread large amounts of hypotheses across the image. Using Stixels attention classification allows to reduce their amount significantly while, at the same time, the classification performance increases.

It also allows to maintain the detection rate constant, while, at the same time, the number of false alarms decreases by almost one order of magnitude [8]. The potential of this proceeding has also been focus of the work of Benenson et al. [5].

7   Summary and Conclusion

This contribution presented a novel vision architecture for understanding complex traffic situations. Each step from pixels over Stixels to objects is based on global optimization in order to achieve both maximum performance and robustness. In particular, real-time SGM is used to compute dense stereo depth maps from rectified image pairs.

The Stixel world is computed from stereo also in a semi-global optimal manner, only ignoring the lateral dependencies of Stixel columns in order to achieve a real-time implementation. The motion estimation is based on the 6D-Vision principle, taking into account the temporal history of the tracked Stixel.

Finally, in order to extract all moving objects, graph cut based optimization is used to find the optimum segmentation of the dynamic Stixel World. As a result we get an extremely robust recognition system with an unprecedented performance. Practice proves the attempted versatility of the Stixel World. It has been successfully used for the initialization of object-specific trackers like the vehicle tracker proposed by Barth [3].

Muffert et al. [21] were able to easily answer the question whether it is safe to enter a roundabout by analyzing the Stixel World computed for a sideways-looking camera system. As shown in [8], Enzweiler et al. used Stixels to speed up their object classifiers by a factor of ten and simultaneously reduced the false positive rate by nearly one order of magnitude.

References

1. Badino, H., Franke, U., Mester, R.: Free space computation using stochastic occupancy grids and dynamic programming. In: Workshop on Dynamical Vision, ICCV, Rio de Janeiro, Brazil (October 2007)
2. Badino, H., Franke, U., Pfeiffer, D.: The Stixel World - A Compact Medium Level Representation of the 3D-World. In: Denzler, J., Notni, G., Süße, H. (eds.) DAGM 2009. LNCS, vol. 5748, pp. 51–60. Springer, Heidelberg (2009)
3. Barth, A., Pfeiffer, D., Franke, U.: Vehicle tracking at urban intersections using dense stereo. In: 3rd Workshop on Behaviour Monitoring and Interpretation, BMI, Ghent, Belgium, pp. 47–58 (November 2009)
4. Bellman, R.: Dynamic Programming. Princeton University Press (1957)
5. Benenson, R., Timofte, R., Van Gool, L.: Stixels estimation without depth map computation. In: IEEE CVVT: E2M at ICCV (November 2011)
6. Boykov, Y., Veksler, O., Zabih, R.: Fast approximate energy minimization via graph cuts. In: ICCV, Kerkyra, Corfu, Greece, pp. 377–384 (September 1999)
7. Elfes, A.E.: Sonar-based real-world mapping and navigation. Journal of Robotics and Automation 3(3), 249–265 (1987)

8. Enzweiler, M., Hummel, M., Pfeiffer, D., Franke, U.: Efficient stixel-based object recognition. In: IEEE Intelligent Vehicles Symposium, Alcalá de Henares, Spain (June 2012)
9. Erbs, F., Franke, U.: Stixmentation - probabilistic stixel based traffic scene labeling. In: BMVC, Guildford, UK. BMVA Press (September 2012)
10. Felzenszwalb, P.F., Veksler, O.: Tiered scene labeling with dynamic programming. In: IEEE CVPR, San Francisco, CA, USA, pp. 3097–3104 (June 2010)
11. Franke, U., Rabe, C., Badino, H., Gehrig, S.: 6D-Vision: Fusion of Stereo and Motion for Robust Environment Perception. In: Kropatsch, W.G., Sablatnig, R., Hanbury, A. (eds.) DAGM 2005. LNCS, vol. 3663, pp. 216–223. Springer, Heidelberg (2005)
12. Gallup, D., Pollefeys, M., Frahm, J.-M.: 3D Reconstruction Using an n-Layer Heightmap. In: Goesele, M., Roth, S., Kuijper, A., Schiele, B., Schindler, K. (eds.) DAGM 2010. LNCS, vol. 6376, pp. 1–10. Springer, Heidelberg (2010)
13. Gehrig, S.K., Eberli, F., Meyer, T.: A Real-Time Low-Power Stereo Vision Engine Using Semi-Global Matching. In: Fritz, M., Schiele, B., Piater, J.H. (eds.) ICVS 2009. LNCS, vol. 5815, pp. 134–143. Springer, Heidelberg (2009)
14. Hirschmüller, H.: Accurate and efficient stereo processing by semi-global matching and mutual information. In: IEEE CVPR, San Diego, CA, USA, pp. 807–814 (June 2005)
15. Hoiem, D., Efros, A.A., Hebert, M.: Geometric context from a single image. In: ICCV, pp. 654–661 (2005)
16. Kolmogorov, V., Rother, C.: Minimizing nonsubmodular functions with graph cuts- a review. IEEE Trans. on PAMI 29(7), 1274–1279 (2007)
17. Kweon, I.S., Kanade, T.: High-resolution terrain map from multiple sensor data. IEEE Trans. on PAMI 14, 278–292 (1992)
18. Lacroix, S., Kyun Jung, I., Mallet, A.: Digital elevation map building from low altitude stereo imagery. In: Int. SIRS (2001)
19. Liu, X., Veksler, O., Samarabandu, J.: Order-preserving moves for graph-cut-based optimization. IEEE Trans. on PAMI 32(7), 1182–1196 (2010)
20. Moravec, H.P.: Robot spatial perception by stereoscopic vision and 3D evidence grids. Technical Report CMU-RI-TR-96-34, Carnegie Mellon University (1996)
21. Muffert, M., Milbich, T., Pfeiffer, D., Franke, U.: May I enter the roundabout? a time-to-contact computation based on stereo-vision. In: IEEE IV, Alcalá de Henares, Spain (June 2012)
22. Oniga, F., Nedevschi, S.: Curb detection for driving assistance systems: A cubic spline-based approach. In: IEEE IV, Baden-Baden, Germany, pp. 945–950 (June 2011)
23. Oniga, F., Nedevschi, S., Meinecke, M.-M., To, T.B.: Road surface and obstacle detection based on elevation maps from dense stereo. In: IEEE ITSC, Seattle, WA, USA (September 2007)
24. Pfeiffer, D., Franke, U.: Efficient representation of traffic scenes by means of dynamic Stixels. In: IEEE IV, San Diego, CA, USA, pp. 217–224 (June 2010)
25. Pfeiffer, D., Franke, U.: Towards a global optimal multi-layer Stixel representation of dense 3D data. In: BMVC, Dundee, Scotland. BMVA Press (August 2011)
26. Scharstein, D., Szeliski, R.: Middlebury online stereo evaluation (2002), http://vision.middlebury.edu/stereo
27. Siegemund, J., Pfeiffer, D., Franke, U., Förstner, W.: Curb reconstruction using conditional random fields. In: IEEE IV, San Diego, CA, USA, pp. 203–210 (June 2010)

Fast Stixel Computation
for Fast Pedestrian Detection

Rodrigo Benenson, Markus Mathias, Radu Timofte, and Luc Van Gool

ESAT-PSI-VISICS/IBBT, KU Leuven, Belgium
firstname.lastname@esat.kuleuven.be

Abstract. Applications using pedestrian detection in street scene require both high speed and quality. Maximal speed is reached when exploiting the geometric information provided by stereo cameras. Yet, extracting useful information at speeds higher than 100 Hz is a non-trivial task. We propose a method to estimate the ground-obstacles boundary (and its distance), without computing a depth map. By properly parametrizing the search space in the image plane we improve the algorithmic performance, and reach speeds of 200 Hz on a desktop CPU. When connected with a state of the art GPU objects detector, we reach high quality detections at the record speed of 165 Hz.

Fig. 1. Fast pedestrian detection pipeline (based on [1]). This paper focuses on speeding up the stixel world estimation (step 1) via algorithmic improvements.

1 Introduction

Fast object detection is of utmost importance in ground mobile robots. The faster the objects are detected and categorized, the faster the robot will react to them, enabling high speed displacement and/or smooth natural motion. False positive detections should be minimized, to avoid unnatural motions; false negative detections should be minimized for safety reasons. On the other hand, the computational budget is restricted due to constrains on power consumption and the need to execute other modules on the same platform.

This tension between speed and quality has motivated a significant amount of research. Recently a new approach for fast pedestrian detection has been proposed [1]. The authors proposed a method for high quality detections at 50 Hz

A. Fusiello et al. (Eds.): ECCV 2012 Ws/Demos, Part III, LNCS 7585, pp. 11–20, 2012.

in the monocular case (using GPU), and proposed to exploit the geometrical information to reach 135 Hz in the stereo case (using GPU + CPU). To reach such high speed in the stereo case, Benenson et al. proposed to skip the usual depth map computations stage, and instead use a direct method to estimate the presence of objects above the ground [2] ("stixel world" estimation [3]). Combining such fast detection method with fast stereo image processing, allows to detect pedestrians in less that 10 milliseconds per image.

In [1] the authors report than the current method is CPU-bound; although GPU detection runs at ∼ 150 Hz, the stereo processing only reaches 135 Hz, becoming the limiting factor. In this paper we revisit the stereo processing method, and show that with a proper re-parametrization, it is possible to reach 200 Hz for the stixel world estimation. This new method enables reaching high quality detections at 165 Hz, and frees CPU resources for additional tasks (e.g. tracking, planning).

1.1   Related Work

The idea of exploiting stereo information to speed-up objects detection has been around since more than fifteen years [4] . Multiple methods for coupling depth maps and objects detection have been proposed [5,6,7,8,9,10,11]. Similarly, free space estimation allows to disregard areas of the image where we know obstacles are not present [12,13].

The vast majority of methods previously proposed compute as a first step a dense (or semi-dense) depth map of the scene, and then use this depth map to infer the presence of objects. When doing this, the depth map computation becomes the speed bottleneck, since it needs to compute much more information than needed ("distance of every pixel in the image" versus "where are the objects?"). Badino et al. introduced the notion of "stixel world", which can be seen as the minimal world model useful to describe the objects, it simply includes a ground plane and objects that "stick out" from the ground [3,2].

Kubota et al. [14] showed that depth maps could be skipped, and the distance to objects could be directly estimated. Benenson et al. [2] then extended this work by showing that height estimation could also be done without depth map computation, and that the stixel world estimated by such an approach is suitable for objects detection [1,15] and for object motion estimation [16].

1.2   Contribution

Although direct stixel world estimation [2] provides a significant speed-up (from ∼ 20 Hz to ∼ 100 Hz), when coupled with state of the art GPU objects detector, it lags behind becoming the speed bottleneck [1]. This is the problem we address in this paper, our **key contribution** is proposing a new parametrization for direct stixel world computation (without depth map) which allows to reach ∼ 200 Hz on CPU without compromising on the detection quality.

All together we reach high quality detections at 165 Hz (CPU+GPU), with the GPU becoming the bottleneck, and freeing CPU resources for other tasks.

In section 2 we describe our stixel world estimation method. Section 3 explains how the stixels are used to accelerate and improve objects detection. Section 4 provides empirical evidence of the improved quality versus speed trade-off, both for stixels computation per se and when coupled with objects detection. We conclude and sketch future work in section 5.

2   Fast Stixel Estimation

The stixel world model can be decomposed in three sets of parameters: the ground plane, the distance to the objects and the objects height.

For objects detection we assume the object height is known and class dependent, thus we focus on ground plane and distance to objects estimation.

Similar to previous work [14,13,2] we first estimate the ground plane (using evidence collected in v-disparity domain[1]) (see section 2.1), and then we use the ground plane to estimate the distance to the objects ("stixels distance"). The key difference of our proposal, is that the distance estimation is formulated directly in the u-v domain, instead of u-disparity as previously done (see section 2.2).

Assumptions. We share the same assumptions than [14,2]. The key assumption is that the camera has negligible roll with respect to the ground plane (pitch and height are estimated). In the current implementation we use a flat ground plane model, but nothing impedes using non-linear models. The object height is assumed known, but the method is robust to fluctuations on the height. Being stereo matching based, the common Lambertian surface assumption is used.

2.1   Ground Plane Estimation

We use the same approach as [2]. The ground plane is estimated using the v-disparity method [6], but the evidence is collected directly from matching left and right image rows at different disparities (instead of computing and projecting a depth map). See figure 2.

Fig. 2. The evidence for the ground plane estimation is computed by matching pixels in the left and right images

---

[1] In this text u refers to the image columns, and v to the image rows.

Given the evidence collected in each row, we extract the disparity with minimal cost per row and then use robust line fitting to find the ground plane. The ground plane model is represented by a function $f_{ground} : V \mapsto D$ that maps every image row v to a specific disparity $d = f_{ground}(v)$.

In order to speed-up computation, instead of collecting evidence for every row below the horizon; we consider computing only one-out-of-N row. This provides significant speed-up without degrading quality (specially when handling large images).

2.2   Stixel Distance Estimation

Previous methods for stixel distance estimation suggested to collect evidence column-wise in the image, and then estimate the distance by solving a dynamic programming problem in the u-disparity domain [14,13,2]. Although effective, this approach has three weaknesses:

Wrong quantization. When concerned about objects detection, we search to answer "where in the image can we expect objects of the class of interest?". When computing in the u-disparity domain, we create a non-homogeneous discretization in the image space (linear grows of ground plane distance, but quadratic grows of disparity distance). The quantization of the objects bottom (v dimension) will be more fine grained near the horizon, and coarser at the bottom of the image. For objects detection we rather have a regular quantization on the vertical axis.

Ignores horizontal gradient. When matching left and right images for different disparities, the information being used are the image gradients aligned to the vertical axis (vertical gradient). The horizontal gradient is completely un-informative for stereo matching. In a sense, the v-disparity cost matrix (see [2]) contains only *half* of the information available in the image.
We expect that the ground-object boundary correlates with the horizontal gradient (i.e. that more often than not, there is a visible boundary at the object bottom). This information should be exploited.

Computes more than needed. Because of the quantization effect discussed above, not only we have undesired quantizations, but also we are computing more than needed. When in the disparity domain, we will reach sub-pixel resolution close to the horizon, causing redundant computations. For objects detection, we only require to compute enough to have a coarse (and unbiased) estimate of the object position in the image.

Sampling Rows and Columns. To solve these problems we propose to *change the parametrization* from the u-disparity domain into directly the u-v domain. We are unaware of any previous work that used such parametrization.

In order to exploit the horizontal gradient information, one could weight the likelihood of a particular boundary candidate by the gradient magnitude at a particular pixel. This would force to consider every pixel below the horizon line. In order to speed-up the evaluation we use an alternative approach. The image is split vertically in multiple row bands, and inside every band, for every image column, the pixel with the maximal horizontal gradient is selected (see figure 3). By only evaluating evidence at the pixel with maximum gradient we significantly reduce the required computation. By selecting the maximal gradient we increase the chances to find the object border accurately. In the possible but unlikely case that the ground has distracting horizontal stripes the incurred error is bounded (by the band height).

The row band i is termed b_i. The particular row selected inside band b_i at stixel q_j is termed $v(q_j, b_i)$. Given the ground plane model we can write $d(q_j, b_i) = f_{ground}(v(q_j, b_i))$.

Objects of interest will in general have an image width larger than one column, thus computing evidence for every column on the image is highly redundant. We allow ourselves to sample evidence each one-out-of-N column, at regular intervals. Each stixel q_j is located at column $u(q_j) = j \cdot stixel\_width$.

By selecting different stixel widths and row band heights, we are able to control the amount of data extracted from the image.

Dynamic Programming Formulation. The goal is to find the optimal row band for each stixel

$$b_s^*(q) = \underset{b(q)}{\operatorname{argmin}} \sum_q c_s(q, b(q)) + \sum_{q_a, q_b} s_s(v(q_a, b(q_a)), v(q_b, b(q_b))) \quad (1)$$

where q_a, q_b are neighbours ($|a - b| = 1$), c_s is the data term and s_s the smoothness term. This problem can efficiently be solved using dynamic programming [14,2].

Data term For each stixel column q and row band b, we calculate the evidence supporting the presence of a stixel in the left image by computing the cost $c_s(q, b)$ ("stixel cost"). The lower the cost the more likely that a stixel is present.

$$c_s(q, b) = c_o(u(q), d(q, b)) + c_g(u(q), d(q, b)) \quad (2)$$

where $c_o(u, d)$ ("object cost"), the cost of a vertical object being present, and $c_g(u, d)$ ("ground cost"), the cost of a supporting ground being present. See figure 3 for an illustration on how these cost are computed. c_o simply sums the evidence along the vertical column, using the expected object height, projected in the image using the distance given by the ground plane estimation. c_g sums the evidence along the ground plane. In an efficient implementation, the ground plane estimate is used to warp the right image such as c_g can be computed using sums over columns between the left image and the warped right image. This warping can be done even with non linear ground plane models. See [2] for more details on c_o and c_g computation.

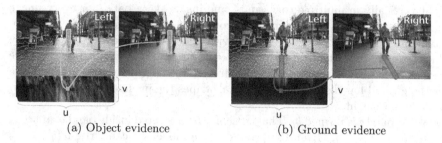

(a) Object evidence   (b) Ground evidence

Fig. 3. The object and ground costs are computed by matching pixels in the left and right images. White dots on the image indicates object-ground boundary candidates, based on horizontal gradient maxima.

Smoothness term The smoothness term s_s enforces to respect the left-right occlusion constraints and promotes ground-object boundaries with few jumps.

$$s_s\left(v_a, v_b\right) = \begin{cases} \infty & \text{if } d\left(v_a\right) < d\left(v_b\right) - 1 \\ c_o\left(u_a, d\left(v_a\right)\right) & \text{if } d\left(v_a\right) \approx d\left(v_b\right) - 1 \\ -w \cdot c_o\left(u_a, d\left(v_a\right)\right) & \text{if } q_a = q_b \\ 0 & \text{if } d\left(v_a\right) > d\left(v_b\right) - 1 \end{cases} \tag{3}$$

The sign $\approx$ in equation 3 indicates that we will consider the lowest q_b where $s_s \neq \infty$ as if $d\left(v_a\right) = d\left(v_b\right) - 1$. w is a free parameter that promotes boundaries with few jumps, we use $w = 0.5$.

2.3   Algorithmic Speed-Up

Solving the dynamic programming problem of equation 1 has a complexity $O\left(Q \cdot B^2\right)$ where Q is the number of stixels in the image, and B is the number of row bands considered. The computation cost of the data term c_s is directly proportional to $Q \cdot B$. The total computational cost of our method is then $O\left(k_a \cdot Q \cdot B^2 + k_b \cdot Q \cdot B + k_c \cdot Q\right)$, where $k_c \cdot Q$ indicates the operations required to find the maximal gradient point for each row band. Reducing B allows to significantly improve the computation time.

In [2] every column of the image and every disparity are considered, typically, 640 columns and 128 disparities. In our implementation, for such case roughly half of the time is spent computing c_s, and half of the time solving the dynamic programming problem. If we consider stixels of width 2 pixels and 50 row bands, the total computation is expected to drop by a factor 7 (assuming $k_a = k_b$ and $k_c \ll k_b$). In section 4 we show how the quality and the effective speed fluctuate with different values for Q and B. However, it can be readily seen that significant speed-ups are achievable with this approach.

It should be noted that, as it is, we only consider objects with their bottom visible in the image. For full object detection this is a desirable property.

Nothing impedes to use the method considering row bands "out of the image" (corresponding to larger disparity values), we only need to propagate the values c_g in the visible area towards the invisible areas.

3 Object Detection Using Stixels

The authors of [1] have kindly provided an early access to their open source release of the (so called) VeryFast detector. When coupled with stixels estimates this detector uses the stixels of the *previous* frame, to guide the detections in the current frame. Given the expected center position of the object (stixel) in the image, and its expected scale; the detector will search around a few pixels up-and-down in the column (e.g. ±30 pixels) and a few scales (e.g. ±5 scales).

The number of windows evaluated is then be number of columns×vertical search range×scales search ranges (e.g. 640×60×10), instead of every column×every row×every scale (e.g. 640 × 480 × 55), which corresponds to a ∼ 20× reduction in the search space. In section 4 we show that using the new "fast" *u-v* stixels estimation has no impact on quality respect to the original stixels estimation method used in [1].

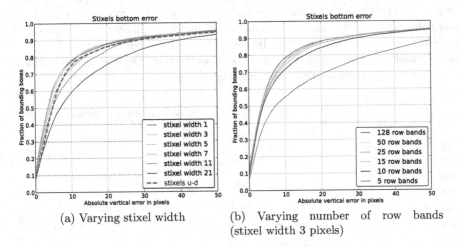

(a) Varying stixel width   (b) Varying number of row bands (stixel width 3 pixels)

Fig. 4. Effect of stixel width and number of row bands on the quality

4 Evaluation

4.1 Stixels Estimation

In comparison to [2] we have introduced a few additional degrees of freedom, which allow a more fine grained control of the quality versus speed trade-off. In figures 4 and 5, we use the same experimental protocol as in [2]. Given the ground truth annotations of the pedestrians in the stereo sequence Bahnhof (999 frames, $\approx$ 7400 annotated bounding boxes), we measure the vertical distance between the estimated stixel bottom (at center column of the annotation) and the bottom of the annotated bounding box. The plots show the cumulative absolute error over the sequence (error versus fraction of bounding boxes below such error).

In figure 4a, we use a very high number of row bands (close to the number of rows below the horizon), and vary the stixel width. We see that up to stixel width of 5 pixels the quality is almost unaffected (since pedestrians are much larger than 5 pixels), but as the width further increases the quality starts to drop. It is interesting to note that computing stixels in u-v domain provides a slight quality improvement with respect to using the u-disparity domain (denominated stixels u-d in figure 4a). This is due to be using the horizontal gradient evidence directly which provides improved robustness to the noise in the ground plane estimate, and bypasses disparity quantization effects.

In figure 4b, we use a stixel width of 3 pixels and vary the number of row bands. Moving from 128 bands to 25 bands provides only a very small drop in quality, yet a significant improvement in speed (see section 2.3). Of course, if the number of bands is too low then quality does drop significantly.

In figure 5a we show the quality impact of using more than one column to cumulate evidence (i.e. not matching a single pixel per row, but pair of pixels, or trio of pixels, etc...). Against the intuition, we see that matching more than one column at a time does not significantly improve quality. This shows that matching only one column already collects the most relevant data from the image (and has the minimal computation cost). Matching too many columns (> 5) creates a blurring effect that degrades the quality.

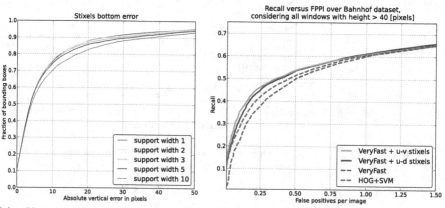

(a) Varying stixel support width   (b) Detection quality of different methods
(stixel width 3 pixels, 25 row bands)

Fig. 5. Stixel and detection quality results

When using a stixel width of 1 pixels and 128 row bands in our u-v stixels implementation we reach 45 Hz on a high-end laptop (4 cores of an Intel

Fig. 6. Some example frames from the result video (see supporting material). Blue lines indicate stixels estimates, boxes mark detected pedestrians.

Core i7-2630QM @ 2.00GHz). From the experiments above we see that using stixel width of 3 pixels, 25 row bands and cumulating evidence along 1 column, provides essentially the same quality as the u-disparity stixels in [2]. Using these parameters we reach 260 Hz, a $2\times$ improvement over [2].

4.2 Object Detection

Stixels estimates can be used to speed-up objects detection. We use the open source `VeryFast` detector from [1] in the same setup that they proposed. We only did minor code optimizations to push further the execution speed by 10%. The key point of this paper is showing that we can make the detection speed GPU bounded instead of CPU bounded as in [1] (thus freeing the CPU for additional tasks).

In figure 5b, we show the detection quality obtained using the traditional `HOG+SVM` detector [17], using the `VeryFast` by itself, `VeryFast` with stixels in the u-disparity domain (`VeryFast + u-d stixels`), and the new `VeryFast` with stixels in u-v domain (`VeryFast + u-v stixels`). It can be seen that the quality is not altered, yet we move from 135 Hz [1] CPU-bound to 165 Hz GPU-bound (CPU side running at 210 Hz), average over 1000 frames on Bahnhof sequence using an Intel Core i7 870 CPU and an Nvidia GeForce GTX 470 GPU. In figure 6 we show some examples of the corresponding stixels and detection quality.

5   Conclusion and Future Work

In this paper we have proposed a new approach for obstacle detection that focuses on computing exactly what we need, and nothing more. We argue that this frugal approach is better than the previous ones because it enables estimating directly what we want ("where are the objects?"), in the domain we want ("where in the image are the objects?"), reaching the speeds we want (as fast as possible).

With our new u-v domain stixels, fast pedestrian detections on stereo image becomes (again) GPU-bound (at 165 Hz). Further speed should then be reached by improving the GPU detector itself, although our initial attempts indicate that this seems a difficult feat. In the current setup higher GPU speed seem easier to reach by hardware updates than by algorithmic modifications. We believe that exploring improvements in quality is a more fruitful direction at this time.

We are also interested in exploiting the high detection speed to build larger systems that employ pedestrian detection as an intermediate step.

Acknowledgement. This work has been partly supported by the Toyota Motor Corporation and the ERC grant COGNIMUND.

References

1. Benenson, R., Mathias, M., Timofte, R., Van Gool, L.: Pedestrian detection at 100 frames per second. In: CVPR (2012)
2. Benenson, R., Timofte, R., Van Gool, L.: Stixels estimation without depthmap computation. In: ICCV, CVVT Workshop (2011)
3. Badino, H., Franke, U., Pfeiffer, D.: The Stixel World - A Compact Medium Level Representation of the 3D-World. In: Denzler, J., Notni, G., Süße, H. (eds.) DAGM 2009. LNCS, vol. 5748, pp. 51–60. Springer, Heidelberg (2009)
4. Franke, U., Kutzbach, I.: Fast stereo based object detection for stop and go traffic. In: IVS (1996)
5. Franke, U., Joos, A.: Real-time stereo vision for urban traffic scene understanding. In: IVS (2000)
6. Labayrade, R., Aubert, D., Tarel, J.P.: Real time obstacle detection on non flat road geometry through 'v-disparity' representation. In: IVS (2002)
7. Nedevschi, S., Danescu, R., Frentiu, D., Marita, T., Oniga, F., Pocol, C., Schmidt, R., Graf, T.: High accuracy stereo vision system for far distance obstacle detection. In: IVS (2004)
8. Hu, Z., Lamosa, F., Uchimura, K.: A complete u-v-disparity study for stereovision based 3D driving environment analysis. In: 3DIM (2005)
9. Seki, A., Okutomi, M.: Robust obstacle detection in general road environment based on road extraction and pose estimation. In: IVS (2006)
10. Bajracharya, M., Moghaddam, B., Howard, A., Brennan, S., Matthies, L.H.: A fast stereo-based system for detecting and tracking pedestrians from a moving vehicle. IJRR (2009)
11. Ess, A., Leibe, B., Schindler, K., Van Gool, L.: Robust multi-person tracking from a mobile platform. PAMI (2009)
12. Okutomi, M., Noguchi, S.: Extraction of road region using stereo images. In: ICPR, vol. 1, pp. 853–856 (1998)
13. Badino, H., Franke, U., Mester, R.: Free space computation using stochastic occupancy grids and dynamic programming. In: ICCV, Workshop on Dynamical Vision (2007)
14. Kubota, S., Nakano, T., Okamoto, Y.: A global optimization algorithm for real-time on-board stereo obstacle detection systems. In: IVS, Turkey (June 2007)
15. Enzweiler, M., Hummel, M., Pfeiffer, D., Franke, U.: Efficient stixel-based object recognition. In: IVS (2012)
16. Günyel, B., Benenson, R., Timofte, R., Van Gool, L.: Stixels Motion Estimation without Optical Flow Computation. In: Fitzgibbon, A., Lazebnik, S., Perona, P., Sato, Y., Schmid, C. (eds.) ECCV 2012, Part VI. LNCS, vol. 7577, pp. 528–539. Springer, Heidelberg (2012)
17. Dalal, N., Triggs, B.: Histograms of oriented gradients for human detection. In: CVPR (2005)

Discovering a Lexicon of Parts and Attributes

Subhransu Maji

Toyota Technological Institute at Chicago,
Chicago, IL 60637, USA
smaji@ttic.edu

Abstract. We propose a framework to discover a lexicon of visual attributes that supports fine-grained visual discrimination. It consists of a novel annotation task where annotators are asked to describe differences between pairs of images. This captures the intuition that for a lexicon to be useful, it should achieve twin goals of discrimination and communication. Next, we show that such comparative text collected for many pairs of images can be analyzed to discover topics that encode *nouns* and *modifiers*, as well as *relations* that encode attributes of parts. The model also provides an ordering of attributes based on their discriminative ability, which can be used to create a shortlist of attributes to collect for a dataset. Experiments on Caltech-UCSD birds, PASCAL VOC person, and a dataset of airplanes, show that the discovered lexicon of parts and their attributes is comparable to those created by experts.

1   Introduction

A lexicon that supports fine-grained visual recognition provides an effective language-based interface for humans to query particular instances of a category. Some successful applications include searching faces with desired attributes [1], shopping websites that support structured search, etc. From the computer vision perspective, such a lexicon can provide insights into which representations are useful for recognition. Indeed, in recent years, vision systems have benefited both in terms of recognition rates and their ability to generalize to new categories by using attributes as an intermediate representation [2,3]. However, to build such systems one requires a large dataset of images annotated with attributes. This work addresses the issue of deciding the set attributes to annotate for an object category, in order to enable fine-grained discrimination.

One may derive such a lexicon from "field guides" – books that help identify particular species of animals, birds, etc. These exist for some categories such as birds, but for a vast majority of object categories, there aren't any such sources. Moreover, even when a field guide is available, it may not be quite suited to the set of images in hand – one may have a field guide for military airplanes, but not for passenger planes or bi-planes. As we scale to thousands of object categories, it becomes desirable that the process of discovering such a lexicon be as automated as possible.

In this work we build on the intuition that a good lexicon should achieve twin goals of communication and discrimination, i.e., it should be easy to describe

A. Fusiello et al. (Eds.): ECCV 2012 Ws/Demos, Part III, LNCS 7585, pp. 21–30, 2012.

list properties
- plane
- has engine
- red color
- has rudder

list differences
propeller plane vs. passenger plane
one engine vs. four engines
red color vs. white color
round rudder vs. pointy rudder

Fig. 1. Fine-grained attributes are better revealed in the discriminative description task (right), than in the traditional description task (left)

instances, as well as sufficient to distinguish instances from one another using the lexicon. To this end we propose a novel annotation task of discriminative description, where one is asked to describe differences between pairs of images. As shown in Figure 1, in our interface, the annotator is shown a pair of images and is asked to describe in free-form English, a few differences between the two. Our annotation task can reveal properties that are more fine-grained than in the traditional annotation task of listing properties of objects, one at a time. Moreover, the frequency with which a certain attribute is used to distinguish pairs within a set provides an indication of its discriminative power. We require that the annotations be structured – each description be of the form "sentence a" vs. "sentence b", where "sentence a" and "sentence b" describe a property of the left and right images respectively. This provides us with a corpus of sentence pairs that can be analyzed to discover a lexicon of parts and attributes using Natural Language Processing (NLP) techniques.

We propose a novel generative model of sentence pairs across the corpus to extract a set of parts, *shared* topics that capture semantic properties such as "color" or "cardinality", as well as relations that encode part-specific attributes. The model also provides an ordering of these attributes based on their frequency within the corpus, which can provide a shortlist of attributes to collect for a dataset. We perform experiments using such annotations collected on Amazon Mechanical Turk [4] for images from Caltech-UCSD birds, PASCAL VOC person, and a dataset of airplane images, and show that the framework can be used to obtain a lexicons of parts and attributes that matches those created by experts.

2   Related Work

The task of discovering a lexicon of visual attributes has received some attention from the computer vision community in recent years. Berg et al. [5] use descriptions of products in shopping websites to mine phrases that appear frequently, which are sorted according to how well a computer vision algorithm can predict them. Parikh et al. [6] discover task-specific attributes with a user in the loop by considering discriminative directions in the data found automatically and asking users to name the variation along that direction. Recently Duan et al. [7] proposed a modification of the latter, which enables discovery of localized attributes such as ours. Both these approaches assume an explicit feature space where good discriminative directions can be easily found. In contrast, we aim to discover visual attributes that directly enable distinction of one instance from another independent of the features, or computer vision pipeline. This may be effective in discovering visual attributes that are otherwise hard to find without an intermediate step of part localization, which on many datasets can be quite difficult. We derive our attributes based on text collected using the proposed annotation task (Section 3), which to our knowledge has not been used previously, and rely on language modeling tools to discover attributes. We show that surface level statistics of the data derived from word alignments of such comparative text can be used to discover a lexicon of parts and attributes.

3 The Discriminative Description Task

Attributes should help to distinguish one instance from another within a category. We use this intuition to design an interface where the primary goal is to extract such attributes. Our annotation task consists of showing annotators pairs of images of the same category and asks them to list 5 visual properties that are different between them in free-form English. Each sentence is required to have the word "vs.", which separates the left and the right property as seen in Figure 1. We also provide a few examples to guide the process. The pairwise comparison encourages annotators to list attributes that distinguish one instance from another. Thus, the lexicon that we elicit from the overall process is likely to be more specialized than what one might otherwise get by collecting properties of the instance one at a time. It also allows us to discover attributes that are relevant to the set of images in hand. For example, if all the planes in our dataset were propeller planes, we would discover attributes that distinguish propeller planes from one another.

The pairwise comparison is a general framework for collecting discriminative properties. In this work we focus on nameable parts and attributes, but with a simple modification of the interface we can also collect evidence for a property that is different by allowing the user to mark such regions in the image. This option might be more suited for categories which have un-nameable parts. One may also obtain even finer grained attributes by repeating the process for pairs of images within a sub-category. This process is natural because it is easier to list differences between objects that are similar as more parts can be put in correspondence and compared.

For a given set of images, one can sample pairs at random. The random sampling strategy biases the discovery process towards those that split the dataset evenly. If a binary attribute is present in a fraction p of the dataset, then the likelihood that it will be revealed in a pairwise comparison is upper bounded by $2p(1 - p)$. We need on average 50 pairs of images to find an attribute that appears on 1% of the dataset. Thus, the pairwise comparison technique is extremely effective in mining discriminative attributes.

4 Discovering a Lexicon of Parts and Attributes

The discriminative description task provides us with pairs of sentences that can be analyzed to discover a lexicon of parts and attributes. The key observation is that in simple forms of comparative text such as those we collect, each sentence pair typically describes only one part and its modifier. As an example, one may describe a difference between a pair of airplane images as "red rudder vs. blue rudder". From this sentence pair, one may infer that the noun that is being described is "rudder", and that it is being modified by "red" and "blue". Moreover, the words "red" and "blue" belong to the same semantic category, which in this case is "color". We propose a generative model of sentence pairs across the corpus that captures this structure. At the top level, topics encode parts and modifiers that are shared across the corpus. Noun topics capture parts, whereas modifier topics capture semantic properties such as "color" or "cardinality". A single noun topic may be modified by several modifier topics, and a single modifier topic may modify several noun topics. The set of attributes, i.e., relations between parts and modifiers can thus be expressed as a bipartite graph between the nouns and modifiers topics.

Given a corpus of sentence pairs $\mathbf{e}_s, \mathbf{f}_s$, the generative model is shown in Figure 2. Each sentence pair is generated according to an *attribute* z_s. The variable z_s encodes a bipartite relation between a *noun* and a *modifier* topic. This is enforced by modeling the topic distribution conditioned on z_s as a multinomial distribution Ω_{z_s} peaked at exactly one each of *noun* and *modifier* topics (see section 4.1). The topics for nouns and modifiers, Γ, are themselves multinomials that denote the probability of word given topic. A word in position i in the left sentence is generated by sampling a topic $t_{s,i}$ conditioned on z_s and a word conditioned on the topic. The right sentence is generated according to an alignment $\mathbf{a}$, which provides the locations of the words in $\mathbf{e}_s$ that generated $\mathbf{f}_s$. Each word in $\mathbf{f}_s$ is generated from the word in $\mathbf{e}_s$ and its topic, at the location given by $\mathbf{a}$, using a topic-specific multinomial Ψ. Let I_s and J_s, denote the lengths of the sth left and right sentences respectively. Then the joint probability of the sentences and latent variables given the parameters $\Theta = \{\theta, \pi, \Omega, \Gamma, \Psi\}$ is given by:

$$P(z_s, \mathbf{e}_s, \mathbf{f}_s, \mathbf{a}_s, \mathbf{t}_s | \Theta) = \prod_{s=1}^{N} P(z_s | \theta) \prod_{i=1}^{I_i} P(t_{s,i} | z_s, \Omega) P(e_{s,i} | t_{s,i}, \Gamma)$$

$$\times \prod_{j=1}^{J_i} P\left(a_j | \pi\right) P\left(f_{s,j} | e_{s,a_j}, t_{s,a_j}, \Psi\right)$$

The generative process for the right sentence $P(\mathbf{f}_s | \mathbf{e}_s, \mathbf{t}_s)$, is similar to the IBM word alignment model [8], popular in machine translation to initialize translation tables across a pair of languages. The starting point for these models is a corpus of sentence pairs in two languages, say *French* and *English*, which are translations of one another. In the simplest IBM model, each word in the French sentence is generated independently from a word in the English sentence according to an alignment vector $\mathbf{a}_s = a_{s,1}, a_{s,2}, \ldots, a_{s,J_s}$, denoting the positions of the word(s) in the English sentence that generated each French word. The joint probability of the alignment vector and the French sentence given the English sentence is:

$$P(\mathbf{f}_s, \mathbf{a}_s | \mathbf{e}_s, I_s, J_s) = \prod_{j=1}^{J_s} P(a_{s,j} | I_s, J_s) P(f_{s,j} | e_{s,a_{s,j}}) \tag{1}$$

Each entry in the alignment vector $a_{s,j} \in \{1, \dots, I_s\}$ is either chosen uniformly at random (IBM 1), or proportional to $\pi(|a_{s,j} - j|)$ (IBM 2). The distribution π is peaked at 0, which encourages words in the same position across a sentence pair to be aligned to one another.

Compared to the IBM models, we have also introduced topics in the source language, which can enable topic-specific word emissions. We also do not model the "NULL" word commonly used in these models since the source and target languages are the same in our setting. This model is related to the BiTAM model proposed by [9], which also models type-specific translations. The difference, however, is that our types (or topics) are attached to the words in the source language and *not* to the alignments.

The generative process for the left sentence is similar to LDA [10] and to its variants such as Correspondence-LDA [11]. The main difference lies in how we model the topics themselves. Our topics encode *nouns* and *modifiers*, and are estimated by relying on the structure of the task to cluster words (described in Section 4.1). In addition the topic proportions in each sentence are constrained to be *bipartite* and *not* drawn from a Dirichlet distribution, which allows us to model part-modifier topic correlations, and thereby discover the relations between parts and their attributes.

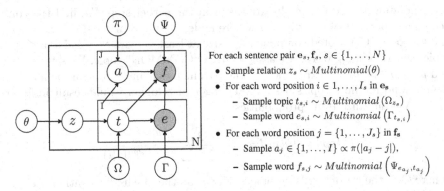

Fig. 2. The generative model of the corpus consisting of sentence pairs $\{\mathbf{e}_s, \mathbf{f}_s\}$

4.1 Initialization and Parameter Estimation

We estimate all the parameters by maximizing the likelihood of the data using EM. Given an estimate of the parameters $\{z_s, \mathbf{t}_s, \mathbf{a}_s, \theta, \pi, \Omega, \Gamma, \Psi\}$, we update one parameter at a time, keeping others fixed, until convergence. Our model has many parameters, and careful initialization is necessary to obtain a good solution. Fortunately, in our case we can initialize the parameters of our model from simpler models which can be easily solved.

Initializing $\pi, \mathbf{a}_s, \Psi$. We use the IBM model 2 in Equation 1 to learn the distortion probabilities π^{ibm} and topic independent Ψ^{ibm}. The alignments are initialized to the most likely ones according to the IBM model. We initialize $\pi \leftarrow \pi^{ibm}$ and $\Psi_{e,f,t} = \Psi^{ibm}_{e,f}$.

Initializing Γ: *noun* and *modifier* Topics. This is a crucial step in our approach. In our application, we wish to learn topics that encode parts and attributes. A possible way of doing this would be to use language-specific knowledge such as part-of-speech tags. However, automatic tagging may not be accurate for words in a new domain, limiting its applicability. We instead use the observation made earlier in this section to initialize noun and modifier topics, i.e., words that repeat across pairs are likely to be from the same noun topic, whereas words that are different are likely to be from the same modifier topic. This provides a domain and perhaps even a language-independent way of characterizing nouns and their modifiers.

To initialize noun topics, we find words i with $f(i) > \tau_p$ and $\Psi_{i,i} > \rho_p$, where $f(i)$ is the number of times the word i appears in the corpus. $\Psi_{i,i}$ characterizes how frequently the word i aligns to itself across sentence pairs. We set $\tau_p = 5$ and $\rho_p = 0.6$, which gives us an initial set of noun topics.

To initialize modifier topics, we construct a similarity matrix between pairs of words $S(i, j) = f(i) \times \Psi^{ibm}_{i,j}$. The matrix S counts the number of times word j is aligned to the word i across the corpus. We zero out the rows and columns corresponding to the words already taken in the earlier step. We find the connected components of the graph G, where nodes i, j are connected if $S(i, j) > \tau_a$ and $\Psi_{i,j} > \rho_a$. Connected components of size at least two are assigned a modifier topic. The remaining words are assigned to a "COMMON" topic. We set $\tau_a = 10$ and $\rho_a = 0.2$ in all our experiments. The parameters ρ and τ control the number of noun and modifier topics desired. Setting τ or ρ higher would result in fewer topics. We initialize topic probabilities:

$$P(topic = t | word = i) = \frac{\sum_{j \in C_t} \Psi^{ibm}(j|i)}{\sum_t \sum_{j \in C_t} \Psi^{ibm}(j|i)} \qquad (2)$$

Where C_t is the set of words in topic t, which can then be used to initialize Γ. As we will see in the experiments section, the process discovers semantic modifier categories such as *color*={*red, blue, green,...*}, *cardinality*={*one, two,...*}, etc., that capture the kinds of variation each part is likely to have.

Initializing Ω, z_s, θ : Bipartite Relations between *nouns* and *modifiers*. The previous step discovers n noun and m modifier topics. We consider relations between all possible choices of noun and modifier topics. In addition, we also consider m relations which correspond to attributes of special part "GLOBAL".

This is to encode relations that describe global properties of the object, such as "gender" for the person category. This leads to a total of $(n + 1) \times m$ relations. For each relation, we initialize a multinomial peaked at the corresponding noun and modifier topics. In addition, the multinomial is allowed a fixed portion of the "COMMON" topic to model words in the sentence that are not from either part and attribute topic. The rest of the values are assigned a small constant value. Given this initialization, we run EM to estimate a mixture of multinomials and memberships. At each M step we ensure that the relations remain bipartite – multinomials are assigned small values for topics other than the ones in the relation and renormalized.

After EM converges, we drop clusters that have fewer than τ members, which is set to 1% of the data in our experiments. We run EM again with the remaining clusters until convergence and initialize z_s, θ, Ω to the values of cluster memberships, frequencies, and estimated multinomial mixture means, respectively.

5   Experiments

We experiment with images from Caltech-UCSD birds, PASCAL VOC person, and a dataset of airplane images. These categories are diverse and contain instances with different attributes. Our experiments were performed on Amazon Mechanical Turk [4] using the interface described in Section 3. For each category, we also provided a few examples of annotations while clearly indicating that the list is not exhaustive. Figure 3 shows example annotations collected using our interface overlaid on the images. Annotators provide natural language descriptions that differentiate the two images. By pairing the same image with others, different properties of the image can be revealed. Thus, our approach may also be used to discover instance-specific attributes that discriminate the instance from others.

The collected annotations can be noisy. These include formatting errors, e.g., empty sentences or sentences without the word "vs." for separation. There is also noise due to different ways of spelling the same word, synonyms, etc. Ignoring sentences with formatting errors typically leaves about $80 - 85\%$ of the sentences.

5.1   Caltech-UCSD Birds

The dataset [12] consists of 200 species of birds and was introduced for fine-grained visual category recognition. We sample 200 images, one random image from each category for our discovery process. For these images we sampled 1600 pairs uniformly at random and collected annotations.

Figure 4(a), shows the learned topics and attributes for birds category. The learned parts for each category are shown on the top row, modifiers on the bottom row, and the bipartite relation between parts and attributes is shown using edges connecting them. The thickness of the edge indicates the frequency of the relation in the dataset. The discovered parts and modifiers correctly refer to parts of the bird such as the *body, beak, wings, tail, head, etc.*, and semantic categories such as *size, color, shape, etc.*, respectively. The most frequent attribute that discriminates birds from one another is the $\{beak\ size\} \leftrightarrow \{small, large\}$, followed by $\{tail\} \leftrightarrow \{long, short, small, ..\}$, i.e. the size of the tail. Other distinguishing features are colors of various body parts such as body, tail and head, and beak shape, such as pointy vs. round, etc. An interesting relation that is discovered is $\{like\} \leftrightarrow \{sparrow, duck, crow, eagle, dove, . . .\}$. Even though we had 200 species of birds, the annotators choose to describe each bird based on their similarity to a commonly-seen set of birds. Similarity to prototypes is a discriminative visual attribute for birds and is often present in field guides.

We compared the attributes discovered by our algorithm to the ones the creators of the Caltech-UCSD birds dataset choose [12]. Out of the 12 parts of birds, which are *forehead, crown, bill, eye, throat, nape, breast, back, wing, belly, leg* and *tail*, we discover 6 of them. We miss parts such as crown and nape, which are sub-parts of the head region and unfamiliar to non-experts. This brings up an important aspect of the problem which is that the lexicon familiar to experts may be quite different from that of annotators commonly available on crowdsourcing platforms such as Amazon Mechanical Turk [4]. Nevertheless, the pairwise comparison is an attractive framework to obtain such lexicons regardless of the expertise of the annotator.

5.2   Airplanes

We collect 200 images from a website of airplane photographs[1]. We sampled 1000 pairs uniformly at random and collected annotations.

Figure 4(b), shows the discovered attributes. Here, the most frequent attribute is the color of the rudder. Our dataset has many passenger planes, and they all tend to have different rudder colors corresponding to different airlines. The number of wheels is the second most distinguishing feature. This actually corresponds to sentence pairs "one front wheel vs. two front wheels", which distinguishes *propeller* and other smaller planes from bigger jet planes. The correct relation is $\{front\ wheel\} \leftrightarrow \{one, two\}$. We instead discover two relations $\{front\} \leftrightarrow \{one\}$ and $\{wheel\} \leftrightarrow \{one\}$, because we don't model phrases. The next most important relation is the facing direction, which roughly distinguishes one half of the dataset from another. Other discovered relations include the shape of the nose $\in \{pointy, round, flat, . . .\}$, kind of the plane $\in \{propeller, passenger, jet, . . .\}$, overall size $\in \{small, big, large, medium\}$, and location of the wing relative to the body. Cardinality affects parts such as wheels, engines and rudders, while color modifies the rudder and body. All these are salient properties that distinguish one airplane from another in our dataset.

5.3   PASCAL VOC Person

A dataset consisting of attributes of people from the PASCAL Visual Object Challenge (VOC) dataset was introduced by Bourdev et al. [3]. We sample 400

---

[1] http://airliners.net

Airplanes   Birds

Fig. 3. Example annotations collected using our interface.

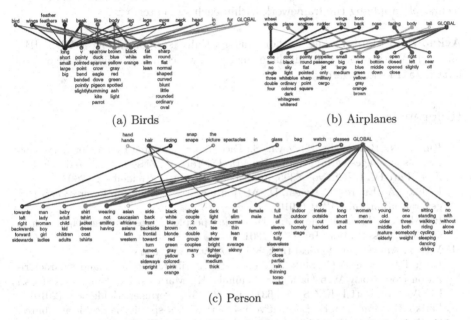

(a) Birds   (b) Airplanes

(c) Person

Fig. 4. Learned *parts* (top row), *modifiers* (bottom row), and *attributes* (edges) for birds, airplanes and person category. The thickness of the edge is proportional to the frequency of the attribute in the corpus.

random images from the training/validation subset of the dataset. For these images we sampled 1600 pairs uniformly at random and collected annotations.

Figure 4(c) shows the discovered attributes for this dataset. We discover attributes such as *gender, hair style, hair length, dress type, wearing glasses, hats, etc* which are present in [3]. In addition, we discover new ones such as the action being performed – sitting, standing, dancing, etc.

6   Conclusion

We propose a framework for discovering a lexicon of fine-grained visual attributes of object categories that achieves the twin goals of communication and discrimination. We show that text generated from pairwise comparisons of instances within object categories provides a rich source of attributes that are discriminative and task-specific by design. We also propose a generative model of the sentence pairs and show that it discovers topics corresponding to parts and modifiers and relations between them on three challenging datasets.

Although in this task we focus on the lexicon aspect, the same interface can be modified so that the user can provide evidence of the difference, for example, by drawing bounding boxes around the region of interest. This can enable discovery of visual parts which are otherwise hard to name. The pairwise comparison framework may be used to discover attributes in a coarse-to-fine manner by recursively applying the framework within each sub-category.

Acknowledgments. The author was partially supported by a 2012 JHU Summer Workshop. The airplane images are courtesy Mick Bajcar and http://airliners.net.

References

1. Kumar, N., Belhumeur, P., Nayar, S.: FaceTracer: A Search Engine for Large Collections of Images with Faces. In: Forsyth, D., Torr, P., Zisserman, A. (eds.) ECCV 2008, Part IV. LNCS, vol. 5305, pp. 340–353. Springer, Heidelberg (2008)
2. Farhadi, A., Endres, I., Hoiem, D.: Attribute-centric recognition for cross-category generalization. In: CVPR (2010)
3. Bourdev, L., Maji, S., Malik, J.: Describing people: A poselet-based approach to attribute classification. In: ICCV (2011)
4. MTurk: Amazon mechanical turk, http://www.mturk.com
5. Berg, T.L., Berg, A.C., Shih, J.: Automatic Attribute Discovery and Characterization from Noisy Web Data. In: Daniilidis, K., Maragos, P., Paragios, N. (eds.) ECCV 2010, Part I. LNCS, vol. 6311, pp. 663–676. Springer, Heidelberg (2010)
6. Parikh, D., Grauman, K.: Interactive discovery of task-specific nameable attributes. In: Workshop on Fine-Grained Visual Categorization, CVPR (2011)
7. Duan, K., Bloomington, I., Parikh, D., Grauman, K.: Discovering localized attributes for fine-grained recognition. In: CVPR (2012)
8. Brown, P.F., Cocke, J., Pietra, S.A.D., Pietra, V.J.D., Jelinek, F., Lafferty, J.D., Mercer, R.L., Roossin, P.S.: A statistical approach to machine translation. Comput. Linguist. (1990)
9. Zhao, B., Xing, E.P.: Bitam: bilingual topic admixture models for word alignment. In: COLING-ACL (2006)
10. Blei, D.M., Ng, A.Y., Jordan, M.I.: Latent dirichlet allocation. J. Mach. Learn. Res. (2003)
11. Blei, D.M., Jordan, M.I.: Modeling annotated data. In: SIGIR (2003)
12. Welinder, P., Branson, S., Mita, T., Wah, C., Schroff, F., Belongie, S., Perona, P.: Caltech-UCSD Birds 200. Technical Report CNS-TR-2010-001, California Institute of Technology (2010)

How Important Are "Deformable Parts" in the Deformable Parts Model?

Santosh K. Divvala, Alexei A. Efros, and Martial Hebert

Robotics Institute, Carnegie Mellon University

Abstract. The Deformable Parts Model (DPM) has recently emerged
as a very useful and popular tool for tackling the intra-category diversity
problem in object detection. In this paper, we summarize the key insights
from our empirical analysis of the important elements constituting this
detector. More specifically, we study the relationship between the role
of deformable parts and the mixture model components within this detector, and understand their relative importance. First, we find that by
increasing the number of components, and switching the initialization
step from their aspect-ratio, left-right flipping heuristics to appearance-
based clustering, considerable improvement in performance is obtained.
But more intriguingly, we observed that with these new components, the
part deformations can now be turned off, yet obtaining results that are
almost on par with the original DPM detector.

1 Introduction

Consider the images of category horse in Figure 1 (row1) from the challenging
PASCAL VOC dataset [1]. Notice the huge variation in the appearance, shape,
pose and camera viewpoint of the different horse instances – there are left and
right-facing horses, horses jumping over a fence in different directions, horses
carrying people in different orientations, close-up shots, etc. How can we build a
high-performing sliding-window detector that can accommodate the rich diversity amongst the horse instances?

Deformable Parts Models (DPM) have recently emerged as a useful and popular tool for tackling this challenge. The recent success of the DPM detector
of Felzenszwalb et al., [2] has drawn attention from the entire vision community towards this tool, and subsequently it has become an integral component
of many classification, segmentation, person layout and action recognition tasks
(thus receiving the lifetime achievement award at the PASCAL VOC challenge).

Why does the DPM detector [2] perform so well? As the name implies, the
main stated contribution of [2] over the HOG detector described in [3] is the
idea of deformable parts. Their secondary contribution is latent discriminative
learning. Tertiary is the idea of multiple components (subcategories). The idea
behind deformable parts is to represent an object model using a lower-resolution
'root' template, and a set of spatially flexible high-resolution 'part' templates.
Each part captures local appearance properties of an object, and the deformations are characterized by links connecting them. Latent discriminative learning

A. Fusiello et al. (Eds.): ECCV 2012 Ws/Demos, Part III, LNCS 7585, pp. 31–40, 2012.

involves an iterative procedure that alternates the parameter estimation step between the known variables (e.g., bounding box location of instances) and the unknown i.e., *latent* variables (e.g., object part locations, instance-component membership). Finally, the idea of subcategories is to segregate object instances into disjoint groups each with a simple (possibly semantically interpretable) theme e.g., frontal vs profile view, or sitting vs standard person, etc, and then learning a separate model per group.

A common belief in the vision community is that the deformable parts is the most critical contribution, then latent discriminative learning, and then subcategories. Although the ordering somewhat reflects the technical novelty (interestingness) of the corresponding tools and the algorithms involved, it is interesting to check whether is that really the order of importance affecting the performance of the detector in practice.

In this paper, we empirically analyze the relative importance of deformable parts and subcategories within the DPM detector. First, we find that (i) by increasing the number of subcategories in the mixture model, and (ii) switching from their aspect-ratio, left-right flipping heuristics to appearance-based clustering, considerable improvement in performance is obtained. But more intriguingly, we observed that with these new subcategories, the part deformations can be turned off, with only minimal performance loss. These observations reveal that the conceptually simpler notion of subcategories is indeed an equally important contribution in the DPM detector. Their careful use can potentially alleviate the need for deformable parts in the DPM detector for many practical applications and object classes.

2   Understanding Subcategories

In order to deal with significant appearance variations that cannot be tackled by the deformable parts, [2] introduced the notion of multiple components i.e., subcategories [4,5,6,7,8] into their detector. The first version of their detector [9] only had a single subcategory. The next version [2] had two subcategories that were obtained by splitting the object instances based on aspect ratio heuristic. In the latest version [10], this number was increased to three, with each subcategory comprising of two bilaterally asymmetric i.e., left-right flipped models (effectively resulting in 6 subcategories). The introduction of each additional subcategory has resulted in significant performance gains (e.g., see slide 23 in [11]).

Given this observation, what happens if we further increase the number of subcategories in their model? In Section 4, we will see that this does not translate to improvement in performance. This is because the aspect-ratio heuristic does not generalize well to a large number of subcategories, and thus fails to provide a good initialization. Nonetheless, it is possible to explore other ways to generate subcategories. For example, subcategories for cars can be based either on object pose (e.g., left-facing, right-facing, frontal), or car manufacturer (e.g., Subaru, Ford, Toyota), or some functional attribute (e.g., sports car, utility vehicle, limousine). Figure 1 illustrates a few popular subcategorization schemes for horses.

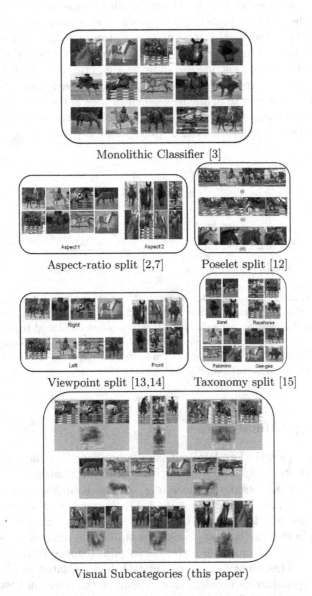

Monolithic Classifier [3]

Aspect-ratio split [2,7]   Poselet split [12]

Viewpoint split [13,14]   Taxonomy split [15]

Visual Subcategories (this paper)

Fig. 1. The standard *monolithic classifier* is trained on all instances together. *Viewpoint split* partitions the data using viewpoint annotations into left, right, and frontal subcategories. *Poselets* clusters the instances based on keypoint annotations in the configuration space. *Taxonomy split* groups instances into subordinate categories using a human-defined semantic taxonomy. *Aspect-ratio split* uses a simple bounding box aspect-ratio heuristic. *Visual subcategories* are obtained using (unsupervised) appearance-based clustering (top: few examples, bottom: mean image).

What is it that the different partitioning schemes are trying to achieve? A closer look at the figures reveals that they are trying to encode the homogeneity in appearance. It is the *visual homogeneity* of instances within each subcategory that simplifies the learning problem leading to better-performing classifiers (Figure. 2). What this suggests is, instead of using semantics or empirical heuristics, one could directly use appearance-based clustering for generating the subcategories. We use this insight to define new subcategories in the DPM detector, and refer to them as *visual* subcategories (in contrast to semantic subcategories that involve either human annotations or object-specific heuristics).

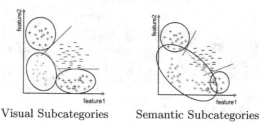

Visual Subcategories   Semantic Subcategories

Fig. 2. A single linear model cannot separate the data well into two classes. (Left) When similar instances (nearby in the feature space) are clustered into subcategories, good models can be learned per subcategory, which when combined together separate the two classes well. (Right) In contrast, a semantic clustering scheme (based on human annotations) also partitions the data but leads to subcategories that are not optimal for learning the category-level classifier.

3 Learning Subcategories

We first briefly review the key details of using subcategories in the DPM detector, and then explain the details specific to their use in our analysis.

Given a set of n labeled instances (e.g., object bounding boxes) $D = (< x_1, y_1 >, \ldots, < x_n, y_n >)$, with $y_i \in \{-1, 1\}$, the goal is to learn a set of K subcategory classifiers to separate the positive instances from the negative instances, wherein each individual classifier is trained on different subsets of the training data. The assignment of instances to subcategories is modeled as a latent variable z. This binary classification task is formulated as the following (latent SVM) optimization problem that minimizes the trade-off between the l_2 regularization term and the hinge loss on the training data [2]:

$$\arg\min_{w} \frac{1}{2} \sum_{k=1}^{K} ||w_k||^2 + C \sum_{i=1}^{n} \epsilon_i, \tag{1}$$

$$y_i . s_i^{z_i} \geqslant 1 - \epsilon_i, \ \epsilon_i \geqslant 0, \tag{2}$$

$$z_i = \arg\max_{k} s_i^k, \tag{3}$$

$$s_i^k = w_k . \phi_k(x_i) + b_k. \tag{4}$$

The parameter C controls the relative weight of the hinge-loss term, w_k denotes the separating hyperplane for the kth subclass, and $\phi_k(.)$ indicates the corresponding feature representation. Since the minimization is semi-convex, the model parameters w_k and the latent variable z are learned using an iterative approach [2].

Initialization. As mentioned earlier, a key step for the success of latent subcategory approach is to generate a good initialization of the subcategories. Our initialization method is to warp all the positive instances to a common feature space $\phi(.)$, and to perform unsupervised clustering in that space. In our experiments, we found the Kmeans clustering algorithm using Euclidean distance function to provide a good initialization.

Calibration. One difficulty in merging subcategory classifiers is to ensure that the scores output by individual SVM classifiers (learned with different data distributions) are calibrated appropriately, so as to suppress the influence of noisy ones. Note that, although the subcategory classifiers are coupled in the latent SVM formulation (1), a careful observation reveals that the classifiers are actually being learned independently. The coupling of classifiers only happens via the latent step (3) (i.e., the assignment of positive and negative instances to the different subcategories). Subsequently the SVM learning per subcategory is independent [2,14].

We address this problem by transforming the output of each SVM classifier by a sigmoid to yield comparable score distributions [16][1](Figure 3). Given a thresholded output score s_i^k for instance i in subcategory k, its calibrated score is defined as

$$g_i^k = \frac{1}{1 + exp(A_k.s_i^k + B_k)},\tag{5}$$

where A_k, B_k are the learned parameters of the logistic loss function $\arg\min_{A_k, B_k} \sum_{i=1}^{n} t_i \log g_i^k + (1 - t_i) \log(1 - g_i^k)$ with $t_i = Or(W_i^k, W_i)$, where $Or(w_1, w_2) = \frac{|w_1 \cap w_2|}{|w_1 \cup w_2|} \in [0, 1]$ indicates the overlap score between two bounding boxes [17], W_i is the ground-truth bounding box for the ith training sample, and W_i^k indicates the predicted bounding box by the kth subcategory. In our experiments, we found this calibration step to help improve the performance (mean A.P. increase of 0.5%).

4   Experimental Analysis

We performed our analysis on the PASCAL VOC 2007 comp3 challenge dataset [1]. We used the standard PASCAL VOC comp3 test protocol, which measures

---

[1] Even though the bias term b_k is used in equation (4) to make the scores of multiple classifiers comparable, we have found that it is possible for some of the subcategories to be very noisy (specifically when K is large and the subcategories have unequal distribution of positives across them), in which case their output scores cannot be compared directly with other, more reliable ones.

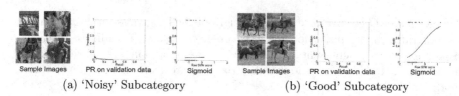

Sample Images   PR on validation data   Sigmoid   Sample Images   PR on validation data   Sigmoid

(a) 'Noisy' Subcategory   (b) 'Good' Subcategory

Fig. 3. The classifier trained on a noisy subcategory (horses with extreme occlusion and confusing texture) performs poorly on the validation dataset. As a result, its influence is suppressed by the sigmoid. While a good subcategory (horses with homogeneous appearance) classifier leads to good performance on the validation data and hence its influence is boosted by the calibration step.

detection performance by average precision (AP) over different recall levels. As our baseline system, we use the latest release of the DPM detector [10] (without the bounding-box prediction and context-rescoring steps). Figure 4 compares the results obtained using the different methods with respect to the baseline for the 20 PASCAL object categories.

The first sub-figure shows the improvements offered by using visual subcategories (with $K=15$) in the DPM detector. The mean relative improvement (over the baseline) across 20 classes is 9.4% (the mean A.P. improves from 0.32 to 0.35). Figure 7 shows the top detections obtained for train category. The individual detectors do a good job at localizing instances of their respective subcategories. In Figure 5, the discovered subcategories for symmetric (pottedplant) and deformable (cat) classes are displayed.

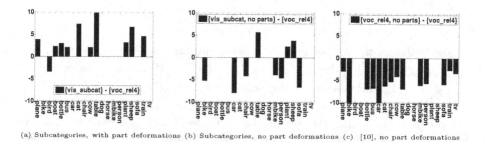

(a) Subcategories, with part deformations (b) Subcategories, no part deformations (c) [10], no part deformations

Fig. 4. Performance difference with respect to the baseline [10] (x-axis: 20 VOC classes, y-axis: difference in A.P.)

Given the high-degree of alignment across the instances within each subcategory, it is interesting to now check the importance of modeling the deformations across the parts within each subcategory. Would a simpler model (without deformations) suffice for training the discriminative detectors? We tested this hypothesis with an experiment by turning off the deformable parts. More specifically, rather than sampling "parts" from the high-resolution HOG template (sampled at twice the spatial resolution relative to the features captured by the root template) and modeling the deformation amongst them, we directly use all the features from the high-resolution template. This update to the DPM detector results in a simple multi-scale (two-level pyramid) representation with the finer resolution catering towards improved feature localization.

Fig. 5. The visual subcategories discovered for pottedplants correspond to different camera viewpoints, while cats are partitioned based on their pose. The baseline system [10] based on the aspect-ratio, left-right flipping heuristic cannot capture such distinctions (as many of the subcategories share the same aspect-ratio and are symmetric).

Figure 4(b) displays the results obtained. We observe that for 11 of the 20 classes (e.g., pottedplants, tvmonitor, trains, etc) there is no difference in performance. For 6 classes (e.g, person, sofa, etc), turning off deformations hurt the performance, while for 3 classes (diningtable, sheep, etc) performance actually improves. On average, using this two-level pyramid representation for the visual subcategories yields a mean A.P. of 0.31 that is almost on par as the full deformable parts baseline (0.32). These observations suggest that, in practice, the relatively simpler concept of visual subcategories is indeed an equally important contribution in the DPM detector. They can potentially alleviate the need for part deformations for many object categories.

Computational Issues. In terms of computational complexity, the two-scale visual subcategory detector ($K=15$) involves one coarse (root) and one fine

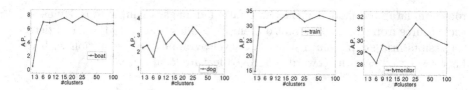

Fig. 6. Variation in detection accuracy as a function of number of subcategories for four distinct VOC2007 classes. The A.P. gradually increases with increasing number of subcategories and stabilizes beyond a point.

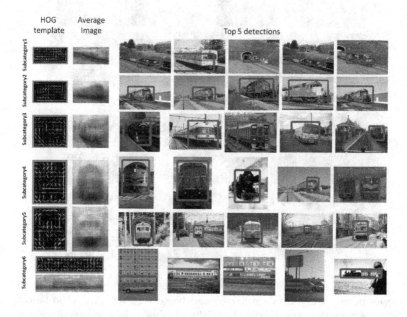

Fig. 7. As the intra-class variance within subcategories is low, the learned detectors perform quite well at localizing instances of their respective subcategories. Notice that for the same aspect-ratio and viewpoint, there are two different subcategories (rows 4,5) discovered for the train category.

resolution template per subcategory, totaling a sum of 30 HOG templates. Whereas the DPM detector has $K=6$ subcategories each with one root and eight part templates, totaling 54 HOG templates, which need to be convolved at test time. In terms of model learning, the DPM detector has the subcategory, as well as the part deformation parameters (six) as latent variables for each of the 24 parts (total of 145 latent variables), while the visual subcategory detector only has the subcategory label as latent. Therefore it not only requires fewer rounds of latent training than required by the DPM detector (leading to faster convergence), but also is less susceptible to getting stuck in a bad local minima. As emphasized in [2], simpler models are preferable, as they can perform better in practice than rich models, which often suffer from difficulties in training.

Number of Subcategories. One important parameter is the number of subcategories K. We analyze the influence of K by using different values ($K = [3, 6, 9, 12, 15, 20, 25, 50, 100]$) for a few classes ('boat', 'dog', 'train', 'tv') on the validation set. We plot the variation in the performance over different K in figure 6. The performance gradually increases with increasing K, but stabilizes around K=15. We used $K = 15$ in all the detection experiments.

Initialization. Proper initialization of subcategories is a key requirement for the success of latent variable models. We analyzed the importance of appearance-based initialization by comparing it with the aspect-ratio based initialization of [2]. Simply increasing the number of subcategories from $K = 6$ to 15 in case of aspect-ratio clustering drops the mean A.P by 1.2%, while appearance-based clustering improves the mean A.P. by 2.3%. (When $K = 6$, aspect-ratio and appearance produced similar result.)

We noticed minimal variation in the final performance on multiple runs with different Kmeans initialization. We found the (latent) discriminative reclustering step helps in cleaning up any *mistakes* of the initialization step. (Also we observed that most of the reclustering happens in the first latent update.)

5   Conclusion

Given that deformable parts can potentially model exponentially large number of object deformations [2], it is expected that their performance would be far more superior and generalizable in comparison to the use of a fixed number of subcategories. However our empirical analysis has surprisingly pointed out that there is only a minimal performance difference between the use of part deformations compared to the use of subcategories. Further, the fact that a simple method (more subcategories, no parts) does almost as well as the relatively more complex method (fewer subcategories, with parts) is informative as the former is conceptually easy to understand and implement, computationally efficient, and generates easily interpretable models.

Acknowledgments. This research was supported by NSF Grant IIS-0905402.

References

1. Everingham, M., Van Gool, L., Williams, C.K.I., Winn, J., Zisserman, A.: The pascal visual object classes challenge (2007),
   http://pascallin.ecs.soton.ac.uk/challenges/VOC
2. Felzenszwalb, P.F., Girshick, R., McAllester, D., Ramanan, D.: Object detection with discriminatively trained part based models. PAMI (2010)
3. Dalal, N., Triggs, B.: Histograms of oriented gradients for human detection. In: Proc. CVPR (2005)
4. Jacobs, R., Jordan, M., Nowlan, S., Hinton, G.: Adaptive mixture of local experts. Neural Computation (1991)

5. Xu, L., Neufeld, J., Larson, B., Schuurmans, D.: Maximum margin clustering. In: NIPS (2005)
6. Seemann, E., Leibe, B., Schiele, B.: Multi-aspect detection of articulated objects. In: CVPR (2006)
7. Park, D., Ramanan, D., Fowlkes, C.: Multiresolution Models for Object Detection. In: Daniilidis, K., Maragos, P., Paragios, N. (eds.) ECCV 2010, Part IV. LNCS, vol. 6314, pp. 241–254. Springer, Heidelberg (2010)
8. Yang, W., Toderici, G.: Discriminative tag learning on youtube videos with latent sub-tags. In: CVPR (2011)
9. Felzenszwalb, P.F., McAllester, D., Ramanan, D.: A discriminatively trained, multiscale, deformable part model. In: CVPR (2008)
10. Felzenszwalb, P.F., Girshick, R.B., McAllester, D.: Discriminatively trained deformable part models, release 4 (2011), http://people.cs.uchicago.edu/~pff/latent-release4/
11. Felzenszwalb, P.F.: Object detection grammars (2011), http://www.cs.brown.edu/~pff/talks/grammar.pdf
12. Bourdev, L., Maji, S., Brox, T., Malik, J.: Detecting People Using Mutually Consistent Poselet Activations. In: Daniilidis, K., Maragos, P., Paragios, N. (eds.) ECCV 2010, Part VI. LNCS, vol. 6316, pp. 168–181. Springer, Heidelberg (2010)
13. Schneiderman, H., Kanade, T.: A statistical method for 3D object detection applied to faces and cars. In: Proc. CVPR, vol. 1, pp. 746–751 (2000)
14. Gu, C., Ren, X.: Discriminative Mixture-of-Templates for Viewpoint Classification. In: Daniilidis, K., Maragos, P., Paragios, N. (eds.) ECCV 2010, Part V. LNCS, vol. 6315, pp. 408–421. Springer, Heidelberg (2010)
15. Deng, J., Dong, W., Socher, R., Li, L.J., Li, K., Fei-Fei, L.: Imagenet: A large-scale hierarchical image database. In: CVPR (2009)
16. Platt, J.C.: Probabilistic outputs for support vector machines and comparisons to regularized likelihood methods. In: Advances in Large Margin Classifiers, pp. 61–74. MIT Press (2000)
17. Alexe, B., Petrescu, V., Ferrari, V.: Exploiting spatial overlap to efficiently compute appearance distances between image windows. In: NIPS (2011)

Bounding Part Scores for Rapid Detection
with Deformable Part Models

Iasonas Kokkinos*

[1] Center for Visual Computing, École Centrale Paris, France
[2] Équipe Galen, INRIA Saclay, Île-de-France, France
[3] Université Paris-Est, LIGM (UMR CNRS), École des Ponts ParisTech, France

Abstract. Computing part scores is the main computational bottleneck in object detection with Deformable Part Models. In this work we introduce an efficient method to obtain bounds on part scores, which we then integrate with deformable model detection. As in [1] we rapidly approximate the inner product between a weight vector and HOG-based features by quantizing the HOG cells onto a codebook and replace their inner product with the lookup of a precomputed score. The novelty in our work consists in combining this lookup-based estimate with the codebook quantization error so as to construct probabilistic bounds to the exact inner product.

In particular we use Chebyshev's inequality to obtain probably correct bounds for the inner product at each image location. We integrate these bounds with both the Dual-Tree Branch-and-Bound work of [2,3] and the Cascade-DPMs of [4]; in both cases the bounds are used in a first phase to conservatively construct a shortlist of locations, for which the exact inner products are subsequently evaluated.

We quantitatively evaluate our method and demonstrate that it allows for approximately a twofold speedup over both [2] and [4] with negligible loss in accuracy.

1 Introduction

Deformable Part Models (DPMs) [5,6,4] combine mathematical rigor with excellent performance, but come with increased computational cost when compared with simpler alternatives such as Bag-of-Word classifiers. In this work we accelerate detection with DPMs: we use the exact same 'mixture-of-DPMs' model as that of [7] and obtain a substantial speedup with negligible and controllable error.

Our work builds on [2,3] where 'Dual Tree Branch-and-Bound' (DTBB) is introduced as an efficient bounding-based method for detection with DPMs. DTBB substantially accelerates the stages following part computation for both single- and multi-category detection, turning their complexity from linear to roughly logarithmic in the image size. However, as highlighted in [8,4] and also mentioned in [2] the computation of part scores is actually the main computational bottleneck for DPMs.

In this work we introduce a method to rapidly compute upper and lower bounds for part scores. We integrate these part bounds in DTBB as well as in Cascade-DPM

---

* This work was supported by grant ANR-10-JCJC-0205.

A. Fusiello et al. (Eds.): ECCV 2012 Ws/Demos, Part III, LNCS 7585, pp. 41–50, 2012.

detection [4]. Our algorithm eventually computes the exact values of the part scores and the correct object score, but only around locations 'shortlisted' by a first bounding stage. This drastically reduces the number of exact score computations performed.

After presenting prior work in Sec. 2, we present our bounding technique in Sec. 3, and describe how we integrate our bounds with DTBB and cascaded detection in Sec. 4; in Sec. 5 we evaluate our method on the PASCAL VOC dataset. Our code is available at http://vision.mas.ecp.fr/Personnel/iasonas/dpms.html.

2 Prior Work on Efficient Object Detection

Cascade algorithms for detection were introduced in the beginning of the previous decade in the context of boosting [9] and coarse-to-fine detection in [10]. Cascades use a sequence of tests to decide about the presence of an object and stop whenever any of those test fails; this reduces the number of image locations where all tests are applied. Cascades use conservative thresholds, set to ensure that the number of false negatives on the training set (and hopefully also the test set) is minimized. This idea has been recently applied to detection with deformable models in [4,8] as well as to pose estimation with more complex structured models in [11], where thresholds are set in a learnable, data-dependent manner.

On the other hand, bounding-based techniques such as Efficient Subwindow Search (ESS) [12] bound the score of a detector within an interval by exploiting properties of its form; this allows to use techniques such as branch-and-bound, or coarse-to-fine search [13] to narrow-down the set of locations containing strong object hypotheses. Bounding-based (admissible) heuristics were used for hierarchical object parsing with A^* in [14], while detection with deformable part models was cast in terms of Branch-and-Bound in [2,3]. More recently, [15] introduced a branch-and-bound method to deal with the more general structured models of [11].

The common idea in the works above is to prune computation when we have evidence that it is not worth pushing it until the end. For DPMs so far this has been done exclusively in 'cascade mode', namely by using empirically set thresholds. In the work of [4] on Cascaded Deformable Part Models (C-DPM) thresholds precomputed on the training set are used to prune computation with minimal possible loss. Specifically the authors observe that the DPM score is obtained gradually as the accumulation of the part scores; after computing the contribution of every part the authors stop the computation if the cumulative sum falls below a conservative (probably correct) threshold. In a similar vein [8] used a coarse-to-fine framework by using the 'root' (whole-object) filter response as a quick test to prune the range of locations where the part filters were evaluated. Again this requires setting a threshold for the root filter and fixing the range over which parts are searched for.

Using the results in our paper we can take an approach complementary to these two works: since we can bound the part scores we do not need to recompute thresholds. In particular for DTBB we approximate the part scores everywhere in a rapid manner and the optimization algorithm determines the subset of locations where the part score estimate is refined. For C-DPM we use our bounding-based technique to perform a rapid (faster than the one in [4]) computation of upper and lower bounds for the root filter and then focus on a subset of part locations while also dynamically pruning the set of candidate object locations.

3 Part Score Bounding

3.1 Score Approximation

We compute part scores as inner products of Histogram-of-Gradient (HOG) [16] features with a part-specific weight vector, trained as in [7]. Denoting by $h[x, f]$ the f-th dimension of the HOG cell located at x, and by $w[y, f]$ the value of the 'part template' (weight vector) for location y and dimension f, the score of a part at x is:

$$s[x] = \sum_{y \in Y} \sum_{f=1}^{F} w[y, f] h[x + y, f], \qquad (1)$$

where Y is a set of displacements and $F = 32$ is the dimensionality of the HOG cell at any point; we skip part indexes for simplicity. For 'part filters' $Y = [0, 5] \times [0, 5]$, so computing the score at any point x requires $36 \cdot 32$ multiplications and summations.

Our goal is to replace these $|Y| \cdot F$ operations with a rapidly computable approximation. By introducing the F-dimensional vectors $\mathbf{w}_y = [w[y, 1], \ldots, w[y, F]]^T$, and $\mathbf{h}_x = [h[x, 1], \ldots, h[x, F]]^T$, we can write the right hand side of Eq. 1 as:

$$s[x] = \sum_{y} \langle \mathbf{w}_y, \mathbf{h}_{x+y} \rangle. \qquad (2)$$

As in [1], we use vector quantization to replace the F multiplications involved in every inner product with a single lookup operation that approximates the final outcome. For this we construct a codebook $\mathcal{C} = \{C_1, \ldots, C_K\}$ for $\mathbf{h}$ with K-means clustering (we use K =256) and create a $K \times |Y|$ array of precomputed values:

$$\Pi[k, y] = \langle C_k, \mathbf{w}_y \rangle, \qquad (3)$$

which gives the score of part-cell y in the presence of an image-cell C_k.

When provided with a new image we quantize its HOG cells with our dictionary, i.e. we associate an index $I[x] = \operatorname{argmin}_k d(C_k, \mathbf{h}_x)$ with every image-cell $\mathbf{h}_x$; in particular we use KD-trees for fast approximate nearest neighbor search [17]. Given x we consider $\mathbf{h}_{i,j} \simeq C_{I[x]}$ and use use this approximation in Eq. 2 to obtain:

$$\langle \mathbf{h}_{x+y}, \mathbf{w}_y \rangle \simeq \langle C_{I[x+y]}, \mathbf{w}_y \rangle = \Pi[I[x + y], y] \qquad (4)$$

$$s[x] \simeq \hat{s}[x] = \sum_{y} \Pi[I[x + y], y], \qquad (5)$$

which exchanges the $|Y| \cdot F$ multiplications and summations of Eq. 2 with $|Y|$ lookup and summation operations. For $F = 32$ this can result in approximately a 30-fold speedup. In practice due to the numerous memory access operations the speedup can be smaller; our implementation is optimized to reduce the number of cache misses, but since the method is rather technical we will report it in a larger version of the paper; we refer to our publicly available code for details.

3.2   Bounding the Approximation Error

We now turn to ways of bounding the inner product score of Eq. 2 in terms of the lookup approximation in Eq. 5, by constructing upper and lower bounds on the approximation error. We first present a deterministic bound which comes from Holder's inequality. As this bound is too loose, it is only useful for presentation, and to introduce the necessary notation; we then provide tighter probabilistic bounds using Chebyshev's inequality.

3.3   A Deterministic Bound Using Holder's Inequality

We denote by $e_x = h_x - C_{I[x]}$ the quantization error for the feature h_x at x; We start by considering the contribution of a single HOG cell, say $x + y$ to the overall score; the approximation error ϵ_{x+y} in Eq. 4 can be expressed in terms of the inner product of e_{x+y} with w_y as follows:

$$\epsilon_{x+y} \doteq \langle h_{x+y}, w_y \rangle - \Pi[I[x + y], y] \tag{6}$$

$$= \langle h_{x+y}, w_y \rangle - \langle C_{I[x+y]}, w_y \rangle = \langle e_{x+y}, w_y \rangle. \tag{7}$$

Holder's inequality states that $\|fg\|_1 \le \|f\|_q \|g\|_p$ for $1/p + 1/q = 1$ and can be used to bound the approximation error in Eq. 7 in terms of the L_2-norms of the quantization error, $\|e_{x+y}\|_2$ and the weight vector $\|w_y\|_2$:

$$|\epsilon_{x+y}| = |\langle w_y, e_{x+y} \rangle| \le \|w_y\|_2 \|e_{x+y}\|_2. \tag{8}$$

This result bounds the approximation error ϵ_{x+y} due to a single HOG cell. Coming to integrating the contributions form the multiple HOG cells, we turn to the approximation error in Eq. 4, which we denote as $\epsilon_x \doteq s[x] - \hat{s}[x] = \sum_y \epsilon_{x+y}$ and bound as follows:

$$|\epsilon_x| \le \sum_y |\epsilon_{x+y}| \le \sum_y \|w_y\|_2 \|e_{x+y}\|_2 \doteq B_x. \tag{9}$$

We note that computing B_x takes only $|Y|$ multiplications and summations: the norm of the quantization error is computed once for the whole image, independently of the number and size of parts, while the norms of the weight vectors can be precomputed.

3.4   A Probabilistic Bound Using Chebyshev's Inequality

Even though rapidly computable, the bound delivered above is too loose to be of practical use. This is due to its generality; as we now show, it can be tightened by exploiting our problem-specific knowledge. In particular the inner product in Eq. 7, $\langle e_{x+y}, w_y \rangle = \sum_f e_{x+y}[f] w_y[f]$ adds up the product of the weight vector and quantization error elements. We know that the distribution of $e_{x+y}[f]$ will be zero-mean and consecutive summands are likely to cancel each other out. The Holder-based bound derived above ignores this and will be valid even if all vector elements have a common sign. As such it gives a bound which is too conservative to be useful.

Instead, we now derive a probabilistic bound that is valid with controllable accuracy. This means that we can tighten the bound at the cost of decreasing its probability of

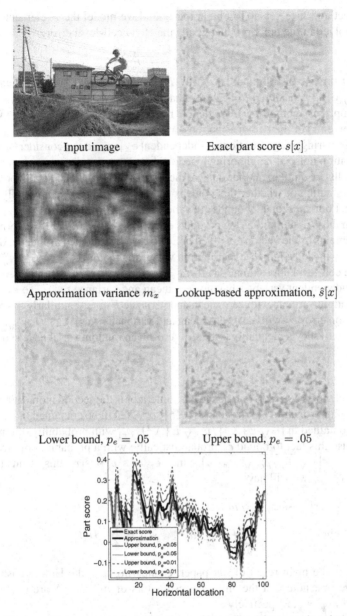

Fig. 1. Illustration of the part score approximation and bounding (please see in color): our goal is to rapidly bound the value of the part score $s[x]$ shown on the top right. The bound we propose in Eq. 12 is formed in terms of two quantities, a lookup-based approximation $\hat{s}[x]$ and an estimate of the approximation error's variance m_x, detailed in Eq. 13 and shown in the second row. These two are combined as in Eq. 12 to form an interval that contains the actual value with a certain probability of error p_e. The values of the lower and upper bounds for $p_e = 0.5$ are visualized in the third row. In the last row we show for an horizontal line through the image the values of the exact score, the approximation, as well as the upper and lower bounds for two different values of p_e. We can observe that for small p_e (higher probability of being correct) the bounds become looser.

being correct and vice versa. To obtain our bound we model the F elements of $\mathbf{e}_{x+y}$ and $\mathbf{w}_y$ involved in the inner product giving the HOG cell-level error:

$$\epsilon_{x+y} = \langle \mathbf{e}_{x+y}, \mathbf{w}_y \rangle \tag{10}$$

as samples from two distributions, $P_{x+y}(\mathbf{e})$, $P_y(\mathbf{w})$ respectively; since $\mathbf{e}$ is quantization error, $P_{x+y}(\mathbf{e})$ is considered to be zero-mean and symmetric around zero; we do not make assumptions about $P_y(\mathbf{w})$. We denote by $m^{\mathbf{e}}_{x+y}$ and $m^{\mathbf{w}}_y$ the respective variances (second moments) of the two distributions. Moreover, we assume that the quantization error at neighboring image locations is independent $\mathbf{e}_{x+y}$; one can consider cases where the quantization noise at neighboring locations has dependencies, e.g. when neighboring HOG cells are similar, and far outside the 'span' of the available codebook; a more thorough evaluation of whether this holds is needed, even though empirically we have observed that our subsequent bounds are valid.

Based on these assumptions, the products $\mathbf{e}_{x+y}[f]\mathbf{w}_y[f], f = 1, \ldots, F$ formed from the f-th elements of the vectors involved in Eq. 10 can be modeled as independent samples of a zero-mean, symmetric distribution with variance $m_{x+y} \doteq m^{\mathbf{e}}_{x+y} m^{\mathbf{w}}_y$. Consequently, the cell-level approximation error ϵ_{x+y} appearing in Eq. 10 can be seen as the sum of F independent variables having zero mean and variance m_{x+y}, so ϵ_{x+y} will in turn be a random variable with zero mean and variance Fm_{x+y}; similarly the part-level approximation error ϵ_x will have zero mean and variance $m_x = \sum_y Fm_{x+y}$.

As per Chebyshev's inequality [18], any zero-mean random variable X satisfies:

$$P(|X| > \alpha) \le \frac{E\{X^2\}}{\alpha^2}, \tag{11}$$

where $E\{\cdot\}$ denotes expectation - hence the numerator is the second moment of X. This means that with probability larger than $E\{X^2\}/\alpha^2$, X will be contained in $[-\alpha, \alpha]$; or, X will be contained in $[-\sqrt{E\{X^2\}/p_e}, \sqrt{E\{X^2\}/p_e}]$ with probability of error p_e.

We can use this fact to bound ϵ_x probabilistically: with a probability of error p_e we will have $\epsilon_x \in [-\sqrt{m_x/p_e}, \sqrt{m_x/p_e}]$. Since $\epsilon_x = s[x] - \hat{s}[x]$, this means that with probability $1 - p_e$ we will have:

$$s[x] \in \left[\hat{s}[x] - \sqrt{m_x/p_e}, \hat{s}[x] + \sqrt{m_x/p_e} \right] \tag{12}$$

$$\text{where} \quad m_x = \sum_y Fm^{\mathbf{e}}_{x+y} m^{\mathbf{w}}_y, \quad \hat{s}[x] = \sum_y \Pi[I[x+y], y]. \tag{13}$$

This bound is the main result of our paper. Comparing it to the Holder-based bound of Eq. 9, we first note that the empirical estimators of $m^{\mathbf{e}}_{x+y}, m^{\mathbf{w}}_y$ are related to the 2-norms of e_{x+y}, $\mathbf{w}_y$, respectively as:

$$m^{\mathbf{e}}_{x+y} = \frac{1}{F} \sum_{f=1}^{F} e^2_{x+y}[f] = \frac{1}{F} \|e_{x+y}\|^2_2 \tag{14}$$

and similarly $m^{\mathbf{w}}_{x+y} = \frac{1}{F}\|\mathbf{w}_{x+y}\|^2_2$. So apart from the root operation computing m_x in Eq. 13 has the same complexity as computing B in Eq. 9. Moreover the length of the interval in Eq. 12 scales proportionally to $\sqrt{|Y|F}$ while in Eq. 9 it scales proportionally to $|Y|F$, which shows that the Chebyshev bound is tighter than the Holder bound.

4   Integration with Deformable Object Detection

We now describe how we integrate the bound obtained above in the Dual-Tree Branch-and-Bound (DTBB) [2] and Cascaded DPM (C-DPM) [4] methods. Due to lack of space we refer to the respective works for algorithm details and provide a high-level, and intuitive outline of the integration, leaving technicalities for a future version.

4.1   Combination with Dual-Tree Branch-and-Bound

The DTBB method described in [2,3] uses bounding-based techniques for detection with DPMs. In particular Branch-and-Bound is used to bypass Generalized Distance Transforms (GDTs) and shown to result in substantial speedups for the part combination phase. However in [2] the part scores are considered to be computed in advance of DTBB, while this is actually the main computational challenge in detection with DPMs. Instead, we now integrate our efficient probabilistic part score bound with DTBB.

In particular, DTBB relies on upper bounding the quantity:

$$\mu_d^s = \max_{x \in X_d} \max_{x' \in X_s'} s[x'] + B[x', x] \tag{15}$$

which indicates the maximal contribution of a set of candidate part points X_s' to a set of candidate object points X_d; $s[x']$ is the appearance term at the candidate part location x' and $B[x', x]$ is the geometric consistency term between x' and the object location x. Since $\max_{x \in X} f[x] + \max_{x \in X} g[x] \geq \max_{x \in X} f[x] + g[x]$, we can bound Eq. 15 as:

$$\mu_d^s \leq \underbrace{\max_{x' \in X_s'} s[x']}_{\overline{S}} + \max_{x \in X_d} \max_{x' \in X_d} B[x', x] \tag{16}$$

A complementary term that emerges [3] is $\lambda_d^s = \min_{x \in X_d} \max_{x' \in X_s} s[x'] + B[x', x]$ which is lower bounded as:

$$\underbrace{\min_{x' \in X_s'} s[x']}_{\underline{S}} + \min_{x \in X_d} \max_{x' \in X_s} B[x', x] \leq \lambda_d^s. \tag{17}$$

The computation of the upper and lower bounds relevant to the geometric term, $B[x', x]$, exploits the fact that X_s, X_d are rectangular, and is detailed in [3]. Coming to the bounds on the unary terms, the approach taken has been to compute the exact part scores at every location $s[x]$ and then obtain $\overline{S}, \underline{S}$. As the domains X_s are organized in a kd-tree the latter maximization can be rapidly performed in a fine-to-coarse manner, but the computation of $s[x]$ was not avoided.

Instead we propose to accelerate the computation of $\overline{S}, \underline{S}$ by initially sidestepping the computation of $s[x]$ using the probabilistic bound of Eq. 13: the terms $\underline{s} = \hat{s}[x] - \sqrt{m_x/p}$ and $\overline{s} = \hat{s}[x] + \sqrt{m_x/p}$ involved in Eq. 13 are with probability $1 - p_e$ lower and upper bounds of $s[x]$ respectively. Based on these we can upper and lower bound S as follows: $\overline{S} = \max_{x' \in X_s'} s[x'] \leq \max_{x' \in X_s'} \overline{s}[x']$ and $\underline{S} = \min_{x' \in X_s'} s[x'] \geq \min_{x' \in X_s'} \underline{s}[x']$, and thereby use $\overline{s}, \underline{s}$ as surrogates for $s[x]$ in DTBB.

A subtlety is that by considering multiple terms when maximizing or minimizing with X_s we increase the probability of violating the (probabilistic) upper and lower bounds. But in practice we are only concerned with the points that give the maximum/minimum, and not the bulk of points contained between them.

We also note that we use $\bar{s}, \underline{s}$ as surrogates for s only in the first phase of DTBB. As soon as Branch-and-Bound converges to singleton intervals (individual pixels), we evaluate the exact part scores, $s[x]$; as we show in the experimental section, this boosts performance when compared to using only the lookup-based approximation. This more elaborate computation however is performed around a drastically reduced set of points, namely around those image locations that survive the first, quick bounding phase. Our method thereby combines the speed of quantization [1] with the accuracy of DTBB [2].

4.2 Combination with Cascaded Deformable Part Models

In [4] the authors exploit the fact that the DPM score is expressed as the accumulation of the part scores to devise a cascaded detection algorithm: after computing the contribution of each part to the overall object score, the computation stops for any location where the sum falls below a conservative (probably correct) threshold.

In order to accelerate the first stage of their algorithm, [4] downproject the HOG features to a lower dimensional space obtained through PCA. This results in fewer multiplications per HOG cell-bin, but can distort the obtained result. The remedy used in [4] is to use separate conservative thresholds for the PCA-based part scores, and estimate them from the training data.

By replacing the PCA-based approximation with the upper bound provided by our method we gain in two ways: first, our method is faster, as for each HOG-cell $x + y$ we use one lookup for $\Pi[I[x + y], y]$ and one multiplication for $\|\mathbf{w}_y\|_2 \|\mathbf{e}_{x+y}\|_2$ instead of 6 multiplications for the PCA-based features. Second, our method does not require gathering additional statistics to compute thresholds, but rather relies on the thresholds computed for the full (32-dimensional) part filters, which only need to be gathered once. This gives us the freedom to explore alternative bounding schemes (e.g. using different codebook construction techniques), without re-running our detector on the training data. Experimentally we verify that the two methods have virtually identical performance.

5   Results

We have validated the merit of our method on the PASCAL VOC'2007 challenge. As we use the exact same models as those in [4] our sole concern is the exactness and speed of the optimization method, and do not address learning issues.

In Fig. 2 we provide precision-recall plots for bicycle detection, in order to demonstrate the impact of our bounding scheme on object detection accuracy; similar results have been obtained for other classes but are omitted for lack of space; they will be included in a larger version of this work.

In all cases 'exact' refers to computations performed using GDTs as in [6]. On the left side, we compare the performance of the PCA-based cascade of [4] with the lookup-based cascade proposed in this work. We observe that if we use the 'raw' lookup-based

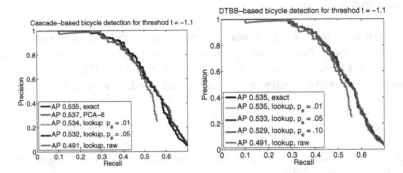

Fig. 2. Precision-Recall curves for bicycle detection using cascade-based (left) and branch-and-bound detection (right). Please see text for details.

Table 1. Means and standard deviation timings, in seconds, of the considered approaches. GDT stands for distance transforms, BB for Dual Tree Branch-and-Bound, CSC for cascade, and LU-{1,5} for lookup-based bounds with $p_e = .01$ and $p_e = .05$ respectively.

	GDTs [6]	BB [2]	BB-LU-5	BB-LU-1	CSC-PCA [4]	CSC-LU-5	CSC-LU-1
Part terms	8.35 ± 0.77	1.69 ± 0.18	0.69 ± 0.03	0.69 ± 0.06	0.00 ± 0.00	0.00 ± 0.00	0.00 ± 0.00
$\theta = -0.5$	0.60 ± 0.05	0.21 ± 0.06	0.47 ± 0.11	1.04 ± 0.25	0.56 ± 0.07	0.19 ± 0.03	0.23 ± 0.04
$\theta = -0.7$	0.60 ± 0.05	0.42 ± 0.10	1.00 ± 0.23	2.33 ± 0.65	0.72 ± 0.09	0.29 ± 0.04	0.36 ± 0.06
$\theta = -1.0$	0.60 ± 0.05	1.31 ± 0.31	3.80 ± 0.90	9.40 ± 2.70	1.04 ± 0.16	0.51 ± 0.10	1.07 ± 0.29

estimate of the part scores, without the related upper and lower bounds, performance drops significantly. However when using bounding intervals to accommodate the 'slack' due to the approximation error the performance directly becomes identical to the PCA-based cascade. However our method does not require additional threshold estimation, and as shown later is faster.

On the right plot we compare the performance of our lookup-based variant of DTBB for different values of p_e; we observe that for small values of p_e the performance is identical with GDTs, but with larger values of p_e performance decreases. Again, this validates the need for incorporating uncertainty in lookup-based approximations. This is consistent with the observations in [1] where performance was observed to drop, even when using a model directly trained with the lookup-based approximation to the features; it is all the more natural that performance drops when using a model trained with the full, clean features and testing with quantized features.

Coming to timing results, we provide in Table I timings gathered from 1000 images of the PASCAL VOC dataset, and averaged over all 20 categories. The first row indicates the time spent to compute part scores by the different methods, and the following rows indicate detection times. We observe that our lookup-based approximations are faster both for DTBB and Cascade Detection for moderate values of the threshold θ; in particular for $\theta = -.7$, or $\theta = -.5$ the lookup-based variant of cascades requires approximately half the time of the PCA-based cascade, and $1/30$ of the time of GDT-based detection. For more conservative threshold values the part score is fully evaluated at more points and the merits of the first fast pass get eliminated.

6   Conclusion

In this work we introduce Chebyshev's inequality to bound part scores in a simple and computationally efficient manner. We demonstrate the merit of our approach by combining the part score bounds with Branch-and-Bound and Cascade detection for deformable part models, which results in substantial speedups without loss in accuracy.

References

1. Vedaldi, A., Zisserman, A.: Sparse Kernel Approximations for Efficient Classification and Detection. In: CVPR (2012)
2. Kokkinos, I.: Rapid deformable object detection using dual-tree branch-and-bound. In: NIPS (2011)
3. Kokkinos, I.: Rapid Deformable Object Detection using Bounding-based Techniques. Technical Report 7940, INRIA (2012)
4. Felzenszwalb, P.F., Girshick, R.B., McAllester, D.A.: Cascade object detection with deformable part models. In: CVPR (2010)
5. Felzenszwalb, P.F., Huttenlocher, D.: Efficient Matching of Pictorial Structures. In: CVPR (2000)
6. Felzenszwalb, P.F., Girshick, R., McAllester, D., Ramanan, D.: Object Detection with Discriminatively Trained Part-Based Models. IEEE T. PAMI (2010)
7. Felzenszwalb, P.F., Girshick, R.B., McAllester, D.: Discriminatively trained deformable part models, release 4,
   http://people.cs.uchicago.edu/~pff/latent-release4/
8. Pedersoli, M., Vedaldi, A., Gonzàlez, J.: A coarse-to-fine approach for fast deformable object detection. In: CVPR (2011)
9. Viola, P., Jones, M.: Rapid Object Detection using a Boosted Cascade of Simple Features. In: CVPR (2001)
10. Fleuret, F., Geman, D.: Coarse-to-fine face detection. IJCV (2001)
11. Sapp, B., Toshev, A., Taskar, B.: Cascaded Models for Articulated Pose Estimation. In: Daniilidis, K., Maragos, P., Paragios, N. (eds.) ECCV 2010, Part II. LNCS, vol. 6312, pp. 406–420. Springer, Heidelberg (2010)
12. Lampert, C., Blaschko, M., Hofmann, T.: Beyond sliding windows: Object localization by efficient subwindow search. In: CVPR (2008)
13. Lampert, C.H.: An efficient divide-and-conquer cascade for nonlinear object detection. In: CVPR (2010)
14. Kokkinos, I., Yuille, A.: HOP: Hierarchical Object Parsing. In: CVPR (2009)
15. Sun, M., Telaprolu, M., Lee, H., Savarese, S.: An efficient branch-and-bound algorithm for optimal human pose estimation. In: CVPR (2012)
16. Dalal, N., Triggs, B.: Histograms of oriented gradients for human detection. In: CVPR, vol. 2, pp. 886–893 (2005)
17. Vedaldi, A., Fulkerson, B.: VLFeat: An open and portable library of computer vision algorithms (2008), http://www.vlfeat.org/
18. Mitzenmacher, M., Upfal, E.: Probability and computing - randomized algorithms and probabilistic analysis. Cambridge University Press (2005)

Learning Compact Visual Attributes
for Large-Scale Image Classification

Yu Su and Frédéric Jurie

GREYC — CNRS UMR 6072, University of Caen Basse-Normandie, Caen, France
{yu.su,frederic.jurie}@unicaen.fr

Abstract. Attributes based image classification has received a lot of attention recently, as an interesting tool to share knowledge across different categories or to produce compact signature of images. However, when high classification performance is expected, state-of-the-art results are typically obtained by combining Fisher Vectors (FV) and Spatial Pyramid Matching (SPM), leading to image signatures with dimensionality up to 262,144 [1]. This is a hindrance to large-scale image classification tasks, for which the attribute based approaches would be more efficient. This paper proposes a new compact way to represent images, based on attributes, which allows to obtain image signatures that are typically 10^3 times smaller than the FV+SPM combination without significant loss of performance. The main idea lies in the definition of intermediate level representation built by learning both image and region level visual attributes. Experiments on three challenging image databases (PASCAL VOC 2007, CalTech256 and SUN-397) validate our method.

1 Introduction

Attribute based image classification [2–6] – in which an image is represented by a set of meaningful visual attributes – has several interesting properties such as the ability to handle large number of categories or the compactness of image representation. For example, in [5], an image is represented by a 2659-d binary vector, each of which corresponds to a visual attribute. However, the attribute based methods typically need a large amount of human efforts, *i.e.* manually defining visual attributes and labeling training images for these attributes. The only exception is [6] which learns both discriminative and nameable visual attributes without labeled training images. But this learning process still includes human supervision and therefore is semi-supervised. Another drawback of visual attributes is their classification performance, which is below or comparable to the simple Bag-of-Words histogram when using the same low-level features.

Indeed, recent literature in image classification have shown that the state-of-the-art results are typically obtained by combining Fisher Vectors (FV) and Spatial Pyramid Matching (SPM) which leads to very high dimensional image signatures. For example, as in [1], the fisher vector for an image is 32,768-d and the final image signature with a three level pyramid ($1 \times 1, 2 \times 2, 3 \times 1$) is is 262,144-d. This is a hindrance to large-scale image classification since storing

A. Fusiello et al. (Eds.): ECCV 2012 Ws/Demos, Part III, LNCS 7585, pp. 51–60, 2012.

high dimensional features for thousands of (or even millions of) images and learning classifiers based on them is very difficult if not impossible. Considering that, many methods were proposed to produce compact image signatures.

SPM [7] divides an images into fixed regions which are not guaranteed to be optimal. Thus, some extensions of SPM were proposed to either learn the positions and sizes of regions [8, 9] or learn a weight for each region [10]. Although these methods produce more compact image signatures than SPM by using less regions, the compression rate is only about 1/4 or 1/2 which is far from enough for large-scale classification tasks. The quantization based techniques were also proposed to compress the high dimensional image signatures (*e.g.* [11–13]). Especially, in [13] the product quantizers (PQ) are adopted to compress the FVs to 1/64 of their original size, without significant loss of performance.

In this work, we propose a novel way to automatically (*i.e.* without any additional annotations) learn both image-level and region-level attributes. The former encode the common visual structures of whole images (corresponding to the 1×1 channel of SPM), while the latter encode the common visual structures of image regions (corresponding to the $2 \times 2, 3 \times 1$ channels of SPM). More specifically, to learn the visual attributes, we first compute descriptors (FVs in our case) for training images or regions randomly sampled from training images. Then we build a small set of prototypes (clusters) from these descriptors and train one classifier per prototype. An image is then encoded by measuring the similarities between its descriptors and the prototypes using the pre-learned prototype classifiers. Since the prototypes usually encode high-level visual structures (see Fig.2), they can be also considered as visual attributes. In the follows, we use the words *attribute* and *prototype* interchangeably. The resultant image signature is called as visual attribute feature (VAF). We show by experiments that, compared with some best known methods, the VAF leads to much better trade-off between compactness and classification performance.

2 Method

Our method has two components: offline learning of image/region attributes and online prediction of them. The former learns a set of attributes from both images and image regions and, based on them, the latter produces compact image signatures. Fig. 1 illustrates how to learn and predict region attributes. The process for image attributes is similar.

2.1 Describing Images and Regions

Recently, Fisher Vector (FV) has shown state-of-the-art performance on image classification. FV characterizes the first and second order differences between the local features and the centers of a Gaussian mixture model (GMM) which is learned on the local features extracted from training images. Given a set of local features $\{x_i : i = 1, \dots, N\}$ extracted from an image or an image region, the FV for the k-th GMM component are computed as:

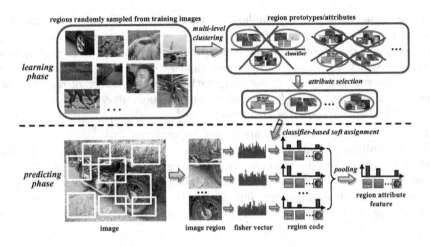

regions randomly sampled from training images   region prototypes/attributes

multi-level clustering

classifier

learning phase

attribute selection

classifier-based soft assignment

predicting phase

pooling

region attribute feature

image   image region   fisher vector   region code

Fig. 1. Learning and prediction of region attributes. See text for details.

$$u_k = \frac{1}{N\sqrt{w_k}} \sum_{i=1}^{N} \gamma_{ik}(\frac{x_i - \mu_k}{\sigma_k}), \quad v_k = \frac{1}{T\sqrt{2w_k}} \sum_{i=1}^{N} \gamma_{ik}[\frac{(x_i - \mu_k)^2}{\sigma_k^2} - 1] \quad (1)$$

where w_k, μ_k, σ_k are the parameters of GMM and γ_{ik} is the soft assignment value. Concatenating both u_k and v_k for all the K components leads to a FV of size $2KD$ where D is the dimension of local features. To speedup the computation of FV, we sparsify the γ_{ik}, *i.e.* set those for which $\gamma_{ik} \approx 0$ to 0. It is worth noting that in this case the FV is still a dense feature vector since the number of GMM components is very small.

In this work, an image is represented by one image-level descriptor and several region-level descriptors. The former is computed by aggregating all the local features from the image into a FV, while the latter are computed by randomly sampling rectangular regions from the image and aggregating the local features within each region into a FV.

2.2 Learning Visual Attributes and Their Predictors

Let $\{f_i : i = 1, \ldots, M\}$ be the FVs extracted from either training images or image regions. Our objective is to obtain a set of visual attributes representing images and regions. We do this by performing spectral clustering [14] on image and region level FVs separately. Each cluster contains visually similar images or regions, and constitutes a visual attribute. In spectral clustering, the FVs are first projected into a low-dimensional manifold by using a similarity matrix of them, and then the traditional k-means is performed on the low-dimensional data to obtain the clusters. Compared with performing k-means directly on the high dimensional FVs, spectral clustering can better capture the intrinsic visual structure of images or regions.

In our implementation, the similarity between two FVs f_i and f_j is computed using a Gaussian kernel $s(f_i, f_j) = \exp(-||f_i - f_j||^2/2\sigma^2)$ where the scaling parameter σ is determined by cross-validation. The visual structures of images or regions, which we aim to capture, can exist at different levels. Thus, in our method, we run the spectral clustering with different number of clusters and aggregate all the so-obtained clusters to form a vocabulary of attributes. We finally have two vocabularies of attributes: $[a_1^g, \ldots, a_{C_g}^g, a_1^l, \ldots, a_{C_l}^l]$, where a^g and a^l are the image and region attributes respectively.

After obtaining visual attributes, we train a classifier (linear SVM in this work) for each of them by the one-vs-rest strategy, producing a set of attribute classifiers $[\phi_1^g, \ldots, \phi_{C_g}^g, \phi_1^l, \ldots, \phi_{C_l}^l]$. The classifier training process is performed for the different clustering levels independently. These attribute classifiers are then used as predictors to produce the attribute features, as described in the next section.

2.3   Generating Visual Attribute Feature

The generation of attribute feature can be considered as an encoding process. The simplest method is the hard assignment in which a vector (FV in our case) is represented by its nearest prototype. The underlying assumption of this strategy is that the vectors satisfy Gaussian mixture distribution and a vector can be represented by a single prototype. To relax this assumption, soft-assignment [15] has been proposed: a vector is assigned to multiple prototypes with assigned values proportional to its similarities to the prototypes. However, this soft-assignment model also assumes the Gaussian mixture distribution of vectors.

In practice, the assumption of Gaussian mixture distribution is not always well satisfied, especially when the dimensionality of feature space is high. In our case, the FVs are much higher dimensional than some common-used local features (e.g. 128-d SIFT). It explains why both the traditional hard-assignment and soft-assignment methods fail to perform well in our case. Thus, we propose in this work a classifier-based soft assignment to encode both image and region descriptors. Specifically, for a descriptor f, its assigned value to an attribute a is computed as

$$\Theta(f, a) = \frac{1}{1 + \exp(-\phi_a(f))} \tag{2}$$

where $\phi_a(f) = w_a^T f + b_a$ is the classifier (linear SVM) of attribute a and the output of ϕ is transformed to $(0, 1)$ by the sigmoid function.

As above mentioned, an image I is represented by an image-level FV and several region-level FVs. For the former, the image signature $\Psi^g(I, a^g)$ is computed by using Eq. (2) directly, i.e. $\Psi^g(I, a^g) = \Theta(f, a^g)$ where f is the image-level FV. For the latter, the image signature is computed by pooling all the encoded image regions:

$$\Psi^l(I, a^l) = \frac{1}{R} \sum_{i=1}^{R} \Theta(f_i, a^l) \tag{3}$$

where f_i is i-th region-level FV extracted from image I and R is the number of regions. Finally, an image is represented by its visual attribute features (VAF):
$A(I) = [\Psi^g(I, a_1^g), \ldots, \Psi^g(I, a_{C_g}^g), \Psi^l(I, a_1^l), \ldots, \Psi^g(I, a_{C_l}^l)]$.

2.4 Producing Compact Image Signature

Since the learned visual attribute have large redundancy, a selection process is needed to get a compact subset of them. Given the original VAF $A = [r_1, ..., r_C]$ obtained in the previous section, a sequential feature selection algorithm (similar to [16]) is used to select a compact subset of features (attributes) with low redundancy. At iteration p, the set A_{p-1}^s of the $p-1$ already selected features is extended by choosing a new feature in $A - A_{p-1}^s$ such as:

$$\hat{r}_p = \underset{r \in A - A_{p-1}^s}{\arg\min} \left(\frac{1}{p-1} \sum_{r_i \in A_{p-1}^s} MI(r, r_i) \right) \quad (4)$$

where $MI(r, r_i)$ is the mutual information between r and r_i which is estimated from the training set. From the information theory point of view, this criterion chooses for each step the feature with the lowest dependence (redundancy) to the set of already selected features. As to A_1^s, in our implementation, it includes a randomly chosen feature.

To get more compact image signature, the A^s is further compressed by using the Locality-Sensitive Hashing (LSH) [17]. Specifically, we draw B random vectors $\{h_b : b = 1, \ldots, B\}$ and represent the image by the sign of $h_b' A^s$ which is a B-bits binary vector.

3 Experiments

3.1 Databases

The proposed method is evaluated on three challenging image databases: PASCAL VOC 2007 [18], Caltech256 [19] and SUN-397 [20].

PASCAL VOC 2007 database contains 9,963 images of 20 object classes. Following the protocol in [18], the performance is measured by the mean Average Precision (mAP) of 20 binary classification tasks.

Caltech256 database contains 256 object categories with about 30K images. Following the protocol in [19], we run the experiments with different numbers of training images per category ($ntrain$=10 and 30). One-vs-rest strategy is used for multiclass classification and the performance is reported as the average classification rate on 256 categories.

SUN-397 database contains 397 scene categories, each of which has at least 100 images collected from the Internet. The experimental setup [20] is similar to that of Caltech256 except that the training images per category is 50.

(a)   (b)   (c)   (d)

Fig. 2. Examples of image prototypes (a) (b) and region prototypes (c) (d)

3.2 Implementation Details

For the local features, we adopt SIFT descriptors extracted on a dense grid of patches over 8 scales separated by a factor 1.2 and the step size is half of the patch-size. The smallest patch size is 16×16 pixels. As in [1], the SIFT descriptors are reduced from 128 to 64 by PCA and modeled by a GMM with 256 components, which results in a FV of 32,768-d ($64 \times 256 \times 2$).

When generating clusters by spectral clustering, 10 different clusterings are done for both image and region level FVs, with the number of clusters varying from 50 to 500 (with an increment of 50), which finally produces 5500 attributes. The train/validation set of PASCAL VOC 2007 is used learn the attribute classifiers and select a compact set of them.

For image classification, the classifier is also learned by linear SVM. The regularization parameter of SVM is also determined on the PASCAL train/validation set. It is worth pointing out that the randomness of the classification performance comes from the randomly sampled image regions, random initialization of attribute selection as well as the randomly selected training images (for CalTech256 and SUN-397 databases). However, in the following experiments, only the averaged performances are reported since the variances in all the experimental settings are no more than 1%.

3.3 Evaluation of Attribute Learning and Prediction

Attribute learning. As above mentioned, the learned prototypes tend to have semantic meanings and therefore can be considered as visual attributes. Fig.2 gives some examples. Specifically, the four prototypes from (a) to (d) can be interpreted as *group of persons*, *animal in the grass*, *vertical structure* and *circular object* respectively. We also compare the spectral clustering with k-means for attribute learning. It can be seen from Fig. 3 that spectral clustering gives better performance no matter how many attributes are selected, which is consistent with our analysis in Section 2.2.

Attribute prediction. In this experiment, we compare the different encoding strategies for attribute prediction as introduced in Section 2.3, *i.e.* traditional distance-based hard/soft assignment and classifier-based hard/soft assignment. Here the classifier-based hard assignment is to assign a image or region descriptor to the attribute with the highest classifier output. It can be seen from Fig. 4 that the classifier-based soft assignment performs best, which validates our analysis

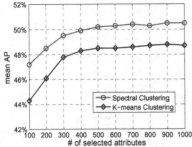
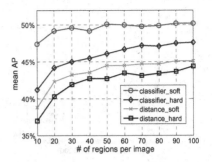
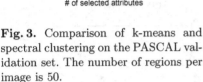

Fig. 3. Comparison of k-means and spectral clustering on the PASCAL validation set. The number of regions per image is 50.

Fig. 4. Comparison of different encoding strategies on the PASCAL validation set. The number of selected attributes is 500.

in Section 2.3. In addition, 50 regions per image gives the best tradeoff between performance and computational cost. Thus, in the following experiments, this parameter is set to 50.

3.4   Evaluation of Real-Valued VAF

In this experiment, we compare the real-valued VAF with the original FV (or BoW histogram) with SPM (1×1, 2×2, 3×1, making a total of 8 channels), as well as other two compact image signatures. The first one is obtained by using PCA to reduce the dimensionality of FV+SPM. The second one is the classemes descriptor [5] which is the output of a large number of weakly trained category classifiers (called as "classemes") on the image. The categories are selected from the LSCOM ontology and the training images are collected by the Bing image search engine. It is worth pointing out that in [5] multiple low-level features (e.g. GIST, HOG and SIFT) are used to learn the classemes. The BoW histogram is built with 1,000 visual words (learned by clustering SIFT features), so its dimensionality with SPM is 8,000.

It can be seen from Fig.5 that the proposed VAF is very compact. Specifically, VAF with 500 dimensions performs slightly worse than the FV+SPM with 262,144 dimensions (less than 3% loss of performance for all the databases). In this case, the compression rate is about 1/500 since both VAF and FV are dense features. With this compact image signature, the time and memory costs for training image classifiers can be greatly reduced. Moreover, the VAF outperforms the PCA reduced feature which validates the effectiveness of representing images by high level visual structures. Compared with the classemes descriptor which can be considered as the image level attribute feature, our method extract both image and region level attributes therefore produce more informative image signature. Besides, the proposed VAF also outperforms the standard BoW histogram.

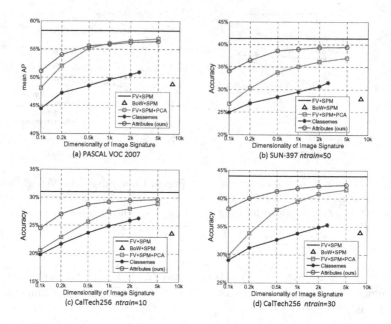

Fig. 5. Comparison of the real-valued VAF with FV+SPM, BoW+SPM, FV+SPM reduced by PCA as well as the classemes descriptor.

3.5   Comparison between Binary VAF and State-of-the-Art

In this experiment, we evaluate the binary VAF which is generated by applying LSH on the selected attribute feature (500-d), and compare them with two state-of-the-art binary image signatures. One is the binary classemes descriptor [5]. The other is the PiCoDes [21] which is learned by explicitly optimizing the performance of classifying 2659 categories randomly sampled from the ImageNet dataset [22]. It can be seen from Fig.6 that the binary VAF outperforms both binary classemes descriptor and PiCoDes except the case of small training samples ($ntrain$=10 on Caltech256 database). Moreover, the VAF is built from single type of local features (*i.e.* SIFT) while both classemes descriptor and PiCoDes are built from multiple types of local features. As to the runtime cost, on a machine with two 3.2GHz CPUs, it takes about 1 second to extract the binary VAF from an image of 500 × 500 pixels, while it takes about 2 seconds to extract binary classemes descriptor or PiCoDes.

Especially, the performance of 4096-bits VAF is almost the same as the 500-d real-valued VAF. In this case, the compression rate relative to the original FV+SPM (with 4 bytes float point for each dimension) is 1/2048 which is much higher than that of product quantizers (1/64) used in [13] to compress the FV.

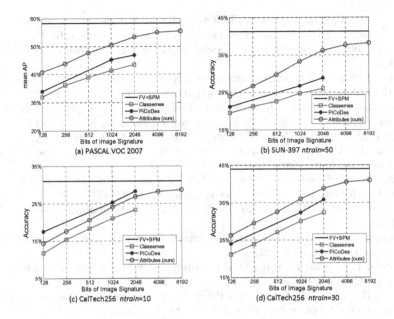

Fig. 6. Comparison of binary VAF with binary classemes descriptor and PiCoDes

4   Conclusions

In this paper, we have introduced compact visual attribute features which encode both image and region level visual structures. Compared with the state-of-the-art fisher vector (with spatial pyramid), the proposed attribute feature is 2048 times smaller with about 3% loss of performance on all the evaluated databases. In the sense of compactness, the proposed attribute feature outperforms the best known methods, e.g. fisher vector with product quantizer [13], classemes descriptor [5] and PiCoDes [21].

It is worth noting that all the learning processes in our method (*e.g.* clustering and classifier training) are performed on PASCAL train/validation set and the learned attributes generalize well for both Caltech256 and SUN-397 databases. Thus, in practice, the visual attributes can be firstly learned in an offline manner and then applied to any classification task. Future works include applying the attribute feature to larger scale image classification (*e.g.* on ImageNet10K [22]) and image retrieval (*e.g.* on Holiday+Flickr1M [23]).

Acknowledgments. This work was partly realized as part of the Quaero Program funded by OSEO, and partly as a part of the ITEA2 RECONSURVE project.

References

1. Perronnin, F., Sánchez, J., Mensink, T.: Improving the Fisher Kernel for Large-Scale Image Classification. In: Daniilidis, K., Maragos, P., Paragios, N. (eds.) ECCV 2010, Part IV. LNCS, vol. 6314, pp. 143–156. Springer, Heidelberg (2010)

2. Li, L., Su, H., Xing, E., Fei-Fei, L.: Object Bank: A High-Level Image Representation for Scene Classification & Semantic Feature Sparsification. In: NIPS (2010)
3. Su, Y., Jurie, F.: Visual word disambiguation by semantic contexts. In: ICCV (2011)
4. Vogel, J., Schiele, B.: Semantic modeling of natural scenes for content-based image retrieval. International Journal on Computer Vision 72, 133–157 (2007)
5. Torresani, L., Szummer, M., Fitzgibbon, A.: Efficient Object Category Recognition Using Classemes. In: Daniilidis, K., Maragos, P., Paragios, N. (eds.) ECCV 2010, Part I. LNCS, vol. 6311, pp. 776–789. Springer, Heidelberg (2010)
6. Parikh, D., Grauman, K.: Interactively building a discriminative vocabulary of nameable attributes. In: CVPR (2011)
7. Lazebnik, S., Schmid, C., Ponce, J.: Beyond bags of features: Spatial pyramid matching for recognizing natural scene categories. In: CVPR (2006)
8. Cao, Y., Wang, C., Li, Z., Zhang, L., Zhang, L.: Spatial-bag-of-features. In: CVPR (2010)
9. Sharma, G., Jurie, F.: Learning discriminative spatial representation for image classification. In: BMVC (2011)
10. Harada, T., Ushiku, Y., Yamashita, Y., Kuniyoshi, Y.: Discriminative spatial pyramid. In: CVPR (2011)
11. Jégou, H., Douze, M., Schmid, C., Pérez, P.: Aggregating local descriptors into a compact image representation. In: CVPR (2010)
12. Perronnin, F., Liu, Y., Sánchez, J., Poirier, H.: Large-scale image retrieval with compressed fisher vectors. In: CVPR (2010)
13. Sanchez, J., Perronnin, F.: High-dimensional signature compression for large-scale image classification. In: CVPR (2011)
14. Ng, A., Jordan, M., Weiss, Y.: On spectral clustering: Analysis and an algorithm. In: NIPS (2001)
15. van Gemert, J., Veenman, C., Smeulders, A., Geusebroek, J.M.: Visual word ambiguity. IEEE Transactions on Pattern Analysis and Machine Intelligence 32, 1271–1283 (2010)
16. Peng, H., Long, F., Ding, C.: Feature selection based on mutual information: criteria of max-dependency, max-relevance, and min-redundancy. IEEE Transactions on Pattern Analysis and Machine Intelligence, 1226–1238 (2005)
17. Charikar, M.: Similarity estimation techniques from rounding algorithms. In: ACM Symposium on Theory of Computing, pp. 380–388 (2002)
18. Everingham, M., Van Gool, L., Williams, C., Winn, J., Zisserman, A.: The PASCAL Visual Object Classes Challenge 2007 results (2007)
19. Griffin, G., Holub, A., Perona, P.: Caltech-256 object category dataset. Technical Report 7694, California Institute of Technology (2007)
20. Xiao, J., Hays, J., Ehinger, K., Oliva, A., Torralba, A.: Sun database: Large-scale scene recognition from abbey to zoo. In: CVPR (2010)
21. Bergamo, A., Torresani, L., Fitzgibbon, A.: Picodes: Learning a compact code for novel-category recognition. In: NIPS (2011)
22. Deng, J., Berg, A.C., Li, K., Fei-Fei, L.: What Does Classifying More Than 10,000 Image Categories Tell Us? In: Daniilidis, K., Maragos, P., Paragios, N. (eds.) ECCV 2010, Part V. LNCS, vol. 6315, pp. 71–84. Springer, Heidelberg (2010)
23. Jegou, H., Douze, M., Schmid, C.: Hamming Embedding and Weak Geometric Consistency for Large Scale Image Search. In: Forsyth, D., Torr, P., Zisserman, A. (eds.) ECCV 2008, Part I. LNCS, vol. 5302, pp. 304–317. Springer, Heidelberg (2008)

Unsupervised Learning of Discriminative Relative Visual Attributes

Shugao Ma[1], Stan Sclaroff[1], and Nazli Ikizler-Cinbis[2]

[1] Department of Computer Science, Boston University
[2] Department of Computer Engineering, Hacettepe University

Abstract. Unsupervised learning of relative visual attributes is important because it is often infeasible for a human annotator to predefine and
manually label all the relative attributes in large datasets. We propose
a method for learning relative visual attributes given a set of images for
each training class. The method is unsupervised in the sense that it does
not require a set of predefined attributes. We formulate the learning as a
mixed-integer programming problem and propose an efficient algorithm
to solve it approximately. Experiments show that the learned attributes
can provide good generalization and tend to be more discriminative than
hand-labeled relative attributes. While in the unsupervised setting the
learned attributes do not have explicit names, many are highly correlated with human annotated attributes and this demonstrates that our
method is able to discover relative attributes automatically.

1 Introduction

There has been increasing interest in visual attribute models for computer vision [1–4]. The key idea is that visual attributes describe properties of entities
and are often shared by many different classes; thus, attribute models learned
on a set of classes can be useful for describing other, previously unseen classes.

Visual attributes can be divided into binary and relative attributes. Previous
studies have mainly focused on binary attributes. Recently, Parikh and Grauman
proposed the use of relative attributes [5], which describe the relative strength
of the presence of a visual attribute. In comparison to binary attributes, relative
attributes are more natural and informative in describing many visual aspects
of objects and scenes.

Attribute learning methods can be divided into supervised and unsupervised
based on the availability of a list of annotated attributes on the training data.
Jointly learning attributes and class models on datasets with labeled attributes
has been widely studied [1–4, 6–9]. All of these methods yield good performance,
particularly with respect to the learned attributes' good generalizability to test
classes that are not present in learning; however, these methods require a human
to predefine the attributes and provide labeled training data.

Supervised learning of attributes has several problems. Firstly, a manually defined set of attributes may be intuitive but not very discriminative for the task
at hand. Secondly, some discriminating attributes may be overlooked or difficult

A. Fusiello et al. (Eds.): ECCV 2012 Ws/Demos, Part III, LNCS 7585, pp. 61–70, 2012.

Fig. 1. Example learned relative attributes for the datasets OSR (top row) and PUB-FIG (bottom row). Each row shows one sample image from each class, presented in order with respect to the learned attribute. In our experiments, the method discovers attributes that are highly correlated with human-labeled attributes: the illustrated attributes highly correlate with human-labeled attributes *Open* and *Young* respectively.

to express in words. Thirdly, attribute labels are produced by annotators' subjective judgements, which may be erroneous [6]. Fourthly, the required human supervision hinders the method's scalability to a large number of attributes.

Other works employ semi-supervised learning of attributes by leveraging information retrieval techniques, e.g., [6, 10–12]. While these techniques reduce the need for annotation, there are two main problems. Firstly, labels from web search or text retrieval tend to be loose and noisy. Secondly, some visual attributes are rarely described by text and are thus hard to learn with these methods.

Another line of work uses active learning to acquire models of attributes. Parikh and Grauman [13] propose a method that automatically identifies binary attributes that are probably *nameable* and asks human annotators to either name the identified attribute or reject it as unnameable. Kovashka, et al. [14] also use active learning to acquire attribute models. Both methods achieve a good balance between the required annotation work and quality of learned attributes; however, they only consider *binary attributes*.

Methods have also been proposed for unsupervised learning of *binary attributes* [2, 4, 12, 15] that provide good generalizability and discriminative properties. However, to the best of our knowledge, there is no previous work on unsupervised learning of *relative attributes*, which is the focus of this paper. Given the demonstrated value of relative attributes and the problems of supervised learning, we would expect our method to be useful. The difficulty in unsupervised learning of relative attributes is that the search space is very large (factorial to the number of classes). Furthemore, certain attributes may only be meaningful to a subset of training classes, depending on whether the strength of the attribute is shared to the same extent among the majority of instances of a class; consequently, the search for relative attributes should also include orderings of subsets of training classes – making the search space even larger.

Contributions: We formulate the unsupervised relative visual attribute learning problem as a mixed integer programming problem and propose an approximation algorithm that performs greedy search in the space of all possible relative attributes. Our method also infers orderings of the relevant training classes with respect to each learned attribute (see examples in Fig. 1). Our experiments on the datasets of [5] show that our automatically learned attributes are discriminative and complementary to hand-labeled relative attributes, and they offer good generalizability to classes that were unseen during training. We also demonstrate that, while in the unsupervised setting the learned attributes do not have explicit semantic names, our method is able to automatically discover all the human annotated attributes for the datasets tested.

2 Automatic Relative Attribute Learning

2.1 Formulation

In training, we are given a set of images $I = \{i\}$ represented by feature vectors $\{x_i\}$ and image class labels $\{c_a\}$. Relative attribute annotations in the form of class orderings are not given; instead, we want to identify those during training along with the set of learned attribute rank functions. To make things simpler, we only consider relative attributes that contain strict pairwise orders. The rank function that we want to learn for each relative attribute a_m is as follows:

$$r_m(x_i^a) = w_m^T x_i^a, \quad s.t. \quad w_m^T x_i^a > w_m^T x_j^b, \; i \in c_a, j \in c_b, c_a \succ c_b, \tag{1}$$

where x_i^a is the feature vector of training image i from class c_a.

Our formulation is based on the one used in [5], and we introduce decision variables to represent missing attribute annotation information. We define $\mu_a = 1$ if the attribute is relevant to c_a otherwise $\mu_a = 0$, and for $\forall a, b, \; a > b$ we define

$$\delta_{ab} = \begin{cases} 1 & c_a \succ c_b \\ -1 & c_a \prec c_b \\ 0 & \mu_a = 0 \vee \mu_b = 0. \end{cases} \tag{2}$$

Intuitively, if an attribute is relevant to more training classes, then it may represent a general attribute that is likely to be relevant to new classes unseen in training. To embody this intuition, we add the ratio of irrelevant classes into the minimization objective. Finally, our formulation for unsupervised relative attribute learning is:

$$\min_{w_m, \xi, \delta, \mu} \quad \frac{1}{2} ||w_m^T||_2^2 + C_1 \sum \xi_{ij,ab}^2 + C_2 (1 - \frac{1}{N} \sum \mu_a) \tag{3}$$

$$s.t. \quad \delta_{ab} w_m^T (x_i^a - x_j^b) \geq min(\mu_a, \mu_b) - \xi_{ij,ab},$$
$$\forall (i, j), i \in c_a, j \in c_b, a > b \tag{4}$$

$$|\delta_{ab} - \delta_{bc}| \geq |\delta_{ab} - \delta_{ac}|, \quad \forall a > b > c, \mu_a = \mu_b = \mu_c = 1 \tag{5}$$

$$|\delta_{ab}| = \mu_a, \quad \forall a \in \{2, \ldots, N\} \tag{6}$$

$$|\delta_{ab}| = \mu_b, \quad \forall b \in \{1, 2, \ldots, N-1\} \tag{7}$$

$$\xi_{ij,ab} \geq 0, \; \delta_{ab} \in \{-1, 0, 1\}, \; \mu_a \in \{0, 1\}. \tag{8}$$

N is the number of training classes, a, b, c are training class indices, and C_1 and C_2 are tradeoff constants among the margin, loss and ratio of irrelevant classes.

For $a > b > c$, constraint (5) requires that if $c_a \succ c_b$, $c_b \succ c_c$ then $c_a \succ c_c$ and if $c_a \prec c_b$, $c_b \prec c_c$ then $c_a \prec c_c$, which enforces that the pairwise orderings between classes do not contradict each other. Constraints (6) and (7) ensure that the value of δ_{ab} is well defined according to (2). For two classes c_a and c_b, if $c_a \succ c_b$ then $\delta_{ab} = 1, \mu_a = \mu_b = 1$ and thus constraint (4) becomes $w_m^T(x_i^a - x_j^b) \geq 1 - \xi_{ij,ab}$; if $c_a \prec c_b$ then $\delta_{ab} = -1, \mu_a = \mu_b = 1$ and constraint (4) becomes $w_m^T(x_i^b - x_j^a) \geq 1 - \xi_{ij,ab}$; if one (or both) of c_a, c_b is irrelevant to the attribute, then one (or both) of μ_a, μ_b becomes zero and (4) reduces to $\xi_{ij,ab} \geq 0$, which essentially removes constraints of irrelevant classes. We note that if the values of μ and δ are fixed (as in the fully supervised setting), then the above reduces to formulation of [5], but considering only strict pairwise orderings.

2.2   Algorithm

The above formulation presents a mixed-integer programming problem and is hard to solve directly. We propose an algorithm to find an effective, approximate solution, which is summarized as follows. At the start of each run of the algorithm we give initial values to μ, δ. Given μ, δ are fixed, we update w_m using an SVM solver. Once w_m is updated, we then fix w_m and update μ, δ. The reduced problem for learning μ, δ is still a mixed integer program, so we propose a greedy algorithm to solve it. The algorithm is run multiple times initialized with every possible pair of classes and each run yields a candidate relative attribute. After learning the set of candidate relative attributes, we remove redundant ones. In our implementation, if the absolute value of the cosine between w_m and w_n is in the range $[0.9, 1]$, then one of the corresponding attributes is removed. Our key ideas in this algorithm are: choosing a broad set of initializations that tend to yield a broad set of useful attributes, and using an efficient algorithm to update μ, δ. More details of our algorithm are given below.

Initialization: At start of the algorithm, we first pick a pair of classes, say c_a and c_b $(a > b)$, and initialize μ and δ as follows:

$$\mu_k = \begin{cases} 1 & k = a \vee k = b \\ 0 & otherwise \end{cases} \qquad \delta_{kh} = \begin{cases} 1 & k = a \wedge h = b \\ 0 & otherwise. \end{cases} \tag{9}$$

Thus, all classes except c_a and c_b are set to be irrelevant to the attribute in this initialization. Additional classes can be discovered as relevant in subsequent iterations. An intuitive explanation for this initialization method is that by making as few assumptions about the initial values of μ, δ as possible, we may consider a broad search space for learning attributes. All possible pairs of classes are used for initialization. As the number of training classes increases, the diversity of the data may also increase, so there may be additional useful relative attributes and the algorithm is run more times to learn these attributes. For a training set of N classes, the total number of class pairs is $\frac{1}{2}N(N-1)$, which is manageable.

Updating w_m: When the values for μ, δ are fixed, learning w_m reduces to a form that is similar to SVM learning but on pairwise difference vectors. We apply a standard SVM solver [16] to learn w_m. To speed up learning, we only generate constraints (4) between classes that are adjacent in the class orderings of that relative attribute. When w_m is learned, we compute the objective value and stop the training if it stops decreasing. If $\mu_a = 1$ for all classes c_a, we also stop training, since no classes remain to be added to the list of relevant classes.

Updating μ, δ: When w_m is fixed, the formulation in Sec. 2.1 is still hard to solve directly. We use a greedy algorithm to solve this problem. At iteration t, we want to pick a class, say c_a, which is labeled as irrelevant by the previous iteration and which will introduce the least additional loss if labeled as relevant at this iteration. We then want to add c_a to the list of relevant classes and update the values of μ, δ accordingly. First, for any class c_b such that $\mu_b^{t-1} = 1$, we compute $m_b^t = \text{median}(\{p_j | p_j = w_m^{tT} x_j^b, j \in c_b\})$. The resulting set of m_b^t will divide the real line into several bins. Then, for any class c_a such that $\mu_a^{t-1} = 0$, we compute the entropy e_a^t of the set $\{p | p = w_m^{tT} x_i^a, i \in c_a\}$ over the histogram of the real line whose bin boundaries are negative infinity, the sorted set of m_b^t, and infinity. Finally, we select the class that has the smallest entropy and add it to the list of relevant classes. This strategy selects the relevant class without explicitly computing the pairwise loss. Although the selected class may not be the class that introduces the least loss under the ranking function, it will introduce low loss because the projections of samples in that class tend to aggregate on the projection line between the medians of projections of relevant classes' samples. After selecting a class c_a to add to the list of relevant classes, we update μ, δ

$$\mu_k^t = \begin{cases} \mu_k^{t-1}, & k \neq a \\ 1, & k = a \end{cases} \tag{10}$$

$$\delta_{kh}^t = \begin{cases} \delta_{kh}^{t-1}, & k \neq a \wedge h \neq a \\ 1, & (k = a \ \wedge \ m_a^t > m_h^t) \ \vee \ (h = a \ \wedge \ m_k^t > m_a^t) \\ -1, & (k = a \ \wedge \ m_a^t < m_h^t) \ \vee \ (h = a \ \wedge \ m_k^t < m_a^t) \\ 0, & (k = a \ \wedge \ \mu_h^t = 0) \ \vee \ (h = a \ \wedge \ \mu_k^t = 0) \end{cases} \tag{11}$$

where m_a^t is the median value of the set $\{p_i | p_i = w_m^{tT} x_i^a, i \in c_a\}$.

3 Experiments

To evaluate our formulation, we used two datasets: the Outdoor Scene Recognition (OSR) Dataset [17] containing 2688 images of 8 categories, and a subset of the Public Figure Face Database (PUBFIG) dataset [4] containing 772 images from 8 random identities (almost 100 images each). This is the same setting provided by the authors of [5] and we used the same features: a 512-D gist [17] descriptor for OSR and a combination of 512-D gist descriptor and 45-D *lab* color histogram for PUBFIG. The train/test split was provided with the datasets.

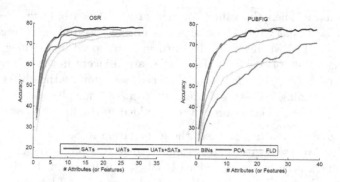

Fig. 2. Multi-class classification results

We conducted experiments that evaluate our learned relative attributes in multi-class classification and K-shot classification. We also conducted an experiment that examines the correlation between our automatically-learned relative attributes and human-labeled relative attributes. Our Matlab implementation will be made available via ftp. The CPU time for attribute learning in Matlab is 127 seconds for OSR and 102 seconds for PUBFIG (28 attributes on each dataset) on a laptop (2.4 GHz Intel Core 2 Duo, 2G memory).

3.1   Multi-class Classification

In this experiment, we trained multi-class SVM classifiers with an RBF kernel by libsvm [18] using: (a) relative attributes learned by our unsupervised algorithm (UATs); (b) relative attributes learned by the supervised algorithm [5] (SATs); (c) combination (UATs+SATs); (d) linear SVM learned between each pair of classes (BINs); (e) PCA; (f) Fisher's Linear Discriminant between every pair of classes (FLD). The latter three are included as baselines of mid-level features. For SATs, we used the attribute values provided by the authors of [5]. 30 images per class were used for training and the others for testing. The classification accuracy was computed as the mean per-class accuracy, i.e., the number of correctly classified test samples *vs.* total number of test samples. Fig. 2 reports classification accuracy as a function of the number of attributes used. For UATs, SATs, BINs and FLD, we ran the experiments 30 times using different attribute (or feature) orders and report the mean. For UATs+SATs, we used all the SATs while varying the number of UATs, according to the reverse order of their correlation to the SATs, with least-correlated UAT added first, as will be explained in Sec. 3.3. For PCA, the principal components are used in order of their eigenvalue (maximum first).

In Fig. 2, it appears that the performance using SATs is limited by the number of labeled attributes: only 6 annotated relative attributes for OSR and 11 for PUBFIG. However, our algorithm learns more attributes: we learned 25 relative attributes for OSR (3 redundant attributes were removed) and 28 for PUB-FIG. We also observe that combining SATs+UATs increases the classification

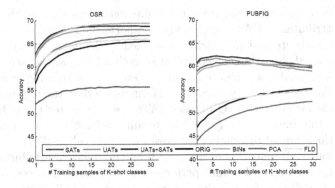

Fig. 3. K-shot classification performance. Total number of classes remains 8.

accuracy over using SATs alone, which shows that the UATs can capture some discriminative information that may be overlooked by humans when labeling the relative attributes. However, the overall performance of UATs+SATs is similar to using only UATs. This is consistent with results reported for binary attributes in [2], and we think it may be due to the high correlation between the labeled relative attributes and some of the relative attributes learned by our algorithm. On both datasets, UATs perform better than mid-level feature baselines. The results show our method performs better than dimensionality reduction techniques PCA and FLD. Note that, our method should not be seen as a dimensionality reduction technique because when the number of classes increases, additional useful attributes may be learned and the resulting attribute space may not be smaller than the raw feature space.

We also compared the ability of BINs and UATs to order the classes, using an entropy criterion similar to the one in Sec. 2.2. The results show that UATs produce class orderings that have lower entropy than for BINs and thus better separate the classes (detailed results are omitted due to space limitations).

3.2 K-Shot Classification

To evaluate the generalizability of learned attributes, we performed K-shot classification. In our setting, 2 classes (we call them *K-shot classes*) were left out and attributes were trained on the other 6 classes. The learned attributes were then used in a 1NN classifier for multi-class classification, with K training images for each K-shot class and all training images for the other classes (30 per class). We plotted the classification accuracy against varying K value for the 1NN classifier. For each possible choice of K-shot classes and choice of K, we repeated the experiment 10 times (each time randomly selecting K training images from each K-shot class) and computed the mean accuracy. We compared 6 image representations: (a) original features (ORIG); (b) SATs; (c) UATs; (d) UATs+SATs; (e) BINs; (f) PCA; (g) FLD. For SATs, we used the code and parameter settings provided by the authors of [5] to learn the attributes.

For PCA, the number of used principal components is set to be the same as number of attributes in UATs+SATs. Fig. 3 reports the results.

The results indicate that the attributes learned by the unsupervised algorithm and the supervised algorithm can complement each other, and also show that the UATs can yield good discrimination even if there are few training examples for a test class. For the OSR dataset, SATs perform worse than the original features (ORIG), while for the PUBFIG dataset SATs preform better than ORIG. We suspect that this may due to the attribute annotations: it is hard to control the quality (in terms of discriminative power and generalizability) of manually labeled attributes. Besides, there are only 6 labeled relative attributes for the OSR dataset, which may also limit performance. Our method discovers a larger set of relative attributes for this dataset, and sidesteps this limitation. When K is small (the more interesting case), UATs perform better than mid-level feature baselines. When K is large, the performances of UATs and BINs are similar, but we emphasize here that comparing to mid-level features, our method is explicitly designed to identifying useful class orderings (Sec. 3.3).

3.3 Correlation Analysis

In this section we analyze the correlation between automatically learned relative attributes and human-labeled relative attributes. For each pair of automatically learned class ordering and manually labeled class ordering, we compute the Kendall Tau correlation:

$$\tau = \frac{n_c - n_d}{\frac{1}{2}n(n-1)} \tag{12}$$

Table 1. Correlation between manually labeled class orderings and automatically learned class orderings. In OSR, classes are coast (C), forest (F), highway (H), inside-city (I), moutain (M), open-country (O), street (S) and tall-building (T). In PUBFIG, classes are Alex Rodriguez (A), Clive Owen (C), Hugh Laurie (H), Jared Leto (J), Miley Cyrus (M), Scarlett Johansson (S), Viggo Mortensen (V) and Zac Efron (Z).

OSR			
Attr. Name	Sem. Attr.	Auto. Learned Attr.	$\hat{\tau}$
natural	T≺I∼S≺H≺C∼O∼M∼F	S≺I≺H≺F≺O	0.89
open	T∼F≺I∼S≺M≺H∼C∼O	T≺F≺S≺O≺C≺H	0.86
perspective	O≺C≺M∼F≺H≺I≺S≺T	O≺F≺H≺I≺S	1
large-objects	F≺O∼M≺I∼S≺H∼C≺T	F≺M≺S≺H≺C≺T	0.97
diagonal-plane	F≺O∼M≺C≺I∼S≺H≺T	F≺O≺M≺I≺H≺S	0.79
close-depth	C≺M≺O≺T∼I∼S∼H∼F	M≺O≺F≺I≺S	0.84
PUBFIG			
Attr. Name	Sem. Attr.	Auto. Learned Attr.	$\hat{\tau}$
Masculine-looking	S≺M≺Z≺V≺J≺A≺H≺C	S≺M≺Z≺A≺H≺C	1
White	A≺C≺H≺Z≺J≺S≺M≺V	A≺Z≺H≺J≺S	0.80
Young	V≺H≺C≺J≺A≺S≺Z≺M	V≺H≺C≺J≺A≺M	1
Smiling	J≺V≺H≺A∼C≺S∼Z≺M	J≺H≺C≺A≺Z	0.95
Chubby	V≺J≺H≺C≺Z≺M≺S≺A	J≺H≺C≺Z≺A≺M	0.87
Visible-forehead	J≺Z≺M≺S≺A∼C∼H∼V	J≺Z≺M≺C≺A≺H	0.89
Bushy-eyebrows	M≺S≺Z≺V≺H≺A≺C≺J	S≺M≺Z≺A≺H≺C	0.73
Narrow-eyes	M≺J≺S≺A≺H≺C≺V≺Z	M≺A≺J≺H≺C	0.80
Pointy-nose	A≺C≺J∼M∼V≺S≺Z≺H	A≺M≺V≺J≺H	0.84
Big-lips	H≺J≺V≺Z≺C≺M≺A≺S	H≺J≺V≺M≺A	1
Round-face	H≺V≺J≺C≺Z≺A≺S≺M	V≺J≺Z≺A≺S	1

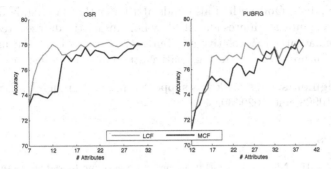

Fig. 4. Multi-class classification by adding unsupervised relative attributes according to the order of their correlation to the labeled relative attributes: LCF - least correlated is added first; MCF - most correlated is added first

where n_c and n_d are the number of concordant and discordant pairs between the two orderings respectively and n is the total number of pairs. The range of τ is in $[-1, 1]$ and it is 1 if the two orderings are the same (-1 if reversely the same). Considering anti-correlation, we used its absolute value: $\hat{\tau} = |\tau|$. Learned class orderings may contain only a subset of classes and in these cases we compute the correlation between the learned class ordering and the corresponding sub-list of the labeled class ordering.

Table 1 shows the results and from it we can see that for all of the human-labeled relative attributes, there are automatically learned relative attributes that are highly correlated with them. One potential application is to learn relative attributes using our unsupervised algorithm before labeling semantic relative attributes, and use these learned attributes as initial guidance for annotation. Furthermore, we observe that some learned relative attributes are not highly correlated with any of the human-labeled relative attributes. These may correspond to attributes that were overlooked by the annotator or hard to be concisely described. We now test the hypothesis that these attributes are indeed useful and can complement the human-labeled relative attributes. In the multi-class classification setting (Sec. 3.1), we start from using all SATs and add UATs one by one, according to their correlation to labeled semantic attributes: (a) most correlated first (MCF); (b) least correlated first (LCF). Fig. 4 shows the results, which validate our hypothesis.

4   Conclusion

We propose a formulation that can efficiently learn relative attributes and infer the training class orderings with respect to each of the learned attributes. The formulation also considers an attribute's relevance to each training class. In our experiments, the learned relative attributes are discriminative and provide good generalizability and classification performance. Compared to supervised learning of relative attributes [5], our algorithm does not need human labeling of attributes and can also learn useful attributes that may be difficult to describe with concise labels. Our method also finds attributes that are highly correlated with all the semantic attributes identified by humans for the datasets tested. The present formulation learns relative attributes at the class level. An interesting direction for future work is learning relative attributes at the instance level.

Acknowledgments. This work was supported in part through US NSF grants 0855065, 0910908, and 1029430.

References

1. Lampert, C.H., Nickisch, H., Harmeling, S.: Learning to detect unseen object classes by between-class attribute transfer. In: CVPR (2009)
2. Farhadi, A., Endres, I., Hoiem, D., Forsyth, D.A.: Describing objects by their attributes. In: CVPR (2009)
3. Farhadi, A., Endres, I., Hoiem, D.: Attribute-centric recognition for cross-category generalization. In: CVPR (2010)
4. Kumar, N., Berg, A.C., Belhumeur, P.N., Nayar, S.K.: Attribute and simile classifiers for face verification. In: ICCV (2009)
5. Parikh, D., Grauman, K.: Relative attributes. In: ICCV (2011)
6. Mahajan, D.K., Sellamanickam, S., Nair, V.: A joint learning framework for attribute models and object descriptions. In: ICCV (2011)
7. Wang, Y., Mori, G.: A Discriminative Latent Model of Object Classes and Attributes. In: Daniilidis, K., Maragos, P., Paragios, N. (eds.) ECCV 2010, Part V. LNCS, vol. 6315, pp. 155–168. Springer, Heidelberg (2010)
8. Yu, X., Aloimonos, Y.: Attribute-Based Transfer Learning for Object Categorization with Zero/One Training Example. In: Daniilidis, K., Maragos, P., Paragios, N. (eds.) ECCV 2010, Part V. LNCS, vol. 6315, pp. 127–140. Springer, Heidelberg (2010)
9. Wang, G., Forsyth, D.A.: Joint learning of visual attributes, object classes and visual saliency. In: ICCV (2009)
10. Ferrari, V., Zisserman, A.: Learning visual attributes. In: NIPS (2007)
11. Berg, T.L., Berg, A.C., Shih, J.: Automatic Attribute Discovery and Characterization from Noisy Web Data. In: Daniilidis, K., Maragos, P., Paragios, N. (eds.) ECCV 2010, Part I. LNCS, vol. 6311, pp. 663–676. Springer, Heidelberg (2010)
12. Rohrbach, M., Stark, M., Szarvas, G., Gurevych, I., Schiele, B.: What helps where - and why? semantic relatedness for knowledge transfer. In: CVPR (2010)
13. Parikh, D., Grauman, K.: Interactively building a discriminative vocabulary of nameable attributes. In: CVPR (2011)
14. Kovashka, A., Vijayanarasimhan, S., Grauman, K.: Actively selecting annotations among objects and attributes. In: ICCV (2011)
15. Torresani, L., Szummer, M., Fitzgibbon, A.: Efficient Object Category Recognition Using Classemes. In: Daniilidis, K., Maragos, P., Paragios, N. (eds.) ECCV 2010, Part I. LNCS, vol. 6311, pp. 776–789. Springer, Heidelberg (2010)
16. Fan, R.E., Chang, K.W., Hsieh, C.J., Wang, X.R., Lin, C.J.: LIBLINEAR: A library for large linear classification. JMLR 9 (2008)
17. Oliva, A., Torralba, A.: Modeling the shape of the scene: A holistic representation of the spatial envelope. IJCV 42(3) (2001)
18. Chang, C.C., Lin, C.J.: LIBSVM: A library for support vector machines. ACM TIST 2, 27:1–27:27 (2011), Software available at http://www.csie.ntu.edu.tw/~cjlin/libsvm

A Method for Online Analysis
of Structured Processes Using Bayesian Filters
and Echo State Networks

Dimitrios I. Kosmopoulos and Fillia Makedon

University of Texas at Arlington,
Computer Science and Engineering, TX 76013, USA
dkosmo@ieee.org, makedon@uta.edu

Abstract. We propose a Bayesian filtering framework for online analysis
of visual structured processes, which can be combined with the Echo
State Network (ESN) to capture prior information. With the proposed
method we mitigate the effective Markovian Behavior of the ESN. We
are able to keep a set of hypotheses about the entire history of behaviors
and to evaluate them online based on new observations. The performance
is evaluated under two complex visual behavior understanding scenarios
using public datasets: a visual process for a kitchen table preparation
and a real life manufacturing process.

1 Introduction

Lately the visual analysis of workflows as part of industrial or other processes
has been gaining momentum, see, e.g., [1], [2], [3], [4], [5]. A workflow is a structured process that occurs repetitively and consists of a sequence of discrete tasks
that need to be recognized. The task order follows some statistically consistent
patterns, which can be modelled as priors.

Our goal is the online labeling of each video frame given a set of available
task labels. The online classification is performed by combining a probabilistic
framework with an online supervised time series classifier such as the Echo State
Network (ESN) [6]. The sole use of a probabilistic framework can only capture
the dynamics between tasks but cannot solve the problem, since we need to know
the statistics of each individual task. On the other hand, the sole use of ESNs
can model adequately each individual task but cannot model accurately the
interaction between tasks because the ESNs have a behavior close to Markovian
(see, e.g., [7]), which is not the case for the sequence of industrial tasks.

Contribution. We present a method to enhance the performace of the ESN
classifier for workflows. Specifically, we combine the advantages of the ESN and of
a probabilistic framework based on particle filtering and we exploit prior knowledge about task dynamics and workflow hierarchy. We aim to show that this
framework works better than (a) a classifier that makes an explicit Markovian
assumption (Hidden Markov Model - HMM) and (b) a classifier that effectively

A. Fusiello et al. (Eds.): ECCV 2012 Ws/Demos, Part III, LNCS 7585, pp. 71–80, 2012.

behaves as a Markovian one (ESN). The approach is applicable to any online classifier that calculates observation probabilities.

2   Related Work

A popular framework for time series analysis is the HMM (see e.g., [8]). It is efficient for application in previously segmented sequences (see e.g., [1]), however when the boundaries of the sequence are not known the search very inefficient [9]. In [10] a dynamic programming algorithm of (restrictive) cost T^3, is used to segment and then classify the sequences. In [11] action sequences are segmented using a margin criterion, however Markovian behavior is assumed.

Here we examine workflows which are composed of tasks and therefore are of hierarchical nature. Typical approaches that exploit the hierarchical structure of time series, are the hierarchical HMMs [12] or the layered hidden Markov model (LHMM) ([13]). Examples of such approaches for visual workflows can be found in [3]. In many workflows, the whole history of tasks is required, because it affects the appearance of future tasks (tasks that are executed are not expected and tasks not already executed are expected to appear later); therefore the Markovian assumption is not correct and this fact motivates methods that relax this assumption. In [14] Rao Blackwell particle filters were used along with a dynamic Bayesian network for tracking of hierarchical events. In [15] a method based on a Bayesian filter and HMMs was proposed for visual analysis. In [16], [17] the utility of particle filters in combination with an HMM is noticed, however, in these works observation predictions are performed, which is different from our online classification problem.

The ESN, see, e.g., [18], is a very promising method for general online classification of time series. It has been proved to be more robust than the HMM (see, e.g., [19], and TDNN [20]. It offers several benefits such as (i) fast and simple learning of many outputs simultaneously, (ii) possibilities of both off-line and on-line learning and testing, (iii) ability to learn complex dynamic behaviors, and (iv) directly dealing with high dimensional input data.

The ESN appears to be an attractive option for analysis of workflows (see e.g., [2]), since it does not make any explicit Markovian assumptions. However, it was shown in [7] that it effectively behaves as a Markovian classifier, i.e., recent states have a far larger influence on the predicted state. Therefore some additional methods are required for workflow analysis, to mitigate this effect.

In [21] an ESN was used to classify a whole sequence after the tasks get completed and segmented. Unlike in [21] here we assign a task label for each frame online, without waiting for the tasks to finish and we do not need to perform any explicit segmentation (thus no related training is required).

3   The Online Classification Framework

We denote as $\mathbf{x}_t$ the state vector including the label l_t from the L classes (tasks) that has to be assigned to frame t. Our goal is to calculate the posterior $p\left(\mathbf{x}_{0:t}|\mathbf{o}_{1:t}\right)$ at every t, given the measurements $\mathbf{o}_{1:t}$(visual observations) up to t. *We emphasize that the* $\mathbf{x}_{0:t}$ *denotes the label sequence for the whole workflow history, and our ultimate goal is to calculate this exact sequence.*

A very attractive option is the ESN, which is a discrete time, continuous state, recurrent neural network proposed in [6]. Learning complexity is kept low while good generalization can be achieved on various dynamic problems. The hidden layer consists of N randomly connected neurons (N is typically in the order of a few hundred or several thousands). If the connectivity is low, this layer provides independent output trajectories. For this reason, the hidden layer is also called a "reservoir". Furthermore, there are neurons which are connected to cycles in the reservoir, so that past states "echo" in the reservoir.

The big advantage of the ESN is that it can be considered as a black box that can label the data sequences in a online fashion, i.e., given a sequence of observations $\mathbf{o}_{1:t}$, it can calculate the label $\mathbf{x}_{t+1}$ for the current observation $\mathbf{o}_{1:t}$ (it is assumed that the nework is trained properly). To mitigate the effectively Markovian behavior of the ESN, i.e., recent states play far more important role, we propose to use particle filters to capture the entire label history. A possible method to calculate $p\left(\mathbf{x}_{0:t}|\mathbf{o}_{1:t}\right)$ is by employing a Bayesian filter, commonly expressed as:

$$p\left(\mathbf{x}_{0:t}|\mathbf{o}_{1:t}\right) = p\left(\mathbf{x}_{0:t-1}|\mathbf{o}_{1:t-1}\right)\frac{p\left(\mathbf{o}_t|\mathbf{x}_{0:t},\mathbf{o}_{1:t-1}\right)p\left(\mathbf{x}_t|\mathbf{x}_{0:t-1},\mathbf{o}_{1:t-1}\right)}{p\left(\mathbf{o}_t|\mathbf{o}_{1:t-1}\right)} \qquad (1)$$

To estimate the fraction term of the right part of equation (1) we proceed as follows. *First*, the term $p\left(\mathbf{o}_t|\mathbf{o}_{1:t-1}\right)$ is independent of the class to which the current observations should be assigned to, so it can be omitted from the following calculations. *Second*, it is reasonable to assume that the current observation $\mathbf{o}_t$ depends only on the current task $\mathbf{x}_t$, so we simplify $p\left(\mathbf{o}_t|\mathbf{x}_{0:t},\mathbf{o}_{1:t-1}\right)$ to $p(\mathbf{o}_t|\mathbf{x}_t)$. *Third*, for the term $p\left(\mathbf{x}_t|\mathbf{x}_{0:t-1},\mathbf{o}_{1:t-1}\right)$ we propose an alternative expression, which is simply $p(\mathbf{x}_t|\mathbf{x}_{0:t-1})$; the latter holds because if the task history is known then the observation history does not affect the appearance of the next task. It is also reasonable to assume that in an industrial setting each task has a duration, which can be expressed by a probabilistic function, which can be learned. Therefore the state vector $\mathbf{x}_t$ is decomposed to $\mathbf{x}_t = (x_t^l, x_t^D)$, where x_t^l is the label of the current observations (in other words the task/class to which the current observations are assigned) and x_t^D is the residual duration of the current task.

Under these assumptions equation (1) simplifies to:

$$p\left(\mathbf{x}_{0:t}|\mathbf{o}_{1:t}\right) \propto p\left(\mathbf{x}_{0:t-1}|\mathbf{o}_{1:t-1}\right) \cdot p\left(\mathbf{o}_t|\mathbf{x}_t\right)p\left(\mathbf{x}_t|\mathbf{x}_{0:t-1}\right) \qquad (2)$$

As observed in equation (2), the posterior probability $p\left(\mathbf{x}_{0:t}|\mathbf{o}_{1:t}\right)$ is proportional to a) the recurrent term $p\left(\mathbf{x}_{0:t-1}|\mathbf{o}_{1:t-1}\right)$, b) the probability $p(\mathbf{o}_t|\mathbf{x}_t)$, which expresses the observation model for each task, i.e., observations probability coming from the time series classifier c) the $p(\mathbf{x}_t|\mathbf{x}_{0:t-1})$, which expresses our a priori knowledge about task duration and transition from one state to another. Given the simplification of the general framework in (2), in the following we propose ways to integrate in a real time classification framework observations from multiple streams (see (b)) and prior knowledge (see (c)).

3.1 Integrating A-Priori Knowledge

The estimation of the probability $p(x_{0:t}|o_{1:t})$ requires the a priori knowledge about task *duration* and *transition* between tasks.

The *duration* d of a task k is stochastic and can be represented as a pdf $p_k(d)$. We used offline trained Gaussian mixture models to represent prior information about expected duration of tasks. In our notation we use the concept of residual duration of a task (the remaining time until the finalization of the task). The residual duration is denoted as x_t^D. As presented in (3) when we first enter task k, x_t^D is set to a value sampled from the pdf $p_k(d')$; then the residual duration decrements to zero. When x_t^D becomes zero then the task will change according to the probabilities given by a decision tree $T_{x_{0:t}}$ (see (4)). $T_{x_{0:t}}$ is a decision

$$P(x_t^D = d'|x_{t-1}^D = d, x_t^l = k) = \begin{cases} p_k(d') & if \ d = 0 \ (reset) \\ \delta(d', d-1) & if \ d > 0 \ (decrement) \end{cases} \tag{3}$$

$$P(x_t^l = j|x_{t-1}^l = i, x_{t-1}^D = d) = \begin{cases} \delta(i,j) & if \ d > 0 \ (same \ task) \\ T_{x_{0:t}} & if \ d = 0 \ (task \ \ transition) \end{cases} \tag{4}$$

tree holding the priors about the *transition* between different tasks given the previous history of tasks. Assume that k_o is the task that appears in order o, given all previous tasks. Then we denote the associated pdf as $p(k_o|k_{0:o-1})$. In case of non zero value for that probability there will be a node at the o-th level of the tree with value equal to k_o; also it will be connected to its parent via an edge of weight equal to $p(k_o|k_{0:o-1})$; the parent (on the $(o-1)$-th level of the tree) has value k_{o-1}. The root of the tree has a virtual task value k_0, while its children indicate the tasks that may start the workflow (the edges are the associated priors). A complete task sequence is represented by a path connecting the root with any of the tree leaves. Given a path P, of L tasks going from k_0 to k_L the probability of $p(P)$ is given by

$$p(P) = \prod_{l=0}^{L} p(k_l|k_{0:l-1}) \tag{5}$$

which is the product of the associated probabilities for all the links in the path. Such a tree can be learned by using a training set of full workflows, and therefore the "legitimate" paths and their probabilities can be specified. More specifically, for each parent node we find the possible successors (descendants) and based on the normalized frequency that a specific child is selected as next task, we assign a probability value to the connecting edge. Since the history of all previous different tasks is maintained by using such a tree, we do not rely on the Markovian assumption. At this point we clarify that $p(k_o|k_{0:o-1})$ by definition indicates only the transitions between different tasks ($k_o \neq k_{o-1}$).

In summary, we devised a representation of $p(\mathbf{x}_t|\mathbf{x}_{t-1})$ by (3), (4), which includes our prior knowledge about the duration and the transition between tasks. That representation is valuable for sampling and hypotheses evaluation, as will be explained in the following.

3.2 Evaluating Hypotheses

The main difficulty of solving equation (2) is that it involves dependencies from previous observations (visual descriptors) and classification (observation assignment to one of the L available classes). To handle the dependencies of the posterior probability $p(\mathbf{x}_{0:t}|\mathbf{o}_{1:t})$ with the previous frame states (i.e., frame classification), we need first to introduce our set of hypotheses and then to validate them under a probabilistic framework.

Let us assume that we have a set of H available hypotheses (particles). A hypothesis describes a particular combination of the classes that the previous frames have been assigned to, in other words it is a particular assignment of labels for $\mathbf{x}_{0:t}$. Every hypothesis is evaluated through the Bayesian filters, which are estimation methods based on simulation and previous observations [22].

Weights are associated to the hypotheses, expressing the significance degree to the modeling process. Therefore given H hypotheses we have H weighted particle trajectories $\left\{ \mathbf{x}_{0:t-1}^{(n)}, w_{0:t-1}^{(n)} \right\}_{n=1}^{H}$. Each of these trajectories approximates the posterior probability $p(\mathbf{x}_{0:t-1}|\mathbf{o}_{1:t-1})$ up to time $t - 1$. The current weight $w_t^{(n)}$ for the nth hypothesis at the current frame t is estimated through the distribution $w_t^{(n)} = p(\mathbf{o}_t|x_t^{(n)})$

We can estimate the weights $w_t^{(n)}$ if we know a hypothesis, i.e., we know the class x_t^l to which observation t belongs, as well as the respective duration x_t^D. The pdf of the weights derives from the ESN output (the L outputs are normalized to express a probability). The hypothesis about the value of $\mathbf{x}_t$ requires a priori knowledge regarding task duration and order of tasks and is generated by sampling the pdf $p(\mathbf{x}_t|\mathbf{x}_{t-1})$ using (3), (4). The related pdfs are estimated offline (see subsection 3.1).

The hidden system state space (current task-related label) is one-dimensional and discrete, with low number of possible values (equals to the number of possible tasks). Also the duration is actually sampled only during task transition and in the other cases the sampling is trivial because it decrements with probability equal to one. Therefore the method is efficient because only a relatively low number of particles is required. An overview is given in Algorithm 1.

4   Experiments and Results

4.1   The Workflow Recognition Dataset

The workflow recognition dataset [23] depicts real workers on the production line and includes tasks of picking several parts from racks and placing them on

Algorithm 1. Proposed Method

{OFFLINE TRAINING}
{Decision tree learning}
$T_{x_{0:t}}$ = LearnTree(AllTaskPaths)
{Supervised task learning through ESN}
for $k = 1$ to $NumberOfTasks$ **do**
  $p_k(d)$ = LearnDuration(AllTaskInstances,k)
end for
esn = TrainESN(TrainingStream, Labels)
{ONLINE CLASSIFICATION FRAMEWORK}
while input==TRUE **do**
  {The loop executes for all t}
  F=AcquireFrame()
  $\mathbf{o}_t$ = ProcessFrame(F); {extraction of observations}
  for $k = 1$ to $NumberOfTasks$ **do**
    $p(\mathbf{o}_t|\mathbf{x}_t = s)$ = CalcObservationProb(esn, $\mathbf{o}_{1,t}, ..., \mathbf{o}_{M,t}$)
  end for
  {for every Hypothesis do}
  for $n = 1$ to H **do**
    $\mathbf{x}_t^{(n)} = Sample\ p\left(\mathbf{x}_t|\mathbf{x}_{0:t-1}^{(n)}\right)$ {use eq. (3), (4) }
    $Weight\ \mathbf{x}_t^{(n)}$ by: $w_t^{'(n)} = p\left(\mathbf{o}_t|\mathbf{x}_t^{(n)}\right)$
  end for
  for $n = 1$ to H **do**
    $Normalize$ the weights by: $w_t^{(n)} = \dfrac{w_t^{'(n)}}{\sum_{n_1=1}^{H} w_t^{'(n_1)}}$
  end for
  Switching-state particles with low weight are set back to previous state.
  for $n = 1$ to H **do**
    Update $p(\mathbf{x}_{0:t}^{(n)}|\mathbf{o}_{1:t})$ {use eq. (2) }
  end for
  The winner is the particle $n_0 : p(\mathbf{x}_{0:t}^{(n_0)}|\mathbf{o}_{1:t}) \geq p(\mathbf{x}_{0:t}^{(n)}|\mathbf{o}_{1:t}), \forall n \in \{1, ..., H\}$
end while

---

a designated cell some meters away, where welding took place. The behaviors (tasks) we were aiming to model are: (1) One worker picks part #1 from rack #1 and places it on the welding cell, (2) Two workers pick part #2a from rack #2 and place it on the welding cell. (3) Two workers pick part #2b from rack #3 and place it on the welding cell. (4) A worker picks up parts #3a and #3b from rack #4 and places them on the welding cell. (5) A worker picks up part #4 from rack #1 and places it on the welding cell. (6) Two workers pick up part #5 from rack #5 and place it on the welding cell. The most common task sequences were 1-2-3-4-5-6, 1-2-3-5-4-6 and 1-2-3-4-6-5.

For our experiments, we have used 20 sequences representing full assembly cycles, each one containing each of the defined behaviors and camera 32 from workflow 1. The length of each sequence ranged from 2000 to 4000 frames. We used the provided annotation. The dataset involves several occlusions and par-

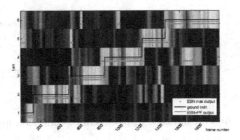

Fig. 1. Heat diagram representing the responses of the 6 ESN outputs for an industrial scenario. Values close to zero are colored deep blue, values close to one are colored red, and intermediate values by the corresponding colors. The maximum outputs are marked by green dots. Superimposed is the ground truth and the ESN+PF response.

tially overlapping views. The features in the dataset were Zernike moments of motion history images with dimension of 31 see, e.g., [1] for details.

The ESN had a linear regression reservoir (changing the ESN type did not favor any of the compared methods) of 500 plain nodes, which was efficient for real time execution, small enough to avoid overfitting and effective. Increasing the number of nodes would result in high memory requirements without real benefit. We had six output nodes, corresponding to six tasks. The median of the last 31 estimations was taken for lower output jitter. We have used the Matlab toolbox provided by the authors [18] using spectral radius 0.60, input scaling 0.3 and smoothing of noise level 0.0003 for optimal results. We trained the ESNs with the entire workflows and applied five-fold cross validation.

For the particle filter we used only 200 particles, which was a good trade-off, and we were able to perform the whole processing at a rate of about 20Hz, the most costly of which was the feature extraction. The confusion matrix per task for a typical case is given in Fig. 2. The learning phase included learning the task durations using a Gaussian mixture model, the task trajectories using a decision tree and the task models using HMMs.

In figure 1 we display the response of the ESN as a heat diagram and we compare it to the ground truth as well as to our ESN+PF approach. More specifically, the 6 outputs of the ESN (corresponding to the six tasks) are normalized, so that they constitute a probability function. Values close to zero are represented by deep blue, values close to one are represented by red, and the intermediate values by the corresponding colors.

The particle that was able to explain best the sequence according to (2) was considered to be the winner. In all cases the work cycle, which consisted of all tasks 1 to 6 was successfully recognized. Clearly our method (ESN+PF) outperforms the simple ESN. The latter tends to assign labels based almost only on the current and the very recent observations ignoring the history of tasks. As expected it behaves efficiently as a Markovian classifier, therefore a task can be misinterpreted as any other task as revealed by in Fig.2. On the contrary the ESN+PF makes estimations which even if not correct they are very close to the currently executed task, giving a better estimation of the executed task sequence.

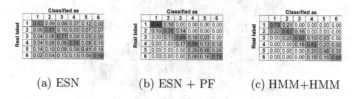

(a) ESN   (b) ESN + PF   (c) HMM+HMM

Fig. 2. The WR dataset: Comparison of confusion matrices

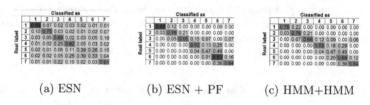

(a) ESN   (b) ESN + PF   (c) HMM+HMM

Fig. 3. The TUM kitchen dataset: Comparison of confusion matrices

The output of the simple ESN was used for the ESN+PF, so the comparison of the two methods is fair.

To show the effect of the invalidity of the Markovian assumption we also used a method based on the HMM. Firstly we *segmented* the sequences into tasks and then we *classified* each segment. For the *segmentation* task we trained an HMM to detect the task transitions, within a time widnow similarly to [21].

As for the classification task, we trained one HMM per task (*L* task-HMMs). Then we defined one HMM for the tested workflows (1 workflow-HMM) in a hierarchical fashion. The states of the workflow-HMM were defined by the detected segments, the emitted observations were the probabilities for each task as provided by the task-HMMs, the transition matrix was given by the transition probabilities between the tasks, and the prior was given by the tasks' priors (same as the ones used for the ESN+PF). Then we run the Viterbi algorithm to find the sequence of tasks for the workflow-HMM. This scheme will be hereafter referred to as HMM+HMM. The performance seems to be inferior to the ESN+PF and the errors stem from the Markovian assumption, the errors in the segmentation (the segmenation accuracy was measured as 14.1 ± 10.3 frames *mean $\pm$ std.*) and the inaccuracies of the observation model.

4.2   The TUM Kitchen Dataset Case

Another workflow application is presented by the TUM kitchen dataset [24] (also publicly available). It contains several instances of a table-setting workflow performed by different subjects, involving the manipulation of objects and the environment. For our purposes we have used the views camera 0 to recognize the following sequential tasks (where different permutations are allowed): (1) Taking a tray and putting it on the table. (2) Taking a napkin and putting it on the table (3) Opening a drawer, taking a fork and putting it on the table (4) Opening a drawer (the same as in 3), taking a knife and putting it on the table (5) Opening a drawer (the same as in 3, 4), taking a spoon and putting it on the table. (6) Opening a shelf, taking out a plate and putting it on the table (7) Opening a shelf, taking out a cup and putting it on the table. The most common task sequences were 1-2-3-4-5-6-7, 1-2-4-5-6-3-7 and 1-2-3-7-4-5-6.

We have used workflows/episodes with IDs: 0_0, 0_1, 0_3, 0_4, 0_6, 0_7, 0_8, 0_9, 0_10, 0_11, 1_0, 1_1, 1_2, 1_3, 1_4, 1_6, 1_7 in a 4-fold cross validation scheme. The ground truth was based on the annotation provided in the dataset. As soon an object was arranged on the table and the subject started heading away from it, we marked that point as the end of the current segment and the beginning of a new one. We also extracted similar features as in the previous application.

The results obtained for the ESN, ESN+PF and HMM+HMM methods (Fig. 3), were similar to the previous application. We note that tasks 4, 5 and 6 bear a great resemblance since they consist in opening the same drawer, picking a similar object (fork, knife, or spoon) and placing it on the table, thus it is quite difficult for a classifier to differentiate among them; that is confirmed by the misclassification rates among tasks 4, 5, 6.

5 Conclusions

We proposed an online framework for behavior recognition in workflows in real-time. We verified the effectively Markovian behavior of the ESN and we showed how to mitigate it by using a priori information, which can be embedded in a set of hypotheses (particles). The a priori information about the tasks sequence gave better results than the conventional ESN. It also gave better results compared to making an explicit Markovian assumption like by using a hierarchy of HMMs.

References

1. Kosmopoulos, D., Chatzis, S.: Robust visual behavior recognition. IEEE Signal Processing Magazine 27, 34–45 (2010)
2. Veres, G., Grabner, H., Middleton, L., Van Gool, L.: Automatic Workflow Monitoring in Industrial Environments. In: Kimmel, R., Klette, R., Sugimoto, A. (eds.) ACCV 2010, Part I. LNCS, vol. 6492, pp. 200–213. Springer, Heidelberg (2011)
3. Padoy, N., Mateus, D., Weinland, D., Berger, M.O., Navab, N.: Workflow Monitoring based on 3D Motion Features. In: Workshop on Video-Oriented Object and Event Classification in Conj. with ICCV 2009, Kyoto, pp. 585–592. IEEE (2009)
4. Behera, A., Cohn, A.G., Hogg, D.C.: Workflow Activity Monitoring Using Dynamics of Pair-Wise Qualitative Spatial Relations. In: Schoeffmann, K., Merialdo, B., Hauptmann, A.G., Ngo, C.-W., Andreopoulos, Y., Breiteneder, C. (eds.) MMM 2012. LNCS, vol. 7131, pp. 196–209. Springer, Heidelberg (2012)
5. Lalos, C., Voulodimos, A., Doulamis, A., Varvarigou, T.: Efficient tracking using a robust motion estimation technique. Mult. Tools and Applications, 1–16 (2012)
6. Jaeger, H.: The echo state approach to analysing and training recurrent neural networks. Technical Report GMD 148, German National Research Center for Information Technology (2001)

7. Gallicchio, C., Micheli, A.: Architectural and markovian factors of echo state networks. Neural Networks 24, 440–456 (2011)
8. Rabiner, L.R.: A tutorial on hidden Markov models and selected applications in speech recognition. Proceedings of the IEEE 77, 257–286 (1989)
9. Eickeler, S., Kosmala, A., Rigoll, G.: Hidden markov model based continuous online gesture recognition. In: ICPR, pp. 1206–1208 (1998)
10. Lv, F., Nevatia, R.: Recognition and Segmentation of 3-D Human Action Using HMM and Multi-class AdaBoost. In: Leonardis, A., Bischof, H., Pinz, A. (eds.) ECCV 2006, Part IV. LNCS, vol. 3954, pp. 359–372. Springer, Heidelberg (2006)
11. Hoai, M., Lan, Z.Z., De la Torre, F.: Joint segmentation and classification of human actions in video. In: IEEE Conference on Computer Vision and Pattern Recognition, CVPR (2011)
12. Fine, S., Singer, Y., Tishby, N.: The hierarchical hidden markov model: Analysis and applications. Machine Learning 32, 41–62 (1998)
13. Oliver, N., Garg, A., Horvitz, E.: Layered representations for learning and inferring office activity from multiple sensory channels. Comput. Vis. Image Underst. 96, 163–180 (2004)
14. Xiaoling, X., Layuan, L.: Real time analysis of situation events for intelligent surveillance. In: International Symposium on Computational Intelligence and Design, ISCID 2008, vol. 2, pp. 122–125 (2008)
15. Kosmopoulos, D.I., Doulamis, N.D., Voulodimos, A.S.: Bayesian filter based behavior recognition in workflows allowing for user feedback. Computer Vision and Image Understanding 3, 422–434 (2012)
16. Zhang, D., Ning, X., Liu, X.: Smc method for online prediction in hidden markov models. Kybernetes 38, 1819–1827 (2009)
17. Fei, H.: A hybrid HMM/particle filter framework for non-rigid hand motion recognition. In: ICASSP, vol. 5, pp. V-889–V-892 (2004)
18. Jaeger, H., Maass, W., Principe, J.: Special issue on echo state networks and liquid state machines. Neural Networks 20, 287–289 (2007)
19. Skowronski, M.D., Harris, J.G.: Automatic speech recognition using a predictive echo state network classifier. Neural Networks 20, 414–423 (2007)
20. Venayagamoorthy, G.K.: Online design of an echo state network based wide area monitor for a multimachine power system. Neural Networks 20, 404–413 (2007); Echo State Networks and Liquid State Machines
21. Voulodimos, A., Kosmopoulos, D., Veres, G., Grabner, H., Van Gool, L., Varvarigou, T.: 2011 special issue: Online classification of visual tasks for industrial workflow monitoring. Neural Netw. 24, 852–860 (2011)
22. Arnaud, D., Simon, G., Christophe, A.: On sequential monte carlo sampling methods for bayesian filtering. Statistics and Computing 10, 197–208 (2000)
23. Voulodimos, A., et al.: A dataset for workflow recognition in industrial scenes. In: IEEE Int. Conference on Image Processing, pp. 3310–3313 (2011)
24. Tenorth, M., Bandouch, J., Beetz, M.: The TUM Kitchen Data Set of Everyday Manipulation Activities for Motion Tracking and Action Recognition. In: THEMIS Workshop, In conj. with ICCV (2009)

Monocular Camera Fall Detection System Exploiting 3D Measures: A Semi-supervised Learning Approach

Konstantinos Makantasis[1], Eftychios Protopapadakis[1], Anastasios Doulamis[1], Lazaros Grammatikopoulos[2], and Christos Stentoumis[3]

[1] Technical University of Crete, 73100 Chania, Greece
{konst.makantasis,eft.protopapadakis}@gmail.com, adoulam@cs.ntua.gr
[2] Technological Educational Institute of Athens, 12210, Athens, Greece
lazaros.pcvg@gmail.com
[3] National Technical University of Athens, 15773, Athens, Greece
cstent@mail.ntua.gr

Abstract. Falls have been reported as the leading cause of injury-related visits to emergency departments and the primary etiology of accidental deaths in elderly. The system presented in this article addresses the fall detection problem through visual cues. The proposed methodology utilize a fast, real-time background subtraction algorithm based on motion information in the scene and capable to operate properly in dynamically changing visual conditions, in order to detect the foreground object and, at the same time, it exploits 3D space's measures, through automatic camera calibration, to increase the robustness of fall detection algorithm which is based on semi-supervised learning. The above system uses a single monocular camera and is characterized by minimal computational cost and memory requirements that make it suitable for real-time large scale implementations.

Keywords: image motion analysis, semisupervised learning, self calibration, fall detection.

1 Introduction

According to medical records, traumas resulting from falls have been reported as the second most common cause of death for the elderly and as the most important problem that hinders these people's ability to live an independent life. Therefore, a major research effort has been conducted for automatically detecting persons' falls, either through the use of specialized equipment, (i.e. accelerometers, floor vibration sensors, gyroscope sensors, barometric pressure sensors, sound sensors) [1-4] or through visual cues by using cameras [5-12].

Techniques based on specialized equipment, require the use of wearable devices that should be attached to the human body and thus their efficiency relies on persons' ability and willingness to wear them. On the other hand, vision based systems, a more research challenging alternative due to the complexity of visual

A. Fusiello et al. (Eds.): ECCV 2012 Ws/Demos, Part III, LNCS 7585, pp. 81–90, 2012.
© Springer-Verlag Berlin Heidelberg 2012

content and the fact that a fall should be discriminated than other ordinary humans' activities (i.e. sitting, lie down), present several advantages. They are installed on buildings and not worn by users, are able to detect multiple events simultaneously and the recorded video can be used for post verification analysis. Towards this direction, the works of [6, 7, 11] exploit foreground object's shape, as well as, its vertical motion velocity to detect a fall incident. The authors of [8] and [5] use a wider set of features along with SVM to detect falls. In system of [12] a classifier, capable to discriminate six indoor human activities, is trained based on knowledge derived from human anatomy body parts ratios. Although, experimental results of the above works show high detection rates none of these exploits 3D information to increase system robustness. A 3D active vision system based on Time of Flight cameras is proposed in [9]. However, the measures that are provided by this type of cameras could be affected by reflectivity objects properties and aliasing effects when the camera-target distance overcomes the non-ambiguity range. In [10] a multi camera system that exploits stereo vision is proposed. 3D processing, though more robust than a 2D image analysis in terms of fall detection and discrimination among falls and other daily activities; requires high computational cost that usually making these systems unsuitable for real-time, large scale implementations.

In this paper, a new innovative approach is presented that exploits, on the one hand, monocular cameras to detect falls in real-time and, on the other, it is capable to exploit actual 3D space's measures, through camera calibration and inverse perspective mapping (IPM), to increase system's robustness for a wider range of camera positions and mountings compared to other 2D fall detection methods ([7, 11]). The fall detection algorithm discriminates fall incidents by using a non-Linear Warning System (nLWS) based on semi-supervised learning. Our system, due to its minimal computational cost and memory requirements, let alone its low financial cost since ordinary low-resolution cameras are used, making it affordable for a large scale.

1.1 Problem Formulation

Fall incidents can be discriminated than other human activities by using human motion and posture analysis. Information about humans' posture can be derived by the height-width ratio; in a 3D space this ratio is smaller in value when a fall event occurs compared to humans in standing position. In addition, as explained in [8] and [5], the ellipse that bounds the foreground object and more specifically the angle of its major semi-axis can provide useful information about human posture. This angle is close to 90° when the human is in standing position and close to 0° after a fall incident. Considering on motion information, the most commonly used feature is vertical motion velocity, which during a sequence of frames can be expressed by Eq.(1)

$$V = \sum_{i=k-m}^{k} h_a(i) - h_a(i-1) \tag{1}$$

$h_a(k)$ stands for the actual height of a human in 3D space at the kth image frame. Vertical motion velocity is calculated for a sequence m of frames and is an estimation of the speed of the motion and also an evident of how severe would be a fall. Instead of humans' projected height, we choose to use their actual height, measured in physical world units (e.g., cm, inches), since: (a) this yields a more robust performance not affected by cases where the human is far away or very close to the camera, (b) actual height can provide information about the moving object, making the system capable to discriminate if the moving object might be a human or something else and (c) system's performance improves for a wider range of camera positions and mountings.

In order to extract all these features, first of all, a foreground extraction algorithm has to be used to extract the foreground object, which initially is unknown (Section 2). Width-height ratio computation requires information about left-most q_{lm}, right-most q_{rm}, top-most q_{tm} and bottom-most q_{bm} points of foreground object, to calculate its projected height and width (Section 2.1), while the bounding ellipse can be approximated by using image moments for the foreground object's area (Section 2.2).

Representation of an object on camera's plane is presented in Fig.1(a). It appears that the actual height of foreground object can be given through Eq.(2), if cameras focal length f, distance Z between the camera and foreground object and foreground object's projected height h_p are known.

$$h_a = Z\,\frac{h_p}{f} \tag{2}$$

h_p can be obtained in the same way as width-height ratio, f can be automatically obtained through camera self-calibration (Section 3) and Z can be obtained through the construction of a reference plane Fig.1(c) that is the orthographic view of the floor Fig.1(b) (Section 3.1).

1.2 Proposed Contribution

The main contributions of the proposed system are:

3D measures exploitation using a single monocular camera. Using a single monocular camera along with the exploitation of 3D measures, give our system the opportunity to detect falls in real-time, like 2D fall detection methods, and to approximate the robustness of 3D ones.

Semi-supervised learning fall detection algorithm. A semi-supervised learning approach, let the fall detection algorithm that exploits a non Linear Warning System (nLWS), to be effectively trained by calling an expert to further refine an initially unsupervised created small subset of labeled samples.

Self calibrated fall detection system. The proposed fall detection system utilizes a self calibration technique, to estimate camera parameters, based on the detection of vanishing points. Using of self-calibration creates a *fully* automatic

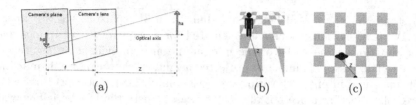

Fig. 1. (a) object representation on camera's plane, (b) floor plane, (c) reference plane

system capable to operate properly without the need of any human user manual configuration.

The rest of this paper is organized as follows: in Section 2 the foreground extraction algorithm is presented along with 2D features extraction, Section 3 presents self calibration method and 3D features extraction, in Section 4 the fall detection algorithm is presented, Section 5 concerns on experimental results and, finally, Section 6 concludes this work.

2   Foreground Extraction and 2D Features

For foreground extraction, we used the technique described in [11], which is based on an iterative scene learning algorithm. This is a lightweight foreground extraction algorithm, with minimal computational cost and memory requirements, capable to operate properly in real-time and in complex, dynamic in terms of visual content and unexpected environments.

It uses the "pyramidal" Lucas-Kanade algorithm to estimate the intensity of motion vectors in a scene, along with their directions, in order to identify humans' movements. Motion information is used as a background updating mechanism, according to which the background is updated at every frame instance by using motion vectors within high motion information areas. If motion vectors' intensity exceeds a threshold then this area is denoted as foreground, otherwise it is denoted as background Fig.2(b).

2.1   Foreground Object's Projected Height-Width Ratio

The first step for width-height ratio computation, is the estimation of foreground object's projected height and width. These two measures can be estimated by the four corners of a minimum bounding box, Fig.2(b), that includes the foreground. The four corners of the minimum bounding box are associated with foreground object's q_{lm}, q_{rm}, q_{tm} and q_{bm} points and thus height width ratio can be expressed by Eq.(3)

$$R = \frac{h_p}{w_p} = \frac{q_{tm} - q_{bm}}{q_{rm} - q_{lm}} \tag{3}$$

where w_p and h_p stand for the projected width and height of foreground object.

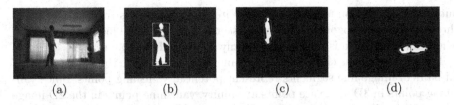

(a)   (b)   (c)   (d)

Fig. 2. (a) original frame, (b) minimum bounding box, (c) approximated ellipse for standing position, (d) approximated ellipse after a fall incident

2.2   Bounding Ellipse Major Semi-axis Angle

For the approximation of an bounding ellipse that includes the foreground object, we based on image moments that can successfully describe objects' properties after segmentation. An ellipse is defined by its center $(\bar{x}, \bar{y})$, its orientation, which is the angle θ of its major semi-axis and the lengths a and b of its major and minor semi-axes.

For a scalar image with pixel intensities $I(x,y)$, spatial image moments are given by

$$M_{ij} = \sum_x \sum_y x^i y^j I(x,y) \quad for\ i,j = 0,1,2,... \tag{4}$$

The center of the ellipse coincides with the center of mass of foreground object and can be obtained by

$$(\bar{x}, \bar{y}) = \{M_{10}/M_{00}, M_{01}/M_{00}\} \tag{5}$$

The orientation θ of the ellipse can be computed with the central moments of second order. Computation of central moments is based on the centroid $(\bar{x}, \bar{y})$ and is given by

$$\mu_{ij} = \sum_x \sum_y (x - \bar{x})^i (y - \bar{y})^j I(x,y) \quad for\ i,j = 0,1,2,... \tag{6}$$

and orientation θ is given by

$$\theta = \frac{1}{2} \arctan\left(\frac{2\mu_{11}}{\mu_{20} - \mu_{02}}\right) \tag{7}$$

Approximated ellipses for standing position and after a fall incident are shown in Fig.2(c)-(d).

3   Camera Self-calibration

Camera calibration is necessary to obtain camera's focal length, which is required for actual human's height approximation. Our system by using a single stationary monocular camera, only a single view of the scene is available. In order to use an automatic calibration technique three finite vanishing points that correspond to three mutually orthogonal planes of the scene are necessary. This can be achieved when camera's plane is not parallel to any of these three planes.

The image plane is chosen as the accumulator space, while the intersections of all pairs of image line segments represent potential vanishing points. Since vanishing points in 3D scene are points at infinity, vanishing points in the 2D image cannot lie on line segments. All potential vanishing points that do not satisfy this constraint are removed. For the rest of them the contribution of every line segment is computed by means of a voting scheme. Next, all potential vanishing points are checked against certain geometrical criteria for the determination of the three dominant vanishing points of mutually orthogonal space directions. Only triplets of vanishing points forming acute triangles are considered (orthogonality criterion) and principal point, orthocenter of the triangle, as well as, computed camera constant should have "reasonable" values (camera criterion). Vanishing point triplets that satisfy these criteria are sorted according to their total score; that with the highest score is chosen as the final triplet of dominant vanishing points.

Radial lens distortion at any image point (x_d, y_d) can be modeled by the first two coefficients of a Taylor series around $r = 0$, where r is the distance between point (x_d, y_d) and principal point (x_o, y_o). Radial lens distortion is given by

$$x_u = x_d + x_d(k_1r^2 + k_2r^4) \quad and \quad y_u = y_d + y_d(k_1r^2 + k_2r^4) \qquad (8)$$

(x_u, y_u) is the undistorted point corresponding to distorted point (x_d, y_d). The observed lines are constraint to converge to their corresponding vanishing point $V(x_v, y_v)$ according to the following equation [13]

$$[x - (x - x_o)(k_1r^2 + k_2r^4) - x_v]cos\phi + [y - (y - y_o)(k_1r^2 + k_2r^4) - y_v]sin\phi = 0 \quad (9)$$

where (x, y) are the image coordinates of an individual point on a line and (x_o, y_o) is the principal point. Coefficients k_1 and k_2 are computed so as the root mean square distance of points (x, y) from the fitted line is minimized. To estimate principal point (x_o, y_o) and camera constant (focal length) c, each pair of orthogonal vanishing points, $\mathbf{v_1}$ and $\mathbf{v_2}$, expressed in homogeneous coordinates, supplies a linear constraint on the entities of conic ω of the form

$$\mathbf{v_1}^T\omega\mathbf{v_2} = 0 \qquad (10)$$

by ignoring image aspect ratio and skewness, ω may be written as:

$$\omega = \begin{bmatrix} 1 & 0 & -x_o \\ 0 & 1 & -y_o \\ -x_o & -y_o & x_o{}^2 + y_o{}^2 + c^2 \end{bmatrix} \qquad (11)$$

3.1   Reference Plane Construction - Height Approximation

For a projective space $\wp^n$ a projective homography is defined as a nonsingular matrix $\mathbf{H}_{(n+1)\mathbf{x}(n+1)}$ with elements belonging to an affine space $\Re^n$, and defined up to a certain scalar value. A point $\mathbf{x}$ is projectively transformed to $\hat{\mathbf{x}}$ as follows:

$$\hat{\mathbf{x}} = \mathbf{H}\mathbf{x}, \quad \mathbf{x}, \hat{\mathbf{x}} \in \wp^n \qquad (12)$$

where $\mathbf{H}$ is the coordinate transformation matrix (homography matrix). According to the IPM algorithm, described in [14], $\hat{\mathbf{x}}$ and $\mathbf{x}$ can be expressed as:

$$\hat{\mathbf{x}} = [\hat{x}\ \hat{y}\ 1] \quad and \quad \mathbf{x} = [x\ y\ 1] \qquad (13)$$

where $x, y, \hat{x}, \hat{y}$ represent Cartesian coordinates on image plane and reference plane respectively and homography matrix $\mathbf{H} = [h_{ij}]$ is a 3x3 matrix, normalized so to have $h_{33} = 1$. Eq.(12) requires at least four non collinear points in order to be solved. By using a known target or ground truth images, a larger set of points can be found and this equation can be solved in a least square sense. This equation represents a perspective transformation, any parallelogram can be transformed to any trapezoid and vice versa.

To approximate the distance Z between foreground object and camera, we use the q_{bm} point. On the reference plane the relation between camera's natural units (pixels) and the units of the physical world (cm) is linear and thus Z is straightforwardly calculated. This results in a simple model and a single solution in which a point in the 3D world (X, Y, W) with actual height h_a is projected on the image plane with projected height h_p in accordance with Eq.(14).

$$h_a = Z\frac{h_p}{c} \qquad (14)$$

The appearance of errors during perspective transformations affects the h_a estimation (Fig.3), as it depends on distance estimation on created reference plane.

Fig. 3. Real height approximation

4 Fall Detection Algorithm

Fall detection algorithm utilizes a non Linear Warning System (nLWS). The nLWS is a feed forward neural network, topologically optimized (i.e. number of hidden layers, neurons, activation function), using an island genetic algorithm. The system's inputs are vectors of size 3x1. The first and second elements are calculated as the change at the angle (degrees) and at the height (cm) for the last four frames, respectively. The third input is the ratio between foreground object's projected height and width (both in pixels). The target outputs were logical values $\in \{0, 1\}$, where 1 suggests that a fall has happened.

System initialization - The training procedure takes place offline. Initially the input vectors are separated in two classes. The separation is performed unsupervised using a similarity based classifier (i.e. kmeans) using various metric distances. A weighted average sum function of the results (for each of the metric distances) is used to decide in which class each frame should be placed. An assumption is made that the fewer-element class describes the possible falls. Subsequently, the following semi-supervised training procedure occurs: initially, the vectors are labeled according to the suggested class. At this stage the training sample for the nLWS is formed and training procedure takes place. Then, for the non-fall class, an expert is summoned to further refine it by removing at random non-fall describing vectors. Finally, the nLWS weights and biases are adapted at the new values. For any given input vector the nLWS output is expected at $[0, 1]$. Values close to 1 mean that it is more likely to observe a fall.

Evaluation Phase - The fall detection mechanism is based on threshold value. Initially, that value is set as the average of the n greatest output prices according to the training sample (n was set at $40 \mapsto 6\%$ of the training set). The vectors are fed one by one at the nLWS. If a score greater than the threshold is achieved then a fall tag is given at the specific input vector. For the following frames the same procedure is followed. If within a range of 10 sequent frames more than 3 positive-fall tags are observed then we have detected a fall (it is assumed that the duration of a fall incident is 3 to 4 frames for real time operation - at least 20fps). That range scheme is based on the input vector creation; similar vectors will be created around the fall time and will produce higher output values.

5   Experimental Results

During the experiments one person simulated falls, in every direction according to the camera position and normal every day activities, that may look like falls but they are not, Fig.4. Self calibration method was compared to calibration method that comes with OpenCV and both algorithms present the same results for radial distortion and camera constant. The fall detection algorithm was tested in dynamically changing visual conditions, including illumination changes, cluttered background and occlusions at a martial arts school in Chania and at a demo room in Trikala municipality for 5 and 9 days respectively.

Our system operates in real-time at 20fps and as experimental results suggest that algorithm detects over 90% of fall incidents and presents very low false positive rate, which is not crucial when post verification video analysis is available. In sample and out of sample algorithm's performance is presented in Fig.5. The performance of fall detection scheme is presented in Table 1(a). Its performance is affected by foreground extraction, and this results to more robust performance for indoor environments, the impact of occlusions is being reduced as camera's height is being increased and in contrast to other approaches (e.g. [8]), its performance is not affected by the direction of falls. Table 1(b) presents false positive rates for different activities. Lie on the floor presents the biggest false positive rate, however, this activity can't be thought as "normal".

(a)   (b)

Fig. 4. (a) falls, (b) normal activities

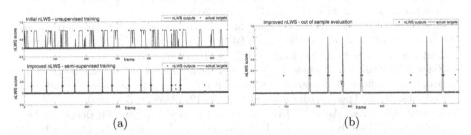

(a)   (b)

Fig. 5. (a) In sample performance, (b) Out of sample performance

Table 1. (a) Performance (b) Total false positive rate divided in regard to activities

(a)   (b)

Camera's height (cm)		Proposed system	Indoor No occlusion	Indoor with occlusion	Outdoor
40	Falls detected	90 %	98 %	76 %	83 %
	Wrong detections	4	2	5	9
220	Falls detected	93 %	97 %	92 %	82 %
	Wrong detections	6	4	7	8
260	Falls detected	97 %	97 %	94 %	82 %
	Wrong detections	3	3	4	6

Activity	False positive
Lie down	62,5%
Sit on floor	25%
Other	12,5%

6   Conclusions

This paper presents a fall detection scheme that exploits 3D measures by using a single monocular camera through camera self-calibration and inverse perspective mapping. The proposed scheme operates in real-time and detects over 90% of fall incidents in complex and dynamically changing visual conditions, while it presents very low false positive rate. Besides the contribution to humans fall problem, significant measures of a 3D scene can be calculated that can reveal much more information which might be useful in different kind of applications.

Acknowledgements. The research leading to these results has been supported by European Union funds and national funds from Greece and Cyprus under the project "POSEIDON: Development of an Intelligent System for Coast Monitoring using Camera Arrays and Sensor Networks" in the context of the inter-regional programme INTERREG (Greece-Cyprus cooperation) - contract agreement K1 3 1017/6/2011.

References

1. Le, T., Pan, R.: Accelerometer-based sensor network for fall detection. In: Biomedical Circuits and Systems Conference, BioCAS, pp. 265–268. IEEE (November 2009)
2. Nyan, M., Tay, F.E., Murugasu, E.: A wearable system for pre-impact fall detection. Journal of Biomechanics 41(16), 3475–3481 (2008)
3. Bianchi, F., Redmond, S., Narayanan, M., Cerutti, S., Lovell, N.: Barometric pressure and triaxial Accelerometry-Based falls event detection. IEEE Trans. on Neural Systems and Rehabilitation Engineering 18(6), 619–627 (2010)
4. Zigel, Y., Litvak, D., Gannot, I.: A method for automatic fall detection of elderly people using floor vibrations and sound - proof of concept on human mimicking doll falls. IEEE Trans. on Biomedical Eng. 56(12), 2858–2867 (2009)
5. Debard, G., Karsmakers, P., Deschodt, M., Vlaeyen, E., Van den Bergh, J., Dejaeger, E., Milisen, K., Goedemé, T., Tuytelaars, T., Vanrumste, B.: Camera based fall detection using multiple features validated with real life video (July 2011)
6. Rougier, C., Meunier, J., St-Arnaud, A., Rousseau, J.: Robust video surveillance for fall detection based on human shape deformation. IEEE Trans. on CSVT (5), 611–622 (2011)
7. Fu, Z., Culurciello, E., Lichtsteiner, P., Delbruck, T.: Fall detection using an address-event temporal contrast vision sensor. In: ISCAS 2008, pp. 424–427 (2008)
8. Foroughi, H., Rezvanian, A., Paziraee, A.: Robust fall detection using human shape and multi-class support vector machine. In: ICVGIP 2008, pp. 413–420 (2008)
9. Diraco, G., Leone, A., Siciliano, P.: An active vision system for fall detection and posture recognition in elderly healthcare. In: DATE 2010, pp. 1536–1541 (2010)
10. Thome, N., Miguet, S., Ambellouis, S.: A Real-Time, multiview fall detection system: A LHMM-Based approach. IEEE Trans. on CSVT 18(11), 1522–1532 (2008)
11. Doulamis, N.: Iterative motion estimation constrained by time and shape for detecting person's falls. In: ACM 3rd Inter. Conference on Pervasive Technologies Related to Assistive Environments, Samos, Greece
12. Qian, H., Mao, Y., Xiang, W., Wang, Z.: Home environment fall detection system based on a cascaded multi-SVM classifier. In: ICARCV 2008, pp. 1567–1572 (2008)
13. Grammatikopoulos, L., Karras, G., Petsa, E.: An automatic approach for camera calibration from vanishing points. ISPRS 62(1), 64–76 (2007)
14. Bevilacqua, A., Gherardi, A., Carozza, L.: Automatic perspective camera calibration based on an incomplete set of chessboard markers. In: Sixth ICVGIP, Bhubaneswar, India, pp. 126–133 (2008)

Person Identification Using Full-Body Motion and Anthropometric Biometrics from Kinect Videos

Brent C. Munsell[1], Andrew Temlyakov[2], Chengzheng Qu[2], and Song Wang[2]

[1] Claflin University, Orangeburg, SC. 29115
[2] University of South Carolina, Columbia, SC. 29208
bmunsell@claflin.edu, {temlyaka,quc,songwang}@cec.sc.edu

Abstract. For person identification, motion and anthropometric biometrics are known to be less sensitive to photometric differences and more robust to obstructions such as glasses, hair, and hats. Existing gait-based methods are based on the accurate identification and acquisition of the gait cycle. This typically requires the subject to repeatedly perform a single action using a costly motion-capture facility, or 2D videos in simple backgrounds where the person can be easily segmented and tracked. For person identification these manufactured requirements limit the use gait-based biometrics in real scenarios that may have a variety of actions with varying levels of complexity. We propose a new person identification method that uses motion and anthropometric biometrics acquired from an inexpensive Kinect RGBD sensor. Different from previous gait-based methods we use all the body joints found by the Kinect SDK to analyze the motion patterns and anthropometric features over the entire track sequence. We show the proposed method can identify people that perform different actions (e.g. walk and run) with varying levels of complexity. When compared to a state-of-the-art gait-based method that uses depth images produced by the Kinect sensor the proposed method demonstrated better person identity performance.

1   Introduction

The development of accurate and efficient person identification methods is a major area of research in the computer vision, biometric, surveillance, and security communities. In general, person identification is typically achieved by measuring and analyzing biologic features, or *biometrics*, where a biometric is some distinguishing characteristic used for recognition. For example, high impact research has been conducted that identify people with similar facial, fingerprint, or iris biometrics [1–6] in 2D images or videos. To date, person identification systems that incorporate one, or more [7, 8], of these biometrics tend to dominate the community. However, the person being identified is usually required to physically touch the sensor, or cooperate with the sensor when acquiring data. Also, in real imagery the accurate identification and location of these biometrics can

A. Fusiello et al. (Eds.): ECCV 2012 Ws/Demos, Part III, LNCS 7585, pp. 91–100, 2012.

be sensitive to photometric differences and obstructions (e.g., glasses, hair, hats) which may severely degrade recognition performance.

To overcome these limitations, person identification methods that use a lower extremity (i.e. below the hips) gait biometric have been proposed that attempt to identify people with similar lower extremity gait kinematics [9–11], stride and cadence [12, 13], and mechanics [14, 15]. Even though these gait-based methods are less restrictive and more robust to obstructions they do require the accurate detection of the motion region, and the coherent segmentation of the object (i.e. person boundary or silhouette) over a specified time sequence to isolate the gait cycle. In [16] the isolated gait cycle is used to construct normalized (i.e. temporally averaged) energy volumes, in [17] the isolated gait cycle is used to align the motion samples, and in [18] gait specific features are normalized using the isolated gait cycle . In real video footage that may have a variety of actions with varying levels of complexity, isolating the gait cycle can be computationally expensive and error prone. If the gait cycle is not properly detected and isolated, gait alignment and normalization errors are likely to be introduced, which may result in very poor recognition performance.

We present a novel person identity method that uses full-body (upper and lower extremity) motion and anthropometric biometrics derived from Kinect videos. The Kinect sensor was chosen because it is an inexpensive, easy-to-use, and accurate 3D motion sensor that is not sensitive to photometric differences. The major contribution is three-fold: 1. We introduce a new motion biometric that examines the coordinated motion of the entire body when a person performs a basic action, 2. The derived motion biometric examines the periodic motion of the tracked joints over the entire track sequence making the proposed motion biometric more robust than those derived by gait-based methods that are sensitive to gait cycle isolation errors, and 3. We introduce an integrated anthropometric biometric to boost biometric authentication if the motion biometric is unable to distinguish two people with similar full-body motion patterns. Unlike existing methods that may use anthropometric data to improve object tracking [18] or pose estimation [17] prior to biometric authentication, the proposed motion and anthropometric biometrics are combined to form a unified person identity classifier.

In the experiments, challenging scenarios are performed that study the subtle difference in motion among 10 different people when they perform 2 basic actions (walking and running). In total we collect 100 short[1] Kinect videos (40 videos for training and 60 for testing) resulting in an average ROC Equal Error Rate and Cumulative Match Curve Rank-1 identification rate of 13% and 90% respectively. Using the same Kinect data set, the proposed method is compared to the Gait Energy Volume (GEV) [16] a state-of- the-art lower extremity gait-based method and the experiments show our method out performs GEV. The remainder of this paper is organized as follows: Section-2 the proposed method is described in detail, Section-3 experiments are performed that evaluate person identity performance, and in Section-4 a brief conclusion is given.

---

[1] Roughly 30 sec of footage at 30 fps

2   Proposed Method

In this section we develop new classification methods that attempt to identify the basic action and identity of unknown persons in Kinect videos. Conceptually, the proposed method is accomplished using the two-stage classification system illustrated in Fig. 1(b). In the first stage, a test Kinect video with an

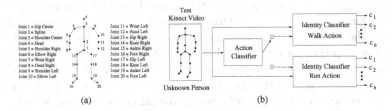

(a)   (b)

Fig. 1. (a) The 20 skeletal joints found using the Kinect SDK. (b) Two-stage classification system where the first stage recognizes the action and the second stage recognizes the identity of an unknown person in a Kinect video.

unknown action is input into a trained action classifier that is capable of recognizing two basic actions: walking and running. To accomplish this, a training set of Kinect videos are collected that capture subjects, with different gender, executing two basic actions. For each frame, in each training video, the normalized 3D locations of the 20 skeletal joints, illustrated in Fig. 1(a), are projected into a high-dimensional space and hyperplanes that best separate the two actions are found by a Support Vector Machine (SVM). Given a test Kinect video the learned hyperplanes allow us to classify each frame in the video and then the unknown action is recognized using a majority vote algorithm.

In the second stage, the test Kinect video is input into an identity classifier matched to the recognized action. For each basic action, we train n human identity classifiers by considering motion patterns and human anthropometric measures for n different people. In particular, the motion biometric is trained using Kinect videos that describe the radial, azimuth, and elevation motion patterns of 20 skeletal joints performing the same action multiple times. Likewise, the anthropometric biometric is trained using the same Kinect videos, however this biometric is a statistical model that describes the proportions between the 20 skeletal joints. Finally, n identity costs $c_1, c_2, \ldots, c_n$ are calculated and the unknown person in the test Kinect video is recognized by finding the score with the smallest value.

2.1   Action Classification

Let $\mathcal{V}^w = \{\mathcal{V}_i^w; \ i = 1, 2, \ldots, m\}$ be a set of walking and $\mathcal{V}^r = \{\mathcal{V}_i^r; \ i = 1, 2, \ldots, m\}$ be a set of running training Kinect videos, where $\mathcal{V}_i^w = (\mathcal{F}_{i1}^w, \mathcal{F}_{i2}^w, \ldots, \mathcal{F}_{in}^w)$ is an ordered sequence of image frames that capture various people performing normal walk actions. Using each frame in $\mathcal{V}_i^w$ a $60 \times n$

dimension skeletal matrix $S_i^w = [s_{i1} \cdots s_{ik} \cdots s_{in}]$ is constructed, where s_{ik} is a column vector that defines the 3D locations of the 20 skeletal joints in the kth frame[2]. This is repeated for each of the m videos in $\mathcal{V}^r$, and the resulting skeletal matrices are concatenated to form one matrix $S = [S_1^w S_2^w \cdots S_m^w S_1^r S_2^r \cdots S_m^r]$ with dimension $60 \times 2nm$. The combined skeletal matrix S is decomposed $\hat{S} = U\Sigma D^T$ into a set of matrices using singular value decomposition, where D is a $2nm \times 2nm$ dimension matrix of right singular vectors, Σ is a $60 \times 2mn$ dimension diagonal matrix of singular values, and U is a 60×60 dimension matrix of left singular vectors. Since most of the singular values are very small or zero, only the 10 largest singular values are considered. Therefore the reduce space is now represented by $\hat{\Sigma}$ that has dimension 10×10, $\hat{D}$ that has dimension $2nm \times 10$, and $\hat{U}$ that has dimension 60×10. The reduced dimension row vectors in $\hat{D}$ are then used to train a multi-class SVM, and because the data is not linearly separable a non-linear Gaussian Radial Basis Function kernel learns the hyperplanes used in classification.

Given a test Kinect video $\mathcal{V}$ the reduced dimension matrices $\hat{\Sigma}$ and $\hat{U}$ are used to insert each frame $\{\mathcal{F}\}_{k=1}^n$ into the space spanned by the row vectors in $\hat{D}$ using $\hat{d}_k = s_k^T \hat{U} \hat{\Sigma}^{-1}$, where vector s_k contains the origin translated 3D locations of the 20 skeletal joints in frame $\mathcal{F}_k$. Once each frame in $\mathcal{V}$ is inserted into the high dimensional space they are labeled as a walk or run action by the trained SVM. The action is then recognized using a majority vote algorithm by determining the action that appears the most among all n frames.

2.2   Identity Classification

Given a test Kinect video of an unknown person X performing a recognized action, the identity cost

$$\min_{\forall P}\{ \Delta_M(X, P) \cdot \Delta_A(X, P) \}$$

is calculated for each person P in the training data set, where $\Delta_M(X, P)$ is the motion difference and $\Delta_A(X, P)$ is the anthropometric difference. The identity of person X is recognized when the person with the least cost is found.

The motion biometric is trained as follows: Let $\mathcal{V}^w = (\mathcal{F}_1^w, \mathcal{F}_2^w, \ldots, \mathcal{F}_n^w)$ be a training Kinect video that captures a person performing the walk action. Like Section-2.1, $S^w = [s_1 \cdots s_k \cdots s_n]$ is constructed using each frame in the video, however column vector s_k now defines the r radius, θ azimuth, and ϕ elevation values of the 20 skeletal joints in the kth frame[3], which is then seperated into three different $20 \times n$ dimension matrices namely: M_r the radius matrix, M_ϕ the elevation matrix, and M_θ the azimuth matrix. Specifically, row vector $r_1 = (r_{11}, r_{12}, \ldots, r_{1n})$ defines the radial motion, $\theta_1 = (\theta_{11}, \theta_{12}, \ldots, \theta_{1n})$ defines

---

[2] Translation differences are removed by picking joint-2 as the origin $(0, 0, 0)$ and the remaining 19 joints are translated relative this joint. E.g., $s_{ik} = ((x_{1k} - x_{2k}), (y_{1k} - y_{2k}), (z_{1k} - z_{2k}), \ldots, (x_{20k} - x_{2k}), (y_{20k} - y_{2k}), (z_{20k} - z_{2k}))^T$

[3] $s_k = (r_{1k}, \theta_{1k}, \phi_{1k}, \ldots, r_{20k}, \theta_{20k}, \phi_{20k})^T$

the angular azimuth motion, and $\phi_1 = (\phi_{11}, \phi_{12}, \ldots, \phi_{1n})$ defines the angular elevation motion of joint-1 when the person executes the walk action.

For each motion matrix, a motion histogram is constructed using Algorithm-1. For example, given M_r and k_f, in *line-2* $\mathbf{h} = (h_1, h_2, \ldots, h_{N/2})$ a $N/2$ dimension vector is created, where F_s is the sampling frequency and h_1 corresponds to $F_s/N = 0.5$ Hz. Likewise, $h_2 = 1$ Hz, $h_3 = 1.5$ Hz and so forth. In *line-5* a N-point Discrete Fourier Transform (DFT) is performed using the radial values in row i, and then in *line-6* a k_f dimension vector $\mathbf{b}$ of bin values are found for the top k_f frequencies that have the largest magnitude (sorted in descending order). In *lines 7-9*, for each frequency bin the corresponding histogram bin is incremented by one, and then on line *line-11* the radial motion histogram is normalized by n the total number of rows in the motion matrix.

Algorithm 1. Histogram(M, k_f)

1: $N \leftarrow 2048$
2: $F_s \leftarrow N/2$
3: $\mathbf{h} \leftarrow zeros(F_s)$
4: **while** $i \leq n$ **do**
5:     $Y \leftarrow | DFT(M(i,:), N) |, i = i + 1$
6:     $\mathbf{b} \leftarrow \text{sort}(Y, k_f)$
7:     **while** $j \leq k_f$ **do**
8:         $\mathbf{h}[\mathbf{b}(j)] \leftarrow \mathbf{h}[\mathbf{b}(j)] + 1, j = j + 1$
9:     **end while**
10: **end while**
11: $\mathbf{h} = \mathbf{h}/n$

For each person in the training data set 6 motion histograms are computed using Algorithm-1 (i.e. 3 histograms for each action). Given X an unknown person not in the training data set, and P a known person in the training data set the motion difference is calculated using

$$\Delta_M(X, P) = 1 - \frac{R(\mathbf{h}_r^x, \mathbf{h}_r^p) + R(\mathbf{h}_\theta^x, \mathbf{h}_\theta^p) + R(\mathbf{h}_\phi^x, \mathbf{h}_\phi^p)}{3}$$

where $R(\cdot)$ is the correlation coefficient, $(\mathbf{h}_r^x, \mathbf{h}_\theta^x, \mathbf{h}_a^a)$ are the motion histograms for X, and $(\mathbf{h}_r^p, \mathbf{h}_\theta^p, \mathbf{h}_\phi^p)$ are the motion histograms for P. The motion difference has a value in $[0\ 1]$, where a value of 0 indicates the two people have identical motion patterns for the recognized action.

The anthropometric biometric is trained as follows: Let $\mathcal{V}^w = (\mathcal{F}_1^w, \mathcal{F}_2^w, \ldots, \mathcal{F}_n^w)$ be a training Kinect video that captures a person performing the walk action. For each frame in the video a 20×20 dimension joint proportion matrix is constructed using the (x, y, z) locations of the 20 skeletal joints. Specifically, joint proportion is calculated by $p_{ab} = \frac{d(a,b)}{d_{total}}$, where $d(a, b)$ is the

Euclidean distance between joints a and b, and $d_{total} = d(1,4)+d(3,8)+d(3,12)+d(1,16)+d(1,20)$ is the total skeletal distance[4]

The resulting joint proportion matrices are concatenated to form one matrix $J = [J_1^w \ J_2^w \ \cdots \ J_n^w]$ that has dimension $20 \times 20n$. A statistical model $\mathcal{N}(\bar{p}, D)$ is constructed using the proportions in J, where $\bar{p}$ is a 20 dimension vector that describes the mean proportions for all 20 joints, and D is a 20×20 covariance matrix that describes proportion variation for all 20 joints. For each person in the training data set 2 anthropometric statistical models are constructed (i.e. one model for each action). Given X an unknown person not in the training data set, and P a known person in the training data set the anthropometric difference is calculated using the well known KL-distance measure

$$\Delta_A(X,P) = \frac{1}{2} \left(\log \frac{|D_p|}{|D_x|} + Tr(D_p^{-1}D_x) + \right.$$
$$\left. (\bar{p}_x - \bar{p}_p)^T \ D_p^{-1} \ (\bar{p}_x - \bar{p}_p) \ - d \right)$$

where $\mathcal{N}(\bar{p}_x, D_x)$ is the anthropometric statistical model for unknown person X, and $\mathcal{N}(\bar{p}_p, D_p)$ is the learned anthropometric statistical model for person P, and $d = 20$ the dimension of the covariance matrix. In general, a small anthropometric difference value indicates the two people have very similar joint proportions for the recognized action.

3   Experiments

In this section experiments are performed that evaluate the proposed system's ability to correctly classify unknown people and their action in Kinect videos. The performance of the proposed method is compared to the Gait Energy Volume (GEV) method [16]. In general, GEV is the 3D extension of the 2D Gait Energy Image (GEI) [19]. Using the depth images, the tracked human silhouettes are segmented and the segmentation results are used to isolate each gait cycle in the video sequence. For each isolated gait cycle the results are aligned and averaged to form the GEV. Principal Component Analysis (PCA) and Multiple Discriminant Analysis (MDA) are used to find a reduced dimension feature vector that well describes the GEV. This unknown feature vector is compared to known feature vectors using a distance based measurement to recognize the identity of the tracked person in the Kinect video. In these experiments we manually identified the gait cycle and then used the recommended settings to perform PCA and MDA dimensionality reduction.

In Section 3.1 we describe the Kinect data sets used to train the action and identity classifiers, and in Section 3.2 we describe the Kinect data sets used to test the accuracy of the system and for performance comparison. Both data sets were collected using a Kinect sensor mounted on a movable cart that faced the person performing the action. During data collection the distance between the apparatus and the subject was roughly 1.5 to 3 meters. Lastly, we evaluate the

---

[4] For example, $p_{18} = (\ d(1,2) + d(2,3) + d(3,5) + d(5,6) + d(6,7) + d(7,8)\ )/d_{total}$.

performance of the action and person identity classifiers in Section 3.3 using the well known Receiver Operating Characteristic (ROC) curve and the Cumulative Match Curve (CMC) [20]. The ROC is also used to evaluate the sensitivity of the method when: 1. only one biometric is used for identity classification, and 2. the number of frequencies k_f (see Section 2.2) used to construct the (r, θ, ϕ) motion histograms are changed over a range of values (*Note: This is the only free parameter in the proposed person identification system*).

3.1   Training Data

The training data set included 10 people, 6 males and 4 females, where each person executed each of the 2 basic actions 2 times. For instance, each person has 4 Kinect videos: 2 walking and 2 running. In total, the training data set has 40 videos. Example 3D skeletons found by the Kinect sensor that illustrate the 2 basic actions are shown in Fig. 2. The activity classifier was trained using all 40 videos. For each walk identity classifier the motion and anthropometric biometrics were trained using the two collections for that person. Likewise, for each run identity classifer the motion and anthropometric biometrics were trained using the two collections for that person. For the 6 male subjects the age range was between 25 and 40 years old, and the height range was roughly between 1.73 and 1.8 meters. For the 4 female subjects the age range was between 25 and 37 years old, and the height range was roughly between 1.55 to 1.6 meters.

Fig. 2. Example training data. *Top row*: example skeletons of a person performing a normal running action. *Bottom row*: example skeletons of a person performing a normal walking action.

3.2   Test Data

Using the same 10 people in the training data set, each person in the test data set executed each of the 2 basic actions 3 times, i.e. each person has 6 Kinect videos: 3 walking and 3 running. In total, the test data set has 60 videos. To make the test data set challenging, each person was asked to perform the additional actions: *First Collection* (least challenging) wear a backpack that contained 20 lbs of books, *Second Collection* (moderately challenging) wear the same 20 lb backpack, and carry an object in their right hand, and *Third Collection* (most challenging) perform the slow moving "S" motion shown in Fig. 3. In general, these collections simulate real scenarios that may be found in public gathering areas such as airports, train stations, or shopping malls.

Fig. 3. Example Third Collection testing data. *Top row:* example skeletons of a person performing the "S" the running action. *Bottom row:* example skeletons of a person performing the "S" walking action.

3.3 Results

Action classification performance using majority vote was 100% for both actions, where action classification performance per video ranges from 50.30% to 100% with the average being 93.47%. The ROC curves in Fig. 4(a) show the Verification Rate (VR) and Equal Error Rate (EER) performance for our method and GEV. This figure also shows the CMC Rank-1 through 6 performance for our method and GEV. For both actions the EER and CMC Rank-1 performance of our method is better than GEV. For the walk and run actions our method shows a 11% and 4% EER increase in performance respectively. For the walk action our method is 90% accurate by Rank-3, whereas GEV is still hovering around 88% by Rank-6, and for the run action the Rank-1 performance of our method is 90% while GEV does not achieve 90% until Rank-3. The ROC curves in this figure also show the motion biometric is not overly sensitive to k_f the number of frequencies used to construct the motion histograms. In fact, the ROC curves show roughly the same performance when k_f is three or five times greater than 10. This suggests the joint motion patterns may be adequately described by the top 10 frequencies with the largest magnitude.

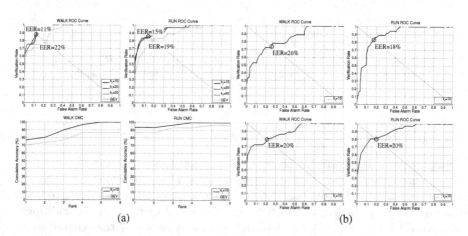

(a)   (b)

Fig. 4. For both actions **(a)** *Top Row:* VR and EER performance comparison between our method ($k_f = 10, 30, 50$) and GEV [16]. *Bottom Row:* CMC Rank-1 through 6 performance comparison between our method ($k_f = 10$) and GEV. **(b)** *Top Row:* VR and EER performance using only the motion biometric ($k_f = 10$). *Bottom Row:* VR and EER performance using only the anthropometric biometric ($k_f = 10$).

Figure 4(b) shows the VR and EER performance when only the motion and anthropometric biometric is used by the identity classifier. As seen in these ROC curves, person identification is more accurate when both biometrics are used by the identity classifier. For the walk action the anthropometric EER performance is slightly better than the motion biometric, which suggests the anthropometric biometric guides the motion biometric. However, for the run action the discriminative power of the motion biometric is high, requiring less help from the anthropometric biometric.

Since the computation complexity of the SVD and SVM algorithms are $\mathcal{O}(pq^2 + p^2q + q^3)$ [21] and $\mathcal{O}(q^2)$ [22] respectively, the computational complexity of the action classifier $\approx \mathcal{O}(q^3)$ where $q = 2mn$. The space complexity of the action classifier is $\mathcal{O}(q^2)$, i.e. the size of the right singular value matrix D. An analysis of Algorithm-1 shows the computational complexity of the identity classifier is $\mathcal{O}(nNlogN)$, and the space complexity of the identity classifier is $\mathcal{O}(n)$, i.e. the column dimension of the radius, azimuth, and elevation matrices. On a 2.4GHz Intel Core 2 Quad CPU, the total time needed to train the action classifier was 32 min, and the time needed to train one identity classifer was 30 ms.

4 Conclusion

In conclusion, a novel person identity method that uses full-body motion and anthropometric biometrics derived from Kinect videos was presented. Different form traditional gait-based methods that attempt to isolate and examine the gait cycle in the video sequence, our method considers the entire track sequence and examines the periodic motion of upper and lower extremity joints found by the Kinect SDK that have the largest contribution to the action being performed. Challenging test data sets where constructed that have a variety of basic actions with varying levels of complexity. Experiments showed that the proposed method has an average ROC EER of 13% and an average CMC Rank-1 identification rate of 90%. Performance comparisons where conducted using a gait-based method that uses depth images produced by the Kinect sensor. The results showed our method to have better performance. Experiments were also conducted to assess the individual sensitivities of the two biometrics, and the results suggest both biometrics are needed for person identification. We also show the motion biometric is not overly sensitive to the number of frequencies used to build the motion histograms.

References

1. Turk, M.A., Pentland, A.P.: Face recognition using eigenfaces. In: IEEE Conference on Computer Vision and Pattern Recognition, pp. 586–591 (1991)
2. Jain, A., Hong, L., Bolle, R.: Online fingerprint verification. IEEE Transactions on Pattern Analysis and Machine Intelligence 19, 302–314 (1997)

3. Ma, L., Tan, T., Wang, Y., Zhang, D.: Personal identification based on iris texture analysis. IEEE Transactions on Pattern Analysis and Machine Intelligence 25, 1519–1533 (2003)
4. Ross, A., Dass, S., Jain, A.: Fingerprint warping using ridge curve correspondences. IEEE Transactions on Pattern Analysis and Machine Intelligence 28, 19–30 (2006)
5. Lu, X., Jain, A.: Deformation modeling for robust 3D face matching. IEEE Transactions on Pattern Analysis and Machine Intelligence 30, 1346–1357 (2008)
6. Pillai, J., Patel, V., Chellappa, R., Ratha, N.: Secure and robust iris recognition using random projections and sparse representations. IEEE Transactions on Pattern Analysis and Machine Intelligence 33, 1877–1893 (2011)
7. Hong, L., Jain, A.: Integrating faces and fingerprints for personal identification. IEEE Transactions on Pattern Analysis and Machine Intelligence 20, 1295–1307 (1998)
8. Chang, K., Bowyer, K., Sarkar, S., Victor, B.: Comparison and combination of ear and face images in appearance-based biometrics. IEEE Transactions on Pattern Analysis and Machine Intelligence 25, 1160–1165 (2003)
9. Murase, H., Sakai, R.: Moving object recognition in eigenspace representation: gait analysis and lip reading. Pattern Recognition Letters 17, 155–162 (1996)
10. Cutler, R., Davis, L.S.: Robust real-time periodic motion detection, analysis, and applications. IEEE Transactions on Pattern Analysis and Machine Intelligence 22, 781–796 (2000)
11. Boyd, J.E., Little, J.J.: Biometric Gait Recognition. In: Tistarelli, M., Bigun, J., Grosso, E. (eds.) Advanced Studies in Biometrics. LNCS, vol. 3161, pp. 19–42. Springer, Heidelberg (2005)
12. Gafurov, D., Helkala, K., Søndrol, T.: Biometric gait authentication using accelerometer sensor. JCP 1, 51–59 (2006)
13. Abdelkader, C.B., Davis, L., Cutler, R.: Stride and cadence as a biometric in automatic person identification and verification. In: IEEE International Conference on Automatic Face and Gesture Recognition, pp. 372–377 (2002)
14. Campbell, L., Bobick, A.: Recognition of human body motion using phase space constraints. In: International Conference on Computer Vision, pp. 624–630 (1995)
15. Little, J., Boyd, J.E.: Recognizing people by their gait: The shape of motion. Videre 1, 1–32 (1996)
16. Sivapalan, S., Chen, D., Denman, S., Sridharan, S., Fookes, C.B.: Gait energy volumes and frontal gait recognition using depth images. In: International Joint Conference on Biometrics (2011)
17. Gu, J., Ding, X., Wang, S., Wu, Y.: Action and gait recognition from recovered 3-D human joints. Trans. Sys. Man Cyber. Part B 40, 1021–1033 (2010)
18. Green, R.D., Guan, L.: Quantifying and recognizing human movement patterns from monocular video images - part ii: Applications to biometrics. IEEE Transactions on Circuits and Systems for Video Technology 14, 179–190 (2003)
19. Han, J., Bhanu, B.: Individual recognition using gait energy image. IEEE Transactions on Pattern Analysis and Machine Intelligence 28, 316–322 (2006)
20. Bolle, R.M., Connell, J.H., Pankanti, S., Ratha, N.K., Senior, A.W.: The relation between the roc curve and the cmc. In: Proceedings of the Fourth IEEE Workshop on Automatic Identification Advanced Technologies, pp. 15–20 (2005)
21. Brand, M.: Incremental Singular Value Decomposition of Uncertain Data with Missing Values. In: Heyden, A., Sparr, G., Nielsen, M., Johansen, P. (eds.) ECCV 2002, Part I. LNCS, vol. 2350, pp. 707–720. Springer, Heidelberg (2002)
22. Fan, R.E., Chen, P.H., Lin, C.J.: Working set selection using second order information for training support vector machines. Journal of Machine Learning Research 6, 1889–1918 (2005)

Spatio-temporal Video Representation with Locality-Constrained Linear Coding

Manal Al Ghamdi, Nouf Al Harbi, and Yoshihiko Gotoh

University of Sheffield, UK

Abstract. This paper presents a spatio-temporal coding technique for a video sequence. The framework is based on a space-time extension of scale-invariant feature transform (SIFT) combined with locality-constrained linear coding (LLC). The coding scheme projects each spatio-temporal descriptor into a local coordinate representation produced by max pooling. The extension is evaluated using human action classification tasks. Experiments with the KTH, Weizmann, UCF sports and Hollywood datasets indicate that the approach is able to produce results comparable to the state-of-the-art.

1 Introduction

There exist numerous applications in the field of computer vision, including video information extraction and retrieval, classification, summarisation, surveillance and human-computer interaction to name a few. A number of techniques have been put forward to progress this area, a rough sketch of which is given in the next section. This paper presents a spatio-temporal extension of the locality-constrained linear coding (LLC) scheme for video classification tasks. In order to detect interest feature points, the dense 2D scale-invariant feature transform (SIFT) is replaced with spatio-temporal SIFT (ST-SIFT). The ST-SIFT is able to extract effectively the significant invariant local points in the spatial and the temporal domains.

The approach consists of two principle stages: The first stage involves transformation of a 3D video signal into spatio-temporal pyramids, followed by extraction of the interest features from spatial and spatio-temporal planes using a ST-SIFT detector. In the second stage, the LLC is applied on the extracted descriptor in order to encode the local descriptors with similar basis from a codebook. The approach is evaluated using a human action classification tasks as a benchmark. To this end, KTH, Weizmann, UCF sports and Hollywood datasets are used in the experiment, resulting in performances comparable to the state-of-the-art. The contributions of this work can be summarised as follows:

* Extension of the current LLC scheme from a 2D image to a spatio-temporal video signal;
* Provision of a robust schema to represent a human action signal;
* Application of the spatio-temporal LLC for human action classification achieving the state-of-the-art performance on several benchmarks.

A. Fusiello et al. (Eds.): ECCV 2012 Ws/Demos, Part III, LNCS 7585, pp. 101–110, 2012.

2   Related Work

There have been a number of visual content based approaches developed in recent years. Harris and Forstner's work on interest point operators and the detection of local structures in space-time was taken up and further developed by Laptev and Lindeberg [1]. The concept of correlating a 2D image to a 3D space-time volume was explored by Shechtman and Irani [2], as this approach facilitates the correlation of dynamic behaviours and actions. Alternatively, the maximisation of mutual information (MMI) was utilised by Lio and Shah [3] in order to pick the best total of words for a bag-of-words algorithm. Identification of natural human behaviour within a variety of different and true-to-life video settings was attempted by Laptev et al. [4], while Klaser et al. [5] used histograms of oriented 3D spatio-temporal gradients to develop a local descriptor.

The work undertaken by Wong and Cipolla [6] made use of information to derive a set of motion recognition interest points; the spatio-temporal interest points with equal time scale-invariant (spatial and temporal) are discussed by Willems et al. [7]. SIFT has been successful in various image processing applications for locally detecting and describing interest points [8]. SIFT extension can be categorised into three groups: (1) extension of the descriptor part only, combined with 2D detectors provided by Scovanner et al. [9], (2) a full 3D spatial extension such as n-SIFT by Cheung and Hamarneh [10], and (3) a combination of different approaches to separately describing motion and appearance as MoSIFT by Chen and Hauptmann [11].

Despite the fact that a variety of algorithms have been suggested to complete the task, several problems remain; the notable one is that, in general, a feature-point method tends to sparsity, with the implication of high complexity levels for the selection of the model and learning. In response to this, a number of approaches were proposed that involved combined features learning techniques, dimensionality reduction approaches and clustering methods. Robust sparse coding (RSC) scheme, for instance, was presented by Yang et al. [12], where sparse coding (SC) was considered as a sparsity-constrained robust regression problem. RSC improved the performance of the original SC and proved its effectiveness in handling facial occlusions.

Developed by Grauman and Darrell [13], the spatial pyramid matching (SPM) used vector quantisation (VQ) to solve a constrained least square problem. The mechanism of the SPM was based on partitioning the input image into sub-regions; local features of each region were extracted using the appropriate descriptor in order to generate descriptor layers. A codebook of M entries was applied to quantise each descriptor and obtain code layers. To achieve the SPM layer, the product of all sub-regions was grouped by averaging and normalising into a histogram. Histograms of all sub-regions were concatenated together in order to generate the final representation of the image. However the SPM method discarded the similarity between similar descriptor; because of the large quantisation error, the VQ code for comparable descriptor could lead to completely different response. More recently Yang et al. [14] developed an extension of the SPM by replacing VQ with SC. It was derived by relaxing the cardinality restriction constraint of VQ, so each descriptor could be encoded by multiple bases. Although SC had shown remarkable effectiveness in representing feature quantisation, it suffered from two limitations: (1) even if there was a simple variation in local features, the response of basis in dictionary could be quite different, (2) it eliminated the interdependence and relationships between local features, which adversely affected the image representation.

In order to overcome these limitations Wang et al. [15] proposed the LLC, utilising K nearest codewords to encode descriptors within the Euclidean space. In LLC, each descriptor was more precisely encoded by different bases, and LLC code was able to detect the interdependence between similar descriptors by sharing bases. By making use of locality constraints, LLC projected descriptors into their respective local coordinate systems. The representational output was then created by max pooling the coordinates of these projections. In conjunction with a linear classifier, this method was a considerable improvement over the non-linear SPM that was traditionally used, giving the best available performance on a number of standard benchmarks. The LLC approach provided (through the objective function) an analytical solution, as opposed to the computational response generated by SC strategies. It also worked efficiently due to its fast approximation method, which involved initially performing a k-nearest neighbour search, allowing a subsequent small constrained least square fitting problem.

3 Spatio-temporal Coding

This section presents the locality constrained spatio-temporal coding technique that considers the locality of the manifold structure in the input space.

3.1 Spatio-temporal SIFT

The ST-SIFT algorithm is developed to represent video content with invariant interest points. These points contain the amount of information sufficient to describe video streams. Most of the previous studies extended the SIFT algorithm spatially to extract the extrema from 3D images [10,11,16] or detect 2D interest points and describe them with a 3D descriptor [9]. The ST-SIFT, on the other hand, detects the spatially distinctive points with sufficient motion information at multi-scales. To achieve the invariance in both space and time, a spatio-temporal difference of Gaussian (DoG) pyramid is calculated first. The common points between three spatial and temporal planes carry vital information. The ST-SIFT algorithm is outlined below.

Spatio-temporal DoG Pyramid. For a video sequence with the frame size of $W \times H$, let $I(x, y, t)$ denote a pixel at location (x, y) in frame t. We construct the Gaussian pyramid of N levels where N is determined from the frame size. G_i $(i = 0, \ldots, N - 1)$ represents each level of the pyramid, where the highest level $G_0(t)$ corresponds to the original video frame sequence. This process leads to the multi-level spatio-temporal Gaussian and the DoG pyramids. Incremental convolution of video signal I with the 3D Gaussian filter G results in the scale space L of the first level:

$$L(x, y, t, \sigma, \tau) = G(x, y, t, \sigma, \tau) * I(x, y, t, \sigma, \tau) \qquad (1)$$

with multiple scales S separated by a constant value of $K = 2^{1/S}$. Following Lowe [8], $S + 3$ scales are generated to guarantee that local extrema detection will cover the complete octave. To produce a lower level the signal is spatially and temporally downsampled with the Gaussian at scales σ and τ. This yields a level with the lower frame rate and frames of the smaller size. The frame size at level G_i is $W/2^i \times H/2^i$, and $G_i(t)$ matches $G_0(2^i t)$ at time t. The next step is to construct a DoG pyramid; for each level in the Gaussian pyramid, a DoG of one lower octave is derived by subtracting the Gaussian of the adjacent scales.

Interest Points Detection. Once the DoG pyramid is constructed, local extrema of the adjacent scales in the xy, xt and yt planes are compared. Lopes *et al.* presented an approach to forming a spatio-temporal volume by stacking a set of frames from a video signal [17]. There are three directions to slice this volume into planes. One can slice through the spatial axis to create xy planes. Alternatively one can create a sequence of planes from the temporal axis combined with either of x or y spatial axis. Extrema are detected from each slice of the spatio-temporal pyramid separately, and the union of common extrema in three directions are selected as interest points. In the end filtering may be applied to remove noisy points and edges.

3.2   Conventional 2D LLC

The LLC is a coding scheme proposed by Wang *et al.* [15] to project individual descriptors onto their respective local-coordinate systems. Locality is more important than sparsity with LLC because, although locality implies sparsity, the reverse does not hold. The use of the locality constraint in favour of the sparsity constraint in LLC has the potential for a number of helpful properties. They may include: (a) better reconstruction: in contrast to a single basis codebook entry that VQ uses to represent each descriptor, LLC employs multiple bases. This means that while in the former approach similar descriptors may have very different codes, in the latter correlations between descriptors can be captured and the bases are shared; (b) locally smooth sparsity: reconstruction error is reduced in LLC through the use of multiple bases — *i.e.*, its explicit locality adaptor makes sure that patches with similarities have correspondingly similar codes; (c) analytical solution: spare coding problems can usually be solved only numerically, whereas LLC allows an analytical derivation.

Let M and K denote the numbers of codebook entries and nearest codewords, computational complexity is reduced to $\mathcal{O}(M+K^2)$ from $\mathcal{O}(M^2)$, where $K \ll M$. A codebook learning step is built into LLC via an 'online method' of learning [15]; B is the initial codebook that has been trained via k-means clustering.

B is then updated in increments as the training descriptors are iterated. For each of these increments, single or small-batch examples x_i are taken up and used to provide the required solution, resulting in the LLC codes associated with the current codebook B. This process takes the forms of a feature selector, since it retains only a set of bases B_i, the corresponding weights of which exceed a pre-set constant and refits x_i but omitting locality constraints. The code thereby generated can be employed to update the basis using a gradient descent. In brief, the LLC algorithm can be summed up in the following distinct steps:

1. Using 2D-SIFT descriptors, the local descriptor is identified within a dense image grid;
2. The local descriptor is translated into SC using LLC's nonlinear descriptor coding;
3. The representational outcome (feature representation) is generated by SC being submitted to multi-scale spatial pyramid max pooling.

There are clear benefits to this approach, *e.g.*, speed, simplicity and scalability, while providing the comparable performance to the SPM with SC [14].

3.3 Spatio-temporal LLC

The approach contains three steps; capturing video events with spatio-temporal local descriptors X, learning the locality-constrained sparse code S, and finally learning and optimising the codebook B (*c.f.*, Figure 1).

Spatio-temporal Interest Points. Interest points are detected using the ST-SIFT detector. To describe the region around the detected points, the 3D-HOG (histogram of oriented gradients) descriptor developed by Scovanner *et al.* [9] is used, calculating the spatio-temporal gradient for each pixel in the given cuboid. The approach leads to local regions that are invariant to scale and location in both the spatial and the temporal domains.

Learning Locality-Constrained Sparse Coding. The approach follows Wang *et al.* [15]; the criteria for the spatio-temporal LLC is

$$\min_{S} \sum_{i=1}^{N} \|x_i - Bs_i\|^2 + \lambda \|d_i \odot s_i\|^2 \quad st. \quad 1^\top s_i = 1, \forall i \tag{2}$$

where $\odot$ is the element-wise multiplication. The locality constrained parameter d_i represents every basis vector with different freedom based on its similarity to the spatio-temporal descriptor x_i:

$$d_i = \exp\left(\frac{dist(x_i, B)}{\sigma}\right) \quad st. \quad dist(x_i, B) = [dist(x_i, b_1), \ldots, dist(x_i, b_M)]^T \tag{3}$$

where $dist(x_i, b_1)$ is the Euclidean distance between the spatio-temporal descriptor and the basis codebook, and σ is the weight to control the locality parameter.

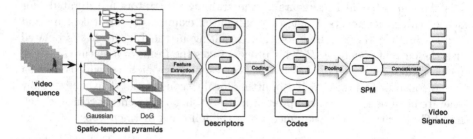

Fig. 1. ST-SIFT is combined with LLC

Codebook Optimisation. Given a set of n-dimensional spatio-temporal descriptors, $x_1, x_2, \ldots, x_m$, we generate an initial codebook using the k-means clustering method. Optimisation is performed so that the product of LLC coefficients and codebook basis should best approximate each spatio-temporal descriptor. The objective function can be defined as [15]:

$$\operatorname*{argmin}_{S,B} \sum_{i=1}^{N} \left\{ \|x_i - Bs_i\|^2 + \lambda\|d_i \odot s_i\|^2 \quad st. \quad 1^\top s_i = 1, \forall i \quad \|b_j\|^2 \leq 1, \forall j \right\}$$

(4)

This is a convex problem in B only or S but not in both together, and can be iteratively solved by the coordinate descent method:

1. Initialise the dictionary B with the codebook generated by clustering:

$$B \leftarrow B_{init}$$

(5)

2. For each spatio-temporal descriptor x_i, compute the new LLC coefficient s_i using the current B:

$$s_i \leftarrow \operatorname*{argmax}_{s} \|x_i - Bs\|^2 + \lambda\|d \odot s\|^2 \quad st. \quad 1^\top s = 1$$

(6)

3. Update the current dictionary only if the computed LLC coefficient value is greater than a predefined threshold:

$$\triangle B_i \leftarrow -2\tilde{s}_i(x_i - B_i\tilde{s}_i), \quad \mu \leftarrow \sqrt{\frac{1}{i}}, \quad B_i \leftarrow B_i - \frac{\mu\triangle B_i}{|\tilde{s}_i|_2}$$

(7)

4. Project the computed dictionary onto the output matrix:

$$B(:, id) \leftarrow proj(B_i)$$

(8)

4   Experiments

We evaluated the spatio-temporal LLC (ST-LLC) using human action classification tasks.

4.1   Implementation

To extract interest points from the spatio-temporal video cube, ST-LLC was built on 2D-LLC based image classifier [15]. Firstly, the spatio-temporal regions around the interest points were described by the 3D-HOG. Publicly available code by Scovanner *et al.* [9] was used. For each interest point the descriptor length was 640-dimensional and was determined by the number of bins to represent angles, θ and ϕ, in the sub-histograms. In the SPM step, the ST-LLC codes were computed for each spatio-temporal sub-region and pooled together using multi-scale max pooling to create the corresponding pooled representation. We used 4×4, 2×2 and 1×1 sub-regions. The pooled features were then concatenated and normalised using ℓ^2-normalisation. The next step was dictionary generation; a sample of the generated descriptors for interest points were clustered to a pre-specified number of visual words. We used Elkan's k-means clustering algorithm from the *VLFeat toolbox* [18], which was faster than the standard Lloyd's k-means. A support vector machine (SVM) classifier was used to learn a model from signatures for each action. We used a one-vs-all trained linear SVM.

4.2   Experimental Setup

Four publicly available human actions datasets were employed for benchmark.

* KTH dataset [19] — six human actions (walking, jogging, running, hand-waiving, boxing and hand-clapping) with each action performed by 25 persons in four different scenarios with monotone background;
* Weizmann data [20] — human actions performed by nine actors in ten action categories: walking, running, jumping, gallop sideways, bending, one-hand-waving, two-hands-waving, jumping in place, jumping jack, and skipping. Each clip contains single person performing an action in static background;
* UCF sports data [21] — more realistic but challenging data collected from broadcast sport videos. Nine actions are publicly available: diving, golf swinging, kicking, lifting, horseback riding, running, skating, swinging, walking;
* Hollywood dataset [4] — samples from 32 real-world movies with human actions. This is a challenging dataset due to its dynamic background and camera motions, categorised to one or more of eight human actions: answer phone, get out car, hand shake, hug person, kiss, sit down, sit up, and stand up. The dataset is divided to a testing set of 211 clips collected from 20 movies and two training sets: '*automatic*' created by script-based action annotation, and '*clean*' labelled manually. We train the classifier using the *clean* training set containing 219 clips.

When constructing a Gaussian pyramid, the number of scales was set to three for each of four levels in the KTH and Weizmann datasets, and three for each of three levels in the UCF sports and Hollywood datasets. A leave-one-out cross validation was used. The following parameters were used: codebook size of 1024 words (the key parameter for dictionary training), the number of neighbours $K = 5$, $\lambda = 500$ in Equation (4) and $\sigma = 100$ in Equation (3).

Table 1. Comparison of ST-LLC and the conventional 2D-LLC

detector	descriptor	coding	KTH	Weizmann	UCF	Hollywood
ST-SIFT	3D-HOG	LLC	100%	100%	88.9%	50.0%
2D-DoG	2D-HOG	LLC	49.7%	48.0%	70.8%	19.4%

4.3 Results

Table 1 shows that the ST-SIFT detector followed by the 3D-HOG descriptor and LLC coding outperformed the conventional 2D-LLC (a combination of the original 2D DoG detector, the 2D-HOG descriptor by Lowe [8], and the spatial LLC). The accuracies with the ST-LLC representation were 100% for KTH, 100% for Weizmann, 88.89% for UCF sports and 50% for Hollywood dataset. This indicates that ST-SIFT with locality-constrained coding is able to (1) capture interest points that have vital information in both the spatial and the temporal domains and to (2) represent events in real video sequences.

4.4 Comparison with the Recent State-of-the-Art

The achieved results of the ST-LLC with the human action classification benchmarks are roughly comparable to the current state-of-the-art. The KTH and the Weizmann data are technically 'solved' datasets, as the classification accuracy of 100% was reported by several groups recently. Sun *et al.* [22] reached 100% for both datasets, while Weinland *et al.* [23], Schindler and Gool [24] and Yeffet and Wolf [25] achieved 100% for the Weizmann data. Previously Yao *et al.* [26] performed 97.8% with the Weizmann using the Hough transform voting framework. Campos *et al.* [27] achieved an accuracy of 96.7% with the Weizmann dataset and 93.5% with the KTH dataset by applying bags-of-words and spatio-temporal shapes to represent human actions. For the KTH data, Chen and Hauptmann [11] reported 95.8% and Wu *et al.* [28] resulted in 95.7%. Gilbert *et al.* [29] achieved 94.5% using a mined dense spatio-temporal features.

For the UCF sports data, the ST-LLC (88.9%) outperform most of the recently reported results including 79.2% by Yeffet and Wolf [25] and 80.0% by Campos *et al.*Wu *et al.* [28] applied a method based on Lagrangian particle trajectories and boosted the accuracy to 89.7%. The ST-LLC is in line with the state-of-the-art results published recently by Sun *et al.* [22] (86.9%), Weinland *et al.* [23] (87.7%) and Yao *et al.* [26] (86.6%). Finally for the Hollywood dataset, to our knowledge, the current best result was produced by Gilbert *et al.* [29] (53.5%) using the hierarchical data mining approach. Other reported results include Chen and Hauptmann [11] (30.9%), Klaser *et al.* [5] (24.7%), Laptev *et al.* [4] (27.0%) and Yeffet and Wolf [25] (36.8%).

5 Conclusion

In this paper we presented a spatio-temporal coding technique based on ST-SIFT descriptor for human action recognition task. The method extended the

LLC approach by utilising the ST-SIFT descriptor to densely extract salient feature points from a 3D signal. This produced a group of distinctive feature points which were invariant to scale, rotation and translation as well as robust to temporal variation. The experimental results showed that LLC with the ST-SIFT outperformed (or at least achieved as good as) the most of state-of-the-art approaches on human action classification benchmarks, including KTH, Weizmann, UCF sports and Hollywood datasets.

Acknowledgements. The first author would like to thank Umm Al-Qura University, Makkah, Saudi Arabia for funding this work as part of her PhD scholarship program.

References

1. Laptev, I.: On space-time interest points. International Journal of Computer Vision, 107–123 (2005)
2. Shechtman, E., Irani, M.: Space-time behavior-based correlation-or-how to tell if two underlying motion fields are similar without computing them? IEEE Trans. Pattern Anal. Mach. Intell., 2045–2056 (2007)
3. Liu, J., Shah, M.: Learning human actions via information maximization. In: IEEE Conference on Computer Vision and Pattern Recognition, CVPR (2008)
4. Laptev, I., Marszalek, M., Schmid, C., Rozenfeld, B.: Learning realistic human actions from movies. In: IEEE Conference on Computer Vision and Pattern Recognition, CVPR, pp. 16:1–16:43 (2008)
5. Klaser, A., Marszałek, M., Schmid, C.: A spatio-temporal descriptor based on 3D-gradients. In: BMVC, pp. 995–1004. British Machine Vision Association (2008)
6. Wong, S., Cipolla, R.: Extracting spatiotemporal interest points using global information. In: IEEE International Conference on Computer Vision, ICCV, pp. 3455–3460 (2007)
7. Willems, G., Tuytelaars, T., Van Gool, L.: An Efficient Dense and Scale-Invariant Spatio-Temporal Interest Point Detector. In: Forsyth, D., Torr, P., Zisserman, A. (eds.) ECCV 2008, Part II. LNCS, vol. 5303, pp. 650–663. Springer, Heidelberg (2008)
8. Lowe, D.G.: Distinctive image features from scale-invariant keypoints. International Journal of Computer Vision, 91–110 (2004)
9. Scovanner, P., Ali, S., Shah, M.: A 3-dimensional sift descriptor and its application to action recognition. In: Proceedings of the international conference on Multimedia, pp. 357–360. ACM (2007)
10. Cheung, W., Hamarneh, G.: N-sift: N-dimensional scale invariant feature transform for matching medical images. In: IEEE International Symposium on Biomedical Imaging: From Nano to Macro, pp. 720–723 (2007)
11. Chen, M.Y., Hauptmann, A.: Mosift: Recognizing human actions in surveillance videos. Transform, 1–16 (2009)
12. Yang, M., Zhang, L., Yang, J., Zhang, D.: Robust sparse coding for face recognition. In: Computer Vision and Pattern Recognition, CVPR, pp. 625–632 (2011)
13. Grauman, K., Darrell, T.: The pyramid match kernel: Discriminative classification with sets of image features. In: IEEE International Conference on Computer Vision, ICCV, pp. 1458–1465 (2005)

14. Yang, J., Yu, K., Gong, Y., Huang, T.: Linear spatial pyramid matching using sparse coding for image classification. In: IEEE Conference on Computer Vision and Pattern Recognition, CVPR, pp. 1794–1801 (2009)
15. Wang, J., Yang, J., Yu, K., Lv, F., Huang, T., Gong, Y.: Locality-constrained linear coding for image classification. In: IEEE Conference on Computer Vision and Pattern Recognition, pp. 3360–3367 (2010)
16. Allaire, S., Kim, J., Breen, S., Jaffray, D., Pekar, V.: Full orientation invariance and improved feature selectivity of 3D sift with application to medical image analysis. In: IEEE Computer Society Conference on Computer Vision and Pattern Recognition Workshops, CVPR (2008)
17. Lopes, A., Oliveira, R., de Almeida, J., de A Araujo, A.: Spatio-temporal frames in a bag-of-visual-features approach for human actions recognition. In: XXII Brazilian Symposium on Computer Graphics and Image Processing, pp. 315–321 (2009)
18. Vedaldi, A., Fulkerson, B.: Vlfeat: an open and portable library of computer vision algorithms. In: Proceedings of the International Conference on Multimedia, pp. 1469–1472. ACM (2010)
19. Schuldt, C., Laptev, I., Caputo, B.: Recognizing human actions: a local svm approach. In: Proceedings of the International Conference on Pattern Recognition, pp. 32–36 (2004)
20. Blank, M., Gorelick, L., Shechtman, E., Irani, M., Basri, R.: Actions as space-time shapes. In: The IEEE International Conference on Computer Vision, ICCV, pp. 1395–1402 (2005)
21. Rodriguez, M., Ahmed, J., Shah, M.: Action mach a spatio-temporal maximum average correlation height filter for action recognition. In: IEEE Conference on Computer Vision and Pattern Recognition, CVPR (2008)
22. Sun, C., Junejo, I.N., Foroosh, H.: Action recognition using rank-1 approximation of joint self-similarity volume. In: IEEE International Conference on Computer Vision, ICCV, pp. 1007–1012 (2011)
23. Weinland, D., Özuysal, M., Fua, P.: Making Action Recognition Robust to Occlusions and Viewpoint Changes. In: Daniilidis, K., Maragos, P., Paragios, N. (eds.) ECCV 2010, Part III. LNCS, vol. 6313, pp. 635–648. Springer, Heidelberg (2010)
24. Schindler, K., Van Gool, L.: Action snippets: How many frames does human action recognition require? In: IEEE Conference on Computer Vision and Pattern Recognition, CVPR (2008)
25. Yeffet, L., Wolf, L.: Local trinary patterns for human action recognition. In: IEEE International Conference on Computer Vision, ICCV, pp. 492–497 (2009)
26. Yao, A., Gall, J., Van Gool, L.: A hough transform-based voting framework for action recognition. In: Computer Vision and Pattern Recognition, CVPR, pp. 2061–2068 (2010)
27. de Campos, T., Barnard, M., Mikolajczyk, K., Kittler, J., Yan, F., Christmas, W., Windridge, D.: An evaluation of bags-of-words and spatio-temporal shapes for action recognition. In: IEEE Workshop on Applications of Computer Vision, WACV, pp. 344–351 (2011)
28. Wu, S., Oreifej, O., Shah, M.: Action recognition in videos acquired by a moving camera using motion decomposition of lagrangian particle trajectories. In: IEEE International Conference on Computer Vision, ICCV, pp. 1419–1426 (2011)
29. Gilbert, A., Illingworth, J., Bowden, R.: Fast realistic multi-action recognition using mined dense spatio-temporal features. In: IEEE International Conference on Computer Vision, ICCV, pp. 925–931 (2009)

Real Time Detection of Social Interactions in Surveillance Video

Paolo Rota, Nicola Conci, and Nicu Sebe

University of Trento, via Sommarive 5, Povo (TN) Italy

Abstract. In this paper we present a novel method to detect the presence of social interactions occurring in a surveillance scenario. The algorithm we propose complements motion features with proxemics cues, so as to link the human motion with the contextual and environmental information. The extracted features are analyzed through a multiclass SVM. Testing has been carried out distinguishing between casual and intentional interactions, where intentional events are further subdivided into normal and abnormal behaviors. The algorithm is validated on benchmark datasets, as well as on a new dataset specifically designed for interactions analysis.

1 Introduction

The research in video surveillance and environmental monitoring has revealed a recent trend in bringing the analysis of the scene to a higher level, shifting the attention from traditional topics, such as tracking and trajectory analysis [1], towards the semantic interpretation of the events occurring in the scene [2,3]. In particular, behavior analysis in terms of action and activity recognition has emerged as a relevant subject of research, especially for classification and anomaly detection purposes. Important contributions to the field have been proposed by Scovanner et al. [4], in which authors learn pedestrian parameters from video data to improve detection and tracking, and by Robertson et al. [5] where human behavior recognition is modeled as a stochastic sequence of actions described by trajectory information and local motion descriptors.

Bringing the analysis to a higher level of interpretation involves understanding the real social relationships undergoing between subjects, thus requiring to extend the analysis domain also to psychology and sociology. To this aim, the proxemics theory can be effectively exploited to observe the human relationships captured by a surveillance camera [6,7].

The goal of proxemics is to measure the social distance between subjects in order to infer interpersonal relationships. In this area, the works by Cristani et al. [8] aim at understanding the social relations among subjects when sharing a common space. The authors detect the so-called F-Formations present in the scene, thus inferring whether an interaction between two or more persons is occurring or not. A recent and relevant approach based on proxemics has been proposed by Zen et al. [9]. The authors identify proxemics cues in order

A. Fusiello et al. (Eds.): ECCV 2012 Ws/Demos, Part III, LNCS 7585, pp. 111–120, 2012.

to discriminate personality traits as *neuroticism* and *extraversion*, and use the collected data to construct the corresponding behavioral model. The acquired data is then used to improve the accuracy of the tracking algorithm. A similar approach has been proposed by Pellegrini et al. [10], using the social force model [11]. The solution proposed in [10] considers each subject as an agent, for which the model of motion has to be optimized, so as to prevent collisions with the other entities moving in the scene. The authors consider every agent as driven by its destination, taking into account, besides position, also additional parameters like velocity and direction of motion. The collected data is then used to build a model to measure the proximity level between the subjects, and to construct an avoidance function. A very recent approach is the work by Cui et al. [12]. The authors extract an *interaction energy potential* to model the relationships ongoing among groups of people. The relationship between the current state of the subject and the corresponding reaction is then used to model normal and abnormal behaviors. The authors also claim that their approach is independent from the adopted tool for human motion segmentation.

A hierarchical approach is instead proposed by [13] where human behavior is described at multiple levels of detail ranging from macro events to low-level actions. Authors exploit the fact that social roles and actions are interdependent one to each other and related to the macro event that is taking place.

In this work we define the interaction as a combination of energy functions that capture the state of a subject in the social context he moves. Since tracking is out of the scope of this work, our goal is to build a classifier to identify and recognize different types of behaviors. A novel aspect we introduce with respect to [10], consists in the insertion of an *intentionality* parameter in the processing chain, targeted at distinguishing between intentional and casual interactions. This term, provided by the proxemics information, is used to weight the interaction patterns acquired in real-time on a sliding window basis. The output of the function is then brought into the Fourier domain, thus removing the temporal correlation of the samples, and eventually fed into an SVM classifier. We have devised three different scenarios: (i) casual interaction, (ii) normal, and (iii) abnormal interaction. The interactions of type (i) refer to non-intentional events, while the type (ii) and (iii) reveal intentional interactions, divided into regular and potentially dangerous events.

The method has been tested on three datasets specifically chosen for human interaction analysis.

2   Methodology

According to the proxemics principles, distances can say a lot about the relationships going on between people, about their intimacy level, making it possible to distinguish between intentional and non-intentional behavioral cues. This information is generally variable in space in time and depends on the location in which a person stands, on the density of people in the area, but also on cultural and religious differences.

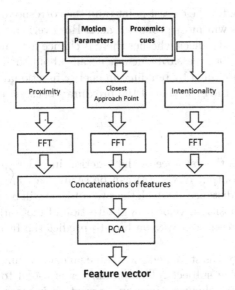

Fig. 1. Flowchart of the proposed architecture

Fig. 1 shows the proposed architecture for social interaction analysis, for which we will provide additional details in the next subsections.

2.1 Proxemics Parameters

In the model we propose, we follow the path covered by Pellegrini et al. [10] in order to capture the salient motion features that can be associated to an interaction. Each subject i is modeled at each time t by a state vector of parameters that takes into account the current position and velocity:

$$S_i(t) = [\mathbf{p}_i(t), \mathbf{v}_i(t)] \tag{1}$$

At each time instant t it is then possible to model the distance between each pair of subjects (i, j) as:

$$d_{ij}^2 = \left\| \mathbf{p}_i + t\mathbf{v}_i - \mathbf{p}_j - t\mathbf{v}_j \right\|^2 \tag{2}$$

By defining $\mathbf{k}_{ij}^t = \mathbf{p}_i^t - \mathbf{p}_j^t$ and $\mathbf{q}_{ij}^t = \mathbf{v}_i^t - \mathbf{v}_j^t$ and applying the derivative with respect to t in Eq. (2), it is possible to find the time instant t^* at which the distance d_{ij}^* between the subjects is minimized.

$$t^* = -\frac{\mathbf{k} \cdot \mathbf{q}}{\left\| \mathbf{q} \right\|^2}, \quad d_{ij}^{*2} = \left\| \mathbf{k} - \frac{\mathbf{k} \cdot \mathbf{q}}{\left\| \mathbf{q} \right\|^2} \mathbf{q}^\top \right\|^2 \tag{3}$$

Eq. (3) is the estimate for the closest point (and the corresponding time instant), at which the subjects will most probably meet. However, this piece of information, although relevant to check whether there is chance for i and j to interact in the next future, does not necessarily include details about their interaction level. An estimate can be obtained by building an energy functional between subjects i and j by measuring the evolution of the proximity between them over time:

$$E_{ij}^c = e^{-\frac{d_{ij}^{*2}}{2\sigma_d^2}} \tag{4}$$

In Eq. (4) σ_d controls the variance of the function in order to make it more or less responsive. The output of Eq. (4) can be seen as a *collision warning*, and represents the closest distance at which the two subjects will be, given the current motion parameters (position, velocity and direction of motion). This element is important because it can be used as a hint to predict the future developments of the interaction.

In line with the previous statement, we define an energy function to model the actual distance between subjects. This parameter is useful to obtain a proper modeling of the social behavior, since an interaction is more likely to happen when two persons are closer rather than when they are far apart from each other.

$$E_{ij}^d = e^{-\frac{\|\mathbf{k}_{ij}^w\|^2}{2\sigma_w^2}} \tag{5}$$

In [10], and for tracking purposes, the authors use the term E_{ij}^d as a weight to model the outcome of Eq. (4) together with another term depending on the angle between the direction of motion of i and the position of j. Our goal is however different, since we want to understand the dynamics of the interaction. Furthermore, the direction information, is in general noisy, particularly in the case of unrestricted video scenes, and for these reasons it has been discarded from out model.

In order to model the intentionality of an interaction, we adopt the so-called *O-space* [14]. The *O-space* consists of a circular area between the subjects, located in the direction of their gaze. It can be seen as the interaction space, namely the area comprised between two people interacting and facing one to each other.

By means of this definition, the *O-Space* can be used as a selectivity criterion, i.e. to inform about the presence of an interaction. The *O-Space* is in general defined as a static and non-deformable area right in front of the person and is not suitable for dynamic motion models, in which interactions can occur also in case the subjects move (e.g. walking together). Therefore, in our proposal we borrow the idea of the *O-space* as an area of attention of the subject, which can be adopted to infer the intentionality (or causality) of an interaction. In our model the *O-space* is positioned along the direction of motion of the subject and its center varies depending on his velocity. This gives us the opportunity of handling also dynamic interactions, and not only static events.

The position of the *O-space* is defined as:

$$Ox = p_x + a_x \Lambda \sin(\theta)$$
$$Oy = p_y - a_y \Lambda \cos(\theta)$$

(6)

where p_x and p_y are the coordinates of the subject, Λ is the displacement of the subject from the previous frame, a_x and a_y are tuning parameters depending on the field of view of the camera, and θ is the absolute direction of motion. The *O-space* area is used to calculate the intentionality component of the interaction, similarly to what we did for the proxemics information:

$$E_{ij}^o = e^{-\frac{\left\|\mathbf{k}_{ij}^o\right\|^2}{2\sigma_o^2}}$$

(7)

where k_{ij}^O is the distance between the *O-space* centers of subject i and j , respectively. This parameter allows to filter out the noisy information collected by the other terms (for example two people very close but facing in opposite directions), thus reducing the chances of false positives returned in the presence of casual interactions of subjects standing nearby. The *O-space* model we have adopted is shown in Fig. 2.

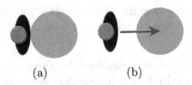

(a)   (b)

Fig. 2. O-space modeling. The figure represents the two cases in which the subject is (a) standing still, and (b) when he is moving from left to right. In the latter case the O-space shifts in the direction of motion proportionally with its velocity.

2.2   Feature Extraction

Following the flow chart in Fig. 1 we collect the proxemics values $E_{ij}^d(t), E_{ij}^c(t),$ $E_{ij}^o(t)$ in a given temporal window (128 samples in our examples), and at each time instant we apply the FFT (Fast Fourier Transform) (8) on the window samples. At this stage, the importance of the FFT is to eliminate the temporal correlation of the samples by only considering the contribution they bring into the interaction in terms of dynamics of that specific event.

$$X_k = \sum_{n=0}^{N-1} x_n e^{-i2\pi k \frac{n}{N}} \quad k = 0, ..., N-1$$

(8)

The next step consists of concatenating the three sets of features to construct the feature vector that will be analyzed by the classifier. This process is carried out at every time instant, resulting in a large number of parameters (128x3).

Therefore, we apply a dimensionality reduction through Principal Component Analysis (PCA). Accordingly, the training set is arranged in a $n \times m$ matrix where n is the number of samples and m the number of features. From the matrix X the eigenvalues of the related zero mean covariance matrix are extracted and the obtained vector is sorted by magnitude in descending order. The first value is the so-called principal component. From eigenvalues vector we can compute eigenvectors $m \times m$ matrix.

$$Y = W_s^T X \qquad (9)$$

As shown in (9) the feature space has now been reduced, restraining the training set to a new matrix of size $n \times s$ where $s < m$ is the number of eigenvectors that we consider as relevant for our analysis.

Now that we have constructed our training set, we adopt a similar procedure for prediction. Each new incoming sample consists of a $1 \times m$ vector that is processed as X in (9) obtaining as output a $1 \times s$ vector. This new vector is the input for the SVM, from which we will classify the type of the ongoing interaction.

2.3   Classification Procedure

After obtaining the reduced feature space, classification is computed using a kernel based SVM. Since the classification output strongly depends on the data used for training, let us briefly see what are the main steps we follow to obtain a reliable training set:

- Select the training videos representing the three classes that we want to classify with the frame-by-frame interaction labeling (manually done in a previous stage);
- Compute the interaction values as presented in Section 2.1 for the whole duration of the video;
- Segment the interaction values in accordance with the labels;
- Run the sliding window over the segmented interaction values, and consider each step as a feature vector;
- Transform each feature vector in the FFT domain and reduce the dimensionality using Principal Component Analysis;
- The resulting arrays consist of the features space for the classifier, which will be tuned by cross validation optimization to estimate the best configuration for the class separation.

It is worth noting that samples for training are picked randomly and in equal number for each class from the dataset, in order to avoid any possible bias in the training and to prevent overfitting of a particular class with respect to the others.

In the test phase the procedure simply consists of collecting the sliding window data at each time step, compute the FFT transform and the PCA decomposition using the training eigenvectors, thus building the new space. Data are then sent to the classifier for the final class prediction.

3   Results

Datasets. To validate our method we have used three different datasets: our own dataset SI (Social Interactions) Dataset [15], a selection of video sequences collection of YouTube CCTV videos (different contexts) and some sequences taken from the BEHAVE database.

The SI Dataset has been acquired to specifically address the topic of interactions analysis, since the number of social interactions occurring in more traditional datasets such as the PETS is limited, making it difficult to obtain sufficient statistical evidence. The set consists of 12 fully annotated video sequences of different length recorded at 25 FPS. Sequences mainly represent regular daily life behaviors such as people chatting, walking together or simply crossing each other. The dataset also includes more critical types of interactions, simulating

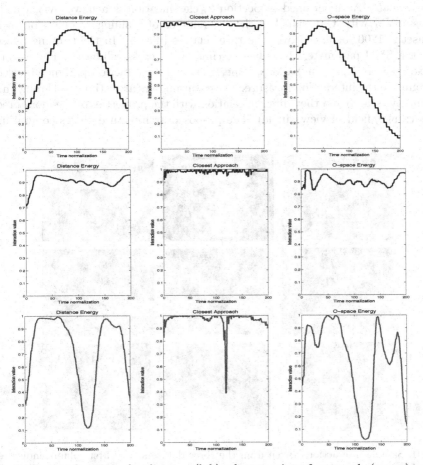

Fig. 3. Energy functions for distance (left), closest point of approach (center), and O-Space (right), in presence of two people crossing (first row), chatting (second row), and fighting (third row)

fights. The video sequences are recorded outdoor, under three different views, for which we will use here only the bird's eye view for similarity with the other datasets. For our experiments, and considering that tracking is out of the scope of this paper, we use the collected ground truth, from which it is possible to extrapolate all the necessary parameters required by our method.

The YouTube dataset is composed by 4 video sequences recorded in as many different locations. This dataset is not homogeneous because the videos come from different sources, with different view angles and different fields of view. For there reasons the videos are very challenging, since they represent real-life situations, and are not acquired with any specific purpose.

From the BEHAVE dataset [16] we have included in the experiments two different segments regarding different behavioral situations. Also here videos are acquired from far range, and are only partially annotated. We have then collected the corresponding ground truth.

Experiments. As mentioned in Section 2, classification is achieved via a multiclass SVM with Gaussian kernel. The number of training samples for each dataset is 1200, balanced over the three classes (400x3). In the training phase the best SVM parameters have been estimated by cross-validation. The testing phase takes as input the SVM parameters and the interaction parameters used to compute the interaction measure. These parameters are estimated through an exhaustive search and they differ in relation with the properties of the monitored area (range, field of view, angle). The proposed architecture allows computing

Fig. 4. Sample interactions taken from the three datasets. The first column indicates casual interactions, the central column refers to normal interactions, while the last column signals the presence of abnormal interactions.

the interaction measure on-line, without waiting for the end of the interaction. In fact, the complexity of the algorithm is negligible, compared to computational resources required for people detection and tracking. In Fig. 3 the energy functions obtained from three different sample sequences are shown.

In terms of numerical results we present two different tables, where it is possible to observe the effectiveness of our approach, especially in unconstrained scenarios, in which the interpretation of the interactions could be problematic. As it can be noticed from Table 1 and Table 2, the algorithm performs in general well especially in detecting the presence of an interaction, in all three datasets used for testing. As far as the class 3 is concerned (anomalous events) and considering the complexity of the task, the improvement given by the O-Space term is considerable (more than 20% in precision) due to the capability of better isolating the interacting subjects. A graphical presentation of the classification process is shown in Fig. 4. Here, each line reports three snapshots taken from the different datasets, each of them representing one of the classes. White lines (left column) indicate that no interaction is currently ongoing, yellow lines (center column) refer to normal interactions, while red lines (right column) indicate the presence of an abnormal event.

Table 1. Performance comparison of the proposed algorithm with and without the O-Space energy on the three datasets

		O-space Method			Without O-space Method		
		Precision	Recall	HitRate	Precision	Recall	HitRate
SI	Casual	93,3%	94,1%		93,5%	91,1%	
	Normal	75,1%	76,1%	88,5%	63,3%	77,5%	86,1%
	Abnormal	55,3%	48,7%		55,4%	45,3%	
Behave	Casual	75,8%	93,8%		75,3%	93,8%	
	Normal	98,0%	93,9%	90,1%	97,7%	94,3%	90,1%
	Abnormal	42,5%	27,5%		43,6%	22,6%	
YouTube	Casual	88,2%	90,2%		66,3%	76,2%	
	Normal	84,4%	80,2%	82,7%	70,9%	43,7%	60,1%
	Abnormal	38,2%	40,3%		11,0%	17,7%	

Table 2. Confusion matrices for the three datasets obtained using the O-Space energy

		Casual	Normal	Abnormal
SI	Casual	94,07%	3,68%	2,25%
	Normal	18,49%	76,17%	5,34%
	Abnormal	37,56%	15,34%	47,10%
Behave	Casual	93,82%	3,53%	2,65%
	Normal	3,98%	93,92%	2,10%
	Abnormal	61,83%	10,92%	27,25%
YouTube	Casual	90,16%	5,00%	4,85%
	Normal	12,74%	80,23%	7,03%
	Abnormal	29,71%	29,92%	40,37%

4 Conclusion

In this paper we have proposed a tool to analyze social interactions in surveillance video, combining traditional metrics based on distance and velocity, and proxemics cues. Proxemics is handled as an intentionality parameter, giving the opportunity to better focus on the events of interest by considering only the moving subjects whose motion patterns demonstrate a will to interact. The method has been evaluated on three different datasets, confirming the viability of the method in recognizing different types of interactions. One of the datasets, specifically designed for social interactions analysis is provided by the authors as an additional contribution of the paper.

References

1. Piotto, N., Conci, N., De Natale, F.: Syntactic matching of trajectories for ambient intelligence applications. IEEE Transactions on Multimedia 11(7), 1266–1275 (2009)
2. Zhang, Y., Ge, W., Chang, M., Liu, X.: Group context learning for event recognition. In: WACV (2010)
3. Turaga, P., Chellappa, R., Subrahmanian, V., Udrea, O.: Machine recognition of human activities: A survey. IEEE Transactions on Circuits and Systems for Video Technology 18(11), 1473–1488 (2008)
4. Scovanner, P., Tappen, M.: Learning pedestrian dynamics from the real world. In: ICCV, pp. 381–388 (2009)
5. Robertson, N., Reid, I.: Behaviour understanding in video: a combined method. In: ICCV, vol. 1 (2005)
6. Hall, E.: The hidden dimension, vol. 6. Doubleday, New York (1966)
7. Hall, E.: The silent language. Anchor (1973)
8. Cristani, M., Bazzani, L., Paggetti, G., Fossati, A., Tosato, D., Del Bue, A., Menegaz, G., Murino, V.: Social interaction discovery by statistical analysis of f-formations. In: Proceedings of British Machine Vision Conference (2011)
9. Zen, G., Lepri, B., Ricci, E., Lanz, O.: Space speaks: towards socially and personality aware visual surveillance. In: MPVA 2010, pp. 37–42. ACM (2010)
10. Pellegrini, S., Ess, A., Schindler, K., Van Gool, L.: You'll never walk alone: Modeling social behavior for multi-target tracking. In: ICCV (2009)
11. Mehran, R., Oyama, A., Shah, M.: Abnormal crowd behavior detection using social force model. In: CVPR (2009)
12. Cui, X., Liu, Q., Gao, M., Metaxas, D.: Abnormal detection using interaction energy potentials. In: CVPR, pp. 3161–3167 (2011)
13. Lan, T., Sigal, L., Mori, G.: Social roles in hierarchical models for human activity recognition. In: CVPR (2012)
14. Cristani, M., Paggetti, G., Vinciarelli, A., Bazzani, L., Menegaz, G., Murino, V.: Towards computational proxemics: Inferring social relations from interpersonal distances. In: SocialCom, pp. 290–297 (2011)
15. Rota, P., Zhang, B., Ullah, H., Conci, N.: Unitn social interactions dataset. University of Trento, Italy (2012), http://mmlab.science.unitn.it/USID/
16. Laghaee, A.: Behave dataset (2007),
    http://homepages.inf.ed.ac.uk/rbf/BEHAVE/

Towards Space-Time Semantics in Two Frames

Karla Brkić[1],*, Axel Pinz[2], Zoran Kalafatić[1], and Siniša Šegvić[1]

[1] University of Zagreb, Faculty of Electrical Engineering and Computing, Croatia
[2] Graz University of Technology, Austria

Abstract. We present a novel, low-level scheme to analyze spatial and temporal change within a local support region. Assuming available region correspondences between two adjacent frames, we divide each region into a regular grid of patches. Depending on the change of an image function inside the patch over time, each patch is assigned weights for the following four labels: "C" for a constant patch, "O" when new information originates from outside the support region, "I" for "inner" changes, and "N" for information from neighboring patches. Our method goes beyond optical flow, as it provides an additional semantic level of understanding the changes in space-time. We demonstrate how our novel "COIN" scheme can be used to categorize local space-time events in image pairs, including locally planar support regions, 3D discontinuities, and virtual vs. real crossings of 3D structures.

1 Introduction

In this paper we focus on discovering scene structure at a very low level (e.g. the level of an interest point or a small image patch), assuming that a temporal sequence of at least two frames is available. Changes in low-level appearance over the course of two frames are encoded in a semantically meaningful descriptor which assigns weights to the following hypotheses: constant, influenced by neighbor, inner change, outer change. Using the descriptor, we are able to reason about coplanarity, discontinuity and general stability of appearance of the region of interest.

Analysis of low-level dynamic structure in video is related to several research strands. One is spatiotemporal texture recognition. There, short video clips are usually represented by generative statistical models [1]. A recent approach [2] attempts to capture the spectrum of dominant image motions which arise for instance when looking at the snow falling in the wind. Each video clip is represented by a 28 bin histogram containing evidence for a small predefined set of image motions, such as e.g. "upward motion of two pixels per frame".

Another related research strand includes the analysis of occluding boundaries and video segmentation [3]. Many of the existing approaches are based on locating contrasting optical flow (e.g. [4, 5]). A promising approach which avoids the

---

* This research has been supported by the University of Zagreb Development Fund and Research Centre for Advanced Cooperative Systems (EU FP7 #285939).

A. Fusiello et al. (Eds.): ECCV 2012 Ws/Demos, Part III, LNCS 7585, pp. 121–130, 2012.

dependence on optical flow has been presented [6]. There, the occluding boundaries are detected as regions with high curvature of spatio-temporal contrast in the frequency domain, much along the lines of the known Harris corner detector.

Finally, our work is related to sparse spatio-temporal features [7–12]. An early treatise of this concept [7], proposes an interest point detector suitable for classifying actions such as eye opening or knee bending. A more advanced implementation of that concept has been proposed in [13], as a generalization of the known HOG detector to the 3D case. A recent approach [14] has demonstrated that sparse spatio-temporal features can be used to detect occlusion boundaries as well.

In this work, we analyze changes in local appearance by dividing the region of interest into a grid of patches and assigning weights to individual hypotheses based on patch histograms in two consecutive frames. We avoid building on top of optical flow, as dense optical flow can not be accurately computed in many cases of practical importance. Optical flow approaches typically optimize some kind of correspondence criterion: if the objective function is multimodal (such as at an aliased texture) it is easy to get stuck at a wrong local maximum. In contrast to the work of Derpanis and Wildes, [2, 6] our approach supports the notion of emergent events of the low level structure in video, and can naturally represent occurrences of uncovered texture behind the occlusion boundaries.

2   The COIN Descriptor

The COIN descriptor is a semantic descriptor of temporal change in local appearance of an image region. The observed region is divided into a regular grid of $m \times n$ patches. The semantic description is obtained by studying patch appearance in two consecutive frames at times t_1 and $t_2 > t_1$.

First, we model patch appearance by histograms of a particular image function. Then, the histogram of each patch in t_2 is compared to the histograms of the patch itself and the 4-neighborhood in t_1. Based on the comparison and the position of the patch itself within the grid, we assign weights to one of the following four hypotheses: C - the patch remained constant in time, O - there is new information in the patch which originated from outside the grid, I - the patch changed "by itself", i.e without outer influence, N - the information in the patch originated from one of its neighbors from the previous frame.

COIN can be calculated for various spatial resolutions in three different scenarios: i) using a fixed grid over entire frames, we want to find semantically interesting structures in a scene; ii) on the level of an interest point, we wish to describe an interest point and answer questions such as is it stable, does it depict a depth discontinuity or a planar surface; iii) on the level of an object of interest, we search for spatio-temporal structure within a bounding box. While case i) is "camera-centered", cases ii) and iii) require frame-to-frame correspondences, established by interest point or object tracking. In this paper we restrict the experimental analysis of the descriptor properties to the level of an interest point, but the descriptor is well-suited to be applied to scenarios i) and iii) as well.

2.1 Calculating Patch Histograms

Without loss of generality, let us assume that we have two bounding boxes around an image region of interest, one taken at time t_1 and another at time $t_2 > t_1$. We denote their widths and heights as (w_1, h_1) and (w_2, h_2), respectively. Each bounding box is divided into a regular grid of $m \times n$ patches. The size of an individual patch within the first boundig box is $(w_1/m, h_1/n)$, while the size of an individual patch within the second bounding box is $(w_2/m, h_2/n)$. We denote the patches within the grid at time t_i as $p_1^{t_i}, p_2^{t_i}, \ldots, p_{m \times n}^{t_i}$. For an illustration, see Fig. 1, depicting COIN calculation on a series of synthetic images. The images, shown in the first row of the figure, consist of a regular grid of diversely colored rectangles. In dividing the images into a regular grid of 5×5 patches, each patch will fall perfectly into one colored rectangle, and will contain a single dominant hue plus the black rectangle border.

For each patch $p_i^{t_1}$ we calculate a patch histogram $H_i^{t_1}$ for a previously chosen image function (hue, value, saturation, or gradient). The same is done for patches $p_j^{t_2}$. This step results in two collections of a total of $m \times n$ histograms (which we call grids of histograms), one obtained in time t_1 and another in time t_2. Each histogram represents a $(w/m) \times (h/n)$-sized subregion of the image ROI. We denote the histogram of i-th patch in time t_j as $H_i^{t_j}$.

After calculating image function histograms, they are normalized so that $\sum b_k = 1$, $b_k \in H_i^{t_j}$, i.e. the values of all histogram bins sum to 1.

2.2 Assigning C, O, I, N Hypotheses

Having calculated an image function histogram of a patch in time t_2, we want to determine what happened to the patch, given its appearance in t_1. To do so, we use three operations: histogram intersection, $H_i \cap H_j$; histogram subtraction, $H_i \backslash H_j$; and histogram mass computation, $\mu(H_i)$. The result of histogram intersection is a new histogram in which the value of each bin is the minimum value from the two intersected histograms. Subtraction is achieved simply by subtracting bin values, and mass computation by summing them.

We adhere to the normalized histograms paradigm adopted so far, and aim at assigning each patch $p_k^{t_2}$ a four-dimensional, COIN function (C, O, I, N), which is normalized, so that $C + O + I + N = 1$. The idea is to first calculate the change in the appearance of the patch histogram which cannot be attributed neither to its appearance in the previous frame nor to one of its neighbors. This change is then labeled as inner or outer, and the remaining mass is distributed to constant and neighbor hypotheses. We start by finding the patch $p_l^{t_1}$ among the patches in 4-neighborhood of $p_k^{t_2}$ for which $\mu(H_k^{t_2} \cap H_l^{t_1})$ is maximal. In other words, for the patch in the current frame, we find the most similar 4-neighbor in the previous frame based on the mass of intersection of their histograms. Note that here we observe only the 4-neighborhood, assuming that we have sufficient spatial and

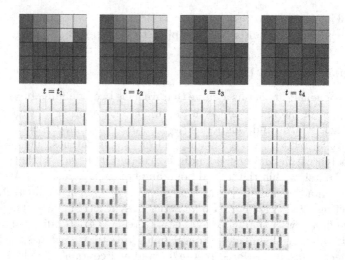

Fig. 1. Our running example explaining all the steps of the COIN calculation process. The descriptor components for each image patch are displayed in different colors and in order: C, O, I, N. C occurs both in transition from frame 1 to frame 2 (they are equivalent), as well as in the red area of the grid in the first three frames. O occurs in the left column of frames 3 and 4. In frame 4, two red patches change to magenta. Magenta was not seen within the grid before, therefore we assign O to the bottom right patch and I to the center patch.

temporal resolution to capture interesting events under that constraint. Next, by intersecting the current and the previous patch histogram, we get what these two histograms have in common. If we then subtract that from the current patch histogram,

$$\Gamma = H_k^{t_2} \backslash (H_k^{t_1} \cap H_k^{t_2}), \qquad (1)$$

what remains is the histogram of change in appearance of the patch. This change either arrived from a neighbor, or the patch was changed by inner/outer influences. We can now compute the joint weight of inner and outer hypotheses,

$$\omega_{IO} = \Gamma \backslash (\Gamma \cap H_l^{t_1}), \qquad (2)$$

following the same logic as in the computation of Γ.

The value $\mu(\omega_{IO})$ is the mass of the total change in appearance of the histogram which cannot be attributed to a neighbor. There are two cases that can happen: (i) there is information which was not seen before, and it originated within the patch itself, or (ii) there is change which originated from outside the bounding box. To distinguish between these cases, we use a prior: a $m \times n$ matrix of values from 0 to 1, where the value α_k at the position of the studied patch k denotes the probability of the inner hypothesis. We usually choose values of α_k to reflect that outer change is more likely to occur closer to the border of the bounding box than inner change. We might, for instance, consider using a Gaussian kernel or a similar matrix. The values of I and O are then:

$$I = \alpha_k \omega_{IO}, \quad O = (1 - \alpha_k)\omega_{IO} \tag{3}$$

As ω_{IO} is always smaller than 1, we can find the rest of the mass which is to be assigned to constant and neighbor hypotheses as:

$$\omega_{CN} = 1 - \omega_{IO} \tag{4}$$

We denote the intersection mass between the histogram of the current patch and the histogram of the previous patch as

$$\omega_C = \mu(H_k^{t_2} \cap H_k^{t_1}), \tag{5}$$

and the intersection mass between the histogram of the current patch and the histogram of the most similar neighbor as

$$\omega_N = \mu(H_k^{t_2} \cap H_l^{t_1}) \tag{6}$$

Both ω_C and ω_N are between 0 and 1. We would like to proportionally distribute the remaining mass ω_{CN} to ω_C and ω_N to obtain the weights of C and N hypotheses. We do so in the following manner:

$$C = \frac{\omega_C}{\omega_C + \omega_N} \omega_{CN}, \text{ and } N = \frac{\omega_N}{\omega_C + \omega_N} \omega_{CN} \tag{7}$$

Following the computation outlined above, we obtain the values C, O, I, N which form the COIN function of the patch $p_k^{t_2}$. By concatenating values of COIN functions for each patch in the grid, we obtain the COIN descriptor. As an example, consider the first two frames in Fig. 1. The two frames are exactly the same. Calculated COIN descriptors between frames are shown in the third row of the figure. They are represented as $m \times n$ 4-bin histograms, where each histogram represents the weights $C, O, I,$ and N. Due to the nature of COIN computation, all weights sum to 1. As the first two frames are equal, we might expect $C = 1$ for all patches of the COIN descriptor, but this is the case just for histogram 10. Notice that every patch except patch 10 has a twin neighbor, i.e a neighbor which looks exactly like it. Therefore, it might be the case that the patch and the neighbor have switched places, even though apparently the image is unchanged. Thus, all patches but patch 10 have $C = N = 0.5$. Patch 10 has no twin neighbors, resulting in $C = 1$. In the two top rows for transitions from frames 2 to 3 and 3 to 4 we see $N = 1$. This is due to colored patches moving to the right. Finally, we see inner and outer change in the second and the third COIN descriptor. In the second COIN, we see that patches near the left edge bring in new information. In the third COIN, we additionally see $I = 1$ in the center patch, outer change in the bottom right corner. Here, we used a simple prior of $\alpha_k = 0$ for all the patches at the border of the bounding box, $\alpha_k = 1$ otherwise. Of course, in real scenarios inner change could also happen at the border of the bounding box (a person suddenly appearing in a window, or a semaphore changing its signal), but this should then be covered by an adequate selection of the prior.

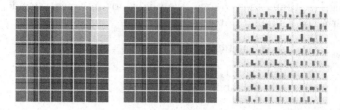

Fig. 2. An 8 × 8 grid superimposed on frames 3 and 4 and the calculated COIN descriptor

3 Experiments

In our experiments, we highlight and analyze various properties of our novel COIN descriptor. We start (3.1) with some more analysis on the synthetic images used in section 2 regarding parameter settings (i.e. grid size). Next (3.2), we present results on real image sequences taken in our lab. In these experiments we concentrate on space-time semantics that can be deduced from COINs. To highlight these semantic aspects of COINs, we have chosen a colorful world that can be well represented by histograms of hue. Finally (3.3), we show results in discriminating different types of low-level structure on a sequence from the DTU Robot Data Set.

3.1 Further Experiments on the Synthetic Image Sequence

In section 2 we used a simple synthetic sequence as our running example. The sequence consists of colored rectangles, and in our previous discussion we used a grid of 5 × 5 patches, which aligned perfectly with the grid present in the image. But what if we were to use a finer grid, where patches would contain multiple colors? Would the underlying behavior still be visible? Fig. 2 illustrates a grid of 8 × 8 patches superimposed on synthetic images in frames 3 and 4, and the COIN descriptor calculated on that grid. All other parameters, including the inner prior, were the same as in the previous example. What is apparent from this simple experiment is that the COIN descriptor generates a semantically correct description of what happens in time even if we use unfavorable grid sizes. In the first column of the 8 × 8 grid we clearly see outer change, the same as in the first column of the 5 × 5 grid (see Fig.1). We can also notice that both the inner and the outer change of red to magenta are still reflected within COIN histograms, although now distributed through four cells in the grid instead of one. This is because magenta rectangles now span through four image patches, insted of corresponding perfectly to a single patch. It is interesting to notice the first two rows within the fifth column of the histogram grid. There, we would expect to see maximum weight assigned to the neighbor hypothesis, but it is instead assigned to the inner and outer hypotheses. If we have a look at the fifth patch in the first row in frame 1, it is mostly light-blue, with a little bit of green. Its first neighbors are either light blue or green, the nearest dark blue neighbor is 2 places in the grid away. In frame 2, the patch receives a lot of dark blue. As we analyze only the 4-neighborhood of the patch, the neighbor hypothesis gets weighted down and the outer hypothesis dominates, which is a reasonable behavior. If undesirable, it could be tuned out by modifying the parameter α_k.

3.2   The Color World Experiments

Verifying that the COIN concept works on simple synthetic images, we moved on to testing it on real images. For that purpose, we created the experimental setup depicted in Fig. 3. The background is an 80×30 cm poster comprised of 1×1 cm squares. While all squares have maximum saturation and value in HSV space, the hue of each is random. In the foreground, we have placed several arrangements of 10×10 cm targets, including homogeneous as well as random colors, holes in a target, and real as well as "virtual" crossings. In all cases, the camera has been translated from right to left, frontoparallel to the background, at a distance of approx. 1 m. In these experiments, the observed behavior of COIN descriptors was very similar to its behavior on synthetic data. Due to space limitations, here we will briefly present just a descriptor of a real crossing and a descriptor of a virtual crossing and discuss how the two might be distinguished.

Fig. 3. Our experimental setup. (left): Camera taking a sequence. (middle and right): Our experimental setup to capture the "real" and "virtual" crossings shown in Fig. 4. The camera is translated parallel to the background target at a distance of 1m, using a focal length of 100 mm and an aperture setting of 22. All targets show random hue patches of maximum saturation and value, foreground targets are 10×10 cm. For the "virtual" crossing (Fig. 4 top), the two targets are placed at 22 cm, and 40 cm in front of the background, while the "real" crossing (Fig. 4 bottom) is placed 15 cm in front of the background.

The top row of Fig. 4 depicts two frames of two textured targets overlapping, and the corresponding COIN descriptor calculated at the point where the targets cross. The overlap is virtual, meaning that in 3D the targets are apart. In contrast, the bottom row of Fig. 4 depicts a case where the targets are touching. Notice that in the case of the virtual crossing the front target is actually occluding the back target as time advances. This means that we would see a lot more

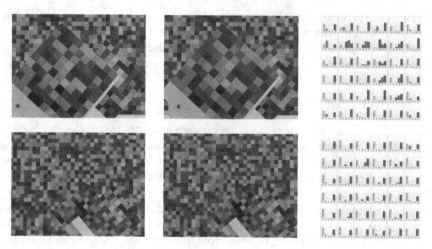

Fig. 4. Two targets which do not overlap in 3D ("virtual crossing", top) and two targets which do overlap in 3D ("real crossing", bottom), along with the corresponding COIN descriptors built around the crossing. The COINs were built over a 6 × 6 grid, using 10-bin hue histograms.

inner change if we *reversed* the sequence. To illustrate, we've included an additional column in our representation of COIN descriptors, which we named I_d, for "inner disappearing". I_d is equal to I of the COIN of the reversed sequence. Our regular I was renamed to I_a, for "inner appearing". In the case of a real crossing, we see dominating constant/neighbor hypotheses at the edge where the targets cross, while in the case of a virtual crossing, we notice the appearance of inner/outer change, which is, as expected, especially prominent with I_d. Based on this finding, we propose a simple measure of the level of spatio-temporal discontinuity:

$$\Sigma_I^{t_2} = \sum \frac{I_a + I_d}{2} \qquad (8)$$

where I_a and I_d are calculated for each patch $p_k^{t_2}$ within the grid at time t_2.

3.3 Experiments on the DTU Robot Data Set

Having found that the COIN descriptor performs well on artificial scenes, we tested whether it can discriminate between 3D discontinuities, coplanarities and virtual crossings. To the best of our knowledge, there are not any publicly available datasets with suitably or similarly labeled video data. However, the recent DTU Robot Data Set by Aanaes et al. [15] consists of 60 scenes and scene surface data obtained from a structured light scan, so it has the potential for automated groundtruth acquisition.

In the experiment reported here, we used the first 49 frames of scene number 14 from the DTU Robot Data Set. We manually labeled ten interesting structures in the scene throughout all 49 frames: three small depth discontinuities, three

Fig. 5. Points selected for manual experimental validation of COIN from the DTU Robot Data Set (#014, frame number 24)

Table 1. Experimental results on classifying point types on the DTU Robot Data Set sequence #14. Point IDs are the same as in Fig. 5.

	small discontinuity			large discontinuity			virtual crossing		coplanarity	
ID	3	4	7	1	8	9	6	5	2	10
Σ_I	0.20	0.19	0.23	0.62	0.63	0.52	0.71	0.39	0.00	0.04

large depth discontinuities, two coplanarities and two virtual crossings, as shown in Fig. 5. Then, COIN descriptors were built using an offset of 5, i.e. between frames 1 and 6, 6 and 11 etc. We used a grid of 5×5 patches and histograms of hue with 10 bins. As a measure of the level of discontinuity within a grid, we used Σ_I (Eq. 8). Table 1 shows the average value of this measure for four different categories of points. We can notice that the smaller and and the larger depth discontinuities as well as coplanarities seem to be well separated by the value of this measure. One virtual crossing has a very large value of $\overline{\Sigma_I}$, while the other has a value in between the values for small and large discontinuities. This is correct, because a virtual crossing is by definition a depth discontinuity. It remains to be seen on a larger dataset whether we will be able to distinguish virtual crossings from other discontinuities using Σ_I only, or whether we will need other more complex measures which would, for instance, take into account the position of the inner change within the grid.

4   Conclusion and Outlook

We have presented a quite novel scheme to describe and detect semantics of local frame-to-frame appearance change. Aiming to extend the success of histogram / appearance based methods in 2D to space-time, we devised a solid mathematical framework for reliable computation of weights assigned to C, O, I, N hypotheses. The applicability of the descriptor was confirmed by our experiments, which have demonstrated how to use COIN for reliable labeling of coplanarity vs. discontinuity and to distinguish between real and virtual crossings.

We plan to investigate the properties of COIN on a larger amount of data, which will be obtained either by automated groundtruth acquisition or manual labeling. We are also interested in using COIN to distinguish other kinds of local structures, e.g. convexities or concavities. Using COINs inside bounding boxes of more complex image events, e.g. articulated object motion, should provide excellent means to classify complex motion patterns. Furthermore, aggregating COINs to sequences of COINs over video might provide a higher semantic level.

References

1. Doretto, G., Chiuso, A., Wu, Y., Soatto, S.: Dynamic textures. Int. J. of Comp. Vis. 51, 91–109 (2003)
2. Derpanis, K., Wildes, R.: Spacetime texture representation and recognition based on a spatiotemporal orientation analysis. IEEE TPAMI (2012)
3. Doulamis, A., Doulamis, N., Ntalianis, K., Kollias, S.: An efficient fully unsupervised video object segmentation scheme using an adaptive neural-network classifier architecture. Trans. Neur. Netw. 14, 616–630 (2003)
4. Ogale, A.S., Fermüller, C., Aloimonos, Y.: Motion segmentation using occlusions. IEEE Trans. Pattern Anal. Mach. Intell. 27, 988–992 (2005)
5. Stein, A.N., Hebert, M.: Local detection of occlusion boundaries in video. Image Vision Comput. 27, 514–522 (2009)
6. Derpanis, K.G., Wildes, R.P.: Detecting Spatiotemporal Structure Boundaries: Beyond Motion Discontinuities. In: Zha, H., Taniguchi, R.-I., Maybank, S. (eds.) ACCV 2009, Part II. LNCS, vol. 5995, pp. 301–312. Springer, Heidelberg (2010)
7. Dollár, P., Rabaud, V., Cottrell, G., Belongie, S.: Behavior recognition via sparse spatio-temporal features. In: VS-PETS (2005)
8. Ke, Y., Sukthankar, R., Hebert, M.: Efficient visual event detection using volumetric features. In: Proc. ICCV, vol. 1, pp. 166–173 (2005)
9. Laptev, I., Lindeberg, T.: Space-time interest points. In: Proc. ICCV (2003)
10. Laptev, I.: On space-time interest points. Int. J. of Comp. Vis. 64, 107–123 (2005)
11. Le, Q.V., Zou, W.Y., Yeung, S.Y., Ng, A.Y.: Learning hierarchical invariant spatio-temporal features for action recognition with independent subspace analysis. In: Proc. CVPR, pp. 3361–3368 (2011)
12. Wang, H., Ullah, M.M., Kläser, A., Laptev, I., Schmid, C.: Evaluation of local spatio-temporal features for action recognition. In: Proc. BMVC, p. 127 (2009)
13. Kläser, A., Marszałek, M., Schmid, C.: A spatio-temporal descriptor based on 3d-gradients. In: Proc. BMVC, pp. 995–1004 (2008)
14. Brkić, K., Pinz, A., Šegvić, S., Kalafatić, Z.: Histogram-Based Description of Local Space-Time Appearance. In: Heyden, A., Kahl, F. (eds.) SCIA 2011. LNCS, vol. 6688, pp. 206–217. Springer, Heidelberg (2011)
15. Aanæs, H., Dahl, A., Steenstrup Pedersen, K.: Interesting interest points. Int. J. of Comp. Vis. 97, 18–35 (2012)

SuperFloxels: A Mid-level Representation for Video Sequences

Avinash Ravichandran[1], Chaohui Wang[1],
Michalis Raptis[2], and Stefano Soatto[1]

[1] Vision Lab, UCLA
[2] Disney Research, Pittsburgh

Abstract. We describe an approach for grouping trajectories extracted from a video that preserves motion discontinuities due, for instance, to occlusions, but not color or intensity boundaries. Our method takes as input trajectories with variable length and onset time, and outputs a membership function as well as an indicator function denoting the *exemplar* trajectory of each group. This can be used for several applications such as compression, segmentation, and background removal.

1 Introduction

We are interested in establishing temporal correspondence in video, for the purpose of later analysis, for instance object or event detection, fine-scale localization, and recognition. In general, we seek a mid-level representation that would facilitate, or at least not jeopardize, semantic analysis, that is the attribution of identities and relations among locations or motions within a video.

Ideally, for every location in the domain of the image, we are interested in establishing its trajectory, or *flow*, in the time interval during which it is visible. Due to occlusions, we have to book-keep points that appear and disappear, and store the trajectory of each visible pixel, along with its color. Even if we neglect the color variability along a trajectory, it is easy to see that such a representation would soon have a complexity far greater than the original data. Therefore, to reduce complexity, we seek to group different trajectories. Since any grouping or segmentation procedure necessarily entails a loss of information, we seek to perform it in a way that causes as little damage as possible.

How do we measure damage? Ideally, by the loss in performance in the semantic analysis task downstream. This loss should be as small as possible. However, since we do not know the "ideal" performance, we can test directly for semantic consistency: If a certain set of locations is known to belong to an object or event at a certain time, we want the subsequent trajectories to also belong to the same object or event for all the time during which they are visible.

Since we do not have an end-to-end system available, our design criterion is to group together trajectories respecting motion discontinuities and occlusion boundaries, but not intensity/color boundaries. In analogy to *superpixels* that aim to preserve the latter, we call our scheme to preserve the former *superfloxels*.

A. Fusiello et al. (Eds.): ECCV 2012 Ws/Demos, Part III, LNCS 7585, pp. 131–140, 2012.
© Springer-Verlag Berlin Heidelberg 2012

Related Work. The most common preprocessing operation performed on videos for the purpose of analysis is segmentation based on motion discontinuities, for the most part based on few temporally adjacent frames [1–3]. Trajectory-based methods have started to take hold more recently [4–10]. Naturally, the longer the temporal window, the richer the temporal context that can be incorporated in the later processing. This improves robustness and enables analysis of subtle cues for instance in traffic model learning [11] and anomaly detection [12].

There are, however, challenges associated with trajectory grouping. First, trajectories often cover only a portion of the frames in the video sequence, due to occlusions, image noise, *etc.* As a result, trajectories have different lengths and their comparison is not straightforward. Second, like any grouping procedure, there is no "right" number of clusters, and one has to accommodate different model complexities in the analysis. Finally, it is important but challenging to preserve occlusion boundaries so that clusters do not cross such boundaries.

Most existing trajectory-based methods ignore one or more of these issues. For example, [4, 5] assume that the number of clusters is known and tra- jectories are projected into different linear motion subspaces of low dimension using an affine camera model. Moreover, [4] requires complete trajectories, a tall order. Other approaches have been proposed to deal with incomplete trajectories, such as subspace separation [5, 6], extrapolation of incomplete trajectories [13], the adoption of Markov Random Field (MRF) formulation [10] as well as explicit clustering formulations [7–9]. Since the intrinsic complexity of the grouping method determines the scale of the problem it can handle, only sparse cases (*i.e*, tens to hundreds of trajectories) were considered in those factorization-based methods [4–6], while non-factorization-based methods [7–10] have been demonstrated with thousands of trajectories.

Among the non-factorization methods, [8] used spectral clustering and a post-processing procedure to deal with object segmentation. On the other hand, [9] used motion saliency to remove background trajectories and obtain the foreground map. A greedy search then partitioned the foreground trajectories based on their motion affinity and topology constraints. Despite promising results, the performance of such an approach relies heavily on the accuracy of the foreground map estimation and the greedy search process provides no optimality guarantee for the clustering. Finally, none except [10] explicitly accounts for occlusions. In the MRF-based formulation in [10], occlusions are modeled based on incomplete trajectories and "T-Junctions". However, discovering "T-Junctions" is still a challenging problem, that relies on local temporal information. Additionally, this method requires the number of clusters to be provided.

Paper Contribution. In this paper, we describe an over-segmentation algorithm that clusters trajectories extracted from a video into *superfloxel*. Each *superfloxel* is denoted by a trajectory that is representative of the cluster of trajectories and serves as a mid-level representation of the video sequences. We achieve this by ensuring that our clustering scheme respects motion and occlusion boundaries and we influence the choice of the cluster centers using such cues. Our approach is not an object segmentation scheme but instead a generic preprocessing framework that can be used for different applications such as activity recognition, object segmentation, *etc.* Our framework does not require multiple initializations or a predefined number of *superfloxels*. Instead, our method automatically determines the number of *superfloxels* by balancing the inter-cluster variation with the proposed prior terms on the cluster centers.

2 Formulation

Let $I : \mathcal{D} \subset \mathbb{R}^2 \times \mathbb{Z}^+ \rightarrow \mathbb{R}^+; (x, t) \mapsto I_t(x)$ be a video sequence, defined on a 2D image domain $\mathcal{D}$ and I_t denotes the image corresponding to frame t. We extract from I a set of trajectories $\mathcal{T} = \{T_i\}_{i=1}^N$, where each trajectory T_i is represented by $x_t^i \in \mathcal{D}$, where $t \in [t_s^i, t_e^i] \subset \mathbb{Z}^+$ denotes the temporal extent of the trajectory, starting at t_s^i and ending at t_e^i. Given these trajectories, we aim to cluster them into K groups (superfloxels) through a membership function, $L : \mathcal{T} \rightarrow [1, K]; T_i \mapsto l_i$ where $K < N$. To this end, the first step is to define a notion of similarity between these trajectories on which we base our clustering.

2.1 Similarity between Trajectories

Given two trajectories T_i and T_j, we are interested in defining a measure of similarity between them. There are several choices for defining such metrics between trajectories such as the spatial distance or the velocity distance which can be defined as follows:

$$d_{spatial}(T_i, T_j)^2 = \sum_{f \in \mathcal{O}(T_i, T_j)} (x_f^i - x_f^j)^2, \tag{1}$$

$$d_{velocity}(T_i, T_j)^2 = \sum_{f, f+1 \in \mathcal{O}(T_i, T_j)} [(x_f^i - x_{f+1}^i) - (x_f^j - x_{f+1}^j)]^2, \tag{2}$$

where $\mathcal{O}(T_i, T_j) = [t_s^i, t_e^i] \cap [t_s^j, t_e^j]$ denotes the temporal overlap between T_i and T_j. Since our goal is to obtain a mid-level representation of the video, we require a grouping that is spatially compact and salient in its motion. Furthermore, we do not want the length of the trajectories to influence the pairwise distances. Considering all these requirements, we propose the following distance:

$$d(T_i, T_j) = \frac{1}{|\mathcal{O}(T_i, T_j)|} d_{spatial}(T_i, T_j)[1 + d_{velocity}(T_i, T_j)]. \tag{3}$$

We add the constant 1 to the velocity distance to ensure that when two trajectories are identical (motion wise), the spatial distance still acts as a weight. We wish to point out that different variations of the velocity distance have been used in the literature where the velocity difference is defined between the locations at time t and $t + t_0$ where $t_0 = 5$ in [8] $t_0 = 3$ in [9]. While this offset could make the distance more robust, manually choosing its value is difficult in practice as it depends on the frame-rate and the motion of objects in the scene.

The trade-off of using the above distance is that while we ensure spatial compactness of our superfloxels, we discount the velocity difference at motion boundaries. Since motion boundaries provide strong cues for separating different objects/parts, we would like our distance to respect them while considering the similarity between two trajectories. Hence, we define the following distance that serves as a penalty for crossing motion boundaries:

$$d_{mb}(T_i, T_j) = \frac{1}{|\mathcal{O}(T_i, T_j)|} \sum_{f \in \mathcal{O}(T_i, T_j)} \int_0^1 B_f(x_f^i + \lambda(x_f^i - x_f^j))d\lambda, \qquad (4)$$

where $B : \mathcal{D} \subset \mathbb{R}^2 \times \mathbb{Z}^+ \to \{0,1\}$; $(x,t) \mapsto B_t(x)$ is the motion boundary at time t. This distance is added to Eq. 3 to yield our final similarity metric.

2.2   Clustering Formulation

In order to provide a useful reduction of data volume, we aim to group all the trajectories into a number of clusters, each called a *superfloxel*. Furthermore, we are interested in selecting an *exemplar* for each superfloxel such that it can best represent the properties of its components. If we assume that we know K, then in order to cluster the data points and obtain the cluster centers that are denoted by $\mathcal{C} = \{C_k\}_{k=1}^K \subset \mathcal{T}$, we minimize the objective function

$$\mathcal{E}(\mathbf{w}, \mathcal{C}) = \sum_{T_i \in \mathcal{T} \setminus \mathcal{C}} \sum_{C_k \in \mathcal{C}} w_{ik} d(T_i, C_k), \qquad (5)$$

such that $w_{ik} \in \{0,1\}$ and $\sum_k w_{ik} = 1$. Each binary variable w_{ik} indicates whether trajectory T_i is assigned to the cluster center C_k or not. Moreover, the constraint $\sum_k w_{ik} = 1$ guarantees that each trajectory will be assigned to exactly one cluster center. However, if we use the same function when K is unknown, the trivial solution to the above minimization is $K = |\mathcal{T}|$. In order to prevent this, we introduce a prior on the choice of cluster centers:

$$\mathcal{E}(\mathbf{w}, \mathcal{C}, K) = \sum_{C_k \in \mathcal{T}} \sum_{T_i \in \mathcal{T} \setminus C_k} w_{ik} d(T_i, C_k) + \sum_{C_k \in \mathcal{T}} w_{kk} \phi(C_k), \qquad (6)$$

where the binary variable w_{kk} indicates whether trajectory C_k is a cluster center or not, defining implicitly the subset $\mathcal{C}$ of the cluster centers and leading the constraint on $\mathbf{w}$ that is $w_{ik} \leq w_{kk}$. The optimization problem of (6) is a Linear Integer program [14, 15], which can be efficiently solved via Linear Program (LP) relaxation. By relaxing the binary variables $\mathbf{w}$ to take non-negative values, the above formulation can be cast as an LP as shown in [14]. More specifically, our clustering formulation is expressed as the following LP:

$$\min_{\mathbf{w}} \sum_{C_k \in \mathcal{T}} \sum_{T_i \in \mathcal{T} \setminus C_k} w_{ik} d(T_i, C_k) + \sum_{C_k \in \mathcal{T}} w_{kk} \phi(C_k)$$
$$\text{subject to: } \sum_k w_{ik} = 1, w_{ik} \leq w_{kk}, w_{ik} \geq 0. \qquad (7)$$

The advantages of such an approach are: 1) it is guaranteed to converge; 2) it does not require initialization of the cluster centers or the number of cluster centers; and 3) we can specify the prior on the selection of the cluster centers. Our choice of prior $\phi(C_k)$ needs to reflect the fact that our clusters have low motion discrepancy and respect motion boundaries. A natural choice is to prevent trajectories that are near the motion boundaries to be chosen as cluster centers. We defer the discussion of the prior until Sect. 4.

3 Applications

The superfloxelization presented above forms our mid-level representation of the video sequence, based on which we can post-process the cluster trajectories for different applications. However, in all the cases, we only need to deal with the cluster centers of superfloxels. This has the following advantages: (1) the computational complexity of the post processing stage is significantly reduced, (2) we are robust to outliers that are present in the trajectories, by grouping the trajectories. We validate our representation by outlining several applications.

Model Selection. Our algorithm automatically selects the number of super-floxels. However, if the number of groups that are present in the video sequence is known, it can be enforced easily by merging superfloxels to the desired number. Given the cluster centers of the superfloxels, we calculate the same distance we use for clustering (Eq. 3). We drop the motion boundary distance since the cluster centers are spread throughout the image. Hence, calculating such a distance is not meaningful in this case. We can then obtain a hierarchical tree representation of these cluster centers via a greedy merging scheme using single linkage. At each step, the pair of superfloxel cluster centers (or group of superfloxels) that have the least distance among them are merged. This process is repeated until there is only one node in the tree (*e.g*, Fig. 2). Once two or more nodes have been merged, the distance between the merged node and any other node is calculated using single linkage: $d(C_i, C_j) = \min_{C_u \in C_i, C_v \in C_j} d(C_u, C_v)$. This tree can be cut to obtain the required number of groups. Our experiments show that this simple merging technique yields in good performance.

Background Removal. For applications such as human activity recognition, trajectory-based methods have shown promising performance [16]. Hence in this case, the superfloxelization could be a useful preprocessing step in order to capture the different parts of the object as well as separate the foreground from the background. Recently, [16] showed that by removing the background trajectories, the performance of recognition algorithm increased on standard activity recognition benchmarks. Although methods such as [17] address the issue of removing the background from freely moving cameras, such methods used the entire set of trajectories that are present in video to determine the background. Hence, such methods are computationally expensive and do not provide a grouping of the remaining trajectories.

Given the cluster centers, we can exploit them to discard the background superfloxels. In order to perform this, for each pair of frames we fit a motion model based on the location of the points of the cluster centers in those frames using RANSAC [18], which determines the trajectories that are inliers and outliers. Repeating this for the different pairs of frames gives us the trajectories that are inliers and that are outliers. The background is then determined by the superfloxels corresponding to the cluster centers that were considered as inliers.

Fig. 1. Visualization of motion cues for a sample sequence. From left to right: original image, the optical flow field and the distance transform on motion boundaries.

4   Implementation Details

The spatial distance and the velocity distance computations are straightforward and can be done very efficiently. For the distance term in Eq. 4 that is defined over a straight line connecting two points, we speed up the computation by using an approximation to the straight line between two points (via Bresenham's algorithm [19]). Furthermore, calculating this distance over all pairs of points is not very meaningful. For instance, if two points that lie far apart in the background, the line between them could pass through motion boundaries corresponding to multiple objects. Hence, we calculate the motion boundary penalty only in a neighborhood around the motion boundaries. Using the distance transform [20] on the motion boundaries, we can quickly determine this neighborhood. Let $d_{B_f}(x)$ denote the distance transform under the motion boundaries B_f at a given time instance f. We calculate $d_{mb}(T_i, T_j)$ if $\forall f \in \mathcal{O}(T_i, T_j)$ $d_{B_f}(x_f^i) \leq 2\tau$ and $d_{B_f}(x_f^j) \leq 2\tau$. The parameter τ that determines the neighborhood around the motion boundaries for which we calculate d_{mb} (Fig. 1).

Notice from Fig. 1 that points close to the edge of the image tend to have a high value. Hence, if we use our prior based on the distance transform, such points will have a higher likelihood of being chosen as cluster centers. In order to prevent this and to ensure that our prior is consistent with our distances between trajectories, we define the prior on the clusters centers as follows:

$$\phi(T_i) = \begin{cases} \gamma & \text{if } \exists f \in [t_s^i, t_e^i] \text{ s.t. } d_{B_f}(x_f^i) < \tau \\ 0 & \text{otherwise.} \end{cases} \tag{8}$$

This biases cluster centers to be chosen further from motion boundaries.

5   Experimental Results

We extracted trajectories using the Large Deformation Optical Flow (LDOF) [21] and the Dense Point Tracker (DPT) [22]. We also experimented with the Sparse Occlusion Optical Flow (SOOF) [23] and DPT to obtain the trajectories. This was motivated by the fact that [23] accounts explicitly for occlusions while calculating the optical flow. Hence, trajectories that are near the occlusion

Table 1. Comparison of Different Algorithms using Different Metrics

Method	Density	Overall Error	Average Error	Over segmentation	# of extracted objects
[8]	3.316	4.861	25.870	0.692	26
[8] + SOOF	3.155	4.961	24.344	0.654	28
Our Method + LDOF	3.316	3.675	**10.175**	27.654	30
Our Method + SOOF	3.155	**2.880**	10.586	30.885	28
Background Merge + LDOF	3.316	7.284	21.971	7.269	27
Background Merge + SOOF	3.155	6.822	23.577	8.538	23

Table 2. Comparison of Different Algorithms using the Trimmed Mean of Metrics

Method	Density	Overall Error	Average Error	Over segmentation	# of extracted objects
[9]	3.22	3.760	22.06	1.150	25
Our Method + LDOF	3.313	3.468	**9.580**	27.500	30
Our Method + SOOF	3.158	**2.510**	10.311	30.833	28
Background Merge + LDOF	3.313	5.711	21.174	6.950	27
Background Merge + SOOF	3.158	4.931	22.763	8.167	23

edges of the moving object can be better tracked. We tested our method on the MOSEG Database [8] which contains 26 sequences of variable length. Each sequence contains a few frames with ground truth annotation. Additionally, this database comes with its own evaluation software for quantitative analysis. We use the same experimental setup as [9], *i.e* we apply our algorithm to the first 50 frames of each sequence and if the sequence contains less than 50 frames we use the entire video sequence. In all our experiments we set $\tau = \gamma = 20$.

Quantitative Results. We report the quantitative results for the different variations of our algorithm as well as that of the baseline [8]. We calculated different metrics such as the overall error, the average error, the over-segmentation index as well as the number of objects that are extracted. The overall error determines if a trajectory is assigned to the correct label. If a cluster spans multiple objects, then the points on one of the objects are considered as errors while determining the overall error. The average error determines the mean error over each region as opposed to the entire image area. The number of objects extracted are regions that have less than 10% error in their clustering assignment. Finally, the over-segmentation determines the number of groups that need to be merged to get the ground truth annotation. The evaluation tool also calculates density which is the measure of the percentage of points that are labeled in the video.

The quantitative results are shown in Table 1. Here we report the mean over all the sequences in the database for the different variations of both the baseline algorithm as well as our methods. From this table it can be seen that the baseline using SOOF produces better results compared to using LDOF. Our method of superfloxelization is better when compared to the baseline in all metrics.

The comparison with [9] is reported in Table 2. Notice that the numbers in this table are different from that of Table 1, because [9] uses a trimmed mean as measures (the top 10% and the bottom 10% of the values are thrown out before

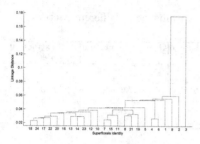

Fig. 2. The superfloxel tree structure obtained using the merging procedure (left) and the superfloxel image locations with numbers indicating their indices (right)

computing the mean). Although we do not endorse this evaluation methodology, for the sake of comparison we report the trimmed mean of our results as well.

Choosing the Number of Superfloxels. We earlier outlined how we can build a tree representation of the superfloxels. The tree structure for one video is shown in Fig. 2. From this figure we can see that the tree structure captures the overall structure of the scene. Note that this tree is only obtained using the cluster centers of the superfloxels. This demonstrates that our cluster centers are good representative candidates of the whole superfloxel. When $K = 2$, the cut of the tree gives us node 3 which corresponds to the entire car as one cluster and the rest of the nodes as the other cluster. We show other examples of choosing the value of K in Fig. 3, which shows that as we increase K the different objects that are present in the scene appear. Once the number of superfloxels that are required becomes more than the number of objects, we start to observe oversegmentation. The advantage of having the superfloxels is that we can now vary K as we like without clustering the entire set of trajectories again.

Background Removal. We have outlined a method to remove the background and show sample results in Fig. 4, which illustrates that our method is able to successfully remove the background in these videos. For a video of 50 frames that contains 16000 trajectories, the background removal after superfloxelization takes about 2 seconds using an unoptimized Matlab implementation. A quantitative analysis was also performed; we determine the background superfloxels and merge it as one group and then apply the quantitative evaluation used for the original superfloxels. The quantitative results are presented in Table 1, which show that while the overall error is increased by this process, the average error and the number of objects is better than the baseline. We notice that using the SOOF optical flow resulted in smaller number of extracted objects. Also, the number of segments that are needed to be merged to obtain the objects is much lower. In all our experiments, we used a homography as the motion model between two frames.

(a) Original Image   (b) K=2   (c) K=3   (d) K=4

Fig. 3. Choosing the number of superfloxels using our tree representation: (a) Original Image; (b, c, d) show the different superfloxels for varying values of K

Fig. 4. Example of background removal. Top row shows the resulting superfloxels, Bottom row shows the background removed using the cluster centers of the superfloxels. Notice that in the last column, the leaf that is moving is not considered as background.

6   Conclusion

Superfloxels are agglomeration of trajectories in video that preserve motion discontinuities. They are designed to be a generic preprocessing step for video analysis. We have shown some sample applications of our framework and its performance. Our approach enables accommodating tracks of different lengths, and produces as a result a collection of groups of tracks that can be further refined in the presence of prior knowledge, for instance on the number of objects in the scene or other prior models. Quantitative comparison on benchmark datasets shows that our method outperforms other methods for trajectory clustering.

Acknowledgments. This work was supported by NSF CCF-0969032, ARO W911NF-11-1-0391 and ONR N000141110863. We thank Nikos Komodakis and Nikos Paragios for providing the clustering code. We also thank Alper Ayvaci for valuable discussions.

References

1. Shi, J., Malik, J.: Normalized cuts and image segmentation. PAMI 22(8) (2000)
2. Kumar, M.P., Torr, P.H.S., Zisserman, A.: Learning layered motion segmentation of video. In: ICCV (2005)
3. Cremers, D., Soatto, S.: Motion competition: a variational approach to piecewise parametric motion segmentation. IJCV 62(3), 249–265 (2005)
4. Yan, J., Pollefeys, M.: A General Framework for Motion Segmentation: Independent, Articulated, Rigid, Non-rigid, Degenerate and Non-degenerate. In: Leonardis, A., Bischof, H., Pinz, A. (eds.) ECCV 2006, Part IV. LNCS, vol. 3954, pp. 94–106. Springer, Heidelberg (2006)
5. Vidal, R., Hartley, R.: Motion segmentation with missing data using powerfactorization and GPCA. In: CVPR (2004)
6. Rao, S., Tron, R., Vidal, R., Ma, Y.: Motion segmentation via robust subspace separation in the presence of outlying, incomplete, or corrupted trajectories. In: CVPR (2008)
7. Fradet, M., Robert, P., Perez, P.: Clustering point trajectories with various lifespans. In: CVMP (2009)
8. Brox, T., Malik, J.: Object Segmentation by Long Term Analysis of Point Trajectories. In: Daniilidis, K., Maragos, P., Paragios, N. (eds.) ECCV 2010, Part V. LNCS, vol. 6315, pp. 282–295. Springer, Heidelberg (2010)
9. Fragkiadaki, K., Shi, J.: Detection free tracking: Exploiting motion and topology for segmenting and tracking under entanglement. In: CVPR (2011)
10. Lezama, J., Alahari, K., Sivic, J., Laptev, I.: Track to the future: Spatio-temporal video segmentation with long-range motion cues. In: CVPR (2011)
11. Wang, X., Tieu, K., Grimson, E.: Learning Semantic Scene Models by Trajectory Analysis. In: Leonardis, A., Bischof, H., Pinz, A. (eds.) ECCV 2006, Part III. LNCS, vol. 3953, pp. 110–123. Springer, Heidelberg (2006)
12. Piciarelli, C., Micheloni, C., Foresti, G.L.: Trajectory-based anomalous event detection. IEEE TCSVT 18(11) (2008)
13. Brostow, G.J., Cipolla, R.: Unsupervised bayesian detection of independent motion in crowds. In: CVPR (2006)
14. Komodakis, N., Paragios, N., Tziritas, G.: Clustering via LP-based stabilities. In: NIPS (2009)
15. Charikar, M., Guha, S., Tardos, É., Shmoys, D.: A constant-factor approximation algorithm for the k-median problem. JCSS 65(1) (2002)
16. Wu, S., Oreifej, O., Shah, M.: Action recognition in videos acquired by a moving camera using motion decomposition of lagrangian particle trajectories. In: ICCV (2011)
17. Sheikh, Y., Javed, O., Kanade, T.: Background subtraction for freely moving cameras. In: ICCV (2009)
18. Fischler, M.A., Bolles, R.C.: Random sample consensus: A paradigm for model fitting with applications to image analysis and automated cartography. Communications of the ACM (6) (1981)
19. Bresenham, J.E.: Algorithm for computer control of a digital plotter. IBM Systems Journal 4(1) (1965)
20. Felzenszwalb, P.F., Huttenlocher, D.P.: Distance transforms of sampled functions. Technical report, Cornell Computing and Information Science (2004)
21. Brox, T., Malik, J.: Large displacement optical flow: Descriptor matching in variational motion estimation. PAMI 33(3) (2011)
22. Sundaram, N., Brox, T., Keutzer, K.: Dense Point Trajectories by GPU-Accelerated Large Displacement Optical Flow. In: Daniilidis, K., Maragos, P., Paragios, N. (eds.) ECCV 2010, Part I. LNCS, vol. 6311, pp. 438–451. Springer, Heidelberg (2010)
23. Ayvaci, A., Raptis, M., Soatto, S.: Sparse occlusion detection with optical flow. IJCV (2011)

Relative Camera Localisation
in Non-overlapping Camera Networks
Using Multiple Trajectories

Vijay John, Gwenn Englebienne, and Ben Krose

Intelligent Autonomous Systems Group,
University of Amsterdam, Amsterdam, Netherlands
{v.c.k.john,g.englebienne,b.j.a.krose}@uva.nl

Abstract. In this article we present an automatic camera calibration algorithm using multiple trajectories in a multiple camera network with non-overlapping field-of-views (FOV). Visible trajectories within a camera FOV are assumed to be measured with respect to the camera local co-ordinate system. Calibration is performed by aligning each camera local co-ordinate system with a pre-defined global co-ordinate system using three steps. Firstly, extrinsic pair-wise calibration parameters are estimated using particle swarm optimisation and Kalman filtering. The resulting pair-wise calibration estimates are used to generate an initial estimate of network calibration parameters, which are corrected to account for accumulation errors using particle swarm optimisation-based local search. Finally, a Bayesian framework with Metropolis algorithm is adopted and the posterior distribution over the network calibration parameters are estimated. We validate our algorithm using studio and synthetic datasets and compare our approach with existing state-of-the-art algorithms.

1 Introduction

Estimation of camera parameters (intrinsic and extrinsic) are essential to perform metric world reconstruction and measure real world distances based on their image projections. The vision problems using camera calibration information include tracking, activity recognition, visual reconstruction etc with applications in security, surveillance, bio-medical analysis, character animation etc [1]. In large environment applications, typically, a network of cameras are deployed with non-overlapping field-of-views (FOV) [2]. Calibration in such a network is difficult without the aid of external calibration objects, usually requiring manual intervention.

In this article, we present an algorithm for extrinsic calibration of non-overlapping FOV camera network. Multiple trajectories of objects defined with respect to a pre-defined global co-ordinate system are termed as global trajectories. Global trajectories visible in a particular camera FOV are measured with respect to the camera co-ordinate system and are termed as local trajectories. Calibration can be performed by aligning local co-ordinate systems with

A. Fusiello et al. (Eds.): ECCV 2012 Ws/Demos, Part III, LNCS 7585, pp. 141–150, 2012.

the global co-ordinate system. However, in order to perform the alignment, the global trajectories need to be derived from the measured local trajectories, but this problem is complicated owing to the lack of overlap between network cameras.

Overview. In our proposed calibration approach, firstly, we consider pair-wise cameras in the network and estimate their extrinsic pair-wise calibration parameters using particle swarm optimisation(PSO)[3] and linear Kalman filter. The estimated pair-wise calibration parameters are used to generate an initial estimate of network calibration parameters, using a weighted directed graph. To account for pair-wise calibration errors, estimated network calibration parameters are corrected using PSO-based local search with forward-backward Kalman filter and K-L divergence based cost function. Finally, a Bayesian framework is formulated to obtain a posterior distribution over the extrinsic network calibration parameter, with priors defined on the corrected network calibration estimate. The likelihood term in our posterior distribution incorporates the trajectory uncertainty obtained using Kalman smoothing. The expected value of calibration parameters are calculated from sequence of samples generated from the posterior distribution using Metropolis algorithm [4], a Markov Chain Monte-Carlo method.

To the best of our knowledge, our work contributes to the state-of-the-art in at least three ways. First, the use of multiple trajectories for extrinsic camera pose estimation in non-overlapping FOV has not been reported. Secondly, we incorporate the uncertainty associated with each trajectory in the Bayesian framework. Thirdly, we automatically initialise the parameter estimation.

The rest of this paper is organised as follows. Section 2 summarizes some of the relevant literature in relation to our work. Section 3 presents our algorithm. Section 4 presents experimental results of our proposed algorithm on our studio dataset and synthetic datasets. Section 5 summarizes our work and suggests future development.

2   Related Work

There are two different classes of camera calibration literature in non-overlapping FOV networks, which we briefly review next. In the first class of literature, external objects are used to aid in calibration, for example, assistive sensors like mirrors [5]. Recently, Micusik et al. [6] use an inertial sensor in their work to obtain a closed-form solution for intrinsic and extrinsic camera parameters.

In the second class of literature, where our proposed algorithm lies, moving objects in camera FOV are used to estimate the parameters. Javed et al. [7] use velocity extrapolation to project FOV of one camera to the other and estimate camera parameters. Later, Rahimi et al. [8] adopted a maximum a posterior (MAP) framework to perform simultaneous tracking and calibration using single estimated trajectories. A linear motion model is used as motion prior and MAP estimates are obtained using Newton-Raphson's method. Nadeem et al. [2] use forward-backward regression to generate trajectories in non-overlapping FOV region, which are used to estimate the parameters. A common feature of the second class of literature is the assumption of linear trajectories with additive noises in the non-overlap region, with additive trajectory noise estimating non-linearity.

3 Camera Calibration Algorithm

In our work, we make the following assumptions, given a network of N non-overlap FOV cameras $\mathbf{c} = \{c^n\}_{n=1}^N$, we assume that each c^n can map image coordinates of k visible trajectory in its FOV to its 2-D local co-ordinate system as $X_k^n = \{\mathbf{x}_k^n(t)\}_{t=1}^T$. Similar to [2,8], we also assume that each camera provides a top-down view of the scene with its optical axis being perpendicular to the ground plane. Next, we assume that data association for multiple trajectories both within a camera FOV and across different camera FOV are available.

The extrinsic network calibration parameters ($\mathbf{M_g}$) that need to be estimated are given as $\mathbf{M_g} = \{\mathbf{m}_g^n\}_{n=1}^N$ where $\mathbf{m}_g^n = [\mathbf{q}_g^n, \theta_g^n]$ contains 2-D translation $\mathbf{q}_g^n = [qx_g^n, qy_g^n]$ and 2-D rotation θ_g^n. An overview of our algorithm is shown in Figure 1(a) and detailed description of steps involved are given below. Additionally, a layout of network and parameters are shown in Figure 1(b).

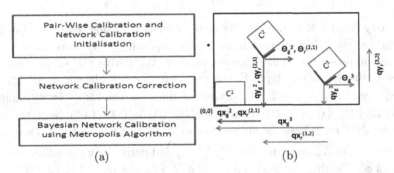

Fig. 1. (a)The overview of our algorithm. (b) A visualisation of camera network layout along with the calibration parameters (network and pair-wise) to be estimated are given.

3.1 Pair-Wise Calibration Parameter Estimation

To estimate pair-wise calibration parameters, represented as $\mathbf{m}_r^{(i,j)}$ for pair (i,j), firstly, camera pairs in the network are selected using FOV exit-entrance time instants. Specifically, cameras c^i and c^j are considered a pair, if a measured local trajectory X_k^i exits c^i at exit time instant t_0 and moves in non-overlap region before entering c^j at entrance time instant t_1, with $j \neq i$, before entering other cameras. The trajectory segments corresponding to camera pair (i,j) and defined in c^i co-ordinate is given as $\overline{X}_k^i = [X_k^i = \{\mathbf{x}_k^i(t)\}_{t=1}^{t_0}, X_k^{(u,i)} = \{\mathbf{x}_k^i(t)\}_{t=t_0+1}^{t_1-1}, \hat{X}_k^i = \{\mathbf{x}_k^i(t)\}_{t=t_1}^T]$, where the segments $X_k^{(u,i)}$ in non-overlap FOV and $\hat{X}_k^i$ need to be estimated. Given the estimated trajectory segments, $\mathbf{m}_r^{(i,j)}$

can then be estimated by aligning $\hat{X}_k^i$ with its corresponding trajectory segment defined in c^j co-ordinate system $(\hat{X}_k^j)$, where correspondence is established using time stamps.

Non-overlap FOV Prediction. To estimate $X_k^{(u,i)}$, a linear Kalman filter is initialised at measurement $(\mathbf{x}_k^i(1))$ and filtered state estimates $Z_k^i = \{\mathbf{z}_k(t)\}_{t=1}^{t_1}$ are obtained, where $\mathbf{z}_k(t) = [z_k^h(t), \dot{z}_k^h(t), z_k^v(t), \dot{z}_k^v(t)]'$ with 2-D position and velocity components. During Kalman filtering, the measurements in non-overlap region are considered missing. It has been shown that for missing measurement in Kalman filter, the ideal estimator at update step $z_{t|t}$ can be replaced with predictor, $z_{t|t-1}$, with the proof of error residual convergence shown in [9]. However, the posterior error covariance $\Sigma_{t|t}$ corresponding to missing measurements gradually increases. Given, the filtered state estimates, $X_k^{(u,i)}$ is extracted from $Z_k^{u,i} = \{\mathbf{z}_k(t)\}_{t=t_0+1}^{t_1}$ using matrix H given in Eqn 1. The Kalman filter's state transition matrix A is also given in Eqn

$$A = \begin{bmatrix} 1 & 1 & 0 & 0 \\ 0 & 1 & 0 & 0 \\ 0 & 0 & 1 & 1 \\ 0 & 0 & 0 & 1 \end{bmatrix} \quad H = \begin{bmatrix} 1 & 0 & 0 & 0 \\ 0 & 0 & 1 & 0 \end{bmatrix} \tag{1}$$

Trajectory Shape Estimation. We next estimate $\hat{X}_k^i$ using relative angles and magnitude (shape) information from its corresponding trajectory in c^j $(\hat{X}_k^j)$, which can improve the calibration estimation. We derive the shape information using the following steps. Firstly, we consider 3-tuple states in $\hat{X}_k^j$, i.e. $\hat{\mathbf{x}}_k^j(t), \hat{\mathbf{x}}_k^j(t+1)$ and $\hat{\mathbf{x}}_k^j(t+2)$ and derive the difference vector (velocity) magnitudes $\hat{\rho}_k^j(t, t+1), \hat{\rho}_k^j(t+1, t+2)$ and angles $\hat{\phi}_k^j(t, t+1), \hat{\phi}_k^j(t+1, t+2)$. Next, the relative angles $\hat{\psi}_k^j(t, t+2)$ between difference vector angles are calculated. Then from the trajectory set $\overline{X}_k^i$, we consider $[X_k^i, X_k^{(u,i)}]$ and derive only the difference vector angles $\hat{\phi}_k^i$. Finally, using all the calculated information, $\hat{X}_k^i = \{\hat{\mathbf{x}}_k(t)\}_{t=t_1+2}^T$ is estimated using Eqn 2 and Eqn 3 in a *for* loop from $t = t_1 \dots T - 2$

$$\hat{\phi}_k^i(t+1, t+2) = \hat{\psi}_k^j(t, t+2) + \hat{\phi}_k^i(t, t+1) \tag{2}$$

$$\hat{\mathbf{x}}_k^i(t+2) = \hat{\mathbf{x}}_k^i(t+1) + \hat{\rho}_k^j(t+1, t+2) \begin{bmatrix} cos(\hat{\phi}_k^i(t+1, t+2)) & 0 \\ 0 & sin(\hat{\phi}_k^i(t+1, t+2)) \end{bmatrix} \tag{3}$$

Note that $\hat{\mathbf{x}}_k^i(t_1 + 1)$ in Eqn 3 is estimated by extending the Kalman filter used in non-overlap prediction.

Particle Swarm Optimisation. We formulate our pair-wise camera calibration estimation as a non-linear optimization problem, that aligns $\hat{X}_k^j$ with $\hat{X}_k^i$, using particle swarm optimisation (PSO) with a distances-based cost function as shown in Equation 4. PSO a non-linear iterative swarm intelligence algorithm [3] comprises of a swarm of candidate particles or states, here pair-wise calibration parameters ($\mathbf{m}_r$), that solves a problem by iteratively improving the candidate particle location in the cost function. We use a inertia-varying PSO [3] that performs a global-to-local search. We refer the readers to [3] for further details. Our pair-wise camera calibration problem is formulated as follows for camera pair (i, j)

$$\hat{\mathbf{m}}_r^{(i,j)} = \underset{\mathbf{m}_r^{(i,j)}}{\mathrm{argmin}} \sqrt{(\hat{X}_k^i - F(\hat{X}_k^j, \mathbf{m}_r^{(i,j)}))^2} \qquad (4)$$

where F(.) represents the function that performs 2D co-ordinate transformation. Our main motivation for incorporating PSO instead of other optimisation algorithm are results obtained by PSO in complex vision problems like articulated tracking [10]. Specifically, PSO has demonstrated automatic initialisation property in addition to constraining the search within pre-defined search limits [3].

Initial Network Calibration Parameter Estimate. An initial estimate of network calibration parameters can be obtained from pair-wise calibration estimates. As done previously [8], we represent the global co-ordinate system at origin of the camera with maximum network connection in the network, for example c^1, and the corresponding unobserved global trajectories are represented as $Y_k = \{\mathbf{y}_k(t)\}_{t=1}^T$. Given this assumption, network calibration parameter can then be calculated from sum of pair-wise calibration parameters i.e. $\mathbf{m}_g^n = \mathbf{m}_r^{(1,j)} + \mathbf{m}_r^{(j,n)}$, with j intermediate cameras. To select the intermediate j cameras, a weighted directed graph is set-up with each node representing a camera and the weighted edges representing a trajectory-connected camera pair. The edge weights are derived from the average time duration taken by trajectories in the non-overlap region between trajectory-connected camera pairs. The edge weights are inversely proportional to the average time duration. Given the weighted directed graph, Djikstra's algorithm is used to calculate the shortest path (j cameras), from which an initial estimate of network calibration parameters are obtained.

3.2   Network Parameters Correction

An inherent problem with calculating the network calibration parameters from pair-wise parameters is the possibility of error accumulation. To account for accumulative errors, a local search is set-up using inertia-varying PSO [3] with forward-backward Kalman filter and K-L divergence based cost function (Eqn 5). Specifically, we consider the transformed set of initial global trajectories $\mathbf{Y} = \{Y_k\}_{k=1}^K$, where the various trajectory segments in Y_k are given as $Y_k = [Y_k^1, \hat{Y}_k^{(u,1)}, \hat{Y}_k^n]$, where $\hat{Y}_k^n$ is the transformed trajectory segment in c^n and $\hat{Y}_k^{(u,1)}$ is the non-overlap segment. Our cost function is designed to align $\hat{Y}_k^n$ with the complete global trajectory using 2-D co-ordinate transformation parameters (PSO state) $\mathbf{M_C} = \{\mathbf{m}_c^n\}_{n=1}^N$. The corrective PSO swarm is initialised around the initial estimate of network calibration parameters.

Cost Function. During PSO optimisation run, for each initial global trajectory, the PSO states in the swarm generate corrected global trajectories, which are evaluated using a forward-backward Kalman filter and K-L divergence based cost function. Specifically, for each corrected global trajectory, a forward Kalman filter is initialised at starting time instant $Y_k(1)$ generating posterior state estimates $p_f^k(t)$. Additionally, a backward Kalman filter is initialised at final time instant $T\ (Y_k(T))$ generating posterior state estimates $p_b^k(t)$ in the reverse direction to forward Kalman filter. Given, the Kalman filter estimates a K-L divergence based cost function is set-up as

$$\hat{\mathbf{M}}_{\mathbf{c}} = \operatorname*{argmin}_{\mathbf{M_c}} \sum_{k=1}^{K} \sum_{t=1}^{T} D_{kl}(p_f^k(t) \| p_b^k(t)) \tag{5}$$

Since our corrective cost function is designed for linear non-overlap global trajectory segments, we automatically select such global trajectories using a threshold based on non-overlap-segment length. Note that this selection is performed only for corrective optimisation. Next, we describe our Bayesian formulation, where $\hat{\mathbf{M}}_{\mathbf{c}}$ is used as priors.

3.3   Bayesian Framework

The extrinsic network calibration parameters $\mathbf{M_g}$ are estimated by formulating a Bayesian framework. Specifically, a posterior distribution over $\mathbf{M_g}$ given as

$$p(\mathbf{M_g}|\mathbf{X}) \propto p(\mathbf{X}|\mathbf{M_g})p(\mathbf{M_g}) \tag{6}$$

The likelihood distribution for the Bayesian formulation is then set up as

$$p(\mathbf{X}|\mathbf{M_g}) = p(F(\mathbf{X}, \mathbf{M_g})) \tag{7}$$

where F(). performs coordinate transformation. To obtain $P(F(\mathbf{X}, \mathbf{M_g}))$, we use the Kalman smoother. First, we consider $F(\mathbf{X}, \mathbf{M_g})$ to be the measurement for state $\mathbf{Z}$. Specifically, the functional form of Kalman smoother is given as follows

$$\mathbf{z}_k(t+1) = A\mathbf{z}_k(t) + w_t \tag{8}$$
$$f(\mathbf{x}_k(t), m_g) = H\mathbf{z}_k(t) + v_t \tag{9}$$
$$\tag{10}$$

where $\mathbf{z}_k(t) = [z_k^h(t), \dot{z}_k^h(t), z_k^v(t), \dot{z}_k^v(t)]'$ is state with 2-D position and velocity, A and H are state transition and measurement matrix given in Eqn 1, w_t and v_t are normally distributed process and measurement noise with zero mean and learnt covariances [11]. Kalman smoothing obtains the state estimate for all $Z_k = \{\mathbf{z}_k(t)\}_{t=1}^{T}$, where the state estimate $\mathbf{z}_k(t)$ at t is given as

$$p(\mathbf{z}_k^n(t)|\{f(\mathbf{x}_k^n(t), \mathbf{m_g})\}_{t=1}^{T}) = \mathcal{N}(\mathbf{z}_k^n(t); \mu_{zk}^n(t), \Sigma_{zk}^n(t)), \tag{11}$$

where $\{f(\mathbf{x}_k^n(t), \mathbf{m_g})\}_{t=1}^{T}$ is the complete measurement. Kalman smoother's posterior state estimate and error covariance at t is given by $\mu_{zk}^n(t)$ and $\Sigma_{zk}^n(t)$. Given the state estimates the likelihood is then formulated as.

$$p(F(\mathbf{X}, \mathbf{M_g})) \propto \prod_{k,n,t \in D} p(F(\mathbf{x}_k^n(t), \mathbf{m_g}^n); H\mu_{zk}^n(t), H\Sigma_{zk}^n(t)H') \tag{12}$$

where D is set of k independent trajectories visible in c^n camera at t, with $(t, n, k) \in D$. Furthermore, 2-D rotation parameter θ_g^n and translation parameters q_g^n in each $\mathbf{m}_g^n$ are considered independent, as a-priori, resulting in posterior distribution represented as.

$$p(\mathbf{M}|\mathbf{X}) \approx \prod_{k,n,t \in D} p(F(\mathbf{x}_k^n(t), \mathbf{m}_g^n); H\mu_{zk}^n(t), H\Sigma_{zk}^n(t)H')p(\theta_g^n)p(q_g^n) \qquad (13)$$

The prior distribution over angles $p(\theta_g^n)$ is a Von-Mises distribution, a circular normal distribution, given in Eqn , where μ and $1 \setminus \kappa$ are analogous to mean and covariance of normal distribution and I_0 is a modified Bessel function of order 0. The translation prior distributions $p(q_g^n)$ are given as Gaussian distributions. The mean of Von-Mises and Gaussian priors are based on corrected network calibration estimates while the covariance is set based on empirical trials.

$$p(\theta|\mu, \kappa) = \frac{e^{\kappa cos(\theta - \mu)}}{2\pi I_0 \kappa} \qquad (14)$$

Finally, to derive the expected value of the network calibration parameters $E(\mathbf{M_g})$, we use Metropolis algorithm [4], a Markov chain Monte carlo method (MCMC), to generate a sequence of samples from the posterior distribution in Equation 6. The proposal distributions for our algorithm are also based on corrected network calibration estimates. Specifically, a Von-Mises angle proposal distribution and Gaussian translation proposal distribution. As is the case with Metropolis algorithms, in our generated sequence of samples, while calculating the expected value, we consider samples after a burn-in period b and only take every s^{th} sample, described in the experiments below, from the sequence of samples.

4   Experimental Results

Our proposed algorithm was validated using our studio dataset as well as a synthetic dataset. To the best of our knowledge, we are the first work to estimate calibration parameters using multiple trajectories, hence for comparative purposes, we could only compare our algorithm with single trajectory algorithm by Rahimi et al. [8], considered as state-of-art in literature.

Studio Dataset
Our studio dataset consists of 3 sequences captured using 5 non-overlapping FOV stereo cameras, capturing @15 Hz mounted on the ceiling to provide a top-down view of the environment. The studio environment, represented an indoor retail shop with $2 - 4$ subjects performing actions simulating a shopping environment. Our in-house tracking software generates the multiple trajectories, on which manual data-association is performed. These manually annotated trajectories function as input to our algorithm. The layout and motion characteristics of our studio is shown in Figure 2, where non-overlap trajectory segments are typically non-linear between c^3 and c^4, while being linear in the remaining non-overlap regions.

Table 1. Comparative calibration errors (mean,std.dev) between our algorithm and MAP [8] (b) Detailed calibration errors (mean,std.dev) of our algorithm on the studio dataset

Algorithm	Studio			Synthetic		
	θ(rad)	qx (m)	qy (m)	θ(rad)	qx (m)	qy (m)
Multiple Track	0.23±0.1	0.46±0.2	0.34±0.2	0.12±0.1	0.31±0.1	0.28±0.2
MAP [8]	0.25±0.1	0.56±0.1	0.39±0.2	0.2±0.1	0.43±0.1	0.36±0.1

(a)

Cam 2			Cam 3		
θ(rad)	qx (m)	qy (m)	θ(rad)	qx (m)	qy (m)
0.24±0.1	0.47±0.3	0.27±0.2	0.24±0.2	0.51±0.2	0.32±0.1
Cam 4			Cam 5		
θ(rad)	qx (m)	qy (m)	θ(rad)	qx (m)	qy (m)
0.26±0.1	0.42±0.2	0.47±0.4	0.23±0.2	0.6±0.4	0.65±0.5

(b)

Algorithm parameters. The location and orientation of the cameras in the network with respect to the global co-ordinate system (pre-defined camera) was measured manually. In the pair-wise calibration estimation, we used 5 particles for 100 iterations, with starting inertia 2.0 and ending inertia 0.1. Additionally, the same initial state or calibration parameter is used for all camera-pairs reflecting automatic initialisation of PSO. In the corrective optimization step, we used 3 particles with same ending inertia and 0.5 starting inertia to simulate a local search [3]. Finally, in our component-wise Metropolis algorithm, the Von-Mises distribution had κ set to 10, while the Gaussian distribution had covariance of 0.1. Furthermore, the burn-in period b was set to 1000, and we sampled every 10 sample (s). The number of time steps in our MCMC method was set to 2500.

Results. As shown in Table 1 and Figure 2, our proposed algorithm is able to accurately estimate the network extrinsic calibration parameters. The average errors reported are obtained using distances between our algorithm's estimates and the ground truth parameters. Note that the average calibration errors in Table 1a (Studio dataset) are based on manually selected single long trajectories, as a result of MAP algorithm limitation [8]. Specifically, [8] require single long trajectory across all camera FOV.

Synthetic Dataset

We have generated sequences from three layouts of non-overlap cameras, *zig-zag*, *diamond* and *square*, with 3 trajectories each. For the algorithm parameters, we utilised the same parameters as used for our studio dataset. The layout and motion characteristics of the synthetic dataset is shown in Figure 2.

Comparison with Rahimi et al.[8]. As shown in Table 1a, our algorithm performs marginally better or similarly to Rahimi et al. [8]. Additionally, our algorithm has demonstrated automatic initialisation. In case of the work by Rahimi et al. [8], based on Newton-Raphson's method, it can be seen that to obtain an optimal calibration estimate a good initialisation of parameters are needed, as wrong initialisation could result in wrong convergence [12]. Finally, on comparing

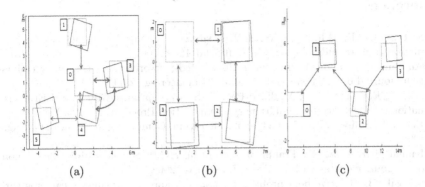

| (a) | (b) | (c) |

Fig. 2. Visualisation of Network Calibration parameter estimates for (a)Studio dataset, (b) Square dataset and (c) Zig-zag dataset. The green box represents ground truth camera position, while black box represents our algorithm's estimate. The motion observed in the non-overlap region between camera pairs is represented by arrows. The global co-ordinate cam is represented by 'O'.

the Bayesian frameworks, [8] obtain the MAP point estimate of the posterior distribution, while we obtain an approximation of the posterior distribution itself.

5   Conclusion and Future Work

We have presented a extrinsic network calibration parameter estimation algorithm for non-overlapping FOV cameras network using multiple trajectories. First, we estimate pair-wise camera calibration parameters using PSO, which are then used to estimate global trajectories. Next, we perform a local search on the global trajectory and correct it. Finally, a Bayesian formulation with Metropolis algorithm is adopted and posterior over calibration parameters are obtained. We demonstrate good calibration accuracies on our studio and synthetic datasets.

Our proposed algorithm obtains good calibration accuracies on our test datasets as observed in Table 1 and Figure 2. However, it can be seen that as the camera distance from global co-ordinate camera increases there is a relative error increase, for example, Cam 4 in Zig Zag dataset (Figure 2c). Similarly, cameras not directly connected to global co-ordinate camera also report relatively higher errors, for example, Cam 5 in our studio dataset (Figure 2a). In our future work, we plan to address this issue, by either adopting a switching linear dynamic model within the Kalman filter for curved trajectory prediction.

Acknowledgments. This work was supported by a grant from Point One UII project PNU10C18 in a collaboration with Philips Research, Eindhoven and Eagle Vision Systems, The Netherlands (EVS). EVS provided the Eagle-Z stereo cameras and tracking software for our experiments with the studio dataset being captured at Philips Research.

References

1. Moeslund, T.B., Hilton, A., Krger, V.: A survey of advances in vision-based human motion capture and analysis. CVIU 104, 90–126 (2006)
2. Anjum, N.: Camera localization in distributed networks using trajectory estimation. Journal of Electrical and Computer Engineering (2011)
3. Shi, Y., Eberhart, R.: A Modified Particle Swarm Optimizer. In: The IEEE International Conference on Evolutionary Computation Proceedings (1998)
4. Beichl, I., Sullivan, F.: The metropolis algorithm. Computing in Science and Engg. (2000)
5. Kumar, R.K., Ilie, A., Frahm, J.M., Pollefeys, M.: Simple calibration of non-overlapping cameras with a mirror. In: CVPR (2008)
6. Micusik, B.: Relative pose problem for non-overlapping surveillance cameras with known gravity vector. In: CVPR (2011)
7. Javed, O., Rasheed, Z., Alatas, O., Shah, M.: Knight: A real time surveillance system for multiple overlapping and non-overlapping cameras. In: ICME (2003)
8. Rahimi, A., Dunagan, B., Darrell, T.: Simultaneous calibration and tracking with a network of non-overlapping sensors. In: CVPR (2004)
9. Chen, G.: A simple treatment for sub-optimal kalman filtering in case of measurement data missing. IEEE Transactions on Aerospace and Electronic Systems (1990)
10. John, V., Trucco, E., Ivekovic, S.: Markerless human articulated tracking using hierarchical particle swarm optimisation. Image Vision Comput. 28, 1530–1547 (2010)
11. Ghahramani, Z., Hinton, G.E.: Parameter estimation for linear dynamical systems. Technical report, University of Toronto (1996)
12. Kelley, C.T.: Solving Nonlinear Equations with Newton's method. Fundamentals of Algorithms (2003)

Detecting Interesting Events
Using Unsupervised Density Ratio Estimation

Yuichi Ito[1,*], Kris M. Kitani[2], James A. Bagnell[2], and Martial Hebert[2]

[1] Nikon Corporation, Shinagawa, Tokyo 140-8601 Japan
[2] Carnegie Mellon University, Pittsburgh, PA 15213 USA

Abstract. Generating meaningful digests of videos by extracting interesting frames remains a difficult task. In this paper, we define interesting events as unusual events which occur rarely in the entire video and we propose a novel interesting event summarization framework based on the technique of *density ratio estimation* recently introduced in machine learning. Our proposed framework is unsupervised and it can be applied to general video sources, including videos from moving cameras. We evaluated the proposed approach on a publicly available dataset in the context of anomalous crowd behavior and with a challenging personal video dataset. We demonstrated competitive performance both in accuracy relative to human annotation and computation time.

Keywords: Video Summarization, Density Ratio Estimation.

1 Introduction

While the amount of video data from personal cameras has been increasing exponentially, the raw content of any long video is often uninformative and only a small portion of the video contains interesting information. A framework that could automatically detect and highlight interesting events within a video would significantly improve the efficiency of video analysis by focusing attention on the most salient content. While it would be impossible to anticipate the interests of the viewer without extensive training data, at least being able to filter out frames of common or uninteresting events would be very valuable. In fact, commercial products, such as Magisto [1] were introduced to address this problem.

We explore an event summarization framework based on an unsupervised classification technique to select frames (Figure 1). We assume that the input video can be described by a nominal distribution of frames, described by visual features, plus a fraction of outlier frames which do not fit the nominal distribution. In that model, the "interesting" frames selected by the algorithm correspond to unusual events which occur rarely in the entire video. This task is particularly well suited to unedited consumer videos which often include large segments of repeating or uninformative material. Importantly, the approach is unsupervised so that the level of interest of a frame is defined relative to the input video rather than relative to some fixed training set which may have little relation with the input video.

---

* This work was done while the author was at Carnegie Mellon University.

A. Fusiello et al. (Eds.): ECCV 2012 Ws/Demos, Part III, LNCS 7585, pp. 151–161, 2012.
© Springer-Verlag Berlin Heidelberg 2012

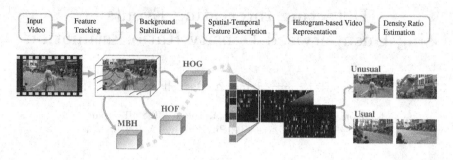

Fig. 1. Overview of our proposed framework

We encode each frame of an input video by a set of quantized spatio-temporal feature descriptors while eliminating the noise due to background motion. This approach is well suited to detecting spatio-temporal salient events. e.g. salient actions, scene changes, etc. We divide the entire set of features from the input video into two sections, and we train a logistic classifier on the corresponding two-class problem, following discriminative density ratio techniques introduced in machine learning [2]. In reality, we use different splits of the video and combine the outputs of the corresponding classifiers to get a combined detection score.

1.1 Related Work

Our task is to detect interesting events from general video sources, which is related to two broad areas of research: video summarization and anomaly detection. There are various event detection approaches in complex visual scenes [3,4]. Most of the approaches for video summarization are based on video skimming, which is a technique to select short video clips. Previous work on video skimming [5] can be classified into two categories: summary oriented and highlight oriented. Summary oriented methods keep the essential part of each shot and generates brief summaries [6,7]. In contrast, the highlight oriented methods only select a few interesting and salient parts of the original video. Movie trailers and highlights of sports events are examples of this type [8]. The latter methods are most closely related to our task. However, defining which video shots to be highlighted is a subjective and difficult process. Detecting unusual events, or "anomalies", is also a key component of video surveillance systems. Although the details vary depending on the specific application, anomaly detection generally involves detecting events which occur rarely using model or saliency based [9,10,11], sparse coding [12], trajectory analysis [13], or HMM models [14].

2   Proposed Method

2.1   Density Ratio Estimation

For the sake of explanation, let us first consider a slightly different problem in which we have two separate videos. One video, called the "reference" or R, does not contain any interesting events. The second video called the "input" video or I, is the one in which we wish to find the interesting events, i.e., the ones that are sufficiently different from R. We also assume that each frame of both videos is represented by a feature vector f. In this setting, the task is to decide whether each frame of I, f_I is unusual, i.e., sufficiently different from the other frames in the video. One natural approach [15] is to model the probability density of the frame features from the reference video $P(f|R)$. One can then classify those frames f_I from I for which $P(f|R)$ is low as interesting or unusual events. This density estimation approach has several major issues. First, density estimation in a high dimensional space is generally a difficult problem and may be, in fact, unnecessary to detect anomalies. In addition, because it is based on the likelihood of feature occurrence in the video, the approach cannot account for the prior frequency of occurrence of any feature value in *any* video.

The alternate approach that we explored is known as density ratio estimation [2]. This approach exploits the insight from machine learning that it is much easier to learn a ratio of two probability densities in a high dimensional space than to learn each separately. This is why density ratio estimation is used in many fields, such as outlier detection [2] and change points detection [16], etc. In this model, we view R and I as training data for a two-class classification problem in which we assign a label $y = +1$ if the frame is classified as originating from R and $y = -1$ if it is classified as originating from I. Under this classification task definition, we can estimate the density ratio $\rho(f) = \frac{P(y=+1|f)}{P(y=-1|f)}$ from all the frames in R and I. For a given frame f_I from I, $\rho(f_I)$ should be close to 0.5 or greater if the frame is not part of an anomalous segment because, by definition, non-anomalous features are similarly distributed between reference and input videos, whereas the probability is close to 0 if the feature comes from an anomalous part of the video. Anomalous segments can then be detected by thresholding $\rho(f)$, or equivalently by thresholding $P(y = +1|f)$ (Figure 2). This approach has the advantage of not relying on restrictive assumptions on a prior distribution of features because it works directly with the posterior distributions. For the same reason, it provides a natural reference decision threshold of 0.5, irrespective of the distribution of features across the videos. It also has the advantage of being a fast classifier and requiring constant time irrespective of the complexity of video. An effective and simple way of estimating $\rho(f)$ is to estimate a logistic classifier from the data in R and I. Under the logistic model:

$$P(y|f;w) = \frac{1}{1 + e^{yw^T f}}, \tag{1}$$

where w is a vector of parameters estimated from the data. Specifically, w is obtained by maximizing the log-likelihood over the training data. Also, we add an L2 regularizer to help control over-fitting, resulting in the overall optimization problem:

$$argmax_w \sum_i P(y_i|f_i; w) - \lambda ||w||^2, \tag{2}$$

where the sum is taken over all the frames in the videos, and λ controls the regularization. We optimize it with stochastic gradient ascent with a decaying

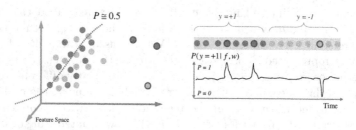

Fig. 2. Using density ratio estimation, e.g., logistic model, for detecting unusual events

learning-rate of $\alpha_t = c/\sqrt{t}$, where c is the step-size and t is the iteration number. In practice we use 100 iteration of the stochastic gradient outer loop. Importantly, this approach is entirely unsupervised.

2.2 Unsupervised Detection from a Single Input Video

The approach presented so far assumed two separate videos, one reference video showing nominal feature distribution and one input video in which we wish to detect the frames that are unusual with respect to the reference video. In our target task, however, we have a single input video from which we need to draw subsets of frames that can be used as reference/input pairs. More precisely, given an input video V with N frames, we separate it into two subsets V^+ and V^- of equal sizes $N/2$. V^+ and V^- are the analogs of R and I in the above introduction, except that they are drawn from a single video. We can then train a two-class classifier using a logistic model as described above, i.e., estimating w such that $P(y|f; w)$ agrees with $y = +1$ on V_+ and -1 on V_-. Those frames with feature vector f that occur frequently in both V_+ and V_- will have a probability $P(y|f; w)$ close to 0.5, while the unusual frames will have probability far from 0.5. This is of course the ideal case. In practice, however, the classifier is not perfect and an approach that is more robust to noise in the classifier is to use the median value M computed over the entire input V instead of 0.5 as reference value. We can then assign a score a_n to each frame n of V as: $a_n = |P(y_n = +1|f_n; w) - M|$.

Ideally, we should train a classifier and evaluate the scores on *all* the possible splits of V. Since this would require an impractically large number of rounds of logistic training, we limit ourselves to three splits corresponding to the following intervals of frames : $V_+ = [1, N/2]$, $V_+ = [N/4, 3N/4]$, $V_+ = [1, N/4] \bigcup [N/2, 3N/4]$. As shown in Figure 3, these three splits provide a good first order coverage of the possible splits of the data. From each split k we can estimate the parameter $w^{(k)}$ of the logistic classifier of the corresponding binary classification problem, as described above, and for each frame n with feature f_n we can estimate the score $a_n^{(k)} = |P(y_n^{(k)} = +1|f_n; w^{(k)}) - M^{(k)}|$, where $M^{(k)}$ is the median value of the probabilities over all the frames. The final score for each frame is obtained by averaging the scores: $a_n = \sum_k a_n^{(k)}$ for frame n. The overall procedure for computing the scores is shown in Table 1. We implemented two ways of using the aggregate scores for detecting the interesting frames. The first approach,

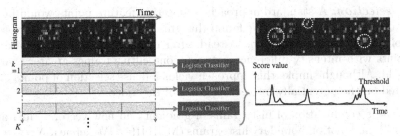

Fig. 3. Top left: Visualization of the feature vector f computed at each frame. Middle left: Three different splits of the input video into +1/-1 classes. Bottom right: Final score obtained by averaging the outputs of the classifiers learned on the three splits (higher value = more interesting frames). Top right: The manually drawn white circles point to feature components that triggered detection of interesting events.

Table 1. Overall algorithm

Proposed Algorithm
Input : video sequence V with N frames with features $\{f_n\}$
Output : $\{a_n, n = 1 \ldots N\}$
for $k=1, \cdots, K$ **do**
1. Generate a split $(V_+^{(k)}, V_-^{(k)})$
2. Give label value to all $\{y_n^{(k)}\}$ based on
$$y_n^{(k)} = \begin{cases} +1 \ (n \in V_+^{(k)}) \\ -1 \ (n \in V_-^{(k)}) \end{cases}$$
3. Estimate parameter $w^{(k)}$ of logistic classifier from $\{f_n\}$, and $\{y_n^{(k)}\}$
4. Estimate the conditional probability $P(y_n^{(k)} = +1 \mid f_n; w^{(k)})$ and median value $M^{(k)}$
5. Calculate and accumulate the distance from median value
$$a_n = a_n + |P(y_n^{(k)} = +1 \mid f_n; w^{(k)}) - M^{(k)}|$$
end

labeled "Proposed1" in the result section, simply thresholds the scores so that frame n is retained if $a_n > \epsilon$. The second approach ("Proposed2") is threshold free and is inspired from the classical SVM calibration procedure from Platt [17]. If M is the median value of a_n over all the frames in V, we define two subsets of frames, V_+^o and V_-^o corresponding to frames with scores below or above the threshold M, respectively. We can then estimate the parameter w_o of a logistic regressor for the split (V_+^o, V_-^o) and we obtain the final classification score by applying this logistic function to the original classification scores.

To compute the feature vector f of a frame, we first select p image points $x_1, ..., x_p$ in the frame and we compute a 576-dimensional descriptor $\hat{f}(x_i)$ at each point. The set of $\hat{f}(.)$ computed over the entire video is quantized into K centers $\hat{f}_j, j = 1, ...K$ The final feature vector f used in the classifier is the K-dimensional histogram of quantized $\hat{f}(.)$ values computed over the video frame. Additional details are as follows:

Point selection: A standard approach to selecting feature points would be to use an interest point detector. We found that this technique generates too sparse a set of points for our approach. Instead, after coarse stabilization, we use all the points with intensity difference between consecutive frames greater than a threshold. Although simple, this approach yields a dense selection of points concentrated on the potentially interesting parts of the video.

$\hat{f}$: We use a combination of histograms of gradient and flow vectors (HoG and HoF [18]), and motion boundary histograms (MBH [19]). We define a $N \times N \times M$ patch around each x_i ,which we divide into $n_\sigma \times n_\sigma \times n_\tau$ cells. In each cell, we compute 1) a 8-bin histogram of gradient direction in that cell; 2) a 8-bin histogram of optical flow, using Farneback's copencv implementation; 3) two 8-bin histograms encoding MBH (MBH uses histograms in the x and y axis, as in [19]). We use M=10, N = 15, $n_\sigma = 3$, $n_\tau = 2$ for a 576-dim descriptor at each point.

Quantization: We quantize $\hat{f}$: using K-means over the set of feature vectors from the entire video. We chose $K = 32$ and verified that performance remains stable over a range of values 16–64 (K is kept constant across the experiments).

Background stabilization: Generally, personal videos tend to include shaky background motion because they are taken by hand-held cameras. This background motion affects the motion descriptors and the performance of the classifier. To minimize this effect, we estimate background motion by calculating a homography between consecutive frames and we align the frames prior to feature computation. We estimate the homography using LMeds by establishing KLT feature correspondences between frames. Since our event descriptors temporally span M = 10 frames, we use stabilization over a 10 frame moving window.

3   Experiments

3.1   Baseline Algorithms

To test the effectiveness of our proposed algorithms, we use two baseline algorithms: One Class Support Vector Machine(OC-SVM), and sparse coding. These were chosen because of their good performance and because they are unsupervised techniques. OC-SVM is representative of outlier detection algorithms based on SVMs, which have produced excellent results in [20]. We used the publicly available implementation of [21], configured with a Gaussian kernel and $\nu = 0.5$. The second baseline is based on sparse reconstructability of query events from a learned dictionary, which is one of the state-of-the-art unusual event detection methods [12]. We used [22] for implementing sparse coding with Nesterov's optimization method with a regularization parameter $\lambda = 10$.

3.2   UMN Dataset

We tested our proposed framework on the publicly available dataset of crowd videos from the UMN dataset [23]. This dataset consists of 11 different scenarios in 3 different scenes of crowd escape scenarios, over a total of 7740 frames. Each

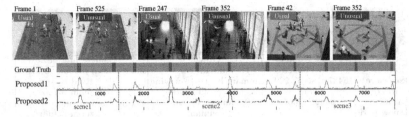

Fig. 4. Example frames of usual(green) and unusual(red) events and the qualitative scoring results of our proposed methods for UMN dataset

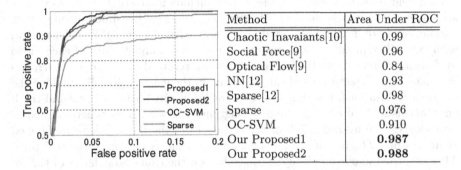

Method	Area Under ROC
Chaotic Inavaiants[10]	0.99
Social Force[9]	0.96
Optical Flow[9]	0.84
NN[12]	0.93
Sparse[12]	0.98
Sparse	0.976
OC-SVM	0.910
Our Proposed1	**0.987**
Our Proposed2	**0.988**

Fig. 5. ROC curve and performance comparison

video consists of an initial section of normal behavior and ends with sequences of unusual behavior (Figure 4). While these videos address a more specific task than our unconstrained detection problem, i.e., they are restricted to crowd motions and explicit "normal" section at the start of each video, they allow us to compare directly with published numbers in a way that does not favor our approach since many of the published techniques are tuned to crowd motions. In Figure 5, the AUC values of our methods outperform most of the other methods and are comparable to [10] and sparse coding [9]. However, our method is a more general solution, because it does not make any assumption about the content of the video, while [10] is specifically designed for anomalies in crowd videos, and [9] assumes that the first part of the video is nominal, i.e., can be used as reference to learn the dictionary, while we allow unusual events to occur anywhere in the video. Descriptor extraction takes about 0.43 second/frame for all the algorithms. Dictionary learning and classification takes 0.41, 0.022, and 0.020 second/frame for Sparse coding, OC-SVM, and our method, respectively, as measured on a single core 2.97 GHz Intel Core i7 PC with 8.0GB memory.

4   Personal Videos

We evaluated our framework using examples that are more representative of consumer videos. We used a dataset acquired in different scenes and locations using

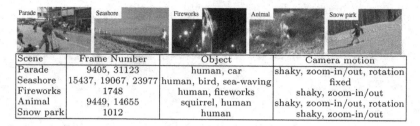

Scene	Frame Number	Object	Camera motion
Parade	9405, 31123	human, car	shaky, zoom-in/out, rotation
Seashore	15437, 19067, 23977	human, bird, sea-waving	fixed
Fireworks	1748	human, fireworks	shaky, zoom-in/out
Animal	9449, 14655	squirrel, human	shaky, zoom-in/out, rotation
Snow park	1012	human	shaky, zoom-in/out

Fig. 6. Personal Video Dataset. The dataset totally include 9 videos on 5 scene.

a hand-held consumer camera[1]. The videos include interesting events as well as long stretches of routine activity. The dataset consists of five different categories: parade, seashore, fireworks, animal , and snow park (Figure 6). In order to deal with variability in human annotations, we generated annotations of each video by fifteen different subjects. The annotators all received the same set of written instructions to detect rare and salient events in the entire video. To combine the multiple annotations, we compare the algorithms with each set of ground truth annotations and we average the resulting performance numbers across annotation sources. On average 17 % of the frames from the input videos are labeled as interesting. The average of all the 15 annotations is shown in Figure 7(top). Although the annotators disagree somewhat on the exact boundaries of the intervals of interest in the video, they do agree strongly on the general locations of the major events. A similar level of consensus is observed on all the annotations from all the videos. Quantitatively, the standard deviation of the length of video labeled as interesting relative to the length of the input video across all labelers is 5%. The score estimated by our Proposed2 algorithm is shown in Figure 7(middle) along with a few sampled framed detected as interesting or common by the algorithm are shown in Figure 7(bottom). In addition to SVM and sparse coding, we compared our proposed framework with two commercial products: Windows Movie Maker(WMM) and Magisto. Magisto [1] is one of most sophisticated video summarization services, which can automatically produce digested videos by using combinations of scene analysis and recognition algorithms. The scoring curve and the annotation averaged over the fifteen annotators are shown in Figure 7. The scores correlate well with human annotation data. It is interesting to note that, around ground truth events, the score decreases as the agreement among human annotators decreases. The overall performance is shown in the ROC and PR curves in Figure 8(b-c). For this dataset, chance performance is at precision 0.17 (maximum F-measure at 0.29.) In addition, Figure 8(a) compares classification performance as the detection threshold varies. This confirms that the performance of our proposed method gradually changes while maintaining higher F-measure value than the other algorithm. This implies that our method can be more easily tuned than the video summarization tools. Similar conclusions can be drawn from Table 2. Our approach outperforms other algorithms based on the area under the PR (average precision) or the ROC curves.

---

[1] The dataset is available at https://sites.google.com/site/yitopaper/

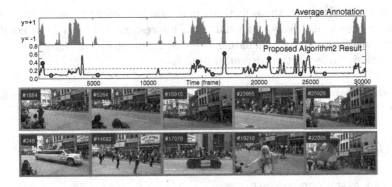

Fig. 7. Performance on one personal video: (Top) Average annotations from human labelers (+1 = interesting and -1 = common); (Middle) score returned by our algorithm (Proposed2) (higher score = more interesting frame); (Bottom) Sampled frames corresponding to the dots in the score curve (Green = common; red = interesting.)

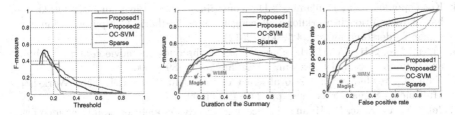

Fig. 8. F-measure as function of detection threshold; (b) Precision/recall curve; (c) ROC curve

Table 2. Quantitative performance comparison

Algorithm	AU-FT	AU-FD	AU-ROC	Highest Precision(Duration)	Highest F-measure(Duration)
WMM	–	–	–	0.26 (0.23)	0.22 (0.23)
Magisto	–	–	–	0.44 (0.14)	0.21 (0.14)
OC-SVM	0.080	0.38	0.54	0.53 (0.09)	0.40 (0.19)
Sparse	0.098	0.36	0.60	0.43 (0.04)	0.41 (0.80)
Proposed1	**0.175**	0.42	0.69	0.53 (0.10)	0.51 (0.38)
Proposed2	0.152	**0.43**	**0.71**	**0.57** (0.15)	**0.54** (0.40)

For reference, we also indicate the highest F-measure and precision reached by each algorithm, along with the corresponding relative duration of the selected part of the video.

5   Conclusion

We proposed a feature-based event summarization method using an unsupervised logistic classifier framework for detecting frames which depart from the overall distribution of frames in the video. We showed promising performance on different types of datasets. In designing this approach, we deliberately limited ourselves to the distribution of low-level features in order to test the feasibility of the method. However, these features may not be sufficient to discern subtle differences that make events unusual. One interesting direction is to combine high-level descriptors, e.g., including the responses of action detectors in the feature descriptor, with the current approach.

Acknowledgement. This work was partially funded by ARL under Agreement W911NF-10-2-0061.

References

1. Magisto, http://www.magisto.com
2. Sugiyama, M., Yamada, M., von Bunaud, P., Suzuki, T., Kanamori, T., Kawanabe, M.: Direct density-ratio estimation with dimensionality reduction via least-squares hetero-distributional subspace search. Neural Networks 24 (2011)
3. Pritch, Y., Rav-Acha, A., Peleg, S.: Nonchronological video synopsis and indexing. IEEE Trans. Pattern Anal. Mach. Intell. 30, 1971–1984 (2008)
4. Kosmopoulos, D.I., Doulamis, N.D., Voulodimos, A.S.: Bayesian filter based behavior recognition in workflows allowing for user feedback. Computer Vision and Image Understanding 116, 422–434 (2012)
5. Li, Y., Lee, S.H., Yeh, C.H., Kuo, C.C.J.: Techniques for movie content analysis and skimming. Signal Processing Magazine 23, 79–89 (2006)
6. Nam, J., Tewfik, A.H.: Video abstract of video. In: Proc. IEEE 3rd Workshop Multimedia Signal Processing, pp. 117–122 (1999)
7. Jolic, N., Petrovic, N., Huang, T.: Scene generative models for adaptive video fast forward. In: Proc. ICIP (2003)
8. Xiong, Z., Radhakrishnan, R., Divakaran, A.: Generation of sports highlights using motion activity in combination with a common audio feature extraction framework. In: Proc. ICIP, vol. 1, pp. I–5–I–8 (2003)
9. Mehran, M.S.R., Oyama, A.: Abnormal crowd behavior detection using social force model. In: Proc. CVPR (2009)
10. Wu, S., Moore, B., Shah, M.: Chaotic invariants of lagrangian particle trajectories for anomaly detection in crowded scenes. In: Proc. CVPR (2010)
11. Seo, H.J., Milanfar, P.: Static and space-time visual saliency detection by self-resemblance. Journal of Vision (2009)
12. Cong, Y., Yuan, J., Liu, J.: Sparse reconstruction cost for abnormal event detection. In: Proc. CVPR (2011)
13. Piciarelli, C., Micheloni, C., Foresti, G.: Trajectory-based anomalous event detection. IEEE Transaction on Circuits and Systems for Video Technology 18 (2008)
14. Zhang, D., Gatica-Perez, D., Bengio, S., McCowan, I.: Semi-supervised adapted hmms for unusual event detection. In: Proc. CVPR (2005)
15. Zhao, M., Saligrama, V.: Anomaly detection with score functions based on nearest neighbor graphs. In: Proc. NIPS (2009)
16. Matsugu, M., Yamanaka, M., Sugiyama, M.: Detection of activities and events without explicit categorization. In: Proc. ICCV Workshop (2011)
17. Platt, J.C.: Probabilistic outputs for support vector machines and comparisons to regularized likelihood methods. In: Advances in Large Margin Classifiers (1999)
18. Laptev, I., Marszalek, M., Schmid, C., Rozenfeld, B.: Learning realistic human actions from movies. In: Proc. CVPR (2008)

19. Dalal, N., Triggs, B., Schmid, C.: Human Detection Using Oriented Histograms of Flow and Appearance. In: Leonardis, A., Bischof, H., Pinz, A. (eds.) ECCV 2006. LNCS, vol. 3952, pp. 428–441. Springer, Heidelberg (2006)
20. Scholkopf, B., Williamson, R., Smola, A., Taylor, J.S., Platt, J.C.: Support vector method for novelty detection. In: Proc. NIPS (2000)
21. Canu, S., Grandvalet, Y., Guigue, V., Rakotomamonjy, A.: Svm and kernel methods matlab toolbox. INSA de Rouen, Rouen, France (2005)
22. Matlab Toolbox,
    http://www.mathworks.com/matlabcentral/fileexchange/16204
23. UMN dataset, http://mha.cs.umn.edu/Movies/

Destination Flow for Crowd Simulation

Stefano Pellegrini[1,*], Jürgen Gall[2], Leonid Sigal[3], and Luc Van Gool[1]

[1] ETH Zurich
[2] MPI for Intelligent Systems
[3] Disney Research Pittsburgh

Abstract. We present a crowd simulation that captures some of the semantics of a specific scene by partly reproducing its motion behaviors, both at a lower level using a steering model and at the higher level of goal selection. To this end, we use and generalize a steering model based on linear velocity prediction, termed LTA. From a goal selection perspective, we reproduce many of the motion behaviors of the scene without explicitly specifying them. Behaviors like "wait at the tram stop" or "stroll-around" are not explicitly modeled, but learned from real examples. To this end, we process real data to extract information that we use in our simulation. As a consequence, we can easily integrate real and virtual agents in a mixed reality simulation. We propose two strategies to achieve this goal and validate the results by a user study.

1 Introduction

The modeling of human crowds is of enormous interest for a multitude of applications, ranging from gaming, over movie effects, to evacuation simulators and urban planning. Humans exhibit a huge variety of motion behaviors that is not trivial to reproduce in virtual characters. Following the terminology of [17], we distinguish among three levels of motion behavior: goal setting, steering and locomotion. In this paper we will focus on goal setting and, partly, on steering.

Our goal is to simulate crowds within a specific context. Depending on the environment there will be different motion patterns. Whereas people may leisurely walk in a park, they probably are quite hasty in a business district. Different environments, which could also be indoor, will also contain different sources, attractors, and sinks where people resp. appear, often go to, or disappear. All these factors must be accounted for when animating a virtual crowd. Manual specification (e.g., scripting) is common, but also very tedious and time consuming. As alternative, data-driven approaches [8,9] extract real trajectories from an actual crowd and use these. Data-driven approaches, however, do not generalize well and are difficult to adapt to scene changes.

In this paper, we therefore propose to combine rule-based steering models with data-driven goal selection to minimize the manual work for animators while still being able to generalize to scene changes. Human steering models have

---

* The authors acknowledge financial support from EC project TANGO (FP7-ICT-249858).

A. Fusiello et al. (Eds.): ECCV 2012 Ws/Demos, Part III, LNCS 7585, pp. 162–171, 2012.
© Springer-Verlag Berlin Heidelberg 2012

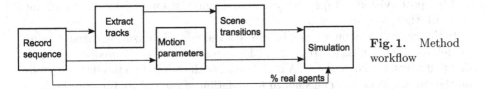

Fig. 1.   Method workflow

been studied for several decades in different disciplines. When building a rule-based steering model, rather than a data-driven approach, one can conveniently integrate this knowledge into simple rules that capture general properties of human low-level motion. These properties are not expected to be valid only in a specific scene. The same model can therefore be employed in different situations by simply adapting the goal selection layer. In this layer, behaviors like "wait at the tram stop", "stroll-around" or "go and grab a coffee" are not explicitly scripted but learned from real examples. This said, user interaction is easy to integrate in the process, and arbitrary behaviors can be chosen.

Our approach only requires a few minutes (5 to 10) of video recording with real people moving in the scene. Their trajectories and group memberships are extracted by means of a semi-automatic tracker similar to the one in [15]. This video data is processed both to analyze lower level properties such as typical personal area [4] and to extract the regions in the scene that are relevant for crowd motion. Based on the extracted trajectories, the *destination flow* between the regions is learned, which is a probabilistic goal selection layer that extends the steering model. To carry out the actual agent motion, we choose to generalize the LTA steering model [14]. In particular, we generalize the avoidance component in that model, add a temporal horizon to the collision anticipation and add the realistic possibility of people walking in groups within the crowd. Finally, in order to maximally benefit from the real trajectories that one might have at one's disposal, we propose the use of mixed crowds, consisting of a blend of real and virtual trajectories.[1] At simulation time, the mix of real vs. virtual people is a free parameter, allowing the user to adapt crowd density (see Fig. 1).

Contributions: The first contribution of the paper is the introduction of the *destination flow*, a probabilistic goal selection layer that extends the steering model. In another contribution this paper proposes two different, possibly combinable, strategies to mix real and individual trajectories in the crowd simulation. Finally, we generalize the LTA steering model to fit our purposes.

2   Related Work

Autonomous agents are an active area of research since a long time[18,5,19,22]. A detailed review can be found in [20].

Steering models have mostly been used for computer graphics animations and to simulate evacuation scenarios. However, other fields, such as robotics [21,24]

---

[1] We will call real agents those crowd members the trajectory of whom is derived directly from captured data, and virtual agents those that are generated by simulation.

and computer vision [1,14] recently developed interest for such models and came out with their own solutions.

In this work we will build upon LTA [14], an energy minimization based steering model. As other models [17,16,13,24], LTA uses a linear velocity prediction, but in different ways. In particular LTA defines a smooth energy function that depends on the subject velocity. The smooth formulation of the energy function leads to a straightforward integration of multiple interactions and additional components (*e.g.* grouping), like for [5]. However, the choice of the next agent velocity does not depend on the absolute value of the function, as in the Social Force model [5], rather on the function shape (*i.e.* the location of the minima), making it easy to design and check the model properties. Also geometric models [24] share this advantage. Contrary to geometric models, however, LTA's energy function is differentiable and efficient gradient minimization techniques can be readily applied. LTA has never been tested before for crowd simulation. In this paper we improve and generalize the model to make it suitable for such purpose.

While the majority of the steering models have focused on individual motion, recently more and more authors propose to include the grouping feature into the simulation [11,12,7]. Using groups, but data-driven, is the approach of [8]. Here, state-velocity pairs are extracted from real data and at simulation time a combination of them is employed in order to simulate group behaviors. Also data-driven, a different kind of microscopic model has been proposed by [9]. This is an example-based model, that uses a database build with real world trajectories. [6] build a model of the crowd structure and motion, learning these features from real data. The crowd animation is carried out by selecting collision free trajectories that are consistent with the formation model. The authors show how models learned from different types of crowd can be combined and result in a blending of the original models.

Closely related to our work, is the study presented in Chapter 6 of [20]. The authors here first describe which scene information could be useful to reproduce a real scene in a simulation. However, the information extraction at this point is manual and requires a customization for each scene. Furthermore, they use real tracked trajectories to extract scene specific velocity fields. The velocity fields are then clustered and virtual agents at simulation time are driven by these fields. Our approach is different in that we compute region of interest and transitions among them, rather than extract velocity fields. This allows us to simulate in a stochastic manner complex scenes, where repetitive behaviors are possible. Last, we study the mixing of real and virtual agents [25] in the reproduced scene.

Another important aspect of an autonomous virtual agent is the goal selection. In [23] the intentions of different types of agents are represented by different flowcharts. In [12], when in the *autonomous mode*, the crowd responds to events following the rules specified by the animator. A Finite State Machine is used to model the goal selection layer both in [2] and in [3]. In these works, the region structure and the transition rules are manually specified. In our paper we reduce the concept of intention, or goal, to that of a destination in space and we let the transitions be learned automatically from the scene.

3   Steering Model

To simulate crowds we use the steering model presented in [14], termed LTA. In this model, the next velocity for an agent is computed by minimizing an energy function that reproduces avoidance and goal-seeking aspects of human walking. The key aspect of the model is that the decision of the next velocity is based on the distance of maximum approach $\mathbf{d}_{ij}$ between pedestrians i and j. In this paper we generalize the model, with parameters λ, in three directions:

- We substitute the isotropic avoidance component I_{ij} of the original formulation with an anisotropic one:

$$I_{ij} = \exp\left(-\mathbf{d}_{ij}^{T}\begin{bmatrix}\lambda_{I,1} & 0 \\ 0 & \lambda_{I,2}\end{bmatrix}\mathbf{d}_{ij}\right). \qquad (1)$$

- We add to the energy function a grouping term to allow representing groups of pedestrians walking together.

$$G_{ij} = \mathbf{d}_{ij}^{T}\begin{bmatrix}\lambda_{G,1} & 0 \\ 0 & \lambda_{G,2}\end{bmatrix}\mathbf{d}_{ij}. \qquad (2)$$

- We introduce a temporal horizon T, to limit the computation of the $\mathbf{d}_{ij}$ to a realistic time interval.

The function that we minimize at each time step[2] for each agent i becomes:

$$E_i = \sum_{j\in\mathcal{V}_i} w_{ij}I_{ij} + \sum_{j\in\mathcal{G}_{ij}\cap\mathcal{V}_i} w_{ij}G_{ij} + S_i\lambda_S + D_i\lambda_D, \qquad (3)$$

where w_{ij}, S_i and D_i are the same weights, speed and destination components as defined in the original paper, $\mathcal{V}_i$ is the set of pedestrians that are visible to subject i and $\mathcal{G}_i$ is the set of subjects that are in the same group of subject i.

4   Scene Transitions

The original LTA assumes that the destination $\mathbf{z}_i^t$ and the desired speed u_i are known for each subject i. In order to be able to mimic the motion patterns in a specific scene, we propose to learn a probabilistic model for these quantities. To this end, we extract the trajectories of real people and the groups from a video with an interactive tracker [15] and label the static objects $\mathcal{O}^t$ manually. We use cameras from the top (Fig. 3) to capture the entire scene and to facilitate the tracker job. We also define a set of scene events, $\mathcal{E}$, and the subset $\mathcal{A}^t \subseteq \mathcal{E}$ of active events at time t. In the following, we assume that $\mathcal{A}^t$ and $\mathcal{E}$ are given.

Based on the trajectories, we model the desired speed u_i by a normal distribution, where mean μ and variance Σ are estimated from the observed velocities. As people do not walk with very low speed, we set an additional threshold of $0.5ms^{-1}$

---

[2] Note that we dropped the time dependency to reduce notational clutter.

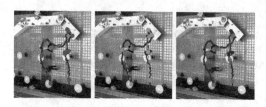

Fig. 2. The approximation of a real trajectory (in blue) for $\kappa = 1$ (red), $\kappa = 10$ (green) and $\kappa = 100$ (magenta). Note how a too small value of κ will introduce too many corners while the large value will miss some.

to avoid slow walkers being sampled from the tail of the speed distribution. In our model, the subjects in the same group share the same desired speed.

To learn the sequence of destinations for each group of subjects, we need to know the *intentional* destination of the recorded pedestrians. To this end, we extract interesting points from the scene by segmenting the trajectories.

4.1   Segmenting the Trajectories

Given a uniformly sampled point trajectory $\mathcal{Q}_i = [\mathbf{p}_i^0 \dots \mathbf{p}_i^T]$, we are interested in a sequence of points, or *corners*, $\mathbf{p}_i^0 \dots \mathbf{p}_i^{t_c} \dots \mathbf{p}_i^T$ that split the trajectory in a sequence of sub-tracks. Each of these sub-tracks specifies a unit of motion that a subject should be able to undertake without any complex path planning operation. Since thresholding the velocity or the curvature of the trajectories turned out not to be robust, the problem is solved by a shortest path search in a graph, as in [10]. The graph is obtained by connecting each $\mathbf{p}_i^t \in \mathcal{Q}_i$ with all subsequent points. The cost of the transition from $\mathbf{p}_i^{t_a}$ to $\mathbf{p}_i^{t_b}$ is defined by

$$\gamma(t_a, t_b) = \kappa + \sum_{t=t_a}^{t_b} ||\mathbf{p}_i^t - (\mathbf{p}_i^{t_a} + \frac{t - t_a}{t_b - t_a}(\mathbf{p}_i^{t_b} - \mathbf{p}_i^{t_a}))||^2 \,, \tag{4}$$

where κ is a fixed cost associated to each split to regularize the number of splits. The summation in Eq. 4 is the cost of approximating the portion of the trajectory from t_a to t_b with a straight line. The impact of the regularizer κ is shown in Fig. 2. We set $\kappa = 10$ in this paper. The corners of a trajectory make the sequence of desired destinations and the movement from one corner to the next is a *transition*. Rather than assigning the corner directly to the scene, we extract R interesting spatial *regions* from the scene and assign a corner to each of them. We distinguish between entrance, exit and transition corners and regions depending on whether they are at the beginning, in the middle or at the end of the trajectories. The corners are distributed within the region according to a distribution ρ_r, with $r = 1 \dots R$.

In our experiments, we use square cells to represent each region as shown in Fig. 3, left. The size of each region cell affects the destination flow. We found a good compromise at $2m$ edge size. We also define two special regions, *create* and *destroy* to handle agents initialization and termination, respectively. Note that the same solution can be used for different kinds of region shapes, not necessarily square cells and user interaction with shape and cell position is straightforward.

The distribution ρ_r is estimated using a kernel density estimate over the region corners, with a normal kernel of $0.2m$ standard deviation.

In this paper, a group of subjects always share the same intention, and therefore the same destination region r. The splitting described in Sec. 4.1 can be generalized to a group of trajectories by simply averaging the transition costs in Eq. 4 of the subjects within the same group. In practice, due to the problems produced by groups that are at the edge of two cells, we count the transitions at the individual level. A region transition $r_a \to r_b$ is therefore defined by a pair of consecutive corners in a subject trajectory. The transition probability $p(r_b|r_a)$ is estimated by the normalized count of the transitions $r_a \to r_b$.

The probabilities, however, can change based on the events that are active. We therefore model the transition probabilities for each active event set $\mathcal{A}^t$ by accumulating in each $p^{\mathcal{A}^t}(r_a|r_b)$ only the transitions that are observed when the corresponding event set is active. We call the set of regions and transitions the *destination flow*.

4.2 Simulation

The simulation of a group g of people starts with a transition from the *create* region to a entrance region r_g, according to the transition probability $p^{\mathcal{A}^t}(r_g|create)$. Every time a new transition r_g is sampled for a group, for each subject i_g a new destination point $\mathbf{z}_{i_g}^t$ is sampled from the destination region r_g, according to the distribution ρ_r. The agent motion to the destination $\mathbf{z}_{i_g}^t$ is demanded to the steering model of Sec. 3. Note that the agents are not performing any navigation task. The destination flow, made mostly of straight paths, partially replaces the navigation task.

A group g reaches the destination when each subject i_g in the group reaches its individual destination point $\mathbf{z}_{i_g}$, e.g. when the distance $d(\mathbf{p}_{i_g}^t, \mathbf{z}_{i_g}^t)$ is small. We define an indicator binary variable n_g^t, that is 1 when the group reached destination, otherwise it is 0. A group selects a new region r_i (possibly the same) at time t only when $n_g^{t-1} = 1$. More formally, the region transitions that determine the motion pattern of simulated pedestrians are modeled as

$$p(r_g^t|r_g^{t-1}, \mathcal{A}^t, n_g^{t-1}) = \begin{cases} \delta_{r_g^t, r_g^{t-1}} & n_g^{t-1} = 0 \\ p^{\mathcal{A}^t}(r_g^t|r_g^{t-1}) & \text{otherwise} \end{cases} \tag{5}$$

where $\delta_{a,b}$ is the Kronecker function that is 1 if $a = b$, and 0 otherwise. The dependencies of the variables described in this section are shown in the graphical model in Fig. 3. Note how the groups share the same quantities.

5 Mixed Reality

Adding real agents to a simulated scene, or the other way around, can be beneficial to enrich the simulation with specific, possibly actor-played, actions. The main problem is that the real agents are not aware of the simulated ones. Simply

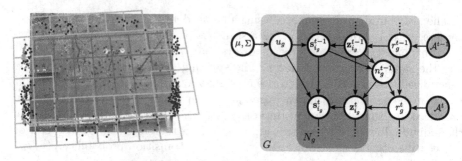

Fig. 3. Left: The grids used for the destination flow. We show the 3 kind of corners: entrance (green), exit (blue) and turn (red). We show the grid for turning points (magenta) and the two overlapping entrance and exit grid (cyan). Empty cells are not shown. **Right:** The dependencies in the goal selection layer. $\mathbf{s}_i^t$ is the state of subject i at time t, given by her position and velocity. Shaded nodes are observed variables.

adding them together will result in general in unlikely configurations, especially when the density of the scene increases. We propose two possible solutions:

Sampling: Sampling from the destination flow is straightforward, as the model dependencies contain no directed cycle; see Fig. 3. Each sample produces a different scene simulation. Therefore we can sample repeatedly until a certain criterion, *e.g.* a minimum number of collisions, is met.

Path-following: Another solution is to allow real agents for small deviations from their real trajectory. We implement this solution by using a path following strategy for each subject. In particular, each real subject at time t becomes a simulated one with her future position at $t+2s$ as destination. The agent desired speed is the average speed in the next 2 seconds. The limited freedom granted by this path following strategy will allow to reduce the number collisions. Note that this strategy can be combined with the previous one.

6   Experiments

Our goal is to reduce to a minimum the amount of manual work for the animator in order to build a realistic simulation of a specific scene. In order to test our algorithm, we need therefore to use real data. We will use three real sequences for our experiments: the *Students* sequence, a ~ 3.5 minutes outdoor sequence has been provided by a third party [9]; the *Meeting* sequence, 10 minutes long, recorded in an indoor during the coffee break of a project meeting; the *Street* sequence [14] contains people walking in the proximity of a tram stop (the event "tram" is active when the tram is at the stop with open doors).

Where not available, the ground truth was extracted with the help of the tracker.

6.1   User Study

To validate the quality of the reproduced scene, we set up a user study. We used 2 different video sequences: Meeting and Street. Three 45s long mixtures of real and virtual agents were generated for these sequences: 0% (purely simulated), 50% and 100% (real sequence without the path-following strategy of Sec. 5). A purely simulated sequence was generated also using a random transition matrix[3]. We call this last simulation the random simulation. For each simulation, the entrance time and the composition of the group was decided by the real sequence. We used a simplified reconstruction of the environment.

Each agent V_i is populated with all the pedestrians within a 10m radius that are connected to i after a Delaunay triangulation and that are in the 180 degrees field of view of i. The interaction parameters were set to match those of the simulated scene. In Fig. 4-center, we report the 2D histograms that show the frequency of the displacement of two subjects, one of which sits in the center of the histogram $\mathbf{p} = \mathbf{0}$ with velocity positive only along the horizontal axis. Left-right symmetry (with respect to the subject in the middle of the histogram) is enforced. These histograms were used to fit the interaction parameters $\lambda_{I,1}, \lambda_{I,2}, \lambda_{G,1}, \lambda_{G,2}$, while we manually set for all the sequences $\lambda_S = 0.3$ and $\lambda_D = 0.03$. To fit the interaction parameters, we use a Gibbs measure interpretation of the energy terms, and we minimize the sum of squared residual between the histogram and

$$(1/Z) \exp\left(-\omega(I(\mathbf{d}) + G(\mathbf{d}))\right) \tag{6}$$

where I and G are from Eq. 1 and Eq. 2, respectively, and Z is a normalizing constant to ensure that Eq. 6 sums to 1. ω is a parameter that is used only for the conversion from energy to probability. Fig. 4-left shows the result of the fitted energy for the Street sequence. The user study was made available to volunteers on the web. The users were given a sample of the original recorded sequence and then they were asked: "The videos below refer to the scenario shown in the video of the previous page. How realistic does it look to you?". The users had to answer with a score from 1 (unrealistic) to 10 (realistic) for each video. 58 people gave an answer for the Meeting sequence, 51 for the Street one.

The results are shown in Fig. 4, left. In the Street sequence, there is no significant difference between the results of the three mixtures ($p > 0.05$), while there is a difference between the score of each of the mixtures and the random simulation ($p < 0.05$). This suggests that the simulated and mixed simulations achieve a realism similar to the one of the real sequence, with integration of real and virtual agents providing opportunity for adding specific, real, possibly unusual, actions.

For the Meeting sequence the real sequence is scored significantly better ($p < 0.05$) than all the others. The random sequence has the lowest average score, but the difference with the other simulated sequences is not significant. In this case, the user does not find the simulated agents as realistic as the real ones, in terms of motion and interactions. We believe that this happens for two reasons. The first is that in the real sequence the transitions are time-dependent, meaning the people in the beginning of the sequence move to the main table and later move to the other part of the scene. Instead, within the event occurrence, our transitions model a stationary process. The second reason is that the environment is dense with static obstacles and standing people. This makes the navigation difficult.

---

[3] We did not allow arbitrary transitions from any region to the *exit* regions.

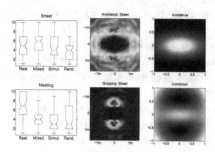

Fig. 4. **Left:** The results of the user study. The central red bar is the median score and the box extends from the 25-th to the 75-th percentile. The dashed lines go to the data points not considered as outliers (red cross). The green cross is the mean score. **Center:** The occupancy histogram for the Street sequence. **Right:** The energy terms after fitting to the histogram.

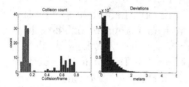

Fig. 5. **Left:** Collisions with path-following strategy (red) and without (blue). **Right:** The real agents' deviation (median $0.33m$) from the original trajectory for one sample, with path-following strategy.

6.2   Mixing Real and Simulated People

As discussed in Sec. 5, an interesting possibility is that of using real and simulated agents in the same simulation. There we proposed 2 possible strategies to achieve such goal. Fig. 5, left, shows the results of the comparison. In detail, we extract 100 sample simulations of the Students sequence, with a 50% mixture, once with and once without the path-following strategy, and for each sample we collect the number of collisions (distance $< 0.4m$) between real and virtual agents. The effect of the path-following strategy in reducing the collisions is evident. This, however, comes at the cost of slight deviations from the real agent original trajectory. This is shown in Fig. 5 right. The path-following strategy should then be preferred when the fidelity of the real agent trajectories is not crucial.

7   Conclusions

Our goal was to produce a model that could adapt to the semantics of a particular scene, and reproduce it with small effort. Once the virtual agents behave similarly to real people, it is easier to integrate them in the same environment. We validated this possibility by conducting a user study.

Even if the goal selection layer is reduced to a destination selection, a series of interesting behaviors emerge. For example, people gather around tables thus forming new groups, even with no notion of group merging in our model. The action of getting in a tram when it comes, is also the pure result of a learned "go-to" behavior. Although probably less visible, the customization of the steering model to the particular scene has been effective in reproducing its features.

Timings. For the Meeting sequence, it took ~ 4 hours to extract tracks and group memberships. All the other processing is carried out in the order of seconds. With our unoptimized code, the simulation of the Students sequence, $215s$ long with an average of 40 agents, requires $117s$ on a single core @2.67GHz.

References

1. Antonini, G., Martinez, S.V., Bierlaire, M., Thiran, J.P.: Behavioral priors for detection and tracking of pedestrians in video sequences. IJCV 69, 159–180 (2006)
2. Barros, L.M., da Silva, A.T., Musse, S.R.: Petrosim: An architecture to manage virtual crowds in panic situations. In: CASA, pp. 111–120 (2004)
3. Braun, A., Bodman, B., Musse, S.R.: Simulating virtual crowds in emergency situations. In: VRST (2005)
4. Gérin-Lajoie, M., Richards, C., McFadyen, B.J.: The negotiation of stationary and moving obstructions during walking: anticipatory locomotor adaptations and preservation of personal space. Motor Control (2005)
5. Helbing, D., Molnár, P.: Social force model for pedestrian dynamics. Phys. Rev. E (1995)
6. Ju, E., Choi, M., Park, M., Lee, J., Lee, K., Takahashi, S.: Morphable crowds. In: SIGGRAPH Asia (2010)
7. Karamouzas, I., Overmars, M.: Simulating the local behaviour of small pedestrian groups. In: VRST (2010)
8. Lee, K.H., Choi, M.G., Hong, Q., Lee, J.: Group behavior from video: a data-driven approach to crowd simulation. In: SCA (2007)
9. Lerner, A., Chrysanthou, Y., Lischinski, D.: Crowds by example. In: EUROGRAPHICS (2007)
10. Mann, R., Jepson, A.D., El-Maraghi, T.: Trajectory segmentation using dynamic programming. In: ICPR (2002)
11. Moussaïd, M., Perozo, N., Garnier, S., Helbing, D., Theraulaz, G.: The walking behaviour of pedestrian social groups and its impact on crowd dynamics. PloS One (2010)
12. Musse, S.R., Thalmann, D.: Hierarchical model for real time simulation of virtual human crowds. TVCG 7 (2001)
13. Ondřej, J., Pettré, J., Olivier, A., Donikian, S.: A synthetic-vision based steering approach for crowd simulation. In: SIGGRAPH (2010)
14. Pellegrini, S., Ess, A., Schindler, K., Van Gool, L.: You'll never walk alone: Modeling social behavior for multi-target tracking. In: ICCV (2009)
15. Pellegrini, S., Ess, A., Van Gool, L.: Improving Data Association by Joint Modeling of Pedestrian Trajectories and Groupings. In: Daniilidis, K., Maragos, P., Paragios, N. (eds.) ECCV 2010, Part I. LNCS, vol. 6311, pp. 452–465. Springer, Heidelberg (2010)
16. Pettré, J., Ondřej, J., Olivier, A., Cretual, A., Donikian, S.: Experiment-based modeling, simulation and validation of interactions between virtual walkers. In: SCA (2009)
17. Reynolds, C.: Steering Behaviors for Autonomous Characters. In: GDC (1999)
18. Reynolds, C.W.: Flocks, herds and schools: A distributed behavioral model. In: SIGGRAPH (1987)
19. Shao, W., Terzopoulos, D.: Autonomous pedestrians. In: SCA (2005)
20. Thalmann, D., Musse, S.R.: Crowd Simulation. Springer (2007)
21. Trautman, P., Krause, A.: Unfreezing the Robot: Navigation in Dense, Interacting Crowds. In: IROS (2010)
22. Treuille, A., Cooper, S., Popović, Z.: Continuum crowds. ACM TOG (2006)
23. Tu, X., Terzopoulos, D.: Artificial fishes: physics, locomotion, perception, behavior. In: SIGGRAPH (1994)
24. van den Berg, J.P., Lin, M.C., Manocha, D.: Reciprocal velocity obstacles for real-time multi-agent navigation. In: ICRA, pp. 1928–1935 (2008)
25. Zhang, Y., Pettré, J., Ondřej, J., Qin, X., Peng, Q., Donikian, S.: Online inserting virtual characters into dynamic video scenes. CAVW 22(6) (2011)

3D Rotation Invariant Decomposition
of Motion Signals

Quentin Barthélemy[1,2], Anthony Larue[1], and Jérôme I. Mars[2]

[1] CEA-LIST, LOAD, 91191 Gif-sur-Yvette, France
{quentin.barthelemy,anthony.larue}@cea.fr
[2] Grenoble-INP, GIPSA-Lab, DIS, 38402 Grenoble, France
jerome.mars@gipsa-lab.grenoble-inp.fr

Abstract. A new model for describing a three-dimensional (3D) trajectory is introduced in this article. The studied object is viewed as a linear combination of rotatable 3D patterns. The resulting model is now 3D rotation invariant (3DRI). Moreover, the temporal patterns are considered as shift-invariant. A novel 3DRI decomposition problem consists of estimating the active patterns, their coefficients, their rotations and their shift parameters. Sparsity allows to select few patterns among multiple ones. Based on the sparse approximation principle, a non-convex optimization called 3DRI matching pursuit (3DRI-MP) is proposed to solve this problem. This algorithm is applied to real and simulated data, and compared in order to evaluate its performances.

Keywords: 3D, motion trajectory, rotation invariant, shift-invariant, matching pursuit, Procrustes, registration.

1 Introduction

In 3D space, a time-varying 3D trajectory composed of N temporal samples is considered. This trajectory is decomposed on elementary patterns and is thus described as the sum of K vectors. Different models can be considered.

In computer vision, Akhter et al. [1] described a non-rigid 3D object of P points as P temporal trajectories of N samples. A single point will be considered in this work. Thus, the 3D trajectory $y \in \mathbb{R}^{3 \times N}$ is defined as:

$$y = \sum_{k=1}^{K} a_k \, \theta_k \,, \tag{1}$$

where $a_k \in \mathbb{R}^{3 \times 1}$ are the coefficients, and $\theta_k \in \mathbb{R}^{1 \times N}$ are the trajectory basis vectors. The trajectory y is the sum of K trajectory basis vectors $\{\theta_k\}_{k=1}^{K}$, as illustrated in Fig. 1 *(top)*. Contrary to its dual model based on a *shape* basis [2], the advantage of a *trajectory* basis [1] is to be defined independently of the data. So, generic basis as fast transforms can be employed with this model. More particularly, discret cosinus transform (DCT) appears to be a well-adapted generic basis to study motion signals (as also noticed in [3]).

A. Fusiello et al. (Eds.): ECCV 2012 Ws/Demos, Part III, LNCS 7585, pp. 172–182, 2012.

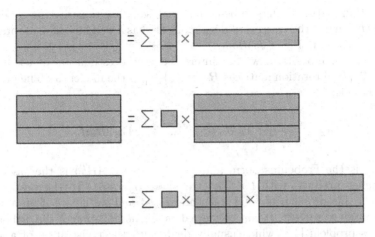

Fig. 1. Illustration of the three models to describe a 3D trajectory. Akter's et al. model *(top)*, Barthélemy's et al. model *(middle)* and the introduced 3DRI model *(bottom)*.

In signal processing, Barthélemy et al. [3] described a multicomponent temporal signal as the sum of multicomponent patterns. They used a redundant basis composed of $M > N$ elements which is called dictionary. In this case, elements of the dictionary are no more called vectors but atoms. Considering here the particular case of tricomponent data, a 3D trajectory of N samples is viewed as the sum of K 3D trajectories. The trajectory $y \in \mathbb{R}^{3 \times N}$ is defined as:

$$y = \sum_{k=1}^{K} x_k\, \phi_k \,, \tag{2}$$

where $x_k \in \mathbb{R}$ are the coefficients, and $\phi_k \in \mathbb{R}^{3 \times N}$ are the 3D atoms. Thereby, as seen in Fig. 1 *(middle)*, the trajectory y is viewed as a weighted sum of K 3D atoms. This model is different from the Akhter model. Indeed, in model (1), each unicomponent trajectory θ_k (1D pattern) is multiplied by three coefficients, one by dimension. In model (2), each tricomponent trajectory ϕ_k (3D pattern) is multiplied by a scale factor. Here, the advantage of using this model is to deal with 3D trajectory patterns $\phi_k \in \mathbb{R}^{3 \times N}$ whose the three components can be different contrary to model (1) which has the same pattern on the three components. The differences between model (1), called *multichannel* framework, and model (2), called *multivariate*, are well detailed in [3].

The purpose of this article is to provide a 3D rotation invariant (3DRI) model. Thus, a rotation matrix $R_k \in \mathbb{R}^{3 \times 3}$ is added to each 3D atoms ϕ_k and model (2) becomes:

$$y = \sum_{k=1}^{K} x_k\, R_k\, \phi_k \,. \tag{3}$$

Each rotation matrix R_k has to be orthogonal, so it has to verify the condition: $R_k R_k^T = Id$. Finally, the trajectory y is represented as a weighted sum of rotatable 3D atoms as seen in Fig. 1 *(bottom)*.

In 3DRI decomposition, we are interested in the estimation of coefficients $x = \{x_k\}_{k=1}^{K}$ and rotation matrices $\boldsymbol{R} = \{R_k\}_{k=1}^{K}$ of the model (3). The problem to solve here is:

$$min_{x,R} \left\| y - \sum_{k=1}^{K} x_k R_k \phi_k \right\|^2 \quad s.t. \ \forall k \in \mathbb{N}_K, R_k R_k^T = Id, \quad (4)$$

where $\|.\|$ is the Frobenius norm and $\langle A, B \rangle = trace(AB^T)$ is the associated matrix inner product, with $(.)^T$ the transpose operator. To the best of our knowledge, this problem has not been addressed and we ignore if an analytic solution exists to solve it. It can be viewed as a generalization of the orthogonal Procrustes problem [4,5] which usually deals with the registration of a single pattern. Moreover, the shift-invariant case will be considered hereafter. Using a sparsity constraint, we propose a nonconvex optimization to solve this more complex problem, based on the matching pursuit (MP) principle. This introduced algorithm is called 3D rotation invariant matching pursuit (3DRI-MP).

We first present existing methods to solve 3D registration problems in Section 2 and then the shift and 3D rotation invariance problem is defined. 3D rotation invariant MP is introduced in Section 3 and is illustrated on real data in Section 4. As validation, experiments on simulation data are shown in Section 5.

2   State of the Art and Problem

In this section, the state of the art in rigid 3D registration is first presented and the shift and 3D rotation invariance problem is then detailed.

2.1   State of the Art in Rigid 3D Registration

In this paragraph, 3D decomposition problems related to problem (4) are mentioned. A rigid transformation composed of a 3D rotation R and a spatial translation T is considered here between the trivariate pattern ϕ and the original signal y. The rigid 3D registration, also called orthogonal Procrustes problem, consists of finding parameters R and T such that:

$$min_{R,T} \| y - R \phi - T \|^2 \quad s.t. \ RR^T = Id. \quad (5)$$

Eggert et al. [4] reviewed the several methods that give an analytical solution to this rigid 3D registration problem: singular value decomposition (SVD), unit quaternions, and orthonormal matrix.

In [5], Gower and Dijksterhuis reviewed multiple different Procrustes problems and many generalizations, notably the generalized Procrustes analysis (GPA) [5]. However, problem (4) is not addressed. Note also that neither the multiview reconstruction problem [6] nor the iterative closest point (ICP) algorithm [7] solve problem (4).

2.2   Shift and 3D Rotation Invariance Problem

In this paragraph, the shift-invariance and the sparse approximation are first detailed, and the shift and 3D rotation invariance problem is then explained.

In the shift-invariant case, we want to sparsely code the signal y as a sum of a few short structures, known as kernels, that are characterized independently of their positions. This model is usually applied to time-series data, and it avoids block effects in the analysis of largely periodic signals and provides a compact kernel dictionary [3]. The L shiftable kernels of the compact dictionary Ψ are replicated at all of the positions, to provide the M atoms of the dictionary Φ. The N samples of the signal y, the residual error ϵ, and the atoms ϕ_m are indexed[1] by t. The kernels $\{\psi_l\}_{l=1}^{L}$ can have different lengths. The kernel $\psi_l(t)$ is shifted in the τ samples to generate the atom $\psi_l(t-\tau)$, and the subset σ_l collects the translations τ of the kernel $\psi_l(t)$. For the few kernels that generate all of the atoms, we have:

$$y(t) = \sum_{m=1}^{M} x_m\,\phi_m(t) + \epsilon(t) = \sum_{l=1}^{L}\sum_{\tau\in\sigma_l} x_{l,\tau}\,\psi_l(t-\tau) + \epsilon(t)\,. \qquad (6)$$

The signal y is thus approximated as a weighted sum of shiftable kernels ψ_l.

Due to shift-invariance, the dictionary Φ is the concatenation of L Toeplitz matrices [3] and is overcomplete. Since $M > N$, the dictionary is redundant and the linear system is thus under-determined and has multiple solutions. The introduction of constraints such as *sparsity* allows the solution to be regularized. The sparse approximation selects only K active atoms among the M possible and computes the associated coefficients vector x to have the better approximation of the signal y. One way to formalize the sparse approximation is:

$$min_x \left\| y(t) - \sum_{l=1}^{L}\sum_{\tau\in\sigma_l} x_{l,\tau}\,\psi_l(t-\tau) \right\|^2 \quad s.t.\ \|x\|_0 \le K\,, \qquad (7)$$

where $K \ll M$ is a constant and $\|x\|_0$ is the number of nonzero elements of vector x. But this problem is NP-hard [8]. So, non-convex pursuits tackle sequentially it such as matching pursuit (MP) [9]. The orthogonal matching pursuit (OMP) [10] assures that coefficients x are the orthogonal projection of the signal over the selected atoms. Using only K active atoms among the M possible, sparsity provides the compactness so much quested by [1]. From the beginning of this paragraph, explanations have been given for univariate signals. But they are extended to trivariate signals by the multivariate OMP (M-OMP) [3] which makes the atoms choice and the coefficients estimation. The introduced model (3) allows atoms to rotate but needs an appropriate approximation method to estimate the associated rotation matrices besides.

---

[1] Note that $a(t)$ and $a(t - t_0)$ do not represent samples, but the signal a and its translation of t_0 samples.

Now combining shift and 3D rotation invariances problems, we obtain the following problem to solve:

$$min_{\boldsymbol{x},\boldsymbol{R}} \left\| y(t) - \sum_{l=1}^{L} \sum_{\tau \in \sigma_l} x_{l,\tau}\, R_{l,\tau}\, \psi_l(t-\tau) \right\|^2$$

$$s.t. \ \|\boldsymbol{x}\|_0 \le K \ and \ \forall l \in \mathbb{N}_L, \forall \tau \in \sigma_l, \ R_{l,\tau} R_{l,\tau}^T = Id\,. \tag{8}$$

More than Eq.(4), Eq.(8) is the real issue that is addressed in this article. Eq.(8) combines Eq.(4) which we ignore if an analytic solution exists and Eq.(7) which is NP-hard. We propose a non-convex optimization to solve this particularly hard problem.

Note that 2DRI-OMP [3] simply tackles Eq.(8) in the 2D case. The presented article can be viewed as a non-trivial 3D extension (without orthogonal projection), that explains the name of the method presented.

3   3D Rotation Invariant Matching Pursuit

In this section, our proposed sparse 3DRI decomposition algorithm is introduced. We first detail the chosen method for the 3D registration, which will be the core of the introduced algorithm. Then, a non-convex optimization based on MP principle is introduced to solve Eq.(8) and is called 3DRI-MP.

3.1   3D Registration by SVD

Registration problem (5) is considered here with a normed trivariate pattern $\phi \in \mathbb{R}^{3 \times N}$, but without spatial translation. The sought parameters are the rotation R and the scale factor x:

$$min_{x,R} \| y - x\,R\,\phi \|^2 \ s.t. \ RR^T = Id\,. \tag{9}$$

For solving this 3D registration problem, the SVD method is chosen among the other possible methods because it is the cheapest and it simply deals with the particular cases of noise and planar patterns [4].

The method chosen is described in Algorithm 1. After having computed the correlation matrix $M_c = y\phi^T \in \mathbb{R}^{3 \times 3}$ (step 1), its SVD is carried out: $(U, \Lambda_1, V) = SVD(M_c)$ (step 2). Defining matrix Λ_2 such that $\Lambda_2 = diag(1, 1, det(UV^T))$, the optimal rotation is: $R = U\Lambda_2 V^T$ (step 3). The correlation value which provides the scale factor is computed such that: $x = trace(R\phi y^T) \ge 0$ (step 4).

```
Algorithm 1 : (x,R) := Reg_SVD (phi,y)
    begin
1:    Mc := y*phi^T ;
2:    (U,Lambda_1,V) := SVD(Mc) ;
3:    R := U*Lambda_2*V^T ;
4:    x := trace(R*phi*y^T) ;
end.
```

3.2 3DRI-MP Description

In this section, the 3DRI-MP is going to be explained step by step. A trivariate signal $y \in \mathbb{R}^{3 \times N}$ and a dictionary $\boldsymbol{\Psi} = \{\psi_l\}_{l=1}^{L}$ of shiftable trivariate normed kernels are considered. Given this redundant trivariate dictionary, 3DRI-MP produces a sparse approximation of the signal y (Algorithm 2).

The initialization (step 1) allocates the studied signal y to the residue ϵ^0. At the current iteration k, the algorithm selects the atom that produces the absolute strongest decrease in the mean square error (MSE) $\left\| \epsilon^{k-1} \right\|^2$. This is equivalent to finding the registered atom that is the most correlated to the residue ϵ^{k-1} (see Appendix). The correlation value $x_{l,\tau}^k = trace(R_{l,\tau}^k \psi_l(t-\tau)\epsilon^{k-1}(t)^T)$ is computed for each shift τ, with $R_{l,\tau}^k$ the optimal rotation matrix to register $\psi_l(t - \tau)$ on $\epsilon^{k-1}(t)$. To carry out this step, algorithm Reg_SVD is applied for each τ and each $l = 1..L$ (step 5), and then, the maximum of the values $x_{l,\tau}^k (\geq 0)$ is searched for to select the optimal atom (step 7), characterized by its kernel index l^k and its position τ^k. Selected atoms form an active dictionary. The vector $\boldsymbol{x}$ accumulates the active (*i.e.* nonzero) coefficients that are the maximum correlation values (step 8). Associated rotation matrices are grouped in $\boldsymbol{R}$ (step 9) and the current residue is computed (step 10).

A threshold on k the number of iterations or a threshold on the relative root MSE (rRMSE) $\left\| \epsilon^k \right\| / \|y\|$ can be used as stopping criteria (step 12). In the end, the 3DRI-OMP provides a K-sparse approximation of y using the K selected active elements:

$$\hat{y}^K = \sum_{k=1}^{K} x_{l^k,\tau^k}^k \, R_{l^k,\tau^k}^k \, \psi_{l^k}(t-\tau^k) \, . \tag{10}$$

Without considering the nonconvexity of the algorithm, if there is no overlap between the selected atoms, 3DRI-MP gives the orthogonal projection of the signal on the active dictionary in Eq. (8). Otherwise, it is suboptimal since atom overlaps generate cross terms that are not treated by 3DRI-MP.

```
Algorithm 2 : (x,R) := 3DRI_MP (y,Psi)
    begin
1:     initialization: k:=1, epsilon^0:=y, x:=[], R:=[] ;
2:     repeat
3:        for l = 1 .. L
4:           3D Registration for each tau:
5:           (x^k_{l,tau}, R^k_{l,tau}) :=
                 Reg_SVD (psi_l(t-tau),epsilon^{k-1}(t)) ;
6:        end for
7:        (l^k,tau^k) := arg max_{l,tau}  x^k_{l,tau} ;
8:        x := x U x^k_{l^k,tau^k} ;
9:        R := R U R^k_{l^k,tau^k} ;
10:       epsilon^k := epsilon^{k-1}
                 - x^k_{l^k,tau^k}*R^k_{l^k,tau^k}*psi_{l^k}(t-tau^k) ;
11:       k := k + 1 ;
```

12:    until stopping criterion
end.

4 Illustration on Real Data

An application of 3DRI-MP on real data is shown in this section. Studied data are
motion signals of French cued speech, which is a gestural language to complement
speech reading [11]. This language associates speech articulation to cues formed
by the hand. To make the acquisition, retroreflective markers are put on the
hand of a skilled cuer. Data are acquired by an optical system which records
the 3D coordinates of the markers. At the end of the acquisition, tricomponent
coordinates are obtained for each marker, and we focus on the one located on
the top on the thumb. Velocity signals $v = [\, v_x \; ; \; v_y \; ; \; v_z \,]^T$ are the inputs of the
3DRI-MP, and a dictionary of $L = 6$ kernels is designed to be adapted to such
data. These few kernels represent the main motion primitives.

The original velocity signal v is plotted in Fig. 2 *(top)*, and is composed
of the three velocity components v_x *(solid blue line)*, v_y *(dashed red)* and v_z
(dotted green). This signal is processed by 3DRI-MP with $K = 10$ iterations and
gives the approximated signal $\hat{v}$ plotted in Fig. 2 *(bottom)*. The rRMSE of this
approximation is 28.8 %. This error is quite high, but the goal is to decompose
the signal on its main motion primitives, and not to code all the variabilities
with numerous small coefficients.

Velocity signals are integrated to have a more visual representation of the
data. The original trajectory associated to the studied signal v is plotted in
Fig. 3 *(top left)*. Now, we are interested by the contributions of the largest
atoms. The trajectory is reconstructed using the contributions of the $K = 5$

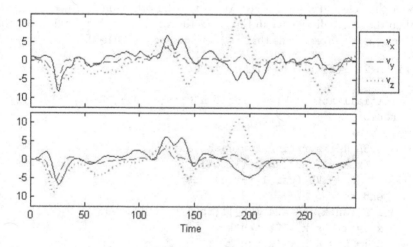

Fig. 2. The original signal *(top)* and its approximation with $K = 10$ atoms *(bottom)*.
Each signal is composed of the three velocity components v_x *(solid blue line)*, v_y *(dashed
red)* and v_z *(dotted green)*

largest coefficients of the 3DRI-MP decomposition. The reconstruction is plotted in Fig. 3 *(top right)*, showing each of the 5 atoms of the approximation. The stars represent the beginning of the kernels trajectories. In Fig. 3 *(top right)*, we remark that kernel $l = 6$ *(dashed red line)* is employed three times with different orientations (and with different coefficients and shifts). This shows the 3D rotation invariance of the 3DRI-MP which provides a good matching of the studied trajectory allowing the kernels rotation. The original trajectory is now randomly rotated in Fig. 3 *(bottom left)*, and it is reconstructed with its $K = 5$

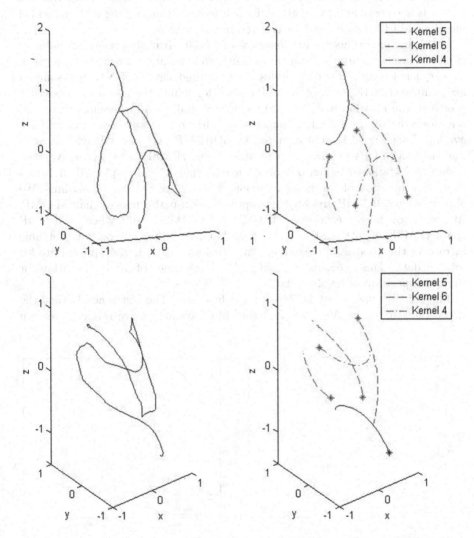

Fig. 3. The original *(resp. rotated)* trajectory *(top left)* *(resp. (bottom left))* and its reconstruction with the contributions of the $K = 5$ largest atoms *(top right)* *(resp. (bottom right))*

largest coefficients in Fig. 3 *(bottom right)*. Recontructions of Fig. 3 *(top right)* and *(bottom right)* are similar, taking into account the rotation: this highlights the rotation robustness of the 3DRI-MP.

5   Comparisons on Simulation Data

In this section, in order to evaluate its performances, 3DRI-MP is applied to simulation data and compared to M-OMP used in a trivariate case. Remark that it is not possible to compare 3DRI-MP to algorithm dealing with model (1) mentioned in Introduction since it is too much different.

In the first experiment, a dictionary Ψ of $L = 50$ trivariate kernels is randomly created: kernels are drawn from white Gaussian noise and they are then normed. The kernels length is $T = 65$ samples. One hundred signals of $N = 1600$ samples are composed of the sum of $K = 15$ atoms, for which the coefficients (strictly positive), the rotation matrices and the kernels indices are randomly drawn on a uniform distribution. Shift parameters are drawn in a way that atoms do not overlap. Each signal is approximated by 3DRI-MP and M-OMP with $K = 15$ iterations in order to recover the 15 atoms. The rRMSE $\|\epsilon^k\|/\|y\|$ is averaged (mean and standard deviation) over the 100 signals and is plotted in Fig. 4 *(left)* as a function of the inner iterations $k = 1..K$ of the two algorithms. We observe that 3DRI-MP gives better approximation performances than M-OMP. At the end of the K iterations, 3DRI-MP has a rRMSE of 0% whereas M-OMP has a rRMSE of 92.0%. The rRMSE of M-OMP is huge since it is not able to recover the good atoms. It shows that this algorithm is not appropriate for rotated data. This experiment highlights the relevance of 3DRI algorithm for the decomposition of revolved data.

The second experiment is close to the first one. The difference is that the signals length is now $N = 250$, and the shift parameters are randomly drawn

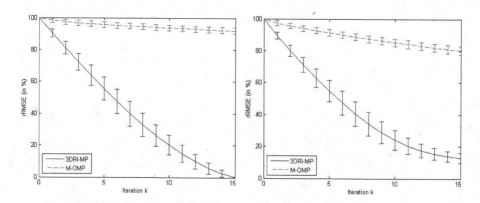

Fig. 4. Comparisons between the performances of 3DRI-MP and M-OMP without *(left)* and with *(right)* atoms overlaps. The rRMSE, averaged over 100 signals, is plotted as a function of the inner iteration k.

on a uniform distribution. As a consequence, the different atoms overlap. In the same way, the averaged rRMSE is plotted in Fig. 4 *(right)* as a function of the inner iterations k. The final rRMSE is 12.8% for 3DRI-MP, that is worse than the first experiment. In fact, when atoms overlap, 3DRI-MP which does not provide the orthogonal projection of Eq. (8) since it does not take into account the cross terms due to overlaps. This experiment shows the need to improve the 3DRI decomposition method. Concerning M-OMP, the final rRMSE is 80.2%, so performances seem to be improved. In fact, it does not recover the atoms better than in the first experiment. Signal energy is more compact since atoms overlap, so M-OMP approximates more energy at each iteration.

6 Conclusion and Prospects

This article has proposed a new model for describing a time-varying 3D object as the sum of rotatable 3D patterns. The considered model combines the 3D rotation invariance (3DRI) and the shift-invariance of the patterns. The introduced 3DRI-MP solves the 3DRI decomposition problem estimating the active atoms, their coefficients, their matrices and their shifts. It has been illustrated on real data and evaluated on simulation data. There are multiple applications in various domains: non-rigid structure-from-motion, 3D curve matching, 3D tracking, gesture representation and analysis and all other processings based on 3DRI decomposition.

The considered prospects are to improve the 3DRI decomposition method for coping with overlaps, to present a dictionary learning algorithm able to learn a kernels dictionary with model (3) and to add a classification step to make gesture recognition.

Acknowledgements. The authors thank F. Elisei from GIPSA-DPC for his explanations about cued speech data (acquired during the RNRT 01/37 ARTUS project).

References

1. Akhter, I., Sheikh, Y., Khan, S., Kanade, T.: Trajectory space: A dual representation for nonrigid structure from motion. IEEE Trans. on Pattern Analysis and Machine Intelligence 33, 1442–1456 (2011)
2. Bregler, C., Hertzmann, A., Biermann, H.: Recovering non-rigid 3D shape from image streams. In: Proc. Computer Vision and Pattern Recognition, CVPR (2000)
3. Barthélemy, Q., Larue, A., Mayoue, A., Mercier, D., Mars, J.: Shift & 2D rotation invariant sparse coding for multivariate signals. IEEE Trans. on Signal Processing 60, 1597–1611 (2012)
4. Eggert, D., Lorusso, A., Fisher, R.: Estimating 3-D rigid body transformations: a comparison of four major algorithms. Machine Vision and Applications 9, 272–290 (1997)
5. Gower, J., Dijksterhuis, G.: Procrustes Problems. Oxford Statistical Science Series (2004)

6. Bergevin, R., Soucy, M., Gagnon, H., Laurendeau, D.: Towards a general multi-view registration technique. IEEE Trans. on Pattern Analysis and Machine Intelligence 18, 540–547 (1996)
7. Besl, P., McKay, H.: A method for registration of 3-D shapes. IEEE Trans. on Pattern Analysis and Machine Intelligence 14, 239–256 (1992)
8. Davis, G.: Adaptive Nonlinear Approximations. PhD thesis, New York University (1994)
9. Mallat, S., Zhang, Z.: Matching pursuits with time-frequency dictionaries. IEEE Trans. on Signal Processing 41, 3397–3415 (1993)
10. Pati, Y., Rezaiifar, R., Krishnaprasad, P.: Orthogonal Matching Pursuit: recursive function approximation with applications to wavelet decomposition. In: Proc. Asilomar Conf. on Signals, Systems and Comput. (1993)
11. Gibert, G., Bailly, G., Beautemps, D., Elisei, F., Brun, R.: Analysis and synthesis of the three-dimensional movements of the head, face, and hand of a speaker using cued speech. Journal of Acoustical Society of America 118, 1144–1153 (2005)

Appendix: Selection Step of 3DRI-MP

Defining the error as: $\epsilon = y - \sum_{m=1}^{M} x_m \, R_m \, \phi_m$, the derivation of the criterion $J = \|\epsilon\|^2 = trace(\epsilon\epsilon^T)$ with respect to x_m gives:

$$\frac{\partial J}{\partial x_m} = -2\, trace(R_m \phi_m \epsilon^T) = -2\, \langle R_m \phi_m, \epsilon \rangle \,, \tag{11}$$

and in the shift-invariant formalism, it provides the selection step of Section 3.2:

$$-\frac{1}{2} \frac{\partial \|\epsilon\|^2}{\partial x_{l,\tau}} = trace(R_{l,\tau} \psi_l(t - \tau)\, \epsilon^T) = \langle R_{l,\tau} \psi_l(t - \tau), \epsilon \rangle \,. \tag{12}$$

Learn to Move: Activity Specific Motion Models for Tracking by Detection*

Thomas Mauthner, Peter M. Roth, and Horst Bischof

Inst. f. Computer Graphics and Vision,
Graz University of Technology, Austria

Abstract. In this paper, we focus on human activity detection, which solves detection, tracking, and recognition jointly. Existing approaches typically use off-the-shelf approaches for detection and tracking, ignoring naturally given prior knowledge. Hence, in this work we present a novel strategy for learning activity specific motion models by feature-to-temporal-displacement relationships. We propose a method based on an augmented version of canonical correlation analysis (AuCCA) for linking high-dimensional features to activity-specific spatial displacements over time. We compare this continuous and discriminative approach to other well established methods in the field of activity recognition and detection. In particular, we first improve activity detections by incorporating temporal forward and backward mappings for regularization of detections. Second, we extend a particle filter framework by using activity-specific motion proposals, allowing for drastically reducing the search space. To show these improvements, we run detailed evaluations on several benchmark data sets, clearly showing the advantages of our activity-specific motion models.

1 Introduction

In the recent past, human action recognition has been of growing interest in Computer Vision, where typical applications include visual surveillance, human computer interaction, and monitoring systems for elderly people. Thus, a variety of approaches have been proposed introducing new features, representations, or classification methods. Since actions can be described as chronological sequences special attention has been paid on how to incorporate temporal information into the feature description. For the basic problem of activity classification per video, global representations are a common choice [1,2]. Different spatio-temporal interest points (STIP) and descriptors were evaluated in [1]; the relationship between spatial and temporal STIPs was additionally explored in [2]. This applies for early datasets with homogeneous backgrounds and single moving objects like [3] as well as for recently collected datasets showing a larger variety of the activities, e.g, [4].

---

* The work was supported by the Austrian Research Promotion Agency (FFG) project SHARE in the IV2Splus program and the Austrian Science Fund (FWF) under the project MASA (P22299).

A. Fusiello et al. (Eds.): ECCV 2012 Ws/Demos, Part III, LNCS 7585, pp. 183–192, 2012.

The problem gets even harder if additionally to classification also detection is considered. This is of relevance if, e.g., several simultaneous activities, background motion, or high inner class variability of backgrounds have to be handled. Previous methods either assumed given tracks from, e.g., background subtraction or general tracking approaches [5,6] and analyzed activities per track or just per frame [7,8]. For linking the latter one in an online manner, particle filter is a favored choice [7,5]. Recently, an offline linking method via graph-based representation has been proposed by [8]. But in general, all these approaches do not take into account the prior knowledge about the correlation of motion and specific activities.

Hence, we propose to learn activity specific motion models in a combined recognition and temporal voting scheme. In particular, we incorporate a temporal displacement voting, which is learned via an augmented canonical correlation analysis (AuCCA), into a regularization for activity detections and a particle filter framework. We compare the thus obtained results to state-of-the-art methods for combined activity classification and voting, namely k-means hierarchies and Hough forest. The main contributions of this paper are:

- an efficient classification and voting framework via AuCCA
- the correction of activity detections via consistency checks
- a particle filter tracker with activity specific motion proposals.

The reminder of the paper is organized as follows. In Section 2, we first define the problem of learning combined classification and temporal displacement voting. We propose our AuCCA approach and show how the idea of temporal displacement voting can be incorporated into other standard learning frameworks. Next, Section 3 depicts the detection and tracking framework and shows how to incorporate the learned temporal motion models. Experimental results are shown in Section 4, where competitive results for activity classification are presented. Moreover, we demonstrate the advantages of learned motion models for unsupervised detection correction and evaluate tracking vs. random-walk and optical flow based models. Finally, Section 5 summarizes the proposed approach and gives an outlook on how AuCCA can be incorporated into other concepts for temporal activity detection linking.

2   Learning of Specific Motion Models

First of all, we describe the general idea of learning motion models via temporal displacements. To allow for combined activity detection/classification we describe an action by a d-dimensional feature vector $x_i \in \mathbb{R}^d$ in a temporal context. Thus, in addition to the corresponding class labels $y_i \in \{1, 2, ..., c\}$ also the temporal offsets for the activity center within in $t + \tau$ frames are given: $\mathbf{d}_i^\tau \in \mathbb{R}^2$. Thus, during training we have a prior knowledge on the object's movement within τ frames.

In the following, we determine three approaches that can be adopted for that purpose: (a) hierarchical k-means clustering, (b) Random Forest (RF), and (c)

Canonical Correlation Analysis (CCA). K-means is an unsupervised generative method not exploiting class labels during training; however, class labels and displacement values can be stored according to the obtained clusters. In contrast, Random Forest (RF) use a discriminative splitting function and can also be extended to train according to displacement values [9]. Canonical Correlation Analysis (CCA) additionally allows for maximizing the correlation between input feature vectors, class labels, and displacement vectors. We start the discussion with the proposed AuCCA exploiting the correlation between the feature vectors and the displacement vectors. Then, for comparison, we extend k-means and RF such that they can also learn the displacement values.

2.1 Augmented Canonical Correlation Analysis (AuCCA)

In general, the goal of Canonical Correlation Analysis (CCA) is to find pairs of directions that maximize the correlation between two random variables [10]. Formally, given two mean normalized random variables $\mathbf{x}$ and $\mathbf{d}$, CCA is defined as the problem of finding a set of two basis vectors $\mathbf{w}_x$ and $\mathbf{w}_d$ such that the correlation between the projections $x' = \mathbf{W}_x^\top \mathbf{x}$ and $d' = \mathbf{W}_d^\top \mathbf{d}$ is maximized. These are obtained by maximizing the correlation coefficient

$$\rho = \frac{\mathbf{w}_x^\top \mathbf{C}_{xd} \mathbf{w}_d}{\mathbf{w}_x^\top \mathbf{C}_{xx} \mathbf{w}_x \mathbf{w}_d^\top \mathbf{C}_{dd} \mathbf{w}_d} , \qquad (1)$$

where $\mathbf{C}_{xx}$ and $\mathbf{C}_{dd}$ are the within-class covariance matrices and $\mathbf{C}_{xd}$ is the between-class covariance matrix. The projections onto $\mathbf{w}_x$ and $\mathbf{w}_d$, i.e., x' and d', are called the *canonical factors*. In our case, we build on an efficient and numerically stable formulation building on an SVD decomposition [11].

Assuming that all input features in $\mathbf{X} \in \mathbb{R}^{d \times n}$ and the corresponding displacement values in $\mathbf{D} \in \mathbb{R}^{2 \times n}$ are given, we can project the training data onto their canonical correlation coefficients: $\mathbf{X}' = \mathbf{W}_x^\top \mathbf{X}$, with $\mathbf{X}' \in \mathbb{R}^{2 \times n}$. We estimate a linear mapping $\mathbf{F}$ from the canonical correlation coefficients to the corresponding displacement values $\mathbf{D}$ using the least square solution of $\mathbf{F} = \mathbf{D} \mathbf{X}'^\top$. This yields a very efficient representation as only $\mathbf{W}_x \in \mathbb{R}^{2 \times d}$ and $\mathbf{F} \in \mathbb{R}^{2 \times 2}$ have to be stored for later evaluations. During testing we estimate the displacements for a given sample vector $\hat{\mathbf{x}}$ by projection onto the canonical space by $\hat{\mathbf{x}}' = \mathbf{W}_x \hat{x}$ and the mapping $\hat{\mathbf{d}} = \mathbf{F}\hat{\mathbf{x}}'$.

The dimensionality of the canonical correlation coefficients is limited by the smaller dimensionality of the correlated training sets $\mathbf{X}$ and $\mathbf{D}$. Thus, too much discriminative information could get lost due to reduced dimensionality. To overcome this problem, Kernel-CCA can be used, which, however, would be computationally much more expensive. Instead, we exploit the additional information given by a multi-class problem and augment the displacement values in each $\mathbf{d}_i$ with a binary label vector $\mathbf{y}_i$ with $\mathbf{y}_i(j) = 1$ for the correct class and 0 otherwise.

The incorporated class information strengthens the correlation between points and the higher dimensional correlation space allows for better representation of the mapping from feature to offset space. Moreover, we get a classifier for free. Fig. 1 depicts the distribution of temporal offsets over all activities in the *UCF-Sports* dataset. The coefficients of standard CCA show directly the distribution in $d = 2$ dimensional space before multiplying with $\mathbf{F}$. The $d = (c + 2)$ dimensional coefficients of AuCCA have been visualized using a metric multidimensional down-scaling to a dimensionality of 2. Due to the high dimensionality of the coefficient space, the spatial offsets cannot directly be seen, but the class specific grouping of AuCCA is demonstrated. Illustrative examples for displacement vectors are shown in Fig. 2.

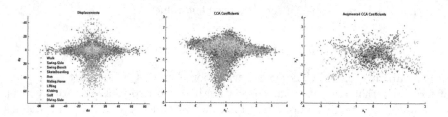

Fig. 1. Distribution of temporal offsets: left: displacement values for UCF sports dataset, color-coded for individual actions; middle: standard 2-dimensional CCA coefficients; right: coefficients of AuCCA, nicely showing the separated classes

2.2 Hierarchical K-Means Clustering

The key idea of hierarchical k-means clustering, also known as Vocabulary Tree, is to recursively split the training data via k-means clustering. This process is repeated recursively until no samples are left in a branch of the hierarchy or the maximum depth L is reached. For each of the thus obtained cluster centers φ (i.e., leaf nodes) we can then estimate a class probability distribution $p(c|\varphi)$. To learn action specific motion models, we additionally store temporal displacement vectors of each training sample in each leaf node φ.

During evaluation, a test sample is traversed down the tree, using depth-first-search, until it reaches a leaf node. Hence, for each sample we get the class probabilities and the temporal displacement values stored in the leaf node. For simplicity we average the displacement values and report the mean d_x, d_y values. An important factor for good generalization and robustness is the use of k-means ensembles, i.e., we split the training set randomly into T subsets, and train T individual k-means hierarchies. Similar to the idea of Random Forests [12,9], this avoids overfitting on the training data and shows better generalization capabilities. During evaluation, a test sample is traversing down all hierarchies and the results of all reached leaves are averaged.

2.3 Random Forests

Hierarchical k-means clustering can be adopted for the intended task by additionally storing the displacement vectors in the leaf nodes. However, the discriminative information given by the class labels is ignored. To also exploit this information Random Forests can be used. In general, a forest consists of an ensemble of T binary decision trees, which are constructed recursively starting from the root node. For each node, binary tests are computed to split the data $\mathbf{X}$ into subsets going to the left or the right branch [13].

Two prominent ways to build a Random Forest are to maximize the information gain [12,13,9] or in addition to minimize the displacement uncertainty (as proposed for the Hough Forest [9]). Maximizing the information gain is equivalent to minimizing the class-label uncertainty. In the second case, samples with similar displacements are grouped together. The decision whether the class-label or displacement uncertainty should be minimized is selected randomly during training. For evaluation, a test sample is traversing down each tree and the results of all reached leaves are averaged. Thus, in contrast to the previous mentioned k-means we have a supervised and discriminative discretization of our feature space.

3   Framework (Building Action Tracks)

This section delineates how the proposed activity-specific motion models learned with AuCCA can be exploited for the task of specific detection and tracking.

3.1   Detection Correction with Forward-Backward Consistency Regularization

The concept of forward-backward mapping is known from key-point tracking or optical flow estimation. Estimating the forward displacement of a small and local image patch $t \to t+1$ should deliver the same result as tracking backward $t+1 \to t$. Section 2 formalized how temporal voting information can be learned for complete object patches, where we are not limited to $t+1$ displacements but can train an arbitrary mapping backward for τ and $-\tau$ frames. Now, we exploit this knowledge to filter out false-positive detections by applying AuCCA displacement mappings for positive detections at time t. We estimate a forward mapping of τ frames, run the detector at the thus proposed positions at $t+\tau$, and map positive detections backward with AuCCA learned for $-\tau$ displacements.

To show the robustness and the generalization capabilities, results from tracking on *Weizmann robust* data are illustrated in Fig. 2. Green and red points visualize positive detections for time t and $t+\tau$, respectively, and colored lines the temporal votings in $\tau = 5$ frames. We can see an accurate voting to the object's center in $+\tau$ frames and how false positive detections are marginalized out by missing backward mappings. We derive a conservative learning framework from this observation for unsupervised mining of new positive and negative samples. We are regularizing over the spatial and temporal neighborhood of positive detections. Detections with no forward-backward consistent detection in their local neighborhood are defined as new negative samples. Detections with a majority of consistent neighbors are defined as new positives while others are seen as neutral and are not used for updating the detector (see Fig. 3).

Fig. 2. Positive detections in frame t with AuCCA forward displacement vectors for $t + \tau$ (left). Detector evaluation of proposed positions at $t + \tau$ and backward displacements for positive detections with consistent backward mapping (right). Green and red bounding boxes show the ground-truth for time t and $t + \tau$, respectively.

3.2 Review of Particle Filter

Particle filtering for tracking [14] provides a probabilistic framework, which maintains multiple hypotheses of the current object state and has proven to yield robust tracking results. The probability distribution of the hidden target state $\mathbf{s}_t$ of the tracked object at time step t is estimated using a set of N_P weighted particles $S_t = \{s_t^i, w_t^i\}$ with $i = 1...N_P$ at time step t and the associated measurements z_t^i. Each particle x_t^i simulates the real hidden state of the object, using the dynamic model $p(s_t^i|s_{t-1}^i)$ and the observation likelihood $p(z_t^i|s_t^i)$. The object state is approximated by a weighted average over this finite set of particles. To avoid a degeneration of the particle set, a re-sampling of the particles is necessary according to their particle weights $w_t^i \approx p(z_t^i|s_t^i)$. For more details we would refer to [14].

3.3 Integrating Intelligent Motion Models

The most important parameters are the number of particles N_P and the choice of the dynamic model $p(s_t^i|s_{t-1}^i)$. The better the motion model the less particles are needed and a small re-sampling rate would indicate a good fit. In addition, the efficiency is increased as the runtime is linear according to the number of particles. A classical choice for the dynamic model would be to use random walks (e.g., used for activity tracking in [5]), where the motion is modeled by Gaussian noise: $s_{t-1}^i + \mathcal{N}(0, \sigma_t)$. Obviously this is very inefficient as no information about the current object motion is incorporated, but a general choice if nothing about the object's behavior is known. A slightly advanced version is to use a constant velocity model, where in addition to Gaussian noise the velocity (u, v) at time $t - 1$ is added to move particles to s_t [7].

None of the previous mentioned approaches takes into account that during tracking of activities prior knowledge about activity specific motion is given. In addition, particle filtering is perfectly suited for incorporating an individual motion model per s_{t-1}^i. Given the learning frameworks presented in Section 2, we can directly integrate their temporal displacement proposals into the motion model. For each particle state s_{t-1}^i, describing a potential position, we can extract a feature vector $\mathbf{x}_{t-1}^i$ and evaluate it using AuCCA, which yields a displacement suggestions $\hat{\mathbf{d}}_i$. If required, also the class labels $\hat{\mathbf{y}}_i$ can be estimated. The transition to s_t^i is modeled by $\hat{\mathbf{d}}_i + \mathcal{N}(0, \sigma_d)$ (in our case we have $\sigma_d \ll \sigma_t$), which is mainly needed for diffusing particle positions after resampling. A corresponding evaluation and a comparison to optical flow and random-walk based motion models is given in the experimental section.

4   Experiments

We selected two commonly known datasets for evaluation of our framework, i.e., *Weizmann*[1] data set [3] and *UCF-Sports*[2] [4]. Both datasets allow for object centered recognition and contain activities with different or alternating motion directions. Please note that we our primary goal was not breaking recognition scores. Especially for the *UCF-Sports* data set global representations on video level show superior results [1]. But this is somehow misleading as the activity defining the label of a video may only occupy a fraction of the video volume. Therefore, global representations are often influenced more by the global motion and a small variability of the background than by the activity itself. Hence, such representations often "solve the dataset" but do not solve the task. We are interested in exploiting the object's motion related to its current activity and in generating detection tracklets throughout videos. We compensate for global camera motion to estimate the real objects motion for training and testing. Otherwise the object centered camera motion gives a too strong prior to evaluate for displacement estimation. Note that for tracking our proposed motion estimation could be combined with global motion in the same way as shown in [7].

4.1   Evaluation of Complexity

We start with a general evaluation of the compared motion estimation models, namely the AuCCA, Random Forest(RF) and the k-means hierarchies (Kmeans). For describing the activities, we used HoG and HoF features for *Weizmann* and in addition bag-of-words histograms describing the spatio-temporal interest points in a local surrounding of the object for *UCF-Sports*. To emphasize the efficient representation using AuCCA, we compare training and evaluation time of a cross validation run on *UCF-Sports*. On average, training CCA and AuCCA takes $32.5sec.$ and $33.3sec$, respectively. In contrast, training a RF with 5 trees of maximum depth 10 takes $1400sec$; training Kmeans with 5 hierarchies with $k = 4$ and maximum depth 5 even $4044sec$. The evaluation of AuCCA is computed in $0.23sec$, where for RF and Kmeans $9sec$ and $20sec$ are required, respectively.

---

[1] http://www.wisdom.weizmann.ac.il/~vision/SpaceTimeActions.html
[2] http://server.cs.ucf.edu/~vision/data.html

4.2   Unsupervised Adaption via Forward-Backward Regularization

We tested our forward-backward consistency regularization for the task of unsupervised scene adaption of an activity detector. We trained a *walking* detector using positive and negative samples from the *Weizmann* dataset via a linear SVM and tested it on the *Weizmann robust* dataset.[3] This less known dataset contains highly cluttered backgrounds and high irregularities within actions, as can be seen in Figs. 2 and 3. Thus, it is perfectly suited to test our approach for robustness. We compare the performance of the originally trained detector (baseline) with the results of forward-backward consistency checked detections (AuCCA regularized), which shows a clear reduction of false positives. The poor performance of the baseline classifier is induced by the lack of meaningful background samples during training. Consistency checks allow for automatic generation of new positive and especially negative training samples, which are incorporated into the update of the detector via bootstrapping, leading to further enhanced detection results (retrained). The results in Fig. 3 show the capability of AuCCA for mining new training samples by exploiting activity specific motions.

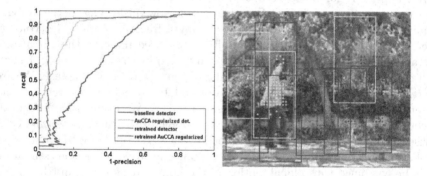

Fig. 3. Results of unsupervised activity detector training using AuCCA forward/backward mapping with $\tau = 5$ (left). Examples of positive (green), neutral (yellow), and negative (red) updates for scene adaption from *Weizmann* to *Weizmann robust* (right).

4.3   Comparison of Motion Estimation and Particle Behavior

The main motivation for this paper was to estimate temporal displacements from high-dimensional training data and to show that this is superior compared to random or optical flow driven motion models. First, we analyze the capabilities of the individual methods proposed in Section 2 compared to optical flow based displacement estimation. Average results for *Weizmann* and *UCF-Sports* are shown in Fig. 4. We trained for displacements from $\tau = 1, ..., 5$ frames, and compare to optical flow with a constant velocity assumption, i.e., the current

---

[3] http://www.wisdom.weizmann.ac.il/ vision/VideoAnalysis/Demos/
SpaceTimeActions/DB/robust-deform.zip

flow at time t is propagated linearly by multiplying with τ. We group together results for static activities like *wave* and *bend* for *Weizmann* and *golf* and *lifting* for *UCF-Sports* and show individual results for the dynamic activities. One can clearly see that optical flow is not a good choice for linking activity detections over several frames. In contrast, the results of the proposed methods are in the same range with only minor deviations.

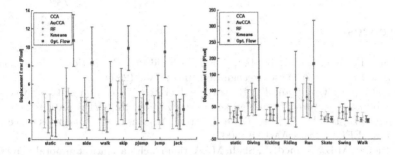

Fig. 4. Average displacement results for *Weizmann* with $\tau = 3$ (left) and for *UCF-Sports* with $\tau = 3$ (right)

For evaluating the applicability of the activity linking approach discussed in Section 3 we compared our activity specific displacements learned with AuCCA and a random walk model. We made two tracking runs on *UCF-Sports*, one with random walk motion model for the particle filter and one with AuCCA motion propositions per particle. To allow for fair comparison, the underlying detector was the same for both runs. This guarantees that particle weights are influenced by the representation. So we only used the displacement values of AuCCA and not the classification results nor the coefficient values. We made two tests with random walk (RW): (a) with set of $N_P = 100$ particles and $\sigma_t = 50$ and (b) with $N_P = 100 \sigma_t = 200$. The AuCCA particle filter used only $N_P = 30$ and $\sigma_d = 25$ to re-sample particles. The average errors to target position for testing on *diving*, *riding*, *run* and *swing-side* where $15.86pix$ for the AuCCA, $12.64pix$ for RW100, and $7.83pix$ for RW200. This shows that our proposed voting scheme is accurate enough and allows for significant smaller particle sets.

5   Conclusion

Most approaches for activity recognition either build on a global image description or assume that the localization of the actor is already given. To overcome these limitations, e.g., if multiple actors are performing multiple actions, combined detection/recognition approaches can be applied. In this work, we addressed this problem by introducing a motion model predicting the spatial displacement over time. In particular, we introduced the idea of augmented Canonical Correlation Analysis (AuCCA), which additionally to image descriptions and discriminative class labels incorporates the correlation of the temporal displacement vectors. The proposed AuCCA allows for unsupervised mining new training samples and post-processing of false positive detections by exploiting activity specific motions. Integrated into a particle filter framework the number of required particles can be drastically reduced. We demonstrated our approach for two publicly available standard benchmark datasets, namely *Weizmann* and *UCF-Sports*, showing competitive results.

References

1. Wang, H., Ullah, M.M., Laptev, A.K.I., Schmid, C.: Evaluation of local spatio-temporal features for action recognition. In: BMVC (2009)
2. Kovashka, A., Grauman, K.: Learning a hierarchy of discriminative space-time neighborhood features for human action recognition. In: CVPR (2010)
3. Gorelick, L., Blank, M., Shechtman, E., Irani, M., Basri, R.: Actions as space-time shapes. IEEE Trans. PAMI 29 (2007)
4. Rodriguez, M.D., Ahmed, J., Shah, M.: Action mach - a spatio-temporal maximum average correlation height filter for action recognition. In: CVPR (2008)
5. Lin, Z., Jiang, Z., Davis, L.S.: Recognizing actions by shape-motion prototype trees. In: ICCV (2009)
6. Burgos-Artizzu, X.P., Dollar, P., Lin, D., Anderson, D.J., Perona, P.: Social behavior recognition in continous video. In: CVPR (2012)
7. Yao, A., Gall, J., van Gool, L.: A hough transform-based voting framework for action recognition. In: CVPR (2010)
8. Khamis, S., Morariu, V.I., Davis, L.S.: A flow model for joint action recognition and identity maintenance. In: CVPR (2012)
9. Gall, J., Lempitsky, V.: Class-specific hough forests for object detection. In: CVPR (2009)
10. Hotelling, H.: Relations between two sets of variates. Biometrika 28, 321–377 (1936)
11. Melzer, T., Reiter, M., Bischof, H.: Appearance models based on kernel canonical correlation analysis. Pattern Recognition 36, 1961–1971 (2003)
12. Breiman, L.: Random forests. Machine Learning (2001)
13. Bosch, A., Zisserman, A., Munoz, X.: Image classification using random forests and ferns. In: ICCV (2007)
14. Arulampalam, S., Maskell, S., Gordon, N., Clapp, T.: A tutorial on particle filters for on-line non-linear/non-gaussian bayesian tracking. IEEE Trans. Signal Processing 50, 174–188 (2002)

Flow Counting Using Realboosted Multi-sized Window Detectors

Håkan Ardö, Mikael Nilsson, and Rikard Berthilsson

Lund University, Cognimatics AB

Abstract. One classic approach to real-time object detection is to use adaboost to a train a set of look up tables of discrete features. By utilizing a discrete feature set, from features such as local binary patterns, efficient classifiers can be designed. However, these classifiers include interpolation operations while scaling the images over various scales. In this work, we propose the use of real valued weak classifiers which are designed on different scales in order to avoid costly interpolations. The use of real valued weak classifiers in combination with the proposed method avoiding interpolation leads to substantially faster detectors compared to baseline detectors. Furthermore, we investigate the speed and detection performance of such classifiers and their impact on tracking performance. Results indicate that the realboost framework combined with the proposed scaling framework achieves an 80% speed up over adaboost with bilinear interpolation.

1 Introduction

Object detection and tracking are central problems to computer vision. Finding objects from a specific object class and keeping track of them is often a first step that other computer vision tasks rely on. It is therefore important to find a solution to the problem that is fast, accurate and robust to the changes that naturally occur in real photographic situations. Preferably the method should also allow for low memory consumption and use only fix-point operations. This is a challenging task that allows the detector to be embedded within modern surveillance cameras that still typically lack floating point units. Concerning speed, most often the number of objects from the object class is several orders of magnitude lower than the number of objects not belonging to the class. This is for example the case for face detection and pedestrian detection. Here, the object classifier normally uses a sliding window that is scaled to different sizes and placed at all possible locations in the image. For each instance, the classifier should output true or false. It follows that the object detection must process several thousands of instances for a single image, and it is desired to process several such images per second.

In this paper we investigate object detectors connected to temporal tracking, in order to perform flow counting. In particular, counting of humans and bicycles. These kind of flow counts are often used by, for example, traffic planers and scientists to asses how public infrastructure is used.

A. Fusiello et al. (Eds.): ECCV 2012 Ws/Demos, Part III, LNCS 7585, pp. 193–202, 2012.

Next section presents the flow counting framework. Section 3 presents the object detection and corresponding classifier design. Section 4 discusses the temporal tracking employed. Section 5 presents experimental results.

2 Flow Counting Framework

The framework utilized here goes from video input to a flow counting report, see Fig. 1. The first step, which typically is the main bottleneck processing-wise, is the object detection. In this paper, we will investigate three classifiers used for object detection. Following the detection is temporal tracking conducted in order to achieve consistency over the temporal domain. The tracker employed is the classical Kalman filter. That means a linear model is used to model the dynamics. It fits nicely when modelling the motion of, for example, bicycles traveling along a straight road. However, it might be a more crude approximation when modelling, for example, the motion of faces in a general video.

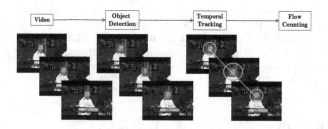

Fig. 1. Overview of framework for track counting in order to estimate flows. Images from Youtube faces database [1].

3 Object Detection

An early and successful approach to construct real-time detectors is to use a sliding window and a cascade of classifiers [2]. The detector use a set of Haar-like features, that can be computed relatively fast by using an integral image. The features are used as weak classifiers to train a cascade of adaboost [3] detectors. One problem is that the integral image requires a lot of memory. Furthermore, the features are sensitive to local changes in lighting. A later and more promising result was achieved by using features with a higher degree of invariance such as local binary patterns (LBP) [4] or local successive mean quantization transform (SMQT) [5,6]. These features take values from some discrete and finite set. Both use a sliding window as above and can be used in cascades. Compared to Haar-like features [2], they do not require any integral image and need fewer operations to compute feature values. Whereas, the detector in presented by Viola and Jones [2] can run on different scales, the LBP detector is however locked to one scale and the image itself has to be resized to different scales.

3.1 Multi-sized Windows

To overcome this resizing limitation we propose to train three differently sized detectors, with 16×16, 20×20 and 25×25 windows, respectively. All three detectors are used to scan the test image at its original size. Then the image is reduced to half its original size and all detectors are used again. This gives more or less the same result as using a single detector and only reducing the image size a factor 1.26 each time, but it operates faster. This is due to the fact that only one third of the image resizing operations have to be performed and, furthermore, no interpolation is needed here as the scale factor is exactly two. Note that these three detectors can be trained simultaneously. Using different window sizes or more than 3 sizes would be possible, but was not investigated. However, note that as the window size gets larger the detector gets somewhat slower. Also, the LBP features are local features and would pick up different things at different scales.

3.2 Boosting Real Valued Functions

The LBP and SMQT methods use features that take values from some discrete and finite set $\mathcal{X}$. For the classical LBP $\mathcal{X} = \{0, 1, \cdots, 255\}$. Using a training set consisting of pairs, $(\mathbf{x}_i, y_i)$, $i = 1, \ldots, m$, where $\mathbf{x}_i = (x_{i,1}, \cdots, x_{i,n}) \in \mathcal{X}^n$ are feature vectors and $y_i \in \{-1, 1\}$ the corresponding labels. Note that the feature vectors consists of n features.

According to the anyboost framework [7], most boosting algorithms can be described as a gradient descent optimization in a function space, $\mathrm{lin}\,(\mathcal{F})$, consisting of all linear combinations of base classifiers $f \in \mathcal{F}$. Here, we will consider the case when $\mathcal{F}$ consists of all real valued lookup tables of a single discrete feature, $\mathcal{X} \to \mathbb{R}$, such as LBP. The values of the lookup table $f_t \in \mathcal{F}$ will be denoted $a_{t,v}$ with $f_t(v) = a_{t,v}$. The table f_t will be used for feature number t and we will use the notation $f_t(\mathbf{x}_i) = f_t(x_{i,t})$.

The objective of the training is to find a detector function, $F \in \mathrm{lin}\,(\mathcal{F})$, that as often as possible, classifies the training data correctly, i.e. $y_i = \mathrm{sign}\,(F(\mathbf{x}_i))$. The final detector is found by minimizing the cost function

$$C(F) = \frac{1}{m} \sum_{i=1}^{m} c(y_i F(\mathbf{x}_i)), \qquad (1)$$

where $c : \mathbb{R} \to \mathbb{R}$ is a non-negative, decreasing function. Different boosting algorithms can be derived by using different cost functions c. Adaboost uses $c(\alpha) = e^{-\alpha}$. Gradient descent is an iterative algorithm that in each iteration updates its current detector function F by finding the direction $f \in \mathcal{F}$ in which $C(F + \epsilon f)$ most rapidly decreases. In the case of adaboost, a line search is performed to find the optimal ϵ, which is used to update the current detector function F.

According to the anyboost framework [7], the optimal direction is found as the function, f, maximizing

$$-\langle \nabla C(F), f \rangle, \qquad (2)$$

where $\langle \cdot, \cdot \rangle$ denotes the inner product

$$\langle F, G \rangle = \sum_{i=1}^{m} F(\mathbf{x}_i) G(\mathbf{x}_i) \tag{3}$$

on $\lin(\mathcal{F})$. This is only true if the optimization is restricted to functions f of unit length, i.e $\langle f, f \rangle = 1$. In the anyboost setting [7], a scaled version of (3) is used so that $\langle f, f \rangle = 1$ for all $f : \mathcal{X}^n \to \{-1, 1\}$, which means that it is not necessary to constrain the optimization. In the present case of $f : \mathcal{X}^n \to \mathbb{R}$ there exists no scaled version of (3) with this property and the constraint has to be considered during the optimization.

By introducing a set of weights or a distribution over the training samples,

$$d_i = \frac{c'(y_i F(\mathbf{x}_i))}{\sum_{i=1}^{m} c'(y_i F(\mathbf{x}_i))}, \tag{4}$$

the target function (2) can be written as (see [7] for details)

$$\frac{1}{m} \sum_{i=1}^{m} y_i f(\mathbf{x}_i) d_i. \tag{5}$$

In the anyboost case where f only takes values in $\{-1, 1\}$, the optimal direction is the one that minimizes the weighted classification error

$$\sum_{i|y_i \hat{f}(\mathbf{x}_i)=-1} d_i. \tag{6}$$

Generalizing this result to the present case where f can take any real value is done in Lemma 2. For each fixed feature x_t, $1 \le t \le n$, Lemma 1 gives the optimal coefficients of f_t. Schapire and Singer [8] have provided the same result in form of a closed form solution for a case that is equivalent to the single feature setting here. That is, given a feature x_t, $1 \le t \le n$, how should the values $a_{t,v} \in \mathbb{R}$ be chosen? In Lemma 1 a different proof based on the anyboost [7] approach is given. This alternative derivation also allow the design of an algorithm for choosing the optimal feature t, $1 \le t \le n$, to add in each iteration, which is presented in Lemma 2.

Lemma 1. *Given a classifier $F(\mathbf{x}) = \sum_t f_t(\mathbf{x})$ and a feature number, $1 \le t \le n$, the coefficients, $a_{t,v}$, of a lookup table, $f_t(v) = a_{t,v}$, that minimizes $C(F + f_t)$ from (1) with $c(\alpha) = e^{-\alpha}$ is given by*

$$a_{t,v} = \frac{1}{2} \log \frac{\sum_{i|x_{i,t}=v,y_i=1} d_i}{\sum_{i|x_{i,t}=v,y_i=-1} d_i}. \tag{7}$$

Proof. To find the coefficients of f_t that minimizes the cost function

$$C(F + f_t) = \sum_{i=1}^{m} c(y_i F(\mathbf{x}_i) + y_i f_t(\mathbf{x}_i)), \tag{8}$$

the terms are reordered and grouped based on the feature value, which leads to

$$C\left(F+f_t\right)=\sum_{v\in\mathcal{X}}\sum_{i|x_{i,t}=v}c\left(y_iF\left(\mathbf{x}_i\right)+y_if_t\left(\mathbf{x}_i\right)\right). \tag{9}$$

Now $f_t\left(\mathbf{x}_i\right)=f_t(v)=a_{t,v}$ is constant with regard to the inner sum. Each term of the outer sum can thus be optimized separately as there are no dependencies between them. Differentiating gives

$$\frac{\partial C}{\partial a_{t,v}}=\sum_{i|x_{i,t}=v}y_ic'\left(y_iF\left(\mathbf{x}_i\right)+y_ia_{t,v}\right). \tag{10}$$

Using the same cost function as adaboost, $c\left(\alpha\right)=e^{-\alpha}$, gives $c'\left(\alpha\right)=-e^{-\alpha}$, and

$$\frac{\partial C}{\partial a_{t,v}}=-\sum_{i|x_{i,t}=v}y_ie^{-y_iF(\mathbf{x}_i)-y_ia_{t,v}}. \tag{11}$$

The sum can be separated into one sum for positive examples and one for negative. The factor depending on $a_{t,v}$ can be factored out, so that

$$\frac{\partial C}{\partial a_{t,v}}=\sum_{i|x_{i,t}=v,y_i=-1}e^{-y_iF(\mathbf{x}_i)}e^{a_{t,v}}-\sum_{i|x_{i,t}=v,y_i=1}e^{-y_iF(\mathbf{x}_i)}e^{-a_{t,v}}. \tag{12}$$

Solving $\frac{\partial C}{\partial a_{t,v}}=0$ for $a_{t,v}$ gives the optimal coefficients,

$$a_{t,v}=\frac{1}{2}\log\frac{\sum_{i|x_{i,t}=v,y_i=1}e^{-y_iF(\mathbf{x}_i)}}{\sum_{i|x_{i,t}=v,y_i=-1}e^{-y_iF(\mathbf{x}_i)}}. \tag{13}$$

Anyboost maintains a set of weights, d_i, or a distribution, over the examples,

$$d_i=\frac{c'\left(y_iF\left(\mathbf{x}_i\right)\right)}{\sum_{i=0}^{m}c'\left(y_iF\left(\mathbf{x}_i\right)\right)}=\frac{e^{-y_iF(\mathbf{x}_i)}}{\sum_{i=0}^{m}e^{-y_iF(\mathbf{x}_i)}}, \tag{14}$$

where the second equality holds for the adaboost cost function. Expressing $a_{t,v}$, by using these weights, concludes the proof.

$\square$

Lemma 2. *The feature number, $1\leq t^*\leq n$, for which the cost function (1) decreases most rapidly is given by*

$$t^*=\operatorname*{argmax}_{1\leq t\leq n}\sum_{v}\frac{\left(\sum_{i|x_{i,t}=v}y_id_i\right)^2}{\sum_{i|x_{i,t}=v}1}. \tag{15}$$

Proof. According to [7] the optimal t is found by maximizing

$$\frac{1}{m}\sum_{i=1}^{m}y_if_t\left(\mathbf{x}_i\right)d_i. \tag{16}$$

In the present setting where f_t can take any real value, the optimization has to be constrained to functions f_t for which $\langle f_t, f_t \rangle = 1$. The factor $1/m$ is constant and does not affect the position of the maximum and can thus be dropped. The terms of the remaining sum can be reordered and grouped based on the feature values, yielding

$$\sum_{v \in \mathcal{X}} \sum_{i | x_{i,t} = v} y_i f_t(\mathbf{x}_i) d_i. \tag{17}$$

The term $f_t(\mathbf{x}_i) = f_t(v) = a_{t,v}$ is constant with respect to the inner sum and can be factored out. That makes the inner sum constant and can be calculated from the current weights and the labels of the training data. The constraint $\langle f_t, f_t \rangle = 1$ implies that $\sum_{i=1}^{m} a_{t,x_{i,t}}^2 = 1$. By denoting the number of training examples with value v on feature t $c_{t,v} = \sum_{i | x_{i,t} = v} 1$, the constraint can be written $\sum_{v \in \mathcal{X}} c_{t,v} a_{t,v}^2 = 1$.

By introducing new coordinates, $\hat{a}_{t,v} = \sqrt{c_{t,v}} a_{t,v}$, it follows that $\|\hat{\mathbf{a}}_t\| = 1$, where $\hat{\mathbf{a}}_t = (\hat{a}_{t,0}, \hat{a}_{t,1}, \cdots)$. Introducing the new coordinates into (17) results in

$$\sum_{v \in \mathcal{X}} \frac{\hat{a}_{t,v}}{\sqrt{c_{t,v}}} \sum_{i | x_{i,t} = v} y_i d_i. \tag{18}$$

Let the inner sum normalized by $\sqrt{c_{t,v}}$ be denoted $b_{t,v}$ and note that it can be divided into negative and positive training samples. It follows that

$$b_{t,v} = \sum_{i | x_{i,t} = v} \frac{y_i d_i}{\sqrt{c_{t,v}}} = \sum_{i | x_{i,t} = v, y_i = 1} \frac{d_i}{\sqrt{c_{t,v}}} - \sum_{i | x_{i,t} = v, y_i = -1} \frac{d_i}{\sqrt{c_{t,v}}}. \tag{19}$$

Equation (18) is the scalar product between the vectors $\hat{\mathbf{a}}_t$ and $\mathbf{b}_t = (b_{t,0}, b_{t,1}, \cdots)$, which can also be written $\|\hat{\mathbf{a}}_t\| \|\mathbf{b}_t\| \cos \phi$, where ϕ is the angle between $\hat{\mathbf{a}}_t$ and $\mathbf{b}_t$. The constraint $\langle f, f \rangle = 1$ implies that $\|\hat{\mathbf{a}}_t\| = 1$. Apart from that, $\hat{\mathbf{a}}_t$ can be chosen freely, which means it can be chosen parallel to $\mathbf{b}_t$ in which case $\cos \phi$ reaches its maximum, 1. The only factor left to maximize is $\|\mathbf{b}_t\|$, which means that the optimal feature t^* can be found by

$$t^* = \underset{t}{\operatorname{argmax}} \|\mathbf{b}_t\|. \tag{20}$$

Substituting $\mathbf{b}_t$ for its definition (19) and removing the outermost square root (which does not affect the position of the maximum) concludes the proof.

$\square$

A detector F can now be trained by iteratively choosing a feature t by using Lemma 2 and then select coefficients $a_{t,v}$ for f_t using Lemma 1. The weights d_i are maintained in the same manner as with adaboost. They are initiated to $1/m$ before the first iteration and then updated using $d_i := d_i e^{-a_{t,x_{i,t}} y_i}$.

4   Temporal Tracking

To count the number of tracks, the single frame detections are tracked across multiple frames. The tracking approach used is based on the Kalman filter.

It maintains one set of confirmed tracks and one set of tentative tracks. Both kind of tracks are maintained using Kalman filters with the position and velocity vectors as state and the position as observation.

The detections from a new frame are first matched to the confirmed tracks using the Hungarian method [9]. The Mahalanobis distance between the observation predicted by the Kalman filter and the detection is used as cost-function. The detections not matching any of those are then matched to the tentative tracks, again using the Hungarian method. New tentative tracks are produced for the detections not matching any existing or tentative tracks.

When enough detections have been assigned to a tentative track it becomes confirmed. If the variance of a track becomes too large it is considered lost and is removed. If such a track was confirmed it is counted and accumulated into the flow count report.

5   Experimental Results

Experiments were performed using a five stage cascade and a 3×3 neighborhood LBP feature and executed on a 2.93 GHz Core 2 Duo. Three detectors were trained using the classical adaboost (with binary weak classifiers) [3], realboost as presented in Section 3.1 and split up SNoW [6]. All three produce detectors of the same form, although the lookup tables produced by the classical adaboost are more restricted as the week classifiers are only allowed the values of -1 or 1 and not any real value as is the case with the other two classifiers. The cascades were formed by requiring a True Positive Rate (TPR) of 99.5% and a False Positive Rate (FPR) of 5% for each step.

5.1   Face Detection

The training data consists of 10620 manually annotated faces and 1713 high resolution images containing no faces. The test data consists of 1183 faces and 191 negative images. The test data described above was used to verify the detection performance of the resulting detector, and the run time was evaluated on a 6000×2585 image[1] Results are shown in Table 1.

Note that the realboost detector has similar accuracy to adaboost or the split up SNoW, but it is more than 60% faster. This is a significant speedup, and stems from the fact that fewer features can be used in the initial steps effectively discarding a lot of negative examples at an early stage. Note that the exact same implementation were used for each of the detectors. The only difference is the values of the lookup-tables and the number of features used in each cascade step.

5.2   CMU+MIT

The three detectors trained on our database was also tested using the CMU+MIT test dataset (set A, B and C), with results presented in Table 2. This dataset

[1] http://www.flickr.com/photos/kitty-kat/6049220331/

Table 1. Results comparing the performance of three different detectors. The number of features used in each stage of the cascade is listed as well as the run time needed to process an image. The true positive rate (TPR) shows the amount of faces detected among the 1183 faces in the training database and the false positive rate (FPR) shows the number of false detections made per mega-pixel.

Training	Size	Features					Run time (s)		TPR	FPR
Adaboost	16×16	59	156	196	196	196	2.81			
	20×20	55	141	264	324	324	2.80	8.17	96.53 %	0.147 %
	25×25	58	139	249	431	418	2.98			
Split Up SNoW	16×16	81	57	44	14	0	3.00			
	20×20	65	64	79	91	25	2.63	8.94	95.86 %	0.071 %
	25×25	101	52	137	180	59	3.74			
Realboost	16×16	36	81	159	196	196	1.76			
	20×20	32	75	128	232	278	1.72	**4.93**	96.28 %	0.136 %
	25×25	37	72	121	180	195	1.85			

contain noisier images as compared to our training dataset, which seams to lead to a high false negative rate as LBP is noise sensitive. However this test confirms the increased speed of the realboost approach, which here is 50% faster than adaboost and 70 % faster than split up SNoW.

Table 2. The detection results from testing the trained detectors on our database on the CMU+MIT database together with the runtime for processing the entire database. In the Prop. columns results from using 3 window sizes and no interpolation, and in the Bilin. columns results from using a single window size and bilinear rescaling are shown.

Training	True Positives		False Negatives		False Positives		Runtime	
	Prop.	Bilin.	Prop.	Bilin.	Prop.	Bilin.	Prop.	Bilin.
adaboost	373	407	137	102	11	4	9.65 s	11.56 s
split up SNoW	333	356	177	154	5	5	10.85 s	14.9 s
realboost	356	403	154	107	9	7	**6.39 s**	7.59 s

5.3   Single Sized Detector

The rescaling approach proposed was compared with the standard approach of using a single window size and rescaling the image using bilinear interpolation. A rescaling factor of $2^{1/3} \approx 1.26$ was used together with a step size of $1/16$ of the window side. This gives approximately the same number of windows tested in both cases. Results on the CMU+MIT dataset is presented in Table 2. Realboost shows a 19 % speedup, split up SNoW 37 %, while adaboost is 20 % faster.

5.4   Tracking Faces

The output of the three detectors described above were passed to the Kalman tracker framework in order to perform face tracking. The Youtube faces [1] database were used for testing. It consists of 3425 video clips with one face trajectory marked out in each clip. In total there are 619139 frames. The tracks produced by the tracker were matched to the ground truth tracks as favorably as possible and the number of frames where the tracker placed the correct object close to the ground truth object were considered correct and counted. The results are presented in Table 3.

Table 3. The number of frames in which the detector detected (Matches) or missed (Misses) the annotated face as well as the same data after tracking. After tracking, the id-number of the detection also has to be correct for a frame to be considered matched.

Training	Detector		Tracker		
	Matches	Misses	Matches	Misses	Runtime
Adaboost	592723	28403	602503	16636	29.54 h
Split Up SNoW	580385	40741	599301	19074	29.17 h
Realboost	589174	31952	601142	17662	**26.16 h**

Note that while the number of frames where the realboost detector misses a face have increased with 11% as compared with the adaboost. However, the number of frames where the tracker misses a face have only increased by 5% as the tracker is able to fill in some missing detections.

5.5   Counting Bicycles

The proposed framework were tested on a bicycle counting scenario where a bicycle road was filmed for two days. The bicycles from the first day were marked manually and the detectors trained on that data. The bicycles from the second day was counted both manually and automatically and the results are compared in Figure 2. Processing 1000 frames required 10.76 s for realboost, 13.25 s for adaboost and 16.97 for the single window bilinear scaled adaboost. The mean absolute counting error over 30 min parts is 17.6 % for realboost, 9.8 % for adaboost and 12.3 % for bilinear scaling.

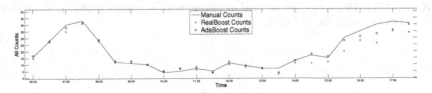

Fig. 2. Comparing automatic and manual bicycle counts

6 Conclusions

In this paper we present a novel approach to speed up real time object detections. This by exploring real valued weak classifiers and detectors with multiple sized windows. Results indicate that the realboost framework archives a 65% speedup over adaboost and a further 19% speedup by utilizing the proposed scaling framework compared to the common bilinear interpolation. In a tracking scenario the proposed solution can run close to 60% faster than standard adaboost implementation, with only a 5.3 percentage points loss in performance.

It should be possible to improve on those results by also optimizing over the window size of the detector, the number of window sizes used as well as the parameters of the Kalman filters. Also, in many flow counting applications, especially traffic studies, somewhat lower accuracy can be compensated for by increasing the amount of measurements.

References

1. Wolf, L., Hassner, T., Maoz, I.: Face recognition in unconstrained videos with matched background similarity. In: IEEE Computer Society Conference on Computer Vision and Pattern Recognition, pp. 529–534 (2011)
2. Viola, P., Jones, M.: Rapid object detection using a boosted cascade of simple features. In: Proceedings of the 2001 IEEE Computer Society Conference on Computer Vision and Pattern Recognition (CVPR), vol. 1, pp. 511–518 (2001)
3. Freund, Y., Schapire, R.E.: A Decision-Theoretic Generalization of On-Line Learning and An Application to Boosting. In: Vitányi, P.M.B. (ed.) EuroCOLT 1995. LNCS, vol. 904, pp. 23–37. Springer, Heidelberg (1995)
4. Ojala, T., Pietikainen, M., Harwood, D.: Performance evaluation of texture measures with classification based on kullback discrimination of distributions. In: Proceedings of the 12th IAPR International Conference on Pattern Recognition - Conference A: Computer Vision Image Processing, vol. 1, pp. 582–585 (October 1994)
5. Nilsson, M., Dahl, M., Claesson, I.: The successive mean quantization transform. In: IEEE International Conference on Acoustics, Speech, and Signal Processing (ICASSP), vol. 4, pp. 429–432 (March 2005)
6. Nilsson, M., Nordberg, J., Claesson, I.: Face detection using local smqt features and split up snow classifier. In: IEEE International Conference on Acoustics, Speech, and Signal Processing (ICASSP) (April 2007)
7. Mason, L., Baxter, J., Bartlett, P.L., Frean, M.R.: Boosting algorithms as gradient descent. In: NIPS, pp. 512–518 (1999)
8. Schapire, R.E., Singer, Y.: Improved boosting algorithms using confidence-rated predictions. Mach. Learn. 37, 297–336 (1999)
9. Kuhn, H.W.: The hungarian method of solving the assignment problem. Naval Res. Logistics Quart. 2, 83–97 (1955)

Dynamic Markov Random Field Model
for Visual Tracking

Daehwan Kim[1], Ki-Hong Kim[1], Gil-Haeng Lee[1], and Daijin Kim[2]

[1] Creative Content Research Laboratory, ETRI, Daejeon, Republic of Korea
{daehwank,kimgh,ghlee}@etri.re.kr
[2] Department of Computer Science and Engineering, POSTECH, Pohang, Republic of Korea
dkim@postech.ac.kr

Abstract. We propose a new dynamic Markov random field (DMRF) model to track a heavily occluded object. The DMRF model is a bidirectional graph which consists of three random variables: hidden, observation, and validity. It temporally prunes invalid nodes and links edges among valid nodes by verifying validities of all nodes. In order to apply the proposed DMRF model to the object tracking framework, we use an image block lattice model exactly correspond to nodes and edges in the DMRF model and utilize the mean-shift belief propagation (MSBP). The proposed object tracking method using the DMRF surprisingly tracks a heavily occluded object even if the occluded region is more than 70~80%. Experimental results show that the proposed tracking method gives good tracking performance even on various tracking image sequences(ex. human and face) with heavy occlusion.

Keywords: Markov random field, Dynamic Markov random field, Visual tracking.

1 Introduction

Visual tracking is an important research topic in the computer vision field since it can be applied to many applications such as surveillance, security system, augmented reality and so on. Although many tracking methods [1] [2] [3] have been proposed, it has still several problems such as pose variations, appearance changes by illumination changes, and temporal or partial occlusion. Especially, tracking heavily occluded objects is one of the most difficult problems due to the lack of their visible area and very similar appearance within the occlusion.

Depth-based tracking methods [4] and [5] track occluded objects using depth information using multiple calibrated images. While these tracking methods tracked occluded objects well, they required additional time to calibrate multiple images and to generate depth images. Appearance-based tracking methods [6] and [3] track occluded objects by searching the object appearance in the input image. Some adaptive appearance-based methods attempt to solve the occlusion problem by statistical analysis [7] [8]. While these tracking methods tracked occluded objects well and were quite insensitive to appearance changes over time, they missed occluded objects when the object appearance was very simple or repetitive.

A. Fusiello et al. (Eds.): ECCV 2012 Ws/Demos, Part III, LNCS 7585, pp. 203–212, 2012.

Most of those visual tracking methods under heavy occlusion only give a rough boundary box or position due to using an estimation way based on velocity or acceleration. So these do not provide exact tracking results. It is originated from non-use of local observation information in small image blocks. However, it is still very difficult to practically use them due to lack of discriminative feature of local image blocks with very similar appearance. Fortunately, a well-encoded prior knowledge [9] [10] [11] can be a good counterproposal to make discrimination of the local feature higher. It is based on constrained pairwiseness of the structured spatial arrangement of nodes in the Markov random field (MRF) model. The MRF parameters are estimated using belief propagation (BP) [12] [13] [14] [9], which is a powerful method for computing marginal distribution of hidden random variables. These methods overcome a difficulty of the multi-modal posterior distribution caused from highly similar appearance. The combination of the MRF and BP gives a good local evidence.

However, it only works when propagations among nodes of the structured layout occur correctly. Heavy occlusion causes a global drift or distortion of the whole object layout by propagating wrongly from nodes corresponding to occluded image blocks. To avoid the bad propagation with keeping the structural layout, it rather prunes the invalid nodes from the graphical structure under such a situation. Figure 1 shows the tracking examples using the conventional MRF-based tracking method [9] with two different image block lattices. The tracking result of using the pruned lattice model is better than the result of using the full lattice model. This informs that there exits effects of nodes corresponded to the occluded image blocks and the propagations from such nodes are unnecessary.

(a)   (b)

Fig. 1. Tracking examples using two different image block lattices. (a) By using human-like lattice model. (b) By using its pruned lattice model.

In this paper, we propose a dynamic Markov random field (DMRF) model that does not propagate bad effects from the invalid nodes by dynamically reconfiguring the graphical structure. The proposed model is represented by adding a validity variable to the conventional MRF model and altering an undirected edge into an bidirectional edge, respectively. The added validity variable determines whether each node is valid or not, and the altered bidirectional edge gives a permission to propagate the messages derived from its neighboring nodes. These make a structured layout of our proposed model be easily re-configured. To efficiently infer the hidden variables of the DMRF model, we use mean-shift belief propagation (MSBP) proposed by [9] to efficiently infer hidden random variables in our DMRF model. Finally, we develop an object tracking algorithm that can track a heavily occluded object even. To evaluate the tracking accuracy of the proposed method, we apply our approach to various object tracking image sequences including occluded human and face.

2 Dynamic Markov Random Field

A DMRF is a bidirectional graph $G = (V, E)$, where V and E represent the set of nodes and edges in the graph, where each node represents a random variable and each edge represents a statistical dependency between random variables by the connected edges. The DMRF model has three random variables: the hidden random variables $\mathbf{x}_i$, $i = 1, 2, \cdots, N$, the observation random variables z_i, $i = 1, 2, \cdots, N$, and the validity variables v_i, $i = 1, 2, \cdots, N$, where N is the number of nodes (Fig. 2).

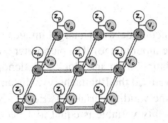

Fig. 2. A graphical structure of DMRF model

We can represent the DMRF in terms of the joint probability as

$$p(\mathbf{x}_1, .., \mathbf{x}_N, z_1, .., z_N, v_1, .., v_N) = \prod_{(i,j) \in E} \psi(x_i, x_j) \prod_{i \in N}^{N} \phi(x_i, z_i, v_i), \qquad (1)$$

where N, $\mathbf{x}_i$, z_i and v_i are the number of nodes, the ith hidden random variable, the ith observation random variable, and the ith validity variable, respectively.

The pairwise compatibility function $\psi(\mathbf{x}_i, \mathbf{x}_j)$ is defined as a measurement of the spring energy between two connected nodes $\mathbf{x}_i$ and $\mathbf{x}_j$. If the value of the pairwise compatibility function becomes large, the two nodes are highly dependent on each other. In this work, we take the pairwise compatibility function as

$$\psi(\mathbf{x}_i, \mathbf{x}_j) = \exp(-\alpha |d(\mathbf{x}_i, \mathbf{x}_j) - d(\mathbf{x}(T_i), \mathbf{x}(T_j))|), \qquad (2)$$

where α adjusts the elasticity of the edge between two nodes, $\mathbf{x}_i$ and $\mathbf{x}_j$ denote the positions of input image blocks for the ith and jth nodes, respectively, $\mathbf{x}(T_i)$ and $\mathbf{x}(T_j)$ denote the positions of template image blocks for the ith and jth nodes, respectively, and $d(\bullet, \bullet)$ is a Euclidean distance between the positions for two nodes.

The joint compatibility function $\phi(\mathbf{x}_i, z_i, v_i)$ associates the probabilistic relation among a hidden random variable $\mathbf{x}_i$, observation random variable z_i, and its validity random variable v_i. In this work, we take the joint compatibility function as

$$\phi(\mathbf{x}_i, z_i, v_i) = 1 - \phi_v(\mathbf{x}_i, v_i)(1 - \phi_o(\mathbf{x}_i, z_i)), \qquad (3)$$

where, $\phi_v(\mathbf{x}_i, v_i)$ and $\phi_o(\mathbf{x}_i, z_i)$ are validity and observation compatibility functions, respectively.

The observation compatibility function $\phi_o(\mathbf{x}_i, z_i)$ is defined as

$$\phi_o(\mathbf{x}_i, z_i) = \exp(-\beta \sum_{j \in W(i)} (I(\mathbf{x}_{i,j}) - T(\mathbf{x}_{i,j}))^2), \tag{4}$$

where I and T denote the image and template image block, respectively, $W(i)$ is the sample with the sample window for the ith node, $\mathbf{x}_{i,j}$ is the jth sample within the sample block for the ith node, and β is a normalizing parameter.

The validity compatibility function $\phi_v(\mathbf{x}_i, v_i)$ is defined as

$$\phi_v(\mathbf{x}_i, v_i) = \begin{cases} 1, \text{ if } \exp(-\gamma d_v(I(\mathbf{x}_{i,j}), T_{i,j},)) > th_v \\ 0, \text{ otherwise} \end{cases} \tag{5}$$

where d_v is the similarity function between a target image template block T_i and $I(\mathbf{x}_i)$ (centered at location $\mathbf{x}_i$ of the input image). The parameter γ adjusts the influence of the validity variable v_i for validating an image block. th_v denotes the threshold value for the validity variable. Here, we used the Bhattacharyya distance as a similarity function. The reason for formulating the validity variable as Eq. (5) is as follows. When a node is valid, the value of the validity variable is equal to 1 because the DMRF should be functioned as the MRF. When a node is invalid, the value of the validity variable is equal to the reciprocal of the joint compatibility function because the right-hand product terms in Eq. (1) should be equal to 1 to make the joint compatibility function ineffective.

There are two well-known inference rules to infer the hidden random variables: Sum-Product and Max-Product rules. We take the Sum-Product rule that are based on discrete belief propagation (DBP) because it is easily computed using the element-wise product of arrays [9]. We modify the existing inference rule to compute the hidden random variables in the DMRF as follows.

2.1 Sum-Product Rule

The sum-product rule computes the marginal posterior probability (belief) as

$$b(\mathbf{x}_i) = k\phi(\mathbf{x}_i, z_i, v_i) \prod_{j \in N_v(i)} m_{j \to i}(\mathbf{x}_i), \tag{6}$$

where k and $N_v(i)$ are a normalization constant and the neighboring valid nodes of the ith node, respectively, and $\phi(\mathbf{x}_i, z_i, v_i)$ is the joint compatibility function derived from only valid nodes between the image block and the template image block.

The message $m_{j \to i}(\mathbf{x}_i)$ passing from the jth node to the ith node is computed recursively as

$$m_{j \to i}(\mathbf{x}_i) = \sum_{\mathbf{x}_j} \phi(\mathbf{x}_j, z_j, v_j)\psi(\mathbf{x}_j, \mathbf{x}_i) \prod_{k \in N_v(j) \backslash i} m_{k \to j}(\mathbf{x}_j), \tag{7}$$

where $N_v(j) \backslash i$ means the neighboring valid nodes of the jth node except the ith node.

The hidden random variable $\mathbf{x}_i$ is computed by summation over the possible states as

$$\mathbf{x}_i = \sum_{\mathbf{x}_i} \mathbf{x}_i b(\mathbf{x}_i), \tag{8}$$

where $b(\mathbf{x}_i)$ is the marginal posterior probability (belief) for the ith node.

2.2 State Inference

We used mean-shift belief propagation (MSBP) [9] [15] to efficiently estimate the state (or belief) of each node. We only evaluate within a discrete local regular grid of samples centered of the previous state because it is hard to evaluate all the possible states of the hidden variable. The message passing is performed to compute a belief for each sample at one iteration. After computing beliefs of all samples, it obtains a new estimated state by doing mean-shift on the samples. It repeats this process until there is no state change. A reader, who want to look for detailed description about the MSBP, refers to the MSBP [9].

3   The Proposed Object Tracking Algorithm

A node is valid if the validity compatibility function $\phi_v(\mathbf{x}_i, v_i)$ is greater than a threshold value. Otherwise, the node is invalid. If the invalid nodes are used for message passing, we may reach the wrong result in the state inference. To reduce the influence of such a wrong propagation, we propose to reconfigure the graphical structure of the DMRF model by pruning invalid nodes, recovering the nodes that are valid frame but were invalid in the previous frame, and reconnecting the neighboring valid nodes of the pruned invalid node. This reconfiguration forces the graphical structure of the DMRF model to be strongly connected.

Fig. 3 shows a typical example of the reconfiguration of the graphical structure of the DMRF model, where (a) represents that two nodes V_j and V_o are connected to each other due to the invalid node V_k and the invalid node V_k only receives messages from the two nodes V_j and V_o, and (b) represents three different situations: (1) two nodes V_q and V_o are connected to each other due to the invalid node V_r and the invalid node V_r only receives messages from the two nodes V_q and V_o, (2) four pairs of two nodes V_q and V_m, V_m and V_j, V_j and V_o and V_o and V_q are connected to each other due to the invalid node V_n and the invalid node V_n only receives the messages from the four nodes V_q, V_m, V_j and V_o and (3) the node V_k is recovered to the valid node and the recovered node V_k can send messages to two neighboring nodes V_j and V_o.

Table 1 summarizes our proposed object tracking algorithm.

4   Experimental Results and Discussion

4.1   Databases and Measures

The proposed object tracking method using the DMRF model was implemented on a Windows PC platform with a 2.83 GHz Intel Core 2 Quad CPU and 8 GB RAM in

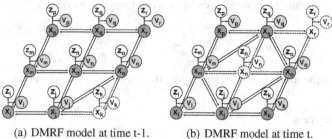

(a) DMRF model at time t-1.   (b) DMRF model at time t.

Fig. 3. A typical example of the graphical structure reconfiguration

Table 1. The proposed object tracking algorithm

Initialization step:
Construct: an image block lattice L by dividing an object into several image blocks.
Set: the initial image block parameters and three function parameters of the lattice L on the first image frame.
- The image block parameters: position $\mathbf{x}_i^1 = (u_i^1, v_i^1)$, width w_i^1, height h_i^1, template image block T_i^1, and relative distance $d(\mathbf{x}_i^1, \mathbf{x}_j^1)$ between image blocks.
- Three function parameters: α, β, and γ in Eqs. (2), (4), and (5).
Tracking step:
Sample: discrete local regular grid positions $\hat{X}^t = \hat{\mathbf{x}}_i{}^t$ centered at the previous state $\mathbf{x}_i^{t-1}$ for each node.
Weight: to the samples by passing the message Eq. (7) and computing the belief Eq. (6).
Mean-shift: on a belief grid of samples and estimate new positions $\mathbf{x}_i^t$ of all image blocks. Repeat this step until there is no state change.
Re-configuration step:
Validate: all nodes of L by thresholding the validity compatibility function $\phi_v(\mathbf{x}_i^t, v_i^t)$.
Prune: all invalid nodes and their outgoing edges. If the invalid node changes to the valid node, the node and its outgoing edges are rehabilitated.
Generate and Connect: temporal edges between two valid neighbor nodes around the pruned invalid node. If the invalid node is rehabilitated, the temporal edges are disconnected and disappeared.

the Matlab 9.0 environment. To evaluate the proposed tracking method, we used 74 different trajectories (70 for human and 4 for face) under heavy occlusions. The 70 human trajectories ($H_1 - H_{70}$) were randomly taken from the CAVIAR database[1], which captured moving people in a a shopping center by a single camera with a resolution of 384 x 288 image and 25 frames per second (fps). Two face trajectories (F_1 and F_2) were taken from the HONDA database [2] , which captured a moving face by a single camera with a resolution of 640 x 480 image and 15 frames per second (fps). Two face trajectories (F_3 and F_4) were captured with the Web-camera in our laboratory with a resolution of 320 x 240 image and 20 frames per second (fps).

We would like to make a comparison and evaluation on the proposed method (named by 'DMRFT') with the three state-of-the-art tracking methods, which are incremental learning-based tracking method (ILT) [7], semi-supervised learning-based tracking method (SST) [8] and Markov random field-based tracking method (MRFT) [9], through the qualitative and quantitative tracking results. We manually initialized the

---

[1] See http://homepages.inf.ed.ac.uk/rbf/CAVIAR

[2] See http://vision.ucsd.edu/ leekc/HondaUCSDVideoDatabase/ HondaUCSD.html .

target objects' position and template image block of them at the first frame. We used two block lattice models for MRFT and DMRFT presented in Figure 4 or 5. We set the parameters α, β, and γ to 0.1, 10, and 1, respectively.

To evaluate the tracking performance between the tracking results and the ground truth, we consider two measures to evaluate the tracking performance: tracking error and tracking accuracy. Tracking error is the average of the distance between the center point of the tracked object and that of the ground truth during the whole frames. Tracking accuracy is an average of the overlap pixels between the boundary box of the tracked object and that of the ground truth during the whole frames as

$$Accuracy = \frac{1}{N} \sum_{t=1}^{N} \frac{R(H_t \cap G_t)}{R(H_t \cup G_t)}, \tag{9}$$

where N denote the number of frames, H_t is the tracked object (bounding box) at the tth frame, G_t is the ground truth (bounding box) at the tth frame, and $R(\bullet)$ is a function to compute the area. Generally, we have a good object tracking result if the tracking accuracy is greater than 70%.

4.2 Quantitative Tracking Results

Human Tracking. We represented each detected human by the DMRF structure with 20 nodes, where each node corresponded to the center position of template image block. Next, we represented the Euclidean distance between the center positions of two neighboring template image blocks as the edge, which is represented by the white line.

Table 2 (a) summarizes the human tracking results in terms of tracking error among the four different tracking methods. The DMRFT outperformed the three existing methods in terms of average tracking error because it could accurately estimate the center position of the DMRF structure from the successful human tracking of partially visible regions and the successful estimation of occluded regions. Table 2 (b) summarizes the human tracking results in terms of tracking accuracy among the four different tracking methods. The DMRFT outperformed the three existing methods in terms of average tracking accuracy because it could keep the DMRF structures of the occluded humans by the successful tracking of partially visible regions and the successful estimation of occluded regions. The average human tracking accuracy of DMRFT using the 70 human trajectories H_1 to H_{70} was 72.1%, which is accepted as a good tracking performance.

Face Tracking. We represented each detected face by a DMRF structure with 26 nodes, where each node corresponds to the center position of template image block. Next, we represented the Euclidean distance between the center positions of two neighboring template blocks as the edge, which is represented by the white line.

Table 3 (a) summarizes the face tracking results in terms of tracking error among the four different tracking methods. The DMRFT outperformed the three existing methods in terms of tracking error because it could accurately estimate the center position of the DMRF structure from the successful face tracking of partially visible regions and the successful estimation of occluded regions. The MRFT has moderate face tracking errors except for the face trajectory F_4 because the tracked faces had not drifted under

Table 2. Comparison of human tracking errors and accuracies using the human trajectories H_1 to H_{70}. E_{H_1} (or A_{H_1}) and $E_{H_{34}}$ (or $A_{H_{34}}$) denote the tracking error (or accuracy) of the human trajectory H_1 and the tracking error (or accuracy) of the human trajectory H_{34}, and $E_{H_{AVG}}$ (or $A_{H_{AVG}}$) denotes the average tracking error (or accuracy) of all human trajectories H_1 to H_{70}.

(a) Tracking error

Tracking Method	Tracking Error		
	E_{H_1}	$E_{H_{34}}$	$E_{H_{AVG}}$
ILT [7]	7.0	8.3	33.7
SST [8]	8.9	146.1	152.2
MRFT [9]	1.1	5.1	19.1
DMRFT	1.0	1.3	3.4

(b) Tracking accuracy

Tracking Method	Tracking Accuracy		
	A_{H_1}	$A_{H_{34}}$	$A_{H_{AVG}}$
ILT [7]	25.1%	34.6%	27.5%
SST [8]	35.0%	31.5%	29.5%
MRFT [9]	61.5%	57.6%	58.4%
DMRFT	70.9%	73.4%	72.1%

heavy occlusion. Table 3 (b) summarizes the face tracking results in terms of tracking accuracy among the four different tracking methods. The DMRFT outperformed the three existing methods in terms of tracking accuracy because it could keep the DMRF structures of the occluded faces by the successful face tracking of partially visible regions and the successful estimation of occluded regions. The face tracking accuracies of DMRFT using the four face trajectories F_1 to F_4 were greater than 70%, which are accepted as good tracking performance.

Table 3. Comparison of face tracking errors and accuracies using the human trajectories F_1 to F_4. E_{F_1} to E_{F_4} (or A_{F_1} to A_{F_4}) denote the face tracking error (or accuracy) of the face trajectory F_1 to F_4, respectively, and $E_{F_{AVG}}$ (or $A_{F_{AVG}}$) denotes the average face tracking error (or accuracy) of all the face trajectories F_1 to F_4.

(a) Tracking error

Tracking Method	Tracking Error				
	E_{F_1}	E_{F_2}	E_{F_3}	E_{F_4}	E_{AVG}
ILT [7]	22.8	1.95	17.4	31.5	23.9
SST [8]	50.0	77.79	63.1	152.9	102.9
MRFT [9]	6.4	1.5	1.0	33.5	15.8
DMRFT	3.4	1.2	0.7	1.6	1.3

(b) Tracking accuracy

Tracking Method	Tracking Accuracy				
	A_{F_1}	A_{F_2}	A_{F_3}	A_{F_4}	$A_{F_{AVG}}$
ILT [7]	60.6%	61.0%	19.8%	14.2%	20.0%
SST [8]	35.0%	41.7%	51.1%	17.2%	34.9%
MRFT [9]	70.8%	66.9%	68.8%	25.4%	49.5%
DMRFT	74.9%	72.6%	71.6%	72.7%	72.3%

4.3　Qualitative Tracking Results

Human Tracking Examples. Fig. 4 shows the human tracking results of the human trajectory H_1 and H_{34} over three different frames, respectively, where the black and white block in the case of (d)(i) and (e)(j) of two figures denote valid and invalid blocks, respectively. The tracking results using ILT and SST failed to track the occluded human because the bounding box had shrunk, drifted or disappeared. The tracking results using MRFT missed the occluded human because the human structure had drifted onto the occluding human due to the occlusion. On the other hand, the tracking results using DMRFT succeeded in tracking the occluded human because it tracked the partially visible regions well and was almost unaffected by the occluded regions.

Face Tracking Examples. Fig. 5 shows the face tracking results of the face trajectory F_2 and F_4 over three different frames, respectively, where the black and white block in the case of (d)(i) and (e)(j) of two figures denote valid and invalid blocks, respectively. The tracking results using ILT and SST failed to track the occluded face because the bounding box had drifted, shrunk or disappeared. The tracking results using MRFT in the Fig. 5(d) was good, but those in the Fig. 5(i) missed the occluded face because the MRF structure of the occluded face had drifted. On the other hand, the tracking results using DMRFT succeeded in tracking the occluded face although the occluding hand passed over the face.

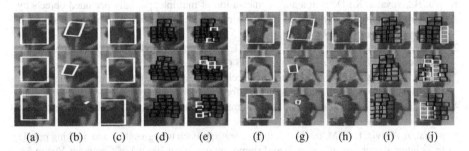

(a) (b) (c) (d) (e) (f) (g) (h) (i) (j)

Fig. 4. Human tracking results of the human trajectory H_1 (a∼e) and H_{34} (f∼j). (a)(f) GT, (b)(g) ILT, (c)(h) SST, (d)(i) MRFT, and (e)(j) DMRFT.

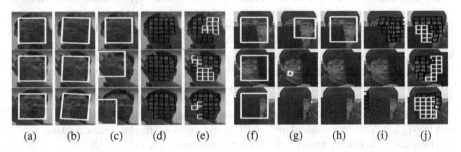

(a) (b) (c) (d) (e) (f) (g) (h) (i) (j)

Fig. 5. Face tracking results of the face trajectory F_2(a∼e) and F_4 (f∼j). (a)(f) GT, (b)(g) ILT, (c)(h) SST, (d)(i) MRFT, and (e)(j) DMRFT.

5   Conclusion

We proposed a new dynamic Markov random field (DMRF) model for tracking an object under severe occlusion. In the visual tracking problem, the conventional Markov random field (MRF) and belief propagation (BP) tackle a multi-modal posterior distribution problem, but it is vulnerable for tracking an heavily occluded object due to wrong propagations from invalid nodes. Especially, their use produces a global drift and distortion of the whole layout with an image block lattice model. However, DMRF, which is a bidirectional graph which consists of three random variables:hidden, observation, and validity, reduce the effect of such wrong propagation by temporally pruning invalid nodes and linking edges among valid nodes. The proposed object tracking method using the DMRF surprisingly tracks a heavily occluded object even though experimenting on various object sequences with severe occlusion.

Acknowledgments. This work was supported by the R&D program of Ministry of Culture, Sports and Tourism (MCST) and Korea Evaluation Institute of Industrial Technology (KEIT) (10039923, Development of Live4D contents platform technology based on expansion of realistic experiential space).

References

1. Wu, B., Nevatia, R.: Detection and segmentation of multiple, partially occluded objects by grouping, merging, assigning part detection responses. International Journal of Computer Vision 82, 185–204 (2009)
2. Senior, A., Hampapur, A., Tian, Y., Brown, L.: Appearance models for occlusion handling. Image and Vision Computing 24, 1233–1243 (2006)
3. Hu, W., Zhou, X., Hu, M., Maybank, S.: Occlusion reasoning for tracking multiple people. IEEE Transactions on Circuits and Systems for Video Technology 19, 114–121 (2009)
4. Zhao, T., Nevatia, R.: Tracking multiple humans in complex situations. IEEE Transactions on Pattern Analysis and Machine Intelligence 26, 1208–1221 (2004)
5. Mittal, A., Davis, L.S.: M2tracker: A multi-view approach to segmenting and tracking people in a cluttered scene using region-based stereo. International Journal of Computer Vision 51, 189–203 (2003)
6. Lin, Z., Davis, L., Doermann, D., Dementhon, D.: An interactive approach to pose-assisted and appearance-based segmentation of humans. In: Proc. of IEEE International Conferenece on Computer Vision, pp. 1–8 (2007)
7. Ross, D., Lim, J., Lin, R.: Incremental learning for robust visual tracking. International Journal of Computer Vision 77, 125–141 (2008)
8. Mei, X., Ling, H.: Beyond semi-supervised tracking: Tracking should be as simple as detection, but not simpler than recognition. In: Proc. of IEEE International Conferenece on Computer Vision Workshop, pp. 1409–1416 (2009)
9. Park, M., Liu, Y., Collins, R.: Efficient mean shift belief propagation for vision tracking. In: Proc. of IEEE Computer Vision and Pattern Recognition, pp. 1–8 (2008)
10. Lin, W., Liu, Y.: A lattice-based mrf model for dynamic near-regular texture tracking. IEEE Transactions on Pattern Analysis and Machine Intelligence 29, 777–792 (2007)
11. Liu, J., Liu, Y.: Multi-target tracking of time-varying spatial patterns. In: Proc. of IEEE Computer Vision and Pattern Recognition, pp. 1839–1846 (2010)
12. Coughlan, J., Huiying, S.: Shape matching with belief propagation: Using dynamic quantization to accomodate occlusion and clutter. In: Proc. of IEEE Computer Vision and Pattern Recognition Workshop (2004)
13. Felzenszwalb, P., Huttenlocher, D.: Efficient belief propagation for early vision. International Journal of Computer Vision 70, 41–54 (2006)
14. Yedidia, J., Freeman, W., Weiss, Y.: Understanding belief propagation and its generalizations. In: International Joint Conference on Artificial Intelligence (2001)
15. Park, M., Brocklehurst, K., Collins, R., Liu, Y.: Deformed lattice detection in real-world images using mean-shift belief propagation. IEEE Transactions on Pattern Analysis and Machine Intelligence 31, 1804–1816 (2009)

Mode Seeking with an Adaptive Distance Measure

Guodong Pan, Lifeng Shang, Dirk Schnieders, and Kwan-Yee K. Wong

Department of Computer Science
The University of Hong Kong
Pokfulam Road, Hong Kong
{gdpan,lfshang,sdirk,kykwong}@cs.hku.hk

Abstract. The mean shift algorithm is a widely used non-parametric clustering algorithm. It has been extended to cluster a mixture of linear subspaces for solving problems in computer vision such as multi-body motion segmentation, etc. Existing methods only work with a set of subspaces, which are computed from samples of observations. However, noises from observations can distort these subspace estimates and influence clustering accuracy. We propose to use both subspaces and observations to improve performance. Furthermore, while these mean shift methods use fixed metrics for computing distances, we prefer an adaptive distance measure. The insight is, we can use temporary modes in a mode seeking process to improve this measure and obtain better performance. In this paper, an adaptive mode seeking algorithm is proposed for clustering linear subspaces. By experiments, the proposed algorithm compares favorably to the state-of-the-art algorithm in terms of clustering accuracy.

Keywords: Mean Shift Algorithm, Metric Learning.

1 Introduction

The mean shift (MS) algorithm is a non-parametric clustering method for finding centers of arbitrarily distributed points in a vector space [1]. Characterized as a gradient ascent algorithm, it has been successfully applied to tackle problems like image segmentation and tracking [1][2].

Recently the MS algorithm has been extended to Grassmann manifolds for clustering linear subspaces [3][4]. A Grassmann manifold is a collection of linear subspaces endowed with a distance measure. A Grassmann point is a linear subspace represented by an orthonormal matrix. If we concatenate columns of this matrix into a long vector, the Grassmann manifold is a surface in a high dimensional space. We will use the terms Grassmann point and linear subspace interchangeably. The basic idea of the MS algorithm over Grassmann manifolds is to compute a set of Grassmann points from samples of observations, find modes or local centers of these Grassmann points, and cluster the points using the modes.

A. Fusiello et al. (Eds.): ECCV 2012 Ws/Demos, Part III, LNCS 7585, pp. 213–222, 2012.

Subbarao and Meer proposed the nonlinear mean shift algorithm [3], which started from a Grassmann point and iteratively moved it by logarithm and exponential mappings. One problem of their method is these mappings are computationally expensive. The intrinsic mean shift (Intrinsic MS) algorithm proposed by Cetingül and Vidal [4] used discrepancy measures and QR decompositions to simplify the computation. Unfortunately, clustering accuracy of both methods is greatly restricted by accuracy of estimation of Grassmann point sets. The accuracy of clustering depends on how well sampled Grassmann points can reflect the underlying density functions. Due to noise, these Grassmann points could deviate very much from the ground truth, and this heavily impairs performance. Actually the sampled points only retrieve part of observation information, and there is much information left behind. Reusing observation information will improve clustering accuracy.

In this paper, we propose a mode seeking algorithm (GOPS MS) to improve accuracy of clustering linear subspaces. It reuses observations as well as linear subspaces. Given a linear subspace, we find observations in this subspace, and encapsulate these observations and the subspace into an entity. This entity is viewed as a point in a **G**rassmann manifold and **O**bservations **P**roduct **S**pace, or simply a GOPS point. We will define a distance measure in GOPS such that, if two linear subspaces are similar, their corresponding GOPS points are close. Equipped with this measure, the GOPS MS performs mode seeking in the GOPS, and linear subspaces are clustered according to these GOPS modes.

In tradition, MS algorithms [5][1][4][3] have fixed distance measures. In a mode seeking process, they use a fixed distance to shift a temporary mode to the next. However, we find a temporary mode actually provides useful information to measure similarity between GOPS points. The proposed GOPS MS is equipped with a distance measure adapted to temporary modes. When this measure is updated with such a mode, distances between similar observations decrease and these observations become more dense (see Figure 1). This facilitates clustering tasks.

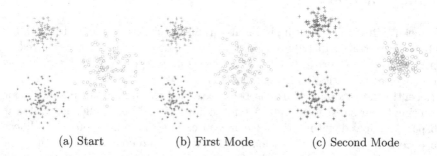

(a) Start   (b) First Mode   (c) Second Mode

Fig. 1. Illustration of change of distances. (a) shows distances between points with an initial distance measure. The right green circles scatter in a large region. (b)(c) show distances between points with distance measures updated by modes. These green circles become more and more dense.

Our algorithm can be applied to many problems in computer vision [4][6][7][8]. In this paper, we apply it to the problems of multi-body motion segmentation, shape categorization and face clustering, and compare it with the Intrinsic MS, a fixed metric algorithm. The corresponding overall clustering accuracy of the proposed algorithm are *99.2%*, *89.5%* and *98.0%*, and better than those of the Intrinsic MS (82.1%, 64.5%, 76.5%).

The rest of the paper is organized as follows. In Sect. 2, Euclidean mean shift is reviewed, from which we will motivate our GOPS MS. In Sect. 3, we construct the GOPS and explain the GOPS MS algorithm. Sect. 4 shows experiments and comparisons with the Intrinsic MS. Conclusion and future work are discussed in Sect. 5.

2   Euclidean Mean Shift

The Euclidean MS algorithm [9] finds local centers of a point set in a Euclidean space, and clusters all points in this set by these centers. If the point set is viewed as sampled points from a density function over the Euclidean space, the local centers are actually modes of this set, which are the points of local maximum density. So this algorithm is also considered as to seek modes and group points sharing the same mode together.

Formally, let a set of observations $x_n \in \mathbb{R}^d, n = 1, \ldots, N$, be points sampled independently from a density function f. The kernel density estimate of f at x, denoted by $\hat{f}(x; h)$, is given by $\hat{f}(x; h) = c \sum_{n=1}^{N} \Phi(u_n^2; h)$, where $\Phi(\cdot)$ is a kernel function, $u_n = ||x - x_n||$ is a distance measure, c is a normalization term, and $h > 0$ is the bandwidth. To locate a mode, the Euclidean MS algorithm seeks next temporary mode $y^{(k+1)}$ by minimizing a sum of weighted distance squares [10]

$$y^{(k+1)} = \arg\min_{y} \sum_{n=1}^{N} ||x_n - y||^2 \psi(||x_n - y^{(k)}||^2; h). \tag{1}$$

where $\psi(u_n; h) = -\nabla\Phi(u_n; h)$. The distance $|| \cdot ||$ play an important role to measure similarity between two points. Although it is a metric, the MS algorithm does not require that. In the next section, we will define a distance measure that is not a metric to compute similarity between points in GOPS. In addition, it is shown in [10] that the convergence of the MS algorithm depends on the convexity of the kernel $\Phi(\cdot)$.

3   Mode Seeking in GOPS

In the following, we construct the GOPS to reuse observations for clustering and explain the GOPS MS algorithm.

3.1   GOPS

The GOPS is a set of GOPS points with a distance measure over it. The GOPS point is an entity including a linear subspace and observations in this subspace, denoted by $G = \{\mathbf{X}, \mathbf{S_X}\}$. Here $\mathbf{X}$ is a $m \times p$ orthonormal matrix indicating a p-dimensional linear subspace in $\mathbb{R}^m$. Each observation is a vector in $\mathbb{R}^m$. And $\mathbf{S_X}$ is an observation set in this subspace, denoted by a $m \times N$ matrix, where N is the number of observations.

Suppose we have two GOPS points $G_1 = \{\mathbf{X}_1, \mathbf{S_{X_1}}\}, G_2 = \{\mathbf{X}_2, \mathbf{S_{X_2}}\}$. The GOPS distance d_{GO} is defined as

$$d_{GO}^2(G_{\mathbf{X}_1}, G_{\mathbf{X}_2}) = c_1 d_G^2(\mathbf{X}_1, \mathbf{X}_2) + c_2 d_{\mathbf{X}_1}^2(\mathbf{S_{X_1}}, \mathbf{S_{X_2}}), \qquad (2)$$

where c_1, c_2 are weights and $d_G, d_{\mathbf{X}_1}$ are defined as follows. The Grassmann distance [4] $d_G^2(\mathbf{X}_1, \mathbf{X}_2)$ computes distance between two linear subspaces as

$$d_G^2(\mathbf{X}_1, \mathbf{X}_2) = p - tr(\mathbf{X}_2^{\mathrm{T}} \mathbf{X}_1 \mathbf{X}_1^{\mathrm{T}} \mathbf{X}_2). \qquad (3)$$

The fit measure $d_{\mathbf{X}_1}^2(\mathbf{S_{X_1}}, \mathbf{S_{X_2}})$ measures how well a linear subspace $\mathbf{X}_1$ fit observations $\mathbf{S_{X_1}}, \mathbf{S_{X_2}}$. Let $\mathbf{I}_m$ be a $m \times m$ identity matrix. The fitness of $\mathbf{X}_1$ to $\mathbf{S_{X_2}}$ is

$$V_{\mathbf{X}_1}^2(\mathbf{S_{X_2}}) = tr(\mathbf{S_{X_2}}^{\mathrm{T}}(\mathbf{I}_m - \mathbf{X}_1 \mathbf{X}_1^{\mathrm{T}})\mathbf{S_{X_2}}), \qquad (4)$$

The fit measure between two GOPS points is defined as

$$d_{\mathbf{X}_1}^2(\mathbf{S_{X_1}}, \mathbf{S_{X_2}}) = \frac{V_{\mathbf{X}_1}^2(\mathbf{S_{X_1}}) + V_{\mathbf{X}_1}^2(\mathbf{S_{X_2}})}{(|\mathbf{S_{X_1}}| + |\mathbf{S_{X_2}}|)^2}, \qquad (5)$$

where $|\mathbf{S}|$ provides the cardinality of $\mathbf{S}$. Since $\mathbf{S_{X_1}}$ lies in $\mathbf{X}_1$, $V_{\mathbf{X}_1}^2(\mathbf{S_{X_1}}) \approx 0$ and the fit measure actually measures the residual of $\mathbf{S_{X_2}}$ to $\mathbf{X}_1$. And $\mathbf{X}_1$ is called the reference subspace of this fit measure.

3.2   Adaptive Mode Seeking

The GOPS MS algorithm is summarized in Algorithm 1. It starts with a GOPS point $G_{\mathbf{Y}^{(1)}} = \{\mathbf{Y}^{(1)}, S_{\mathbf{Y}^{(1)}}\}$, sets $\mathbf{Y}^{(1)}$ as the reference subspace of the fit

---

Algorithm 1. Adaptive Mode Seeking

Input: A set of linear subspaces $\mathbf{X}_n, n = 1, 2, ..., N$, an observation set $\mathbf{S}$;
Output: A clustering of subspaces;
Algorithm:
for Each $\mathbf{X}_n$ **do**
   Compute observations $\mathbf{S_{X_n}}$ in $\mathbf{X}_n$ by subset selection;
   $\mathbf{Y} = \mathbf{X}_n$ and $\mathbf{S_Y} = \mathbf{S_{X_n}}$;
   repeat
      Update $\mathbf{Y}$ by fixing $\mathbf{S_Y}$ and solving Equation (7);
      Update $\mathbf{S_Y}$ using subset selection with the updated $\mathbf{Y}$;
   until $\mathbf{Y}, \mathbf{S_Y}$ changes little;
end for
Group together GOPS points sharing their modes.

---

measure (5) and computes its distances with other points $d_{GO}(G_{\mathbf{Y}^{(k)}}, G_{\mathbf{X}_n})$, $n = 1, \cdots, N$. We follow (1) and locate the next temporary mode $G_{\mathbf{Y}^{(k+1)}}$ by

$$G_{\mathbf{Y}^{(k+1)}} = \arg\min_{G_{\mathbf{Y}}} \sum_{n=1}^{N} d_{GO}^2(G_{\mathbf{Y}}, G_{\mathbf{X}_n}) w_n(G_{\mathbf{Y}^{(k)}}), \qquad (6)$$

where

$$w_n(G_{\mathbf{Y}^{(k)}}) = \psi(d_{GO}^2(G_{\mathbf{Y}^{(k)}}, G_{\mathbf{X}_n}); h).$$

The equation (6) is simplified by substituting (2) into (6) (see supplementary material), and yields

$$G_{\mathbf{Y}^{(k+1)}} = \arg\min_{G_{\mathbf{Y}}} ||\mathbf{Y}\mathbf{Y}^{\mathrm{T}} - \mathbf{C}^{(k)}||_F^2, \qquad (7)$$

where

$$\mathbf{C}^{(k)} = \sum_{n=1}^{N} w_n(G_{\mathbf{Y}^{(k)}})(c_1 \mathbf{X}_n \mathbf{X}_n^{\mathrm{T}} + c_2 [\mathbf{S}_{\mathbf{Y}} \mathbf{S}_{\mathbf{X}_n}][\mathbf{S}_{\mathbf{Y}} \mathbf{S}_{\mathbf{X}_n}]^{\mathrm{T}}). \qquad (8)$$

The notion $[\mathbf{S}_{\mathbf{Y}} \mathbf{S}_{\mathbf{X}_n}]$ stands for making a matrix by putting columns of $\mathbf{S}_{\mathbf{X}_n}$ after those of $\mathbf{S}_{\mathbf{Y}}$.

The two components of $G_{\mathbf{Y}^{(k+1)}}$ are computed by fixing one and updating the other respectively. First we fix $\mathbf{S}_{\mathbf{Y}} = \mathbf{S}_{\mathbf{Y}^{(k)}}$ in (8). Since $\mathbf{Y}\mathbf{Y}^{\mathrm{T}}$ is the closest rank-p matrix to $\mathbf{C}^{(k)}$ under Frobenius norm, following [11], we decompose $\mathbf{C}^{(k)} = \mathbf{U}\mathbf{D}\mathbf{V}^{\mathrm{T}}$ with singular value decomposition (SVD) and set $\mathbf{Y}^{(k+1)} = \mathbf{U}(:, 1:p)$ (i.e., the columns of $\mathbf{U}$ associated with the p-largest eigenvalues). The $\mathbf{S}_{\mathbf{Y}^{(k+1)}}$ is updated by performing subset selection introduced later.

The subspace $\mathbf{Y}^{(k+1)}$ is a low dimensional representation of the column space of $\mathbf{C}^{(k)}$. Since those GOPS points $G_{\mathbf{X}_n}$ close to $G_{\mathbf{Y}^{(k)}}$ have large weights in Equation (8), $\mathbf{Y}^{(k+1)}$ essentially fits to observation sets $\mathbf{S}_{\mathbf{X}_n}$ close to $\mathbf{Y}^{(k)}$. Intuitively, we use more observations roughly in $\mathbf{Y}^{(k)}$ to refine estimation of linear subspace. Therefore, $\mathbf{Y}^{(k+1)}$ is more accurate than $\mathbf{Y}^{(k)}$.

To compute the next mode $\mathbf{Y}^{(k+2)}$, we reset the fit measure's reference subspace to the temporary mode $\mathbf{Y}^{(k+1)}$ and repeat above. Since the fit measure (5) is adapted to $\mathbf{Y}^{(k+1)}$, the GOPS distance (2) is updated accordingly. To see why this adaptive distance measure improves clustering accuracy, notice that $\mathbf{Y}^{(k+1)}$ fits better than $\mathbf{Y}^{(k)}$ to observation components of GOPS points near $\mathbf{Y}^{(k)}$. The fit measure between these points becomes smaller. Therefore, those GOPS points are more close and dense as illustrated in Figure 1. This makes clustering tasks easier. We will keep on updating $G_{\mathbf{Y}^{(k+1)}}$ until there is no more change. A mode is then obtained.

3.3   Subset Selection

The observation set $\mathbf{S}_{\mathbf{Y}^{(k+1)}}$ is updated by performing subset selection with $\mathbf{Y}^{(k+1)}$. Suppose observations are generated from a model and have Gaussian noises. According to [12], a normalization of their residual to the model, called the studentized residual, follows a student's t distribution. We will apply t-tests to these residuals to find a subset of observations lying in $\mathbf{Y}^{(k+1)}$. This process is called subset selection. Before this, let us see how to compute the scalar studentized residual of a linear regression model. Given N scalar observations $\mathbf{S} \in \mathbb{R}^{1 \times N}$, N explanatory d-dimensional vectors $\mathbf{Q} \in \mathbb{R}^{p \times N}$, a Gaussian noise $\epsilon \sim N(0, \sigma^2 I)$ and a regression coefficient vector $\mathbf{X} \in \mathbb{R}^{1 \times p}$ such that $\mathbf{S} = \mathbf{XQ} + \epsilon$, the studentized residual for an observation $\mathbf{S}_{(n)}$ is defined as

$$t_{(n)} = \frac{\mathbf{S}_{(n)} - \mathbf{XQ}_{(n)}}{\hat{\sigma}_n \sqrt{(1 - \mathbf{V}_{(n,n)})}}, \tag{9}$$

where $\mathbf{S}_{(n)}$ is the n-th element of $\mathbf{S}$, $\mathbf{Q}_{(n)}$ is the n-th column of $\mathbf{Q}$, $\hat{\sigma}_n$ is the estimated variance, $\mathbf{V} = \mathbf{Q}^\mathrm{T}(\mathbf{QQ}^\mathrm{T})^{-1}\mathbf{Q}$ and $\mathbf{V}_{(n,n)}$ is the n-th diagonal element of $\mathbf{V}$.

Our model has two major differences compared with the linear regression model above. First, $\mathbf{S}_{(n)}$ is a m-dimensional vector instead of a scalar. Second, our model is a mixture model rather than a single one. Unfortunately, it is unknown if a vector residual follows a t distribution or others, and, if multi-variable tests are proper. We adapt the testing as follows. Firstly, we perform the t test for each dimension of $\mathbf{S}_{(n)}$. If any dimension of $\mathbf{S}_{(n)}$ cannot pass the test, $\mathbf{S}_{(n)}$ is rejected. Secondly, a portion of observations is utilized to estimate variances. The detail is described in Algorithm 2. To guarantee the convergence of GOPS MS, we select the largest size subset $\mathbf{S}_{\mathbf{Y}^{(k+1)}}$ from subset selection such that the cost function (7) decreases.

Algorithm 2. Subset Selection Algorithm

Input: A linear subspace $\mathbf{X} \in \mathbb{R}^{m \times p}$, observations $\mathbf{S_X} \in \mathbb{R}^{m \times N}$ in $\mathbf{X}$, and a single observation $S_{(h)} \in \mathbb{R}^m$;

Output: if $S_{(h)}$ lies in $\mathbf{X}$;

Algorithm:

Let $\mathbf{Q} = \mathbf{X}^\mathrm{T}\mathbf{S_X}$ and $Q_{(h)} = \mathbf{X}^\mathrm{T}S_{(h)}$;

Compute a residual vector $\mathbf{E} = \mathbf{S_X} - \mathbf{XQ}$ and sort the norm of each column of $\mathbf{E}$ increasingly;

Select W columns of $\mathbf{E}$ with the smallest norms;

Estimate j-th dimension's variance using these columns by $\hat{\sigma}_{(j,i)} = \frac{\sum_{i=1}^{W} \mathbf{E}_{(j,i)}}{M - p}$;

Compute a score $t_{(j,h)}$ for $S_{(h)}$'s j-th dimension by (9);

Perform the t test of $t_{(j,h)}$ with the degree of freedom $W - p - 1$ at the significance level of 5%;

If any dimension of $S_{(h)}$ fails this test, $S_{(h)}$ does not lies in $\mathbf{X}$.

---

4 Experiments

In this section, we describe experimental setup and apply the GOPS MS to problems of multi-body motion segmentation, affine shape categorization, and face clustering.

4.1 Experiments Setting

In all experiments, we construct GOPS points as follows. For each observation, we find its p nearest neighbors $\mathbf{S_X} \in \mathbb{R}^{m \times p}$ in Euclidean space. Here p is the rank of a linear subspace. Perform SVD on $\mathbf{S_X} = \bar{\mathbf{U}}\bar{\mathbf{D}}\bar{\mathbf{V}}^T$ and take $\bar{\mathbf{U}}(:, 1 : p)$ as a Grassmann point $\mathbf{X}$. The set $\mathbf{S_X}$ is taken as observations in $\mathbf{X}$. The weight c_1, c_2 in d_{GO} is set by $c_1 = 1 - \lambda$ and $c_2 = \lambda$. For all applications, we set $\lambda = 0.9$. The Epanechnikov kernel [5] is selected to compute $w_n(\cdot)$. In subset selection, we use $W = 0.1N$, where N is the number of observations.

Given the number of clusters, the proposed algorithm is compared with the Intrinsic MS [4] in terms of clustering accuracy. The clustering accuracy is measured by the missing rate, which is the ratio of the number of points incorrectly clustered to the total.

Fig. 2. (a)(b) **Results for multi-body motion segmentation** Features of the same color belong to the same group. The segmentation for these examples are 100% correct. The results are better viewed on a screen. **(c) Missing rates of multi-body motion segmentation for ten examples in [4].**

4.2 Multi-body Motion Segmentation

Multi-body motion segmentation is an essential problem for reconstructing or understanding a dynamic scene with multiple rigidly moving objects. In this task, trajectories of image features are segmented using their motion similarity without knowing the moving object number. Observations are trajectories represented by vectors in $\mathbb{R}^{2F}$, where F denotes number of frames. Under affine camera models, each motion is a 4 dimensional linear subspace in $\mathbb{R}^{2F}$ [4].

The GOPS corresponds to the Motion-Trajectory space. To compare with the Intrinsic MS, we apply the GOPS MS to the ten examples of the Hopkins155

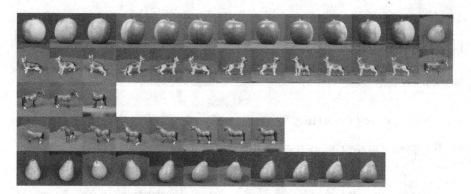

Fig. 3. Shape categorization results of GOPS MS The images in the second and third rows belong to the dog category. Images in each other row are clustered into one category.

database selected by the Intrinsic MS. Some results are shown in Figure 2 (a)(b). The comparison of the GOPS MS and the Intrinsic MS is shown in Figure 2 (c). The average missing rate of GOPS MS is 0.8% and better than that of Intrinsic MS, which is 17.9%.

4.3 Affine Shape Categorization

Shape representation and analysis play an important role in object recognition, gait recognition and image registration. Landmark based shape analysis, which represents a shape by landmark points on its contour, is a popular approach for shape representation. The affine shape space method [8] models shapes as affine transformations of a base shape. Given a base shape represented by a $m \times 2$ matrix $\mathbf{B}$, the shape space is the set $\mathbb{P} = \{\mathbf{P}|\mathbf{P} = \mathbf{B}\mathbf{A}\}$, where $\mathbf{A}$ is any 2×2 full rank matrix. Each shape space is mapped to a linear subspace spanned by $\mathbf{B}$. The study of affine shape spaces boils down to a study of the points on the Grassmann manifold.

Affine shape categorization attempts to group shapes generated from the same base shape $\mathbf{B}$ together. To perform the GOPS MS, we reformulate the affine shape space as

$$\mathbf{P} = \begin{bmatrix} \mathbf{x}\,\mathbf{y}\,0\,0 \\ 0\,0\,\mathbf{x}\,\mathbf{y} \end{bmatrix} \begin{bmatrix} A_{11}^1 & \cdots & A_{11}^N \\ A_{21}^1 & \cdots & A_{21}^N \\ A_{12}^1 & \cdots & A_{12}^N \\ A_{22}^1 & \cdots & A_{22}^N \end{bmatrix}. \tag{10}$$

Here $\mathbf{P}$ is a $2m \times N$ matrix, which includes N shapes and m landmarks for each shape. x, y are the X-coordinates and Y-coordinates of a base shape $\mathbf{B} = \begin{bmatrix} \mathbf{x}\,\mathbf{y} \end{bmatrix}$. $A_{i,j}^n$ is the element of the i-th row j-th column of an affine transformation $\mathbf{A}^n$. In this application, we use the database ETH-80 [13] as a benchmark. The database ETH-80 includes eight categories of objects. We select four categories and twelve images for each category for categorization.

We follow [14] to extract landmarks. After locating the outmost contour of every image, we take the pixel with the smallest x and y coordinate as a starting point, order the pixels on contour anti-clockwisely and sample 200 landmarks uniformly. Principal component analysis (PCA) is applied to project these shapes onto a subspace of 25 dimensions for computational efficiency. Then the GOPS MS is performed. Our results are shown in Figure 3. The missing rate of GOPS MS is 10.4%, which is better than 35.4% of the Intrinsic MS.

4.4 Face Clustering under Varying Illumination

Given a set of face images taken under varying illumination conditions, face clustering attempts to cluster these images corresponding to the same face. By assuming human faces are Lambertian objects, these images are approximately lying in a low-dimensional subspace [7]. Hence this problem can be solved by the GOPS MS.

We carry on experiments with the Yale Faces B database [15]. This database consists of photos of 10 faces taken under 9 different poses and 64 different illumination conditions. We follow [6] and select nine subsets of the ten faces as examples for clustering. For computational efficiency, these images are down sampled to 120×160 pixels and principal component analysis (PCA) is applied to further reduce each image into a 25-dimensional vector. Table 1 summarizes the missing rates for both algorithms. Compared with the Intrinsic MS algorithm, our algorithm outperforms it for all the examples.

Table 1. Missing rates for face clustering Numbers in this table refer to the missing rate (%). Each example is a combination of photos of attendees. For simplicity, we use (1,5,8) to stand for a collection of photos of NO.1, NO.5 and NO.8 attendees. These selected combinations are Id1: (5,8), Id2: (1,5,8), Id3: (1,5,8,10), Id4: (1,4,5,8,10), Id5: (1,2,4,5,8,10), Id6: (1,2,4,5,7,8,10), Id7: (1,2,4,5,7,8,9,10), Id8: (1,2,3,4,5,7,8,9,10), Id9: (1,2,3,4,5,6,7,8,9,10).

Example Id	(1)	(2)	(3)	(4)	(5)	(6)	(7)	(8)	(9)	Mean
GOPS	2.5	0	1.1	0	0.7	0.4	4.5	1.0	7.2	1.95
Intrinsic	28.4	0	18.2	24.0	38.4	20.3	19.5	30.4	31.8	23.4

5 Conclusion

In this paper, we propose a mode seeking algorithm using observations and linear subspaces to improve accuracy of clustering linear subspaces. As a mode seeking process goes on, the distance measure in use is updated by temporary modes. Distances between similar linear subspaces are decreasing with the updated measure. This facilitates our clustering task. The proposed algorithm can be applied to many computer vision problems, and we demonstrate its effectiveness for multi-body motion segmentation, shape categorization and face clustering. The experimental results show this algorithm improves the clustering accuracy significantly compared with the state-of-the-art Intrinsic MS algorithm.

References

1. Comaniciu, D., Meer, P.: Mean shift: a robust approach toward feature space analysis. IEEE Transactions on Pattern Analysis and Machine Intelligence 24, 603–619 (2002)
2. Comaniciu, D., Ramesh, V., Meer, P.: Kernel-based object tracking. IEEE Transactions on Pattern Analysis and Machine Intelligence 25, 564–577 (2003)
3. Subbarao, R., Meer, P.: Nonlinear mean shift over riemannian manifolds. International Journal of Computer Vision 84(1), 1–20 (2009)
4. Çetingül, H., Vidal, R.: Intrinsic mean shift for clustering on stiefel and grassmann manifolds. In: IEEE Conference on Computer Vision and Pattern Recognition, pp. 1896–1902 (2009)
5. Cheng, Y.: Mean shift, mode seeking, and clustering. IEEE Transactions on Pattern Analysis and Machine Intelligence 17(10), 790–799 (1995)
6. Vidal, R.: A tutorial on subspace clustering. IEEE Signal Processing Magazine (to appear)
7. Ho, J., Yang, M.H., Lim, J., Leem, K.C., Kriegman, D.: Clustering appearances of objects under varying illumination conditions. In: IEEE Conference on Computer Vision and Pattern Recognition, pp. 11–18 (2003)
8. Turaga, P., Veeraraghavan, A., Chellappa, R.: Statistical analysis on stiefel and grassmann manifolds with applications in computer vision. In: IEEE Conference on Computer Vision and Pattern Recognition, pp. 1–8 (2008)
9. Fukunaga, K., Hostetler, L.: The estimation of the gradient of a density function, with applications in pattern recognition. IEEE Transactions on Information Theory 21, 32–40 (1975)
10. Sheikh, Y., Khan, E., Kanade, T.: Mode-seeking by medoidshifts. In: IEEE International Conference on Computer Vision, pp. 1–8 (2007)
11. Absil, P.A., Mahony, R., Sepulchre, R.: Optimization algorithms on matrix manifolds. Princeton University Press (2007)
12. Cook, R.D., Weisberg, S.: Residuals and Influence in Regression. Chapman and Hall, New York (1982)
13. Leibe, B., Schiele, B.: Analyzing appearance and contour based methods for object categorization. In: IEEE Conference on Computer Vision and Pattern Recognition, vol. 2, pp. 409–415 (2003)
14. Ling, H., Jacobs, D.W.: Shape classification using the inner-distance. IEEE Transactions on Pattern Analysis and Machine Intelligence 29(2), 286–299 (2007)
15. Georghiades, A., Belhumeur, P., Kriegman, D.: From few to many: Generative models for recognition under variable pose and illumination. In: IEEE Computer Society Conference on Automatic Face and Gesture Recognition, pp. 277–284 (2000)

Constrained Clustering
with Local Constraint Propagation

Ping He*, Xiaohua Xu, and Ling Chen

Department of Computer Science, College of Information Engineering,
Yangzhou University, Yangzhou 225000, China
{angeletx,arterx,yzulchen}@gmail.com

Abstract. We consider the problem of multi-class constrained clustering given pairwise constraints, which specify the pairs of data belonging to the same or different clusters. In this paper, we present a new
constrained clustering algorithm, Local Constraint Propagation (LCP),
which can propagate the influence of each pairwise constraint to the
unconstrained data with sufficient smoothness. It not only reveals the
underlying structures of the clusters, but also integrates the influence of
all the pairwise constraints on every data point. Promising experiments
on image segmentations demonstrate the effectiveness of our method.

Keywords: constrained clustering, constraint propagation, image segmentation.

1 Introduction

Many real-world clustering applications suffer from the problem of clustering ambiguity, which refers to multiple reasonable partitions for one clustering problem.
Since each data usually contains several different semantic concepts, the clustering can be performed from different aspects or in different granularities. In
such cases, the goodness of a clustering result to a great extent depends on the
expectation of the users.

To avoid the clustering ambiguity and improve the clustering accuracy, constrained clustering provides an implicit way to indicate the user-desired contents
by specifying the pairs of data that belong to the same cluster (must-link constraints) and the pairs of data that belong to different clusters (cannot-link
constraints) [1]. A common difficulty of the existing constrained clustering algorithms is how to utilize the limited but informative pairwise constraints [2].

Generally, the various constrained clustering approaches can be classified into
two lines. The first line adapts the unsupervised methods, including k-means
[3], all-pairs shortest path [4], Gaussian mixtures models [5], Gaussian process
[6] and Spectral clustering[7][8][9][10], to satisfy the pairwise constraints in a
smaller subset of solution space with additional requirements. Among them,

---

* This research was supported in part by the NFS of China under Grant Nos. 61003180
and 61070047, NSF of Education Department of Jiangsu Province under contract
09KJB200013 and NSF of Jiangsu Province under contract BK2010318.

A. Fusiello et al. (Eds.): ECCV 2012 Ws/Demos, Part III, LNCS 7585, pp. 223–232, 2012.

some algorithms ignore the impact of the pairwise constraints on the unconstrained data, while the others either fail to handle the cannot-link constraints, or have problem in dealt with the multi-class clustering tasks.

The second line of the constrained clustering algorithms derives an appropriate metric to adjust the must-linked data close and the cannot-linked data faraway [11][12]. Its difficulty lies in how to determine the scope of the metric. Li et al. [2] learn a global metric to spread the influence of each pairwise constraint to the whole data set uniformly. However, it is contradictory to our intuition that a pairwise constraint should exert greater influence on the nearby edges than on the distant edges, just like a stone thrown into a lake. Bilenko et al. [13] suggest to learn a local metric for each cluster, and demonstrate its superiority over the global metric learned on the whole data set. Nevertheless, there are two drawbacks of this method. One is that it requires sufficient pairwise constraints to obtain a reliable estimation of the local metrics. The other is that the "one metric for one cluster" assumption may not hold true for all the data sets. A more attractive idea is to learn the influence range of each pairwise constraint adaptively without any parameter estimation.

In this paper, we propose a Local Constraint Propagation (LCP) algorithm, which propagates the influence of the pairwise constraints to the unconstrained data in proportion to their similarities with the constrained data. To this end, we first determine the degree of influence that each unconstrained object receives from the constrained objects using the label propagation technique [14]. Then an intermediate structure, called "component", is defined to include the factional data points that are affected by a constrained data point as well as itself. The advantage of introducing the components is that they not only help to find out the influence range of each pairwise constraint (i.e. the components that the pair of constrained objects belong to) without parameter estimation, but also reveal some underlying structures of the clusters. Therefore, we can easily expand the influence of the pairwise constraints by directly enforcing them on the related components. In the end, LCP combines all the influence from the different pairwise constraints into a cluster indicating matrix.

The remainder of this paper is organized as follows. We first introduce the label propagation technique in section 2, and then present our algorithm LCP in section 3. They are followed by the performance evaluation in section 4. Section 5 concludes the whole paper.

2   Label Propagation

Label propagation is a well-known transductive learning algorithm [14]. Given a data set $\mathcal{S} = (\mathcal{X}_l, \mathcal{Y}_l) \cup \mathcal{X}_u$, where $\mathcal{X}_l = \{x_1, \cdots, x_l\}$ is the labeled data subset, $\mathcal{Y}_l = \{y_1, \cdots, y_l\}$ is the label subset of $\mathcal{X}_l$, $\mathcal{X}_u = \{x_{l+1}, \cdots, x_n\}$ is the unlabeled data subset, the aim of transductive learning is to predict $\mathcal{Y}_u$, the label subset of $\mathcal{X}_u$.

Suppose such a random walk, in which each data represents a different state of a Markov chain. $\mathcal{X}_l$ is set the absorbing states, $\mathcal{X}_u$ is set the transitive states.

There are n particles starting from n different states. They move from state s_i to state s_j with probability p_{ij}. If any particle reaches one of the absorbing states, it would be trapped; otherwise, it continues moving. The random walk stops when all the particles are absorbed.

In correspondence to the partition of $\mathcal{X}_l$ and $\mathcal{X}_u$, the transition probability matrix P is organized as follow,

$$P = \begin{bmatrix} P_{ll} & P_{lu} \\ P_{ul} & P_{uu} \end{bmatrix} \tag{1}$$

where P_{ll} and P_{uu} record the transition probabilities from $\mathcal{X}_l$ and $\mathcal{X}_u$ to themselves, while P_{lu} and P_{ul} record the transition probabilities between $\mathcal{X}_l$ and $\mathcal{X}_u$. The stationary distributions of the random walk is computed by

$$\hat{Y}^{t+1} = P\hat{Y}^t \quad \text{and} \quad \hat{Y} = \hat{Y}^\infty \tag{2}$$

Each column of $\hat{Y}_{n \times l}$ records the probabilities of all the particles absorbed by a different absorbing state when arriving stationary distribution.

To solve eq. (2), $\hat{Y}$ is partitioned into two parts,

$$\hat{Y} = \begin{bmatrix} \hat{Y}_l \\ \hat{Y}_u \end{bmatrix} \tag{3}$$

$\hat{Y}_l$ is called the class indicating matrix of $\mathcal{X}_l$, while $\hat{Y}_u$ is called the class indicating matrix of $\mathcal{X}_u$. Since $\mathcal{Y}_l$ is already known, we can determine $\hat{Y}_l$ in advance: $\hat{y}_{ij} = 1$ iff $y_i = j$, otherwise, $\hat{y}_{ij} = 0$. The converged solution of $\hat{Y}_u$ can be proved

$$\hat{Y}_u = (I - P_{uu})^{-1} P_{ul} \hat{Y}_l \tag{4}$$

In the end, each data is assigned with the class label that it most probably belongs to, i.e. $y_i = \arg\max_j \hat{y}_{ij}$.

3   Local Constraint Propagation

Assume that each data is a vertex on a graph. If we view transductive learning as a vertex-constrained problem, then constrained clustering is an edge-constrained problem, which is more difficult to deal with.

In constrained clustering, an unlabeled data set $\mathcal{X}$ and a pairwise constraint set $\mathcal{C} = \{\mathcal{C}_= \cup \mathcal{C}_{\neq}\}$ are provided. $\mathcal{C}_=$ is the must-link constraint subset, and $\mathcal{C}_{\neq}$ is the cannot-link constraint subset. Both $\mathcal{X}$ and $\mathcal{C}$ are mapped onto a graph $\mathcal{G} = (\mathcal{V}, W)$, where $\mathcal{V} = \{v_1, \cdots, v_n\}$ is the vertex set, v_i corresponds to x_i, W is the similarity matrix of $\mathcal{V}$. The must-link constraint $(v_i, v_j, =) \in \mathcal{C}_=$ indicates that v_i and v_j belong to the same cluster, while the cannot-link constraint $(v_i, v_j, \neq) \in \mathcal{C}_{\neq}$ indicates that v_i and v_j belong to different clusters. The goal of constrained clustering is to partition $\mathcal{V}$ into p clusters and satisfy $\mathcal{C}$ as much as possible.

In this section, we propose a new constrained clustering algorithm, named Local Constraint Propagation (LCP), to deal with typical multi-class constrained clustering problems given must-link and/or cannot-link constraints. LCP first determines the influence range of each constrained vertex by constructing components. Then it expands the influence of the pairwise constraints by enforcing them on the components. Finally, LCP combines the influence of all the pairwise constraints into a cluster indicating matrix.

3.1 Component Construction

First of all, we propose a q/q^{-1} modification strategy on W to keep the transition probabilities of the vertex-level random walk consistent with the pairwise constraints. The modified similarity matrix is defined

$$\tilde{W} = (\tilde{w}(i,j))_{n \times n} \tag{5}$$

in which

$$\tilde{w}(i,j) = \begin{cases} w(i,j)^q & \text{if } \exists \, (v_i, v_j, =) \in \mathcal{C}_= \\ w(i,j)^{\frac{1}{q}} & \text{if } \exists \, (v_i, v_j, \neq) \in \mathcal{C}_{\neq} \\ w(i,j) & \text{otherwise} \end{cases} \tag{6}$$

Its corresponding transition probability matrix is

$$P = \tilde{D}^{-1} \tilde{W} \tag{7}$$

where $\tilde{D} = \text{diag}(\tilde{W} \mathbf{1}_n)$ is the diagonal degree matrix. The parameter $q \in (0, 1]$ in eq. (6) controls the power of the increase and the decrease of the original similarities. Since we assume that the elements of W are within the range of $(0, 1]^1$, the value of q indicates the degree of the original similarities that can be remained on the constrained edges: a larger q preserves more original similarity, while a smaller q integrates more supervision. When $q \to 0$, the q/q^{-1} strategy sets the similarities of must-linked edges with 1 and the similarities of cannot-linked edges with 0. When $q = 1$, the q/q^{-1} strategy keeps the original similarities unchanged. Compared with the existing 1/0 and reward/penalty strategies [9][10], our method has the advantage of not only avoiding the extreme modifications like 1/0, but also keeping the modified similarities within the range of $[0, 1]$.

Let $\mathcal{V}_c$ be the vertex subset constrained by the pairwise constraints,

$$\mathcal{V}_c \stackrel{\text{def}}{=} \{ v_i, v_j \mid \exists \, (v_i, v_j, =) \in \mathcal{C}_= \text{ or } (v_i, v_j, \neq) \in \mathcal{C}_{\neq} \} \tag{8}$$

$\mathcal{V}_u$ be the unconstrained vertex set,

$$\mathcal{V}_u \stackrel{\text{def}}{=} \mathcal{V} \setminus \mathcal{V}_c \tag{9}$$

We set $\mathcal{V}_c$ as the absorbing boundary of the vertex-level random walk, and the unconstrained vertices in $\mathcal{V}_u$ as the transitive states. Then label propagation is used to determine the influence of each constrained vertex on every unconstrained vertex. A $n \times |\mathcal{V}_c|$ matrix F is constructed to include the influence of

---

[1] If there exists $w(i,j) > 1$, then normalization needs to be performed in advance.

each constrained vertex exerted on all the vertices including $\mathcal{V}_c$ and $\mathcal{V}_u$. Similar to the class indicating matrix in eq. (3), F is partitioned into two parts,

$$F = \begin{bmatrix} F_c \\ F_u \end{bmatrix} \tag{10}$$

where the subscript c indicates the constrained vertex subset $\mathcal{V}_c$, while the subscript u indicates the unconstrained vertex subset $\mathcal{V}_u$. The transition probability matrix P is reorganized accordingly,

$$P = \begin{bmatrix} P_{cc} & P_{cu} \\ P_{uc} & P_{uu} \end{bmatrix} \tag{11}$$

where P_{cc}, P_{uu}, P_{cu} and P_{uc} are the transition probability sub-matrices within or between $\mathcal{V}_c$ and $\mathcal{V}_u$. Moreover, we assume that each constrained vertex is independent from the influence of the other constrained vertices, which leads to

$$F_c = F_c^0 = I \tag{12}$$

According to the converged solution in eq. (4), the propagated influence of $\mathcal{V}_c$ on $\mathcal{V}_u$ is

$$F_u = (I - P_{uu})^{-1} P_{cu} \tag{13}$$

We define an intermediate structure between the fine-grained vertex and the coarse-grained cluster, called "component", as the union of the fractional vertices affected by each constrained vertex (including itself). We call F the component indicating matrix, because the ith row of F includes the probabilities of vertex v_i belonging to the different components. Let $\mathcal{T}$ represent the set of the components, $|\mathcal{T}|$ represent the number of the components. The jth component $\mathcal{T}_j$ is composed of every vertex v_i whose degree of the component membership $f_{ij} > 0$.

$$\mathcal{T}_j = \{ f_{ij} \cdot v_i \mid f_{ij} > 0 \} \tag{14}$$

3.2 Component Clustering

Now consider a higher-level random walk on the constructed components. Suppose that $\mathcal{T}_1, \mathcal{T}_2, \cdots, \mathcal{T}_{|T|}$ respectively denote the $|\mathcal{T}|$ components. The pairwise component similarity matrix W_c is defined

$$W_c = F^T \tilde{W} F \tag{15}$$

whose element

$$\begin{aligned} w_c(\alpha, \beta) &= \sum_{i=1}^{n} \sum_{j=1}^{n} f_{i\alpha} f_{j\beta} \tilde{w}_{ij} \\ &= f_{\cdot\alpha}^T \tilde{W} f_{\cdot\beta} \end{aligned} \tag{16}$$

is the weighted sum of the pairwise vertex similarities, and the weight equals to the probability of the vertices belonging to the specified pair of components. Furthermore, we define the normalized component similarity matrix as

$$\bar{W}_c = D_c^{-\frac{1}{2}} W_c D_c^{-\frac{1}{2}} \tag{17}$$

where $D_c = \text{diag}(W_c \mathbf{1}_{|\mathcal{T}|})$ is the diagonal degree matrix of the components. It ensures that the elements of $\bar{W}_c$ are within the range of $[0, 1]$.

To expand the influence of the pairwise constraints to the unconstrained vertices, we directly enforce $\mathcal{C}$ on $\bar{W}_c$ with the q/q^{-1} modification strategy. The modified normalized component similarity matrix is

$$\tilde{W}_c = (\tilde{w}_c(\alpha, \beta))_{|\mathcal{T}| \times |\mathcal{T}|} \tag{18}$$

whose element

$$\tilde{w}_c(\alpha, \beta) = \begin{cases} \tilde{w}_c(\alpha, \beta)^q & \text{if } \exists (v^\alpha, v^\beta, =) \in \mathcal{C}_= \\ \tilde{w}_c(\alpha, \beta)^{\frac{1}{q}} & \text{if } \exists (v^\alpha, v^\beta, \neq) \in \mathcal{C}_{\neq} \\ \tilde{w}_c(\alpha, \beta) & \text{otherwise} \end{cases} \tag{19}$$

in which v^α and v^β are respectively the constrained vertices in $\mathcal{T}_\alpha$ and $\mathcal{T}_\beta$.

After the constraint propagation, the transition probability matrix of the component-level random walk becomes

$$P_c = \tilde{D}_c^{-1} \tilde{W}_c \tag{20}$$

where $\tilde{D}_c = \text{diag}(\tilde{W}_c \mathbf{1}_{|\mathcal{T}|})$. Melia et al. [15] proved that the cluster partition that minimize the transition probabilities among the different clusters is the same one as that minimize the normalized cut [16]. By using the spectral relaxation technique, we can obtain an approximately optimal solution to the normalized cut,

$$U = [u_1 \ u_2 \ \cdots \ u_p] \tag{21}$$

where $u_1, u_2, \cdots, u_p$ satisfy that

$$P_c u_i = \lambda_i u_i \tag{22}$$

λ_i is the ith maximal eigenvalue of P_c. We call U the cluster indicating matrix of the components, because the ith row of U contains the cluster membership of the ith component.

Finally, the influence of all the pairwise constraints propagated through different components is combined on every single vertex. We multiply the component indicating matrix of the vertices ($F_{n \times |\mathcal{T}|}$) and the cluster indicating matrix of the components ($U_{|\mathcal{T}| \times p}$), to get the cluster indicating matrix of the vertices.

$$G_{n \times p} = FU \tag{23}$$

The cluster assignment of each vertex is obtained by projecting the row vectors of U onto a unit hypersphere [17],

$$\tilde{G} = \text{diag}(\text{diag}(GG^T))^{-\frac{1}{2}} G \tag{24}$$

and then applying k-means algorithm on it.

4   Experiments

In this section, we evaluate the clustering performance of Local Constraint Propagation (LCP) algorithm in comparison with three most related spectral constrained clustering algorithms, including Spectral Learning (SL) [9], SS-Kernel-Kmeans (SSKK) [10], and Constrained Clustering with Spectral Regularization (CCSR) [2] on image segmentations.

Among the three compared algorithms, SL replaces the similarities of the must-linked vertices with 1 and the similarities of the cannot-linked vertices with 0, followed by the spectral clustering performed on the modified similarity matrix. SSKK has a similar paradigm of SL. Its main difference from SL is that it adds a reward to the similarities of the must-linked vertices and subtracts a penalty from the similarities of the cannot-linked vertices. CCSR transforms all the data into the spectral space, and learns a global metric that makes the similarity matrix most consistent with the pairwise constraints using semi-definite optimization.

All the four constrained clustering algorithms are implemented in Matlab. Each of them is provided with the same graphs. The similarity of each pair of pixels is measured by the magnitude of their intervening contours [16],

$$w_{ij} = e^{-\max_{x \in \text{line}(i,j)} \|\text{edge}(\mathrm{x})\|^2 / \sigma_e}, \tag{25}$$

where $\text{line}(i, j)$ is a straight line that connects the ith and j^{th} pixels, $\text{edge}(x)$ is the magnitude of the intervening contour at location x, σ_e is set one tenth of the maximal edge magnitude on graph. To ensure the sparsity of the similarity matrices, we only allow each pixel to connect with its neighboring pixels within a circle of radius $r = 10$.

In the implementation of our LCP algorithm, we infer the transitive closure of the pairwise constraints to replace the original $\mathcal{C}$ for information utilization[3]. The parameter q of the q/q^{-1} similarity modification strategy is set 0.01. Due to the large number of pixels in images, it is inefficient to compute the component indicating submatrix F_u with the converged solution (eq. (13)), whose time complexity is $O((n - |\mathcal{T}|)^3)$. To overcome this shortcoming, we adopt a more time-saving approach, i.e. compute F_u with the state transition equation $F_u^{t+1} = P_{uc}F_c^t + P_{uu}F_u^t$ (derived from $F^{t+1} = PF^t$) iteratively. Since the sparse transition probability matrix has at most r^2 non-zeros elements in each row, and the number of the constrained pixels ($|\mathcal{T}|$) is negligible compared with the number of all the pixels (n), it can be proved that the time complexity of the iterative computation of F_u is approximately $O(n)$.

4.1   Experimental Results

We select five natural color images from the Berkeley Segmentation Database [18] and scale them to 170×113 pixels. Different pairwise constraints are provided to bias the extraction target towards the various desired contents (see the first column in Fig. 1). The first three tasks respectively aim to localize the worm,

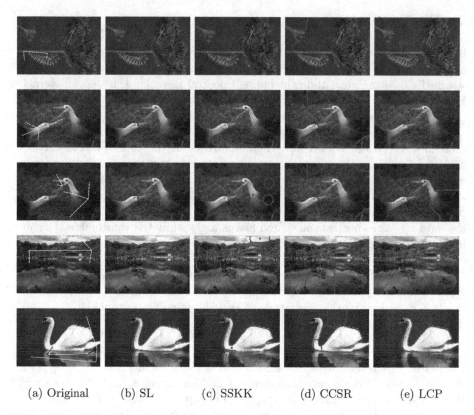

(a) Original   (b) SL   (c) SSKK   (d) CCSR   (e) LCP

Fig. 1. Segmentation results on image segmentations given both must-link (solid lines) and cannot-link (dashed lines) constraints

the left bird and the right bird from the same input image, while the last two images try to differentiate the sky, the trees, the house and the swan from their reflections in the lake and the background.

Fig. 1 compares the segmentation results of the constrained clustering algorithms. LCP is demonstrated superior to the other methods by producing the exact segmentation results indicated by the pairwise constraints. We explain its success through the components constructed around the constrained vertices illustrated in Fig. 2. In each subfigure of Fig. 2, a light is placed on the constrained vertex to illuminate the unconstrained vertices in proportion to their probabilities of belonging to the same component. Since each image is composed of several local image elements corresponding to different contents or subjects, the components constructed by LCP are the ideal approximations of the image elements, if not their fragments. The automatic recognition of the local image elements, combined with the enforcement of the pairwise constraints on the elements, reduces the complex constrained image segmentations to the simple clustering of the limited number of image elements.

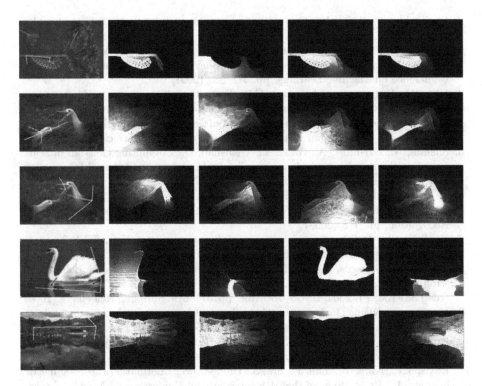

Fig. 2. The components constructed around the constrained vertices by LCP (Because of the different numbers of the constrained vertices in Fig. 1, we only select part of the components for illustration.). The brighter a pixel, the higher the probability it belongs to the component.

5   Conclusion

A new constrained clustering algorithm named Local Constraint Propagation is proposed and demonstrated. Compared with the previous methods, our approach is featured in the following aspects. (1) LCP adaptively determine the influence range of each constrained vertex, called "component", which not only provides valuable insight to the underlying structures of the clusters, but also enables the enforcement of the pairwise constraints on a wider range. (2) LCP expands the influence of the pairwise constraints within the components locally and proportionally, instead of spreading them to the whole data set globally and uniformly. (3) LCP requires no estimation of the global or local metrics during the constraint propagation.

References

1. Basu, S., Davidson, I., Wagstaff, K.L.: Constrained Clustering: Advances in Algorithms, Theory, and Applications. Chapman and Hall/CRC (2008)

2. Li, Z., Liu, J., Tang, X.: Constrained clustering via spectral regularization. In: Proceeding of Computer Vision and Pattern Recognition 2009, pp. 421–428 (2009)
3. Wagstaff, K., Cardie, C., Rogers, S., Schroedl, S.: Constrained k-means clustering with background knowledge. In: Proceedings of the Eighteenth International Conference on Machine Learning, pp. 577–584 (2001)
4. Klein, D., Kamvar, S.D., Manning, C.D.: From instance-level constraints to space-level constraints: Making the most of prior knowledge in data clustering. In: Proceedings of the Nineteenth International Conference on Machine Learning, ICML 2002, pp. 307–314. Morgan Kaufmann Publishers Inc., San Francisco (2002)
5. Shental, N., Bar-hillel, A., Hertz, T., Weinshall, D.: Computing gaussian mixture models with em using equivalence constraints. In: Advances in Neural Information Processing Systems, vol. 16, pp. 465–472. MIT Press (2003)
6. Lu, Z., Carreira-Perpinan, M.: Constrained spectral clustering through affinity propagation. In: Proceedings of IEEE Conference on Computer Vision and Pattern Recognition, pp. 1–8 (2008)
7. Yu, S.X., Shi, J.: Segmentation given partial grouping constraints. IEEE Transactions on Pattern Analysis and Machine Intelligence 26, 173–180 (2004)
8. De Bie, T., Suykens, J.A.K., De Moor, B.: Learning from General Label Constraints. In: Fred, A., Caelli, T.M., Duin, R.P.W., Campilho, A.C., de Ridder, D. (eds.) SSPR&SPR 2004. LNCS, vol. 3138, pp. 671–679. Springer, Heidelberg (2004)
9. Kamvar, S., Klein, D., Manning, C.D.: Spectral learning. In: International Joint Conference on Artificial Intelligence 2003, pp. 561–566 (2003)
10. Kulis, B., Basu, S., Dhillon, I., Mooney, R.: Semi-supervised graph clustering: A kernel approach. Machine Learning 74, 1–22 (2009)
11. Davis, J.V., Kulis, B., Jain, P., Sra, S., Dhillon, I.S.: Information-theoretic metric learning. In: Proceedings of the 24th International Conference on Machine Learning, ICML 2007, pp. 209–216. ACM, New York (2007)
12. Liu, W., Ma, S., Tao, D., Liu, J., Liu, P.: Semi-supervised sparse metric learning using alternating linearization optimization. In: Proceedings of the 16th ACM SIGKDD International Conference on Knowledge Discovery and Data Mining, KDD 2010, pp. 1139–1148. ACM, New York (2010)
13. Bilenko, M., Basu, S., Mooney, R.: Integrating constraints and metric learning in semi-supervised clustering. In: Proceeding of 21st International Conference on Machine Learning, Banff, Canada, pp. 81–88 (2004)
14. Zhu, X., Ghahramani, Z., Lafferty, J.: Semi-supervised learning using gaussian fields and harmonic functions. In: The 20th International Conference on Machine Learning, ICML, pp. 912–919 (2003)
15. Meila, M., Shi, J.: A random walks view of spectral segmentation. In: Proceeding of International Workshop on AI and, Statistics, AISTATS, pp. 873–879 (2001)
16. Shi, J., Malik, J.: Normalized cuts and image segmentation. IEEE Transactions on Pattern Analysis and Machine Intelligence, PAMI (2000)
17. Ng, A., Jordan, M., Weiss, Y.: On spectral clustering: Analysis and an algorithm. In: Advances in Neural Information Processing Systems, vol. 14, pp. 849–856. MIT Press (2001)
18. Martin, D., Fowlkes, C., Tal, D., Malik, J.: A database of human segmented natural images and its application to evaluating segmentation algorithms and measuring ecological statistics. In: ICCV (2001)

Occlusion Handling in Video Segmentation via Predictive Feedback

Jeremie Papon, Alexey Abramov, and Florentin Wörgötter

Bernstein Center for Computational Neuroscience (BCCN)
III Physikalisches Institut - Biophysik, Georg-August University of Göttingen

Abstract. We present a method for unsupervised on-line dense video segmentation which utilizes sequential Bayesian estimation techniques to resolve partial and full occlusions. Consistent labeling through occlusions is vital for applications which move from low-level object labels to high-level semantic knowledge - tasks such as activity recognition or robot control. The proposed method forms a predictive loop between segmentation and tracking, with tracking predictions used to seed the segmentation kernel, and segmentation results used to update tracked models. All segmented labels are tracked, without the use of a-priori models, using parallel color-histogram particle filters. Predictions are combined into a probabilistic representation of image labels, a realization of which is used to seed segmentation. A simulated annealing relaxation process allows the realization to converge to a minimal energy segmented image. Found segments are subsequently used to repopulate the particle sets, closing the loop. Results on the Cranfield benchmark sequence demonstrate that the prediction mechanism allows on-line segmentation to maintain temporally consistent labels through partial & full occlusions, significant appearance changes, and rapid erratic movements. Additionally, we show that tracking performance matches state-of-the art tracking methods on several challenging benchmark sequences.

1 Introduction

Unsupervised image segmentation attempts to cluster pixels into regions which represent the objects present in an image frame without human intervention. Unsupervised video object segmentation (VOS) extends this idea by linking pixels in time as well as space, to generate spatio-temporal clusters. Unfortunately, the addition of the temporal domain brings new challenges; pixels which should be grouped across time may not be continuously visible from frame to frame, as in the case of partial or full occlusions.

To overcome this, we use a novel predictive feedback mechanism which combines Bayesian tracking and VOS to preserve object labels. In this feedback mechanism, multiple particle filters in parallel track object labels, generating a prediction for segmentation, which relaxes this prediction to match the current scene. The relaxed segmentation result is then used to update the particle filters. This loop permits permanence of arbitrary objects through full occlusions.

A. Fusiello et al. (Eds.): ECCV 2012 Ws/Demos, Part III, LNCS 7585, pp. 233–242, 2012.

There are many existing video object segmentation (VOS) methods, but we shall only review here methods which meet three criteria; on-line (the algorithm may only use past data), dense (every pixel is assigned to a spatio-temporal cluster), and unsupervised. Several state-of-the-art segmentation algorithms meet these requirements: Multiple hypothesis video segmentation (MHVS) from superpixel flows [1], Propagation, validation, and aggregation (PVA) of a preceding graph [2], and Matching images under unstable segmentations [3]. Of these methods, none are able to handle full occlusions; in fact only MHVS considers occlusions, and it is only able to handle partial occlusions for a few frames, and does not consider full occlusions. Even state of the art off-line methods such as that of Brendel and Todorovic [4] only handle partial occlusions, claiming that "complete occlusions ... require higher-level reasoning".

Bayesian predictive filters (such as Particle filters) are a broad, well-established field in target tracking [5]. While effective for tracking, these methods generally depend on fixed models with a small dimensional state-space, and are unable to deal with the high-dimensionality of VOS. A recent method [6] uses graph cuts to extract segmentations, and a dynamical model to form predictions which guide successive segmentations. It formally models visible and occluded parts of the tracked objects, and so does not scale well with an increasing number of objects, and thus is better suited to extracting the silhouettes of a few objects than performing a full segmentation. Other methods, such as [7], are limited in that they require pre-computed models which are calibrated to a ground plane in order to resolve occlusions.

The paper is organized as follows. Section 2 presents the proposed algorithm; Section 2.1 gives an overview of the segmentation kernel used, and Section 2.2 discusses the predictive framework. Section 3 consists of experimental results in a specific scenario and comparison to state of the art tracking methods. Finally, Section 4 describes current limitations of the algorithm, discusses future work, and concludes.

2 Proposed Algorithm

We shall first give an overview of the algorithm (depicted in Figure 1). To begin, segmentation is performed on the first frame F_{t_0} to generate an initial set of labels S_{t_0}. This is used to generate initial sets of particles, each of which contains a map of an object. Color histogram features are then generated for each object (as in [8]) and particles are initialized with randomly distributed initial velocities. Thus each object k at initial time t_0 from the segmentation is specified by a set of N_k particles $X_{t_0}^{k,1:N_k}$, each of which contains a representation of the object, specified by a pixel existence map M, a reference color histogram $\hat{q}$ calculated from $F_{t_0} \cap M_{t_0}^{k,n}$, a position shift vector p_{t_0}, and a velocity vector v_{t_0}.

Particles are then propagated in time independently, shifting their existence maps to new regions of the image. These shifted maps are used to generate new measured color histograms q_{t_0+1}, which are evaluated to determine particle weights. The set of particles for object k, $X_{t_0+1}^{k,1:N_k}$, is then combined to create

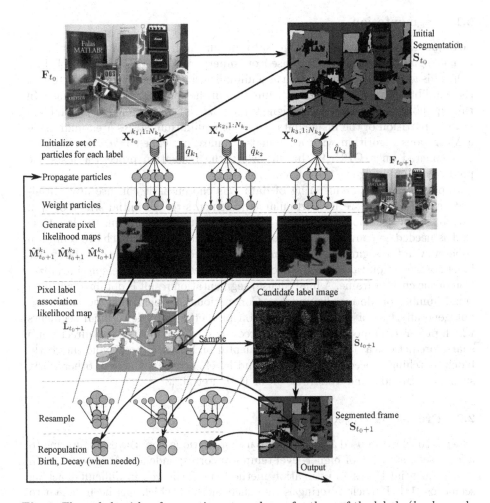

Fig. 1. Flow of algorithm for one time step, shown for three of the labels (k_1, k_2, and k_3). For description see Section 2.

an overall object pixel likelihood map $\hat{\mathbf{M}}_{t_0+1}^{k}$. The pixel likelihood maps for all objects are then used to generate a label association likelihood map $\hat{\mathbf{L}}_{t_0+1}$, where each pixel in the map is a PDF specifying the probability of the pixel belonging to each object k.

The label association likelihood map is then sampled using a per-pixel selection procedure (as described in Section 2.2) to generate a candidate label image, $\tilde{\mathbf{S}}_{t_0+1}$. This is used as the initialization for the Metropolis-Hastings algorithm with annealing of Abramov et al. [9], which updates the labels iteratively until an equilibrium segmented state is reached. The segmentation result, $\mathbf{S}_{t_0+1}$ is subsequently used to update the set of particles via three mechanisms; birth, decay, and repopulation, which are described in Section 2.2.

2.1 Segmentation

To adjust the candidate label image $\tilde{\mathbf{S}}_t$ to the current frame $\mathbf{F}_t$, we use a real-time image segmentation algorithm based on superparamagnetic clustering of data [10]. This formulates segmentation as a minimization problem which seeks to find the equilibrium states of the energy function in the superparamagnetic phase. In this equilibrium state regions of aligned spins (labels) coexist and correspond to a natural partition of the image data [10]. The equilibrium states are found using a Metropolis algorithm with a simulated annealing, called *relaxation process*, implemented on a GPU [9]. In this work, the relaxation process adjusts the predicted label image to the current frame.

Superparamagnetic clustering of data was chosen as it can use any initialization state; there are no particular requirements to the initial states of spin variables, and the closer the initial states are to the equilibrium, the less time that is needed to converge. This property makes it possible to achieve temporal coherency in the segmentation of temporally adjacent frames by using the sparse label configuration taken from the candidate label image for the spin initialization of the current frame. A final (dense) segmentation result is obtained within a small number of Metropolis updates. Conventional segmentation methods cannot generally turn a sparse segmentation prediction into dense final segments which preserve temporal coherence. Moreover, since the method can directly use sparse predictions as the seed of the segmentation kernel, we can avoid the costly block-matching procedure required to find label correspondences in other work, such as in Brendel and Todorovic [4] or Hedau et al. [3].

2.2 Predicting Object Labels

The goal of the proposed algorithm is to use predictions from Bayesian filtering to inform segmentation of higher-level temporal correspondences. It is well known that sequential Bayesian estimation methods perform well in difficult tracking scenarios [11]. Particle filtering is one such method which has been shown to approximate the optimal tracking solution well, even in complex multi-target scenarios with strong nonlinearities [5]. In this section we describe how particle filtering can be used to predict pixel associations in order to seed segmentation labels.

Parallel Particle Filters. The predictive portion of the method uses multiple Sequential Importance Resampling (SIR) filters in parallel to track multiple objects simultaneously. Objects are assumed independent and interaction between labels is not considered within the filters. Particles are first propagated using a constant velocity dynamic model, and their predicted existence maps $\tilde{\mathbf{M}}^{k,n}$ are used to generate a measured histogram, q_t. Particles are weighted based on the Bhattacharyya distance between the reference histogram $\hat{q}$ for the particle and the measured histogram q_t, and then normalized as a set for each label k. Systematic resampling is used to prevent particle degeneracy, due to its speed and good empirical performance [11].

The resulting distributions from the weighting procedure are used to generate object pixel likelihood maps for each label, $\hat{\mathbf{M}}_{t+1}^k$, which are then combined into the label association likelihood map $\hat{\mathbf{L}}_t$ (as described in the next sections), which can then be relaxed to produce a final segmented output, $\mathbf{S}_t$.

Label Image Generation. The middle portion of Figure 1 depicts how the candidate label image, $\tilde{\mathbf{S}}_t$, is generated. The candidate label image is a summary of the accumulated knowledge of the particle filters; it is a prediction of what the segmented scene should look like. That is to say, it is a pixel-wise realization of the label association likelihood map $\hat{\mathbf{L}}_t$, which is constructed by combining the object pixel likelihood maps $\hat{\mathbf{M}}_t^k$ (which approximate the posteriors of the particle sets). $\tilde{\mathbf{S}}_t$ is the seed of the segmentation kernel, which uses pixel values from $\mathbf{F}_t$ to perform the relaxation process and generate a dense label image.

Object Pixel Likelihood Maps. The object pixel likelihood map for a particular object k is the weighted sum of the pixel existence maps of all of its labels,

$$\hat{\mathbf{M}}_t^k = \sum_{n=1}^{N_k} w_t^{k,n} \mathbf{M}^{k,n}. \tag{1}$$

Because the weights have been normalized, the pixel values in $\hat{\mathbf{M}}_t^k$ will be in the range $[0, 1]$. High pixel values will occur in regions which are present in the existence maps of highly weighted particles, or alternatively, are present in many particles with average weight.

Label Association Likelihood Map. The label association likelihood map $\hat{\mathbf{L}}_t$ is a combination of all the object pixel likelihood maps, such that each pixel contains a discrete probability distribution giving the likelihood of the pixel belonging to a certain label. Additionally, a likelihood, p_0, for the pixel belonging to no label is inserted to allow pixels where no label has high likelihood to remain unlabeled in $\tilde{\mathbf{S}}_t$. More formally,

$$\hat{\mathbf{L}}_t = \bigcup_{n=1}^K \hat{\mathbf{M}}_t^n + p_0. \tag{2}$$

Each pixel of $\hat{\mathbf{L}}_t$ is then normalized, such that the sum of the discrete probabilities sums to one. The candidate label image can then be generated by taking a realization of $\hat{\mathbf{L}}_t$ to select pixel label values. An example of the result of this process, $\tilde{\mathbf{S}}_t$, can be seen in Figure 1.

Particle Birth, Repopulation, and Decay. A key feature of the method is use of segmentation results $\mathbf{S}_t$ to update the particle sets. This allows the creation of new object labels, adaptation to changing object appearance, and elimination of objects which are no longer observed. This is accomplished via three mechanisms; birth, repopulation, and decay.

Birth occurs when a label which has not existed previously is found in the segmentation output S_t. It consists of generating a set of particles X^k for the new label using S_t to initialize an existence map M_t^k and $\{F_t \cap M_t^k\}$ to calculate a reference color histogram $\hat{q}_t^k$. Decay occurs when a label is not found in the segmentation output, $k \notin S_t$. Particles are selected from k using random sampling, at a rate determined by the decay rate λ_d, and are pruned; they are no longer considered when filtering k. If the number of active particles for a label falls below a certain threshold, N_{min}, then the set of particles for the label is deleted, and the object is no longer tracked.

Repopulation allows the pixel likelihood map for an object, $\hat{M}^k$, to adapt over time to the changing appearance of the object. Every iteration, all previously existing object labels which are found in S_t are repopulated by replacing some particles in the set with particles generated from S_t and F_t. Particles are chosen for replacement using stratified sampling, at a rate specified by parameter λ_r. The repopulation mechanism gradually modifies the object "model" through the addition of particles which have an updated existence map and color histogram (coming from the segmentation result). Note that there is no explicit model for the objects shape, only a pixel likelihood map generated at each time step by weighting an objects constituent particles using the current image frame.

Occlusion Handling. Occlusion relationships are handled naturally, since foreground objects will tend to have a strong peak in their weight distribution, corresponding to those particles which align properly with F_t. Objects they occlude will have a flat particle weight distribution, since there will exist no shifted existence map which contains a color distribution which matches the reference histogram exactly. This is due to the fact that the occluding objects and objects surrounding the occluded object have color distributions which differ from the occluded object. Let us assume foreground object j is contained by occluded object k, that is

$$M_t^{j,n} \subset M_t^{k,n}. \tag{3}$$

We also assume that the number of particles is sufficiently large such that

$$\exists\, M_t^{j,n} \in M_t^j : hist(F_t \cap M_t^{j,n}) \approx \hat{q}^{j,n}. \tag{4}$$

If the objects have different color distributions then from (3) and (4)

$$\nexists\, M_t^{k,n} \in M_t^k : hist(F_t \cap M_t^{k,n}) \approx \hat{q}^{k,n} \tag{5}$$

therefore

$$min_{1:N_j}\{\Delta(\hat{q}^{j,n}, hist(F_t \cap M_t^{j,n}))\} <$$
$$min_{1:N_k}\{\Delta(\hat{q}^{k,n}, hist(F_t \cap M_t^{k,n}))\} \tag{6}$$

and thus

$$max_{1:N_j}\{w_t^{j,n}\} > max_{1:N_k}\{w_t^{k,n}\}. \tag{7}$$

This means that in the label association likelihood map $\hat{\mathbf{L}}_t$, the occluding object will have a higher likelihood then the occluded. The candidate label image, $\tilde{\mathbf{S}}_t$ will therefore tend to favor occluding object labels, which will dominate the occluded object label during the segmentation relaxation process.

3 Experimental Results

In order to evaluate performance, we demonstrate occlusion-handling in the context of the Cranfield benchmark, a test scenario used in robotics research to evaluate ability to plan and execute goals. The benchmark consists of building a "widget" consisting of several simple parts such as pegs. In this work, we segment a recording of a human constructing the Cranfield benchmark in order to demonstrate the ability to distill meaningful semantic information from object labels. We emphasize meaningful because the recording contains many occlusions, which cause all other state-of-the-art VOS methods to lose track of labels, spoiling the semantic information contained in the segmentation result (for instance, if a peg changes label when occluded by a hand). In all tests, we employ no learned or a-priori specified models and use 100 particles per label (this runs at 10fps at 640x480 with a GPU implementation).

Figure 2 (see supplementary material for full video) shows the ability of the algorithm to handle full and partial occlusions in the Cranfield sequence. Objects which are temporarily occluded by the hand regain their original labels once they are no longer occluded. Additionally, as objects deform (for instance, as a peg is rotated), tracking successfully maintains their correct labels, while segmentation and repopulation adapt the masks to their changing appearance.

The visual quality of segmentation results are not evaluated here as they have been presented in [9]. Additionally, we do not evaluate other VOS methods, as it is clearly stated in the literature that they fail under partial [2] and full [4,1] occlusions (see supplementary material for an example). Instead, we evaluate the algorithm from a pure tracking standpoint, as these methods are currently able to cope with full occlusions. We compare to the state of the art on several challenging video tracking benchmark sequences which are available online[1]. Results are compared to PROST [12], MilTrack [13], FragTrack [14], and ORF [15]. Details concerning the parameters used for the above algorithms in the benchmarking can be found in [12].

In order to compare with the other methods, we needed to output a tracking rectangle for each frame - we simply used the bounding box of the tracked label. This was compared to ground-truth using two measures; Euclidean distance and the PASCAL-challenge based score proposed in [12]. The latter compares the area of intersection of the ground truth and tracked box with the union of the same. When this is greater than 0.5, the object is considered successfully tracked. Table 1 gives our results and the results for the other methods.

---

[1] http://gpu4vision.icg.tugraz.at/index.php?content=subsites/ prost/prost.php

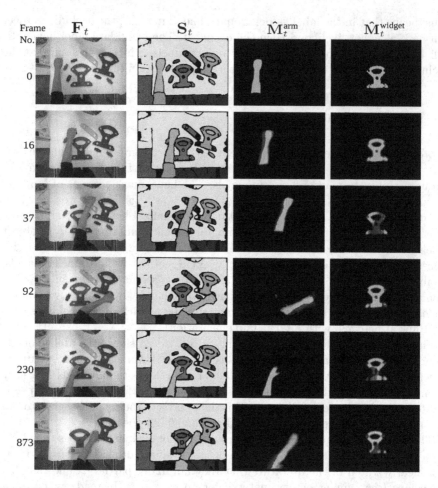

Fig. 2. Output frames from the *Cranfield* sequence, in which objects are completely occluded by an arm, and change in appearance when manipulated. Labels are clearly maintained through partial and full occlusions, as well as through manipulations and changes in appearance. F_t-Original frames. S_t-Segmentation output. $\hat{M}_t^{arm}$ & $\hat{M}_t^{widget}$-Object pixel likelihood maps for the arm and widget base plate labels. Intensity represents the sum of the normalized weights of the set of particles.

Table 1. PROST dataset benchmark results. Numbers given are average pixel error (APE) and PASCAL scores, given as APE | PASCAL

Sequence	PROST	MIL	Frag	ORF	Segmenting-PF
Lemming	25.1 | 70.5	14.9 | 83.6	82.8 | 54.9	166.3 | 17.2	19.8 | 73.9
Box	13.0 | 90.6	104.6 | 24.5	57.4 | 61.4	145.4 | 28.3	114.1 | 7.5
Liquor	21.5 | 85.4	165.1 | 20.6	30.7 | 79.9	67.3 | 53.6	25.5 | 54.2
Board	39.0 | 75.0	51.2 | 67.9	90.1 | 67.9	154.5 | 10.0	30.9 | 71.4

Testing showed that, when certain assumptions hold, our algorithm performs on par with, and in some cases outperforms, state of the art tracking algorithms. This is the case for the *liquor*, *lemming*, and *board* sequences. In the *lemming* sequence (shown in supplementary material), our algorithm outperforms the other methods in cases of occlusion, especially when the tracked object is fully occluded. While other methods offer false positives and erroneous tracks, our method decays the label for the object and avoids proposing incorrect tracking solutions. In addition to showing the strengths of our method, a weakness was also highlighted by the benchmark sequences. The *box* sequence demonstrated the limitations of using unsupervised color-based segmentation to initialize the objects to track. In the sequence, the object to track contains strong color differences, which are segmented into different initial regions. As the object moves around, the particles for these regions are attracted to other objects it passes over which have similar color. This will be addressed in future work, which will use a measurement model more heavily weighted on geometric information rather than color.

4   Conclusion

This paper presented a method for performing on-line, dense, unsupervised video segmentation which uses feedback to handle occlusions. Results showed that the method is able to resolve occlusion relations between objects without explicitly modeling them, and by doing so can maintain consistent labels for objects, even through partial or full occlusions. Additionally, the method is able to adapt to rapidly changing appearance of tracked objects, producing consistent segmentations over lengthy video sequences. The combination of these in an unsupervised online algorithm enables new robotics research, as it allows extraction of semantic information directly from segmented labels. This semantic information (how objects interact with eachother) could be used to bootstrap unsupervised learning algorithms and generate plans for complex tasks - such as building the Cranfield benchmark.

Future work will address the limitations of the measurement model by the addition of geometric features extracted from point cloud data. Additionally, movement of labels while occluded is an area of open research; currently, the algorithm will diffuse particles following the most recent velocity vector (before occlusion), and does not associate occluded particles with the motion of the occluder. Finally, we should note that this work shows the need for a standardized video benchmark which evaluates segmentation performance in complex scenarios (such as movement while occluded). In particular, the community needs to select a set of complex scenarios, and come to a consensus as to what constitutes "correct" labeling of them.

Acknowledgments. The research leading to these results has received funding from the European Community's Seventh Framework Programme FP7/2007-2013 (Specific Programme Cooperation, Theme 3, Information and Communication Technologies) under grant agreement no. 270273, Xperience and grant agreement no. 269959, Intellact.

References

1. Vazquez-Reina, A., Avidan, S., Pfister, H., Miller, E.: Multiple Hypothesis Video Segmentation from Superpixel Flows. In: Daniilidis, K., Maragos, P., Paragios, N. (eds.) ECCV 2010, Part V. LNCS, vol. 6315, pp. 268–281. Springer, Heidelberg (2010)
2. Liu, S., Dong, G., Yan, C.H., Ong, S.H.: Video segmentation: Propagation, validation and aggregation of a preceding graph. In: IEEE Conference on Computer Vision and Pattern Recognition, CVPR (2008)
3. Hedau, V., Arora, H., Ahuja, N.: Matching images under unstable segmentations. In: IEEE Conference on Computer Vision and Pattern Recognition, CVPR (2008)
4. Brendel, W., Todorovic, S.: Video object segmentation by tracking regions. In: IEEE International Conference on Computer Vision, ICCV (2009)
5. Vermaak, J., Godsill, S., Perez, P.: Monte carlo filtering for multi target tracking and data association. IEEE Transactions on Aerospace and Electronic Systems 41, 309–332 (2005)
6. Papadakis, N., Bugeau, A.: Tracking with occlusions via graph cuts. IEEE Transactions on Pattern Analysis and Machine Intelligence 33, 144–157 (2011)
7. Ablavsky, V., Thangali, A., Sclaroff, S.: Layered graphical models for tracking partially-occluded objects. In: IEEE Conference on Computer Vision and Pattern Recognition, CVPR (2008)
8. Pérez, P., Hue, C., Vermaak, J., Gangnet, M.: Color-Based Probabilistic Tracking. In: Heyden, A., Sparr, G., Nielsen, M., Johansen, P. (eds.) ECCV 2002, Part I. LNCS, vol. 2350, pp. 661–675. Springer, Heidelberg (2002)
9. Abramov, A., Pauwels, K., Papon, J., Wörgötter, F., Dellen, B.: Real-time segmentation of stereo videos on a portable system with a mobile gpu. IEEE Transactions on Circuits and Systems for Video Technology (in press)
10. Blatt, M., Wiseman, S., Domany, E.: Superparamagnetic clustering of data. Physical Review Letters 76, 3251–3254 (1996)
11. Doucet, A., De Freitas, N., Gordon, N. (eds.): Sequential Monte Carlo methods in practice (2001)
12. Santner, J., Leistner, C., Saffari, A., Pock, T., Bischof, H.: Prost: Parallel robust online simple tracking. In: IEEE Conference on Computer Vision and Pattern Recognition, CVPR (2010)
13. Babenko, B., Yang, M.H., Belongie, S.: Visual tracking with online multiple instance learning. In: IEEE Conference on Computer Vision and Pattern Recognition, CVPR (2009)
14. Adam, A., Rivlin, E., Shimshoni, I.: Robust fragments-based tracking using the integral histogram. In: IEEE Conference on Computer Vision and Pattern Recognition, CVPR (2006)
15. Saffari, A., Leistner, C., Santner, J., Godec, M., Bischof, H.: On-line random forests. In: IEEE International Conference on Computer Vision Workshops, ICCV Workshops (2009)

Collective Activity Localization
with Contextual Spatial Pyramid

Shigeyuki Odashima, Masamichi Shimosaka, Takuhiro Kaneko,
Rui Fukui, and Tomomasa Sato

The University of Tokyo, Tokyo, Japan
{odashima,simosaka,kaneko,fukui,tsato}@ics.t.u-tokyo.ac.jp

Abstract. In this paper, we propose an activity localization method
with contextual information of person relationships. Activity localization is a task to determine "who participates to an activity group", such
as detecting "walking in a group" or "talking in a group". Usage of
contextual information has been providing promising results in the previous activity recognition methods, however, the contextual information
has been limited to the local information extracted from one person
or only two people relationship. We propose a new context descriptor
named "contextual spatial pyramid model (CSPM)", which represents
the global relationships extracted from the whole of activities in single
images. CSPM encodes useful relationships for activity localization, such
as "facing each other". The experimental result shows CSPM improve
activity localization performance, therefore CSPM provides strong contextual cues for activity recognition in complex scenes.

1 Introduction

Recognizing human activities from images has been a challenging task. Since
the most of traditional vision-based human activity recognition works have been
focused on single-person activities (e.g. [1, 2]) , several recent works [3–7] are
tackling for activities with multiple-people interactions (called "collective activity"). The collective activities are such as "crossing the road", "queuing" and so
on. The most of the former works have focused on image/video sequence classification task [4, 7], which determines the particular image or video sequence
contains the activity or not, and several works focus on activity classification
task on each person [3–6]. However, the former works do not handle "who participates in the same activity group", such as "talking in two groups" (Figure
1(a)). The task of "detecting and localizing collective activities" is able to be
formulated as a form similar to the object localization tasks [8,9]. In this paper,
we focus on the collective activity localization.

Collective activity recognition (including collective activity classification and
localization) is difficult because sometimes people in different activity have
similar appearance (Figure 1(b)). Therefore, the most of former approaches use
contextual information. The former works can be categorized into following two
approaches: by unary relationships [3,4,6,7] and by pairwise relationships [4,5,10]
(Figure 2(a)). Unary relationships are information extracted from the near region

A. Fusiello et al. (Eds.): ECCV 2012 Ws/Demos, Part III, LNCS 7585, pp. 243–252, 2012.

Fig. 1. Collective activity localization. (a) Examples of activity groups. Though individual activity are the same, people belong to different groups (left: two walking groups, right: two talking groups). Activity localization is a task to determine these activity groups. (b) Difficulty of collective activity recognition. Though "queuing" activity and "talking" activity are different activity, people in these activities look similar if you see individual people.

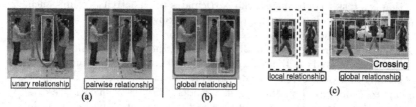

Fig. 2. Relationships in collective activities. (a) Local relationships and (b) global relationship in the collective activity. Though the former works mainly use local relationships, the proposed method focuses global relationship extracted from the whole of single activities. (c) An example of global relationship in collective activities. Since "crossing" activity is locally seen as "walking" activity, distinguishing crossing from walking only by local relationship is hard because of this ambiguity. On the other hand, global relationship provides several important cues which is difficult to acquire by local relationships (e.g. in "crossing" activity, people in "walking" to opposite direction exist on the both side of the activity group).

of a person or image point, such as how people near a focused person look like. Pairwise relationships are information of two focused people, such as in "queuing" activity, people are facing in same direction. However, these approaches use only local information, i.e. one-person or two-people relationships, so global information from whole participants of the activity has been ignored (Figure 2(b)). The global information extracted from whole activity participants would be useful for activity localization, for example, "talking" activity needs "facing each other". At the same time, the global relationships are useful for recognizing activities: though a "crossing" activity is locally seen as "walking" activity, "crossing" and "walking" can be distinguished by using person layout of the whole of an activity (Figure 2(c)). This paper introduces a new context descriptor named "contextual spatial pyramid model (CSPM)", which extracts global relationships from whole participants in single activity. Thanks to its representation similar to spatial pyramids [11], CSPM is able to encode global people layout in an activity (e.g. "facing each other"), therefore CSPM provides a strong cue for activity localization. We show how CSPM improves activity localization performance with the experimental results.

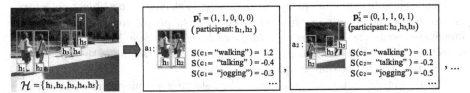

Fig. 3. Activity localization model. An activity window is defined by participants of the activity. The proposed method enumerates possible activity windows composed by subsets of detected people, and assigns score to the activity windows.

1.1 Related Work

Contextual information is widely used in object detection [12], human-object interaction recognition [13–15] and collective activity recognition [3, 4, 6, 7, 10]. Though the contextual information is useful for recognition, the most of previous works have focused only on local relationships. The methods with whole activity appearance [14, 16] are close to our approach. However, though the methods use only whole appearance information as global relationship, our method is explicitly able to include much richer contextual information, such as "facing each other".

Though pairwise relationship is widely used as an contextual information (e.g. [4, 10, 12, 13, 15]), a recent work [4] reports that not all possible pairwise relationships are useful for activity recognition. Therefore, several recent works estimate the hidden structure of person relationships to improve activity classification accuracy [4, 5]. These hidden structure can be interpreted as "who are related in the scene", i.e. "who participates in the same activity" or "who are related in the target activity". Our method estimates the structure by detecting activity groups and by extracting sufficient relationships from the whole of an activity group, therefore the proposed method can be regarded as an extension of these structure-inference based methods.

Here we summarize the main contributions of this paper. (1) Collective activity *localization*: the most of works in collective activity recognition have focused on image-level or single-person activity classification. Since several works [6, 7] mention activity localization in collective activity recognition tasks, they do not give localization performance evaluations. We present an activity localization model from multiple person detections, also we give performance evaluation of activity localization methods. (2) A new context descriptor extracted from the whole of an activity: we present a new context descriptor named contextual spatial pyramid model (CSPM). CSPM provides rich contextual cue for activity localization (e.g. person layout in the whole of an activity).

2   Modeling Activity Localization

In this section, we introduce our activity localization model. Inspired by sliding window classifiers, the proposed method enumerates possible person groups (activity windows), and assigns scores to them (Figure 3).

The method first detects people in the image (Felzenszwalb's object detectors [9] are employed in our experiment). Assume N_p people are detected in the image. We write the kth detected person as $h_k \in \mathcal{H}$, where $\mathcal{H}$ represents set of detected people. The location l_{h_k} of h_k is given by a rectangle on the image, i.e. its left, top, right, bottom $(x_{l,h_k}, y_{t,h_k}, x_{r,h_k}, y_{b,h_k})$.

The ith activity window a_i is defined by selecting activity participants from $\mathcal{H}$. The activity participants $\mathbf{p}_i$ of the activity window a_i can be written as $\mathbf{p_i}^\mathsf{T} = (p_{i1}, p_{i2}, ..., p_{iN_p})$. $p_{ik} \in \{1, 0\}$ is the indicator variable, which represents the kth person h_k is the participant of activity window a_i or not. The location l_{a_i} of ith activity window a_i is defined as the rectangle which surrounds the all participants of a_i.

Activity localization is the task to compute score that an activity window belongs to an activity category c. Our method computes scores by features extracted from each person (unary features) and features extracted from the whole of the activity (group features). The score $S(c_i = c)$ when the activity window a_i belongs to an activity category c is computed as follows:

$$S(c_i = c) = \sum_{k \in \mathcal{P}_i} \mathbf{w}_u(c)^\mathsf{T} \phi_u(h_k) + \mathbf{w}_g(c)^\mathsf{T} \phi_g(a_i) \tag{1}$$

where $\phi_u(h_k)$, and $\phi_g(a_i)$ depict the unary features of the person h_k and the group features of the activity window a_i, respectively. $\mathcal{P}_i \in \{1, ..., N_p\}$ is the set of indices where $p_{ik} = 1$. Roughly speaking, the first term of Eq.(1) represents the appearances of people in an activity group, and the second term represents the global relationships in an activity group. To detect activities on a image, the method enumerates the activity windows with scores over a threshold in each activity category.

Eq.(1) can be rewritten as a linear SVM form (e.g. [17]):

$$S(c_i = c) = \mathbf{w}(c)^\mathsf{T} \phi(a_i) \tag{2}$$

where $\mathbf{w}(c)^\mathsf{T} = (\mathbf{w}_u(c)^\mathsf{T}, \mathbf{w}_g(c)^\mathsf{T})$ and $\phi(c)^\mathsf{T} = (\sum_{k \in \mathcal{P}_i} \phi_u(h_k)^\mathsf{T}, \phi_g(a_i)^\mathsf{T})$.

Implementation: By the scoring procedure, we usually get multiple overlapping detections for each instance of an activity. We apply greedy nonmaximum suppression procedure [9] for activity windows in the same activity category with 50% over overlap.

Our method needs to compute $N_c(2^{N_p} - 1)$ scores when N_c activity categories are defined. This computation is NP-hard. However, the person detector is reliable and N_p is not so large in our application, so we can enumerate all activities in our study. Also, we empirically find that the effect of the maximum N_p is low if the value is not too small, because detecting all people in the crowded situation is infeasible due to occlusions. We set max $N_p = 10$ for computational efficiency. Note that search techniques such as branch-and-bound or $\mathbf{A}^*$ would be able to applied for general cases.

3   Contextual Feature Descriptors

In this section, we introduce contextual feature descriptors of the proposed method. To compute scores, we extract unary features and group features from activity participants. Rather than directly using certain raw features (e.g. HOG features [8]), we use contextual features, i.e. action classification scores of each person, etc. Action denotes a simple, atomic posture performed by a single person (e.g. standing and facing right, etc.). Action classification scores are computed by pre-trained SVM classifier based on HOG features extracted from detected people's bounding boxes.

Unary Features: $\phi_u(h_k)^{\mathsf{T}} = (\phi_u^{\mathrm{a}}(h_k)^{\mathsf{T}}, \phi_u^{\mathrm{pd}}(h_k)^{\mathsf{T}}, 1)$. $\phi_u^{\mathrm{a}}(h_k)$ is a feature generated by action scores, $\phi_u^{\mathrm{pd}}(h_k) \in \mathbb{R}$ is person detection score of the person detector [9], 1 is bias term.

In this work, we employ 2 types of features as $\phi_u^{\mathrm{a}}(h_k)$. The first feature is bag-of-word style feature $\phi_u^{\mathrm{bow}}(h_k) \in \mathbb{R}^K$ [4], where K is the number of action categories. $\phi_u^{\mathrm{bow}}(h_k)$ of the person h_k is computed as follows:

$$\phi_u^{\mathrm{bow}}(h_k)^{\mathsf{T}} = (S_{1k}, ..., S_{Kk}) \tag{3}$$

where $S_{ik} \in \mathbb{R}$ represents person h_k's classification score of ith action. $\phi_u^{\mathrm{bow}}(h_k)$ represents the focal person's posture information by histogram representation.

The second feature is action context (AC) descriptor [4] $\phi_u^{\mathrm{ac}}(h_k) \in \mathbb{R}^{3K}$ in an image. The original AC descriptor encodes both of spatial information and temporal information, we employ spatial information only, to detect activities in each image independently. $\phi_u^{\mathrm{ac}}(h_k)$ of a person h_k is computed as follows:

$$\phi_u^{\mathrm{ac}}(h_k)^{\mathsf{T}} = (S_{1k}, ..., S_{Kk}, \max_{m \in \mathcal{N}_1(h_k)} S_{1m}, ..., \max_{m \in \mathcal{N}_1(h_k)} S_{Km},$$
$$\max_{m \in \mathcal{N}_2(h_k)} S_{1m}, ..., \max_{m \in \mathcal{N}_2(h_k)} S_{Km}) \tag{4}$$

where $\mathcal{N}_1(h_k)$ and $\mathcal{N}_2(h_k)$ are "sub-context regions" of kth person (in this work, we define $\mathcal{N}_1(h_k)$ and $\mathcal{N}_2(h_k)$ as circles of 0.5h and 2h respectively (h is person h_k's height), according to Lan's parameter [4]). $\phi_u^{\mathrm{ac}}(h_k)$ can capture the information of people nearby as well as the focal person's posture information.

Group Features: $\phi_g(a_i)^{\mathsf{T}} = (\phi_g^{\mathrm{cspm}}(a_i)^{\mathsf{T}}, 1)$. $\phi_g^{\mathrm{cspm}}(a_i) \in \mathbb{R}^{KN_{\mathrm{cd}}}$ represents features in activity window a_i extracted by contextual spatial pyramid model. N_{cd} is the number of subregions of CSPM. Figure 4(a) represents an overview of CSPM. To handle people layouts, $\phi_g^{\mathrm{cspm}}(a_i)$ has representations similar to spatial pyramids [11]. $\phi_g^{\mathrm{cspm}}(a_i)$ represents action layout in the activity window a_i by computing bag-of-words like features in the subregions (e.g. in "talking" activity, right-facing persons are on the left side and left-facing persons are on the right side). $\phi_g^{\mathrm{cspm}}(a_i)$ is computed as the following average-pooling representation:

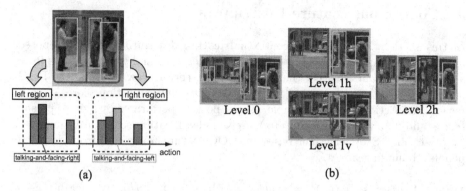

(a)   (b)

Fig. 4. Contextual spatial pyramid model (CSPM). (a) An overview of CSPM. CSPM encodes global relationships of an activity, by extracting action scores of participants in the subregions. For example, if "talking-and-facing-right" score is high in the left region and "talking-and-facing-left" score is high in the right region, the overall feature represents "talking and facing each other". (b) Spatial pyramid representations. In this work, CSPM takes regions with different separation level (total $N_{cd} = 9$ subregions).

$$\phi_g^{\mathrm{cspm}}(a_i)^{\mathsf{T}} = (\frac{1}{M_{\mathcal{R}_1}} \sum_{m\in\mathcal{R}_1(a_i)} S_{1m}, ..., \frac{1}{M_{\mathcal{R}_1}} \sum_{m\in\mathcal{R}_1(a_i)} S_{Km}, ...,$$

$$\frac{1}{M_{\mathcal{R}_{N_{cd}}}} \sum_{m\in\mathcal{R}_{N_{cd}}(a_i)} S_{1m}, ..., \frac{1}{M_{\mathcal{R}_{N_{cd}}}} \sum_{m\in\mathcal{R}_{N_{cd}}(a_i)} S_{Km}) \qquad (5)$$

where $\mathcal{R}_j(a_i)$ is the jth subregion in the spatial pyramid and $M_{\mathcal{R}_j}$ is the number of people in the jth subregion. The proposed method regards the person h_k is in the subregion $\mathcal{R}_j(a_i)$ if h_k participates the activity window a_i (i.e. $p_{ik} = 1$) and if h_k's bounding box intersects subregion $\mathcal{R}_j(a_i)$. If the subregion $\mathcal{R}_j(a_i)$ contains no people, the bin values of the subregion are set to zero.

$\phi_g^{\mathrm{cspm}}(a_i)$ is generated by extracting actions of participants in each subregion, so each bin value of CSPM represents global relationships of an activity group. For example, if the participants of an activity group are globally "facing each other", the bin values of "facing-right" in the left region and "facing-left" in the right region will be high. Therefore, CSPM descriptor can encode global interactions between people in an activity group.

Figure 4 shows the spatial pyramid representation of $\phi_g^{\mathrm{cspm}}(a_i)$. $\phi_g^{\mathrm{cspm}}(a_i)$ takes subregions from level 0, 1h, 1v and 2h ($N_{cd} = 9$).

4   Experiment

We demonstrate our method on the extended version [6] of the collective activity dataset [3]. The dataset contains 72 annotated video clips acquired by low resolution hand held cameras. In the original dataset, all the people in every tenth frame of the videos are assigned one of the following seven activity categories: crossing,

Collective Activity Localization with Contextual Spatial Pyramid 249

Table 1. Per-class and mean average precision (AP) scores on the collective activity dataset. Left: baseline with bag-of-words style features (BoWS), right: baseline with action context (AC) descriptors. The **bold** scores represent best scores in each baseline setting, the *italic* scores represent lower scores than baseline scores. CSPM improves mean AP scores in both of BoWS and AC feature settings.

Class	BoWS	BoWS + CSPM
Crossing	0.090	**0.104**
Dancing	0.215	**0.697**
Jogging	0.426	**0.429**
Queuing	0.115	**0.216**
Talking	0.107	**0.381**
Waiting	0.065	**0.097**
Walking	0.020	**0.053**
Mean AP	0.148	**0.282**

Class	AC	AC + CSPM
Crossing	**0.144**	*0.099*
Dancing	0.353	**0.734**
Jogging	**0.439**	*0.430*
Queuing	0.044	**0.122**
Talking	0.046	**0.087**
Waiting	0.093	**0.125**
Walking	0.021	**0.046**
Mean AP	0.163	**0.235**

waiting, queuing, walking, talking, dancing and jogging, and one of the following eight pose categories: right, front-right, front, front-left, left, back-left, back and back-right. Following Lan's definition [4], we define 56 action labels (7 activity labels × 8 pose labels) by combining the pose and activity information, i.e. the action labels include crossing and facing right, crossing and facing front-right, etc. Note that actions are intermediate outputs: action classification scores are used only for feature descriptions. We define ground truth activities on each image, by assigning people participating to the activity and the activities' category. We select one fourth of the video clips to form the test set, and the rest of the video clips are used for training (total 2943 training images and 882 test images). Following PASCAL VOC Challenge's localization criteria [18], the detected activity is considered as a correct detection if the overlap ratio between the bounding box of detected activity and the bounding box of ground truth activity exceeds 50%.

Results: To evaluate our feature model, we compare localization accuracy with several feature settings: unary features only (with bag-of-words style features (ϕ_g^{bow}) and with AC features (ϕ_g^{ac}) : variant of [4]) and unary features and CSPM (with ϕ_g^{bow} and with ϕ_g^{ac}). We define "unary features only" feature set (i.e. local relationships only) as baseline, and evaluate effectiveness of CSPM.

We compute precision-recall curves and the average precision (AP) scores across activity classes. We show the precision-recall curves in Figure 5 and the comparison of AP scores in Table 1. As seen in Table 1, the proposed CSPM descriptor improves localization performance in all activity categories when bag-of-words style features are used as unary features (Table 1 left), and improves localization performance in 5 activity categories when action context descriptors are used as unary features (Table 1 right). Also, CSPM descriptor improve mean AP scores of activity categories in both baseline settings, therefore this result shows CSPM provides useful cues for activity localization.

In the all feature settings, methods with CSPM record highest AP scores in 5 activity categories (with BoWS, 3 categories: queuing, talking, walking, and with

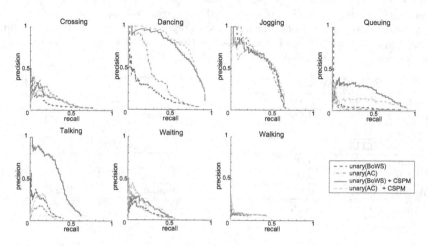

Fig. 5. Precision-recall curves (best viewed in color)

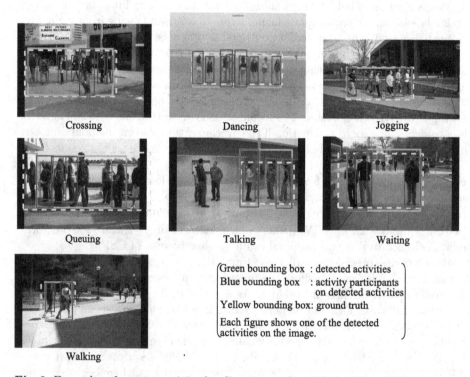

Fig. 6. Examples of correct activity localization results with BoWS + CSPM feature setting (best viewed in color).

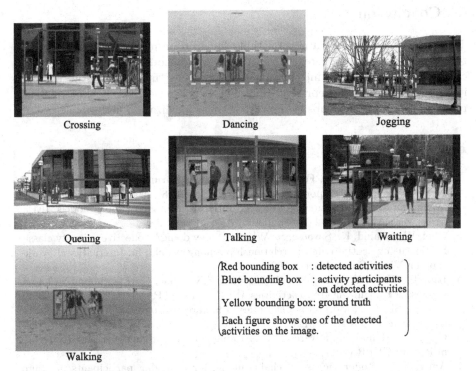

Crossing   Dancing   Jogging

Queuing   Talking   Waiting

Red bounding box   : detected activities
Blue bounding box   : activity participants
                      on detected activities
Yellow bounding box: ground truth

Each figure shows one of the detected
activities on the image.

Walking

Fig. 7. Examples of failed activity localization results with BoWS + CSPM feature setting (best viewed in color). Several detection results are treated failed detections due to localization failure (crossing, dancing, jogging, talking).

AC, 2 categories: dancing, waiting), and the method with AC descriptor only records highest AP scores in 2 activity categories (crossing, jogging). Though AP score decreases with CSPM descriptor in several activity categories when the AC descriptor is used as baseline, it is because that AC and CSPM represent different information in the activity groups. Though AC descriptor is a strong descriptor (especially people in the scene participate in single activity, such as "crossing" activity), the AC descriptor encodes person relationships regardless of the activity group, therefore the AC descriptor may encode relationships inconsistent with CSPM descriptors. More efficient feature combination is one of the future works. We visualize the localization results in Figure 6 (correct detections) and Figure 7 (false detections).

Though the proposed method of mean AP scores (roughly 26%) is lower than precision scores on the state-of-the-art result of *person*-level classification or *image*-level classification, it is because that activity localization task is much more difficult. The localization task needs determining the "people in the same activity" in addition to determining activity labels (e.g. in Figure 7, detection results of crossing, dancing, jogging, talking are treated false detections due to localization failure though the detected activities contain ground truth activities), so the activity localization task is a difficult task compared with activity *classification* task.

5 Conclusion

This paper has described a novel activity localization method with a new context descriptor named contextual spatial pyramid model (CSPM). CSPM encodes rich global relationships in an activity (such as "facing each other"), with its spatial-pyramid-like representation. The experimental result shows CSPM provides useful relationships to improve activity localization performance.

References

1. Niebles, J.C., Wang, H., Fei-Fei, L.: Unsupervised learning of human action categories using spatial-temporal words. IJCV 79, 299–318 (2008)
2. Wang, Y., Mori, G.: Human action recognition by semilatent topic models. IEEE Trans. on PAMI 31, 1762–1774 (2009)
3. Choi, W., Shahid, K., Savaese, S.: What are they doing?: collective acitivity classification using spatio-temporal relationship among people. In: International Workshop on Visual Surveillance (2009)
4. Lan, T., Wang, Y., Yang, W., Robinovitch, S.N., Mori, G.: Discriminative latent models for recognizing group activities. IEEE Trans. on PAMI 34, 1549–1562 (2012)
5. Lan, T., Sigal, L., Mori, G.: Social roles in hierarchical models for human activity recognition. In: CVPR (2012)
6. Choi, W., Shahid, K., Savarese, S.: Learning context for collective activity recognition. In: CVPR (2011)
7. Amer, M.R., Todorovic, S.: A chains model for localizing participants of group activities in videos. In: ICCV (2011)
8. Dalal, N., Triggs, B.: Histograms of oriented gradients for human detection. In: CVPR (2005)
9. Felzenszwalb, P.F., Girshick, R.B., McAllester, D., Ramanan, D.: Object detection with discriminatively trained part based models. IEEE Trans. on PAMI 32, 1627–1645 (2010)
10. Ryoo, M.S., Aggarwal, J.K.: Spatio-temporal relationship match: video structure comparison for recognition of complex human activities. In: ICCV (2009)
11. Lazebnik, S., Schmid, C., Ponce, J.: Beyond bags of features: spatial pyramid matching for recognizing natural scene categories. In: CVPR (2006)
12. Desai, C., Ramanan, D., Fowlkes, C.: Discriminative models for multi-class object layout. In: ICCV (2009)
13. Gupta, A., Kembhavi, A., Davis, L.: Observing human-object interactions: using spatial and functional compatibility for recognition. IEEE Trans. on PAMI 31, 1775–1789 (2009)
14. Sadeghi, M.A., Farhadi, A.: Recognition using visual phrases. In: CVPR (2011)
15. Yao, B., Khosla, A., Fei-Fei, L.: Classifying actions and measuring action similarity by modeling the mutual context of objects and human poses. In: ICML (2011)
16. Amer, M.R., Todorovic, S.: Sum-product networks for modeling activities with stochastic structure. In: CVPR (2012)
17. Fan, R.E., Chang, K.W., Hsieh, C.J., Wang, X.R., Lin, C.J.: LIBLINEAR: a library for large linear classification. JMLR 9, 1871–1874 (2008)
18. Everingham, M., Williams, C.K.I., Winn, J., Zisserman, A.: The PASCAL visual object classes (VOC) challenge. IJCV 88, 303–338 (2010)

Viewpoint Invariant Collective Activity Recognition with Relative Action Context

Takuhiro Kaneko, Masamichi Shimosaka, Shigeyuki Odashima,
Rui Fukui, and Tomomasa Sato

The University of Tokyo, Japan
{kaneko,simosaka,odashima,fukui,tsato}@ics.t.u-tokyo.ac.jp

Abstract. This paper presents an approach for collective activity recognition. Collective activities are activities performed by multiple persons, such as queueing in a line and talking together. To recognize them, the action context (AC) descriptor [1] encodes the "apparent" relation (e.g. a group crossing and facing "right"), however this representation is sensitive to viewpoint change. We instead propose a novel feature representation called the *relative action context (RAC) descriptor* that encodes the "relative" relation (e.g. a group crossing and facing the "same" direction). This representation is viewpoint invariant and complementary to AC; hence we employ a simplified combinational classifier. This paper also introduces two methods to accelerate performance. First, to make the contexts robust to various situations, we apply post processes. Second, to reduce local classification failures, we regularize the classification using fully connected CRFs. Experimental results show that our method is applicable to various scenes and outperforms state-of-the art methods.

1 Introduction

Collective activity recognition is one of the most challenging tasks in computer vision. Since collective activities (e.g. queueing in a line, talking together or waiting by a street intersection) are performed by multiple persons, it is often hard to differentiate them only by appearance of the individual. Hence, recent works exploit the contextual information of nearby people [1–8]

When exploiting the contextual information of nearby people, it is required to answer the following question: "How to describe human relationship?" To answer the question, the action context (AC) descriptor [1] represents "apparent" relation (e.g. two persons who are queuing and facing "left" as shown in Figure 1). Such an apparent relation descriptor is suitable when appearance is specific to the target activity. For example, a waiting group is more likely observed from an anterior view rather than from a right view in an image. However, an apparent relation descriptor is sensitive to viewpoint change. To solve the problem, we develop a novel "relative" relation descriptor called the *relative action context (RAC) descriptor*. A relative relation descriptor encodes relative relation (e.g. two persons who are queuing and facing the "same" direction as illustrated in Figure 1), therefore, it contains invariance under viewpoint change

A. Fusiello et al. (Eds.): ECCV 2012 Ws/Demos, Part III, LNCS 7585, pp. 253–262, 2012.
© Springer-Verlag Berlin Heidelberg 2012

Queuing and facing left for both persons ≠ Queuing and facing back-right for both persons

Queuing and facing should be the same direction

Fig. 1. How to describe human relationship? There are two approaches to describe human relationship: an apparent relation descriptor that encodes apparent relation in an image (e.g. queuing and facing "left", queuing and facing "back-right"), and a relative relation descriptor that encodes relative relation (e.g. queuing and facing the "same" direction). The former can encode appearance specific to the target activity, however, it is sensitive to viewpoint change, while the latter is robust to viewpoint change as well as consistent within the same category of collective activity.

as well as consistency within the same category of collective activity. Note that Choi *et al.* [4, 5] also propose relative relation descriptor, however, these methods exploit only poses (e.g. facing right) rather than actions (e.g. "talking" and facing right); hence they cannot encode apparent differences between activities. Furthermore, since AC and RAC descriptors represent human relation from a different standpoint and they are complementary, we employ a simplified combinational classifier, so as to obtain stable performance in various scenes.

We also introduce two methods to accelerate performance. First, to make the contexts robust to various situations, we apply the following two post processes: threshold processing and Gaussian filtering. When extracting a histogram-style context, Yang *et al.* [9] use sparse coding that not only allows the representation to capture salient properties of images but also achieves lower quantization error, so as to outperform the recent works [10, 11]. Inspired by [9], we use threshold processing to extracts salient properties from noisy contexts, and employ Gaussian filtering to relax quantization errors. Notice that recent works [9–11] use unsupervised histogram derived from the bag-of-words representation, while our work uses supervised histogram calculated by a multiclass classifier.

Second, we employ fully connected CRFs [7, 12, 13] to obtain the consistency in a group. Unlike recent works that optimize collective activity recognition via graph structures [2–6], our model assumes that all the persons in a frame are related, and describes their relationship as potentials that vary depending on the scale of features, in order to handle various group shapes. Our model has similarities to [7], however differs from it in exploiting the data in only the current frame rather than those in the entire video, so as to apply online applications.

In summary, the contributions of this paper are 1) to develop a novel relative relation descriptor called the *relative action context (RAC) descriptor* that is invariant under viewpoint change; 2) to employ a simplified combinational classifier of AC and RAC descriptors to obtain stable performance in various scenes;

3) to make the contexts robust to various situations using simple post processes; 4) to obtain robustness to local classification failures using fully connected CRFs that assume all the relationships among the people in a frame. Experimental results show that our proposed method not only applies to various scenes but also outperforms state-of-the art methods [1, 4, 5, 7].

2 Group Context Descriptor

This section first explains an apparent relation descriptor (section 2.1), then presents a novel relative relation descriptor called the *relative action context (RAC) descriptor* (section 2.2), and finally examines how to combine the apparent relation descriptor and the relative relation descriptor (section 2.3).

2.1 Apparent Relation Descriptor

An apparent relation descriptor encodes apparent human relationship on images. For example, there exists a queuing group on an image, the group is more likely seen from a right view rather than from an anterior view. In this case, it is important to describe the appearance that persons queuing and facing to the right extend transversally. Such apparent relations are useful when the apparent relations are specific to the target activity. Our model uses the action context (AC) descriptor [1] to represent apparent relation.

AC descriptor is per-person descriptor, and each descriptor is calculated by concatenating the following two feature descriptors: one is the action descriptor that represents the action of the focal person, and the other is the context descriptor that captures the behavior of nearby people, as illustrated in Figure 2.

The action descriptor has a bag-of-words style. Instead of using raw person descriptors (e.g. HOG [14]), we describe the action descriptor generated by outputs of a multiclass SVM classifier associated with action labels. Using the score returned by the SVM classifier, the i-th person is represented as the following K-dimensional vector: $F_i = [S_{1i}, S_{2i}, ..., S_{Ki}]$, where K is the number of action classes, and S_{ki} is the score of classifying the i-th person to the k-th action class.

After the action descriptor is computed for each person, the context descriptor is calculated by integrating the action descriptor of nearby people in the "context region", as illustrated in Figure 2. The context region is further divided into M regions (called "sub-context regions") in space and time, then the context descriptor is represented as the following $M \times K$ dimensional vector:

$$C_i = [D_{1i}, ..., D_{Mi}]$$
$$= \left[\max_{j \in \mathcal{N}_1(i)} S_{1j}, ..., \max_{j \in \mathcal{N}_1(i)} S_{Kj}, ..., \max_{j \in \mathcal{N}_M(i)} S_{1j}, ..., \max_{j \in \mathcal{N}_M(i)} S_{Kj} \right], \quad (1)$$

where D_{mi} is called the "sub-context descriptor" representing the context in the m-th sub-context region of the i-th person, and $\mathcal{N}_m(i)$ indicates the indices of people in the sub-context region.

Finally, the AC descriptor of i-th person A_i is computed by concatenating its action descriptor F_i and its context descriptor C_i: $A_i = [F_i, C_i]$.

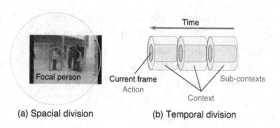

(a) Spacial division   (b) Temporal division

Fig. 2. Illustration of AC descriptor. AC descriptor is calculated by concatenating its action descriptor and its context descriptor. The context region is further divided into sub-context regions in (a) space and (b) time.

2.2 Relative Relation Descriptor

A relative relation descriptor encodes relative relationship between the focal person and others. For example, when the focal person is facing right and another person is facing left, the relative relation is defined as facing the "opposite" direction. This descriptor cannot represent apparent relations specific to the target activity, however, it contains invariance under viewpoint change (e.g, camera rotation), and consistency within the same collective activity.

Similarly to [2], we define actions by concatenating poses and activities (e.g. talking and facing right). This means that the action descriptor and the sub-context descriptor are $K(= U \times V)$ dimensional vectors, where U is the number of activity classes and V is the number of pose classes. Using U and V, we redefine the action descriptor F_i, and the sub-context descriptor D_{mi} in Section 2.1:

$$
\begin{aligned}
F_i &= [S_{1i}, S_{2i}, ..., S_{Ki}] \\
&= [S_{11i}, S_{12i}, ..., S_{uvi}, ..., S_{UVi}],
\end{aligned} \tag{2}
$$

$$
\begin{aligned}
D_{mi} &= \left[\max_{j \in \mathcal{N}_m(i)} S_{1j}, ..., \max_{j \in \mathcal{N}_m(i)} S_{Kj} \right] \\
&= \left[\max_{j \in \mathcal{N}_m(i)} S_{11j}, \max_{j \in \mathcal{N}_m(i)} S_{12j}, ..., \max_{j \in \mathcal{N}_m(i)} S_{uvj}, ..., \max_{j \in \mathcal{N}_m(i)} S_{UVj} \right]. \tag{3}
\end{aligned}
$$

Our proposed descriptor (the *relative action context (RAC) descriptor*) is calculated by shifting AC descriptor based on the pose of the focal person, as shown in Figure 3. First, the pose of the i-th person $\hat{v}_i$ is calculated from the person descriptor (e.g. HOG [14]) using a multiclass classifier. In terms of the pose $\hat{v}_i$, the i-th person's relative action descriptor $\hat{F}_i$ and the relative sub-context descriptor $\hat{D}_{mi}$ are defined as

$$
\begin{aligned}
\hat{F}_i &= \big[S_{1\hat{v}_i i}, ..., S_{1Vi}, S_{11i}, ..., S_{1(\hat{v}_i-1)i}, ..., \\
&\quad S_{U\hat{v}_i i}, ..., S_{UVi}, S_{U1i}, ..., S_{U(\hat{v}_i-1)i} \big], \tag{4}
\end{aligned}
$$

$$
\begin{aligned}
\hat{D}_{mi} &= \Big[\max_{j \in \mathcal{N}_m(i)} S_{1\hat{v}_i j}, ..., \max_{j \in \mathcal{N}_m(i)} S_{1Vj}, \max_{j \in \mathcal{N}_m(i)} S_{11j}, \max_{j \in \mathcal{N}_m(i)} S_{1(\hat{v}_i-1)j}, ..., \\
&\quad \max_{j \in \mathcal{N}_m(i)} S_{U\hat{v}_i j}, ..., \max_{j \in \mathcal{N}_m(i)} S_{UVj}, \max_{j \in \mathcal{N}_m(i)} S_{U1j}, \max_{j \in \mathcal{N}_m(i)} S_{U(\hat{v}_i-1)j} \Big]. \tag{5}
\end{aligned}
$$

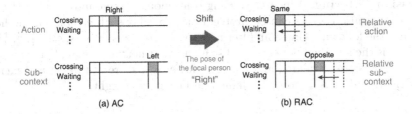

(a) AC   (b) RAC

Fig. 3. Illustration of a method for constructing RAC descriptor from AC descriptor. RAC descriptor is calculating by shifting AC descriptor based on the pose of the focal person. When the focal person is facing right and another person is facing left in AC descriptor, another person is defined as facing the "opposite" direction in RAC descriptor.

The relative context descriptor of i-th person $\hat{C}_i$ is computed by concatenating its relative sub-context descriptor: $\hat{C}_i = [\hat{D}_{1i}, ..., \hat{D}_{Mi}]$. Finally, the RAC descriptor of i-th person R_i is computed by concatenating its relative action descriptor $\hat{F}_i$ and its relative context descriptor $\hat{C}_i$: $R_i = [\hat{F}_i, \hat{C}_i]$.

2.3 Combination of Descriptors

After extracting the apparent relation descriptor (AC descriptor) and the relative relation descriptor (RAC descriptor), we transform them into probabilities via softmax transformation, and combine them via the MAX rule [15]:

$$\hat{y}_i = \arg \max_{y_i} P_i(y_i) \quad \text{s.t.} \quad P_i(y_i) = \max_k P_i(y_i|d_k), \tag{6}$$

where $P_i(y_i)$ is the probability that the activity of the i-th person is y_i, $P_i(y_i|d_1)$ is the probability calculated from the apparent relation descriptor, $P_i(y_i|d_2)$ is the probability computed from the relative relation descriptor.

3   Methods to Accelerate Performance

3.1   Post Processes: Context Conversion

In order to make a histogram-style context (e.g. A_i, R_i) robust to various situations, we employ the following two post processes: threshold processing that allows the representation to capture the salient properties from noisy context; Gaussian processing that reduces quantization errors.

Threshold Processing: Given a histogram-style context, we execute the following threshold processing to each score s: $\hat{s} = s$ (if $s > \alpha$) or 0 (otherwise), where α is a threshold. Threshold processing makes the contexts sparse and allows the representation to be specialized. In implementation, we define $\alpha = 0$. A_i and R_i are the scores returned by the SVM classifiers, therefore, this threshold value implies that we exploit only the properties of present actions.

Gaussian Filtering: When converting continuous volume into quantized volume, quantization errors can be problematic. To relax such errors, our method executes the following Gaussian filtering to each score s: $\hat{s} = [s_l, s, s_r] \cdot [\frac{1}{4}, \frac{2}{4}, \frac{1}{4}]^T$, where s_l is the left neighbor score and s_r is the right neighbor score. For example, when s is a score of talking and facing right, s_l is a score of talking and facing back-right, and s_r is a score of talking and facing front-right.

3.2   Regularization Using Fully Connected CRFs

In order to reduce local classification failures, we impose smoothness by applying fully connected CRFs [7, 12, 13]. In particular, our model not defines human relation as heuristic but assumes that all the persons in a frame are related and describes their relation as potential that vary depending on the scale of features, so as to apply various group shapes. The observed data of the detected persons are defined as $\boldsymbol{x} = \{x_1, ..., x_N\}$, where x_i is the observed data of the i-th person and N is the number of detected persons in a frame. Let the corresponding activity labels be defined as $\boldsymbol{y} = \{y_1, ..., y_N\}$. A conditional random field $(\boldsymbol{x}, \boldsymbol{y})$ is characterized by a Gibbs distribution: $P(\boldsymbol{y}|\boldsymbol{x}) = \frac{1}{Z(\boldsymbol{x})} \exp(-E(\boldsymbol{y}))$, where $Z(\boldsymbol{x})$ is the partition function, and $E(\boldsymbol{y})$ is the Gibbs energy:

$$E(\boldsymbol{y}) = \sum_i \psi_u(y_i) + \sum_i \sum_{j>i} \psi_p(y_i, y_j), \tag{7}$$

where $\psi_u(y_i)$ is the unary potential and $\psi_p(y_i, y_j)$ is the pairwise potential.

The unary potential $\psi_u(y_i)$ is defined as $\psi_u(y_i) = -\log(P_i(y_i))$, where $P_i(y_i)$ is the probability that the activity of the i-th person is y_i. The pairwise potential is defined in terms of the positions p_i and p_j, and weight w:

$$\psi_p(y_i, y_j) = w\mu(y_i, y_j) \exp\left(-\frac{|p_i - p_j|^2}{2\theta^2}\right), \tag{8}$$

where $\mu(y_i, y_j)$ is the label compatibility function given by Potts model [16]: $\mu(y_i, y_j) = [y_i \neq y_j]$. Note that we normalize positions by the minimum height of all the persons in a frame, and describe human relationship as relative value rather than absolute value, to obtain robustness to a difference in perspective.

Our model defines the pairwise potential as Gaussian kernel, therefore, in inference, it is possible to apply highly efficient approximated inference algorithm via mean field approximation and high-dimensional filtering [12]. This reduces the calculation cost to linear to the number of the detected persons N. In learning, the kernel parameters w, θ are estimated. Due to non-convexity of kernel width θ on log-loss criterion, it is hard to optimize it globally, therefore, we use grid search from the training set with cross-validation.

4   Experiments

Collective Activity Dataset: We evaluate our model on the collective activity dataset [4]. This dataset consists of 44 short videos of crossing, waiting, queueing, walking and talking. The videos were recorded under realistic conditions, including camera shaking, background clutter and transient mutual occlusions of persons. All the persons in every 10th frame are labeled with the ground truth: pose, activity and bounding box information. We use the same leave-one-video-out scheme described in [1, 4, 5, 7], and report activity recognition results on a per-person basis. We use a linear SVM (e.g. LIBLINEAR [17]) as a classifier, and its parameters are set according to cross-validation in the training set.

Evaluation of the Group Context Descriptors: To evaluate our proposed group context descriptors, we demonstrate the two experiments: (1) comparison among the three group context descriptors (AC descriptor, RAC descriptor, and the combination of them), (2) comparison among the post processes (threshold processing and Gaussian filtering). Note that the focus of these experiments is evaluating each factor of group context descriptors. In this evaluation, we assume that persons are detected without errors, i.e., use ground-truth person locations.

The quantitative results are summarized in Table 1. Since the test set is imbalanced about activity classes and the difficulty of recognition is different among videos, we report overall, mean per-class and mean per-video accuracies. The quantitative results are competitive between AC descriptor and RAC descriptor in Table 1, however, the applicable scenes are different as presented in Figure 4. When apparently similar groups exist in the training data, AC descriptor is useful, however, when viewpoint change occurs, RAC descriptor is more useful. The combination of AC and RAC descriptors can handle both applicable scenes as illustrated in the top three rows of Figure 4, and exceeds AC and RAC descriptors in terms of number, as shown in Table 1. However, it is hard to handle the scene where the multiple groups are overlapping as shown in the bottom row of Figure 4. Note that we also evaluated other combination methods such as the MIN, Product, Sum rules [15], and an SVM classifier for the AC and RAC descriptors: $[A_i, R_i]$. All of them performed slightly worse than our approach.

To evaluate our proposed post processes, we compare classification accuracies with and without threshold processing or Gaussian filtering, in Table 1. Both AC and RAC descriptors have the highest accuracies using Gaussian filtering after threshold processing. This implies that relaxing quantization errors after extracting salient properties is the most effective. We also evaluated the other smoothness method such as mean filtering: $\hat{s} = [s_l, s, s_r] \cdot [\frac{1}{3}, \frac{1}{3}, \frac{1}{3}]^T$. It performed worse than our approach because it smoothens properties to excess.

Comparison with State-of-the-Art Methods: We also compare our method with the recent methods [1, 4, 5, 7]. To compare fairly, we apply the pedestrian detector in [18] to detect the persons, similarly to [1, 4, 5, 7]. Experimental results are shown in Table 2 and Figure 5. Here, we report the regularizing classification result using CRFs. It exceeds the result without CRFs, since this model reduces local classification failures. Note that the approach of [7] needs the data in the entire video to obtain the spatial and temporal consistency, and the approach of [5] needs the 3D trajectory data of each person to apply 3D MRF, while our method does not need the surplus data.

Table 1. Comparison of group context descriptors: AC descriptor (the first row to the fifth row), RAC descriptor (the sixth row to the tenth row), and the combination of them (the eleventh row to the twelfth row). Comparison of post processes: threshold processing and Gaussian filtering. The characters T, G, TG, GT indicate threshold processing, Gaussian filtering, Gaussian filtering after threshold processing, and threshold processing after Gaussian filtering.

Method	Overall	Mean per-class	Mean per-video
AC	71.1	69.0	63.3
AC + T	73.0	71.2	64.7
AC + G	71.5	69.3	64.0
AC + TG	**74.0**	**72.2**	**66.3**
AC + GT	73.0	70.9	64.9
RAC	71.4	69.4	65.0
RAC + T	72.3	70.4	66.6
RAC + G	72.5	70.7	66.4
RAC + TG	**73.1**	**71.4**	**67.4**
RAC + GT	72.6	70.8	66.8
Combination (AC + RAC)	73.2	71.2	66.4
Combination (AC + TG) + (RAC + TG)	**75.1**	**73.1**	**68.6**

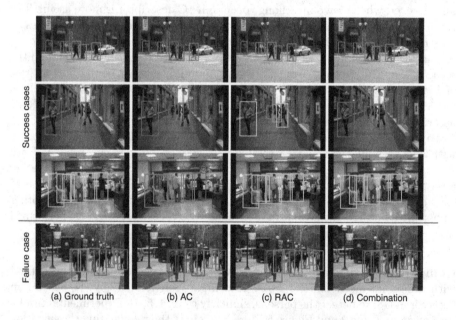

Fig. 4. Qualitative results of collective activities recognition using group context descriptors: (a) ground truth, (b) AC descriptor, (c) RAC descriptor, (d) the combination of them. The labels C (magenta), S (blue), Q (cyan), W (red), T (green) indicate crossing, waiting, queueing, walking and talking. Top three rows show examples of successful classification and a bottom row shows examples of false classification.

Table 2. Comparison of activity classification accuracies using different methods. Top eight rows show the results using only group context descriptors, and bottom four rows show the results regularized by graph structures. Our apparent relation descriptor (AC + TG) outperforms state-of-the art apparent descriptor (AC in [1]). Our relative relation descriptor (RAC + TG) also exceeds state-of-the art relative descriptors (STV in [4] and RSTV in [5]). Moreover, the combination of them surpasses them.

Method	Mean per-class
HOG	50.0
STV in [4]	64.3
RSTV in [5]	67.2
AC in [7]	67.4
AC in [1]	68.2
RAC + TG	68.5
AC + TG	71.3
Combination	**71.9**
STV + MC in [4]	65.9
RSTV + MRF in [5]	70.9
AC + FC-CRF in [7]	72.2
Combination + CRF	**73.2**

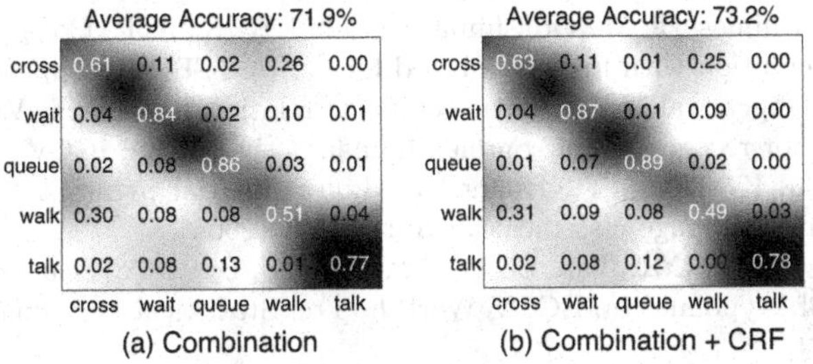

(a) Combination   (b) Combination + CRF

Fig. 5. Confusion matrices for activity classification with and without CRFs: (a) the result with the combination of AC + TG and RAC + TG, and (b) the result with the combination + CRF. In the confusion matrices, rows represent ground truths and columns represent predictions. Each row is normalized to sum to 1. Note that walking vs crossing is still ambiguous in our model, because these activities often depend on not human relationship but environmental settings: a sidewalk or a pedestrian crossing.

5   Conclusion

This paper has described the novel relative relation descriptor called RAC descriptor, as against an apparent relation descriptor such as AC descriptor. Owing to its "relative" relation description, the proposed RAC descriptor is viewpoint invariant and consistent within the same category of collective activity. AC and RAC descriptors are complementary in human relation representation; hence we employ a simplified combinational classifier, so as to obtain stable performance in various scenes. We also introduce two methods to improve performance. One is post processes that make the contexts robust to various situations, and the other is regularizing classification by fully connected CRFs that assume all the relationships among the people in a frame. Finally, our experimental results on the collective activity dataset demonstrate that our method recognizes collective activity stably in various scenes and outperforms state-of-the art methods.

References

1. Lan, T., Wang, Y., Mori, G.: Retrieving actions in group contexts. In: International Workshop on Sign Gesture Activity (2010)
2. Lan, T., Wang, Y., Yang, W., Mori, G.: Beyond actions: Discriminative models for contextual group activities. In: Adv. in NIPS 23 (2010)
3. Lan, T., Sigal, L., Mori, G.: Social roles in hierarchical models for human activity recognition. In: CVPR (2012)
4. Choi, W., Shahid, K., Savarese, S.: What are they doing?: Collective activity classification using spatio-temporal relationship among people. In: International Workshop on Visual Surveillance (2009)
5. Choi, W., Shahid, K., Savarese, S.: Learning context for collective activity recognition. In: CVPR (2011)
6. Amer, M.R., Todorovic, S.: A chains model for localizing participants of group activities in videos. In: ICCV (2011)
7. Kaneko, T., Shimosaka, M., Odashima, S., Fukui, R., Sato, T.: Consistent collective activity recognition with fully connected CRFs. In: ICPR (to appear, 2012)
8. Ryoo, M.S., Aggarwal, J.K.: Spatio-temporal relationship match: Video structure comparison for recognition of complex human activities. In: ICCV (2009)
9. Yang, J., Yu, K., Gong, Y., Huang, T.: Linear spatial pyramid matching using sparse coding for image classification. In: CVPR (2009)
10. Csurka, G., Dance, C.R., Fan, L., Willamowski, J., Bray, C.: Visual categorization with bags of keypoints. In: ECCV Workshop on Statistical Learning in Computer Vision (2004)
11. Lazebnik, S., Schmid, C., Ponce, J.: Beyond bags of features: Spatial pyramid matching for recognizing natural scene categories. In: CVPR (2006)
12. Krähenbühl, P., Koltun, V.: Efficient inference in fully connected CRFs with Gaussian edge potentials. In: Adv. in NIPS 24 (2011)
13. Zhang, Y., Chen, T.: Efficient inference for fully-connected CRFs with stationarity. In: CVPR (2012)
14. Dalal, N., Triggs, B.: Histogram of oriented gradients for human detection. In: CVPR (2005)
15. Hatef, M., Duin, R.P., Matas, J.: On combining classifiers. PAMI 20, 226–239 (1998)
16. Boykov, Y.Y., Jolly, M.P.: Interactive graph cuts for optimal boundary and region segmentation of objects in n-d images. In: ICCV (2001)
17. Fan, R.E., Chang, K.W., Hsieh, C.J., Wang, X.R., Lin, C.J.: LIBLINEAR: A library for large linear classification. Journal of Machine Learning Research 9, 1871–1874 (2008)
18. Felzenszwalb, P., McAllester, D., Ramanan, D.: A discriminatively trained, multiscale, deformable part model. In: CVPR (2008)

On Recognizing Actions in Still Images
via Multiple Features

Fadime Sener[1], Cagdas Bas[2], and Nazli Ikizler-Cinbis[2]

[1] Computer Engineering Department, Bilkent University, Ankara, Turkey
[2] Computer Engineering Department, Hacettepe University, Ankara, Turkey

Abstract. We propose a multi-cue based approach for recognizing human actions in still images, where relevant object regions are discovered and utilized in a weakly supervised manner. Our approach does not require any explicitly trained object detector or part/attribute annotation. Instead, a multiple instance learning approach is used over sets of object hypotheses in order to represent objects relevant to the actions. We test our method on the extensive Stanford 40 Actions dataset [1] and achieve significant performance gain compared to the state-of-the-art. Our results show that using multiple object hypotheses within multiple instance learning is effective for human action recognition in still images and such an object representation is suitable for using in conjunction with other visual features.

1 Introduction

Recognizing actions in still images has recently gained attention in the vision community due to its large applicability to various domains. In news photographs, for example, it is especially important to understand what the people are doing from a retrieval point of view.

As opposed to motion and appearance in videos, still images convey the action information via the pose of the person and the surrounding object/scene context. Objects are especially important cues for identifying the type of the action. Previous studies verify this observation [2–4] and show that identification of objects play an important role in action recognition.

In this paper, we approach the problem of identifying related objects from a weakly supervised point of view and explore the effect of using Multiple Instance Learning(MIL) for finding the candidate object regions and their corresponding effect in recognition. Our approach does not use any explicit object detector, or part/attribute annotation during training. Instead, multiple object hypotheses are generated via objectness measure [5]. We then utilize a MIL classifier for learning the related object(s) amongst the noisy set of object region candidates.

Besides the features extracted from candidate object regions, we evaluate various features that can be utilized for effective recognition of actions in still images. In our evaluation, we consider facial features in addition to features extracted within person regions and also features that describe the global image

A. Fusiello et al. (Eds.): ECCV 2012 Ws/Demos, Part III, LNCS 7585, pp. 263–272, 2012.

characteristics. We evaluate how much each proposed representation contribute to the recognition of particular actions.

We test our approach on the Stanford 40 actions dataset [1]. Our results show that the MIL framework over the candidate object hypotheses is quite successful and achieves better recognition performance compared to the state-of-the-art part and attributes based model of [1].

The remaining of the paper is organized as follows: We first review the related literature over the subject in Section 2. Then, we present the various features utilized for recognizing actions in still images, especially the MIL approach for objects in 3. In Section 4, we present the extensive evaluation of the features in the Stanford 40 actions [1] dataset. Section 5 finalizes the discussion with the conclusions and possible future directions.

2   Related Work

Human action recognition has been an active research area for computer vision for a while. For an extensive review, the interested reader can refer to one of the recent surveys over the subject [6, 7] and the references therein. Most of the existing work focuses on action recognition in videos, which makes use of motion cues and temporal information [8]. Action recognition in still images, however, is a more challenging problem, due to the lack of motion information and the difficulty of foreground subject segmentation.

In comparison to the large amount of work available for action recognition in videos, action recognition in still images is a less studied problem and is recently gaining attention. Wang, et al. [9] utilize deformable template matching for computing the distance between human poses and grouping similar poses. Thurau and Hlavac [10] use non-negative matrix factorization on pose primitives, where the pose primitives are learnt from non-cluttered videos and applied to images for finding the closest pose. In [11], the pose models are learnt from action images and those models are applied to classify actions in videos.

In more recent work, Yao and Fei Fei [12] have looked into the relationship between poses and objects and model the interactions using grouplet features. Object-person interactions are explored in other works such as [2, 3, 13, 14]. Delaitre et al. [15] has studied the use of bag-of-features and part-based representations using structural SVMs. Later on, Yao et al. [16] explore the use of random forests with discriminative decision trees. In their most recent work, Yao et al. [1] propose a part and attribute based model, which makes use of explicit object detectors for aiding action recognition in still images.

Prest et al. [4] also propose weakly supervised learning of human-object interactions. In [4], the objects having similar relative location with respect to the person are searched for the most recurring configuration for each action. For each image, their formulation is restricted to select one object window, whereas in our MIL approach, more than one object region can contribute to the recognition of the actions. Moreover, we do not enforce any spatial constraint for the objects and allow contributing object windows to come from any region of the image.

Fig. 1. Candidate object regions found by objectness measure [5]. The person bounding box is shown in blue and object regions are in red. Candidate object regions form the instances of the corresponding MIL bags.

3 Multiple Features for Actions in Still Images

3.1 Multiple Instance Learning for Candidate Object Regions

In order to recognize actions in still images, the related objects can be particularly important. In this paper, instead of using explicit object detectors, we investigate whether we can automatically learn potential object regions that can boost action recognition performance. For this reason, we extract several candidate object regions and use these object regions in a Multiple Instance Learning(MIL) framework.

We assume that the objects that the people are interacting with are visually salient objects. We use objectness measure [5] for finding visually salient regions within the image. Objectness measure uses several cues (such as multi-scale saliency, color contrast, edge density, etc.) in an image to identify regions for generic objects. We use this measure to identify candidate object hypotheses. Figure 1 shows example images. As it can be seen, in some images, objectness measure is able to locate objects of interest such as rowing boat. However, this measure also generates some noisy regions that do not include any related object.

In our implementation, we sample 100 windows from each image based on their objectness measure, i.e, the probability of containing an object. The authors of [5] recommend sampling 1000 image windows to cover all possible objects, but it would be very costly for the scalability of the approach. Therefore, we limit the sampling to 100 windows. We then extract dense SIFT feature vectors from each of these windows, and describe each via its bag-of-words representation using $2 \times 2 + 1 \times 1$ spatial tiling. The used codebook size is 1000 and the final feature vector dimensionality is 5000.

After sampling 100 windows from each image, we use k-means over the appearance feature vectors and group these 100 windows into 10 clusters. We use the cluster centers as our representation of candidate object regions. This step reduces the number of candidate object regions and also focuses on more condensed regions of potential objects. It is also likely that this clustering step smooths out the effect of the noise within candidate object regions.

As a result, we obtain multiple candidate regions from each image, some of which are likely to contain relevant objects for particular actions. However, we do not know which of these regions are related to the action. This case is particularly suitable for Multiple Instance Learning (MIL), since there are several candidate regions where some of them are noisy and some of them could potentially include related contextual object for the action. In the traditional supervised learning, the learning procedure works over instances x_i and their corresponding labels y_i. In contrast, multiple instance learning operates over bags of instances, where each bag B_i is composed of multiple instances x_{ij}. In our formulation, each image can be considered as a *"bag"* of possible object regions and each extracted candidate object region is a corresponding *"instance"* inside the bag. A bag B_i is labeled as positive, if at least one of the instances x_{ij} within the bag is known to be positive, whereas it is labeled as negative, if all the instances are known to be negative. This form of learning is referred as "semi-supervised" (or "weakly supervised"), since the labels for the individual instances (in our case, individual object regions) are not available, and only labels of the bags are given.

Given the extracted candidate bounding boxes, we adopt Multiple Instance Learning with Instance Selection (MILES) [17] algorithm for learning the related object regions. MILES algorithm works by embedding the original feature space x, to the instance domain $\mathbf{m}(B)$. Each bag corresponds to an image and therefore has an associated label $Y_i \in A$, where $A = \{a_1, ..., a_M\}$ is the possible set of M actions. Each bag is represented by its similarity to each of the instances in the dataset. In our formulation, since the number of images and number of windows extracted from each image is high, we can cluster the instances and find the "concept instances" for a more scalable representation. The similarity between bag $\mathbf{B}_i$ and a concept instance c_l is defined as

$$s(c_l, \mathbf{B}_i) = \max_j \exp\left(-\frac{D(x_{ij}, c_l)}{\sigma}\right), \tag{1}$$

where $D(x_{ij}, c_l)$ measures the distance between a concept instance c_l and a bag instance x_{ij} and σ is the bandwidth parameter. We use the Euclidean distance for D and for the concept instances c_l, we either use all the object regions or cluster the instances via k-means and use the cluster centers as c_l for each action. We evaluate the effect of this clustering in the experiments section.

Each bag can then be represented in terms of its similarities to each of these target concepts and this mapped representation $\mathbf{m}(B_i)$ can be written as

$$\mathbf{m}(B_i) = [s(c_1, B_i), s(c_2, B_i), \ldots, s(c_N, B_i)]^T. \tag{2}$$

Using this embedded representation, we then train an L2-regularized SVM with RBF kernel for each action class in a one-vs-all manner.

3.2   Facial Features for Action Recognition

For quite a number of actions, facial features can be an indicator of the ongoing action. For example, for catching action, the person can be looking into some direction focusing on the thrown object. Similarly, the objects around the face can be a cue for the actions such as talking on the phone, brushing teeth, and so on. Based on this observation, we investigate the effect of facial features for generic action recognition in still images. In [18], it has been shown that facial

Fig. 2. The first three images show the person bounding boxes and the face detector outputs, and the latter ones shows face regions determined wrt person bounding boxes

features can be useful in interaction recognition, and here we investigate their effect to generic actions.

With this intuition, we run a face detector [19] and for images in which the faces are detected, we extract an extended bounding box around the face area as shown in Fig. 2. For the images in which no face is detected, we use the top region of the person bounding box as the face area. From these regions, we extract dense SIFT [20] features and employ bag-of-words. We cluster the face images and form a codebook using k-means ($k = 1000$). Then using 2×2 spatial tiling, we extract the codeword histograms from each of the spatial bins. We also concatenate the bag-of-words histogram of the overall face region, hence the final feature vector size becomes 5000.

3.3 Additional Features

We also include additional features which are frequently used for action recognition to our evaluation framework. For this purpose, we extract the Histogram of Oriented Gradient(HOG) features from the person regions in the image. Furthermore, bag-of-words(BoW) representations extracted from person bounding boxes have also been evaluated. For this purpose, similar to BoW extracted around the faces, the SIFT features are densely extracted from the person regions and k-means clustering (with $k = 1000$) is applied to form the corresponding codebook. Then, 3×3 spatial binning is applied and all the codebook histograms from each spatial bin are concatenated with the global histogram extracted from the whole person region. In the end, the final feature vector for person BoW representation is 10000 dimensional.

In addition to the features extracted from the person region, we also consider the features from the original image and form the BoW representation from the whole image. This is also extracted in a similar manner to person BoW, where $3 \times 3 + 1 \times 1$ spatial tiling is used and the resulting feature vectors from each spatial bin are concatenated altogether to form a 10000-dimensional vector.

4 Experiments

4.1 Datasets and Experimental Setup

In the experiments, we use the Stanford 40 Actions dataset [1], which contains 40 actions and 180-300 images for each action. We use the same train/test split

Fig. 3. An example execution of the MIL framework (best viewed in color). Amongst the 10 example object regions extracted by [5] from the training set, the top 3 regions that contribute to the classification are shown in green, cyan and blue respectively.

provided, which includes 4000 train images and 5532 test images. The bounding boxes for the people doing the action are provided with the dataset. In our experiments, we use these bounding boxes in extracting person/face HoG and BoW features, both in the train and test phases, simulating the case with a perfect person detector, as in [15].

We train a one-vs-all SVM classifier for each of the feature representations separately. The final classification scores are obtained by linearly combining individual classifier confidences giving an equal weight for each feature representation.

4.2 Performance of the Individual Features

Example object/image regions that are discovered by the MIL training stage are shown in Fig. 3. For the visualization purposes, number of candidate object regions in this example run is limited to 10 and the top regions mapped to the most contributing concept instances are displayed. As it can be seen, the algorithm is quite successful in discovering the related object regions. In the "cooking" image, the dish region is discovered, whereas in "walking the dog" example, the dog is successfully located. The MIL method also finds the person region as a top contributing region in most of the cases.

In Table 1, we evaluate the effect of the clustering individual instances versus using all instances in the objectness-based MIL formulation. While the clustering provides a scalable representation that requires much less time (clustering with $k = 300$ runs ~ 14 times faster than no clustering case), using all the candidate object regions for instance embedding produces far more effective results in terms of the classification performance.

We then evaluate the performance of the individual features. Accuracy and mean Average Precision(mAP) values achieved by using individual features are

Table 1. Accuracy and mean average precision(mAP) achieved by our MIL approach

	accuracy	mAP
objectMIL ($k = 300$)	37.08	34.03
objectMIL ($k = 1000$)	46.78	46.01
objectMIL (no clustering)	**51.34**	**51.80**

Table 2. Accuracy and mean average precision(mAP) of individual features and the combinations

	accuracy	mAP
personHOG	24.75	19.35
personBoW	28.56	21.53
faceHOG	14.01	10.37
faceBoW	17.93	13.83
imgBoW	33.51	26.32
objectMIL	51.34	51.80
imgBoW+objectMIL	52.30	52.23
All(w/o objectMIL)	41.47	36.63
All	**55.93**	**55.55**
Yao [1]	NA	45.7

shown in Table 2. As it can be seen, the best performance is obtained using our MIL framework over the candidate object regions. This demonstrates that without explicit object detectors, we can extract useful information from the candidate object regions generated, in a weakly supervised manner by means of the multiple instance learning formulation.

Person-based features are also informative. Interestingly, performance of the BoW extracted from the whole image is higher than BoW extracted from the person bounding boxes only. This indicates that, the overall image contains more information than the person bounding box itself and the context information accompanying the person is useful for action recognition.

Figure 4 shows the performance of the individual features with respect to each action. Overall, the combination of all the features works the best for most of the actions. Interestingly, for some actions such as "climbing, rowing a boat, smoking and using computer" the performance of the proposed MIL framework performs better than using all features. BoW features over the facial region works best for the actions like "climbing, rowing a boat, playing violin, jumping, watching TV, shooting an arrow, brushing teeth". This is not surprising, since in these actions either the facial expression is representative of the action or the related object is closer to the face area. For "climbing, riding a horse, rowing a boat, playing guitar, riding a bike, playing violin, jumping, throwing frisby, running, applauding, holding an umbrella" kind of actions, HoG features around the face area are even more informative than the BoW counterpart. This may be due to the importance of orientation of faces in these type of actions.

4.3 Comparison to State-of-the-Art

We compare our method to the state-of-the-art method of Yao et al [1] in Table 2 and Figure 5. Yao et al.'s method is based on part and attribute representation, where each image is represented via a sparse set of "*action bases*". These action bases are defined as the high level interactions between individual action attributes and action parts. In this respect, the attributes that describe an action

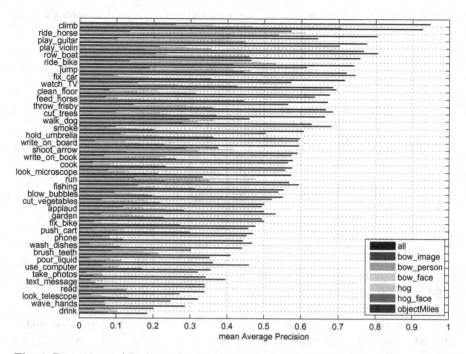

Fig. 4. Per action mAPs for each of the features (best viewed in color and magnified). Overall, combining all the features' responses works the best. For some actions, the performance of object MIL approach is even better than the combination.

are annotated and a discriminative binary classifier is trained for each action attribute. Moreover, each part is modeled by the output of an object detector (pre-trained on ImageNet data) or a pre-trained poselet detector [21].

In Table 2, imgBoW+objectMIL result shows the performance of our method without using any person bounding box information and All shows the performance of the proposed method using all features described in Section 3. Compared to the state-of-the-art result of Yao et. al [1], our method achieves significantly better results, while using much less supervision. Even without assuming the availability of a person detector, the objectness-based MIL method combined with image BoW features provide ∼ 6.5% performance improvement in this extensive dataset.

Looking at Fig. 5, we observe that our method outperforms the parts and attributes method of [1] for most of the actions, especially for "climbing, playing guitar, playing violin, fixing a car, cooking, smoking, cooking, applauding, phoning, taking photos, texting message" actions. This indicates that without using any explicit object/part detector, our method is able to discover the recurring objects or image regions that contribute to the recognition. On the contrary, [1] outperforms our method especially in "riding a horse, rowing a boat, riding a bike, walking the dog, shooting an arrow, fishing, holding an umbrella, running"

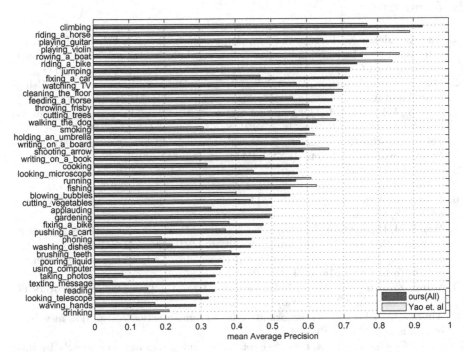

Fig. 5. Comparison of the proposed approach with that of Yao et al. [1] in terms of classification performance of the individual action classes

actions. This may be due to the success of the explicit detectors in locating certain objects and also due to the shared nature of the attribute classifiers.

5   Conclusions and Discussion

In this paper, we have proposed a method that leverages the candidate object regions in a weakly unsupervised manner via Multiple Instance Learning and evaluated the performance of this method in combination with other visual features for human action recognition in still images. Our experimental results show that the proposed MIL framework is suitable for extracting the relevant object information, without the need for explicit object detectors. We have achieved better classification performance compared to the state-of-the-art on the extensive Stanford 40 actions still image dataset.

Our findings indicate possible future directions, particularly, using richer representations over salient object regions and improving weakly supervised learning of relevant objects.

Acknowledgments. This work was supported by a Google Research Award.

References

1. Yao, B., Jiang, X., Khosla, A., Lin, A.L., Guibas, L.J., Fei-Fei, L.: Human action recognition by learning bases of action attributes and parts. In: International Conference on Computer Vision (ICCV), Barcelona, Spain (November 2011)
2. Gupta, A., Kembhavi, A., Davis, L.S.: Observing human-object interactions: Using spatial and functional compatibility for recognition. TPAMI 31, 1775–1789 (2009)
3. Yao, B., Fei-Fei, L.: Modeling mutual context of object and human pose in human-object interaction activities. In: CVPR, San Francisco, CA (June 2010)
4. Prest, A., Schmid, C., Ferrari, V.: Weakly supervised learning of interactions between humans and objects. IEEE TPAMI 34, 601–614 (2012)
5. Alexe, B., Deselaers, T., Ferrari, V.: What is an object? In: IEEE Conf. on Computer Vision and Pattern Recognition, San Francisco, USA (2010)
6. Poppe, R.: A survey on vision-based human action recognition. Image Vision Computing 28, 976–990 (2010)
7. Weinland, D., Ronfard, R., Boyer, E.: A survey of vision-based methods for action representation, segmentation and recognition. CVIU 115, 224–241 (2011)
8. Laptev, I., Marszalek, M., Schmid, C., Rozenfeld, B.: Learning realistic human actions from movies. In: CVPR (2008)
9. Wang, Y., Jiang, H., Drew, M.S., Li, Z.N., Mori, G.: Unsupervised discovery of action classes. In: CVPR (2006)
10. Thurau, C., Hlavac, V.: Pose primitive based human action recognition in videos or still images. In: CVPR (2008)
11. Ikizler-Cinbis, N., Cinbis, R.G., Sclaroff, S.: Learning actions from the web. In: Int. Conf. on Computer Vision (2009)
12. Yao, B., Fei-Fei, L.: Grouplet: a structured image representation for recognizing human and object interactions. In: The Twenty-Third IEEE Conference on Computer Vision and Pattern Recognition, San Francisco, CA (June 2010)
13. Desai, C., Ramanan, D., Fowlkes, C.: Discriminative models for static human-object interactions. In: Workshop on Structured Models in Computer Vision (2010)
14. Delaitre, V., Sivic, J., Laptev, I.: Learning person-object interactions for action recognition in still images. In: NIPS (2011)
15. Delaitre, V., Laptev, I., Sivic, J.: Recognizing human actions in still images: a study of bag-of-features and part-based representations. In: BMVC (2010)
16. Yao, B., Khosla, A., Fei-Fei, L.: Combining randomization and discrimination for fine-grained image categorization. In: CVPR, Springs, USA (June 2011)
17. Chen, Y., Bi, J., Wang, J.Z.: Miles: Multiple-instance learning via embedded instance selection. IEEE TPAMI 28, 1931–1947 (2006)
18. Patron-Perez, A., Marszalek, M., Reid, I., Zisserman, A.: High five: Recognising human interactions in tv shows. In: British Machine Vision Conference (2010)
19. Viola, P., Jones, M.: Rapid object detection using a boosted cascade of simple features. In: CVPR (2001)
20. Lowe, D.G.: Distinctive image features from scale-invariant keypoints. Int. J. Comput. Vision 60, 91–110 (2004)
21. Bourdev, L., Malik, J.: Poselets: Body part detectors trained using 3D human pose annotations. In: ICCV (2009)

Tighter Relaxations for Higher-Order Models Based on Generalized Roof Duality

Johan Fredriksson, Carl Olsson, Petter Strandmark, and Fredrik Kahl

Centre for Mathematical Sciences, Lund University, Sweden
http://www.maths.lth.se/vision/

Abstract. Many problems in computer vision can be turned into a large-scale boolean optimization problem, which is in general NP-hard. In this paper, we further develop one of the most successful approaches, namely roof duality, for approximately solving such problems for higher-order models. Two new methods that can be applied independently or in combination are investigated. The first one is based on constructing relaxations using generators of the submodular function cone. In the second method, it is shown that the roof dual bound can be applied in an iterated way in order to obtain a tighter relaxation. We also provide experimental results that demonstrate better performance with respect to the state-of-the-art, both in terms of improved bounds and the number of optimally assigned variables.

1 Introduction

Discrete energy minimization methods have become the golden standard for many computer vision and machine learning problems. Their ability to compute globally optimal solutions or strong relaxations makes them suitable for a large class of problems such as dense matching/stereo, segmentation, image synthesis [1]. Often formulations with pair-wise cliques are used to incorporate length regularization [2]. In this case graph cuts are able to compute optimal or guaranteed near optimal solutions for binary and multi-class problems [3].

The modeling power of pair-wise cliques is however limited and there has been an increasing interest in higher-order interactions. For example, to avoid the well known shrinking bias of length or area based approaches, curvature regularization which requires higher-order models is considered in [4, 5]. Other examples are [6] where approximate belief propagation is used for inference of a higher-order learned model, [7] where second order smoothness priors are used for stereo and [8] which uses a higher-order model for texture restoration. Even potentials where the cliques involve all variables have been considered [9].

In this paper we are interested in minimizing energies with higher-order interactions. Specifically, we will consider the quartic case (4th order energies), but in principle our methods can be applied to interactions of any order. Our work builds on the generalized roof duality methods presented in [10–12]. Here it is shown that a lower bound on the minimum of an nth order pseudo-boolean

A. Fusiello et al. (Eds.): ECCV 2012 Ws/Demos, Part III, LNCS 7585, pp. 273–282, 2012.

function can be found by performing a maximization over a set of nth order symmetric submodular pseudo-boolean functions. In practice however, determining whether a function is submodular is co-NP complete if $n \geq 4$ [13]. Therefore searching over the set of submodular functions is difficult. We propose to circumvent this problem by optimizing over positive linear combinations of a set of generators (or extreme rays). The idea of generators was first introduced in [12]. In this paper, even though the resulting function space is only a subset of all submodular functions, we show for $4th$ order models that optimizing over this subset yields significantly better results than previously published methods.

We also present a method for improving the lower bound and increasing the number of persistent variables based on a symmetric extension of the original objective function. The approach is iterative and is guaranteed to produce at least the lower bound of the roof dual. A similar approach was developed in [14] for the special case of quadratic pseudo-boolean functions.

Related Work. In recent years a number of strategies for optimizing higher-order energies have been proposed. In [15, 16] dual decomposition is used and move-making algorithms are proposed in [17, 18]. Furthermore, linear programming approaches have been considered [19] as well as belief propagation [6].

Our approach is based on max-flow/min-cut methods which are considered to be state-of-the-art for quadratic polynomials [1]. To handle higher-order interactions, reduction techniques have been developed [20–22]. In [20], a roof duality framework is presented based on reduction, but at the same time, the authors note that their roof duality bound depends on which reductions are applied. In contrast our work is based on [10, 12] which introduce a framework that works directly on the higher-order potentials.

The extension method has similarities to the probing method of [1] in the sense that both methods fixate one variable at the time and re-run the max-flow computations for the modified graph. However, we need only to fixate a variable once whereas probing requires fixating a variable to both 0 and 1. The methods can be used in combination for tighter relaxations.

2   Generalized Roof Duality

In this section we will briefly state some of the results from [12] that serve as a basis for our methods. The basic problem is that of minimizing a pseudo-boolean polynomial $f : \{0,1\}^n \mapsto \mathbb{R}$ of degree m. Since this problem is in general NP-hard the following family of relaxations is considered:

$$l(g) := \min_{(x,y) \in \{0,1\}^{2n}} g(x, y) \tag{1}$$

$$\text{s.t.} \quad g \text{ is submodular} \tag{2}$$

$$g(x, \bar{x}) = f(x) \tag{3}$$

$$g(x, y) = g(\bar{y}, \bar{x}). \tag{4}$$

Here the notation $\bar{x} = (1 - x_1, 1 - x_2, \ldots, 1 - x_n)$ is used. Note that the relaxation g has twice the number of variables, that is, $g : \{0,1\}^{2n} \mapsto \mathbb{R}$. A function g satisfying the last condition $g(x, y) = g(\bar{y}, \bar{x})$ is said to be *symmetric*. It can be seen that $l(g)$ is a lower bound on the minimum of f for any feasible g. Furthermore, [10] shows persistency of the minimizers of g: if $x_i^* = \bar{y}_i^*$ for a minimizer (x^*, y^*) of g then any minimizer z^* of f must have $z_i^* = x_i^*$. Hence, persistency can be used to determine the optimal assignment of a single variable.

The goal is now to find the strongest possible bound $l(g)$, that is, to maximize $l(g)$ over the set of feasible functions. To avoid solving the max-min problem, [12] proposes the following procedure:

1. Find $g^* \in \text{argmax } g(0, 0)$, where the maximum is taken over all functions g fulfilling (2)-(4).
2. Compute a minimizer $(x^*, y^*) \in \text{argmin } g^*(x, y)$.
3. If (x^*, y^*) is not identically zero, use persistency to simplify f and goto 1. Otherwise, stop.

The above procedure can be proved to provide a solution that gives a bound which is equal to or higher than $\max l(g)$. It turns out that if f is a quadratic pseudo-boolean function, then the obtained maximum bound is the same as the roof dual bound. Furthermore, for the cubic case ($m = 3$) it is shown that the maximization of $g(0, 0)$ can be computed using linear programming.

Unfortunately, when $m > 3$ determining whether a given polynomial is submodular is co-NP-complete. One way of avoiding this problem is to restrict the space of functions in the maximization of $g(0, 0)$ to a subset that is easy to generate. Ideally this set should be selected so that the maximum lower bound is not weakened too much. Next we will show how to use a set of generators to approximate the set of feasible functions well in the quartic case ($m = 4$).

3   Generators for Submodular Functions

The submodular symmetric functions of degree 4 form a cone. In this section we will construct a basis for a subcone that enables us to optimize over it efficiently. The elements of the basis are called *generators* and each submodular symmetric function can be written as a linear combination (with positive coefficients) of the generators. Unfortunately, not all generators of degree 4 can be optimized using max-flow/min-cut algorithms. Therefore we have to settle for optimizing over a subset of the cone.

The generators of the submodular (non-symmetric) cone are given in [23] for $n = 4$. There are 10 generator classes, however, one of the classes cannot be optimized using max-flow/min-cut [24]. For each generator $e(x_i, x_j, x_k, x_l)$ in the remaining 9 classes, we can construct a symmetric generator as

$$e(x_i, x_j, x_k, x_l) + e(\bar{y}_i, \bar{y}_j, \bar{y}_k, \bar{y}_l). \tag{5}$$

Such a generator can only generate monomials with either x-variables or y-variables. Therefore, we also incorporate generators where x- and y-variables have switched places, such as

$$e(y_i, x_j, x_k, x_l) + e(\bar{x}_i, \bar{y}_j, \bar{y}_k, \bar{y}_l). \tag{6}$$

The procedure gives 132 quartic generators for each combination of indices i, j, k, l. The same procedure can be applied to the lower order generators which result in 8 cubic generators for each i, j, k and 2 quadratic for each i, j.

In order to generate the roof dual bound we need to be able to maximize $g(\mathbf{0}, \mathbf{0})$ over feasible functions g. Given the generators above we can construct symmetric submodular functions from positive linear combinations

$$g(\boldsymbol{x}, \boldsymbol{y}) = \sum_{i=1}^{k} \alpha_i e_i(\boldsymbol{x}, \boldsymbol{y}), \quad \alpha_i \geq 0, \tag{7}$$

where $\{e_i\}_{i=1}^{k}$ are all of our generators. Moreover, by identifying coefficients, the constraint $g(\boldsymbol{x}, \bar{\boldsymbol{x}}) = f(\boldsymbol{x})$ can be implemented as a linear system of equations $A\boldsymbol{\alpha} = \boldsymbol{a}$, where $\boldsymbol{\alpha}$ is a vector containing all the coefficients α_i in the linear combination (7). Therefore the maximization of $g(\mathbf{0}, \mathbf{0})$ can be formulated as the linear program

$$\max \boldsymbol{c}^T \boldsymbol{\alpha} \tag{8}$$
$$\text{s.t. } A\boldsymbol{\alpha} = \boldsymbol{a} \tag{9}$$
$$\boldsymbol{\alpha} \geq \mathbf{0}, \tag{10}$$

where the vector $\boldsymbol{c}$ contains the coefficients for $e_i(\mathbf{0}, \mathbf{0})$.

In [11], a completely different way is used to construct g, not using generators. It can be shown that the feasible set of functions in this construction is a strict subset of the function cone generated by our generators.

4   Symmetric Extension

In order to improve the lower bound and increase the number of persistencies of $f : \{0, 1\}^n \to \mathbb{R}$, we will extend $f(\boldsymbol{x})$ by introducing an additional variable x_0. Let $\phi : \{0, 1\}^{n+1} \to \mathbb{R}$ be the extension of $f(\boldsymbol{x})$ such that

$$\phi(\boldsymbol{x}, x_0) = x_0 f(\boldsymbol{x}) + \bar{x}_0 f(\bar{\boldsymbol{x}}). \tag{11}$$

By construction we have $\phi(\boldsymbol{x}, 1) = f(\boldsymbol{x})$ and $\phi(\bar{\boldsymbol{x}}, 0) = f(\boldsymbol{x})$. The function ϕ is symmetric in the sense that $\phi(\boldsymbol{x}, x_0) = \phi(\bar{\boldsymbol{x}}, \bar{x}_0)$ and therefore

$$\min_{\boldsymbol{x}} f(\boldsymbol{x}) = \min_{x_0=1} \phi(\boldsymbol{x}, x_0) = \min_{x_0=0} \phi(\boldsymbol{x}, x_0). \tag{12}$$

It is easy to see that the same holds for any other variable x_k, $k = 1, \ldots, n$,

$$\min_{\boldsymbol{x}} f(\boldsymbol{x}) = \min_{x_k=1} \phi(\boldsymbol{x}, x_0) = \min_{x_k=0} \phi(\boldsymbol{x}, x_0). \tag{13}$$

The key observation is that if we can determine the optimal value of any of the variables for $\min_{x_k=1} \phi(\boldsymbol{x}, x_0)$ through persistency, then we can simplify the original problem $\min f(\boldsymbol{x})$.

Lemma 1. *If*

$$(\boldsymbol{x}^*, x_0^*) \in \operatorname{argmin}_{x_k=1} \phi(\boldsymbol{x}, x_0) \Rightarrow x_i^* = 1 \tag{14}$$

for some $i \neq k$, then, for every

$$\boldsymbol{z}^* \in \operatorname{argmin} f(\boldsymbol{z}) \Rightarrow z_k^* = z_i^*. \tag{15}$$

Proof. Let us assume that (14) holds but there is some solution $\boldsymbol{z}^*$ with $z_k^* \neq z_i^*$ and $f(\boldsymbol{z}^*) = \min f(\boldsymbol{z})$. We get two cases; either $z_k^* = 1$ or $z_k^* = 0$.

If $z_k^* = 1$ then we have

$$\phi(\boldsymbol{z}^*, 1) = f(\boldsymbol{z}^*) = \min f(\boldsymbol{z}) = \min_{x_k=1} \phi(\boldsymbol{x}, x_0). \tag{16}$$

Therefore $(\boldsymbol{z}^*, 1) \in \operatorname{argmin}_{x_k=1} \phi(\boldsymbol{x}, x_0)$ but $z_i^* = \bar{z}_k^* = 0$ contradicting (14).

If $z_k^* = 0$ then we have

$$\phi(\bar{\boldsymbol{z}}^*, 0) = \phi(\boldsymbol{z}^*, 1) = f(\boldsymbol{z}^*) = \min f(\boldsymbol{z}) = \min_{x_k=1} \phi(\boldsymbol{x}, x_0). \tag{17}$$

Therefore $(\bar{\boldsymbol{z}}^*, 0) \in \operatorname{argmin}_{x_k=1} \phi(\boldsymbol{x}, x_0)$ but $\bar{z}_i^* = z_k^* = 0$ contradicting (14).

Hence, we can reduce the number of variables of our original problem for each persistency obtained from the fixations of the symmetric extension. In case we can additionally determine x_0^*, the following stronger result holds.

Corollary 1. *If*

$$(\boldsymbol{x}^*, x_0^*) \in \operatorname{argmin}_{x_k=1} \phi(\boldsymbol{x}, x_0) \Rightarrow x_i^* = x_0^* = 1 \tag{18}$$

for some $i \neq k$, then, for every

$$\boldsymbol{z}^* \in \operatorname{argmin} f(\boldsymbol{z}) \Rightarrow z_k^* = z_i^* = 1. \tag{19}$$

Proof. Suppose (18) holds and there is a solution $\boldsymbol{z}^*$ with $z_i^* = 0$. First $z_i^* = z_k^*$ according to the Lemma 1. Then

$$\phi(\bar{\boldsymbol{z}}^*, 0) = \phi(\boldsymbol{z}^*, 1) = f(\boldsymbol{z}^*) = \min f(\boldsymbol{z}) = \min_{x_k=1} \phi(\boldsymbol{x}, x_0). \tag{20}$$

Therefore $(\bar{\boldsymbol{z}}^*, 0) \in \operatorname{argmin}_{x_k=1} \phi(\boldsymbol{x}, x_0)$ but $z_0^* = 0$ contradicting (18).

In Lemma 1 and Corollary 1 we have only considered the cases when $x_i^* = 1$ is persistent. Similar results can of course be derived when $x_i^* = 0$ is persistent. We summarize the results in Table 1.

To reduce the number of variables in f we use generalized roof duality to determine persistencies of $\min_{x_k=1} \phi(\boldsymbol{x}, x_0)$. Depending on which of the variables we fix to be one, different reductions can be obtained. Our approach is to

Table 1. Persistency in $\min_{x_k=1} \phi(x, x_0)$ and the resulting reductions in f

persistency of x_0^*	persistency of x_i^*	reductions in $f(z)$
-	$x_i^* = 1$	$z_k = z_i$
-	$x_i^* = 0$	$z_k = \bar{z}_i$
$x_0^* = 0$	$x_i^* = 1$	$z_k = z_i = 0$
$x_0^* = 0$	$x_i^* = 0$	$z_k = \bar{z}_i = 0$
$x_0^* = 1$	$x_i^* = 1$	$z_k = z_i = 1$
$x_0^* = 1$	$x_i^* = 0$	$z_k = \bar{z}_i = 1$

go through all the possible fixations systematically and reduce f as soon as a persistency is obtained. We summarize our algorithm below.

1. Construct $\phi(x, x_0)$ and set lower bound $l := -\infty$.
2. For $k = 0, \ldots, n$ do
   (i) Compute persistencies and lower bound l_k of $\min_{x_k=1} \phi(x, x_0)$.
   (ii) Reduce f using the persistencies and Table 1.
   (iii) Update the lower bound $l := \max(l, l_k)$.

The fixation $x_k = 1$ for $k = 0$ corresponds to the original function f as $\phi(x, 1) = f(x)$ and therefore the procedure will always give at least as many persistencies as the usual procedure. Note that no additional persistencies are obtained if one were to fixate $x_k = 0$ due to symmetry.

5   Experiments

In this section we will describe some challenging optimization problems in order to test and compare the performance of the proposed methods. We will use the methods listed in Table 2.

Table 2. Abbreviations for the different methods

RD	Standard roof duality [1]
GRD	Generalized Roof Duality (GRD) as in [12]
GRD-gen	GRD using generators (Section 3)
GRD-ext	GRD-gen in combination with symmetric extension (Section 4)
Fix et al.	The reductions proposed in [25]
HOCR	The reductions proposed in [22]

5.1   Segmentation with Curvature Regularization

We first present a segmentation experiment where higher order cliques model the curvature regularization. A discretized version of the following energy is used:

$$E(S) = \int_S f(x) \, dx + \int_{\partial S} (\rho + \sigma \kappa(s)^2) ds. \tag{21}$$

Here $f(\mathbf{x})$ is the cost of assigning $\mathbf{x}$ to the interior of S and the second term is a combined length and curvature regularizer. We will use the pseudo-boolean optimization approach suggested in [5] for an 8-connected grid which requires quartic interactions. The construction can be understood by examining Figure 1. The boolean variables x_a, x_b, x_c and x_d are assigned interior or exterior. The two arrows will contribute to the curvature if and only if both of them are on the boundary, that is, $x_a \neq x_b$ and $x_c \neq x_d$. This can be encoded using the quartic term

$$b_{ij}\Big(x_a x_c(1 - x_b)(1 - x_d) + (1 - x_a)(1 - x_c)x_b x_d\Big), \qquad (22)$$

where b_{ij} is the contributed curvature penalization.

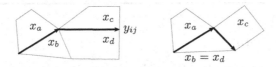

Fig. 1. Examples of four incident region variables x_a, x_b, x_c and x_d in an arbitrary mesh. The region variables may coincide for some edge pairs.

We use the cameraman as a test image, Figure 2. The unary data costs for the foreground and background are set to $\lambda(1 - I(\mathbf{x}))$ and $\lambda I(\mathbf{x})$, respectively, where $I(\mathbf{x}) \in [0, 1]$ is the gray scale value at position $\mathbf{x}$ and $\lambda = 75$. The length and curvature weights are set to $\rho = 1$ and $\sigma = \{1, 2\}$, respectively. Experimental data are collected in Table 3.

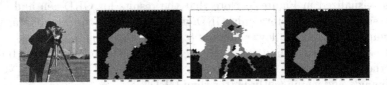

Fig. 2. Input image and the results for GRD, GRD-gen, and Fix et al. Unlabeled variables are colored black. The HOCR method returned no assigned variables.

None of the methods are able to produce a complete labeling which indicates the difficulty of the problem. The resulting (incomplete) segmentations for $\sigma = 1$ are plotted in Figure 2. Note that GRD-gen outperforms the competitors with more than 3 times as many assigned variables for $\sigma = 1$ and it is the only method to assign labels for $\sigma = 2$. While the runtime for GRD-gen was much faster than GRD it was considerably slower than both of the other methods. The GRD-gen method has potential for this problem but the approximation tightness needs to be improved in order to beat state-of-the-art based on LP relaxations [5].

Table 3. Results for the curvature experiments

$\sigma = 1$	Assigned variables	Runtime [s]	Lower bounds
GRD	20.8%	5050	4.24×10^4
GRD-gen	76.5%	1080	8.29×10^4
Fix et al.	16.0%	1.00	4.54×10^4
HOCR	0.00%	1.00	-7.42×10^4

$\sigma = 2$	Assigned variables	Runtime [s]	Lower bounds
GRD	0.00%	10300	-0.48×10^5
GRD-gen	34.4%	4995	0.719×10^5
Fix et al.	0.00%	1.00	-0.38×10^5
HOCR	0.00%	1.00	-2.872×10^5

5.2 Synthetic Data

In the final experiment, we test the various methods on synthetically generated polynomials with random coefficients:

$$f(x) = \sum_{(i,j,k,l) \in T} f_{ijkl}(x_i, x_j, x_k, x_l), \tag{23}$$

where $T \subseteq \{1 \dots n\}^4$ is a random set of quadruples and each f_{ijkl} is a fourth degree polynomial with its coefficient picked uniformly from $[-100, 100]$. The persistency results for problem instances with $n = 1000$, $|T| = \{50, 100, 200, 300\}$ are given in Table 4. The persistency distributions for $n = 1000$, $|T| = 300$ are also visualized in Figure 3. Note that the results for GRD-gen and GRD-ext are similar and therefore only GRD-gen is present in the left diagram. We also compare the relative lower bounds $(\ell - \ell_{GRD})/|\ell_{GRD}|$, where ℓ_{GRD} is the generalized roof dual bound for $f(x)$, see Table 5. The relative lower bounds follow the same trend as the persistency, GRD-gen and GRD-ext give similar lower bounds and significantly better than GRD.

Table 4. Results for the synthetic experiments

Assigned variables	$|T| = 50$	Runtime [s]	$|T| = 100$	Runtime [s]	$|T| = 300$	Runtime [s]
GRD-ext	74.5%	3.95	73.6%	17.9	68.3%	430
GRD-gen	73.6%	0.06	72.9%	0.10	66.5%	0.61
GRD	59.1%	0.06	56.3%	0.12	48.0%	1.01
Fix et al.	34.8%	0.00	33.2%	0.00	23.7%	0.01
HOCR	23.0%	0.00	21.4%	0.00	14.5%	0.01

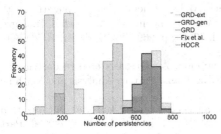

Fig. 3. Average persistency for the synthetic experiments with $|T| = 300$.

Table 5. Relative lower for the synthetic experiments with $|T| = 300$.

Rel. bounds	Min	Median	Max
GRD-ext	5.9%	7.7%	10.1%
GRD-gen	5.6%	7.5%	9.4%
GRD	0.0%	0.0%	0.0%
Fix et al.	−14.0%	−16.3%	−18.0%
HOCR	−44.6%	−48.9%	−52.6%

6 Discussion

Two new methods have been investigated with the objective to improve the performance of the well-known roof dual bound for pseudo-boolean optimization. We have experimentally demonstrated that (i) constructing submodular relaxations using generators significantly outperforms previously published methods and that (ii) applying the roof dual in an iterated manner does lead to stronger bounds and more persistencies, but may not be worth-while for the problems considered unless the extra computational cost can be drastically reduced.

We are currently working on improving the running times for the two methods. Most of the time is spent on the LP for constructing the relaxation. In [12], a heuristic scheme for GRD which completely avoids the LP is presented without any significant loss in relaxation performance. Essentially the same heuristics can be applied to GRD based on generators. Further, the max-flow computations in each step of the extension method are typically very similar. Therefore, reusing flows is a likely to speed up the computations.

Acknowledgments. This work was funded by the Swedish Foundation for Strategic Research through the programmes *Future Research Leaders* and *Wearable Visual Information Systems* and by the European Research Council through the programme *GlobalVision*.

References

1. Kolmogorov, V., Rother, C.: Minimizing nonsubmodular functions with graph cuts - a review. IEEE Trans. Pattern Anal. Mach. Intell. 29, 1274–1279 (2007)
2. Boykov, Y., Kolmogorov, V.: Computing geodesics and minimal surfaces via graph cuts. In: Int. Conf. Computer Vision, Nice, France (2003)
3. Boykov, Y., Veksler, O., Zabih, R.: Fast approximate energy minimization via graph cuts. IEEE Trans. Pattern Anal. Mach. Intell. 23, 1222–1239 (2001)
4. Schoenemann, T., Kahl, F., Cremers, D.: Curvature regularity for region-based image segmentation and inpainting: A linear programming relaxation. In: Int. Conf. Computer Vision, Kyoto, Japan (2009)
5. Strandmark, P., Kahl, F.: Curvature Regularization for Curves and Surfaces in a Global Optimization Framework. In: Boykov, Y., Kahl, F., Lempitsky, V., Schmidt, F.R. (eds.) EMMCVPR 2011. LNCS, vol. 6819, pp. 205–218. Springer, Heidelberg (2011)

6. Lan, X., Roth, S., Huttenlocher, D., Black, M.J.: Efficient Belief Propagation with Learned Higher-Order Markov Random Fields. In: Leonardis, A., Bischof, H., Pinz, A. (eds.) ECCV 2006, Part II. LNCS, vol. 3952, pp. 269–282. Springer, Heidelberg (2006)
7. Woodford, O., Torr, P.H., Reid, I., Fitzgibbon, A.: Global stereo reconstruction under second-order smoothness priors. IEEE Trans. Pattern Analysis and Machine Intelligence 31, 2115–2128 (2009)
8. Cremers, D., Grady, L.: Statistical Priors for Efficient Combinatorial Optimization Via Graph Cuts. In: Leonardis, A., Bischof, H., Pinz, A. (eds.) ECCV 2006, Part III. LNCS, vol. 3953, pp. 263–274. Springer, Heidelberg (2006)
9. Nowozin, S., Lampert, C.H.: Global interactions in random field models: A potential function ensuring connectedness. SIAM J. Imaging Sciences 3, 1048–1074 (2010)
10. Kolmogorov, V.: Generalized roof duality and bisubmodular functions. In: Neural Information Processing Systems (2010)
11. Kahl, F., Strandmark, P.: Generalized roof duality for pseudo-boolean optimization. In: Int. Conf. Computer Vision, Barcelona, Spain (2011)
12. Kahl, F., Strandmark, P.: Generalized roof duality. Discrete Appl. Math. (to appear, 2012)
13. Crama, Y.: Recognition problems for special classes of polynomials in 0-1 variables. Math. Programming 44, 139–155 (1989)
14. Boros, E., Hammer, P., Sun, R., Tavares, G.: A max-flow approach to improved lower bounds for quadratic unconstrained binary optimization (QUBO). Discrete Optimization 5, 501–529 (2008)
15. Komodakis, N., Paragios, N.: Beyond pairwise energies: Efficient optimization for higher-order MRFs. In: Conf. Computer Vision and Pattern Recognition, Miami, USA (2009)
16. Strandmark, P., Kahl, F.: Parallel and distributed graph cuts by dual decomposition. In: Conf. Computer Vision and Pattern Recognition, San Francisco, USA (2010)
17. Kohli, P., Kumar, M.P., Torr, P.: P^3 & beyond: Move making algorithms for solving higher order functions. IEEE Trans. Pattern Analysis and Machine Intelligence 31, 1645–1656 (2009)
18. Lempitsky, V., Rother, C., Roth, S., Blake, A.: Fusion moves for Markov random field optimization. IEEE Trans. Pattern Analysis and Machine Intelligence 32, 1392–1405 (2010)
19. Werner, T.: High-arity interactions, polyhedral relaxations, and cutting plane algorithm for MAP-MRF. In: Conf. Computer Vision and Pattern Recognition, Anchorage, USA (2008)
20. Lu, S., Williams, A.: Roof duality for polynomial 0-1 optimization. Math. Programming 37, 357–360 (1987)
21. Freedman, D., Drineas, P.: Energy minimization via graph cuts: Settling what is possible. In: Conf. Computer Vision and Pattern Recognition, San Diego, USA (2005)
22. Ishikawa, H.: Transformation of general binary MRF minimization to the first order case. IEEE Trans. Pattern Anal. Mach. Intell. 33, 1234–1249 (2011)
23. Promislow, S.D., Young, V.R.: Supermodular functions on finite lattices. Order 22, 389–413 (2005)
24. Živný, S., Cohen, D.A., Jeavons, P.G.: The expressive power of binary submodular functions. Discrete Appl. Math. 157, 3347–3358 (2009)
25. Fix, A., Grubner, A., Boros, E., Zabih, R.: A graph cut algorithm for higher-order markov random fields. In: Int. Conf. Computer Vision, Barcelona, Spain (2011)

Approximate Envelope Minimization
for Curvature Regularity

Stefan Heber, Rene Ranftl, and Thomas Pock

Institute for Computer Graphics and Vision, Graz University of Technology
Inffeldgasse 16, A-8010 Graz, Austria
{stefan.heber,ranftl,pock}@icg.tugraz.at
http://www.icg.tu-graz.ac.at

Abstract. We propose a method for minimizing a non-convex function, which can be split up into a sum of simple functions. The key idea of the method is the approximation of the convex envelopes of the simple functions, which leads to a convex approximation of the original function. A solution is obtained by minimizing this convex approximation. Cost functions, which fulfill such a splitting property are ubiquitous in computer vision, therefore we explain the method based on such a problem, namely the non-convex problem of binary image segmentation based on *Euler's Elastica*.

Keywords: Curvature, segmentation, convex conjugate, convex envelope.

1 Introduction

Many problems in computer vision such as image restoration, image segmentation, stereo and motion can be formulated as energy minimization problems. The energy functions to be minimized can be developed in different settings. In a MRF setting, the energy can be derived from the maximum a posteriori (MAP) formulation on a discrete graph with a node set representing the image pixels, and an edge set defining the pixel interactions to measure smoothness. In a variational setting, images are interpreted as continuous functions, and differential operators are used to measure smoothness of the functions. Although, both methods are very different in their theoretical background, they have in common that in the end one has to solve a numerical optimization problem. Hence, their success largely depends on the ability of the underlying numerical algorithm to find a solution close to the global optimizer.

Energies that can be solved globally are rare in computer vision. If the label set is binary and the pairwise terms are submodular, the energies can be minimized globally by computing a minimum cut [6,12] on the graph. The equivalent formulation in a variational setting is given by the total variation. See [3] for detailed relationships. Multi-label problems can not be solved globally in general. A remarkable exception is the case where the label set is ordered linearly and the pairwise terms are convex functions. It has been shown in [8] that this class of problems can be solved exactly by computing a minimum cut on an extended graph in higher dimensions. In a variational setting, it has been shown that the same class of energies can be minimized globally by solving a minimal surface problem in higher dimensions [16].

A. Fusiello et al. (Eds.): ECCV 2012 Ws/Demos, Part III, LNCS 7585, pp. 283–292, 2012.

Recently, higher order terms have attracted a lot of attention in the MRF community, because of their ability to model complex interactions between image pixels. Minimizing higher order terms is even harder than minimizing pairwise terms. One possibility is to apply reduction schemes such as the one presented in [9] to transform the higher order terms into pairwise terms and to subsequently make use of certain relaxation techniques such as QPBO [7,17,10] to solve the transformed energy. Although, the transformed energy is in general non-submodular, QPBO can still compute a partially optimal solution. Another possibility is to solve the higher order problem directly [10]. It is also possible to use linear programming (LP) relaxation techniques which can turn the problem into a tractable linear programming problem. This approach has been originally presented in [19] and has been extended and improved over the years in various ways *e.g.* [18,22,14].

In this paper, we propose a method for minimizing general non-convex energies, and we will discuss it based on the task of binary image segmentation with length and curvature regularization. Such curvature-based models have attained considerable attention in recent years, due to psychophysical experiments on contour completion [11]. These experiments pointed out, that curvature plays an important role in human perception. Thus, there is an increasing interest to incorporate curvature information as a prior to various imaging problems. Unfortunately, such curvature depending functionals are hard to minimize, due to their strong non-convexity.

In principal, any non-convex energy could be minimized by computing its convex envelope and by minimizing the convex envelope instead. However, computing the convex envelope is not tractable for most problems. Therefore, we propose to minimize an approximated convex envelope, which is computed by splitting the energy into combinatorially tractable parts, and then globally minimize the sum of the convex envelopes of those parts. Note, that the main idea of splitting the problem into appropriate subproblems is similar to the dual decomposition technique, which was used in [13] to address discrete MRF-based optimization problems in computer vision.

The paper is organized as follows. In Section 2 we will describe the task of binary image segmentation with length and curvature regularization, and we will show how to split up the according cost function into a set of simple functions. In Section 3 we will show how to minimize such type of functions. In Section 4 we will present some results and in the last section we will finally give a short conclusion.

2 Binary Image Segmentation with Curvature Regularity

The task of binary image segmentation is to divide the domain $\Omega \subset \mathbb{R}^2$ of a given image $I : \Omega \to \mathbb{R}$ into foreground R and background $\Omega \setminus R$ by minimizing the functional

$$f(R) = \lambda \int_R d(x)dx + \int_{\partial R} \left(\alpha + \beta \left|\kappa_{\partial R}(x)\right|^p\right) d\mathcal{H}^1(x) , \qquad (1)$$

where $d(x) = d_\Omega(x) - d_{\Omega \setminus R}(x)$. d_Ω and $d_{\Omega \setminus R}$ are functions, that depend on the input image I, and $\kappa_{\partial R}$ is the curvature of the boundary of R. Thus, the first integral in (1) represents the data-term weighted by λ. The second integral is Mumford's elastica curve model [15], where α weights the boundary length and β the curvature.

In what follows we will discretize $f(R)$ and split it into a finite sum of local functions $f_i(R)$, $1 \leqslant i \leqslant m$. Therefore, we have to divide our image domain Ω into a set of non-overlapping basic regions, called a cell-complex. Next, we define m local neighborhoods N_i, that are sets of connected basic regions and satisfy $\bigcup_{i=1}^{m} N_i = \Omega$.

In order to discretize the energy $f(R)$ we choose an arbitrary planar graph $G = (V, E)$ covering Ω with a vertex-set V and an edge-set E. The face-set F of the graph G defines the set of basic regions. Hence, the discrete version of (1) can be defined as

$$f_D(R) = \lambda \sum_{k=1}^{|F|} R_k d_k + \sum_{j=1}^{|V|} \left(\alpha\, l_j(\pi_j(R)) + \beta\, \kappa_j(\pi_j(R)) \right) , \tag{2}$$

where $R \in \{0, 1\}^{|F|}$ and each element R_k indicates if the basic region F_k is part of the foreground or not. $d \in \mathbb{R}^{|F|}$ contains the data-term for each basic region, and l_j and κ_j are functions calculating the length and curvature costs at each vertex V_j. Note, that for calculating the regularization costs for V_j we only need those elements of R, that correspond to the adjacent regions of V_j. Therefore, we select the according elements of R with a linear operator π_j. Now, we define for each neighborhood N_i a function

$$f_i(R) = \lambda \sum_{k=1}^{|F|} \chi_{N_i}(F_k)\, c_{ik}\, R_k\, d_k \tag{3}$$

$$+ \sum_{j=1}^{|V|} \chi_{\hat{N}_i}(V_j)\, \hat{c}_{ij} \left(\alpha\, l_j(\pi_j(R)) + \beta\, \kappa_j(\pi_j(R)) \right) ,$$

where $\hat{N}_i$ is the set of interior vertices of the neighborhood N_i, c_{ik} and $\hat{c}_{ij}$ are positive normalization coefficients satisfying

$$\sum_{i=1}^{m} \chi_{N_i}(F_k)\, c_{ik} = \sum_{i=1}^{m} \chi_{\hat{N}_i}(V_j)\, \hat{c}_{ij} = 1 . \tag{4}$$

As a result we can write (2) as a sum of simple functions $f_i(R)$.

$$f_D(R) = \sum_{i=1}^{m} f_i(R) \tag{5}$$

Now we explain how the functions l_j and κ_j calculate the regularization costs for the vertex V_j by an example. Consider the situation sketched in Fig. 1(a). Here, the gray regions belong to the foreground and the white regions belong to the background. Thus, the node V_1 belongs to the boundary of R with length cost $l_1(R_1, \ldots, R_5) = \frac{1}{2}(|e_1| + |e_4|)$, where $|e|$ is the length of the edge e. The division by two is necessary to get the correct length, when summing up over all vertices.

To measure the curvature we use a discrete formulation introduced by Bruckstein et al. [2]. Hence, in the case at hand, shown in Fig. 1(a), the curvature cost is

$$\kappa_1(R_1, \ldots, R_5) = \frac{\phi^p_{e_1, e_4}}{\min\{|e_1|, |e_4|\}^{p-1}} , \tag{6}$$

where ϕ_{e_1, e_4} is the angle between e_1 and e_4.

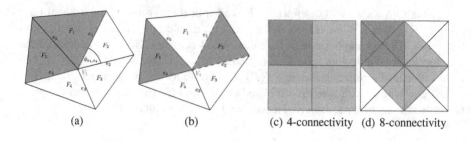

(a)   (b)   (c) 4-connectivity (d) 8-connectivity

Fig. 1. (a) and (b) show two foreground/background configurations for the adjacent regions of a vertex V_1. Such configurations are used to assign regularization costs to the vertex V_1. (a) shows a common boundary and (b) a situation where two boundary segments meet in a single vertex. (c) and (d) illustrate possible neighborhoods N_i (blue regions) and their corresponding interior vertices $\hat{N}_i$ (marked by purple dots), for 4- and 8-connectivity. These neighborhoods are defined for each pixel in the image, where a single pixel is indicated by the dark blue region.

The regularization costs are precomputed for certain configurations of R_k within a neighborhood N_i. Note that in the case where all adjacent regions of a vertex belong to either foreground or background the regularization cost vanishes. Configurations where different boundary segments meet at a single vertex (compare Fig. 1(b)) can be treated separately, *i.e.* we can calculate reasonable regularization cost, or we can also exclude such configurations by setting the costs to infinity. Thus, with our approach we can avoid problems with self-intersecting boundaries, present in the approach of Schoenemann *et al.* [20,21]. Furthermore, we can calculate the correct boundary cost for each configuration, including those, where boundaries meet at a single vertex. Such configurations are *e.g.* incorrectly handled in the 3-clique strategy presented by El-Zehiry and Grady [5].

Finally, Fig. 1(c) and 1(d) show some possibilities to define the cell-complex and the according neighborhoods.

3 Approximate Envelope Minimization

We are given the following minimization problem

$$\min_{x \in X} f(x), \quad \text{with} \quad f(x) = \sum_{i=1}^{m} \left(\tilde{f}_{A_i} \circ \pi_{A_i} \right)(x) , \tag{7}$$

where X is the n dimensional Euclidean space $\mathbb{R}^n$ and $f : X \to \mathbb{R}$ is a non-convex function. Moreover, the function $f(x)$ fulfills a certain splitting property, which allows us to rewrite it as the sum of functions $f_{A_i}(x) := (\tilde{f}_i \circ \pi_{A_i})(x)$. Here $\tilde{f}_{A_i} : X_{A_i} \to \mathbb{R}$ is a function defined on an appropriate subspace $X_{A_i} \subseteq X$. Each subspace X_{A_i} is implicitly defined according to an ordered index set $A_i = \{k_1, \ldots, k_{l_{A_i}}\}$ via the mapping $\pi_{A_i} : X \to X_{A_i}$,

$$\pi_{A_i}(x) := \left(x[k_1], \ldots, x[k_{l_{A_i}}] \right)^T , \tag{8}$$

where $x[t]$ is the tth element of x. Furthermore, we define the following pseudo re-projection $\pi^+_{A_i} : X_{A_i} \to X$

$$\pi^+_{A_i}(x) := y \in X, \text{ with } y[s] = \begin{cases} x[r] & \text{if } s \in A_i \text{ and } r = |\{k \leqslant s \mid k \in A_i\}| \\ 0 & \text{else}, \end{cases} \quad (9)$$

where $|A|$ denotes the cardinality of the set A, and we assume that

$$X = \left\{ \pi^+_{A_i}(x_{A_i}) \mid x_{A_i} \in X_{A_i}, 1 \leqslant i \leqslant m \right\} . \quad (10)$$

It is essential for our approach that the domain of a single function $\tilde{f}_{A_i}$ is much smaller than the domain of the function f. Further, note that the convex conjugate f^* and bi-conjugate f^{**} are by definition convex functions since they are written through a point-wise supremum over affine functions. Thus, it is clear that the minimizer of the non-convex optimization problem (7) can be computed by minimizing the convex envelope f^{**} instead. Unfortunately, computing f^{**} is intractable in many situations and hence there is not much hope to find a closed form expression for f^{**}. However, there is hope that we can compute a weaker approximation to the *true* convex envelope by allowing for some simplifications. The key idea is presented in Proposition 1.

Proposition 1. *Given the definitions above, the following inequality holds*

$$f^{**}(x) = \left(\sum_{i=1}^{m} \tilde{f}_{A_i} \circ \pi_{A_i} \right)^{**}(x) \geqslant \sum_{i=1}^{m} \left(\tilde{f}^{**}_{A_i} \circ \pi_{A_i} \right)(x) =: \bar{f}(x) . \quad (11)$$

Proof. See supplementary material. □

Proposition 1 basically shows, that a weaker (less tight) envelope $\bar{f}(x)$ is obtained by computing the sum of the bi-conjugate functions instead of the bi-conjugate of the sum. On the one hand, the expected advantage of the former is that the functions $\tilde{f}^{**}_{A_i}$ might be much easier to compute than $\left(\sum_{i=1}^{m} \tilde{f}_{A_i} \right)^{**}$. On the other hand, the quality of the relaxation depends on the splitting of f.

3.1   The Approximate Convex Envelope

As indicated by the task stated in Section 2, many problems in computer vision suggest a natural splitting of the energy, which is mainly motivated by the fact that energies are usually modeled by defining the interaction between certain elements in a local neighborhood. Thus each function $\tilde{f}_{A_i}$ in (7) can be defined to model the interaction in one specific neighborhood.

Moreover, based on a given splitting one can improve the relaxation by grouping certain functions f_{A_i} together to a new function f_{G_j}, *i.e.* summing up the according functions $\tilde{f}_{A_i}$. Note, that this grouping strategy improves the relaxation, but simultaneously increases the combinatorial complexity. In the following, we will work with an approximation to the true convex envelope given by

$$\hat{f}(x) = \sum_{j=1}^{\hat{m}} \left(\tilde{f}^{**}_{G_j} \circ \pi_{G_j} \right)(x) . \quad (12)$$

By using Proposition 1, one can easily verify, that the following inequalities hold for all $x \in X$.

$$f^{**}(x) \geqslant \hat{f}(x) \geqslant \bar{f}(x) \tag{13}$$

Hence, instead of minimizing f or f^{**}, we propose to minimize $\hat{f}$. The resulting minimization problem can be rewritten as the following saddle-point problem.

$$\min_{x \in X} \hat{f}(x) = \min_{x} \sum_{j=1}^{\hat{m}} \tilde{f}_{G_j}^{**} \left(\pi_{G_j}(x) \right) = \min_{x} \max_{y} \sum_{j=1}^{\hat{m}} \langle \pi_{G_j}(x), y_{G_j} \rangle - \tilde{f}_{G_j}^{*}(y_{G_j}) , \tag{14}$$

where $y = (y_{G_1}, \ldots, y_{G_{\hat{m}}})^{\mathrm{T}}$ and $y_{G_j} \in X_{G_j}^{*}$. In order to solve (14), it is crucial to handle the $\tilde{f}_{G_j}^{*}$ functions, which can be done in various ways. For simplicity we will use a polyhedral approximation which is explained in Section 3.2.

3.2 Polyhedral Approximations

In many interesting cases we do not expect that we will find an explicit formula for the conjugate functions $\tilde{f}_{G_j}^{*}$. Hence, we need to find an implicit representation. The key comes through the following inequality, which is provided by the definition of the convex conjugate. Given a function g and its convex conjugate g^{*}, one has for any x, $y \in X$

$$g^{*}(y) \geqslant \langle x, y \rangle - g(x) . \tag{15}$$

By definition equality is reached by taking the supremum over x of the right hand side. Let us now interpret the above inequality in terms of the epigraphs of g and g^{*}. Let (x, s) be a point in the epigraph of g. Then one has for any (y, t) in the epigraph of g^{*}

$$t \geqslant \langle x, y \rangle - s . \tag{16}$$

In other words, we can refine a polyhedral approximation of g^{*} by successively sampling points from the epigraph of g, and by adding inequality constraints as denoted in (16). Clearly, the largest (and hence most successful) constraints will be generated by taking points on the graph of g, *i.e.* points $(x, g(x))$. The idea is now to obtain an approximation of g^{*} by computing a finite number of points $\{(x_i, g_i), 1 \leqslant i \leqslant k\}$ on the graph of g. As shown above, we can generate a set of constraints of the form

$$t \geqslant \langle x_i, y \rangle - g_i \quad \text{for} \quad 1 \leqslant i \leqslant k . \tag{17}$$

Of course, the more constraints we add, the better the approximation will be. Note, that in the case of discrete multi-labeling problems the domain X is already finite. Thus, by taking all points in X as sampling points, we obtain an exact representation.

3.3 Linear Programming Formulation

Now we propose a relaxed version of the saddle-point problem described in (14) by using polyhedral approximations according to (17). By approximating each $\tilde{f}_{G_j}^{*}(x)$ in (14) one obtains the following relaxation

$$\min_{x} \max_{y,t} \sum_{j=1}^{n} \langle \pi_{G_j}(x), y_{G_j} \rangle - t_{G_j} \qquad (18)$$

$$\text{s.t. } t_{G_j} \geqslant \left\langle s^i_{G_j}, y_{G_j} \right\rangle - f_{G_j}(s^i_{G_j}), \text{ for } 1 \leqslant i \leqslant k_{G_j}, \ 1 \leqslant j \leqslant n,$$

where $t = (t_1, \ldots t_n)^{\mathrm{T}}$, and $s^i_{G_j}$ denotes the ith sampling position of the group G_j. By introducing Lagrange multipliers $\mu(s^i_{G_j})$ for each constraint we can identify the t_{G_j} variables as Lagrange multipliers for $\sum_{i=1}^{k_{G_j}} \mu(s^i_{G_j}) = 1$. Thus, the vector μ^j, which contains all elements of μ, that belong to the jth group, has to be on the standard k_{G_j}-dimensional unit simplex $S_{k_{G_j}}$. In a final step, we identify the y_{G_j} variables as Lagrange multipliers for $\pi_{G_j}(x) = \sum_{i=1}^{k_{G_j}} s^i_{G_j} \mu(s^i_{G_j})$ and rewrite (18) as

$$\min_{x,\mu} \sum_{j=1}^{n} \sum_{i=1}^{k_j} f_{G_j}(s^i_{G_j}) \mu(s^i_{G_j}) \qquad (19)$$

$$\text{s.t. } \mu^j \in S_{k_{G_j}}, \quad \pi_{G_j}(x) = \sum_{i=1}^{k_{G_j}} s^i_{G_j} \mu(s^i_{G_j}), \quad 1 \leqslant j \leqslant n.$$

By taking a closer look at (19), one can see, that the solution x is obtained as a collection of convex combinations of sampling positions within the groups. Furthermore, due to the definition of $\pi_{G_j}(x)$ these convex combinations have to coincide with the solutions of neighboring groups for elements, where their domains intersect.

The LP in (19) shows an interesting connection to the Shlezinger relaxation [19], which had been generalized by Werner et al. [23]. The only differences are the so called marginalization constraints obtained by discretizing the label space, which has not been done in the proposed method.

3.4 Primal-Dual Algorithm

In this section we describe how to solve the saddle-point problem (14) via the primal-dual approach described by Chambolle and Pock [4]. Therefore, it will be convenient to introduce a linear assembling operator A, such that $Ay = \sum_{j=1}^{\hat{m}} \pi^+_{G_j}(y_{G_j})$. By using this operator, we can rewrite (14) as

$$\min_{x} \max_{y} \langle Ay, x \rangle - \sum_{j=1}^{\hat{m}} f^*_{G_j}(y_{G_j}). \qquad (20)$$

A numerical algorithm to solve the above saddle-point problem is given by

$$\begin{cases} x^{k+1} = (x^k - \tau A y^k) \\ \bar{x}^{k+1} = x^{k+1} + \theta(x^{k+1} - x^k) \\ y^{k+1}_{G_j} = (\mathrm{id} + \sigma \partial f^*_{G_j})^{-1} \left(y^k_{G_j} + \sigma \left[A^* \bar{x}^{k+1} \right]_j \right) \quad \forall 1 \leqslant j \leqslant \hat{m}, \end{cases} \qquad (21)$$

where τ and σ are chosen such that $\tau\sigma\|A\|^2 < 1$ and $\theta \in [0, 1]$.

Thus, the only interesting thing to show is the calculation of the resolvent operator $(I + \sigma \partial f^*_{G_j})^{-1}(z)$, which is defined as the solution of

$$\underset{w}{\text{argmin}} \frac{\|w - z\|^2}{2\sigma} + f^*_{G_j}(w) . \tag{22}$$

By using the polyhedral approximation (17), we can rewrite (22) as

$$\underset{w,t}{\min} \frac{\|w - z\|^2}{2\sigma} + t \tag{23}$$

$$\text{s.t.} \ \left\langle s^i_{G_j}, w \right\rangle - f_{G_j}(s^i_{G_j}) - t \leqslant 0 , \ \forall 1 \leqslant i \leqslant k_{G_j} .$$

Introducing Lagrange multipliers $\mu = (\mu(s^1_{G_j}), \ldots, \mu(s^{k_{G_j}}_{G_j}))^{\mathrm{T}}$ for the inequality constraints, we arrive at

$$\underset{w,t}{\min} \underset{\mu \geqslant 0}{\max} \frac{\|w - z\|^2}{2\sigma} + t + \sum_{i=1}^{k_{G_j}} \left(\left\langle s^i_{G_j}, w \right\rangle - f_{G_j}(s^i_{G_j}) - t \right) \mu(s^i_{G_j}) . \tag{24}$$

Thus, minimizers in w are characterized by

$$w = z - \sigma \sum_{i=1}^{k_{G_j}} s^i_{G_j} \, \mu(s^i_{G_j}) . \tag{25}$$

By substituting this relation into the proximal map (24), we can get rid of w, and we see that t itself is just a Lagrange multiplier for $\sum_{i=1}^{k_{G_j}} \mu(s^i_{G_j}) = 1$, *i.e.* μ has to be in the standard k_{G_j}-dimensional unit simplex $S_{k_{G_j}}$. Hence we obtain

$$\underset{\mu \in S_{k_{G_j}}}{\min} \frac{\sigma}{2} \left\| \sum_{i=1}^{k_{G_j}} s^i_{G_j} \, \mu(s^i_{G_j}) - \frac{z}{\sigma} \right\|^2 + \sum_{i=1}^{k_{G_j}} f_{G_j}(s^i_{G_j}) \, \mu(s^i_{G_j}) , \tag{26}$$

which is a simplex constrained quadratic program, that can be solved *e.g.* with the FISTA algorithm presented by Beck and Teboulle [1].

Compared to the minimization strategy presented in Section 3.3, the quadratic program is defined point-wise, thus the μ variables need not to be saved for the entire set of neighborhoods, yielding a memory-efficient algorithm.

4   Results

In this section we present some experimental results for our example task of binary image segmentation based on Mumford's elastica curve model [15].

Here the data term in (2) is computed as $d = (I - \mu_f)^2 - (I - \mu_b)^2$, where I is the input image and $\mu_{f,b}$ are the mean values of the foreground and background. We set $\lambda = 1$ and evaluate the results for different α and β configurations (compare Fig. 2).

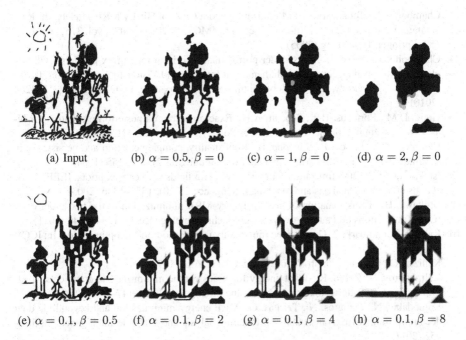

(a) Input   (b) $\alpha = 0.5, \beta = 0$ (c) $\alpha = 1, \beta = 0$ (d) $\alpha = 2, \beta = 0$

(e) $\alpha = 0.1, \beta = 0.5$ (f) $\alpha = 0.1, \beta = 2$ (g) $\alpha = 0.1, \beta = 4$ (h) $\alpha = 0.1, \beta = 8$

Fig. 2. Segmentation results for the Don Quixote image by Pablo Picasso (256×216 px) using a cell-complex, that corresponds to a 8-connected graph in graph cut frameworks (compare Fig. 1(d)). We set $\lambda = 1$ and show results for different α and β values. The processing time is between 1 and 5 minutes, depending on the strength of the regularization.

As expected the segmentation results with curvature regularity ($\beta \neq 0$) favor certain directions, and lead to polygonal structures. Moreover, one can see that the curvature regularization tends to preserve elongated structures, whereas the length regularization tries to remove them.

5   Conclusion

In this paper we proposed a novel approach for minimizing non-convex functions, that fulfill a certain splitting property. As such functions are ubiquitous in computer vision, the proposed approach is applicable to a broad class of problems. Moreover, we demonstrated the general applicability of the approach on the task of binary image segmentation based on Mumford's elastica curve model [15].

References

1. Beck, A., Teboulle, M.: A fast iterative shrinkage-thresholding algorithm for linear inverse problems. SIAM Journal on Imaging Sciences 2(1), 183 (2009)
2. Bruckstein, A.M., Netravali, A.N., Richardson, T.J.: Epi-convergence of discrete elastica. Applicable Analysis 79, 137–171 (2001)

3. Chambolle, A.: Total Variation Minimization and a Class of Binary MRF Models. In: Rangarajan, A., Vemuri, B.C., Yuille, A.L. (eds.) EMMCVPR 2005. LNCS, vol. 3757, pp. 136–152. Springer, Heidelberg (2005)
4. Chambolle, A., Pock, T.: A first-order primal-dual algorithm for convex problems with applications to imaging. Journal of Mathematical Imaging and Vision 40(1), 120–145 (2010)
5. El-Zehiry, N.Y., Grady, L.: Fast global optimization of curvature. In: CVPR, pp. 3257–3264 (2010)
6. Greig, D.M., Porteous, B.T., Seheult, A.H.: Exact maximum a posteriori estimation for binary images. Journal of the Royal Statistics Society 51(Series B), 271–279 (1989)
7. Hammer, P.L., Hansen, P., Simeone, B.: Roof duality, complementation and persistency in quadratic 0-1 optimization. Mathematical Programming 28(2), 121–155 (1984)
8. Ishikawa, H.: Exact optimization for markov random fields with convex priors. IEEE Transactions on Pattern Analysis and Machine Intelligence 25(10), 1333–1336 (2003)
9. Ishikawa, H.: Transformation of general binary MRF minimization to the first-order case. IEEE Transactions on Pattern Analysis and Machine Intelligence 33, 1234–1249 (2011)
10. Kahl, F., Strandmark, P.: Generalized roof duality for pseudo-boolean optimization. In: ICCV (2011)
11. Kanizsa, G.: Organization in Vision. Praeger, New York (1979)
12. Kolmogorov, V., Zabih, R.: What energy functions can be minimized via graph cuts. IEEE Transactions on Pattern Analysis and Machine Intelligence 26(2), 147–159 (2004)
13. Komodakis, N., Paragios, N., Tziritas, G.: MRF energy minimization and beyond via dual decomposition. IEEE Transactions on Pattern Analysis and Machine Intelligence 33, 531–552 (2011)
14. Komodakis, N., Tziritas, G.: A new framework for approximate labeling via graph cuts. In: ICCV, pp. 1018–1025 (2005)
15. Mumford, D.: Elastica and computer vision. In: Algebraic Geometry and Its Applications, pp. 491–506 (1994)
16. Pock, T., Cremers, D., Bischof, H., Chambolle, A.: Global solutions of variational models with convex regularization. SIAM Journal on Imaging Sciences 3(4), 1122–1145 (2010)
17. Rother, C., Kolmogorov, V., Lempitsky, V., Szummer, M.: Optimizing binary MRFs via extended roof duality. In: CVPR, pp. 1–8 (2007)
18. Schlesinger, D., Flach, B.: Transforming an arbitrary minsum problem into a binary one. Technical Report TUD-FI06-01, Dresden University of Technology (2006)
19. Schlesinger, M.: Syntactic analysis of two-dimensional visual signals in noisy conditions. Kibernetika 4, 113–130 (1976) (in Russian)
20. Schoenemann, T., Kahl, F., Cremers, D.: Curvature regularity for region-based image segmentation and inpainting: A linear programming relaxation. In: ICCV, September 29-October 2, pp. 17–23 (2009)
21. Schoenemann, T., Kahl, F., Masnou, S., Cremers, D.: A linear framework for region-based image segmentation and inpainting involving curvature penalization. International Journal of Computer Vision (to appear, 2012)
22. Werner, T.: A linear programming approach to max-sum problem: A review. IEEE Transactions on Pattern Analysis and Machine Intelligence 29(7), 1165–1179 (2007)
23. Werner, T.: Revisiting the linear programming relaxation approach to gibbs energy minimization and weighted constraint satisfaction. IEEE Trans. Pattern Anal. Mach. Intell. 32(8), 1474–1488 (2010)

Relating Things and Stuff by High-Order Potential Modeling

Byung-soo Kim[1,*], Min Sun[1,*], Pushmeet Kohli[2], and Silvio Savarese[1]

[1] University of Michigan, Ann Arbor, U.S.A
[2] Microsoft Research Cambridge, UK

Abstract. In the last few years, substantially different approaches have been adopted for segmenting and detecting "things" (object categories that have a well defined shape such as people and cars) and "stuff" (object categories which have an amorphous spatial extent such as grass and sky). This paper proposes a framework for scene understanding that relates both things and stuff by using a novel way of modeling high order potentials. This representation allows us to enforce labelling consistency between hypotheses of detected objects (things) and image segments (stuff) in a single graphical model. We show that an efficient graph-cut algorithm can be used to perform maximum a posteriori (MAP) inference in this model. We evaluate our method on the Stanford dataset [1] by comparing it against state-of-the-art methods for object segmentation and detection.

1 Introduction

The last decade has seen the development of a number of methods for object detection, segmentation and scene understanding. These methods can be divided into two broad categories: methods that attempt to model and detect object categories that have distinct shape properties such as cars or humans (*things*), and methods that seek to model and identify object categories whose internal structure and spatial support are more heterogeneous such as grass or sky (*stuff*). In the first category, we find that methods based on pictorial structures [2] or generalized Hough transform [3,4] work best. These representations are appropriate for capturing shape or structural properties of *things*, and typically parameterize the object hypothesis by a bounding box. The second category of methods aim at segmenting the image into semantically consistent regions [5,6,7] and work well for *stuff*, like sky or road.

Recently, researchers have proposed methods to jointly detect *things* and segment *stuff*. Gould et al. [8] proposed a random field model incorporating both stuff-stuff, thing-stuff, and thing-horizon relationships. However, MAP inference on their model is computationally expensive and typically takes around five minutes per image. To overcome this limitation, some authors have proposed inference procedures which iteratively solve different visual tasks (e.g., detection,

---

* Equal contributions.

A. Fusiello et al. (Eds.): ECCV 2012 Ws/Demos, Part III, LNCS 7585, pp. 293–304, 2012.

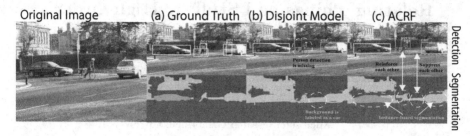

Fig. 1. Our goal is to segment the image into things (e.g., cars, humans, etc) and stuff (e.g., road, sky, etc) by combining segmentation (bottom) with object detection (top). Notice that our final ACRF recovers missing detections, and corrects mistaken segment labels since an object hypothesis and segments are reinforced or suppressed from the novel higher-order potential. At the top of each column, we show the top 3 probable bounding boxes, where light and dark boxes denote the confidence ranking from high to low, and dashed lines are used to indicate false detections. Segmentation results are shown in each bottom column, where we highlight our instance-based segmentation in (c)-bottom, where different colors represent different object instances. Notice that our final ACRF captures the key relationships and recovers many missing detections and segmentation labels by jointly reinforcing or suppressing each other. Thing-Stuff relationships are indicated by arrows connecting a bounding box and segments.

segmentation, occlusion reasoning, etc) using the outputs of state-of-the-art detection or segmentation methods as the input feature [9,10,11]. The drawback of these inference procedures is that different objective functions are optimized independently without guaranteeing that a joint solution is reached and that performances are improved at each iteration.

Ladicky et al. [12] introduce a higher-order potential to incorporate thing-stuff relationships and demonstrate that the information from object detection can be used to improve the segmentation performance. Their higher-order potential is designed so that an efficient graph-cut algorithm can be used to solve the MAP inference problem. However, the model of [12] encourages the labels of the segments to be the same as the label of the detection only when a detection is encountered. When a detection is not found, the labels of the segments are encourage to take labels other than the particular label of the detection. Therefore, the consistency of the object detections and segment labels is only weakly enforced. Finally, both [12,13] cannot be used to assign segments to object instances (i.e., object instances of same class cannot be distinguished in a labeling space.). On the contrary, our proposed model can address both issues.

We propose a novel framework for jointly detecting things and segmenting stuff by using a novel way of modeling high order potentials. Our contributions are three-fold. Firstly, the model enables to segment objects in expanded labeling space where classes as well as instances can be distinguished (see color coded segments in Fig. 1(c)) by associating segments of thing categories to instance-specific labels. Secondly, the higher-order potential enforces two types of consistency (i.e., reinforcement and suppression) between an object hypothesis and

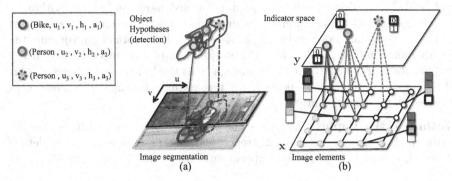

Fig. 2. Our Augmented CRF model (ACRF). In panel (a), we show an image and the indicator variables corresponding to the different object hypotheses present in it. Notice there are two person instance hypotheses in this example. The blue indicator is correct (solid-circle) and the purple indicator is mistaken (dash-circle). In panel (b), the figure shows the label space of the segmentation variables **X** and the indicator variables **Y** using the color-coded column. The interaction between variables are represented using edges. Notice that the dash-edges denote the indicator variable is turned off and suppresses the corresponding label in **X**, and the solid-edges denote the indicator variable is turned on and reinforces the corresponding label in **X**.

segments. As seen in Fig. 1(b), detections typically do not agree with the segmentation results if the detection and segmentation are applied separately. However, in our model the person segments are reinforced by a strong person detection, and the mistaken car segments are suppressed by a weak car detection from the background (Fig. 1(c)). Finally, the special design of the higher-order potential allows efficient inference which takes a few seconds per image in average using graph-cut.

Augmented CRF. Our framework extends the basic conditional random field (CRF) formulations for scene segmentation (i.e., stuff recognition) [14,6] by introducing the concept of an object instance hypothesis (Fig. 2-Top). Each hypothesis is described by object categorical label l, and 2D bounding box (u, v, h, a), where (u, v) denotes the 2D location and (h, a) denote the height and aspect ratio. We refer to our model as the augmented CRF, or ACRF, to highlight the newly added object hypothesis indicator variables. The indicator variables can take only two states, 0 or 1, which represents the absence or presence of an object instance hypothesis, respectively. The edges between two layers of ACRF highlight that labelling consistency between object detection and segment labels is enforced (Fig. 2).

Learning. We formulate the problem of learning these costs as a Structured SVM (SSVM) [15] learning problem with two types of loss functions related to the segmentation loss and detection loss, respectively (see Sec. 4 for details).

MAP Inference. Jointly estimating the segmentation variables X and object indicator variables Y (Fig. 2(c)) is challenging due to the intrinsic difference of the variable space and the presence of high-order potentials between things and stuff. We design an efficient graph-cut-based move making algorithm by combining state-of-the-art discrete optimization techniques. Our method is based on the α-expansion move making approach [16], which works by projecting the energy minimization problem of segmentation variables X into a binary energy minimization problem to have the same space as the indicator variables Y. Our MAP inference algorithm takes only a few seconds per image in average as opposed to five minutes in [8].

Outline of the Paper. The rest of the paper is organized as follows. We describe the model representation, inference, learning, and implementation details in Sec. 2, 3, and 4, respectively. Experimental results are given in Sec. 5.

2   Augmented CRF

Object segmentation, like other image labelling problems, is commonly formulated using Conditional Random Fields (CRF). The conventional CRF model is defined over a set of random variables $X = \{x_i\}$, $i \in \mathcal{V}$ where $\mathcal{V}$ represents the set of image elements, which could be pixels, patches, super-pixels, etc (Fig. 2 (b)-Bottom). Each random variable x_i is assigned to a label from a discrete label space **L**, which for the task of object-category segmentation, is considered the set $\mathcal{L}$ of object categories such as grass, road, car and people.

The energy (or cost) function $E(X)$ of the CRF is the negative logarithm of the joint posterior distribution of the model and has the following common form: $E(X) = -\log P(X|\mathcal{E}) = -\log \phi_{eRF}(X|\mathcal{E}) + \mathrm{K} = \sum_{c \in \mathcal{C}^X} \psi_c(X_c) + \mathrm{K}$, where $\mathcal{E}$ is the given evidence from the image and any additional information (e.g., object property lists), $\phi_{eRF}(X|\mathcal{E})$ takes the form of a higher order CRF model defined over image elements. $\phi_{eRF}(X|\mathcal{E})$ can be decomposed into potential ψ_c which is a cost function defined over a set of element variables (called a clique) X_c indexed by $c \in \mathcal{C}^X$, $\mathcal{C}^X$ is the set of cliques for image elements, and K is a constant related to the partition function. The problem of finding the most probable or maximum a posteriori (MAP) assignment of the CRF model is equivalent to solving the following discrete optimization problem: $X^* = \arg\min_{X \in \mathcal{L}^{|\mathcal{V}|}} E(X)$.

The standard CRF model mostly relies on bottom-up information. It is constructed using unary potentials based on local classifiers and smoothness potentials defined over pairs of neighboring pixels. Higher-order potentials such as the ones used in [6] reinforce labels of groups of image elements to be the same. This classic representation for object segmentation has led to excellent results for the stuff object categories, but has failed to replicate the same level of performance on the thing object categories.

In addition to the variables representing image elements, our model contains a set of indicator variables (later referred as indicators) $Y = \{y_j \in \{0, 1\}\}$ for every possible configuration $j \in \hat{\mathcal{Q}}$ of an object (Fig. 2 (c)-Top). The configuration set $\hat{\mathcal{Q}}$ is a Cartesian product of the space of all possible object category labels $\mathcal{L}$, all possible 2D bounding boxes in the image. For example, a configuration $j \in \hat{\mathcal{Q}}$ specifies that an instance of the object category $l_j \in \mathcal{L}$ exists at location (u_j, v_j) with height h_j and aspect ratio a_j in the image. We also associate each object instance with a segmentation mask $\mathcal{V}_j$ which is the set of image elements associated with the object (see technical report [17]).

As mentioned earlier, variables X representing the image elements in the classical CRF formulation for object segmentation take values for the set of object categories $\mathcal{L}$ only. In contrast, in our framework, these variables take values from a set of all possible object configuration $x_i \in \mathbf{L} = \hat{\mathcal{Q}}$ (refer as *augmented labeling space*). On the one hand, this allows us to obtain segmentations of individual instances of particular object categories which the classical CRF formulations are unable to handle. On the other hand, the space of all possible detections $\hat{\mathcal{Q}}$ is clearly huge, which makes learning and inference much more challenging. We will come back to this issue later.

The joint posterior distribution of the segmentation X and indicator variables Y can be written as: $P(X, Y|\mathcal{E}) \propto \phi_{eRF}(X|\mathcal{E}) \, \phi_{con}(X, Y|\mathcal{E})$. The potential function ϕ_{con} enforces that the segmentation and indicator variables take values which are consistent with each other (Fig. 2 (b)). The term is formally defined as: $\phi_{con}(X, Y|\mathcal{E}) = \prod_{j \in \hat{\mathcal{Q}}} e^{\Phi(y_j, X)}$, Hence, the model energy can be written as:

$$E(X, Y) = \sum_{c \in \mathcal{C}^X} \psi_c(X_c) + \sum_{j \in \hat{\mathcal{Q}}} \Phi(y_j, X) . \tag{1}$$

The first term of the energy function is defined in a manner similar to [6]. We now describe other terms of the energy function in detail in the following subsection.

Implicit Representation of Inactive Object Configurations. It is easy to see that the space of all possible configuration space $\hat{\mathcal{Q}}$ is huge, which would make learning and performing inference in the above model completely infeasible. However, in real world images, only a few possible configurations are actually present. Thus, most indicator variables y_j, $j \in \hat{\mathcal{Q}}$ are inactive (take value 0), and similarly the label set for the segmentation variables is typically quite small. We use an object detector that has been trained on achieving high recall rate to generate the set of *plausible* object configuration space $\mathcal{Q}$ instances that are likely to be present in any given image. In this way, we reduce the problem into a manageable size so that the inference algorithm can handle it in practice.

2.1 Relating Object Hypotheses Y and Segments X

The function $\Phi(y_j, X)$ is a likelihood term that enforces consistency in the assignments of the jth indicator variable y_j and a set of segmentation variables X. It is formally defined as:

$$\Phi(y_j, X) = \begin{cases} \inf & \text{if } y_j \neq \delta_j(X) \\ \gamma_{l_j} \cdot |\mathcal{V}_j| & \text{if } y_j = \delta_j(X) = 1 \\ 0 & \text{if } y_j = \delta_j(X) = 0 \end{cases} , \tag{2}$$

where j is any possible object configuration in $\mathcal{Q}$, the function $\delta_j(X)$ indicates whether the indicator j shares a consistent object category label with image elements in $\mathcal{V}_j$, and is defined as:

$$\delta_j(X) = \begin{cases} 1 & \text{if } R_j(X) = \frac{|\mathcal{V}_j(X)|}{|\mathcal{V}_j|} \geq R(l_j) \\ 0 & \text{otherwise} \end{cases}, \qquad (3)$$

where $|\mathcal{V}_j(X)| = |\{i; x_i = l_j \text{ for } i \in \mathcal{V}_j\}|$ is the number of elements in $\mathcal{V}_j$ assigned with label l_j, $|\mathcal{V}_j|$ is the total number of elements in $\mathcal{V}_j$, $R_j(X)$ is the consistency percentage, and $R(l_j) \in [0\ 1]$ is an object category-specific consistency threshold. Hence, the first condition in the above function ensures that $y_j = 1$ if and only if the detection j shares an object label with at least $R(l_j)$ percent of the pixels (or image element) in $\mathcal{V}_j$ (i.e. $R_j(X) \geq R(l_j)$). The remaining conditions in Eq. 2 shows that if the detection is considered correct by our model, the energy is penalized by $\gamma_j \cdot |\mathcal{V}_j|$, where γ_j is inversely proportional to the detection confidence.

3   Inference

We now show that the MAP inference problem in our ACRF model can be solved by minimizing the energy function using an efficient graph cut based expansion move making algorithm [16].

Standard move making algorithms repeatedly project the energy minimization problem into a smaller subspace in which a sub-problem is efficiently solvable. Solving this sub-problem produces a change to the solution (referred to as a move) which results in a solution having lower or equal energy. The *optimal* move leads to the largest possible decrease in the energy.

The *expansion* move algorithm projects the problem into a Boolean label sub-problem. In an α-expansion move, every segmentation variable X can either retain its current label or transit to the label α. One iteration of the algorithm involves making moves for all α in $\mathcal{L}$ successively. Under the assumption that the projection of the energy is pairwise and submodular, it can be exactly solved using graph cuts [18,19]. We derive graph construction only for energy terms related to indicator variables Y, for all other terms, the constructions are introduced in [6,16].

The energy terms related to the instance indicator variables are $\Phi(y_j, X)$ in Eq. 2. We observe that, when $y_j = 1$

$$\Phi(y_j, X) = \begin{cases} \inf & \text{if } \delta_j(X) = 0 \\ \gamma_j & \text{if } \delta_j(X) = 1 \end{cases} \approx \gamma_j \frac{1 - R_j(X)}{1 - R(l_j)}. \qquad (4)$$

When $y_j = 0$

$$\Phi(y_j, X) = \begin{cases} \inf & \text{if } \delta_j(X) = 1 \\ 0 & \text{if } \delta_j(X) = 0 \end{cases} \approx \gamma_j \frac{R_j(X)}{R(l_j)}. \qquad (5)$$

Hence, $\Phi(y_j, X)$ can be approximated by

$$\Phi(y_j, X) = \gamma_j (y_j \frac{1 - R_j(X)}{1 - R(l_j)} + (1 - y_j) \frac{R_j(X)}{R(l_j)}). \qquad (6)$$

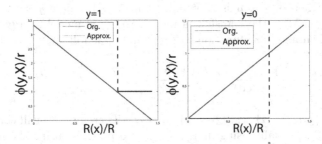

Fig. 3. Comparison between the original function $\Phi(y, X)$ (blue line) and the approximated function (red lines) in Eq. 5 and 4. The left panel shows the case when $y = 1$. The right panel shows the case when $y = 0$. Notice the dash blue lines indicate the sharp transition from finite values to infinite values.

The effect of the approximation in Eq. 5 and 4 are shown in Fig. 3. Instead of imposing an infinite cost when $\delta(X) \neq y$, our approximation imposes an cost which is linearly proportional to the consistency percentage $R(X)$. When $y = 1$, the ratio between the consistency percentage and the consistency threshold $R(X)/R(l)$ are *reinforced* to be large, which means the more elements in X labeled as l the better (Fig. 3-Left). On the contrary, When $y = 0$, the ratio between the consistency percentage and the consistency threshold $R(X)/R(l)$ are *suppressed* to be small, which means the less elements in X labeled as l the better (Fig. 3-Right). In the next section, we show that the approximated higher-order potential becomes pair-wise and submodular when applying the standard transformation function for the α-expansion move.

3.1 α-Expansion Move Energy

We first define the transformation function $T_\alpha(x_i; t_i)$ for the α-expansion move which transforms the label of a random variable x_i as:

$$T_\alpha(x_i; t_i) = \begin{cases} \alpha, & \text{if } t_i = 0 \\ x_i, & \text{if } t_i = 1 \end{cases} \tag{7}$$

The corresponding α-expansion move energy for the term in Eq. 6 can be written as: $\Phi(y_j, T_\alpha(X; T)) =$

$$\begin{cases} \gamma_j \left(\frac{y_j}{1 - R(l_j)} (1 - R_j(X) + \sum_{i \in \mathcal{V}_j(X)} \frac{(1-t_i)}{|\mathcal{V}_j|}) \right. \\ \left. + \frac{1 - y_j}{R(l_j)} (\sum_{i \in \mathcal{V}_j(X)} \frac{(t_i)}{|\mathcal{V}_j|}) \right), \text{if } \alpha \neq l_j \\ \gamma_j \left(\frac{1 - y_j}{R(l_j)} (R_j(X) + \sum_{i \in \mathcal{V}_j \setminus \mathcal{V}_j(X)} \frac{(1-t_i)}{|\mathcal{V}_j|}) \right. \\ \left. + \frac{y_j}{1 - R(l_j)} (\sum_{i \in \mathcal{V}_j \setminus \mathcal{V}_j(X)} \frac{(t_i)}{|\mathcal{V}_j|}) \right), \text{if } \alpha = l_j \end{cases} \tag{8}$$

where $T = \{t_i\}$ and $\mathcal{V}_j \setminus \mathcal{V}_j(X)$ is the remaining set of elements in $\mathcal{V}_j$ with labels (i.e.,$\{x_i \neq l_j; i \in \mathcal{V}_j\}$). Notice that when $\alpha \neq l_j$ the function is submodular in

(y_j, t_i), but when $\alpha = l_j$ it is submodular in $(\overline{y}_j, t_i)$, where $\overline{y}_j = 1 - y_j$ is the negation of y_j. After the transformation, the original model energy becomes a pairwise and submodular function of T, Y, and $\overline{Y}$ as follows,

$$E(T, Y, \overline{Y}) = \sum_{c \in \mathcal{C}^X} \psi_c(T_c) + \sum_{j \in \hat{\mathcal{Q}}_1} \Phi(y_j, T) + \sum_{j \in \hat{\mathcal{Q}}_2} \Phi(\overline{y}_j, T) . \tag{9}$$

where $\hat{\mathcal{Q}}_1 = \{y_j; l_j \neq \alpha\}$ and $\hat{\mathcal{Q}}_1 = \{y_j; l_j = \alpha\}$. Therefore, we will construct the graph using T, partially using indicator y_j, and partially using the negation of indicator $\overline{y}_j$ depending on whether $l_j = \alpha$.

4 Learning

The full CRF model in Eq. 1 contains several terms. In order to balance the importance of different terms, we introduce a set of linear weights for each term as follows,

$$W^T \Psi(X.Y) = \sum_{c \in \mathcal{C}} w_c \psi_c(X_c) + \sum_{j \in \mathcal{Q}_1} w^u(l_j)(\Phi(y_j, X)) \tag{10}$$

where w_c models weights for unary, pair-wise, and higher-order terms in X, and $w^u(l)$ is the object category specific weight for the consistency potential between Y and X.

Assume that a set of example images, ground truth segment object category labels, and ground truth object bounding boxes $\{I^n, X^n, Y^n\}_{n=1,...,N}$ are given. The SSVM problem is as follows,

$$\min_{W, \xi \geq 0} W^T W + C \sum_n \xi^n(X, Y) \tag{11}$$

$$\text{s.t.} \quad \xi^n(X, Y) = \max_{X, Y}(\triangle(X, Y; X^n, Y^n) + W^T \Psi(X^n, Y^n) - W^T \Psi(X, Y)), \forall n ,$$

where W concatenates all the model parameters which are linearly related to the potentials $\Psi(X, Y)$; C controls the relative weight of the sum of the violated terms $\{\xi^n(X, Y)\}$ with respect to the regularization term; $\triangle(X, Y; X^n, Y^n)$ is the loss function that generates large loss when the X or Y is very different from X^n or Y^n. The designed loss functions and the algorithm we used to solve this optimization problem are described in the technical report [17].

The remaining model parameters are set as follows. The object category-specific $R(l)$ in Eq. 2 are estimated using the median values observed in training data.

5 Experiments

We compare our full ACRF model with [1,20,21,12,13] on Stanford Background (refer as Stanford) dataset [1]. As opposed to other datasets, such as MSRC [14], Stanford dataset contains a large number of cluttered scenes and "things"

(a) Global Accuracy					
[1]	[21]	[20]	[13]	[12]	ACRF
76.4	76.9	77.5	80.0	80.2	**82.0**

(b)	Background	Car	Person	Motor-bike	Bus	Boat	Cow	Sheep	Bi-cycle	Global	Avg.
CRF	77.4	49.1	39.9	15.3	76.3	18.9	65.0	70.4	17.3	79.9	47.7
ACRF	77.1	56.7	61.7	9.3	69.7	36.9	88.1	62.8	64.2	82.0	58.5

Fig. 4. Segmentation performance comparison on the Stanford dataset. (a) Global segmentation accuracy of our ACRF model compared with state-of-the-art methods, where "Global" is the overall percentage of pixels correctly classified. (b) System analysis of our model. The CRF row shows the results by using only the stuff-stuff relationship component (first term in Eq. 1) of our ACRF model. The last row shows results of the full ACRF model. Notice "Avg." is the average of the percentage over eight foreground classes and one background class.

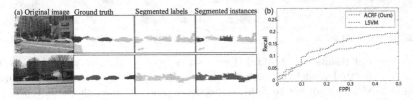

Fig. 5. (a) Typical thing segmentation results on the Stanford dataset. Notice that our model can obtain instance-based segmentations (last column) due to the ability to reason in the augmented labeling space $\hat{Q}$. (b) Recall v.s. FPPI curves of our ACRF and LSVM on Stanford dataset. Our ACRF achieves better recall at different FPPI values.

object instances per image which makes segmenting and detecting "things" to particularly challenging tasks.

For the experiments below, we use the same pre-trained LSVM detectors [2] to obtain a set of object-instance hypotheses for "things" categories (e.g., car, person, and bike). The object depths are inferred by combining both cues from the size and the bottom positions of the object bounding boxes similar to [22,10]. The responses from off-the-shelf stuff classifiers are used as the unary stuff potentials in our model. We model different types of pair-wise stuff relationships using a codebook representation similar to [23].

Stanford Dataset. Stanford dataset [1] contains 715 images from challenging urban and rural scenes. On top of 8 background ("stuff") categories, we annotate 9 foreground ("things") object categories - car, person, motorbike, bus, boat, cow, sheep, bicycle, others. We follow the 5-fold cross-validation scheme which splits the data into different 572 training and 143 test images. We use the same STAIR Vision Library [24] used in [1] to obtain the stuff unary potentials. Pixel-wise segmentation performance are shown in Fig. 4. Our ACRF model outperforms all state-of-the-art methods [20,1,21,12,13] [1] (Fig. 4(a)). A system analysis of our model (Fig. 4(b)) shows that the performances of most foreground classes (five out of eight) are significantly improved when additional components are added on top of the baseline CRF model, while the performance

---

[1] We implement [12,13] by ourselves and evaluate the performance.

302   B. Kim et al.

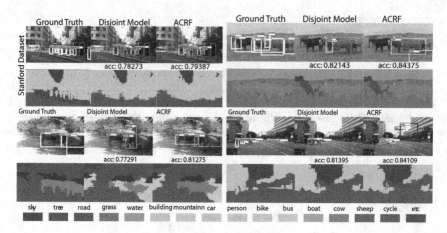

Fig. 6. Typical results on Stanford. Every set of results compare ground truth annotation, disjointed model (disjointedly applied object detection and segmentation), CRF+Det, ACRF, from left to right, respectively. The odd rows show the top K object hypotheses (color-coded bounding boxes representing the confidence ranking from light to dark), where K is the number of recalled objects in the ACRF result. The even rows show the segmentation results (color-code as shown at the bottom).

of the background classes remain almost unchanged. As a result, the full ACRF model obtains the best performance for six out of eight foreground classes and a 10.8% average improvement over the baseline model. Typical results are shown in Fig. 6-Top. We highlight that our model can generate object instance-based segmentations due to the ability to reason in the *augmented labeling space* $\hat{Q}$ (Fig. 5(a)). Our method can predict the numbers of object instances per image accuractely with an average errors of 0.27.

Another advantage of using our model is the ability to improve detection accuracy. We measured detection performance in terms of Recall v.s. False Positive Per Image (FPPI) in Fig. 5(b), where detection results from 5-fold validations are accumulated and shown in one curve. The performance of the proposed model is compared with the pre-trained LSVM [2]. Our model achieves consistent higher recall than the LSVM baseline as shown in Fig. 5(b).

6   Conclusion

We have presented a unified CRF-based framework for jointly detecting and segmenting "things" and "stuff" categories in natural images. We have shown that our framework incorporates in a coherent fashion various types of (geometrical and semantic) contextual relationships by introducing a novel high order potential model. Our new formulation generalizes previous results based on CRF where the focus was only to reinforce agreement between detections and segmentations. We have quantitatively and qualitatively demonstrated that our method: i) produces better segmentation results than state-of-the art on the Stanford dataset; ii) improves the recall of object instances on Stanford dataset.

Acknowledgements. We acknowledge the support of the Gigascale Systems Research Center and NSF CPS grant #0931474.

References

1. Gould, S., Fulton, R., Koller, D.: Decomposing a scene into geometric and semantically consistent regions. In: ICCV (2009)
2. Felzenszwalb, P., McAllester, D., Ramanan, D.: A discriminatively trained, multi-scale, deformable part model. In: CVPR (2008)
3. Leibe, B., Leonardis, A., Schiele, B.: Combined object categorization and segmentation with an implicit shape model. In: ECCV Workshop on Statistical Learning in Computer Vision (2004)
4. Gall, J., Lempitsky, V.: Class-specific hough forests for object detection. In: CVPR (2009)
5. He, X., Zemel, R.S., Carreira-Perpiñán, M.Á.: Multiscale conditional random fields for image labeling. In: CVPR (2004)
6. Kohli, P., Ladicky, L., Torr, P.H.: Robust higher order potentials for enforcing label consistency. In: CVPR (2008)
7. Shotton, J., Blake, A., Cipolla, R.: Semantic texton forests for image categorization and segmentation. In: CVPR (2008)
8. Gould, S., Gao, T., Koller, D.: Region-based segmentation and object detection. In: NIPS (2009)
9. Heitz, G., Gould, S., Saxena, A., Koller, D.: Cascaded classification models: Combining models for holistic scene understanding. In: NIPS (2008)
10. Sun, M., Bao, S.Y., Savarese, S.: Geometrical context feedback loop. IJCV (2012)
11. Hoiem, D., Efros, A.A., Hebert, M.: Closing the loop on scene interpretation. In: CVPR (2008)
12. Ladický, L., Sturgess, P., Alahari, K., Russell, C., Torr, P.H.S.: What, Where and How Many? Combining Object Detectors and CRFs. In: Daniilidis, K., Maragos, P., Paragios, N. (eds.) ECCV 2010, Part IV. LNCS, vol. 6314, pp. 424–437. Springer, Heidelberg (2010)
13. Ladicky, L., Russell, C., Kohli, P., Torr, P.H.S.: Graph Cut Based Inference with Co-occurrence Statistics. In: Daniilidis, K., Maragos, P., Paragios, N. (eds.) ECCV 2010, Part V. LNCS, vol. 6315, pp. 239–253. Springer, Heidelberg (2010)
14. Shotton, J., Winn, J., Rother, C., Criminisi, A.: *TextonBoost*: Joint Appearance, Shape and Context Modeling for Multi-class Object Recognition and Segmentation. In: Leonardis, A., Bischof, H., Pinz, A. (eds.) ECCV 2006, Part I. LNCS, vol. 3951, pp. 1–15. Springer, Heidelberg (2006)
15. Tsochantaridis, I., Hofmann, T., Joachims, T., Altun, Y.: Support vector learning for interdependent and structured output spaces. In: ICML (2004)
16. Boykov, Y., Veksler, O., Zabih, R.: Fast approximate energy minimization via graph cuts. PAMI (2001)
17. Kim, B., Sun, M., Kohli, P., Savarese, S.: Relating things and stuff by high-order potential modeling. Technical report (2012), http://www.eecs.umich.edu/vision/ACRFproj.html
18. Boros, E., Hammer, P.: Pseudo-boolean optimization. Discrete Applied Mathematics (2002)
19. Kolmogorov, V., Zabih, R.: What energy functions can be minimized via graph cuts. PAMI (2004)

20. Tighe, J., Lazebnik, S.: SuperParsing: Scalable Nonparametric Image Parsing with Superpixels. In: Daniilidis, K., Maragos, P., Paragios, N. (eds.) ECCV 2010, Part V. LNCS, vol. 6315, pp. 352–365. Springer, Heidelberg (2010)
21. Munoz, D., Bagnell, J.A., Hebert, M.: Stacked Hierarchical Labeling. In: Daniilidis, K., Maragos, P., Paragios, N. (eds.) ECCV 2010, Part VI. LNCS, vol. 6316, pp. 57–70. Springer, Heidelberg (2010)
22. Hoiem, D., Efros, A.A., Hebert, M.: Putting objects in perspective. In: CVPR (2006)
23. Bosch, X.B., Gonfaus, J.M., van de Weijer, J., Bagdanov, A.D., Serrat, J., Gonzàlez, J.: Harmony potentials for joint classification and segmentation. In: CVPR (2010)
24. Gould, S., Russakovsky, O., Goodfellow, I., Baumstarck, P., Ng, A., Koller, D.: The stair vision library (v2.3) (2009)

Submodular Relaxation for MRFs with High-Order Potentials

Anton Osokin and Dmitry Vetrov

Moscow State University, Russia
anton.osokin@gmail.com, vetrovd@yandex.ru

Abstract. In the paper we propose a novel dual decomposition scheme for approximate MAP-inference in Markov Random Fields with sparse high-order potentials, i.e. potentials encouraging relatively a small number of variable configurations. We construct a Lagrangian dual of the problem in such a way that it can be efficiently evaluated by minimizing a submodular function with a min-cut/max-flow algorithm. We show the equivalence of this relaxation to a specific type of linear program and derive the conditions under which it is equivalent to generally tighter LP-relaxation solved in [1]. Unlike the latter our relaxation has significantly less dual variables and hence is much easier to solve. We demonstrate its faster convergence on several synthetic and real problems.

Keywords: Markov random fields, energy minimization, MAP-inference, dual decomposition, high-order potentials.

1 Introduction

Markov random fields (MRFs) are a popular approach for analyzing interdependent data. Its main advantage is the ability to express the joint distribution over the whole set of hidden variables in terms of a product of potentials usually depending on small subsets of the variables. Small-order MRFs became very wide-spread in many tasks that arise in computer vision mainly for regularization purposes since they allowed to take the context (or neighborhood) into account. However, recently it has been shown that the use of high-order terms can improve the accuracy in many vision problems (see, e.g. [2]).

One of the most important tasks in any MRF is the search of most probable configuration, also known as MAP-inference. In this paper we will describe this task in terms of minimizing the negative log-likelihood of MRF (energy).

Recently, the minimization of MRF energies with high-order potentials has attracted a lot of attention. One line of research is to develop reductions of general high-order energies to equivalent pairwise ones. The drawback of this approach is that the resulting minimization problem can be exponentially large [3]. However, for some classes of high-order potentials this transformation can be performed efficiently: Rother et al. in [4] show that sparse or pattern-based potentials (potentials that encourage small number of predefined node configurations) can be efficiently transformed into pairwise ones.

A. Fusiello et al. (Eds.): ECCV 2012 Ws/Demos, Part III, LNCS 7585, pp. 305–314, 2012.

A popular way to minimize energies with high-order potentials without a reduction is applying a specialized version of α-expansion algorithm [5] that takes those potentials into account on each expansion-step. This approach can be applied only for specific type of high-order potentials: $\mathcal{P}^n$ Potts potentials [6] and their robust version [2] encourage all the nodes in a specific area to take the same label, label costs [7] penalize the total number of labels used in the solution. Although sometimes being efficient in practice this approach usually does not give any guarantees on the solution and can get stuck in local minima.

Another approach to minimizing energies with high-order potentials is to generalize the dual decomposition scheme proposed in [8]. The most obvious generalization adds a subproblem per each high-order potential (in what follows we refer to this approach by clique-wise decomposition, CWD)[1]. As any dual decomposition method CWD ends up with a convex non-smooth dual problem and is guaranteed to solve a specific LP-relaxation of the initial problem. The main drawback of CWD is its high computational complexity induced by two factors: the dual problem is non-smooth and its dimensionality is high. Komodakis and Paragios in [1] show that in case of pattern-based potentials it is possible to cleverly combine multiple high-order potentials in one subproblem and thus improve both the convergence speed and tightness of the relaxation.

In all dual decomposition methods the final optimization problem is convex but non-smooth and thus quite difficult to solve. The most standard way to tackle it is to use different subgradient-based schemes (see [8] for review). This methods are intuitive, produce almost zero computational overhead, but are not robust and are very sensitive to parameter choice. Finding better ways to optimize the dual is an area of active research (see e.g. [9,10]).

In this paper we try to reduce the dimensionality of the dual problem and thus make it easier to solve. We propose a quite general framework that is based on a Lagrangian decomposition that extends recently proposed Submodular Decomposition method (SMD) [11]. Our approach in theory deals with arbitrary high-order potentials but is practical only for pattern-based potentials and their robust versions (including (robust) $\mathcal{P}^n$ Potts and label costs). We provide the theoretical analysis of our approach and its empirical evaluation.

The rest of the paper is organized as follows: we present submodular relaxation algorithm in section 2; section 3 explores its theoretical properties including convergence points, persistency property and considers an important special case of permuted $\mathcal{P}^n$ Potts potentials; in section 4 we provide experiments and and finish with a conclusion in section 5.

2   Submodular Relaxation

Consider hypergraph $\mathcal{G} = (\mathcal{V}, \mathcal{C})$ where $\mathcal{V}$ is a set of nodes and $\mathcal{C}$ is a set of hyperedges. Let $x_i \in \{1, \ldots, K\} = \mathcal{K}$, $i \in \mathcal{V}$ be a discrete variable (label) associated with each node. Consider a problem of minimizing the following energy (negative log-likelihood of an MRF up to a constant):

---

[1] In [1] this approach was referred to as "generic optimization".

$$E(X) = \sum_{i \in \mathcal{V}} \phi_i(x_i) + \sum_{c \in \mathcal{C}} \phi_c(\boldsymbol{x}_c), \tag{1}$$

where $\phi_i(x_i)$, $\phi_c(\boldsymbol{x}_c)$ are unary and high-order potentials, $\boldsymbol{x}_c = (x_{i_1^c}, \ldots, x_{i_{L(c)}^c})$ is a labeling of nodes incident to hyperedge c; $L(c)$ stands for the order of hyperedge c. Energy (1) can be rewritten in terms of indicator variables $y_{ik} \in \{0,1\}$ ($y_{ik} = 1 \iff x_i = k$):

$$E(Y) = \sum_{i \in \mathcal{V}} \sum_{k=1}^{K} \phi_i(k) y_{ik} + \sum_{c \in \mathcal{C}} \sum_{\boldsymbol{k} \in \mathcal{K}^{L(c)}} \phi_c(\boldsymbol{k}) \prod_{l=1}^{L(c)} y_{i_l^c k_l}. \tag{2}$$

Unconstrained minimization of energy (1) over multi-label variables X is equivalent to minimization of energy (2) over binary variables Y under consistency constraints:

$$\sum_{k=1}^{K} y_{ik} = 1, \ \forall i \in \mathcal{V}. \tag{3}$$

Note that by adding constant term we may always ensure $\phi_c(\boldsymbol{k}) \leq 0$ for all c. In this case we can use identity $\left(- \prod_{l=1}^{L} y_{i_l}\right) = \min_{z \in \{0,1\}} \left((L-1)z - \sum_{l=1}^{L} y_{i_l} z\right)$ to transform high-order energy (2) into pairwise energy in such a way that $\min_{Y \in (3)} E(Y) = \min_{Z,Y:Y \in (3)} E(Y, Z)$.[2]

Note that for general high-order potentials $\phi_c(\boldsymbol{x}_c)$ function $E(Y, Z)$ depends on exponentially many variables Z. In what follows we assume the pattern-based (or sparse) form of $\phi_c(\boldsymbol{x}_c)$, i.e. most of values are equal to zero and others are negative. Specifically, denote labelings of potential c that we encourage by $\mathcal{D}^c = \{\boldsymbol{d}^c\} = \{(d_1^c, \ldots, d_{L(c)}^c)\}$.[3] Using this notation $E(Y, Z)$ can be written as follows:

$$E(Y, Z) = \sum_{i \in \mathcal{V}} \sum_{k=1}^{K} \phi_i(k) y_{ik} - \sum_{c \in \mathcal{C}} \sum_{\boldsymbol{d}^c \in \mathcal{D}^c} \phi_c(\boldsymbol{d}^c) \left((L(c) - 1) z_{c, \boldsymbol{d}^c} - \sum_{l=1}^{L(c)} y_{i_l^c d_l^c} z_{c, \boldsymbol{d}^c} \right). \tag{4}$$

Energy $E(Y, Z)$ is submodular w.r.t. variables Y and Z and thus in absence of additional constraints can be efficiently minimized by min-cut/max-flow algorithms [12]. Adding and relaxing constraints (3) to the minimization of (4) gives us the following Lagrangian dual:

$$D(\Lambda) = \min_{Y,Z \in \{0,1\}} L(Y, Z, \Lambda) = \min_{Y,Z \in \{0,1\}} \left(E(Y, Z) + \sum_{i \in \mathcal{V}} \lambda_i \left(\sum_{k=1}^{K} y_{ik} - 1 \right) \right). \tag{5}$$

---

[2] This transformation of binary high-order function (2) is in fact equivalent to a special case Type-II binary transformation of [4], but in this form it was proposed much earlier (see e.g. [3] for review).

[3] All the remaining derivations in this section can be generalized to a robust version of pattern based potentials using robust Type-II transformation of [4].

Function $D(\Lambda)$ is a lower bound on energy (1) and is concave but non-smooth. Thus, it can be maximized e.g. by subgradient algorithms. Note that $L(Y, Z, \Lambda)$ remains submodular w.r.t. (Y, Z) for all Λ allowing us to efficiently evaluate D at any point. We refer to this approach as submodular relaxation (SMR).

It is worth emphasizing that in contrast to CWD and PatB methods of [1] number of dual variables in our approach does not depend on the number of high-order potentials (always equals to $|\mathcal{V}|$). In CWD dual there are $K \sum_{c \in \mathcal{C}} L(c)$ variables. PatB reduces this number by combining multiple high-order potentials in one subproblem but will still have in at least in a factor of K more variables than SMR for the case when high-order potentials densely cover all variables. SMR can be naturally combined with SMD [11] and include pairwise potentials without the increase of the number of dual variables but for both CWD and PatB this modification will require additional subproblems thus increasing the dimensionality of the dual even further.

3   Theoretical Properties

In this section we explore some properties of the relaxation that is solved by maximizing lower bound $D(\Lambda)$ and address some practical issues of its application to inference problems.

3.1   General Case

Theorem 1. *Maximum of the SMR dual function $D(\Lambda)$ (5) is equal to the solution of the following linear program:*

$$\min_{Y,Z} Q(Y, Z) \tag{6}$$

$$s.t. \quad y_{ik}, z_{c,\boldsymbol{d}^c} \in [0, 1], \quad \forall i \in \mathcal{V}, k \in \mathcal{K}, c \in \mathcal{C}, \boldsymbol{d}^c \in \mathcal{D}^c \tag{7}$$

$$z_l^{c,\boldsymbol{d}^c} \leq z_{c,\boldsymbol{d}^c}, \quad z_l^{c,\boldsymbol{d}^c} \leq y_{i_l^c d_l^c}, \quad \forall c \in \mathcal{C}, \boldsymbol{d}^c \in \mathcal{D}^c, \forall l = 1, \ldots, L(c) \tag{8}$$

$$\sum_{k=1}^{K} y_{ik} = 1, \quad \forall i \in \mathcal{V} \tag{9}$$

where the target function $Q(Y, Z)$ is defined as follows:

$$Q(Y, Z) = \sum_{i \in \mathcal{V}} \sum_{k=1}^{K} \phi_i(k) y_{ik} - \sum_{c \in \mathcal{C}} \sum_{\boldsymbol{d}^c \in \mathcal{D}^c} \phi_c(\boldsymbol{d}^c) \left((L(c) - 1) z_{c,\boldsymbol{d}^c} - \sum_{l=1}^{L(c)} z_l^{c,\boldsymbol{d}^c} \right).$$

Proof. Denote

$$R(\Lambda) = \min_{Y,Z \in (7),(8)} \left(Q(Y, Z) + \sum_{i \in \mathcal{V}} \lambda_i \left(\sum_{k=1}^{K} y_{ik} - 1 \right) \right).$$

Recall that $\phi_c(\boldsymbol{d}^c) \leq 0$. In this case problem (6), (7), (8) is equivalent to the standard (Schlesinger's) LP-relaxation of binary submodular energy (4) which is known to be tight (see, e.g. [13]) and hence $R(\Lambda) = D(\Lambda)$. Consider $\Lambda^* = \arg\max R(\Lambda)$. Due to the strong duality in LP problems there exist primal and dual variables such that

$$(\Lambda^*, Y^*, Z^*) = \arg\max_{\Lambda} \min_{Y,Z\in(7),(8)} \left(Q(Y,Z) + \sum_{i\in\mathcal{V}} \lambda_i^* \left(\sum_{k=1}^{K} y_{ik} - 1 \right) \right)$$

$$= \arg\min_{Y,Z\in(7),(8)} \max_{\Lambda} \left(Q(Y,Z) + \sum_{i\in\mathcal{V}} \lambda_i^* \left(\sum_{k=1}^{K} y_{ik} - 1 \right) \right).$$

This implies that (Y^*, Z^*) satisfy (9), i.e. $R(\Lambda^*)$ is equal to the solution of the problem (6)—(9). Finally, equality $R(\Lambda^*) = D(\Lambda^*)$ completes the proof.

3.2   Permuted $\mathcal{P}^n$ Potts

Relaxation (6)-(9) is not the best possible LP-relaxation of initial problem. In [1] the authors formulated a tighter relaxation with additional constraint responsible for marginalization of higher order potential w.r.t all but one variable:

$$\sum_{\mathbf{k}\in\mathcal{K}^{L(c)}:\ k_l=k_0} z_l^{c,k} = y_{i_l^c k_0}, \quad \forall c \in \mathcal{C},\ k_0 \in \mathcal{K},\ l = 1,\dots,L(c). \quad (10)$$

Definition 1. *A higher order potential is called permuted* $\mathcal{P}^n$ *Potts iff*

$$\forall c \in \mathcal{C}\ \forall i \in c\ \forall \mathbf{d}', \mathbf{d}'' \in \mathcal{D}^c:\quad \mathbf{d}' \neq \mathbf{d}'' \Rightarrow d_i' \neq d_i''.$$

In permuted $\mathcal{P}^n$ Potts potentials all preferable configurations differ from each other in all variables. $\mathcal{P}^n$ Potts potential described in [6] is a special case.

Theorem 2. *If all higher-order potentials are permuted* $\mathcal{P}^n$ *Potts, then the maximum of dual function* (5) *is equal to the solution of LP* (6)-(10).

Proof. The proof follows from the fact that in the case of permuted $\mathcal{P}^n$ potential for each i_l^c and for each $k \in \mathcal{K}$ there exists no more than one $\mathbf{d}^c \in \mathcal{D}^c$ such that $d_l^c = k$. But each single $z_l^{c,\mathbf{d}^c} = y_{i_l^c k_l}$ due to (8) and negative sign of $\phi_c(\mathbf{d}^c)$.

3.3   Consistency

Now examine the properties of point $\Lambda^* = \arg\max D(\Lambda)$. Denote

$$Z_{ik}(\Lambda) = \text{Arg}\min_{y_{ik}} \left[\min_{Y\setminus\{y_{ik}\},Z} L(Y,Z,\Lambda) \right].$$

Definition 2. *Point* Λ *is a weak agreement point if*

$$\forall i \in \mathcal{V}\ \exists k: \{1\} \subseteq Z_{ik}(\Lambda),\ \forall k' \neq k, \{0\} \subseteq Z_{ik'}(\Lambda).$$

Informally this definition means that at weak agreement point Λ means for each node i of MRF there is at least one label k such that there exists unconstrained minimum of $L(Y, Z, \Lambda)$ w.r.t. $Y, Z \in \{0, 1\}$ such that $y_{ik} = 1$ and there exist optimal configurations where all other $y_{ik'} = 0$.

Theorem 3. *Point Λ^* satisfies weak agreement.*

The proof is performed by contradiction and is almost identical to the proof of theorem 4 in [11].

Definition 3. *For a weak agreement point Λ define a strong agreement set:*

$$S(\Lambda) = \left\{ i \in \mathcal{V} \mid |Z_{ik}(\Lambda)| = 1 \ \forall k \right\}.$$

For any node from the strong agreement set the consistent labeling (i.e. labeling that satisfies (3)) can be restored from $Z_{ik}(\Lambda)$. It is easy to show that if $S(\Lambda) = \mathcal{V}$ then $D(\Lambda)$ is equal to the optimal solution of (2) and the optimal labeling can be extracted uniquely from $Z_{ik}(\Lambda)$. A more interesting question is whether there exists optimal labeling such that for each node from $S(\Lambda^*)$ its labeling equals the one obtained from $Z_{ik}(\Lambda)$ (so-called, persistency property). Unfortunately, the answer is generally negative even for maximal cliques of size two (see the supplementary material [4] for a counter-example).

Note that this result is similar to the analogous result for tree-reweighted message passing (TRW) for pairwise MRFs. In [13] it was proven that for binary problems $(K = 2)$ persistency holds for nodes strongly labeled with TRW, but for $K > 2$ it does not hold. If $K = 2$ in pairwise MRF SMR is equivalent to QPBO [14] method for which persistency is well-known to hold.

3.4   Getting a Primal Solution

Due to the lack of persistency property the question of a getting primal solution after solving the dual is not trivial. We suggest the following post-processing procedure. First assign $y_{ik} = 1$ if $\{1\} \subseteq Z_{ik}(\Lambda)$ and $\nexists k' < k : \{1\} \subseteq Z_{ik'}(\Lambda)$ and $y_{ik} = 0$ otherwise. Define

$$\hat{Y}_c = \arg\min_{\sum_{k=1}^{K} y_{ik}=1} \left(\sum_{k=1}^{K} \sum_{i \in c} (\phi_i(k) + \lambda_i^*) y_{ik} + \sum_{d^c \in \mathcal{D}^c} \phi_c(d^c) \prod_{l=1}^{L(c)} y_{i_l^c d_l^c} \right).$$

For each $c \in \mathcal{C}$ try to improve the current labeling Y by setting $Y_c = \hat{Y}_c$. If $E(Y)$ is reduced we change the current labeling. Then we switch to next c until all hyperedges have been considered. The process is repeated several times. This procedure is similar to Iterated Conditional Modes and therefore we refer to it as ICM.

---

[4] http://bayesgroup.ru/wp-content/uploads/2012/01/
SMR_HiPot12_supplementary.pdf

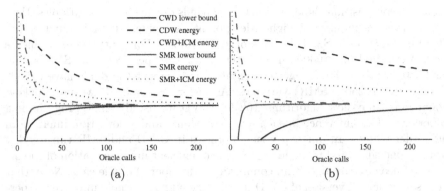

Fig. 1. Energies/lower bounds produced by SMR and CWD on synthetic datasets. All blue curves correspond to CWD, red curves – to SMR; solid lines show the lower bounds, dashed lines — energies obtained via random agreement of the subproblems, dotted lines – energies after 1 cycle of greedy improving via ICM (see sec. 3.4). (a) corresponds to the dataset with high-order potentials of size 50, (b) – of size 500.

4   Experiments

In this section we present an empirical evaluation of SMR compare it against CWD. We also evaluate the effect ICM-based postprocessing scheme on both methods. We perform the comparison on two synthetic sets of energies and one energy acquired from an image segmentation problem.

Both synthetic datasets consist of 20 energies depending on 10-label variables that form 4-neighborhood grids graphs of 50x50 nodes. All unary potentials are generated from gaussian distribution $\mathcal{N}(0, 10)$. The pairwise potentials are all Potts: $0.1|c_{ij}|[x_i \neq x_j]$, where $c_{ij} \sim \mathcal{N}(0, 1)$. Afterwards we add 50 $\mathcal{P}^n$ Potts potentials. For the first experiment we add potentials connecting random 50 nodes each, for the second experiment – 500 random nodes each. The costs of the potentials are generated from the uniform distribution on the segment $[0, 100]$.

As an image segmentation problem we take segmentation of image (fig. 3a) into three classes: "fern", "ground", "grass". For each class we select a small region (seeds) and fit a Gaussian mixture distribution with 5 components to colors of selected pixels in CIELUV color-space. Negative log-densities form unary terms, pairwise terms are Potts with weight 1, high-order potentials are posed on mean-shift superpixels computed with EDISON[5] system [15] with default parameters, the weight of high-order potentials is 100.

In SMR we minimize submodular functions using Boykov-Kolmogorov max-flow/min-cut algorithm [16][6]. To implement CWD we make the following decomposition of the energy: all pairwise potentials are separated into vertical and horizontal chains, each high-order potential forms a separate subproblem, unary potentials are evenly distributed between the horizontal and the vertical forests.

---

[5] http://coewww.rutgers.edu/riul/research/code/EDISON/

[6] http://pub.ist.ac.at/~vnk/software/maxflow-v3.02.src.tar.gz

In such decomposition the dual function depends on $|\mathcal{V}|K(1+h)$ variables. Here h is an average number of high-order potentials incident to individual nodes. The dual function in SMR depends on $|\mathcal{V}|$ variables. For synthetic experiments the CWD's dual has 50000 and 275000 variables respectively, the SMR's dual has 2500 variables. For image segmentation experiment the duals have 675000 (CWD) and 112500 (SMR) variables. As an oracle for SMR we use Boykov-Kolmogorov max-flow algorithm [16]; for CWD we use dynamic programming to perform MAP-inference in each row and column and follow [1] in inferring in high-order cliques. In our experiments oracles in CWD and SMR run roughly for the same time, and to exclude the issue of efficient implementation of the oracles we measure the algorithm complexity in number of oracle calls. Note, that more sophisticated version of CWD, PatB [1], could potentially improve the performance only when the high-order potentials intersect. For our first synthetic dataset high-order potentials almost do not intersect, for image segmentation example the do not intersect at all.

An important part of experimental comparison is the choice of the optimization method used to solve the dual problems. Originally [1] discusses two strategies: subgradient ascent and averaging of min-marginals. Min-marginal averaging corresponds to coordinate ascent and can get stuck in arbitrary poor coordinate-wise optimum of the dual [17,11]. Subgradient ascent technics are in theory guaranteed to converge to the optimum but our experiments (confirmed by the recent research [9]) show that the subgradient schemes are unstable and sensitive to parameter choice, and their convergence can be very slow. To exclude the aspect of parameter choice in all experiments we use an off-the-shelf HANSO optimization system v2.01[7]. HANSO system consists of a specific version of BFGS algorithm that is applicable to non-differentiable functions [18] and a robust gradient sampling method [19] that is used to adjust the solution at the end of the process. The computation overhead for HANSO system (time spent not on evaluating the function, but on inner manipulations) is non-zero and increases with the growth of the dimensionality of dual variables, but in all our experiments it spends less than 5% of total running time. We are aware that recently there've been much research in developing fast and robust methods to solve such duals (e.g. [9,10]). We believe that at least some of these technics can be applied to improve SMR as well and leave this as future work.

Figures 1 and 2 present the evaluation on synthetic and segmentation datasets. Figure 3 shows the initial image (a),(b) and the resulting segmentation with (c) and without (d),(e) high-order terms. In all cases we observed that SMR converges faster than CWD in terms of the value of the dual and obtains better primal discrete solution. Our experiments show that ICM postprocessing greatly helps CWD but has very little effect on SMR, even slowing it down in terms of time.

---

[7] http://www.cs.nyu.edu/overton/software/hanso/

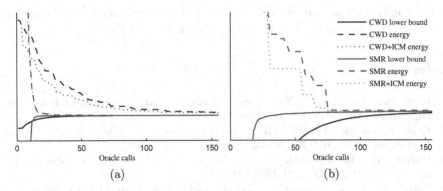

(a)   (b)

Fig. 2. Comparison of SMR and CWD on the image segmentation experiment. Both plots show energies/lower bounds against number of oracle calls. (b) is a zoomed version of (a). Note that both SMR and CWD were able to achieve the global maximum of the lower bound, and SMR was able to retrieve the global minimum of the initial energy as well (the duality gap is zero).

Fig. 3. (a) – the initial image; (b) – the zoomed part of the initial image; (c) – the result of SMR with high-order cliques, SMR found the global minimum; (d),(e) - the results of segmentation without high-order potentials, computed with α-expansion algorithm.

5   Conclusion

In the paper we suggest a new type of approximate inference algorithm for the case of sparse higher-order potentials that encourage few configurations of variables. Our method (SMR) is based on relaxation of the energy by making it submodular. Such relaxation corresponds to the solution of specific LP-relaxation of the discrete problem. Although in general this relaxation is less tight then clique-wise decomposition (CWD) we have derived an important case when they are equivalent. In comparison to CWD and its improved version PatB our method (SMR) requires less Lagrangian multipliers, converges faster and the process of obtaining primal solutions is easier. These properties make SMR a promising tool for training and MAP-inference in MRFs with higher order potentials.

Acknowledgments. This work was supported by the Russian Foundation for Basic Research (projects 12-01-00938, 12-01-31254, 12-01-33085).

References

1. Komodakis, N., Paragios, N.: Beyond pairwise energies: Efficient optimization for higher-order MRFs. In: CVPR (2009)
2. Kohli, P., Ladický, L., Torr, P.H.S.: Robust higher order potentials for enforcing label consistency. IJCV 82, 302–324 (2009)
3. Ishikawa, H.: Transformation of general binary MRF minimization to the first order case. IEEE TPAMI 33, 1234–1249 (2011)
4. Rother, C., Kohli, P., Feng, W., Jia, J.: Minimizing sparse higher order energy functions of discrete variables. In: CVPR (2009)
5. Boykov, Y., Veksler, O., Zabih, R.: Fast approximate energy minimization via graph cuts. IEEE TPAMI 23, 1222–1239 (2001)
6. Kohli, P., Kumar, M.P., Torr, P.: $\mathcal{P}^3$&Beyond: Move making algorithms for solving higher order functions. IEEE TPAMI 31, 1645–1656 (2008)
7. Delong, A., Osokin, A., Isack, H., Boykov, Y.: Fast approximate energy minimization with label costs. IJCV 96, 1–27 (2012)
8. Komodakis, N., Paragios, N., Tziritas, G.: MRF energy minimization and beyond via dual decomposition. IEEE TPAMI 33, 531–552 (2010)
9. Kappes, J.H., Savchynskyy, B., Schnörr, C.: A bundle approach to efficient MAP-inference by lagrangian relaxation. In: CVPR (2012)
10. Komodakis, N.: Towards More Efficient and Effective LP-Based Algorithms for MRF Optimization. In: Daniilidis, K., Maragos, P., Paragios, N. (eds.) ECCV 2010, Part II. LNCS, vol. 6312, pp. 520–534. Springer, Heidelberg (2010)
11. Osokin, A., Vetrov, D., Kolmogorov, V.: Submodular decomposition framework for inference in associative Markov networks with global constraints. In: CVPR (2011)
12. Boros, E., Hammer, P.L.: Pseudo-boolean optimization. Discrete Appl. Math. 123, 155–225 (2002)
13. Kolmogorov, V., Wainwright, M.: On the optimality of tree-reweighted max-product message passing. In: UAI (2005)
14. Kolmogorov, V., Rother, C.: Minimizing non-submodular functions with graph cuts – a review. IEEE TPAMI 29, 1274–1279 (2007)
15. Christoudias, C., Georgescu, B., Meer, P.: Synergism in low-level vision. In: CVPR (2002)
16. Boykov, Y., Kolmogorov, V.: An experimental comparison of min-cut/max-flow algorithms for energy minimization in vision. IEEE TPAMI 26, 1124–1137 (2004)
17. Kolmogorov, V.: Convergent tree-reweighted message passing for energy minimization. IEEE TPAMI 28, 1568–1583 (2006)
18. Lewis, A., Overton, M.: Nonsmooth optimization via BFGS. SIAM J. Optimization (2008)
19. Burke, J., Lewis, A., Overton, M.: A robust gradient sampling algorithm for non-smooth, nonconvex optimization. SIAM J. Optimization 15, 751–779 (2005)

Adjacency Matrix Construction
Using Sparse Coding for Label Propagation

Haixia Zheng, Horace H.S. Ip, and Liang Tao

Centre for Innovative Applications of Internet and Multimedia Technologies
(AIMtech Centre), Department of Computer Science,
City University of Hong Kong, Kowloon, Hong Kong
{hxzheng2,liangtao3}@student.cityu.edu.hk,
cship@cityu.edu.hk

Abstract. Graph-based semi-supervised learning algorithms have attracted increasing attentions recently due to their superior performance in dealing with abundant unlabeled data and limited labeled data via the label propagation. The principle issue of constructing a graph is how to accurately measure the similarity between two data examples. In this paper, we propose a novel approach to measure the similarities among data points by means of the local linear reconstruction of their corresponding sparse codes. Clearly, the sparse codes of data examples not only preserve their local manifold semantics but can significantly boost the discriminative power among different classes. Moreover, the sparse property helps to dramatically reduce the intensive computation and storage requirements. The experimental results over the well-known dataset Caltech-101 demonstrate that our proposed similarity measurement method delivers better performance of the label propagation.

1 Introduction

The issues faced by many practical applications in pattern recognition are that only a few labeled data are available and large amounts of data remain unlabeled. Since it is quite expensive and time consuming to label data whereas unlabeled data can be easier to obtain. How to efficiently combine abundant unlabeled data and limited labeled data is an important research field, which is the main aim of semi-supervised learning techniques [1].

In the past decade, the graph-based semi-supervised learning approaches have aroused considerable interests as they can generate elegant mathematical formulation through label propagation and are easy to be implemented . The graph-based semi-supervised learning approaches build the whole dataset as a graph where the vertices represent the data and the edges represent the pairwise relationships. Zhu et al. [2] utilized the harmonic property of Gaussian random field over the graph for semi-supervised learning. Belkin [3] learned a regression function that fits the labels at labeled data and at the same time maintains smoothness over the data manifold expressed by the graph. Zhou et al. [4] proposed to conduct semi-supervised learning with the local and global consistency.

A. Fusiello et al. (Eds.): ECCV 2012 Ws/Demos, Part III, LNCS 7585, pp. 315–323, 2012.
© Springer-Verlag Berlin Heidelberg 2012

Delalleu et al. [5] proposed a nonparametric inductive function which makes label prediction based on a subset of samples and then truncates the graph Laplacian with the selected subset and its connection to the rest samples. Zhang et al. [6] applied the Nyström approximation to the huge graph adjacency (or affinity) matrix. Fergus et al. [7] specified the label prediction function using smooth eigenvectors of the graph Laplacian which are calculated by a numerical method. Liu et al. [8] constructed a tractable large graph via a small number of anchor points, and predicted the label for each data point as a locally weighted average of the labels on anchor points.

However, the performance of these graph-based semi-supervised learning approaches relies heavily on the adjacency matrix construction. Each entry in adjacency matrix denotes the weight of the corresponding edge, which specifies the similarity between the two data samples. A number of methods have been proposed to construct the adjacency matrix. The simplest method to measure the similarity of data points is to use the Euclidean distances between them. A straightforward extension is the K-Nearest Neighbor (KNN) [9], in which only the edges between a data point and its K-Nearest Neighbors have non-zero weights. Another widely used method is using Gaussian Kernel Similarity [4] to compute the edge weights of the graph. Roweis et al. [10] first proposed to reconstruct the sample from its neighboring points and utilize the local linear reconstruction coefficients as graph weights. Cheng et al. [11] measured the similarities among data points by decomposing each data point as a L_1 sparse linear combination of the rest of the data points. Hence, all these adjacency matrix construction methods are using the original high-dimension data points and are thus relatively computationally expensive.

In this paper, we compute the similarities among the data points based on their low dimensional sparse codes. The key idea is that their sparse codes of data points not only preserve their local manifold structures but can improve the discriminative power among different classes. Further, the sparse property also helps to reduce the intensive computation and storage requirements. Therefore, this approach is much easier to scale up for the large scale dataset. We evaluate the proposed approach on the popular dataset Caltech-101 for the image categorization task. The experimental results indicate that the proposed algorithm significantly improves label propagation performance.

2   Adjacency Matrix Construction Using Sparse Coding

In this section, we will present the adjacency matrix construction algorithm. Let $X = \{x_1, x_2, \cdots, x_n\}$ denote the whole dataset. The goal is to construct the adjacency matrix $W = [W_{ij}]_{n \times n}$, where W_{ij} denotes the similarity between the data x_i and x_j. It can be achieved by the following two steps:

2.1   Calculate Their Sparse Codes of All the Data

Sparse coding provides a class of algorithms for finding succinct representation of data. Given a large number of input data, sparse coding algorithms can automatically compute a small number of representative patterns which are called basis set and the original data space can be represented by appropriate combination of basis set. Therefore, the high dimensionality of the original data can be reduced to the low dimensions of its sparse coding representation. Another important property of sparse coding method is that it usually produces a sparse representation of the data. Such a representation encodes much of the data using few active components, which makes the encoding easy to interpret and at the same time saves the store space and computational time.

For the dataset $X = \{x_1, x_2, \cdots, x_n\} \subset \mathbb{R}^m$, the optimization equation to compute sparse codes is:

$$\min_{A,B} \sum_{i=1}^{n} (\|x_i - B\alpha_i\|^2 + \lambda\phi(\alpha_i)), \tag{1}$$

where $B = [b_1, \cdots, b_p] \in \mathbb{R}^{m \times p}$ is the basis set, also called dictionary; $A = [\alpha_1, \cdots, \alpha_n] \in \mathbb{R}^{p \times n}$ is the sparse codes set for X, and most entries in A are zeros; λ is regularization parameter and sets to be 0.15 in our experiments; $\phi(\alpha_i)$ is regularization function.

Usually, $\phi(\alpha_i)$ is set to be $\mathbb{L}_1$ penalty function $\|\alpha_i\|_1$, because $\mathbb{L}_1$ penalty yields a sparse solution for α_i and can be robust to irrelevant features [12,13]. But this does not consider the inherent domain knowledge embedded in the data itself.

In our algorithm, we set $\phi(\alpha_i)$ to be locality constraint regularization $\alpha_i^T E_i \alpha_i$, where E_i is a $p \times p$ diagonal matrix with its (j,j)-element equal to $\exp(\|x_i - b_j\|_2/\delta)$ and δ is used to adjust the weight decay speed for the locality constraint. It should be noted that locality is more essential than sparsity, as locality must lead to sparsity but not necessary vice versa [14,15].

This optimization problem for Eq. (1) is not jointly convex for basis set B and sparse codes A simultaneously. But the sparse coding problem is convex for basis set B when sparse codes A is fixed, and is also convex for sparse codes A when basis set B is fixed. Similar to [12,13], we can minimize the objective function with respect to basis set B and sparse codes A alternatively.

When sparse codes A is fixed, the Eq. (2) with respect to dictionary B can be solved using incremental codebook optimization method [15]:

$$\begin{aligned} &\min_B \sum_{i=1}^{n} (\|x_i - B\alpha_i\|^2 + \lambda\alpha_i^T E_i \alpha_i) \\ &\text{s.t.} \quad \sum_{i=1}^{p} \|b_i\| \leq 1 \end{aligned} \tag{2}$$

To handle the scale issue associated with the dictionary, we add extra normalization constraints $\|b_i\| \leq 1$ $(i = 1, \cdots, p)$ into the above optimization.

When basis set B is fixed, the formula can be reduced to:

$$\min_A \sum_{i=1}^{n} (\|x_i - B\alpha_i\|^2 + \lambda\alpha_i^T E_i \alpha_i) \tag{3}$$

We can optimize every α_i alternatively and do not consider all the sparse codes $A = [\alpha_1, \cdots, \alpha_n]$ simultaneously. That is, when we focus on α_i, the other sparse codes are fixed. Then we can get the analytical closed-form solution of Eq. (3) with respect to α_i as follows:

$$\alpha_i^* = \arg\min_{\alpha_i} \sum_{i=1}^n (\|x_i - B\alpha_i\|^2 + \lambda \alpha_i^T E_i \alpha_i)$$
$$= (B^T B + \lambda E_i)\backslash(B^T x_i) \tag{4}$$

2.2   Construct Adjacency Matrix Based on Their Sparse Codes

The weight W_{ij} is conventionally calculated using Gaussian Kernel Similarity as

$$W_{ij} = \begin{cases} \exp\left(-\|\alpha_i - \alpha_j\|^2/2\sigma^2\right), & i \neq j \\ 0, & i = j \end{cases} \tag{5}$$

However, the major shortcoming using Gaussian Kernel Similarity method is that even a small perturbation of variable σ will make its performance dramatically different, and there is no reliable way to determine the optimal value of parameters especially when the amount of labeled data is rather small [8,16].

Similar to [10,16], we specify the similarity between two data points through geometric reconstruction. With the consideration that the sparse codes of data points not only preserve their local manifold structures but can boost the discriminative power among different classes, and that the sparse property can also help to reduce the computation cost, we assign the weights of adjacency matrix through local linear reconstruction coefficients of their sparse codes. Therefore, the objective is

$$\min_W \sum_{i=1}^n \|\alpha_i - \sum_{j:\alpha_j \in N(\alpha_i)} W_{ij}\alpha_j\|^2,$$
$$\text{s.t.} \quad W_{ij} \geq 0 \text{ and } \sum_{j:\alpha_j \in N(\alpha_i)} W_{ij} = 1 \tag{6}$$

in which $N(\alpha_i)$ represents the neighborhood of α_i, and W_{ij} is the contribution of α_j to α_i. Obviously, the more similar α_j to α_i, the larger W_{ij} will be. Especially, when $\alpha_i = \alpha_k \in N(\alpha_i)$, then $W_{ik} = 1$ and $W_{ij} = 0$ $(j \neq k, \alpha_j \in N(\alpha_i))$ is the optimal solution. Therefore, W_{ij} can be used to measure how similar α_j to α_i.

The reconstruction weights W_{ij} in Eq. (6) can be solved using the standard quadratic programming (QP) [16]. More importantly, the optimized regression weights in Eq. (6) are much sparser. After all the reconstruction weights W_{ij} are solved, we can obtain a sparse adjacency matrix $W = [W_{ij}]_{n \times n}$. In order to ensure adjacency matrix W is symmetric, we then set $W = (W + W^T)/2$.

3   The Framework of Label Propagation

Given a data set $\mathcal{X} = \{x_1, \cdots, x_l, x_{l+1}, \cdots, x_n\} \subset \mathbb{R}^m$ and a label set $\mathcal{L} = \{1, \cdots, c\}$, the first l data $x_i (i \leq l)$ are labeled as $y_i \in \mathcal{L}$ and the remaining data $x_i (l + 1 \leq i \leq n)$ are unlabeled. The goal is to predict the label of the unlabeled data through label propagation. Let F denote the set of $n \times c$ matrices with nonnegative entries. Matrix $F = [F_1^T, \cdots, F_n^T]^T \in \mathcal{F}$ corresponds to a classification on the dataset $\mathcal{X}$ by labeling each point x_i as the label $y_i = \arg \max_{j \leq c} F_{ij}$. We can understand F as a vectorial function $F : \mathcal{X} \mapsto \mathbb{R}^c$ which assigns a vector F_i to each data x_i. Define a $n \times c$ matrix $Y \in \mathcal{F}$ with $Y_{ij} = 1$ if x_i is labeled as $y_i = j$ and $Y_{ij} = 0$ otherwise. Clearly, Y is consistent with the initial labels according to decision rule [4]. The algorithm can be summarized as follows:

(1) Compute the sparse codes $A = [\alpha_1, \cdots, \alpha_n]$ for all the data $\mathcal{X} = \{x_1, \cdots, x_l, x_{l+1}, \cdots, x_n\}$ through Eq. (4).
(2) Construct the adjacency matrix $W = [W_{ij}]_{n \times n}$ by solving the Eq. (6), and set $W = (W + W^T)/2$ to ensure W is symmetric.
(3) Iterate $F(t + 1) = \gamma W F(t) + (1 - \gamma)Y$ until convergence, where γ is a parameter and set to be 0.75 in our evaluations.
(4) Let F^* denote the limit the sequence $\{F(t)\}$. Label each data x_i as a label $y_i = \arg\max_{j \leq c} F_{ij}$.

According to [16], the above algorithm will converge to

$$F^* = (1 - \gamma)(\mathbf{I} - \gamma W)^{-1} Y, \qquad (7)$$

in which $\mathbf{I}$ is the identity matrix of order n.

4   The Regularization Framework

We can derive our algorithm from a regularization framework. The cost function associated with F can be defined as follows:

$$Q(F) = \frac{1}{2}(\sum_{i=1}^{n} \sum_{j:\alpha_j N(\alpha_i)} W_{ij} \|F_i - F_j\|^2 + \mu \sum_{i=1}^{n} \|F_i - Y_i\|^2) \qquad (8)$$

where $\mu > 0$ is the regularization parameter. The first term is the smoothness constraint, which means that a good classifying function should not change too much between nearby points. The second term of the formula is the fitting constraint, which means a good classifying function should not change too much from the initial label assignment [4]. Note that the fitting constraint term contains labeled and unlabeled data. Differentiate $Q(F)$ with respect to F, we have

$$\frac{\partial Q(F)}{\partial F} = (\mathbf{I} - W)F + \mu(F - Y) \qquad (9)$$

Then we can easily get the optimal solution of Eq. (8) by setting Eq. (9) to zero:

$$F = (1 - \gamma)(\mathbf{I} - \gamma W)^{-1} Y \qquad (10)$$

where $\gamma = 1/(1 + \mu)$. It can be observed that Eq. (10) is equal to the Eq. (7) —the closed form expression of the above iteration algorithm.

5   Experiments

First, we evaluate the performance of our algorithm over the widely-used dataset Caltech 101 [17]. The Caltech-101 dataset contains 9144 images in 101 classes (including airplanes, cameras, chairs, etc.) with significant variance in shape. The number of images per category varies from 31 to 800. Most images are medium resolution, i.e. about 300×300 pixels. Following the common experiment setup for Caltech-101 suggested by the original dataset [17] and also used by many other researchers [18], for each category we partitioned the whole dataset into 5, 10, 15, 20, 25 and 30 training images and the rest are test images. After that, we measured the performance using average accuracy over 102 classes (i.e. 101 classes and a 'background' class).

Our implementations utilizes a single descriptor type, the popular SIFT descriptor, as in [19,20]. The SIFT descriptors extracted from 16×16 pixel patches were densely sampled from each image in the whole dataset on a grid with step size of 8 pixels. All the image features are quantized into 2048 clusters. In our experiments the images were all preprocessed into gray scale, and resized to be no larger than 300×300 pixels with preserved aspect ratio.

Following the common benchmarking procedures, we repeat the experimental process by 10 times with different random selected training and test images to obtain reliable results. The average of per-category recognition rates were recorded for each run. Finally, we report our results by the average of all the recognition rates. We also compared our result with several existing approaches. Detailed comparison results are shown in Fig. 1.

In Fig. 1, it can be seen that our proposed approach outperforms other existing state-of-the-art image categorization algorithms at least 1.04% (15 training images per category). Our approach can achieve up to 2.34% of performance

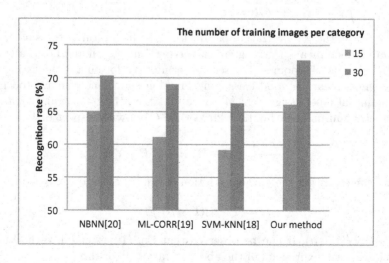

Fig. 1. Image categorization performance comparison on Caltech-101 dataset

Fig. 2. Image classes with higher recognition rate

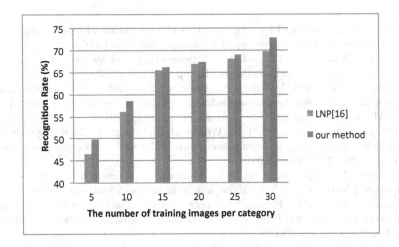

Fig. 3. Performance comparison between our method and LNP

improvement with 30 training images per category. At the same time, we can observe the recognition rate growing with the number of training images per category due to the benefit of growing supervisory information of training data. As illustrated in Fig. 2, with 15 training images per category, the recognition rate of higher than 75% is obtained in five classes.

To further evaluate the effectiveness of our proposed adjacency matrix algorithm, we compare our algorithm with the Linear Neighborhood Propagation (LNP) [16], which computes the weights of affinity matrix based on local linear reconstruction of original high-dimension data points. As shown in Fig. 3, our algorithm outperforms Linear Neighborhood Propagation [16]. Importantly, the adjacency matrix constructed by means of sparse codes will be much sparser than that based on original high-dimension data, thus the computation cost and storage space will be reduced.

6 Conclusion

We propose a novel affinity matrix construction approach for label propagation through the local linear reconstruction of their sparse codes. The proposed algorithm takes into consideration that sparse codes of data samples not only preserve their local manifold structures but can boost the discriminative power among different classes. Additionally, the sparse property leads to requires less computation cost and storage overhead. The experimental evaluations demonstrate that effectiveness of our proposed method is fully comparable with the LNP [16].

References

1. Zhu, X.: Semi-supervised learning literature survey. Technical report, Department of Computer Sciences, University of Wisconsin, Madison (2005)
2. Zhu, X., Ghahramani, Z., Lafferty, J.: Semi-supervised learning using gaussian fields and harmonic functions. In: ICML, pp. 912–919 (2003)
3. Belkin, M., Matveeva, I., Niyogi, P.: Regularization and Semi-supervised Learning on Large Graphs. In: Shawe-Taylor, J., Singer, Y. (eds.) COLT 2004. LNCS (LNAI), vol. 3120, pp. 624–638. Springer, Heidelberg (2004)
4. Zhou, D., Bousquet, O., Lal, T.N., Weston, J., Schölkopf, B.: Learning with local and global consistency. In: Advances in Neural Information Processing Systems 16, pp. 321–328. MIT Press (2004)
5. Delalleau, O., Bengio, Y., Roux, N.L.: Nonparametric function induction in semi-supervised learning. In: Proc. Artificial Intelligence and Statistics (2005)
6. Zhang, K., Kwok, J.T., Parvin, B.: Prototype vector machine for large scale semi-supervised learning. In: Proceedings of the 26th Annual International Conference on Machine Learning (2009)
7. Fergus, R., Weiss, Y., Torralba, A.: Semi-Supervised Learning in Gigantic Image Collections. In: Neural Information Processing Systems (2009)
8. Liu, W., He, J., Chang, S.F.: Large Graph Construction for Scalable Semi-Supervised Learning. In: International Conference on Machine Learning, pp. 679–686 (2010)
9. Belkin, M., Niyogi, P.: Laplacian Eigenmaps for Dimensionality Reduction and Data Representation. Neural Computation, 1373–1396 (2003)
10. Roweis, S.T., Saul, L.K.: Nonlinear dimensionality reduction by locally linear embedding. Science, 2323–2326 (2000)
11. Cheng, H., Liu, Z., Yang, J.: Sparsity induced similarity measure for label propagation. In: International Conference on Computer Vision, pp. 317–324 (2009)
12. Lee, H., Battle, A., Raina, R., Ng, A.Y.: Efficient sparse coding algorithms. In: Neural Information Processing Systems, pp. 801–808 (2006)
13. Mairal, J., Bach, F., Ponce, J., Sapiro, G.: Online dictionary learning for sparse coding. In: International Conference on Machine Learning, pp. 689–696 (2009)

14. Lu, Z., Peng, Y.: Latent semantic learning by efficient sparse coding with hypergraph regularization. In: Burgard, W., Roth, D. (eds.) AAAI (2011)
15. Wang, J., Yang, J., Yu, K., Lv, F., Huang, T.S., Gong, Y.: Locality-constrained Linear Coding for image classification. In: Computer Vision and Pattern Recognition, pp. 3360–3367 (2010)
16. Wang, F., Zhang, C.: Label propagation through linear neighborhoods. In: International Conference on Machine Learning, pp. 985–992 (2006)
17. Fei-Fei, L., Fergus, R., Perona, P.: Learning Generative Visual Models from Few Training Examples: An Incremental Bayesian Approach Tested on 101 Object Categories. In: Computer Vision and Pattern Recognition (2004)
18. Zhang, H., Berg, A.C., Maire, M., Malik, J.: SVM-KNN: Discriminative Nearest Neighbor Classification for Visual Category Recognition. In: Computer Vision and Pattern Recognition, vol. 2, pp. 2126–2136 (2006)
19. Jain, P., Kulis, B., Grauman, K.: Fast image search for learned metrics. In: Computer Vision and Pattern Recognition (2008)
20. Boiman, O., Shechtman, E., Irani, M.: In defense of Nearest-Neighbor based image classification. In: Computer Vision and Pattern Recognition (2008)

Climbing: A Unified Approach for Global Constraints on Hierarchical Segmentation

Bangalore Ravi Kiran, Jean Serra, and Jean Cousty

Université Paris-Est, Laboratoire d'Informatique Gaspard-Monge, A3SI, ESIEE

Abstract. The paper deals with global constraints for hierarchical segmentations. The proposed framework associates, with an input image, a hierarchy of segmentations and an energy, and the subsequent optimization problem. It is the first paper that compiles the different global constraints and unifies them as *Climbing energies*. The transition from global optimization to local optimization is attained by the h-increasingness property, which allows to compare parent and child partition energies in hierarchies. The laws of composition of such energies are established and examples are given over the Berkeley Dataset for colour and texture segmentation.

1 Motivation

There have been multiple approaches to image segmentation by global constraint models. Some of them emphasize the use of seeds, e.g. the labels in graph-cuts, or the markers in watersheds. In addition, they view the space as a one scale structure. This line of thought is illustrated by the search for a maximum flow in a directed graph, or by the optimization of a conditional random field(CRF). At the opposite end, other segmentation approaches emphasize the scaling of the space by means of hierarchies, and attach less importance to labelling questions, in a first step at least.

The present paper is devoted to this second type of global constraints. A hierarchy, or pyramid, of image segmentations is classically understood as a series of progressive simplified versions of an initial image, which result in increasing partitions of the space. In the following, we do not aim to focus on the methods for obtaining pyramids of segmentation, and consider rather the whole hierarchies as a starting point [1]. Indeed, a multi-scale image description can rarely be considered as an end in itself. It often requires to be completed by some energy function that allows us to formalize optima, and to summarizes a hierarchy into some "optimal cut". Three questions arise then, namely:

---

[1] The main techniques for hierarchical segmentation include functional minimizations of Mumford and Shah type, semi-groups of morphological filters, and progressive floodings on watersheds [1]. In addition, the learning strategies for segmentation, as developed by [2], or by [3], among others, lead to very significant hierarchies. One can also quote [4] where Mumford and Shah functional is modified by shape descriptors.

A. Fusiello et al. (Eds.): ECCV 2012 Ws/Demos, Part III, LNCS 7585, pp. 324–334, 2012.

1. given a hierarchy H of partitions and a an energy ω on the partial partitions, how to combine the classes of this hierarchy for obtaining a new partition that minimizes ω, and which can be determined easily, in one ascending pass for example? In other words, how to characterize the convenient energies?
2. most of the segmentations involve several features (colour, shape, size, etc.), which give birth to several energies ω. How to combine them?
3. when one energy ω depends on an integer j, i.e. $\omega = \omega^j$, how to generate a sequence of minimum partitions that increase with j, which therefore should form a minimum hierarchy?

These questions have been taken up by several authors, for many years, and by various methods. The most popular energies ω for hierarchical partitions derive from that of Mumford and Shah, in which a term of fidelity to the data is summed up with a term of boundary regularization. The optimization turns out to be a trade off between these two constraints. The method initiated by Ph. Salembier and L. Garrido for generating thumbnails is of this type [5]. They interpret the best cut as the most accurate image simplification for a given compression rate. The approach has been extended to additive energies by L.Guigues et al [6]. It is always assumed, in all these studies, that the energy of any partial partition equals the sum of the energies of its classes, which considerably simplifies the combinatorial complexity, and answers the above two questions 1 and 3.

However, one can wonder whether additivity is the very underlying cause of the nice properties, since P. Soille's constraint connectivity [7], though non linear, satisfies similar properties. It is also the case for F. Zanoguerra's lasso, which labels a foreground inside a given contour [8]. In these two cases, the addition is replaced by the supremum operation. Finally, one finds in literature a third type of energy, illustrated by Akçay and Aksoy, in [9] which holds on nodes only, and no longer on partial partitions. And again, it yields to best cuts, which are accessed in one pass.

Is there a common denominator to all these approaches, more comprehensive than just additivity? For solving problem 1 above, the alternative and simpler condition of $h-$increasingness (for hierarchical increasingness), proposed in [10] encompasses all above energy optimizations. But does it suffice for solving the two other points? This will be the matter of this paper, where the three above questions correspond to the next three sections, followed by a few examples.

Going back to the comparison between hierarchies, and CRF and graph min-cuts methods, one can notice that:

1. The CRFs and min-cut max-flow formulation represent spatial interaction between pixels which is restricted in a unitary neighbourhood, and the increased complexity may not be always advantageous [11].
2. Hierarchical methods provide a lower combinatorial complexity while supplying intuitive segmentations. In addition, the construction of a hierarchy and of the ulterior energy ω may use independent pieces of information (e.g. in section 5, luminance based energy, versus chrominance and texture) .

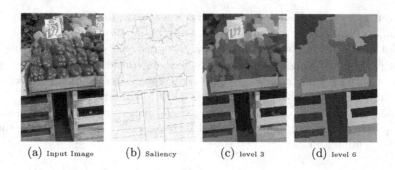

(a) Input Image   (b) Saliency   (c) level 3   (d) level 6

Fig. 1. Saliency map and hierarchy of segmentations at few levels and their child-parent correspondences

3. Indirectly, the hierarchical clustering induces larger and larger neighbourhoods. This helps to differentiate textures at various scales, to progressively localize a significant detail, and to optimize image compression.

1.1 Notation and Terms

The space under study (euclidean R^n, digital Z^n, or otherwise) is denoted by E. A partition $\pi(S)$ associated with a set $S \in \mathcal{P}(E)$ is called *partial partition* of E of support S [12]. The family of all partial partitions of set E is denoted by $\mathcal{D}(E)$, or simply by $\mathcal{D}$. A hierarchy H is a finite chain of partitions π_i, i.e.

$$H = \{\pi_i, 0 \leq i \leq n \mid i \leq k \leq n \Rightarrow \pi_i \leq \pi_k\}, \tag{1}$$

where π_n is the partition $\{E\}$ of E in a single class.

The partitions of a hierarchy may be represented by their classes, or by the saliency map of the edges[13],[1], as depicted in Figure 1, or again by a family tree where each node of bifurcation is a class S, as depicted in Figure 2. The classes of π_{i-1} at level $i-1$ which are included in class S_i are said to be *the sons* of S_i. Denote by $\mathcal{S}(H)$ the set of all classes S of all partitions involved in H. Clearly, the descendants of each S form in turn a hierarchy $H(S)$ of summit S, which is included in the complete hierarchy $H = H(E)$.

Cuts in a hierarchy Any partition π of E whose classes are taken in $\mathcal{S}$ defines a *cut* π in a hierarchy H. The set of all cuts of E is denoted by $\Pi(E) = \Pi$. Every "horizontal" section $\pi_i(H)$ at level i is obviously a cut, but several levels can cooperate in a same cut, such as $\pi(S_1)$ and $\pi(S_2)$, drawn with thick dotted lines in Figure 2. Similarly, the partition $\pi(S_1) \sqcup \pi(S_2)$ generates a cut of $H(E)$. The symbol $\sqcup$ is used here for expressing that groups of classes are concatenated. Let $\Pi(S)$ be the family of all cuts of $H(S)$.

2 Hierarchical Increasingness

This section is a reminder of [10] when the h-increasingness was introduced first.

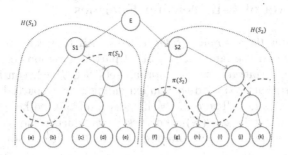

Fig. 2. The hierarchy: S_1 and S_2 are the nodes sons of E, and $H(S_1)$ and $H(S_1)$ are the associated sub-hierarchies. π_1 and π_2 are cuts of $H(S_1)$ and $H(S_1)$ respectively, and $\pi_1 \sqcup \pi_2$ is a cut of E.

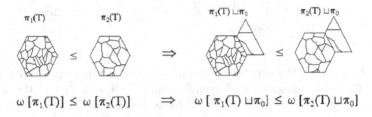

$$\omega\,[\pi_1(\mathrm{T})] \leq \omega\,[\pi_2(\mathrm{T})] \quad \Rightarrow \quad \omega\,[\,\pi_1(\mathrm{T})\sqcup\pi_0] \leq \omega\,[\pi_2(\mathrm{T})\sqcup\pi_0]$$

Fig. 3. Hierachical increasingness

Cuts of minimum energy and h-increasingness An energy $\omega : \mathcal{D}(E) \to \mathbb{R}^+$ is a non negative numerical function over the family $\mathcal{D}(E)$ of all partial partitions of set E, and an *optimal cut* $\pi^* \in \Pi(E)$ of E, is one that minimizes ω, i.e. such that $\omega(\pi^*) = \inf\{\omega(\pi) \mid \pi \in \Pi(E)\}$.

Proposition 1. *Let π_1 and π_2 be two partial partitions of same support, and π_0 be a partial partition disjoint from π_1 and π_2. An energy ω on $\mathcal{D}(E)$ is said to be hierarchically increasing, or h-increasing, in $\mathcal{D}(E)$ when, $\pi_0, \pi_1, \pi_2 \in \mathcal{D}(E)$, π_0 disjoint of π_1 and π_2, we have*

$$\omega(\pi_1) \leq \omega(\pi_2) \quad \Rightarrow \quad \omega(\pi_1 \sqcup \pi_0) \leq \omega(\pi_2 \sqcup \pi_0). \tag{2}$$

Let $H \in \mathcal{H}$ be a finite hierarchy, and ω be an energy on $\mathcal{D}(E)$. Consider a node S of H with p sons $T_1..T_p$ of minimum cuts $\pi_1^*, ..\pi_p^*$. The largest cut of minimum energy of summit S is either the cut

$$\pi_1^* \sqcup \pi_2^* .. \sqcup \pi_p^*, \tag{3}$$

or the partition of S into a unique class, if and only if S is h-increasing (proof given in [14]).

Implication (2) is illustrated in Figure 3. The condition of h-increasingness yields a dynamic program for finding the optimum cut $\pi^*(H)$ in one pass i.e. each node of the hierarchy is read only once [6], [14].

3   Generation of h-Increasing Energies

Composition from the energies of the classes. An easy way to obtain a h-increasing energy on the family $\mathcal{D}(E)$ of all partial partitions of E consists in taking, firstly, an arbitrary energy ω on all sets $S \in \mathcal{P}(E)$, considered as one class partial partitions $\{S\}$, and then in extending ω to all partial partitions by some law of composition. The h-increasingness is introduced here by the law of composition, and not by $\omega[\mathcal{P}(E)]$. The first laws which come to mind are, of course, addition, supremum, and infimum, and indeed we can state

Proposition 2. *Let E be a set and $\omega : \mathcal{P}(E) \to \mathbb{R}^+$ an arbitrary energy defined on $\mathcal{P}(E)$, and let $\pi \in \mathcal{D}(E)$ be a partial partition of classes $\{S_i, 1 \leq i \leq n\}$. Then the three extensions of ω to the partial partitions $\mathcal{D}(E)$*

$$\omega(\pi) = \bigvee_i \omega(S_i), \quad \omega(\pi) = \bigwedge_i \omega(S_i), \quad and \quad \omega(\pi) = \sum_i \omega(S_i), \tag{4}$$

are h-increasing energies.

Here, $\bigvee$ and $\bigwedge$ are the supremum and infimum operators respectively. The second rel.(4) encompasses that of Mumford and Shah, and that of the separable energies [6] [5]. The energies composed by suprema appear in [7] [8]. A number of other laws are compatible with h-increasingness. One could use the product of energies, the difference sup-inf, the quadratic sum, and their combinations. Moreover, one choose an ω dependent on more than one class, on the proximity of the edges, on another hierarchy, etc..

Lattice of h-increasing energies. The h−increasing energies can be combined in several manners. For example, if $\{\omega_i, i \in I\}$ stands for a family of sum-generated energies, and for a family $\{\lambda_i, i \in I\}$ of non negative weights, then the weighed sum $\omega = \sum \lambda_i \omega_i$ turns out to be h−increasing, and sum-generated.

  Similarly, the class $\mathcal{L}_\vee$ of the $\vee$-generated h−increasing energies $\{\omega_i, i \in I\}$ is closed under weighted supremum, i.e. $\omega = \vee \lambda_i \omega_i \in \mathcal{L}_\vee$. Moreover, $\omega_{\min} \in \mathcal{L}_\vee$ for $\omega_{\min}(\pi) = 0, \forall \pi \in \mathcal{D}(E)$. Therefore $\mathcal{L}_\vee$ turns out to be a lattice for the usual numerical ordering. Note that the $\vee$, paradoxically, expresses the intersection of criteria. For example take, in a color pyramid, the energy:

$$\omega_1(S) = 0 \text{ if the range of the luminance in } S \text{ is } < k_1, \quad \omega_1(S) = 1 \text{ if not,}$$

$$\omega_2(S) = 0 \text{ if the range of the saturation in } S \text{ is } < k_2, \quad \omega_2(S) = 1 \text{ if not,}$$

$$\omega_3(S) = 0 \text{ if the area of } S \text{ is } \geq k_3, \quad \omega_3(S) = 1 \text{ if not.}$$

Then the energy $\vee \omega_i(S) = 0$ when S is not too small, and constant enough in luminance and saturation.

Energies by refinement. Up to now, we have associated an energy with each subset X of E, and then extended it to each partial partition π of the space by some law of composition of the classes X of π. But the goal of h−increasingness

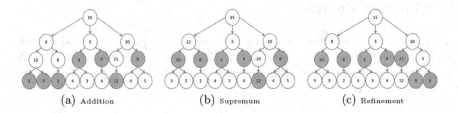

(a) Addition   (b) Supremum   (c) Refinement

Fig. 4. Optimal Cuts by the 3 different composition of energies, (a) (Salambier-Guigues) addition - The value $f(x)$ at node x is compared to the sum $g(x)$ of the values of its sons. When $f(x) < g(x)$, then one keeps $f(x)$ When not, one replaces node x by its sons. The optimal cut is the union of the largest kept nodes. (b) (Soille-Grazzini) supremum- The values of $f(x)$ decrease along the hierarchy. A node is maintained when $f(x) \leq k$ The optimal cut is the union of the largest kept nodes. (c) (Akçay-Aksoy) Refinement - $\omega(S) \leq \omega(S\prime)$ when 1) $S \subseteq S\prime$ 2) $f(S) \leq f(S\prime)$ The optimal cut at point x is the largest node which is more energetic than all its descendants Or, when none, it is the leaf that contains point x.

does not demand we know the energy of all partial partitions. It suffices indeed to be able to order the energies, which can be obtained from the usual ordering by refinement on partitions. Allocate an energy $\mu(S)$ to each node of a hierarchy H, where μ takes its values in a partially ordered set M.

Definition 1. *The node S is said to be less energetic, in terms of refinement, than S', and one writes $S \preccurlyeq S'$, when*

$$S \preccurlyeq S' \quad \Leftrightarrow \quad S \supseteq S' \ and \ \mu(S) \geq \mu(S') \qquad S \ , \ S' \in \mathcal{P}(E), \ \mu \in M. \quad (5)$$

The partial partition π is less energetic than π', and one writes $\pi \preccurlyeq \pi'$, when

1. *both π and π' have the same support Supp*
2. *for all points $x \in Supp$, one has $S(x) \preccurlyeq S'(x)$.*

The energy ω associated with π is obviously $h-$increasing. Therefore there exists a minimum cut. For finding its node at point x, one starts from the set $\mathcal{S}(x) = \{S_i(x), 1 \leq i \leq n\}$ of all classes containing x. It admits an element $S_{i_0}(x)$ of smallest energy, where either $i_0 = \sup\{i : \mu(S_i) \leq \mu(S_{i-1}), 1 \leq i \leq n\}$, or $i_0 = 1$. Unlike the additive and the $\vee$-generated energies, this one accepts that, among several "brothers", some be minimum nodes and not others. One may find an example of energy by refinement, due to [9]. They study airborne multi bands images and take (up to a small change) $\mu(S) = -$ Area $(S) \times$ (mean of all standard deviations of all bands in S)

Any index of similarity can be used for μ. For example, take $\mu(S) = 0$ when all sons of S have similar areas, or similar colour histograms, etc.. Then the supremum $\vee\{\mu_r, 1 \leq r \leq p\}$ of such binary texture energies is still of the same type (i.e. $\mu(S) = \vee\mu_r(S) = 0$ when all $\mu_r(S) = 0$ and $\mu(S) = 1$ when not), and it represents the *intersection* of all criteria μ_r.

4 Climbing Energies

The usual energies are often given by finite sequences $\{\omega^j, 1 \leq j \leq p\}$ that depend on a positive index, or parameter, j. Therefore, the processing of hierarchy H results in a sequence of p optimum cuts π^{j*}, of labels $1 \leq j \leq p$. A priori, the π^{j*} are not ordered, but if they were, i.e. if

$$j \leq k \quad \Rightarrow \quad \pi^{j*} \leq \pi^{k*}, \qquad j, k \in J, \tag{6}$$

then we should obtain a nice progressive simplification of the optimum cuts. For getting it, we need to combine h-increasingness with the supplementary axiom (7) of *scale increasingness*, which results in the following *climbing energies*.

Definition 2. *We call* climbing energy *any family* $\{\omega^j, 1 \leq j \leq p\}$ *of energies over* $\widetilde{\Pi}$ *which satisfies the three following axioms, valid for* $\omega^j, 1 \leq j \leq p$ *and for all* $\pi \in \Pi(S)$, $S \in \mathcal{S}$

- *i) each* ω^j *is* h-increasing,
- *ii) each* ω^j *admits a* single *optimum cutting,*
- *iii) the* $\{\omega^j\}$ *are scale increasingness, i.e. for* $j \leq k$, *each support* $S \in \mathcal{S}$ *and each partition* $\pi \in \Pi(S)$, *we have that*

$$j \leq k \quad and \quad \omega^j(S) \leq \omega^j(\pi) \Rightarrow \omega^k(S) \leq \omega^k(\pi), \qquad \pi \in \Pi(S), \quad S \in \mathcal{S}. \tag{7}$$

Axiom i) and ii) allow us to compare the same energy at two different levels, whereas iii) compares two different energies at the same level. The relation (7) means that, as j increases, the ω^j's preserve the sense of energetic differences between the nodes of hierarchy H and their partial partitions. In particular, all energies of the type $\omega^j = j\omega$ are scale increasing. The climbing energies satisfy the very nice property to order the optimum cuts with respect to the parameter j:

Theorem 1. *Let* $\{\omega^j, 1 \leq j \leq p\}$ *be a family of energies, and let* π^{j*} *(resp.* π^{k*}*) be the optimum cut of hierarchy* H *according to the energy* ω^j *(resp.* ω^k*). The family* $\{\pi^{j*}, 1 \leq j \leq p\}$ *of the optimum cuts generates a unique hierarchy* H^* *of partitions, i.e.*

$$j \leq k \quad \Rightarrow \quad \pi^{j*} \leq \pi^{k*}, \qquad 1 \leq j \leq k \leq p \tag{8}$$

if and only if the family $\{\omega^j\}$ *is a climbing energy (proof given in [14]).*

Such a family is climbing in two senses: for each j the energy climbs pyramid H up to its best cut (h-increasingness), and as j varies, it generates a new pyramid to be climbed (scale-increasingness). The question of unicity of the optimal cuts is not handled here, but here in [14].

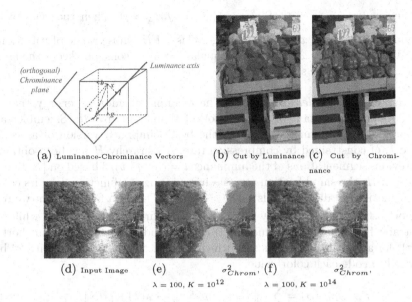

(a) Luminance-Chrominance Vectors   (b) Cut by Luminance (c) Cut by Chromi-nance

(d) Input Image   (e) $\quad\quad\quad \sigma^2_{Chrom},$ (f) $\quad\quad\quad \sigma^2_{Chrom},$
$\lambda = 100, K = 10^{12}$ $\quad\quad\quad$ $\lambda = 100, K = 10^{14}$

Fig. 5. In the RGB space, a colour vector $\overrightarrow{x}$ (r, g, b) can be decomposed in its two orthogonal projections on the grey axis, namely $\overrightarrow{l}$ of components $(l/3, l/3, l/3)$, and on the chromatic plane orthogonal to the grey axis at the origin, namely $\overrightarrow{c}$ of components $(3/\sqrt{2})(2r - g - b, 2g - b - r, 2b - r - g)$. We have $\overrightarrow{x} = \overrightarrow{l} + \overrightarrow{c}$. (d), (e) and (f) Optimal cut that enhances texture by parameters: $\sigma^2_{Lum}, \sigma^2_{Chrom}$ refers to whether the Energy function was composed on variance of the partial partitions Luminance or Chrominance. λ the scale parameter, K constant that normalizes the variance of areas of set of children with respect to global energy of the children belonging a given parent

5   Examples

In all cases below, the energies depend on a scalar parameter k such that the families $\{\omega^k\}$ are climbing.

Supremum composed binary energies . The simplest energies are the binary ones, which take values 1 and 0 only. We firstly observe that the relation $\pi \sqsubseteq \pi_1$, where $\pi_1 = \pi \sqcup \pi'$ is made of the classes of π plus other ones, is an ordering. A binary energy ω such that for all $\pi, \pi_0, \pi_1, \pi_2 \in \mathcal{D}(E)$

$$\omega \text{ is } \sqsubseteq\text{-increasing, i.e. } \omega(\pi) = 1 \quad \Rightarrow \quad \omega(\pi \sqcup \pi_0) = 1$$

$$\omega(\pi_1) = \omega(\pi_2) = 0 \quad \Rightarrow \quad \omega(\pi_1 \sqcup \pi_0) = \omega(\pi_2 \sqcup \pi_0),$$

is obviously h-increasing, and conversely. The Soille-Grazzini minimization provides an example of this type. A numerical function f is now associated with hierarchy H. Consider the range of variation $\delta(S) = \max\{f(x), x \in S\} - \min\{f(x), x \in S\}$ of f inside set S, and the h-increasing binary energy $\omega^k(\langle S \rangle) = 0$ when $\delta(S) \leq k$, and $\omega^k(\langle S \rangle) = 1$ when not. Compose ω according the law of the supremum, i.e. $\pi = \sqcup \langle S_i \rangle \Rightarrow \omega^k(\pi) = \bigvee_i \omega^k(\langle S_i \rangle)$. Then the class of the optimum cut at point $x \in E$ is the larger class of H whose range of variation is $\leq j$. When the energy ω^k of a father equals that of its sons, one keeps the father when $\omega^k = 0$, and the sons when not.

Additive energies under constraint. The example of additive energy that we now develop is a variant of the creation of thumbnails by Ph. Salembier and L. Garrido [5]. We aim to generate "the best" simplified version of a colour image f, of constrained by compression rate. A hierarchy H has been obtained by previous segmentations of the luminance $l = (r+g+b)/3$ based on [1]. In each class S of H, the simplification consists in replacing the function f by its colour mean (mean over all 3 channels) $\mu(S) = \frac{\Sigma_{x \in S} x}{card(S)}$. The data fidelity term(we refer in short as $\omega_\mu(\pi)$) is given by L_2 norm by the first functional in 9 while the constraint function (second functional) i.e. The coding cost(we refer in short as $\omega_\partial(\pi)$) for a frontier element is $\simeq 2$, which is given, for the whole S, with 24 bits assigned to code each color value.

$$\omega_{lum}(S) = \sum_{x \in S} \| l(x) - m(S) \|^2 + \lambda(24 + | \partial S |), \tag{9}$$

Here we separate the colour image into 2 components the luminance vector which gives the gray scale, and its complementary chrominance plane as shown in 5(a). The principle idea here is to show that the non negative energy described per partition and the actual hierarchies of partitions are well separated entities in this framework, and thus multiple constraint functions to optimize over a hierarchy of partitions generated from a different function over the image space.

$$\omega_{chrom}(S) = \sum_{x \in S} \| c(x) - m(S) \|^2 + \lambda(24 + | \partial S |) + \sum_{S\prime \in siblings(S)} \frac{K}{\sigma^2(Area(S\prime))}, \tag{10}$$

Thus here in (10) we observe that the class variance is now calculated over the chrominance function of the image, which simplifies the image while keeping partitions which minimize the variance of the chrominance vector c. According to Lagrange formalism, the total energy of class S is as shown. Classically one reaches the minimum under constraint $\omega(S)$ by means of a system of partial derivatives. Now remarkably our approach replaces the computation of derivatives by a *climbing*. Indeed we can access the energy of a cut π by summing up that of its classes, which leads to $\omega(\pi) = \omega_\mu(\pi) + \lambda^j \omega_\partial(\pi)$. The cost $\omega_\partial(\pi)$ decreases as λ^j increases, therefore we can climb the pyramid of the best cuts and stop (thus optimal λ) when the constraint is satisfied.

Intuitively, texture features are formulated into this multi-scale framework where the optimal scale parameter combines the effect of chrominance and structure of texture into one global energy function, thus showing the flexibility of the framework. The third term in (10) decreases when any child in the hierarchy whose siblings have low variance of component areas with respect to each other. This is done also with the constraint that the variance of the chrominance vector is reduced over the partitions of pyramid produced from the luminance vector l. The lattice of h-increasing energies extends this concept to energies whose optimal cuts can be combined or recomposed again using the supremum of the partitions, as explained earlier in the section - "lattice if h-increasing energies".

6   Conclusion

The primary contributions of this theoretical paper were :

1. Defining an novel non negative global *climbing energy* that helps perform an optimization over the hierarchy of segmentations, that generate *optimal* segmentations by the classical Mumford shah functional, and compiling other energies used to combine partitions from hierarchies, in the literature.
2. Obtaining the conditions for a general class of energies to be h-increasing.
3. Demonstrating how to formulate multiple constraint functions over the image space and obtained different optimal segmentations. An example with colour image segmentation and Texture enhancement are shown.

The results in this paper are thus not necessarily to be restricted to the point of view of global constraints but belong to the theoretical results of optimization over scale increasing pyramids of partitions.

References

1. Cousty, J., Najman, L.: Incremental Algorithm for Hierarchical Minimum Spanning Forests and Saliency of Watershed Cuts. In: Soille, P., Pesaresi, M., Ouzounis, G.K. (eds.) ISMM 2011. LNCS, vol. 6671, pp. 272–283. Springer, Heidelberg (2011)
2. Arbelaez, P., Maire, M., Fowlkes, C., Malik, J.: Contour detection and hierarchical image segmentation. IEEE Trans. Pattern Anal. Mach. Intell. 33, 898–916 (2011)
3. Russell, B.C., Freeman, W.T., Efros, A.A., Sivic, J., Zisserman, A.: Using multiple segmentations to discover objects and their extent in image collections. In: Proceedings of the 2006 IEEE CVPR, vol. 2, pp. 1605–1614 (2006)
4. Cardelino, J., Caselles, V., Bertalmío, M., Randall, G.: A contrario hierarchical image segmentation. In: ICIP, pp. 4041–4044 (2009)
5. Salembier, P., Garrido, L.: Binary partition tree as an efficient representation for image processing, segmentation, and information retrieval. IEEE Transactions on Image Processing 9, 561–576 (2000)
6. Guigues, L., Cocquerez, J.P., Men, H.L.: Scale-sets image analysis. International Journal of Computer Vision 68, 289–317 (2006)
7. Soille, P.: Constrained connectivity for hierarchical image partitioning and simplification. IEEE Transactions on Pattern Analysis and Machine Intelligence 30, 1132–1145 (2008)
8. Zanoguera, M.F., Marcotegui, B., Meyer, F.: A toolbox for interactive segmentation based on nested partitions. In: ICIP (1), pp. 21–25 (1999)
9. Akcay, H.G., Aksoy, S.: Automatic detection of geospatial objects using multiple hierarchical segmentations. IEEE T. Geoscience and Remote Sensing 46, 2097–2111 (2008)

10. Serra, J.: Hierarchies and Optima. In: Debled-Rennesson, I., Domenjoud, E., Kerautret, B., Even, P. (eds.) DGCI 2011. LNCS, vol. 6607, pp. 35–46. Springer, Heidelberg (2011)
11. Lucchi, A., Li, Y., Bosch, X.B., Smith, K., Fua, P.: Are spatial and global constraints really necessary for segmentation? In: ICCV, pp. 9–16 (2011)
12. Ronse, C.: Partial partitions, partial connections and connective segmentation. J. Math. Imaging Vis. 32, 97–125 (2008)
13. Najman, L., Schmitt, M.: Geodesic saliency of watershed contours and hierarchical segmentation. IEEE Trans. Pattern Anal. Mach. Intell. 18, 1163–1173 (1996)
14. Serra, J., Kiran, B.R.: Climbing on pyramids. CoRR abs/1204.5383 (2012)

Hierarchical Late Fusion
for Concept Detection in Videos

Sabin Tiberius Strat[1,4], Alexandre Benoit[1], Hervé Bredin[2],
Georges Quénot[3], and Patrick Lambert[1]

[1] LISTIC - Université de Savoie, Annecy, France
http://www.polytech.univ-savoie.fr/index.php?id=listic-accueil
[2] Université Paris-Sud / CNRS-LIMSI, Orsay, France
http://www.limsi.fr/
[3] Laboratory of Informatics of Grenoble, France
http://www.liglab.fr/?lang=en
[4] IPAL - University "POLITEHNICA" of Bucharest
http://alpha.imag.pub.ro/en/home_page.html

Abstract. We deal with the issue of combining dozens of classifiers
into a better one, for concept detection in videos. We compare three
fusion approaches that share a common structure: they all start with a
classifier clustering stage, continue with an intra-cluster fusion and end
with an inter-cluster fusion. The main difference between them comes
from the first stage. The first approach relies on a priori knowledge about
the internals of each classifier (low-level descriptors and classification
algorithm) to group the set of available classifiers by similarity. The
second and third approaches obtain classifier similarity measures directly
from their output and group them using agglomerative clustering for the
second approach and community detection for the third one.

Keywords: late fusion, hierarchical, semantic concepts, video, semantic
indexing.

1 Introduction

Semantic indexing, as defined in the TRECVid evaluation campaign, consists in
automatically detecting the presence of visual concepts in pre-segmented video
shots [1] and returning a ranked list of shots the most likely to contain a given
concept. Judging from the performance obtained by the best system in 2010
(with a mean inferred average precision on 30 concepts of 0.090), there is still
a long way to go to solve this problem [2]. Some concepts appear to be much
easier to detect than others and no single classifier emerges as *the one* that
systematically (for any concept) outperforms the others. Therefore, for the sake
of universality, many systems rely on the combination of a large (up to 100+)
set of classifiers. They usually differ in the type of descriptors (color, texture,
or bag of visual words, etc.) and/or in the machine learning algorithm (support
vector machine or k nearest neighbors, for instance) they rely upon.

A. Fusiello et al. (Eds.): ECCV 2012 Ws/Demos, Part III, LNCS 7585, pp. 335–344, 2012.
© Springer-Verlag Berlin Heidelberg 2012

This paper focuses on the last step of this common semantic indexing pipeline: the late fusion of available classifiers. Let K be the number of classifiers and N the number of video shots.

Each classifier $k \in \{1 \ldots K\}$ provides scores $\mathbf{x}_k = [x_{k1}, \ldots, x_{kN}]$ indicating the likelihood for each shot $n \in \{1 \ldots N\}$ to contain the requested concept. The objective is to find a combination function $\mathbf{f}$ so that the resulting classifier $\mathbf{x} = \mathbf{f}(\mathbf{x}_1, \ldots, \mathbf{x}_K)$ is better than any of its components, and as good as possible.

When looking for an effective combination of classifiers, several questions arise. Should we use them all in the fusion process, or just the best ones? Does combining two classifiers always yield better results than the two of them taken separately? Should we weigh them differently in case one is much better than the other? Tackling a similar problem, *Ng and Kantor* [3] proposed a method to predict the effectiveness of their fusion approach and concluded that "[...] *schemes with dissimilar outputs but comparable performance are more likely to give rise to effective naive data fusion*". There are multiple ways of measuring this similarity between two classifiers i and j. One of them is the Spearman rank correlation coefficient ρ_{ij}:

$$\rho_{ij} = \frac{\sum_{n=1}^{n=N} (r_{in} - \overline{r_i})(r_{jn} - \overline{r_j})}{\sqrt{\sum_{n=1}^{n=N} (r_{in} - \overline{r_i})^2 \sum_{n=1}^{n=N} (r_{jn} - \overline{r_j})^2}} \tag{1}$$

where r_{kn} is the rank of shot n according to classifier k: $r_{kn} = 1$ (resp. N) for the shot whose value x_{kn} is the maximum (resp. minimum). ρ_{ij} ranges from -1 (one ranking is the exact opposite of the other one) to 1 (rankings are identical). $\rho_{ij} = 0$ can be understood as classifiers being independent from each other.

Figure 1 uses a *spring layout* to represent this similarity measure for 90 classifiers trained for the concept *Computers*. Each classifier is represented by a node and similar classifiers (higher value of ρ_{ij}) are positioned closer to each other. It appears that some kind of community structure naturally emerges, with several groups of classifiers being more strongly connected internally than with the outside of their group. This is partly due to the low-level descriptors used internally by the classifiers (the type of descriptor is denoted by the shape of the nodes). For instance, classifiers based on color (circles) seem to agglutinate, as do classifiers based on audio features (diamonds). Finally, the size of items is directly proportional to the performance of the corresponding classifier. Therefore, best performing classifiers (i.e. larger items) also tend to agglutinate as they provide rankings that are closer to the reality – therefore closer to each other.

In this paper, we compare three fusion approaches that rely on these observations and share a common structure described in Figure 2. They all begin with a classifier clustering stage, continue with an intra-cluster fusion and end with an inter-cluster fusion.

Section 2 describes the first approach that relies on manually grouping classifiers of similar origin, in a hierarchic manner. The second and third approaches, described in Sections 3 and 4, group classifiers automatically according to their output scores, either iteratively in an agglomerative fashion, or based on a

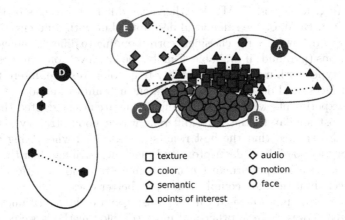

Fig. 1. Similarity of classifiers trained for detection of concept *Computers*. Each node represents a classifier, and edges represent the similarity between them (we only display some of the edges). The dotted edges represent classifiers which derive from the same descriptor, but have a different machine learning algorithm.

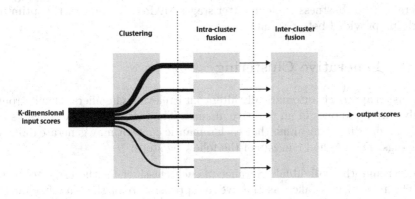

Fig. 2. Overview of the proposed late fusion approaches, sharing a common structure: a classifier clustering stage, an intra-cluster fusion and finally an inter-cluster fusion

community detection algorithm respectively. Experiments and results are described in Section 5.

2   Manual Hierarchy

The manual hierarchy was designed according to a high level knowledge about the descriptors and the classifiers. The main principle considered is to fuse first descriptors or classifiers that are expected to be closer considering their nature or principle of operation. The manual hierarchy incorporates more levels than the automatic ones, with branches with different depths. In practice, we fused first the output of all the available machine learning algorithms for each descriptor (e.g. kNN and SVM). We then fuse different variants of the same descriptor (e.g. BOW of the same local descriptor but with different dictionary sizes). Afterwards, we fuse the classifiers corresponding to different image spatial decompositions (pyramid) if available. Finally, the last level concerns descriptors of different types within the same modality (e.g. color, texture, interest points, percepts or faces) and descriptors from different modalities (audio and visual).

Various experiments with manually defined hierarchies suggested that going from the most similar to the most different was a good strategy. These experiments also showed that the best results are obtained when using as many combinations as possible of descriptors and machine learning algorithms. Even combinations with low performance can contribute to a global performance increase, especially if they are complementary to better ones.

Late fusion was performed at all levels using a weighted arithmetic mean of normalized scores. Several other and more complex methods were tried but produced no or very small improvements. Three weighting strategies were considered: uniform (simple arithmetic mean), MAP based (simple function of the MAP of the different inputs), and direct optimization by cross-validation. Cross-validation experiments showed that in the early stages, uniform weighting was preferable for robustness while in latter stages MAP-based or directly optimized weighting provided better results.

3   Agglomerative Clustering

This fusion approach automatically filters out irrelevant classifiers, then it groups highly-correlated ones in an iterative manner. The target semantic concepts are treated individually, meaning that each semantic concept may generate different groupings. The method consists of the following steps:

1. determine the individual relevance of each classifier for the target concept. The relevance is taken as the average precision α of the classifier for the target concept on the training dataset, normalized by the proportion of true positives in the training dataset.
2. retain only classifiers with a relevance higher than 1 (better than random classification). Additionally, the classifiers must have at least 1/8th of the relevance of the best one, so as not to "pollute" the good classifiers with bad ones.
3. Some of the retained classifiers are highly correlated, so we look for the pair with the maximum correlation and fuse it into a single classifier. We update the correlation between the resulting classifier and the remaining ones.
4. The previous step is repeated many times, until a sufficiently correlated pair can no longer be found. This has a dimensionality-reduction effect and also helps to reduce the classification "noise".

The correlation measure used is the correlation coefficient of the raw classification scores. We consider a pair of attributes as correlated if *(a)* the correlation coefficient for all video shots is at least 0.75, to ensure that the two classifiers give similar information on a global scale, and *(b)*, the correlation between the scores for just the positive shots must be at least 0.65, to ensure that the positives tend to be classified in the same way. We add the second constraint because in TRECVid, most of the target concepts have very few positives, and otherwise, the classification scores on the negatives would dominate the correlation.

Now, the resulting classifiers are again filtered based on their average precision on the training set, using the same criteria as before. Afterwards, this approach separates into two versions, which are detailed below.

First Version: Weighted Average. The individual relevances of each remaining classifier are used as weights for a weighted arithmetic mean, thus obtaining the final classification score. We have not used this version in the official TRECVid 2011 submissions, because previous tests have indicated that the second version should be better (however with a different performance metric).

In the end, because all the previous steps consisted of selections and averaging, without any normalisation operations as those in section 4, this approach is in fact a weighted arithmetic mean, with a more elaborate way of choosing the weights.

Second Version: PCA and Nearest-Neighbors. In this version, we continue with a Principal Component Analysis (PCA) to further eliminate correlation and reduce the dimensionality of the problem. We retain the first 1, 2, 3, 4 and 5 most important dimensions, and on each of these choices independently, we apply a neighborhood-based fusion strategy, as follows: for a test shot, we count the positives and negatives from the training base in a volume of radius d around it. This radius is taken as an average distance between training shots. If no neighbors are present within the volume, we consider the shot as a positive, based on the assumption that because positives are generally much rarer than negatives, they are unable to densely cover their entire corresponding space.

Because experiments on cross-validation have shown that we cannot predict the optimal number of dimensions to take after PCA, the last step consists in averaging the classification scores obtained with 1, 2, 3, 4 and 5 dimensions.

This version has been used to generate two official submissions for TRECVid 2011, the details of which will be given in Section 5.

4   Community Detection

This last fusion approach is very similar to the previous one. The main difference relies in the way classifier clusters are discovered.

We define the agreement $A_{ij} = \max(0, \rho_{ij})$ between two classifiers i and j, where ρ_{ij} is the Spearman rank correlation coefficient given in equation 1. A complete undirected graph $\mathcal{G}$ is constructed with one node per classifier. Each pair of classifiers (i, j) is connected by an undirected edge, whose weight is directly proportional to A_{ij}. A simplified representation of such a graph is given in Fig. 1.

We rely on the so-called *Louvain* approach for automatic community detection proposed by *Blondel et al.*, and apply it on graph $\mathcal{G}$. It is a heuristic method that is based on the maximization of modularity $\mathcal{Q}$:

$$Q = \frac{1}{\sum\limits_{i,j} A_{ij}} \sum\limits_{i,j} \left[A_{ij} - \frac{\sum\limits_k A_{ik} \sum\limits_k A_{kj}}{\sum\limits_{i,j} A_{ij}} \right] \delta_{ij} \tag{2}$$

where $\delta_{ij} = 1$ if classifiers i and j are members of the same community, 0 otherwise. $\mathcal{Q}$ can be seen as a measure of the quality of the detected communities. It increases when communities have stronger intra-community and weaker inter-community edges [4]. For a detailed description and analysis of the algorithm, we refer the interested reader to [5].

With no objective groundtruth to compare with, it is difficult to evaluate the detected communities. However, looking at Fig. 1 and the five detected communities (A to E), it seems that the *Louvain* algorithm did a good job at finding communities related to the nature of the low-level descriptors on which classifiers are based. In particular, a dotted edge between a pair of classifiers indicates that they are based on the very same descriptors and they only differ in the machine learning algorithm they rely on. None of these pairs is split into two different communities.

After the clustering stage, classifiers from each community are combined by simple sum of normalized scores, in order to obtain one new classifier per community. The normalization strategy is presented further below. These new classifiers are expected to be at least as good as the best of their components and can sometimes lead to much better performance.

Since they come from different communities, these new *community classifiers* are very likely to output very dissimilar scores and rankings. They are combined using a weighted sum fusion of normalized scores:

$$\mathbf{x} = \sum\limits_{c=1}^{c=C} \alpha_c \widehat{\mathbf{x}_c} \tag{3}$$

where the weights α_c are in fact the average precisions of each of these new *community classifiers*. They are estimated using a development set.

Both fusion steps rely on normalized scores. We investigated multiple normalization techniques (min/max, σ/μ, TanH) but only report on the one that proved to be the best, TanH normalization [6]:

$$\widehat{x_{kn}} = \frac{1}{2} \left\{ \tanh \left[0.01 \left(\frac{x_{kn} - \mu_k}{\sigma_k} \right) \right] + 1 \right\} \tag{4}$$

where μ_k and σ_k) are respectively the mean and standard deviation of scores provided by classifier k on test set.

5   Experiments

The fusion approaches are tested on the TRECVid 2011 dataset. We train our algorithms on the official development collection, and we evaluate the performances on the official test collection.

5.1   Input Classifiers

The input classification scores are obtained by applying supervised classification algorithms on multidimensional descriptors extracted from the video shots. We use a battery of multidimensional descriptors such as various color histograms, Gabor transforms, spatio-temporal interest points, SIFT or SURF Bag-of-Words, face tracks, presence of mid-level semantic concepts, audio spectral profiles, histograms of Local Binary Patterns etc. Most of the descriptors have several versions, obtained by varying the extraction parameters (such as the number of bins when performing clustering, the spatial pyramid decomposition etc.).

Additionally, we apply power transformations on the multidimensional descriptors in order to optimize the data distribution before doing the supervised classification. We selected an optimal power coefficient for each descriptor by cross-validation on the training set.

The supervised classification algorithms are either a k-Nearest Neighbor (KNN) or a multiple Support Vector Machine (MSVM). By combining descriptors with different power transformations with the supervised classifiers, we obtain sets of classification scores which we call *KNNG, KNNC, KNNB, MSVM* and *ALLC*.

The KNN scores are relatively fast to compute, as the nearest-neighbors need to be determined only once for all target semantic concepts. This is important, because finding neighbors in a large collection and with many dimensions is a computationally-expensive operation. Only the counting of positives and negatives among neighbors needs to be done for each concept individually, but this is trivial. The optimization of the KNN hyper parameters can be done either at the individual target concept level (KNNC) or globally (KNNG). By partitioning the development set, the latter was found to be more robust and the late fusion of both (KNNB) was found to be better than both in almost all cases.

The MSVM classifiers are generated only using the optimal power transformation for the 49 available descriptors. ALLC, being the average of KNNB and MSVM, also has 49 classifiers, being slightly better than both KNNB and MSVM. However, because the MSVM supervised classification is much more computationally-demanding (and because it needs to be done for each concept separately), only a subset of MSVM and ALLC scores was available for the official submissions of TRECVID.

5.2   Submissions

The official submissions consist of a *Manual hierarchy fusion* with all the available classifiers, two *Agglomerative clustering fusions (second version)*, one applied on the KNNB and one on the KNNC classifiers, and a *Community detection fusion* applied on the KNNC/KNNG sets. Additionally, we apply a video shot re-ranking strategy based on temporal coherence, which further increases performances. The MSVM and ALLC classifiers, even though they are better than KNN, were only used for the *Manual hierarchy fusion*, because they were not all ready before the submission deadline.

Because the number of permitted official submissions per team was limited to 5, we extend our study with unofficial experiments. For these, all the MSVM and ALLC scores are now available for input.

As a reference for comparison, we take, for each semantic concept individually, its best classifier in cross-validation on the training set. We complement this reference with the arithmetic mean, either with equal weights for all classifiers, or weighted for each semantic concept individually by the average precision obtained by a classifier for that concept. We also experimented in earlier stages with a geometric mean of the input classifiers and with a rank fusion, but these last two approaches give very similar results to the arithmetic mean.

5.3   Results and Comparison

The results obtained by the various fusions are summarised in Table 1.

Among our official submissions, the *Manual hierarchy fusion* is the best. This is partly due to the fact that manually grouping classifiers obtained in a similar manner ensures more homogeneous properties within a group. The rest of the performance increase of the manual hierarchy is due to the inclusion of some of the MSVM and ALLC classifiers (which are better than KNN), even if they were not all available at that time. This submission ranked 8th among all submissions from all participants in the task.

Table 1. Performance of fusion approaches. We display the Mean Average Precisions (mAvgPrec), and also the rankings of the official submissions among all Semantic Indexing task participants. The first four rows are official TRECVid submissions, which did not benefit from the complete MSVM and ALLC sets of classifiers. The other rows are unofficial experiments, when the MSVM and ALLC sets were complete.

Fusion	Applied on	mAvgPrec	+ re-rank
Manual hierarchy	ALLC	0.1454	0.1529 (#8)
Agglomerative clustering (v2)	KNNB		0.1194 (#25)
Agglomerative clustering (v2)	KNNC		0.1142 (#30)
Community detection	KNNC/KNNG	0.1341 (#17)	0.1387 (#15)
Best classifier	KNNB		0.1146
Best classifier	ALLC	0.1178	0.1332
Arithmetic Mean	KNNB		0.1381
Arithmetic Mean	ALLC	0.1415	0.1481
Weighted Mean	ALLC	0.1419	0.1491
Agglomerative clustering (v1)	KNNB		0.1423
Agglomerative clustering (v1)	ALLC	0.1457	0.1520
Agglomerative clustering (v2)	ALLC	0.1332	0.1444
Community detection	ALLC	0.1438	

The *Community detection* applied on the KNNC/KNNG sets ranked 15th and 25th (with and without temporal re-ranking respectively) in the official hierarchy, while the *Agglomerative clustering fusions (second version)* ranked 25th for KNNB and 30th for KNNC, which situates it close to the middle of the official hierarchy.

Looking also at the unofficial experiments, a first thing to notice is that all of the methods outperform the *Best classifier* baseline, if they are applied on the same dataset and all of them either use, or do not use, the temporal re-ranking. The *Community detection* using KNNC/KNNG outperforms the *Best classifier* on KNNB (KNNB is the fusion of KNNC and KNNG) by a good margin of 21% if using the temporal re-ranking, while the *Agglomerative clustering (v.2)* of KNNB achieves a small margin of 4%.

Regarding the addition of temporal re-ranking, we do not display the average precision for all methods, but we confirm that it improves the results for all fusions. The performance boost is especially obvious for the *Best classifier* approach, where, using the ALLC input scores, we increase the average precision by 13%.

For the automatic clustering approaches applied on ALLC, the *Agglomerative clustering (first version)* is the best, outperforming the *Best classifier* by 23%, followed by the *Community detection* (22%), and finally by the *Agglomerative clustering (second version)* (13%). However, the performance of the arithmetic mean, either simple or weighted, is not to be ignored. The margins by which the *Agglomerative clustering (v.1)* and the *Community detection* outperform the simple arithmetic mean are much lower: 3% and 1.6% respectively, while the *Agglomerative clustering (second version)* actually performs worst. The weighted arithmetic mean, with weights given by the individual relevance of attributes, gives very similar results.

Considering the simplicity of the arithmetic mean, the processing time constraints need to be taken into account when deciding whether or not the performance boost of a more complex fusion method is worth the effort. Already, the simple arithmetic mean manages to improve on the *Best classifier* by a margin of 20%.

6   Conclusion and Future Work

In this paper, we proposed several ways of combining dozens of input classifiers into better ones, and applied them in the context of the *TRECVid 2011 Semantic Indexing* task. We have shown that all of the methods outperform taking the best classifier for each concept, and they are all better than an arithmetic mean, except the second version of agglomerative clustering, which was optimized based on different criteria. The performance boost of the more complex methods however, needs to be balanced with the computational complexity, as the arithmetic mean is very close in performance.

In the future, we plan to experiment with combining the three fusion approaches presented, and also using various score normalisation strategies at different levels of the algorithm.

Acknowledgments. This work was supported by the Quaero Program and the QCompere project, respectively funded by OSEO (French State agency for innovation) and ANR (French national research agency). The authors would also like to thank the members of the IRIM consortium for the classifier scores used throughout the experiments described in this paper.

References

1. Smeaton, A.F., Over, P., Kraaij, W.: High-Level Feature Detection from Video in TRECVid: a 5-Year Retrospective of Achievements. In: Divakaran, A. (ed.) Multimedia Content Analysis, Theory and Applications, pp. 151–174. Springer, Berlin (2009)
2. Snoek, C.G.M., van de Sande, K.E.A., de Rooij, O., Huurnink, B., Gavves, E., Odijk, D., de Rijke, M., Gevers, T., Worring, M., Koelma, D.C., Smeulders, A.W.M.: The MediaMill TRECVID 2010 Semantic Video Search Engine. In: Proceedings of the 8th TRECVID Workshop, Gaithersburg, USA (2010)
3. Ng, K.B., Kantor, P.B.: Predicting the Effectiveness of Naive Data Fusion on the Basis of System Characteristics. Journal of the American Society for Information Science 51, 1177–1189 (2000)
4. Newman, M.E.J.: Modularity and Community Structure in Networks. Proceedings of the National Academy of Sciences of the United States of America 103, 8577–8582 (2006)
5. Blondel, V.D., Guillaume, J.L., Lambiotte, R., Lefebvre, E.: Fast Unfolding of Communities in Large Networks. Journal of Statistical Mechanics: Theory and Experiment 2008, P10008 (2008)
6. Ross, A.A., Nandakumar, K., Jain, A.K.: Handbook of Multibiometrics. International Series on Biometrics. Springer-Verlag New York, Inc., Secaucus (2006)

Fast and Adaptive Deep Fusion Learning
for Detecting Visual Objects

Nikolaos Doulamis[1] and Anastasios Doulamis[2]

[1] National Technical University of Athens,
9 Heroon Polytechnious Str. 15773, Zografou, Athens, Greece
[2] Technical University of Crete, University Campus, Chania, Greece.
{ndoulam,adoulam}@cs.ntua.gr

Abstract. Currently, object tracking/detection is based on a "shallow learning" paradigm; they locally process features to build an object model and then they apply adaptive methodologies to estimate model parameters. However, such an approach presents the drawback of losing the "whole picture information" required to maintain a stable tracking for long time and high visual changes. To overcome these obstacles, we need a "deep" information fusion framework. Deep learning is a new emerging research area that simulates the efficiency and robustness by which the humans' brain represents information; it deeply propagates data into complex hierarchies. However, implementing a deep fusion learning paradigm in a machine presents research challenges mainly due to the highly non-linear structures involved and the "curse of dimensionality". Another difficulty which is critical in computer vision applications is that learning should be self adapted to guarantee stable object detection over long time spans. In this paper, we propose a novel fast (in real-time) and adaptive information fusion strategy that exploits the deep learning paradigm. The proposed framework integrates optimization strategies able to update in real-time the non-linear model parameters according in a way to trust, as much as possible, the current changes of the environment, while providing a minimal degradation of the previous gained experience.

1   Introduction

The current object detection methods exploit a "shallow learning paradigm"; they locally process and map features to build an object model and then they apply adaptive learning methods to estimate model parameters [1]. However, the use of local features inherently presents the drawback of losing the "whole picture information" resulting in several mismatches (see Fig. 1a). Although attempts have been recently proposed to solve this critical aspect through global optimization strategies [2], it seems that there is no a unified mathematical framework that allows "deep" information fusion under a fast (in real-time) and adaptive way (robust to environmental visual changes). The current approaches present the drawback that the training procedures are highly unstable; we need several implementation cycles to conclude to a stable solution.

A. Fusiello et al. (Eds.): ECCV 2012 Ws/Demos, Part III, LNCS 7585, pp. 345–354, 2012.

However, the main difficulty in implementing such a deep information fusion algorithm is the so called "curse of dimensionality", i.e., the learning complexity exponentially grows with a linear increase in the dimensionality of the data. To make things worse, the data should be related with highly non-linear associations, which present additional research challenges to be optimized and adapted under real-time constraints. This is the reason why until now only shallow learning paradigms have been adopted in computer vision.

Although multi-layer learning models have been known for many years ago, they could not been trained well due to the fact that the performance of the existing training algorithms is significantly deteriorated for large number of hidden layers. This drawback was alleviated, to an extent, when a reasonably efficient, new learning algorithm was introduced by Hinton et al. [3], opening new frontiers for the use of deep structures. However, even with these significant contributions, deep information fusion learning lacks self adaptability which is a critical aspect in computer vision; object tracking for very long time periods encounters abrupt and high visual changes (see Fig.1(b)-(d)). For this reason, semi-supervised learning strategies (SSL) have been investigated as an efficient learning paradigm to increase the reliability of object tracking [1] using, however, shallow boosting mechanisms. However, again semi-supervision (e.g., simple inclusion of unlabelled) does not face the inherent problem of instability and time consuming training process which is presented in deep, non-linear structures.

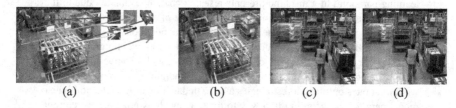

    (a)   (b)   (c)   (d)

Fig. 1. (a) The deep learning paradigm; local processing looses the 'whole picture information. Although one could discriminate the content of the whole image, it is impossible to understand where the six sub-images come from. (b,c) The self training necessity; It is impossible for the tracker to remain stable for both images due to background/foreground changes. Thus, we need self-training mechanisms; For example, the green (blue) regions are selected as confident background (foreground) from the pool of unlabelled data by exploiting motion information (see Fig.1c). (d) The final tracking after several adaptation cycles.

1.1 Previous Works

Recently a great effort has been dedicated to handle object tracking as a classification problem [4]. However, these approaches exploit no adaptable mechanisms to update the performance of the classifier and thus the structure of the model remains fixed. One of the first approaches towards an adaptable classification for object tracking have been presented in [5], [6]. These works, however, do not face efficiently the general trade-off between model stability and adaptability. A highly specific model significantly increases the reliability of the tracker to capture the target but looses adaptability. On the other hand, a highly general model copes with the legitimate changes in appearance but with a cost in reliability. To cope with these problems, Matthews et al. [7] propose an updated template algorithm that avoids the "drifting" inherent. Other methods exploit the semi-supervised paradigm [1], [8] a co-training strategy [9], a combination of generative and discriminative trackers [10] or finally coupled layered visual models [11].

The realization that local information sometimes is not enough to make a correct decision led to the development of global optimization trackers. These trackers operate on larger time scales and make use of high-level reasoning to re-solve ambiguities. Examples are the use of a minimum cost graph matching that runs the Hungarian algorithm [12]. Other works handle the problem as a minimum flow cost problem [13], [2]. However, in case that the background / foreground significantly change, there is no way to estimate matches for long time periods forcing the algorithm to fail.

1.2   Contribution

In this paper, we propose a novel mathematical framework which permits fast and adaptive information fusion over deep learning structures. Very few works have been proposed in the literature that exploit conventional (i.e., non-adaptive) deep learning strategies in computer vision/image processing applications. The [3] demonstrates the efficiency of deep learning on simple image recognition while [14] addresses the 3D based object recognition problem. The use of conditional Deep Belief and Convolutional Networks for video sequence and human motion synthesis was reported in [15], [16]. However, none of the aforementioned approaches adopt an adaptive and fast deep learning strategy; therefore they cannot be applied in real-life application scenarios where dynamic and abrupt changes of the environment are encountered.

The proposed methodology assumes that few labeled data are first used to train multi-layered deep structures and then the "parameters" of the architecture are dynamically updated as new unlabelled data come to adjust the performance of the deep structures to the statistical characteristics of the new data. In this way, we are able to deal with the trade-off regarding adaptability versus stability. The proposed adaptable deep learning architectures are able to perform stable tracking even in complex environmental conditions, while retains the adaptable behavior of the tracker. The proposed framework incorporates highly non-linear models but simultaneously integrates optimization strategies able to update in real-time the non-linear model parameters according in a way to trust, as much as possible, the current changes of the environment, while providing a minimal degradation of the previous gained experience.

2   Problem Formulation

In the deep learning paradigm, a region instead of a single pixel value is used as input in object modeling. In particular, we consider the object detection problem as the estimation of a multi-valued non-linear function $\mathbf{h}(\cdot)$ that maps features of the region s

[we denote the respective feature map as $\mathbf{x}(s)$] with a probability vector $\hat{\mathbf{d}}$ (an estimate of the actual probability vector $\mathbf{d}$). Vector $\hat{\mathbf{d}}$ assigns a region s to one of the M available objects.

$$\hat{\mathbf{d}}(s) \approx \mathbf{h}_q(\mathbf{x}(s)) \tag{1}$$

where subscript q refers to the total parameters' space of the non-linear model $\mathbf{h}(\cdot)$. In the following, we assume, for simplicity, a two-class object detection problem. Then, the probability vector $\hat{\mathbf{d}}$ becomes scalar $d(s)$ and non-linear model as $h(\cdot)$. Extension to an M class object detection problem can be performed straightforwardedly.

The main difficulty in implementing Eq. (1) is that $h(\cdot)$ is actually unknown. Using concepts from functional analysis and assuming some simple restrictions regarding the continuity of $h(\cdot)$, we can model the $h(\cdot)$ as a finite sum of known functional components.

$$\hat{d}(s) \approx \phi(\mathbf{w}_N^T \cdot \mathbf{u}^{(N)}) \tag{2a}$$

$$\text{with } \mathbf{u}^{(l)} = \varphi\left(\mathbf{W}_{l-1}^T \cdot \mathbf{u}^{(l-1)}\right), \ l = 1,2,..., N \ \text{ and } \ \mathbf{u}^{(0)} = \mathbf{x}(s) \tag{2b}$$

In Eq. (2) $\varphi(\cdot)$ is a known vector-valued functional component which should be bounded, continuous and monotonically increasing. In our case, we select function $\phi(\cdot)$ as the sigmoid function. Vector $\mathbf{w}_l$ are coefficients that weigh the non-linear transformations $\mathbf{u}$ of the input feature map $\mathbf{x}(s)$. Matrix $\mathbf{W}_0$ represents the weighted coefficients used for the initial transformation of $\mathbf{x}(s)$. l indicates the layer of the deep representation.

2.1   Limitations of Conventional Re-training

Although Eq. (2) is a robust mathematical framework for object modeling using deep architectures, the main difficulty results from the efficiency of the algorithm used to approximate the unknown coefficients $\mathbf{W}_l$ with $l=1,...,N\text{-}1$ and $\mathbf{w}_N$. In the following, for simplicity we denote all these coefficients as q. Under a supervised framework, a least squared steepest descent approach is usually applied to estimate the unknown coefficients q. However, in complex non-linear relationships and in case of a considerable number of input variables, there are multiple local minima in the error surface. Thus, it is quite possible the optimization to be trapped into local minima instead of global one. Another difficulty is that real-world applications are dynamic processes. The probabilistic characteristics of the data change through time while the collection effort for the labeled data is enormous and arduous. Furthermore, training a multi-layer structure on the use of only labeled data often leads to poor performance since adaptability is not permitted. Thus, supervised learning even though deep architectures are used, is not sufficient to address a stable object tracking for very long time spans, where usually abrupt and high visual changes take place. To address this problem, in this paper, we propose the mathematical framework of a fast and adaptive deep information fusing learning strategy and apply it to automatically update the behaviour of a tracker in a way to trust as much as possible, the current visual changes, while minimally degrading the already gained experience.

3   The Adaptive and Fast Deep Fusion Paradigm

Traditional classifiers use only labeled data (feature and label pairs) to train. Due to the nature of computer vision applications labeled data are difficult to obtain. This is due to the fact that it requires a specialist to label the data, which is not practically feasible especially under real-time video supervision processes. On the other hand, unlabeled data is abundant and can be easily collected. In this paper, we exploit this feature by letting the aforementioned deep learning structure to automatically self-adapt to the current conditions of the environment (dynamic changes of the visual scene conditions). Thus, the initially trained deep models can be enhanced, through the proposed adaptive strategy learning.

Let us now formulate the adaptive deep fusion framework. We assume that we have an incomplete (approximate) object model $h_{q_{in}}(\cdot)$ the parameters of which q_{in} have been estimated using for example a supervised training phase. Let us now assume that at a time $t+T$ we process the image $I(t+T)$ and extract a set of unlabeled features $x_i^u(s)$ for regions $s \subseteq I(t+T)$. Then, our target is to refine the object function $h_{q_{in}}(\cdot)$ from the incomplete model coefficients q_{in} to a new more accurate (updated) model, i.e., $h_{q_{in}}(\cdot) \rightarrow h_{q_{ad}}(\cdot)$, exploiting the unlabeled data $x_i^u(s)$.

In particular, initially, from the pool of unlabeled data U we estimate a very small set of samples of high confidence $C \subset U$ to belong to the objects of interest. Actually set C describes the current knowledge of the environment (see Section 4). Assuming a two-class object detection problem, set C can be exclusively divided into two sub-sets $C = C_1 \cup C_2$; where C_1 (C_2) refers to the foreground (background) object.

$$h_{q_{ad}}(x_i^u) \approx B \ \forall x_i^u \in C \ \text{ where } \ B = \begin{cases} 0 \ \forall x_i^u \in C_1 \\ 1 \ \forall x_i^u \in C_2 \end{cases} \tag{3}$$

Eq. (3) means that after the adaptation the new coefficients q_{in} should be updated so that they trust as much as possible the most confident unlabeled data.

We also assume that a small perturbation of the coefficient space is sufficient to get an adequate modification of the model function. Therefore, we have that

$$q_{ad} = q_{in} + dq \ \text{ or equivalently} \tag{4}$$

$$W_l^{ad} = W_l^{in} + dW_l \ \text{ for } l=1,..,N\text{-}1 \text{ and } w_N^{ad} = w_N^{in} + dw_N \tag{5}$$

where dq, $d\mathbf{w}_N$, $d\mathbf{W}_l$ refers to a small perturbation of the coefficients space.

3.1   The Proposed Adaptive and Fast Retraining Strategy

Assuming a small perturbation for the coefficients, we can linearize Eq. (3) on the use of first order Taylor series expansion. This way, we can linearly express the unknown coefficients $d\mathbf{w}_N$ and $d\mathbf{W}_l$ as a function of the weights before adaptation $\mathbf{W}_l^{in}$ and $\mathbf{w}_N^{in}$. Then, the following theorem can be proven.

Theorem 1: The constraint of (3) under the assumption of (5) is decomposed to a system of linear equations of the form $\mathbf{c} = \sum_l a_l^T \cdot vec(d\mathbf{W}_l)$, where vector $\mathbf{c}$ and vectors, a_l depends only on the previous known coefficients, $\mathbf{W}_l^{in}$ and $\mathbf{w}_N^{in}$; $vec(\cdot)$ is an operator that forms a vector from a matrix by stacking up all of the matrix elements.

Vector $\mathbf{c}$ expresses the differences between the multi-layer output after and before the adaptation. In other words, it provides an estimate of how much the classifier should be modified to trust the current visual properties (trust the current conditions). Vectors a_l are more complex relationships of the previous coefficients q_{in}. However, usually, a very small set of confident unlabeled data is selected to reduce error accumulation in tracking. Thus, the number of unknowns of the linear system of Theorem 1 is greater than the number of equations. To handle this problem, an additional constraint is introduced to restrict the solution of (3) on a feasible space. In our case, we assume that the norm $\|dq\|$ should undergone a minimal modification.

$$\min\|dq\| \tag{6}$$

The minimization of Eq. (6) subject to the constraint of Eq. (3) is in fact a convex minimization problem subject to linear constraints. Among several applicable techniques, the reduced gradient method has been selected due to its cost effectiveness.

4   Confident Data Selection

The purpose of this section is to automatically evaluate the unlabelled data so that the most confident ones are detected. This is an independent mechanism compared with the deep learning process; it exploits apart from the output of the object model (through the deep learning structure) additional criteria coming from moving coherency. It is worth noting that this process is not a classification framework, but an automatic way to train with unlabeled data. Let us form a graph $G = (V, E)$, the vertices of which corresponds to a set of selected unlabelled samples while the edge expresses a distance confident metric between two samples. In particular, let $e_{i,j}$ denote the graph edge between the node i and the node j. Then, graph edges should reflect the likelihood of the two samples to belong to the same object.

$$e_{i,j} = corr\big(\mathbf{x}(s_i), \mathbf{x}(s_j)\big) \cdot XNOR(\hat{d}(\mathbf{x}(s_i)), \hat{d}(\mathbf{x}(s_j))) \tag{7}$$

Eq. (7) expresses that the two samples present high likelihood to belong to the same objet class if their features present the same properties and the respective outputs of the initial (before updating) object model also present consistency. In case, we refer to foreground extraction applications, we can enrich (7) with additional constraints. For example, the likelihood that the two pixels belong to the foreground object is temporality constrained by the motion information. Thus, we have

$$Te_{i,j} = e_{i,j} \cdot AND(\vartheta(\mathbf{x}(s_i)), \vartheta(\mathbf{x}(s_j))) \tag{8}$$

To select the most confident unlabelled data, we partition the graph using spectral clustering algorithm.

5   Real-World Experiments

The experiments have been conducted using four public datasets; PETS2007 (a conference room), PETS2006 (a metro station) and two views of SCOVIS [19] depicting industrial workflows. Wide overlapped windows of 64x64 pixels have been chosen as regions s. Within this area, the MPEG-7 descriptors, such as Scalable Color, Dominant Color, and the Color Structure are used as features, which are fed into a 3-layer deep structure to perform tracking, each comprises of 10 neurons. In the rest, we focus on a foreground / background separation problem. The initial weights was estimated based on a training set of 320, 230, 570 samples for PETS2007, PETS2006 and SCOVIS dataset.

To estimate the most confident unlabelled data, we exploit the motion activity of the scene, estimated by Lucas-Kanade optical flow on selecting good features. For acceleration, we activate the adaptation strategy only in case where significant motion activity is encountered and we skip for the selection data of similar feature properties.

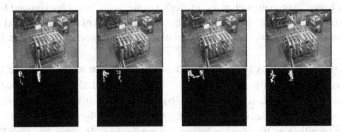

Fig. 2. Background changes effect. From left to Right: a,b) Two workers' detection of small size on complex background, c) tracking failure due to background change (workers move a car equipment), d) background content correction and accurate foreground detection by adaptation.

Initially, we present the results regarding SCOVIS dataset due to its complexity. To demonstrate tracker stability, we apply the proposed algorithm on more than

20,000 frames of SCOVIS other than the ones used in the training set. Within this long span of test sequence, several complex environmental changes occur which present challenges to maintain a stable object tracking. In particular, Fig. 2 presents a scene where a slight background change takes place; a car equipment is moving by the workers. As is observed, the tracker consistently detects the two workers. However, in Fig. 2c, the equipment is erroneously considered part of the tracking objects but as the algorithm runs and more unlabelled data are exploited, the proposed deep structure unlearns the error and sets the equipment as background (Fig. 2d).

Fig. 3. Occlusions effect. From left to Right: a) The left worker is partially occluded and the tracker stably detects this, b) the left worker re-appears, c) again the left worker is occluded, d) the two workers overlaps each other, e) both workers are partially occluded.

Fig. 4. Tracking effect over long time spans. a) One of the two workers disappears from the scene, while the background has changed from Fig. 3. b) Welding fire in the background; tracking efficiency under illumination changes. c) Active camera effect; the background has significantly changed; stable tracking after several adaptation cycles. d,e) new foreground enters the scene, stable tracking after several iterations, through the second worker is missed in Fig 4e.

Fig. 3 shows five frames of another part of the sequence to demonstrate the effect on occlusions. In Fig. 3a, the left worker is partially extracted since he is occluded by the rack. Then, he is tracked again (Fig. 3b) while he is again occluded in Fig. 3c. Similar performance is observed for the other frames. In Fig. 4a, we observe the stability of the algorithm as the worker leaves the scene. Fig. 4b show the stability of the algorithm for high illumination changes (fire welding). Finally, the last two frame presents tracking performance for long time spans where background has significantly change and new foreground object enter the scene. After several adaptation cycles stable tracking is encountered.

We then objectively evaluate and compare our scheme with other methods. The evaluation was performed using four segments of the SCOVIS sequence of different visual properties, which are merged together to form one sequence. Fig. 5 shows the confident error as the ratio of the XOR of the tracked and ground truth mask over ground truth. In Fig. 5, we have compared the results with the on-line SVM [10], the Semi Boost [8], the Students-t [18] and the Gaussian [17] tracking. For fair comparison, we have modified the algorithms to use the same confident unlabelled data. We observe that our algorithm better handles the problem of adaptability vs. stability in terms of providing well enough generative models which can simultaneously specialize well to visual changes. Table 1 shows the average confidence over the four examined video sequences of our method and the four compared ones.

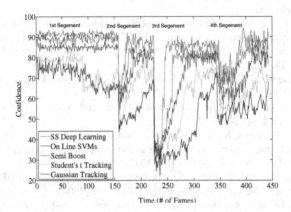

Fig. 5. Comparison of the proposed algorithm with other adaptable tracking methodologies over a merged of difference scene segments of SCOVIS dataset. We observe that the proposed algorithm is more stable in terms of adaptability and tracking accuracy.

Table 1. Average tracking confidence over different datasets and methods

Sequences	SSL Deep Learning	On Line SVM	Semi Boost	Student's t Distribution	Gaussian Tracking
SCOVIS Cam 32	85.22%	76.28%	80.32%	65.99%	58.02%
SCOVIS Cam 34	84.64%	74.66%	79.73%	65.23%	57.57%
PETS2007	88.33%	82.22%	84.44%	79.55%	74.54%
PETS2006	90.12%	87.33%	89.12%	83.22%	80.18%

6   Conclusions

In this paper, we introduced a semi-supervised deep learning algorithm for stable long time object tracking in real-time. We exploited perturbation theory with optimization strategies to efficiently self-adapt non-linear deep structures in a way to trust as much as possible the current visual properties, while simultaneously providing a minimal degradation of the already gained experience. We have tested the proposed semi-supervised deep learning under quite complex video footages, where several occlusions, illumination changes, background / foreground content modification are encountered.

Acknowledgements: The research leading to these results has been supported by European Union funds and national funds from Greece and Cyprus under the project "POSEIDON: Development of an Intelligent System for Coast Monitoring using Camera Arrays and Sensor Networks" in the context of the inter-regional programme INTERREG (Greece-Cyprus cooperation) - contract agreement K1 3 10–17/6/2011.

References

[1] Stalder, S., Grabner, H., van Gool, L.: Beyond semi-supervised tracking: Tracking should be as simple as detection, but not simpler than recognition. In: Proc. of IEEE ICCV, pp. 1409–1416 (2009)

[2] Henriques, J.F., Caseiro, R., Batista, J.: Globally optimal solution to multi-object tracking with merged measurements. In: Proc. of IEEE ICCV, pp. 2470–2477 (2011)

[3] Hinton, G., Osindero, S., Teh, Y.: A fast learning algorithm for deep belief nets. Neural Computation 18, 1527–1554 (2006)

[4] Lepetit, V., Lagger, P., Fua, P.: Randomized trees for real-time keypoint recognition. In: Proc. IEEE CVPR, vol. 2, pp. 775–781 (2005)

[5] Collins, R.T., Liu, Y.: On-line selection of discriminative tracking features. In: Proc. of IEEE ICCV, vol. 1, pp. 346–352 (2003)

[6] Doulamis, A., Ntalianis, K., Doulamis, N., Kollias, S.: An Efficient Fully-Unsupervised Video Object Segmentation Scheme Using an Adaptive Neural Network Classifier Architecture. IEEE Trans. on NNs 14(3), 616–630 (2003)

[7] Matthews, L., Ishikawa, T., Baker, S.: The template update problem. IEEE Trans. on Pattern Analysis and Machine Intelligence 26(6), 810–815 (2004)

[8] Grabner, H., Leistner, C., Bischof, H.: Semi-supervised On-Line Boosting for Robust Tracking. In: Forsyth, D., Torr, P., Zisserman, A. (eds.) ECCV 2008, Part I. LNCS, vol. 5302, pp. 234–247. Springer, Heidelberg (2008)

[9] Tang, F., Brennan, S., Zhao, Q., Tao, H.: Co-tracking using semi-supervised support vector machines. In: Proc. of IEEE ICCV, pp. 1–8 (2007)

[10] Yu, Q., Dinh, T.B., Medioni, G.: Online Tracking and Reacquisition Using Co-trained Generative and Discriminative Trackers. In: Forsyth, D., Torr, P., Zisserman, A. (eds.) ECCV 2008, Part II. LNCS, vol. 5303, pp. 678–691. Springer, Heidelberg (2008)

[11] Cehovin, L., Kristan, M., Leonardis, A.: An adaptive coupled-layer visual model for robust visual tracking. In: Proc. of IEEE ICCV, pp. 1363–1370 (2011)

[12] Xing, J., Ai, H., Lao, S.: Multi-object tracking through occlusions by local tracklets filtering and global tracklets association with detection responses. In: IEEE Conference on Computer Vision and Pattern Recognition Workshops, pp. 1200–1207 (2009)

[13] Zhang, L., Yuan, L., Nevatia, R.: Global data association for multi-object tracking using network flows. In: Proc. of IEEE CVPR, pp. 1–8 (2008)

[14] Nair, V., Hinton, G.: 3-D object recognition with deep belief nets. In: Proc. NIPS (2009)

[15] Taylor, G., Hinton, G.E., Roweis, S.: Modeling human motion using binary latent variables. In: Proc. NIPS (2007)

[16] Schulz, H., Behnke, S.: Object-Class Segmentation using Deep Convolutional Neural Networks. In: Proc. of DAGM Workshop, Frankfurt (August 2011)

[17] Stauffer, C., Grimson, W.E.L.: Adaptive background mixture models for real-time tracking. In: Proc. of IEEE CVPR, Fort Colins, CO (June 1999)

[18] Moghaddam, Z., Piccardi, M.: Robust density modelling using the student's t-distribution for human action recognition. In: Proc. of IEEE ICIP, pp. 3261–3264 (2011)

[19] Voulodimos, A., Kosmopoulos, D.I., Vasileiou, G., Sardis, E., Doulamis, A.D., Anagnostopoulos, V., Lalos, C., Varvarigou, T.A.: A dataset for workflow recognition in industrial scenes. In: Proc. of IEEE ICIP, pp. 3249–3252 (2011)

Hybrid Pooling Fusion in the BoW Pipeline

Marc Law, Nicolas Thome, and Matthieu Cord

LIP6, UPMC - Sorbonne University, Paris, France
{Marc.Law,Nicolas.Thome,Matthieu.Cord}@lip6.fr

Abstract. In the context of object and scene recognition, state-of-the-art performances are obtained with Bag of Words (BoW) models of mid-level representations computed from dense sampled local descriptors (*e.g.* SIFT). Several methods to combine low-level features and to set mid-level parameters have been evaluated recently for image classification.

In this paper, we further investigate the impact of the main parameters in the BoW pipeline. We show that an adequate combination of several low (sampling rate, multiscale) and mid level (codebook size, normalization) parameters is decisive to reach good performances. Based on this analysis, we propose a merging scheme exploiting the specificities of edge-based descriptors. Low and high-contrast regions are pooled separately and combined to provide a powerful representation of images. Sucessful experiments are provided on the Caltech-101 and Scene-15 datasets.

1   Introduction and Related Work

Image classification is one of the most challenging problems in computer vision. Indeed, the prediction of complex semantic categories, such as scenes or objects, from the pixel level, is still a very hard task. Two main breakthroughs have been reached in the last decade to achieve this goal. The first one is the design of discriminative low-level local features, such as SIFT [1]. The second one is the emergence of mid-level representations inspired from the text retrieval community, based on the Bag of Words (BoW) model [2].

In the BoW model, converting the set of local descriptors into the final image representation is performed by a succession of two steps: coding and pooling. In the original BoW model, coding consists in hard assigning each local descriptor to the closest visual word, while pooling averages the local descriptor projections. One important limitation of the visual BoW model is the lack of spatial information. The most popular extension to overcome this problem is the Spatial Pyramid Scheme [3]. In addition, many efforts have been recently devoted to improve coding and pooling [4]. To attenuate the quantization loss, soft assignment attempts to smoothly distribute features to the codewords [5, 6]. In sparse coding approaches [7–9], there is an explicit minimization of the feature reconstruction error, along with a regularization prior that encourages sparse solutions. Different pooling strategies have also been studied. Max pooling is a promising alternative to sum pooling [6–10], especially when linear classifiers are used. Therefore, the combination of sparse coding, spatial pyramids and max-pooling is often regarded as the strategy leading to state-of-the-art performances.

A. Fusiello et al. (Eds.): ECCV 2012 Ws/Demos, Part III, LNCS 7585, pp. 355–364, 2012.

In this paper, we first investigate the BoW pipeline in terms of parameter setting and feature combination for classification. We do believe that such an analysis should help clarify the real difference between mid-level representations for a classification purpose. Based on this study, we also introduce an early fusion [11] method that takes into account and distinguishes low-contrast regions from high-contrast regions in images. Low-contrast regions are usually either completely removed and ignored from the mid-level representation of images, either processed as any common feature. The idea is to exploit occurrence statistics of low-contrast regions and combine them with classical recognition methods applied on high contrast regions. The fusion we propose does not exploit low-level features of different natures (such as combining edge-based, color, metadata descriptors...) but processes low-level features differently with regard to their gradient magnitude. We focus our experiments on the Caltech-101 [12] and Scene-15 [3] datasets, where most of state-of-the art methods improving over the BoW model have been evaluated. The remainder of the paper decomposes as follows. Section 2 presents the classification pipeline evaluated in the paper. In Section 3, we specifically study the pooling fusion of low and high contrast regions. With local edge-based descriptors (e.g. SIFT), the feature normalization process is likely to produce noisy features: we analyze the use of a thresholding procedure used in VLFEAT [13] to overcome this problem. In addition, we propose novel coding and pooling methods that are well adapted for handling low-constrast regions. Section 4 provides a systematic evaluation of the impact on classification performances of the different parameters studied in the paper.

2   Classification Pipeline

Fig. 1 illustrates the whole classification pipeline studied in this paper. Local features are first extracted in the input image, and encoded into an off-line trained dictionary. The codes are then pooled to generate the image signature. This mid-level representation is ultimately normalized before training the classifier. Each block of the figure is detailed in the following sections.

2.1   Low-Level Feature Extraction

The first step of the BoW framework is the feature extraction. We follow a regular grid-based sampling strategy, that proves to be superior to other sparse or random samplings for classification tasks [14]. SIFT features are computed because

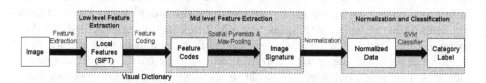

Fig. 1. BoW pipeline for classification

of their excellent performances attested in various datasets. In the sampling process, two parameters have a strong impact on classification performances:
– **Sampling Density**. The denser the sampling is, the better the performances get. The density is set through the spatial stride parameter. In published papers [6–9], the stride is usually set to 8 pixels[1].
– **Monoscale Versus Multiscale Features**. It is known [15] that using multiscale features increases the amount of low-level information for generating the mid-levels signatures, and thus favorably impacts performances. Wang *et al.* [8] evaluate their method (LLC) in a multiscale setting, making the comparison with respect to other methods that use monoscale features somehow unfair.

2.2   Mid-level Coding and Pooling Scheme

Let $\mathbf{X} = (\mathbf{x}_1, \ldots, \mathbf{x}_i, \ldots, \mathbf{x}_N)$ be the set of local descriptors in an image. In the BoW model, the mid-level signature generation first requires a set of codewords $\mathbf{b}_i \in \mathbb{R}^d$ (d is the local descriptor's dimensionality). Let $\mathbf{B} = (\mathbf{b}_1, \ldots, \mathbf{b}_j, \ldots, \mathbf{b}_M)$ denote the resulting visual dictionary. Usually, $\mathbf{B}$ is learned using an unsupervised clustering algorithm applied on local descriptors randomly selected from an image dataset, providing a set of M clusters with centers $\mathbf{b}_j$.

In [15], several mid-level representations including different coding and pooling methods are evaluated. In this paper, we focus our re-implementation on one specific method: the Localized Soft Coding (LSC) approach [6]. Indeed, LSC proves to be a very competitive method, reaching very good results in Caltech-101 and Scene-15 databases[2]. Specifically, LSC is shown to be comparable or superior to sparse coding methods, *e.g.* [7–9], while the encoding is significantly faster since no optimization is involved. Note that LSC is used with linear classifiers (see Section 2.3), making the representation adequate for dealing with large-scale problems. In LSC [6], the encoding $u_{i,j}$ of $\mathbf{x}_i$ to $\mathbf{b}_j$ is computed as follows using the k-nearest neighbors $\mathcal{N}_k(\mathbf{x}_i)$:

$$u_{i,j} = \frac{e^{-\beta \hat{d}(\mathbf{x}_i, \mathbf{b}_j)}}{\sum\limits_{l=1}^{M} e^{-\beta \hat{d}(\mathbf{x}_i, \mathbf{b}_l)}} \qquad \hat{d}(\mathbf{x}_i, \mathbf{b}_j) = \begin{cases} d(\mathbf{x}_i, \mathbf{b}_j) & \text{if } \mathbf{b}_j \in \mathcal{N}_k(\mathbf{x}_i) \\ \infty & \text{otherwise} \end{cases} \qquad (1)$$

$\hat{d}(\mathbf{x}_i, \mathbf{b}_j)$ is the "localized" distance between $\mathbf{x}_i$ and $\mathbf{b}_j$, *i.e.* we encode a local descriptor $\mathbf{x}_i$ only on its k-nearest neighbors. From the Localized Soft Coding

---

[1] However, in the provided source codes for evaluation, the sampling is often set to lower values (*e.g.* 6 pixels)(http://www.ifp.illinois.edu/~jyang29/ScSPM.htm or http://users.cecs.anu.edu.au/~lingqiao/). Compared to the value of 8 pixels, the performances decrease of about $1 \sim 2\%$, making some reported results in published papers over-estimated.

[2] Note that from personal communication with the authors, we discover that the performances of 74% in [6] in the Caltech-101 dataset have been obtained with a wrong evaluation metric. The level of performances that can be obtained with the setup depicted in [6] is about 70% (see Section 4). However, the conclusion regarding the relative performances of LSC with respect to sparse coding remains valid.

strategy leading to $u_{i,j}$ codes, *max pooling* is used to generate the final image signature $\mathbf{Z} = \{z_j\}_{j\in\{1;M\}}$ and $z_j = \max\limits_{i\in\{1;N\}} u_{i,j}$. In addition, spatial information is incorporated using a linear version [7] of the Spatial Pyramid Matching (SPM) Scheme [3]: signatures are computed in a multi-resolution spatial grid with three levels 1×1, 2×2 and 4×4. At the mid-level representation stage, the main parameter impacting accuracy is definitively M, the dictionary size.

2.3 Normalization and Learning

Once spatial pyramids are computed, we use linear SVMs to solve the supervised learning problem. The signature normalization is questionable. In [15], ℓ_2-normalization is applied, because this processing is claimed to be optimal with linear SVMs [16]. On the other hand, normalizing the data may discard relevant information for the classification task. For that reason, some authors report that ℓ_2-normalization negatively impacts performances, and therefore choose not performing any normalization, as in LSC [6] or in the sparse coding work of [17].

We use for all experiments the ℓ_2-regularized ℓ_1-loss support vector classification solver of the LibLinear library [18]. The C parameter of the SVM can be determined on a validation set, we set it to 10^5 because we did not observe improvement nor decline of accuracy for large values of C.

3 Pooling Fusion of Low and High Contrast Regions

Originally, local descriptors like SIFT [1] have been used to describe the visual content around keypoints. The keypoints are generally detected as high saliency image areas, where the contrast in the considered region is large, making the extraction of egde-based descriptors relevant. However, when a dense sampling strategy is used, the feature extraction becomes problematic because edge-based feature extraction is prone to noise in low contrast areas. This drawback is worsen with SIFT descriptors that are ℓ_2-normalized in order to gain robustness to illumination variations: in the dense sampling setup, this normalization might make (noisy) descriptors be close to descriptors with very large gradient magnitude.

To better deal with low-contrast areas in the BoW classification pipeline, we propose the following improvements: defining visual stop features (Section 3.1), and specific coding and pooling methods for low-contrast regions (Section 3.2).

3.1 Visual Stop Feature: Thresholding Low Contrast Patches

In the context of image retrieval, Sivic and Zisserman [2] define **visual stop words** as the most frequent visual words in images that need to be removed from the feature representation. With the SIFT computation in low contrast patches, we are concerned about a specific type of problematic features that we call **visual stop features** since they arise at the feature extraction step (before the BoW computation). To overcome the problem of noisy SIFT computation,

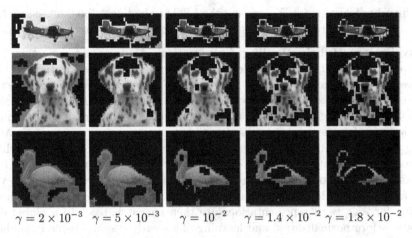

$$\gamma = 2 \times 10^{-3} \quad \gamma = 5 \times 10^{-3} \quad \gamma = 10^{-2} \quad \gamma = 1.4 \times 10^{-2} \quad \gamma = 1.8 \times 10^{-2}$$

Fig. 2. Visualization of the visual stop features (regions filled in black) depending on the threshold γ applied to the SIFT descriptor norm

we propose to threshold the descriptor norm magnitude. Let us consider a given SIFT feature $\mathbf{x}$ extracted in some region of an image. We apply the following post-processing to $\mathbf{x}$ so that the output of the feature computation is $\mathbf{x_p}$:

$$\mathbf{x_p} = 0 \text{ if } ||\mathbf{x}|| < \gamma \quad \text{and} \quad \mathbf{x_p} = \mathbf{x}/||\mathbf{x}|| \text{ otherwise} \qquad (2)$$

This post-processing for the SIFT computation is performed in some publicly available libraries, *e.g.* VLFEAT [13]. The idea is to set the descriptors corresponding to low contrast regions to a default value (*e.g.* 0), and not normalizing them in this case. This thresholding is dedicated to filter out the noisy feature computation by assigning a constant value to "roughly" homogeneous regions. The parameter γ defines the threshold up to which a region is considered homogeneous. In a given image $\mathcal{I}$, we denote as $\mathcal{X}_s$ the set of stop features: $\mathcal{X}_s = \{\mathbf{x} \in \mathcal{I} \ / \ ||\mathbf{x}|| < \gamma\}$. Contrarily, the set of non-homogeneous regions $\mathcal{X}_m$ fulfills: $\mathcal{X}_m = \{\mathbf{x} \in \mathcal{I} \ / \ ||\mathbf{x}|| \geq \gamma\}$. Fig. 2 illustrates some examples of visual stop features (filled in black) depending on γ, in Caltech-101. We notice that patches with lowest magnitude mostly do not belong to the object to be recognized, supporting the relevance of the applied post-processing. We propose in the next subsection a specific modeling, in the BoW framework, of stop features.

3.2   Hybrid Image Representation

New Dictionary Training & Feature Coding. First, we propose to identify a specific word in the dictionary ($\mathbf{b_0}$) to represent homogeneous regions. During codebook training, we learn the $M-1$ remaining codewords, ($\mathbf{b_1}, ..., \mathbf{b_{M-1}}$), thus excluding stop features when randomly sampling descriptors in the database. Second, during feature encoding, we propose to hard assign each visual stop feature to the specific word corresponding to homogeneous regions ($\mathbf{b_0}$).

For the other features, $i.e.$ $\mathcal{X}_m$, we use the LSC method described in Section 2.2, encoding each feature on the $M - 1$ "non-homogeneous" codewords elements.

Early Fusion: Hybrid Pooling Aggregation. As described in Section 2.2, max pooling is used with LSC because it achieves better classification performances than average pooling. For visual stop features, however, since hard assignment is performed, the corresponding pooled value z_0 for the word representing homogeneous regions b_0 using max pooling would be binary. Thus, it would only account for the presence/absence of homogeneous regions in the image. Using average pooling instead seems more appropriate: the pooled value then incorporates a statistic estimation of the ratio of low-contrast regions in the image, that is much more informative than the binary presence/absence value. We thus follow an hybrid pooling strategy, using average pooling for $\mathcal{X}_s$ and max pooling for $\mathcal{X}_m$. Both representations are then concatenated into a global descriptor before normalization and learning. This early fusion scheme is applied in each bin of the SPM pyramid indepently.

Our hybrid pooling BOW pipeline has the following advantages: (1) The codebook can be learned only for features of $\mathcal{X}_m$, resulting in a richer representation of $\mathcal{F}_m$ for the same number of training samples; (2) The hard assignment to b_0 for $\mathcal{X}_s$ is relevant since the each homogeneous region should not be encoded in the "non-homogeneous" codewords; (3) The encoding of $\mathcal{X}_s$ is substantially faster than using the standard LSC method, since the automatic assignment avoids the (approximate) nearest neighbor search that dominates the computational time; (4) The average pooling strategy applied to the homogeneous codeword b_0 incorporates a richer information about the ratio of homogeneous regions in the image. This feature, that must vary among different classes, can therefore be capitalized on when training the classifier.

4 Experiments

Before evaluating our hybrid method, we first report an exhaustive quality assessment of the BoW strategy.

4.1 Datasets and Experimental Setup

Experiments are proposed on two widely used datasets: Caltech-101 [12] and Scene-15 [3]. Caltech-101 is a dataset of 9144 images containing 101 object classes and a background class. Scene-15 contains 4485 images of 15 scene categories.

A fixed number of images per category (30 for Caltech-101 and 100 for Scene-15) is selected to train models and all the remaining images are used for test. The performance is measured as the average classification accuracy across all classes over 100 splits. All the images are resized to have a maximum between width and height set to 300 pixels.

Like Chatfield et $al.$ [15], we only extract SIFT descriptors. We use a spatial stride of between 3 and 8 pixels (corresponding to the sampling density), and at 4 scales for the multiscale, defined by setting the width of the SIFT spatial bins to 4, 6, 8 and 10 pixels respectively. The default spatial stride is 3 pixels. When referring to monoscale, we set the width of the spatial bins to 4 pixels, with a default spatial stride of 8 pixels. SIFT descriptors are computed with the vl_phow command included in the VLFEAT toolbox [13], version 0.9.14, for the following experiments (Subsection 4.2). Apart from the stride and scale parameters, the default options are used. In Subsection 4.3, monoscale patches are extracted with the default vl_dsift command designed for monoscale extraction.

For LSC implementation, Liu *et al.* [6] use $\beta = 1/(2\sigma^2) = 10$ (Eq 1) with normalized features. Since VLFEAT feature norms are 512, we set $\sigma \simeq 115$ and the number of nearest neighbors $k = 10$ (Eq 1) to be consistent with [6].

4.2   BoW Pipeline Evaluation

We study in Table 1 the results of the BoW pipeline using the LSC coding method for Caltech-101 dataset. The main parameters studied are the codebook size, the spatial stride, the mono/multiscale strategy, and the normalization.

Table 1. Classification results on Caltech-101 dataset with 30 training images per class

Spatial Stride	Scaling	Codebook size	Accuracy (no norm)	Acc. (ℓ_2-norm)
8	monoscale	800	70.07 ± 0.96	70.46 ± 1.04
6	monoscale	800	71.64 ± 0.99	72.01 ± 0.96
3	monoscale	800	72.45 ± 1.05	72.73 ± 0.99
8	monoscale	1700	71.67 ± 0.93	71.95 ± 0.90
8	monoscale	3300	72.13 ± 0.99	72.50 ± 0.97
8	multiscale	800	73.35 ± 0.89	73.83 ± 0.96
8	multiscale	1700	75.34 ± 0.92	75.97 ± 0.86
8	multiscale	3300	76.91 ± 0.98	77.02 ± 0.94
3	multiscale	800	73.81 ± 0.95	73.99 ± 0.86
3	multiscale	1700	75.72 ± 1.13	76.00 ± 0.94
3	multiscale	3300	77.23 ± 1.02	77.47 ± 0.99
3	multiscale	6500	78.00 ± 1.05	78.46 ± 0.95

Table 2. Classification results on Scene-15 dataset with 100 training images per class

Spatial Stride	Scaling	Codebook size	Acc. (no norm)	Acc. (ℓ_2-norm)
8	monoscale	1000	78.72 ± 0.62	78.96 ± 0.60
6	monoscale	1000	79.53 ± 0.65	79.74 ± 0.65
3	monoscale	1000	79.74 ± 0.61	80.05 ± 0.67
8	monoscale	1700	79.98 ± 0.61	80.29 ± 0.58
8	monoscale	3400	80.61 ± 0.61	81.16 ± 0.57
8	multiscale	1000	79.59 ± 0.63	80.12 ± 0.56
8	multiscale	1700	80.91 ± 0.56	81.25 ± 0.54
8	multiscale	3400	82.01 ± 0.72	82.39 ± 0.60
3	multiscale	1000	79.74 ± 0.60	80.14 ± 0.59
3	multiscale	1700	81.03 ± 0.65	81.23 ± 0.60
3	multiscale	3400	82.17 ± 0.73	82.42 ± 0.59
3	multiscale	6800	82.66 ± 0.62	83.44 ± 0.55

We selected the most important combinations between all the possibilities. First, one can notice that multiscale is always above monoscale results. In monoscale setup, we do not investigate too many combinations. The best results are 72.73% for a small spatial stride with normalization. The codebook size of 3300 also gives good results. Compared to the classical performance of 64% of the BoW SPM [3], it is remarkable to see how a careful parametrization including normalization of a BoW soft pipeline may boost the performances up to 9%.

These trends are fully confirmed in the multiscale setting. The best score of 78.46% is obtained with a small spatial stride of 3, multiscale, and a dictionary of size 6500 with ℓ_2-normalization. The soft BoW pipeline outperforms the advanced methods presented in [15], the Fisher Kernel method (reported at 77.78%), and the LLC (reported at 76.95%) with the same multiscale setup and a codebook of 8000 words (for LLC). It is also above the score of Boureau [17], where the best result reported using sparse coding is 77.3%. They use a very high dimensional image representation and a costly sparse coding optimization, with a monoscale scheme but a two-step aggregating SIFT features.

Table 2 reports the experimental results on Scene-15. They are all consistent with the experiments on Caltech-101. The best result of 83.44% is also obtained for a multiscale scheme, a small spatial stride of 3, and a large dictionary of size 6800 with normalization. This score is still slightly better than the Boureau one of 83.3% [17], but remains below state-of-the-art results for that database.

These experiments confirm that the parameters mentioned in Section 2 may significantly improve the recognition. A small spatial stride with multiscale, a large codebook and a proper normalization of the spatial pyramid is the winning cocktail for the BoW pipeline. However, the accuracy improvement is more impressive for Caltech-101 (reaching very high performances) than for Scene-15.

4.3   Evaluation of Our Strategy

We evaluate here the classification performances of our early fusion detailed in Section 3. First, we study the impact of γ (Eq 2). Fig. 3(a) shows the evolution of the classification performances depending on γ on Caltech-101 database, in both monoscale and multiscale settings. The results are largely impacted when γ varies: the performances can be improved up to 3% for the monoscale setup using $\gamma \simeq 10^{-2}$ compared to the default value. The same trend appears for the multiscale setting. For Scene-15 dataset (Fig. 3(b)), the conclusion differs: in a multiscale setting the performances can be slightly improved, whereas the best result is obtained for $\gamma = 0$ with monoscale features. This may be explained by the fact that in object recognition (particularly on Caltech-101), the patches with lowest magnitude usually do not describe the object to be recognized and belong to the background (see Fig. 2).

Second, we evaluate the specific encoding and pooling method for low contrast regions described in Section 3.2. We provide two gradual evaluations (see Fig. 4). The proposed changes improve performances in Caltech-101 database, in both monoscale (Fig. 4(a)) and multiscale setting (Fig. 4(b)). For the multiscale setup, the performances are in addition more robust to γ variations. For the monoscale

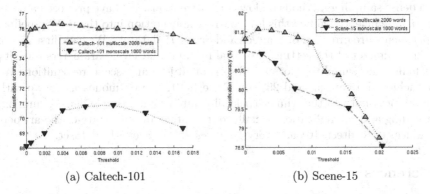

(a) Caltech-101   (b) Scene-15

Fig. 3. Accuracy of the normalized LSC model as the threshold under which features are set to 0 varies (a) on Caltech-101, (b) on Scene-15

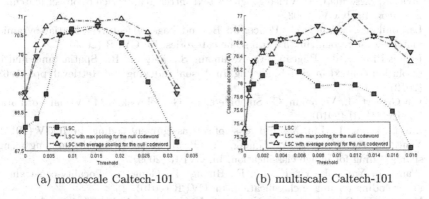

(a) monoscale Caltech-101   (b) multiscale Caltech-101

Fig. 4. Accuracy of the normalized LSC strategies on Caltech-101 (a) monoscale setup with a codebook of 1000 words, (b) multiscale setup with a codebook of 2000 words

setup, the average pooling outperforms the max pooling method, validating the idea that enriching the homogeneous regions pooling with a non-binary value can favorably impact performances. This is not the case in the multiscale experiments, probably because fewer homogeneous regions are extracted in such a setup (due to the increase of the region size), making the statistical estimate of the homogeneous regions ratio less reliable.

Finally, if we use the best setting of parameters with a codebook of 10^4 words, we obtain the score of **79.07±0.83%** on Caltech-101 dataset and **83.83±0.59%** on Scene-15 with our fusion scheme over low/high contrast regions. To the best of our knowledge, this performance on the Caltech-101 benchmark is above all previously published results for a single descriptor type and linear classification.

5   Conclusions

The BoW strategy is still very competitive for image classification. In this paper, we have investigated some early fusion methods to deal with artifacts inherited from dense sampling methods on low contrast regions. We have proposed a novel scheme to efficiently embed this low contrast information into the BoW pipeline. Experiments are provided on Caltech and Scene-15 datasets. We have first shown the great impact of the setting of several low and mid level parameters (density and multiscale sampling, normalization) for object and scene recognition. We have achieved a gain around 20% on Caltech-101 from a monoscale setup with a small dictionary to the winner cocktail combining multiscale dense sampling, soft coding and normalization. Finally, our strategy obtains state-of-the-art performances on Caltech-101 and very good results on Scene-15 dataset.

References

1. Lowe, D.: Distinctive image features from scale-invariant keypoints. IJCV 60, 91–110 (2004)
2. Sivic, J., Zisserman, A.: Video google: A text retrieval approach to object matching in videos. In: ICCV (2003)
3. Lazebnik, S., Schmid, C., Ponce, J.: Beyond bags of features: Spatial pyramid matching for recognizing natural scene categories. In: CVPR (2006)
4. Benois-Pineau, J., Bugeau, A., Karaman, S., Mégret, R.: Spatial and multi-resolution context in visual indexing. In: Visual Indexing and Retrieval, pp. 41–63 (2012)
5. van Gemert, J., Veenman, C., Smeulders, A., Geusebroek, J.M.: Visual word ambiguity. PAMI (2010)
6. Liu, L., Wang, L., Liu, X.: In defense of soft-assignment coding. In: ICCV (2011)
7. Yang, J., Yu, K., Gong, Y., Huang, T.: Linear spatial pyramid matching using sparse coding for image classification. In: CVPR (2009)
8. Wang, J., Yang, J., Yu, K., Lv, F., Huang, T., Gong, Y.: Locality-constrained linear coding for image classification. In: CVPR (2010)
9. Boureau, Y., Bach, F., LeCun, Y., Ponce, J.: Learning mid-level features for recognition. In: CVPR (2010)
10. Boureau, Y., Ponce, J., LeCun, Y.: A theoretical analysis of feature pooling in vision algorithms. In: ICML (2010)
11. Snoek, C., Worring, M., Hauptmann, A.: Learning rich semantics from news video archives by style analysis. TOMCCAP 2 (2006)
12. Fei-Fei, L., Fergus, R., Perona, P.: Learning generative visual models from few training examples: an incremental bayesian approach tested on 101 object categories. In: CVPR Workshop on GMBV (2004)
13. Vedaldi, A., Fulkerson, B.: VLFeat: An open and portable library of computer vision algorithms (2008), http://www.vlfeat.org/
14. Fei-Fei, L.: A bayesian hierarchical model for learning natural scene categories. In: CVPR (2005)
15. Chatfield, K., Lempitsky, V., Vedaldi, A., Zisserman, A.: The devil is in the details: an evaluation of recent feature encoding methods. In: BMVC (2011)
16. Vedaldi, A., Zisserman, A.: Efficient additive kernels via explicit feature maps. PAMI 34 (2011)
17. Boureau, Y., Le Roux, N., Bach, F., Ponce, J., LeCun, Y.: Ask the locals: multi-way local pooling for image recognition. In: ICCV (2011)
18. Fan, R.E., Chang, K.W., Hsieh, C.J., Wang, X.R., Lin, C.J.: LIBLINEAR: A library for large linear classification. JMLR 9 (2008)

Joint Sparsity-Based Robust Multimodal Biometrics Recognition

Sumit Shekhar[1], Vishal M. Patel[1], Nasser M. Nasrabadi[2], and Rama Chellappa[1]

[1] University of Maryland, College Park, USA
[2] Army Research Lab, Adelphi, USA

Abstract. Traditional biometric recognition systems rely on a single biometric signature for authentication. While the advantage of using multiple sources of information for establishing the identity has been widely recognized, computational models for multimodal biometrics recognition have only recently received attention. We propose a novel multimodal multivariate sparse representation method for multimodal biometrics recognition, which represents the test data by a sparse linear combination of training data, while constraining the observations from different modalities of the test subject to share their sparse representations. Thus, we simultaneously take into account correlations as well as coupling information between biometric modalities. Furthermore, the model is modified to make it robust to noise and occlusion. The resulting optimization problem is solved using an efficient alternative direction method. Experiments on a challenging public dataset show that our method compares favorably with competing fusion-based methods.

1 Introduction

Unimodal biometric systems rely on the evidence of a single source of information such as a single iris or fingerprint or face for authentication. Unfortunately these systems often have to deal with some of the following inevitable problems [1]: (a) Noisy data (b) Non-universality: the biometric system based on a single source of evidence may not be able to capture meaningful data from some users. (c) Intra-class variations: in the case of iris recognition a user who wears artificial contact lenses with various patterns can cause these variations. (d) Spoof attack: hand signature forgery is an example of this type of attack. It has been observed that some of the limitations of unimodal biometric systems can be addressed by deploying multimodal biometric systems that essentially integrate the evidence presented by multiple sources of information such as iris, fingerprints and face.

Classification in multibiometric systems is done by fusing information from different modalities. The information fusion can be done at different levels, which can be broadly divided into feature level, score level and rank/decision level fusion. Due to preservation of raw information, feature level fusion can be more discriminative than score or decision level fusion [2]. But, there have been very little effort in exploring feature level fusion in the biometric community. This is because of the different output formats of different sensors, which result in features with different dimensions. Often the features have large dimensions, and

A. Fusiello et al. (Eds.): ECCV 2012 Ws/Demos, Part III, LNCS 7585, pp. 365–374, 2012.

fusion becomes difficult at feature level. The prevalent method is feature concatenation, which has been used for different multibiometric settings [3, 4]. However, in many scenarios, each modality produces high-dimensional features. In such cases, the method is both impractical and non-robust. It also cannot exploit the constraint that features of different modalities should share the identities.

In recent years, theories of Sparse Representation (SR) and Compressed Sensing (CS) have emerged as powerful tools for efficiently processing data. This has led to a resurgence in interest in the principles of SR and CS for biometrics recognition. See [5, 6] and the references therein for a survey of biometrics recognition algorithms using SR and CS. Motivated by the success of SR in unimodal biometric recognition, we propose a joint sparsity-based algorithm for multimodal biometrics recognition. Our method is based on the well known regularized regression method, multi-task multivariate Lasso [7, 8]. Figure. 1 presents an overview of our method.

This paper makes the following contributions:

- We present a robust feature level fusion algorithm for multibiometric recognition tasks. Through the proposed joint sparse framework, we can easily handle different dimensions of different modalities by forcing the different features to interact through their sparse coefficients. Further, the proposed algorithm can efficiently handle large dimensional feature vectors.
- We make the classification robust to occlusion and noise by introducing an error term into the optimization framework.
- The algorithm is easily generalizable to handle multiple test inputs from a modality.

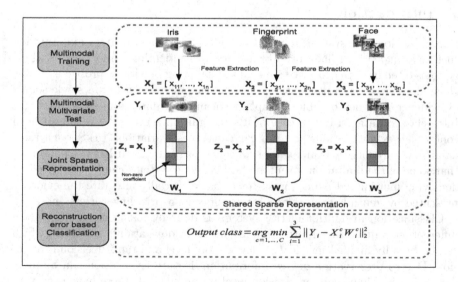

Fig. 1. Overview of our algorithm

2 Joint Sparsity-Based Multimodal Biometrics Recognition

Consider a multimodal C-class classification problem with D different biometric traits. Suppose there are p_i training samples in each biometric trait. For each biometric trait $i = 1, \ldots, D$, we denote

$$\mathbf{X}^i = [\mathbf{X}_1^i, \mathbf{X}_2^i, \ldots, \mathbf{X}_C^i]$$

as an $n \times p_i$ dictionary of training samples consisting of C sub-dictionaries $\mathbf{X}_k^i$'s corresponding to C different classes. Each sub-dictionary

$$\mathbf{X}_j^i = [\mathbf{x}_{j,1}^i, \mathbf{x}_{j,2}^i, \ldots, \mathbf{x}_{j,p_j}^i] \in \mathbb{R}^{n \times p_j}$$

represents a set of training data from the ith modality labeled with the jth class. Note that n is the feature dimension of each sample and there are p_j number of training samples in class j. Hence, there are a total of $p = \sum_{j=1}^{C} p_j$ many samples in the dictionary $\mathbf{X}_C^i$. In multimodal biometrics recognition problem given a test samples (matrix) $\mathbf{Y}$, which consists of D different modalities $\{\mathbf{Y}^1, \mathbf{Y}^2, \ldots, \mathbf{Y}^D\}$ where each sample $\mathbf{Y}^i$ consists of d_i observations $\mathbf{Y}^i = [\mathbf{y}_1^i, \mathbf{y}_2^i, \ldots, \mathbf{y}_d^i] \in \mathbb{R}^{n \times d_i}$, the objective is to identify the class to which a test sample $\mathbf{Y}$ belongs to. In what follows, we present a multimodal multivariate sparse representation-based algorithm for this problem [7–9].

2.1 Multimodal Multivariate Sparse Representation

We want to exploit the joint sparsity of coefficients from different biometrics modalities to make a joint decision. To simplify this model, let us consider a bimodal classification problem where the test sample $\mathbf{Y} = [\mathbf{Y}^1, \mathbf{Y}^2]$ consists of two different modalities such as iris and face. Suppose that $\mathbf{Y}^1$ belongs to the jth class. Then, it can be reconstructed by a linear combination of the atoms in the sub-dictionary $\mathbf{X}_j^1$. That is, $\mathbf{Y}^1 = \mathbf{X}^1 \boldsymbol{\Gamma}^1 + \mathbf{N}^1$, where $\boldsymbol{\Gamma}^1$ is a sparse matrix with only p_j nonzero rows associated with the jth class and $\mathbf{N}^1$ is the noise matrix. Similarly, since $\mathbf{Y}^2$ represents the same subject, it belongs to the same class and can be represented by training samples in $\mathbf{X}_j^2$ with different set of coefficients $\boldsymbol{\Gamma}_j^2$. Thus, we can write $\mathbf{Y}^2 = \mathbf{X}^2 \boldsymbol{\Gamma}^2 + \mathbf{N}^2$, where $\boldsymbol{\Gamma}^2$ is a sparse matrix that has the same sparsity pattern as $\boldsymbol{\Gamma}^1$. If we let $\boldsymbol{\Gamma} = [\boldsymbol{\Gamma}^1, \boldsymbol{\Gamma}^2]$, then $\boldsymbol{\Gamma}$ is a sparse matrix with only p_j nonzeros rows.

In the more general case where we have D modalities, if we denote $\{\mathbf{Y}^i\}_{i=1}^D$ as a set of D observations each consisting of d_i samples from each modality and let $\boldsymbol{\Gamma} = [\boldsymbol{\Gamma}^1, \boldsymbol{\Gamma}^2, \ldots, \boldsymbol{\Gamma}^D] \in \mathbb{R}^{p \times d}$ be the matrix formed by concatenating the coefficient matrices with $d = \sum_{i=1}^D d_i$, then we can seek the row-sparse matrix $\boldsymbol{\Gamma}$ by solving the following ℓ_1/ℓ_q-regularized least square problem

$$\hat{\boldsymbol{\Gamma}} = \arg\min_{\boldsymbol{\Gamma}} \frac{1}{2} \sum_{i=1}^{D} \|\mathbf{Y}^i - \mathbf{X}^i \boldsymbol{\Gamma}^i\|_F^2 + \lambda \|\boldsymbol{\Gamma}\|_{1,q} \tag{1}$$

where λ is a positive parameter and q is set greater than 1 to make the optimization problem convex. Here, $\|\boldsymbol{\Gamma}\|_{1,q}$ is a norm defined as $\|\boldsymbol{\Gamma}\|_{1,q} = \sum_{k=1}^{p} \|\gamma^k\|_q$ where γ^k's are the row vectors of $\boldsymbol{\Gamma}$ and $\|\mathbf{Y}\|_F$ is the Frobenius norm of matrix $\mathbf{Y}$ defined as $\|\mathbf{Y}\|_F = \sqrt{\sum_{i,j} Y_{i,j}^2}$. Once $\hat{\boldsymbol{\Gamma}}$ is obtained, the class label associated with an observed vector is then declared as the one that produces the smallest approximation error

$$\hat{j} = \arg\min_j \sum_{i=1}^{D} \|\mathbf{Y}^i - \mathbf{X}^i \delta_j^i(\boldsymbol{\Gamma}^i)\|_F^2, \tag{2}$$

where δ_j^i is the matrix indicator function defined by keeping rows corresponding to the jth class and setting all other rows equal to zero. Note that the optimization problem (1) reduces to the conventional Lasso [10] when $D = 1$ and $d = 1$. For $D = 1$ (1), it is equivalent to multivariate Lasso [7].

2.2   Robust Multimodal Multivariate Sparse Representation

In this section, we consider a more general problem where the data is contaminated by noise. In this case, the observation model can be modeled as

$$\mathbf{Y}^i = \mathbf{X}^i \boldsymbol{\Gamma}^i + \mathbf{Z}^i + \mathbf{N}^i, \quad i = 1, \ldots D, \tag{3}$$

where $\mathbf{N}^i$ is a small dense additive noise and $\mathbf{Z}^i \in \mathbb{R}^{n \times d_i}$ is a matrix of background noise (occlusion) with arbitrarily large magnitude. One can assume that each $\mathbf{Z}^i$ is sparsely represented in some basis $\mathbf{B}^i \in \mathbb{R}^{n \times m^i}$. That is, $\mathbf{Z}^i = \mathbf{B}^i \boldsymbol{\Lambda}^i$ for some sparse matrices $\boldsymbol{\Lambda}^i \in \mathbb{R}^{m_i \times d_i}$. Hence, (3) can be rewritten as

$$\mathbf{Y}^i = \mathbf{X}^i \boldsymbol{\Gamma}^i + \mathbf{B}^i \boldsymbol{\Lambda}^i + \mathbf{N}^i, \quad i = 1, \ldots D, \tag{4}$$

With this model, one can simultaneously recover the coefficients $\boldsymbol{\Gamma}^i$ and $\boldsymbol{\Lambda}^i$ by taking advantage of that fact that $\boldsymbol{\Lambda}^i$ are sparse

$$\hat{\boldsymbol{\Gamma}}, \hat{\boldsymbol{\Lambda}} = \arg\min_{\boldsymbol{\Gamma}, \boldsymbol{\Lambda}} \frac{1}{2} \sum_{i=1}^{D} \|\mathbf{Y}^i - \mathbf{X}^i \boldsymbol{\Gamma}^i - \mathbf{B}^i \boldsymbol{\Lambda}^i\|_F^2 +$$

$$\lambda_1 \|\boldsymbol{\Gamma}\|_{1,q} + \lambda_2 \|\boldsymbol{\Lambda}\|_1, \tag{5}$$

where λ_1 and λ_2 are positive parameters and $\boldsymbol{\Lambda} = [\boldsymbol{\Lambda}^1, \boldsymbol{\Lambda}^2, \ldots, \boldsymbol{\Lambda}^D]$ is the sparse coefficient matrix corresponding to occlusion. The ℓ_1-norm of matrix $\boldsymbol{\Lambda}$ is defined as $\|\boldsymbol{\Lambda}\|_1 = \sum_{i,j} |\Lambda_{i,j}|$. Note that the idea of exploiting the sparsity of occlusion term has been studied by Wright *et al.* [5].

Once $\boldsymbol{\Gamma}, \boldsymbol{\Lambda}$ are computed, the effect of occlusion can be removed by setting $\tilde{\mathbf{Y}}^i = \mathbf{Y}^i - \mathbf{B}^i \boldsymbol{\Lambda}^i$. One can then declare the class label associated to an observed vector as

$$\hat{j} = \arg\min_j \sum_{i=1}^{D} \|\mathbf{Y}^i - \mathbf{X}^i \delta_j^i(\boldsymbol{\Gamma}^i) - \mathbf{B}^i \boldsymbol{\Lambda}^i\|_F^2. \tag{6}$$

2.3   Optimization Algorithm

In this section, we present an algorithm to solve (5) based on the classical alternating direction method of multipliers (ADMM) [11], [12]. Note that the optimization problem (1) can be solved by setting λ_2 equal to zero. Let

$$\mathcal{C}(\boldsymbol{\Gamma}, \boldsymbol{\Lambda}) = \frac{1}{2} \sum_{i=1}^{D} \|\mathbf{Y}^i - \mathbf{X}^i \boldsymbol{\Gamma}^i - \mathbf{B}^i \boldsymbol{\Lambda}^i\|_F^2.$$

In ADMM the idea is to decouple $\mathcal{C}(\boldsymbol{\Gamma}, \boldsymbol{\Lambda}), \|\boldsymbol{\Gamma}\|_{1,q}$ and $\|\boldsymbol{\Lambda}\|_1$ by introducing auxiliary variables to reformulate the problem into a constrained optimization problem

$$\min_{\boldsymbol{\Gamma}, \boldsymbol{\Lambda}, \mathbf{U}, \mathbf{V}} \mathcal{C}(\boldsymbol{\Gamma}, \boldsymbol{\Lambda}) + \lambda_1 \|\mathbf{V}\|_{1,q} + \lambda_2 \|\mathbf{U}\|_1 \quad \text{s. t.}$$

$$\boldsymbol{\Gamma} = \mathbf{V}, \boldsymbol{\Lambda} = \mathbf{U}. \tag{7}$$

Since, (7) is an equally constrained problem, the Augmented Lagrangian method (ALM)[11] can be used to solve the problem. This can be done by minimizing the augmented lagrangian function $f_{\alpha_{\Gamma}, \alpha_{\Lambda}}(\boldsymbol{\Gamma}, \boldsymbol{\Lambda}, \mathbf{V}, \mathbf{U}; \mathbf{A}_{\Lambda}, \mathbf{A}_{\Gamma})$ defined as

$$\mathcal{C}(\boldsymbol{\Gamma}, \boldsymbol{\Lambda}) + \lambda_2 \|\mathbf{U}\|_1 + \langle \mathbf{A}_{\Lambda}, \boldsymbol{\Lambda} - \mathbf{U} \rangle + \frac{\alpha_{\Lambda}}{2} \|\boldsymbol{\Lambda} - \mathbf{U}\|_F^2 +$$

$$\lambda_1 \|\mathbf{V}\|_{1,q} + \langle \mathbf{A}_{\Gamma}, \boldsymbol{\Gamma} - \mathbf{V} \rangle + \frac{\alpha_{\Gamma}}{2} \|\boldsymbol{\Gamma} - \mathbf{V}\|_F^2, \tag{8}$$

where $\mathbf{A}_{\Lambda}$ and $\mathbf{A}_{\Gamma}$ are the multipliers of the two linear constraints, and $\alpha_{\Lambda}, \alpha_{\Gamma}$ are the positive penalty parameters. The ALM algorithm solves $f_{\alpha_{\Gamma}, \alpha_{\Lambda}}(\boldsymbol{\Gamma}, \boldsymbol{\Lambda}, \mathbf{V}, \mathbf{U}; \mathbf{A}_{\Lambda}, \mathbf{A}_{\Gamma})$ with respect to $\boldsymbol{\Gamma}, \boldsymbol{\Lambda}, \mathbf{U}$ and $\mathbf{V}$ jointly, keeping $\mathbf{A}_{\Gamma}$ and $\mathbf{A}_{\Lambda}$ fixed and then updating $\mathbf{A}_{\Gamma}$ and $\mathbf{A}_{\Lambda}$ keeping the remaining variables fixed. Due to the separable structure of the objective function $f_{\alpha_{\Gamma}, \alpha_{\Lambda}}$, one can further simplify the problem by minimizing $f_{\alpha_{\Gamma}, \alpha_{\Lambda}}$ with respect to variables $\boldsymbol{\Gamma}, \boldsymbol{\Lambda}, \mathbf{U}$ and $\mathbf{V}$, separately. Different steps of the algorithm are given in Algorithm 1. In what follows, we describe each of the suboptimization problems in detail.

Algorithm 1: Alternating Direction Method of Multipliers (ADMM).

Initialize: $\boldsymbol{\Gamma}_0, \mathbf{U}_0, \mathbf{V}_0, \mathbf{A}_{\Lambda,0}, \mathbf{A}_{\Gamma,0}, \alpha_{\Gamma}, \alpha_{\Lambda}$

While not converged do

1. $\boldsymbol{\Gamma}_{t+1} = \arg\min_{\boldsymbol{\Gamma}} f_{\alpha_{\Gamma}, \alpha_{\Lambda}}(\boldsymbol{\Gamma}, \boldsymbol{\Lambda}_t, \mathbf{U}_t, \mathbf{V}_t; \mathbf{A}_{\Gamma,t}, \mathbf{A}_{\Lambda,t})$
2. $\boldsymbol{\Lambda}_{t+1} = \arg\min_{\boldsymbol{\Lambda}} f_{\alpha_{\Gamma}, \alpha_{\Lambda}}(\boldsymbol{\Gamma}_{t+1}, \boldsymbol{\Lambda}, \mathbf{U}_t, \mathbf{V}_t; \mathbf{A}_{\Gamma,t}, \mathbf{A}_{\Lambda,t})$
3. $\mathbf{U}_{t+1} = \arg\min_{\mathbf{U}} f_{\alpha_{\Gamma}, \alpha_{\Lambda}}(\boldsymbol{\Gamma}_{t+1}, \boldsymbol{\Lambda}_{t+1}, \mathbf{U}, \mathbf{V}_t; \mathbf{A}_{\Gamma,t}, \mathbf{A}_{\Lambda,t})$
4. $\mathbf{V}_{t+1} = \arg\min_{\mathbf{V}} f_{\alpha_{\Gamma}, \alpha_{\Lambda}}(\boldsymbol{\Gamma}_{t+1}, \boldsymbol{\Lambda}_{t+1}, \mathbf{U}_{t+1}, \mathbf{V}; \mathbf{A}_{\Gamma,t}, \mathbf{A}_{\Lambda,t})$
5. $\mathbf{A}_{\Gamma,t+1} \doteq \mathbf{A}_{\Gamma,t} + \alpha_{\Lambda}(\boldsymbol{\Gamma}_{t+1} - \mathbf{U}_{t+1})$
6. $\mathbf{A}_{\Lambda,t+1} \doteq \mathbf{A}_{\Lambda,t} + \alpha_{\Gamma}(\boldsymbol{\Gamma}_{t+1} - \mathbf{V}_{t+1})$

Update Step for Γ: The first suboptimization problem involves the minimization of $f_{\alpha_\Gamma, \alpha_\Lambda}(\Gamma, \Lambda, \mathbf{V}, \mathbf{U}; \mathbf{A}_\Lambda, \mathbf{A}_\Gamma)$ with respect to Γ. It has the quadratic structure, which is easy to solve by setting the first-order derivative equal to zero, and has the following solution

$$\Gamma_{t+1}^i = (\mathbf{X}^{i^T}\mathbf{X}^i + \alpha_\Gamma \mathbf{I})^{-1}(\mathbf{X}^{i^T}(\mathbf{Y}^i - \Lambda_t^i) + \alpha_\Gamma \mathbf{V}_t^i + \mathbf{A}_{V,t}^i),$$

where $\mathbf{I}$ is $p \times p$ identity matrix and $\Lambda_t^i, \mathbf{V}_t^i$ and $\mathbf{A}_{V,t}^i$ are submatrices of $\Lambda_t, \mathbf{V}_t$ and $\mathbf{A}_{V,t}$, respectively.

Update Step for Λ: The second suboptimization problem is similar in nature, whose solution is given below

$$\Lambda_{t+1}^i = (1 + \alpha_\Lambda)^{-1}(\mathbf{Y}^i - \mathbf{X}^i \Gamma_{t+1}^i + \alpha_\Lambda \mathbf{U}_t^i - \mathbf{A}_{\Lambda,t}^i),$$

where $\mathbf{U}_t^i$ and $\mathbf{A}_{\Lambda,t}^i$ are submatrices of $\mathbf{U}_t$ and $\mathbf{A}_{\Lambda,t}$, respectively.

Update step for $\mathbf{U}$: The third suboptimization problem is with respect to $\mathbf{U}$, which is the standard ℓ_1 minimization problem which can be recast as

$$\min_{\mathbf{U}} \frac{1}{2}\|\Lambda_{t+1} + \alpha_\Lambda^{-1}\mathbf{A}_{\Lambda,t} - \mathbf{U}\|_F^2 + \frac{\lambda_2}{\alpha_\Lambda}\|\mathbf{U}\|_1. \tag{9}$$

Equation (9) is the well-known shrinkage problem whose solution is given by

$$\mathbf{U}_{t+1} = \mathcal{S}\left(\Lambda_{t+1} + \alpha_\Lambda^{-1}\mathbf{A}_{\Lambda,t}, \frac{\lambda_2}{\alpha_\Lambda}\right),$$

where $\mathcal{S}(a,b) = sgn(a)(|a| - b)$ for $|a| \geq b$ and zero otherwise.

Update Step for $\mathbf{V}$: The final suboptimization problem is with respect to $\mathbf{V}$ and can be formulated as

$$\min_{\mathbf{V}} \frac{1}{2}\|\Gamma_{t+1} + \alpha_\Gamma^{-1}\mathbf{A}_{\Gamma,t} - \mathbf{V}\|_F^2 + \frac{\lambda_1}{\alpha_\Gamma}\|\mathbf{V}\|_{1,q}. \tag{10}$$

Due to the separable structure of (10), it can be solved by minimizing with respect to each row of $\mathbf{V}$ separately. Let $\gamma_{i,t+1}, \mathbf{a}_{\Gamma,i,t}$ and $\mathbf{v}_{i,t+1}$ be rows of matrices $\Gamma_{t+1}, \mathbf{A}_{\Gamma,t}$ and $\mathbf{V}_{t+1}$, respectively. Then for each $i = 1, \ldots, p$ we solve the following sub-problem

$$\mathbf{v}_{i,t+1} = \arg\min_{\mathbf{v}} \frac{1}{2}\|\mathbf{z} - \mathbf{v}\|_2^2 + \eta\|\mathbf{v}\|_q, \tag{11}$$

where $\mathbf{z} = \gamma_{i,t+1} - \mathbf{a}_{\Gamma,i,t}\alpha_\Gamma^{-1}$ and $\eta = \frac{\lambda_1}{\lambda_2}$. One can derive the solution for (11) for any q. In this paper, we only focus on the case when $q = 2$. The solution of (11) has the following form

$$\mathbf{v}_{i,t+1} = \left(1 - \frac{\eta}{\|\mathbf{z}\|_2}\right)_+ \mathbf{z},$$

where $(\mathbf{v})_+$ is a vector with entries receiving values $\max(v_i, 0)$.

Our algorithm for multimodal biometrics recognition is summarized in Algorithm 2.

Algorithm 2: Sparse Multimodal Biometrics Recognition (SMBR).

Input: Training samples $\{\mathbf{X_i}\}_{i=1}^{D}$, test sample $\{\mathbf{Y_i}\}_{i=1}^{D}$, Occlusion basis $\{\mathbf{B}\}_{i=1}^{D}$
Procedure: Obtain $\hat{\boldsymbol{\Gamma}}$ and $\hat{\boldsymbol{\Lambda}}$ by solving

$$\hat{\boldsymbol{\Gamma}}, \hat{\boldsymbol{\Lambda}} = \arg\min_{\boldsymbol{\Gamma}, \boldsymbol{\Lambda}} \frac{1}{2} \sum_{i=1}^{D} \|\mathbf{Y}^i - \mathbf{X}^i \boldsymbol{\Gamma}^i - \mathbf{B}^i \boldsymbol{\Lambda}^i\|_F^2 + \lambda_1 \|\boldsymbol{\Gamma}\|_{1,q} + \lambda_2 \|\boldsymbol{\Lambda}\|_1,$$

Output: $\texttt{identity}(\mathbf{Y}) = \arg\min_j \sum_{i=1}^{D} \|\mathbf{Y}^i - \mathbf{X}^i \delta_j^i(\hat{\boldsymbol{\Gamma}}^i) - \mathbf{B}^i \hat{\boldsymbol{\Lambda}}^i\|_F^2.$

---

3   Experiments

We evaluated our algorithm for different multi-biometric settings. We tested on a publicly available dataset - the WVU Multimodal dataset [13]. The WVU dataset is one of the few publicly available datasets which allows fusion at image level, hence the proposed feature level fusion technique can be tested. In all the experiments, $\mathbf{B}_i$ was set to be identity for convenience, *i.e.*, we consider error to be sparse in image domain.

3.1   WVU Multimodal Dataset

WVU multimodal dataset is a comprehensive collection of different biometric modalities such as fingerprint, iris, palmprint, hand geometry and voice from subjects of different age, gender and ethnicity. It is a challenging dataset and many of these samples are of poor quality corrupted with blur, occlusion and sensor noise as shown in Figure 2. Out of these, we chose iris and fingerprint modalities for testing the algorithm, giving a total of 6 modalities (4 fingerprint + 2 iris). The evaluation was done on a common subset of 219 subjects having samples in all the modalities.

Fig. 2. Examples of challenging images from the WVU Multimodal dataset, suffering from various artifacts as sensor noise, blur, occlusion and poor acquisition

Preprocessing. Robust pre-processing of images was done before feature extraction. Iris images were segmented following the recent method proposed in [14]. Following the segmentation, 25×240 iris templates were formed by resampling using the publicly available code of Masek *et al.* [15]. Fingerprint images were enhanced using the filtering based methods described in [16], and then the core point was detected using the enhanced images [17]. Features were then extracted around the detected core point.

Feature Extraction. Gabor features were extracted on the processed images as they have been shown to give good performance on both fingerprints [17] and iris [15]. For fingerprints, the processed images were convolved with Gabor filters at 8 different orientations. Circular tesselations were extracted around the core point for all filtered images. The mean values for each sector were concatenated to form 3600×1 feature vectors. For iris, the templates were convovled with a log-Gabor filter, and vectorized to give 6000×1 dimensional feature.

Experimental Set-up. The dataset was randomly divided into 4 training samples per class (1 sample here is 1 data sample each from 6 modalities) and the rest 519 for testing. The recognition result was averaged over 5 runs. The proposed methods were compared with compared with state-of-the-art classification methods such as sparse logistic regression (SLR) [18] and SVM [19]. Although these methods give superior performance on individual modalities, they cannot handle multimodal data. One possible way to handle multimodal data is to use feature concatenation. But, this resulted in feature vectors of size 26400×1 when all 6 modalities are used, and is not useful. Hence, two techniques were explored for fusion. In the first technique, a score-based fusion was followed where the probability outputs for test sample of each modality, $\{y_i\}_{i=1}^6$ were added together to give the final score vector. Classification was based upon the final score values. For the second technique, the subject chosen by the maximum number of modalities was taken to be from the correct class.

Observations. The recognition performances of SMBR-WE (without error) and SMBR-E (with error) were compared with linear SVM and linear SLR classification methods. In the experiments, λ_1 and λ_2 were set to 0.01. Figures 3 and Table 1 demonstrate recognition performance of different methods on three fusion settings - (1) two irises, (2) four fingerprints and (3) all combined.

Table 1. Rank one recognition performance for WVU Multimodal dataset

	SMBR-WE	SMBR-E	SLR-Sum	SLR-Major	SVM-Sum	SVM-Major
4 Fingerprints	**97.9**	97.6	96.3	74.2	90.0	73.0
2 Irises	76.5	**78.2**	72.7	64.2	62.8	49.3
Overall	**98.7**	98.6	97.6	84.4	94.9	81.3

Comparsion of Methods: Clearly, the proposed SMBR approach outperforms existing techniques for all the fusion settings. Both SMBR-E and SMBR-WE have similar performance, though the latter seems to give a slightly better performance. This may be due to the penalty on the sparse error, though the error

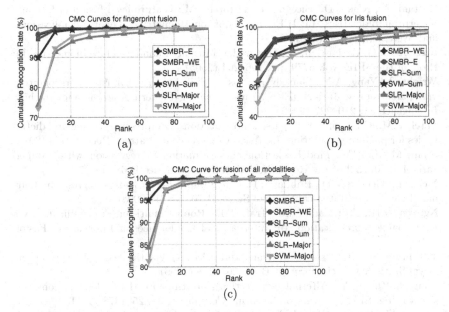

Fig. 3. CMC (Cumulative Match Curve) for multimodal fusion using (a) four finger-prints, (b) two irises and (c) all modalities

may not be sparse in image domain. Further, sum-based fusion shows a superior performance over voting-based methods, and SLR performs better than SVM on all the modalities. However, by jointly classifiying all the modalities, SMBR achieves the best performance.

4   Conclusion

We have proposed a novel multimodel multivariate joint sparsity-based algo-rithm for multimodal biometrics recognition. The algorithm is robust as it ex-plicitly accounts for both noise and occlusion. An efficient algorithm based on alternative direction was proposed for solving the optimization problem. Vari-ous experiments show that our method is robust and significantly improves the overall recognition accuracy.

Acknowledgment. The work of SS, VMP and RC was partially supported by a MURI grant from the Army Research Office under the Grant W911NF-09-1-0383.

References

1. Ross, A., Jain, A.K.: Multimodal biometrics: an overview. In: Proc. European Signal Processing Conference, pp. 1221–1224 (2004)
2. Klausner, A., Tengg, A., Rinner, B.: Vehicle classification on multi-sensor smart cameras using feature- and decision-fusion. In: IEEE Conf. Dist. Smart Cameras, pp. 67–74 (2007)

3. Rattani, A., Kisku, D., Bicego, M., Tistarelli, M.: Feature level fusion of face and fingerprint biometrics. In: IEEE Int. Conf. on Biometrics: Theory, Applications, and Systems, pp. 1–6 (2007)
4. Ross, A.A., Govindarajan, R.: Feature level fusion of hand and face biometrics. In: Proc. of the SPIE, vol. 5779, pp. 196–204 (2005)
5. Wright, J., Yang, A.Y., Ganesh, A., Sastry, S.S., Ma, Y.: Robust face recognition via sparse representation. IEEE Transactions on Pattern Analysis and Machine Intelligence 31, 210–227 (2009)
6. Patel, V.M., Chellappa, R.: Sparse representations, compressive sensing and dictionaries for pattern recognition. In: Asian Conference on Pattern Recognition (2010)
7. Yuan, M., Lin, Y.: Model selection and estimation in regression with grouped variables. Journal of the Royal Statistical Society: Series B 68, 49–67 (2006)
8. Meier, L., Geer, S.V.D., Bhlmann, P.: The group lasso for logistic regression. Journal of the Royal Statistical Society: Series B 70, 53–71 (2008)
9. Nguyen, N.H., Nasrabadi, N.M., Tran, T.D.: Robust multi-sensor classification via joint sparse representation. In: International Conference on Information Fusion (2011)
10. Tibshirani, R.: Regression shrinkage and selection via the lasso. Journal of the Royal Statistical Society: Series B 58, 267–288 (1996)
11. Yang, J., Zhang, Y.: Alternating direction algorithms for l1 problems in compressive sensing. SIAM Journal on Scientific Computing 33, 250–278 (2011)
12. Afonso, M., Bioucas-Dias, J., Figueiredo, M.: An augmented lagrangian approach to the constrained optimization formulation of imaging inverse problems. IEEE Transactions on Image Processing 20, 681–695 (2011)
13. Crihalmeanu, S., Ross, A., Schuckers, S., Hornak, L.: A protocol for multibiometric data acquisition, storage and dissemination. Technical Report, WVU, Lane Department of Computer Science and Electrical Engineering (2007)
14. Pundlik, S., Woodard, D., Birchfield, S.: Non-ideal iris segmentation using graph cuts. In: IEEE CVPR Workshop, pp. 1–6 (2008)
15. Masek, L.: Recognition of human iris patterns for biometric identification. Technical report, The University of Western Australia (2003)
16. Chikkerur, S., Wu, C., Govindaraju, V.: A systematic approach for feature extraction in fingerprint images. In: Int. Conference on Bioinformatics and its Applications, p. 344 (2004)
17. Jain, A., Prabhakar, S., Hong, L., Pankanti, S.: Filterbank-based fingerprint matching. IEEE Transactions on Image Processing 9, 846–859 (2000)
18. Krishnapuram, B., Carin, L., Figueiredo, M., Hartemink, A.: Sparse multinomial logistic regression: fast algorithms and generalization bounds. IEEE Transactions on Pattern Analysis and Machine Intelligence 27, 957–968 (2005)
19. Burges, C.J.: A tutorial on support vector machines for pattern recognition. Data Mining and Knowledge Discovery 2, 121–167 (1998)

GPS-Based Multi-viewpoint Integration for Anticipative Scene Analysis

Kohji Kamejima

Osaka Institute of Technology, Faculty of Information Science and Technology,
1-79-1 Kitayama, Hirakata 573-0196 Japan,
kamejima@is.oit.ac.jp
http://www.is.oit.ac.jp/~kamejima

Abstract. A multi-viewpoint integration scheme is introduced to recognize scene features *prior to* physical access. In this schematics, chromatic complexity of vehicle's- and bird's-eye-views of roadway scenes are matched to extend GPS tracks towards possible destinations. Saliency patterns arising in destination images are anticipatively extracted to control the focus of inherent and machine vision to what to be analyzed.

Keywords: Multi-viewpoint Image, Scene Analysis, Chromatic Complexity, GPS Signal Processing, Image Saliency.

1 Introductory Remarks

By networking on-board vision system with global positioning and earth observation systems, we can localize landmark objects in distant scenes along roadway patterns to be followed. This implies that a multitude of intelligent vehicles can be exploited for over-the-horizon cooperation of the maneuvering processes; the scene images provided by probe vehicles are re-used by future visitors as anticipative visualization of landmarks to be recognized. Such augmented perception can be utilized as the basis of spontaneous coordination of participant vehicles through the localization [8] and regulation [9] of maneuvering processes. To activate the localization and/or regulation processes, the future visitors should retrieve the probed images along feasible trajectories and anticipatively control the focus of recognition.

Within the framework of the the satellite-roadway-vehicle networking, we can implement an access path to 'future' scenes as illustrated in Fig. 1; a scene image is matched with a local section of satellite image including GPS track; detected roadway pattern is extended towards possible destinations to observe landmark distribution in the probed scenes *prior to* physical access. It has been pointed out that image features can be organized to extract saliency distribution including various types of objects-to-be-observed [3,7]. However, due to significant discrepancy of photographing conditions, it is not easy to predict what will be observed in the future scenes through the analysis of the probed images; based on such ill conditioned observation, in many practical situations, the on-vehicle vision are

A. Fusiello et al. (Eds.): ECCV 2012 Ws/Demos, Part III, LNCS 7585, pp. 375–384, 2012.

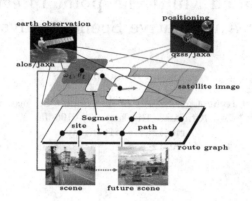

Fig. 1. Schematics of Anticipative Scene Analysis

required to yield a man readable visualization to maintain the consistency of the over-the-horizon maneuvering processes. Noticing that human's inherent vision is endowed with not-yet-explicated focusing mechanism in chromatic diversity, in this paper, we consider saliency based integration of multi-viewpoint images connected by GPS tracks.

2   GPS Tracking on Satellite Image

Suppose that bird's-eye-views and perspectives of roadway scenes are jointly captured through the earth observation systems and on-vehicle cameras, respectively, to generate multi-viewpoint images on an image plane Ω endowed with longitude-latitude or camera specific coordinate system. Let GPS tracks be identified with stochastic processes to be segmented in terms of 2D vectors $v_t = (\omega_t, \theta_t)$, $t = 0, 1, 2, \ldots, k$, with origin ω_t and direction θ_t. By nondeterministically associating a sequence of v_t within GPS residual [4], we have a noisy observation of not-yet-identified roadway pattern on a cut of satellite image.

To correct the GPS residual, the scene image captured at ω_t is matched with a local section of the satellite image. In this association process, first, an open space in a roadway area is recognized in the scene image and scanned to collect a set of color samples $S = \{ f_i^{\mathrm{RGB}}, i = 1, 2, \ldots \}$ with size $\|S\|$. Let the pixel value f^{RGB} be mapped into the positive part of a unit sphere; through the mapping $\phi\left(f^{\mathrm{RGB}}\right) = f^{\mathrm{RGB}}/\left|f^{\mathrm{RGB}}\right|$, we can evaluate the local complexity of the sample S in terms of 2D Gaussian measure

$$g_\alpha\left(\phi_i|\phi_j\right) = \frac{1}{2\pi\alpha} \exp\left[-\frac{|\phi_i - \phi_j|^2}{2\alpha}\right]. \tag{1}$$

Define local similarity by $R_S = e^{-\sigma_{\phi\phi}^2/2\alpha}/2\pi\alpha$ based on the following statistics

$$\sigma_{\phi\phi}^2 = \frac{1}{\|S\|(\|S\|-1)} \times \sum_{f_i^{RGB}, f_j^{RGB} \in S, f_i^{RGB} \neq f_j^{RGB}} |\phi(f_i^{RGB}) - \phi(f_j^{RGB})|^2 .$$

By selecting the representatives $f_{i*}^{RGB} \in S$ with respect to the equivalence criterion R_S, we have a palette $\mathfrak{s} = \{f_{i*}^{RGB}\}$ to nondeterministically re-draw the essential part of the roadway area. Let the consistency of a pixel f_ω^{RGB}, $\omega \in \Omega$ with $\mathfrak{s}$ be evaluated in the locally Gaussian space as follows:

$$\max_{f_j^{RGB} \in \mathfrak{s}} g_\alpha \left[\phi(f_\omega^{RGB}) | \phi(f_j^{RGB})\right] > R_S \Rightarrow f_\omega^{RGB} \overset{R_S}{\sim} \mathfrak{s}. \tag{2}$$

To associate the bird's eye view with the perspective of the vehicle, a local section including ω_t is scanned to generate another palette $\check{\mathfrak{s}} = \{\check{f}_i^{RGB}\}$. By applying the association rule (2), we have an estimate of the roadway palette:

$$\hat{\mathfrak{s}} = \left\{\hat{f}_i^{RGB} \overset{R_S}{\sim} \check{\mathfrak{s}} \mid \hat{f}_i^{RGB} = f_i^{RGB} + (\bar{\check{\mathfrak{s}}} - \bar{\mathfrak{s}}), \quad f_i^{RGB} \in \mathfrak{s}\right\}, \tag{3}$$

where $\bar{\mathfrak{s}}$ and $\bar{\check{\mathfrak{s}}}$ designate mean colors of $\mathfrak{s}$ and $\check{\mathfrak{s}}$, respectively. In (3), the spectral shift due to the disparity of photographing conditions are compensated via the mean value adaptation; samples from the exterior of the not-yet-identified roadway area are eliminated as non-equivalent pixels. By evaluating the consistency within the bird's eye view in terms of $(\hat{\mathfrak{s}}, g_\alpha)$-information, thus, we can apply Hough voting to roadway pattern detection; $v_t(\omega_t, \theta_t)$ is adapted to $\hat{v}_t(\hat{\omega}_t, \hat{\theta}_t)$ spanning significant chromatic discrepancy between scene- and satellite images.

An example of experimental results of roadway pattern detection is shown in Fig. 2; a GPS track from the 'gateway' to the 'branch' is marked on the satellite image in terms of v_t-sequence in (b); a perspective image at the branch is captured by the camera to generate the palette $\mathfrak{s}$ on a sampling area indicated in (a); the palette $\mathfrak{s}$ is adapted to $\check{\mathfrak{s}}$ extracted from the satellite image as illustrated in (c); resulted estimate $\hat{\mathfrak{s}}$ is applied to detect a segment of the roadway pattern at the branch area. As indicated in (d), the segment was allocated along really existing roadway patterns; furthermore, by iterating the segmentation process, a 'robotic probe' was deployed to simulate the $\hat{\theta}_t$-sequence of a GPS track towards the 'cross' as indicated in (e); thus, the GPS tracks was extended to connect possible destinations. By invoking experimental results using various complex roadway scenes, we can simulate feasible trajectories of 1.3–1.9 km length towards future scenes [5]; via the adaptation-and-elimination process (3), 1/2,000–1/2,500 of color samples are used in the Hough voting process; in the adaptation process shown in (c), the complexity of roadway area is finally represented by 29 feature colors.

3   GPS-Based Graph Generation

Suppose that possible destinations $N = \{n_i^d, i = 1, 2, \dots\}$ are localized in the satellite image. By identifying the simulated GPS track with a route graph

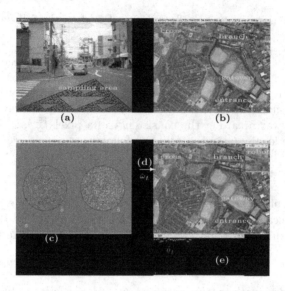

Fig. 2. GPS Track Extension via Multi-viewpoint Association

spanning the distribution of N, we can extract a image of 'future' scenes which has been captured by probe vehicles. To implement efficient search scheme, we introduce a dynamic matching algorithm in a stochastic sense.

Conditional Brownian Motion Model: Let a landmark $n \in N$ be localized at $n_\perp \in \Omega$ and consider the probability distribution to capture 2D Brownian motion with origin landmark n at time σ, i.e.,

$$g_\sigma(\omega|n) = \frac{1}{2\pi\sigma} \exp\left[-\frac{|\omega - n_\perp|^2}{2\sigma}\right]. \tag{4}$$

Noticing the following approximation

$$g_\sigma(\omega|n) - \delta_{n_\perp} = \int_0^\sigma \frac{1}{2} \Delta g_s(\omega|n)ds \sim \frac{\sigma}{2} \Delta g_\sigma(\omega|n),$$

and extending the representation (4) to the distribution of the localization image $\chi_N = \frac{1}{\|N\|} \sum_{n \in N} \delta_{n_\perp}$, we have the following probability distribution to finally capture at least one Brownian motion shifted from N:

$$\frac{\sigma}{2} \Delta\varphi_\sigma(\omega|N) + [\chi_N - \varphi_\sigma(\omega|N)] = 0. \tag{5}$$

By identifying the information arising from the landmarks $N - n$ with independent noisy background, we have the following decomposition:

$$\varphi_\sigma(\omega|N) = g_\sigma(\omega|n) + \chi_\Omega, \tag{6}$$

where χ_Ω denotes the uniform distribution standing for the background noise.

Dynamic Detection: Let the origin be randomly re-selected in each unit time interval. In such a situation, the probability to capture a Brownian motion iteratively conditioned until time $t > 0$ is given by

$$\tilde{g}_t^n(\omega|N) = \left(\frac{1}{\|N\|}\right)^t g_t(\omega|n) = e^{-\rho t} g_t(\omega|n), \qquad \rho = \log\|N\|. \qquad (7)$$

Thus, we can apply the dynamic likelihood test [10] to the identification of the segment $\hat{v}_t$ with the conditional Brownian motion process. To this end, first, the variation is evaluated as follows:

$$d\varphi_t = -\nabla\varphi_\sigma(\hat{\omega}_t|N)^T \hat{v}_t dt. \qquad (8)$$

Noticing $\varphi_\sigma \sim g_\sigma$ within the area $|\omega - \hat{n}_\perp| < \sqrt{\sigma_N}$ and

$$\nabla g_\sigma(\omega|n) = -\frac{1}{\sigma}(\omega - \hat{n}_\perp) g_\sigma(\omega|n),$$

next, we have the following stochastic differential:

$$d\tilde{\varphi}_t = \frac{d\varphi_t}{\varphi_t} = \tilde{\phi}_t dt + \sqrt{\sigma_w} dw_t,$$

where $\tilde{\phi}_t = (\omega - \hat{n}_\perp)^T \hat{v}_t$ and the fluctuation due to the background distribution χ_Ω is simulated in terms of Wiener process w_t with $\sqrt{\sigma_w}$. By modifying the Wiener measure in terms of the iteration factor $e^{-\rho t}$ induced in (7) and noticing that the likelihood ratio satisfies the stochastic differential equation

$$\frac{d\Lambda_t}{\Lambda_t} = \frac{\tilde{\phi}_t}{\sigma_w} d\tilde{\varphi}_t - \rho dt, \qquad (9)$$

finally, the nearest localization $\hat{n}_\perp$ can be detected in a rectangle $d\hat{\Omega}_t$ with diagonal vertexes $\hat{\omega}_t$ and $\check{\omega}_t$ given by

$$\check{\omega}_t = \hat{\omega}_t + 2\sqrt{-2\sigma \log\left[\frac{\varphi_\sigma}{\varphi_{max}}\right]} \frac{\nabla\varphi_\sigma}{|\nabla\varphi_\sigma|}, \qquad (10)$$

where $\varphi_{max} = \max_{\omega \in \Omega} \varphi_\sigma(\omega|N)$. The estimation process (10) is activated at each segment $\hat{v}_t$ consistent with one of $g_\sigma(\omega|n)$, $n \in N$; this implies that the landmark search process is controlled by the dynamical system (9) to confine within a restricted region $d\hat{\Omega}_t$.

The performance of the detection scheme is illustrated in Fig. 3 where a series of GPS track data (v_t) is matched with landmark set; in this case, the distribution of 18 landmarks are allocated in a cut of satellite image of 640×480 resolution to yield the field information φ_σ in subwindow (a) where the GPS track consisting of 336 $\hat{v}_t$-vectors is matched with φ_σ. The transition of Λ_t is displayed in (b); in this subwindow, the level of background noise χ_Ω and $d\hat{\Omega}_t$-generation time are indicated by thin white line and large white circles, respectively; the scene image of the latest landmark is displayed in the subwindow (c). Throughout the GPS track analysis, a route graph spanning 5 landmarks was generated as an access path to the future scenes along roadway pattern.

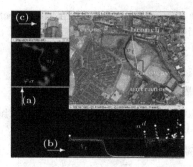

Fig. 3. GPS-based Route Graph Generation

4   Saliency Indexing for Scene Feature Detection

In many practical roadway scenes, various types of objects to be recognized are randomly distributed in complex background. This implies that the probed images should be articulated into a not-yet-identified set of landmark objects to adapt the on-vehicle vision to the future scenes. To this end, the probe vehicles are required to recognize the diversity of naturally complex scenes in terms of transferable information.

It should be noted that the perception of chromatic diversity is essentially mental processes supported by stochastic neuronal dynamics [2]. To visualize the performance of the mental process, let the chromatic diversity of naturally complex scenes be represented in a linear color space

$$\Gamma \ni \gamma = e^{\mathrm{RGB}}\phi, \qquad e^{\mathrm{RGB}} = \begin{bmatrix} e^{\mathrm{R}} & e^{\mathrm{G}} & e^{\mathrm{B}} \end{bmatrix},$$

where $e^{(\cdot)} = \begin{bmatrix} \cos\theta_{(\cdot)} & \sin\theta_{(\cdot)} \end{bmatrix}^T$ with $\theta_{\mathrm{R}} = \pi/2, \theta_{\mathrm{G(B)}} = \theta_{\mathrm{R}} + (-)2\pi/3$. In this color space, the chromatic diversity is visualized as a random aggregation of δ-measure $\chi_{\mathfrak{s}} = \sum_{\phi \in \mathfrak{s}} \delta_{\gamma(\phi)}$ as well as the N-allocation. By identifying the distribution $\chi_{\mathfrak{s}}$ with a degenerate version of a not-yet-identified fractal attractor, we can design a set of fixed points of an iterated function system [1]; through the adaptation of the fractal dynamics to a non-degraded version of the distribution $\chi_{\mathfrak{s}}$, a global features, called *as-is* primaries $\hat{\Pi} = \{ \hat{\pi}_i \}$ [6], are recognized.

According to the fractal visualization of the color perception process, the chromatic diversity spanning the roadway scenes should be accepted via parametric restoration of a fractal attractor; hence, the complexity of 'neuronal computation' can be evaluated in terms of the *as-is* primary. To this end, first, the probability of the neuronal photopigment selection is evaluated by $p(\phi|\hat{\pi}_i) = (\phi^T \hat{\pi}_i)^2$. Next, the *a posteriori* probability of the neuronal selection under the observation ϕ is evaluated by

$$p\left(\hat{\pi}_i|\phi\right) = p\left(\phi|\hat{\pi}_i\right) \frac{p\left(\hat{\pi}_i\right)}{\sum\limits_{\hat{\pi}_i \in \hat{\Pi}} p\left(\phi|\hat{\pi}_i\right) p\left(\hat{\pi}_i\right)}, \qquad p\left(\hat{\pi}_i\right) = \frac{1}{\|\hat{\Pi}\|}.$$

As the result, finally, we can index the complexity of the neuronal process in terms of the Shannon's entropy:

$$\mathcal{S}_\phi = - \sum_{\hat{\pi}_i \in \hat{\Pi}} p\left(\hat{\pi}_i|\phi\right) \log p\left(\hat{\pi}_i|\phi\right), \tag{11}$$

The complexity index (11) is applied to the extraction of saliency distribution in roadway scenes as demonstrated in Fig 4; the fluctuation of γ-representation arising in the scene image Fig. 2(a) is displayed in (c); resulted distribution χ_s is identified with a fractal attractor to specify a scene specific deviation of the primary as indicated in (b). By using the evaluation (11), the following pixel-wise filter is designed and applied to the distribution $\phi\left(f^{\mathrm{RGB}}\right)$ at $\omega \in \Omega$:

$$\psi_\omega = 1 - \exp\left[-\frac{1}{2}\left(\frac{\log\|\hat{\Pi}\| - \mathcal{S}_{\phi_\omega}}{\log\|\hat{\Pi}\| - \mathcal{S}_m}\right)^2\right], \tag{12}$$

where $\mathcal{S}_m$ designates the mean value of $\mathcal{S}_{\phi_\omega}$ on entire Ω. In this filtering, the computational cost for neuronal color preference is evaluated in terms of $\mathcal{S}_\phi$ to emphasize the 'easy-to-select' pixels. As demonstrated in the main window, Fig. 4(a), the ψ_ω-filtering is effective to extract random distribution of landmarks to be noted by on-vehicle vision and inherent perception as well. The result of RGB-based recognition is displayed in Fig. 5 where the ψ-distribution is evaluated in terms of conventional RGB primary; the comparison with the RGB-based recognition demonstrates that the *as-is* primary based saliency distribution provides more sensitive filter to 'low-keyed' landmarks, in particular. Thus, we can exploit the *as-is* primary to control the focus of the on-vehicle vision.

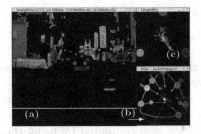

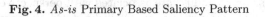

Fig. 4. *As-is* Primary Based Saliency Pattern   **Fig. 5.** RGB-based Recognition

5 Transferability of *As-is* Primary

To support the over-the-horizon cooperation, the *as-is* primary should be transferred to future visitors spanning significant discrepancy of photographing conditions and object allocation. The robustness of the *as-is* primary is demonstrated trough experimental studies. Figure 6 indicates a part of recognition results where the *as-is* primary extracted in the branch scene, Fig 2(a), is applied to various perspectives of the cross scene; these results shows that the *as-is* primary can be transferred to distant scenes spanning considerable discrepancy in photographing conditions and physical degeneration processes. Figure 7 illustrates another results where the *as-is* primary extracted in previously probed image of cross scene; these results demonstrates that the *as-is* primary provided by probe vehicles can be re-used by future visitors to the scenes.

cross-1: f_ω^{RGB} from branch: $\psi_\omega f_\omega^{\mathrm{RGB}}$ cross-2: f_ω^{RGB} from branch: $\psi_\omega f_\omega^{\mathrm{RGB}}$

cross-3: f_ω^{RGB} from branch: $\psi_\omega f_\omega^{\mathrm{RGB}}$ cross-4: f_ω^{RGB} from branch: $\psi_\omega f_\omega^{\mathrm{RGB}}$

Fig. 6. Transferability of *As-is* Primary: branch→cross

The effectiveness and transferability of the *as-is* primary is evaluated in terms of the complexity arising in the saliency distribution $(\cdot)$ given by

$$\mathcal{S}_{(\cdot)} = -\frac{1}{C_{(\cdot)}} \int_\Omega (\cdot)_\omega \log(\cdot)_\omega d\omega + \log C_{(\cdot)}, \qquad (13)$$

where $C_{(\cdot)}$ denotes the normalization constant. The experimental results are summarized in Table 1 where the reduction of the computational complexity is evaluated in terms of the difference between the Shannon's entropy with respect to the uniform distribution $\mathcal{S}_\emptyset$, i.e., $d\mathcal{S}_{(\cdot)} = \mathcal{S}_\emptyset - \mathcal{S}_{(\cdot)}$. In this table, saliency distribution and the gray level distribution are invoked to yield $\mathcal{S}_\psi$ and $\mathcal{S}_G$ via the evaluation (13), respectively; the distribution ψ is computed by using the *as-is* primary detected in each scene image; ψ^b and ψ^p are associated with perspective images transferred from branch and cross-p scenes, respectively; $\psi^\triangle$ designates the saliency distribution based on RGB primary. As shown in this table, the ψ_ω-filter well concentrate the information distributed in the image plane into a set

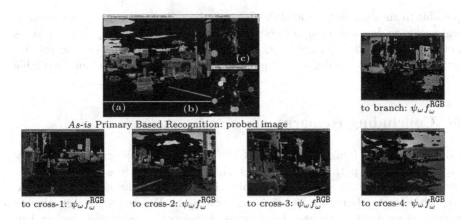

As-is Primary Based Recognition: probed image

to branch: $\psi_\omega f_\omega^{RGB}$

to cross-1: $\psi_\omega f_\omega^{RGB}$ to cross-2: $\psi_\omega f_\omega^{RGB}$ to cross-3: $\psi_\omega f_\omega^{RGB}$ to cross-4: $\psi_\omega f_\omega^{RGB}$

Fig. 7. Transferability of *As-is* Primary: probe→visitor

of saliency patterns to reduce the essential length of focus control programs to $e^{-1.3} - e^{-0.42}$ of random search in image plane; by this concentration, on-vehicle vision can reduce the delay to activate object recognition processes no less than $30\% - 72\%$ of focus control based on gray level distribution. The comparison of dS_ψ- and dS_{ψ^b}-results implies that future visitors can concentrate the focusing area to 6–68% of saliency patterns in destination images via the prediction by using observed scene image; this implies that the forward transfer of the *as-is* primary along the simulated GPS track yields a efficient focus control to scene-transversal object images; while the reference to probed image can be exploited as an effective backup in the sampling-based palette generation. In comparison with the RGB based complexity reduction, the saliency indexing based on native- and/or transferred *as-is* primary was proved to maintain sensitivity to considerably 'low-keyed' object images.

Table 1. Relative Complexity Reduction

scene	dS_ψ	dS_{ψ^b}	dS_{ψ^p}	$dS_{\psi\triangle}$	$\lVert \hat{\Pi} \rVert$	dS_G
branch	1.342628	–	0.310515	1.435720	7	0.080535
cross-1	0.583304	0.640835	0.514303	2.276305	8	0.138044
cross-2	0.829417	0.900230	0.474707	1.828937	4	0.162454
cross-3	0.421347	0.947673	0.454722	1.576738	4	0.182304
cross-4	0.434097	0.542789	0.290063	0.577541	5	0.131293
probed	0.587654	1.315543	–	2.084636	7	0.115865

As demonstrated in Fig. 4, we can exploit the ψ_ω-filter for the extraction of the saliency distribution including various types of objects to be observed; in contrast with the conventional method, resulted $\psi_\omega f_\omega^{RGB}$-pattern is controllable in terms of the *as-is* primary. The transferability of the *as-is* primary makes it possible to anticipatively control the focus on the saliency patterns *prior to* physical access as demonstrated in Figs. 6 and 7. Despite that the ψ_ω distribution is not sufficient for unique identification of natural objects, we can significantly reduce the complexity of decision steps by machine vision exhibiting man readable visualization.

6 Concluding Remarks

Complexity-based image analysis and GPS-based route graph generation jointly provide an access path to destination images through satellite-roadway-vehicle network. By simulating neuronal computation process of chromatic diversity in terms of a fractal dynamics, the *as-is* primary can be detected to extract saliency patterns in noisy background. Experimental results demonstrated that we can recognize and transfer the *as-is* primary to control the focus of machine vision to various types of man readable saliency patterns.

References

1. Barnsley, M.F., Demko, S.: Iterated function systems and the global construction of fractals. The Proceedings of the Royal Society of London A-399, 243–275 (1985)
2. Ebner, M.: Color Constancy. John Wiley and Sons, West Sussex (2007)
3. Itti, L., Kock, C., Niebur, E.: A model of saliency-based visual attention for rapid scene analysis. IEEE Transactions on Pattern Analysis and Machine Intelligence PAMI-20(11), 1254–1259 (1998)
4. Kamejima, K.: GPS/GNSS residual analysis via competitive-growth modeling of ionosphere dynamics. In: Signal Processing XIII: Proceedings of the 13th European Signal Processing Conference (EUSIPCO 2005), Antalya, Turkey, pp. WedAmOR4–2(4 pages). EURASIP (2005)
5. Kamejima, K.: Generation and adaptation of transferable roadway model for anticipative road following on satellite-roadway-vehicle network. SICE Journal of Control, Measurement, and System Integration 4(2), 97–104 (2011)
6. Kamejima, K.: Multi-fractal articulation of environmental saliency for contextual visualization of naturally complex scenes. International Journal of Innovative Computing, Information and Control 8(3B), 2233–2248 (2012)
7. Kwak, S., Ko, B., Byun, H.: Automatic salient-object extraction using the contrast map and salient points. In: Proceedings Pacific-Rim Conference on Multimedia, pp. II:138–II:145 (2004)
8. Tan, H.-S., Huang, J.: DGPS-based vehicle-to-vehicle cooperative collision warning: Engineering feasibility viewpoints. IEEE Transactions on Intelligent Transportation Systems ITS-7(4), 415–428 (2006)
9. Wang, J., Schroedl, S., Mezger, K., Ortloff, R., Joos, A., Passegger, T.: Lane keeping based on location technology. IEEE Transactions on Intelligent Transportation Systems ITS-6(3), 351–356 (2005)
10. Wong, E.: Stochastic Processes in Information and Dynamical Systems. McGraw-Hill, New York (1971)

Fusion of Speech, Faces and Text for Person Identification in TV Broadcast

Hervé Bredin[1], Johann Poignant[2], Makarand Tapaswi[3], Guillaume Fortier[4],
Viet Bac Le[5], Thibault Napoleon[6], Hua Gao[3], Claude Barras[1], Sophie Rosset[1],
Laurent Besacier[2], Jakob Verbeek[4], Georges Quénot[2], Frédéric Jurie[6],
and Hazim Kemal Ekenel[3]

[1] Univ Paris-Sud / CNRS-LIMSI UPR 3251, BP 133, F-91403 Orsay, France
[2] UJF-Grenoble 1 / UPMF-Grenoble 2 / Grenoble INP / CNRS-LIG UMR 5217,
F-38041 Grenoble, France
[3] Karlsruher Institut fur Technologie, Karlsruhe, Germany
[4] INRIA Rhone-Alpes, 655 Avenue de lEurope, F-38330 Montbonnot, France
[5] Vocapia Research, 3 rue Jean Rostand, Parc Orsay Université, F-91400 Orsay,
France
[6] Université de Caen / GREYC UMR 6072, F-14050 Caen Cedex, France

Abstract. The REPERE challenge is a project aiming at the evaluation of systems for supervised and unsupervised multimodal recognition of people in TV broadcast. In this paper, we describe, evaluate and discuss QCOMPERE consortium submissions to the 2012 REPERE evaluation campaign dry-run. Speaker identification (and face recognition) can be greatly improved when combined with name detection through video optical character recognition. Moreover, we show that unsupervised multimodal person recognition systems can achieve performance nearly as good as supervised monomodal ones (with several hundreds of identity models).

1 Introduction

Over the years, a growing amount of multimedia data has been produced and made available, fostering the need for automatic processing systems allowing efficient search into multimedia archives.

Person recognition is one of the main keys for structuring a video document. Face recognition in images or videos [1] and speaker identification in audio [2] are already very active research fields in this domain.

As illustrated in Figure 1, the REPERE challenge[1] aims at gathering four communities (face recognition, speaker identification, optical character recognition and named entity detection) towards the same goal: multimodal person recognition in TV broadcast. It takes the form of an annual evaluation campaign and debriefing workshop.

---

[1] http://www.defi-repere.fr

A. Fusiello et al. (Eds.): ECCV 2012 Ws/Demos, Part III, LNCS 7585, pp. 385–394, 2012.

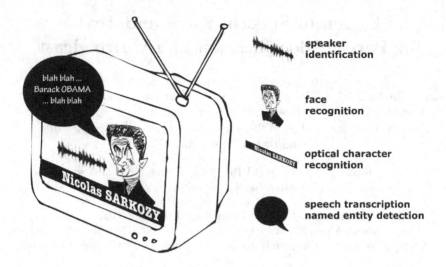

Fig. 1. One identity, four modalities

In this paper we describe QCOMPERE consortium submissions to the 2012 REPERE evaluation campaign dry-run. The REPERE corpus and evaluation protocol is described in Section 2. Mono-modal person recognition components are introduced in Section 3, while Section 4 is dedicated to their supervised and unsupervised combination. Finally, results are reported and discussed in Section 5.

2   The REPERE Challenge

The REPERE evaluation campaign dry-run was organized in January 2012. We first describe the corresponding REPERE corpus which is meant to be extended throughout the duration of the project, with a final total of 60 hours of annotated videos. Then, the main tasks and the corresponding evaluation metric are quickly summarized.

2.1   Corpus

The 2012 REPERE corpus contains a total of 6 hours of annotated videos recorded from 2 French TV channels (BFMTV and LCP) and 7 different TV shows (TV news and talk shows). It is divided into development and test sets (3 hours each). Annotations are provided for four main modalities:

Speaker. Each speech turn is described with its start and end timestamps and the normalized speaker identity (e.g. Nicolas_SARKOZY).

Head. Each head track is described with its appearance and disappearance timestamps and the associated normalized identity.

Written. Every overlaid text box is transcribed with its appearance and disappearance timestamps and written person names are tagged with the normalized identity.

Spoken. Each speech turn is transcribed and spoken person names are tagged with the normalized identity (e.g. `Barack_OBAMA`).

People whose identity cannot be infered from the rest of the video (and who are not famous people) are tagged as such in a consistent way (e.g. `Unknown_1` ≠ `Unknown_2`). Moreover, a set $\mathcal{F}$ of video frames was sampled (one every 10 seconds on average) and annotated more precisely with the position of each face and overlaid text bounding boxes.

2.2   Main Tasks

The main objective of the REPERE challenge is to answer the two following questions at any instant of the video:

$$\text{``who is speaking?''} \quad \text{``who is seen?''}$$

While the former question can be seen as the usual speaker diarization and tracking problem, the latter cannot be reduced to basic face recognition. As a matter of fact, a person who is seen from the back must also be recognized if a human could infer his/her identity from the context.

In the context of the REPERE challenge, we distinguish mono- and multimodal conditions as well as supervised and unsupervised person identification.

In the **mono-modal** case, only the raw acoustic signal can be used to detect and identify speakers (using its automatic transcription is not allowed). Similarly, visual person recognition cannot rely on name detection in overlaid text, for instance. On the other hand, in the **multi-modal** case, any of the four modalities (speaker, head, written or spoken) can be used to answer both questions.

In the **supervised** case, any previously trained identity model can be used to recognize a person. However, these models are strictly forbidden in the **unsupervised** conditions: person names can only be inferred from the **written** and **spoken** modalities. Therefore, any unsupervised method is – by design – multi-modal.

2.3   Estimated Global Error Rate

Though the whole test set is processed, evaluation is only performed on the annotated frames $\mathcal{F}$. For each frame f, let us denote #total(f) the number of persons in the reference. The hypothesis proposed by an automatic system can make three types of errors:

False Alarms (#fa) when it contains more persons than there actually are in the reference.

Missed Detections (#miss) when it contains less persons than there actually are in the reference.

Confusion (#conf) when the detected identity is wrong. For evaluation purposes, and because unknown people cannot – by definition – be recognized in any way, they are excluded from the scoring.

The Estimated Global Error Rate (EGER) is defined by:

$$\text{EGER} = \frac{\sum\limits_{f \in \mathcal{F}} \#\text{conf}(f) + \#\text{fa}(f) + \#\text{miss}(f)}{\sum\limits_{f \in \mathcal{F}} \#\text{total}(f)}$$

3   Monomodal Components

3.1   Who Is Speaking?

Speaker diarization is the process of partitioning the audio stream into homogeneous clusters without prior knowledge of the speaker voices. Our system SD relies on two steps: agglomerative clustering based on the BIC criterion to provide pure clusters followed by a second clustering stage using more complex models and cross-likelihood ratio (CLR) as distance between clusters [3].

```
audio ──▶ │ speaker diarization │ ─SD─▶ │ GSV/SVM speaker identification │ ──▶ S1
                                        │ GMM/UBM speaker identification │ ──▶ S2
```

Unsupervised speaker diarization is followed by a cluster-wise **speaker identification**. We implemented two systems [4]. The GSV-SVM system S1 uses the supervector made of the concatenation of the UBM-adapted GMM means to train one Support Vector Machine classifier per speaker. Our baseline system S2 follows the standard GMM-UBM paradigm. For both systems, each cluster is scored against all gender-matching speaker models, and the best scoring model is chosen if its score is higher than the decision threshold.

Three data sources were used for training 535 different speaker models in our experiments: the REPERE development set, the ETAPE[2] evaluation data and French radio data annotated into politicians speaking times.

3.2   Who Is Seen?

Figure below summarizes how our two submissions to the monomodal face recognition REPERE task are built and differ from each other.

Face detection and tracking is achieved using a detector-based face tracker in a particle-filter framework [5]. Face tracks are first initialized by scanning the first frame of every shot, and the subsequent fifth frame, using frontal, half-profile

---

[2] http://www.afcp-parole.org/etape.html

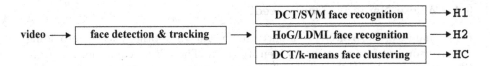

and profile face detectors – making face detection independent of the initial pose. Tracking is performed in an online manner, using the state of the previous frame to infer the location and head pose of the faces in the current frame. Head pose is explicitly incorporated in the continuous tracked state (alongside face position and size) as the head yaw-angle. A total of 11 yaw-angle-dependent face detectors are combined to score each particle of a track.

Features used in H1 are based on a local appearance-based approach [6]. Each face is normalized to a canonical pose and size and then split into 8×8 blocks. The top five Discrete Cosine Transform (DCT) coefficients are stored for each block. For recognition, one-vs-all second order polynomial kernel SVMs are trained for each person in the development set. Normalized classification scores are then accumulated over each track to obtain face identity scores in the range from 0 to 1.

In H2 approach, nine facial points located around the eyes, nose and mouth are automatically detected [7]. Each of them is described by a 490-dimensional HOG descriptor [8], yielding a 4410-dimensional feature vector per face. Logistic discriminant metric learning [9] is then used to project this vector into a 200-dimensional feature vector space where the ℓ_2 distance is combined with a nearest neighbor classifier for face recognition.

Alongside these supervised face recognition approaches, a **face clustering** system HC is also implemented for later use in multimodal unsupervised face recognition. It uses DCT-based descriptors from H1. Seven representative face samples are extracted from each face track using k-means algorithm. Then, hierarchical agglomerative clustering is performed until the elbow point of the distortion curve is reached – in order to get pure clusters.

3.3   Whose Name Is Written?

As illustrated in Figure 1, voice and appearance are not the only sources of information available to identify a person on TV. Hence, guests or reporters are sometimes introduced to the viewer using overlaid text containing their name.

A video OCR system was designed to automatically extract this information, which is especially useful in an unsupervised framework [10]. Overlaid text boxes are first detected using a coarse-to-fine approach with temporal tracking. Then, Google Tesseract open-source OCR system provides one transcription for every corresponding frames. They are finally combined to produce one single better transcription for each text box.

Using the shows from the development set and a list of famous people names extracted from Wikipedia, we were also able to extract the positions most likely used by each type of show to introduce a person. Only the detected names at these positions are used in later fusion.

3.4   Whose Name Is Pronounced?

Person names are also often pronounced by the anchor or other guests – providing a fourth source of information to identify them. Though we could not integrate this information in the final system in time for the first campaign, we did develop a system aiming at extracting these names.

First, a state-of-the-art speech-to-text system (STT) based on statistical modeling techniques [11] is used to automatically obtain the speech transcription. Then, a named entity recognition system NE [12] automatically detects several kind of named entities in the STT output, including the <pers> entity that is of interest in this work. It has a tree structure that is summarized in Figure 2.

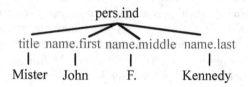

Fig. 2. Structured person entity

For precision concerns, we only detect <pers> entities for which both a first name and a last name are available (regardless of their order) – thus leaving room for great future improvement.

4   Multimodal Fusion

Once all monomodal components have been run on a video, their outputs can be combined to improve the overall person recognition performance. Figure 3 draws up their list, along with two slightly modified versions of OCR: extended to the whole speech turns (OCR$^+$) or speaker diarization clusters (OCR*).

4.1   Supervised Person Recognition

Since each modality relies on its own temporal segmentation, the first step consists in aligning the various timelines onto the finest common segmentation. The final decision is taken at this segmentation granularity. For each resulting segment S, a list of possible identities is built based on the output of all modalities. For each hypothesis identity P, a set of features is extracted:

- Does the name of P appear in OCR? in OCR$^+$? in OCR*?
- Duration of appearance of the name of P in OCR$^+$, in OCR*.
- Duration of appearance of any name in OCR$^+$, in OCR*.
- Their ratio.
- Speaker recognition scores for identity P provided by S1 and S2.
- Their difference to the best scores of any other identity.

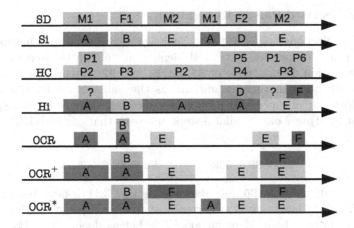

Fig. 3. Several annotation timelines

- Is $\mathcal{P}$ the most likely identity according to S1 or S2?
- Do the gender of $\mathcal{P}$ and the detected gender of the speaker cluster match?

Two additional features were added for face recognition:

- Face recognition scores for identity $\mathcal{P}$ provided by H1 and H2.
- Is $\mathcal{P}$ the most likely identity according to H1 or H2?

Based on these features, we trained several classifiers using Weka[3] to answer to the following question:

"is $\mathcal{P}$ speaking (or seen) for the duration of $\mathcal{S}$?"

Since these features can be either boolean or (unbounded) float, several classifiers insensitive to numerical types were used. As shown in Table 1, the best classifier for each task was selected using 2-fold cross-validation on the development set.

Table 1. Estimated Global Error Rate on development set

Classifier	Speaker	Head	Classifier	Speaker	Head
NaiveBayes	32.49	66.42	J48	28.20	63.12
RBFNetwork	32.12	65.61	ADTree	27.82	62.31
RandomTree	31.09	66.55	NBTree	26.98	64.73
RandomForest	29.41	**61.63**	MultilayerPerceptron	**26.24**	63.86

The best performance was obtained using multi-layer perceptron for `speaker` identification and random forest for its `face` counterpart. The identity with the highest score is selected for the `speaker` task and the N-best hypotheses for the `head` task – where N is the number of detected heads.

---

[3] http://www.cs.waikato.ac.nz/ml/weka

4.2 Unsupervised Person Recognition

As stated in Section 2, the REPERE challenge also includes an unsupervised track, for which no previously trained identity model can be used to perform person recognition. Hence, none of S1, S2, H1 and H2 systems can be used for people identification in these conditions, as they all rely on trained identity models. Both our unsupervised person identification systems Su (for speaker) and Hu (for head) rely on a similar 3-steps approach that can be schematized as follows:

$$Su = SD \otimes OCR \qquad Hu = HC \otimes OCR$$

First, speaker diarization (SD, introduced in Section 3.1) or face clustering (HC, from Section 3.2) labels every occurrence of the same person with a unique anonymous tag (e.g. head#1 or speaker#2). Let us denote $\mathcal{K} = \{k_1, \ldots, k_L\}$ the set of L resulting (speaker or face) clusters. Then, OCR (from Section 3.3) provides a short list of M possible names $\mathcal{N} = \{n_1, \ldots, n_M\}$. Finally, each person cluster (speaker or face) k is renamed after the name $\widehat{n}$ with the largest co-occurrence duration C_{kn}. In case a cluster has no co-occurring name, its tag is set to Unknown:

$$\forall k \in \mathcal{K}, \quad \widehat{n_k} = \begin{cases} \underset{n \in \mathcal{N}}{\operatorname{argmax}} C_{kn} & \text{if } \exists\, n \in \mathcal{N} \text{ such that } C_{kn} > 0, \\ \text{Unknown} & \text{otherwise.} \end{cases}$$

Note that this approach can lead to the propagation of one name n to multiple clusters. It does not blindly trust the speaker diarization or face clustering systems. In particular, it assumes that they may produce over-segmented clusters (for instance, split speech turns from one speaker into two or more clusters) that can be merged afterwards.

5 Results

Table 2 summarizes the performance of both mono- and multi-modal approaches, as well as of the unsupervised ones.

Table 2. Estimated Global Error Rate

Conditions	Speaker	Head
Supervised & monomodal	S1 — 48.1% S2 — 51.4%	H1 — 77.4% H2 — 82.5%
Supervised & multimodal	Ss — 25.8%	Hs — 61.5%
Unsupervised	Su — 52.2%	Hu — 68.0%

As expected, S1 (based on GSV-SVM) brings significant improvement (-3.3% EGER) over the simpler system S2 (based on GMM/UBM) for mono-modal speaker recognition. Why mono-modal **speaker** approaches (EGER $\approx 50\%$)

Table 3. Number of persons with trained identity model & best possible performance for a monomodal supervised person recognition oracle

	# persons	# modeled	Oracle EGER
Speaker	116	57 (49%)	33.8%
Head	145	50 (34%)	50.8%

Table 4. Is unsupervised recognition even possible? Number of persons whose name is written at least once & oracle performance

	# persons	# written	Oracle EGER
Speaker	116	74 (64%)	41.7%
Head	145	82 (56%)	32.5%

work much better than their **head** counterpart (EGER $\approx 80\%$) can be explained by looking at Table 3. Indeed, only one third of known persons in test set actually had a previously trained head model (vs. 49% for speaker recognition). Even an *oracle* capable of correctly identifying any previously modeled person (from the development set) could not reach better performance than 50% for head-based people recognition.

One of the most interesting contribution of this paper is the improvement brought by multi-modal fusion of the **written** modality with **speaker** and **head** ones: around 20% absolute EGER decrease for both of them (Ss vs. S1, and Hs vs. H1).

Finally, the other major result highlighted in this paper is that multi-modal unsupervised person recognition can achieve performance as good as monomodal supervised approaches (Su vs. S1 and Hu vs. H1). Yet, Table 4 shows that one can expect much better performance from Su and Hu. An *oracle* capable of giving the correct name to a person – as long as his/her name appears at least once during the show – can indeed reach around 42% (respectively 32%) EGER, when relying on perfect **speaker** diarization (resp. **head** clustering) and perfect **written** name detection.

6   Conclusion

In this paper, we described, evaluated and discussed QCOMPERE consortium submissions to the 2012 REPERE evaluation campaign dry-run. We showed that speaker identification (and face recognition) can be greatly improved when combined with name detection through video optical character recognition; and that unsupervised multimodal person recognition systems can achieve performance nearly as good as supervised monomodal ones.

Yet, there is plenty of room for improvement – in particular for our face recognition algorithms that showed their limits on this particular type of videos.

Moreover, the **spoken** modality has not yet been added to the game. It might indeed be very useful, especially in the unsupervised conditions: talk-show anchors, for instance, tend to introduce their guest by pronouncing their name. These are issues we will address for next year REPERE evaluation campaign.

Acknowledgment. This work was partly realized as part of the Quaero Program and the QCOMPERE project, respectively funded by OSEO (French State agency for innovation) and ANR (French national research agency).

References

1. Zhao, W., Chellappa, R., Phillips, P.J., Rosenfeld, A.: Face Recognition: a Literature Survey. ACM Comput. Surv. 35(4), 399–458 (2003)
2. Bimbot, F., Bonastre, J.F., Fredouille, C., Gravier, G., Magrin-Chagnolleau, I., Meignier, S., Merlin, T., Ortega-García, J., Petrovska-Delacrétaz, D., Reynolds, D.A.: A Tutorial on Text-Independent Speaker Verification. EURASIP J. Appl. Signal Process. 2004, 430–451 (2004)
3. Barras, C., Zhu, X., Meignier, S., Gauvain, J.L.: Multi-Stage Speaker Diarization of Broadcast News. IEEE Transactions on Audio, Speech and Language Processing 14(5), 1505–1512 (2006)
4. Le, V.B., Barras, C., Ferràs, M.: On the use of GSV-SVM for Speaker Diarization and Tracking. In: Proc. Odyssey 2010 - The Speaker and Language Recognition Workshop, Brno, Czech Republic, pp. 146–150 (June 2010)
5. Baeuml, M., Bernardin, K., Fischer, M., Ekenel, H., Stiefelhagen, R.: Multi-Pose Face Recognition for Person Retrieval in Camera Networks. In: Advanced Video and Signal-based Surveillance (2010)
6. Ekenel, H., Stiefelhagen, R.: Analysis of Local Appearance Based Face Recognition: Effects of Feature Selection and Feature Normalization. In: CVPR Biometrics Workshop (2006)
7. Everingham, M., Sivic, J., Zisserman, A.: "Hello! My name is... Buffy" – Automatic Naming of Characters in TV video. In: British Machine Vision Conference (2006)
8. Dalal, N., Triggs, B.: Histograms of Oriented Gradients for Human Detection. In: International Conference on Computer Vision & Pattern Recognition, pp. 886–893 (2005)
9. Guillaumin, M., Mensink, T., Verbeek, J., Schmid, C.: Face Recognition from Caption-based Supervision. International Journal of Computer Vision 96(1), 64–82 (2012)
10. Poignant, J., Besacier, L., Quénot, G., Thollard, F.: From Text Detection in Videos to Person Identification. In: IEEE ICME, Melbourne, Australia (2012)
11. Gauvain, J., Lamel, L., Adda, G.: The LIMSI Broadcast News Transcription System. Speech Communication 37(1-2), 89–109 (2002)
12. Dinarelli, M., Rosset, S.: Models Cascade for Tree-Structured Named Entity Detection. In: Proceedings of International Joint Conference of Natural Language Processing (IJCNLP), Chiang Mai, Thailand (November 2011)

Explicit Performance Metric Optimization for Fusion-Based Video Retrieval*

Ilseo Kim[1], Sangmin Oh[2], Byungki Byun[3],[**], A.G. Amitha Perera[2], and Chin-Hui Lee[1]

[1] Georgia Institute of Technology
[2] Kitware Inc.,
[3] Microsoft

Abstract. We present a learning framework for fusion-based video retrieval system, which explicitly optimizes given performance metrics. Real-world computer vision systems serve sophisticated user needs, and domain-specific performance metrics are used to monitor the success of such systems. However, the conventional approach for learning under such circumstances is to blindly minimize standard error rates and hope the targeted performance metrics improve, which is clearly suboptimal. In this work, a novel scheme to directly optimize such targeted performance metrics during learning is developed and presented. Our experimental results on two large consumer video archives are promising and showcase the benefits of the proposed approach.

1 Introduction

In many computer vision problems, the success of the learning algorithms is measured by domain- and application-specific performance metrics that simulate the real-world needs. One example is video retrieval, where diverse performance metrics are used to measure the quality of the system as well as the potential user experience. For example, [1,2] uses precision of top ranked retrieval results; TRECVID multimedia event detection (MED) task [3] prefers the ratio of 12.5:1 between probability of miss and false alarm; and [4] uses F-1 score. However, most learning methods optimize error rate, not the domain-specific performance measure, potentially yielding suboptimal solutions.

Another imperative aspect of real-world computer vision systems is the ability to fuse multiple features. The benefits of fusion have been clearly demonstrated in recent literature. For example, for video retrieval, [2,4] use multiple audio visual

---

* This work was supported by the Intelligence Advanced Research Projects Activity (IARPA) via Department of Interior National Business Center contract number D11PC20069. The U.S. Government is authorized to reproduce and distribute reprints for Governmental purposes notwithstanding any copyright thereon. Disclaimer: The views and conclusions contained herein are those of the authors and should not be interpreted as necessarily representing the official policies or endorsements, either expressed or implied, of IARPA, DOI/NBC, or the U.S. Government.
** The third author contributed to this work while he was with Georgia Institute of Technology.

A. Fusiello et al. (Eds.): ECCV 2012 Ws/Demos, Part III, LNCS 7585, pp. 395–405, 2012.
© Springer-Verlag Berlin Heidelberg 2012

cues, and [1,5,4] incorporate even text features from tags or the video webpages. However, most of these techniques use the traditional hinge loss error function during their learning process and have not attempted to directly optimize their preferred performance metrics.

In this work, we propose a learning framework which is able to directly optimize specific performance metrics, and demonstrate its value in effectively fusing multiple features. First, we introduce a systematic learning framework to *directly* optimize specific performance metrics beyond simple error rates. This direct optimization means that we can avoid the prolonged parameter search process typically required when the target metrics are optimized indirectly. Second, we apply our learning framework to fusion classifiers for consumer video retrieval problems. We show that our approach can learn competitive fusion classifiers while simultaneously optimizing given performance metrics. Our experiments on challenging video datasets show promising results.

2   Related Work

With our focus on optimizing performance metrics for fusion classifiers in consumer video retrieval, there are three areas of related work.

Performance Metric Optimization. Learning with explicit performance metric optimization has been mostly studied in machine learning community, albeit sparsely. [6] is a good reference and discusses optimization of a few performance metrics for SVM and boosting. However, most of them use elements of discrete search, different from our straightforward continuous optimization. Pareto criteria was introduced for multiple performance metric optimization [7]; however, Pareto criteria only provides partial ordering between multiple metrics, and joint optimization or complex metrics are not supported. In contrast, the basis of our approach, maximal figure-of-merit (MFoM), is a general framework which has been applied to problems such as text categorization, e.g., [8]. This work provides the first study on incorporating MFoM framework for audio-visual fusion for video retrieval, and presents the first principled approach to explicitly optimize the criteria in Sec. 3.

Fusion. An example fusion method is multiple kernel learning (MKL) [9]. In MKL, because a final fusion classifier is trained using all features jointly from early stages, it can be categorized as an 'early fusion' method. However, MKL does not systematically support the optimization of particular performance metrics, and reported results are not always competitive [10]. Other examples include the use of boosting for fusion [11,10]. A variant of LP-Boost introduced in [10] is more related to our work in terms of overall 'late fusion' architecture.

Fusion-Based Consumer Video Retrieval. The fusion of multi-modal features for consumer video retrieval is an on-going area of research. For example, [2] introduced CCV dataset and showcase a benchmark system which uses SVM as a fusion classifier. [4] introduces a retrieval system which improves performance by incorporating manually designed semantic hierarchy. [5,1] presents tag recommendation approaches on YouTube videos. For collaborative competition, TRECVID [3] runs an MED track and disseminates large datasets annually.

3 Explicit Performance Metric Optimization

In this section, we show how our approach explicitly optimizes targeted performance metrics. The novel elements are in the details of incorporating the performance metric into the objective function of a learning framework. For clarity, this paper focuses on our chosen metric; however, the derivation can be easily extended to other metrics of interest.

3.1 Evaluation Metric for Real-World Video Retrieval

In real-world retrieval tasks, the performance metrics that capture user desires can differ widely. For example, for a 'Google search', the important metric may be precision of the top-N. For a statistical analysis problem, on the other hand, recall may be the most important factor. In general, a large class of these metrics can be thought of as the weighted combinations of the probabilities of missed detections (P_{MD}) and false alarms (P_{FA}) at a particular operating point.

In this paper, we focus on the weighted sum of P_{MD} and P_{FA} at a particular ratio, wihch is suggested by the TRECVID MED tasks. Concretely, the goal is:

$$\text{Minimize } S_\tau = P_{MD} + \tau \times P_{FA} \quad \text{s.t.} \quad \frac{P_{MD}}{P_{FA}} = \tau. \tag{1}$$

In the following, we explain our approach with regards to this particular metric. However, we note again that the framework is more general, and can be easily applied to other metrics such as rankings, F_1 or average precision.

To optimize the metric in Eq. 1, a standard scheme is to learn a model with its own learning objectives and adjust detection thresholds until the desired ratio of $P_{MD}/P_{FA} = \tau$ is met where the metric S_τ will be computed. With this approach, however, there is no guarantee that the learning procedure will focus on improving performance at particular operating points. Our solution described in the following sections provides a principled approach to achieve such a goal.

3.2 Maximal-Figure-of-Merit (MFoM) Framework

Our learning task is formulated within a discriminative framework. Let $T = \{(x, y) \mid x \in R^D, y \in C\}$ be a set of training data, where x is a D-dimensional sample and y is a class label $C = \{C_+, C_-\}$, i.e., positive and negative.

Let $d(x; \Lambda) \in (-\infty, \infty)$ be a *class confidence function* which indicates the confidence that a sample x belongs to the positive class, C_+, where a large positive value corresponds to a high confidence. Given $d(\cdot)$ and Λ, the decision rule for a sample x is defined as *accept* $x \in C_+$ if $d(x; \Lambda) > 0$, and *reject* otherwise. Our goal is to learn the parameters Λ to optimize the targeted metric.

The core ideas of our MFoM-based learning approach are two-fold. First, we exploit the fact that most performance metrics and their sub-components, such as P_{MD} and P_{FA} in Eq. 1, can be expressed as a combination of the four sub-metrics from a confusion matrix: true positive (TP), false positive (FP), true negative (TN), and false negative (FN). Second, we approximate a target metric such as S_τ in Eq. 1, that is based on discrete error counts with a parameterized continuous and differentiable loss function $L(T; \Lambda)$.

In particular, the four sub-metrics are approximated as continuous functions using (truncated) sigmoid functions $\sigma(\cdot)$, which approaches one for high confidence for a positive class C_+, or approaches zero otherwise. In detail, the four approximated sub-metrics are expressed as follows:

$$\widehat{TP} = \sum_{(x,y)|y\in C_+} \sigma(d(x;\Lambda)), \quad \widehat{FN} = \sum_{(x,y)|y\in C_+} \left(1 - \sigma(d(x;\Lambda))\right) \quad (2)$$

$$\widehat{FP} = \sum_{(x,y)|y\in C_-} \sigma(d(x;\Lambda)), \quad \widehat{TN} = \sum_{(x,y)|y\in C_-} \left(1 - \sigma(d(x;\Lambda))\right)$$

where the sigmoid function, $\sigma(z) = \left(1 + \exp(-\alpha \cdot z)\right)^{-1}$, is parameterized by a positive constant α. Then, the overall loss function L is formulated from approximate sub-metrics ($\widehat{\cdot}$) using a mapping function $f(\cdot)$ as follows:

$$S_\tau \approx L(T; \Lambda) = f\left(\widehat{TP}, \widehat{FP}, \widehat{TN}, \widehat{FN}|\Lambda\right) \quad (3)$$

The role of the mapping function f is to reconstruct the loss function L accurately from sub-metrics. In fact, if the given target metric is a simple combination of sub-metrics, a precise mapping f is possible; e.g., for the F_1 metric where $F_1 = 2TP/(2TP + FN + FP)$. In some cases, however, the loss function may involve complex conditions such as the ratio constraint in Eq. 1, which needs approximation. We discuss this issue further in Sec. 3.3.

Finally, the optimal parameter Λ_{opt} that minimizes $L(T; \Lambda)$ is learned by the generalized probabilistic descent (GPD) [12] algorithms.

In all, there are three steps needed for the MFoM framework to be properly used for problems at hand. First, an appropriate parameterized class-confidence function $d(x; \Lambda)$ needs to be defined. The class of linear discriminant functions (LDF) is used in this work; but, in general, any parameterized function can be used [8] such as a kernelized discriminant function. Second, a good mapping function f needs to be designed to simulate the target metric. Finally, an effective constant α which controls the slope of the sigmoid function needs to be selected. The larger α is, the more accurate the approximations in Eq. 2. However, the smaller α is, the smoother the overall approximation in Eq. 3. In practice, we observed that the choice of α affects convergence speed, rather than accuracy, for most datasets with reasonable sizes.

3.3   Strategies for Complex Target Metric Approximation

In this section, we present how a good mapping function f in Eq. 3 can be designed to yield an accurate continous loss function $L(T; \Lambda)$ for a given target metric, with focus on the example metric introduced in Eq. 1.

For cases where complex target metrics prohibit the use of precise mapping function f, our proposed method is to approximate the target metric as a combination of simpler sub-functions. This usually involves a set of parameters Γ which control the relative weights of sub-functions. Optimal values for Γ may

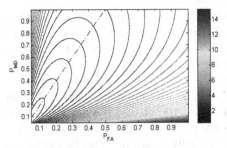

Fig. 1. Iso-contour curves of the loss function $L(T; \Lambda)$ defined in Eq. 4 when $\tau = 2$ and $\gamma = 1$. The dashed straight line corresponds to a iso-ratio $P_{MD}/P_{FA} = 2$.

be found through analytic approaches by minimizing the divergence between the resulting approximation f and the given target metric. On the other hand, good values for Γ can be found through cross validation as well. In fact, a more complex scheme of dynamically varying Γ during learning can be beneficial. For example, in Eq. 1, an optimal value for Γ may differ according to varying values of P_{MD} and P_{FA} during learning steps. The investigation of diverse detailed learning strategies is beyond the scope of this work, so we focus on illustrating these ideas on a concrete example below.

For the example target metric in Eq. 3, a linear sub-function for weighted error rate $\left[\widehat{P_{MD}} + \tau \times \widehat{P_{FA}}\right]$ can be incorporated in a straightforward manner where the approximations $\widehat{P_{MD}}$ and $\widehat{P_{FA}}$ are set to be equal to $\widehat{FN}$ and $\widehat{FP}$ (in Eq. 2) divided by the total number of positive and negative samples respectively. In addition, our mapping function should be designed to prefer user-specified target ratio τ between P_{MD} and P_{FA}. To enforce such a ratio constraint, we include a sub-function $R\left(\tau, P_{MD}/P_{FA}\right)$ which monotonically increases loss with respect to the difference between a target ratio τ and the exhibited ratio $\widehat{P_{MD}}/\widehat{P_{FA}}$. By incorporating both terms with a weighting parameter $\Gamma = \gamma$, the loss function $L(T; \Lambda)$ that approximates Eq. 1 is finally defined as:

$$L(T; \Lambda) = \left[\widehat{P_{MD}} + \tau \times \widehat{P_{FA}}\right] + \gamma \times \left[R\left(\tau, \widehat{P_{MD}}/\widehat{P_{FA}}\right)\right] \quad (4)$$

With small γ, learning focuses more on minimizing the error rate; however, the learned model is less likely to show a desired target error ratio τ, since the minimum value of the weighted error rate could be derived by reducing P_{FA} and sacrificing P_{MD}, especially when τ is large. On the other hand, with large γ, learning will focus more on meeting target error ratio, and less on decreasing error rates. In this work, we set γ to a fixed constant by searching through cross-validation; this has shown promising results.

Among many options for the ratio constraint approximation term R, we found the following form to work well and used it in this work:

$$R\left(\tau, \widehat{P_{MD}}/\widehat{P_{FA}}\right) = \left\{\log(\tau) - \log\left(\frac{\widehat{P_{MD}}}{\widehat{P_{FA}}}\right)\right\}^2 \quad (5)$$

The logarithmic squared form used above provides a computational advantage in that overall gradients can be easily computed as a sum of two terms (i.e., the gradients of P_{MD} and P_{FA}), avoiding the complications potentially caused by the direct use of division P_{MD}/P_{FA}.

To showcase the quality of the approximation in Eq. 4, Fig. 1 illustrates the iso-contour curves of the loss function, along with the iso-error ratio line (dashed). It can be clearly seen that the designed loss function is correlated with and declines towards the iso-error ratio line. This implies that the minimum value of the loss function defined in Eq. 4 can be found near the iso-error ratio line and left-bottom of the plot through the gradient descent procedures.

4   Late Score Fusion Framework

Our fusion-based video retrieval architecture is formulated within the *late fusion* paradigm. By late fusion, we mean that scores are computed independently by multiple base classifiers, one per feature type, and fusion classification is conducted on the computed scores. We use the MFoM approach to learn the fusion classifier parameters while explicitly optimizing target performance metrics.

4.1   Training Discriminative Score Fusion

During training, each base classifier is trained in a one-vs-all manner as well, and is used to generate a single score for the target class. For base classifiers, we used SVMs and their estimated probabilities as base classifier scores.

For a fusion classifier, we used MFoM learning scheme and adopted LDF as our class-confidence function as $d(x; \Lambda) = \sum_j \omega_j x_j + \omega_0$, where x is the score vector from base classifiers. Accordingly, MFoM systematically learns the weights for each score dimension for the target class, while explicitly optimizing the desired performance metric. This way, the fusion classifier becomes confident when multiple base classifier scores are high, and vice versa.

4.2   Additional Non-target Class Scores for Fusion Classifiers

To improve the performance of the fusion classifier further, we have investigated the use of additional non-target base classifier scores as inputs for 1-vs-All fusion classifiers, and observed consistent improvement in the final fusion classification. For example, we can incorporate the output by a base classifier trained for *Birthday party* for the training of a fusion system for the target class of *Wedding*. In this scheme, our fusion classifier uses $(M \times K)$-dimensional discriminative scores as its inputs, where there are K features and M base classifiers available. We believe the improvement is obtained because a fusion classifier systematically incorporates the correlation among event classes. Negative correlation as well as positive correlation could be helpful to acquire more discriminant power, i.e., high probabilities of outdoor event classes infer low confidence on indoor event classes. Fig. 5 illustrates the learned model parameters of fusion classifiers for

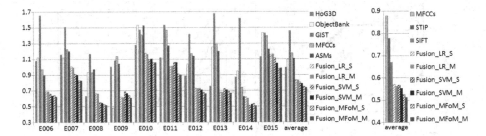

Fig. 2. Comparison of performance metrics (lower is better). Results by base classifiers, LR-, SVM-, and MFoM-based fusion with only target class scores ('_S') and additional non-target class scores ('_M') are shown; **(Left)** 10 classes and average from TRECVID 2011 MED and **(Right)** Average of 20 classes from the CCV dataset.

the 10 test event classes from TRECVID 2011 MED. The details of this experimental results, in addition to the comparison of performance with and without the use of non-target scores illustrated in Fig. 2 are described in Sec. 5.

5 Experiments and Result Analysis

We have applied the proposed framework on two challenging large-scale consumer video datasets including TRECVID '11 MED [3] and Columbia Consumer Video (CCV) [2] datasets. Both the size and complexity of the datasets are beyond other alternatives such as YouTube Sports [11] or Holywood datasets [13].

Our proposed methods are compared against other standard fusion techniques [10,4] based on logistic regression (LR) and linear SVM. We also compare fusion results with and without non-target base classifier scores, as discussed in Sec. 4.2. For all experiments, performance measure in Eq. 1 has been used, with $\tau = 12.5$ for TRECVID '11 MED and $\tau = 10$ for the CCV dataset. For the training of comparative approaches, we have assigned the weights equal to τ to positive samples. Operating points were selected on the training performance curves where the specified ratio τ is satisfied. Finally, the performance metrics are computed at the selected operating points.

5.1 Results on TRECVID 2011 MED Dataset

TRECVID 2011 MED corpus [3] provides an excellent test-bed for real-world video retrieval problems due to its large size (45K video clips) and huge inter- and intra-class content variability. For the MED task, there are 10 annotated event classes: E006-*Birthday party*, E007-*Changing a vehicle tire*, E008-*Flashmob gathering*, E009-*Getting a vehicle unstuck*, E010-*Grooming an animal*, E011-*Making a sandwich*, E012-*Parade*, E013-*Parkour*, E014-*Repairing an appliance*, and E015-*Working on a sewing project*.

Features and Base Classifiers. We used five types of features in our experiments: HoG3D [14], Object Bank (OB) [15], GIST [16], MFCCs [17], and ASMs

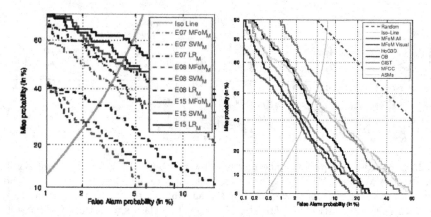

Fig. 3. (Left) Comparison among the fusion results for E007, E008, and E015. MFoM outperforms SVM and LR, especially along with the isoline of $P_{FA} : P_{MD} = 1 : 12.5$. **(Right)** Comparison among the results by the base and fusion classifiers for E012.

[17]. HoG3D is designed to be a low-level feature which captures texture and motion within videos, while OB consists of 177 semantic object detectors. MFCCs and ASMs are low- or mid-level audio features. For HoG3D, MFCC, and ASMs, we aggregated them into a clip-level bag-of-words feature, and learned a SVM with a histogram intersection kernel (HIK). For OB, we aggregated the features using max-pooling across multiple frames, and learned a linear SVM. For GIST, we learned a linear SVM using per-frame features, and performed clip-level classification by averaging the scores over multiple frames (Note this paper is not focused on the specifics of the base classifiers, but rather on their fusion).

Comparison of Fusion Performance on the Target Metric. The overall performance is summarized in Fig. 2(Left) where lower bars indicate superior performance. For training of different fusion classifiers (MFoM, SVM, LR), identical base classifier scores were used where the results with and without non-target class scores are denoted by postfixes _M and _S respectively. It can be observed that Fusion_MFoM_M (S_τ=0.7374) achieves the best performance consistently across all events, where it shows meaningful improvement of relatively 12.9% on average, against Fusion_LR_M (S_τ=0.8326) and 7.3% from Fusion_SVM_M (S_τ=0.7916). A similar result holds when using only target-class scores (_S).

The benefits of explicit performance metric optimization by our methods can be examined in more detail by looking at the the detection error tradeoff (DET) curves [18] for three test event classes shown in Fig. 3(Left). For the three event classes, the DET curves of the proposed MFoM approach (red) is superior or comparable to the other approaches. The remaining seven event classes showed similar patterns. However, while MFoM performs better than the other methods around the operating point, it is not always better away from the operating point (e.g. E15 (solid) and E07 (dot-dash)). This is not unexpected, since the goal of our approach is to explicitly improve performance at the operating point.

In terms of training parameters, the MFoM fusion classifiers were trained with the following parameters: $\alpha = 30$, and $\gamma = 0.2 \sim 0.4$. γ varies across classes, and was determined by cross-validation. Similar cross validation schemes were used to identify optimal parameters for SVM and LR.

Performance of Base Classifiers and the Effect of Fusion. Among the individual features shown in Fig. 2(Left), HoG3D shows the best performance on average, especially for events with temporal dynamics, such as E012. Next, OB is followed, which is competitive for relatively static classes, such as E011. Notably, audio features are competitive for audio-rich events such as E006.

All the fusion methods consistently outperform base classifiers, showing the clear benefits of fusion. For example, Fig. 3(Right) illustrates the effect of fusion by the proposed algorithm for E012 in the DET plot. It is notable that the fusion of the visual features (blue line) is better than the individual visual features (HoG3D, OB, and GIST). Furthermore, the final fusion result (red line) is improved by additionally incorporating the audio features.

For a qualitative assessment, Fig. 4 shows the top retrieved results for E011 from the proposed fusion approach and the two base classifiers. It is interesting to see that the two visual features seem complementary. HoG3D captures textures of scenes as well as temporal dynamics, while OB outputs responses from object detectors. Accordingly, some of the top results by HoG3D are mainly triggered by only textures such as roads or plain background, while most of the top results by OB contain a vehicle in the middle. Combining textures of scenes and responses from object detectors, the fusion results show much better performance that mostly have a vehicle object and a consistency in spatio-temporal dynamics.

Model Parameters and Effect of Additional Non-target Class Scores. The learned model parameters of our MFoM fusion scheme are illustrated in Fig. 5. Each row represents 50-dimensional LDF parameters, which is composed of the weights for the 10-dimensional scores from each feature block. A high positive value indicates strong positive correlation of the corresponding score element to a target class, while a negative value implies a negative correlation. Diagonal structures are observed because base classifiers learned for the same target class are more discriminative, as expected. It is also interesting to see correlations between different event types. For example, the fusion classifier for E011 (row 6) shows positive correlation with ObjectBank base classifiers (column 11) for E006, perhaps because both events frequently occur in dining rooms.

5.2   Results on Columbia Consumer Video dataset

As the second dataset, we applied the proposed fusion scheme on Columbia Consumer Video (CCV) dataset [2], which is another publicly available large-scale consumer video dataset. It includes 9,317 consumer videos in 20 complex event classes. In addition, it provides 3 types of precomputed bag-of-words features for SIFT, STIP [13], and MFCC.

We conducted identical experiments on CCV dataset. For all three types of features, base classifiers are learned using HIK SVMs. Then, LR-, SVM-, MFoM-

Top 30 results by fusion

Top 10 results by HoG3D

Top 10 results by OB

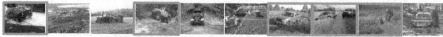

Fig. 4. Top 30 results by the proposed fusion algorithm, top 10 results by HoG3D and OB; sorted from top-left to botom-right. True positives are marked with green boxes.

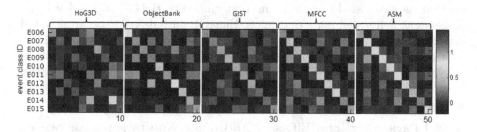

Fig. 5. Learned model parameters of LDF for the event classes E006–E015 on the MED dataset. Each row is the 50-dimensional model parameter of one-versus-all fusion classifiers for every event. Each column corresponds to one of 50 base classifiers.

based fusion classifiers were learned on top of the identical base classifiers. Experimental results on CCV dataset are summarized on Fig. 2(Right). Patterns identical to the results on TRECVID dataset has been observed for all 20 event classes. For brevity, only the average performance across all classes is shown here. Overall, there is an average gain of 10.1% and 6.3% achieved by MFoM fusion (MFoM_M, S_τ=0.5208), over the LR fusion method (LR_M, S_τ=0.5637) and the SVM fusion method (SVM_M, S_τ=0.5536), respectively.

6   Conclusion

In this work, we have presented our novel late-fusion framework for video retrieval, which explicitly optimizes given performance metrics. In particular, we showcased an effective approximation scheme for the important class of weighted metrics which can include sub-metrics such as P_{MD} and P_{FA}, and requirements for an operating point. Our experimental results on two large consumer video archives are promising, and suggest that our approach will add value for real-world computer vision applications with sophisticated user needs.

Acknowledgement. We thank Anthony Hoogs, Greg Mori, Arash Vahdat, Zhi Feng Huang, Weilong Yang, Scott McCloskey, and Ben Miller for helpful discussion and sharing features used in this work.

References

1. Toderici, G., Aradhye, H., Pasca, M., Sbaiz, L., Yagnik, J.: Finding meaning on youtube: Tag recommendation and category discovery. In: CVPR (2010)
2. Jiang, Y.G., Ye, G., Chang, S.F., Ellis, D., Loui, A.C.: Consumer video understanding: A benchmark database and an evaluation of human and machine performance. In: ACM ICMR (2011)
3. Smeaton, A.F., Over, P., Kraaij, W.: Evaluation campaigns and trecvid. In: ACM MIR (2006)
4. Wang, Z., Zhao, M., Song, Y., Kumar, S., Li, B.: Youtubecat: Learning to categorize wild web videos. In: CVPR (2010)
5. Yang, W., Toderici, G.: Discriminative tag learning on youtube videos with latent sub-tags. In: CVPR (2011)
6. Joachims, T.: A support vector method for multivariate performance measures. In: ICML (2005)
7. Calonder, M., Lepetit, V., Fua, P.: Pareto-optimal Dictionaries for Signatures. In: CVPR (2010)
8. Gao, S., Wu, W., Lee, C.H., Chua, T.S.: A mfom learning approach to robust multiclass multi-label text categorization. In: ICML (2004)
9. Varma, M., Ray, D.: Learning the discriminative power-invariance trade-off. In: ICCV (2007)
10. Gehler, P.V., Nowozin, S.: On feature combination for multiclass object classification. In: IEEE International Conference on Computer Vision, ICCV (2009)
11. Liu, J., Luo, J., Shah, M.: Recognizing realistic actions from videos in the wild. In: CVPR (2009)
12. Katagiri, S., Juang, B.H., Lee, C.H.: Pattern recognition using a family of design algorithm based upon the generalized probabilistic descent method. Proc. of the IEEE, 2345–2373 (1998)
13. Laptev, I., Marszalek, M., Schmid, C., Rozenfeld, B.: Learning realistic human actions from movies. In: CVPR (2008)
14. Kläser, A., Marszalek, M., Schmid, C.: A spatio-temporal descriptor based on 3D-gradients. In: BMVC (2008)
15. Li, L.J., Su, H., Xing, E.P., Fei-Fei, L.: Object bank: A high-level image representation for scene classification and semantic feature sparsification. In: Proceedings of the Neural Information Processing Systems, NIPS (2010)
16. Oliva, A., Torralba, A.: Modeling the shape of the scene: a holistic representation of the spatial envelope 42, 145–175 (2001)
17. Lee, C.H., Soong, F., Juan, B.H.: A segment model based approach to speech recognition. In: ICASSP (1988)
18. Martin, A.F., Doddington, G., Kamm, T., Ordowski, M., Przybocki, M.: The DET curve in assessment of detection task performance. In: Eurospeech (1997)

Unsupervised Classemes

Claudio Cusano[1], Riccardo Satta[2], and Simone Santini[3,*]

[1] Department of Informatics, Systems and Communication (DISCo), Università degli Studi di Milano-Bicocca, Viale Sarca 336, 20126 Milano, Italy
[2] Department of Electrical and Electronic Engineering, Università di Cagliari, Italy
[3] Escuela Politécnica Superior, Universidad Autónoma de Madrid, Spain

Abstract. In this paper we present a new model of *semantic* features that, unlike previously presented methods, does not rely on the presence of a labeled training data base, as the creation of the feature extraction function is done in an unsupervised manner.

We test these features on an unsupervised classification (clustering) task, and show that they outperform primitive (low-level) features, and that have performance comparable to that of supervised semantic features, which are much more expensive to determine relying on the presence of a labeled training set to train the feature extraction function.

1 Introduction

Several authors have proposed, in the last few years, the use of class information in the definition of features or, to say it in a nother way, the definition of features based not only on the image data but also on certain, limited, semantic information. The general schema of these features is as follows. Consider a reference database of images $D = \{x_1, \ldots, x_n\}$, and a reference partition of D into classes (according to some semantically meaningful criterion), $\mathcal{D}$, with $\mathcal{D} = \{D_1, \ldots, D_q\}$, $\bigcup_i D_i = D$, and for all $i \neq j$, $D_i \cap D_j = \emptyset$. The subsets D_i may or may not have associated labels. Also, let $\mathcal{I}$ be a space of images, and $\phi : \mathcal{I} \to X$ a feature extractor function from images to a suitable feature space X.

These features and the reference data base are used to train, in a supervised way, q classifiers $C_1, \ldots C_q$ with $C_i : X \to [0, 1]$ determining the degree to which the feature vector X belongs to the category i. The outputs of these classifiers are then used, in combination with the low level feature extractor ϕ, to create a semantic feature vector for an unknown image x. That is, an image is represented by the q-dimensional vector

$$F(x) = [C_1(\phi(x)), \ldots, C_q(\phi(x))] \tag{1}$$

we call $F : \mathcal{I} \to [0, 1]^q$ a *supervised semantic* feature extraction function. This general scheme is sometimes implemented with a slight modification, which has

---

* The authos was supported in part by the *Ministerio de Educación y Ciencia* under the grant N. TIN2011-28538-C02, *Novelty, diversity, context and time: new dimensions in next-generation information retrieval and recommender systems.*

A. Fusiello et al. (Eds.): ECCV 2012 Ws/Demos, Part III, LNCS 7585, pp. 406–415, 2012.

been shown to improve perfoamance in certain cases. The feature space X is partitioned into p parts (the nature of this partition depends on the specific method used), and q classifiers corresponding to the q categories are trained separately on these p partitions. In this case, the feature vector will have dimension pq. The recent literature proposes several instantiations of this general scheme. Vogel and Schiele presented an image representation formed by local semantic descriptions [18]. They classify local image regions into semantic concept classes such as water, rocks, or foliage. Images are represented through the frequency of occurrence of these local concepts. Li *et al.* [12] in their *object bank* system use 177 object recognizers at 12 different scales, over 21 image regions, obtaining a vector of $177 \times 12 \times 21 = 44,604$ components.

Ciocca *et al.* presented an image descriptor, that they called "prosemantic features", based on the output of a number of image classifiers [3]. The feature vector is created, by concatenating the output of 56 different soft classifiers trained to identify 14 different classes on the basis of four different low-level features.

Torresani *et al.* [17] presented a descriptor composed of the output of 2,659 classifiers trained to recognized scene-level visual concepts (called "classemes") taken from the LSCOM ontology [13].

In [4] we tested these *supervised* features against a representative sample of *primitive* features (low-level features extracted directly fom the images) on an unsupervised classification task. We wanted to test whether the use of supervised learning in the feature definition phase would help in the unsupervised classification of hitherto unseen classes. We performed tests on three different data bases: the Simplicity data set [19] (a subset of the Corel data set), the GIST scene data set [14], and Li and Fei-Fei's event data set [11]. The results were that supervised features outperform primitive ones in all the unsupervised classification tasks. The relative merits of the three types of features that were tested (classemes, prosemantic, object bank) are more debatable and depend on the data set on which we are testing, but the advantage of using semantic information in order to define the features have been clearly estabished.

The work in this paper begins with an important observation from [17]:

> It is not required or expected that these base categories will provide useful semantic labels [...]. On the contrary, we work on the assumption that modern category recognizers are essentially quite dumb: so a `swimmer` recognizer looks mainly for water texture, and the `bomber␣plane` recognizer contains some tuning for the "C" shapes corresponding to the airplane nose and perhaps the "V" shapes at the wing and tail. [..] The true building blocks are not the classeme labels that we can see, but their underlying dumb components, which we cannot.

If this observation is correct, then the class labels (that is, the *a priori* division into semantically defined classes) adds nothing, in the best scenario, to the classifiers. In the worst scenario, the use of an *a priori* division can actually be counterproductive, as class divisions might cut across the *underlying dumb components* that are what the classifiers really identify. For example, the existence of two classes, `airplane` and `bird` forces the classifiers to disregard the "C" shape of the nose, which is a feature common to two classes. A classifier not forced to distinguish between planes and birds could make a better use of this important low-level clue.

In this paper we propose to replace the *supervised* classification used to train the classifiers $C_1, \ldots, C_q$ with *unsupervised* classification, in which the only external constraint is the number of classes q, which determines the dimension of the semantic feature space. We see two main advantages in this: on the one hand, it will be possible to derive the feature computing function using an *unlabeled* training set, rather than a labeled one as it is the case for supervised features. On the other hand, we hope that the classifiers will "latch" directly to the significant visual cues that determine the structure of the training set rather than having categories imposed from outside.

2   Unsupervised Classeme

Our method is a simple modification of the supervised (semantic) feature extraction. We are given a training data set D and, possibly, a desired dimensionality q. The method operates as follows:

i) define a *low-level* feature extractor $\phi : \mathcal{I} \to X$ for a suitable low-level feature space X;

ii) use a clustering algorithm on the feature space X to divide the data base D into q classes $D_1, \ldots, D_q$;

iii) use the classes $D_1, \ldots, D_q$ as ground truth in order to train q classifiers $C_1, \ldots, C_q$ with outputs in $[0, 1]$ to recognize the classes.

iv) define the *unsupervised classemes* feature vector for an image x as

$$U(x) = [C_1(\phi(x)), \ldots, C_q(\phi(x))] \tag{2}$$

with $U : \mathcal{I} \to [0, 1]^q$.

The value q can either be a design parameter (this is the case of our tests, in which we used a k-means clustering algorithm for the first unsupervised clustering) or be determined automatically by the system if a clustering algorithm is used that autonomously determines the number of classes (such as affinity propagation [7] of hierarchical clustering [20]). This possibility adds flexibility to the use of these features: if the design calls for a feature vector of a specific size, then the designer can use k-means, thus establishing the number of classes and therefore the size of the vector. Otherwise, the designer can use a clustering algorithm without a predefined number of clusers and let the system determine the size of the feature vector based on the characteristics of the training set.

Note that although the classifiers $C_1, \ldots, C_q$ are trained using a supervised algorithm, the method, as a whole, is unsupervised. This gives it an important advantage with respect to supervised semantic features, as the determination of the feature extraction function doesn't need a labeled data base.

2.1   Implementation Details

In the tests that we propose in this paper, we used four feature sets: a RGB histogram, the first and second YUV moments on a 9×9 subdivision, an edge direction histograms (EDH) computed on a 8×8 subdivision, and bag of SIFT descriptors. Each one of the four features was considered separately. Moreover, each of the feature spaces was partitioned in four sub-spaces, and classifiers were trained separately for each one of them (e.g. the 512 bin RGB histogram was divided in four sub-histograms of 128 bins each), except the YUV block-histogram, which was partitioned in three sub-spaces. In the end, the feature space was partitioned in $p = 4 + 4 + 4 + 3 = 15$ sub-spaces.

Each sub-space of the partition resulted in q clusters (so that we have a total of $15q$ clusters, which is also the dimension of the final feature vector). The number of clusters was 5 or 10 depending on the test (see below), giving us feature vectors of size 150 or 75.

For each sub-space of the partition, we trained classifiers to recognize the q classes derived from the clusters, using for each cluster a one-vs-all training (samples from the selected cluster are used as positive examples, and samples from all the others are used as negative examples, subsampling the negative classes so as to obtain a balanced set). The classifiers $C_1, \ldots, C_{15q}$ were SVM with Gaussian kernels.

3   The Comparison Methods

We have compared our unsupervised classemes with ten other features on an unsupervised classification problem, three *supervised* methods, and seven primitive features.

3.1   Classemes

Torresani *et al.* use as feature vector the output of a large number of weakly trained object category classifiers [17].

In terms of our schema, the low level space X was composed of Color GIST [15], Pyramid of Histograms of Oriented Gradients [5], Pyramid self-similarity [1], and bag of SIFT descriptors. The space was not partitioned. A large number of classifiers ($q = 2659$) was trained on categories taken from the LSCOM ontology [13]. Each classifier has been trained one-vs-all on a category with the LP-β multi-kernel algorithm [8].

Classemes has been presented as a descriptor for image retrieval. Torresani *et al.* have shown that classification accuracy on object category recognition is comparable with the state of the art, but with a computational cost orders of magnitude lower.

3.2   Prosemantic Features

Prosemantic features are based on the classification of images into a set of 14 categories ($q = 14$): animals, city, close-up, desert, flowers, forest, indoor, mountain, night, people, rural, sea, street, and sunset. Some classes describe the image at a scene level (city, close-up, desert, forest, indoor, mountain, night, rural, sea, street, sunset), while other describe the main subject of the picture (animals, flowers, people).

The low-level feature space X is defined by four low-level features. The space is partitioned by features, that is, for each class, four different classifiers are defined, each one based on one of the four low-level categories ($p = 4$).

Each classifier has been independently trained on images downloaded from various image search engines with different parameters. The classifiers' output was normalized by a linear transformation

$$\phi'_{c,p}(x) = a_{c,p}\phi_{c,p}(x) + b_{c,p},\tag{3}$$

where the parameters $a_{c,p}$ and $b_{c,p}$ are determined by a logistic regression which maps the score of the classifier to an estimate of the posterior probability

$$p(c|x) \simeq (1 + \exp(-\phi'_{c,p}(x)))^{-1}.\tag{4}$$

3.3   Object Bank

Object Bank is an image representation constructed from the responses of many object detectors, which can be viewed as a "generalized object convolution" [12]. Two state-of-the-art detectors are used: the latent SVM object detectors [6] for most of the blobby objects such as tables, cars, humans, etc, and a texture classifier [9] for more texture-based objects such as sky, road, sand, etc.

A large number of object detectors are run across an image at different scales. Each scale and each detector yield an initial response map of the image. The authors used 177 object detectors at 12 detection scales. Each response map is then aggregated according to a spatial pyramid of three levels ($1 + 4 + 16 = 21$ regions). The final descriptor is thus composed of $177 \times 12 \times 21 = 44,604$ components ($q = 44,604$).

The authors evaluated the object bank descriptor in the context of scene categorization. By using linear classifiers, they obtained a significant improvement against low-level representations on a variety of data sets.

3.4   Primitive Features

We also compared our feature vector with seven state of the art primitive features. We considered three descriptors defined by the MPEG-7 standard–namely the Scalable Color Descrptor (SCD), the Color Layout Descriptor (CLD), and the Edge Histogram Descriptor (EHD) [16]–the Color and Edge Directivity Descriptor (CEDD) [2], the Gist features [14], bag of features [21], and the spatial pyramid representation [10].

4   The Data Sets

We tested these feature vectors for unsupervised classification on three data bases representative of different situations common in the applications. The first experiment has been conducted on the Simplicity data set [19], which is a subset of the COREL data set, formed by ten categories containing 100 images each. It can be considered an "easy" data set, since the ten categories are clearly distinct, with little or no ambiguity. On the one hand, this restricts the significance of the experimentation, but on the other hand, it makes the results more reliable (since there is only a single, reasonable way of dividing the data in ten meaningful clusters).

The second group of tests was done on the scene recognition data set collected by Oliva and Torralba [14] to evaluate features and methods for scene classification. This data set contains eight outdoor scene categories: coast, mountain, forest, open country, street, inside city, tall buildings and highways, for a total of 2,688 images (260–410 images per class). With respect to the Simplicity data set, there is less inter-class variability, and are therefore the classes are expected to be harder to separate.

The third data set considered contains images of eight different classes of events [11]. This data set has been collected in order to evaluate event classification methods. It is composed of 1,579 images (eight classes, 137–250 images per class) showing people performing various sport activities (rock climbing, rowing, badminton, bocce, croquet, polo, sailing, and snowboarding). Of the three data sets, this is undoubtedly the most challenging, as events can't be classified only at a scene level, but object detection and pose recognition are often required.

5   The Tests

For each of the three data bases that we are using, we have a ground truth with a definite number of categories (ten for Simplicity, eight for the Torralba data base and for the Event data set). Since our purpose here was to test the features, we avoided possible instabilities deriving from the performance of the clustering algorithm by using k-means, where k was set to the same number of classes as the ground truth. In the following, to avoid confusion, we shall refer to the classes discovered by the clustering algorithm as *u-classes*, and to the actual (ground truth) classes as *g-classes*.

In order to compute the classification rate, for each one of the u-classes obtained by the clustering algorithm, we determine which one of the g-classes is most represented, and assign that u-class to it. This entails that several u-classes can be taken as representatives of the same g-class. In this case, all images of the g-class classified in either of the u-classes is taken as correct. An example of this can be seen in table 2 (matrix on the bottom-left), which shows the confusion matrix for the classeme features on the Simplicity data set. In both u-classes 6 and 7, the most represented g-class is *Horses*, so both these u-classes are considered as representatives of Horses, and both the 44 images of horses in u-class 6 and the 43 images in u-class 7 are considered as correct classifications. On the other hand, it may happen that a g-class is not the most represented class in any u-class. This is the case, in the same matrix, of the class *Elephants*. In this case, all elephant images are considered misclassified.

Table 1. Summary of the classification results for the ten methods on the three test data bases

Feature	Simplicity	Scene	Events
Unsupervised classemes	81.7	65.0	57.0
Classemes	65.0	76.4	62.0
Prosemantic	73.7	78.3	64.9
Object Bank	57.8	70.0	43.1
GIST	33.7	57.1	46.2
Bag of SIFT	49.0	39.1	36.6
Spatial Pyramid	47.4	43.0	36.7
CEDD	62.2	38.3	40.4
SCD	42.3	27.1	27.9
CLD	54.1	32.1	32.1
EHD	50.4	59.5	49.6

The results are summarized in table 1. A first general observation is that unsupervised classemes work better than supervised semantic on the Simplicity data base and slightly worse on the scene and event data base. In any case, they outperform all primitive features. Apart from the better performance of unsupervised classemes on the Simplicity data base, this is in line with what one can intuitively expect: unsupervised classemes use more information than primitive features (they use a training set of images) but less than supervised (they don't need a labeled data set), and their performance is placed accordingly. Nevertheless, in some cases, unsupervised classemes can outperform semantic features, despite the absence of labels.

In order to analyze more closely these differences, we show, in tables 2–4 the confusion matrices for unsupervised and supervised semantic features. If we consider again Torresani's observation reported in the introduction, it is clear that unsupervised classemes *lock-in* to the most salient visual features independently of the presence of labels, and form clusters based on these salient features, while supervised features have to find a compromise between salient visual features and the labels that are given to them. If we compare unsupervised classemes with prosemantic on the Simplicity data base, we notice, for instance, the 68 misclassifications of prosemantics between Africa people and Food. Some pictures of Africa people have a color structure similar to pictures of food, so the labeling would in this case give indications contrary to the visual features, and this probably provokes the creation of weaker classifiers (viz. classifiers with a narrower margin). The same happens in the case of classemes between horses and elephants, to the extent that the g-category *Elephants* disappears, and two u-categories are assigned to *Horse*. On the other hand, in the scene data base, we see that, in spite of the lower overall performances, unsupervised classemes correctly identify all the g-classes, although in some cases there is considerable confusion, such as between the classes. Consider, for example, the classes *Mountain* and *open country*. What brings down the performance of

Table 2. Confusion matrices for unsupervised classemes, Prosemantic, classemes, and Object Bank features on the **Simplicity** data base

Class	Unsupervised classemes										Prosemantic									
	1	2	3	4	5	6	7	8	9	10	1	2	3	4	5	6	7	8	9	10
Africa people	79	-	-	7	-	1	6	3	3	1	2	-	6	-	68	4	-	18	-	2
Buses	-	93	-	1	-	-	1	5	-	-	94	-	-	-	-	-	5	1	-	-
Dinosaurs	-	-	100	-	-	-	-	-	-	-	-	-	100	-	-	-	-	-	-	-
Elephants	3	-	-	77	-	-	19	-	-	1	-	-	61	-	3	11	-	9	14	2
Flowers	3	-	-	1	87	2	-	1	6	-	-	-	-	99	1	-	-	-	-	-
Food	4	-	-	15	2	75	-	1	2	1	-	5	1	11	71	-	-	12	-	-
Horses	-	-	-	-	-	-	97	1	2	-	-	-	-	-	-	88	-	12	-	-
Monuments	6	1	-	8	2	-	3	67	9	4	9	-	4	1	1	56	23	4	1	
Mountains	1	-	-	5	-	-	4	2	74	14	-	-	7	-	-	-	3	1	77	12
Sea	2	-	-	7	-	-	2	4	17	68	1	-	6	-	3	-	5	7	10	68

Class	Classemes										Object Bank									
	1	2	3	4	5	6	7	8	9	10	1	2	3	4	5	6	7	8	9	10
Africa people	61	-	-	14	8	10	-	5	1	1	32	1	-	9	-	41	8	2	6	1
Buses	-	92	-	-	-	-	6	2	-	-	-	97	-	1	-	-	2	-	-	-
Dinosaurs	-	-	98	-	-	-	-	-	-	-	-	-	99	-	-	-	-	-	-	1
Elephants	14	-	-	-	1	42	7	3	33	-	1	-	-	42	-	1	18	5	14	19
Flowers	5	-	-	91	4	-	-	-	-	-	6	-	-	-	58	36	-	-	-	-
Food	15	-	-	6	65	4	-	-	10	-	10	-	1	4	2	56	-	-	25	2
Horses	4	-	-	-	-	44	43	4	5	-	2	-	-	5	-	-	66	8	18	1
Monuments	4	2	1	-	3	5	-	64	20	1	12	8	2	13	-	4	2	39	13	7
Mountains	2	-	1	1	3	31	-	1	47	14	4	-	-	37	-	1	3	2	31	22
Sea	1	-	-	1	5	4	-	3	41	45	1	-	-	20	-	2	2	3	14	58

Table 3. Confusion matrices for the unsupervised classemes, Prosemantic, classemes, and Object Bank features on the **Scene** data base

Class	Unsupervised classemes								Prosemantic							
	1	2	3	4	5	6	7	8	1	2	3	4	5	6	7	8
Coast	224	3	68	5	19	37	2	2	294	2	14	-	27	20	-	3
Forest	-	311	-	-	4	13	-	-	-	291	-	1	26	10	-	-
Highway	51	3	158	18	5	8	13	4	8	1	206	7	4	12	14	8
Inside city	8	2	1	185	2	2	38	70	-	-	5	178	-	2	84	39
Mountain	10	36	9	3	260	53	1	2	9	9	2	-	332	22	-	-
Open country	36	96	20	2	54	197	3	2	24	32	4	-	54	294	2	-
Street	-	-	3	43	12	2	203	29	-	-	5	32	2	1	245	7
Tall building	3	6	15	72	28	11	12	209	2	-	2	53	9	1	25	264

Class	Classemes								Object Bank							
	1	2	3	4	5	6	7	8	1	2	3	4	5	6	7	8
Coast	201	3	92	-	1	62	-	2	254	3	1	2	41	58	1	-
Forest	-	312	-	-	14	2	-	-	-	302	-	23	-	-	3	-
Highway	21	-	202	9	5	15	8	-	129	-	6	5	22	86	12	-
Inside City	1	-	-	249	-	-	51	7	3	-	241	-	-	3	27	34
Mountain	4	17	6	-	274	71	2	-	4	29	-	253	31	47	8	2
Open Country	11	19	57	-	46	276	-	1	37	13	-	54	205	98	3	-
Street	-	-	1	30	-	-	259	2	1	2	9	4	-	9	248	19
Tall Building	-	4	-	26	1	-	45	280	-	4	53	6	-	1	12	280

unsupervised classemes is in this cases the presence of g-classes poorly separated from the visual point of view. Many images of *Mountain* do satisfy the visual conditions to be considered *open country* and, in the absence of a label that forces the two g-classes to be separated, they form similar clusters, leading to the rlatively high confusion between the two g-classes. Many cases of high-confusion in unsupervised classemes can be ascribed to the presence of classes poorly separable from the visual point of view, with many images that could belong to one or the other (Forest vs. open country, street vs. inside city vs. tall building, etc.). In this case, the supervised features have the advantage that the presence of the label forces the classifiers to focus on certain visual features rather ignoring others (e.g. the classifier of *tall building* is forced to concentrate on long vertical lines). In the event data base, most methods work rather poorly, as many classes are not distinguishable based on the general characteristics of the scene, their identification depending on the presence of specific objects (such as the presence of a mallet to distinguish *croquet* from *bocce*).

Table 4. Confusion matrices for unsupervised classemes, Prosemantic, classemes, and Object Bank features on the **Event** data base

Class	Unsupervised classemes								Prosemantic							
	1	2	3	4	5	6	7	8	1	2	3	4	5	6	7	8
Rock climbing	171	2	3	6	5	2	2	3	170	1	-	-	5	3	-	15
Rowing	3	165	12	6	32	14	8	10	5	156	6	2	9	25	42	5
Badminton	3	14	89	67	5	13	4	5	1	3	168	6	2	14	3	3
Bocce	38	1	15	13	50	13	1	6	10	1	15	15	60	28	2	6
Croquet	24	2	65	13	109	13	-	10	3	2	12	109	76	31	-	3
Polo	4	2	8	52	29	83	-	4	5	1	19	56	13	82	-	6
Sailing	5	23	5	9	7	1	115	25	-	16	5	-	4	5	126	34
Snowboarding	21	5	7	15	20	8	9	115	12	13	1	-	5	11	10	138

Class	Classemes								Object Bank							
	1	2	3	4	5	6	7	8	1	2	3	4	5	6	7	8
Rock climbing	158	-	-	27	-	3	1	5	97	78	-	-	-	5	3	11
Rowing	1	187	6	19	19	8	4	6	2	1	106	76	17	5	3	40
Badminton	-	1	150	5	28	7	-	9	-	-	14	4	145	17	8	12
Bocce	7	2	8	82	15	21	1	1	7	7	4	4	16	17	54	28
Croquet	15	2	1	88	83	44	-	3	5	9	22	44	15	73	38	30
Polo	5	3	14	29	36	90	3	2	2	1	11	29	24	49	42	24
Sailing	-	15	2	5	12	5	146	5	-	2	28	43	41	43	28	5
Snowboarding	8	10	3	44	13	14	21	77	27	5	8	16	15	14	63	42

6   Conclusions

We have presented a new model of *semantic* features that, unlike previous methods, does not rely on the presence of a labeled training data base, as the creation of the feature extraction function is done in an unsupervised way.

We have compared our features with three supervised semantic features and seven primitive ones, showing that the performance of unsupervised classemes is definitely better than that of primitive features and of the same order as that of supervised ones. Given the broad availability of large collections of non labeled images, we believe that the method presented here represents a viable alternative to primitive features and supervised semantic features.

References

1. Bosch, A., Zisserman, A., Munoz, X.: Image classification using rois and multiple kernel learning. International Journal of Computer Vision 2008, 1–25 (2008)
2. Chatzichristofis, S.A., Boutalis, Y.S.: CEDD: Color and Edge Directivity Descriptor: A Compact Descriptor for Image Indexing and Retrieval. In: Gasteratos, A., Vincze, M., Tsotsos, J.K. (eds.) ICVS 2008. LNCS, vol. 5008, pp. 312–322. Springer, Heidelberg (2008)
3. Ciocca, G., Cusano, C., Santini, S., Schettini, R.: Prosemantic Features for Content-Based Image Retrieval. In: Detyniecki, M., García-Serrano, A., Nürnberger, A. (eds.) AMR 2009. LNCS, vol. 6535, pp. 87–100. Springer, Heidelberg (2011)
4. Ciocca, G., Cusano, C., Santini, S., Schettini, R.: Supervised features for unsupervised image categorization. IEEE Transactions on Pattern Analysis and Machine Intelligence (submitted, 2012)
5. Dalal, N., Triggs, B.: Histograms of oriented gradients for human detection. In: IEEE Computer Society Conference on Computer Vision and Pattern Recognition, CVPR 2005, vol. 1, pp. 886–893 (2005)

6. Felzenszwalb, P.F., Girshick, R.B., McAllester, D., Ramanan, D.: Object detection with discriminatively trained part-based models. IEEE Transactions on Pattern Analysis and Machine Intelligence 32(9), 1627–1645 (2010)

7. Frey, B.J., Dueck, D.: Clustering by passing messages between data points. Science 315(5814), 972–976 (2007)

8. Gehler, P., Nowozin, S.: On feature combination for multiclass object classification. In: 2009 IEEE 12th International Conference on Computer Vision, pp. 221–228 (2009)

9. Hoiem, D., Efros, A.A., Hebert, M.: Automatic photo pop-up 24(3), 577–584 (2005)

10. Lazebnik, S., Schmid, C., Ponce, J.: Beyond bags of features: Spatial pyramid matching for recognizing natural scene categories. In: 2006 IEEE Computer Society Conference on Computer Vision and Pattern Recognition, vol. 2, pp. 2169–2178 (2006)

11. Li, L.J., Fei-Fei, L.: What, where and who? classifying events by scene and object recognition. In: Proc. IEEE Int'l Conf. Computer Vision, pp. 1–8 (2007)

12. Li, L.J., Su, H., Xing, E.P., Fei-Fei, L.: Object bank: A high-level image representation for scene classification and semantic feature sparsification. In: Advances in Neural Information Processing Systems (2010)

13. Naphade, M., Smith, J.R., Tesic, J., Chang, S.F., Hsu, W., Kennedy, L., Hauptmann, A., Curtis, J.: Large-scale concept ontology for multimedia. IEEE Multimedia 13(3), 86–91 (2006)

14. Oliva, A., Torralba, A.: Modeling the shape of the scene: A holistic representation of the spatial envelope. Int'l J. Computer Vision 42(3), 145–175 (2001)

15. Oliva, A., Torralba, A.: Building the gist of a scene: The role of global image features in recognition. Progress in Brain Research 155, 23–36 (2006)

16. Sikora, T.: The MPEG-7 visual standard for content description-an overview. IEEE Trans. Circuits and Systems for Video Technology 11(6), 696–702 (2001)

17. Torresani, L., Szummer, M., Fitzgibbon, A.: Efficient Object Category Recognition Using Classemes. In: Daniilidis, K., Maragos, P., Paragios, N. (eds.) ECCV 2010, Part I. LNCS, vol. 6311, pp. 776–789. Springer, Heidelberg (2010)

18. Vogel, J., Schiele, B.: Semantic modeling of natural scenes for content-based image retrieval. International Journal of Computer Vision 72(2), 133–157 (2007)

19. Wang, J.Z., Li, J., Wiederhold, G.: Simplicity: Semantics-sensitive integrated matching for picture libraries. IEEE Trans. Pattern Analysis and Machine Intelligence 23(9), 947–963 (2001)

20. Ward Jr., J.H.: Hierarchical grouping to optimize an objective function. J. the Am. Statistical Assoc. 58(301), 236–244 (1963)

21. Zhang, J., Marszalek, M., Lazebnik, S., Schmid, C.: Local features and kernels for classification of texture and object categories: A comprehensive study. International Journal of Computer Vision 73(2), 213–238 (2007)

A Benchmarking Campaign for the Multimodal Detection of Violent Scenes in Movies

Claire-Hélène Demarty[1], Cédric Penet[1], Guillaume Gravier[2],
and Mohammad Soleymani[3]

[1] Technicolor, 1 ave de Belle-Fontaine, 35576 Cesson-Sévigné, France
[2] CNRS/IRISA, Campus de Universitaire de Beaulieu, 263 Avenue du Général
Leclerc, 35042 Rennes, France
[3] Department of Computing, Imperial College London, SW7 2AZ, London, United
Kingdom

Abstract. We present an international benchmark on the detection of
violent scenes in movies, implemented as a part of the multimedia benchmarking initiative MediaEval 2011. The task consists in detecting portions of movies where physical violence is present from the automatic
analysis of the video, sound and subtitle tracks. A dataset of 15 Hollywood movies was carefully annotated and divided into a development set
and a test set containing 3 movies. Annotation strategies and resolution
of borderline cases are discussed at length in the paper. Results from
29 runs submitted by the 6 participating sites are analyzed. The first
year's results are promising, but considering the use case, there is still
a large room for improvement. The detailed analysis of the 2011 benchmark brings valuable insight for the implementation of future evaluation
on violent scenes detection in movies.

1 Introduction

MediaEval[1] is a benchmarking initiative dedicated to evaluating new algorithms
for multimedia access and retrieval. MediaEval emphasizes the multimodal character of the data (speech, audio, visual content, tags, users, context, etc). As a
track of MediaEval, the Affect Task - Violent Scenes Detection - involves automatic detection of violent segments in movies. This challenge derives from a
use case at Technicolor[2]. Technicolor is a provider of services in multimedia entertainment, and solutions, in particular, in the field of helping users select the
most appropriate content, according to, for example, their profile. Given this,
a particular use case arises which involves helping users choose movies that are
suitable for children in their family, by previewing the parts of the movies (i.e.,
scenes or segments) that include the most violent moments.

In the literature, violent scenes detection in movies has received very little attention so far. Monomodal static approaches were initially proposed [1,2].

---

[1] http://www.multimediaeval.org/
[2] http://www.technicolor.com

A. Fusiello et al. (Eds.): ECCV 2012 Ws/Demos, Part III, LNCS 7585, pp. 416–425, 2012.
© Springer-Verlag Berlin Heidelberg 2012

Multimodality has been recently considered in [3,4]. However, the main draw-backs of all these methods lie in the lack of a standard definition of violence and of standard databases. For example, a dataset of 20 minutes is used in [5], a 200-clip collection of scenes from action movies is considered in [6]. In [2,7], four movies are considered for training and testing. Hence the need for a dedicated benchmark for violent scenes detection is beneficial to provide a consistent and substantial dataset, together with a common definition of violence and with evaluation protocols and metrics.

The choice of the targeted content, i.e., Hollywood movies, raises additional challenges which are not addressed in similar evaluation tasks, for example in the TRECVid Surveillance Event Detection or Multimedia Event Detection Evaluation Tracks[3]. Indeed, systems will have to cope with content of very different genres and special montage effects, which may alter the events to detect. The affect task of MediaEval 2011 therefore constitutes a first attempt to address all these needs.

The paper provides an overview of the 2011 task. Its main contributions are: first, the provision of a definition of violence in movies, second, the description of a comprehensive dataset of 15 Hollywood movies together with their annotations, and valuable insights on the elaboration of the dataset and annotation strategies. Last, this paper reports on the collective effort of the organizers and participants to detect the violent segments in movies. Section 2 details the chosen definition of violence, the task definition and the dataset and evaluation protocols and metrics. In Section 3, results of the benchmark are reported with a short comparative description of the systems. The paper concludes in section 4, with a summary of the lessons learned and directions for a future benchmark.

2   Task Description

The 2011 Affect Task required participants to deploy multimodal approaches to automatically detect portions of movies depicting violence. This calls for a clear definition of violence that serves as a basis for annotating data for the benchmark.

2.1   Towards a Definition of Violence

The notion of violence remains highly subjective as it depends on viewers. The World Health Organization (WHO) defines violence as [8]: "*The intentional use of physical force or power, threatened or actual, against oneself, another person, or against a group or community, that either results in or has a high likelihood of resulting in injury, death, psychological harm, maldevelopment, or deprivation*". According to the WHO, three types of violence can be distinguished, namely, self-inflicted, interpersonal, and collective [9]. Each category is divided according to characteristics related to the setting and nature of violence, e.g., physical,

---

[3] http://www.nist.gov/itl/iad/mig/sed.cfm

sexual, psychological, and deprivation or neglect. In the context of movies and television, Kriegel [10] defines violence on TV as an *"unregulated force that affects the physical or psychological integrity to challenge the humanity of an individual with the purpose of domination or destruction"*. These definitions only focus on intentional actions and, as such, do not include accidents, which are of interest in the use case considered, as they also result in potentially shocking gory and graphic scenes, e.g., a bloody crash. We therefore adopted an extended definition of violence that includes accidents while being as objective as possible and reducing the complexity of the annotation task. In MediaEval, violence is defined as "physical violence or accident resulting in human injury or pain". Violent events are therefore limited to physical violence, verbal or psychological violence being intentionally excluded.

Even though we attempted to narrow the field of violent events down to a set of events as objectively violent as possible, there are still some borderline cases. First of all, sticking to this definition leads to the rejection of some shots in which the results of some physical violence are shown but not the violent act itself. For example, shots in which one can see a dead body with a lot of injuries and blood were not annotated as violent. On the contrary, a character simply slapping another one in the face is considered as a violent action according to the task definition. Other events defined as 'intent to kill', in which one sees somebody shooting somebody else for example with the clear intent to kill, but the targeted person escapes with no injury, were also discussed and finally not kept in the violent set. On the contrary, scenes where the shooter is not visible but where shooting at someone is obvious from the audio, e.g., one can hear the gunshot possibly with screams afterward, were annotated as violent. Interestingly, such scenes emphasize the multimodal characteristic of the task. Shots showing actions resulting in pain but with no intent to be violent or, on the contrary, with the aim of helping rather than harming, e.g., segments showing surgery without anesthesia, fit into the definition and were therefore deemed violent. Another borderline case keenly discussed was shots showing the destruction of a whole city or the explosion of a moving tank. Technically speaking, these shots do not show any proof of people death or injury, though one can reasonably assume that the city or the tank were not empty at the time of destruction. Consequently, such cases, where pain or injury is implicit, were annotated as violent. Finally, shots showing the violent action and the result of the action itself happen to be separated by several non violent shots. In this case, the entire segment was annotated as violent if the duration between the two violent shots (action and result) was short enough (less than two seconds).

2.2 Data Description

In line with the considered use case, the dataset consisted of 15 Hollywood movies from a comprehensive range of genres, from extremely violent to movies without violence. From these 15 movies, the 12 following ones were designated as development data: *Armageddon, Billy Elliot, Eragon, Harry Potter and the*

Order of the Phoenix[4], *I am Legend, Leon, Midnight Express, Pirates of the Caribbean and the Curse of the Black Pearl*[5], *Reservoir Dogs, Saving Private Ryan, The Sixth Sense, the Wicker Man.* The three following movies were used as test set: *Kill Bill 1, The Bourne Identity* and *the Wizard of Oz.*

Table 1. Movie dataset (Dev. set: first 12 movies; test set: last 3 movies).

Movie	Duration	Shot length	Violence Duration (%)	Violent Shots (%)
Armageddon	8680.16	3562	14.03	14.6
Billy Elliot	6349.44	1236	5.14	4.21
Eragon	5985.44	1663	11.02	16.6
Harry Potter 5	7953.52	1891	10.46	13.43
I am Legend	5779.92	1547	12.75	20.43
Leon	6344.56	1547	4.3	7.24
Midnight Express	6961.04	1677	7.28	11.15
Pirates Carib. 1	8239.4	2534	11.3	12.47
Reservoir Dogs	5712.96	856	11.55	12.38
Saving Private Ryan	9751.0	2494	12.92	18.81
The Sixth Sense	6178.04	963	1.34	2.80
The Wicker Man	5870.44	1638	8.36	6.72
Total	**83805.9**	**21608**	**9.52**	**12.7**
Kill Bill	5626.6	1597	17.4	24.8
The Bourne Identity	5877.6	1995	7.5	9.3
The Wizard of Oz	5415.7	908	5.5	5.0
Total	**16919.9**	**4500**	**10.2**	**14.0**

Statistics on violent scenes in each movie are provided in Table 1. The development dataset represents a total of 21,608 shots—as given by automatic shot segmentation developed internally at Technicolor—for a total duration of 83,800 seconds. Violent content corresponds to 9.5% of the total duration and 12.7% of the shots, pointing out the fact that violent segments are not scarce in the database. We tried to respect the genre repartition (from extremely violent to non violent) both in the development and evaluation sets. This appears in the provided statistics, as some movies such as *Billy Elliot* or *The Wizard of Oz* contain a smaller proportion of violent shots (around 5%). The choice we made for the definition of violence impacts the proportion of annotated violence in some movies such as *The Sixth Sense* where violent shots amount to only 2.8% of the duration. However, the movie contains several shocking scenes of dead people which do not fit the definition of violence that we adopted. In a similar manner, psychological violence, such as what may be found in *Billy Elliot*, was also not annotated, which also explains the small number of violent shots in this particular movie.

---

[4] Harry Potter 5
[5] Pirates Carib. 1

The violent scenes dataset[6] was created by seven human assessors. In addition to segments containing physical violence (with the above definition), annotations also include high-level concepts for the visual modality. For violent segments, the annotation was conducted using a 3-step process, with the same so-called 'master annotators' for all movies. A first master annotator extracted all violent segments. A second master annotator reviewed the annotated segments and possibly missed segments according to his/her own judgment. Disagreements were discussed on a case by case basis, the third master annotator making the final decision in case of an unresolved disagreement. Each annotated violent segment contained a single action, whenever possible. In the case of overlapping actions, the corresponding global segment was proposed as a whole. This was indicated in the annotation files by adding the tag "multiple action scene". The boundaries of each violent segment were defined at the frame level, i.e., indicating the start and end frame numbers.

The high-level video concepts were annotated through a simpler process, involving only two annotators. Each movie was first processed by an annotator and then reviewed by one of the master annotator. Seven visual concepts are provided: *presence of blood, fights, presence of fire, presence of guns, presence of cold weapons, car chases and gory scenes.* For the benchmark, participants had the option to carry out detection of the high-level concepts. However, concept detection is not among the task's goals and these high-level concept annotations were only provided on the development set. Each of these high-level concepts followed the same annotation format as for violent segments, i.e., starting and ending frame numbers and possibly some additional tags which provide further details. For blood annotations, a tag in each segment specifies the proportion of the screen covered in blood. Four tags were considered for fights: only two people fighting, a small group of people (roughly less than 10), large group of people (more than 10), distant attack (i.e., no real fight but somebody is shot or attacked at distance). As for the presence of fire, anything from big fires and explosions to fire coming out of a gun while shooting, a candle, a cigarette lighter, a cigarette, or sparks was annotated, e.g., a space shuttle taking off also generates fire and receives a fire label. An additional tag may indicate special colors of the fire (i.e., not yellow or orange). If a segment of video showed the presence of firearms (respectively cold weapons) it was annotated by any type of (parts of) guns (respectively cold weapons) or assimilated arms. Annotations of gory scenes are more difficult. In the present task, they are indicating graphic images of bloodletting and/or tissue damage. It includes horror or war representations. As this is also a subjective and difficult notion to define, some additional segments showing disgusting mutants or creatures are annotated as gore. In this case, additional tags describing the event/scene are added.

---

[6] The annotations, shot detections and key frames for this task were made available by Technicolor. The dataset can be obtained after signing the User Agreement form, available on the website (http://www.multimediaeval.org).

In addition to the video data, automatically generated shot boundaries with their corresponding key frames, as detected by Technicolor's software, were also provided with each movie.

2.3 Evaluation Rules

Due to copyright issues, the video content was not distributed and participants were required to buy the DVDs. We provided the online store's URLs for the DVDs which were used for annotations. This was done to ensure that every participant can access the exact, same version of the movies. Participants were allowed to use all information automatically extracted from the DVDs, including visual and auditory material as well as subtitles. English was the chosen language for both the audio and subtitles channels. The use of any other data, not included in the DVD (web sites, synopsis, etc.) was not allowed.

Two types of runs were initially considered in MediaEval 2011, a mandatory shot classification run and an optional segment detection one. The shot classification run consisted in classifying each shot provided by Technicolor's shot segmentation software as violent or not, optionally with a confidence score—the higher the score, the more likely the violence. The segment detection run involved detection of the violent segment boundaries, regardless of the shot segmentation provided.

For official ranking of the systems, system comparison was based on a detection cost function weighting false alarms (FA) and missed detections (MI), according to

$$C = C_{fa}P_{fa} + C_{miss}P_{miss} \qquad (1)$$

where the costs $C_{fa} = 1$ and $C_{miss} = 10$ are arbitrarily defined to reflect (a) the prior probability of the situation and (b) the cost of making an error. P_{fa} and P_{miss} are respectively the FA (false positive) and MI (false negative) rates given the system's output and the reference annotation. In the shot classification, the FA and MI rates were calculated on a per shot basis while, in the segment level run, they were computed on a per unit of time basis, i.e., durations of both references and detected segments are compared. This cost function is called 'MediaEval cost' in the following. To avoid only evaluating systems at given operating points and enable full comparison of systems, we also used detection error trade-off (DET) curves whenever possible, plotting P_{fa} as a function of P_{miss} given a segmentation and a confidence score for each segment. Note that in the segment detection run, DET curves are possible only for systems returning a dense segmentation (a list of segments that spans the entire video): segments not present in the output list are considered as non violent for all thresholds.

3 Results

The Affect Task on Violent Scenes Detection was proposed in MediaEval as a pilot for the first year. Thirteen teams, corresponding to 16 research groups considering joint submission proposals, declared interest in the task. Finally, six teams registered and completed the task, representing four different countries, for a grand total of 29 runs submitted (see Table 2). From the number of groups interested and the number of participants, the Affect task has proved to be of interest for the research community. This was confirmed by the active mailing list, which also denoted more a collaborative spirit between the teams than a competitive one, as promoted by MediaEval campaigns. All participants submitted runs for the required shot classification task and none to the optional segment detection. Results are summarized in Table 2.

Table 2. Participation and results (DYN: University of Toulon; NII: National Institute of Informatics; TUB: Technical University of Berlin; UGE: University of Geneva; LIG: Laboratoire d'Informatique de Grenoble; TI: joint participation Technicolor-INRIA. The MediaEval cost value corresponds to the best run per participant, according to this metric. MAP: mean average precision. (*) task organizers.

Part.	Country	# Runs	Med. Cost	MAP
DYN	France	2	6.46	0.08
NII	Japan	6	1.00	0.18
TUB	Germany	3	1.26	0.12
UGE*	Switzerland	5	2.00	0.17
LIG	France	1	7.93	0.04
TI*	France	12	0.76	0.25

The 29 submissions mostly correspond to 6 different systems which can be grouped in three main categories. Two participants (NII [11] and LIG [12]) treated the problem of violent scenes detection as a concept detection problem, applying generic systems developed for TRECVid evaluations to violent scenes detection, potentially with specific tuning. Both sites used classic video only features, computed on the keyframes provided, based on color, textures, edges, either local (interest points) or global, and classic classifiers. One participant (DYNI [13]) proposed a classifier-free technique exploiting only two low-level audio and video features, computed on each successive frame, both measuring the activity within a shot. After a late fusion process, decision was taken by comparison with a threshold. The last group of participants (TUB [14] , UGE [15] and TI [16]) built dedicated supervised classification systems for the task of violent scenes detection. Different classifiers were used from SVM, Bayesian networks to linear or quadratic discriminant analysis. All used multimodal features, either audio-video or audio-video-textual features (UGE). Features were computed globally for each shot (UGE, TI) or on the provided keyframes (TUB). Both early (TUB, UGE, TI) or late (TI) fusions were used, together with a temporal integration of the decisions at the output of the classifiers (UGE, TI).

Based on the results achieved by the different systems, one may draw some tentative conclusions about the global characteristics that were more likely to be useful for violence detection. Local video features (SIFT-like), as used by LIG, NII and TUB, did not add a lot of information to the systems. On the contrary, taking advantage of different modalities seems to improve performance. This is confirmed by comparing the two runs from DYNI, and the TI runs among which monomodal or multimodal configurations were submitted. Although results do not prove their action in one way or another, it also seems of interest to use temporal integration. This was carried out in different manners in the systems, either by using contextual features, i.e., features at different times, or by temporal smoothing or aggregation of the decisions at the output of the chain.

4   Lessons Learned

One goal of this task proposal was to provide a shared framework for violence detection systems for videos. Having the same database and annotations, and the same definition of the violent events is already a significant step towards building of such a framework. However, many lessons were learned from the implementation of the task as a pilot in MediaEval 2011.

Globally, it should first be noted from Table 2 that the overall performances of the proposed systems are not good enough to satisfy the requirements of a real-life commercial product. This means that the problem of automatically detecting violent scenes is still far from being solved and needs further attention.

Figure 1 shows the evolution of the detection error curves. These curves were build using the scores provided by all but one participant. On each of them, only the best run per participant, according to the MediaEval cost, was kept. Instead of giving an evaluation of the systems at different operating points, Figure 1 proposes a more complete comparison. Additionally, it should be noted that the ordering of the systems differs according to the chosen metric.

From Table 2, the metric also appears to be excessively biased towards MI errors or, equivalently, towards high recall at the expense of precision. A ratio of 10 between the FA and MI rates turned out to be so high that it leads to classifying all the scenes into the violent class for some systems (NII). Indeed, classifying all shots as violent results in a MediaEval cost value of 1 which is in most cases lower than what automatic systems obtained. This conclusion calls for a review of the metric in the future, towards a less biased criterion but still reflecting the Technicolor use case.

The definition of violence in the last campaign was chosen to satisfy a need of objectivity in the events, but does not cover all the violent scenes in the context of the Technicolor use case. With such a definition, some actions, e.g., one hurting himself accidentally against a chair, belong to the class of events to detect, despite their minor violent content. Conversely shocking scenes of dead or severely injured people will not be counted as violent. This emphasizes the need for further improvement of the current definition in the future campaigns. Another drawback of this definition is that it complicates the choice of relevant features for the task. For example, the presence of blood which could be a decisive feature is no longer enough to recognize a scene as violent.

A relatively large and standard dataset of movies for violence detection has been developed. The developed dataset is roughly four times larger than the

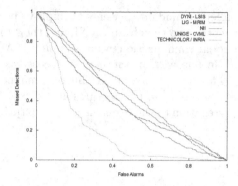

Fig. 1. False alarms vs. missed detections for each best run per participant. The best runs were selected according to the MediaEval cost values.

largest reported dataset in the literature. But even 15 movies is still not large enough to cover the variety of violent scenes in movies. First, violent events remain relatively rare (10% of the dataset). Second, because of the large variation between existing violent actions or events, in a dataset with 15 movies, there are only few similar violent excerpts. Therefore, the development of a larger dataset is certainly beneficial.

5   Conclusions

The Affect Task on Violent Scenes Detection in the context of the MediaEval 2011 benchmarking initiative has been presented. As a pilot task, this first year reached its objective: a common definition of the events to detect, together with a standard dataset and its associated ground truth were proposed, leading to a first solid basis for further research on this topic. Detailing this set-up to the research community was the main contribution of this paper. The task also successfully attracted participants, showing that this task and its open issues are interesting for multimedia indexing and discovery research community. For MediaEval 2012, the task will be further developed, with improvements in the task definition, dataset and the chosen evaluation metrics.

Acknowledgement. We would like to thank all the task participants and other contributors whose combined efforts contributed to make this first year run successful, especially our annotators who did a tedious but nevertheless necessary and valuable job. We also greatly appreciate our participants for giving us consent to describe their systems and results in this paper.

References

1. Pikrakis, A., Giannakopoulos, T., Theodoridis, S.: Gunshot detection in audio streams from movies by means of dynamic programming and Bayesian networks. In: Int. Conf. on Accoustic, Speech and Signal Processing, pp. 21–24 (2008)
2. Chen, L.H., Su, C.W., Weng, C.F., Liao, H.Y.M.: Action Scene Detection With Support Vector Machines. Journal of Multimedia 4, 248–253 (2009)
3. Giannakopoulos, T., Makris, A., Kosmopoulos, D., Perantonis, S., Theodoridis, S.: Audio-Visual Fusion for Detecting Violent Scenes in Videos. In: Konstantopoulos, S., Perantonis, S., Karkaletsis, V., Spyropoulos, C.D., Vouros, G. (eds.) SETN 2010. LNCS, vol. 6040, pp. 91–100. Springer, Heidelberg (2010)
4. Gong, Y., Wang, W., Jiang, S., Huang, Q., Gao, W.: Detecting Violent Scenes in Movies by Auditory and Visual Cues. In: Huang, Y.-M.R., Xu, C., Cheng, K.-S., Yang, J.-F.K., Swamy, M.N.S., Li, S., Ding, J.-W. (eds.) PCM 2008. LNCS, vol. 5353, pp. 317–326. Springer, Heidelberg (2008)
5. Giannakopoulos, T., Kosmopoulos, D.I., Aristidou, A., Theodoridis, S.: Violence Content Classification Using Audio Features. In: Antoniou, G., Potamias, G., Spyropoulos, C., Plexousakis, D. (eds.) SETN 2006. LNCS (LNAI), vol. 3955, pp. 502–507. Springer, Heidelberg (2006)
6. Bermejo Nievas, E., Deniz Suarez, O., Bueno García, G., Sukthankar, R.: Violence Detection in Video Using Computer Vision Techniques. In: Real, P., Diaz-Pernil, D., Molina-Abril, H., Berciano, A., Kropatsch, W. (eds.) CAIP 2011, Part II. LNCS, vol. 6855, pp. 332–339. Springer, Heidelberg (2011)
7. Chen, L.H., Hsu, H.W., Wang, L.Y., Su, C.W.: Violence detection in movies. In: 2011 Eighth International Conference on Computer Graphics, Imaging and Visualization (CGIV), pp. 119–124 (2011)
8. Violence: a public health priority. Technical report, World Health Organization, Geneva, Switzerland (1996) WHO/EHA/SPI.POA.2
9. Krug, E.G., Mercy, J.A., Dahlberg, L.L., Zwi, A.B.: The world report on violence and health. The Lancet 360, 1083–1088 (2002)
10. Kriegel, B.: La violence à la télévision. Rapport de la mission d'évaluation, d'analyse et de propositions relative aux représentations violentes à la télévision. Technical report, Ministère de la Culture et de la Communication, Paris, France (2003)
11. Lam, V., Le, D.D., Satoh, S., Duong, D.A.: Nii, japan at mediaeval 2011 violent scenes detection task. In: Multimedia Benchmark Workshop, MediaEval 2011 (2011)
12. Safadi, B., Quenot, G.: Lig at mediaeval 2011 affect task: use of a generic method. In: Multimedia Benchmark Workshop, MediaEval 2011 (2011)
13. Glotin, H., Razik, J., Paris, S., Prevot, J.M.: Real-time entropic unsupervised violent scenes detection in hollywood movies - dyni @ mediaeval affect task 2011. In: Multimedia Benchmark Workshop, MediaEval 2011 (2011)
14. Acar, E., Spiegel, S., Albayrak, S.: Mediaeval 2011 affect task: Violent scene detection combining audio and visual features with svm. In: Multimedia Benchmark Workshop, MediaEval 2011 (2011)
15. Gninkoun, G., Soleymani, M.: Automatic violence scenes detection: A multi-modal approach. In: Multimedia Benchmark Workshop, MediaEval 2011 (2011)
16. Penet, C., Demarty, C.H., Gravier, G., Gros, P.: Technicolor and inria/irisa at mediaeval 2011: learning temporal modality integration with bayesian networks. In: Multimedia Benchmark Workshop, MediaEval 2011. CEUR Workshop Proceedings, vol. 807. CEUR-WS.org (2011)

A Selective Weighted Late Fusion
for Visual Concept Recognition

Ningning Liu, Emmanuel Dellandrea, Chao Zhu,
Charles-Edmond Bichot, and Liming Chen

Université de Lyon, CNRS,
Ecole Centrale de Lyon, LIRIS, UMR5205, F-69622, France
{ningning.liu,emmanuel.dellandrea,chao.zhu,
charles-edmond.bichot,liming.chen}@ec-lyon.fr

Abstract. We propose in this paper a novel multimodal approach to automatically predict the visual concepts of images through an effective fusion of visual and textual features. It relies on a Selective Weighted Late Fusion (SWLF) scheme which, in optimizing an overall Mean interpolated Average Precision (MiAP), learns to automatically select and weight the best experts for each visual concept to be recognized. Experiments were conducted on the MIR Flickr image collection within the ImageCLEF 2011 Photo Annotation challenge. The results have brought to the fore the effectiveness of SWLF as it achieved a MiAP of 43.69 % for the detection of the 99 visual concepts which ranked 2nd out of the 79 submitted runs, while our new variant of SWLF allows to reach a MiAP of 43.93 %.

Keywords: Visual concept recognition, multimodality, feature fusion.

1 Introduction

Machine-based recognition of visual concepts aims at automatically recognizing high-level visual semantic concepts (HLSC), including scenes (e.g., indoor, outdoor, landscape, *etc.*), objects (car, animal, person, *etc.*), events (travel, work, *etc.*), or even emotions (melancholic, happy, *etc.*). It proves to be extremely challenging because of large intra-class variations and inter-class similarities, clutter, occlusion and pose changes. The past decade has witnessed tremendous efforts from the research communities as testified the multiple challenges in the field, e.g., Pascal VOC [1], TRECVID [2] and ImageCLEF [3]. Most approaches to visual concept recognition (VCR) have so far focused on appropriate visual content description, and have featured a dominant bag-of-visual-words (BoVW) representation along with local SIFT descriptors. Meanwhile, increasing works in literature have discovered the wealth of semantic meanings conveyed by the abundant textual captions associated with images [4]. Therefore, multimodal approaches are proposed for VCR by making joint use of user textual tags and visual descriptions to bridge the gap between HLSC and low-level visual features. The work presented in this paper is in that line and targets an effective feature fusion scheme for VCR.

A. Fusiello et al. (Eds.): ECCV 2012 Ws/Demos, Part III, LNCS 7585, pp. 426–435, 2012.

As far as multimodal approaches are concerned, it requires a fusion strategy to combine information from multiple sources, *e.g.*, visual stream and sound stream for video analysis [5], textual and visual content for multimedia information retrieval [6], *etc.* This fusion can be carried out at feature level [7], namely *early fusion*, or at score level [8], *i.e. late fusion*, or even at some intermediate level, *e.g.*, such as kernel level [9]. While early fusion is straightforward and simply consists of concatenating the features extracted from various information sources into a single representation, its disadvantage is also well known: the curse of dimensionality and the difficulty in combining features of different natures into a common homogeneous representation. As a result, late fusion strategies, which consist of integrating the scores as delivered by the classifiers on various features through a fixed combination rule, *e.g.*, sum, are the preferred fusion method in literature [10,11]. They not only provide a trade-off between preservation of information and computational efficiency but also consistently yield better performance as compared to early fusion methods [5]. Furthermore, a comprehensive comparative study of various combination rules, *e.g.*, sum, product, max, min, median, and majority voting, by Kittler *et al.* [12], suggests that the sum rule is much less sensitive to the error of individual classifiers when estimating posterior class probability.

The proposed fusion scheme, namely Selective Weighted Late Fusion (SWLF), falls into the category of late fusion strategies. Specifically, when different features, *e.g.*, visual ones and textual ones, can be used for VCR, SWLF learns to automatically select and weight the best experts to be fused for each visual concept to be recognized. The proposed SWLF builds on two simple insights. First, the score delivered by a feature, *i.e.* expert, should be weighted by its intrinsic quality for the classification problem at hand. Second, in a multi-label scenario where several visual concepts may be assigned to an image, different visual concepts may require different features which best recognize them. For instance, the "sky" concept may greatly require global color descriptors, while the best feature to recognize a concept like street could be a segment-based feature for capturing straight lines of buildings. Furthermore, we also propose three different variants of SWLF which are compared using data provided by the ImageCLEF 2011 photo annotation task. The experimental results demonstrate the effectiveness of the proposed approach.

The rest of this paper is organized as follows. The proposed fusion scheme, SWLF, is presented in section 2. The experiments we have conducted to evaluate SWLF are described in section 3. Finally, we conclude and give some insight on the future work in section 4.

2   Selective Weighted Late Fusion

The proposed SWLF scheme has a learning phase which requires a training dataset for the selection of the best experts and their corresponding weights for each visual concept. Specifically, given a training dataset, we divide it into two disjoint parts composed of a training set and a validation set. For each visual concept, a binary classifier (concept versus no concept) is trained, which is also called *expert* in the subsequent, for each type of features using the data in the training set. Thus, for each concept, we generate as many experts as the number of different types of features. The quality of each expert can then be evaluated through a quality metric using the data in the validation set. In this work, the quality metric is chosen to be the interpolated Average Precision (iAP). The higher iAP is for a given expert, the more weight should be given to the score delivered by that expert for the late fusion. Concretely, given a visual concept k, the quality metrics, *i.e.* iAP, produced by all the experts are first normalized into w_k^i. To perform a late fusion of all these experts at score level, the *sum of weighted scores* is then computed as in (1):

$$score : z_k = \sum_{i=1}^{N} (w_k^i * y_k^i), \tag{1}$$

where y_k^i represents the score of the ith expert for the concept k, and w_k^i stands for the normalized iAP performance of the feature f_i on the validation dataset. In the subsequent, late fusion through (1) is called *weighted score* rule.

For the purpose of comparison, we also consider three other score level fusion schemes, namely "min", "max" or "mean" respectively expressed as $min : z_k = min(y_k^1, y_k^2, ..., y_k^N)$, $max : z_k = max(y_k^1, y_k^2, ..., y_k^N)$, $mean : z_k = \frac{1}{N} \sum_{i=1}^{N} y_k^i$.

Actually, these three fusion rules can have very simple interpretation. The *min* fusion rule is the consensus voting. A visual concept is recognized only if all the experts recognize it. The *max* rule can be called alternative voting. A visual concept is recognized as long as one expert has recognized it. Finally, the *mean* rule can be assimilated as the majority voting where a concept is recognized if the majority of the experts recognize it.

In practice, one discovers that the late fusion of all the experts leads to a decrease in the global classification accuracy, *i.e.* the mean iAP over the whole set of visual concepts. The reason could be that some of features so far proposed can be noisy and irrelevant to a certain number of visual concepts, thus disturbing the learning process and lowering the generalization skill of the learnt expert on the unseen data. For this purpose, we further implement the SWLF scheme inspired by a wrapper feature selection method, namely the SFS method (Sequential Forward Selection) [13], which firstly initializes an empty set, and at each step the feature that gives the highest correct classification rate along with the features already included is added to the set of selected experts to be fused. More specifically, for each visual concept, all the experts are sorted in a decreasing order according to their iAP. At a given iteration N, the only first N experts are used for late fusion and their performance is evaluated over the data of the validation set. N is increased until the overall classification accuracy measured in terms of MiAP starts to decrease.

2.1   The Learning Algorithm of SWLF

The learning procedure of the SWLF algorithm can be defined as follows:

Selective Weighted Late Fusion (SWLF) algorithm for training

Input: Training dataset T (of size N_T) and validation dataset V (of size N_V).
Output: Set of N experts for the K concepts $\{C_k^n\}$ and the corresponding set of weights $\{\omega_k^n\}$ with $n \in [1, N]$ and $k \in [1, K]$.
Initialization: $N = 1$, $MiAP_{max} = 0$.

- Extract M types of features from T and V
- For each concept $k = 1$ to K
  - For each type of feature $i = 1$ to M
    1. Train the expert C_k^i using T
    2. Compute ω_k^i as the iAP of C_k^i using V
  - Sort the ω_k^i in descending order and denote the order as $j^1, j^2, ..., j^M$
    to form $W_k = \{\omega_k^{j^1}, \omega_k^{j^2}, ..., \omega_k^{j^M}\}$ and the corresponding set of experts
    $E_k = \{C_k^{j^1}, C_k^{j^2}, ..., C_k^{j^M}\}$
- For the number of experts $n = 2$ to M
  - For each concept $k = 1$ to K
    1. Select the first n experts from $E_k : E_k^n = \{C_k^1, C_k^2, ..., C_k^n\}$
    2. Select the first n weights from $W_k : W_k^n = \{\omega_k^1, \omega_k^2, ..., \omega_k^n\}$
    3. For $j = 1$ to n : Normalise $\omega_k^{j'} = \omega_k^j / \sum_{i=1}^n \omega_k^i$
    4. Combine the first n experts into a fused expert, using the *weighted score*
       rule through (1): $z_k = \sum_{j=1}^n \omega_k^{j'} . y_k^j$ where y_k^j is the output of C_k^j
    5. Compute $MiAP_k^n$ of the fused expert on the validation set V
  - Compute $MiAP = 1/K . \sum_{k=1}^K MiAP_k^n$
  - If $MiAP > MiAP_{max}$
    * Then $MiAP_{max} = MiAP$, $N = n$
    * Else break

2.2 The Variants of SWLF

As the number of experts N is the same for each concept in the above algorithm, this version of SWLF is called *SWLF_FN* (fixed N). However, several variants can be built upon SWLF. Indeed, instead of fixing the same number of experts N for all concepts, it is possible to select the number of experts on a per-concept basis. Thus the number of experts can be different for each concept. We have also implemented this variant denoted *SWLF_VN* (variable N) in the following. Another variant concerns the way the experts are selected at each iteration. Instead of adding the nth best expert at iteration n to the set of previously selected $n - 1$ experts, one can also select the expert which yields the best combination of n experts, in terms of $MiAP$, once added to the set of $n - 1$ experts already selected at the previous iteration. This variant is denoted *SWLF_SFS* in the following as the selection scheme is inspired from the feature selection method "Sequential Feature Selection" [13] generally used for early fusion of features.

3   Experiments

In order to allow a comparison of our method with those among the most recent ones in the visual concept recognition domain, we carried out experiments on the MIR Flickr image collection that was used within the ImageCLEF 2011 Photo Annotation Challenge [3]. The goal of this challenge was to automatically annotate images according to 99 visual concepts. The database is a subset of MIRFLICKR-1M image collection from thousands of real world users under a creative common license. It is split into a training set of 8,000 images and a test set of 10,000 images. Each image is provided with a textual description (user tags).

The measure we have considered to evaluate the classification performance is the Mean interpolated Average Precision (MiAP) that is also used in ImageCLEF 2011 Photo Annotation Challenge.

3.1   The Features

More and more, images are provided with textual resources such as Exif data, legends, tags. These data can be easily obtained on the sharing websites such as Flickr[1], which is the data source of the MIRFLICKR-1M, and the textual descriptions are a rich source of semantic information that is interesting to consider for the purpose of image classification and retrieval.

Therefore, in order to describe images for further classification, we propose to use not only visual features extracted from the image, but also textual features extracted from the textual resources associated with images. These features are briefly presented in the next subsections.

Visual Features. As the concepts to be detected in images can be characterized by many different visual properties, we extract a rich set of features. Indeed, we consider low-level features based on color, texture, shape, being local or global, as well as mid-level features related to aesthetic and affective image properties. The color features are moments and histograms computed with several different color spaces such as RGB and HSV. The texture features are based on cooccurrences [14] and on different variants of Local Binary Patterns (LBP) using several scales and color spaces [15]. Shape feature are histograms of image line orientations extracted from Hough transform [16]. Several variants of SIFT features are also extracted using a dense grid and different color spaces [17]. Among the mid-level features, we extract aesthetic features proposed in [18] and [19] as well as affective features related to color harmony and dynamism [20].

In total, we extract 24 visual feature sets of various dimensions ranging from 1 for color harmony to 4000 for each of the SIFT variants (the size of the codebook).

Textual Features. The textual resources associated with images can take many forms. We consider in this paper that images are provided with a set of words

---
[1] http://www.flickr.com/

(or tags), as it is the case with the MIR Flickr image collection that we use in our experiments.

Our goal here is to extract a semantic information from this text. To do so, we use a feature that is defined as a histogram of textual concepts towards a vocabulary or dictionary where each bin of this histogram represents a concept of the dictionary, whereas its value is the accumulation of the contribution of each word within the text document toward the underlying concept according to a semantic similarity measure provided by Wordnet ontology [21]. For instance, the bin associated with the concept "rain" of the dictionary can be activated by tags such as "water", "liquid", "precipitation", "dripping liquid", "monsoon", etc..

As several dictionaries and semantic similarity measures are conceivable, we extract 10 variants of this textual histogram feature leading to a total of 10 textual features.

3.2 Experimental Setup

The initial training dataset, provided by ImageClef 2011 for the photo annotation challenge, was first divided into a training set (50%, 4005 images) and a validation set (50%, 3995 images), and balanced the positive samples of most concepts as half for training and half for validation. The proposed features, both textual and visual, were then extracted from the training and validation sets. Support Vector Machines (SVM) [22] were chosen as classifiers (or experts) for their effectiveness both in terms of computation complexity and classification accuracy. A SVM expert was trained for each concept and each type of features, as described in section 2. Following J. Zhang et $al.$ [23], we used χ^2 kernel for histogram-based features and RBF kernels for the other features. The RBF and χ^2 kernel functions are defined by: $K_{rbf}(F, F') = exp^{-\frac{1}{2\sigma^2}\|(F-F')\|^2}$ and $K_{\chi^2}(F, F') = exp^{\frac{1}{I}\sum_{i=1}^{n}\frac{(F_i-F_i')^2}{F_i+F_i'}}$ where F and F' are the feature vectors, n is their size, I is the parameter for normalizing the distances which was set at the average value of the training set, and σ was set at $\sqrt{n/2}$.

We made use of the LibSVM library [24] as SVM implementation (C-Support Vector Classification). The tuning of the different parameters for each SVM expert was performed empirically according to our experiments, in which the weight of negative class ("-w-1") was set at 1, and the weight for positive class ("-w1") was optimized on the validation set using a range of 1 through 30.

In the following, we give results of SWLF on the validation set which is a part of the training set provided for the ImageCLEF 2011 challenge, but also on the test set on which participants were evaluated as it has been released after the competition.

3.3 Experimental Results

The fusion schemes we propose in this paper have been used to combine the 24 visual and 10 textual features presented in section 3.1, and applied to MIR Flickr image collection. Figure 1 presents the MiAP performance achieved by the basic SWLF scheme, SWLF_FN, using the "score" rule for combining experts which is compared with the standard fusion operators "min", "max" and "mean". These results are given on both the validation and test sets and show the evolution of the MiAP as N, the number of features to be fused, is increased from 1 to 34.

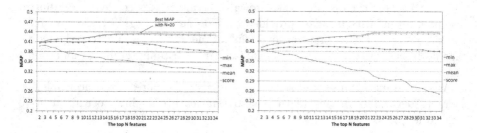

Fig. 1. The MiAP performance of SWLF_FN using different rules ("min", "max", "mean" and "score") for fusing visual and textual features using the validation set (a) and the test set (b).

As we can see from Figure 1 (a), the max and min-based SWLF_FN schemes tend to decrease the MiAP when the number of features to be fused, N, is successively increased from 1 to 34. On the contrary, the performance of weighted score and mean-based SWLF_FN schemes keep increasing until N reaches 20 and then stays stable. These results demonstrate that the weighted score and mean-based SWLF schemes perform consistently better than the max and min-based fusion rules. While close to each other, the weighted score-based SWLF_FN scheme performs slightly better than the mean-based SWLF_FN scheme. Figure 1 (b) presents the results obtained using the test set. We can observe that the results are very close to those obtained using the validation set, which proves the very good generalization skill of SWLF_FN, particularly when using "mean" and "score" fusion rules.

Table 1. The MiAP obtained by SWLF_FN, SWLF_VN and SWLF_SFS on the validation and test sets

Method	MiAP on the validation set	MiAP on the test set
SWLF_FN(N=20)	43.55 %	42.71 %
SWLF_FN(N=22)	43.53 %	43.69 %
SWLF_VN	44.51 %	38.61 %
SWLF_SFS	44.03 %	43.93 %

A comparison of the MiAP obtained by the three SWLF variants (SWLF_FN, SWLF_VN and SWLF_SFS) is provided in Table 1. It confirms the good generalization skill of SWLF since the MiAP obtained on the test set is very similar as

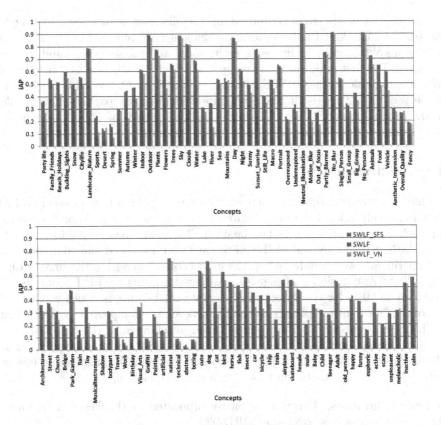

Fig. 2. The iAP obtained by SWLF_FN, SWLF_VN and SWLF_SFS for the 99 concepts of ImageCLEF 2011 Photo Annotation challenge

the one obtained on the validation set. The best result is obtained by SWLF_SFS with a MiAP of 43.93 % on the test set, closely followed by SWLF_FN (with $N = 22$) with a MiAP of 43.69 %. SWLF_VN is the least efficient among SWLF variants. Indeed, although it performs slightly better than SWLF_FN and SWLF_SFS on the validation set, its performance drops by more than 5 % on the test set. This tends to suggest that SWLF_VN, in optimizing the iAP on a per class-basis, is more prone to overfitting than SWLF_FN and SWLF_SFS, thus leading to a more severe performance drop on unseen data (test dataset).

Figure 2 presents the iAP obtained by SWLF_FN, SWLF_VN and SWLF_SFS for each of the 99 concepts that had to be detected within the ImageCLEF 2011 Photo Annotation challenge. One can notice that the slight superiority of SWLF_SFS over SWLF_FN based on the global MiAP is respected for most of the concepts, as well as the lower results obtained by SWLF_VN. This Figure also shows that some concepts are very well detected such as "Neutral_Illumination", "Outdoor", "Sky" with an iAP around 90 % whereas some are very difficult to detect such as "Abstract", "Boring", "Work" with an iAP lower than 10 %.

The results of the runs submitted by the different teams participating to the ImageCLEF 2011 Photo Annotation challenge are reported in [3]. The best results are obtained by teams using multimodal approaches (visual and textual features). The first rank was obtained by TUBFI with a MiAP of 44.3 % followed by our submission using SWLF_FN with a MiAP of 43.7 % (this is given in Table 2 of [3]). This result has been improved after our participation thanks to the proposition of SWLF_SFS which displays a MiAP of 43.9 %, proving its effectiveness for combining visual and textual features.

4   Conclusion

We have presented in this paper a novel Selective Weighted Late Fusion (SWLF) that iteratively selects the best features and weights the corresponding scores for each concept at hand to be classified. Three variants of SWLF, namely SWLF_FN, SWLF_VN and SWLF_SFS, have been proposed and compared.

Experiments were conducted on the image collection within the ImageCLEF 2011 Photo Annotation challenge. Our submission using SWLF_FN obtained a MiAP of 43.69 % for the detection of the 99 visual concepts which ranked 2nd out of the 79 submitted runs. This results has even been improved by the variant SWLF_SFS developed after our participation, reaching a MiAP of 43.93%.

The experimental results have also shown that SWLF, in efficiently fusing visual and textual features, displays a very good generalization ability on unseen data for the image annotation task with a multi-label scenario.

Acknowledgments. This work is partly supported by the french ANR under the project VideoSense ANR-09-CORD-026.

References

1. Everingham, M., Van Gool, L.J., Williams, C.K.I., Winn, J.M., Zisserman, A.: The pascal visual object classes (voc) challenge. Int. J. Comput. Vision, 303–338 (2010)
2. Smeaton, A.F., Over, P., Kraaij, W.: Evaluation campaigns and trecvid. In: MIR 2006: Proceedings of the 8th ACM International Workshop on Multimedia Information Retrieval, pp. 321–330 (2006)
3. Nowak, S., Nagel, K., Liebetrau, J.: The clef 2011 photo annotation and concept-based retrieval tasks. In: CLEF Workshop Notebook Paper (2011)
4. Guillaumin, M., Verbeek, J.J., Schmid, C.: Multimodal semi-supervised learning for image classification. In: CVPR, pp. 902–909 (2010)
5. Snoek, C.G.M., Worring, M., Smeulders, A.W.M.: Early versus late fusion in semantic video analysis. In: Proceedings of the 13th Annual ACM International Conference on Multimedia, pp. 399–402 (2005)
6. Ah-Pine, J., Bressan, M., Clinchant, S., Csurka, G., Hoppenot, Y., Renders, J.M.: Crossing textual and visual content in different application scenarios. Multimedia Tools and Applications 42, 31–56 (2009)
7. Snoek, C.G.M., Worring, M., Geusebroek, J.M., Koelma, D.C., Seinstra, F.J.: The mediamill trecvid 2004 semantic video search engine. In: Proceedings of the TRECVID Workshop (2004)

8. Westerveld, T., Vries, A.P.D., van Ballegooij, A., de Jong, F., Hiemstra, D.: A probabilistic multimedia retrieval model and its evaluation. EURASIP Journal on Applied Signal Processing 2003, 186–198 (2003)
9. Binder, A., Samek, W., Kloft, M., Müller, C., Müller, K.R., Kawanabe, M.: The joint submission of the tu berlin and fraunhofer first (tubfi) to the imageclef2011 photo annotation task. In: CLEF Workshop Notebook Paper (2011)
10. Wu, Y., Chang, E.Y., Chang, K.C.C., Smith, J.R.: Optimal multimodal fusion for multimedia data analysis. In: Proceedings of the 12th Annual ACM International Conference on Multimedia, pp. 572–579 (2004)
11. Znaidia, A., Borgne, H.L., Popescu, A.: Cea list's participation to visual concept detection task of imageclef 2011. In: CLEF Workshop Notebook Paper (2011)
12. Kittler, J., Hatef, M., Duin, R.P.W., Matas, J.: On combining classifiers. IEEE Trans. Pattern Anal. Mach. Intell. 20, 226–239 (1998)
13. Pudil, P., Novovičová, J., Kittler, J.: Floating search methods in feature selection. Pattern Recogn. Lett. 15, 1119–1125 (1994)
14. Haralick, R.M.: Statistical and structural approaches to texture. Proceedings of the IEEE 67, 786–804 (1979)
15. Zhu, C., Bichot, C.E., Chen, L.: Multi-scale color local binary patterns for visual object classes recognition. In: ICPR, pp. 3065–3068 (2010)
16. Pujol, A., Chen, L.: Line segment based edge feature using hough transform. In: The Seventh IASTED International Conference on Visualization, Imaging and Image Processing, VIIP 2007, pp. 201–206 (2007)
17. van de Sande, K.E.A., Gevers, T., Snoek, C.G.M.: Evaluating color descriptors for object and scene recognition. IEEE Trans. Pattern Anal. Mach. Intell. 32, 1582–1596 (2010)
18. Ke, Y., Tang, X., Jing, F.: The design of high-level features for photo quality assessment. In: CVPR, vol. 1, pp. 419–426 (June 2006)
19. Datta, R., Li, J., Wang, J.Z.: Content-based image retrieval: approaches and trends of the new age. In: Multimedia Information Retrieval, pp. 253–262 (2005)
20. Dellandréa, E., Liu, N., Chen, L.: Classification of affective semantics in images based on discrete and dimensional models of emotions. In: International Workshop on Content-Based Multimedia Indexing (CBMI), pp. 99–104 (June 2010)
21. Miller, G.A.: Wordnet: A lexical database for english. Communications of the ACM 38, 39–41 (1995)
22. Vapnik, V.N.: The Nature of Statistical Learning Theory. Springer New York Inc., New York (1995)
23. Zhang, J., Lazebnik, S., Schmid, C.: Local features and kernels for classification of texture and object categories: a comprehensive study. Int. J. Comput. Vision 73, 213–238 (2007)
24. Chang, C.C., Lin, C.J.: LIBSVM: A library for support vector machines. ACM Transactions on Intelligent Systems and Technology 2, 1–27 (2011)

Fusion of Multiple Visual Cues for Visual Saliency Extraction from Wearable Camera Settings with Strong Motion

Hugo Boujut[1], Jenny Benois-Pineau[1], and Remi Megret[2]

[1] University of Bordeaux, LaBRI, UMR 5800, F-33400 Talence, France
{hugo.boujut,benois-p}@labri.fr
[2] University of Bordeaux, IMS, UMR 5218, F-33400 Talence, France
remi.megret@ims-bordeaux.fr

Abstract. In this paper we are interested in the saliency of visual content from wearable cameras. The subjective saliency in wearable video is studied first due to the psycho-visual experience on this content. Then the method for objective saliency map computation with a specific contribution based on geometrical saliency is proposed. Fusion of spatial, temporal and geometric cues in an objective saliency map is realized by the multiplicative operator. Resulting objective saliency maps are evaluated against the subjective maps with promising results, highlighting interesting performance of proposed geometric saliency model.

1 Introduction

Since recently, the focus of attention in video content understanding, presentation, and assessment has moved toward incorporating of visual saliency information to drive local analysis process. Hence in the paper from A. Benoit [1], the task is to classify animated movies from low motion content. The *global* saliency is therefore expressed by rhythm and other motion descriptors. In another task such as content viewing on a mobile screen, the most salient regions are selected according to the perceptual model of L. Itti and C. Koch [2]. If we simplify the concept of saliency to its very basic definition, we can reasonably say that visual saliency is what attracts human gaze. Numerous psycho-visual studies which have been conducted since the last quarter of 20th century uncovered some factors influencing it. Considering only signal features, the sensitivity to color contrasts, contours, orientation and motion observed in image plane has been stated by numerous authors [3,4]. Nevertheless, only these features are not sufficient to delimit the area in the image plane which is the strongest gaze attractor. In [5], the author states, for still images, that *observers show a marked tendency to fixate the center of the screen when viewing scenes on computer monitors*. The authors of [6] come to the same conclusion for dynamic general video content such as movies and Hollywood trailers. This is why the authors of [7] propose the third cue which is the geometrical saliency modelled by a 2D Gaussian located at the image center. While signal based cues remain valuable

A. Fusiello et al. (Eds.): ECCV 2012 Ws/Demos, Part III, LNCS 7585, pp. 436–445, 2012.

saliency indicators, we claim that geometrical saliency depends on global motion and camera settings in the dynamic scene. Nowadays, the attention of computer vision community is more and more turned to the new forms of video content: such as wearable video cameras, or "egocentric" view of the world [8,9]. Some attempts to identify visual saliency mainly on the basis of the frequency of repetition of visual objects and regions in the wearable video content have recently been made in [10]. We are specifically interested in building visual saliency maps by fusion of all cues in the pixel domain for the case of "egocentric" video content recorded with wearable cameras. Hence in this paper, we propose an automatic method of spatio-temporal saliency extraction for wearable camera videos with a specific accent on geometrical saliency dependent on strong wearable camera motion. We evaluate the proposed method with regard to subjective saliency maps obtained from gaze tracking.

The rest of the paper is organized as follows. In section 2 we will introduce the context and motivation of our work. In section 3 we report the method and our psycho-visual experiments for reference subjective saliency map construction. The objective saliency map will be presented in Section 4. The evaluation of the latter will be described in Section 5. Section 6 will conclude our work and outline its perspectives.

2 Motivations

The context of actual work is the multi-disciplinary research on Alzheimer disease [11,12]. The goal here is to ensure an objective assessment of the capacity of patients to conduct the IADL (Instrumental Activities of Daily Living). In [11] the framework for video monitoring with wearable camera was designed. The wearable camera is fixed in an ergonomic position on the patient's shoulder (see Fig. 1) and the recording is realized at patient's home. The computer vision task consists in an automatic recognition and indexing of IADLS from a taxonomy proposed to patients in each recording. We seek to limit the automatic analysis of the observed dynamic scene to the area of interest which is visually salient for the medical practitioner. Hence in the next section we study the subjective saliency of this type of content. Then we propose an automatic, objective saliency model from video data and assess it with regard to the built subjective saliency ground truth.

3 Subjective Saliency Map

In this section we present our approach for subjective saliency extraction on wearable video.

3.1 Eye-Tracker Experiment

The subjective saliency maps expressing user attention are obtained on the basis of psycho-visual experiment consisting in measuring the gaze positions on videos

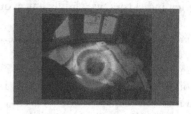

Fig. 1. Wearable camera setup   **Fig. 2.** Subjective saliency map example

from wearable video camera. The map of the visual attention has to be built on each frame of these videos. Videos from wearable camera differ from *traditional* video scenes: the camera films the user point of view, including his hands. Unlike *traditional* videos, wearable camera videos have a very high temporal activity due to the strong ego-motion of the wearer.

The gaze positions are recorded with an eye-tracker. We used HS-VET 250Hz from Cambridge Research Systems Ltd. This device is able to record 250 eye positions per second. The videos we display in this experiment have a frame-rate of 29.97 frames per second. A total of 28 videos filming the activities of daily living of patients and healthy volunteers are displayed to each participant of the experiment. This represents 17 minutes and 30 seconds of video. The resolution of the videos is 1280x960 pixels and the storage format is raw YUV 4:2:0. The experiment conditions and the experiment room is compliant to the recommendation ITU-R BT.500-11 [13]. Videos are displayed on a 23 inches LCD monitor with a native resolution of 1920x1080 pixels. To avoid image distortions, videos are not resized to screen resolution. A mid-gray frame is inserted around the displayed video. 25 participants were gathered for this experiment, 10 women and 15 men. For 5 participants some problems occurred in the eye-tracking recording process. So we decided to exclude these 5 records.

After looking at gaze position records on video frames, we stated that gaze anticipated camera motion and user actions. This phenomenon has been already reported by M. Land et al. in [14]. They state that *visual fixation does precede motor manipulation, putting eye movements in the vanguard of each motor act, rather than as adjuncts to it.*

Nevertheless, gaze positions cannot directly be applied as *ground truth* to compare automatic saliency model we aim at. They must be processed in order to get the subjective saliency map. The next section describes how to build subjective saliency maps from gaze tracking records.

3.2   Subjective Saliency Map Build Method

Any *objective* human visual perception model has to be validated and evaluated with regard to a *ground truth*. The *ground truth* is the *subjective* saliency in this case. The subjective saliency is built from eye position measurements. There are two reasons for which eye positions cannot be directly used to represent the visual attention. First, the eye positions are only spots on the frame and do not represent the field of view. Secondly, to get accurate results, the saliency map is not built with the eye tracking data from one subject, but from many subjects. So the subjective saliency map should provide an information about the density of eye positions.

The method proposed by D. S. Wooding [15] fulfils these two constraints. In the case of video sequences, the method is applied on each frame I of a video sequence K. The process result is a subjective saliency map $S_{subj}(I)$ for each frame I. With this method, the saliency map is computed in three steps. In the first step, for each eye measure m of frame I, a two dimensional Gaussian is applied at the center of the eye measure $(x_0, y_0)_m$. The two dimensional Gaussian depicts the fovea projection on the screen. The fovea is the central retina part where the vision is the most accurate. In the *Sensibility to Light* [16] book chapter from D.C. Hood and M.A. Finkelstein (1986), the authors stated that the fovea covers an area from 1.5° to 2° in diameter at the retina center. D.S. Wooding proposed to set the Gaussian spread σ to an angle of 2°.

For the eye measure m of the frame I, a partial saliency map $S_{subj}(I, m)$ is computed (1).

$$S_{subj}(I, m) = Ae^{-\left(\frac{(x-x_{0_m})^2}{2\sigma_x^2} + \frac{(y-y_{0_m})^2}{2\sigma_y^2}\right)}$$

(1)

with $\sigma_x = \sigma_y = \sigma$ and $A = 1$

Then, at the second step, all the partial saliency maps $S_{subj}(I, m)$ of frame $S_i I$ are added into $S_{subj}\prime(I)$ (2).

$$S_{subj}\prime(I) = \sum_{m=0}^{N_I} S_{subj}(I, m)$$

(2)

where N_I is the number of eye measures recorded on all the subjects for the frame I. Finally, at the third step, the saliency map $S_{subj}\prime(I)$ is normalized by the highest value $argmax$ of $S_{subj}\prime(I)$. The normalized subjective saliency map is stored in $S_{subj}(I)$. An example of a subjective saliency map is presented in Fig. 2. Subjective saliency maps cannot be used for real-world applications in video analysis, as requiring psycho-visual experiments for each video to process. We are thus interested in an automatic *objective* saliency maps. The subjective saliency maps will be used as the ground truth to asses the objective maps automatically built.

4   Objective Saliency Map

To delimit the area of video analysis in video frames to the regions which are potentially interesting to human observers we need to model visual saliency on the basis of video signal features. Here we follow the results of community research we reported in Section 1 proposing fusion of spatial, temporal and geometric cues. We extend the state-of-the art approaches by a specific modelling of geometrical saliency and propose multiplicative fusion of all three cues.

4.1   Spatial Saliency Map

The spatial saliency map S_{sp} is mainly based on color contrasts [17]. We used the method from O. Brouard, V. Ricordel and D. Barba [7]. The spatial saliency map extraction is based on seven color contrast descriptors. These descriptors are computed in the HSI color space. On the contrary to RGB color system, the HSI color space is well suited to describe color interpretation by humans. The spatial saliency is defined according to the following seven local color contrasts V in the HSI domain : the *Contrast of Saturation*, *Contrast of Intensity*, *Contrast of Hue*, *Contrast of Opponents*, *Contrast of Warm and Cold Colors*, *Dominance of Warm Colors*, and *Dominance of Brightness and Saturation*.

The spatial saliency value $S'_{sp}(I, i)$ for pixel i from frame I is computed by mean fusion operator from seven color contrast descriptors (3) :

$$S'_{sp}(I, i) = \frac{1}{7} \sum_{\varsigma=1}^{7} V_{\varsigma}(I, i) \qquad (3)$$

Finally, $S'_{sp}(I, i)$ is normalized between 0 and 1 to $S_{sp}(I, i)$ according to its maximum value.

4.2   Temporal Saliency Map

The objective spatio-temporal saliency map model requires a temporal saliency dimension. This section will describe how to build temporal saliency maps. The temporal saliency map S_t models the attraction of attention to motion singularities in a scene. The visual attention is not grabbed by the motion itself. The gaze is attracted by the motion difference between the *real* motion scene and the global motion scene. The motion difference is called the residual motion. O. Brouard et al. [7] and S. Marat [18] propose a temporal saliency map model that takes advantage of the residual motion. In this paper, we have implemented the model from O. Brouard et al. [7].

The temporal saliency map is computed in three steps. The first one is the optical flow estimation. Then the global motion is estimated in order to get the residual motion. Finally a psycho-visual filter is applied on the residual motion.

To compute the optical flow, we have applied the Lucas Kanade method from OpenCV library [19]. The optical flow was sparsely computed on 4x4 blocks, as good results were reported in [20] when using 4×4 macro-block motion vectors from the H.264 AVC compressed stream. The next step in temporal saliency computation is the global motion estimation.

The goal here is to estimate a global motion model to differentiate then local motion from camera motion. In this work, we follow the preliminary study from [20] and use a complete first order affine model (4) :

$$\begin{aligned} dx_i &= a_1 + a_2 x + a_3 y \\ dy_i &= a_4 + a_5 x + a_6 y \end{aligned} \qquad (4)$$

Here $\theta = (a_1, a_2, \ldots, a_6)^T$ is the parameter vector of the global model (4) and $(dx_i, dy_i)^T$ is the motion vector of a block. To estimate this model, we used robust least square estimator presented in [21]. We denote this motion vector $\boldsymbol{V}_\theta(I, i)$. Our goal is now to extract the local motion in video frames i.e. residual motion with regard to model (4). We denote the macro-block optical flow motion vector $\boldsymbol{V}_c(I, i)$. The residual motion $\boldsymbol{V}_r(I, i)$ is computed as a difference between block motion vectors and estimated global motion vectors.

Finally, the temporal saliency map $S_t(I, i)$ is computed by filtering the amount of residual motion in the frame. The authors of [7] reported, as established by S. Daly, that the human eye cannot follow objects with a velocity higher than $80°/s$ [22]. In this case, the saliency is null. S. Daly has also demonstrated that the saliency reaches its maximum with motion values between $6°/s$ and $30°/s$. According to this psycho-visual constraints, the filter proposed in [7] is given by (5).

$$S_t(s_i) = \begin{cases} \frac{1}{6}\boldsymbol{V}_r(I, i), & \text{if } 0 \le \boldsymbol{V}_r(I, i) < \boldsymbol{v}_1 \\ 1, & \text{if } \boldsymbol{v}_1 \le \boldsymbol{V}_r(I, i) < \boldsymbol{v}_2 \\ -\frac{1}{50}\boldsymbol{V}_r(I, i) + \frac{8}{5}, & \text{if } \boldsymbol{v}_2 \le \boldsymbol{V}_r(I, i) < \boldsymbol{v}_{max} \\ 0, & \text{if } \boldsymbol{v}_{max} \le \boldsymbol{V}_r(I, i) \end{cases} \quad (5)$$

with $\boldsymbol{v}_1 = 6°/s$, $\boldsymbol{v}_2 = 30°/s$ and $\boldsymbol{v}_{max} = 80°/s$. We follow this filtering scheme in temporal saliency map computation.

4.3 Geometric Saliency Map

As stated in the introduction, many studies have showed that the observers are attracted by the screen center. In [7], the geometrical saliency map is a 2D Gaussian located at the screen center with a spread $\sigma_x = \sigma_y = 5°$. In our psycho-visual experiments we stated that in a shoulder-fixed wearable camera video the gaze is always located in the first upper third of video frames, see the scattered plot of subjective saliency peaks in Fig. 3. Therefore, we have set the 2D Gaussian center at $x_0 = \frac{width}{2}$ and $y_0 = \frac{height}{3}$. The geometrical saliency S_g map equation is given by (6).

$$S_g(I) = e^{-\left(\frac{(x-x_0)^2}{2\sigma_x^2} + \frac{(y-y_0)^2}{2\sigma_y^2}\right)} \quad (6)$$

However, this attraction may change with the camera motion. This is explained by the anticipation phenomenon [14], see section 3.1. Hence we propose to simulate this phenomenon by moving the 2D Gaussian centred on initial "geometric saliency point" in the direction of the camera motion projected in the image plane. A rough approximation of this projection is the motion of image center computed with the global motion estimation model, equation (4), where $x = \frac{width}{2}$ and $y = \frac{height}{2}$.

4.4 Saliency Map Fusion

In the previous sections we explained how to compute spatial temporal and geometric saliency maps. In this section we describe the method that merges

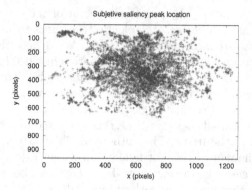

Fig. 3. Scattered plot of subjective saliency peaks for all database frames

these three saliency maps in the target *objective* saliency map. The fusion result is a spatio-temporal-geometric saliency map. In [20], several fusion methods for the spatio-temporal saliency without geometric component were proposed. We have tested these fusion methods on wearable video database. The results show that the multiplicative fusion performs the best. So for the full spatio-temporal-geometric saliency we compute multiplicative S^{mul}_{sp-t-g} (7).

$$S^{mul}_{sp-t-g}(I) = S_{sp}(I) \times S_t(I) \times S_g(I) \tag{7}$$

5 Evaluation

5.1 Normalized Scanpath Saliency

In this section, we compare the *objective* spatio-temporal saliency maps with *subjective* saliency map obtained from gaze tracking S_{subj}.

Here, we use the Normalized Scanpath Saliency (NSS) metric that was proposed in [18]. The NSS is a Z-Score that expresses the divergence of the subjective saliency maps from the objective saliency maps. The NSS computation for a frame I is depicted by (8). Here, S^N_{obj} denotes the objective saliency map S_{obj} normalized to have a zero mean and a unit standard deviation, $\bar{X}$ means an average. When $\overline{S_{subj} \times S^N_{obj}}$ is higher than the average objective saliency, the NSS is positive; it means that the gaze locations are inside the saliency depicted by the objective saliency map. In other words, higher the NSS is, more objective and subjective saliency maps are similar.

$$NSS = \frac{\overline{S_{subj} \times S^N_{obj}} - \overline{S_{obj}}}{\sigma(S_{obj})} \tag{8}$$

The NSS score for a video sequence is obtained by computing the average of NSS for all frames as in [18]. Then the overall NSS score on each video database is the average NSS of all video sequences. Results are presented in the next section.

5.2 Results

In this section, we compare the correlation of three automatic saliency maps with the subjective saliency. These three saliency maps are the spatio-temporal saliency map, the spatio-temporal-geometrical without camera motion, and the proposed method the spatio-temporal-geometrical with camera motion, expressing the anticipation phenomenon. The 28 video sequences described in Section 2 from wearable cameras are all characterized by strong camera motion which is up to 50 pixels magnitude in the center of frames. As it can be seen from the Fig. 4 the proposed method with moving of geometrical Gaussian almost systematically outperforms the base-line spatio-temporal saliency model and the spatio-temporal-geometrical saliency with a fixed Gaussian. For few sequences (e.g. number 2), the performance is poorer than obtained by geometric saliency with a fixed Gaussian. In these visual scenes, the distractors appear in the field of view. The resulting subjective saliency map then contains multiple maxima due to the unequal perception of scenes by the subjects. This is more "semantic saliency" phenomenon (faces, etc) which can not be handled with the proposed model. The average NSS on the whole database also shows the interest of proposed moving geometrical saliency. The mean NSS scores are respectively 1.832 for spatio-temporal, 2.607 for spatio-temporal with still geometrical Gaussian, and 2.791 with moving geometrical Gaussian. Which means 52.37% improvement of correspondence with subjective visual saliency map, which was our goal.

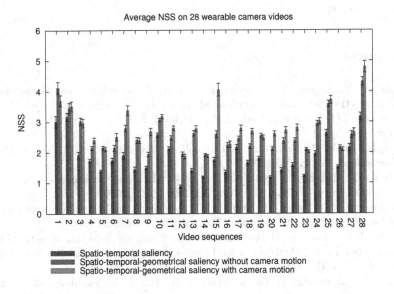

Fig. 4. Average NSS computed on 28 videos from a wearable camera

6   Conclusion

Hence in this work we proposed new objective visual saliency model and computation method by fusing spatial, temporal and geometric cues in video frames. The method was proposed for video with a strong motion recorded with cameras worn by subjects in the context of recording of Instrumental Activities of Daily Living. To our knowledge, this is the first attempt to define saliency in such a content taking into account psycho-visual models known for other types of traditional video content. First of all, conducting psycho-visual experiment on a representative set of test subjects, we stated the anticipation phenomenon in gaze positioning which was obviously transmitted to the subjective saliency map built according to Wooding method. While in previous research, the geometrical saliency was systematically frame centred, we recorded experimental evidence of the dependence of the geometric saliency of camera fixation on a body. Finally, in order to incorporate the anticipation phenomenon into the automatic construction of objective saliency map we expressed it by moving geometric saliency Gaussian in direction of camera motion projected into the image plane. These results are encouraging. In some video sequences moving of geometric Gaussian allows to improve the NSS up to 40% compared to fixed Gaussian and up-to 50% compared to base-line spatio-temporal psycho-visual saliency model. In the future of this work we will work on incorporating distractors and on saliency -based feature weighting in the problem of scene recognition.

Acknowledgments. This research is supported by the EU FP7 PI Dem@Care project #288199.

References

1. Ionescu, B., Vertan, C., Lambert, P., Benoit, A.: A color-action perceptual approach to the classification of animated movies. In: Proceedings of the 1st ACM International Conference on Multimedia Retrieval, ICMR 2011, pp. 10:1–10:8. ACM, New York (2011)
2. Itti, L., Koch, C.: Computational modelling of visual attention. Nature Review Neuroscience 2, 194–203 (2001)
3. Itti, L.: Quantifying the contribution of low-level saliency to human eye movements in dynamic scenes. Visual Cognition 12, 1093–1123 (2005)
4. Le Meur, O., Le Callet, P., Barba, D.: Predicting visual fixations on video based on low-level video features. Vision Research 47, 1057–1092 (2007)
5. Tatler, B.W.: The central fixation bias in scene viewing: Selecting an optimal viewing position independently of motor biases and image feature distributions. Journal of Vision 7, 1–17 (2007)
6. Dorr, M., Martinetz, T., Gegenfurtner, K.R., Barth, E.: Variability of eye movements when viewing dynamic natural scenes. Journal of Vision 10 (2010)
7. Brouard, O., Ricordel, V., Barba, D.: Cartes de Saillance Spatio-Temporelle basées Contrastes de Couleur et Mouvement Relatif. In: Compression et Representation des Signaux Audiovisuels, CORESA 2009, Toulouse, France, 6 pages (2009)

8. Lee, Y.J., Ghosh, J., Grauman, K.: Discovering important people and objects for egocentric video summarization. In: Proceedings of the IEEE Conference on Computer Vision and Pattern Recognition, CVPR 2012, pp. 1–8 (2012)
9. Starner, T., Schiele, B., Pentland, A.: Visual contextual awareness in wearable computing. In: ISWC, pp. 50–57 (1998)
10. Ren, X., Philipose, M.: Egocentric recognition of handled objects: Benchmark and analysis. In: Computer Vision and Pattern Recognition Workshop, pp. 1–8 (2009)
11. Karaman, S., Benois-Pineau, J., Mégret, R., Dovgalecs, V., Dartigues, J.F., Gaëstel, Y.: Human Daily Activities Indexing in Videos from Wearable Cameras for Monitoring of Patients with Dementia Diseases. In: ICPR 2010, Istanbul, Turquie, pp. 4113–4116 (2010) ANR-09-BLAN-0165-02
12. Szolgay, D., Benois-Pineau, J., Mégret, R., Gaëstel, Y., Dartigues, J.F.: Detection of moving foreground objects in videos with strong camera motion. Pattern Analysis and Applications 14, 311–328 (2011)
13. International Telecommunication Union: Methodology for the subjective assessment of the quality of television pictures. Recommendation BT.500-11, International Telecommunication Union (2002)
14. Land, M., Mennie, N., Rusted, J.: The roles of vision and eye movements in the control of activities of daily living. Perception 28, 1311–1328 (1999)
15. Wooding, D.: Eye movements of large populations: Ii. Deriving regions of interest, coverage, and similarity using fixation maps. Behavior Research Methods 34, 518–528 (2002), doi:10.3758/BF03195481
16. Hood, D.C., Finkelstein, M.A.: Sensitivity to light. In: Boff, K.R., Kaufman, L., Thomas, J.P. (eds.) Handbook of Perception and Human Performance. Sensory processes and perception, vol. 1, pp. 5-1–5-66. John Wiley & Sons, New York (1986)
17. Aziz, M., Mertsching, B.: Fast and robust generation of feature maps for region-based visual attention. IEEE Transactions on Image Processing 17, 633–644 (2008)
18. Marat, S., Ho Phuoc, T., Granjon, L., Guyader, N., Pellerin, D., Guérin-Dugué, A.: Modelling spatio-temporal saliency to predict gaze direction for short videos. International Journal of Computer Vision 82, 231–243 (2009), Département Images et Signal
19. Bouguet, J.Y.: Pyramidal implementation of the lucas kanade feature tracker. Intel Corporation, Microprocessor Research Labs (2000)
20. Boujut, H., Benois-Pineau, J., Ahmed, T., Hadar, O., Bonnet, P.: A metric for no-reference video quality assessment for hd tv delivery based on saliency maps. In: 2011 IEEE International Conference on Multimedia and Expo (ICME), pp. 1–5 (2011)
21. Kraemer, P., Benois-Pineau, J., Domenger, J.P.: Scene Similarity Measure for Video Content Segmentation in the Framework of Rough Indexing Paradigm, Espagne, pp. 141–155 (2004)
22. Daly, S.J.: Engineering observations from spatiovelocity and spatiotemporal visual models. In: IS&T/SPIE Conference on Human Vision and Electronic Imaging III, vol. 3299, pp. 180–191 (1998)

Enhancing Semantic Features with Compositional Analysis for Scene Recognition

Miriam Redi and Bernard Merialdo

EURECOM, Sophia Antipolis
2229 Route de Cretes
Sophia Antipolis
{redi,merialdo}@eurecom.fr

Abstract. Scene recognition systems are generally based on features that represent the image semantics by modeling the content depicted in a given image. In this paper we propose a framework for scene recognition that goes beyond the mere visual content analysis by exploiting a new cue for categorization: the image *composition*, namely its photographic style and layout. We extract information about the image composition by storing the values of affective, aesthetic and artistic features in a *compositional vector*. We verify the discriminative power of our *compositional vector* for scene categorization by using it for the classification of images from various, diverse, large scale scene understanding datasets. We then combine the compositional features with traditional semantic features in a complete scene recognition framework. Results show that, due to the complementarity of compositional and semantic features, scene categorization systems indeed benefit from the incorporation of descriptors representing the image photographic layout (+ 13-15% over semantic-only categorization).

1 Introduction

The automatic recognition of visual scenes is a typical, non-trivial computer vision task. The aim is to automatically identify the place where a given image has been captured, or, for example, the type of environment in which a robot is navigating. The general approach is to build a statistical model that can distinguish between pre-defined image classes given a low-dimensional description of the image input, namely a feature vector (here also *signature* or *descriptor*).

Fig. 1. Similar images share similar compositional attributes: depth of field for monuments, point of view for sports field, contrast for natural scenes, level of details and order for indoor scenes.

A. Fusiello et al. (Eds.): ECCV 2012 Ws/Demos, Part III, LNCS 7585, pp. 446–455, 2012.

One of the main elements influencing the effectiveness of categorization frameworks is indeed the composition of the descriptors used for categorization, because it represents the visual content of the image, i.e. its *semantics*, and semantic analysis is of crucial importance for the identification of the scene category. In scene recognition literature, semantic features are extracted to analyze the image content using either local analysis, based on local interest point descriptors [1] aggregated into a compact image representation [2], or global analysis [3], where general properties of the image, such as color or texture distribution, are summarized into a single descriptor.

Semantic information is without discussion the primary cue for scene identification. However, there exists another important source of information regarding the image scene, namely its *composition*, that could be helpful to recognize the scene category. It has been indeed extensively studied and verified in photography theory [4] that the composition of an image and the content depicted are closely related. We understand here as image composition a combination of aesthetic, affective and artistic components that concur in creating its photographic style, intent [5] and layout. How is this related to scene identification? For example, intuitively it is more likely than an image with a high level of symmetry depicts a non-natural scene (e.g. a building), or that a picture with high level of detail comes from indoor environments. Moreover, as proved in [6], groups of semantically similar images can share the same compositional attributes (e.g. same point of view and depth of field for buildings or sport fields, same color contrast for natural outdoor scenes, see Figure 1).

Given these observations, in this paper we explore the role of compositional attributes for scene recognition using a computational approach. This work represents one of the first attempts of verifying the discriminative ability of compositional features for scene categorization. We design a categorization system that incorporates affective, aesthetic and artistic features, and combines them with traditional semantic descriptors for scene classification. The fusion of such different, discriminative and complementary sources of information about the scene attributes brings a substantial improvement of the scene categorization performances, compared to systems based on semantic features only.

While in literature [7] compositional attributes are generally related to the simple image layout (**aesthetic** attributes, e.g. rules of thirds), here we extend this definition to include **affective** (emotional) and **artistic** attributes that can help characterizing the "intent" [5] of the photographer when composing a given picture. Arranging pictures is not only about applying objective rules, but it is also about following an artistic, intuitive process and convey intentions, meanings and emotions [5]. In order to properly describe the image composition, we therefore extract a set of features from three closely related domains, namely computational aesthetics [8,9] , affective image analysis [10] and artwork analysis [11], and collect them into a single *compositional descriptor*. Many of the features we extract have been proved to be discriminative in their respective domains, but here, we test their discriminative ability for scene classification. In addition to existing features, e.g. low depth of field indicators [8], or color names

[10], we implement two new compositional features: our own version of "image uniqueness", namely a measure evaluating the novelty of the image content, and our own formula to determine image "symmetry". Moreover, we also extract popular semantic features such as the Saliency Moments [12] and the Bag of Words [2]. Then, for both sources of information (compositional+semantic), we use Support Vector Machines to model the feature space and predict the scene category. We then experiment with different fusion methods (early, late) to combine the semantic and compositional information extracted with such features.

We test the effectiveness of our *compositional descriptor* for scene classification using a variety of challenging datasets [13,3,14], including the SUN [14] dataset, that contains around 400 categories of very diverse scenes. We first use our compositional vector as a stand-alone descriptor and we verify that compositional features carry discriminative power for scene categorization. Moreover, we show that, by summarizing the image layout properties into an image descriptor for classification, we introduce a new, complementary source of information regarding the scene characteristics. Therefore, when we combine our descriptor with traditional semantic features in a complete scene categorization system, we increase the classification accuracy of a semantic feature-only system by 13-15% for both small-scale [13,3] and large-scale [14] scene understanding datasets.

The remainder of this paper is organized as follows: in Sec. 2 we outline the state of the art methods related to compositional scene analysis; we then show in Sec. 3 the details of our scene categorization framework embedding compositional and semantic features; finally, we validate our hypothesis with some experimental results in Section 4.

2   Related Work

Compositional features as we understand them have been used in literature for aesthetic, affective or artistic image analysis. Aesthetic image analysis aim at building systems that automatically define the beauty degree of an image: for example, Datta et al. in [8] extract features that model photography rules using a computational approach to predict subjective aesthetic scores for photographs; such model is improved in [15] by adding saliency information in the aesthetic degree prediction framework. In affective image analysis, the aim is to automatically define the type of emotions that a given image arouses: in [16], specific color-based features are designed for affective analysis and in [10], a pool of features arising from psychology and art, and related to the image composition, is proposed to infer the emotions generated by digital images. In art image analysis, specific computational features (e.g. complexity, shape of segments) are designed to investigate patterns in paintings [11] or to assess artwork quality [17].

The interaction between semantic and compositional information has been studied before to improve the modeling of aesthetic/artistic properties of digital images. For example, in [7] semantic concepts are detected in order to enhance the prediction of image aesthetic and interestingness degrees; another approach that combines computational aesthetics with semantic information is proposed

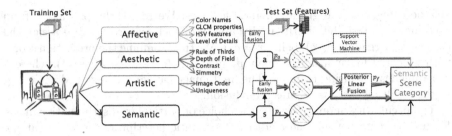

Fig. 2. Combining compositional and semantic attributes for scene recognition

by Obrador et al. [9], that build a set of category-based models for beauty degree prediction; moreover, in [18], painting annotation performances are improved by adding semantic analysis in the artwork understanding framework.

While the relation between semantics and composition has been investigated to improve aesthetic/artistic/emotional analysis, few works have explored the other way around: are compositional features useful for semantic analysis? In this paper, we address this question by combining typical stylistic features with semantic descriptor for scene classification. To our knowledge, the only related work that addresses the same question is the one presented by Van Gemert [6], that generalize the spatial pyramid descriptor aggregator by incorporating photographic style attributes for object recognition. Our work differs from the one in [6] because (1) we focus on a different problem, namely scene categorization rather than object recognition, testing on a variety of challenging databases (2) we test the effectiveness of the actual compositional feature for scene recognition, rather than being inspired from photographic style to modify an existing algorithm.

3   Analyzing Compositional Attributes for Scene Recognition

Scene recognition systems automatically categorize a given image into a predefined set of semantic classes corresponding to different scenery situations. In our approach, we exploit for this purpose the informativeness regarding image composition and photographic style typical of aesthetic, artistic and affective image features. We then combine them with the discriminative traditional semantic features in a complete scene categorization system that predicts an image class based on such diverse sources of information.

Our general framework is basically a traditional image categorization/retrieval framework (see Fig. 2): based on compositional image features, for each category, we learn a model from the training images with Support Vector Machines (SVMs). Similarly, we train a set of SVMs (one for each class) using a set of semantic features. In the test phase, for a new image, given both compositional and semantic features and the models previously computed, we obtain, for each category c, $p_a(c)$ i.e. the category score given compositional features, and $p_s(c)$, i.e. the category score given semantic features. We retain the prediction from each model to test the discriminative ability of each feature, and we assign the category as $\arg\max_c p_x(c)$, being $x = a, s$. We then combine the prediction scores with weighted linear fusion, namely $p_f(c) = \lambda(p_a(c)) - (1 - \lambda)(p_s(c))$, where λ is a value learnt during training. The final image category is assigned according to the resulting category scores after fusion.

The peculiarity of our system is the choice of particular, discriminative image features that go beyond the traditional semantic descriptors for scene categorization by evaluating not only the content but also the compositional style of the image. In the remainder of this Section, we therefore focus on the analysis of the compositional features we extract from the image, together with some insights about the type of semantic analysis we perform to complete the scene recognition task.

3.1   Compositional Features: Aesthetic, Affective and Artistic Features

Previous works in computational image composition [9,7] understands it as a set of objective rules for constructing the image layout. For example, compositional attributes have been defined for aesthetic scene analysis as *"characteristics related to the layout of an image that indicate how closely the image follows photographic rules of composition"* [7]. Here, we extend this concept to include features describing image emotional and artistic traits. As Freeman states in [5] *"So far we have been concerned with the vocabulary of grammar and composition, but the process usually begins with purpose - a general or specific idea of what kind of image a photographer wants"*. In order to model the photographer's "intent" as defined by Freeman, we summarize the image composition using affective attributes, that describe the emotions that a given image arouses through affective measures, and artistic attributes, that determine, for example, the "uniqueness" of a given image.

In order to effectively describe the image photographic and artistic composition, we therefore design a compositional descriptor of 43 features coming from emotion-based image recognition, computational aesthetics, and painting analysis. For each image/frame, we extract our compositional 43-d feature vector $a = \{a(i)\}_{i=1}^{43}$, as follows:

Color names, a(1-9). Similar to [10] we count the amount of 9 different common colors in the image: different color combinations are used from artists/photographers to arouse different emotions.

GLCM properties, a(10-19). Gray-level co-occurrence matrices [19] are efficient ways to infer the image texture properties, which are of crucial importance to determine the affective content of a given image. Here, similar to [10], we fill our feature vector with the properties of correlation, homogeneity, energy, entropy and dissimilarity inferred from the GLCM matrix of a given image.

HSV features, a(20-25). After transforming the image into HSV space, we take the mean of hue, saturation and brightness, and compute *pleasure, arousal* and *dominance* features according to [10].

Level of detail, a(26). We measure image homogeneity from [10] based on the number of segments resulting after waterfall segmentation.

Rule of thirds, a(27-29). We evaluate how much the image follows the photography rule of thirds by taking the mean of Hue, Saturation and Brightness of the image inner rectangle, as in [8].

Low depth of field, a(30-38). The depth of field measures the ranges of distances from the observer that appear acceptably sharp in a scene. We extract low DoF indicators using wavelet coefficients as described in [8].

Contrast, a(39). As in [20], we extract the contrast Michelson measure [21].

Image Order, a(40,41). According to Birkhoff [22], image beauty can be found in the ratio between order and complexity. Following this theory, image (in particular, arts and painting) order is computed in [11] using an information theory approach. We compute here the image order using Shannon Entropy and Kologomorov Complexity approaches proposed in [11].

Symmetry, a(42). Image Symmetry is a very important element to define the image layout. We define our own symmetry feature: We extract the Edge Histogram Descriptor [23] on both the left half and the right half of the image (but inverting major and minor diagonals in the right half), and retain the difference between the resulting histograms as the amount of symmetry in the image.

Uniqueness, a(43). How much an image represents a novelty compared to known information, how much is an image unique, i.e. it differs from the common image behavior? this variable can tell much about the artistic content of an image. We propose a new solution to address this question. We define the common image behavior according to the "1/f law" [24], saying that the average amplitude spectrum of a set of images obeys a $1/f$ distribution. We measure the uniqueness by computing the Euclidean distance between the average spectrum of the images in the database and the spectrum of each image.

We finally normalize all the features in the range [0,1] and combine them into our compositional vector.

3.2 Semantic Features

The core of the discriminative power of our scene recognition system is still the set of semantic features for categorization. Here, we select to compute a powerful global feature for scene recognition, namely the Saliency Moments (SM) descriptor. The SM has been proved in [12] to outperform existing features for image categorization and retrieval and it was effectively used in various Trecvid runs (e.g. [25]) due to its complementarity with the state of the art image descriptors. The SM descriptor exploits the informativeness of the saliency distribution in a given image and computes a fast, low dimensional gist of the image through visual attention information summary. First, the spectral saliency map [26] is extracted. Such spectral signal is then sampled using Gabor Filters: the resulting Saliency Components are then decomposed into smaller regions, then mean and higher order statistics are calculated for each region and stored in the final 462-d feature vector $s = \{s(l)\}_{l=1}^{462}$.

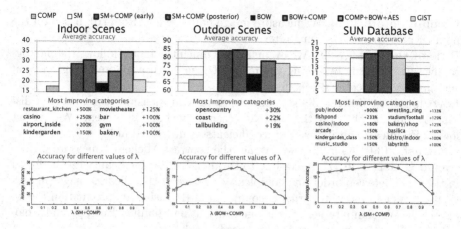

Fig. 3. Results of large scale and small scale scene recognition

Moreover, for indoor and outdoor scene recognition, we extract also a sematic feature based on local image descriptors aggregation, namely the Bag-of-Words (BOW) feature. The BOW model [2] is one of the most used approaches for semantic indexing and image retrieval. In this approach, local descriptors as SIFT [1] are computed to describe the surroundings of salient [27] or densely sampled [28] points. Each image is then mapped into a fixed length signature through a visual codebook computed by clustering the local descriptors in the training set. We chose this feature for its high discriminative ability and its complementarity to global features such as SM and our compositional feature.

4   Experimental Results

In order to test the effectiveness of the proposed approach, and verify the usefulness of aesthetic and affective features for semantic indexing, we use our framework for two scene recognition tasks: small scale categorization and large scale categorization. For the first task, we use two very popular benchmarking datasets for indoor [13] and outdoor [3] scene recognition, while for large scale scene recognition, we test our system on the challenging SUN database [14].

For each database, we first compute the classification accuracy given the model built using each semantic feature (i.e. "BOW" or "SM" in Fig. 3). We then look at the classification performances resulting from using our compositional feature ("COMP") as a stand-alone descriptor. Furthermore, we show the effectiveness of the combination of aesthetic and compositional features by first fusing semantic and aesthetic features in a single, early fused descriptor (e.g. "SM+COMP (early)"). Finally, we combine the predictions of the single-descriptor-based models with posterior linear fusion. We fix the parameter λ for fusion and show the resulting, improved, performances (e.g. "SM+COMP (posterior)" in Fig. 3). For all descriptors and datasets proposed, we learn the feature space through a multiclass SVM with Radial Basis Function Kernel and we evaluate the performances by average multiclass accuracy.

4.1   Small Scale Scene Recognition

Automatic classification of images into scene categories is performed here using the proposed framework over two small scale dataset for indoor and outdoor scene recognition.

Outdoor Scenes

The Outdoor Scenes Dataset was first introduced in [3] to evaluate the performances of a very popular descriptor for scene categorization, namely the Gist descriptor. It is composed of 2600 color images spanning 8 categories of natural outdoor scenes. In order to perform our experiments, we split the outdoor scene dataset into 100 images per class for training and the rest for testing, as proposed in [3]. For this dataset, we compute both the SM and the BOW descriptors, and combine them with the compositional descriptor proposed in this work.

Results show that, by combining aesthetic, affective and artistic features in our compositional descriptor ("COMP") we obtain an effective descriptor (68% of accuracy VS 12.5% of a random classifiers) for outdoor scene recognition. Moreover, we can see that, while its combination with the SM descriptor does not bring much improvement[1], its fusion with the BOW features increases the performances of the BOW-only classification by 11%.

Indoor Scenes

The Indoor Scenes Dataset,was proposed in [13] as a new, unique database for indoor scene recognition, collecting around 15000 images from various sources, and considering 67 different image categories related to indoor environments. For our experiments, we split this datasets as proposed in [13]: for each class, we retain 20 images for testing and the rest for training. Again, for this small-scale database we compute both SM and BOW and we combine it with the aesthetic/artistic/affective feature vector.

Results in this task clearly highlight the effectiveness of compositional features for scene recognition: while the accuracy of the compositional descriptor alone is not as good as semantic features (around 17% vs. 26% of SM), but still more than 10 times better than a random classifier ($\sim$ 1,4%), the scenario changes when we combine it with traditional semantic features. As a matter of fact, both the early (+ 8%) and the posterior (+ 15%) fusion with the Saliency Moment descriptor successfully enhance the final scene recognition performances. Similar, more evident behavior when we combine the compositional features with the BOW descriptor: such fusion brings an improvement of 30 % compared to BOW-only classification. Being BOW and SM complementary, and being both complementary to compositional features, we also tried to combine the predictions resulting from the three stand-alone models using posterior linear fusion. The improvement over the classification based on SM (i.e. the most performing stand-alone descriptor) in this case is more than 20%, suggesting that introducing compositional features in the pool of existing semantic features is a promising cue for indoor scene recognition.

---

[1] This is because SM is an extremely effective descriptor by itself for outdoor scenes, and because it contains already some compositional information related to saliency

Large Scale Scene Recognition

Finally, we present our results for large scale scene recognition over the challenging SUN database, proposed in [14] as a complete dataset for scene understanding, with a variety of indoor and outdoor scene environments, spanning 899 categories for more than 130,000 images. As in [14], for benchmarking purposes, we select a pool of 397 scenes out of the categories proposed, and we use a subset of the SUN dataset consisting 10 folds that contains, for each category, 50 images for test and 50 for training. Results are obtained by averaging the performances of the descriptors over the 10 partitions considered. In order to test the effectiveness of our approach, we compute here the SM descriptor and combine it with the compositional feature we propose.

Results on this dataset follow the same pattern of the previously analyzed experiments: the combination of the SM with aesthetic/affective features brings an improvement of 8% with early fusion and 13% with late fusion compared to the SM-only classification, thus confirming the discriminative ability and the complementarity of aesthetic and compositional features for scene recognition even on a large scale.

5   Conclusions

This work represents a first attempt of combining semantic, artistic, affective, and emotional image analysis in a unique framework for scene recognition. We showed with our results that categorization systems benefit from the incorporation of compositional features. The current system can be improved by experimenting with different types of fusion or by designing a set of category-specific compositional vectors, which can be constructed based on the discriminative ability of each feature of each class.

References

1. Lowe, D.: Distinctive image features from scale-invariant keypoints. International Journal of Computer Vision 60, 91–110 (2004)
2. Csurka, G., Dance, C., Fan, L., Willamowski, J., Bray, C.: Visual categorization with bags of keypoints. In: Workshop on Statistical Learning in Computer Vision, ECCV, vol. 1, p. 22. Citeseer (2004)
3. Oliva, A., Torralba, A.: Modeling the shape of the scene: A holistic representation of the spatial envelope. International Journal of Computer Vision 42 (2001)
4. Krages, B.: Photography: the art of composition. Allworth Pr. (2005)
5. Freeman, M.: The photographer's eye: composition and design for better digital photos. Focal Pr. (2007)
6. van Gemert, J.: Exploiting photographic style for category-level image classification by generalizing the spatial pyramid. In: Proceedings of the 1st ACM International Conference on Multimedia Retrieval, p. 14. ACM (2011)
7. Dhar, S., Ordonez, V., Berg, T.: High level describable attributes for predicting aesthetics and interestingness. In: 2011 IEEE Conference on Computer Vision and Pattern Recognition (CVPR), pp. 1657–1664. IEEE (2011)

8. Datta, R., Joshi, D., Li, J., Wang, J.Z.: Studying Aesthetics in Photographic Images Using a Computational Approach. In: Leonardis, A., Bischof, H., Pinz, A. (eds.) ECCV 2006. LNCS, vol. 3953, pp. 288–301. Springer, Heidelberg (2006)
9. Obrador, P., Saad, M.A., Suryanarayan, P., Oliver, N.: Towards Category-Based Aesthetic Models of Photographs. In: Schoeffmann, K., Merialdo, B., Hauptmann, A.G., Ngo, C.-W., Andreopoulos, Y., Breiteneder, C. (eds.) MMM 2012. LNCS, vol. 7131, pp. 63–76. Springer, Heidelberg (2012)
10. Machajdik, J., Hanbury, A.: Affective image classification using features inspired by psychology and art theory. In: Proceedings of the International Conference on Multimedia, pp. 83–92. ACM (2010)
11. Rigau, J., Feixas, M., Sbert, M.: Conceptualizing birkhoff's aesthetic measure using shannon entropy and kolmogorov complexity. In: Computational Aesthetics in Graphics, Visualization, and Imaging (2007)
12. Redi, M., Merialdo, B.: Saliency moments for image categorization. In: Proceedings of the 1st ACM International Conference on Multimedia Retrieval, ICMR 2011 (2011)
13. Quattoni, A., Torralba, A.: Recognizing indoor scenes. In: IEEE Conference on Computer Vision and Pattern Recognition (2009)
14. Xiao, J., Hays, J., Ehinger, K., Oliva, A., Torralba, A.: Sun database: Large-scale scene recognition from abbey to zoo. In: 2010 IEEE Conference on Computer Vision and Pattern Recognition (CVPR), pp. 3485–3492. IEEE (2010)
15. Wong, L., Low, K.: Saliency-enhanced image aesthetics class prediction. In: 2009 16th IEEE International Conference on Image Processing (ICIP). IEEE (2009)
16. Wang, W., Yu, Y.: Image emotional semantic query based on color semantic description. In: Proceedings of 2005 International Conference on Machine Learning and Cybernetics, vol. 7, pp. 4571–4576. IEEE (2005)
17. Li, C., Chen, T.: Aesthetic visual quality assessment of paintings. IEEE Journal of Selected Topics in Signal Processing 3, 236–252 (2009)
18. Leslie, L., Chua, T., Ramesh, J.: Annotation of paintings with high-level semantic concepts using transductive inference and ontology-based concept disambiguation. In: Proceedings of the 15th International Conference on Multimedia. ACM (2007)
19. Haralick, R.M., Shapiro, L.G.: Computer and Robot Vision, 1st edn. Addison-Wesley Longman Publishing Co., Inc., Boston (1992)
20. Desnoyer, M., Wettergreen, D.: Aesthetic image classification for autonomous agents. In: Proc. ICPR. Citeseer (2010)
21. Michelson, A.: Studies in optics. Dover Pubns. (1995)
22. Birkhoff, G.: Aesthetic measure (1933)
23. Won, C., Park, D., Park, S.: Efficient use of mpeg-7 edge histogram descriptor. Etri Journal 24, 23–30 (2002)
24. Ruderman, D.: The statistics of natural images. Network: Computation in Neural Systems 5, 517–548 (1994)
25. Delezoide, B., Precioso, F., Redi, M., Merialdo, B., Granjon, L., Pellerin, D., Rombaut, M., Jégou, H., Vieux, R., Mansencal, B., et al.: Irim at trecvid 2011: Semantic indexing and instance search. TREC Online Proceedings (2011)
26. Hou, X., Zhang, L.: Saliency detection: A spectral residual approach. In: IEEE Conference on Computer Vision and Pattern Recognition, CVPR 2007. IEEE (2007)
27. Fergus, R., Perona, P., Zisserman, A.: Object class recognition by unsupervised scale-invariant learning. In: Proceedings of the 2003 IEEE Computer Society Conference on Computer Vision and Pattern Recognition, vol. 2. IEEE (2003)
28. Fei-Fei, L., Perona, P.: A bayesian hierarchical model for learning natural scene categories. In: IEEE Computer Society Conference on Computer Vision and Pattern Recognition, CVPR 2005, vol. 2, pp. 524–531. IEEE (2005)

Object Reading:
Text Recognition for Object Recognition

Sezer Karaoglu, Jan C. van Gemert, and Theo Gevers

Intelligent Systems Lab Amsterdam (ISLA), University of Amsterdam,
Science Park 904, 1098 XH, Amsterdam, The Netherlands

Abstract. We propose to use text recognition to aid in visual object
class recognition. To this end we first propose a new algorithm for text
detection in natural images. The proposed text detection is based on
saliency cues and a context fusion step. The algorithm does not need
any parameter tuning and can deal with varying imaging conditions. We
evaluate three different tasks: 1. Scene text recognition, where we increase
the state-of-the-art by 0.17 on the ICDAR 2003 dataset. 2. Saliency based
object recognition, where we outperform other state-of-the-art saliency
methods for object recognition on the PASCAL VOC 2011 dataset. 3.
Object recognition with the aid of recognized text, where we are the first
to report multi-modal results on the IMET set. Results show that text
helps for object class recognition if the text is not uniquely coupled to
individual object instances.

1 Introduction

Text in natural scenes typically adds semantic information to the scene. For
example, text adds identification on the brand or type of a product, it specifies
which buildings serve food, and gives directions by road signs. In this paper,
we propose to exploit this semantic relationship between text and the scene to
improve automatic object recognition where visual cues may not prove sufficient.

Traditional optical character recognition (OCR) systems are well-suited for
documents however their performance drastically drops when applied to natural scene images. The challenges for OCR include an unknown background
and varying text sizes, styles and orientations. Moreover, the imaging conditions
are often unknown, which adds sensitivity to specular reflections, shadows, occlusion, (motion) blur and resolution. To overcome such issues, we propose to
rely on visual saliency for detecting text regions in the image. Color invariants
and curvature saliency allows robustness to imaging conditions, whereas context
information gathered by text distribution statistics addresses the background.
Unlike state-of-the-art text detection methods [1,2] we do not rely on any heuristics nor on a learning phase. Therefore, the proposed method can detect a-priori
unseen text styles at any orientation and scale. Moreover, we show that the proposed saliency method is not limited to text, and can also be applied for generic
object recognition.

A. Fusiello et al. (Eds.): ECCV 2012 Ws/Demos, Part III, LNCS 7585, pp. 456–465, 2012.

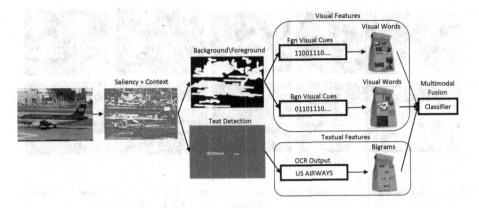

Fig. 1. Visual saliency is used for object recognition and for text detection. The detected text is converted to characters and words, which in turn are used in a bag-of-character-bigrams text classifier. This text classifier is combined with a bag-of-visual-words image representation

The contributions of this paper are twofold. First, we propose a novel saliency method with a context integration step that can be used both for text and object recognition. Second, we integrate saliency into a full end-to-end text detection and recognition pipeline that incorporates recognized text in the visual scene for image classification. In figure 1 we show an overview of our approach.

2   Related Work

Learning-based approaches for classifying text regions [1,3,4] typically use Histogram of Gradients (HOG), edge density or contrast features. Such features are computationally expensive since they require an exhaustive scale and spatial search. Moreover, the necessity of a learning phase makes these systems language dependent. They require a new classifier for each different language or text style and are therefore not robust for unknown sets of text structures. Our approach does not require any learning and is compatible with any a-priori unknown languages and text styles.

Other approaches without a learning phase use heuristics to exploit the geometric and structural properties of text. Such properties are typically based on connected components (CC) and include a stroke width transform [2], component size or distribution of gradients. A threshold is typically used to classify regions as text. However, relying on thresholds makes these approaches sensitive to changing conditions such as text font, text orientation and unknown languages. In this paper we introduce a novel contextual guidance approach to prevent using any predefined thresholds.

Texts in natural scenes are typically designed to attract attention. The work of Judd et al. [5] show that scene texts receive many eye fixations and psychophysical experiments done by Wang and Pomplun [6] confirm that text is

Fig. 2. An example of the saliency maps. (a) Original, (b) Color Boosting, (c) Curvature Shape Saliency (d) Context guided Saliency and (e) Final output.

salient. Other work [7] compares different saliency methods to show that such methods may be used to locate scene text. All this research evaluates existing visual attention models for text detection to show that scene text is salient. In this paper, we introduce a new visual attention model to improve text detection.

The work done by Zhu et al. [8] is the most similar to ours. The authors exploit information from text regions in natural scenes to improve object/scene classification accuracy. The authors combine visual features extracted from the full image with features extracted only from detected text regions. We, in contrast, truly recognize the text from images rather than investigating the visual features extracted from text regions.

3 Saliency and Context Cues for Text Detection

We propose text detection based on saliency cues. Such cues prevent an exhaustive spatial and scale search over all possible regions. We focus on color and curvature saliency cues, and rely on context information to bind them.

Color Boosting Saliency. Texts often have a uniform distinct color that makes them stand out from their surroundings. The distinctiveness of the local color information is commonly ignored by most of the saliency detectors. Previous methods [7,9] mainly focus on obtaining gradient information only from the luminance channel. To add color to general image gradients, Van de Weijer et al. [10] use information theory to boost color information by replacing gradient strength with information content. Let $f_x = (O_{1x}, O_{2x}, O_{3x})^T$ be the spatial image derivatives in the x dimension where O_1 stands for the first opponent color channel, then information theory relates the information content I as $I(f_x) = -\log(p(f_x))$, where $p(f_x)$ is the probability of the spatial derivative. We integrate color boosting to enhance the saliency of text color transitions. In figure 2b we show an example of color boosting applied to texts.

Curvature Saliency. Color boosting saliency is not sensitive to colorless edge transitions, see the top image in figure 2b. Consequently, we aim for a shape-based saliency approach in addition to color boosting saliency. To this end, we employ curvature saliency (D) as used in the work by Valenti et al. [11], defined by $D = \sqrt{f_{I,xx}^2 + f_{I,xy}^2 + f_{I,yy}^2}$, where $f_{I,xx}$ and $f_{I,yy}$ stand for the second-order derivatives of the intensity image $f_I(x,y)$ in the x and y dimensions, respectively. Due to the contrast between text and its background, text regions strongly respond to curvature saliency.

Contextual Priors. We remove non-text regions which are mistakenly detected by color boosting and curvature saliency maps by contextual priming. We analyzed the spatial occurrence probability of text in natural scene images from the ICDAR 2003[1] text locating competition training set. The occurrence probability for a given location is calculated by counting the presence of text for that location in the full training set. The spatial occurrence probability of text in the ICDAR dataset shows that the regions in the center of the image space are most likely to be text, see figure 3. This may be due to the fact that interesting objects are tend to be placed in the center of the images by human photographers.

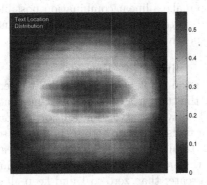

Fig. 3. Spatial occurrence probability of text in the ICDAR 2003 training dataset

Since text is generally present in the image center, we base our contextual integration step on connectivity of the background. Specifically, we aim to connect all background regions with the help of the text occurrence probability map. We build a non-text map for each image, by connecting the non-text regions with conditional dilation. Conditional dilation (δ) is a morphological operation which can be defined as $\delta_B(\gamma|S) \triangleq (\gamma \oplus B) \cap S$, where B, γ and S are the structuring

---

[1] http://algoval.essex.ac.uk/icdar/

Original   Binarized   Output   Original   Binarized   Output

Fig. 4. System output illustrating robustness to highlights and shadows

element, mask image and reference image (gray level input image), respectively. The structuring dilation element is chosen as 3-by-3 square to preserve small characters. This operation is executed iteratively

$$\rho_B^-(\gamma|S) \triangleq \bigcup_{n=1}^{\infty} \delta_B^n(\gamma|S), \text{ until } \gamma_{n+1} = \delta_B(\gamma_n|S) \iff \gamma_n \neq \gamma_{n+1} . \quad (1)$$

For the γ seed points we use the zero-probability spatial locations of the IC-DAR 2003 training set as shown in figure 3. Conditional dilation uses simple subtraction operations to remove non-text regions from both the color and the curvature saliency maps. In this way, we avoid an exhaustive search for character recognition. In figure 2, we show an example of such contextual integration.

Feature Integration. The color boosting and curvature maps are individually reconstructed with the help of conditional dilation. The maps are normalized to a fixed range $[0, 1]$ to make a linear combination possible. The linear weights of curvature and color boosting saliency for linear combination are empirically obtained as 3 and 1 respectively.

Noise Removal and Refinement. For noise removal we follow Zhang and Kasturi [12] who divide the whole range of gradient orientation $[0, 2\pi)$ into 4 bins. The authors show that text is a closed region and contains all four gradient directions regardless of text type or style. The authors use only those pixels where the Canny edge detector finds an edge response, making it sensitive to the Canny edge detector response. To alleviate this, we use all CC regions. To extract CCs on the saliency maps, the saliency maps are converted into binary images by setting saliency values greater than zero to 1 and keep all others at 0.

The binarized and filtered saliency map is further processed to fill the holes within text regions and enlarged with morphological dilation. The conditional dilation is again applied to these enlarged regions to extract well-formed text masks. The zeros of our binarized saliency map are chosen as seeds of starting of equation 1 while the reference image S is chosen as gray level input image. At the end of the process we have one pair of text saliency map. One saliency map for text regions darker than their surroundings and another one for lighter text regions. The returned saliency maps are our final text detection output. For the system evaluation we feed the OCR system with these saliency maps. These outputs can be used for precise text localization or as input to other text recognition systems. In figure 4 we show an example of the proposed text detection method.

Table 1. Character and word recognition results on ICDAR 2003 dataset

Method	Character	Word				
	Matched	Precision	Recall	F-Score	Time	Dictionary
TESS		0.35	0.18	0.27	**0.21s**	-
ABBYY	0.37	**0.71**	0.32	0.52	1.9s	-
Neumann and Matas'10 [3]	0.67	0.42	0.39	0.40	0.36s	-
Neumann and Matas'11 [13]		0.42	0.41	0.41	0.83s	-
Wang et al. [1]		0.45	0.54	0.51	15s	+
Our Method (Opponent)	0.21	0.47	0.24	0.36	7.2s	-
Our Method (Intensity)	0.62	0.64	0.52	**0.58**	7.2s	-
Our Method (Combination)	**0.68**	0.51	**0.59**	0.55	11.6s	-

4   Results and Discussion

4.1   Character and Word Recognition Results

The text recognition is evaluated on the ICDAR Robust Reading Competition. We compare against five other pipelines: 1. Neumann and Matas [3]. 2. An extension of Neumann and Matas [13]. 3. A dictionary-based approach by Wang et al. [1]. 4. ABBYY FineReader[2], a leading commercial OCR engine. 5. An open source OCR engine Tessaract[3] (TESS). The output of our saliency map is given as input to an OCR system without any text localization. Although TESS can perform in real time, we choose ABBYY because of its superior accuracy. We follow [3] and evaluate precision, recall, f-score, time, and the use of a dictionary. In addition, we also compare character vs. word recognition.

We present our results in table 1. In this table we also evaluate the saliency maps in opponent color space and in intensity-only. The conversion from RGB color space to opponent color space produces low resolution at the chromatic channels. Therefore, connectivity within a character for opponent color space is sometimes broken by the conditional dilation. This may explain why the intensity based saliency method outperforms the opponent color based saliency map. Note that the combined results improve over the-state-of-the-art.

The method of Wang et al. [1] creates word list dictionaries for every image from the ground truth vocabulary and the authors refine their OCR results using the smallest edit distance to the created word lists. This helps them to reduce the number of false positives and also to increase the true positives for this system. However, creating these lists cannot be generalized beyond the training set. Our system does not use any word list, and improve precision and recall of [1] with 7% and 5%, respectively. The algorithm of Neumann and Matas [13] also does not use any word list. The results show that we increase their baseline score by 17%. Note that the accuracy of text recognition from our text segmentation

---

[2] http://finereader.abbyy.com
[3] http://code.google.com/p/tesseract-ocr/

masks is highly dependent on the OCR software. Even though the characters are precisely detected, the ABBYY OCR system could not always recognize the characters. Better recognition results can be obtained with a better OCR system.

4.2   Object Recognition Results

The proposed saliency method for text detection can be applied to generic object detection. To this end, the context guided saliency map is directly used for foreground/background separation. The scene borders are selected as seeds in equation 1. The full process is repeated in the same way as done for text detection, until the refinement step. We evaluate object recognition on the trainval classification set of the Pascal VOC[4] 2011. We report average precision scores as is commonly done for this set and repeat our experiment three times to obtain standard deviation scores to validate significance testing. As the classification baseline we use the popular bag of visual words (BOW) scheme. For features we use SIFT and the visual word vocabulary size is 4000 which is created per training set for each of the 3 splits with K-means on $500K$ randomly sampled SIFT features. For classification, we use the histogram intersection kernel in libsvm and use its built in cross-validation method to tune the C parameter.

We compare our saliency method in an object recognition task against three state of the art saliency detection algorithms. One is the curvature shape saliency method [11]. The second saliency detector is based on frequency, color and luminance and outperforms other approaches in an object segmentation task [14]. The last saliency method is a recent method based on multi-scale contrast, center surround histogram, and color spatial distributions [15].

To incorporate the saliency methods in the BOW scheme we follow the generalized spatial pyramid scheme by Van Gemert [16]. The traditional spatial pyramid [17] builds correspondences by quantizing the absolute position of an image feature in disjoint equivalence classes. The generalized spatial pyramid scheme of [16] allows us to use the same approach, only for more general equivalence classes based on saliency. We quantize the saliency-score in disjoint equivalence classes, and create correspondences between these equivalence classes. If saliency values range between $[0, \ldots, 1)$ then an example of two disjoint equivalence classes (low and high saliency) is given by $\left\{ [0, \ldots, \frac{1}{2}), [\frac{1}{2}, \ldots, 1) \right\}$. Each image feature can be assigned to an equivalence class depending on its average amount of saliency. Note that we create equivalence classes based on saliency, keeping non-salient regions in a class of their own. Hence, our approach retains features that are non-salient. If they are consistently non-salient within an object category, such features will still aid in object classification.

We show the classification results per category in figure 5c. Since we use the scene borders as seeds our method does not work as well for object that touch the border, such as *bus*, *diningtable* and *chair*. We do best for categories where objects are strongly edged, and do not touch the border such as *aeroplane*, *bird*, *bicycle*, *cat*, *motorbike* and *tvmonitor*. The mean average precision scores in increasing order are: baseline: 0.429, Freq: 0.438, Signature: 0.443, Shape:

---

[4] http://pascallin.ecs.soton.ac.uk/challenges/VOC/

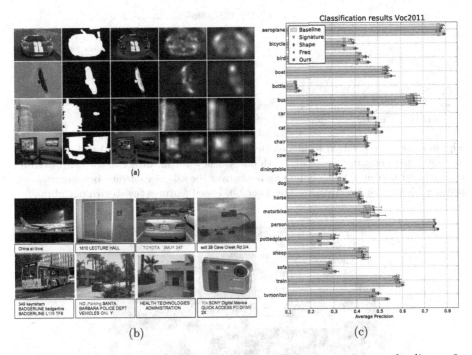

Fig. 5. (a) Original image and four saliency methods: 1. our proposed saliency, 2. Frequency based [14], Shape saliency [11] and Signature saliency [15]. (b) IMET dataset original images and OCR output; red chars are not recognized. (c) Classification results on the Pascal VOC 2011 for the BOW baseline and the four saliency methods.

0.452, and ours: 0.462. Hence, our saliency method, which is designed with text detection in mind, outperforms other state-of-the-art saliency methods for object recognition, generalizing beyond the domain of text detection.

4.3 Multi-modal Object Recognition Results

We evaluate multi-modal object recognition based on visual features fused with text recognition on the IMET dataset [8]. This dataset consists of around 2,000 images, in 8 categories. The image set contains several natural images with text somewhere in them, see figure 5(b) for some examples. As the baseline we again use the BOW model with SIFT features. For the text recognition we use a bag-of-bigrams. We again use a histogram intersection kernel and tune the C parameter with cross-validation. We fuse the visual kernel with the OCR kernel by a simple addition. We identify two setups for text recognition: 1. the most realistic, where we feed our saliency output to the OCR; 2. feed the saliency output of the ground truth boxes to the OCR. This allows us to evaluate the effect of correct text localization.

The classification scores per category are given in figure 6. The text-only results perform the worst. Of the text-only results the OCR with the ground truth bounding box over our saliency map is better than directly feeding the

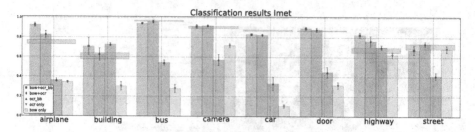

Fig. 6. Image classification results on the IMET dataset for the BOW baseline, and the four OCR methods; ocr: text only, with our saliency output direct to the OCR ocr_bb: text only, with ground truth bounding boxes over the saliency output, bow+ocr: visual features fused with ocr features, bow+ocr_bb: visual features fused with ocr_bb.

Fig. 7. Yellow dashes and boxes denote our output. The red boxes are not recognized.

saliency map to the OCR. Only in the categories *camera* and *street* is the raw OCR better. This is because there are more actual text regions in the image than given by the ground truth. Generally, the results show that adding text to visual features helps. Only for *car* the results decrease, because the unique text on one license plate text does not generalize to other license plates. The MAP scores, in increasing accuracy are ocr: 0.422, ocr_bb: 0.512, bow: 0.779, bow+ocr: 0.816, bow+ocr_bb: 0.839. The dataset is well suited for visual information as indicated by the high baseline BOW score. However, we improve the visual-only score by 6% with fusing text information.

As a possible application we show in figure 7 our system's output on a Google image of the class *building*, where the text adds significant semantic information.

5   Conclusion

We propose to use text in natural images to aid visual classification. To detect the text in a natural image, we propose a new saliency method that is based on low-level cues and novel contextual information integration. We show that this saliency method outperforms the state-of-the-art end-to-end scene text recognition scores with 0.17 on standard ICDAR 2003 datatset. Moreover, our saliency method outperforms other state-of-the art saliency methods for object recognition in the PASCAL VOC 2011 dataset. On the IMET dataset, we show that text recognition from natural scene images helps object classification if there is text in the image, and if the text is not too specific to a single object.

References

1. Wang, K., Babenko, B., Belongie, S.: End-to-end scene text recognition. In: ICCV (2011)
2. Epshtein, B., Ofek, E., Wexler, Y.: Detecting text in natural scenes with stroke width transform. In: CVPR, pp. 2963–2970 (2010)
3. Neumann, L., Matas, J.: A Method for Text Localization and Recognition in Real-World Images. In: Kimmel, R., Klette, R., Sugimoto, A. (eds.) ACCV 2010, Part III. LNCS, vol. 6494, pp. 770–783. Springer, Heidelberg (2011)
4. Wang, K., Rescorla, E., Shacham, H., Belongie, S.: Openscan: A fully transparent optical scan voting system. In: Electronic Voting Technology Workshop (2010)
5. Judd, T., Ehinger, K.A., Durand, F., Torralba, A.: Learning to predict where humans look. In: ICCV, pp. 2106–2113 (2009)
6. Wang, H.C., Pomplun, M.: The attraction of visual attention to texts in real-world scenes. In: CogSci 2011 (2011)
7. Shahab, A., Shafait, F., Dengel, A., Uchida, S.: How salient is scene text? In: IAPR International Workshop on Document Analysis Systems (2012)
8. Zhu, Q., Yeh, M.C., Cheng, K.T.: Multimodal fusion using learned text concepts for image categorization. In: ACM MM (2006)
9. Uchida, S., Shigeyoshi, Y., Kunishige, Y., Feng, Y.: A keypoint-based approach toward scenery character detection. In: ICDAR, pp. 819–823 (2011)
10. van de Weijer, J., Gevers, T., Bagdanov, A.D.: Boosting color saliency in image feature detection. TPAMI 28, 150–156 (2006)
11. Valenti, R., Sebe, N., Gevers, T.: Image saliency by isocentric curvedness and color. In: ICCV, pp. 2185–2192 (2009)
12. Zhang, J., Kasturi, R.: Text detection using edge gradient and graph spectrum. In: ICPR, pp. 3979–3982 (2010)
13. Neumann, L., Matas, J.: Text localization in real-world images using efficiently pruned exhaustive search. In: ICDAR, pp. 687–691 (2011)
14. Achanta, R., Hemami, S., Estrada, F., Susstrunk, S.: Frequency-tuned Salient Region Detection. In: CVPR (2009)
15. Liu, T., Yuan, Z., Sun, J., Wang, J., Zheng, N., Tang, X., Shum, H.Y.: Learning to detect a salient object. TPAMI 33 (2011)
16. van Gemert, J.C.: Exploiting photographic style for category-level image classification by generalizing the spatial pyramid. In: ICMR (2011)
17. Lazebnik, S., Schmid, C., Ponce, J.: Beyond bags of features: Spatial pyramid matching for recognizing natural scene categories. In: CVPR (2006)

Bayesian Multimodal Fusion in Forensic Applications*

Virginia Fernandez Arguedas, Qianni Zhang, and Ebroul Izquierdo

Multimedia and Vision Research Group
School of Electronic Engineering and Computer Science
Queen Mary, University of London
Mile End Road, E1 4NS, London, UK
{virginia.fernandez,qianni.zhang,ebroul.izquierdo}@eecs.qmul.ac.uk

Abstract. The public location of CCTV cameras and their connexion with public safety demand high robustness and reliability from surveillance systems. This paper focuses on the development of a multimodal fusion technique which exploits the benefits of a Bayesian inference scheme to enhance surveillance systems' reliability. Additionally, an automatic object classifier is proposed based on the multimodal fusion technique, addressing semantic indexing and classification for forensic applications. The proposed Bayesian-based Multimodal Fusion technique, and particularly, the proposed object classifier are evaluated against two state-of-the-art automatic object classifiers on the i-LIDS surveillance dataset.

1 Introduction

The recent outbreak of vandalism, accidents and criminal activities, has affected the general public's concern about security. Nowadays, higher safety levels and new security measures are demanded. Monitoring private areas (i.e. shopping malls) and public environments prone to vandalism (i.e. bus stations) has become a crucial task generating a great growth of deployed surveillance systems. The enormous amount of information recorded daily for monitoring purposes is typically controlled by surveillance operators and removed some time later due to storage space limitation. Besides, the lack of pre-processing of the video data increases the complexity of the forensic search and restrains the evolution towards autonomous surveillance systems.

Existing limitations of surveillance video systems demand the development of automatic and smart surveillance solutions to detect and classify objects and events. Despite the huge interest in real-time surveillance applications, accurate object indexing and classification techniques are demanded to improve post-investigations and tackle efficient surveillance object and event storage by using semantic indexing/classification.

Over the past several decades, many different approaches have been proposed to automatically represent objects or concepts in videos. Numerous features

---

* The research was partially supported by the European Commission under contract FP7-SEC 261743 VideoSense.

A. Fusiello et al. (Eds.): ECCV 2012 Ws/Demos, Part III, LNCS 7585, pp. 466–475, 2012.
© Springer-Verlag Berlin Heidelberg 2012

analysing visual appearance, motion, shape or temporal evolution have been proposed and selected depending on their performance for diverse applications [1]. Single features or inputs are capable of obtaining high accuracy results and tackle specific problems, i.e. object detection. However, the use of complementary information increases the accuracy of the overall decision making process and enhances the possibilities and capabilities of different systems to perform more sophisticated tasks, i.e. object classification, speaker identification, etc. Multimodal fusion research was motivated for the exploitation of complementary resources/inputs to enhance the system performance; gaining much attention in research areas such as machine learning, pattern recognition and multimedia analysis.

Typically surveillance applications are affected by several restrictions such as low quality images or environmental factors. The public location of surveillance cameras, usually in un-controlled environments, affects not only the quality of the images but also the availability of the image itself. Such constraints limit the range of multimodal fusion techniques, demanding a method capable of dealing with lack of information as well as the presence of uncertainty. The close relationship between surveillance applications and safety demands high robustness and their continuous-working mode.

Two contributions are presented in this paper. Firstly, a Bayesian inference scheme able to fuse several diverse-nature cues is presented, providing a multimodal fusion technique capable of handling the absence of information and the presence of uncertainty. Secondly, a surveillance object classifier exploiting the benefits of the proposed Bayesian multimodal fusion approach is proposed based on the analysis of visual and temporal information.

The remainder of this paper is organised as follows. In Section 2, an exhaustive study of the existing multimodal fusion techniques and their impact on surveillance applications is presented. The proposed Bayesian-based multimodal fusion technique is further detailed in Section 3, while Section 4 presents the proposed surveillance object classifier developed based on the proposed Bayesian inference scheme to enhance the classifier performance in situations of absent information. Experimental results and the performance evaluation of the proposed Bayesian-based object classifier against state-of-the-art object classifiers are presented in Section 5. Whilst, Section 6 draws conclusions and presents the potential future work.

2   Literature Review

The variety of media, features or partial decisions provide a wide range of options to address specific tasks. However, the different characteristics of the modalities involved in any analysis hinder the combination for several reasons including, (i) the particular format acquisition of different media, (ii) the confidence level associated to each data depending on the task under analysis, (iii) the independent protection of each type of data and (iv) the different processing times related to the different type of media streams. Multimodal fusion techniques can be performed at different levels, tackling such constraints from different angles, distinguishing mainly two, feature and decision level [2].

Feature-level multimodal fusion includes all the approaches which combine the available input data before performing the objective task. In this case, the number of features extracted from different modalities must be combined in a unique vector (output) which will be considered as a unique input by the objective task. The main advantages of the feature-level multimodal fusion techniques consist of the need for a unique learning phase for the combined feature vector and the possibility to take advantage of the correlation between multiple features from different modalities [3]. On the other hand, feature-level multimodal fusion presents several disadvantages (i) the difficulty to learn cross-correlation amongst features increases with the number of different media considered, (ii) the feature format should be the same before their fusion and (iii) the synchronisation between features is more complex due to their different modalities [4]. Moreover, Zhang et Izquierdo demonstrated the fundamental need of considering the different nature of the features prior to their fusion, admitting that features "existing" in different feature spaces could not be combined in a linear manner without further consideration [5].

Decision-level multimodal fusion proposes to individually analyse each input, providing local decisions. Those decisions are then combined using a fusion unit to make a fused decision vector that is analysed to obtain a final decision, considering such decisions as the output of the fusion technique. Unlike feature level fusion techniques, decision level multimodal fusion techniques benefit from unique representation despite the use of the multiple media modalities; easing their fusion, the scalability of the system and enabling the use of different and the most suitable techniques to obtain partial solutions. However, the acquisition of partial solutions prevents the considering of the features correlation and is affected by the individual learning process associated to each feature.

In the last few years, multimedia researchers have developed numerous multimodal fusion techniques to perform various multimedia analysis tasks. Some of the most well-known fusion techniques include (i) linear weighted fusion [6,7], (ii) Support Vector Machines (SVM) [8,9], (iii) Bayesian inference [10,11], (iv) Dempster-Shafer theory [12] and (v) Neural Networks [13,14]. In surveillance, automatic object classification is an active research field due to the dependence of the event detection and classification techniques prior to this step.

Typically, surveillance object classifiers are based on binary decisions. For instance, in [15], the authors compute high dimensional features based on edges and use *SVM* to detect human regions. While, Paisitkriangkrai et al. [16] propose a pedestrian detection algorithm based on local feature extraction and SVM classifiers. Within binary classification, several vehicle classification techniques used SVMs to map the detected objects into different categories [17,18]. The former [17] proposes a vehicle classifier where the features to model each object are extracted using Independent Component Analysis while SVM is used to categorise each vehicle into a semantic class. While the latter [18] classifies vehicles in night time traffic using SVMs over their eigenspaces. However, several approaches propose object classification using a probabilistic framework based on Bayesian Networks, Neural Networks or Hidden Markov Models (HMM) [19,20]. In [19], a multi-class vehicle classification system is presented based on the analysis of rear-side view images. Authors classify the vehicles into four classes including Sedan, Pickup truck, SUV/Minivan and unknown, extracting a set of features to build a feature vector which later is processed by a Hybrid Dynamic Bayesian Network. Zhang et al. addressed the problem of automatic object classification for surveillance videos focusing on traffic monitoring [21]. Their approach consists on the application of Adaboost for feature selection and classification formulation. The classification stage consists of the weighted combination of several weak classifiers. Additionally, generative models like HMM and Graph Models have also been used for object recognition. For instance, in [20], a new detection and recognition method for moving objects is proposed. The authors apply temporal difference for moving object detection, use the discrete wavelet transformation technique to extract the feature vectors and conduct object recognition using HMMs. Finally, in [22], the authors present an empirical performance comparison between several classifiers, such as SVM, Bayesian Network Classifiers or Decision Trees, based on a feature vector built with smoothed discrete cosine transform (DCT) features, 2D moment-based features, horizontal and vertical projection and morphological features, to classify objects in real-world video surveillance scenes.

3   Bayesian-Based Multimodal Fusion

The all-pervasive presence of CCTV cameras, their location in public uncontrolled areas and the strict relationship with safety and security demand a high reliability and continuous work of any surveillance application despite the absence of limited information. Consequently, in this paper, a Bayesian-based multimodal fusion technique is proposed to probabilistically combine diverse-nature cues while addressing the absence of information and the presence of uncertainty by the means of inferring information from previously acquired knowledge.

Bayesian Networks enable the robust integration and combination of multiple diverse-nature sources of information applying rules of probability theory. Fusion techniques based on Bayesian Networks benefit from three fundamental advantages. First, the Bayesian inference method allows the combination of multimodal information due to its possibility of adaptation as the information evolves as well as its capability to apply subjective or estimated probabilities when empirical data is absent [2]. Secondly, the hierarchical structure provides flexibility and scalability, facilitating not only the inclusion of additional information, but also enabling the degradation of the a-posteriori probability in case of the absence of a certain cue/s. Finally, Bayesian Networks allow domain knowledge to be embedded in the structure and parameters of the networks, allowing the adjustment of the fusion technique to the domain and scenario's requirements.

The proposed Bayesian-based multimodal fusion technique provides a probabilistic framework capable of combining multimodal cues at the decision-level, unifying the output of several modules to provide a unique output in the decision-making process. In addition to the advantages provided by the Bayesian Networks, the proposed multimodal fusion technique benefits from (i) the normalised and unique representation of the information despite the multiple media modalities considered within the analysis and (ii) the combination of different nature features considering their own feature space and unique metrics.

The topology applied in the proposed Bayesian-based multimodal fusion technique is shown in Figure 1. The multimodal cues to combine are independent and can be derived from different inputs, i.e. video, metadata, sound. Considering the decision-level fusion as a classification problem, the Bayesian inference scheme can be formulated using the maximum a-posteriori criterion (MAP):

$$D = argmax_i\{P(C_i|F_1, F_2, ..., F_L)\} = argmax_i\{\prod_{j=1}^{L} P(F_j|C_i)P(C_i)\} =$$

$$= argmax_i \begin{pmatrix} \prod_{j=1}^{L} P(F_j|C_1)P(C_1) \\ \prod_{j=1}^{L} P(F_j|C_2)P(C_2) \\ \vdots \\ \prod_{j=1}^{L} P(F_j|C_N)P(C_N) \end{pmatrix}$$

where $P(C_i|F_1, F_2, ..., F_L)$ defines the probability of a concept C_i to be the final decision undertaken by the classifier, D, considering all the individual partial decisions provided by individual classifiers; F_j are the individual classifiers that provide partial decisions to the Bayesian inference scheme; $P(C_i)$ represent the a-priori probability of the i concept; L defines the amount of partial decisions incorporated in the multimodal fusion and N represents the number of concepts involved in the classification problem.

Regarding the conditional probability matrices connecting each partial decision to the network, shown in Figure 1, Bayesian Networks allow specification according to the scenario and application. Consequently, the relationships among the analysed cues can be set manually or learned from training data.

4   Bayesian-Based Object Classifier for Forensic Applications

In order to evaluate the proposed Bayesian-based Multimodal Fusion technique, a surveillance object classifier framework based on the proposed Bayesian inference scheme is presented. The scalable hierarchical structure of the Bayesian-based Multimodal Fusion technique allows the incorporation of various classifiers, enabling a high level of flexibility and adaptation to the scenario under analysis in the form of a-priori probabilities.

Two baseline classifiers provide partial decisions to the proposed decision-level multimodal fusion for the classification of moving objects detected in outdoor surveillance videos monitoring urban scenarios. First, a set of visual features are extracted and combined using a feature-level multimodal fusion technique which preserves the non-linearity of the different feature spaces, as detailed in

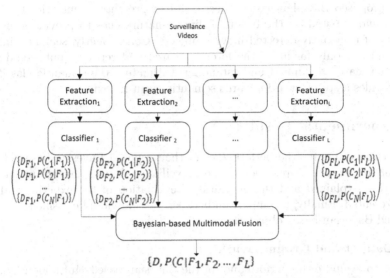

Fig. 1. Bayesian-based object classifier framework

[23]. Secondly, a set of features describing the object's temporal evolution and behaviour are extracted and combined using a behavioural fuzzy classifier, as detailed in [24]. Each of the partial decisions corresponds to an input to the Bayesian inference scheme and represents a classification decision accompanied by a certainty value on the classification. The Bayesian inference scheme is employed to combine the partial decisions considering also the knowledge acquired from the scenario under analysis.

Each individual classifier provides a partial decision coupled together with a conditional probability matrix describing the probability of a detected moving object, or observation O_k, to belong to each of the semantic concepts, $C_i, i = 1, ..., N$, considered within the classification scenario:

$$\begin{pmatrix} P(C_1|F_1) & P(C_1|F_2) \\ P(C_2|F_1) & P(C_2|F_2) \\ ... & ... \\ P(C_N|F_1) & P(C_N|F_2) \end{pmatrix}$$

where Fj represents each of the individual classifiers whose decisions are fused applying Bayes' probabilistic rules. Each partial decision could perform automatic object classification. However, the integration of several features, derived from different and uncorrelated media, addresses higher robustness, stability, flexibility and adaptation towards the scenario under analysis.

Bayesian Networks enable the continuous work of the multimodal classifier due to their reliability in the presence of missing evidence, either partially or completely. The Bayesian inference scheme allows the system to classify any observation despite the lack of partial decisions, but rigorously decreases the certainty on the classification accordingly.

The proposed Bayesian-based object classifier presents a semantic classification technique based on the fusion of diverse-nature cues to provide semantic indexing of previously detected moving objects. Consequently, semantic indexing would not only facilitate the forensic search and retrieval but would also adapt the search to human understanding. Ultimately the semantic classification provides a step forward towards semantic event indexing.

5   Experimental Results

This section evaluates the performance of the proposed Bayesian-based object classifier for forensic applications. The surveillance dataset and ground truth are further explained and the quantitative evaluation of the experimental results presented. Finally, a comparison between the individual classifiers and the proposed Bayesian-based object classifier is detailed.

5.1   Dataset and Ground Truth

In order to evaluate the performance of the Bayesian-based Multimodal Fusion technique, the proposed Bayesian-based object classifier has been applied to a variety of outdoor video sequences belonging to the i-LIDS dataset[1], provided by the U.K. Home Office. The video sequences recorded under realistic conditions are provided for different scenarios. Our study focuses on urban environments; therefore, the dataset under analysis is Parked Vehicle Detection. Through a careful examination of the dataset, two semantic object categories were noted to be highly repetitive in the sequences, namely Person and Vehicle. The proposed Bayesian-based Object Classifier categorises each moving object detected within the surveillance video as *person, vehicle* or *unknown*.

To study the efficiency of the Bayesian-based Multimodal Fusion technique, a ground truth has been manually annotated. A total of 1567 objects were included, 6% were person while 50% were vehicle. Due to the imposed guidelines for the manual annotation, objects presenting certain constraints such as small blob size, partial occlusion of the object over 50% or multiple objects coexisting in a blob, were annotated as *unknown*. The proposed approach automatically classifies objects according to the partial decisions provided by independent classifiers, analysing diverse-nature cues, and inferring information in the presence of (either partially or completely) missing evidence.

5.2   Quantitative Performance Evaluation

To evaluate the performance of the proposed Bayesian-based object classifier and, ultimately, the performance of the Bayesian-based Multimodal Fusion technique, we assumed a tracking algorithm fed the individual classifiers with detected moving objects or observations. Two individual classifiers based on the extraction of visual and temporal information, respectively, categorise each observation into one of the two semantic concepts defined for the scenario. A conditional probability matrix is calculated by each individual classifier and passed

---

[1] Imagery Library for Intelligent Detection Systems, i-LIDS. http://ilids.co.uk

to the Bayesian inference scheme. The Bayesian-based Multimodal Fusion technique combines the different partial decisions to achieve a unique classification considering diverse-nature cues while preserving their individual feature spaces and metrics. The obtained results are shown in Table 1.

Table 1. Performance evaluation of the proposed Bayesian-based object classifier

Concepts		True Positive	True Negative	False Positive	False negative
Vehicle	Observations	619	31	16	17
	%	97	66	34	3
Person	Observations	31	619	17	16
	%	66	97	3	34

Typically, in surveillance applications, there are two fundamental objectives: (i) to achieve a high true positive rate balanced with a low false negative rate which reveals the capability of the classifier to detect the desired concepts and (ii) to maintain a low false positive rate in order to avoid false alarms within the surveillance application. The results provided by the Bayesian-based object classifier (refer to table 1) reveal, for the semantic concept Vehicle, a high rate of true positive detections coupled with a low false negative rate, 97% and 3%, respectively, while maintaining a moderate rate of false positive detection, 34%. The semantic concept Person presents lower true positive and false negative rate, 66% and 34%, respectively, while scoring a remarkable false positive rate, 3%. The results, both the false positive rates for vehicles and the true positive rate for person, are directly affected by the sparseness of the concept person within the ground truth.

The main objective of this paper was to present a multimodal fusion technique which would allow the integration of various different-nature features independently of which media were they derived from, to benefit from (i) the representability provided by each feature, (ii) their un-correlation in order to cover a bigger spectrum, and (iii) the robustness acquired by the system due to the consideration of multiple partial decisions rather than relying in a single decision. In order to demonstrate the improvement on the performance, the proposed Bayesian-based object classifier is compared with the individual classifiers which provided the partial decisions (refer to table 2).

According to the comparative results shown in Table 2, the proposed Bayesian-based object classifier outperforms both individual classifiers. While independent classifiers, based on visual and temporal features, achieve a true positive rate of 77% and 79% respectively, this is exceeded by the Bayesian object classifier in 20% for the semantic concept Vehicle. However, the improvement undertaken by the proposed fusion approach is smaller, increasing the true positive rate by 2% and 9% for the visual and temporal features classifiers. Similarly, the other rates (true negative, false positive and false negative) present improvements whenever the Bayesian-based object classifier is applied compared to the results provided by the independent classifiers. Finally, detailed analysis reveals that

Table 2. Performance comparison between the proposed classifier and the two intermediate state-of-the-art classifiers

Concepts		True Positive	True Negative	False Positive	False Negative
Vehicle	Visual Features [23](%)	77	64	36	23
	Temporal Features [24](%)	79	57	43	21
	Bayesian (%)	97	66	34	3
Person	Visual Features [23](%)	64	77	23	36
	Temporal Features [24](%)	57	79	21	43
	Bayesian (%)	66	97	3	34

the proposed multimodal fusion enhances the object classification procedure, increasing positive detection while reducing false alarms.

6   Conclusions and Future Work

In this paper, a probabilistic multimodal fusion technique was proposed to integrate diverse-nature cues in surveillance applications. In order to evaluate the fusion technique, a Bayesian-based object classification framework was presented. The main objective was to create a scalable technique which allowed the probabilistic combination of multiple features while preserving their nature. The proposed Bayesian inference scheme addressed the, partial or total, absence of information, by degrading the classification results accordingly. The proposed object classifier combined the decisions provided by two state-of-the-art object classifiers in a probabilistic framework which also considered the scenario a-priori knowledge. The proposed approach outperformed both state-of-the-art classifiers, demonstrating the benefits of combining uncorrelated features to improve the classification results and to enhance the robustness of the classification framework.

Considering the dependence of the event classifiers on the object classification results, in the future, we plan to use the Bayesian-based Multimodal Fusion technique to combine classification results, arisen from various object classifiers, to perform event detection and classification.

References

1. Fernandez Arguedas, V., Zhang, Q., Chandramouli, K., Izquierdo, E.: Vision Based Semantic Analysis of Surveillance Videos. In: Anagnostopoulos, I.E., Bieliková, M., Mylonas, P., Tsapatsoulis, N. (eds.) Semantic Hyper/Multi-media Adaptation. SCI, vol. 418, pp. 83–126. Springer, Heidelberg (2012)
2. Atrey, P., Hossain, M., El Saddik, A., Kankanhalli, M.: Multimodal fusion for multimedia analysis: a survey. Multimedia Systems 16, 345–379 (2010)
3. Snoek, C., Worring, M., Smeulders, A.: Early versus late fusion in semantic video analysis. In: ACM Multimedia (2005)

4. Wu, Z., Cai, L., Meng, H.: Multi-level Fusion of Audio and Visual Features for Speaker Identification. In: Zhang, D., Jain, A.K. (eds.) ICB 2005. LNCS, vol. 3832, pp. 493–499. Springer, Heidelberg (2005)
5. Zhang, Q., Izquierdo, E.: Combining low-level features for semantic inference in image retrieval. EURASIP Journal on Advances in Signal Processing 12 (2007)
6. Jaffre, G., Pinquier, J.: Autdio/video fusion: a preprocessing step for multimodal person identification. In: MMUA (2006)
7. Kankanhalli, M., Wang, J., Jain, R.: Experiential sampling in multimedia systems. IEEE Transactions on Multimedia 8, 937–946 (2006)
8. Nirmala, D., Paul, B., Vaidehi, V.: A novel multimodal image fusion method using shift invariant discrete wavelet transform and support vector machines. In: ICRTIT, pp. 932–937 (2011)
9. Arsic, D., Schuller, B., Rigoll, G.: Suspicious behavior detection in public transport by fusion of low-level video descriptors. In: ICME, pp. 2018–2021 (2007)
10. Bahlmann, C., Zhu, Y., Ramesh, V., Pellkofer, M., Koehler, T.: A system for traffic sign detection, tracking, and recognition using color, shape, and motion information. In: IEEE Intelligent Vehicles Symposium, pp. 255–260. IEEE (2005)
11. Meuter, M., Nunn, C., Görmer, S., Müller-Schneiders, S., Kummert, A.: A decision fusion and reasoning module for a traffic sign recognition system. IEEE Transactions on Intelligent Transportation Systems, 1–9 (2011)
12. Klausner, A., Tengg, A., Rinner, B.: Vehicle classification on multi-sensor smart cameras using feature-and decision-fusion. In: ICDSC, pp. 67–74. IEEE (2007)
13. Xiao, J., Wang, X.: Study on traffic flow prediction using rbf neural network. In: ICMLC, vol. 5, pp. 2672–2675 (2004)
14. Ozkurt, C., Camci, F.: Automatic traffic density estimation and vehicle classification for traffic surveillance systems using neural networks. Mathematical and Computational Applications 14, 187 (2010)
15. Dalal, N., Triggs, B.: Histograms of oriented gradients for human detection. In: CVPR, vol. 1, pp. 886–893. IEEE (2005)
16. Paisitkriangkrai, S., Shen, C., Zhang, J.: Performance evaluation of local features in human classification and detection. IET Computer Vision 2, 236–246 (2008)
17. Chen, X., Zhang, C.: Vehicle Classification from Traffic Surveillance Videos at a Finer Granularity. In: Cham, T.-J., Cai, J., Dorai, C., Rajan, D., Chua, T.-S., Chia, L.-T. (eds.) MMM 2007. LNCS, vol. 4351, pp. 772–781. Springer, Heidelberg (2006)
18. Thi, T., Robert, K., Lu, S., Zhang, J.: Vehicle classification at nighttime using eigenspaces and support vector machine. In: ICISP, vol. 2, pp. 422–426. IEEE (2008)
19. Kafai, M., Bhanu, B.: Dynamic bayesian networks for vehicle classification in video. IEEE Transactions on Industrial Informatics, 1 (2012)
20. Cho, W., Kim, S., Ahn, G.: Detection and recognition of moving objects using the temporal difference method and the hidden markov model. In: CSAE, vol. 4, pp. 119–123 (2011)
21. Zhang, Z., Li, M., Huang, K., Tan, T.: Boosting local feature descriptors for automatic objects classification in traffic scene surveillance. In: ICPR, pp. 1–4 (2008)
22. Gurwicz, Y., Yehezkel, R., Lachover, B.: Multiclass object classification for real-time video surveillance systems. Pattern Recognition Letters (2011)
23. Fernandez Arguedas, V., Zhang, Q., Chandramouli, K., Izquierdo, E.: Multi-feature fusion for surveillance video indexing. In: WIAMIS. IEEE (2011)
24. Fernandez Arguedas, V., Izquierdo, E.: Object classification based on behaviour patterns. In: ICDP (2011)

Noise Modelling and Uncertainty Propagation for TOF Sensors

Amira Belhedi[1,2,3], Adrien Bartoli[2], Steve Bourgeois[1], Kamel Hamrouni[3], Patrick Sayd[1], and Vincent Gay-Bellile[1]

[1] CEA, LIST, LVIC
[2] Clermont Université, Université d'Auvergne, ISIT
[3] Université de Tunis El Manar, ENIT, SITI
{amira.belhedi,Vincent.Gay-Bellile,Steve.Bourgeois,Patrick.Sayd}@cea.fr,
adrien.bartoli@gmail.com, kamel.hamrouni@enit.rnu.tn

Abstract. Time-of-Flight (TOF) cameras are active real time depth sensors. One issue of TOF sensors is measurement noise. In this paper, we present a method for providing the uncertainty associated to 3D TOF measurements based on noise modelling. Measurement uncertainty is the combination of pixel detection error and sensor noise. First, a detailed noise characterization is presented. Then, a continuous model which gives the noise's standard deviation for each depth-pixel is proposed. Finally, a closed-form approximation of 3D uncertainty from 2D pixel detection error is presented. An applicative example is provided that shows the use of our 3D uncertainty modelling on real data.

1 Introduction

Time-of-Flight (TOF) cameras open new possibilities in fields such as 3D reconstruction, Augmented Reality and video-surveillance since they provide depth information in real-time and at high frame-rates. They are based on the emission of a modulated infrared light which is thereafter reflected by the objects in the scene. The signal's phase shift φ is determined and thus the depth value d by a TOF approach [1]. The depth value, at each pixel, is given by $d = \frac{c\varphi}{4\pi\omega}$, where c is the speed of light and ω is the modulation frequency. This technology has several limitations, one of them being measurement noise. During the past years, some works [2–5] have been devoted to enhancing the depth images captured by a TOF sensor by handling the noise. However, there have been no studies of noise that provides the TOF measurements uncertainty.

In this paper, we characterize the noise distribution as Gaussian (Section 2). We show that its standard deviation varies according to the pixel position and the depth. We propose a continuous noise modelling which gives the noise's standard deviation for each depth-pixel (Section 3). Our model uses a 3D smoothing spline, known as a 3D Thin-Plate Spline, known to work well to model complex variations. Generally speaking, a measurement is meaningful only if its uncertainty can be compute as well. We present a method for providing 3D uncertainty for TOF sensors (Section 4). The 3D uncertainty in TOF measurements is the

A. Fusiello et al. (Eds.): ECCV 2012 Ws/Demos, Part III, LNCS 7585, pp. 476–485, 2012.
© Springer-Verlag Berlin Heidelberg 2012

combination of pixel detection error and sensor noise. We describe how errors in 2D measurements propagate to error in the 3D measurements, and hence we are able to compute a confidence interval on any 3D measurement, *i.e.* a quantitative assessment of accuracy. The proposed method is a closed-form approximation from 2D pixel detection error and a continuous depth noise model. The work has a variety of applications. We present an applicative example in Section 5.

Notation. A 2D point $\mathbf{p}$ (pixel) is the 2-vector defined as $\mathbf{p}^{\mathsf{T}} = (u \quad v)$ with $(u \quad v)$ the pixel coordinates, a 2.5D point $\mathbf{q}$ (depth-pixel) is the 3-vector defined as $\mathbf{q}^{\mathsf{T}} = (u \quad v \quad d)$ with d the associated depth and the corresponding 3D point in the camera coordinate frame is $\mathbf{Q}^{\mathsf{T}} = (X \quad Y \quad Z)$.

2   Noise Characterization

The noise characterization is based on the study of the variation on the depth-pixel measurements for several TOF images taken in the same conditions. Images of a white wall were acquired at 7 depths from 0.9 m to 7.4 m. At each depth, 100 depth images were recorded. To characterize the noise distribution, we used the technique of normal probability plot [6]. The data are plotted against a theoretical normal distribution in such a way that the points should form an approximate straight line. Departures from this straight line indicate departures from normality. An example corresponding to a depth-pixel (Figure 5) shows that the scatter follows approximately straight lines. To verify graphically the normality of the noise distribution for more pixels, the images' centers are considered. Their associated histograms showing the distribution of the depth measurements are plotted in Figure 1. These histograms, as can be graphically seen, follow a Gaussian distribution. After the graphical verification, a more robust Gaussian test was used. The Lilliefors (adaptation of the Kolmogorov-Smirnov [1]) tests the null hypothesis that the data comes from a distribution in the normal family. The test returns the logical value $h = 1$ if it rejects the null hypothesis, otherwise it returns $h = 0$. This test is performed for each pixel of the 7 depths, then the median and mean value of h for all pixels are computed. The median value is equal to 0 and the mean value is also 'near' zero (equal to 0.1472). These values confirm that the TOF noise follows a Gaussian distribution to a good extent. We are now interested in noise variation according to pixel position and depth. The standard deviation σ is calculated for each pixel of the 7 images. Figure 2 present σ values at each pixel for an approximative depth $d = 4.23m$. As can be clearly seen, σ increases away from the image center (5 to 7 mm) to the image boundaries (7 to 27 mm). The highest accuracy is achieved at the image center where the illumination of the observed object is at its highest value. The same phenomenon is observed for the other 6 depths. The standard deviation dependency on the depth is shown in Figure 3. The σ at each pixel of the 7 depths is calculated and plotted against the depths values. σ increases with depth and

---

[1] The Kolmogorov-Smirnov test is used to decide if a sample comes from a population with a specific distribution.

varies approximately from 0 to 40 mm (the mean value of σ is 8 mm) as shown in Figure 4. The noise's standard deviation gives an information about the accuracy of measurement. This information is essential in any application, since it denotes the degree to which a measurement result will represent the true value. The calculated standard deviation from the 7 depths is however not sufficient. In practice, it is important to have a continuous noise modelling.

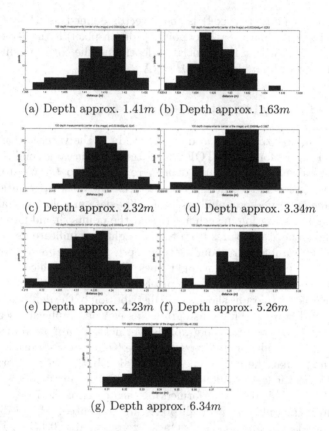

(a) Depth approx. 1.41m (b) Depth approx. 1.63m

(c) Depth approx. 2.32m   (d) Depth approx. 3.34m

(e) Depth approx. 4.23m (f) Depth approx. 5.26m

(g) Depth approx. 6.34m

Fig. 1. Noise's standard deviation distribution graphs. Each graph represents the distribution of the 100 depth measurements of the image center (of a white wall). Graphically, these histograms correspond to Gaussian distribution, as confirmed by the Kolmogorov-Smirnov test.

3 A Continuous Noise Modelling

The TOF noise has a Gaussian distribution, thus, the proposed noise modelling is based on standard deviation. The noise's standard deviation depends on both the pixel position and the depth. These variations cannot be well modelled by a simple constant or linear function. A more complex model is needed. It must also provide continuity, since it must give for each depth-pixel (2.5D point)

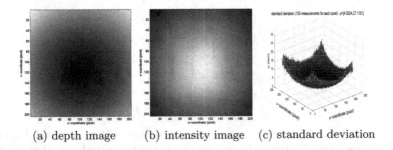

(a) depth image   (b) intensity image   (c) standard deviation

Fig. 2. Standard deviation σ (c) of a depth image (a) (of a white wall (b) at approx. 4.23 m) measured at each pixel. It is calculated out of 100 depth measurements at each pixel. σ increases from the image center (5 to 7 mm) to the image boundaries (7 to 27 mm).

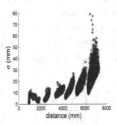

Fig. 3. The standard deviation calculated at each pixel of the 7 depths (of a white wall). σ is calculated out of 100 depth measurements at each pixel.

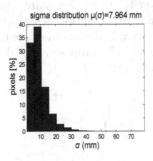

Fig. 4. Distribution of standard deviation calculated at each pixel of the 7 depths (of a white wall). σ is calculated out of 100 depth measurements at each pixel. σ increases with depth from 0 to 40 mm with a mean value equal to 8 mm.

the associated noise's standard deviation. A 3D Thin-Plate-Spline function is therefore chosen, since it verifies all these conditions. The 3D-TPS $\mathbb{R}^3 \to \mathbb{R}$ is a smooth function [7] known to be an efficient approximation to several types of deformation that minimizes the 'bending energy'. It is flexible, controlled by l 3D centers $\mathbf{c}_k$ ($\mathbf{c}_k \in \mathbb{R}^3, k = 1, \ldots, l$) that may be placed anywhere in space

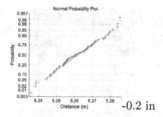

-0.2 in

Fig. 5. Normal probability plot corresponding to a depth-pixel. The scatter (plotted in blue) follows approximatively the straight line of the theoretical normal distribution (plotted in red).

and is driven by assigning target values α_k to the l 3D centers c_k. It is usually parametrized by an $l + 4$ coefficient vector $\mathbf{h}^\mathsf{T} = (\ \mathbf{w}^\mathsf{T} \quad \mathbf{a}^\mathsf{T}\ )$ computed from the target vector α (described in the following) and a regularization parameter $\lambda \in \mathbb{R}^+$. There are l coefficients in $\mathbf{w}$ and 4 coefficients in $\mathbf{a}$. The coefficients in $\mathbf{w}$ must satisfy $\check{\mathsf{P}}^\mathsf{T}\mathbf{w} = \mathbf{0}$, where the kth row of $\check{\mathsf{P}}^\mathsf{T}$ is given by $(\mathbf{c}_k^\mathsf{T}\ 1)$. These 4 'side-conditions' ensure that the TPS has square integrable second derivatives. Let $\boldsymbol{\ell}_\mathbf{q}^\mathsf{T} = ((d(\mathbf{q}, \mathbf{c}_1))\ \cdots\ (d(\mathbf{q}, \mathbf{c}_l))\ \mathbf{q}^\mathsf{T}\ 1)$, the 3D-TPS at a point $\mathbf{q}$ is given by:

$$\omega(\mathbf{q}, \mathbf{h}) = \boldsymbol{\ell}_\mathbf{q}^\mathsf{T}\mathbf{h} = \left(\sum_{k=1}^{l} \mathbf{w}_k d(\mathbf{q}, \mathbf{c}_k)\right) + \mathbf{a}^\mathsf{T}\check{\mathbf{q}}. \tag{1}$$

where $d(\mathbf{q}, \mathbf{c}_k)$ is the distance between $\mathbf{q}$ and $\mathbf{c}_k$.

We use the 3D-TPS to model the Gaussian noise's standard deviation by defining a set of l centers positioned throughout the working volume (Figure 6). This parametric function is chosen for many reasons. First, it efficiently approximates the noise's standard deviation being considered as a deformation. Second, it limits the memory requirement, in fact, only the $l+4$ parameters and the l centers have to be saved. The proposed model is based on the standard deviation and defined by the function f:

$$f: \quad \Omega \quad \rightarrow \mathbb{R}$$
$$\begin{pmatrix} u \\ v \\ d \end{pmatrix} \rightarrow \sigma, \tag{2}$$

where $\Omega \subset \mathbb{R}^3$, $\Omega = [u_{min}; u_{max}] \times [v_{min}; v_{max}] \times [d_{min}; d_{max}]$ and σ is a scalar that represents the standard deviation. $f(\mathbf{q}) \overset{\text{def}}{=} \boldsymbol{\ell}_\mathbf{q}^\mathsf{T}\mathbf{h}$ and f lies in $L^2(\psi)$ [2]. The $l + 4$ TPS coefficients in $\mathbf{h}$ are computed from the target σ_k (the standard deviation). Applying the TPS Equation (1) to the center c_r with target values σ_r gives:

$$\left(\sum_{k=1}^{l} \mathbf{w}_k d(\mathbf{c}_r, \mathbf{c}_k)\right) + \mathbf{a}^\mathsf{T}\check{\mathbf{c}}_r = \sigma_r. \tag{3}$$

---

[2] The Hilbert space of square-integrable functions.

Combining the equations obtained for all the l centers with the side-conditions in a single matrix equation gives:

$$\underbrace{\begin{pmatrix} K_\lambda & P \\ P^T & 0 \end{pmatrix}}_{D} \underbrace{\begin{pmatrix} w \\ a \end{pmatrix}}_{h} = \begin{pmatrix} \sigma \\ 0 \end{pmatrix} \text{ with } K_\lambda = \begin{cases} \lambda & r = k \\ d(c_r, c_k) & r \neq k. \end{cases} \tag{4}$$

In practice, we set λ to some small value such as $\lambda = 10^{-4}$, to ensure that K_λ and thus D are well conditioned. This is a linear system, the TPS coefficients in h are thus easily solved.

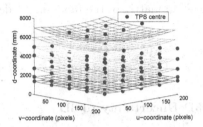

Fig. 6. The 7 depth images plotted together with the 3D TPS centers

4   Propagating Pixel Uncertainty to 3D

Pixel detection and extraction, whether manual or automatic, can only be performed to a finite accuracy. In addition to pixel detection error, depth-pixel extracted from TOF images are subject to sensor noise. One objective here is to consider how these errors propagate through the measurement formulas in order to quantify the uncertainty on the final 3D measurements. This is based on noise modelling. We concentrate in geometric measurements like object width and height, although, the method is not limited to those. This is achieved by using a first order error analysis. From pixels detected or clicked in the image, we want to estimate the geometric measurement and its uncertainty by propagating the uncertainty from the 2D point p to a 3D point Q. We proceed in three steps: the first one is the uncertainty propagation from 2D (a pixel p) to 2.5D (q), the second one is the uncertainty propagation from 2.5D (corresponding point q) to 3D (corresponding point Q) and the third one is the uncertainty propagation from 3D to the final geometric measurement.

4.1   Propagating Pixel Uncertainty to 2.5D

The uncertainty of a 2D point p is the click or the detection error. This error is defined by the variance matrix on p denoted by Σ^P (2×2 matrix). We suppose that Σ^P is given. We define the transformation $T1$ between p and q:

$$T1: \quad \Gamma \quad \rightarrow \Omega$$

$$\begin{pmatrix} u \\ v \end{pmatrix} \rightarrow \begin{pmatrix} u \\ v \\ d \end{pmatrix}, \tag{5}$$

where $d = d(u,v)$ and $\Gamma = [u_{min}; u_{max}] \times [v_{min}; v_{max}]$ defined by the image resolution.

A first order approximation for the variance-covariance matrix Σ^q_{inter} of $\mathbf{q}$ is given by:

$$\Sigma^q_{inter} = J_{T1} \Sigma^P J_{T1}^T, \tag{6}$$

where J is the 3×2 Jacobian matrix of the function $T1$ defined as:

$$J_{T1} = \begin{pmatrix} 1 & 0 \\ 0 & 1 \\ d(u+1,v) - d(u,v) & d(u,v+1) - d(u,v) \end{pmatrix}, \tag{7}$$

4.2 Propagating 2.5D Uncertainty to 3D

In addition to the uncertainty of a 2D point detection, there is the uncertainty of the depth measurement. It is defined by the standard deviation σ modelled by the 3D TPS function f (Equation (2)). Incorporating the depth variance σ^2 in the variance-covariance matrix Σ^q_{inter} gives:

$$\Sigma^q = \Sigma^q_{inter} + \begin{pmatrix} 0 & 0 & 0 \\ 0 & 0 & 0 \\ 0 & 0 & \sigma^2 \end{pmatrix}, \tag{8}$$

We show in the following that a transformation $T2$ exists between the two spaces. We assume that the camera's intrinsic parameters are known. Thus, the transformation from $\mathbf{q}$ to $\mathbf{Q}$ in the metric space can be estimated (as shown in the Figure 7). We call $(c_u \quad c_v)$ the optical center on the sensor array, f_c the camera focal length, $(d_u \quad d_v)$ the pixel pitch in the u (resp.

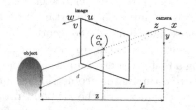

Fig. 7. 2.5D point $\mathbf{q}$ versus 3D point $\mathbf{Q}$

v) direction. Neglecting lens distortion, the transformation between $\mathbf{q}$ and $\mathbf{Q}$ is given by:

$$T2: \quad \Omega \quad \rightarrow \psi$$

$$\begin{pmatrix} u \\ v \\ d \end{pmatrix} \rightarrow \begin{pmatrix} X \\ Y \\ Z \end{pmatrix} \text{ with } \begin{cases} X = Z \frac{(u - c_u) d_u}{f_c} \\ Y = Z \frac{(v - c_v) d_v}{f_c} \\ Z = d \frac{f_c}{\sqrt{f_c^2 + ((u - c_u) d_u)^2 + ((v - c_v) d_v)^2}} \end{cases} \tag{9}$$

where ψ is a subset of $\mathbb{R}^3$: $\psi = [X_{min}; X_{max}] \times [Y_{min}; Y_{max}] \times [Z_{min}; Z_{max}]$. A first order approximation of he variance-covariance matrix $\Sigma^{\mathbf{Q}}$ of $T2$ is given by:

$$\Sigma^{\mathbf{Q}} = \mathsf{J}_{T2}\Sigma^{\mathbf{q}}\mathsf{J}_{T2}{}^{\mathsf{T}}, \tag{10}$$

where J_{T2} is the 3×3 Jacobian matrix of the function $T2$.

4.3   Propagating 3D Uncertainty to Distance Measurement

When making measurements between 3D points $\mathbf{Q}_i$, uncertainty arises from the uncertain localisation of the 3D points modelled by their associated variance-covariance matrix $\Sigma^{\mathbf{Q}_i}$. Here, we are concerned with measurement of the distance between two 3D points. Given two points $\mathbf{Q}_1, \mathbf{Q}_2$ and their associated variance-covariance matrices $\Sigma^{\mathbf{Q}_1}$ and $\Sigma^{\mathbf{Q}_2}$, the distance between $\mathbf{Q}_1$ and $\mathbf{Q}_2$ is defined by the function D:

$$D: \quad \psi^2 \quad \rightarrow \mathbb{R}$$
$$\begin{pmatrix} \mathbf{Q}_1 \\ \mathbf{Q}_2 \end{pmatrix} \rightarrow \|\overrightarrow{\mathbf{Q}_1\mathbf{Q}_2}\|_2. \tag{11}$$

Assuming a statistical independence between $\mathbf{Q}_1$ and $\mathbf{Q}_2$, a first order approximation of the variance σ_D^2 is given by:

$$\sigma_D^2 = \mathsf{J}_D \begin{pmatrix} \Sigma^{\mathbf{Q}_1} & 0 \\ 0 & \Sigma^{\mathbf{Q}_2} \end{pmatrix} \mathsf{J}_D{}^{\mathsf{T}}, \tag{12}$$

where J_D is the 1×6 Jacobian matrix of the function D.

5   Applicative Example

We give a simple example of use of our uncertainty modelling on real data. The TOF camera used is a PMD CamCube2 with a resolution of 204×204 pixels [8]. It is assumed to be calibrated (its internal parameters are known). The example consists in measuring the width and the height of a calibration checkerboard. These measurements are obtained from the 4 points clicked on the image $\mathbf{p}_1, \mathbf{p}_2$ and $\mathbf{p}_3, \mathbf{p}_4$ (see Figure 8(b)). For each 2D point $(\mathbf{p}_i)_{i=1}^4$, the $\Sigma^{\mathbf{P}_i}$ is computed: multiple-clicks are performed and the standard deviation in each direction (u, v) is computed. Then, the corresponding 3D point $(\mathbf{Q}_i)_{i=1}^4$ and their covariance-variance matrix $(\Sigma^{\mathbf{q}_i})_{i=1}^4$ and $(\Sigma^{\mathbf{Q}_i})_{i=1}^4$ are computed as explained in Section 4. The first point $\mathbf{p}_1$ is considered as an example to present the uncertainty propagation. The covariance matrices $\Sigma^{\mathbf{P}_1}$, $\Sigma^{\mathbf{q}_1}$ and $\Sigma^{\mathbf{Q}_1}$ are:

$$\Sigma^{\mathbf{P}_1} = \begin{pmatrix} 2.5^2 & 0 \\ 0 & 1.7^2 \end{pmatrix} \quad \Sigma^{\mathbf{q}_1} = \begin{pmatrix} 6 & 0 & 24.7 \\ 0 & 2.9 & 1.3 \\ 24.7 & 1.3 & 154.3 \end{pmatrix} \quad \Sigma^{\mathbf{Q}_1} = \begin{pmatrix} 286.3 & -64.4 & 230.2 \\ -64.5 & 202.9 & -7.9 \\ 230.2 & -7.9 & 275 \end{pmatrix}.$$

From these matrices, the uncertainty ellipse of $\mathbf{p}_1$ (Figure 8(c)) and the uncertainty ellipsoids of $\mathbf{q}_1$ (Figure 8(d)) and $\mathbf{Q}_1$ (Figure 8(e)) are drawn. Then, the checkerboard width $D(\mathbf{Q}_1, \mathbf{Q}_2)$ and height $D(\mathbf{Q}_3, \mathbf{Q}_4)$ values are computed from Equation (11). Their values are respectively equal to $h = 1250$ mm and $w = 906mm$, the ground truth are respectively 1200 mm and 900 mm. The error between measured and ground truth distances is not only due to sensor noise. The TOF camera are subject to depth distortion [9–11]. There are several causes for depth distortion, one of them is the called *systematic error*. In this paper, this latter is corrected [12]. After width and height computation, their variance values are computed from Equation (12) and the uncertainty (which is equal to standard deviation) are deduced. They are respectively equal to $\sigma_h{=}28.4$ mm and $\sigma_w{=}17.9$ mm. Note that ground truth values fall within the confidence intervals $[h - 2\sigma_h; h + 2\sigma_h]$ and $[w - \sigma_w; w + \sigma_w]$ with levels of confidence [3] equal to 95% and 68%.

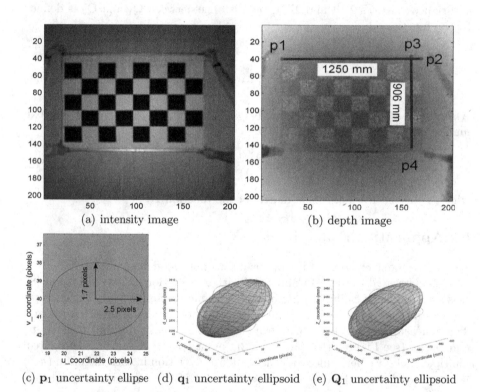

(a) intensity image   (b) depth image

(c) $\mathbf{p}_1$ uncertainty ellipse   (d) $\mathbf{q}_1$ uncertainty ellipsoid   (e) $\mathbf{Q}_1$ uncertainty ellipsoid

Fig. 8. Measuring the checkerboard width and height from depth-pixels: (a) the intensity image and (b) the depth image corrected for radial distortion. Computed width and height are respectively equal to $1250 \pm 28.4mm$ and $906 \pm 17.9mm$. The computed (c) uncertainty ellipse of $\mathbf{p}_1$ and uncertainty ellipsoid of (d) $\mathbf{q}_1$ and (e) $\mathbf{Q}_1$ are presented. The associated uncertainly ellipses are drawn in blue around the ellipsoids.

---

[3] The level of confidence would indicate the probability that the confidence interval contains the ground truth value. Not that greater levels of confidence give larger confidence intervals, and hence less precise estimates of the parameter.

6 Conclusion

We have characterized the noise distribution of TOF sensors as Gaussian. A 3D Thin-Plate-Spline is used as a noise's standard deviation model. A method that approximates the uncertainty associated to TOF measurements is proposed. A simple example on real data demonstrate an application of the proposed approach. Future work will improve the robustness of TOF algorithms using the uncertainty information. It would also be interesting to test the proposed approach for the Kinect sensor.

References

1. Lange, R.: 3D Time-of-Flight distance measurement with custom solid-state image sensors in CMOS/CCD-technology. PhD thesis, University of Siegen, Germany (2000)
2. Kim, S.Y., Cho, J.H., Koschan, A., Abidi, M.A.: Spatial and temporal enhancement of depth images captured by a time-of-flight depth sensor. In: ICPR (2010)
3. Kim, S.M., Cha, J., Ryu, J., Lee, K.H.: Depth video enhancement for haptic interaction using a smooth surface reconstruction. IEICE - Trans. Inf. Syst. E89-D, 37–44 (2006)
4. Cho, J.H., Chang, I.Y., Kim, S., Lee, K.: Depth image processing technique for representing human actors in 3dtv using single depth camera. In: 3DTV (2007)
5. Zhu, J., Wang, L., Yang, R., Davis, J.: Fusion of time-of-flight depth and stereo for high accuracy depth maps. In: CVPR (2008)
6. Chambers, J.M., Cleveland, W.S., Kliener, B., Tukey, P.A.: Graphical Methods for Data Analysis. Wadsworth (1983)
7. May, S., Droeschel, D., Holz, D., Fuchs, S.: Three-dimensional mapping with time-of-flight cameras. J. Field Robot. 26, 934–964 (2009)
8. PMDTechnologies: Pmd[vision]camcube 3.0 (2009),
   http://www.pmdtec.com/products-services/pmdvisionr-cameras/pmdvisionr-camcube-20/
9. Karel, W., Dorninger, P., Pfeifer, N.: In situ determination of range camera quality parameters by segmentation. In: Opt. 3D Meas. Tech. (2007)
10. Guömundsson, S.A., Aanæs, H., Larsen, R.: Environmental effects on measurement uncertainties of Time-of-Fight cameras. In: ISSCS (2007)
11. Weyer, C.A., Bae, K.H., Lim, K., Lichti, D.D.: Extensive metric performance evaluation of a 3D range camera. In: ISPRS (2008)
12. Belhedi, A., Bourgeois, S., Gay-Bellile, V., Sayd, P., Bartoli, A., Hamrouni, K.: Non-parametric depth calibration of a tof camera. In: ICIP (2012)

Single Color One-Shot Scan Using Topology Information

Hiroshi Kawasaki[1], Hitoshi Masuyama[1], Ryusuke Sagawa[2], and Ryo Furukawa[3]

[1] Kagoshima University, Kagoshima, Japan
[2] AIST, Tsukuba, Japan
[3] Hiroshima City University, Hiroshima, Japan

Abstract. In this paper, we propose a new technique to achieve one-shot scan using single color and static pattern projector; such a method is ideal for acquisition of a moving object. Since a projector-camera systems generally have uncertainties on retrieving correspondences between the captured image and the projected pattern, many solutions have been proposed. Especially for one-shot scan, which means that only a single image is used for reconstruction, positional information of a pixel on the projected pattern should be encoded by spatial and/or color information. Although color information is frequently used for encoding, it is severely affected by texture and material of the object. In this paper, we propose a technique to solve the problem by using topological information instead of colors. Our technique successfully realizes one-shot scan with monochrome pattern.

1 Introduction

Importance of shape capture of moving objects is rapidly increasing. For example, recently, inexpensive scanning devices developed for entertainment purposes made a great success to achieve the device-free interface [1]. Because their purpose of the scanner is mainly on a motion capture, their accuracy and density are relatively low, compared to existing range sensors for industrial purposes. If high accuracy with dense resolution is realized on such scanners, they become more useful for various purposes, *e.g.*, medical application and fluid analysis.

There are several methods exist for capturing moving objects with active scanning techniques, such as stereo based methods or time-of-flight (TOF) methods. Especially, structured-light stereo methods are suitable for capturing moving objects and have been widely researched [1–4]. Structured-light methods are usually categorized into two types: temporal-encoding and spatial-encoding methods. Since the spatial-encoding method just requires a single input for reconstruction (*a.k.a.* one-shot scan), it is ideal for capturing moving objects. Therefore, many researches have been conducted with spatial-encoding methods [5]. However, since they require certain areas to encode the position of the pixel of the projected pattern, the resolution tends to be low and reconstruction becomes unstable with an inevitable turbulence of color. One efficient way to encode information on the surface of the object is to use an epipolar geometry. By using

A. Fusiello et al. (Eds.): ECCV 2012 Ws/Demos, Part III, LNCS 7585, pp. 486–495, 2012.
© Springer-Verlag Berlin Heidelberg 2012

it, ambiguity can be decreased from 2D to 1D and stability can be improved drastically. To use the epipolar constraint, stripe pattern which is perpendicular to the epipolar line is commonly used [6–8]. Grid pattern is also used to increase the stability [9, 3, 10]. Although such approaches greatly ease the problem, since color information is easily affected by texture, material and lighting conditions, results are still unstable in a real scene.

To avoid color problems, several methods are proposed for efficient spatial encoding without using colors, such as dot patterns or grid patterns [1]. Even though, there still remain several problems, *i.e.*, inaccuracy by short base line and sparse reconstruction. In this paper, we propose a one-shot scanning method which can solve the aforementioned problems with the following approaches.

Topology Information for Wide Base-Line Stereo: To increase the stability on retrieving correspondences, we propose a topology information instead of color information. We use a graph representation for the pattern and the nodes can be used as features that can be distinguished by, for example, the order of nodes (the number of edges connected to the nodes). Since the topology information is preserved during geometric transformation, robust correspondences with wide base-line can be realized.

Geometric Information for Dense Reconstruction: Topology information can only be applied sparsely on the pattern, we use geometric information to increase the density of reconstruction. As for the implementation, a small window is used to calculate matching scores using geometric information for each pixel. Unlike the topology information, the matching score is sensitive to the geometric transformation, we also estimate the surface normal for each pixel. Although such pixels are reconstructed unstably, a global optimization technique is conducted.

Global Optimization to Decrease Wrong Reconstruction: Since the technique is based on stereo, MRF based global optimization technique can be applied. In our method, the matching scores of each pixel especially with geometric information tend to have several local minima; such multiple candidates are efficiently solved by global optimization. We use belief propagation method in the paper.

2   Related Work

Triangulation based methods (*e.g.*, light-sectioning method or stereo method) and time-of-flight(TOF) based methods are widely known for active measurement. Since many TOF based systems use point lasers, they are not suitable to capture the entire scene in a short period of time. To capture dynamic scenes, some TOF devices project temporally-modulated light patterns and acquire a depth image at once by using a special 2D image sensor[11]. However, the present systems are easily disturbed by other light sources and the resolution is low.

With regard to triangulation based methods, many methods use point or line lasers and a scene is scanned by sweeping the lights. This type is unsuitable for dynamic scenes, because sweeping takes a time. Using area light sources, such as video projector, is a simple solution to reduce the time to scan. However, unlike

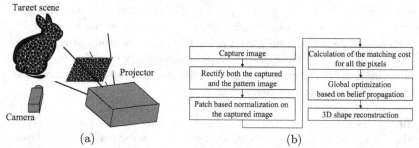

Fig. 1. (a) System configuration where a graph-based pattern is projected from the projector and captured by the camera, and (b) an algorithm overview

a point or a line light sources, there is an ambiguity on correspondences. For solution, typically two methods are known, *i.e.*, temporal-encoding or spatial-encoding methods[6].

In a temporal-encoding method, multiple patterns of illuminations are projected, and the correspondence information is encoded in the temporal modulations. Thus, it is essentially unsuitable for acquiring dynamic scenes. However, some methods are proposed to resolve the problem; by capturing with high frequencies [12–14]. Although it is reported that some works can capture around 100 FPS by combining motion compensation, since these methods require multiple frames, the quality of the results is degraded if object moves fast.

A spatial-encoding method uses a static pattern and usually requires just a single image, and thus, it is suitable to capture dynamic scenes. However, since information should be encoded in certain areas of the pattern, the resolution tends to be low. Moreover, correspondences are not stably determined because the patterns are distorted due to the color or the shapes of the object surface. Many methods have been proposed to solve the problems; *e.g.*, using multiple lines with globally-unique color combinations [15, 16], dotted lines with unique modulations of dots [17, 18], 2D area information for encoding [19, 1], or connections of grid patterns [20, 2–4]. However, no method has achieved a sufficient performance in all aspects of precision, resolution, and stability.

In the paper, we propose a simple technique to solve the aforementioned problems using the new pattern which uses topology information. With our technique, all the problems are not solved, however, some promising aspects can be shown for future direction of one-shot scan with single color.

3   Overview and System Settings

Our system consists of a single projector and a camera. The projector casts a static pattern as shown in Fig.1(a). The pattern consists of lines (edges) and intersections (nodes) which make a graph representation (details are described in Sec.4). Since the pattern is static, no synchronization is required.

Overview of our algorithm is shown in Fig.1(b). First, we rectify both the captured image and the projected pattern. Then, we normalize the captured

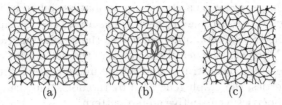

Fig. 2. Graph pattern generated by Penrose tiling: (a) a basic pattern, (b) a basic pattern that is modified so that thin rhombuses (one of them is marked by a red ellipse) are enlarged, and (c) a pattern in which the positions of the nodes are disturbed to reduce the repetition of similar patterns

image for better calculation of the matching cost. In this process, since environmental lighting condition and texture is not uniform, adaptive normalization is applied. In the next step, matching costs are calculated for each pixel. We also estimate the surface normal in this step. Using the cost, global optimization is conducted using BP. Finally, the depths for all the pixels are reconstructed using the estimated disparity for each pixel.

4   Topology Preserving Pattern

In one-shot active stereo, the pattern projected to the target is important to achieve sufficient performances. The pattern is projected to the target surface and observed by the camera. The observed pattern is deformed by the geometries of the surface. The local deformation of this process can be represented as 3D homographies by regarding the local surface as a small plane (a patch).

One of the patterns whose geometric property is not changed under 2D homography is a line. However, a simple line does not have much geometric features, thus, it is not appropriate for a pattern for stereo matching as it is. One of the possible solution for this is to use a pattern for a planar graph (graph that can be embedded in the plane without intersecting edges) with an appropriate geometric complexity.

For a planar graph as a pattern, one important feature is the number of edges that are connected to each of the nodes (orders of the nodes), or edge connections between the nodes. Those features are topological properties of the graph which does not change under 2D homographies. In the present work, we propose to use a pattern generated by Penrose tiling[21], which has plenty of such features.

Penrose tiling is a kind of tiling (filling a plane with some geometric shapes without overlaps nor gaps) that can be generated by a small number of tiles. The generated patten is known to have no translational symmetry. Among several kinds of Penrose tiling, we use a pattern that are generated by two kinds of rhombuses[21] (rhombus tiling). The generation can be easily achieved using a recursive algorithm. An example of rhombus tiling is shown in Fig.2(a).

If orders of nodes are regarded as features, a graph that includes nodes with many kinds of orders has more distinctive features. However, if an order of a node is too large (*i.e.*, too many edges are connected to the node), some of the edges may easily become indistinguishable under deformation caused by homographies. About the proposed pattern, the orders of nodes are 3, 4, or 5. This means that, although this graph has several orders of nodes, the maximum order of a node is limited to be 5. Moreover, the density of nodes in the pattern is uniform. This is useful to achieve dense reconstruction at actual measurement. From the above-mentioned properties, the graph generated by rhombus tiling can be considered to have good properties as an active stereo pattern.

The minimum angle of corners of the rhombuses, which is shown in Fig.2(a), is as small as 36 degrees; such a narrow angle is inappropriate for the pattern, because the two edges of the corners may become difficult to distinguish by some homographic deformations. In this work, we modified positions of the nodes so that the minimum angle of corners is increased. To achieve this, we assume repulsive forces between the nodes of the graph that would be generated if all the nodes had the same electrical charges. Then, we move each nodes following the resultant forces. As a result, the distances between the nodes becomes more uniform, the thin rhombus becomes thicker as shown in Fig.2(b), and the properties of the pattern is improved.

Another effective technique is disturbing the repetition of similar patterns. As a simple implementation, we slightly move each nodes randomly as shown in Fig.2(c).

5   Reconstruction by Stereo with Regularization

In our method, reconstruction process consists of mainly two parts. The first one is a matching cost calculation part and the other is a global optimization part.

As the input for reconstruction process, first, we rectify both the captured image and the projected pattern so that the cost calculation process can be conducted along a horizontal line. Then, disparity search range for the cost calculation is defined by considering the in-focus range of the projector; it is usually 10% length of the distance between the projector and the target. After all the matching costs for all the disparities along all the horizontal lines are calculated, global optimization is applied to get the final 3D shape.

5.1   Matching Cost Calculation

Patch Based Normalization. Since a captured image contains both bright and dark areas, preprocessing is required before cost calculation to retrieve the reliable matching cost. Since the pattern consists of only lines, one may consider that the line detection can be a solution. It is true and that can be used as the normalization process, however, the algorithm itself is still under research. Furthermore, a line detection algorithm basically loses some important information for matching cost, such as sub-pixel information with gray-scale intensity. Therefore, we take another approach to preserve those information. In this paper, we apply window based normalization for local areas. The following linear transformation is conducted for each window defined for each target pixel.

$$I_{new}(x) = (I_{org}(x) - I_{low}) \frac{255}{I_{high} - I_{low}}. \tag{1}$$

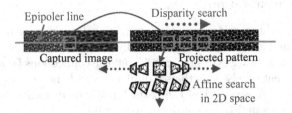

Fig. 3. Matching cost calculation algorithm

In the equation, I_{low} and I_{high} represent the lowest and highest value in each window. The window size is defined so as to two times larger than the window size for the matching cost calculation.

Matching Cost Calculation with Surface Orientation Estimation. For passive stereo, there are a few techniques considering the orientation of the surface of the object [22]. This is natural because high frequency features (higher than window size) do not exist frequently in the actual scene and color information is sufficient to retrieve good correspondences. Whereas in active stereo, since high frequency patterns are intentionally projected to the object to increase the stability and density of the captured image, the patterns are severely distorted by the surface orientation, which should be resolved.

In this paper, we calculate the matching cost using SSD with a small window and the size of the window is defined so that at least one intersection point is included. In such case, the window size is relatively small compared to the image size, and thus, pattern distortion caused by the orientation of the surface can be represented by affine transformation with two DOFs. Since each window contains at least three lines which share the intersection point, pattern is always unique under affine transformations. Therefore, we can estimate the surface orientation for each point independently. In our method, instead of applying optimization technique to find the solution, we conduct full search to estimate the parameter. There are mainly two reasons for this. First, since topology pattern has several local minima, simple optimization techniques, such as the least descent method, sometimes fail. Secondly, because the patch size is small, the number of variety of pattern transformation could be small. Therefore, for actual implementation, we precompute the pattern with a limited number of affine transformation and find the best match to estimate the surface normal. In our experiment, we find that total 42 patterns (6 and 7 for each parameter) are sufficient to produce enough quality. Fig.3 show the cost calculation process and the SSD value is calculated by the following equation.

$$SSD(x, d) = \arg \min_{\mathbf{a}} \sum_{x' \in W(x+d)} (I_c(x') - I_p(H_\mathbf{a}(x')))^2, \qquad (2)$$

where d is a disparity, $W(x)$ is the rectangular patch around x, and $H_a(x')$ is the affine transformation with parameter $\mathbf{a}$. $I_c(\cdot)$ and $I_p(\cdot)$ are the intensities of the camera and projector images, respectively.

5.2 Global Optimization

Once all the matching costs are calculated, global optimization is applied to eliminate the small noise which is produced by the self-similarity of the patterns. The captured image consists of pixel $p \in V$ and the connections $(p, q) \in U$, where p and q are adjacent pixels, V is the set of pixels, and U is the set of connections of adjacent pixels. A pixel p has the costs for all the disparities $d_p \in D_p$. We define the energy to find the disparity map as follows:

$$E(D) = \sum_{p \in V} D_p(d_p) + \sum_{(p,q) \in U} W_{pq}(d_p, d_q), \qquad (3)$$

where $D = \{d_p | p \in V\}$. $D_p(d_p)$ is the data term of assigning a pixel to disparity d_p. $W_{pq}(d_p, d_q)$ is the regularization term of assigning disparity d_p and d_q to neighboring pixel points. The data term is the SSD calculated by the method described in previous section. The regularization term is defined as follows

$$W_{pq}(d_p, d_q) = |d_p - d_q| \qquad (4)$$

The energy is minimized based on belief propagation [23] in this paper.

6 Experiment

We applied a camera of 1600×1200 pixels, a projector of 1024×768 pixels and a PC with Intel Core i7 2.93GHz/NVIDIAGeForce 580GTX.

First, we show the effectiveness of the proposed topology pattern by comparing with several different patterns. Fig.4 shows the results and table 1 shows the RMSEs from the fitted planes, corner angles, and the number of reconstructed points. As shown in table 1, case (a) was inaccurate and small in the number

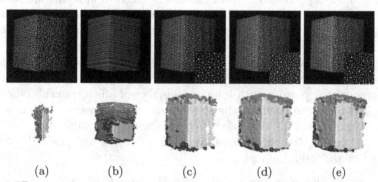

| (a)   (b)   (c)   (d)   (e) |

Fig. 4. 3D reconstruction results. The top row images are inputs, and the bottom row images are results: (a) the result of a random dot pattern, (b) a grid pattern, (c) a pattern generated from the rhombus tiling(see Fig.2(a)), (d) the rhombus tiling weakly disturbed by noise, and (e) the rhombus tiling strongly disturbed by noise(see Fig.2(c)).

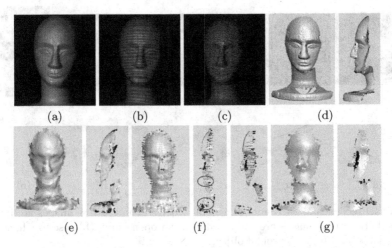

Fig. 5. Comparison of other methods: (a) a target object, (b) the object projected by a grid pattern [3], (c) by the proposed pattern, (d) the result of phase-shift as a ground truth, (e) the result of Kinect, (f) the result from (b), and (g) the result from (c)

of reconstruction and case (b) was inaccurate in the corner angle (actually, the global position itself was incorrect). In the proposed methods, the number of reconstructed points increased as the randomness was added to the pattern. Therefore, we can conclude that our topology preserving pattern is a promising approach as a single-colored active one-shot scan, and that adding randomness to the pattern can improve performances.

Table 1. RMSEs(m) from fitted planes, corner angles, and the number of reconstructed points for results shown in Fig.4

	(a)random	(b)grid	(c)penrose	(d)penrose r1	(e)penrose r2
RMSE(m)	0.0023	0.0016	0.0018	0.0016	0.0016
Corner angle(deg.)	59.5	58.5	92.0	91.9	91.9
Number of points	10583	31154	26340	28934	28986

Next, the accuracy of the proposed method was evaluated by capturing the head of the figure as shown in Fig.5. The size of the object was 0.25m high and the distance from the camera was about 0.6m. In Fig.5, results by different methods are shown: (d) the temporal-encoding method by projecting phase-shift pattern, (e) Kinect, (f) the spatial-encoding method by projecting single color grid pattern [3], and (g) the proposed method. Since the temporal-encoding method (d) has an advantage in terms of accuracy, we used it as the ground truth for evaluation. In figure (f), we put two results; the left one is the result with wrong connections between the face and the neck indicated by the red circle, which inevitably occurs on grid pattern [3] and the right where such wrong connections are cut. The differences between points are calculated by using a

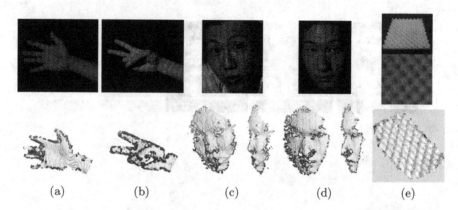

(a)   (b)   (c)   (d)   (e)

Fig. 6. 3D reconstruction results of general objects. The top row images are inputs, and the bottom row images are the results: (a) an open hand, (b) a scissor hand, (c) and (d) faces, and (e) a sinusoidal object.

method proposed by Cignoni [24]. The RMSEs from ground truth are (e) 0.4mm, (f) left 2.3mm, (f) right 0.09mm, and (g) 0.07mm, respectively. We can confirm that the propose method (g) gave the best performance. However, the number of the reconstructed points is smaller than other methods. We consider that this is mainly because our method does not use the information of the connection of the pattern. This is our future work to solve the problem. Calculation time of our method was around 1min. to 5min. per image. Speeding up the calculation time is also our important future work.

Finally, we show the results of more general objects. Fig.6 show the results of the captured scenes of hands, faces and a sinusoidal object, respectively. Since the proposed method is one-shot method, it can generate 3D shapes even if the target object is not static. Here, you can see some noises near the boundary of the shapes. We consider that this is because surface normals near occluding boundaries are wrongly estimated.

7   Conclusion

In this paper, efficient and dense 3D reconstruction method from a single image using single-colored static pattern is proposed. The method utilizes topology information to achieve wider base-line with stable reconstruction compared to the previous methods. We also propose a geometric information to increase the density by solving the affine transformation of the pattern. At the final reconstruction step, BP technique is used to integrate both topology information and geometry based techniques. In the experiments, we evaluated the accuracy of our method compared to the state-of-the-art one-shot scan techniques and proves the strength of our method. Several directions of the future research are presented.

References

1. Microsoft: Xbox 360 Kinect (2010), http://www.xbox.com/en-US/kinect
2. Kawasaki, H., Furukawa, R., Sagawa, R., Yagi, Y.: Dynamic scene shape reconstruction using a single structured light pattern. In: CVPR, pp. 1–8 (2008)
3. Sagawa, R., Ota, Y., Yagi, Y., Furukawa, R., Asada, N., Kawasaki, H.: Dense 3d reconstruction method using a single pattern for fast moving object. In: ICCV (2009)
4. Ulusoy, A.O., Calakli, F., Taubin, G.: One-shot scanning using de bruijn spaced grids. In: The 7th IEEE Conf. 3DIM (2009)
5. Salvi, J., Pages, J., Batlle, J.: Pattern codification strategies in structured light systems. Pattern Recognition 37, 827–849 (2004)
6. Salvi, J., Batlle, J., Mouaddib, E.M.: A robust-coded pattern projection for dynamic 3D scene measurement. Pattern Recognition 19, 1055–1065 (1998)
7. Je, C., Lee, S.-W., Park, R.-H.: High-Contrast Color-Stripe Pattern for Rapid Structured-Light Range Imaging. In: Pajdla, T., Matas, J. (eds.) ECCV 2004, Part I. LNCS, vol. 3021, pp. 95–107. Springer, Heidelberg (2004)
8. Zhang, L., Curless, B., Seitz, S.: Rapid shape acquisition using color structured light and multi-pass dynamic programming. In: 3DPVT, pp. 24–36 (2002)
9. Furukawa, Y., Ponce, J.: Dense 3D motion capture from synchronized video streams. In: CVPR (2008)
10. Sagawa, R., Kawasaki, H., Furukawa, R., Kiyota, S.: Dense one-shot 3D reconstruction by detecting continuous regions with parallel line projection. In: ICCV (2011)
11. Canesta, Inc.: CanestaVision EP Development Kit (2010), http://www.canesta.com/devkit.html
12. Rusinkiewicz, S., Hall-Holt, O., Levoy, M.: Real-time 3D model acquisition. In: Proc. SIGGRAPH, pp. 438–446 (2002)
13. Weise, T., Leibe, B., Van Gool, L.: Fast 3D scanning with automatic motion compensation. In: CVPR (2007)
14. Narasimhan, S.G., Koppal, S.J., Yamazaki, S.: Temporal Dithering of Illumination for Fast Active Vision. In: Forsyth, D., Torr, P., Zisserman, A. (eds.) ECCV 2008, Part IV. LNCS, vol. 5305, pp. 830–844. Springer, Heidelberg (2008)
15. Tajima, J., Iwakawa, M.: 3-D data acquisition by rainbow range finder. In: ICPR, pp. 309–313 (1990)
16. Zhang, S., Huang, P.: High-resolution, real-time 3D shape acquisition. In: Proc. Conference on Computer Vision and Pattern Recognition Workshop, p. 28 (2004)
17. Maruyama, M., Abe, S.: Range sensing by projecting multiple slits with random cuts. In: SPIE Optics, Illumination, and Image Sensing for Machine Vision IV, vol. 1194, pp. 216–224 (1989)
18. Artec: United States Patent Application 2009005924 (2007j)
19. Vuylsteke, P., Oosterlinck, A.: Range image acquisition with a single binary-encoded light pattern. IEEE Trans. on PAMI 12, 148–164 (1990)
20. Koninckx, T., Van Gool, L.: Real-time range acquisition by adaptive structured light. IEEE Transaction Pattern Analysis Machine Intelligence 28, 432–445 (2006)
21. Gardner, M.: Penrose Tiles to Trapdoor Ciphers. Cambridge University Press (1997)
22. Furukawa, Y., Ponce, J.: Accurate, dense, and robust multi-view stereopsis. In: CVPR (2007)
23. Felzenszwalb, P., Huttenlocher, D.: Efficient belief propagation for early vision. IJCV 70, 41–54 (2006)
24. Cignoni, P., Rocchini, C., Scopigno, R.: Metro: measuring error on simplified surfaces. Computer Graphics Forum 17, 167–174 (1998)

View Planning Approach for Automatic 3D Digitization of Unknown Objects

Souhaiel Khalfaoui, Ralph Seulin, Yohan Fougerolle, and David Fofi

Le2i Laboratory, UMR-CNRS 6306, University of Burgundy,
71200 Le Creusot, France
{souhaiel.khalfaoui,ralph.seulin,
yohan.fougerolle,david.fofi}@u-bourgogne.fr
http://www.le2i.cnrs.fr

Abstract. This paper addresses the view planning problem for the digitization of 3D objects without prior knowledge on their shape and presents a novel surface approach for the Next Best View (NBV) computation. The proposed method uses the concept of Mass Vector Chains (MVC) to define the global orientation of the scanned part. All of the viewpoints satisfying an orientation constraint are clustered using the Mean Shift technique to construct a first set of candidates for the NBV. Then, a weight is assigned to each mode according to the elementary orientations of its different descriptors. The NBV is chosen among the modes with the highest weights and which comply with the robotics constraints. Eventually, our method is generic since it is applicable to all kinds of scanners. Experiments applying a digitization cell demonstrate the feasibility and the efficiency of the approach which leads to an intuitive and fast 3D acquisition while moving efficiently the ranging device.

Keywords: 3D Digitization, Automation, Automatic Scanning, View Planning, Next Best View, Non-Model-Based Method.

1 Introduction

3D models are widely used in many applications such as industrial inspection, computer games, and augmented reality. The 3D model can be generated either artificially by computer assisted designed (CAD) technique or by digitization. The manual 3D acquisition process is very time consuming for human operator since the viewpoints (scanner positions) are selected by a specialized human operator. The quality of the final result strongly depends on the selected viewpoints and thus on the human expertise. Therefore, it is necessary to define a new digitization strategy of objects that minimizes the impact of the human factor. This independence can be obtained by automating the digitization process. When we address the problem of fully automatic 3D digitization of unknown objects, *Next-Best-View (NBV) planning* is an important approach for the automation procedure. The first goal of view planning is to determine an optimal

A. Fusiello et al. (Eds.): ECCV 2012 Ws/Demos, Part III, LNCS 7585, pp. 496–505, 2012.

positioning of the measuring sensor and to complete the digitization using previous views while minimizing the number of acquisitions. The automation of the 3D acquisition process requires the knowledge of the different components of the measuring system (scanner, positioning system, etc.). Thus, automatic scanning can be decomposed into two phases: the determination of the different poses (position and orientation) and the sensor trajectory generation from previous poses to achieve the next optimal location.

The goal of this work is to automatically generate a complete 3D model of unknown and complex objects by developing an information-driven approach. Therefore, we introduce a novel NBV strategy based on the evolution of the scanned part orientation. Our method enables fast and complete 3D reconstruction while moving efficiently the scanner. By generating a set of potential views, our technique ensures proper avoidance of unreachable configurations. This paper is organized as follows. In the next section we discuss the related work and briefly define the benchmark methods that will be used to evaluate our approach. In section 3 we introduce our NBV planning method followed by experimental results in section 4. We conclude in section 5.

2   Related Work

Scott et al. [1] provided a complete survey paper about the view planning problem in the last few decades. The developed non-model-based methods to compute the best views can be classified into two main approaches: volumetric methods and surface methods.

Volumetric approaches are based on the analysis and the knowledge of the workspace state and use voxelization to represent occupied and empty areas. *Abidi* [2] adapted the concept of entropy in information theory to the problem of volumetric modeling of an unknown object. A utility function is proposed to qualify the amount of acquired data at each stage of the the acquisition process. The local maximum of this function determines the NBV. One advantage is that there is no restriction on the shape, size, and the location of the object. *Reed* [3] proposed an automatic method in two phases: a modelling phase that constructs a coarse surface mesh from fixed positions, and a planning phase that analyses the model to calculate the next sensor position. *Reed* determined the visibility volume which is the volume of the space in which a sensor has a direct view on a particular target. Determining the NBV requires the consideration of three constraints (sensor visibility constraint, occlusion constraint, and sensor positioning constraint) which are associated with different volumes. *Massios and Fisher* [4] introduced a quality criterion in addition to the visibility criterion to improve the overall quality of the acquired data. A voxel representation is used to label voxels as: empty, seen, unseen, or Occlusion Plane. The application of the sensor positioning constraints to the coarse model of the object will determine areas of possible views. This volumetric representation is then projected onto the visibility sphere and the quality criterion is applied to evaluate each view. The direction with the best result is selected. An extension of this algorithm was proposed by *Munkelt et al.* [5] and is composed of two phases. A first initialization phase during which the algorithm maximizes the number of visible voxels respecting a given quality. The second phase maximizes the number of occluded and visible voxels. The stopping criterion of this algorithm is a redundancy rate above a predefined threshold. *Connolly* [6] used an *octree* structure to subdivide the space. The determination of the NBV requires an update of this structure that contains four types of node: parent, empty, occupied, and unseen. Two algorithms were proposed: the Planetarium and the Normal algorithm. The Planetarium searches for the area with maximum unseen voxels and detects occlusions caused by the *occupied* voxels. The Normal algorithm performs a counting of the normals of the *unseen* voxels that have *empty* neighbors, resulting on a viewing vector.

The Surface methods use the surface representation of the model to obtain cues about the regions of missing data. *Maver and Bajcsy* [7] used the model edges to compute the occluded area of each view which was described as a polygon and assumed to be planar. Each edge was classified as active or inactive. A histogram representation of the occluding region and the camera angle was then used to select the next scanning direction. The method proposed by *Kok-lim Low* [8] takes into account several constraints for the view planning (Acquisition and Quality constraints). From a first acquisition, a partial model of the scene is created. The acquired surfaces are labelled *real*. The determination of NBV involves assessing the cost of a view for various constraints. The view with the highest score is chosen as the NBV. The view planning is completed if all the views have a score below a predefined threshold. *Yuan* [9] introduced the concept of Mass Vector Chains (MVC) to characterize closed models. A MVC is defined as the sum of the normal vectors of all surface patches weighted by its projected area in the normal's direction. It was demonstrated that for closed model, the sum of the MVC (Mass Vector Sum (MVS)) is null. The existence of holes in the model causes the MVS to be not null. The opposite of the vector MVS is used as the NBV to complete the model. The algorithm stops only if the object is closed, hence complete. Thus, this method can not be used in the case of complex objects (holes, narrow cavities, etc.). *He and Li* [10] have added a termination condition using a threshold variation of the surface. The sensor characteristics such as desired resolution, scanning resolution, field of view, and working distance were also included to optimize the scanning process. *Loriot* [11] established a rapid method composed of two steps. The first phase is based on the MVC approach. The second phase aims to acquire non-digitized areas. This method is very expensive in robot's movements, especially in the first phase of the algorithm as the method of the MVC supports many round trips around the object. Furthermore, this approach does not take into account the distribution of views in the work space since some viewpoints are particularly close to each other. *Kriegel et al.* [12] determines the candidates for the NBV by calculating points and normals of an estimated quadratic from the different boundaries of the acquired data. This method does not work with large objects or objects that have very sharp angles at the edges. *Khalfaoui et al.* [13] presented a new method based on the evolution of the bounding box of the object during the acquisition process which is based on an arbitrary number of positions computed uniformly using a mid point subdivision. For each step the new data are independent of what was previously acquired. The only information which links two successive acquisitions is the size of the bounding box and not the geometry of the scanned part, which avoids expensive computations on acquired data and leads to a simple and intuitive algorithm.

We reviewed two main approaches: volumetric and surface based methods. For our automation strategy we adopt the surface representation which is more intuitive and simple since it uses directly the characteristics of the acquired data to decide about the NBV. Among the reviewed surface-based methods, we will particularly use MVC [11] and Bounding Box [13] methods for benchmark. The comparison between the different methods will be based on the coverage rate, the number of acquisition, their distribution around the object, and the length of the scanner trajectory.

3   Proposed Method

A large number of views improves the accuracy of the resulting model but increases the acquisition time and the 3D data redundancy. Our goal is to reduce the number of acquisitions while moving the scanner efficiently and to avoid heuristic approaches. The proposed NBV solution is inspired by the human behaviour. When people are given objects they have not seen before, they focus on the edge of the first seen surface, and then they rotate it in order to discover its unseen parts.

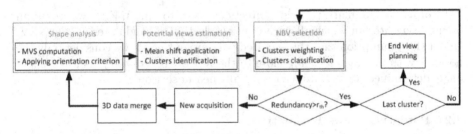

Fig. 1. Flowchart of the proposed method

The developed method is based on the analysis of the orientation of the acquired data at each step of the acquisition process since we assume no prior knowledge about the object shape. The different orientations of the elementary surface patches are classified to determine a set of potential NBVs, so several positioning alternatives of the ranging device, ensuring proper avoidance of robotic singularities and unreachable positions. The next view direction will be chosen between the candidates which satisfy all the constraints of our system. The main stages of the next best view procedure, illustrated in figure 1, are described in detail in the following for the ith step of the acquisition process.

3.1   Shape Analysis

The next view planning is generated incrementally using the latest acquired data. At each step of the acquisition process, all the previously acquired surfaces are merged to obtain a global surface mesh Sh^i. The resulting model is then analyzed to determine its characteristics. The main orientation of the scanned parts, MVS^i, is extracted using the MVC technique [9]. The elementary orientation of each surface patch is also calculated and saved in a global orientation vector θ^i. One key main idea of our algorithm is to consider only bounded displacements around the last position of the scanner. The MVS^i of the rough model changes according to the newly acquired part of the object. Indeed, the addition of new data at the ith step changes the main orientation of the merged parts at the $(i-1)^{th}$ step. As shown in figures 2.b and 2.c, the new candidate to the NBV is selected to cover a portion of the data already scanned to guarantee successful registration due to surface overlap.

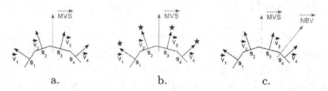

      a.   b.   c.

Fig. 2. Next Best View estimation: a) Mass Vector Sum (MVS) determination b) NBV candidates for our method c) Possible NBV

In order to eliminate the view directions close to the MVS^i, we apply an orientation criterion which allows an initial selection of candidates for the NBV. Under the assumption that the acquired data are not noisy, we consider only the normals with an angle $\theta^i > \theta^i_{th}$ close to the MVS^i direction. θ^i_{th} is a threshold angle determined at each iteration as explained in section 4.

3.2   Potential Views Estimation

After the application of the orientation criterion, all the views have the same probability of being selected for the next acquisition. We then apply the *Mean Shift* technique [14] to cluster all the potential views. The Mean Shift algorithm is an iterative and non-parametric algorithm whose main idea is to treat the data in the n-dimensional space as an empirical function of a probability density where dense regions in the space correspond to local maxima or clusters of this distribution. The data associated with the same fixed point are considered members of the same cluster. Each mode is a six-dimensional vector describing the pose of the scanner (Fig. 3). So there is no decorrelation between the position indicator and orientation in determining a potential view direction. Once the set of potential views is computed, the algorithm decide about the optimal next pose of the scanner head.

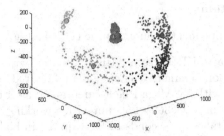

Fig. 3. Determination of four main modes using the *Mean Shift* technique

3.3 NBV Selection

The developed method focuses on the completion of the 3D reconstruction. Since the goal is to explore unseen parts, a weight w_k^i is assigned to each possible view direction k and is determined among its orientation close to the MVS^i as follows:

$$w_k^i = \frac{\theta_k^i}{\theta_{max}^i} \tag{1}$$

where θ_{max}^i is the maximum angle value in the orientation vector θ^i. Let assume that the ith clustering step identifies j main clusters $C^{i,l}$, $l = 1 : j$. The assigned weight $W^{i,l}$ to the lth cluster is determined by summing the elementary weights of the different viewpoints belonging to the same set. The weight is calculated as follows:

$$W^{i,l} = \frac{1}{n^{i,l}} \sum_{k=1}^{n^{i,l}} w_k^{i,l} \tag{2}$$

where $n^{i,l}$ is the number of descriptors forming the set of the cluster $C^{i,l}$. The clusters are sorted according to their weights and the NBV is the one with the highest score. The algorithm switches the NBV from the high weighted cluster to the next one if the redundancy rate is larger than a limit value r_{th}. The stopping criterion is a set of NBVs that ensures a high redundancy between two successive acquisitions.

4 Experiments

In our experiments, we used the following values for the parameters of the next best view generation algorithm. For the threshold angle we choose $\theta_{th}^i = \theta_{median}^i$, which is the median value of the orientation vector θ^i, since it increases after each acquisition and is less sensitive to noisy data. The amount of new acquired data is set to 3%, which yields to a redundancy threshold of $r_{th} = 97\%$.

4.1 Physical System

The algorithm was implemented on a robotic cell (see Fig. 4.a) composed of:

- a 6 DoF robotic arm KR16, from KUKA Roboter, with 6 rotational joints.
- a fringes projection scanner, CometV, manufactured by Steinbichler Optotechnik GmbH with 1.4 Mega Pixels camera and a set of lenses that yields a working volume of $480 \times 360 \times 250$ mm with a working distance of 850 mm. Each acquisition takes 3.5 seconds to be acquired in high quality mode.
- a turntable mounted with its rotational axis vertically and is controlled directly by the robot controller.

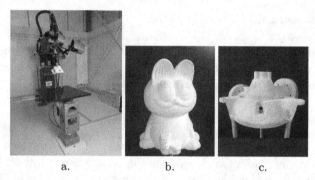

a.   b.   c.

Fig. 4. Experimental setup: a) Robotic cell b) Garfield bust c) Pump-support

4.2 Results

We present the results obtained for two objects with different geometries with three benchmark methods: Bounding Box [13], MVC [11], and the proposed method. The first one is Garfield bust, shown in figure 4.b, which has a form similar to a sphere and its size is $192 \times 180 \times 217$ mm. The second object is a complex industrial Pum-support (see figure 4.c) which has a medium size of $250 \times 234 \times 145$ mm and presents many concavities and occluded parts.

Table 1 summarizes the different performances of benchmark methods and figures 5 and 6 show respectively the scanner trajectories and the evolution of the completeness rate during the acquisition process. The Bounding Box method is characterized by its simplicity and it leads to a high coverage rate for both models, but needs a large number of acquisitions ($NA = 24$). Although the objects have different geometries, the scanner trajectories are similar. For some acquisitions, the arbitrarily distribution of the viewpoints causes a registration problem since the amount of common information between two successive acquisitions is not sufficient for the pre-alignment. As shown in figure 6.a and 6.b, the evolution of the coverage rate by bounding box for both objects is almost linear because of the uniform distribution of the viewpoints, which yields to an equal amount of new information at each stage of the acquisition process.

The MVC method also ensures a high coverage rate of the objects surfaces. However, this method is very expensive in robot's movements, even for simple

Table 1. Comparison of the methods: NA and CR and TL and ET are respectively the number of acquisitions, the Coverage Rate, the Trajectory Length and the Execution Time

Evaluation grid		– –	–	+	++
Method Object		MVC	BBox	New method	
Garfield	NA	28	24	13	
	CR (%)	99.3	99.7	99.6	
	TL (m)	22.1	14.73	8.95	
	ET (mn)	47.2	12.5	13.2	
Pump-support	NA	26	24	12	
	CR (%)	97.9	98.1	98.2	
	TL (m)	24.1	14.5	10.32	
	ET (mn)	45.6	12.2	13.8	

Bounding Box   MVC   New method

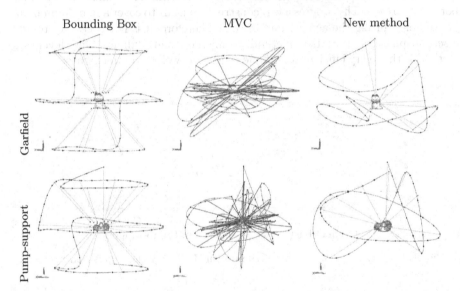

Fig. 5. Trajectories of the scanner during the acquisition process of Garfield and Pump-support using the benchmark methods

objects, especially in the first phase of the algorithm as it supports many round trips around the object which yields to many holes in the resulting model. So, several acquisitions are necessary to complete the few amount of missing data. As illustrated in figure 6.b, the MVC performs as a naive approach while scanning complex objects as the pump-support. As shown in figure 5, the scanner trajectory proves that the MVC does not take into account the distribution of views in the work space since some viewpoints are particularly close to each other. Moreover, both methods, Bounding Box and MVC, do not take into account the physical limitations of the acquisition system such as geometric limitations and singularities of a robotic system since they generate only one NBV at each iteration. Our method overcomes these problems while ensuring a high coverage rate for both objects. As shown in table 1, the number of acquisition is considerably reduced (2×) and the ranging device is moved efficiently around the object along an optimal trajectory (see figure 5) which ensures a progressive and continuous exploration of its different parts. In addition, the proposed technique, contrary to the MVC method, is not sensitive to the initialization step. Indeed, the latter approach constrains the initialization since the first position must be on the sides and not top to the object to overcome collisions with the positioning system. Moreover, our method overcomes the unreachable positions since it computes a set of optimal poses for acquisition. As demonstrated in figure 5, the viewpoints are well distributed around the object which ensures a high coverage of its surface without increasing the 3D data redundancy. Therefore, this method is less expensive in robot's movements and the scanner trajectory is the well optimised which make the acquisition faster. As illustrated in figures 6.a and 6.b, a complete 3D reconstruction of the object surface is achieved with a minimum number of scans for both test objects. The progressive reconstruction leads to cover a maximum number of holes during the acquisition process. Therefore, it is not necessary to add a second phase, as the MVC method, to fill the resulting holes. The developed method is then very efficient for simple objects as well as complex ones.

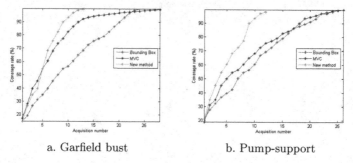

a. Garfield bust   b. Pump-support

Fig. 6. Evolution of the completeness rate (in %) during the acquisition process

5   Conclusions and Future Works

This paper describe an automatic and general surface-based NBV approach. The algorithm does not require any prior knowledge of the object shape. The view planning is based on the analysis of the elementary orientations of the acquired surface patches. A clustering step allows the determination of a set of potential views for acquisition. Using the orientation information, a weight is assigned to each mode and the NBV is the one with the high score. The comparison of our method with a naive method, Bounding Box, and a more advanced technique, the MVC method, confirms the efficiency of our approach while obtaining better results. The method creates the surface of the object by generating viewpoints similar to human intuition and is characterized by its simplicity. This approach permits the determination of a scanner trajectory taking into account the unreachable positions since it computes a set of potential views at each iteration.

The very good results obtained with our method motivate us to explore another interesting direction for future work which is the digitization of large objects or environments.

Acknowledgments. This work was done within the framework of the LE2I laboratory and financially supported by the *Regional Council of Burgundy*. The authors would like to thank *Mr. Mickaël Provost*, Head of *Vecteo company* (*www.vecteo.com*), for his technical support and effective collaboration.

References

1. Scott, W.R., Roth, G., Rivest, J.F.: View planning for automated three-dimensional object reconstruction and inspection. ACM Computing Surveys 35, 64–96 (2003)
2. Abidi, B.: Automatic sensor placement. In: SPIE Conf. on Intelligent Robots and Computer Vision XIV, Philadelphia, PA, vol. 2588, pp. 387–398 (1995)
3. Reed, M.K.: Solid Model Acquisition from Range Imagery. PhD thesis, Columbia University (1998)
4. Massios, N.A., Fisher, R.B.: A best next view selection algorithm incorporating a quality criterion. In: Proceedings of British Machine Vision Conference, BMVC (1998)
5. Munkelt, C., Denzler, J., Kuhmstedt, P.: Incorporation of a-priori information in planning the next best view. In: Proceedings of the ISPRS Commission V Symposium 'Image Engineering and Vision Metrology', Aachen, pp. 261–268 (2006)
6. Connolly, C.I.: The determination of next best views. In: Proceedings of the International Conference on Robotics and Automation, St. Louis, Mo, USA, vol. 2, pp. 432–435. IEEE Computer Society (1985)
7. Maver, J., Bajcsy, R.: Occlusions as a guide for planning the next view. IEEE Transactions on Pattern Analysis and Machine Intelligence 15, 417–433 (1993)
8. Low, K.L.: An adaptive hierarchical next-best-view algorithm for 3D reconstruction of indoor scenes. Technical report, Proceedings of 14th Pacific Conference on Computer Graphics and Applications, Pacific Graphics (2006)
9. Yuan, X.: A mechanism of automatic 3D object modeling. IEEE Transactions on Pattern Analysis and Machine Intelligence 17, 307–311 (1995)
10. He, B.W., Li, Y.F.: A next-best-view method with self-termination in active modeling of 3D objects. In: IROS 2006, pp. 5345–5350 (2006)
11. Loriot, B., Seulin, R., Gorria, P.: Non-model based method for an automation of 3D acquisition and post-processing. Electronics Letters on Computer Vision and Analysis 7, 67–82 (2008)
12. Kriegel, K., Bodenmüller, T., Suppa, M., Hirzinger, G.: A Surface-Based Next-Best-view approach for automated 3D model completion of unknown objects. In: Proceedings of the IEEE International Conference on Robotics and Automation (2011)
13. Khalfaoui, S., Aigueperse, A., Seulin, R., Fougerolle, Y., Fofi, D.: Fully automatic 3D digitization of unknown objects using progressive data bounding box. In: Proceedings of SPIE Electronic Imaging, San Francisco, California, p. 829011 (2012)
14. Comaniciu, D., Meer, P.: Mean shift: A robust approach toward feature space analysis. IEEE Transactions on Pattern Analysis and Machine Intelligence 24, 603–619 (2002)

Depth Enhancement by Fusion for Passive and Active Sensing[*]

Frederic Garcia[1], Djamila Aouada[1], Hashim Kemal Abdella[1,2], Thomas Solignac[3], Bruno Mirbach[3], and Björn Ottersten[1]

[1] Interdisciplinary Centre for Security, Reliability and Trust
Universtity of Luxembourg
{frederic.garcia,djamila.aouada,bjorn.ottersten}@uni.lu
[2] Université de Bourgogne
hashim-kemal_abdella@etu.u-bourgogne.fr
[3] Advanced Engineering - IEE S.A.
{thomas.solignac,bruno.mirbach}@iee.lu

Abstract. This paper presents a general refinement procedure that enhances any given depth map obtained by passive or active sensing. Given a depth map, either estimated by triangulation methods or directly provided by the sensing system, and its corresponding 2-D image, we correct the depth values by separately treating regions with undesired effects such as empty holes, texture copying or edge blurring due to homogeneous regions, occlusions, and shadowing. In this work, we use recent depth enhancement filters intended for Time-of-Flight cameras, and adapt them to alternative depth sensing modalities, both active using an RGB-D camera and passive using a dense stereo camera. To that end, we propose specific masks to tackle areas in the scene that require a special treatment. Our experimental results show that such areas are satisfactorily handled by replacing erroneous depth measurements with accurate ones.

Keywords: depth enhancement, data fusion, passive sensing, active sensing.

1 Introduction

The demand to achieve an autonomous system that is capable of understanding the shape and location of objects in a scene has been growing in recent years. Hence the demand for a quality depth estimation is today one of the active research areas in computer vision. Triangulation methods are commonly used for depth perception, either using stereopsis or stereo vision [1]; the classic implementation of passive sensing, or in the case of active sensing by laser or structured light techniques [2]. It is known that regardless whether the sensing system is passive or active, triangulation methods can be quite time consuming

---

[*] This work was supported by the National Research Fund, Luxembourg, under the CORE project C11/BM/1204105/FAVE/Ottersten.

A. Fusiello et al. (Eds.): ECCV 2012 Ws/Demos, Part III, LNCS 7585, pp. 506–515, 2012.
© Springer-Verlag Berlin Heidelberg 2012

as they have to cope either with the correspondence problem in the first case [1], or to process several encoded illumination patterns in the second case. Current advances in technology have greatly helped to significantly overcome this problem and stereo cameras such as the Bumblebee® XB3 from Point Grey Research or consumer depth cameras such as the recently appeared Microsft Kinect are able to provide high-resolution depth maps in real-time. However, such sensing systems are based on triangulation techniques and thus, they are linked to the baseline between the two cameras or camera plus light source, which yields to occlusions or shadowing, and creates erroneous regions during depth estimation.

We propose to look into approaches of fusion by filtering tested and proven on Time-of-Flight (ToF) cameras [3–6]. Our main goal is to generalize such approach and define a global framework that may be adapted to other active sensors, specifically an RGB-D consumer camera, but also to more traditional passive ones, such as a dense stereo camera. The filtering is based on the concept of fusing the depth map with a guidance or a reference image (or images), usually taken as the matching 2-D image. This guidance image is used to correct unreliable depth regions. In this paper, we will design confidence measures, adequate to the considered sensor, to incorporate to the filter in order to indicate those areas within the initial depth map that require special attention.

The remainder of the paper is organized as follows: Section 2 presents the general framework of depth enhancement by fusion filters. In Section 3, we show how to apply these same filters to a stereo camera, then to a consumer RGB-D camera; hence, illustrating how this depth enhancement framework is generic. Section 4, presents the results of the proposed depth enhancement approach by data fusion in both modalities. Finally, concluding remarks are given in Section 5.

2   Problem Statement and Background

The idea of considering a guidance 2-D image to improve the quality of its corresponding depth map was first introduced by Kopf *et. al* in [7], where they presented the Joint Bilateral Upsampling (JBU) filter, an extension of the bilateral filter [8] that considers two different data sources within the kernel of the filter. Their work was first intended to compute a solution for image analysis and enhancement tasks, such as tone mapping or colourization through a downsampled version of the data. This idea was later applied for depth map enhancement in the context of real-time matting as presented by Crabb et al. [9]. The JBU filter enhances an initial depth map $\mathbf{D}$ to the higher resolution of a corresponding 2-D guidance image $\mathbf{I}$, as follows

$$\mathbf{J_1(p)} = \frac{\sum_{\mathbf{q} \in N(\mathbf{p})} f_{\mathbf{S}}(\mathbf{p}, \mathbf{q}) f_{\mathbf{I}}(\mathbf{I(p)}, \mathbf{I(q)}) \mathbf{D(q)}}{\sum_{\mathbf{q} \in N(\mathbf{p})} f_{\mathbf{S}}(\mathbf{p}, \mathbf{q}) f_{\mathbf{I}}(\mathbf{I(p)}, \mathbf{I(q)})}, \tag{1}$$

where $N(\mathbf{p})$ is the neighbourhood at the pixel indexed by the position vector $\mathbf{p} = (i, j)^T$, with i and j indicating the row, respectively column corresponding to the pixel position. This non-iterative filter formulation is a weighted average of the local neighbourhood samples, where the weights are computed based on spatial and radiometric distances between the centre of the considered sample and the neighbouring samples. Thus, its kernel is decomposed into a spatial weighting term $f_S(\cdot)$ that applies to the pixel position $\mathbf{p}$, and a range weighting term $f_I(\cdot)$ that applies to the pixel value $\mathbf{I}(\mathbf{q})$. The weighting functions $f_S(\cdot)$ and $f_I(\cdot)$ are generally chosen to be Gaussian functions with standard deviations σ_S and σ_I, respectively. Nevertheless, according to the bilateral filter principle, the fundamental heuristic assumptions about the relationship between depth and intensity data, may lead to erroneous copying of 2-D texture into actually smooth geometries within the depth map. Furthermore, a second unwanted artefact known as edge blurring appears along depth edges that have no corresponding edges in the 2-D image, i.e., in situations where objects on either side of a depth discontinuity have a similar colour. In order to cope with these issues, Garcia et. al [4] proposed a new fusion filter known as Pixel Weighted Average Strategy (PWAS). The PWAS filter extends the expression in (1) by an additional factor, to which they refer as the credibility map, that indicates unreliable regions within the depth maps obtained using a Time-of-Flight (ToF) camera. These regions require a special treatment. Thus, for a given depth map $\mathbf{D}$, a credibility map $\mathbf{Q}$, and a guiding intensity image $\mathbf{I}$, the enhanced depth map $\mathbf{J_2}$ resulting from PWAS filtering is defined as follows

$$\mathbf{J_2}(\mathbf{p}) = \frac{\sum_{\mathbf{q} \in N(\mathbf{p})} f_S(\mathbf{p}, \mathbf{q}) f_I(\mathbf{I}(\mathbf{p}), \mathbf{I}(\mathbf{q})) \mathbf{Q}(\mathbf{q}) \mathbf{D}(\mathbf{q})}{\sum_{\mathbf{q} \in N(\mathbf{p})} f_S(\mathbf{p}, \mathbf{q}) f_I(\mathbf{I}(\mathbf{p}), \mathbf{I}(\mathbf{q})) \mathbf{Q}(\mathbf{q})}. \tag{2}$$

with

$$\mathbf{Q}(\mathbf{p}) = \exp\left(\frac{-(\nabla \mathbf{D}(\mathbf{p}))^2}{2\sigma_{\mathbf{Q}}^2}\right), \tag{3}$$

where $\nabla \mathbf{D}$ is the gradient of the given depth map $\mathbf{D}$. Although the PWAS filter copes well with the edge blurring artifact, texture copying is still not fully solved within the enhanced depth maps. In order to significantly reduce this artifact, the same authors proposed in [5] the Unified Multi-Lateral (UML) filter. The UML filter combines two PWAS filters where the output $\mathbf{J_3}$ of the second one has both spatial and range kernels acting onto the same data source $\mathbf{D}$. In addition, they suggested to use the credibility map $\mathbf{Q}$ as a blending function, i.e., $\beta = \mathbf{Q}$, hence, depth pixels with high reliability are not influenced by the 2-D data avoiding texture copying as follows

$$\mathbf{J_4}(\mathbf{p}) = (1 - \beta(\mathbf{p})) \cdot \mathbf{J_2}(\mathbf{p}) + \beta(\mathbf{p}) \cdot \mathbf{J_3}(\mathbf{p}), \tag{4}$$

and

$$\mathbf{J_3}(\mathbf{p}) = \frac{\sum_{\mathbf{q} \in N(\mathbf{p})} f_S(\mathbf{p}, \mathbf{q}) f_D(\mathbf{D}(\mathbf{p}), \mathbf{D}(\mathbf{q})) \mathbf{Q}(\mathbf{q}) \mathbf{D}(\mathbf{q})}{\sum_{\mathbf{q} \in N(\mathbf{p})} f_S(\mathbf{p}, \mathbf{q}) f_D(\mathbf{D}(\mathbf{p}), \mathbf{D}(\mathbf{q})) \mathbf{Q}(\mathbf{q})}. \tag{5}$$

The kernel f_D is another Gaussian function with a different standard deviation σ_D.

3   Proposed Depth Enhancement Framework

It is well known that the estimation of depth using triangulation approaches entails to cope with the correspondence problem [1], *i.e.*, find feature-correspondence pairs between the two images in the case of passive systems, or detect the projected features in the case of active systems [2]. Problems in passive sensing arise when there are homogeneous regions in the scene, which prevents to find a correspondence between the two images or, in active sensing, when the light power of the projected pattern is not enough to be reflected back to the sensor. Furthermore, since both active and passive triangulation methods require a baseline for depth estimation, occlusion and shadowing are two additional drawbacks to overcome. In summary, depth maps obtained from triangulation approaches are unreliable in object boundaries, and in occluded or homogeneous regions. In order to deal with such regions, we propose to fuse these estimated depth maps with their corresponding 2-D images, *i.e.*, the images that were previously used to detect feature-correspondence pairs. In what follows, we propose to generalize state-of-the-art filters used in ToF depth enhancement and apply them to other passive and active sensors. This goes through identifying the regions that suffer from artifacts and require special treatment. Dealing with these regions requires defining the adequate credibility maps for each sensor.

3.1   Application to Passive Sensing

We consider a stereo setup for passive sensing with two initial 2-D images; left image $\mathbf{I}_l$ and right image $\mathbf{I}_r$. The depth map $\mathbf{D}$ is defined by finding the dense correspondence between $\mathbf{I}_l$ and $\mathbf{I}_r$. We adapt the depth enhancement filters presented in Section 2 to depth maps obtained using passing sensing by considering different kinds of credibility maps or masks. Similarly to ToF depth maps, object boundaries are represented by a *boundary map* $\mathbf{Q_b}$, which corresponds to the credibility map in (3) ($\mathbf{Q_b} = \mathbf{Q}$). However, the edges in the estimated depth map $\mathbf{D}$ may be misaligned with their corresponding edges in the 2-D image. Therefore, we propose to dilate $\mathbf{Q_b}$ according to the gradient strength. To that end, we first bin the gradient into five levels. Then, pixels with the highest gradient are dilated strongly while those with the lowest gradient undergo a minimum dilation. Bin centres and levels of dilation are manually tuned.

The second type of credibility map is the *occlusion map* $\mathbf{Q_o}$, which is determined through left/right consistency check [10]. In left/right consistency check, after obtaining the disparity relative to the right image, a comparison is made between the left disparity $\mathbf{D}_l$ and the right one $\mathbf{D}_r$. In this comparison, corresponding pixels are supposed to have the same value, and pixels which deviate from this assumption are considered as occluded in either views. Therefore, the occlusion mask $\mathbf{Q_o}$ is defined as

$$\mathbf{Q_o}(\mathbf{p}) = \exp\left(\frac{-\|\mathbf{D}_l(\mathbf{p}) - \mathbf{D}_r\big(\mathbf{p} + \mathbf{D}_l(\mathbf{p})\big)\|^2}{2\sigma_{\mathbf{o}}^2}\right). \tag{6}$$

Homogeneous regions are also another source of unreliability. In [11], the characteristics of correlation cost at each pixel is analysed for determining a *homogeneity mask* $\mathbf{Q_h}$. Accordingly, pixels in homogeneous regions have a flat correlation cost, while repetitive patterns give rise to a cost function with multiple minima. The cost function C is computed at $\mathbf{p}$ for all possible disparity values. It has a first minimum value at depth d_1 and a second minimum at d_2, with corresponding costs $C(\mathbf{p}, d_1)$ and $C(\mathbf{p}, d_2)$, respectively. These costs are used to define $\mathbf{Q_h}$ as

$$\mathbf{Q_h}(\mathbf{p}) = 1 - \exp\left(\frac{-\left(\frac{C(\mathbf{p},d_2)-C(\mathbf{p},d_1)}{C(\mathbf{p},d_1)}\right)^2}{2\sigma_\mathbf{h}^2}\right), \tag{7}$$

where $\sigma_\mathbf{b}$, $\sigma_\mathbf{o}$, and $\sigma_\mathbf{h}$ are empirically defined parameters.

As a final credibility map for stereo depth enhancement, we propose the following combined one:

$$\mathbf{Q}(\mathbf{p}) = \mathbf{Q_b}(\mathbf{p}) \cdot \mathbf{Q_o}(\mathbf{p}) \cdot \mathbf{Q_h}(\mathbf{p}). \tag{8}$$

3.2   Application to Active Sensing

We herein consider a consumer RGB-D camera as an active sensor, where a depth map $\mathbf{D}$ is acquired simultaneously to a perfectly matching 2-D image $\mathbf{I}$. In contrast to ToF cameras, depth measurements given by RGB-D cameras are known to be much less influenced by noise. This, in turn, allows us to avoid the second PWAS filtering $\mathbf{J_3}$ in (4) as it can be directly replaced by the acquired depth map $\mathbf{D}$, *i.e.*,

$$\mathbf{J_5}(\mathbf{p}) = \left(1 - \beta(\mathbf{p})\right) \cdot \mathbf{J_2}(\mathbf{p}) + \beta(\mathbf{p}) \cdot \mathbf{D}(\mathbf{p}). \tag{9}$$

By doing so, reliable depth measurements are not smoothed and the complexity of the UML filter is comparable to the one of the PWAS filter, which guarantees a real-time performance. However, we realise that if we follow the recommendations of Garcia *et. al* [5] and we set the blending function β equal to the credibility map $\mathbf{Q}$, edge blurring will appear when filtering low reliable depth pixels if no 2-D edge is present. Indeed, this situation occurs when foreground and background objects share the same intensity value, which often occurs when considering grayscale images. Hence, we propose to not rely on the 2-D guidance image when depth measurements have a low reliability, *i.e.*, $\mathbf{Q_D} < \tau_\mathbf{D}$ ($\mathbf{Q_D} = \mathbf{Q}$, defined in (3)), and no corresponding 2-D edge, *i.e.*, $\mathbf{Q_I} > \tau_\mathbf{I}$. $\mathbf{Q_I}$ is defined analogously to $\mathbf{Q_D}$ but considering $\nabla\mathbf{I}$. The constants $\tau_\mathbf{I}$ and $\tau_\mathbf{D}$ are empirically chosen thresholds. We therefore generalise the blending function β in (9) as follows

$$\beta(\mathbf{p}) = \left(u_\mathbf{I}(\mathbf{p}) \cdot u_\mathbf{D}(\mathbf{p})\right) + \mathbf{Q_D}(\mathbf{p}) \cdot \left(1 - u_\mathbf{I}(\mathbf{p}) \cdot u_\mathbf{D}(\mathbf{p})\right), \tag{10}$$

with

$$u_\mathbf{I}(\mathbf{p}) = u\left(\mathbf{Q_I}(\mathbf{p}) - \tau_\mathbf{I}\right) \quad \text{and} \quad u_\mathbf{D}(\mathbf{p}) = u\left(\tau_\mathbf{D} - \mathbf{Q_D}(\mathbf{p})\right), \tag{11}$$

being the function $u(\cdot)$ a step function.

Though bilateral filtering is known to be time consuming, its latest fast implementations based on data quantization and downsampling [12, 13], also applicable to both PWAS and UML filters as demonstrated in [5], enable a high-performance. Thus, in order to ensure a real-time performance, we propose to downsample by a factor of s the credibility maps $\mathbf{Q_D}$ and $\mathbf{Q_I}$ preserving such regions that require special treatment. To that end, we keep the most significant pixel value within each downsampled block of size $(s \times s)$ in the resulting low resolution image $\mathbf{Q} \downarrow_s$, i.e.,

$$\mathbf{Q} \downarrow_s (\mathbf{p}) = \min_{\mathbf{q}} \mathbf{Q}(\mathbf{q}) \text{ s.t. } \|\mathbf{q} - (\mathbf{p} + \mathbf{s})\| < \sqrt{2}s \text{ and } \mathbf{s} = (s, s)^T. \quad (12)$$

4   Experimental results

The proposed enhancement method has been evaluated using three main evaluation metrics: Root Mean Square (RMS), Percentage of Bad Matching Pixels (PBMP), and Structural SIMilarity (SSIM) [14, 15]. RMS is the simplest and the most widely used evaluation technique; yet, criticized for not representing the perceived visual quality [15]. We also found out that RMS value has an exaggeration when there are some pixels with a higher depth deviation. PBMP based evaluation is the common way of comparing depth estimation techniques. It envelopes a threshold to determine the quality of pixels' depth. Mostly this threshold is set to one, which makes any pixel with a deviation slightly greater than one to be set as bad. Our proposed fusion filter has a smoothing effect which will unarguably cause this deviation, making PBMP an inappropriate quality metric. Hence, we prefer to base our evaluation mostly on SSIM, which tries to compare two images based on the luminance, contrast and structural similarity [15].

4.1   Passive Sensing

The results in Table 1 present the quantitative evaluation of the proposed approach applied on the Teddy scene from the Middlebury dataset [16] shown in

Table 1. Quantitative evaluation using the three evaluation metrics on Teddy image sets

Depth map		Evaluation (best - bad)		
		RMS(0 - 1)	PBMP(0 - 100)	SSIM(1 - 0)
Initial		0.3732	13.9253	0.9689
PWAS	Q_h	0.3974	15.7890	0.9842
	Q_b	0.3792	14.3799	0.9843
	Q_o	0.4468	19.9613	0.9844
	Q	0.3688	13.5980	0.9849
JBU		0.4606	21.2127	0.9822

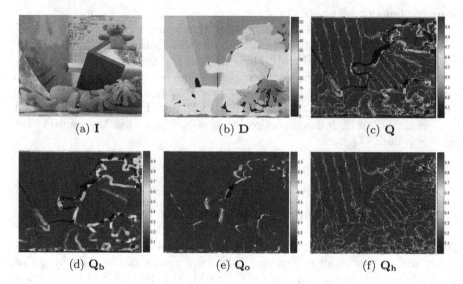

(a) **I**   (b) **D**   (c) **Q**

(d) **Q_b**   (e) **Q_o**   (f) **Q_h**

Fig. 1. Input data and proposed unreliability maps

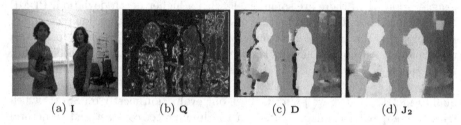

(a) **I**   (b) **Q**   (c) **D**   (d) **J₂**

Fig. 2. Application of our proposed enhancement technique on stereo data acquired by a Bumblebee® XB3 camera

Fig. 1. The scene contains an intensity image and its corresponding disparity map, from which we have generated a depth map as a ground truth using the also provided system specifications. It is clear that PWAS filter using **Q** enhances the initial disparity (obtained using Matlab's disparity function) in all the metrics. However, individual masks show improvements in one measure while there is a degradation in the other. We can also observe that the JBU output is lower than that of PWAS filter. Most importantly, the PBMP and RMS measures are very bad for JBU filter which is due to the smoothing effect of the filter in regions which were perfect in the initial disparity. This effect is slightly controlled by the credibility map in PWAS filtering.

We have also tested the proposed technique on our own recordings using a Bumblebee® XB3 camera [17]. Fig. 2 shows the result using one of these recordings. The reference image **I** is shown in Fig. 2a while the acquired depth map **D** is shown in Fig. 2c. The two people in **D** can be well identified without much extension of boundaries; however, most of the occluded background regions (to the left of each person) and homogeneous regions (top right part of the image) appear to be unreliable. These regions are identified using the three masks defined in Section 3.1. The credibility map $\mathbf{Q}$ shown in in Fig. 2b is the combination of these masks. Fig. 2d shows the enhanced depth map $\mathbf{J_2}$ that results from the proposed fusion filter. As can be observed, the PWAS filter improves the given depth map except around the left person's elbow, the top right of the image and next to the face of the person in the right. This is due to large holes created on the credibility map due to illumination variation and extended textureless surfaces. The PWAS filter can fill small holes, but it is impossible to handle a hole bigger than the fusion window.

4.2 Active Sensing

For the evaluation of our approach on the modality of active sensing we have considered data captured using the Kinect camera. Fig. 3 is a visual example of the credibility maps proposed in Section 3.2 computed on the acquired depth map $\mathbf{D}$ and the corresponding guidance image $\mathbf{I}$, shown in Fig. 3e and Fig. 3a, respectively. Fig. 3d is the downsampled version of $\mathbf{u_I}$, which indicates the presence of a 2-D edge while Fig. 3g corresponds to the downsampled version of $\mathbf{Q_D}$, indicating the presence of a depth edge. The proposed blending function β is shown in Fig. 3h. Note that low-reliability depth pixels in $\mathbf{Q_D} \downarrow_s$ that have no correspondence 2-D edge in $\mathbf{u_I} \downarrow_s$ has been setted to the maximum confidence value in β. The enhanced depth map $\mathbf{J_5}$ that results from the proposed approach is shown Fig. 4b. Table 2 compares the SSIM evaluation of the proposed approach with state-of-the-art depth enhancement methods. For this comparison, we consider only those pixels from $\mathbf{D}$ that have a defined depth value. Thus,

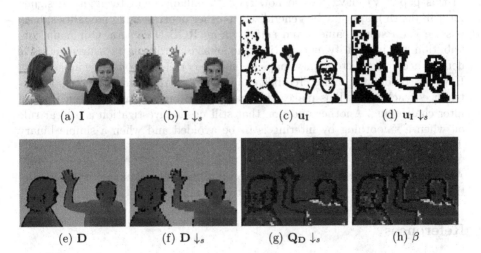

(a) $\mathbf{I}$ (b) $\mathbf{I}\downarrow_s$ (c) $\mathbf{u_I}$ (d) $\mathbf{u_I}\downarrow_s$

(e) $\mathbf{D}$ (f) $\mathbf{D}\downarrow_s$ (g) $\mathbf{Q_D}\downarrow_s$ (h) β

Fig. 3. Input data and proposed credibility and blending masks

(a) **D**   (b) **J₅**

Fig. 4. (a) Initial depth map acquired by the Kinect camera. Black areas indicate non-valid (occluded or shadow) pixels. (b) Enhanced depth map using the proposed approach in (9)

Table 2. Quantitative evaluation using the SSIM evaluation metric on the Kinect data presented in Fig. 3

	JBU filter	PWAS filter	UML filter	Proposed approach
SSIM(1 - 0)	0.73	0.83	0.83	0.86

occlusion or shadowing regions have not been considered. As can be observed, the depth measurements of the enhanced depth map using our approach are closer to the ones of the acquired depth map.

5   Conclusions

In this paper, we have showed how a depth enhancement technique designed for ToF depth maps may be generalized to other depth sensing modalities, both passive via a stereo camera and active via an RGB-D camera. Our main contribution was in identifying each time the areas of erroneous measurements. We defined accordingly credibility maps to enforce corrections on these areas only. However, by defining more credibility maps, more empirical parameters are introduced each time. This makes the practical automated usage of such fusion filter challenging. Another question that still needs investigation is a clear rule on when a smoothing by filtering is to be avoided and when a simple binary decision is to be undertaken as in (10).

Acknowledgements. We would like to thank Isabelle Chesnay and Cecile Petit, for posing in our experiments for active sensing.

References

1. Hartley, R., Zisserman, A.: Multiple View Geometry in Computer Vision, 2nd edn. Cambridge University Press (2003)

2. Salvi, J., Fernandez, S., Pribanic, T., Llado, X.: A state of the art in structured light patterns for surface profilometry. Pattern Recognition 43, 2666–2680 (2010)

3. Chan, D., Buisman, H., Theobalt, C., Thrun, S.: A noise-aware filter for real-time depth upsampling. In: Workshop on Multi-camera and Multi-modal Sensor Fusion Algorithms and Applications, ECCVW (2008)

4. Garcia, F., Mirbach, B., Ottersten, B., Grandidier, F., Cuesta, A.: Pixel Weighted Average Strategy for Depth Sensor Data Fusion. In: International Conference on Image Processing (ICIP), pp. 2805–2808 (2010)

5. Garcia, F., Aouada, D., Mirbach, B., Solignac, T., Ottersten, B.: A New Multi-lateral Filter for Real-Time Depth Enhancement. In: Advanced Video and Signal-Based Surveillance, AVSS (2011)

6. Min, D., Lu, J., Minh, N.D.: Depth Video Enhancement Based on Weighted Mode Filtering. IEEE Transactions on Image Processing (TIP) 21, 1176–1190 (2012)

7. Kopf, J., Cohen, M., Lischinski, D., Uyttendaele, M.: Joint bilateral upsampling. In: SIGGRAPH 2007: ACM SIGGRAPH 2007 papers, p. 96. ACM, New York (2007)

8. Tomasi, C., Manduchi, R.: Bilateral filtering for gray and color images. In: ICCV, pp. 839–846 (1998)

9. Crabb, R., Tracey, C., Puranik, A., Davis, J.: Real-time foreground segmentation via range and color imaging. In: IEEE Computer Society Conference on Computer Vision and Pattern Recognition (CVPR), pp. 1–5 (2008)

10. Benhimane, S., Malis, E.: Real-time image-based tracking of planes using efficient second-order minimization. In: IEEE IROS, vol. 1, pp. 943–948 (2004)

11. Hirschmuller, H.: Real-time correlation-based stereo vision with reduced border errors. IJCV 47(1/2/3), 229–246 (2002)

12. Yang, Q., Tan, K.H., Ahuja, N.: Real-time O(1) bilateral filtering. In: IEEE Computer Society Conference on Computer Vision and Pattern Recognition (CVPR), pp. 557–564 (2009)

13. Paris, S., Durand, F.: A fast approximation of the bilateral filter using a signal processing approach. International Journal of Computer Vision 81, 24–52 (2009)

14. Scharstein, D., Szeliski, R.: A taxonomy and evaluation of dense two-frame stereo correspondence algorithms. International Journal of Computer Vision 47, 7–42 (2002)

15. Wang, Z., Bovik, A.C., Sheikh, H.R., Simoncelli, E.P.: Image quality assessment: From error visibility to structural similarity. In: IEEE TIP, vol. 13-4, pp. 600–612 (2004)

16. Middlebury Stereo Datasets (2011), http://vision.middlebury.edu/stereo/data/

17. Point Grey Research, Inc. (2011), http://www.ptgrey.com

2.1 Depth Estimation of Frames in Image Sequences Using Motion Occlusions

Guillem Palou and Philippe Salembier

Technical University of Catalonia (UPC),
Dept. of Signal Theory and Communications, Barcelona, Spain
{guillem.palou,philippe.salembier}@upc.edu

Abstract. This paper proposes a system to depth order regions of a frame belonging to a monocular image sequence. For a given frame, regions are ordered according to their relative depth using the previous and following frames. The algorithm estimates occluded and disoccluded pixels belonging to the central frame. Afterwards, a Binary Partition Tree (BPT) is constructed to obtain a hierarchical, region based representation of the image. The final depth partition is obtained by means of energy minimization on the BPT. To achieve a global depth ordering from local occlusion cues, a depth order graph is constructed and used to eliminate contradictory local cues. Results of the system are evaluated and compared with state of the art figure/ground labeling systems on several datasets, showing promising results.

1 Introduction

Depth perception in human vision emerges from several depth cues. Normally, humans estimate depth accurately making use of both eyes, inferring (subconsciously) disparity between two views. However, when only one point of view is available, it is also possible to estimate the scene structure to some extent. This is done by the so called monocular depth cues. In static images, T-junctions or convexity cues may be detected in specific image areas and provide depth order information. If a temporal dimension is introduced, motion information can also be used to get depth information. Occlusion of moving objects, size changes or motion parallax are used in the human brain to structure the scene [1].

Nowadays, a strong research activity is focusing on depth maps generation, mainly motivated by the film industry. However, most of the published approaches make use of two (or more) points of view to compute the disparity as it offers a reliable cue for depth estimation [2]. Disparity needs at least two images captured at the same time instant but, sometimes, this requirement cannot be fulfilled. For example, current handheld cameras have only one objective. Moreover, a large amount of material has already been acquired as monocular sequences and needs to be converted. In such cases, depth perception should be inferred only through monocular cues. Although monocular cues are less reliable than stereo cues, humans can do this task with ease.

A. Fusiello et al. (Eds.): ECCV 2012 Ws/Demos, Part III, LNCS 7585, pp. 516–525, 2012.
© Springer-Verlag Berlin Heidelberg 2012

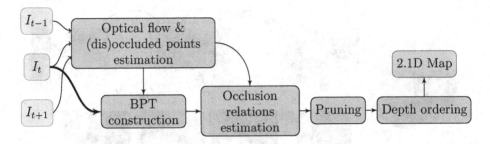

Fig. 1. Scheme of the proposed system. From three consecutive frames of a sequence (green blocks), a 2.1D map is estimated (red block)

The 2.1D model is an intermediate state between 2D images and full/absolute 3D maps, representing the image as a partition with its regions ordered by its relative depth. State of the art depth ordering systems on monocular sequences focus on the extraction of foreground regions from the background. Although this may be appropriate for some applications, more information can be extracted from an image sequence. The approach in [3] provides a pseudo-depth estimation to detect occlusion boundaries from optical flow. References [4,5] estimate a layered image representation of the scene. Whereas, references [6,7] attempt to retrieve a full depth map from a monocular image sequence, under some assumptions/restrictions about the scene structure which may not be fulfilled in typical sequences. The work [8] assigns figure/ground (f/g) labels to detected occlusion boundaries. f/g labeling provides a quantitative measure of depth ordering, as it assigns a local depth gradient at each occlusion boundary. Although f/g labeling is an interesting field of study, it does not offer a dense depth representation.

A good monocular cue to determine a 2.1D map of the scene is motion occlusion. When objects move, background regions (dis)appear, creating occlusions. Humans use these occlusions to detect the relative depth between scene regions. The proposed work assesses the performance of these cues in a fully automated system. To this end, the process is divided as shown in Figure 1 and presented as follows. First, the optical flow is used in Section 2 to introduce motion information for the BPT [9] construction and in Section 3 to estimate (dis)occluded points. Next, to find both occlusion relations and a partition of the current frame, the energy minimization technique described in Section 4 is used. Lastly, the regions of this partition are ordered, generating a 2.1D map. Results compared with [8] are exposed in Section 5.

2   Optical Flow and Image Representation

As shown in Figure 2, to determine the depth order of frame I_t, the previous I_{t-1} and following I_{t+1} frames are used. Forward $\boldsymbol{w}^{t-1,t}$, $\boldsymbol{w}^{t,t+1}$ and backward flows $\boldsymbol{w}^{t,t-1}$, $\boldsymbol{w}^{t+1,t}$ can be estimated using [10]. For two given temporal indices a, b, the optical flow vector $\boldsymbol{w}^{a,b}$ maps each pixel of I_a to one pixel in I_b.

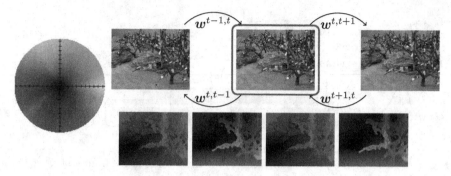

Fig. 2. Left: color code used to represent optical flow values. Three consecutive frames are presented in the top row, I_{t-1} ,I_t in red and I_{t+1}. In the bottom row, from left to right, the $w^{t-1,t}$,$w^{t,t-1}$,$w^{t,t+1}$,$w^{t+1,t}$ flows are shown.

Once the optical flows are computed, a BPT is built [11]. The BPT begins with an initial partition (here a partition where each pixel forms a region). Iteratively, the two most similar neighboring regions according to a predefined distance are merged and the process is repeated until only one region is left. The BPT describes a set of regions organized in a tree structure and this hierarchical structure represents the inclusion relationship between regions. Although the construction process is an active field of study, it is not the main purpose of this paper and we chose the distance defined in [11] to build the BPT: the region distance is defined using color, area, shape and motion information.

3   Motion Occlusions from Optical Flow

When only one point of view is available, humans take profit of monocular depth cues to retrieve the scene structure: motion parallax and motion occlusions. Motion parallax assumes still scenes, and it is able to retrieve the absolute depth. Occlusions may work in dynamic scenes but only offer insights about relative depth. Since motion occlusions appear in more situations and do not make any assumptions, they are selected here. Motion occlusions can be detected with several approaches [12,13]. In this work, however, a different approach is followed as it gave better results in practice.

Using three frames I_{t-1}, I_t, I_{t+1}, it is possible to detect pixels becoming occluded from I_t to I_{t+1} and pixels becoming visible (disoccluded) from I_{t-1} to I_t. To detect motion occlusions, the optical flow between an image pair (I_t, I_q) is used with $q = t \pm 1$. To obtain occluded pixels $q = t + 1$, while disoccluded are obtained when $q = t - 1$.

Flow estimation attempts to find a matching for each pixel between two frames. If a pixel is visible in both frames, the flow estimation is likely to find the true matching. If, however, the pixel becomes (dis)occluded, the matching will not be against its true peer. In the case of occlusion, two pixels p_a and p_b in I_t will be matched with the same pixel p_m in frame I_q:

$$p_a + w^{t,q}(p_a) = p_b + w^{t,q}(p_b) = p_m \qquad (1)$$

Equation (1) implicitly tells that either p_a or p_b is occluded. It is likely that the non occluded pixel neighborhood is highly correlated in both frames. Therefore, to decide which one is the occluded pixel, a patch distance is computed:

$$D(p_x, p_m) = \sum_{d \in \Gamma} (I_q(p_m + d) - I_t(p_x + d))^2 \qquad (2)$$

with $p_x = p_a$ or p_b. The pixel with maximum $D(p_x, p_m)$ value is decided to be the occluded pixel. The neighborhood Γ is a 5×5 square window centered at p_x but results are similar with windows of size 3×3 or 7×7.

Occluded and disoccluded pixels may be useful to some extent (e.g. to improve optical flow estimation, [12]). To retrieve a 2.1D map, an (dis)occluded-(dis)occluding relation is needed to create a depth order. (Dis)occluding pixels are pixels in I_t that will be in front of their (dis)occluded peer in I_q. Therefore, using these relations it is possible to order different regions in the frame according to depth. In the proposed system, occlusion relations estimation is postponed until the BPT representation is available, see Section 4.1. The reason to do so is because raw estimated optical flows are not reliable in occluded points. Nevertheless, with the knowledge of region information it is possible to fit optical flow models to regions and provide confident optical flow values even for (dis)occluded points.

4   Depth Order Retrieval

Once the optical flow is estimated and the BPT is constructed, the last step of the system is to retrieve a suitable partition to depth order its regions. There are many ways to obtain a partition from a hierarchical representation [14,15,9]. In this work an energy minimization strategy is proposed. The complete process comprises two energy minimization steps to find the final partition. Since raw optical flows are not reliable at (dis)occluded points, a first step allows us to find a partition P_f where an optical flow model is fitted in each region. When the occlusion relations are estimated, the second step finds a second partition P_d attempting to maintain occluded-occluding pairs in different regions. The final stage of the system relates regions in P_d according to their relative depth.

Obtaining P_f and P_d is performed using the same energy minimization algorithm. For this reason, the general algorithm is presented first in Section 4.1 and then it is particularized for each step in the following subsections.

4.1   General Energy Minimization on BPTs

A partition P, can be represented by a vector x of binary variables $x_i = \{0, 1\}$ with $i = 1..N$, one for each region R_i forming the BPT. If $x_i = 1$, R_i is in the partition, otherwise $x_i = 0$. Although there are a total of 2^N possible vectors,

---

Algorithm 1. Optimal Partition Selection

function OPTIMALSUBTREE(Region R_i)
    $R_l, R_r \leftarrow (\text{LEFTCHILD}(R_i), \text{RIGHTCHILD}(R_i))$
    $(c_i, o_i) \leftarrow (E_r(R_i), R_i)$
    $(o_l, c_l) \leftarrow \text{OPTIMALSUBTREE}(R_l)$
    $(o_r, c_r) \leftarrow \text{OPTIMALSUBTREE}(R_r)$
    if $c_i < c_r + c_l$ **then**
        $\text{OPTIMALSUBTREE}(R_i) \leftarrow (o_i, c_i)$
    else
        $\text{OPTIMALSUBTREE}(R_i) \leftarrow (o_l \bigcup o_r, c_l + c_r)$
    end if
end function

---

only a reduced subset may represent a partition, as shown in Figure 3. A given vector x is a valid vector if one, and only one, region in every BPT branch has $x_i = 1$. A branch is the sequence of regions from a leaf to the root of the tree. Intuitively speaking, if a region R_i is forming the partition P ($x_i = 1$), no other region R_j enclosed or enclosing R_i may have $x_j = 1$. This can be expressed as a linear constraint A on the vector x. A is provided for the case in Figure 3:

$$Ax = 1 \qquad \begin{pmatrix} 1\,0\,0\,0\,1\,0\,1 \\ 0\,1\,0\,0\,1\,0\,1 \\ 0\,0\,1\,0\,0\,1\,1 \\ 0\,0\,0\,1\,0\,1\,1 \end{pmatrix} x = 1 \qquad (3)$$

Where 1 is a vector containing all ones. The proposed optimization scheme finds a partition that minimizes energy functions of the type:

$$x^* = \arg\min_x E(x) = \arg\min_x \sum_{R_i \in BPT} E_r(R_i) x_i \qquad (4)$$

$$s.t. \qquad Ax = 1 \qquad x_i = \{0, 1\} \qquad (5)$$

where $E_r(R_i)$ is a function that depends only of the internal characteristics of the region (mean color or shape, for example). If that is the case, Algorithm 1 uses dynamic programming (Viterbi like) to find the optimal x^*.

Fitting the Flows and Finding Occlusion Relations. As stated in Section 3, the algorithm [10] does not provide reliable flow values at (dis)occluded points. Therefore, to be able to determine consistent occlusion relations, the flow in non-occluded areas is extrapolated to these points by finding a partition P_f and estimating a parametric projective model [16] in each region. The set of regions that best fits to these models is computed using Algorithm 1 with $E_r(R_i)$:

$$E_r(R_i) = \sum_{q=t\pm 1} \sum_{x,y \in R_i} \left| w^{t,q}(x, y) - \widetilde{w}_{R_i}^{t,q}(x, y) \right| + \lambda_f \qquad (6)$$

Valid $\boldsymbol{x} = (x_1, \ldots, x_7)^T$:

$\boldsymbol{x}_1 = (1,1,1,1,0,0,0)^T$
$\boldsymbol{x}_2 = (0,0,1,1,1,0,0)^T$
$x_3 = (1,1,0,0,0,1,0)^T$
$\boldsymbol{x}_4 = (0,0,0,0,1,1,0)^T$
$\boldsymbol{x}_5 = (0,0,0,0,0,0,1)^T$

Not valid:

$\boldsymbol{x}_I = (1,1,0,0,1,0,0)^T$

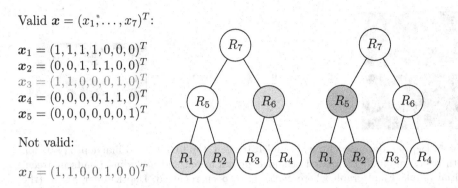

Fig. 3. Right: list of all the possible prunings and the invalid pruning of the rightmost figure. Center: Small BPT with green nodes marked forming the pruning $\boldsymbol{x}_3$. Right: Same BPT, but the marked nodes form an invalid pruning $\boldsymbol{x}_I$.

Fig. 4. From left to right. Keyframe with the region borders overlaid in white. Forward and backward estimated flows (top, bottom respectively) and modeled flows. Keyframe with occluded (red) and occluding (green) pixels overlaid.

The modeled flow $\widetilde{\boldsymbol{w}}_{R_i}^{t,q}$ is estimated by robust regression [17] for each region R_i. The constant $\lambda_f = 4 \times 10^3$ is used to prevent oversegmentation and was found experimentally and proved not to be crucial in the overall system performance.

Occlusion relations estimation. With the partition P_f and a flow model available for each region, occlusion relations can be reliably estimated. The (dis)occluding pixel is the forward mapping from I_t to I_q using $\widetilde{\boldsymbol{w}}_{R_i}^{t,q}$, back-projected to image I_t using $\boldsymbol{w}^{q,t}$. $q = t-1, t+1$ for disocclusions and occlusions relations respectively:

$$\boldsymbol{p}_o = \boldsymbol{p}_u + \widetilde{\boldsymbol{w}}_{R_i}^{t,q}(\boldsymbol{p}_u) + \boldsymbol{w}^{q,t}(\boldsymbol{p}_u + \widetilde{\boldsymbol{w}}_{R_i}^{t,q}(\boldsymbol{p}_u)) \tag{7}$$

with $\boldsymbol{p}_u \in R_i$. Flow fitting and occlusion relations are shown in Figure 4.

Finding the Final Depth Regions. Once the motion flows are modeled for each region of P_f, occlusion relations can be estimated using (7). Since each relation comprises two different pixels $(\boldsymbol{p}_u, \boldsymbol{p}_o)$, we can use the region information in the BPT to propagate these relations to obtain occlusion relations between

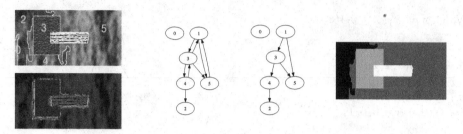

Fig. 5. Depth ordering example. From left to right, top to bottom. Final depth partition with region number. Estimated occluded points in red and occluding points in green. Initial graph. Final graph where cycles have been removed. Depth order image (the brighter the region, the closer).

regions. Therefore, given a partition P, if $\boldsymbol{p}_u$ is in a region R_i and $\boldsymbol{p}_o$ is in a different region R_j, we can conclude that R_j is in front of R_i. However, if both pixels belong to the same region, no relation can be established, since a region cannot be in front of itself. As a result, the pruning idea is to obtain a partition P_d (generally different from P_f) from the BPT which maintains occluded-occluding pairs in different regions, keeping a simple partition. The Algorithm 1 is also used with energy function:

$$E_r(R_i) = \sum_{(\boldsymbol{p}_u, \boldsymbol{p}_o) \in R_i} \frac{1}{N_o} + \lambda_o \qquad (8)$$

Where N_o is the total number of estimated occlusion relations. Equation (8) establishes a compromise between the number of occlusion relations kept and the simplicity (the number of regions) of the partition. To avoid oversegmented solutions for P_d, $\lambda_o = 4 \times 10^{-3}$ is introduced.

4.2 Depth Ordering

Once the final partition D is obtained with the energy defined in (8), a graph $G = (V, E)$ is constructed to allow a global reasoning about local depth cues to be done and in particular to deal with conflicting depth information. The vertices V represent the regions of D and the edges E represent occlusion relations between regions. An edge $e_i = (v_a, v_b, p_i)$ goes from node v_a to node v_b if there are occlusion relations between region R_a and region R_b. The weight $p_i = N_{ab}/N_o$ where N_{ab} is the number of occlusion relations between both regions.

To be able to determine a depth order between regions, G should be acyclic. To this purpose, the algorithm defined in [11] is used. It iteratively finds low confident occlusion relations and breaks cycles. Once all cycles have been removed in G, a topological partial sort [18] is applied and each region is assigned a depth order. Regions which have no depth relation, are assigned the depth of their most similar adjacent region according to the distance in the BPT construction. The complete process is illustrated in Figure 5 with a simple example.

Fig. 6. Results on the CMU dataset. From left to right, for the two columns. 1) Keyframe image and 2) image with occlusion relations (green occluding, red occluded). 3) estimated depth partition, with white regions meaning closer and black meaning further. 4) Figure/ground assignment on contours with green and red overlaid marking figure and ground regions, respectively.

Table 1. Our method vs. [8] on the percentage of correct f/g assignments

Dataset	CMU	BDS
[8]	83.8 %	68.6 %
Proposed system	88.0 %	92.5 %

5   Results

The evaluation of the system is performed at keyframes of several sequences, comparing the assigned f/g contours against the ground-truth assignments. When two depth planes meet, the part of the contour belonging to the closest region is assigned figure, or ground otherwise, see Figure 6. The datasets are the Carneige Mellon Dataset (CMU) [19] and the Berkeley Dataset (BDS) [8]. Results contain sequences with ground-truth data (30 for the CMU, 42 for the BDS). Table 1 shows the percentage of correct f/g assignments on detected contours.

It can be seen in Table 1 that the proposed system outperforms the one presented in [8], showing that motion occlusions are a reliable cue for depth ordering. Results of depth ordering can be seen in Figures 6 and 7, showing that motion occlusions may work over a variety of situations: static scenes, moving foregrounds, moving background or even multiple moving objects.

It is interesting to take a closer look at results in Figure 6 and the occlusion-relation estimation, shown in the second column for each image. In spite of the simplicity of the optical flow estimation algorithm, occlusion points were reliably estimated. Modeling the flows with a projective model provides reliable flow information and proved to be a crucial step for occlusion relations estimation.

Fig. 7. Results on some of the sequences of the BDS dataset. For each column, the right image corresponds to the keyframe with figure/ground assignments on contours overlaid. The left image correspond to the final depth ordered partition.

6   Conclusions

In this work, a system inferring the relative depth order of the different regions of a frame relying only on motion occlusion has been described. Combining a variational approach for optical flow estimation and a region based representation of the image we have developed a reliable system to detect occlusion relations and to create depth ordered partitions using only these depth cues. Comparison with the state of the art shows that motion occlusions are very reliable cues. The presented approach, although using only motion information to detect boundaries, achieves better results on f/g assignment than [8] which is considered as the state of the art in f/g assignment.

There are many possible extensions to the proposed system. First, to provide more occlusion information on a given frame, a bigger temporal window could be used to retrieve motion occlusions. Second, we can take profit of other monocular depth cues, such as T-junctions and convexity to help on motionless depth relations. Although state of the art results on these cues [11] show that they are less reliable than motion occlusions, they could be a good complement to the system. We believe also that occlusions caused by motions can be propagated throughout the sequence to infer a consistent depth ordering across multiple frames. Since results on single frames are promising, sequence depth ordering seems plausible.

References

1. Ono, M.E., Rivest, J., Ono, H.: Depth perception as a function of motion parallax and absolute-distance information. Journal of Experimental Psychology: Human Perception and Performance 12, 331–337 (1986)
2. Qian, N., Qian, D.N.: Binocular disparity and the perception of depth. Neuron 18, 359–368 (1997)

3. He, X., Yuille, A.: Occlusion Boundary Detection Using Pseudo-depth. In: Daniilidis, K., Maragos, P., Paragios, N. (eds.) ECCV 2010, Part IV. LNCS, vol. 6314, pp. 539–552. Springer, Heidelberg (2010)
4. Turetken, E., Alatan, A.A.: Temporally consistent layer depth ordering via pixel voting for pseudo 3D representation. In: Proc. 3DTV Conf.: The True Vision - Capture, Transmission and Display of 3D Video, pp. 1–4 (2009)
5. Chang, J.Y., Cheng, C.C., Chien, S.Y., Chen, L.G.: Relative depth layer extraction for monoscopic video by use of multidimensional filter. In: Proc. IEEE Int. Multimedia and Expo. Conf., 221–224 (2006)
6. Li, P., Farin, D., Gunnewiek, R.K., de With, P.H.N.: On creating depth maps from monoscopic video using structure from motion. In: 27th Symposium on Information Theory in the Benelux, pp. 508–515 (2006)
7. Zhang, G., Jia, J., Wong, T.T., Bao, H.: Consistent depth maps recovery from a video sequence. IEEE Trans. Pattern Anal. Mach. Intell. 31, 974–988 (2009)
8. Sundberg, P., Brox, T., Maire, M., Arbelaez, P., Malik, J.: Occlusion boundary detection and figure/ground assignment from optical flow. In: IEEE Int. Conf. on Computer Vision and Pattern Recognition (CVPR), Colorado Springs, CO (2011)
9. Salembier, P., Garrido, L.: Binary partition tree as an efficient representation for image processing, segmentation, and information retrieval. IEEE Trans. on Image Processing 9, 561–576 (2000)
10. Brox, T., Bruhn, A., Papenberg, N., Weickert, J.: High Accuracy Optical Flow Estimation Based on a Theory for Warping. In: Pajdla, T., Matas, J. (eds.) ECCV 2004, Part IV. LNCS, vol. 3024, pp. 25–36. Springer, Heidelberg (2004)
11. Palou, G., Salembier, P.: From local occlusion cues to global depth estimation. In: IEEE Int. Conf. on Acoustics Speech and Signal Processing, Kyoto, Japan (2012)
12. Sun, D., Sudderth, E., Black, M.J.: Layered Image Motion with Explicit Occlusions, Temporal Consistency, and Depth Ordering. In: Lafferty, J.D., Williams, C.K.I., Shawe-Taylor, J., Zemel, R.S., Culotta, A. (eds.) Advances in Neural Information Processing Systems, vol. 23. Curran Associates, Inc. (2010)
13. Alvarez, L., Deriche, R., Papadopoulo, T., Sánchez, J.: Symmetrical dense optical flow estimation with occlusions detection. Int. Journal of Computer Vision 75, 371–385 (2007), doi:10.1007/s11263-007-0041-4
14. Calderero, F., Marques, F.: Region merging techniques using information theory statistical measures. IEEE Trans. on Image Processing 19, 1567–1586 (2010)
15. Vilaplana, V., Marques, F., Salembier, P.: Binary partition trees for object detection. IEEE Trans. on Image Processing 17, 2201–2216 (2008)
16. Kanatani, K.: Transformation of optical flow by camera rotation. IEEE Trans. on Pattern Analysis and Machine Intelligence 10, 131–143 (1988)
17. Andersen, R.: Modern methods for robust regression. Quantitative applications in the social sciences, vol. 152. Sage Publications (2008)
18. Cormen, T.H., Leiserson, C.E., Rivest, R.L., Stein, C.: Introduction to Algorithms, 2nd revised edn. The MIT Press (2001)
19. Stein, A.: Occlusion Boundaries: Low-Level Detection to High-Level Reasoning. PhD thesis, Robotics Institute, Carnegie Mellon University, Pittsburgh, PA (2008)

Joint Spatio-temporal Depth Features Fusion Framework for 3D Structure Estimation in Urban Environment

Mohamad Motasem Nawaf and Alain Trémeau

Laboratoire Hubert Curien UMR CNRS 5516
Université Jean Monnet, Saint-Etienne, France
firstname.[midname.]lastname@univ-st-etienne.fr

Abstract. We present a novel approach to improve 3D structure estimation from an image stream in urban scenes. We consider a particular setup where the camera is installed on a moving vehicle. Applying traditional structure from motion (SfM) technique in this case generates poor estimation of the 3d structure due to several reasons such as texture-less images, small baseline variations and dominant forward camera motion. Our idea is to introduce the monocular depth cues that exist in a single image, and add time constraints on the estimated 3D structure. We assume that our scene is made up of small planar patches which are obtained using over-segmentation method, and our goal is to estimate the 3D positioning for each of these planes. We propose a fusion framework that employs Markov Random Field (MRF) model to integrate both spatial and temporal depth information. An advantage of our model is that it performs well even in the absence of some depth information. Spatial depth information is obtained through a global and local feature extraction method inspired by Saxena et al. [1]. Temporal depth information is obtained via sparse optical flow based structure from motion approach. That allows decreasing the estimation ambiguity by forcing some constraints on camera motion. Finally, we apply a fusion scheme to create unique 3D structure estimation.

1 Introduction

Estimating the 3D structure of a scene from 2D image stream is one of the most popular problems within computer vision. It is referred to as structure from motion (SfM) or 3D reconstruction from video sequence [2]. SfM has been applied in several applications [2] such as robot navigation, obstacle avoidance, entertainments, driver assistance, reverse engineering and modelling, etc.

In our work, we focus on the problem of estimating the 3D structure from a video taken by a camera installed on a moving vehicle in urban environments. This setup leads possibly to create 3D maps of our world. However, the dominant forward motion of the camera from one side, and the texture-less scenes that are present generally in urban environment produce an erroneous depth recovery. The forward camera motion could result degenerated configurations

A. Fusiello et al. (Eds.): ECCV 2012 Ws/Demos, Part III, LNCS 7585, pp. 526–535, 2012.
© Springer-Verlag Berlin Heidelberg 2012

for a naturally ill-posed problem, or mathematically, a large number of local minima during the minimization of the reprojection error [3], that results in inaccurate camera relative motion estimation. Moreover, the limited lifetime of tracked feature points prevents using general optimization methods such as in traditional SfM. Additionally, forward motion restricts features matching due to non-homogeneous scale changes of image objects, especially those aligned parallel to camera movement.

In the proposed method, we suggest to benefit from the monocular cues (e.g. spatial depth information) to improve 3D depth estimation. We believe that such spatial depth information are complementary to temporal information. For instance, given a blue patch located at the top of an image, an SfM technique will probably fail to compute the depth due to the difficult matching problem, while the monocular depth estimation method (supervised learning) will assign it a large depth value as it will be considered as a sky with high probability.

Similar to other works [1][4][5], we consider that our world is made up of small planar patches, and the relationship between each two patches is either connected, planar or occluded. Based upon these considerations, the goal is to estimate the plane parameters where each patch lies. These patches are obtained from the image using over-segmentation method [6] or what is called superpixels segmentation. In order to fuse both temporal and monocular depth information, and also to handle the interactive relationship between superpixels, we proposed to use an MRF model similar to the one used in [1]. However, we extend the model by adding new terms to include temporal depth information computed using a modified SfM technique. Moreover we benefit from the limited Degrees of Freedom (DoF) of camera motion (which is such of the vehicle) to improve relative motion estimation, and in return, the depth estimation.

Spatial depth information is obtained using an improved version of the method proposed in [1], which estimates the depth from a single image. The method employs an MRF model that is composed of two terms; one integrates a broad set of local and global features, while the other handles the neighbouring relationship between superpixels based on occlusion boundaries. In our method, we compute occlusion boundaries from motion [7] to obtain more reliable results than using a single image as in the aforementioned method. Therefore, it is expected to have better reconstruction, even before integrating the temporal depth information.

To perform SfM, which represents temporal depth information, we use optical flow based technique that allows forcing some constraints on camera motion (which has limited DoF). Moreover, it is proved to have better depth estimation for small baseline distances and forward camera motion [6]. Here, we compute a sparse optical flow using an improved method of Lucase-Kanade with multiresolution and subpixel accuracy, results are refined thanks to camera motion estimation. Based on the famous optical flow equation [6], we obtain the depth for set of points in the image. Hence we can add some constraints on the position of scene patches to whom these points belong.

Outline of the Paper: In section 2 we give an overview of various methods for depth estimation using; video sequences, single image, and then combined spatio-temporal methods. In section 3 we introduce the MRF model that integrates SfM with the monocular depth estimation, and we explain its potential functions, parameters learning and inference. In section 4 we conclude our work and we discuss the advantages of the proposed method.

2   Related Works

In computer vision, structure from motion (SfM) has taken a great attention by researchers, it is considered as one of the well-studied problems. However, most of the efforts are focused on a certain number of aspects. For instance, improving feature points matching [8], formalize better constraints to improve relative camera pose estimation [9][10], robust methods for outliers rejection [11], linear/non-linear reprojection error optimization and bundle adjustment [10], formalize a set of constraints on more than two frames [9]. Most of these contributions do only consider temporal information that results from image stream variation with respect to time, without trying to analyse the monocular depth cues that are present in every single image.

From another side, several monocular cues that exist in a single image have been exploited by researchers, that includes; vanishing points and horizon line [9], shades, shadows, haze, patterns and structure [12]. Unfortunately, most of these cues are not present in all kinds of images, and they require specific settings. In contrast, we are looking to provide a general spatial depth estimation approach to be integrated with temporal depth estimation as mentioned earlier. Hence, we target a new generation (since last decade) of methods that perform 2D to 3D conversion using a single image. Generally these methods have no constrains and are based on the use of exhaustive feature extraction and probabilistic models to learn depth. An early approach attempts to estimate general depth of an image is proposed in [13] which employs Fourier spectrum to compute a global spectral signature of a scene to estimate the average depth of the image scene. Later on, an innovative attempt to perform 3D reconstruction from one image is proposed in [14]. Where first the image is over-segmented into superpixels, then each superpixel is classified as ground, sky or vertical. It employs a wide set of colour, texture, location, shape and edge features for training. Finally, the vertical region is "cut and folded" in order to create a rough 3D model. Although this method has been improved later by considering some geometric subclasses (centre, left, right, etc.) [15], the "ground-vertical" world assumption does not apply for wide range of images. More general method is proposed in [5] which estimates the depth from a single image based on some predicted semantic labels (sky, tree, road, etc.) using multi-class pixel-wise image labelling model. Then, the computed labels guide the 3D estimation by establishing a possible order and positioning of image objects. Another general approach has been proposed in [1] which does not have initial assumption about scene's structure. It proceed by over-segmenting the image similar to [14]. The absolute depth of each image patch is estimated based on learning an MRF model, where a variety of features that capture local and contextual information is employed. We see later how a part of our work is inspired by this method.

In the context of combining both spatial and temporal depth information (as we aim), a method that combines SfM with a simultaneous segmentation and object recognition is proposed in [16], it targets road scene understanding. The task is achieved through a conditional random field model (CRF) which consists of pixel-wise potential functions that incorporate motion and appearance features. The author claims that it overcomes the effect of small baseline variations. In our method, we perform direct depth estimation rather than object recognition. However, similar to [16], our method is also supervised learning oriented, we benefit from computed features to capture contextual information and learn depth. Another approach with the same context is a semantic structure from motion approach [17] which is based on a probabilistic model. The proposed model incorporates object recognition with 3D pose and location estimation tasks. Also it involves potential functions that represent the interaction between objects, points and regions. In comparison with our approach, we use small planar patches [4] to model the world rather than the pixel-wise approach used in [16] as we think they better describe the world around us. Our idea is also supported by the experimental results in [18].

3   Spatio-temporal Depth Fusion Framework

In this section, we first introduce some notations. Then we explain how we compute spatial and temporal depth features. After that, we discuss estimating occlusion boundaries that play an important role in our model. Next, we introduce our proposed framework as an MRF model that incorporates several terms related to spatial and temporal depth features. Finally we show how we estimate the parameters from a given dataset and perform the inference for a new input.

3.1   Image Representation

As mentioned earlier, we assume that the world is composed of planar patches, and the obtained superpixels are their *one-to-many* 2D projection. This assumption represents a good estimate if the number of computed superpixels is large enough. We obtain the superpixels from an image by using an over-segmentation algorithm [6]. We represent the image as a set of superpixels $\mathbf{S}^t = \{S_1^t, S_2^t, ..., S_n^t\}$, where S_i^t defines superpixel i at time t. We define $\alpha_i^t \in \mathbb{R}^3$ the plane parameters associated to S_i^t such that for a given point $x \in \mathbb{R}^3$ on the plane satisfies $\alpha_i^t x = 1$. Our aim is to find the plane parameters for all superpixels in the image stream.

3.2   Spatial Depth Features

Spatial features for supervised depth estimation have not achieved much success compared to other computer vision domains such as object recognition and classification. Although the problem of monocular vision had been well studied in human vision (even before computers appear) and many monocular depth cues that human uses have been identified, however, it was not possible to obtain explicit depth representative measurements such as in stereo vision. Recently, there were several attempts to infer image 3D structure using spatial features and supervised learning [1][5][16]. In our method, we proceed in similar way, in order to capture texture information, the input image is filtered with a set of texture energies and gradient detectors (~20 filters) [18]. Then by using superpixel segmentation image as a mask, we compute the filter response for each superpixel by summing its pixels in the filtered image. We refer the reader to [18] for more details. In order to capture general information, the aforementioned step is repeated for multiple scales of the image. Also, to add contextual information, e.g. texture variations, each superpixel feature vector includes the features of its neighbouring superpixels. Additionally, the formed feature vector includes colour, location, and shape features as they provide representative depth source for fixed camera configuration and urban environment. For instance, recognizing the sky and the ground. These features are computed as shown in table 1 in [14]. We donate X_i^t the feature vector for superpixel S_i^t.

3.3   Temporal Depth Features

In this subsection, we first describe some mathematical foundations and camera model. Then we explain how to perform sparse depth estimation which will be integrated in the probabilistic model given in subsection 3.5.

We use a monocular camera mounted on a moving vehicle. We assume that

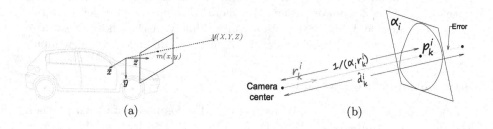

(a)   (b)

Fig. 1. (a) Acquiring geometry: Camera installed on a moving vehicle with Z axis coincides with forward motion direction. (b) Illustration for how to compute the error in depth between the estimated value and the depth for a given α_i

the Z axis of the camera coincides with the forward motion of the vehicle as shown in figure 1(a). Based on pin-hole camera model and camera coordinate system, a given $3D$ point $M(X, Y, Z)$ is projected on the $2D$ image as $m(x, y)$ by a perspective projection:

$$\begin{bmatrix} x \\ y \end{bmatrix} = \frac{f}{Z} \begin{bmatrix} X \\ Y \end{bmatrix} \tag{1}$$

When the vehicle moves, which is equivalent to fixed camera and moving world, the relationship between the velocity of a 3D point $[\dot{X}\dot{Y}\dot{Z}]^T$ and the velocity of its 2D projection $[\dot{x}\ \dot{y}]^T$ is given as the time derivative of equation 1. Then, based on the well-known optical flow equation $\dot{X} = -T - \Omega \times X$, and assuming a rigid scene, we decompose the 3D velocity into translational T and rotational velocity Ω [2]. Hence we obtain equation 2 which is the essence of most optical flow based SfM methods

$$\begin{bmatrix} \dot{x} \\ \dot{y} \end{bmatrix} = \frac{1}{Z} \begin{bmatrix} -f & 0 & x \\ 0 & -f & y \end{bmatrix} \cdot \begin{bmatrix} T_x \\ T_y \\ T_z \end{bmatrix} + \begin{bmatrix} xy/f & -f-(x^2/f) & -y \\ f+(y^2/f) & -xy/f & x \end{bmatrix} \begin{bmatrix} \Omega_x \\ \Omega_y \\ \Omega_z \end{bmatrix} \quad (2)$$

Based on this equation, we proceed in computing a sparse depth. We estimate the relative camera motion between two adjacent frames by first performing SIFT feature points matching [8]. Next we estimate the fundamental matrix using RANSAC [11] and bundle adjustment. Then, given camera intrinsic parameters, we can obtain the Essential matrix that encodes the rotation and translation between the two scenes. Which represent also the relative camera motion parameters $[T\ \Omega]$. The left hand side of equation 2 is basically the optical flow computed between two frames. In our implementation it is obtained using the well-known Lucas-Kanade with multi resolution and sub-pixel accuracy. Moreover, we benefit from the estimated Fundamental matrix to reject outliers in the optical flow. At this point, we could compute an approximate depth for the selected feature points.

Besides, given the specific camera setup as shown in figure 1(a), the motion of the camera is not totally free in the 3D space (motion of a vehicle). Therefore, we could add some constraints that express the feasible relative camera motion between two frames. For instance, limitation in T_y and Ω_z velocities. However, due to the absence of essential physical quantities, precise constraints on camera (or vehicle) motion could not be established theoretically. Instead, we evaluate experimentally possible camera transactions estimated from a set of video sequences acquired in different scenarios. As a result, we could establish some roles to spot outliers in the newly computed values for relative camera motion $[T\ \Omega]$. This way we improve the relative camera motion estimation in our case as we regularly have degenerated configurations (due to small baseline variations and dominant forward motion as mentioned earlier).

3.4   Occlusion Boundaries Estimation

When the camera translates, close objects move faster than far objects, and hence this causes to change the visibility of some objects in the scene. Although this phenomenon is considered as a problem in computer vision, it provides an important source of information about 3D scene structure. In our approach, we benefit from motion to infer occlusion boundaries. We use the method proposed in [7] to generate a soft occlusion boundaries map from two consecutive image frames. The method is based on supervised training of an occlusion detector thanks to a set of visual features selected by a Random Forest (RF) based model. Since occlusion boundaries lie close to surfaces edges, we use the classifier output as an indicator to the relationship between two superpixels if they are connected or occluded. Hence we add a penalty term in our MRF that forces the connectivity between superpixels. This term is inversely-proportional to the obtained occlusion indicator.

3.5   MRF for Depth Fusion

Markov Random Field (MRF) is becoming increasingly popular for modelling 3D world structure [1][5] due to its flexibility in terms of adding appearance constraints and contextual information. In our problem, we formulate our depth fusion as an MRF model that incorporates certain constraints with variable weights so they are jointly respected. Furthermore, we preserve the convexity of our problem such as in [1] to allow solving it through a linear program rather than probabilistic approaches for less computation time. We have seen earlier how to obtain temporal depth information, monocular features and occlusion boundaries. Figure 2 shows a simplified process flow for the proposed framework. We formulate our energy function which includes all of these terms as:

$$E(\alpha^t | X^t, O, \hat{D}, \alpha^{t-1}; \theta) = \underbrace{\sum_i \psi_i(\alpha_i^t)}_{\substack{\text{spatial depth} \\ \text{term}}} + \underbrace{\sum_{ij} \psi_{ij}(\alpha_i^t, \alpha_j^t)}_{\substack{\text{connectivity} \\ \text{term}}} + \underbrace{\sum_{ik} \phi_{ik}(\alpha_i^t, \hat{d}_k^i)}_{\substack{\text{temporal depth} \\ \text{term}}} + \underbrace{\sum_i \phi_i(\alpha_i^t, \alpha_i^{t-1})}_{\substack{\text{time consistency} \\ \text{term}}}$$

$$(3)$$

Where the superscripts t and $t-1$ refer to current and previous frames. X is the set of superpixels feature vectors. O is a map of occlusion boundaries computed from the frames t and $t-1$. The estimated sparse depth is $\hat{D}$, while $\hat{d}_k^i$ is the estimated depth value for pixel k in superpixel i. α_i is superpixel i plane's parameters and α is the set of parameters for all superpixels. θ are the learned monocular depth parameters. We now proceed in describing each term in our model (In the first three terms we will drop down the superscript of frame indicator t as they are the same).

Spatial Depth Term. This term is responsible for penalizing the difference between the computed plane parameters and the one estimated from spatial depth features (based on the learned parameters θ). It is given by the accumulated error for all pixels in the superpixel. See [18] P36-37 for details. For simplification, let's define a function $\delta(d_k^i, \hat{d}_k^i)$ that represents one point fractional depth error between an estimated value $\hat{d}_j^i$ and actual value d_j^i given plane parameters α_i. This potential function is given as

$$\psi_i(\alpha_i) = \beta_1 \sum_j \nu_k^i \delta(d_k^i, \hat{d}_k^i) \tag{4}$$

Where ν_k^i is a learned parameter that indicates the reliability of a feature vector X_k^i in estimating the depth for a given point p_k^i, see [1] for more details. β_1 is a weighting constant.

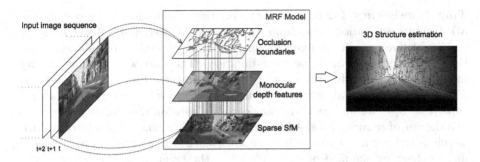

Fig. 2. Graphical representation of our MRF; it takes as input an image sequence. Occlusion boundaries and sparse SfM are estimated from two frames t and $t+1$, while monocular depth features are extracted from the current frame t, the MRF model integrate this information in order to produce a joint result for 3D structure estimation

Connectivity Prior. This term is based on the map of occlusion boundaries explained earlier. For each two adjacent superpixels, we compute an occlusion boundary indicator by summing up all pixels located at the common border in the estimated map. The obtained occlusion indicators are normalized so that they are in the range $[0..1]$. We refer o_{ij} for the indicator between superpixels i and j. The potential function is computed for each two neighbouring superpixels by choosing two adjacent pixels from each. The function penalizes the difference in distance between each of them to the camera. We have

$$\psi_{ij}(\alpha_i, \alpha_j) = \beta_2 \, o_{ij} \sum_{k=l=1}^{2} \delta(d_k^i, d_l^j) \tag{5}$$

Where β_2 is a weighting constant. This potential function forces neighbouring superpixels to be connected only if they are not occluded with the help of occlusion indicator o_{ij}. In comparison with the original method [1], we drop down the co-planarity constraint as we believe that the included temporal information and estimating occlusion boundaries indicator for motion provide an important source of depth information about plane orientation. Therefore, we do not mislead the estimation procedure with such approximation.

Temporal Depth Term. This term enforces some constraints that are established from the set of points where the depth is known. It is evident that with three non-collinear points we can obtain plane parameters α_i. However, to consider less or more number of points, we formulate this potential function to penalize the error between the estimated depth $\hat{d}_k^i$ for a point $p_k^i \in S_i$, and the computed depth given plane parameters α_i. Figure 1 (b) shows how this error is computed. Hence we have

$$\phi_{ik}(\alpha_i, \hat{d}_k^i) = \beta_3(\hat{d}_k^i - 1/\alpha_i^\top r_k^i) \tag{6}$$

Where β_3 is a weighting constant. we compute absolute depth error rather than fractional error since SfM is more confident than spatial depth estimation.

Time Consistency Term. In case of more than two frames, the quality of the 3D structure estimation varies from one frame to another, and it depends highly on the relative camera motion components (larger T_x and T_y translational motions results in better 3D structure estimation). Therefore we add some penalty in order to guide depth estimation at time t given the estimation at time $t-1$. This smooths the overall estimated structure variations in time. Hence, for each superpixel S_i^{t-1} we find its correspondence S_i^t based on the motion parameters and the size of common area. Additionally, we consider some visual features such as colour and texture. Eventually some superpixels will not have correspondence due to changing the field of view. We select the point p_k^i at the centre of the S_i^{t-1} and we form a ray from camera centre to this point. This ray intersects with superpixel S_i^t at point $p_k^{i'}$. The formulated potential function penalizes the distance across the ray between the two points

$$\phi_i(\alpha_i^t, \alpha_i^{t-1}) = \beta_4 \delta(d_k^{i'}, \hat{d}_k^i) \qquad (7)$$

Here β_4 is smoothness term. We intend to use only one point to leave some freedom in plane orientation and for better 3D reconstruction refinement.

3.6 Parameters Learning and Inference

In our MRF formulation we preserve the convexity as all terms are linear or L_1 norm, which is solved using linear program. To learn the parameters, we first proceed with the first two terms of equation 3. We assume unity value for the parameters β_1 and β_2. The two parameters θ and ν are learned individually [18] using a dataset with ground-truth. For the rest of the parameters, β_1 and β_2 defines how the method is spatially oriented, while large β_3 turns the method into conventional SfM. β_4 allows previous estimation to influence the current one. Hence the weighting constants $\beta_{1..4}$ depends on the context, although they could be learned through cross-validation.

4 Discussion and Conclusion

We have presented a novel framework to perform 3D structure estimation from image sequence, which combines both spatial and temporal depth information to provide more reliable reconstruction. Temporal depth features are obtained using a sparse optical flow based structure from motion technique. The spatial depth features are obtained through a broad global and local feature extraction phase that tries to capture monocular depth cues. Both approaches have been tested independently on a wide set of images and proved to have good performance (see [19] [20] for comparison). This is why we believe that our joint approach gives better 3D structure estimation. Or at least, a performance similar to SfM technique (when the weight β_3 is assigned a large value). Additionally, it is adapted to our context where we regularly encounter a failure of certain depth source. For instance, in case of pure rotation in SfM or abnormal colors and appearance for some objects in spatial depth estimation.

References

1. Saxena, A., Sun, M., Ng, A.: Learning 3-d scene structure from a single still image. In: IEEE 11th International Conference on Computer Vision, ICCV 2007, pp. 1–8. IEEE (2007)
2. Aanæs, H.: Methods for structure from motion. IMM, Informatik og Matematisk Modellering, Danmarks Tekniske Universitet (2003)
3. Vedaldi, A., Guidi, G., Soatto, S.: Moving forward in structure from motion. In: IEEE Conference on CVPR 2007, pp. 1–7. IEEE (2007)
4. Saxena, A., Chung, S., Ng, A.: 3-d depth reconstruction from a single still image. International Journal of Computer Vision 76, 53–69 (2008)
5. Liu, B., Gould, S., Koller, D.: Single image depth estimation from predicted semantic labels. In: IEEE Conference on CVPR, pp. 1253–1260. IEEE (2010)
6. Felzenszwalb, P., Huttenlocher, D.: Efficient graph-based image segmentation. International Journal of Computer Vision 59, 167–181 (2004)
7. Humayun, A., Mac Aodha, O., Brostow, G.: Learning to find occlusion regions. In: IEEE Conference on CVPR 2011, pp. 2161–2168. IEEE (2011)
8. Lowe, D.: Distinctive image features from scale-invariant keypoints. International Journal of Computer Vision 60, 91–110 (2004)
9. Hartley, R., Zisserman, A., Ebrary, I.: Multiple view geometry in computer vision, vol. 2. Cambridge Univ. Press (2003)
10. Triggs, B., McLauchlan, P.F., Hartley, R.I., Fitzgibbon, A.W.: Bundle Adjustment – A Modern Synthesis. In: Triggs, B., Zisserman, A., Szeliski, R. (eds.) ICCV-WS 1999. LNCS, vol. 1883, pp. 298–372. Springer, Heidelberg (2000)
11. Fischler, M., Bolles, R.: Random sample consensus: a paradigm for model fitting with applications to image analysis and automated cartography. Communications of the ACM 24, 381–395 (1981)
12. Lindeberg, T., Garding, J.: Shape from texture from a multi-scale perspective. In: Fourth International Conference on Computer Vision, pp. 683–691. IEEE (1993)
13. Torralba, A., Oliva, A.: Depth estimation from image structure. IEEE Transactions on Pattern Analysis and Machine Intelligence 24, 1226–1238 (2002)
14. Hoiem, D., Efros, A., Hebert, M.: Automatic photo pop-up. ACM Transactions on Graphics 24, 577–584 (2005)
15. Hoiem, D., Efros, A., Hebert, M.: Recovering surface layout from an image. International Journal of Computer Vision 75, 151–172 (2007)
16. Sturgess, P., Alahari, K., Ladicky, L., Torr, P.: Combining appearance and structure from motion features for road scene understanding (2009)
17. Bao, S., Savarese, S.: Semantic structure from motion. In: 2011 IEEE Conference on Computer Vision and Pattern Recognition (CVPR), pp. 2025–2032. IEEE (2011)
18. Saxena, A.: Monocular depth perception and robotic grasping of novel objects. Stanford University (2009)
19. Saxena, A.: State-of-the-art results of the depth prediction from single image. Website (2012), http://make3d.cs.cornell.edu/results_stateoftheart.html
20. Civera, J., Davison, A., Montiel, J.: Structure from Motion Using the Extended Kalman Filter, vol. 75. Springer (2011)

A Virtual Environment Tool for Benchmarking Face Analysis Systems

Mauricio Correa[1,2], Javier Ruiz-del-Solar[1,2], and Rodrigo Verschae[2]

[1] Department of Electrical Engineering, Universidad de Chile
[2] Advanced Mining Technology Center, Universidad de Chile
{macorrea,jruizd}@ing.uchile, rodrigo@verschae.org

Abstract. In this article, a virtual environment for realistic testing of face analysis systems under uncontrolled conditions is proposed. The key elements of this tool are a simulator, and real face and background images taken under real-world conditions with different acquisition conditions, such as indoor or outdoor illumination. Inside the virtual environment, an observing agent, the one with the ability to recognize and detect faces, can navigate and observe the face images, at different distances, and angles. During the face analysis process, the agent can actively change its viewpoint and relative distance to the faces in order to improve the recognition results. The virtual environment provides all behaviors to the agent (navigation, positioning, face's image composing under different angles, etc.), except the ones related with the analysis of faces (detection, recognition, pose estimation, etc.). In addition we describe different kinds of experiments that can be implemented for quantifying the face analysis capabilities of agents and provide usage example of the proposed tool in evaluating a face recognition system in a service robot.

Keywords: Face analysis, Face Recognition, Face Recognition Benchmark, Evaluation Methodologies, Virtual Simulation Environment, Simulator.

1 Introduction

Face analysis plays an important role in building HRI (Human-Robot Interaction). Human detection and human identification based on face information are key abilities of intelligent machines whose purpose is to interact with humans. Face analysis is also very important in security applications in dynamic environment, such as security cameras at airports. Evaluating face analysis systems for such environments and conditions is not straightforward, in particular in the cases when the recognition system uses active vision mechanisms to change its viewpoint or position in the scene.

A very important aspect in the development of face analysis methodologies is the use of suitable databases, and evaluation and training methodologies. For instance, the very well known FERET database [9], has been very important in the development of face recognition algorithms for controlled environments in the last years. However, neither FERET nor other relatively new databases such as LFW [5], CAS-PEAL [4] and FRGC [10][8], among others [1][2][3], are able to provide real-world testing conditions for evaluating face recognition systems that include the use of innovative

A. Fusiello et al. (Eds.): ECCV 2012 Ws/Demos, Part III, LNCS 7585, pp. 536–546, 2012.

mechanisms such as spatiotemporal context and active vision, which are required in applications that consider the dynamic interaction with humans in the real world. Even the use of video face databases does not allow testing the use of those ideas. The use of a simulator could allow accomplishing this (viewpoint changes). However, a simulator is not able to generate faces and backgrounds that looks real/natural enough, which is a condition for the realistic testing of face recognition systems.

Nevertheless, the combined used of a simulation tool with real face and background images taken under real-world conditions could allow accomplishing the goal of providing a tool for testing face recognition systems under uncontrolled conditions. In this case, more than providing a database and a testing procedure, the idea would be to supply a virtual environment that offers a database of real face images, a simulated virtual environment, a simulated agent moving in that environment, dynamic image's acquisition conditions, active vision mechanisms, predefined benchmark problems, and an evaluation methodology. The main goal of this paper is to provide such a virtual environment. In this environment: persons are located at different positions and orientations, where the face images are previously acquired under different pitch and yaw angles -- in-plane rotations can be simulated by software --, in indoor and outdoor variable lighting conditions. Inside this environment, an observing agent, the one with the ability to recognize faces, can navigate and observe the real face images (with real background information), at different distances, angles (yaw, pitch, and roll) and with indoor or outdoor illumination. During the recognition process the agent can actively change its viewpoint to improve the face recognition results. In addition, different kinds of agents and agents' trajectories can be simulated, such as an agent navigating in an scene with people looking in different directions (mimicking a home environment), an agent performing a circular scanning (such as in a security checkpoint), or a person approaching to a security camera.

The proposed virtual environment could be of high interest in the development and testing of applications related with the visual analysis of human faces. It allows comparing, quantifying, training and validating face analysis capabilities of agents, and in general intelligent machines, under exactly equal working conditions. In the current communication we focus on face recognition, although its use in others face analysis problems is straightforward. The simulator will be made available for academic use in the near future.

This article is organized as follows. In the following subsection, related work in face databases and evaluation methodologies is outlined. In Section 2, the proposed virtual environment is described, as well as the functionality that the agent should provide. An example of the application of this tool is presented in Section 3. Finally, we conclude in Section 4.

Related Work

The availability of standard databases, benchmarks, and evaluation methodologies is crucial for the appropriate comparison of face recognition systems. There is a large amount of face databases and associated evaluation methodologies that consider different number of persons, camera sensors, and image acquisition conditions, and that are suited to test different aspects of the face recognition problem such us illumination invariance, aging, expression invariance, etc. Basic information about face databases can be found in [2][11].

The FERET database [9] and its associated evaluation methodology is a standard choice for evaluating face recognition algorithms under controlled conditions. Other popular databases used with the same purpose are Yale Face Database [12] and BioID [13]. Other databases such the AR Face Database [14] and the University of Notre Dame Biometrics Database [15] include faces with different facial expressions, illumination conditions, and occlusions. However, from our point of view, all of them are far from considering real-world conditions.

The Yale Face Database B [16] and PIE [17] are the most utilized databases to test the performance of algorithms under variable illumination conditions. Yale Face contains 5,760 single light source images of 10 subjects, each seen under 576 viewing conditions (9 poses x 64 illumination conditions). For every subject in a particular pose, an image with ambient (background) illumination was also captured. PIE is a database containing 41,368 images of 68 people, each person under 13 different poses, 43 different illumination conditions, and with 4 different expressions. Both databases consider only indoor illumination.

The LFW database [5] consists of 13,233 images faces of 5,749 different persons, obtained from news images by means of a face detector. There are no eyes/fiducial point annotations; the faces were just aligned using the output of the face detector. The images have a very large degree of variability in the face's pose, expression, age, race, and background. However, due to LFW images are obtained from news, which in general are taken by professional photographers, they are obtained under good illumination conditions, and mostly in indoors.

FRGC ver2.0 database [8] consists of 50,000 face images divided into training and validation sets. The validation set consists of data from 4,003 subject sessions. A subject session consists of controlled and uncontrolled images. The uncontrolled images were taken in varying illumination conditions in indoors and outdoors. Each set of uncontrolled images contains two expressions, smiling and neutral.

2   Proposed Simulation and Testing Tool

The proposed simulator allows that an observing agent navigate inside a virtual environment (VE), and observe a set of persons. The faces of each of these persons are previously scanned under different yaw and pitch angles, and under different indoor and outdoor illumination conditions. This allows that every time that the agent observes a person's face at a given distance and viewpoint inside the VE, the corresponding images/observations can be composed using real faces and background images, instead of being generated by the simulator.

Image Acquisition and Database Construction

Real face images are acquired at different yaw and pitch angles using a CCD camera mounted in a rotating structure (see Fig. 1a). The person under scan is in a still position, while the camera, placed at the same height than the person's face and at a fixed distance of 140 cm, rotates in the axial plane (the camera height is adjustable). An encoder placed in the rotation axis calculates the face's yaw angle. There are not restrictions on the person's facial expression. The system is able to acquire images with a resolution of 1°. However, in this first version, images are taken every 2°.

The scanning process takes 25 seconds, and we use a 1280 x 960 pixels CCD camera (DFK 41BU02 model). In the frontal image, the face's size is about 200x250 pixels.

Variations in pitch are obtained by repeating the described process with the different required pitch angles. In each case, the camera height is maintained, but the person looks at a different reference points in the vertical axis, which are located at 160 cm in front of the person (see Fig. 1a). In our experience, pitch angles of -15°, 0°, and 15° give account of typical human face variations. In addition, background images for each location, camera-height, and yaw-pitch angle combination are taken with the acquisition device, in order to be able to compose the final real images to be shown to the agent. In Fig. 1(c-d) are shown some images taken with the device.

(a)   (b)   (c) Yaw: 90°, Pitch: -15   (d) Yaw: 0° Pitch: 15,
                                               Outdoor   Indoor

Fig. 1. (a) Diagram of the acquisition system. (b) The system operating in outdoors.

It is important to remark that the acquisition device is portable (it does not require any special installation), and therefore it can be used at different places. Thus, the whole acquisition process can be carried out at different locations (street environment, laboratory environment, mall environment, etc.). In our case we use at least two different locations for each person, one indoor (laboratory with windows), and one outdoors (gardens inside our school's campus).

With the acquired images a face database containing 50 persons is built. For each person, 726 registered face images (121x3x2) are stored. The yaw angle range is -120° to 120°, with a resolution of 2°, which gives 121 images. For each different yaw, 3 different pitch angles are considered (-15°, 0°, and 15°). For each yaw-pitch combination, indoor and outdoor images are taken. In addition, background images corresponding to the different yaw-pitch angles, place and camera-height combinations are also stored in the database.

Virtual Environment and Agent Navigation

By means of the acquired image DB, a virtual environment is implemented (See Fig 2). A virtual environment is defined by N subjects on a Global Map. An observing agent with the ability to analyze (e.g. detect and recognize) faces has the possibility of navigating and making observations inside this scenario. In the virtual scenario, the simulator can generate faces at different distances, angles and light conditions (indoors or outdoors). During the face recognition process, the agent can move in the map to change its point of view and distance to the subject using methods of active vision in order to modify its observations and improve its face recognition results.

The virtual environment offers all the functions that the agent could have in a real scenario (navigation, positioning), and generates images observed by the agent at a given time, images that can contain faces at different angles, etc.

Given (X_A, Y_A, θ_A), where (X_A, Y_A) is the current position of the agent and (θ_A) the current orientation of the agent in the Global Map, for navigating in the environment, the agent can position itself using the following functions provided by the navigation module of the virtual scenario:

- $MoveAgent(\Delta x, \Delta y)$ commands the agent to move in the Global Map relative to its current position. The final pose of the agent would be $(X_A + \Delta x, Y_A + \Delta y, \theta_A)$.
- $TurnAgent(\Delta \theta)$ commands the agent to turn in the Global Map relative to its current orientation. The final pose of the agent would be $(X_A, Y_A, \theta_A + \Delta \theta)$.
- $SetAgentPosition(x, y, \theta)$ allows the agent to set its position in the Global Map. The final pose of the agent would be (x, y, θ).

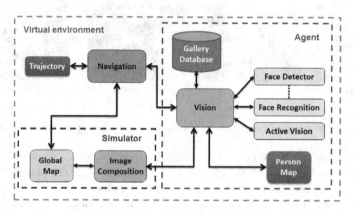

Fig. 2. Diagram of the virtual environment

Given the relative position and orientation between the agent and the observed subject (information stored in the Global Map), the simulator generates the corresponding image as seen from the agent's point of view. The image generation processes more than a rendering process is an image composition process, in which real face and background images, acquired using the device described previously, are used to compose the scene as observed by the agent. This is implemented by the *Image Composition* module. This module reads from the Global Map the position and pose of the agent, as well as the position and pose of the subjects and generates the observation for the agent. Subject's out-of-plane rotations are restricted to the available face images in the sagittal and lateral planes, while there are no restrictions for in-plane rotations. If desired, the simulator can also generate noisy observations, considering the uncertainness in the movement of the agent. Every time the agent changes its pose, the simulator generates/composes the corresponding images if is required by the vision module. For instance, Figure 3 shows a given sequence of agent poses, and the corresponding images composed by the simulator.

The agent, at any given, can navigate to the next point on a defined trajectory (if it is using one) or use active vision to modify its observations and improve face recognition results. Different trajectories are implemented, and described below.

The virtual environment provides to the agent a *Person Map* to store information of the different individuals detected within the environment, thought the agent can use its own implementation. The main idea of this module is to store the position of subjects, and to use the information when a person has been detected and included in the Person Map. Given a Global Map and a detected face in a generated image, the distance from the person to the agent is estimated. Using the agent's current position and this estimation, the position of the subject on the global map is estimated. Then, each detected person is stored at $(X_i, Y_i, \theta_i, E_i)$ with, (X_i, Y_i) position on the map, θ_i the pose and E_i is the estimation error of the position.

In addition, the virtual environment provides a *Gallery* module that the agent can use to store face information of the subjects seen so far (and the corresponding ID in the Person Map) in order to perform the recognition. This gallery can be build online or offline depending on the experiment being performed.

The *Trajectory* module allows to define different kinds of movements the agent can perform in the virtual environment, allowing to define different kinds of scenarios. It is implemented has a sequence of points (X_i, Y_i) that the agent has to flow or that the agent can use as reference.

(a) $x = 100, y = -60, \theta = -30$ (b) $x = 60, y = 65, \theta = 48$ (c) Agent in different
                                                                                positions and observed face

Fig. 3. Example of agent's positioning (c), and observations composed by the simulator. The agent is located in (a) and moves to position (b); both generated images are shown.

Details about the *Trajectory* module are given below.

Some face analysis modules (face detection, face recognition, face alignment, face gender classification, etc.) and the active vision module are available in the virtual environment, but can be redefined by the user to evaluate their own modules. For example, if the user wants to evaluate a face recognition module, he can make use of face detector that uses the ground truth (perfect face detection), one that uses a Viola&Jones detector [19] or one implemented by the user himself.

Trajectory Generation

The virtual environment provides three different kinds of trajectories: constrained navigation, predefined navigation and free navigation. Constrained navigation is used to simulate agents that cannot actively move in the environment. Predefined navigation simulates agents that can move freely, but that have a predefined route that could be followed or not. Free navigation allows the agent to move freely and it does not provide any predefined route to the agent.

- Constrained navigation: the agent must follow a predefined constrained trajectory. Five kinds of these trajectories are provided (see Figure 4 (a-e)):
    a) Frontal: the agent approaches the subject having a frontal view of him.
    b) Site-to-side: the agent moves perpendicular to an imaginary line coming from the observed person.

c) Circular: the agent moves around a person at a fixed distance.

d) Strafe: This movement is a mix of Frontal and Side-to-side. The agent moves with respect to an imaginary line that is not perpendicular to the frontal view of the subject. The movement does not maintains a fixed distance as the agent is approachs the subject.

e) Random: the agent places randomly in front of the subject, positioning inside a rectangle in front of the subject.

- Predefined navigation with active vision: the agent follows a predefined trajectory, but it can position itself freely at any position in the map (Fig. 4 (f)).
- Free navigation: the agent can move freely in the map.

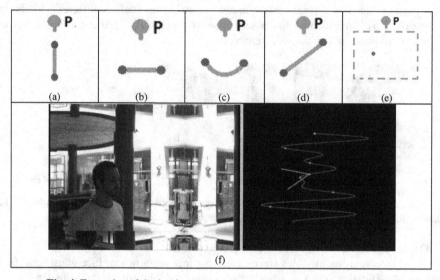

Fig. 4. Examples of the implemented trajectories. See main text for details.

Using these trajectories it is possible to simulate different kinds of scenarios, such as a service robot navigating in a house, a static security camera (with moving subjects), or a scanning device performing a circular moving around the subject. In addition we have included the option of simulating occlusions in the maps.

3   Testing Methodology

In order to recognize faces properly, the agent needs to have the following modules:

1. *Face Detection*: The agent detects a face (i.e. the face region) in a given image.
2. *Face Pose Estimation*: The agent estimates the face's angular pose in the lateral, sagittal and coronal plane.
3. *Active Vision*: Using information about the detected face and its pose, and information observed in the input images, the agent can take actions in order to change its viewpoint for improving face's perception.

4. *Face Recognition*: The identity of the person contained in the face image is determined. The module can include abilities such as face alignment or illumination compensation.

5. Other modules could be also used. For example a gender classifier could be also evaluated, thought this functionality has not been implemented yet (the database has the required information). Age and race classification in not available and would require capturing a new database.

The virtual environment already provides some well-known state of the art methods that can be used for some of these modules. Among others, it provides interfaces for the OpenCV Viola&Jones face detector, an LBP-based face recognition, as well as perfect face and eye detection using the ground truth. Face pose estimation is also provided using the ground truth.

Usage Example: Evaluating a Face Recognition Algorithm

As an example, we evaluate a face recognition algorithm used by an agent corresponding to a robot moving in an environment with 10 persons. The face recognition method to be evaluated corresponds to a local-matching face recognition that is well suited for robot application because of its processing speed. It is based on histograms of LBP (Local Binary Patterns) features [18]. Following [7], histogram intersection (HI) is used as similarity measure. The face images are scaled to 81x150 pixels and divided into 40 regions to compute the LBP histograms.

The number of persons (N) in the first experiments was set to 10 in order to reduce the computational cost, and also considering that this number is enough to evaluate the modules; recall that the same subject may be observed in many frames. In the last two experiments, 20 persons were considered. The experiments are respited 10 times considering a different subjects of the 50 subjects of the DB.

The height of the agent is fixed and equal to the base height of the persons (160 cm). The height of subjects follows a uniform distribution in [136, 184] cm, i.e. a 15% variation around the agent's height.

With respect to how the gallery is constructed, we consider two testing modes:

- *Offline Gallery Mode*: The VE generates a face gallery before the recognition process starts. The gallery contains one image of each person to be recognized. The gallery's images are frontal pictures (no rotations in any plane), taken under indoor illumination conditions. This is the standard operation mode.

- *Online Gallery Mode*: There is no gallery. The agent needs to cross two times the virtual scenario. In the first round, it should create the gallery online. In the second round, the subjects change position in the scene, and the gallery is used for recognition. In both rounds, the agent sees the person's faces at variable distance and angles, in indoor or outdoor illumination conditions. The subjects pose and the illumination conditions are randomly chosen in all cases.

We consider the case of predefined trajectories. With respect to how the agent moves, we consider two cases: with and without the use of active vision. In both cases we consider the use of online and offline gallery DB, which gives 8 cases in total.

In all experiments, the map settings are the same in order to compare the different combinations. Each experiment is repeated 10 times, considering different trajectories (see Fig 4(f) for an example) and different subjects selected randomly out of the 50 subjects in the database. Table I shows the obtained results. The first, second and third columns show which face detector was used, whether the active vision module was used and how the gallery database was build. The fourth column displays the number of subjects added to the gallery database (normally when the gallery is build online, there are some false detections); the fifth column shows the rate of number of subjects correctly detected while traversing the environment; the sixth column shows the face recognition rate out of all subjects in the scene; and the seventh column shows the face recognition rate considering only the detected subjects.

From the first two rows of the table we can that the Person Map module is used, the recognition rate improves from 78.41% to 86.77%. This is because the same subject is not added more than one time to the map, and at the same time there are less false detections. In all the other results (following row in the table) the Person Map is used. From the table it can also be observed that using the active vision module allows, among other things, to build a better gallery database (when the gallery database is built online), and to improve the recognition rate. When the database is built offline, using active vision improves the recognition rate from 86.77% to 92.92% on average.

Table 1. Evaluation of a Face Recognition system based on LBP features [18]

(*) It does not use Person Map. (+) 20 subjects are present in the scene; otherwise there are 10 subjects.						
Face Detection	Active Vision	Gallery Database	Persons added to the gallery	Persons correctly detected [%]	Recognition [%] (out of all subjects in the scene)	Recognition [%] (out of the detected subjects)
Viola&Jones	No	Offline	10.0	84.0%	----	78.4% (*)
Viola&Jones	No	Offline	10.0	84.0%	73.0%	86.8%
Viola&Jones	No	Online	14.8	84.0%	59.0%	70.2%
Viola&Jones	Yes	Offline	10.0	84.0%	78.0%	92.9%
Viola&Jones	Yes	Online	12.2	84.0%	73.0%	86.9%
Ground Truth	Yes	Offline	10.0	100.0%	92.0%	92.0%
Ground Truth	Yes	Online	10.0	100.0%	90.0%	90.0%
Viola&Jones	No	Offline	20.0 (+)	91.8%	83.0%	90.5%
Viola&Jones	Yes	Offline	20.0 (+)	91.8%	87.5%	95.7%

4   Conclusions and Projections

A virtual environment for testing face detection and recognition systems under uncontrolled conditions is proposed. The testing tool combines the use of a simulator with real face and background images taken under real-world conditions. Inside the virtual environment, an agent navigates and observes real face images, at different distances and angles, and with indoor or outdoor illumination. During the face detection and recognition process, the agent can actively change its viewpoint and relative distance to the faces in order to improve the recognition results. This tool allows evaluating multiple face analysis methods.

The applicability of the proposed tool is validated with an example; a face recognition method, namely histograms of LBP features [18], is evaluated in an agent corresponding to a robot moving in an environment with 10 subjects. In this example the face recognition performance is evaluated in two cases: when the gallery is build online and offline. Also, the use of active vision mechanisms is favorably compared to the use of a static trajectory that the agent cannot modify. The results validate our hypothesis that the use of active vision mechanisms improves largely the whole face recognition process, especially in the case of large out-of-plane face rotations.

This tool is useful for testing face analysis systems, in particular for comparing different face detection and recognition systems under similar conditions (e.g. using a similar active vision approach). In addition other face analysis subsystems can be also evaluated. For example a gender classifier, a face pose estimator, or an eye detector could be evaluated (our DB has the required information). In the future, age and race classification could be also implemented, but it would require extending the database.

Acknowledgments. This work was financed by the FONDECYT Postdoctoral Program Grant N. 3120218 and by the FONDECYT program Grant N. 1090250.

References

[1] Abate, A.F., Nappi, M., Riccio, D., Sabatino, G.: 2D and 3D face recognition: A survey. Pattern Recognition Letters 28, 1885–1906 (2007)

[2] Face Recognition Home Page, http://www.face-rec.org/databases/ (available on June 4, 2012)

[3] BeFIT - Benchmarking Facial Image Analysis Technologies home page, http://fipa.cs.kit.edu/412.php (avalilable on July 5, 2012)

[4] Gao, W., Cao, B., Shan, S., Chen, X., Zhou, D., Zhang, X., Zhao, D.: The CAS-PEAL Large-Scale Chinese Face Database and Baseline Evaluations. Trans. Sys. Man Cyber. Part A 38(1), 149–161 (2008)

[5] Labeled Faces in the Wild Database, http://vis-www.cs.umass.edu/lfw/index.html (available on June 5, 2012)

[6] Huang, G.B., Ramesh, M., Berg, T., Learned-Miller, E.: Labeled Faces in the Wild: A Database for Studying Face Recognition in Unconstrained Environments. University of Massachusetts, Amherst, Technical Report 07-49 (October 2007)

[7] Ruiz-del-Solar, J., Verschae, R., Correa, M.: Recognition of Faces in Unconstrained Environments: A Comparative Study. EURASIP Journal on Advances in Signal Processing 2009, Article ID 184617, 19 pages (2009)

[8] Face Recognition Grand Challenge, Official website public site, http://www.frvt.org/FRGC/ (available on June 30, 2010)

[9] Phillips, P.J., Wechsler, H., Huang, J., Rauss, P.: The FERET database and evaluation procedure for face recognition algorithms. Image and Vision Computing J. 16(5), 295–306 (1998)

[10] Phillips, P.J., Flynn, P., Scruggs, T., Bowyer, K., Chang, J., Hoffman, K., Marques, J., Min, J., Worek, W.: Overview of the Face Recognition Grand Challenge. In: Proc. of the IEEE Conf. Computer Vision and Pattern Recognition – CVPR 2005, vol. 1, pp. 947–954 (2005)

[11] Gross, R.: Face Databases. In: Li, S., Jain, A.K. (eds.) Handbook of Face Recognition, pp. 301–327. Springer (2005)

[12] Yale University Face Image Database public site, http://cvc.yale.edu/projects/yalefaces/yalefaces.html (available on June 5, 2012)

[13] BioID Face Database public site,
http://www.humanscan.de/support/downloads/facedb.php (available on June 5, 2012)

[14] AR Face Database public site,
http://cobweb.ecn.purdue.edu/~aleix/aleix_face_DB.html (available on June 30, 2010)

[15] Flynn, P.J., Bowyer, K.W., Phillips, P.J.: Assessment of time dependency in face recognition: An initial study. In: Audio and Video-Based Biometric Person Authentication, pp. 44–51 (2003)

[16] Yale Face Database B. Public site,
http://cvc.yale.edu/projects/yalefacesB/yalefacesB.html (available on June 30, 2010)

[17] PIE Database. Basic information,
http://www.ri.cmu.edu/projects/project_418.html (available on June 30, 2010)

[18] Ahonen, T., Hadid, A., Pietikainen, M.: Face Description with Local Binary Patterns: Application to Face Recognition. IEEE Trans. on Patt. Analysis and Machine Intell. 28(12), 2037–2041 (2006)

[19] Viola, P., Jones, M.: Robust Real-Time Face Detection. Int. J. Comput. Vision 57(2), 137–154 (2004)

An Open Source Framework for Standardized Comparisons of Face Recognition Algorithms

Manuel Günther, Roy Wallace, and Sébastien Marcel

Idiap Research Institute
Rue Marconi 19
CH - 1920 Martigny

Abstract. In this paper we introduce the facereclib, the first software library that allows to compare a variety of face recognition algorithms on most of the known facial image databases and that permits rapid prototyping of novel ideas and testing of meta-parameters of face recognition algorithms. The facereclib is built on the open source signal processing and machine learning library Bob. It uses well-specified face recognition protocols to ensure that results are comparable and reproducible. We show that the face recognition algorithms implemented in Bob as well as third party face recognition libraries can be used to run face recognition experiments within the framework of the facereclib. As a proof of concept, we execute four different state-of-the-art face recognition algorithms: local Gabor binary pattern histogram sequences (LGBPHS), Gabor graph comparisons with a Gabor phase based similarity measure, inter-session variability modeling (ISV) of DCT block features, and the linear discriminant analysis on two different color channels (LDA-IR) on two different databases: The Good, The Bad, and The Ugly, and the BANCA database, in all cases using their fixed protocols. The results show that there is not one face recognition algorithm that outperforms all others, but rather that the results are strongly dependent on the employed database.

1 Introduction

Over the last few decades, a great variety of face recognition algorithms have been proposed. To show their advantage over other existing algorithms, face recognition experiments have typically been executed on one or more publicly available facial image databases [1,2,3,4,5,6,7,8]. Unfortunately, often these databases are not accompanied by strict experimental protocols or the protocols that are provided are *biased*. A protocol for an image database defines which of the images within this database should be used for *training* the algorithms, which are for *enrolling* models and which images are finally used as *probes*. In a biased protocol, the identities used for training and for testing overlap, whereas in unbiased protocols training and testing identities are disjoint. For real-world scenarios, training and testing identities should be disjoint since it is impractical to retrain the algorithms each time a model of a new identity should be enrolled, and it is more realistic that imposters are unknown to the system.

A. Fusiello et al. (Eds.): ECCV 2012 Ws/Demos, Part III, LNCS 7585, pp. 547–556, 2012.

Often, face recognition algorithms are tested only on a few of the available databases and only those results that are superior to some baseline results are published. Regrettably, published results are, thus, usually not comparable. Additionally, often the results of other researchers can not be reproduced since they do not publish all of the meta-parameters of their algorithms. Hence, face recognition surveys like [9,10,11,12,13] can only report the results of other researchers, so "it is really difficult to declare a winner algorithm" [9] since "different papers may use different parts of the database for their experiments" [13]. In an attempt to categorize the algorithms, [10] used a more advanced evaluation of the methods, but still they had to rely on the results published by the authors of the surveyed papers because they could not reproduce them themselves.

Some institutions already tried to provide an open source interface in which different algorithms can be tested, for example the CSU Face Identification Evaluation System [14]. Unfortunately, this library is not sufficient since:

1) the implemented algorithms are already outdated,
2) new algorithms must be implemented in their specific C environment, and
3) the main focus of the library is on the FERET image database [1].

Other comparisons of face recognition algorithms were done by the *face recognition vendor tests* (FRVT) [15,16,17] and similar tests held by the *National Institute for Standards and Technology* (NIST). Though these vendor tests already provide a fair comparison, unfortunately they are designed to compare commercial algorithms and, hence, the methodologies used by the participating vendors are usually kept secret. The results of such tests are, thus, largely useless for researchers who are interested in establishing what are the state-of-the-art face recognition techniques and expanding on the best performing methods.

The contribution of this paper is to present the *facereclib*, which is, to the best of our knowledge, the first tool to dependably compare face recognition algorithms that:

1) relies solely on open source software – all results are reproducible and there are no hidden tricks,
2) utilizes fixed protocols for most of the commonly used image databases – the generated results are, hence, comparable to previously and subsequently published results,
3) supports a broad variety of state-of-the-art face recognition algorithms,
4) allows the easy integration of already existing source code, and
5) permits rapid prototyping of novel ideas and testing meta-parameters of existing algorithms – an ideal playground for researchers.

The facereclib is a satellite package[1] of the recently released open source signal processing and machine learning toolbox *Bob* [18][2], which is written in C++

---

[1] Facereclib, the face recognition satellite package of Bob, will soon be available at http://github.com/idiap/bob/wiki/Satellite-Packages

[2] Bob is open sourced under a GPL v3 license. To download Bob, please visit http://www.idiap.ch/software/bob

and Python and itself contains an implementation of many face recognition algorithms and database protocols. Since the facereclib is also implemented in Python, it is easy to integrate other software. To show that capability, in this paper we incorporate one algorithm from the CSU Face Recognition Resources [19].

The facereclib is created for a fast design and execution of face recognition experiments. It includes Python scripts that take as arguments configuration files for:

1) the employed database, its protocol, and the location of the image files,
2) the parametrization of image alignment and preprocessing,
3) the type and the variation of the extracted features, and
4) the face recognition algorithm and its meta-parameters.

Additionally, a standardized evaluation of the results is provided. This makes it easy for researchers to follow the evaluation protocols since they do not have to implement them themselves, and we hope to encourage researchers to produce comparable results.

To illustrate the potential of the facereclib, we execute four representative face recognition experiments. We apply three state-of-the-art face recognition algorithms from Bob: *local Gabor binary pattern histogram sequences* [20] (LGBPHS), *Gabor graphs* [21] with a Gabor phase based similarity measure [22], and *inter-session variability modeling* (ISV) [23] on *discrete cosine transform* (DCT) block features, as well as one algorithm taken from the CSU Face Recognition Resources [19]: LDA-IR. These algorithms are tested on two popular and challenging facial image databases: *The Good, The Bad, and The Ugly* (GBU) [5] and the *BANCA* [24] database. All face recognition experiments are run using our facereclib. It assures that the recognition results are directly comparable since exactly the same processing chain is executed. Furthermore, all parameters of all steps of the processing chain are given in the configuration files and, importantly, the recognition results are reproducible.

The remainder of this paper is structured as follows: In Section 2 we give a short overview of the features and the algorithms that are used in this paper. Section 3 describes the image databases and the protocols that we consider. Section 4 presents experimental results, while Section 5 ends with a discussion of what we have achieved in this paper.

2   Algorithms

Face recognition algorithms can typically be described in three stages: *training*, *enrollment* and *deployment*. During training, face recognition algorithms adjust their parameters to fit a given set of training images. In enrollment, one or more images per identity are used to generate a *model* for each *client*. During deployment, an unseen *probe* image is compared to one or more of the models, and a *score* for each model/probe pair is computed. When the score exceeds a certain carefully selected threshold, the pair is accepted as a *client claim*, or it is rejected as an *imposter claim*.

The algorithms used in this paper cover a representative set of state-of-the-art approaches to semi-automatic face recognition. Since the aim of this paper is to compare face recognition algorithms rather than face detectors, hand-labeled eye positions were used to geometrically normalize the faces, throughout.

2.1   LDA-IR from CSU

Firstly, we consider the LDA-IR algorithm taken from [19], which extracts the *I layer* of YIQ color space and the *red channel* of RGB color space from 65 × 75 pixel images. After preprocessing, each of these images is projected into a PCA subspace, then an LDA subspace, both of which are always trained on the training set of the respective database. The Euclidean distance is used for comparison of feature vectors.

2.2   Algorithms from Bob

The algorithms below all work with 64 × 80 gray-level images, with eye positions at $(16, 16)$ and $(48, 16)$, and preprocessed with the Tan & Triggs algorithm [25].

Local Gabor Binary Pattern Histogram Sequences (LGBPHS) [20].
Using this algorithm, *local binary pattern* (LBP) histograms are calculated for non-overlapping 8×8 pixel blocks, after convolution with a set of 40 Gabor wavelets. The histograms of all blocks from all wavelets are concatenated into one long vector (188,800 dimensions) and these vectors are compared using the χ^2 measure. The Gabor wavelets are used in the common 8 orientations and 5 scales [21] while the size of the enveloping Gaussian was set to $\sigma = \sqrt{2}\pi$. For LBP extraction, we use uniform circular LBPs with 8 neighbors and in radius of 2 pixels (i. e. $LBP_{8,2}^{u2}$, see [26]).

Gabor Graphs with Gabor Phase Based Similarity [22]. This algorithm compares Gabor jets assembled in grid graphs. Both the magnitude and phase of the Gabor wavelet responses are used. The node positions of the grid graph correspond to the centers of the histogram blocks, leading to 80 Gabor jets per image. The Gabor wavelets are the same as those described for LGBPHS above. Gabor graphs are compared using the average similarity of corresponding Gabor jets, where Gabor jets are compared with the similarity measure S_{n+C} from [22].

Inter-session Variability Modeling (ISV) [23]. Local discrete cosine transform (DCT) features are sampled from overlapping 12×12 pixel blocks, resulting in 3657 feature vectors per image. Pixels are first normalized to zero mean and unit variance within each block. The 45 lowest frequency DCT coefficients form the feature vector for each block and these are normalized to zero mean and unit variance per image as in [27]. In the training stage of ISV, a *universal background model* (UBM) [28] is estimated, followed by a linear subspace (160 dimensions) that models the effects of within-class variability. Enrollment of a client involves adaptation of the UBM to a client-specific *Gaussian mixture model* (GMM).

To compare a probe image to a client's model, a likelihood ratio is calculated with respect to the UBM.

3   Databases, Protocols, and Evaluation Metrics

To estimate how database dependent the tested algorithms are, all algorithms are evaluated on two recent and challenging image databases. Face recognition protocols can be divided into *identification* and *verification* protocols. The two databases that we use are accompanied by face verification protocols.

3.1   The Good, The Bad, and The Ugly Database

The Good, The Bad, and The Ugly database (GBU) [5] includes high resolution images that were taken in uncontrolled illumination conditions, but all faces in the images are frontal. The GBU database defines training sets in four different sizes. Here we used the "x8" set to train the LDA-IR and the smaller "x2" for training the UBM and the ISV subspace[3]. The GBU database provides three different face verification protocols: the Good, the Bad, and the Ugly protocol. In each protocol, models are enrolled using a single image (there exist several models per client), and pairs of probe images and models are defined, which are used to compute the *false acceptance rate* (FAR) and the *correct acceptance rate* (CAR) curves. To evaluate the results of two algorithms, the *receiver operating characteristic* (ROC) curves are compared and if a single number is required, the CAR at FAR=0.1% is reported [17]. Please note that more accurate algorithms produce higher CAR values.

3.2   The BANCA Database

The second database is the BANCA database [24]. Here we use its P protocol. The BANCA database includes medium resolution images taken under controlled and uncontrolled illumination conditions. The poses of the faces are near-frontal. The protocols of BANCA define three sets: a training set, a development set, and a test set. The training set is used to train the LDA-IR and ISV algorithms. The development and test sets are split up into images that are used for model enrollment, and probe images. Probes are compared to the enrolled models in order to compute scores.

The scores of the development set are used to compute a score threshold θ_{dev}, which is applied to the test set in order to compute the final verification result. In this paper, the threshold is set at the *equal error rate* (EER), i.e., where the FAR and the FRR[4] curves of the development set intersect. On the test set, the *half total error rate* (HTER) is reported:

$$\text{HTER}_{\text{test}}(\theta_{\text{dev}}) = \frac{\text{FAR}_{\text{test}}(\theta_{\text{dev}}) + \text{FRR}_{\text{test}}(\theta_{\text{dev}})}{2}. \qquad (1)$$

---

[3] Neither the LGBPHS nor the Gabor graphs algorithm needs a training phase.

[4] The *false rejection rate* (FRR) can be computed as 100% - CAR.

The EER$_{dev}$ and HTER$_{eval}$ measures are error measures. Hence, the better the algorithm performs, the lower the values are.

In contrast to the GBU protocols, BANCA provides several images per client to enroll the models. For enrollment using LGBPHS, the average histogram of the enrollment images is used, while for Gabor graphs and LDA-IR, all images are stored, and the maximum of the similarities of the probe image to all enrollment images is computed. For ISV, the features of all enrollment images are used to enroll the client specific ISV model.

4   Experiments

For a fair comparison of the algorithms in Section 2, we use the implementations in Bob for preprocessing, except for LDA-IR that defines its own preprocessing [19]. Further, facereclib and Bob were used throughout to compute the scores and generate the ROC curves and the EER/HTER results.

4.1   The Good, The Bad, and The Ugly

The ROC curves for the experiments on the GBU database are given in Figure 1, while the corresponding CARs at FAR=0.1% are reported in Table 1. Unsurprisingly, all algorithms work relatively well on the Good protocol, which is the most simple one. Noticeably, the ISV and LDA-IR algorithms, which made use of the training set, are better than the others, which did not. In contrast, on the Bad and Ugly protocols the algorithms perform much worse. Here, the

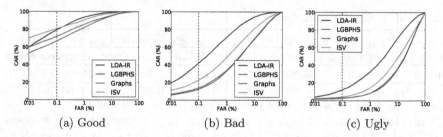

(a) Good   (b) Bad   (c) Ugly

Fig. 1. This figure shows ROC curves for the experiments on the GBU database, for (a) the Good, (b) the Bad, and (c) the Ugly protocol. The curves are displayed with a logarithmic FAR axis.

Table 1. This table details the resulting correct acceptance rates (CAR) at false acceptance rate (FAR) 0.1% on the GBU database

	LDA-IR	LGBPHS	Gabor graphs	ISV
Good	79.2%	66.6%	71.9%	80.5%
Bad	41.8%	12.3%	13.7%	22.5%
Ugly	12.3%	2.7%	3.1%	4.3%

LDA-IR algorithm works best, presumably since it is the only algorithm that uses a parametrization that is optimized for those protocols [19].

4.2 BANCA

The results on the BANCA database are reported in Table 2. Unlike on the GBU database, here the LDA-IR algorithm performs much worse than the other algorithms, which could be because the meta-parameters of LDA-IR are not optimized for this database, whereas, e. g., ISV was developed using BANCA in the initial work of [23]. Of the algorithms from Bob, ISV outperforms the LGBPHS and Gabor graphs slightly. Hence, in contrast to results on the GBU database, utilizing the training set of the BANCA database seems to give somewhat less of an advantage over the non-trained algorithms. It is also worth noting that ISV is the only one of the algorithms that is designed to make use of multiple enrollment images, which are used according to the BANCA protocol, in a principled way.

Table 2. This table presents the verification results of experiments performed on the BANCA database. It includes the equal error rates (EER) on the development set and the half total error rates (HTER) on the test set.

	LDA-IR	LGBPHS	Gabor graphs	ISV
EER	26.2%	13.2%	11.7%	10.0%
HTER	27.2%	16.1%	12.4%	10.9%

5 Conclusion

In this paper we have shown the capabilities of the Bob software library and its new satellite package facereclib to produce a fair comparison of open source face recognition systems. We used the facereclib to perform face verification experiments on the GBU and BANCA databases, using the unbiased protocols that are provided with them and implemented in Bob. It is important to note that interfaces to other image databases like FRGC [6], SCface [29], MOBIO [8], LFW [4], and AT&T [3] (to name only a few) including their fixed protocols are also available, and running experiments on these databases is as easy as changing one command line option.

In this paper, the facereclib was used to compute and compare results of three different face recognition algorithms implemented in Bob, as well as an algorithm implemented in another open source face recognition library that was integrated into the same experimental framework. The results of the algorithm comparison show that there is no one face recognition algorithm that outperforms all others, but rather that the results clearly depend on the image database and even on the protocol that is used. It also is beneficial to use meta-parameters that are optimized to a specific database. From the tested algorithms that are implemented in Bob, here the ISV algorithm performed the best overall, while both Gabor-based algorithms are approximately equal.

In this paper, we have not exhaustively shown the results of all of the face recognition algorithms that are implemented in Bob, for example we skipped the pure *eigenface* approach [30], the *Bayesian intrapersonal/extrapersonal classifier* [31,32], and *probabilistic LDA* (PLDA) [33]. Additionally, we have not tuned any parameter of any algorithm. Hence, the experiments performed in this paper surely provide a proof of concept and a good basis for observing initial trends, but they are not sufficient to judge the tested algorithms.

In future work, we will use facereclib to perform a deeper comparative analysis of algorithms that has never been done before and that is clearly needed. We will run the algorithms on more databases. We will also test different image preprocessing steps, different parameters, different feature comparison functions, and different combinations of features and algorithms. Furthermore, we will also test the impact of automatically detected faces, and the transferability of optimal parameters between image databases.

The results provided by this paper have successfully demonstrated the use of the proposed open source software framework facereclib to compare face recognition algorithms on standardized database protocols. Such a framework is critical to promote reproducible research and leads the way to deeper understanding of the state-of-the-art in this field into the future. For authors of other algorithms, Bob provides a platform to contribute new feature types, new face recognition algorithms, new database protocols, and other innovations to the face recognition community.

By the way: thanks to the facereclib and Bob, all experiments for this paper were designed, run, and evaluated in only three days.

Acknowledgements. The research leading to these results has received funding from the European Community's FP7 under grant agreements 238803 (BBfor2: bbfor2.net) and 284989 (BEAT: beat-eu.org). We want to thank the developers of Bob for their great work, and David S. Bolme for providing the source code of the CSU Face Recognition Resources.

References

1. Phillips, P., Rauss, P., Der, S.: FERET (face recognition technology) recognition algorithm development and test results. Technical report, Army Research Lab (1996)
2. Gao, W., Cao, B., Shan, S., Chen, X., Zhou, D., Zhang, X., Zhao, D.: The CAS-PEAL large-scale Chinese face database and baseline evaluations. IEEE Transactions on Systems, Man, and Cybernetics 38, 149–161 (2008)
3. AT&T Laboratories Cambridge: AT&T database of faces (2004),
   http://www.cl.cam.ac.uk/research/dtg/attarchive/facedatabase.html
4. Huang, G.B., Ramesh, M., Berg, T., Learned-Miller, E.: Labeled faces in the wild: A database for studying face recognition in unconstrained environments. Technical report, University of Massachusetts, Amherst (2007)

5. Phillips, P.J., Beveridge, J.R., Draper, B.A., Givens, G.H., O'Toole, A.J., Bolme, D.S., Dunlop, J.P., Lui, Y.M., Sahibzada, H., Weimer, S.: An introduction to the good, the bad, & the ugly face recognition challenge problem. In: Ninth IEEE International Conference on Automatic Face and Gesture Recognition, pp. 346–353 (2011)
6. Phillips, P., Flynn, P., Scruggs, T., Bowyer, K., Worek, W.: Preliminary face recognition grand challenge results. In: Proceedings of the 7th International Conference on Automatic Face and Gesture Recognition, pp. 15–24 (2006)
7. Messer, K., Matas, J., Kittler, J., Luettin, J., Maître, G.: XM2VTSDB: the extended M2VTS database. In: Proceedings of the Second International Conference on Audio- and Video-Based Biometric Person Authentication (1999)
8. McCool, C., Marcel, S., Hadid, A., Pietikainen, M., Matejka, P., Cernocky, J., Poh, N., Kittler, J., Larcher, A., Levy, C., Matrouf, D., Bonastre, J.F., Tresadern, P., Cootes, T.: Bi-modal person recognition on a mobile phone: using mobile phone data. In: IEEE ICME Workshop on Hot Topics in Mobile Multimedia (2012)
9. Tan, X., Chen, S., Zhang, Z.: Face recognition from a single image per person: A survey. Pattern Recognition 39, 1725–1745 (2006)
10. Serrano, Á., de Diego, I.M., Conde, C., Cabello, E.: Recent advances in face biometrics with Gabor wavelets: A review. Pattern Recognition Letters 31, 372–381 (2010)
11. Huang, D., Member, S., Shan, C., Ardabilian, M., Wang, Y., Chen, L.: Local binary patterns and its application to facial image analysis: A survey. IEEE Transactions on Systems Man and Cybernetics Part C Applications and Reviews 41, 765–781 (2011)
12. Jafri, R., Arabnia, H.R.: A survey of face recognition techniques. Journal of Information Processing Systems 5, 41–68 (2009)
13. Shen, L., Bai, L.: A review on Gabor wavelets for face recognition. Pattern Analysis and Applications 9, 273–292 (2006)
14. Beveridge, R., Bolme, D., Teixeira, M., Draper, B.: The CSU face identification evaluation system user's guide version 5.0. Technical report, Colorado State University (2003)
15. Blackburn, D., Bone, M., Phillips, P.: Face recognition vendor test 2000: evaluation report. Technical report, National Institute of Standards and Technology (2001)
16. Phillips, P., Grother, P., Micheals, R., Blackburn, D., Tabassi, E., Bone, M.: Face recognition vendor test 2002: evaluation report. Technical report, National Institute of Standards and Technology (2003)
17. Phillips, P., Scruggs, T., O'Toole, A., Flynn, P., Bowyer, K., Schott, C., Sharpe, M.: FRVT 2006 and ICE 2006 large-scale results. Technical report, National Institute of Standards and Technology (2007)
18. Anjos, A., Shafey, L.E., Wallace, R., Günther, M., McCool, C., Marcel, S.: Bob: a free signal processing and machine learning toolbox for researchers. In: 20th ACM Conference on Multimedia Systems. ACM Press (2012)
19. Beveridge, R., Bolme, D.S.: CSU Face Recognition Resources (2011), http://www.cs.colostate.edu/facerec/algorithms/baselines2011.php
20. Zhang, W., Shan, S., Gao, W., Chen, X., Zhang, H.: Local Gabor binary pattern histogram sequence (LGBPHS): A novel non-statistical model for face representation and recognition. In: IEEE International Conference on Computer Vision, vol. 1, pp. 786–791 (2005)
21. Wiskott, L., Fellous, J.M., Krüger, N., Malsburg, C.: Face recognition by elastic bunch graph matching. IEEE Transactions on Pattern Analysis and Machine Intelligence 19, 775–779 (1997)

22. Günther, M., Haufe, D., Würtz, R.P.: Face Recognition with Disparity Corrected Gabor Phase Differences. In: Villa, A.E.P., Duch, W., Érdi, P., Masulli, F., Palm, G. (eds.) ICANN 2012, Part I. LNCS, vol. 7552, pp. 411–418. Springer, Heidelberg (2012)
23. Wallace, R., McLareñ, M., McCool, C., Marcel, S.: Inter-session variability modelling and joint factor analysis for face authentication. In: International Joint Conference on Biometrics (2011)
24. Bailly-Baillière, E., Bengio, S., Bimbot, F., Hamouz, M., Kittler, J., Mariéthoz, J., Matas, J., Messer, K., Popovici, V., Porée, F., Ruiz, B., Thiran, J.P.: The BANCA Database and Evaluation Protocol. In: Kittler, J., Nixon, M.S. (eds.) AVBPA 2003. LNCS, vol. 2688, pp. 625–638. Springer, Heidelberg (2003)
25. Tan, X., Triggs, B.: Enhanced local texture feature sets for face recognition under difficult lighting conditions. IEEE Transactions on Image Processing 19, 1635–1650 (2010)
26. Ahonen, T., Hadid, A., Pietikäinen, M.: Face Recognition with Local Binary Patterns. In: Pajdla, T., Matas, J. (eds.) ECCV 2004, Part I. LNCS, vol. 3021, pp. 469–481. Springer, Heidelberg (2004)
27. Wallace, R., McLaren, M., McCool, C., Marcel, S.: Cross-pollination of normalisation techniques from speaker to face authentication using Gaussian mixture models. IEEE Transactions on Information Forensics and Security (2012)
28. Reynolds, D.A., Quatieri, T.F., Dunn, R.B.: Speaker verification using adapted Gaussian mixture models. Digital Signal Processing 10, 19–41 (2000)
29. Grgic, M., Delac, K., Grgic, S.: SCface - surveillance cameras face database. Multimedia Tools and Applications 51, 863–879 (2011)
30. Turk, M., Pentland, A.: Eigenfaces for recognition. Journal of Cognitive Neuroscience 3, 71–86 (1991)
31. Moghaddam, B., Wahid, W., Pentland, A.: Beyond eigenfaces: Probabilistic matching for face recognition. In: IEEE International Conference on Automatic Face and Gesture Recognition, pp. 30–35 (1998)
32. Günther, M., Würtz, R.P.: Face detection and recognition using maximum likelihood classifiers on Gabor graphs. International Journal of Pattern Recognition and Artificial Intelligence 23, 433–461 (2009)
33. Prince, S.J.D.: Probabilistic linear discriminant analysis for inferences about identity. In: Proceedings of the International Conference on Computer Vision (2007)

Adaptive Registration
for Occlusion Robust 3D Face Recognition

Nese Alyuz[1], Berk Gokberk[2], and Lale Akarun[1]

[1] Department of Computer Engineering, Boğaziçi University, Istanbul, Turkey,
{nese.alyuz,akarun}@boun.edu.tr
[2] Department of Electrical Engineering Mathematics and Computer Science,
University of Twente, The Netherlands,
b.gokberk@utwente.nl

Abstract. Occlusions over facial surfaces cause performance degradation for face registration and recognition systems. In this work, we propose an occlusion-resistant three-dimensional face registration method. First, the nose area is detected on a probe face using curvedness-weighted convex shape index map. Then, probable eye and mouth patches are detected and checked for validity. An adaptive model is constructed by selecting valid patches of the average face model. Finally, registration is handled with the Iterative Closest Point algorithm, where the adaptive model is used as the reference. The UMB-DB face database is used to evaluate the registration system: The nose detector has 100% and 93.90% accuracy, for the non-occluded and occluded images, respectively. A simple global depth-based recognition experiment is done to evaluate the registration performance: Our adaptive model-based registration scheme improves rank-1 recognition rate by 16%, when compared with the nose-based alignment approach.

Keywords: 3D face registration, regional face registration, face registration under occlusion.

1 Introduction

Face is a preferred biometric, due to its contactless acquisition and applicability to non-cooperative scenarios. Recent studies have shown that in the three-dimensional (3D) domain; challenges such as illumination and pose can be better handled. However, dealing with extreme occlusion variations remains a challenging task. When occlusions are present, 3D face registration algorithms fail to provide accurate facial point correspondences due to occluding surface points. The resulting alignment between facial surfaces is usually incorrect, leading to low recognition rates.

There are only a few studies dealing with the occluded 3D face recognition problem. In [1], a face recognition system composed of occlusion detection and restoration stages is proposed. However, experiments are conducted on synthetic occlusions. Initially, the non-occluded facial surfaces are registered using manually annotated landmark points, and then the artificial occlusions are added. In [2], a 3D face detection algorithm is proposed to deal with partially occluded faces where inner eye corners and the nose tip are detected based on curvature information. Then, a set of candidate triplets are

A. Fusiello et al. (Eds.): ECCV 2012 Ws/Demos, Part III, LNCS 7585, pp. 557–566, 2012.

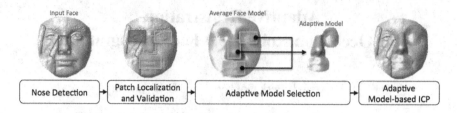

Fig. 1. Diagram of the proposed registration method

formed and registered to the average face using a variant of the ICP. In [3], an occlusion invariant 3D face recognizer is proposed, which employs a nose-based face registration. The nose region is first localized using curvature information and faces are then aligned to a generic nose model. Both in [2] and [3], registration is only dependent on the nasal area, which can be insufficient for a fine alignment. There are other studies regarding partial or regional matching of 3D surfaces: In [4], a partial ICP approach is proposed, in which a subset of nearest point pairs are utilized to calculate the alignment. In [5], a two phase registration scheme is implemented, where the faces are initially registered to a whole face model, and subsequently separate regional registrations are obtained. In [6], a similar regional approach is employed, where a large set of regional alignments are performed. In [7], a semi-rigid region composed of forehead and nose area is utilized for alignment. Although in [4–7] the aim is to improve the alignment, these methods are developed to deal with surface deformations caused by expression variations. Hence, they are not applicable to occlusion variations.

In this work, we propose an occlusion invariant 3D facial registration method. We handle registration by an adaptive model-based approach which assumes partial visibility of the nose. Prior to registration, nose detection is employed and is used to locate eye and mouth patches. Detected patches are then evaluated for their validity. The corresponding valid (occlusion-free) patches of the average face model are selected to construct an adaptive face model. ICP alignment with the adaptive model is able to discard the occluded surface points for point matching. Experiments on the UMB-DB [8] database, show that the adaptive registration attains better registration and identification accuracy under occlusion variations when compared to the nose-based scheme of [3].

2   Proposed Registration System

The proposed face registration system has three phases: (1) nose detection via curvature maps, providing an initialization for fine registration; (2) facial patch localization and validation to form an adaptive face model; (3) model based fine registration via ICP. The overall diagram of the system is given in Figure 1. Details about each phase are given in the following subsections.

2.1   Nose Detection

For rigid alignment of 3D surfaces, Iterative Closest Point (ICP) algorithm [9] is a widely used method. However, like many of the other iterative approaches, performance of ICP relies greatly on the initial conditions. Therefore, an initial alignment should be provided, which will be improved in further iterations. For the surface initialization, most of the 3D face recognition systems depend on accurate localization of facial landmark points [10], [11], [12]. However, when occlusions are present over the facial surface, localization of fiducial points fails. Since facial occlusions may occur over the nose area, our nose detector assumes partial visibility of the complete nose structure with the help of local nasal surface sub-patches (See Section 2.2 for further details).

The nose detection algorithm [3] utilizes surface curvature information, which provides an advantage due to its rotation and translation invariance. Two curvature maps are computed for a given surface, namely the shape index map and the curvedness map. These measures of the local surface, was introduced in [13], computed using the maximum (κ_{max}) and the minimum (κ_{min}) curvatures. The transformation separates components that are dependent or independent of scale [14]. Scale-independent components, such as shape index, provide the distinction between spherical and cylindrical surfaces. On the other hand, the scale-dependent components, such as curvedness, give the magnitude of the curvature. The shape index value $SI(i)$ at surface point i can be computed from κ_{max} and κ_{min}:

$$SI(i) = \frac{1}{2} - \frac{1}{\pi}tan^{-1}\frac{\kappa_{max}(i) + \kappa_{min}(i)}{\kappa_{max}(i) - \kappa_{min}(i)} \tag{1}$$

The shape index map SI takes values in $[0, 1]$ and provides a smooth transition between concave ($0 < SI(i) < 0.5$) and convex ($0.5 < SI(i) < 1$) shapes. As the scale-dependent counterpart of shape index, curvedness measures the rate of curvature at each point:

$$C(i) = \sqrt{\frac{\kappa_{min}(i)^2 + \kappa_{max}(i)^2}{2}}. \tag{2}$$

A planar surface will have a curvedness of zero, whereas a non-planar surface will have a curvedness value proportional to its rate of curvature. The nose detector first constructs shape index and curvedness maps. Since nose is a convex structure, the SI map is thresholded (by 0.5) to eliminate concave regions. The convex SI map, denoted as SI_{cx}, is defined as

$$SI_{cx}(i) = \begin{cases} 0 & \text{if } SI(i) < 0.5 \\ SI(i) & \text{otherwise.} \end{cases} \tag{3}$$

After concave regions are eliminated, SI_{cx} is weighted with curvedness [15] to integrate scale-dependent and scale-independent components:

$$WSI(i) = SI_{cx}(i) * C(i) \tag{4}$$

Here, WSI denotes the curvedness-weighted convex shape index. In Figure 2, the maps constructed at each step are given for an example facial image. The maps illustrated are: SI, SI_{cx}, C, and WSI.

As illustrated in Figure 2, the nose region appears as a distinct fork-shaped structure in the WSI map. To locate the nose area, template matching is employed. For the construction of the nose template, an average face model is created by the Thin Plate Spline

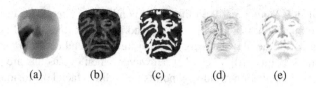

(a)   (b)   (c)   (d)   (e)

Fig. 2. Curvature maps utilized for nose detection are illustrated on an example image: (a) depth image, (b) shape index, (c) convex shape index, (d) curvedness, and (e) weighted convex shape index.

warping, where a set of registered non-occluded neutral training images are used [16]. Then, the average nose model is obtained by manually cropping the face model. The WSI map for the nose model is constructed to serve as the nose template. Given a test image, template matching is performed by normalized cross-correlation, and the region which mostly resembles the nose structure is located.

2.2 Patch Selection and Adaptive Registration

In [3], only local nose regions were considered for occlusion invariant registration. After nose detection, the probe surface was registered using an average nose-region model. However, this approach has shortcomings. Relying solely on the nasal region for the overall face alignment might be suboptimal; especially if the borders of the nose region are affected by occlusions. Additionally, any problems on the nose surface structure, either due to acquisition errors or uncommon nose shapes, may lead to inaccurate facial surface registration. Here, we propose to utilize an adaptive face model. The idea is to adaptively detect and include other non-occluded facial regions such as eyes and mouth automatically to form an adaptive face model for registration. For instance, if the left side of a face is occluded by a hand (See Figure 1), our adaptive face model will automatically be constructed using the non-occluded regions such as right eye, mouth and nose. Then, combined regional models are used for alignment estimation instead of using only the nasal region.

Using the detected location of the nose area, we find other patch locations. In Figure 3, the patch division scheme is shown on the first image. However, not all of the facial patches are beneficial for registration. Therefore, we use a subset of these patches. The patches we use are: nose, left/right eye, and mouth. We also have sub-patches such as left/right nose halves, upper/lower nose halves. Hierarchical division of patches into sub-patches enables us to discard regions where occlusion artifacts are present. To construct average patch models, initially an average face model is generated using the method of [16]. Afterwards, for each patch, an average patch model is constructed by cropping the average face model. From each model, the WSI map is computed to define the patch template. Using these templates, corresponding patch regions on a given face are detected via template matching based on normalized cross correlation. To limit the search space for the localization of each patch, we compute the probable patch center of a probe face using the relative displacements vectors between patch centers of the average face model. Additionally, a predefined bounding box around each patch center is utilized. Due to occlusions over the face, some patches will not be visible and cannot

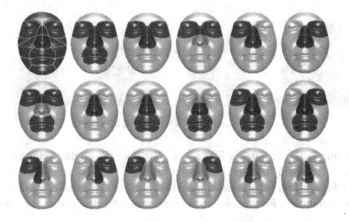

Fig. 3. Facial patches and the adaptive models utilized in registration are given. The first image shows the division scheme utilized for patch construction. To construct the adaptive models, combination of nose, eye, and mouth patches are considered.

be located correctly. Therefore, in order to determine the validity of each patch, thresholding is applied on template matching scores. The thresholds used for patch validity are calculated from patches of a separate non-occluded neutral database, namely the neutral subset of the FRGC v.2 [17]. The probe patches that have dissimilarity scores below the threshold define the valid parts. Here, the patch localization and validation steps are not used to detect patches of the probe face to be used in registration. The validity information of patches are only used for the model selection: The respective valid patches selected from the average face model to constitute the adaptive patch-based model for the respective probe face. In Figure 3, the 17 adaptive models utilized in the registration process are shown (the first image was included to show patch division scheme). After adaptive model construction, the whole probe surface is aligned to the adaptive model via ICP, where ICP estimates the alignment parameters using only the non-occluded regions. Hence, the overall registration approach becomes insensitive to occlusions.

3   Experimental Results

3.1   Databases

In our experiments, we have used two face databases: (1) The FRGCv2 [17], including non-occluded acquisitions; (2) The UMB-DB 3D database [8], including expression and large range of occlusion variations. The FRGCv2 is used for the construction of the average face and patch models, and for the determination of threshold values used for validity check over template matching scores. This database consists of 4007 scans and we use only the neutral faces (2365 scans of 466 subjects). The UMB-DB database is acquired from 142 subjects with a total of 1473 scans. The non-occluded acquisitions include four facial expressions. The number of non-occluded scans is 883, and 441 of

Fig. 4. Sample faces from the UMB-DB

these are neutral. The remaining 590 scans constitute the challenging occlusion subset. The occlusions can be caused by hair, eyeglasses, hands, hats, scarves, and other objects (see Figure 4 for images taken from [8] and Table 1 second column for the number of scan variations). For the occluded faces, ground truth occlusion masks are also available.

3.2 Nose Detection Accuracy

We have located nose regions automatically in the whole UMB-DB database and inspected the results visually. In Table 1, the number of correct detections are given in the third column. The nose regions in the non-occluded scans are successfully located. In the occluded subset, the nose detector obtains high performance with a detection performance of 93.90%. Our nose detector is quite robust to occlusions: In 245 of the 590 occluded images, the nose area was occluded and for 75% of the incorrectly detected 36 images, the nose area was more than 50% occluded. Even for the scarf occlusions, where the nose area is not visible, the detection rate is quite high (92.72%). In Figure 5, some detection examples of challenging occlusions are given. Our detection rates are similar to the face detection results provided in [8] (553 detections out of 590). We also applied our detection algorithm on the FRGCv2, where the nose areas are detected with 100% accuracy (by visual inspection) both on the neutral subset (2365 scans) and the non-neutral subset (1642 scans). As stated earlier, it is sufficient for us to detect the nose area approximately since the subsequent ICP registration handles fine registration using patch-based adaptive models.

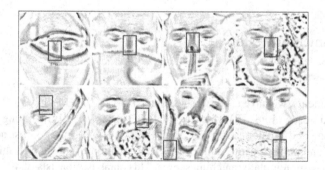

Fig. 5. Correct (first row) and incorrect (second row) nose detections.

Table 1. Nose detection performances on the UMB-DB database

Acquisition Type	Sample Count	Detected Noses (Detection Rates)
Neutral (Gallery)	142	142 (100.00%)
Neutral (Probe)	299	299 (100.00%)
Non-neutral	442	442 (100.00%)
Occlusion	590	554 (93.90%)
Occlusion Type		
Scarf	151	140 (92.72%)
Glasses	75	74 (98.67%)
Hair	33	27 (81.82%)
Hand	165	152 (92.12%)
Hat	183	181 (98.91%)
Other	38	33 (86.84%)

3.3 Patch Validation and Selection Accuracy

After nose detection, the patches of a probe face are estimated and checked for validity. Using validated patches, the corresponding model of the probe face is constructed adaptively. The thresholds used for patch validation are determined from the template matching scores of the FRGCv2 neutral subset. These thresholds are used to set patch validity flags of the UMB-DB scans. When the model selection results are analyzed, it is seen that in 77 out of 590 occlusion scans, the model selection is erroneous. In 36 of the 77 errors, the nose detection prior to patch validation fails. In the other 41 scans, some of the patches are selected incorrectly: These errors appear mostly in the mouth area.

3.4 Registration Accuracy

To evaluate the registration performance, we have constructed a simple recognition experiment. As facial features, we have used depth images: The depth images are obtained by resampling the surfaces from a regular grid, which enables sufficient computation of distances using only the z coordinates. To evaluate the performance of registration, ground truth masks are employed, where non-occluded parts are annotated for the UMB-DB occlusion variations. Using these masks, the occluding parts are discarded from the registered depth images. Then, a depth-based classifier is employed: the averaged l_1-norm between occlusion-removed probe and gallery depth images are computed and 1-nearest neighbor classification is performed. The identification experiment is conducted with three different registration approaches: (1) global face model-based ICP, as a baseline approach; (2) nose model-based ICP, which was previously used in [3]; and (3) the proposed adaptive model-based registration. In Table 2, recognition rates for the UMB-DB database are given in the columns labeled by "manual occlusion removal". The gallery set contains first neutral scan of each of the 142 subjects.

When the identification results (with manual occlusion removal) in Table 2 are analyzed, it is clear that using a larger model is beneficial for the non-occluded scans: For the neutral and non-neutral subsets, best performances are obtained when the whole face model is utilized. The adaptive model based registration has comparable results

Table 2. Identification performances on the UMB-DB database. The reported baseline identification accuracy for the occlusion subset of this database is 56.50% [8].

	Recognition Rates(%)			
Acquisition	Manual Occlusion Removal			Automatic Identification
Type	*Face Model*	*Nose Model*	*Adaptive Model*	*Adaptive Model*
Neutral (Probe)	98.66	88.63	97.32	96.99
Non-neutral	71.49	67.87	70.14	82.35
Occlusion	44.58	48.98	65.08	67.63
Occlusion Type				
Scarf	21.85	28.48	41.72	41.72
Glasses	84.00	64.00	80.00	88.00
Hair	54.55	48.48	66.67	66.67
Hand	16.36	32.12	58.79	63.64
Hat	63.40	73.77	83.61	81.42
Other	28.95	52.63	60.53	68.64

with the facial model, even though the adaptive model has at least 47.7% fewer surface points. This shows that the patch regions provide sufficient information for registration. It is also clear that the adaptive model based registration is superior to the face or nose model based ICP, when faces have occlusions. The face model based registration is not successful on occluded faces (44.58%). By comparing classification results, we clearly see the advantage of the adaptive model (65.08%) over the nose model (48.98%). Furthermore, analysis of performances for different occlusion types are included in Table 2. In most of the scarf occlusions, the lower half of the face including the nose area is occluded. Therefore using a face or a nose model cannot provide acceptable registration. However, for the adaptive approach, the valid eye patches are used and the identification rate is improved. In the hair, hand, and hat occlusions, the adaptive model is always better than face and nose model registrations. In comparison, the nose model covers a much smaller area, and is less prone to occlusions. However, even a small portion of an occlusion appearing in the nasal area will affect the final registration significantly. When valid eye and mouth regions are included in the model, alignment disruptions will be corrected. For the eyeglasses case, the registration scheme depending on a face model is slightly better than the adaptive method since glasses can sometimes invalidate the eye regions.

It should be stressed that depth-based identification performances with manually removed occlusions are only provided to indicate the relative standing of the registration approaches. A recognition approach based on a more advanced representation method is expected to give better recognition performance. We are continuing our studies to develop such an approach. However, we have obtained preliminary occlusion-invariant automatic classification results, where the adaptive model of the probe face is used to define the validity mask for classification. The respective valid points on the probe and gallery faces are then used to compute dissimilarity values. This system is automatic, since no manually labeled occlusion masks are considered. The identification rates of the fully automatic system are given in the last column of Table 2. It is clear that, for the neutral scans, it is beneficial to use the whole face. However, for non-neutral and occlusion scans, automatically defining valid regions and using them at the classification phase by the adaptive model is beneficial: It achieves even better identification rates

(67.32%) than by using manually removed occlusions (65.08%). Our automatic identification results are also better than the results presented in [8] where the PCA-based classifier attains 56.50% identification rate on restored faces after occlusion removal.

4 Conclusion

In this work, we have proposed a 3D face registration system which is robust to occlusions: For the experiments, we have used the challenging UMB-DB, which is reported to have a baseline identification accuracy of 56.50% [8]. Our experiments show that the adaptive model based registration is beneficial for occluded faces: Noses on the non-occluded scans can be detected with 100% accuracy, whereas for the occluded scans, the performance of the nose detector is still very high (93.90%). With an identification experiment, we have shown that, under extreme occlusions, face and nose model-based registrations fail. The proposed scheme, on the other hand, is able to cope with occlusions: The depth-based classifier on occlusion-removed faces shows an improvement of 16%: from 48.98% (nose model) to 65.08% (adaptive model). The preliminary automatic identification results show that it is beneficial to use the adaptive model regions for classification.

References

1. Colombo, A., Cusano, C., Schettini, R.: Three-dimensional occlusion detection and restoration of partially occluded faces. Journal of Mathematical Imaging and Vision 40, 105–119 (2011)
2. Colombo, A., Cusano, C., Schettini, R.: Gappy PCA Classification for Occlusion Tolerant 3D Face Detection. Journal of Mathematical Imaging and Vision 35, 193–207 (2009)
3. Alyuz, N., Gokberk, B., Spreeuwers, L., Veldhuis, R., Akarun, L.: Robust 3D Face Recognition in the Presence of Realistic Occlusions. In: International Conference on Biometrics (2012)
4. Wang, Y., Pan, G., Wu, Z., Wang, Y.: Exploring Facial Expression Effects in 3D Face Recognition Using Partial ICP. In: Narayanan, P.J., Nayar, S.K., Shum, H.-Y. (eds.) ACCV 2006, Part I. LNCS, vol. 3851, pp. 581–590. Springer, Heidelberg (2006)
5. Alyuz, N., Gokberk, B., Akarun, L.: A 3D face recognition system for expression and occlusion invariance. In: International Conference on Biometrics: Theory, Applications and Systems (BTAS), pp. 1–7 (2008)
6. Faltemier, T., Bowyer, K., Flynn, P.: A region ensemble for 3-D face recognition. IEEE Trans. on Information Forensics and Security 3, 62–73 (2008)
7. Al-Osaimi, F., Bennamoun, M., Mian, A.: An expression deformation approach to non-rigid 3D face recognition. International Journal of Computer Vision 81, 302–316 (2009)
8. Colombo, A., Cusano, C., Schettini, R.: UMB-DB: A Database of Partially Occluded 3D Faces. In: ICCV Workshops, pp. 2113–2119 (2011)
9. Besl, P.J., McKay, H.D.: A method for registration of 3D shapes. IEEE Trans. PAMI 14, 239–256 (1992)
10. Lu, X., Jain, A., Colbry, D.: Matching 2.5D face scans to 3D models. IEEE Trans. PAMI 28, 31–43 (2006)
11. Chang, K., Bowyer, W., Flynn, P.: Multiple nose region matching for 3D face recognition under varying facial expression. IEEE Trans. PAMI 28, 1695–1700 (2006)

12. Colombo, A., Cusano, C., Schettini, R.: 3D face detection using curvature analysis. Pattern Recogn 39, 444–455 (2006)
13. Koenderink, J., van Doorn, A.: Surface shape and curvature scales. Image and Vision Computing 10, 557–564 (1992)
14. Tittle, J., Perotti, V.: The perception of shape and curvedness from binocular stereopsis and structure from motion. Attention, Perception, & Psychophysics 59, 1167–1179 (1997)
15. Lo, T., Siebert, J.: Sift keypoint descriptors for range image analysis. In: Annals of the BMVA X, pp. 1–18 (2009)
16. Salah, A.A., Alyuz, N., Akarun, L.: Registration of 3D face scans with average face models. Journal of Electronic Imaging 17 (2008)
17. Phillips, P., Flynn, P., Scruggs, T., Bowyer, K., Chang, J., Hoffman, K., Marques, J., Min, J., Worek, W.: Overview of the face recognition grand challenge. In: CVPR, vol. 1, pp. 947–954 (2005)

Robust and Computationally Efficient Face Detection Using Gaussian Derivative Features of Higher Orders

John A. Ruiz-Hernandez[1], James L. Crowley[2], Claudine Combe[2], Augustin Lux[2], and Matti Pietikäinen[1]

[1] Center for Machine Vision Research - University of Oulu, Finland
{john.ruiz,matti.pietikainen}@ee.oulu.fi
[2] INRIA Grenoble-Rhône-Alpes Research Center, France
{james.crowley,claudine.combe,augustin.lux}@inria.fr

Abstract. In this paper, we show that a cascade of classifiers using Gaussian derivatives features up to fourth order can be used efficiently to improve the detection performance and robustness as well when compared with the popular approaches using Haar-like features or using Gaussian derivatives of lower order. We also present a new training method that structures the cascade detection so as to use the least expensive derivatives in the initial stages, so as to reduce the overall computational cost of detection. We demonstrate these improvements with experiments using two publicly available datasets (MIT+CMU and FDDB), in the face detection problem, in addition we perform several experiment to show the robustness of Gaussian derivatives when several transformations are presented in the image.

Keywords: Higher-Order Gaussian Derivatives, Cascade of Classifiers, Face Detection, Half-Octave Gaussian Pyramid.

1 Introduction

Improvements in the cascades of classifiers to deal with the constraints of speed and robustness can be performed in two different ways, optimizing the cascade learning algorithm or finding a more robust set of features. In this paper we propose a combination of these two techniques. In a first time, to address this limitation, we have explored the use of a cascade detector using Gaussian derivative features of higher order, computed in real time with a half-octave Gaussian pyramid [1] as was proposed by Ruiz-Hernandez et al. [2]. We have found that including derivative features up to the fourth order in the cascade can reduce the overall computational cost, while providing improved robustness to image plane rotation and as well as extend detection to lower resolution images. Gaussian derivative features also make it possible to structure the detection cascade in a manner that further reduces computational cost by using lower cost features in the lower levels of the cascade where the great majority of empty face sub-windows are rejected. We will take profit of this property to propose a new

A. Fusiello et al. (Eds.): ECCV 2012 Ws/Demos, Part III, LNCS 7585, pp. 567–577, 2012.

training algorithm that takes into account the computational cost of each derivative order.

1.1   Principal Contributions

- We propose a speed-optimized cascade framework which takes into account the computational complexity of Gaussian derivatives and the local appearance information provided by different derivative orders to select its adequate position in the cascade.
- Use of Gaussian derivatives up to the fourth order are considered in a cascade of classifiers. Despite its high sensitivity to noise, experiments show that inclusion of higher order derivatives improves detection rates.
- We propose a new metric to compute computational load based on the number of requests to the image representation which is more suitable for evaluating feature performance in face detection.
- We perform several experiments for comparing the performance between Gaussian derivative features and Haar-like features when the input image is modified by different transformations such as contrast, noise and rotation.

To present and develop our hypothesis, this paper is organized as follows: Related works and theoretical background are reviewed in Section 1.2. A cascade framework for training speed-optimized cascades of Gaussian derivatives features is presented in Section 2 and experimental results are presented in Sections 3. Section 4 closes the paper with some concluding remarks.

1.2   Related Work and Theoretical Background

In this section we provide review of previous works related with these paper. For a more comprehensive summary of works in face detection we refer the reader to [3] and recently to [4].

A number of researchers have recently proposed methods to improve detection speed by using different feature types in the same cascade. Meynet et al. [5] proposed a cascade in which the first five nodes were composed of Haar-like features followed by nodes composed of anisotropic Gaussian filters. Xiaohua et al. [6] have explored the use of Haar-like features in the first nodes followed by nodes computed using an approximation of Gabor filters computed from an integral image. Roy and Marcel [7] proposed Haar Local Binary Patterns and Yan et al. [8] Locally assembled Binary features. Ruiz-Hernandez et al. [2] proposed to use Gaussian derivatives features up to the second order with some promising results, nevertheless the the paper does not propose to use higher derivatives orders, in addition, there is no intention to find an optimization method that takes into account the computational cost of each derivative order or a large experimental protocol to show the performance of their approach. Despite the detection speed and robustness improvements in the approaches above mentioned, the use of multiple image representations to perform a single task can pose serious problems in embedded systems because of tight constraints on available memory and computing. Using a Gaussian Pyramid to compute Gaussian derivatives can avoid such problems by providing image features of increasing complexity from a single underlying image representation, besides Gaussian derivatives can be used as image representation in a complex processing pipeline for embedded facial analysis and biometrics systems.

1.3 Computational Cost of Cascade Classifiers

A quantitative measure for the run-time computational cost has been proposed by Brubaker et al. [9]. This measure, referred to as "Computation load", captures the computational cost for classifying a sub-window with the node, including the cost of features belonging to previous nodes.

$$E[T_i] = r_i \sum_{k=1}^{i} M_k \quad where \quad r_i = (i - p_i) \prod_{j=1}^{i-1} p_j \tag{1}$$

Where $E[T_i]$ is the expected computational load for an stage i in the cascade, M_k is the number of features in the node k, p_i is the fraction of sub-windows rejected by the node i and r_i is the fraction of the *decided sub-windows* in the node i.

Brubaker et al. [9] defined the *decided sub-windows* for a node i as the sub-windows that are not passed on to a following node, either because they have been rejected as non-face, or because they have been accepted as a face in the case of a terminal node.

1.4 Computational Cost with Different Types of Features

As shown in Equation 1 the computational load is calculated based in the number of features applied by layer. To extend this concept to compare cascades with different types of features, we propose to use the number of requests for features per mode R_k.

$$E[T_i] = r_i \sum_{k=1}^{i} R_k \tag{2}$$

A *request* is defined as a simple memory access made by the cascade to the image representation such as an integral image or a Half-Octave pyramid. Multiple requests may be necessaries to compute a simple feature in the node k of the cascade.

1.5 Gaussian Derivatives as a Feature Set

The choice of feature set has an important impact on detection rate as well as the scan speed of a cascade detector. We have explored a feature space composed by derivative orders up to four. Derivatives are computed at four different orientations $\theta = \{0, \pi/4, \pi/2, 3\pi/4\}$ in a 24×24 pixel window for all the real sample positions available in a Gaussian pyramid of three levels $\sigma = \left\{ \sqrt{2}, 2, 2\sqrt{2} \right\}$. In this way, a 24×24 pixel window gives rise to 8064 possible derivative features.

To test the performance of Gaussian derivatives features, we defined four different feature sets as shown in Table 1. We trained four cascades (one for each feature set) using the algorithms and the training set explained in preceding sections. Each cascade is composed of 21 nodes, except for the cascade trained with the feature set number 3 that has 22. For each trained cascade, we measure the node performance as the false negative rate in the validation set for each node in each cascade and we show the results in Figure 1, the experiment demonstrate that adding high-order Gaussian derivatives reduces the false negative rate for a given node during the training process. In this experiment, the false positive rate in the first three nodes is similar in all the feature sets and then for deeper nodes the inclusion of higher derivative orders dramatically improve the node-performances.

The node performance measure is useful because it directly compares the ability of each feature set to achieve the node-learning goal with a small number of features per node and number of nodes in the cascade.

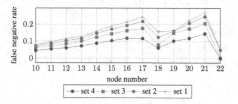

Fig. 1. Node performances for the four cascades trained with the feature sets shown in Table 1. The false negative error rate decreases as the derivative order rises, especially for deeper nodes in the cascade.

Table 1. Four different feature sets using different Gaussian derivative orders at pyramid levels of $\sigma = \left\{ \sqrt{2}, 2, 2\sqrt{2} \right\}$ and orientations $\theta = \left\{ 0, \pi/4, \pi/2, 3\pi/4 \right\}$

Feature Set ($\mathcal{F}_s$)	Derivative Orders	Total
$s = 1$	First Order	1792
$s = 2$	Up to the Second Order	4032
$s = 3$	Up to the Third Order	5824
$s = 4$	Up to the fourth Order	8064

2   Learning Speed-Optimized Cascades

In the preceding section, we have observed the effects of adding Gaussian derivative features up to fourth order in the cascade framework. We have observed that a strong improvement is obtained in the deeper nodes of the cascade. At the same time, higher order derivatives have a slightly higher computational cost. Thus lower computational cost, it appears reasonable to restrict higher order derivatives to deeper levels of the cascade. In this section we explore this hypothesis. Well structured derivatives with scale invariant impulse responses can be computed as sums and differences of adjacent pyramid samples [1]. In such a representation, first order features may be seen as responding to edge-like information, second order features to blob like structures, while higher order derivatives respond to more complex patterns of appearance. The cascade of classifiers framework can exploit such a representation by using less expensive lower order derivative to reject the large majority of empty windows in the lower levels of the cascade, and applying more expensive higher order derivatives in the deeper nodes.

From this hypothesis, we should expect that Gaussian derivatives features of lower order, less expensive derivative features will perform well in the first nodes when not much information is necessary to discriminate a face from non-face while the more expensive higher order features would be useful in deeper nodes where the difference between a face and a background image becomes more difficult to discriminate. The following experiments confirm this hypothesis. Our proposed optimization-framework is summarized in Algorithm 1.

Algorithm 1. The speed-optimized cascade framework

Giving a set of positive examples $\mathcal{P}$, a set of initial negative examples $\mathcal{N}$, a set of positive validation examples $\mathcal{V}$, a set of bootstrapping negative examples $\mathcal{D}$, a training learn goal $\mathcal{G}$, a training learn goal per layer $\mathcal{G}_\mathcal{L}$ and an ensemble of s feature sets $\mathcal{F} = (F_1, F_2, F_3....F_s)$, a value p which represents the desired starting position in the ensemble of feature sets ($p \leq s$);

output: The output is a cascade $H = (H_1, H_2, H_3, ..., H_n)$

initialization: $i \leftarrow 0, H \leftarrow 0$;

repeat

> $i \leftarrow i + 1$;
> *Node Learning* { Learn H_i using $\mathcal{P}$, $\mathcal{F}_p$ and $\mathcal{N}$, add H_i to H};
> Run the current node H_i on $\mathcal{V}$ to compute d_i;
> **while** $(d_i < \mathcal{G}_\mathcal{L}) \wedge (p < s)$ **do**
>> $p \leftarrow p + 1$;
>> *Node Learning* { Learn H_i using $\mathcal{P}$, $\mathcal{F}_p$ and $\mathcal{N}$, add H_i to H};
>> Run the current node H_i on $\mathcal{V}$ to compute d_i;
> **end**
> Remove correctly classified non-face patches from $\mathcal{N}$;
> Run the current cascade H on $\mathcal{D}$, add any false detection to $\mathcal{N}$ until $\mathcal{N}$ reaches the same size as the initial set.;

until *The learning goal $\mathcal{G}$ is satisfied*;

The Node-learning step is composed by two algorithms used in this paper to train the cascades :

- Adaboost [10] to find the best set of T features $\mathbf{h} = (h_1, h_2, \cdots, h_T)$ from a high dimensional feature set, giving this set of features, a feature vector for a training z sample can be build as $\mathbf{h}(\mathbf{z}) = (h_1(\mathbf{z}), h_2(\mathbf{z}), \cdots, h_T(\mathbf{z}))$
- LAC (Linear Asymmetric Classifier) [11] to provide an optimal linear strong classifier to accomplish node-learning, while providing the best trade-off between performance and computational cost, for further details please consult [11].

3   Experimental Results

3.1   Experimental Protocols

We performed several experiments to explore the performance of Gaussian derivatives for the face detection problem. Experiments were constructed to test sensitivity to image degradation, as well as performance with different data sets (MIT+CMU and FDDB) and variation in computational load of different feature sets.

Sensitivity Analysis: we constructed a data set to test sensitivity, where images from the LFW dataset [12] are degraded by rotation, blurring, additive Gaussian noise and contrast to evaluate the influence of such factors on detection rate. We applied all the cascades in our experiments to each image in the degraded dataset. For the transformation parameters, we record the detection rate over the set of images and the number of eventual false positives.

- **Rotation** Each image is rotated sequentially by an angle varying between -25 and +25 degrees with an steep of 3 degrees.
- **Blurring** : A Gaussian smoothing filter with scales ranging from 0 to 10 is applied to each image.
- **Noise**: Gaussian white noise with mean 0 and standard deviation between 0 and 0.2 is added to each image.
- **Contrast**: For each image, the pixel intensities I_p are modified as stated by $I_p = \alpha I_m + (1 - \alpha)I_p$, where I_m is the mean intensity of the image and α is a parameter varying from -2 to 1.0.

Comparative Results in Test Datasets: The performance of the cascade is commonly measured by a ROC (Receptive Operator Curve) calculated with an evaluation dataset. In all our experiments we resize the sliding window by a factor $s = 1.20$ which is a common value used in face detection benchmarks. Finally, we compare all our results with a cascade of Haar-like features to show the performance of our approach compared with the state-of-the-art methods using the FDDB [13] and the popular MIT+CMU [14] datasets.

The FDDB dataset is composed by 2845 images with a total of 5171 faces, which are organized in ten-fold testing sets. The implementation-software of the algorithms for matching detections and annotations in this dataset are publicly available[1]. From this software, a detection is scored taking into account $S(d_i, l_j) = {}^{area(l_j) \cap area(d_i)}/_{area(l_j) \cup area(d_i)}$ where d_i and l_j are the rectangle for the detected face and the rectangle of the ground truth respectively.

Two different types of ROC curves could be computed using the above mentioned score. The first one is the discrete score curve, where only the detection scores superior to 0.5 are used an the second is the continuous score curves where all the possible detections scores are included.

---

[1] http://vis-www.cs.umass.edu/fddb

3.2   Sensitivity Results

The results of experiments with the sensitivity test data set are shown in Figure 2.

The sensitivity to rotation can be observed in Figure 2a. In this case the cascade constructed with Gaussian derivatives outperforms that of Haar features. The detection rate for cascades of Gaussian derivatives is 100% for angles between -13 and +5 degrees and decreases significantly for larger rotations, while detection with Haar features is very sensitive to image plane rotation, maintaining a rate of 100% only for angles between -3 and +3 degrees. The number of false positives for this experiment was zero in all the cases.

The results of the influence of blurring are reported in Figure 2b. Notice that the detection rate remains 100% for blurring noise with a standard deviation of 8.3 and decreases slowly for larger standard deviations. The cascade of Haar features maintains a detection rate of 100% only out to standard deviations of 5 and then rapidly decreases. Thus we can conclude that Gaussian derivatives are less sensitive to image blur. No false positive were observed in this experiment.

Tolerance to contrast is reported in Figure 2c. Cascades of Gaussian derivatives and Haar-features cascade provide similar sensitivity, with a slight improvement for Haar-features. In this experiment, no normalisation to illumination was performed. However, subsequent experiments using illumination normalization showed no noticeable improvements.

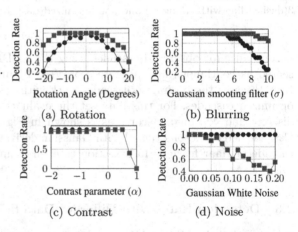

(a) Rotation

(b) Blurring

(c) Contrast

(d) Noise

Fig. 2. Results of comparing a non-optimized cascade of Gaussian derivatives (squares) with a cascade of Haar features (circles) in the sensitivity testing dataset.

The influence of additive image noise is reported in Figure 2d. In this case, the cascade of Haar features outperforms Gaussian Derivatives, maintaining a 100% of detection rate (no false positive) for all the standard deviation values used in the Gaussian noise, compared with the cascade of Gaussian derivatives that maintains 100% of detection rate only for values lower than 0.028 (one false positive for a value of 0.06) and decreases slowly as the noise increases. This results can be explained by the sensitivity to noise of third and fourth order Gaussian derivatives.

For most of data sets tested, Gaussian derivatives out-perform Haar-like features in detection rate. For example, Figure 3 shows results of detection

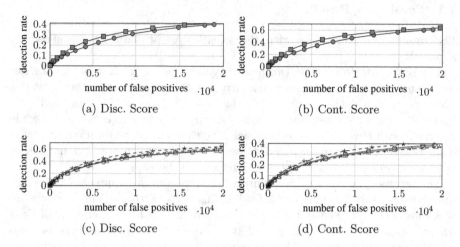

(a) Disc. Score

(b) Cont. Score

(c) Disc. Score

(d) Cont. Score

Fig. 3. ((a) and (b)) Performance comparison of a non-optimized cascades of Gaussian derivatives features (squares) with a Haar-features cascade (circles) in the FDDB face dataset. ((c) and (d)) Performance comparison of speed-optimized cascades of Gaussian derivatives features in the FDDB face dataset ($p = 1$(squares), $p = 2$(circles), $p = 3$(dashed line with triangles) and non-optimized(dashed line with stars)).

performance for optimized cascades using the FDDB data set. Results are presented as continuous and discrete scores(see Figures 3c and 3d respectively). In both cases the optimized cascades work with a similar performance as non-optimized cascades. For this data set the evaluation was performed using the discrete and continuous scores as is shown in Figures 3a and 3b respectively. Cascade detectors constructed with Gaussian derivative features outperform the cascade of Haar features in detection rate (area under the ROC) by almost a 8%.

3.3 Detection Rates with Different Data Sets

Results using the MIT+CMU face data are shown in Table 2. In this case, the Haar-like features perform better than Gaussian derivatives. We believe that this reflects the conditions under which this data set has been constructed. The MIT+CMU face data set is composed of many images that were scanned from newspapers, thereby introducing high levels of additive noise from both the rendering process used in newspapers. In addition, aliasing is apparent in some images due to a low-quality scanning process. Such noise is not characteristic of that obtained with modern digital cameras. Aliasing is rarely seen with digital cameras, because digital cameras almost always use intentional blurring in front of the CCD to avoid aliasing, finally, some of the facial images in this dataset are draws of faces without any textural information, such kind of images could be considered as a false positive in any biometric or security system.

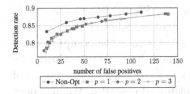

Fig. 4. ROC's of optimized-speed cascades of Gaussian derivatives features in the CMU+MIT face dataset

Table 2. A comparison of detection rates on the CMU+MIT data set for several standard detectors

Method	False Positives								
	6	10	31	46	50	65	78	95	167
Garcia and Delakis [15]	-	0.905	0.915	-	-	0.923	-	-	0.931
Li and Zhang [16]	-	0.836	0.902	-	-	-	-	-	-
Luo [17]	0.866	0.874	0.903	-	0.911	-	-	-	-
Viola and Jones [18]	-	0.783	0.852	-	0.888	0.898	0.901	0.908	0.918
Wu et al [11]	-	-	0.906	0.915	0.917	0.920	0.923	0.926	0.933
Gaussian Derivatives	-	0.833	0.859	0.869	0.870	0.874	0.878	0.883	0.906

3.4 Results on Test Data Sets (Optimized)

In Figure 4, we present the results of performance using the MIT+CMU face data set, as we can see, the cascades trained using the speed optimized framework continues to operate satisfactorily compared with the non-optimized cascades, in terms of detection rate and false positive rate.

3.5 Results on Computational Load (Optimized)

Figure 5 shows the results of measurement of computational load for the speed-optimized cascades using the FDDB dataset. In all cases, despite the similar number of feature requests made to the pyramid (see Figure 5e), the optimized

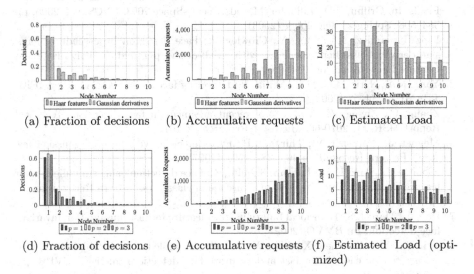

(a) Fraction of decisions   (b) Accumulative requests   (c) Estimated Load

(d) Fraction of decisions   (e) Accumulative requests   (f) Estimated Load (optimized)

Fig. 5. (c) Computational Load comparison between a cascade of Haar features and a non-optimized cascade of Gaussian derivatives. The estimated load in a cascade with Gaussian is reduced, specially in the first nodes. (f) Computational Load comparisons in the optimized-cascade framework for different values of p

cascades increase the number of decisions taken (see Figure 5d), especially in earlier nodes where the number of sub-windows to visit is higher and the number of features is lower. This experiment also demonstrates that the computational load for the optimized cascades is decreased by almost half compared with the non-optimized cascades (see Figure 5f). Thus we can expect a gain of a factor of two in detection speed compared with the non-optimized cascades. We also note that a decrease in the number of nodes necessary to accomplish learning for the optimized cascades trained using $p = 2$.

4   Conclusions

In this paper, we have reported results with experiments with the use of Gaussian derivatives features to detect faces in images. We have shown that Gaussian derivatives outperform in more realistic data sets as the FDDB face data set where the images are similar to these produced by the digital cameras used in mobile telephones and devices. In addition, we have demonstrated the robustness of detection using Gaussian derivatives features to image variations as rotation, blurring, noise and contrast using the sensitivity test data set. We have compared all of our results with these obtained with a cascade of Haar features.

References

1. Crowley, J.L., Riff, O.: Fast Computation of Scale Normalised Gaussian Receptive Fields. In: Griffin, L.D., Lillholm, M. (eds.) Scale-Space 2003. LNCS, vol. 2695, pp. 584–598. Springer, Heidelberg (2003)
2. Ruiz-Hernandez, J.A., Lux, A., Crowley, J.: Face detection by cascade of gaussian derivates classifiers calculated with a half-octave pyramid. In: IEEE Face and Gesture Recognition, pp. 1–6 (2008)
3. Yang, M.H., Kriegman, D.J., Ahuja, N.: Detecting faces in images: A survey. IEEE TPAMI 24, 34–58 (2002)
4. Zhang, C., Zhang, Z.: A survey of recent advances in face detection. Technical Report MSR-TR-2010-66, Microsoft Research (2010)
5. Meynet, J., Popovici, V., Thiran, J.P.: Face detection with boosted gaussian features. Pattern Recognition 40, 2283–2291 (2007)
6. Xiaohua, L., Lam, K.M., Lansun, S., Jiliu, Z.: Face detection using simplified gabor features and hierarchical regions in a cascade of classifiers. Pattern Recognition 30, 717–728 (2009)
7. Roy, A., Marcel, S.: Haar local binary pattern feature for fast illumination invariant face detection. In: BMVC (2009)
8. Yan, S., Shan, S., Chen, X., Gao, W.: Locally assembled binary (lab) feature with feature-centric cascade for fast and accurate face detection. In: IEEE CVPR, pp. 1–7 (2008)
9. Brubaker, S.C., Wu, J., Sun, J., Mullin, M.D., Rehg, J.M.: On the design of cascades of boosted ensembles for face detection. IJCV 77, 65–86 (2008)
10. Freund, Y., Schapire, R.E.: A decision-theoretic generalization of on-line learning and an application to boosting. J. Comput. Syst. Sci. 55, 119–139 (1997)

11. Wu, J., Brubaker, S., Mullin, M., Rehg, J.: Fast asymmetric learning for cascade face detection. IEEE TPAMI 30, 369–382 (2008)
12. Huang, G.B., Ramesh, M., Berg, T., Learned-Miller, E.: Labeled faces in the wild: A database for studying face recognition in unconstrained environments. Technical Report 07-49, University of Massachusetts, Amherst (2007)
13. Jain, V., Learned-Miller, E.: Fddb: A benchmark for face detection in unconstrained settings. Technical Report UM-CS-2010-009, University of Massachusetts, Amherst (2010)
14. Rowley, H., Baluja, S., Kanade, T.: Rotation invariant neural network-based face detection. In: IEEE CVPR (1998)
15. Garcia, C., Delakis, M.: Convolutional face finder: A neural architecture for fast and robust face detection. IEEE TPAMI 26, 1408–1423 (2004)
16. Li, S.Z., Zhang, Z.: Floatboost learning and statistical face detection. IEEE TPAMI 26, 1112–1123 (2004)
17. Luo, H.: Optimization design of cascaded classifiers. In: IEEE CVPR, pp. 480–485 (2005)
18. Viola, P., Jones, M.J.: Robust real-time face detection. IJCV 57, 137–154 (2004)

Multi-view Facial Expression Recognition Analysis with Generic Sparse Coding Feature

Usman Tariq[1], Jianchao Yang[1,2], and Thomas S. Huang[1]

[1] Department of Electrical and Computer Engineering,
Coordinated Science Laboratory,
and Beckman Institute for Advanced Science and Technology,
University of Illinois at Urbana-Champaign, Urbana, IL 61801, USA
[2] Adobe Systems Incorporated, San Jose, CA 95110, USA
{utariq2,jyang29,huang}@ifp.illinois.edu
http://www.illinois.edu, http://www.adobe.com

Abstract. Expression recognition from non-frontal faces is a challenging research area with growing interest. This paper works with a generic sparse coding feature, inspired from object recognition, for multi-view facial expression recognition. Our extensive experiments on face images with seven pan angles and five tilt angles, rendered from the BU-3DFE database, achieve state-of-the-art results. We achieve a recognition rate of 69.1% on all images with four expression intensity levels, and a recognition performance of 76.1% on images with the strongest expression intensity. We then also present detailed analysis of the variations in expression recognition performance for various pose changes.

1 Introduction

The increasing applications of facial expression recognition, especially those in Human Computer Interaction, have attracted a great amount of research work in this area in the past decade. However, much of the literature focuses on expression recognition from frontal or near-frontal face images [1, 2]. Expression recognition from non-frontal faces is much more challenging. It is also of more practical utility, since it is not trivial in real applications to always have a frontal face. Nonetheless, there are only a handful of works in the literature working with non-frontal faces. There has been experimental evidence in both face recognition and Psychology that non-frontal faces may achieve better recognition performance than frontal ones [2–4]. However, there has not been much effort on a detailed analysis of the effect of large pose variations (both pan and tilt angles) on the expression recognition performance. This paper, apart from achieving state-of-the-art results, also attempts to fill in these gaps.

1.1 Related Works

Most existing works focus on recognizing six basic expressions that are universal and recognizable across different cultures. These include anger (AN), fear (FE), disgust

A. Fusiello et al. (Eds.): ECCV 2012 Ws/Demos, Part III, LNCS 7585, pp. 578–588, 2012.

(DI), sad (SA), happy (HA) and surprise (SU) [2]. Some of the notable works in expression recognition focusing on frontal or near-frontal faces include [5–13]. For a comprehensive survey of the works in expression recognition please refer to [1] and [14]. In the following, we shall briefly review the papers that concentrate on non-frontal view facial expression recognition.

The works on non-frontal view expression recognition can be classified based upon the types of features employed. Some works use geometric features, e.g., Hu et al. [15] and Rudovic et al. [16, 17] use displacement or mapping of manually labeled key points to the neutral or frontal face views of the same subject. Whereas, some researchers extract various low-level features (e.g., SIFT) on pre-labeled landmark points and use them for further processing [2]. Some of such works include those by Hu et al. [18] and Zheng et al. [19].

Note that the aforementioned approaches require the facial key-points location information, which needs to be pre-labeled. However, in real applications, key-points need to be automatically detected, which is a big challenge itself in the case of non-frontal faces. To address this issue, there have been some attempts which do not require key-point locations; they rather extract dense features on detected faces[1]. The prominent examples in this category include works by Moore and Bowden [20, 21], Zheng et al. [22] and Tang et al. [23]. Moore and Bowden [20, 21] extract LBP features and its variants from non-overlapping patches. While, Zheng et al. [22] and Tang et al. [23] extract dense SIFT features on overlapping image patches. Zheng et al. [22] use regional covariance matrices for the image-level representation. Tang et al. [23], after dense feature extraction, represent the images with super vectors which are learnt based on ergodic hidden markov models (HMM).

It is worthwhile to mention that the BU3D-FE database [24] has become the de-facto standard for works in this area. Many works use five pan angle views rendered from the database (0°, 30°, 45°, 60° and 90°) [15, 18–21]. However, in real-world situations, we have variations in both pan and tilt angles. Thus, in more recent works [22, 23], people are working with a range of both pan and tilt angles.

Unlike many previous works, our work neither requires key-point localization nor needs a neutral face. We work with 35 views rendered from the BU-3DFE database (combination from 7 pan angles and 5 tilt angles). Unlike [22] and [23], we use all the four expression intensity levels. This work beats the state-of-the-art performance in the same experimental setting as [22] and [23]. Apart from performing better, it also does a significant analysis on the effect of pose and intensity variations on expression recognition results. To our best knowledge, such analysis has not been done before in the literature for such a wide range of pan and tilt angle views. This gives valuable insights to the the multi-view expression recognition problem.

In the following, we first describe the BU-3DFE database used in this work in Section 2. Then we present the generic sparse coding feature from object recognition in Section 3. Multi-view expression recognition experiments are conducted in Section 4. And we present detailed discussions of the results in Section 5. Finally, Section 6 concludes our paper.

---

[1] Extraction of dense features essentially implies computing features on an entire image region from overlapping or non-overlapping image patches.

2 Database

The database used in this work is the publicly available BU3D-FE database [24]. It has 3D face scan and associated texture images of 100 subjects, each performing 6 expressions at four intensity levels. The facial expressions presented in this database include anger (AN), disgust (DI), fear (FE), happy (HA), sad (SA) and surprise (SU). Each subject also has a neutral face scan. Thus, there are a total of 2500 3D faces. The dataset is quite diverse and contains subjects of both gender with various races. Interested readers are referred to [24] for further details.

We used an openGL based tool from the database creators to render multiple views. We generated views with seven pan angles ($0°$, $±15°$, $±30°$, $±45°$) and five tilt angles ($0°$, $±15°$, $±30°$). These views were generated for each subject with 6 expressions and 4 intensity levels, resulting in an image dataset with $5 \times 7 \times \times 6 \times 4 \times 100 = 84000$ images. Some sample images of a subject in various pan and tilt angles are shown in Figure 1.

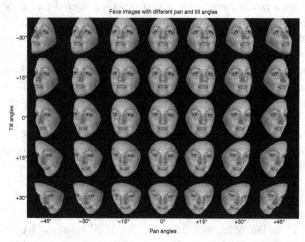

Fig. 1. Rendered facial images of a subject with various pan and tilt angles

3 The Generic Sparse Coding Feature

Recently, much progress has been made in learning mid-level feature representations for image classification [25–28]. These approaches typically follow a common pipeline that consists of three computational modules:

1. *Local feature extraction*: Local descriptors (e.g., raw patches, SIFT or HOG) are extracted from image patches densely sampled from the image to capture the local statistics.
2. *Descriptor encoding*: Each local descriptor is transformed into some code with desired properties (e.g., hard or soft vector quantization [28], LLC [27] or sparse coding [26]), such as compactness, sparseness, or statistical independence.

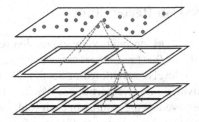

Fig. 2. Spatial pyramid structure for representing the image

3. *Spatial feature pooling*: The codes are then pooled (e.g., averaging [25] or taking the maximum [26, 27]) over different spatial locations across multiple spatial scales to obtain the image level feature representation.

With these mid-level feature representations, state-of-the-art recognition performances have been reported in object recognition and scene classification tasks on benchmark datasets, such as Caltech-101 [29], Caltech-256 [30] and Scene 15 [25]. In this work, we follow the line of mid-level feature learning and apply the image categorization technique for multiple view facial expression analysis. Specifically, we follow the ScSPM work [26] for building the facial image feature representation by max pooling the sparse codes of the local descriptors in a spatial pyramid. The following briefly describes the procedure for building feature representation based on sparse coding.

First, we densely extract local descriptors from the image, and represent the image as sets of local descriptors in a three level spatial pyramid $\mathbf{X} = \left[X_{11}^0, X_{11}^1, X_{12}^1, ..., Y_{44}^2\right]$, where X_{ij}^s is a matrix containing local descriptors from the (i, j)-th spatial block in the s-th spatial scale. As shown in Figure 2, on the s-th image spatial scale, there are 2^s evenly divided spatial blocks in total. Given the dictionary D offline trained [31] from randomly sampled descriptors, we encode the local descriptors into sparse codes by

$$\hat{Z}_{ij}^s = \arg\min_Z \|X_{ij}^s - DZ\|_2^2 + \lambda \|Z\|_1, \tag{1}$$

where the ℓ^1-norm enforces sparsity of the representation and λ controls the sparsity penalty. After encoding all local descriptors into sparse codes, we can similarly represent these sparse codes in the spatial pyramid $\mathbf{S} = \left[\hat{Z}_{11}^0, \hat{Z}_{11}^1, \hat{Z}_{12}^1, ..., \hat{Z}_{44}^2\right]$. The final feature representation is obtained by max pooling over the sparse codes in each spatial block across different spatial scales, i.e.,

$$\beta = \left[\beta_{ij}^s\right], \quad \beta_{ij}^s = \max(|\hat{Z}_{ij}^s|), \tag{2}$$

where β is a concatenation of β_{ij}^s over all (i, j, s) and the "max" operation is performed over each row of $\hat{Z}_{ij}^s$. As shown in [26], max pooling in conjunction with sparse coding works well with linear classifiers, achieving surprisingly good results on image classification tasks. The framework is also backed up by biophysical evidences in the visual cortex (V1) [32].

4 Multi-view Expression Recognition

In this section we detail our work on multi-view expression recognition. We conduct extensive experiments on the 84,000 face images extracted from the BU-3DFE database in 35 views with 4 intensity levels (as outlined in Section 2). The 100 subjects in the database, are randomly divided into five partitions. We do 5-fold cross validation on the 84,000 images and then average the results. In each fold, images from four subject partitions (80% subjects) are used as training and images from the remaining partition (20% subjects) are used as testing. Thus we ensure that the training and testing datasets do not simultaneously contain images from the same subject. We first extract dense SIFT features from images on a regular grid with step size of 3 pixels in both horizontal and vertical directions. Then a randomly sampled subset of these SIFT features is used to train the dictionary, $\mathbf{D} \in \mathbb{R}^{128 \times 1024}$. This dictionary is then used to sparsely encode the SIFT features extracted from each image, from which max pooling is applied to obtain the image-level representation.

We choose to adopt a 'universal' approach for classification, as in [22] and [23]. For such an approach, in essence, the classifier is trained on the entire training set with all the poses. Thus the 'universal' approach does not require a pose detection step in testing. This not only saves computation but also avoids possible pose estimation errors. We used linear SVM [33] as the classifier. Its computational complexity is $O(n)$ in training and constant in testing. Thus, it can scale up well with large scale datasets.

The overall recognition accuracy for 5-fold cross-validation, averaged across all the subjects, expressions, intensity levels and poses, comes out to be **69.1%**. The respective class confusion matrix is shown in Table 1. The effect of varying expression intensities on expression recognition, averaged for all the poses is plotted in Figure 3. The effects of variations in pan and tilt angles on expression recognition performance are shown in Figure 4. Similarly the effects of variations in pan and tilt angles for various expression intensity levels are shown in Figure 5. Figure 6, on the other hand, shows the effect of the simultaneous variations of pan and tilt angles on the average recognition performance.

Note that no other previous work in the literature experimented with all the expression intensity levels and all the subjects for the aforementioned pan and tilt angles.

Table 1. Classification confusion matrix for over-all recognition performance averaged over all poses and expression intensity levels

Overall classification		Predicted					
		AN	DI	FE	HA	SA	SU
Ground Truth	AN	**64.2**	8.4	4.1	2.2	18.1	3.1
	DI	10.9	**70.1**	5.8	3.9	5.2	4.3
	FE	7.5	9.5	**51.1**	13.7	9.5	8.7
	HA	2.1	4.3	9.4	**81.2**	1.7	1.4
	SA	19.6	5.2	7.2	2.3	**63.4**	2.3
	SU	1.8	3.0	4.7	3.0	2.6	**85.0**

Table 2. Performance comparison with previous works on the strongest expression intensity

Zheng et al [22]	Tang et al. [23]	Ours
68.2%	75.3%	**76.1%**

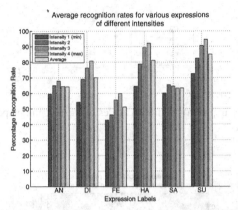

Fig. 3. Recognition performance for various expressions with different intensities

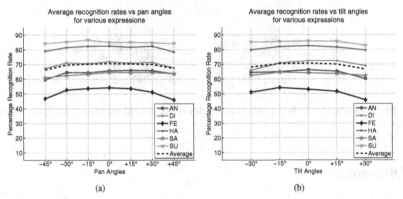

| (a) | (b) |

Fig. 4. Effects of changes in pan (a) and tilt (b) angles on the recognition performance of various expressions

Zheng et al. [22] and Tang et al. [23] follow the same experimental setting of 5-fold cross validation with the same set of pan and tilt angle views, but only focus on the strongest expression intensity level. Hence their image dataset consists of 21,000 images. To fairly compare the performance of this work to those of [22] and [23], we repeat the experiments on the strongest expression intensity level. The comparison of our results with those of [22] and [23] is given in Table 2.

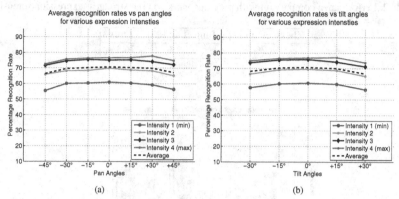

(a)   (b)

Fig. 5. Effects of changes in pan (a) and tilt (b) angles on the recognition performance of various expression intensity levels

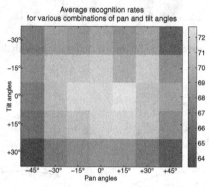

Fig. 6. Effects of changes in both pan and tilt angles on the overall expression recognition performance

5   Discussions

Our work with multi-view expression recognition shows promising results compared to the other state-of-the-art works. Unlike [22] and [23], we experiment with all the four expression intensity levels, which is harder compared to working with just the strongest expression intensity level. This can also be observed from Figures 3 and 5 that the most subtle expressions are the most difficult ones to recognize.

We intend to address a series of questions in this work. For instance, we consider whether the recognition performance is affected in the same manner across different expressions with change in their intensity level. Please refer to Figure 3 for this purpose. It displays the recognition rates for various expressions of different intensities, averaged across all the pan and tilt angle views. It can be observed that the recognition performance of the disgust (DI), fear (FE), happy (HA) and surprise (SU) expressions increases with the increase of expression intensity levels. However, this trend is not strictly followed for the anger (AN) and sad (SA) expressions. Note that the variations in the recognition performance from the least intense (level 1) to the most intense (level 4) anger and sad expressions is much smaller compared to the other expressions. This may stem from the reason that it may be harder for the subjects to display such expressions in varying intensity levels.

Another point to analyze is how does the variation in pan or tilt angles affects the recognition performance. Please consider Figures 4 and 5 for this purpose. Note that here, the results are averaged across the all the intensity levels, across corresponding tilt angles in Figure 4(a) and across the respective pan angles in Figure 4(b); similarly, the recognition rates are averaged across all the expressions, across corresponding tilt angles in Figure 5(a) and across the respective pan angles in Figure 5(b). One may note that, the average expression recognition performance has its maximum value on $0°$ pan or tilt angle. There is a slight performance drop up till $\pm30°$ pan angle (Figures 4(a) and 5(a)) and beyond that the performance drop is more significant. Similarly the average performance drop beyond $\pm15°$ tilt angle (Figures 4(b) and 5(b)) is more significant. Thus, the frontal and near-frontal views give better average recognition performance.

Then we can ask how do individual expressions respond to change in pan or tilt angles. In Figure 4, one can observe that there are three 'clusters' of curves. The first cluster has only the fear expression performance. It is significantly worse compared to the other expressions for all the variations in pose (in pan or tilt angles). This may be due to greater variation in expressing fear amongst the subjects. The other group of curves giving similar performance are for disgust, anger and sad expressions. And the group of curves giving the best performance is for the happy and surprise expressions. One can note from these figures that the negative expressions (fear, anger, disgust, sad) perform significantly worse than the positive ones, for all the variations in pan and tilt angles. One can also make some interesting observations from the variation in tilt angles in Figure 4(b). For instance, for the fear and anger expressions, $-30°$ tilt angle view give better performance compared to $+30°$ tilt angle view. For the disgust expression, however, the positive tilt angle views give better performance compared to the negative tilt angle views. For the other expressions, the trend is approximately symmetric.

We can also analyze the effect of change in pan and tilt angles on individual intensity levels. One can notice from Figure 5 that the curves for the four intensity levels are more or less parallel, meaning thereby that the individual intensities are affected more or less similarly with the change in pan or tilt angles. The two strongest expression intensity levels perform significantly better than the other two, for all the pan or tilt angle variations. However, in real life situations, the expressions are subtle, in general, thus posing a harder research problem for recognition. The third strongest expression intensity still performs significantly better than the most subtle expression intensity level. The expression intensities, in general, achieve a maximum recognition rate at $0°$ pan or tilt angle. There is also a significant performance dip at pose angles beyond $\pm30°$ pan or $\pm15°$ tilt, for all the expression intensities.

Similarly, to address the variation of both pan and tilt angles on average recognition performance please refer to Figure 6. Please note that each 'box' in this figure, gives the average recognition performance of 2400 images in the corresponding pan and tilt angle view combination. Also note that there is a significant performance decrease beyond $\pm30°$ pan and $\pm15°$ tilt angle view. Other than that, the performance seems more or less comparable (in the middle). The view with $15°$ pan and $0°$ tilt gives the best performance. However, it is very close to the frontal view performance.

6   Concluding Remarks

Our work sets a new state-of-the-art for multi-view facial expression recognition on the BU3D-FE database. We also provide a detailed analysis of variations in expression recognition performance with changes in a range of pan angles, tilt angles and both. Such an in-depth analysis is the first of its kind with such a wide range of pan and tilt angle variations. This can aid in designing various expression recognition systems. Also, unlike many other works, the approach used in this work neither requires any key point detection nor does it need a neutral face, and thus is more suitable for practical purposes.

Acknowledgments. This work was partly supported by Intel under the Avascholar project of the Illinois-Intel Parallelism Center (I2PC), by the Project from committee on science and technology of Chongqing (Grant No. cstc2011ggC0042) and by a research grant from Cisco.

References

1. Zeng, Z., Pantic, M., Roisman, G.I., Huang, T.S.: A survey of affect recognition methods: Audio, visual, and spontaneous expressions. IEEE Transactions on Pattern Analysis and Machine Intelligence 31, 39–58 (2009)
2. Zheng, W., Tang, H., Huang, T.S.: Emotion recognition from non-frontal facial images. In: Konar, A., Chakraborty, A. (eds.) Advances in Emotion Recognition. Wiley (in press, 2012)
3. Bruce, V., Valentine, T., Baddeley, A.: The basis of the 3/4 view advantage in face recognition. Applied Cognitive Psychology 1, 109–120 (1987)
4. Liu, X., Chen, T., Rittscher, J.: Optimal pose for face recognition. In: Proceedings of the IEEE Computer Society Conference on Computer Vision and Pattern Recognition, vol. 2, pp. 1439–1446 (2006)
5. Pantic, M., Bartlett, M.S.: Machine analysis of facial expressions. In: Delac, K., Grgic, M. (eds.) Face Recognition, pp. 377–416. I-Tech Education and Publishing (2007)
6. Lucey, S., Ashraf, A.B., Cohen, J.F.: Investigating spontaneous facial action recognition through aam representations of the face. In: Delac, K., Grgic, M. (eds.) Face Recognition, pp. 275–286. I-Tech Education and Publishing (2007)
7. Chang, Y., Hu, C., Feris, R., Turk, M.: Manifold based analysis of facial expression. Image and Vision Computing 24, 605–614 (2006)
8. Valstar, M.F., Gunes, H., Pantic, M.: How to distinguish posed from spontaneous smiles using geometric features. In: Proceedings of the 9th International Conference on Multimodal Interfaces, ICMI 2007, pp. 38–45 (2007)
9. Anderson, K., McOwan, P.W.: A real-time automated system for the recognition of human facial expressions. IEEE Transactions on Systems, Man, and Cybernetics, Part B: Cybernetics 36, 96–105 (2006)

10. Valstar, M., Pantic, M., Patras, I.: Motion history for facial action detection in video. In: Conference Proceedings - IEEE International Conference on Systems, Man and Cybernetics, vol. 1, pp. 635–640 (2004)
11. Dhall, A., Asthana, A., Goecke, R., Gedeon, T.: Emotion recognition using phog and lpq features. In: 2011 IEEE International Conference on Automatic Face and Gesture Recognition and Workshops, FG 2011, pp. 878–883 (2011)
12. Zeng, Z., Tu, J., Pianfetti Jr., B.M., Huang, T.S.: Audio-visual affective expression recognition through multistream fused hmm. IEEE Transactions on Multimedia 10, 570–577 (2008)
13. Tian, Y., Kanade, T., Cohn, J.F.: Recognizing action units for facial expression analysis. IEEE Transactions on Pattern Analysis and Machine Intelligence 23, 97–115 (2001)
14. Fasel, B., Luettin, J.: Automatic facial expression analysis: A survey. Pattern Recognition 36, 259–275 (2003)
15. Hu, Y., Zeng, Z., Yin, L., Wei, X., Tu, J., Huang, T.S.: A study of non-frontal-view facial expressions recognition. In: Proceedings - International Conference on Pattern Recognition (2008)
16. Rudovic, O., Patras, I., Pantic, M.: Regression-based multi-view facial expression recognition. In: Proceedings - International Conference on Pattern Recognition, pp. 4121–4124 (2010)
17. Rudovic, O., Patras, I., Pantic, M.: Coupled Gaussian Process Regression for Pose-Invariant Facial Expression Recognition. In: Daniilidis, K., Maragos, P., Paragios, N. (eds.) ECCV 2010, Part II. LNCS, vol. 6312, pp. 350–363. Springer, Heidelberg (2010)
18. Hu, Y., Zeng, Z., Yin, L., Wei, X., Zhou, X., Huang, T.S.: Multi-view facial expression recognition. In: 2008 8th IEEE International Conference on Automatic Face and Gesture Recognition, FG 2008 (2008)
19. Zheng, W., Tang, H., Lin, Z., Huang, T.S.: A novel approach to expression recognition from non-frontal face images. In: Proceedings of the IEEE International Conference on Computer Vision, pp. 1901–1908 (2009)
20. Moore, S., Bowden, R.: The effects of pose on facial expression recognition. In: British Machine Vision Conference (2009)
21. Moore, S., Bowden, R.: Local binary patterns for multi-view facial expression recognition. Computer Vision and Image Understanding 115, 541–558 (2011)
22. Zheng, W., Tang, H., Lin, Z., Huang, T.S.: Emotion Recognition from Arbitrary View Facial Images. In: Daniilidis, K., Maragos, P., Paragios, N. (eds.) ECCV 2010, Part VI. LNCS, vol. 6316, pp. 490–503. Springer, Heidelberg (2010)
23. Tang, H., Hasegawa-Johnson, M., Huang, T.: Non-frontal view facial expression recognition based on ergodic hidden markov model supervectors. In: 2010 IEEE International Conference on Multimedia and Expo., ICME 2010, pp. 1202–1207 (2010)
24. Yin, L., Wei, X., Sun, Y., Wang, J., Rosato, M.J.: A 3D facial expression database for facial behavior research. In: FGR 2006: Proceedings of the 7th International Conference on Automatic Face and Gesture Recognition, vol. 2006, pp. 211–216 (2006)
25. Lazebnik, S., Schmid, C., Ponce, J.: Beyond bags of features: Spatial pyramid matching for recognizing natural scene categories. In: Proceedings of the IEEE Computer Society Conference on Computer Vision and Pattern Recognition, vol. 2, pp. 2169–2178 (2006)
26. Yang, J., Yu, K., Gong, Y., Huang, T.: Linear spatial pyramid matching using sparse coding for image classification. In: 2009 IEEE Computer Society Conference on Computer Vision and Pattern Recognition Workshops, CVPR Workshops 2009, pp. 1794–1801 (2009)
27. Wang, J., Yang, J., Yu, K., Gong, Y., Huang, T.: Locality-constrained linear coding for image classification. In: IEEE Conference on Computer Vision and Pattern Recognition (2009)
28. Boureau, Y.L., Bach, F., LeCun, Y., Ponce, J.: Learning mid-level features for recognition. In: IEEE Conference on Computer Vision and Pattern Recognition (2010)

29. Fei-Fei, L., Fergus, R., Perona, P.: Learning generative visual models from few training examples: An incremental bayesian approach tested on 101 object categories. Computer Vision and Image Understanding 106, 59–70 (2007)
30. Griffin, G., Holub, A., Perona, P.: Caltech-256 object category dataset. Technical Report 7694, California Institute of Technology (2007)
31. Lee, H., Battle, A., Raina, R., Ng, A.Y.: Efficient sparse coding algorithms. In: NIPS, pp. 801–808 (2007)
32. Serre, T., Wolf, L., Poggio, T.: Object recognition with features inspired by visual cortex. In: Proceedings of the IEEE Computer Society Conference on Computer Vision and Pattern Recognition, vol. 2, pp. 994–1000 (2005)
33. Fan, R.E., Chang, K.W., Hsieh, C.J., Wang, X.R., Lin, C.J.: LIBLINEAR: A library for large linear classification. Journal of Machine Learning Research 9, 1871–1874 (2008)

Real-Time Image Registration of RGB Webcams and Colorless 3D Time-of-Flight Cameras

Juan D. Gomez, Guido Bologna, and Thierry Pun

University of Geneva, Computer Science Department, Switzerland
{juan.gomez,guido.bologna,thierry.pun}@unige.ch

Abstract. In line with the boom of 3D movies and cutting edge technologies, range cameras are increasingly common. Among others, time-of-flight (TOF) cameras give it the ability to capture three-dimensional images that reveal object's distances. A shortcoming of these sensors however, lies in that the majority does not provide color information (not even gray). Therefore they are useless in computer vision applications for which color is crucial. The PMD [vision] ® CamCube 3.0 is one example of an expensive colorless TOF camera. In this work, we attempt the addition of color to this camera by means of inexpensive resources. A regular webcam is stuck on top of the CamCube and its color images are registered into the TOF distance maps. To get this done, we developed an algorithm to enable real-time registration based solely on depth. Thus, this algorithm requires neither intrinsic parameters nor mono-calibration of none of the cameras. We finally show a tracking application in which a stumble is foretold if an object approaches following a threatening trajectory.

1 Introduction

After long waiting, the first operational model of 3D-cameras based on the time-of-flight principle became available on the market. The colorless nature of these cameras however, has prevented the computer-vision community from using this technology. This is because while depth is very often an important feature, color (at least gray) is made always essential in computer vision. Indeed, cost-efficient solutions have come recently to alleviate this drawback. The Microsoft Kinect 3D sensor is an example of cheap TOF cameras that provide full color. Notwithstanding, this fun-only camera is indoor operational only. Besides, the accuracy of its distance images is found drastically diminished. Therefore, TOF 3D-cameras such as the PMD CamCube, continue to be highly desirable for solving unconstrained problems in natural environments.

This work introduces a method for the addition of color to the PMD CamCube camera. Furthermore, this technique can be extended to any another TOF sensor. Given that prices of these cameras still fall far from affordable, we use inexpensive resources to achieve this purpose. A regular webcam is only needed to turn the PMD CamCube operational in applications where the treatment of color and depth together is a must. We implement an online algorithm that matches color images from the webcam with distance images acquired with the TOF sensor in parallel. This algorithm estimates a shift function that in turn describes the misalignment of both

A. Fusiello et al. (Eds.): ECCV 2012 Ws/Demos, Part III, LNCS 7585, pp. 589–592, 2012.

Fig. 1. Apparatuses coupled in this work: The TOF sensor (PMD[vision] ® CamCube 3.0) and the web-cam (HD Webcam C525 Logitech)

coordinates systems. Therefore, we are able to remove the spatial variations between images caused during acquisition to build a 4-dimensions image (red, green, blue, depth).

Finally in this paper, we present an application aimed to identify which would be an obstacle only if its trajectory points straight to the camera after detection. For this application we combine depth-based segmentation with in-color tracking methods. Currently, this is an alerting method used to prevent users from stumbling in a navigation aid for visually impaired persons [1].

2   Image Registration

Here we aim at removing variations between images from both sources (TOF sensor and webcam) due to the differences in acquisition (points of view) which cause the images to be misaligned (their coordinates systems do not match). To register images, a spatial transformation is found which will remove these variations. This transformation has to be calculated once and needs no re-calculation unless the cameras have been decoupled. Once the images are aligned, color and time-of-flight-based distances can be merged into one 4-dimentions image. Our method aimed to approximate such a transformation, falls back on the seminal idea presented in [3]. The authors state that depth measured in stereo vision systems (two cameras closely embed) is discretized into parallel planes (one for each disparity value). Therefore, we assume that while shifts of coordinates between images (where all the depth planes are captured) cannot be described with a single number, shifts between local planes coordinates can certainly be. Our method that calculates all this numbers using planer regressions is described as follows:

- Several objects at different distances are placed in front of the cameras along the TOF range.
- A shot of the scene covering all the objects is captured using both cameras at the same time (one color and one distance/depth image).
- As many landmarks as possible are selected in the color image, as well as their peers in the counterpart distance image. Each landmark then, provides the x and y

coordinates of a point into the color image, into the distance image, and also its own depth D (obtained as well from the distance image).

- Based on this set of landmarks (samples from now on) we can estimate a relation that describes the shift of the coordinates in function of depth (D). We calculate a function per coordinate, this linear function estimates the shift traced from a coordinate into the depth image (x_d, y_d) to its shifted peer into the color image (x_c, y_c): $ShiftX(x_d, D)$ and $ShiftY(y_d, D)$. So that, $ShiftX + x_d = x_c$ and $ShiftY + y_d = y_c$ for a given D.

Once we retrieve the parameters of the two shift functions by interpolation of the samples, we go though every pixel in the distance image and recover its shifted position in the color image (Fig. 2). A one-to-one correspondence between images is then applied. We apply this correspondence using an efficient programming method based on matrixes calculation. Thus, we are able to attain performances up to 0.004 seconds for each image pair. Same method has to be repeated over each pair of images as long as a video is being shot.

Fig. 2. (top-left) Webcam-provided color image. **(top-right)** TOF-provided distance image (resized to fit top-left size). **(bottom-left)** A blended image showing the registration of (top-left) into (top-right). **(bottom-right)** A blended image showing the registration of (top-left) into the rectified version of (top-right) using our algorithm.

3   Application to Obstacle Analysis in Aided Navigation

There are many applications that merely use spatial awareness to meet a goal (e.g., automotive sensors, shapes analysis, robotic). Another gamut of applications however, cannot dispense with color to work properly. For instance, in this application we aim at detecting an approaching obstacle, yet we would like also to trace his trajectory so as to avoid a potential stumble. While this first task relies solely on the TOF attributes, the latter certainly needs of tracking and/or object detection algorithms. Typically, this sort of algorithms falls back on color to achieve the purpose. In this work, we detect a potential obstacle and estimate how likely that is going to lead to a stumble, as follows:

- A riskiness plane P with thickness t is fixed at certain depth d.
- We constantly scan P to detect whether or not an object appears on it (i.e. a cluster of pixels with distance d and greater that a tolerance in the TOF image).
- If an object happened to be detected, we retrieve 15 color images from the webcam back in time (time in which the object traveled from deeper planes).
- We use a short-term tracker (e.g. Lukas-Kanade [2]) to backtrack the object over this set of frames starting from within a bounding box fixed on the position of the TOF-based detection.
- Once the path of the object has been traced, we estimate its trajectory from P up to the camera plane. If a stumble with the camera is likely, we activate an alarm that evidences the hazard of the situation. We do not launch any warning otherwise.

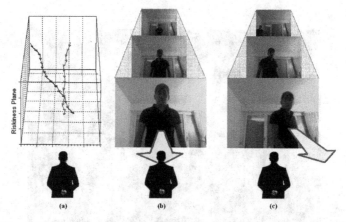

Fig. 3. (a) The resultant path that an object traces up to the riskiness plane, from deeper planes. This path has been backtracked using a short-term tracker algorithm. Red vectors represent an object approaching directly over the user (b). Blue vectors belong to an object with diagonal trajectory (c). In turn, (b) and (c) are illustrative representations that explain both situations by showing some samples of the backtracked sequences. For (b) a stumble is expected whereas, for (c) no stumble is likely. Therefore, only (b) produces a warning alarm.

References

1. Bologna, G., Deville, B., Gomez, J., Pun, T.: Toward local and global perception modules for vision substitution. Neurocomputing 74(8), 1182–1190 (2010)
2. Lucas, B., Kanade, T.: An iterative image registration technique with an application to stereo vision. In: Proc. DARPA, Image Understanding Workshop (1981)
3. De-Maeztu, L., Mattoccia, S., Villanueva, A., Cabeza, R.: Linear stereo matching. In: Proc. ICCV, International Conference on Computer Vision (2011)

Technical Demonstration on Model Based Training, Detection and Pose Estimation of Texture-Less 3D Objects in Heavily Cluttered Scenes

Stefan Hinterstoisser[1], Vincent Lepetit[2], Slobodan Ilic[1], Stefan Holzer[1], Kurt Konolige[3], Gary Bradski[3], and Nassir Navab[1]

[1] Department of Computer Science, CAMP,
Technische Universität München (TUM), Germany
{hinterst,slobodan.ilic,holzers,navab}@in.tum.de
[2] Ecole Polytechnique Federale de Lausanne (EPFL),
Computer Vision Laboratory, Switzerland
vincent.lepetit@epfl.ch
[3] Industrial Perception Inc., USA
{kurt,gary}@industrial-perception.com

Abstract. In this technical demonstration, we will show our framework of automatic modeling, detection, and tracking of arbitrary texture-less 3D objects with a Kinect. The detection is mainly based on the recent template-based LINEMOD approach [1] while the automatic template learning from reconstructed 3D models, the fast pose estimation and the quick and robust false positive removal is a novel addition.

In this demonstration, we will show each step of our pipeline, starting with the fast reconstruction of arbitrary 3D objects, followed by the automatic learning and the robust detection and pose estimation of the reconstructed objects in real-time. As we will show, this makes our framework suitable for object manipulation e.g. in robotics applications.

1 Introduction

Many current vision applications, such as pedestrian tracking, dense SLAM [2], or object detection [1], can be made more robust through the addition of depth information. In this work, we focus on object detection for Robotics and Machine Vision, where it is important to efficiently and robustly detect objects and estimate their 3D poses, for manipulation or inspection tasks. Our approach is based on LINEMOD [1], an efficient method that exploits both depth and color images to capture the appearance and 3D shape of the object in a set of templates covering different views of an object. Because the viewpoint of each template is known, it provides a coarse estimate of the pose of the object when it is detected.

However, the initial version of LINEMOD [1] has some disadvantages. First, templates are learned online, which is difficult to control and results in spotty

A. Fusiello et al. (Eds.): ECCV 2012 Ws/Demos, Part III, LNCS 7585, pp. 593–596, 2012.

Fig. 1. 15 different texture-less 3D objects are simultaneously detected with our approach under different poses on heavy cluttered background with partial occlusion. Each detected object is augmented with its 3D model. We also show the corresponding coordinate systems. **See supplemental video.**

Fig. 2. In this figure, we show the simple reconstruction of the "cat" model. On the left hand side, we see the reconstructed 3D model whereas on the right hand side we augment the real object with the reconstruction.

Fig. 3. The reconstructed 3D models of the 15 different texture-less 3D objects detected in Figs. 1 and 4.

Fig. 4. 15 different texture-less 3D objects are simultaneously detected under different poses on heavy cluttered background with partial occlusion and illumination changes. Each detected object is augmented with its 3D model. We also show the corresponding coordinate systems. **See also the supplemental video.**

coverage of viewpoints. Second, the pose output by LINEMOD is only approximately correct, since a template covers a range of views around its viewpoint. And finally, the performance of LINEMOD, while extremely good, still suffers from the presence of false positives.

In this technical demonstration, we show the result of our most recent work [3] where we overcome these disadvantages, and create a system based on LINEMOD for the automatic modeling, detection, and tracking of 3D objects with RGBD sensors. Our main insight is that a 3D model of the object can be exploited to remedy these deficiencies. Note that accurate 3D models can now be created very quickly [2,4,5,6], and requiring a 3D model beforehand is not a disadvantage anymore. For industrial applications, a detailed 3D model often exists before the real object is even created. In this demonstration, we will use our own model creation framework to show that an appropriate 3D model can be created very easily and very quickly.

Given such a 3D model of an object, we will show the automatic template learning where templates are generated which cover a full view hemisphere of regularly sampled viewpoints of the 3D model. During this learning, the templates are defined only with the most useful appearance and depth information, which allows us to speed up the template detection stage. In addition, we will also show in this demonstration that the 3D model can be used to obtain a fine estimate of the object pose, starting from the one provided by the templates. Together with a simple test based on color, this allows us to remove false positives, by checking if the object under the recovered pose aligns well with the depth map. The end result is a system that significantly improves the original LINEMOD implementation in performance, while providing accurate pose for applications.

To show the computational efficiency of our framework we will perform our technical demonstration on a standard notebook with an Intel i7-2820QM processor with 2.3 GHz and 8 GB of RAM.

In short, we will demonstrate a 3D reconstruction, detection and pose estimation framework that is easy to deploy, reliable, and fast enough to run in real-time.

References

1. Hinterstoisser, S., Holzer, S., Cagniart, C., Ilic, S., Konolige, K., Navab, N., Lepetit, V.: Multimodal Templates for Real-Time Detection of Texture-Less Objects in Heavily Cluttered Scenes. In: ICCV (2011)
2. Newcombe, R.A., Izadi, S., Hilliges, O., Molyneaux, D., Kim, D., Davison, A.J., Kohli, P., Shotton, J., Hodges, S., Fitzgibbon, A.: KinectFusion: Real-Time Dense Surface Mapping and Tracking. In: ISMAR (2011)
3. Anonymous, Authors: Anonymous Title. In: submitted to ACCV (2012)
4. Pan, Q., Reitmayr, G., Drummond, T.: ProFORMA: Probabilistic Feature-based On-line Rapid Model Acquisition. In: BMVC (2009)
5. Weise, T., Wismer, T., Leibe, B., Van Gool, L.: In-hand Scanning with Online Loop Closure. In: International Workshop on 3-D Digital Imaging and Modeling (2009)
6. Newcombe, R.A., Lovegrove, S.J., Davison, A.J.: DTAM: Dense Tracking and Mapping in Real-Time. In: ICCV (2011)

FaceHugger: The ALIEN Tracker Applied to Faces

Federico Pernici

MICC - University Of Florence, Italy

Abstract. This paper proposes an online tracking method which has been inspired by studying the effects of Scale Invariant Feature Transform (SIFT) when applied to objects assumed to be flat even though they are not. The consequent deviation from flatness induces *nuisance factors* that act on the feature representation in a manner for which no general local invariants can be computed, such as in the case of occlusion, sensor quantization and casting shadows. However, if features are over-represented, they can provide the necessary information to build online, a robust object/context discriminative classifier. This is achieved based on weakly aligned *multiple instance* local features in a sense that will be made clear in the rest of this paper. According to this observation, we present a non parametric online tracking by detection approach that yields state of the art performance.

Specific tests on video sequences of faces show excellent long-term tracking performance in unconstrained videos.

1 Introduction

Tracking is a fundamental problem in computer vision. Several aspects of this difficult task have been considered in literature. Generally speaking, difficulties arise depending on the type of information that have to be tracked: 3D pose, imaged 2D location, imaged 2D shape, 3D shape, imaged 2D articulated body shape, 3D articulated body shape, etc. (see [1] for a review and a classification). Besides dealing with the inherent difficulties related to the specific information of interest, effective methods must also provide robust object representation coping with nuisance factors that affect the image formation process. Illumination, viewpoint, shadows, occlusion and clutter have indeed little to do[1] with the tracking of the physical quantities we are interested in. Further complexity is generated by objects or cameras themselves. For example objects may have non-rigid shape such as in the case of faces or may be made of translucent or reflective materials and camera sensors may suffer from the effects of noise, sensor quantization and motion blur.

In addition to these intrinsic problems, practical requirements such as: 1) long-term tracking; 2) object reacquisition after total occlusion and 3) the amount of partial occlusion at which to successfully track an object, may hinder the accomplishment of the tracking task. In some applications, the object to be tracked is known in advance and it is possible to incorporate specific prior knowledge when designing the tracker to alleviate some of these issues [2]. However, the general case of tracking arbitrary objects by simply specifying a *single (one-shot) training example at runtime*, is a challenging

---

[1] Indeed their relationships are too complex to be estimated.

A. Fusiello et al. (Eds.): ECCV 2012 Ws/Demos, Part III, LNCS 7585, pp. 597–601, 2012.

open problem which deserves particular attention. In this scenario, the tracker must be able to model the appearance of the object on-the-fly by generating and labeling image features and learning the model of the object appearance. This basic formulation naturally leads to the semi-supervised learning procedure.

2 Related Work

Despite all the difficulties we introduced so far, a number of methods has been developed in which tracking is considered as simple as 2D image bounding box localization and what is really tracked is indeed the non-stationary image appearance of the object, irrespective of its imaged 3D physical quantities: [3–8].

In a recent quantitative comparison [10], among others, three methods emerged distinguishing for their positive performance and for their algorithmic design and image representation peculiarity: [5, 7, 8]. Their main differences rely on how they consider *the template update problem* which primarily impacts on the drift of the tracker [11]. Babenko et al. [8] address the problem by building an evolving boosting classifier that tracks bags of image patches. Kalal et al.[7] combine a optic flow tracker with an online random forest as introduced in [6]. In Mei and Ling [5] the tracking problem is formulated as finding a sparse representation of the object candidate combining trivial templates which are primarily responsible for the presence and the absence of certain object image patches. We argue that positive performance is intrinsically in the multiview appearance representation which allows overcoming the feature invariance and/or feature selection based on machine learning methods. MILTrack [8], for example, adopting bag of image patches can cope for misalignment and occlusion by adding novel examples as new instances for object representation. Based on this general observation, we propose a technique principally motivated by local feature invariance and by the underlying image formation process. It comprises multiple instances of local features combined with a global shape prior, expressed in terms of a 2D similarity transformation and it approximates object surfaces as nearly planar for which SIFT matching (or other local scale invariant features) has proven to be effective in the solution of the problem [12]. Conscious of the limits of local features invariance, 3D shape deviations from planarity and their interactions with shadow and occlusion are (over)-represented through multiple instances of the same features after a weak alignment along the object template (see Fig.1(a) and 1(b)). For this motivation we call our method ALIEN, Appearance Learning In Evidential Nuisance, since it is based on the physical observation that if the object is reasonably convex, known critical nuisance factors which cannot be neutralized, can be managed based on multiple instances of features selected and updated according to a weak global shape model. This novel representation is exploited in a discriminative background/foreground online tracking (by detection) method which performs feature selection and feature update. The resulting technique allows tracking to continue under severe visibility artifacts. In our demo we build on the ALIEN method to develop a face tracking application in which face re-detection is exploited to distinguish face identities when objects move in and out of the field of view. We call our application FaceHugger, since it "sticks" firmly to the face even in unrestricted viewing conditions.

3   The ALIEN Tracker

Given a bounding box defining an object of interest, our goal is to automatically and unambiguously determine which image features are the most useful in discriminating between the object and the rest of the imaged scene. The main components of our method are two nearest neighbor classifiers (NN); one for the object under tracking and the other for its context. The two classifiers are non-parametric defined in terms of the set of visual features they represent. The object classifier $\mathcal{T}_t$ represents object shape and appearance at time t by a number of features $N_\mathcal{T}$ as: $\mathcal{T}_t = \{(\mathbf{p}_i, \mathbf{d}_i)\}_{i=1}^{N_\mathcal{T}}$, where $\mathbf{p} \in \mathbb{R}^2$ is a point location in the object reference template with its associated image patch descriptor $\mathbf{d} \in \mathbb{R}^n$ as illustrated in Fig. 1(b). The second classifier $\mathcal{C}_t$ defines

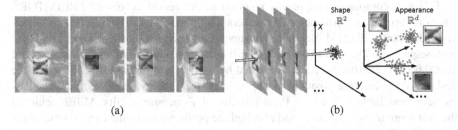

(a)   (b)

Fig. 1. The weakly aligned multi-instance local features concept in the case of tracking a face. (a): Four frames from the *trellis-sequence* [3] with highlighted appearance variations in a particular object region susceptible to self-occlusions and shadows. (b): Region representation after weak alignment. Feature locations describing 2D shape in the xy-coordinate system of the object template are shown with their associated appearance descriptors (128D).

the contextual appearance surrounding, in space and time, the object and is composed of only the appearance component (i.e. standard bag of features representation): $\mathcal{C}_t = \{\mathbf{d}_i\}_{i=1}^{N_\mathcal{C}}$, where $N_\mathcal{C}$ is the number of features and $\mathbf{d} \in \mathbb{R}^n$ is the associated visual descriptor. We use SIFT [12] as the features for both the classifiers, however any scale invariant representation can be plugged in. The final object detector, that will be detailed elsewhere, is composed by the tight interplay between the sets $\mathcal{T}_t$, $\mathcal{C}_t$ and the object state $\mathbf{x}_t$. The detector returns $p(y = 1|\mathcal{S}_t)$ where $\mathcal{S}_t = \{(\mathbf{p}_i, \mathbf{d}_i)\}_{i=1}^{N_S}$ is the set of features extracted from an image search area $\mathbf{S}_t$ and y is a binary variable indicating the presence or the absence of the object of interest in that image region. Detector response is evaluated with a greedy strategy, to also obtain the tracker state. The tracker state $\mathbf{x}_t$ at time t includes the parameters to specify imaged object center location (x_t, y_t), scale s_t and the rotation angle θ_t with respect to the initial bounding box provided at time $t = 0$. Once the tracker state is estimated, we proceed to update the object/context appearance model. To this aim local features inside the Oriented Bounding Box OBB$(\hat{\mathbf{x}}_t)$ region, defined by the tracker state, are labeled as belonging to the object. While for context, we use the features belonging to the annular region surrounding the object accumulated over a time window of length l. Suppose that the classifier is evaluating its response in the estimated search area $\mathbf{S}_t$ at time t, our goal is to perform object detection and object appearance update using the representation we introduced. To this end, the following three points are explicitly addressed by the method and detailed elsewhere for lack of space: (1) *Feature distinctiveness*. Descriptors alone are ambiguous because they can be interpreted as a valid description for both the object and its surround context. An analogous effect is produced by the inherent shape limit of the bounding box. (2) *Not up to date appearance*. Appearance must be updated according to the novel information provided by the detected object in the current image. (3) *Occlusion*. Occlusion must be detected in order to avoid updating the wrong appearance contaminating the object template.

4 Experimental Results: ALIEN vs. Predator

ALIEN was compared with results reported in the recent developed PREDATOR[2], which reports on performance of 5 trackers: Online Boosting (OB) [13], Semisupervised Boosting (SB) [14], Beyond Semisupervised (BS) [15], MIL [8] and CoGD [4] on 9 sequences. The sequences include full occlusion and two of them contain about 10000 frames. Performance are dominated by ALIEN and PREDATOR [7] which are designed for object reacquisition. As in [7], the performance was assessed using the Pascal Score and Table 1 shows the Precision, Recall, F-measure results. ALIEN achieved the best score in the sequences and matched the performance of the current state of the art method [7].

Table 1. ALIEN in comparison to results reported in [7] (Precision/Recall/F-measure). Bold numbers indicate the best score, italic numbers indicate the second best.

Sequence	Frames	OB [13]	SB [14]	BS [15]	MIL [8]	CoGD[4]	TLD [7]	ALIEN
David	761	0.01 / 0.01 / 0.01	0.27 / 0.27 / 0.27	0.16 / 0.12 / 0.13	0.06 / 0.06 / 0.06	0.99 / 0.99 / 0.99	**1.00 / 1.00 / 1.00**	0.99 / 0.98 / 0.99
Jumping	313	0.41 / 0.04 / 0.08	0.14 / 0.08 / 0.10	0.06 / 0.05 / 0.05	0.37 / 0.37 / 0.37	**1.00 / 0.99 / 1.00**	0.99 / 0.99 / 0.99	0.99 / 0.87 / 0.92
Pedestrian 1	140	0.36 / 0.09 / 0.14	0.20 / 0.14 / 0.16	0.10 / 0.04 / 0.05	0.42 / 0.42 / 0.42	0.99 / 0.99 / 0.99	**1.00 / 1.00 / 1.00**	1.00 / 1.00 / 1.00
Pedestrian 2	338	0.74 / 0.12 / 0.21	0.55 / 0.46 / 0.50	1.00 / 0.02 / 0.04	0.10 / 0.12 / 0.11	0.71 / 0.90 / 0.79	*0.89 / 0.92 / 0.91*	**0.93 / 0.92 / 0.93**
Pedestrian 3	184	1.00 / 0.33 / 0.49	0.41 / 0.33 / 0.36	0.81 / 0.40 / 0.54	0.49 / 0.58 / 0.53	0.84 / 0.99 / 0.91	**0.99 / 1.00 / 0.99**	*1.00 / 0.90 / 0.95*
Car	945	0.89 / 0.57 / 0.69	1.00 / 0.67 / 0.80	0.99 / 0.56 / 0.72	0.11 / 0.12 / 0.11	0.91 / 0.92 / 0.91	*0.92 / 0.97 / 0.94*	**0.95 / 1.00 / 0.98**
Motocross	2665	0.13 / 0.00 / 0.00	0.01 / 0.00 / 0.00	0.14 / 0.00 / 0.00	0.02 / 0.01 / 0.01	0.80 / 0.26 / 0.39	**0.67 / 0.58 / 0.62**	*0.49 / 0.58 / 0.54*
Volkswagen	8576	0.04 / 0.00 / 0.00	0.00 / 0.00 / 0.00	0.00 / 0.00 / 0.00	0.26 / 0.03 / 0.05	0.41 / 0.03 / 0.06	*0.54 / 0.64 / 0.59*	**0.99 / 0.70 / 0.82**
Carchase	9928	0.73 / 0.03 / 0.05	0.79 / 0.04 / 0.08	0.38 / 0.09 / 0.14	0.49 / 0.03 / 0.05	0.87 / 0.04 / 0.08	*0.50 / 0.40 / 0.45*	**0.73 / 0.68 / 0.70**
mean	-	0.40 / 0.10 / 0.15	0.30 / 0.18 / 0.20	0.33 / 0.11 / 0.15	0.21 / 0.15 / 0.15	0.68 / 0.55 / 0.55	*0.68 / 0.68 / 0.68*	**0.73 / 0.69 / 0.71**

5 Conclusion

In this paper, we have presented the main features of a method to track an unknown object in long video sequences under complex interactions between illumination, occlusion and object/camera motion. A real-time implementation of the framework has been evaluated under a publicly available dataset with an extensive set of experiments. Superiority of our approach with respect to state of the art methods was reported.

---

[2] Tracking-Learning-Detection (TLD) tracker [7] has been advertised under the name Predator.

References

1. Yilmaz, A., Javed, O., Shah, M.: Object tracking: A survey. ACM Computing Surveys 38, 13 (2006)
2. Lepetit, V., Fua, P.: Monocular model-based 3d tracking of rigid objects. Found. Trends. Comput. Graph. Vis. 1, 1–89 (2005)
3. Ross, D.A., Lim, J., Lin, R.S., Yang, M.H.: Incremental learning for robust visual tracking. Int. J. Comput. Vision 77, 125–141 (2008)
4. Yu, Q., Dinh, T.B., Medioni, G.G.: Online Tracking and Reacquisition Using Co-trained Generative and Discriminative Trackers. In: Forsyth, D., Torr, P., Zisserman, A. (eds.) ECCV 2008, Part II. LNCS, vol. 5303, pp. 678–691. Springer, Heidelberg (2008)
5. Mei, X., Ling, H.: Robust visual tracking using l1 minimization. In: ICCV 2009, pp. 1436–1443 (2009)
6. Santner, J., Leistner, C., Saffari, A., Pock, T., Bischof, H.: Prost: Parallel robust online simple tracking. In: 2010 IEEE Conference on Computer Vision and Pattern Recognition (CVPR), pp. 723–730 (2010)
7. Kalal, Z., Matas, J., Mikolajczyk, K.: P-n learning: Bootstrapping binary classifiers by structural constraints. In: 2010 IEEE Conference on Computer Vision and Pattern Recognition, CVPR (2010)
8. Babenko, B., Yang, M.H., Belongie, S.: Robust object tracking with online multiple instance learning. IEEE Transactions on Pattern Analysis and Machine Intelligence 33, 1619–1632 (2011)
9. Dinh, T.B., Vo, N., Medioni, G.: Context tracker: Exploring supporters and distracters in unconstrained environments. In: 2011 IEEE Conference on Computer Vision and Pattern Recognition, CVPR (2011)
10. Wang, Q., Chen, F., Xu, W., Yang, M.H.: An experimental comparison of online object tracking algorithms. In: Proceedings of SPIE: Image and Signal Processing Track (2011)
11. Matthews, I., Ishikawa, T., Baker, S.: The template update problem. In: Proceedings of the British Machine Vision Conference (2003)
12. Lowe, D.G.: Distinctive image features from scale-invariant keypoints. International Journal of Computer Vision 60, 91–110 (2004)
13. Grabner, H., Bischof, H.: On-line boosting and vision. In: 2006 IEEE Computer Society Conference on Computer Vision and Pattern Recognition, vol. 1, pp. 260–267 (2006)
14. Grabner, H., Leistner, C., Bischof, H.: Semi-supervised On-Line Boosting for Robust Tracking. In: Forsyth, D., Torr, P., Zisserman, A. (eds.) ECCV 2008, Part I. LNCS, vol. 5302, pp. 234–247. Springer, Heidelberg (2008)
15. Stalder, S., Grabner, H., Van Gool, L.: Beyond semi-supervised tracking: Tracking should be as simple as detection, but not simpler than recognition. In: OLCV 2009: 3rd On-line learning for Computer Vision Workshop (2009)

INTAIRACT: Joint Hand Gesture and Fingertip Classification for Touchless Interaction

Xavier Suau, Marcel Alcoverro, Adolfo Lopez-Mendez,
Javier Ruiz-Hidalgo, and Josep Casas

Universitat Politècnica de Catalunya

Abstract. In this demo we present *intAIRact*, an online hand-based touchless interaction system. Interactions are based on easy-to-learn hand gestures, that combined with translations and rotations render a user friendly and highly configurable system. The main advantage with respect to existing approaches is that we are able to robustly locate and identify fingertips. Hence, we are able to employ a simple but powerful alphabet of gestures not only by determining the number of visible fingers in a gesture, but also which fingers are being observed. To achieve such a system we propose a novel method that jointly infers hand gestures and fingertip locations using a single depth image from a consumer depth camera. Our approach is based on a novel descriptor for depth data, the Oriented Radial Distribution (ORD) [1]. On the one hand, we exploit the ORD for robust classification of hand gestures by means of efficient *k-NN* retrieval. On the other hand, maxima of the ORD are used to perform structured inference of fingertip locations. The proposed method outperforms other state-of-the-art approaches both in gesture recognition and fingertip localization. An implementation of the ORD extraction on a GPU yields a real-time demo running at approximately 17fps on a single laptop.

1 Introduction

Until recent years, interaction between humans and computer systems has been driven through specific devices (*i.e.* mouse, keyboard). Such device-dependency turns interaction into a non-natural dialog between humans and machines. Hand gesturing is an interesting way to provide a more immersive and intuitive interaction. Recent consumer depth cameras provide pixel-wise depth information in real-time opening the door to new research directions in the field of Natural User Interfaces (NUI). Our proposal uses this kind of camera as input (*i.e.* Kinect), not requiring any other specific display nor hardware.

Combining a basic set of fingertip configurations with simple hand motion has proven to be successful with modern trackpad devices [2]. Our idea is to extend such paradigm to the touch-less world, providing a more immersive experience than physical trackpads.

A. Fusiello et al. (Eds.): ECCV 2012 Ws/Demos, Part III, LNCS 7585, pp. 602–606, 2012.

The proposed demonstration enables the user to interact with virtual objects by means of combining easy hand motion with finger configurations and movements. Such approach renders a different interaction than recent systems based only on motion [3] or hand pose [4,5], which usually result in complex and difficult to memorize alphabets. For example, a *show menu* command may be performed by showing four fingers combined with a global vertical movement of the hand (as in [2]), while with the reference methods, a specific hand gesture must be assigned to the command.

We believe that exploiting hand gestures in combination with simple motions will have a much higher user acceptance, enabling more commands using an easy and small set of hand gestures. Such strategy allows a highly scalable and configurable interaction. Furthermore, this renders a more tractable hand analysis problem, as one does not necessarily need to estimate the full hand pose. However, fingertip localization must be performed, not being only a problem of detecting the *number* of fingertips in the current input image but *which* fingers (and fingertips) are visible and *where* they are located. Intra-gesture variations (*i.e.* rotation and translation) are also considered, strongly increasing the robustness of the system.

Quantitative results are obtained through evaluation with a recent 3D feature benchmark, revealing the convenience of using ORD for hand gesture classification. Fingertip localization results are compared to a state-of-the-art Random Forest approach.

Even if this demo is focused on interactivity with virtual objects, the system may be extended to a large number of applications. Gaming, creative design, control of CAD environments or musical applications are just some examples.

2 Technical Overview

We propose a novel use of the Oriented Radial Distribution (ORD) feature, presented by Suau *et al.* [1]. The 3D point cloud obtained from a Kinect sensor is our input data. The ORD feature characterizes a point cloud in such a way that its end-effectors are given an elevated ORD value, providing a high contrast between flat and extremal zones. Therefore, ORD is suitable to both globally characterize the structure of a hand gesture and to locally locate its end-effectors (generally fingers). A two-step method is proposed, namely hand gesture classification and fingertip localization, which are obtained with a single ORD calculation on GPU (see Fig. 1). The hand gesture classification step is performed using a k-Nearest Neighbors (k-NN) search on a template dataset. A graph-matching algorithm is used to infer finger locations from the fingertip annotation of the recognized gesture, taking advantage of the ORD structure of the hand under analysis. To automatically annotate the fingertip locations in the training images, we recorded several sequences using a colored glove. This procedure enables an easy extraction of the ground-truth fingertip locations during the training phase. Note that the glove is used only for annotation purposes, as in test time no glove is required.

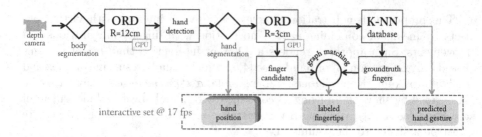

Fig. 1. Technical scheme of the *intAIRact* demo. An *interactive set* containing the last hand positions, hand gesture and fingertip locations is obtained at each frame (17 *fps*).

Fig. 2. Samples of the annotated dataset. We show two examples per gesture (columns), emphasizing that gestures are performed with rotations and translations, resulting in a challenging classification problem (for example, observe the variability of gesture 4). Label 0 corresponds to *no gesture* (*i.e.* other gestures, transitions). The colored glove is only used in the training phase.

Demonstration Operation. We design our system to trigger events as a function of the inferred hand gesture, the fingertip locations and hand trajectory at time t. As a result, we have a user-friendly and scalable touchless interaction, since different events can be triggered by rather subtle changes of any of the mentioned elements. As an example, in our application we define the events *Show/Hide Object Menu* as the set {Gesture 4, fingertips up, hand going up/down}, i.e., two different events are triggered by just a change of one element, the hand trajectory. However, the possibilities of this *interactive set* go beyond that; fingertip locations allow us to compute hand rotations for different gestures. Consequently, a user can trigger a high number of events by remembering 9 gestures and combining them with simple translations and rotations.

3   Quantitative Results

Besides qualitative results (see video), we provide some figures to point out the classification results evaluated against reference methods. A dataset consisting of 4 users performing 9 gestures is used (Fig. 2). Two recordings per user are provided for training purposes, each clip containing between 3000-6000 frames.

Hand Gesture Classification Results. A benchmark consisting of various 3D features (Depth, Curvature, 3DSC [6], VFH [7] and SHOT [8]) is considered in order to evaluate the performance of ORD regarding the classification task. ORD achieves a classification F-Measure of 85.8%. The best result in the benchmark is achieved by the depth feature (67.7%) followed by VFH (49.9%). Therefore, the ORD feature largely outperforms the benchmark, also pointing that depth-based features (ORD and depth) are more convenient for analyzing depth data than 3D based features.

Classification with ORD is also evaluated with small training datasets, obtained as reduced versions of the full dataset by Euclidean clustering. The proposed method successfully tolerates drastic reductions of the training dataset, showing an F-Measure degradation of about 6% with a dataset reduction ×10.

Fingertip Localization Results. To evaluate the proposed algorithm, we implement a fingertip localization method using Random Forests (RF). The RF method is based on the successful system for detecting body parts from range data proposed by Shotton et al. [9]. We use very similar depth-invariant features, but in addition to depth data, we include the ORD feature, which slightly increases the average finger localization accuracy from 58% to 60%. However, the proposed Nearest Neighbor + Graph Matching finger localization method improves the reference RF approach by 8%, achieving an accuracy of 68%.

Computational Performance. The demonstration is carried out on an Intel Core2 Duo CPU E7400 @ 2.80GHz. To calculate the ORD feature, we have coded a parallel implementation on a NVIDIA GeForce GTX 295 GPU, performing about $70 - 140\times$ faster than the implementation in [1]. The complete demonstration setup performs in real-time, at a frame-rate of about $17\,fps$. A frame-rate of $16\,fps$ is achieved by [10]. However, our proposal delivers fingertip positions in addition to hand gestures.

References

1. Suau, X., Ruiz-Hidalgo, J., Casas, J.R.: Oriented Radial Distribution on Depth Data: Appication to the Detection of End-Effectors. In: ICASSP (2012)
2. Apple Inc.: Magic Trackpad (2012)
3. Suau, X., Ruiz-Hidalgo, J., Casas, J.R.: Real-Time Head and Hand Tracking based on 2.5D data. Transactions on Multimedia, 1 (2012)
4. Keskin, C., Kırac, F., Kara, Y.E., Akarun, L.: Real Time Hand Pose Estimation using Depth Sensors. In: ICCV-CDC4CV, pp. 1228–1234 (2011)
5. Minnen, D., Zafrulla, Z.: Towards robust cross-user hand tracking and shape recognition. In: ICCV-CDC4CV, Oblong Industries, Los Angeles, CA, USA (2011)
6. Frome, A., Huber, D., Kolluri, R., Bülow, T., Malik, J.: Recognizing Objects in Range Data Using Regional Point Descriptors. In: Pajdla, T., Matas, J. (eds.) ECCV 2004, Part III. LNCS, vol. 3023, pp. 224–237. Springer, Heidelberg (2004)
7. Rusu, R., Bradski, G., Thibaux, R., Hsu, J.: Fast 3D recognition and pose using the viewpoint feature histogram. In: IROS, pp. 2155–2162 (2010)

8. Tombari, F., Salti, S., Di Stefano, L.: Unique Signatures of Histograms for Local Surface Description. In: Daniilidis, K., Maragos, P., Paragios, N. (eds.) ECCV 2010, Part III. LNCS, vol. 6313, pp. 356–369. Springer, Heidelberg (2010)
9. Shotton, J., Fitzgibbon, A., Cook, M., Sharp, T., Finocchio, M., Moore, R., Kipman, A., Blake, A.: Real-Time Human Pose Recognition in Parts from Single Depth Images. In: CVPR, pp. 1297–1304 (2011)
10. Uebersax, D., Gall, J., Van den Bergh, M., Van Gool, L.: Real-time Sign Language Letter and Word Recognition from Depth Data. In: ICCV-HCI, pp. 1–8 (2011)

Fast and Precise Template Matching Based on Oriented Gradients

Yoshinori Konishi, Yasuyo Kotake, Yoshihisa Ijiri, and Masato Kawade

OMRON Corporation,
9-1 Kizugawadai, Kizugawa-city, Kyoto 619-0283, Japan
{ykoni,kotake,joyport,kawade}@ari.ncl.omron.co.jp

Abstract. In this paper we propose a fast template matching method which can handle various types of objects. In our method the discretized orientations of image gradients which are robust to illumination changes and clutterd backgrounds are used as features. The features are binary represented and they can be matched very fast using bitwise operations. Furthermore, the rotated and resized templates those have similar feature vectors are clustered to one template and the total number of templates are greatly reduced, which boosts the detection speed. The experimental results show that our method can detect target objects (the search space includes translation, ±180 deg rotation, and ±50% scale change) with sub-pixel accracy in real-time.

Keywords: template matching, oriented gradients, ICP.

1 Introduction

Template matching has been widely used for object detections both in academic researches and in real-world applications such as factory automations and medical image processings. But there still remain many problems about processing time, preciseness of the detected results, and robustness.

Although the similarity measures based on pixel values (e.g. normalized cross correlation) have been frequently used for template matching, they are sensitive to illumination changes, noise and blur. Edge-based template matchings (e.g. based on Chamfer distance) are relatively robust to these disturbances. However, they tend to generate many false positives in cluttered backgrounds and the edge extraction is relatively slow. In recent years, object detections based on local feature descriptors such as SIFT and SURF were proposed. They are fast and robust to some deformations, but they can not handle low-textured objects.

Steger et al. [1] proposed occlusion, clutter, illumination invariant similarity measure based on the dot products of image gradient vectors. Hinterstoisser et al. [2] have developed this similarity measure and proposed novel Dominant Orientation Template (DOT). DOT uses only the dominant orientations in squared regions for matching, so it is robust to small image transformations and deformations. The binary representations of the discretized orientations make matching of DOT very fast. However, DOT has some drawbacks: 1) DOT uses a same

A. Fusiello et al. (Eds.): ECCV 2012 Ws/Demos, Part III, LNCS 7585, pp. 607–610, 2012.

Fig. 1. Left: Training image. Middle: Oriented gradients. The eight different colors indicate the different orientations. Right: The extracted edges by Canny edge detector.

rectangular ROI for all rotated and resized templates, so its performance degrades under rotations and scale changes of target objects. 2) The features of DOT include the regions where there is no reliable gradient. Therefore, it tends to generate many false positives in simple backgrounds if the target objects do not have many reliable gradients. 3) The dominant orientations in a squared region (7×7 pix used in their paper) are too coarse to detect precise positions of target objects.

We propose the real-time template matching method which can handle various types of objects (e.g., various shapes, textured and texture-less) and can detect objects with sub-pixel accuracy under various conditions such as illumination changes, noise, and cluttered backgrounds.

2   Proposed Approach

2.1   Template Generation

First, image pyramids of a training image (Fig. 1 Left) are generated and image gradients are caluculated by Sobel filter. Next, the gradients whose intensities are greater than some threshold value are chosen and the angles of the gradient vectors are discretized into 8 orientations (Fig. 1 Middle).

The orientation features are represented as one byte data in which the bit corresponding to the orientation (0,1,...,7) is set to 1. The orientation features and their positions relative to the center of ROI are retained as a template (T in Eq. 1). Rotated and resized templates are also generated by calculating oriented gradients in the rotated and resized training images. We rotate the image by 1 degree from 0 to 360 and resize it by 2% from 50% to 150%. The total number of templates amounts to 18,360 (= m).

$$T_i = \{x_j, y_j, ori_j | j = 1, ..., n\}, i = 1, ..., m \tag{1}$$

One of the most important factor affecting detection speed is the number of templates used for matching. To reduce the number of templates, those have similar feature vectors are integrated to one template. First, the feature vectors of the templates whose rotation angles and scales are similar are matched each other using the matching function of Eq. 2. Next, the feature vectors of the templates those have high matching scores are joined. Different orientations at

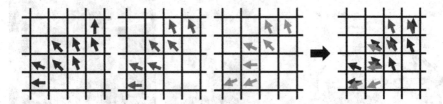

Fig. 2. Template integration. The left 3 panels show original templates which have discretized orientation features. The rightmost panel shows the newly integrated template from 3 original templates.

a same position are integrated by bitwise ADD operation. Figure 2 shows this integration process. In many cases, the total number of templates are reduced from 18,360 to about 1,000.

Edges are extracted in the training image by Canny edge detector (Fig. 1 Right). The positions and the normal vectors of the edge points are added to the template for fine registration of the object positions.

2.2 Detection

In test images, the target objects are detected according to the following procedures: 1) Image pyramids are generated and the discretized orintations of gradients are caluculated at each pyramid level. 2) Object positions are detected based on the similarity measure (Eq. 2) through coarse to fine strategy. 3) The detected results at the lowest pyramid level (x-y positions, rotation angles, and scales of the target objects) are further optimized using ICP [3].

The similarity measure used in detections is defined as the sum of the results of δ function.

$$s(x,y) = \sum_{j=1}^{n} \delta(ori^{I}_{(x+x_j, y+y_j)} \in ori^{T'}_{j}) \tag{2}$$

The δ function returns 1 when the orientation of the test image (I) corresponds to the one of the orientations of the integrated template (T').

$$\delta(ori^{I} \in ori^{T'}) = \begin{cases} 1 & ori^{I} \otimes ori^{T'} > 0 \\ 0 & otherwise \end{cases} \tag{3}$$

The δ function is computed by bitwise AND operations (the symbol $\otimes$) those are much faster than arithmetic operations. This calculation can be much faster by using SIMD instructions. For example, matching of 16 features is done by 1 instruction when using 128-bit register of the Intel SSE instruction set.

3 Experimental Results

Two experiments were done to evaluate our proposed method. One was to evaluate detection rate and speed. The other was to evaluate the precision of the detected results.

Fig. 3. Typical examples of detection results under various conditions. The green rectangles show the bounding boxes of the detected objects and the red lines show the top of them. Left: Cluttered backgrounds. Middle: Illumination change. Right: Perspective distortion.

Table 1. The root mean square errors (RMSE) between the detectied results and the ground truth

x (pix)	y (pix)	rotation (deg)	scale (%)
0.018	0.019	0.011	0.140

For the first experiment, we prepared VGA size (640×480) images of 20 kinds of objects. For each kind of object, 10 objects were placed randomly and taken images under illumination changes, cluttered backgrounds and perspective distortions. A total of 880 images were collected. The image under normal condition was used for training. The typical examples of the detection results are shown in Figure 3. The averaged detection rate was 92.2 % for 8800 objects in all images and the averaged detection time was 23.4 ms on PC (Core i7 870 2.93GHz CPU, 16GB RAM).

To evaluate the precision of the detected xy-positions in the second experiment, we used 3 kinds of objects and their images were taken during they were moved by 0.1 pix using a XY-stage. Digitally rotated and resized images were used for evaluation of the detected rotation angles and scales. The root mean squared errors (RMSE) between the detected results and the ground truth were shown in Table 1. This shows our method can detect target objects with sub-pixel accuracy.

References

1. Steger, C.: Occlusion, Clutter, and Illumination Invariant Object Recognition. In: International Archives of Photogrammetry and Remote Sensing, vol. XXXIV, part3A, pp. 345–350 (2002)
2. Hinterstoisser, S., Lepetit, V., Illic, S., Fua, P., Navab, N.: Dominant Orientation Templates for Real-Time Detection of Texture-Less Objects. In: IEEE Conf. Computer Vision and Pattern Recognition (2010)
3. Zhang, Z.: Iterative Point Matching for Registration of Free-Form Curves and Surfaces. International Journal of Computer Vision 13(2), 119–152 (1994)

Object Categorization Based on a Supervised Mean Shift Algorithm

Ruo Du[1], Qiang Wu[1], Xiangjian He[1], and Jie Yang[2]

[1] University of Technology, Sydney, Australia
[2] Shanghai Jiaotong University, China

Abstract. In this work, we present a C++ implementation of object categorization with the bag-of-word (BoW) framework. Unlike typical BoW models which consider the whole area of an image as the region of interest (ROI) for visual codebook generation, our implementation only considers the regions of target objects as ROIs and the unrelated backgrounds will be excluded for generating codebook. This is achieved by a supervised mean shift algorithm. Our work is on the benchmark SIVAL dataset and utilizes a Maximum Margin Supervised Topic Model for classification. The final performance of our work is quite encouraging.

1 Introduction

In the past decade, the bag-of-words (BoW) model, which originated from natural language processing and information retrieval, has been well recognized as a state-of-the-art method in various visual classification tasks. It has been adopted and proved to work surprisingly well in various applications, e.g., object categorization [1], scene classification [2][3], action recognition [4], human pose estimation [5], visual recognition [6] and so on. In this work, we present a C++ implementation of the BoW model which follows the classic steps:

1. Feature extraction.
2. Codebook generation.
3. Feature coding and pooling.
4. Classification.

In codebook generation step, traditional approach often considers the whole area of an image as the region of interest (ROI) and uses clustering to generate the visual words. This may be all right when the whole image area contains available clues, e.g., in natural scene classification. However, for many other applications, e.g., object categorization which involves determining whether or not an image contains a specific category of objects, only the regions of target objects are ROIs and the backgrounds are noise. In this case, traditional approach will cause that many noise words from background are included in the final codebook. Those noise words will degrade the later classification especially when the backgrounds of images in the training dataset are quite similar. To address this issue, we develop a new clustering, supervised mean shift, which can generate codebook from the target object areas in an multiple-instance learning manner.

A. Fusiello et al. (Eds.): ECCV 2012 Ws/Demos, Part III, LNCS 7585, pp. 611–614, 2012.

In classification, we utilize the maximum entropy discrimination latent Dirichlet allocation (MedLDA) [7] that has been reported being comparable with or outperforming other LDA-based methods [7] and SVMs (with limited or medium scale of training data) [8].

In addition, we save the output of each of the steps and such output is the input for next step. Therefore, every step of the BoW model can be checked and verified. A sample experiment of object categorization is conducted on SIVAL dataset (obtained from *http://www.cse.wustl.edu/accio/*) and accuracy is quite encouraging.

2   The BoW Implementation

Our implementation is modularized and each of the steps can be extended easily.

2.1   Feature Extraction

Feature extraction is to get visual words from the images. Our demo provides sparse and dense feature extractions. For spare feature extraction, we use Rob Hess's SIFT [9] implementation[1] to get the visual words for each image. Each of the SIFT descriptors is a visual word. Similarly, for dense feature extraction, we implement the HOG [10] to get visual words. The step length of HOG scanning window is decided by users. The extracted visual words for each image form a matrix. Each column of the matrix represents a words and such matrix is stored by means of an XML file.

2.2   Codebook Generation

In this step, we firstly generate codebook for every single category, then combine all the category codebooks into the final codebook. To cluster all the visual words in a category, we treat the visual words extracted from the images containing target object as positive data and visual words extracted from other images as negative data, then utilize a supervised mean shift [11] to generate the category codebook. The final codebook is generated by combining all the category codebooks and saved as a matrix (columns are words) through an XML file. Here, $X = \{\mathbf{x}_1, \mathbf{x}_2, \ldots, \mathbf{x}_M\}$ denotes the final codebook.

2.3   Feature Coding and Pooling

Our goal of this step is to convert an image I into a new feature vector W for training classifiers. Here, $I = \{\mathbf{v}_1, \mathbf{v}_2, \ldots, \mathbf{v}_N\}$, and $\mathbf{v}_i$ is an extracted visual word. $W = \{w_1, w_2, \ldots, w_M\}$, and w_i represents the frequency of codebook's i-th word $\mathbf{x}_i$ that occurs in the image I, and M is the size of codebook. Our demo provides two schemes for feature pooling and users can choose either scheme according to the natures of training datasets.

---

[1] Codes are downloaded from http://blogs.oregonstate.edu/hess/code/sift/

1. Sum scheme:

$$w_i = \sum_{j=1}^{N} K_\sigma \left(D(\mathbf{v}_j, \mathbf{x}_i) \right) \tag{1}$$

2. Max scheme:

$$w_i = \max \left(K_\sigma \left(D(\mathbf{v}_1, \mathbf{x}_i) \right), \ldots, K_\sigma \left(D(\mathbf{v}_N, \mathbf{x}_i) \right) \right). \tag{2}$$

In (1) and (2), K_σ is a normalized kernel and $D(\mathbf{v}, \mathbf{x})$ is the distance between $\mathbf{v}$ and $\mathbf{x}$.

2.4 Classification

In the classification step, we use a topic model, maximum entropy discrimination latent Dirichlet allocation (MedLDA) [7], which has been reported outperforming other LDA-based methods. To generate the document data, we first calculate the feature vector W for each image I using previous steps, then we multiply W with a integer M (the size of the codebook) and round up all the entries of $M \cdot W$, finally, all the document data are fed into the MedLDA model to train the parameters of this topic model. The classification results are stored in a text file showing the classification accuracy of the classified labels against ground truth.

3 Demo Performance on SIVAL Dataset

We test our demo on the benchmark SIVAL dataset. SIVAL dataset includes 25 different image categories with 60 images for each category. The categories consist of images of single objects photographed against diverse backgrounds. The objects may occur anywhere spatially in an image and also may be photographed at a wide-angle or close up. To save the running time, we adjust the image size to 300 pixels and keep the height ratio.

In feature extraction, we detect SIFT key points as the visual words and each word is represented as a 128-d vector. In codebook generation, we use supervised mean shift. We also use K-means to generate the codebook for experimental comparison. In feature coding and pooling, we choose the Max Scheme to generate

Table 1. Classification accuracy (in %) comparisons among different methods over 30 runs on the SIVAL. Our demo using supervised mean shift outperforms most methods except GMIL. However, GMIL utilized the manual segmentation information and our demo does not need segmentation but detects interest points automatically.

	Demo_S[a]	Demo_K[b]	GMIL [12]	RMISSL [13]	ACCIO! [16]	ACCIO!+EM [13]	SIMPLIcity [14]	SBN [15]
Average	78.6	51.1	82.0	74.8	74.6	50.3	57.9	53.9

[a] Our demo with Supervised Mean Shift for codebook generation
[b] Our demo with K-means for codebook generation

the features for images. Finally, the MedLDA model is learned for multi-class classification. We repeatedly conduct experiments for 30 runs on the 25-category dataset. The average of the experimental results are compared with other state-of-the-art works on the same dataset. The comparison methods include GMIL [12], RMISSL [13], SIMPLIcity [14], SBN (Single-bolb with Neighbors) [15], aC-CIO! [16] and ACCIO!+EM [13]. Table 1 indicates the accuracy comparison among different methods over 30 runs on the SIVAL dataset.

4   Conclusion

In this paper, we have described an C++ implementation of BoW for visual categorization. Our implementation is highly modularized and can be easily extended. The experiments have showed that our implementation is comparable with the state-of-the-art methods.

References

1. Csurka, G., Dance, C.R., Fan, L., Willamowski, J., Bray, C.: Visual categorization with bags of keypoints. In: ECCV, pp. 1–22 (2004)
2. Fei-fei, L., Perona, P.: A bayesian hierarchical model for learning natural scene categories. In: CVPR, pp. 524–531 (2005)
3. Lazebnik, S., Schmid, C., Ponce, J.: Beyond bags of features: Spatial pyramid matching for recognizing natural scene categories. In: CVPR, pp. 2169–2178 (2006)
4. Laptev, I., Marszalek, M., Schmid, C., Rozenfeld, B., Rennes, I., Grenoble, I.I., Ljk, L.: Learning realistic human actions from movies. In: CVPR (2008)
5. Ning, H., Xu, W., Gong, Y., Huang, T.: Discriminative learning of visual words for 3d human pose estimation. In: CVPR, pp. 1–8 (2008)
6. Donahue, J., Grauman, K.: Annotator rationales for visual recognition. In: ICCV, pp. 1395–1402 (2011)
7. Zhu, J., Ahmed, A., Xing, E.P.: Medlda: maximum margin supervised topic models for regression and classification. In: ICML, pp. 1257–1264 (2009)
8. Rubin, T.N., Chambers, A., Smyth, P., Steyvers, M.: Statistical topic models for multi-label document classification. Machine Learning, 48–55 (in press, 2012)
9. Lowe, D.G.: Distinctive image features from scale-invariant keypoints. IJCV (2003)
10. Dalal, N., Triggs, B.: Histograms of oriented gradients for human detection. In: CVPR, pp. 886–893 (2005)
11. Du, R., Wang, S., Wu, Q., He, X.: Learn concepts in multiple-instance learning with diverse density framework using supervised mean shift. In: DICTA, pp. 643–648 (2010)
12. Wang, C., Zhang, L., Zhang, H.J.: Graph-based multiple-instance learning for object-based image retrieval. In: ACM MIR, pp. 156–163 (2008)
13. Rahmani, R., Goldman, S.A.: Missl: Multiple-instance semi-supervised learning. In: ICML, pp. 705–712 (2006)
14. Wang, J.Z., Li, J., Wiederhold, G.: Simplicity: Semantics-sensitive integrated matching for picture libraries. TPAMI 23, 947–963 (2001)
15. Maron, O., Ratan, A.L.: Multiple-instance learning for natural scene classification. In: ICML, pp. 341–349 (1998)
16. Rahmani, R., Goldman, S.A., Zhang, H., Krettek, J., Fritts, J.E.: Localized content based image retrieval. In: ACM SIGMM International Workshop on Multimedia Information Retrieval, MIR 2005, pp. 227–236 (2005)

3D Gesture Touchless Control Based on Real-Time Stereo Matching

Chao-Kang Liao, Chi-Hao Wu, Ching-Chun Hsiao, Po-Kuan Huang,
Tung-Yang Lin, and Hsu-Ting Lin

Imec Taiwan Innovation Center, Hsinchu, Taiwan
{ck.liao,eddy.wu,claire.hsiao,pk.huang,
tony.lin,christine.lin}@imec-tw.tw

Abstract. In this demonstration a real-time three-dimension gesture control system is reported. It consists with an FPGA board for the depth extraction from stereo camera and a PC with gesture recognition software followed by user interface examples. Application of this technology includes TV remote control, vendor machine interface, or other outdoor touchless control, etc. With optimization on both chip-area and operating clock rate, the stereo matching in FPGA yields a frame rate up to 60 FPS at a resolution of Full HD 1080i. Thus, the system makes the real-time gesture control practical.

1 Introduction

Human-machine interface is the way for people to interact with machines. A good user interface would be appreciated when it is intuitive, highly reliable, and requires less learning period as compared to traditional ways. In recent years, Microsoft Kinect® in cooperating with PrimeSense depth extraction technology has successfully introduced to the world a whole new human-machine interface by using gesture control. Although the Kinect is produced to majorly aim to gaming market, its novelty successfully catches attention to other applications [1]. However, in most of the cases under strong infrared interference (i.e., outdoor environment), the depth measurement with active infrared image becomes difficult since the infrared laser grid would be disturbed by external infrared noise and leads to be unreadable [2].

In this real-time demonstration, we proposed a stereo-matching based gesture control system as another solution to approach the gesture human-machine interface. In this system a stereo camera is used to mimic human eyes to capture pair images with a baseline. Depth information is extracted from the stereo images as the same way for people to sense the distance from their eyes [3]. An efficient stereo matching process performing disparity searching is equipped following the camera to result in a quality depth map. The depth map is sent to the next gesture recognition step for the post processing. Since the shape of the object on the depth map is given without smoothing distortion the following gesture control process performs a reliable recognition on users arm and body. On the other hand, the proposed gesture control process is performed by taking the depth map with the original two-dimensional image as the input

A. Fusiello et al. (Eds.): ECCV 2012 Ws/Demos, Part III, LNCS 7585, pp. 615–618, 2012.

sources. It is designed to have two major functions as for the demonstration. One is a generic and multi-functional interface similar to the regular PC mouse. The other one is three-dimensional (3D) gesture painter.

2   System Apparatus

Figure 1 shows the system apparatus of the demo. A stereo camcorder (Sony HDR-TD10) was equipped as the video source. It is set to output side-by-side FullHD format from its HDMI output. This HDMI output is connected to an FPGA evaluation board (Terasic DE3) equipped with Altera stratix III via its HDMI 1.4 daughter board (HDMI-HSTC 1.4) as an adapter between HDMI to HSTC. The FPGA is programmed with Verilog script for the proposed stereo matching engine to have an output depth map with corresponding stereo images back to the HDMI daughter board.

The gesture recognition is built in the PC with Matlab code for demonstration. The output depth image from FPGA board is captured by a high-speed frame grabber (Unigraf UFG-05 4E) at 30 FPS. In the PC, the gesture recognition process converts the depth map and the image to 3D coordinate regarding to the user pointing finger as the 3D mouse control. The position is used to programmatically mimic the PC mouse movement and click event. Furthermore, a writing brush program using the 3D position information shows another real-time demonstration of this achievement. This program is designed to emphasize the usage of depth data as additional information.

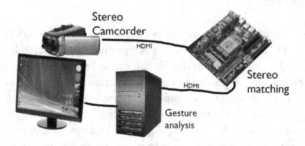

Fig. 1. Real-time system apparatus of the gesture control

2.1   Stereo Matching

Figure 2 presents the schematic of stereo matching algorithm. First of all, a color transformation has been introduced to convert the image from RGB space to only the luminance. Census transform is used to extract necessary image characters from those gray scale data. It downsizes the data again to become several representing bits for each pixel. After the data conversion, these census data are sent to 128 separated matching engines. Each engine results in a cost value for their disparity; thus, the 128 engines generate 128 cost values simultaneously and respectively. This parallel process makes the system more time efficiency; that is, short system latency is achieved. Disparity generator as the next stage takes these cost values into account to result in the depth map. This generator takes also the original image to enhance the object edge on the depth map in order to complete the object shape. Finally, a general 3-by-3 image median filter is adapted to take out pepper-salt noise of the depth map.

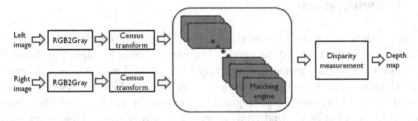

Fig. 2. The schematic of the stereo matching

The performance of this real-time system is optimized from both the efficient algorithm and the hardware architecture approaches. The reachable frame rate is determined by the maximum internal clock frequency of the chip, which is defined by the input pixel clock rate of this video source. In this case, the FPGA is doable to run at a frame rate of 60 FPS with a Full HD 1080i resolution; that is, a pixel clock as well as the system clock is at 62.2MHz. With a fixed measurable disparity range, the system has been built to have a reasonable logic gate count of ~400k gates (estimated based on TSMC 90nm process), yields a resolution up to Full HD. Furthermore, the depth quality has been optimized with restricted image data without referring from other former or later frames (without time averaging). This makes the system no need to the DRAM and keeps the latency of the whole system in dozens of scanlines.

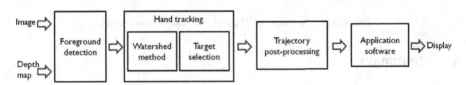

Fig. 3. Flowchart of gesture recognition process

2.2   Gesture Recognition

Following the stereo matching system, the result video stream of the depth image with its corresponding gray image is connected to the frame grabber on PC, in which a MATLAB program acts as an application platform. The gesture analysis is adapted with sequential processes as listed in Figure 3.

First of all, foreground detection is set to extract the moving foreground object based on an adaptive threshold derived from the depth histogram result. In most of the cases, the foreground distinguishes the user hand from the body. Following the foreground subtraction, the segmented foreground is further processed to extract the finger tip. A watershed method with Kalman filtering prediction is used to acquire the initial 3D position of the finger tip. This 3D position is then filtered by a bank of adaptive low pass filters in order to smooth the finger tracking trajectory. The measured 3D position is used to update the mouse cursor movement and the click-event.

3   Demonstrations

Two major demonstrations are introduced. The 3D gesture mouse with the painter treats the user finger tip to be the cursor. The cursor moves by rapidly updating the new position detected from the gesture analysis. In general mouse moves on the 2D plane, which is set to be parallel to the monitor as shown in Figure 4. Two depth thresholds tr1 and tr2 are used to distinguish the actions "activation" and "click-event" respectively from the users. Under this control scenario, a typical mouse function is achieved. In additional to the typical mouse function, a writing brush is also conducted in this demo. This function is similar to the windows painter but with additional brush stroke. If the user moves his hand toward the camera resulting in a greater depth, the brush stroke increases and the drawing line becomes thicker.

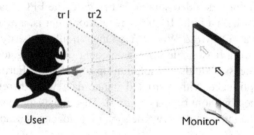

Fig. 4. The schematic of 3D gesture mouse demonstration

4   Summary

The proposed real-time demonstration shows the capability of our stereo matching and its gesture control applications. Compared to our previous achievement, the proposed stereo matching is designed with less background noise and better performance on object edges and is suitable for gesture recognition. The applications are presented as an intuition user interface for user to have real-time 3D control experience.

References

1. Motion sensing technology, http://www.pickar.caltech.edu/e103/
2. Hartfiel, A., Tung, J., Fakih, A., Hoey, J., Poupart, P.: 3D Pose tracking of walker users' lower limb with a structured-light camera on a moving platform. In: 24th IEEE Computer Vision and Pattern Recognition Workshops, Colorado Springs, pp. 29–36 (2011)
3. Yi, G.Y., Yeh, H.C., Vanmeerbeeck, G., Zhang, K., Lafruit, G.: Real-time depth extraction and viewpoint interpolation on FPGA. In: 5th ACM/IEEE International Conference on Distributed Smart Cameras, Ghent, pp. 264–267 (2011)

A Real-Time Scene Text to Speech System

Lukáš Neumann and Jiří Matas

Centre for Machine Perception, Department of Cybernetics
Czech Technical University, Prague, Czech Republic
{neumalu1,matas}@cmp.felk.cvut.cz
http://textspotter.felk.cvut.cz/

Abstract. An end-to-end real-time scene text localization and recognition method is demonstrated. The method localizes textual content in images, a video or a webcam stream, performs character recognition (OCR) and "reads" it out loud using a text-to-speech engine. The method has been recently published, achieves state-of-the-art results on public datasets and is able to recognize different fonts and scripts including non-latin ones.

The real-time performance is achieved by posing the character detection problem as an efficient sequential selection from the set of Extremal Regions (ERs) which has a linear computation complexity in the number of pixels in the image. Robustness to blur, noise and illumination and color variations is also demonstrated. Finally, we show effects of various control parameters.

1 Introduction

Text localization and recognition in real-world (scene) images is an open problem which has been receiving significant attention by the computer vision community. Localizing text in an image is potentially a computationally very expensive task as generally any of the 2^N subsets can correspond to text (where N is the number of pixels). Numerous methods have been recently published [1,2,3,4,5,6], however they only focus on text localization and their performance is not real-time.

In this demonstration, we present a recently published end-to-end real-time[1] text localization and recognition method [7], which achieves state-of-the-art results on standard datasets (see Figure 2). The real-time performance is achieved by posing the character detection problem as an efficient sequential selection from the set of Extremal Regions (ERs). The ER detector is robust against blur, low contrast and illumination, color and texture variation. Its complexity is $O(2pN)$, where p denotes number of channels (projections) used. The method is able to recognize different fonts and scripts including non-latin ones (see Figure 3).

---

[1] We consider a text recognition method real-time if the processing time is comparable with the time it would take a human to read the text.

A. Fusiello et al. (Eds.): ECCV 2012 Ws/Demos, Part III, LNCS 7585, pp. 619–622, 2012.

2   Method Description

In the first stage of the classification, the probability of each ER being a character is estimated using features calculated with $O(1)$ complexity and only ERs with locally maximal probability are selected for the second stage, where the classification is improved using more computationally expensive features. A highly efficient exhaustive search with feedback loops [8] is then applied to group ERs into words, select the most probable character segmentation and perform character recognition (OCR).

Each frame of the webcam video stream is processed independently and text from subsequent frames is aggregated. If the same word is recognized in the same place of the image (with some tolerance) in sufficient number of subsequent frames, it is considered as detected and it is passed to the speech engine (see Figure 1).

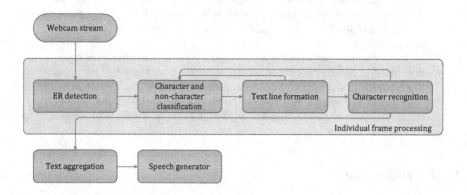

Fig. 1. Stages of the demonstrated method. Each frame is processed independently and text is aggregated for subsequent frames.

3   Application Interface

The demo application interface consists of two independent dialogs: a control console and an output window (see Figure 4). In the control console, a user can select source to be processed (a directory, a single file or a webcam stream), set control parameters and select output mode of the method. The control parameters demonstrate different configurations of the method, such as the trade-off between speed and quality with increasing number of projections. Each output mode shows different stage of the processing and user is thus able to see the role of each module incorporated in the demonstrated method (see Figure 5).

Current work includes porting the method on mobile devices and improving visualization capabilities.

Fig. 2. Text localization and recognition examples on the ICDAR 2011 dataset. Notice the robustness against reflections and lines passing through the text (bottom-left)

Fig. 3. Text localization and recognition output example on non-latin script

Fig. 4. Application interface. Control console (left) and output window (right)

(a)   (b)   (c)

Fig. 5. Application output modes. Class-Specific Extremal Regions (a). Character Extremal Regions (b). Resulting Segmentation (c).

4   Conclusions

An end-to-end text localization and recognition system will be presented. The method is real-time and it achieves state-of-the-art results on standard datasets.

Acknowledgments. The authors were supported by the Czech Science Foundation Project GACR P103/12/G084 and by the CTU Prague student project SGS11/125/OHK3/2T/13.

References

1. Jung-Jin, L., Lee, P.H., Lee, S.W., Yuille, A., Koch, C.: Adaboost for text detection in natural scene. In: ICDAR 2011, pp. 429–434 (2011)
2. Chen, X., Yuille, A.L.: Detecting and reading text in natural scenes. In: CVPR, vol. 2, pp. 366–373 (2004)
3. Lienhart, R., Wernicke, A.: Localizing and segmenting text in images and videos. Circuits and Systems for Video Technology 12, 256–268 (2002)
4. Pan, Y.F., Hou, X., Liu, C.L.: Text localization in natural scene images based on conditional random field. In: ICDAR 2009, pp. 6–10. IEEE Computer Society (2009)
5. Epshtein, B., Ofek, E., Wexler, Y.: Detecting text in natural scenes with stroke width transform. In: CVPR 2010, pp. 2963–2970 (2010)
6. Zhang, J., Kasturi, R.: Character Energy and Link Energy-Based Text Extraction in Scene Images. In: Kimmel, R., Klette, R., Sugimoto, A. (eds.) ACCV 2010, Part II. LNCS, vol. 6493, pp. 308–320. Springer, Heidelberg (2011)
7. Neumann, L., Matas, J.: Real-time scene text localization and recognition. In: CVPR 2012 (to appear, 2012)
8. Neumann, L., Matas, J.: Text localization in real-world images using efficiently pruned exhaustive search. In: ICDAR 2011, pp. 687–691 (2011)

Face-Based Illuminant Estimation

Simone Bianco and Raimondo Schettini

University of Milano-Bicocca
DISCo - Department of Informatics, Systems and Comunication

Abstract. In this work we show that it is possible to use skin tones to estimate the illuminant color. We use a face detector to find faces in the scene, and the corresponding skin colors to estimate the chromaticity of the illuminant. The method, that has been presented at CVPR 2012 [1] is based on two observations: first, skin colors tend to form a cluster in the color space, making it a cue to estimate the illuminant in the scene; second, many photographic images are portraits or contain people. If no faces are detected, the input image is processed with a low-level illuminant estimation algorithm automatically selected according to [2]. The method will be demonstrated on a public dataset of images in RAW format [3], and on images acquired live during the demo.

1 Introduction

Computational color constancy aims to estimate the actual color in an acquired scene disregarding its illuminant. Many illuminant estimation solutions have been proposed in the last few years, although it is known that the problem addressed is actually ill-posed as its solution lacks uniqueness and stability. In this work, we investigate how illuminant estimation can be performed exploiting the color statistics extracted from the faces automatically detected in the image. This work is based on the following observation [1]: skin colors provide enough and reliable information to estimate the scene illuminant and suggest the use of faces to detect skin areas. Skin colors tend to form a cluster in various color spaces and we have shown that the diversity between the gamut of skin pixels of the detected faces and the skin canonical gamut can be affordably used to estimate the scene illuminant. This observation is supported by the fact that consumer photos are very often of faces, and face detection is a technology that has been already integrated in digital cameras with very affordable results.

2 The Proposed Approach

In this work we propose a new method to estimate the scene illuminant using faces: more exactly, we detect faces in the image and extract the skin color information using a rough skin detector. Our method is based on the assumption that skin colors form a sufficiently compact cluster in the color space in order to represent a valid clue for illuminant estimation [1]. Our approach applies gamut

A. Fusiello et al. (Eds.): ECCV 2012 Ws/Demos, Part III, LNCS 7585, pp. 623–626, 2012.

mapping to skin pixels only: the illuminant is estimated as the mapping that can be applied to the gamut of the skin colors in the input image, resulting in a gamut that lies completely within the skin canonical gamut. The Gamut Mapping assumes that for a given illuminant, one observes only a limited gamut of colors [4]. It has a training phase in which a canonical illuminant is chosen and the canonical gamut is computed observing as many surfaces under the canonical illuminant as possible. Given an input image with an unknown illuminant, its gamut is computed and the illuminant is estimated as the mapping that can be applied to the gamut of the input image, resulting in a gamut that lies completely within the canonical gamut and produces the most colorful scene.

The first step is the computation of the skin canonical gamut S_C: this is the convex hull of the skin colors of different people acquired under the chosen canonical illuminant. Given an input image for which we want to estimate the illuminant, in which F faces are present, the masks $u_f(x, y)$, $f = 1, \ldots, F$, are obtained:

$$u_f(x, y) = \begin{cases} 1 \text{ if } (x, y) \in \text{face no. } f \land \text{ is a skin pixel} \\ 0 \text{ otherwise} \end{cases}, \tag{1}$$

i.e. $u_f(x, y)$ assumes the value 1 only on the pixels inside the $f-$th detected face area, being classified as skin pixels. The extracted skin colors $\textbf{\textit{skin}}_f$ are then computed as

$$\textbf{\textit{skin}}_f = \{\boldsymbol{\rho}(x, y) : u_f(x, y) = 1\}, \tag{2}$$

Once we have extracted the skin colors for each detected face, these are converted into the YC_bC_r color space and luminance normalized, such that the average luminance $\overline{Y} = 0.5$. The skin gamut S_I is then computed as the convex hull of the converted values of all detected faces. The set of feasible mappings $\mathcal{M}$ is then determined: it consists of all mappings that can be applied to the skin gamut S_I of the input image and that result in a gamut that lies completely within the skin canonical gamut S_C:

$$\mathcal{M} = \{\mathcal{M}_i : \mathcal{M}_i S_I \in S_C\} \tag{3}$$

In this work each transformation $\mathcal{M}_i$ is be modeled by a diagonal mapping or von Kries model. The illuminant color is then estimated as the inverse of the average of the feasible set [5].

Once we have estimated the illuminant color , given the choice of diagonal mappings, each pixel in the image is color corrected using the von Kries model.

The operation flowchart of the proposed method is reported in Figure 1. The face detector module is run on the input image to detect any faces. If no faces are detected, the input image may be processed with any other state-of-the-art illuminant estimation algorithm. If one or more faces are detected, a skin detection module is run on the detected faces to filter out any non-skin and unreliable pixels.

Looping on all the faces detected, the first step of the skin detection is the conversion of the detected face pixels in the HSV color space. Then a technique

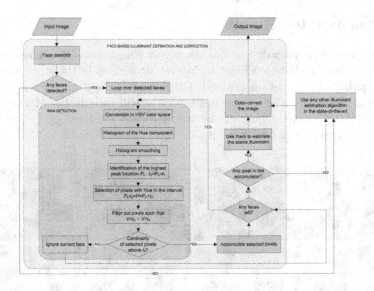

Fig. 1. The operation flowchart of the proposed method

based on scale-space histogram filtering [6] is used to identify the highest peak location and width of the histogram of the hue component, within the hue interval corresponding to feasible skin colors.

The highest peak location P_h and width $2w$ are identified within the hue interval corresponding to feasible skin colors, i.e. $P_h \in [t_0 \ t_1]$. Then only those pixels satisfying the condition $P_h - w < H < P_h + w$ are selected. This condition permits to implement a sort of adaptive skin detector, since the selected hue interval depends on the current peak location P_h. Any unreliable skin pixel as being too dark or too bright, and thus potentially clipped, is filtered out if it satisfies the condition $V < t_2 \lor V > t_3$. If the cardinality of the remaining skin pixels, normalized for the total number of pixels in the detected face, is above the threshold t_4, they are converted into the YC_bC_r color space where they are luminance normalized as previously described, and then they are added in an accumulator.

When the looping on all the faces detected is finished, the accumulator is analyzed: if it is non-empty, the color coordinates of the skin pixels in it are used to estimate the scene illuminant by first computing the skin gamut S_I and then using the skin-based gamut mapping; otherwise the scene illuminant can be estimated using any other state-of-the-art illuminant estimation algorithm. Given the illuminant estimation, the input image is then color corrected to give the final output image.

It should be noted that the proposed method in the present form makes it possible to discard faces with an unnatural mixing illuminant condition (such as when the face is under a colored umbrella) due to the feasibility check on the hues.

3   Demonstrated Results

The method will be visually and quantitatively compared with a large number of low-level, intermediate level and high-level algorithms in the state of the art [7] on a public dataset of images in RAW format [3], and on images acquired live during the demo. The images acquired live will include the Macbeth ColorChecker (MCC) chart, which will be automatically localized [8], to accurately estimate the ground truth illuminant.

Fig. 2. Example of the image in the portrait dataset on which the proposed algorithm makes the two highest angular error. Left to right: original image; ideal correction based on the MCC; correction with the proposed algorithm; correction with the Gamut Mapping algorithm.

References

1. Bianco, S., Schettini, R.: Color constancy using faces. In: IEEE Conf. on Computer Vision and Pattern Recognition, pp. 65–72 (2012)
2. Bianco, S., Ciocca, G., Cusano, C., Schettini, R.: Automatic color constancy algorithm selection and combination. Pattern Recognition 43, 695–705 (2010)
3. Gehler, P., Rother, C., Blake, A., Minka, T., Sharp, T.: Bayesian color constancy revisited. In: IEEE Conf. on Computer Vision and Pattern Recognition, pp. 1–8 (2008)
4. Forsyth, D.A.: A novel algorithm for color constancy. International Journal of Computer Vision 5, 5–36 (1990)
5. Barnard, K.: Improvements to Gamut Mapping Colour Constancy Algorithms. In: Vernon, D. (ed.) ECCV 2000, Part I. LNCS, vol. 1842, pp. 390–403. Springer, Heidelberg (2000)
6. Witkin, A.: Scale-space filtering: a new approach to multi-scale description. In: IEEE International Conf. on Acoustics, Speech, and Signal Processing, vol. 9, pp. 150–153 (1984)
7. Gijsenij, A., Gevers, T., van de Weijer, J.: Computational color constancy: survey and experiments. IEEE Transactions on Image Processing 20, 2475–2489 (2011)
8. Bianco, S., Cusano, C.: Color Target Localization under Varying Illumination Conditions. In: Schettini, R., Tominaga, S., Trémeau, A. (eds.) CCIW 2011. LNCS, vol. 6626, pp. 245–255. Springer, Heidelberg (2011)

Object-Layout-Aware Image Retrieval for Personal Album Management

Mengyou Li[1,2,*], Zheng Song[1,*], Qiang Chen[1], Liang Lin[2],
Zhongyang Huang[3], and Shuicheng Yan[1]

[1] National University of Singapore
[2] Sun Yat-Sen University
[3] Panasonic Singapore Laboratory

Abstract. This demo shows a real-time object-layout-aware image retrieval system for personal album management. The query of the system
is image's object layout and the system retrieves images based on the
layout similarity of concerned objects in the query.

Using automatic object localization algorithms, we propose to index
the personal album with the object positions and scales in the 2D image
plane, which can reflect their layout in 3D scene and hence be used to
measure the object layout similarity.

To query from the database, the users need describe their query by
placing objects onto a canvas and configuring the position and scale of
the objects. Then the system searches the album database and returns
photos with the similar object layout. This system can facilitate people
in finding the photos of which they have impression on the layout of
certain objects.

Keywords: Object Layout, Image Search, Photo Search.

1 Introduction

While more and more visual recognition techniques are integrated into image
retrieval system, most systems still index the database at image level, namely
only provide tags about the whole image instead of detailed descriptions such as
object location, human-object interaction, etc.

However, there is growing need in sensing semantically meaningful objects
in the images and searching by the layout of human and key objects. In this
proposed system, we adopt the recent works on object localization [1] and present
an image search technique effectively utilizing object interactional information.

In our demo system, we first apply object localization algorithms to the images
and extend the previous image-level indexing scheme to an object-level indexing
scheme. We also propose to extend the visual recognition topics to quite a few
daily objects and consequently build comprehensive object-level descriptions to
the images.

---

* Equal contributions.

A. Fusiello et al. (Eds.): ECCV 2012 Ws/Demos, Part III, LNCS 7585, pp. 627–630, 2012.

To achieve the proposed new system, we require the users provide the expected object layout positions and scales in the 2D image geometry in order to reproduce the 3D layout of objects in the image scene. This requirement is consistent with common sense since if one person remember the image content, it can always memorize the layout of the content as well. It provides more flexibility for users to define the images as "how it looks like".

Using the layout of objects as the query is also an appropriate compensation to the current yet not accurate object localization algorithms. To integrate object localization with object layout search, we set a low threshold to the object localization algorithm to produce high recall yet high false positive rate detection results. Then we simultaneously match the positions and scales of all the objects in the query with the detected objects in the database images and find the most confident combinations of the detection results.

2   Client Interface

As the prevalence of tablet mobile devices, the specialized search interface on such devices will be more convenient for personal purpose album management and image browsing. In this demo, we develop the search client based on Android devices.

The interface of the proposed search client is shown in Figure 1. To construct a query, users need place the key objects on the canvas, move them to the desired location, and zoom them to the desired size. Then the system can automatically return the specified photos.

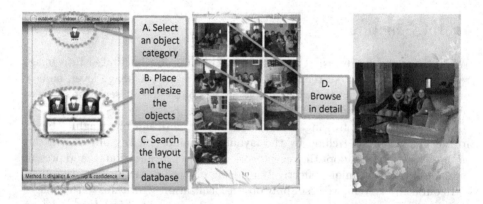

Fig. 1. Interface of the search client. The user first draws the object layout as the query, then search and browse the matched images.

3   Database and Indexing

To index the images with object layout information, an automatic object localization algorithm is applied to all images in the photo database. In our current
system, we use the 20 kinds of objects introduced by the Pascal VOC Challenge [2], and use one state-of-the-art object detector [1] trained on the VOC
dataset.

The object localization algorithm estimates the object positions, scales and
confidences of existence in each image. Then this information is interpreted into
image indices and saved to the database for the object-layout-aware image retrieval.

In detail, the following information will be stored in the database table for
each image:

- The number of detected objects for each class
- The confidence of each detected object instance, which is normalized to [0,1]
- The detected rectangle bounding box of each detected object instance

And note that the bounding box coordinate is represented by the ratio of the
coordinates to the image size in order to normalize all images. For example, let
width and *height* be the width and height of the original image and (x_1, y_1)
be the top-left coordinate of detected bounding box (all above are measured in
pixels), then the stored bounding box top-left coordinate will be $(\frac{x_1}{width}, \frac{y_1}{height})$.

The computation of the object localization algorithm consumes much computer resource. Thus this database construction step should be done off-line on
the server side.

4   Image Retrieval

As aforementioned, each query consists of the names, positions and the sizes
of the expected objects. The search target of the system is to find images with
similar object layout.

Providing a query, the system first retrieves all the images with similar kind
and amount of objects. Then the system calculates the distance and overlap
between the matched objects in the query and the retrieved images to score
the images. For each matched object i, $distance(i)$ is the distance between the
object center point in the query and the retrieved images. And $overlap(i)$ is
the intersection area of the object in the query and retrieved images. With such
elements, the score used for ordering the result photos can be calculated as
Equation 1:

$$score = \sum_{i=1}^{N} (A \times overlap(i) + B \times (1 - distance(i))) \times confidence(i), \qquad (1)$$

while A and B are constant coefficients to control the weight of overlap and
distance. In this demo, we set A = B = 1.

The retrieval result is sorted with descending order of the scores and returned
to the search client. Some example retrieval results are shown in Figure 2.

Fig. 2. Example Results. The experiment is performed on the VOC [2] image database. For each result, the left image is the user query and the right are top retrieved images.

5   Future Work

In the future, we plan to introduce different significance of objects. For example, if we search for a bicycle and a person, the bicycle may have a higher weight, while the person may have the lower one, because persons are found in most photos and might not be the key object. Thus we plan to use machine learning to get a series of weight parameters indicating the significant of the objects, which can lead to a better searching result according with human perception.

References

1. Zhu, L., Chen, Y., Torralba, A., Freeman, W., Yuille, A.: Latent Hierarchical Structural Learning for Object Detection. In: CVPR (2011)
2. Everingham, M., Van Gool, L., Williams, C.K.I., Winn, J., Zisserman, A.: The Pascal Visual Object Classes (VOC) Challenge. IJCV 88, 303–338 (2010)

A Human vs. Machine Challenge
in Fashion Color Classification

Costantino Grana, Daniele Borghesani, and Rita Cucchiara

Università degli Studi di Modena e Reggio Emilia,
Facoltà di Ingegneria "Enzo Ferrari"

Abstract. For this demo, we present a set of stark applications designed
to evaluate the performance of a color similarity retrieval system against
human operators performance in the same tasks. The proposed series of
tests give some interesting insights about the perception of color classes
and the reliability of manual annotation in the fashion context.

Keywords: Human-Machine Interaction, Image Retrieval, Color Analysis, Evaluation.

1 Introduction

Image analysis in the context of clothing and fashion can improve the user experience within Internet shopping (assisting the end-user in the process of searching the desired garments), as well as the quality control of manual annotations, impacting positively on the perception of the quality of the company itself. However properties like color or texture, as well as the very different garments available in the fashion community, are often not clearly distinguishable, even for a human operator. Color in particular is strictly related to its perception, being influenced by nuances, illumination, gamma correction of the screen etc., as well as cultural background of operators and customers, or advertising rules used to improve the product appealing neglecting objective color reproduction.

In this demo, we show simple applications for collecting color evaluations from human operators and compare them to machine outputs, exploiting also deceptive strategies to emphasize biases of operators' judgments.

2 Brief System Description

After a first background removal, the system presents two main modules. A *phototype detection* module first classifies images according to the shooting type by means of a Random Forest classification [1] using histogram projections over x and y. Then, according to the shooting type, the *Interest Garment Selection* module removes both skin and additional garments and accessories to obtain a clear picture of the object of interest: it is a segmentation problem, with an automatic initialization inferred by geometric constraints learned from the dataset. The segmentation was performed exploiting a Gaussian Mixture Models

A. Fusiello et al. (Eds.): ECCV 2012 Ws/Demos, Part III, LNCS 7585, pp. 631–634, 2012.

in color domain, using the iterative energy minimization approach proposed in the GrabCut algorithm [2]. This iterative procedure aims at minimizing by minimum cut the following Gibbs energy:

$$E(\alpha, k, \theta, z) = U(\alpha, k, \theta, z) + V(\alpha, z) \tag{1}$$

where α is the current segmentation mask ($\alpha_n \in \{0, 1\}$), k is a vector, with $k_n \in \{1, \ldots K\}$, assigning to each pixel a unique GMM component, one component either from the background or the foreground model. θ is the set of parameters of the GMM, and z is the image pixels.

Once obtained the mask of the interesting garment, a color histogram with adaptive binning [3] (trained upon the color classes available in our dataset) is computed and used for color retrieval and classification.

3   Discussion

In collaboration with a worldwide leader in fashion e-commerce, we collected a dataset for fashion retrieval and color classification: 60204 images of different garments and accessories, divided into mannequin shootings (23%), models (52%) and still life (25%). The fashion retailer provided a color category for each image, ranging in a set of 60 nuances unevenly distributed in the color space.

In the usual workflow our partner detailed us, the picture of the garment is taken in an arranged room; then a human operator checks the photo *and* the real garment in his hands, assigning a color category within the company database. If we analyze this entire situation, we can easily highlight a number of inaccuracies. The initial photo is taken in a controlled but not calibrated context, so we cannot access to the sRGB color values: a color checker would solve the problem, but this requires a change in the production workflow that, even if endorsed by the company, would not solve the problem with the thousands of images already taken. An operator assigns a color category in a different working place, with a different environmental illumination and therefore a different perception of the color, either for the real thing and the digital reproduction on his computer screen. Moreover, given the enormous amount of garments processed every day, usually it is a one-operator-only opinion.

At last, we end up dealing with a highly confused annotation, and the problem is particularly relevant for two reasons. Firstly the efficiency of color description: we need to know even a very small but as-objective-as-possible subset to train the color classification with; secondly, performance evaluation: we cannot evaluate effectively its performance if a significant part of the dataset is inconsistent.

The problem became initially clear collecting data using the application in Fig. 1(a). Given an initial query depicted in the center of the view, we asked to select which one is believed the most similar. On its left and on its right, randomly, the nearest neighbor within the original color class and the one within the entire dataset is depicted. In the 55% of cases the operator chooses the automatic classification, while in the remaining 45% he preferred the original annotation, with a consistent drop in favor of automatic annotation if the median

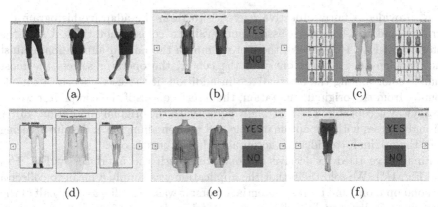

Fig. 1. Screenshots of the very minimal applications proposed in this demo. The rude design is due to our prevailing testing purposes as well as the need to adapt to our partners' production context.

of the query class is presented (78% against 22%). The interclass variance is therefore considerable.

The annotation correction process started asking operators a very limited set $\tilde{R}$ of samples for each nuance. This procedure was completely manual, and led to the definition of a pantone: the idea is to substitute the usually adopted set of uniform color patches with a set of full garments, thus holding a more comprehensive description of color. Then we selected an initial subset of 10000 images (*color reference*, R) whose segmentation mask correctness has been manually verified (using UI of Fig. 1(b)). We employed an active learning framework [4] to assist the user in this task: for each combination of features and classifiers we tested (GMM, dominant color and RGB histogram with Random Forest or SVM, etc...), we performed a first rank of the results based on the feature distance, then a re-rank based on the difference between the first-ranked and the second-ranked elements. Using the interface in Fig. 1(c), with the query at the center and samples from $\tilde{R}$ around, we therefore asked operators' opinion for those garments in which the classifier is more confused about. By keeping only results with higher level of concordance between operators, we obtained a cleaner dataset of 5029 images.

For the final refinement, using again the interface of Fig. 1(a), we asked opinions to operators, but this time we presented them only samples coming from the R, logging how many times a single sample is used in a choice concordant to the automatic segmentation Q_A and instead how many times it is used in a choice concordant to the original annotation Q_Y. We found out that only a fraction of the color reference is actually used (44%, 2258 images), and for each image I a reliability factor C_I has been computed as:

$$C_I = Q_A / (Q_A + Q_Y) \tag{2}$$

Setting an empirical threshold of 0.7, we could reduce the color reference R' down to 897 images.

R' provided a fairly objective reference to train the adaptive histogram descriptor and to be used to assign and evaluate color annotations. Using the interface of Fig. 1(d) we can therefore compare the human annotation against the machine one: given a query in the center, the operator selects the most similar color among the alternatives; in addition, if the user chooses a sample coming from the original annotation, the interface asks if the competitor would be anyway acceptable. 13.3% strongly agrees with the original annotation, 45.7% strongly agrees with the automatic one and the remaining 50%, despite agreeing with the original, considers as acceptable the automatic one.

Finally, we tried to deceive the operators with the interfaces in Fig. 1(e) and Fig. 1(f). We told them that the application was simply a mean to collect a "second opinion" and correct potential errors: it was a half lie, as only half of the displayed results actually belonged to the original annotation, while the others were the outputs of the automatic system. The operators were thus implicitly biased towards the displayed results believing them all the original annotation. Averaging the results on different random subsets and operators, we found out that they agree with themselves in 74.5% of the cases, while they agree with the automatic system similarly in 71.1% of the cases.

4   Conclusions

In our experience, the automatic classification by color in the fashion context, even if based on the digital representation only and without color calibration, is capable of reaching the same reliability of a human operator employed in the same task. Despite the problem remains strongly ill-posed, or perhaps precisely because of this, we can conclude that a good segmentation algorithm and a good color feature can compete with humans in the process of color annotation in such datasets, guaranteeing at the same time a dramatic reduction of the processing times within the company workflow.

References

1. Breiman, L.: Random forests. Machine Learning 45, 5–32 (2001)
2. Rother, C., Kolmogorov, V., Blake, A.: "GrabCut": interactive foreground extraction using iterated graph cuts. In: ACM SIGGRAPH, pp. 309–314 (2004)
3. Grana, C., Borghesani, D., Cucchiara, R.: Class-based color bag of words for fashion retrieval. In: IEEE International Conference on Multimedia and Expo., Melbourne, Austrialia (2012)
4. Lewis, D.D., Gale, W.A.: A sequential algorithm for training text classifiers. In: ACM SIGIR Conference on Research and Development in Information Retrieval, pp. 3–12 (1994)

Understanding Road Scenes Using Visual Cues and GPS Information

Jose M. Alvarez[1,*], Felipe Lumbreras[1], Antonio M. Lopez[1], and Theo Gevers[1,2]

[1] Computer Vision Center, Universitat Autònoma de Barcelona, Barcelona, Spain
[2] Faculty of Science, University of Amsterdam. Amsterdam, The Netherlands

Abstract. Understanding road scenes is important in computer vision with different applications to improve road safety (e.g., advanced driver assistance systems) and to develop autonomous driving systems (e.g., Google driver-less vehicle). Current vision–based approaches rely on the robust combination of different technologies including color and texture recognition, object detection, scene context understanding. However, the performance of these approaches drops-off in complex acquisition conditions with reduced visibility (e.g., dusk, dawn, night) or adverse weather conditions (e.g., rainy, snowy, foggy). In these adverse situations any prior information about the scene is relevant to constraint the process. Therefore, in this demo we show a novel approach to obtain on–line prior information about the road ahead a moving vehicle to improve road scene understanding algorithms. This combination exploits the robustness of digital databases and the adaptation of algorithms based on visual information acquired in real time. Experimental results in challenging road scenarios show the applicability of the algorithm to improve vision–based road scene understanding algorithms. Furthermore, the algorithm can also be applied to correct imprecise road information in the database.

1 Introduction

Understanding road scenes using visual information is a fundamental problem of computer vision [1,2] and also an important component within autonomous driving systems (e.g., Google driver–less car) to improve road safety. Visual information has many advantages over other kinds of information obtained by active sensors (e.g., acoustic, laser, radar–based) including higher resolution, richness of features (color, texture), low cost, easy aesthetic integration, non–intrusive nature and not causing inter–vehicle interference. Vision–based road scene understanding is usually approached as a robust combination of different technologies including color and texture [3], structure from motion [4], object detection [2], scene context understanding. However, the performance of these approaches drops-off in complex acquisition conditions with reduced visibility

---

* This work was supported by Spanish Government under Research Program Consolider Ingenio 2010: MIPRCV (CSD200700018) and MINECO Projects TRA2011-29454-C03-01, TIN2011-25606 and TIN2011-29494-C03-02.

A. Fusiello et al. (Eds.): ECCV 2012 Ws/Demos, Part III, LNCS 7585, pp. 635–638, 2012.
© Springer-Verlag Berlin Heidelberg 2012

(e.g., dusk, dawn, night) or adverse weather conditions (e.g., rainy, snowy, foggy), see Fig. 1. In these adverse situations prior information about the scene is relevant to constraint the process.

Fig. 1. The performance of vision–based road scene understanding algorithms drops–off in complex scenarios including reduced visibility or adverse weather conditions

In this demo we show how to extract on–line road information from digital road databases to generate a road prior and improve the performance of vision–based road scene understanding algorithms. These road databases do not rely on visual information and thus, they are robust to lighting variations or weather conditions. Therefore, their combination exploits the robustness of digital databases and the adaptation of algorithms based on visual information acquired in real time. More precisely, we focus on detecting road areas in challenging scenarios (e.g., tunnels and snowy roads). These road areas are used to discard large image areas (and thus, speed–up scene understanding algorithms) and to impose geometrical constraints on objects in the scene for better road scene understanding. The key idea of the proposed algorithm is extracting road information (e.g., type of road, number of lanes, possible intersections) at the vehicle location from a digital database based on GPS signal. This road information and the inherent localization uncertainty and possible road database errors are modeled and projected into the driver's view (e.g., the image plane of the on–board camera). Experimental results in challenging road scenarios (e.g., tunnels, dusk, snowy) show the applicability of the algorithm to improve vision–based road scene understanding algorithms. We provide qualitative road segmentation results by combining visual cues with the proposed on–line road prior algorithm. Nevertheless, the extension to perform semantic road scene understanding is straightforward. Furthermore, the algorithm can also be applied to correct imprecise road information in the database.

2   On–Line Road Priors for Road Scene Understanding

A road prior can be defined as a two–dimensional array where each bin denotes the probability of the corresponding input image pixel depicting the road surface. These priors can be included in vision-based algorithms to constraint the process and improve their performance. Therefore, we introduce a novel algorithm to estimate road priors on–line using information available in Geographical Information Systems (GIS). Our proposal for obtaining road scene information is based on the algorithm proposed in [5] and depicted in Fig. 2. First, GPS information is used to localize the vehicle in a map and to retrieve road information

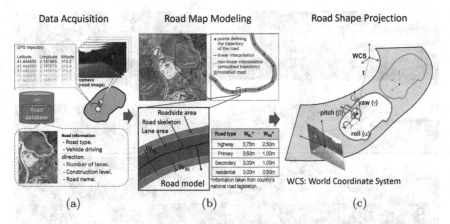

Fig. 2. Algorithm to estimate road priors on–line using geographical information systems. (a) Acquisition platform consisting of an on–board camera and a GPS antenna. The road database provides geographical information and road attributes such as road type (motorway, path, trunk, primary road, secondary road), road name, maximum speed or one or two ways. (b) Road map modeling based on a synthetic road model. (c) Road shape projection: the birds' view is projected into the camera image plane taking into account the uncertainty in the GPS signal and possible errors in the road database. WCS stands for World Coordinate System.

from the database within the surrounding area (Fig. 2a). Then, the road map and the inherent localization uncertainty and possible errors in the database are modeled (Fig. 2b) and projected onto points in the image plane of the on–board camera (the 2D driver's view), see Fig. 2c. To this end, we first build a road map using a set of junctions (points) connected by piece–wise straight lines. Then, this map is modeled using a synthetic road model consisting of a drivable area per lane and two roadsides. Finally, localization error is modeled by projecting multiple instances of the map onto the image plane.

3   Experiments

Experiments are conducted on different geo–referenced image sequences acquired in real–world scenarios (urban, highway, tunnels, dusk, snowy) using an on–board camera and a standard GPS antenna to show the applicability of the proposed algorithm to improve vision–based road scene understanding algorithms. Thus, the combination exploits the robustness of digital databases and the adaptation of algorithms based on visual information acquired in real time. In particular, we provide qualitative road segmentation results by combining visual cues [3] with the proposed on–line road prior algorithm. Nevertheless, the extension to perform semantic road scene understanding [2] is straightforward. Example results road detection combining visual cues and on–line priors are shown in Fig. 3. As shown, road priors are recovered despite the most adverse visibility conditions. Then, visual cues are used to refine the result and discard non–drivable road areas.

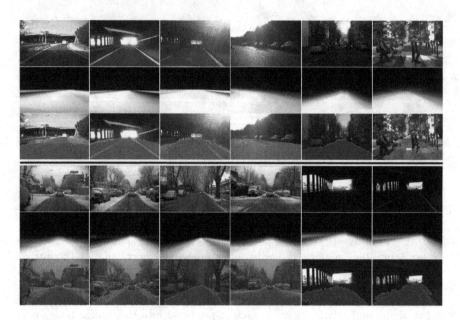

Fig. 3. Experimental results. First and fourth rows: input images. Second and fifth rows: on–line road priors results. Third and sixth rows: example road segmentation results combining on–line priors and visual information.

Finally, an additional potential application of the proposed algorithm is to correct imprecise road information in the database. To this end, road segmentation results can be post–processed to extract the skeleton of the road and then, estimate the road trajectory according to GPS information.

References

1. Zhang, C., Wang, L., Yang, R.: Semantic Segmentation of Urban Scenes Using Dense Depth Maps. In: Daniilidis, K., Maragos, P., Paragios, N. (eds.) ECCV 2010, Part IV. LNCS, vol. 6314, pp. 708–721. Springer, Heidelberg (2010)
2. Ladicky, L., Sturgess, P., Russell, C., Sengupta, S., Bastanlar, Y., Clocksin, W., Torr, P.: Joint optimization for object class segmentation and dense stereo reconstruction. IJCV, 1–12 (2011)
3. Alvarez, J.M., Gevers, T., Lopez, A.M.: 3d scene priors for road detection. In: CVPR 2010, pp. 57–64 (2010)
4. Sturgess, P., Alahari, K., Ladicky, L., Torr, P.H.S.: Combining appearance and structure from motion features for road scene understanding. In: BMVC 2009 (2009)
5. Alvarez, J.M., Gevers, T., Lopez, A.M.: Combining context cues and priors for road detection. Under review in PAMI (2011)

The Leiden Augmented Reality System (LARS)

Qi Zhang and Michael S. Lew

LIACS Media Lab, Leiden University, Leiden, The Netherlands
{lim,mlew}@liacs.nl

Abstract. Most augmented reality toolkits require special markers to be used. In our system any designated object in the environment can be used instead of special markers. Furthermore, our system was designed to work with low contrast surfaces (such as the wrinkles on the hands of the users). We used a constellation of maximally discriminative salient points derived from the environment to position a 3D rendered entity. These salient features are combined with local texture to give greater detection stability which results in less jitter to the user. We present a real time system which has sufficiently low computational requirements that it works with typical hardware found on modern laptops, tablets, and smartphones.

Keywords: augmented reality, visual analysis, interfaces, HCI.

1 Introduction

Augmented reality (AR) systems have the potential to change every facet of our daily lives, from reading the news to new interactive search interfaces [4], from playing games to understanding scientific theories and results [1]. Augmented reality seeks to add additional information to reality frequently though visual and/or audio overlays. In this work we demonstrate a research-level tool called LARS, the Leiden Augmented Reality System which is designed to work with low memory devices on common objects in the user's environment including the user's hands.

In most popular augmented reality toolkits, the systems can typically place a correctly oriented and scaled 3D object on a special marker. In the case of the AR Toolkit [1], the markers are binary patterns which are optimized for their visual analysis algorithms.

In many situations, it is not trivial to have the right binary marker on hand. Instead it can be more practical to use any object which is nearby (markerless), from a book, to a cup, or even one's hand. Related research is ongoing and has used diverse features (i.e. SIFT) [5-9] and techniques [1].

2 Leiden Augmented Reality System (LARS)

To overcome the limitations of binary printed markers, we turn to the paradigm of salient points combined with high performance nearest neighbor algorithms.

A. Fusiello et al. (Eds.): ECCV 2012 Ws/Demos, Part III, LNCS 7585, pp. 639–642, 2012.

We designed our system to use two different salient point algorithms: SIFT [2] and MOD [3] and give some comments of our own experiences in using them for real time interaction. Due to space limitations, a thorough introduction and analysis are beyond the scope of this paper.

The SIFT algorithm was designed by David Lowe and has been widely used in object recognition. It is known to be a good salient point algorithm and is probably the most frequently used benchmark for new salient point detectors. It was initially designed to be "shift-invariant" as per the name and has good performance in a wide variety of applications [2]. A recent augmented reality system which uses SIFT points with good results was discussed by Lima, et al. [5].

The MOD algorithm [3] was designed at Leiden University to overcome several challenges in the SIFT approach. First, the SIFT algorithm requires substantial memory per image, from 100KB to 1MB depending on the number of salient points it finds. Second, the SIFT algorithm is a static, generic, grayscale salient point detector. The user can not easily optimize it for particular contexts. An example would be where the user wants to find more salient points on the clouds in an image as opposed to the landscape. The SIFT algorithm will find the salient points close to the high contrast edges in the landscape.

The MOD algorithm allows the user to indicate what the interesting parts of an image are and it will select the best combination of salient and texture features to maximize the discriminatory power of the salient points in that region. For our system, we implemented the Harris corner detector [9], wavelet salient point detection [3], and the SUSAN interest point detector[9]. For representing the local textures, we chose optimized Gabor filters [10], LBP [3], and Laws[10]. The positional surface is found in LARS as follows:

(1)   User labels part of an object in his environment as a positional surface
(2) U = set of salient positions are extracted from the user labeled region based on all salient point detectors
(3) B = set of salient positions not from the labeled region
(4) M = Select set of discriminative (based on translation, rotation, and non-marked salient point information) salient and texture features based on U as compared to B according to the MOD approach [3].
(5) V = set of salient points are extracted from each captured frame using M
(6)   If there is a near planar transformation from U to V, then mark region with a green rectangle and display the 3D object (Blender or PDB object) with location, pose and scale relative to green rectangle.

3   Experiments

For our experiments, we captured a total of 200 videos: 20 (3 minutes per video for a total of 600 minutes) videos (5 contexts: slow movement, medium movement, fast movement, fronto-planar orientation, oblique orientation; with each context at 4 lighting levels) per object for 10 common office objects (book1 (Spellman Files), book2 (Digital Image Processing), greeting card, CD (the label side), cup, hand, journal, keyboard, desk phone, smartphone). A 5 year old PC (512MB memory, 2.4 Ghz AMD64 X2 processor) and a Logitech Quickcam Pro 9000 webcam were used.

Table 1 displays a comparison between the MOD and SIFT for our system over a set of 10 common office objects (book, phone, cup, hand, etc.). The framerate measures the frames per second of LARS. The Jitter is a typical problem in interactive augmented reality systems and is meant to measure the fine grain error in interactive usage. It was measured using the average pixel distance error of the bounding box for the graphical object from the correct position. The tracking error is meant to capture gross tracking errors and was measured as the probability that the system would make large errors for which we set a threshold at 10%.

Table 1. Comparison between MOD and SIFT in LARS

	Framerate	Jitter Error (% pixel dist.)	Tracking Error
SIFT	14.3	2.79	0.058
MOD	24.9	1.44	0.037

We designed LARS to support two widespread graphical formats: Blender and PDB. The Blender (http://www.blender.org) format is a common 3D graphics format for an open source 3D graphics editing program. Among its features is the ability to take as input dozens of 3D formats and output them to others. The PDB format is a widely used 3D molecular data format. An example of our system displaying DNA using a book as a positional surface (shown as green rectangle) is in Fig. 1.

 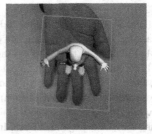

Fig. 1. DNA on a book as positional surface (left) or using a hand (right)

From our experiments, we found that the SIFT algorithm does not find sufficient salient points to allow the stable positioning of the 3D object. The integration of texture features allows low contrast ridges (wrinkles on a hand or texture pattern on a box) to be used as the positioning surface as shown in Fig. 1.

On average over the set of test videos, the MOD approach significantly outperformed SIFT. However, in certain cases both methods performed poorly such as the combination of both low lighting and low contrast objects.

4   Conclusions

Many popular augmented reality toolkits require the usage of special markers for placement of the 3D graphical objects. We presented a real time interactive system which allows the usage of nearby objects to be used to position and orient the augmented reality entities using MOD salient points which integrate texture features to allow low contrast regions to be used as positional surfaces. In our tests, the MOD approach had better jitter and tracking error than SIFT and is currently being actively used for scientific visualization within the Faculty of Science at Leiden University.

Acknowledgments. Leiden University, Helios Technologies and NWO supported this project.

References

1. Fuhrt, B.: Handbook of Augmented Reality. Springer, New York (2011)
2. Lowe, D.: Distinctive image features from scale-invariant keypoints. International Journal of Computer Vision 60(2), 91–110 (2004)
3. Oerlemans, A., Lew, M.S.: Minimum explanation complexity for MOD based visual concept detection. In: Proc. ACM International Conference on Multimedia Information Retrieval (2010)
4. Thomee, B., Lew, M.S.: Interactive search in image retrieval: a survey. International Journal of Multimedia Information Retrieval 1(2) (2011)
5. Lima, J., Pinheiro, P., Teichrieb, V., Kelner, J.: Markerless Tracking Solutions for Augmented Reality on the Web. In: Proc. of IEEE Symposium on Virtual and Augmented Reality (2010)
6. Lee, A., Lee, J., Lee, S., Choi, J.: Markerless augmented reality system based on planar object tracking. In: Proc. of Frontiers of Computer Vision (2011)
7. Maidi, M., Preda, M., van Hung Le: Markerless tracking for mobile augmented reality. In: Proc. of IEEE Int. Conference on Signal and Image Processing Applications (2011)
8. Cho, H., Jung, J., Cho, K., Seo, Y., Yang, H.: AR postcard: the augmented reality system with a postcard. In: Proc. of ACM International Conference on Virtual Reality Continuum and Its Applications in Industry (2011)
9. Tuytelaars, T., Mikolajczyk, K.: Local Invariant Feature Detectors: A Survey. Foundations and Trends in Computer Graphics and Vision 3(3) (2007)
10. Melendez, J., Puig, D., Garcia, M.A.: Comparative Evaluation of Classical Methods, Optimized Gabor Filters and LBP for Texture Feature Selection and Classification. In: Kropatsch, W.G., Kampel, M., Hanbury, A. (eds.) CAIP 2007. LNCS, vol. 4673, pp. 912–920. Springer, Heidelberg (2007)

Prosemantic Image Retrieval

Gianluigi Ciocca[1], Claudio Cusano[1], Simone Santini[2], and Raimondo Schettini[1]

[1] Università degli Studi di Milano-Bicocca,
viale Sarca 336, 20131 Milano, Italy
[2] Universidad Autónoma de Madrid,
C/ Tomas y Valiente 11, 28049 Madrid, Spain

Abstract. In this technical demonstration we present a content-based image retrieval system based on the 'query by example' paradigm. The system effectiveness will be proved for both category and target search on two standard image databases, even without a "good" initial example and ancillary information, such as device metadata, text annotations, etc. These results are obtained by incorporating in the system our recently proposed prosemantic features coupled with a relevance feedback mechanism, and by maximizing novelty and diversity in the result sets.

1 Introduction

In this technical demonstration we present a content-based image retrieval system based on the 'query by example' paradigm. Searches are performed on the basis of pictorial information only and, therefore, the system is aimed at those cases where ancillary information, such as device metadata, text annotations, etc., are missing or unreliable.

It is widely known that the gap between the pictorial features and the image's semantics makes it difficult for purely content-based retrieval systems to obtain satisfactory results. We addressed this problem by incorporating in the system the results of our recent investigation on this topic. First, images are described by *prosemantic features*. These are high-level features which have shown a remarkable capability of capturing the semantic similarity between the images [1]. To further improve the understanding of the user's aims, the queries are processed by *relevance feedback*. The user provides examples of relevant images, and the system iteratively redefines its result depending on the selected images by inferring the case-specific query semantics [1]. By exploiting this mechanism, the user can easily move through the feature space toward the intended goal. However, in some cases relevance feedback fails to converge to the desired images. This happens, for instance, when there are large groups of very similar images: if the user inadvertently drives the system into one of these he would not be able to select different images to move on towards its goal. This is a problem even when the images found are relevant with respect to the query. In fact, when the result set is too homogeneous the user is left without a clear representation of the variety of images that could match his query. We addressed this issue by including an algorithm which selects the final images by optimizing both their relevance with respect to the query as well as their degree of novelty and diversity [2].

A. Fusiello et al. (Eds.): ECCV 2012 Ws/Demos, Part III, LNCS 7585, pp. 643–646, 2012.

2   Incorporating User Needs

For the purpose of this demo, we use the retrieval functionalities of the QuickLook[2] system. The system's framework is based on the feature vector model and support a relevance feedback mechanism [1]. By exploiting the statistical analysis of the image feature distributions of the retrieved items the user has judged relevant, or not relevant, the system is able to identify what features the user has taken into account (and to what extent) in formulating his judgment. The use of this information is twofold: to reformulate the user's query and to modify the image similarity measure.

The query is computed from the feature values that mostly agree with the user selection, while the outliers are removed from the computation (*query refinement*). Let R_+ be the set of relevant images, and $x_I^{(f)}(k)$ be the k-th value of the f-th feature of image I, the components of the query Q are computed as the average of the elements in the following sets:

$$Y_k^{(f)} = \{x_I^{(f)}(k) : \ | \ x_I^{(f)}(k) - x_{\bar{Q}}^{(f)}(k) \ | \leq 3\sigma_k^{(f)}, I \in R_+\}, \qquad (1)$$

where $\bar{Q}$ is the average of the features in R_+ and $\sigma_k^{(f)}$ is the standard deviation of the k-th values in the f-th feature. Image dissimilarity is assessed using a weighed sum of dissimilarities between image features. The influence of relevant features is accentuated while the influence of non-relevant features is damped (*feature reweighing*) by analyzing the relevant and non-relevant images. Let R_- the set of non relevant images. The f-th feature weight is computed as:

$$w^{(f)} = \frac{1}{\epsilon + \mu_+^{(f)}} - \alpha \frac{1}{\epsilon + \mu_*^{(f)}}, \qquad (2)$$

where ϵ and α are positive constants, $\mu_+^{(f)}$ is the average of the dissimilarities computed on the f-th feature between each pair of images in R_+, and $\mu_*^{(f)}$ the average of the dissimilarities computed on the f-th feature between each image in R_+ and each image in R_-. Negative weights are set to 0.

3   Prosemantic Features

Prosemantic features are high-level features which have been designed to represent images by means of their affinity with respect to a given set of semantic categories [1]. The features define a semantic space where new concepts may be represented as a combination of the known categories. In our previous work we have shown that prosemantic features are more suitable for content-based retrieval than traditional low-level features. Their effectiveness derives from their capability of encoding semantic properties of the images which allow a better match against the users intuition about the similarity of the images.

Prosemantic features are obtained from the classification of images into a very small set of 14 categories: animals, city, close-up, desert, flowers, forest, indoor, mountain, night, people, rural, sea, street, and sunset. Some classes describe the image at a scene level (city, close-up, desert, forest, indoor, mountain, night, rural, sea, street, sunset), while other describe the main subject of the picture (animals, flowers, people).

For each class, several SVM classifiers are trained by using different low-level features (RGB histogram, first and second YUV moments on a 9×9 subdivision, edge direction histograms (EDH) computed on a 8×8 subdivision, and bag of SIFT descriptors). Given an image, each classifier $\phi_{c,p}$ provides a membership value which indicates how much that image is compatible with the class c from the point of view of the visual property p. Given a new image x the prosemantic feature vector ψ is obtained by concatenating the membership values: $\psi(x) = (\phi_{1,RGB}(x),\ \phi_{1,YUV}(x),\ \phi_{1,EDH}(x),\ \phi_{1,SIFT}(x),\dots,\ \phi_{14,RGB}(x),$ $\phi_{14,YUV}(x),\ \phi_{14,EDH}(x),\ \phi_{14,SIFT}(x))$.

Instead of endowing the prosemantic feature space with a specific similarity measure, we let the relevance feedback mechanism to weight each component on the basis of the interaction with the user.

4   Novelty and Diversity

Image databases may include several nearly duplicated images that contain more or less the same information. If one of these images is very relevant with respect to the query, it is likely that all of them will be, and that the result set will be composed of very similar images. Although formally relevant, each of these images adds little information to what one already has with just one of them.

To address this issue, the information retrieval community introduced the concepts of *diversity* and *novelty*. Diversity is the notion that allows the result set to deal with queries which can have several interpretations. Given an interpretation of the query there may be different aspects in which the user may be interested. An image is novel to the extent in which it covers aspects of a query not covered by other images in the result set, that is, to the extent in which images are not redundant.

To maximize novelty and diversity, we implemented two variants of the algorithm described in [2]. Given a query q and a set of images $D = \{d_1, \dots, d_N\}$ the algorithm iteratively builds a sequence of response sets $R_1, \dots, R_K$ where: (i) R_1 contains the most relevant image as returned by the search engine; and (ii) R_{k+1} is obtained by adding to R_k the image $d \in D \setminus R_k$ which maximizes the novelty/diversity score $s(d|q, R_k)$. The algorithm continues until the desired number K of images has been selected. For the scoring function we considered two of the models described in [2]. In the probabilistic model the score of an image is equal to the probability that the image is about the same topic as the query and that, at the same time, no image in the current result set is about the same topic. This corresponds to the definition:

$$s_p(d|q, R) = \sum_{c=1}^{14} P(c|q)P(c|d) \prod_{d' \in R} \left(1 - \sum_{c=1}^{14} P(c|q)P(c|d') \right), \qquad (3)$$

where $P(c|d)$ denotes an estimate of the probability (see [2] for more details) that the image d is about the concept c, and where c is used to denote the 14 concepts from which prosemantic features are defined. In the fuzzy model the score function of d is the truth value of the statement *there is a topic in the query for which d is relevant, and no image in the current result set is relevant for that topic*. The truth value is computed by the scoring function:

$$s_f(d|q, R) = \max_{1 \leq c \leq 14} \left\{ \min \left\{ \mu(c, q), \mu(c, d), 1 - \max_{d' \in R} \mu(c, d') \right\} \right\}, \qquad (4)$$

where the value of $\mu(c, d)$ is derived from prosemantic features and corresponds to the truth value of the statement *the image d is relevant for the topic c*.

5   Demo

The demo will allow attendees to verify the effectiveness of the use of the prosemantic features and the novelty/diversity image selection within the QuickLook[2] image retrieval system. The image search with the prosemantic features will be possible with or without leverage of the relevance feedback mechanism. Moreover, category-based or target-based searches can be performed. The user can start a search by choosing an image from the initial displayed ones or from a random selection. As initial query can be selected either a single image or a set of relevant and not relevant images. After submitting the query the system reorder the retrieved images based on their similarities with the query. If the user is not satisfied with the results, more examples of relevant and not relevant images can be added and the retrieval process can be iterated as many times are required to obtain a satisfactory results. Any time during the retrieval process the user can choose to activate the novelty/diversity image selection. The system retrieve a set of new images related to the query and the user can either start a new query or add examples chosen from this new set. This is particularly useful when no suitable examples can be readily selected.

To test the proposed system on heterogeneous image collections, we have included in the system several image data sets. Among them we have included a subset of the Benchathlon data set including 1875 typical consumer photographs. Another data set is the MIR Flickr image collection which consists of 25000 images downloaded from the social photography site Flickr. Having been selected on the basis of their interestingness rating, the data set is composed of original and high-quality photographies.

References

1. Ciocca, G., Cusano, C., Santini, S., Schettini, R.: Halfway through the semantic gap: prosemantic features for image retrieval. Inf. Sciences 181, 4943–4958 (2011)
2. Santini, S., Cusano, C., Schettini, R.: Diversity and novelty in multimedia search. In: ACM Multimedia 2012 (submitted, 2012)

LZM in Action:
Realtime Face Recognition System

Evangelos Sarıyanidi[1], Birkan Tunç[2], and Muhittin Gökmen[3]

[1] Control Engineering Department,
[2] Informatics Institute,
[3] Computer Engineering Department,
Istanbul Technical University

Abstract. In this technical demonstration, we introduce a real time face detection and recognition prototype. The proposed system can work with different image sources such as still images, videos from web cameras , and videos from ip cameras. The captured images are firstly processed by a cascaded classifier of Modified Census Transform (MCT) features to detect the faces. Then, facial features are detected inside the face region. These features are used to align and crop the face patches. Detection phase can be considerably improved by incorporating a tracking scheme to increase the hit rate while decreasing the false alarm rate. The registered faces are recognized using a novel method called Local Zernike Moments (LZM). A probabilistic decision step is employed in the final inference phase to provide a confidence margin. Introducing new identities via system's user interface is considerably simple since the system does not require retraining after each new identity.

1 Introduction

This demonstration introduces a real time face detection and recognition system which is developed to provide a solution to the face recognition problem against changing poses, illumination and facial expressions. The system consists of four interconnected blocks to perform (1) face detection, (2) face tracking, (3) face alignment and cropping, and (4) face recognition. The output of the final block is processed in a final probabilistic decision step to provide a recognition result along with a confidence margin.

The first block finds the faces present in a given image. The classifier used in this step is based on Modified Census Transform (MCT) [1]. The face scanning procedure is introduced in [2]. The detected face rectangles are used as the inputs of the second block to initiate a tracking process. Tracking provides a smooth transition between successive frames while decreasing the false alarm rate considerably by eliminating most of false alarms detected which are detected on single frames. The face alignment and cropping is performed in the third block by detecting facial features inside each face rectangle. MCT-based cascades are employed to detect facial features like eyes, mouth, and nose as they are used to detect faces. Each detected face is aligned according to a base patch and then cropped to provide a region of interest.

A. Fusiello et al. (Eds.): ECCV 2012 Ws/Demos, Part III, LNCS 7585, pp. 647–650, 2012.
© Springer-Verlag Berlin Heidelberg 2012

In the final block face recognition is performed using Local Zernike Moment (LZM) histograms [3]. Several moment components are calculated. These components are partitioned into subregions to get orientation-phase histograms inside each subregion. Recognition is performed using these histograms. The diagram of the proposed system is given in Figure 1.

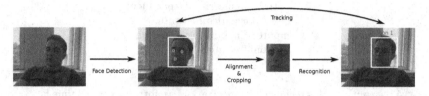

Fig. 1. Illustration of the proposed system

2   Face Detection

The face detection is performed using the features obtained through MCT transformation [1]. A strong face/non-face classifier is constructed by cascading 4 AdaBoost classifiers that use MCT-based features as weak classifiers. Multiscale face-detection is achieved by constructing a Gaussian image pyramid and searching for faces across each level of this pyramid using coarse sampling [2]. Multiview face detection is achieved by training three separate face/non-face classifiers for each pose: left profile, frontal, right profile. Each classifier is practically robust against 30° of in-plane rotation ([−15°, +15°]). Two additional classifiers are trained for each pose to handle in-plane rotation within the ranges of [−45°, −15°] and [+15°, +45°], covering 90° of in-plane rotation in total.

3   Tracking

Kalman filtering-based tracking is employed in order to link the faces in time domain. A face model is assigned for each face, and its location is updated at each frame with the location of the relevant new detection if exists. Face tracking also helps maintaining a smooth transition between frames, and eliminating many false alarms that appear on single frames.

4   Facial Feature Detection and Face Alignment

The faces must be aligned with a sufficient accuracy before they are sent to the recognition process. In order to register the faces, first, the eyes are detected within the face. Then, the faces are de-rotated so that the eyes are aligned. Next, the mouth is detected inside the de-rotated face and finally, the face is cropped using the locations of the eyes and the mouth. MCT based classifiers are used for facial feature detection, as they are used for face detection.

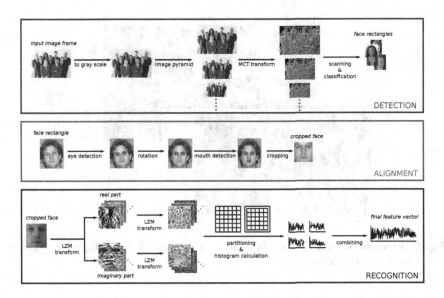

Fig. 2. Detailed diagrams corresponding to different tasks

5   Recognition

The LZM representation is used to perform face recognition. According to this technique, face images are first decomposed into a set of complex moment components using the LZM transformation. Once the moment components are obtained, they are partitioned into subregions and the phase-magnitude histograms are computed at each subregion of each component. The final feature vectors are obtained by simply concatenating all of the local phase-magnitude histograms. Once the feature vectors of the faces are obtained, they are compared using L_1 norm.

Fig. 3. A screenshot from face matching mode. The detailed matching results are displayed when the interested face rectangle is selected.

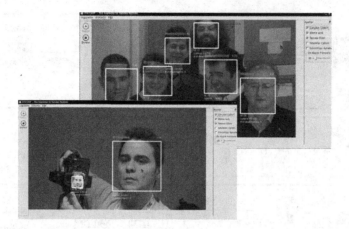

Fig. 4. Screenshots from the realtime mode. The detailed matching results are displayed next to each face rectangle.

6   Real-Life Results

The system is developed as a desktop application which can be run on regular PCs. Two different modes are available to perform recognition on still images and videos. Figure 3 and Figure 4 demonstrate example usages.

References

1. Fröba, B., Ernst, A.: Face detection with the modified census transform. In: Proceedings of the Sixth IEEE International Conference on Automatic Face and Gesture Recognition, pp. 91–96. IEEE Computer Society, Washington, DC (2004)
2. Sarıyanidi, E., Tek, S.C., Gökmen, M.: Efficient face detection using coarse sampling. In: Conference on Signal Processing and Communications Applications (SIU), Turkey (2011)
3. Sarıyanidi, E., Dağlı, V., Tek, S.C., Tunç, B., Gökmen, M.: Local zernike moments: A new representation for face recognition. In: International Conference on Image Processing, ICIP (accepted, 2012)

Using 3D Models for Real-Time Facial Feature Tracking, Pose Estimation, and Expression Monitoring

Angela Caunce and Tim Cootes

Imaging Science and Biomedical Engineering, The University of Manchester, UK

Abstract. We present an application which uses 3D statistical shape models to track a subject in real time using a single fixed camera. The system can handle large pose variation; variable illumination; occlusion; glasses. Since the models are 3D, the application can report pose information which may be vital in a safety context such as driving attentiveness. Two models are used in tandem, one for identity and one for facial actions, enabling the system to also estimate the user's behavioural state at a basic level. The system works directly on the captured images, with no pre-processing, and tracks the facial features using simple template matching and boundary detection. The parameters of the identity model adapt over time to the model subspace occupied by the subject, and this allows the second model to describe simple actions such as eye, brow, and mouth movement. The parameters of the actions model are then used to identify smiling, frowning, talking, and blinking using simple linear discriminants.

1 Introduction

One of the aims in tracking the head and facial features is to obtain information on the activity and attitude of the subject. This could help to identify critical or dangerous situations. Although 2D models have been used with great success to localise and analyse features of the face [1-3], in some unconstrained scenarios with large pose variation or occlusion this approach may be limited. As a consequence, authors have been experimenting with augmented 2D [4, 5] and 3D [6]. A 3D model requires less training data than its 2D counterpart, because of pose invariance, and is able to report critical pose information directly without additional calculation. In [7] the authors showed that their 3D method outperformed an established 2D approach on out of plane rotations and in [8] they extended this for preliminary behaviour analysis and showed that blinks could be detected in a real-world driving scenario with an accuracy of 89%. To do this they used two sparse statistical point models of the whole face: one which captured the identity of the subject and one which was able to describe a small set of facial actions. We have adapted this system to work in real-time to track a subject in front of a single camera (Fig 1). It can also process pre-recorded video which is treated as if it is live input. The application can handle large rotations; variable illumination; blurring; occlusion; and glasses (Figure 2). Since the system uses two models it can isolate the identity of the subject from their actions. This enables us to process the parameters of the actions model to make a preliminary

A. Fusiello et al. (Eds.): ECCV 2012 Ws/Demos, Part III, LNCS 7585, pp. 651–654, 2012.

assessment of the subject's behavioural state. By training linear discriminant vectors from parameters gathered from labeled examples we can identify a number of states such as smiling; frowning; and blinking.

Fig. 1. The system works in real-time using a single camera. The camera window shows the search result; the mesh window follows the pose and actions of the face; the state window indicates face behavior; and the graph shows the behavior history including a record of heading and pitch (red and blue curves respectively).

2   Search Method

The search method uses two sparse 3D statistical models of the form:

$$\mathbf{x} = \overline{\mathbf{x}} + \mathbf{Pb} \tag{1}$$

Where each example $\mathbf{x}$ is represented by a vector of n 3D co-ordinates $(x_1,\ y_1,\ z_1,$ $.......x_n,\ y_n,\ z_n)$. Each is expressed in (1) as the mean vector, $\overline{\mathbf{x}}$, plus a linear combination of the principle components, $\mathbf{P}$, with coefficients, $\mathbf{b}$.

One of the two models is built from 'identity' training data, i.e. data from 923 individuals, with a close to neutral expression, eyes open, and mouth closed. The other is built from a small set of facial actions created from a neutral base. Unlike other approaches which use a combined model strategy [9, 10], these two models are used in an alternating process to localise the features of the face and to provide a basic representation of some simple behaviours. Therefore, at each iteration of the algorithm, both models are fitted in sequence to the same target before moving on to the next. In addition the mean and variance of the identity model parameters are monitored over time and the model is restricted to a subspace described by the latest estimate. See [8] for further details.

Most of the target points are located using an independent local template matching at each model point. There are 238 points in the model and those facing front can search with a small (5x5) view based texture patch using normalized correlation to find the best location. This has the advantage of providing some robustness to illumination variation over the face and between images. The patches are extracted from a mean texture generated from 913 subjects. The population variation in texture is not modelled. Those points at approximately 90 degrees to the viewpoint search along the surface normal for the strongest edge. Once the target points are established the whole model is fitted using the active shape model fitting method in [11] extended to 3D, assuming an orthogonal projection. The search is conducted at three resolutions, starting at the lowest, and is completed at each resolution before moving onto the next. Initialisation is achieved using the Viola-Jones (V-J) face detector [12]. This occurs once at the start and again only when the search fails during the sequence.

Fig. 2. The system can handle occlusion; extreme rotation; variable illumination; blurring; and glasses

3   Identifying the Facial States

The models were used to search a data set of 401 still images where the 103 subjects each adopted some or all expressions selected from: eyes closed; smile; neutral; frown; and surprise. The results were enhanced by merging them with a ground truth markup around the eyes and mouth. Finally the two shape models were re-fitted to these combined results to give a final set of action parameters for each example. After grouping these parameters by facial action and/or expression, they were used to build a set of two-class linear discriminant vectors (2) for: eyes closed; mouth open; neutral; smiling; and frowning. In each case the opposite group was all examples not showing the characteristic.

$$\hat{\mathbf{w}} = \mathbf{S}_W^{-1}(\mathbf{m}_1 - \mathbf{m}_2); \qquad \mathbf{S}_W = \mathbf{S}_1 + \mathbf{S}_2 \qquad (2)$$

where $\mathbf{S}_i$ is a scatter matrix, $\mathbf{S}_W$ is the within groups scatter, and $\mathbf{m}_i$ is the mean vector of class i. To make a classification on a new input frame the set of action parameters is projected onto the discriminant vectors and compared to some thresholds. These thresholds were estimated by projecting all known examples onto all vectors and observing the separation value of the groups in each case. The mood states are prioritised by testing for smiling first, then neutral, then frowning. Blinking and talking are considered independently as they can co-occur with any of the others.

4   Summary

We present a system which uses 3D shape models to track and analyse the face in real-time in challenging situations, including large rotations and occlusion.

Acknowledgements. The 3D data was provided by Genemation Ltd. The project is funded by Toyota Motor Europe.

References

1. Belhumeur, P.N., Jacobs, D.W., Kriegman, D.J., Kumar, N.: Localizing Parts of Faces Using a Consensus of Exemplars. In: Computer Vision and Pattern Recognition, pp. 545–552 (2011)
2. Cristinacce, D., Cootes, T.F.: Automatic feature localisation with constrained local models. Pattern Recognition 41, 3054–3067 (2007)
3. Valstar, M., Martinez, B., Binefa, X., Pantic, M.: Facial Point Detection Using Boosted Regression and Graph Models. In: Computer Vision and Pattern Recognition, pp. 2729–2736 (2010)
4. Vogler, C., Li, Z., Kanaujia, A., Goldenstein, S., Metaxas, D.: The Best of Both Worlds: Combining 3D Deformable Models with Active Shape Models. In: International Conference on Computer Vision, pp. 1–7 (2007)
5. Xiao, J., Baker, S., Matthews, I., Kanade, T.: Real-Time Combined 2D+3D Active Appearance Models. In: Conference on Computer Vision and Pattern Recognition, vol. 2, pp. 535–542 (2004)
6. Romdhani, S., Ho, J., Vetter, T., Kriegman, D.J.: Face Recognition Using 3-D Models: Pose and Illumination. Proceedings of the IEEE 94, 1977–1999 (2006)
7. Caunce, A., Cristinacce, D., Taylor, C., Cootes, T.: Locating Facial Features and Pose Estimation Using a 3D Shape Model. In: Bebis, G., Boyle, R., Parvin, B., Koracin, D., Kuno, Y., Wang, J., Wang, J.-X., Wang, J., Pajarola, R., Lindstrom, P., Hinkenjann, A., Encarnação, M.L., Silva, C.T., Coming, D. (eds.) ISVC 2009, Part I. LNCS, vol. 5875, pp. 750–761. Springer, Heidelberg (2009)
8. Caunce, A., Taylor, C., Cootes, T.: Adding Facial Actions into 3D Model Search to Analyse Behaviour in an Unconstrained Environment. In: Bebis, G., Boyle, R., Parvin, B., Koracin, D., Chung, R., Hammoud, R., Hussain, M., Kar-Han, T., Crawfis, R., Thalmann, D., Kao, D., Avila, L. (eds.) ISVC 2010, Part I. LNCS, vol. 6453, pp. 132–142. Springer, Heidelberg (2010)
9. Amberg, B., Knothe, R., Vetter, T.: Expression Invariant 3D Face Recognition with a Morphable Model. In: International Conference on Automatic Face Gesture Recognition, Amsterdam, pp. 1–6 (2008)
10. Basso, C., Vetter, T.: Registration of Expressions Data Using a 3D Morphable Model. Journal of Multimedia 1, 37–45 (2006)
11. Cootes, T.F., Cooper, D.H., Taylor, C.J., Graham, J.: Active Shape Models - Their Training and Application. Computer Vision and Image Understanding 61, 38–59 (1995)
12. Viola, P., Jones, M.J.: Robust Real-Time Face Detection. International Journal of Computer Vision 57, 137–154 (2004)

Instant Scene Recognition on Mobile Platform

Sebastiano Battiato[1], Giovanni Maria Farinella[1],
Mirko Guarnera[2], Daniele Ravì[1], and Valeria Tomaselli[2]

[1] Image Processing Laboratory, University of Catania, Italy
{battiato,gfarinella,ravi}@dmi.unict.it
[2] Advanced System Technology, STMicroelectronics, Catania, Italy
{mirko.guarnera,valeria.tomaselli}@st.com

Abstract. Scene recognition is extremely useful to improve different
tasks involved in the Image Generation Pipeline of single sensor mobile
devices (e.g., white balancing, autoexposure, etc). This demo showcases
our scene recognition engine implemented on a Nokia N900 smartphone.
The engine exploits an image representation directly obtainable in the
IGP of mobile devices. The demo works in realtime and it is able to
discriminate among different classes of scenes. The framework is built
by employing the FCam API to have an easy and precise control of
the mobile digital camera. Each acquired image (or frame of a video)
is holistically represented starting from the statistics collected on DCT
domain. This allow instant and "free of charge" feature extraction process
since the DCT is always computed into the IGP of a mobile for storage
purposes (i.e., JPEG or MPEG format). A SVM classifier is used to
perform the final inference about the context of the scene.

Keywords: Scene Recognition, DCT Features, FCam, Mobile Platform.

1 Introduction

Before shooting a photo, it is common practice to set focus, exposure and white
balance taking into account the visual content of the observed scene. Clearly,
a software engine able to automatically infer information about the category of
a scene is extremely helpful to drive different tasks performed by single-sensor
imaging devices during acquisition time (e.g., autofocus, autoExposure, white
balance, etc.) or during post-acquisition time (e.g., image enhancement, image
coding). For instance, the results reported in [1] demonstrate that the tuning of
color constancy algorithms by taking into account the results of a scene classification engine (i.e., indoor vs outdoor) is useful to improve the quality of the
final generated image. The need for the development of effective solution for
scene recognition systems to be embedded in consumer imaging devices domain
is confirmed by the growing interest of consumer devices industry which are including those capabilities in their products (e.g., Nikon, Canon, etc.). Different
problems should be considered in transferring the ability of scene recognition
into the IGP of a single imaging devices domain: memory limitation, low computational power, as well as the input data format to be used in scene recognition
task (e.g., RAW, JPEG).

A. Fusiello et al. (Eds.): ECCV 2012 Ws/Demos, Part III, LNCS 7585, pp. 655–658, 2012.
© Springer-Verlag Berlin Heidelberg 2012

In a recent work [2] we have proposed a scene recognition engine working in compressed and constrained domain. It exploits DCT features, fully compatible with the JPEG format (commonly used in consumer digital cameras). The decoding of the images is not necessary in extracting the features used to represent the scene. Local features are extracted by using simple operations directly in compressed DCT domain. Bank of Filters or extra information (eg., visual vocabulary) are not used during features extraction and image representation. The scenes are recognized at superordinate level of description (e.g., Natural vs Artificial, In vs Out, Open vs Closed) through a simple discriminative classifier. A very compact low dimensional vector of parameters is to be stored to perform final inference.

In [3] we have exploited distributions of textons on spatial hierarchy for scene classification at both, basic and superordinate level of description.

Building on [2,3] and considering the shape of the DCT coefficient distributions [4] to discriminate among different classes of scenes, this demo showcases our scene recognition engine implemented on a Nokia N900 smartphone. Although the limited resources of the hand-held device, the demo works in real-time and it is able to accurately discriminate among different classes of scenes. The features used for image representation can be retrieved directly in the IGP of a single sensor device. The outcome of the engine can be used to improve the different tasks involved into the IGP. The recognition results closely match state-of-the-art methods in terms of recognition accuracy.

2   Smartphone and Development Tools

Computational photography has been hampered, in the past, by the lack of a portable and programmable camera. In [5], a new open architecture and API for this kind of cameras has been introduced: the Frankencamera. One implementation of this architecture is embedded in the Nokia N900. This smartphone is equipped with a high-end OAP3430 ARM Cortex A8, running at 600 MHz, and runs the Maemo Linux distribution. The GPU is a PowerVR SGX 530, which supports OpenGL ES2.0. The system has 256 MB of dedicated high performance RAM (Mobile DDR) paired with access to 768 MB swap space managed by the OS, having a total of 1GB of virtual memory. The N900 has a five-megapixel Toshiba ET8EK8 image sensor, and it can capture full-resolution images at 12 frames per second, and VGA resolution at 30 frames per second. Since the Maemo OS is based on GNU Linux-kernel, developing for the N900 is similar to programming for any Linux device. Standard C++ code can be written using Qt, which creates applications that can be cross-compiled for different platforms. Programmers interact with the architecture by means of the "FCam" API, which allows to have access to the low level algorithms and data (e.g., lens position, exposure, gain, white balance, etc.). All the concepts of the FCam API (i.e., shots, sensors, frames and devices) are extensively described in [5,6].

The proposed demo implements our scene categorization method by processing the video stream grabbed by the device obtained through the "FCam" API.

(a)   (b)

Fig. 1. (a) Recognition example of the engine implemented on the Nokia N900. (b) The GUI for tagging new images acquired with the Nokia N900.

The scene recognition engine is written exploiting also the OpenCV [7] and the LibSVM Libraries [8].

3 Demo and Beyond

We demonstrate a scene recognition engine operating on a Nokia N900 hand-held device. The demo works in realtime and it is able to discriminate among 8 different classes of scenes at basic level of description: *Tall Building, Inside City, Street, Highway, Coast, Open Country, Mountain, Forest.*

We build on [2], where DCT features are used to build distributions of local dominant orientation (LDO) to discriminate at superordinate level of description. In this demo, rather than using LDO, the images are represented by encoding the shape of the DCT coefficients distributions [4] on a spatial hierarchy [3]. We consider only a subset of the 64 coefficients of each 8×8 DCT block of the image in order to capture both, edge features and textures. DCT information can be straight extracted during IGP of the device by allowing instant and "free of charge" feature extraction process since the 8×8 DCT representation of an image is always computed during the image generation for storage purposes (e.g., JPEG format). A SVM classifier is employed to perform the final inference about the context of the scene (Fig. 1(a)).

A user interface for tagging new images has been also realized to allow the user in populating the training dataset with new samples (e.g., for incremental learning purposes). Thanks to the FCam API, the tagging tool acquires not only images in their native CFA format (i.e., RAW), but also some useful statistics related to the shot (focus distance, estimated illumination temperature, exposure time, etc), that we are collecting to further improve the scene classification engine (Fig. 1(b)). The semantic categories of scenes that have been chosen for ground truth annotation are inspired to the ones proposed in [9].

4 Experimental Results

In table 1 we report the results obtained by our method on the 8 Scene Categories Dataset proposed by Oliva and Torralba in [9].

Table 1. Results obtained by our method on the 8 Scene Categories Dataset [9]

Confusion Matrix	Tall Building	Inside City	Street	Highway	Coast	Open Country	Mountain	Forest
Tall Building	0.88	0.07	0.00	0.01	0.01	0.00	0.01	0.02
Inside City	0.07	0.87	0.04	0.02	0.00	0.00	0.00	0.00
Street	0.03	0.04	0.89	0.02	0.00	0.01	0.01	0.01
Highway	0.00	0.03	0.02	0.82	0.07	0.03	0.03	0.00
Coast	0.00	0.00	0.00	0.02	0.85	0.11	0.01	0.01
Open Country	0.00	0.00	0.01	0.02	0.15	0.74	0.05	0.03
Mountain	0.01	0.00	0.00	0.01	0.02	0.05	0.85	0.06
Forest	0.00	0.00	0.00	0.00	0.00	0.02	0.05	0.93

The recognition results closely match state-of-the-art methods in terms of recognition accuracy. The results in Table 1 can be compared with respect to the ones obtained by employing the GIST descriptor [9] reported at the following URL: http://people.csail.mit.edu/torralba/code/spatialenvelope/. One should not overlook that our recognition engine has no computational overhead for feature extraction since it works with simple features that are directly computed in the IGP of mobile single sensor devices. This highly reduce the complexity of the scene recognition system.

Acknowledgments. The authors would like to thanks Nokia Research Center Palo Alto for providing the N900 smartphones.

References

1. Bianco, S., Ciocca, G., Cusano, C., Schettini, R.: Improving color constancy using indoor - outdoor image classification. IEEE Transactions on Image Processing 17, 2381–2392 (2008)
2. Farinella, G.M., Battiato, S.: Scene classification in compressed and constrained domain. IET Computer Vision 5, 320–334 (2011)
3. Battiato, S., Farinella, G.M., Gallo, G., Ravì, D.: Exploiting textons distributions on spatial hierarchy for scene classification. Journal on Image and Video Processing 2010, 7:1–7:13 (2010)
4. Lam, E., Goodman, J.: A mathematical analysis of the dct coefficient distributions for images. IEEE Transactions on Image Processing 9, 1661–1666 (2000)
5. Adams, A., Talvala, E.V., Park, S.H., Jacobs, D.E., Ajdin, B., Gelfand, N., Dolson, J., Vaquero, D., Baek, J., Tico, M., Lensch, H.P.A., Matusik, W., Pulli, K., Horowitz, M., Levoy, M.: The frankencamera: an experimental platform for computational photography. ACM Transactions on Graphics - Proceedings of ACM SIGGRAPH 2010 29, 29:1–29:12 (2010)
6. FCam Garage: FCam API (2012), http://fcam.garage.maemo.org/
7. Willow Garage: OpenCV: Open source computer vision library (2012), http://opencv.willowgarage.com/wiki/
8. Chang, C.C., Lin, C.J.: LIBSVM: A library for support vector machines (2012), http://www.csie.ntu.edu.tw/~cjlin/libsvm/
9. Oliva, A., Torralba, A.: Modeling the shape of the scene: a holistic representation of the spatial envelope. International Journal of Computer Vision 42, 145–175 (2001)

Adasens Advanced Driver Assistance Systems Live Demo

Noel Trujillo, Chrystoph Toll, Daniele Sciretti, Silvia Sanchez, Andrej Ritter, Christian Kaes, Vrushali Jedhe, Gabriela Jager, Daniel Danch, Alessandro Colombo, Sebastian Carreño, and Josep Aulinas

Adasens Automotive - FICOSA

Abstract. Computer Vision is starting to play a major role in Automotive Industry. FICOSA-Adasens Automotive is developing Advanced Driver Assistance Systems (ADAS). ADAS are systems that help the driver with the aim to increase car and road safety. In this context, Adasens is proposing a live show consisting of a fully operational stereo vision obstacle detector on-board of an Adasens demo car.

1   Introduction

Advanced Driver Assistance Systems (ADAS) make use of computer vision techniques to increase safety on roads. ADAS are used to identify lanes, recognise traffic signs or detect obstacles, among many other functionalities. The aim of these functionalities is to help drivers and increase vulnerable road users (VRU) safety.

Adasens Automotive is developing integral ADAS solutions. Adasens solutions do not only involve software, but also hardware design. The scope of this paper is to present significant results of Adasens ADAS solutions by the means of a live demo. Adasens vision team is designing, prototyping and implementing real time computer vision solutions, which are then optimized by Adasens embedded team. At this stage, Adasens is presenting a demo car, with fully installed and operational ADAS solutions.

More precisely, the proposal for this demo is to show the functionalities of the stereo system on-board of the demo car. These functionalities consist of 3D obstacle detection and tracking. These functions are part of passive safety systems, which means that these are only used as systems that inform the driver. Notice that no active control systems will be presented during this demo, such as automatic breaking systems or obstacle avoidance systems.

This demo proposal is structured as follows: Section 2 presents a brief summary on state-of-the-art ADAS solutions, focusing on stereo based obstacle detection systems. Section 3 describes Adasens system and solution. Section 4 summarizes what the demo will consist of.

2   State of the Art ADAS Solutions

The evolution of digital cameras in the last ten to twenty years has boosted research on camera based ADAS solutions. Several important examples are already

A. Fusiello et al. (Eds.): ECCV 2012 Ws/Demos, Part III, LNCS 7585, pp. 659–662, 2012.
© Springer-Verlag Berlin Heidelberg 2012

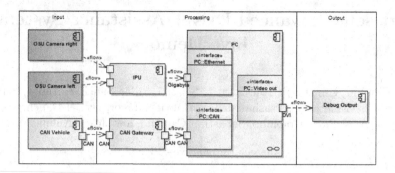

Fig. 1. Adasens system schematics

present in the market, for instance, Mobileye [1]and Continental systems [2]. Most of this systems use a single camera, but the use of stereo systems is becoming more popular. One can find in the literature stereo based ADAS proposals. The solution presented in [3] for heavy vehicles is aimed to detect obstacles from the top of a VOLVO truck. More recently, Daimler R&D team presented the so called 6D vision system [4,5], which consists of a stereo system capable of conveying 3D perception to perceive and identify potential risks. Mobileye has its own stereo approach, called stereo-assist [6] and Continental is developing stereo vision ADAS solutions [7]. In addition, several automakers are already presenting stereo solutions which will be coming soon in the market. For instance, Subaru recently presented its EyeSight driver assistance system [8], which is expected to be in the marked in 2013.

3   Adasens System

In this demo, Adasens is presenting a system composed of:

- Adasens Optical Sensor Unit (OSU) in charge of capturing the scene.
- Adasens Image Processing Unit (IPU) in charge of synchronizing left and right image of the stereo rig.
- On-board Personal Computer (PC) in charge of the high level computer vision computations.
- Adasens Debug Visualization Interface (DVI) in charge of presenting the results in a comprehensible manner.

These components are interconnected as depicted in Figure 1. The two OSUs that form a stereo rig are located in the frontal wind shield. This stereo rig acquires the data which is then pre-processed in the IPU and sent via Ethernet to the PC. The PC performs high level computer vision algorithms such as:

- Image rectification
- Stereo matching
- Stereo triangulation

- Ground segmentation
- 3D segmentation
- Tracking

The conjunction of these algorithms produces significant results. These results are used by functionalities nowadays highly demanded, for instance:

- Lane Departure Warning System (LDW).
- Adaptive Cruise Control (ACC).
- Forward Collision Warning (FCW).
- Pedestrian Protection System.
- Parking Assistance System (PAS)
- Traffic sign recognition (TSR)

4 The Demo

Adasens aims to show the features of its forward looking stereo vision system, with special focus on the obstacle detection functionality. The system is installed and operational on-board of Adasens demo car. The proposed demo consists of a on-site test of the demo car at low speed, where the audience will have the chance to understand Adasens algorithms. In order to give an extensive comprehension of the real time stereo based obstacle detector, Adasens visualization tool will allow the audience to observe the performance of the functionalities under different settings. Figure 2 shows the output of the system at a given frame. This figure presents four sub-windows:

- Top-left image shows the disparity map.
- Bottom-left image shows the 3D clusters.
- Middle image shows a top view of the scene. Every cluster estimated position is plotted with respect to the vehicle.
- Right image is the rectified left image of the stereo rig. Bounding boxes are drawn on top of detected obstacles.

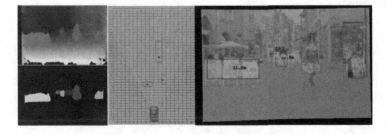

Fig. 2. Example of the Adasens debug visualization

References

1. Mobileye: Technology, http://www.mobileye.com/technology/ (last retrieved: May 2012)
2. Continental AC: Advanced Driver Assistance Systems, http://www.conti-online.com/generator/www/de/en/continental/automotive/themes/commercial_vehicles/safety/adas/index_en.html (last retrieved: May 2012)
3. Bertozzi, M., Broggi, A., Medici, P., Porta, P.P., Sjögren, A.: Stereo vision-based start-inhibit for heavy goods vehicles. In: Procs. IEEE Intelligent Vehicles Symposium 2006, Tokyo, Japan, pp. 350–355 (2006)
4. Wedel, A., Rabe, C., Vaudrey, T., Brox, T., Franke, U., Cremers, D.: Efficient Dense Scene Flow from Sparse or Dense Stereo Data. In: Forsyth, D., Torr, P., Zisserman, A. (eds.) ECCV 2008, Part I. LNCS, vol. 5302, pp. 739–751. Springer, Heidelberg (2008)
5. Rabe, C., Müller, T., Wedel, A., Franke, U.: Dense, Robust, and Accurate Motion Field Estimation from Stereo Image Sequences in Real-Time. In: Daniilidis, K., Maragos, P., Paragios, N. (eds.) ECCV 2010, Part IV. LNCS, vol. 6314, pp. 582–595. Springer, Heidelberg (2010)
6. Stein, G.P., Gdalyahu, Y., Shashua, A.: Stereo-assist: Top-down stereo for driver assistance systems. In: Intelligent Vehicles Symposium, pp. 723–730 (2010)
7. Continental Press Release: Two Eyes Are Better than One – the Stereo Camera Reliably Recognizes Pedestrians and Crossing Traffic (April 2011), http://www.conti-online.com/generator/www/com/en/continental/pressportal/themes/press_releases/3_automotive_group/chassis_safety/press_releases/pr_20110504_stereo_camera_en.html
8. Schriber, R.: Subaru Uses Stereo 3D Tech in New EyeSight ADAS (March 2012), http://www.thetruthaboutcars.com/2012/03/subaru-uses-stereo-3d-tech-in-new-eyesight-adas/

Real-Time 3D Motion Capture by Monocular Vision and Virtual Rendering

David Antonio Gómez Jáuregui and Patrick Horain

Institut Mines-Télécom, Télécom SudParis, 9 rue Charles Fourier,
91011 Evry Cedex, France
David_Gomez1380@yahoo.com.mx, Patrick.Horain@Telecom-Sudparis.eu

Abstract. Avatars in networked 3D virtual environments allow users to interact over the Internet and to get some feeling of virtual telepresence. However, avatar control may be tedious. Motion capture systems based on 3D sensors have recently reached the consumer market, but webcams and camera-phones are more widespread and cheaper. The proposed demonstration aims at animating a user's avatar from real time 3D motion capture by monoscopic computer vision, thus allowing virtual telepresence to anyone using a personal computer with a webcam or a camera-phone. This kind of immersion allows new gesture-based communication channels to be opened in a virtual inhabited 3D space.

Keywords: 3D motion capture, monocular vision, 3D/2D registration, particle filtering, real-time computer vision.

1 Introduction

Avatars in 3D virtual environments allow to enhance remote users' mutual perception by mimicking their motion in real-time. This contributes to gesture-based communication in a virtual inhabited 3D environment [1].

Such an interface relies on real-time user-friendly motion capture. Classical sensors (e.g. data gloves, magnetic sensors or optical markers) require to be attached on the performer's body and limbs. Instead, computer vision allows an inexpensive and practical approach [2], [3]. We focus on 3D human motion capture in real-time without markers. It is still a challenge because of the ambiguities resulting of the lack of depth information, of possible partial occlusion of the body limbs, of the high number of degrees of freedom and of the varying cloth of a person. We focus on 3D human motion capture in real-time without markers. It is still a challenge because of the ambiguities resulting of the lack of depth information, of possible partial occlusion of the body limbs, of the high number of degrees of freedom and of the varying cloth of a person. Webcams are very low-cost and widespread consumer devices, in contrast to recent 3D sensors (e.g. time-of-flight cameras [4] or Kinect [5]) which are non-standard extensions to personal computers. Even mobile devices can capture a video stream and have it sent (through the Internet) and processed on a remote computer.

A. Fusiello et al. (Eds.): ECCV 2012 Ws/Demos, Part III, LNCS 7585, pp. 663–666, 2012.

In this demonstration, we animate a user's avatar from real-time 3D motion capture by monoscopic vision with consumer hardware. We use cameras that come with many personal computers (webcams) or mobile devices (smart phones) (Figure 1).

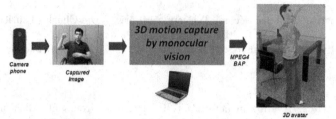

Fig. 1. Animating a 3D avatar from real-time 3D motion capture by monocular vision with consumer hardware

2   Real-Time Model-Based 3D Motion Capture

Our system works by registering a 3D articulated upper-body model to an input video stream. A vector of position and joint angles parameters fully defines the model pose. Registration consists in searching for the best match, with respect to those parameters, between primitives extracted from the 3D model and those from the captured image (Figure 2).

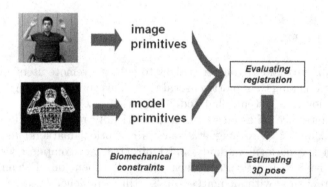

Fig. 2. The implemented approach for 3D motion capture

Our motion capture system is divided into two main stages: initialization and tracking. In the first step, the appearance of the background and the user are learnt, and registration is used to adjust the morphology of the 3D model to the user.

In the tracking step, the pose of the 3D body model that optimally matches the input image is searched iteratively. Biomechanical constraints allow to discard poses that are physically unreachable by the human body [6]. At each video frame, the iterative registration process is initialized at the pose estimated at the previous frames. We extract image features (color regions and edges) from the input video sequence and estimate the 3D pose that best matches them in real-time [6]. Monocular ambiguities due to the lack of depth information are handled in a particle filter framework enhanced with heuristics, under the constraint of real-time computation [7]. Here, we have developed a more sophisticated particle filter algorithm to reduce the number of particles (3D pose hypotheses) required for monocular 3D motion capture. It integrates a number of heuristics and search strategies into the CONDENSATION [8] approach to guide particles toward highly probable solutions. First, in the resampling step, children particles are selected and grouped according to their parents weights using a weight-based resampling heuristic. Then, in the prediction step, large groups of particles are guided toward maximums of the posterior density using local optimization while small group of particles are diffused randomly in the pose space. Ambiguities from monocular images are handled by computing new samples by kinematic flipping [9]. A hierarchical partitioned sampling is used to diffuse particles more efficiently based on motion observations. 3D poses are described using end-effector position to better model uncertainty in depth direction. Finally, evaluation of particles is accelerated by a parallelized GPU implementation. Our real-time particle filter algorithm that combines all the previous heuristics did significantly improved the tracking robustness and accuracy using as little as 200 particles in 20 degrees of freedom state space. Finally, the best particle (3D pose) obtained at each image is encoded in the MPEG-4 BAP format [10]. BAP parameters are sent through a TCP/IP socket connection to a local or remote computer where the 3D collaborative virtual environment application is installed (Figure 3).

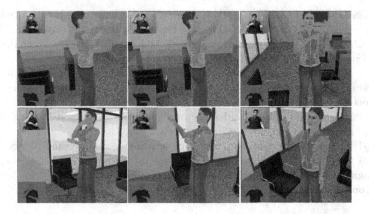

Fig. 3. Real-time 3D motion capture by computer vision and virtual rendering. For each captured image (top left inlays), the 3D model is projected with the pose that best matches the primitives (bottom left inlays). The virtual avatar (OpenSpace3D [11]) renders the captured gestures.

3   Conclusion and Future Work

We have developed an inexpensive system for robust real-time upper-body motion capture from monocular images using consumer hardware with a single camera. This system can be used for gestural communication in a 3D virtual environment in order to reinforce user interaction and the feeling of telepresence. Other potential applications include gesture-based human-computer interaction for networked virtual environments, home video monitoring of fragile elder people, human-robot interaction, multi-modal interfaces, etc.

References

1. Horain, P., Marques Soares, J., Rai, P.K., Bideau, A.: Virtually enhancing the perception of user actions. In: 15th International Conference on Artificial Reality and Telexistence (ICAT 2005), Christchurch, New Zealand, pp. 245–246 (2005)
2. Moeslund, T., Hilton, A., Kruger, V.: A survey of advances in vision-based human motion capture and analysis. Computer Vision and Image Understanding 104, 90–126 (2006)
3. Poppe, R.W.: Vision-based human motion analysis: An overview. Computer Vision and Image Understanding 108, 4–18 (2007)
4. Lindner, M., Schiller, I., Kolb, A., Koch, R.: Time-of-flight sensor calibration for accurate range sensing. Computer Vision and Image Understanding 114, 1318–1328 (2010)
5. Microsoft: Kinect - xbox.com (2011)
6. Gomez Jáuregui, D.A., Horain, P.: Region-Based *vs.* Edge-Based Registration for 3D Motion Capture by Real Time Monoscopic Vision. In: Gagalowicz, A., Philips, W. (eds.) MIRAGE 2009. LNCS, vol. 5496, pp. 344–355. Springer, Heidelberg (2009)
7. Gomez Jáuregui, D.A., Horain, P., Rajagopal, M.K., Karri, S.S.K.: Real-time particle filtering with heuristics for 3D motion capture by monocular vision. In: Proceedings of the 2010 IEEE International Workshop on Multimedia Signal Processing (MMSP 2010), Saint-Malo, France, pp. 139–144 (2010)
8. Isard, M., Blake, A.: Condensation - conditional density propagation for visual tracking. IJCV: International Journal of Computer Vision 29, 5–28 (1998)
9. Sminchisescu, C., Triggs, B.: Kinematic jump processes for monocular 3D human tracking. In: International Conference on Computer Vision and Pattern Recognition, Madison, WI, pp. 69–76 (2003)
10. ISO/IEC 14996-2: Information technology-coding of audio-visual objects-part 2: visual (2001)
11. I-Maginer: Open source platform for 3D environments (2010), www.openspace3d.com

A Tai Chi Training System Based on Fast Skeleton Matching Algorithm

Yu Jin, Xiaoxiang Hu, and GangShan Wu*

State Key Laboratory for Novel Software Technology
Nanjing University, Nanjing 210046, China
{jinyu,huxiaoxiang}@smail.nju.edu.cn, gswu@nju.edu.cn

Abstract. In this paper, we introduce a Tai Chi training system based on Microsoft's Kinect, which automatically evaluates a user's performance and provides real-time feedback for the user to refine his current posture. A novel method to measure posture is also described. The experimental results are promising, demonstrating the effectiveness of our approach.

Keywords: Tai Chi Training System, Kinect, Skeleton Matching.

1 Introduction

After Microsoft released its Kinect, many applications based on Kinect have being emerging, such as dancer's performance system[2], human detection[1], etc. One distinct advantage of the Kinect is that, besides color map data, it could also provide depth map data and skeleton position data. Most of these existing applications utilized these special data to implement their ideas.

In this paper, we also present a Kinect-based system which can help a Tai Chi trainee to improve his performance. The system can evaluate a Tai Chi trainee's performance automatically and provide feedback on how to correct the trainee's current posture in real-time. The underlying mechanism of our evaluation system is measuring the difference between the trainee's posture and the standard one by matching their skeleton. The main challenge is to find an effective skeleton matching algorithm. In hence, we propose a new method to measure the difference between two skeleton frames.

2 System Overview

Our system can help a Tai Chi trainee to improve his performance. The user is supposed to follow the standard video to play Tai Chi, and the system, at the same time, will provide feedback to the user to refine his posture. The flow chart of our method is shown in Fig. 1. The Kinect outputs the user's data,

* Work on this paper was supported by National High-Tech Research and Development Plan of China under Grant No.2011AA01A202.

A. Fusiello et al. (Eds.): ECCV 2012 Ws/Demos, Part III, LNCS 7585, pp. 667–670, 2012.
© Springer-Verlag Berlin Heidelberg 2012

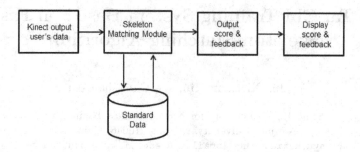

Fig. 1. System Flow Chart

which includes color images, depth images and joint positions. Then the skeleton matching module, taking as input the joint positions of the user and the ones from standard data, outputs the similarity score and feedback to the user.

2.1 Methodology

In our system, we simply compare the user's current posture to the standard one that is being displayed. A skeleton matching algorithm is applied to get the similarity score and feedback for every frame of user's posture. Furthermore, an overall score of user's performance is calculated as the weighted means of all frame's scores. The weight of frame depends on the importance of the corresponding posture.

2.2 Similarity Evaluation

The core of the matching algorithm is how to measure the difference between two skeleton frames. The methods used in [2,3] process all joint as a whole, which makes it hard to know the difference contributed by each joint. In order to measure the skeleton distance separately by each joint, we introduce a novel method here.

We measure the similarity between two skeleton frames on the base of joint angles rather than joint positions, to avoid a calibration procedure which is usually used to eliminate the errors caused by the difference between people's body shapes. Furthermore, measurement with angle is easier to provide precise feedback than measurement with position, because the former's relativity distribute the total distance to each joint. We know that the rotational degrees of freedom (RDOF) of joints are not the same, that is the shoulder joints and hip joints have three RDOF, the elbow joints and knee joints have one RDOF, so we measure these two kinds of joints in different ways. We use axis-angle as measurement for the three RDOF joints and difference of intersection angles for the one RDOF ones. We externally use one angle to measure the difference of spine's rotation angles.

The whole similarity between two skeleton frames is calculated as the weighted mean of the score of nine joints (L/R shoulder, L/R elbow, L/R Hip, L/R knee, spine). The weights are determined by the importance of every joint in the evaluation criteria. The movement distance is calculated as the following formula:

$$S = \sum_{i=1}^{4} \alpha_i J_S^i + \sum_{j=1}^{4} \beta_j J_e^j + \gamma J_{sp} \tag{1}$$

Where J_S^i and α_i are the score weight of the i-th joint that has 3 RDOF, J_e^j and β_j are the score and weight of the j-th joint that has 1 RDOF, and J_{sp} and γ are the score and weight of spine joint.

3   System Evaluation

3.1   Graphic User Interface

The GUI is shown in Fig. 2. It provides 1) Standard video, 2) User's video, 3) User's skeleton map, 4) the instantaneous score and overall score, 5) Weights setting, 6) Angle difference, 7) System information, 8) Control buttons. In 2) and 3), joints with errors over a threshold are highlighted with red. The yellow lines through the 3 RDOF joints in 2) are the axises. The red indication "Extend" and "Bend" near the 1 RDOF joints are correction advices. The button "search" helps user to find which section a fragment of movement belongs to. After the use, the system will switch to playback mode when "playback" is pressed.

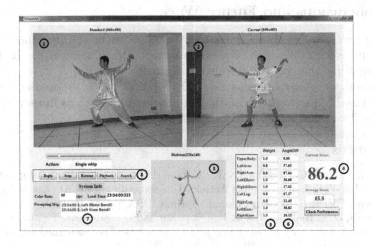

Fig. 2. GUI of the system

3.2   Experimental Result

In order to evaluate the effectiveness of our system, we use the human's scoring as the benchmark, then compare the system's result with the benchmark. We choose a user as our test case whose performance is judged by the system and three observers respectively. For each frame of the performance, scores are given. We compute the average of the observer's scores and compare it with that from system. The results are shown in Fig. 3. According to the figure, the two curves have the same trend, demonstrating that the system's results are comparable and the adopted methodology is effective.

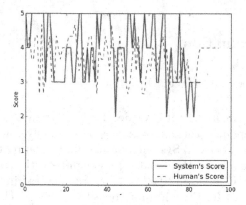

Fig. 3. Results

4   Conclusions and Future Work

In this paper, we introduced a Tai Chi training system and described a novel method measuring difference between skeleton frames. The experimental results were promising, showing effectiveness of our methodology.

In future, we plan to present user 3D visualization, so the feedback will be clearer. Besides, more criteria of Tai Chi performance, such as fluency of movements, will be taken into consideration in our system.

References

1. Xia, L., Chen, C.C., Aggarwal, J.K.: Human detection using depth information by kinect. In: Workshop on Human Activity Understanding from 3D Data in Conjunction with CVPR (HAU3D), Colorado Springs, USA, pp. 15–22 (2011)
2. Alexiadis, D.S., Kelly, P., Daras, P., O'Connor, N.E., Boubekeur, T., Moussa, M.B.: Evaluating a dancer's performance using kinect-based skeleton tracking. In: ACM Multimedia, pp. 659–662 (2011)
3. Xu, F., Liu, Y.B., Stoll, C., Tompkin, J., Bharaj, G., Dai, Q.H., Seidel, H.P., Kautz, J., Theobalt, C.: Video-based characters: creating new human performances from a multi-view video database. ACM Trans. Graph., 32:1–32:10 (2011)

Emotion Mirror: A Novel Intervention for Autism Based on Real-Time Expression Recognition

David Deriso[1], Joshua Susskind[1], Lauren Krieger[2], and Marian Bartlett[1]

[1] Institute for Neural Computation, University of California, San Diego
[2] Dept of Film, Television, and Digital Media, University of California, Los Angeles
{deriso,jmsusskind,laurenkriegerart}@gmail.com,
mbartlett @ucsd.edu

Abstract. Facial expression perception and production are crucial for social functioning. Children with autism spectrum disorders (ASD) are impaired in their ability to produce and perceive dynamic facial expressions, which may contribute to social deficits. Here we present a novel intervention system for improving facial expression perception and production in children with ASD based on computer vision. We present a live demo of the Emotion Mirror, a game where the children make facial expressions of basic emotions (anger, disgust, fear, happiness, sadness, and surprise) that are "mirrored" by a cartoon character on the screen who responds dynamically in real-time. In the reverse mirror condition, the character makes an expression and children are rewarded when they successfully copy the expression of the character. This application demonstrates a novel intersection of computer vision and medicine enabled by real-time facial expression processing.

1   Introduction

Recent advances in automated facial expression recognition technology open new possibilities for clinical research, including assessment and interventions. Children with autism spectrum disorders (ASD) are impaired in their ability to produce [1] and perceive dynamic facial expressions [2]. This demo stems from a multidisciplinary research effort to develop and evaluate a computer assisted intervention system to enhance the facial expression skills of children with ASD that merges the expertise of researchers in computer vision, face perception, autism, and social neuroscience. Advanced computer vision technology can now be leveraged in the investigation of the facial expression perception and production deficits in children with ASD. This technology can be used to quantify deficits in a way that was impractical with previously existing methods, and to create real-time interventions aimed at reducing production and perception deficits.

Here we present a live demo of an intervention game developed for this project called the Emotion Mirror. This is an intervention focused on expression production, which provides real-time feedback on the child's own expressions. The goal is to improve the child's facial expression displays, and also to link motor movement with perception in order to recruit the motor system in the recognition and understanding of the

A. Fusiello et al. (Eds.): ECCV 2012 Ws/Demos, Part III, LNCS 7585, pp. 671–674, 2012.
© Springer-Verlag Berlin Heidelberg 2012

emotion. A body of research in cognitive neuroscience has linked expression perception with motor production systems in the brain, and it has been proposed that a dysfunction in the mirror neuron system may underlie social deficits in autism. e.g. [3].

2   The Computer Expression Recognition Toolbox

The facial expression recognition engine behind the Emotion Mirror is the Computer Expression Recognition Toolbox (CERT) [4]. CERT is a fully automated system for measuring facial expressions in real time [4]. CERT automatically codes the intensity of 6 expressions of basic emotion, 3 dimensions of head pose (yaw, pitch, and roll, as well as the 20 facial actions from the Facial Action Coding System (FACS) [5] most related to emotion.   FACS is a system for objectively coding facial expressions in terms of elemental movements, called action units (AUs), which roughly correspond with individual facial muscle movements. The technical approach to CERT is an appearance-based discriminative approach. Such approaches have proven highly robust and fast for face detection and tracking (e.g. [6]), and have enabled real-time facial expression applications. See [4] for more information on system design and benchmark performance measures. CERT operates in real time at approximately 12-15 frames per second, and is available for academic use.

3   The Emotion Mirror

The emotion mirror is an intervention game in which an avatar responds to facial expression of the subject in real-time. In one condition, the character mirrors the participant's expression ('it mimics you'). The participant is prompted to make one of 6 expressions, and when the expression is successfully produced, the character mirrors the participant's expression. In the reverse condition ('you mimic it') the subject copies the character's expression. As the participant approximates the expression of the character, an ice-cream cone grows by increasing in units of scoops and toppings. A softmax competition between CERT's six expressions of basic emotion and neutral mediates the matching signal between the prompted emotion and that of the participant. This matching signal drives the character's expression intensity in 'it mimics you' and the height of the ice cream in 'you mimic it' in proportion to the participant's expression intensity.

The game includes a selection of engaging animated characters that range in visual complexity.   It is well known that children with ASD tend to be more comfortable with visually simple displays, and are more comfortable with robots and animals than with human faces. The avatars in the intervention game therefore range from animals, to outer-space creatures, to a more realistic human avatar for which children can choose gender, skin color, and hair color to match their own. See Figure 2. The task knits expressive production and perception as it is the participant's own face that drives the expressions shown on the avatar, and provides feedback and practice in facial expression mirroring behaviors.

Fig. 1. Emotion Mirror: An avatar responds to facial expressions of the subject in real-time

4   Intervention Design

The intervention design is a mobile, low cost, platform to improve facial expression production in children with ASD. The hardware for the platform consists of a laptop computer equipped with an integrated Web camera. The software components for the intervention platform consist of (1) CERT (Computer Expression Recognition Toolbox), a program for computer vision based recognition of facial expressions, (2) EMOTION MIRROR: An intervention game written in Adobe Flash, (3) RUBIOS: a library of message passing functions to facilitate inter-process communication between the different software components (Figure 1).

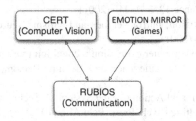

Fig. 2. Structure of the software components of the intervention platform

5   Discussion

Recent advances in computer vision open new avenues for computer assisted intervention programs that target critical skills for social interaction, including the timing, morphology and dynamics of facial expressions. Such systems enable investigations into the learning of facial expression production that were previously not possible. The Emotion Mirror presents pioneering work to develop an engaging intervention system for facial expression processing based on automatic facial expression recognition technology. Importantly, this intervention links motor production with perception in a real-time feedback system.

Expression understanding may span multiple brain structures [7], which must communicate and pass activation through time. Disorders of temporal processing at any level of this system, whether it is in perception, production, or passing of activation between brain structures, could disrupt this system and hence disrupt emotion understanding. Temporal processing deficits have been demonstrated in autism, and may underlie a range of impairments [8]. Together, this suggests that social processing interventions should tap multiple processes, not individually, but together and at the right temporal intervals. Recent technology from computer vision and animation opens up new possibilities for intervention systems that link perception, production, and reward on timescales related to social responding. Such technology contributes not only to potential treatments, but also to the study of learning and plasticity in perception and production systems, and to understanding the cognitive neuroscience of emotion [9].

Acknowledgements. Support for this work was provided by NIH grant NIMH- RC1 MH088633 and NSF grant SBE-0542013. Any opinions, findings, conclusions or recommendations expressed in this material do not necessarily reflect the views of the National Science Foundation.

References

1. McIntosh, D., et al.: When the social mirror breaks ... Developmental Science 9, 295–302 (2006)
2. Adolphs, R., Sears, L., Piven, J.: Abnormal processing of social information from faces in autism. J. Cog. Neuroscience 13, 232–240 (2001)
3. Williams, J., et al.: Imitation, mirror neurons and autism. Neuroscience & Biobehavioral Reviews 25(4), 287–295 (2001)
4. Littlewort, G., et al.: The computer expression recognition toolbox (CERT). In: IEEE International Conference on Automatic Face and Gesture Recognition, pp. 298–305. IEEE Xplore (2011)
5. Ekman, P., Friesen, W.: Facial Action Coding System: A Technique for the Measurement of Facial Movement. Consulting Psych. Press, Palo Alto (1978)
6. Viola, P., Jones, M.: Robust real-time face detection. J. Computer Vision 57(2), 137–154 (2004)
7. Niedenthal, P.M., Mermillod, M., Maringer, M., Hess, U.: The Simulation of Smiles (SIMS) Model: Embodied Simulation and the Meaning of Facial Expression. Behavioral and Brain Sciences 33(6), 417–433 (2010)
8. Gepner, B., Féron, F.: Autism: a world changing too fast for a mis-wired brain? Neurosci. Biobehav. Rev. 33(8), 1227–1242 (2009)
9. Bartlett, M.: Emotion simulation and expression understanding: A case for time. Invited commentary on Niedenthal et al. Behavioral and Brain Sciences 33(6), 435-436 (2010)

Unsupervised Activity Analysis and Monitoring Algorithms for Effective Surveillance Systems

Jean-Marc Odobez[1], Cyril Carincotte[2], Rémi Emonet[1], Erwan Jouneau[2], Sofia Zaidenberg[3], Bertrand Ravera[4], Francois Bremond[3], and Andrea Grifoni[5]

[1] Idiap Research Institute
[2] Multitel
[3] INRIA
[4] Thales Communication
[5] Thales Italia

Abstract. In this demonstration, we will show the different modules related to the automatic surveillance prototype developed in the context of the EU VANAHEIM project. Several components will be demonstrated on real data from the Torino metro. First, different unsupervised activity modeling algorithms that capture recurrent activities from long recordings will be illustrated. A contrario, they provide unusualless measures that can be used to select the most interesting streams to be displayed in control rooms. Second, different scene analysis algorithms will be demonstrated, ranging from left-luggage detection to the automatic identification of groups and their tracking. Third, a set of situationnal reporting methods (flow and count monitoring in escalators and at platforms as well as human presence at lift) that provide a global view of the activity in the metro station and are displayed on maps or along with analyzed video streams. Finally, an offline activity discovery tool based on long term recordings. All algorithms are integrated into a Video Management Solution using an innovative VideoWall module that will be demonstrated as well.

1 Introduction

The demonstration will show different modules developed in the EU VANAHEIM project[1] and that have been exhibited in the Turin Automated Metros security room to participants of the EXPO Ferroviaria fair that was held in Torino at the end of March[2]). The modules feature different innovative surveillance algorithms developed within the project that can increase the effectiveness of existing public transport surveillance systems. The modules are summarized below.

2 Activity Modeling for Stream Selection

There is an ever increasing number of sensors deployed in the real world, being it in large scale sensor networks or closed-circuit television (CCTV) networks.

---

[1] http://www.vanaheim-project.eu
[2] http://www.expoferroviaria.com/eng/page.cfm/link=57

A. Fusiello et al. (Eds.): ECCV 2012 Ws/Demos, Part III, LNCS 7585, pp. 675–678, 2012.

Exploitation of these cameras fulfil several needs, safety, security, or efficiency, e.g., through the identification of typical flux and detection of congestion that can be communicated appropriately to users.

However, most of the time, surveillance network videos are never watched, simply due to the odds: a control room may have 28 monitors to supervise more than 1100 cameras as in our case, and thus the probability to watch the right streams at the right time is therefore very limited. Thus, along with top-down user-based protocols for visualizing and browsing the video networks and the detection of predefined event, bottom-up automatic and content-based selection systems that provide surveillance operators with the most salient and informative data streams could can provide a useful tool to address the selection of streams to be displayed and watched.

The proposed demonstration will address this issue, and show the results of recently published algorithms on unsupervised content-base stream activity modeling and abnormality level estimation [1–4].

Audio Stream Analysis. Audio is a complementary modality that can easily be coupled with video for surveillance and scene understanding. This topic was addressed in the VANAHEIM project for the detection of abnormal audio events. In public transportation context, the acoustic environment is complex, and can be viewed as a superposition of many single audio events that are considered as normal (people discussing, trains arrivals and departures, silences, etc.). In this view, normal audio ambiance models are estimated in an unsupervised way using models such as Gaussian Mixture Models or One Class Support Vector Machines [5]. The demonstrator will also illustrate these methods with several kinds of abnormal events mixed with real audio ambiances.

3   Scene Analysis Algorithms

In a second step, different scene analysis algorithms will be demonstrated. These will range from multi-object tracking [6] or the extraction of behavioral cue like body and head pose through coupled adaptive learning [7], that will be illustrated on real video from offline processing, to real-time processing algorithms like those described below.

Static-Luggage Detection. The algorithm relies on a multi-layer background subtraction method [8] by distinguishing recent background layers from old and long term background layers and foreground regions. It is enhanced by a human-detection algorithm [9] to remove false alarms due to people waiting and hence remaining static for quite some time.

Group Detection and Behavior Analysis. The demonstration will show real-time group detection and tracking in metro data from various views and detected events corresponding to predefined behaviors of interest. The group detection and tracking method works by first tracking mobile objects and then grouping them recursively over time maintaining a spatial and temporal group coherence, using proximity as well as walking similarity (based on speed and direction) [10]. Group behavior is analyzed according to predefined formal scenarios operating on properties of tracked groups [11] .

Flow Monitoring. Several crowd characterization approaches will be shown based on crowd density estimation through interest point extraction and tracking or occupancy rate estimation.

4   Situational Reporting

Finally, a full set of methods that provide estimates of people locations and numbers according to the different camera settings: people flow counting in escalators; people density at platforms and human presence at lift achieved using straight human detection methods [12], and, whenever possible, multi-object tracking relying on Probabilistic Occupancy Maps (POM). All the computed information is back-projected in real time on the infrastructure map of Turin metro or on individual scene views, providing the operators with synthetic views of the metro occupancy and activity.

5   People Activity Discovery Tool

Finally, an offline line tool that aims at analyzing long term recording will be demonstrated. It aims at three different tasks summarized below: i) learning of (floor) activity zones within the scene; ii) learning of activity classes, and iii) calculation of activity statistics. The learning of these activities is done online [13].

The Zone Discovery task consists in identifying the scene activity zones corresponding to entry/exit zones, waiting zones and zones where people interact with the station equipment (i.e. vending machine areas). The processing is done on-line, analyzing video chunks of one hour as they become available. Roughly explained the process is as follows. Stopping points from mobile objects are detected by trajectory analysis and clustered to find a first set of activity zones. The zones that overlap are merged together to get one single activity zone, and activity zones are updated on-line with the analysis of long term data.

Learning of activity classes is a higher level analysis process to extract the main activity patterns of people in the station. It works by linking low-level tracking to the previous learned zones. The whole activity observed from the scene can then be reported following the behaviors (mobiles inside a zone, or moving from one zone to another one) inferred from the learned zones, and build activities that are the combination of all zone-based inferred behaviors.

Based on activity zones and activity patterns, descriptive statistics can be calculated such as the mean occupancy of a zone, the mean time spent in a zone and how zone occupancy changes over time. Similarly, the most common (frequent) activity patterns can be extracted as well as rare activities.

6   Demonstrator

The demonstrator consists of a professional Video Management Solution developed by Thales Italia, where all the analytics modules developed for the

VANAHEIM project have been integrated. The user of the system can easily launch any available algorithm, select the audio or video stream to use, and configure the graphical overlay (videowall) where to show the analytics' results. Given that no live feed can be provided, algorithms will be applied (with online processing) on 26 real data streams pre-recorded from one of the metro stations in Torino.

References

1. Emonet, R., Varadarajan, J., Odobez, J.M.: Extracting and locating temporal motifs in video scenes using a hierarchical non parametric bayesian model. In: CVPR (2011)
2. Emonet, R., Varadarajan, J., Odobez, J.M.: Multi-camera Open Space Human Activity Discovery for Anomaly Detection. In: IEEE International Conference on Advanced Video and Signal-Based Surveillancei AVSS (2011)
3. Jouneau, E., Carincotte, C.: Particle-based tracking model for automatic anomaly detection. In: International Conference on Image Processing (2011)
4. Jouneau, E., Carincotte, C.: Mono versus multi-view tracking-based model for automatic scene activity modeling and anomaly detection. In: IEEE Int. Conf. on Advanced Video and Signal-Based Surveillance, AVSS (2011)
5. Lecomte, S., Lengellé, R., Richard, C., Capman, F., Ravera, B.: Abnormal events detection using unsupervised one-class svm - application to audio surveillance and evaluation. In: IEEE Int. Conf. on Advanced Video and Signal-Based Surveillance (2011)
6. Heili, A., Chen, C., Odobez, J.: Detection-based multi-human tracking using a crf model. In: ICCV Workshop Visual Surveillance (2011)
7. Chen, C., Odobez, J.M.: We are not contortionists: coupled adaptive learning for head and body orientation estimation in surveillance video. In: CVPR (2012)
8. Yao, J., Odobez, J.M.: Multi-layer background subtraction based on color and texture. In: IEEE International Conference on Computer Vision and Pattern Recognition, pp. 1–8 (June 2007)
9. Yao, J., Odobez, J.M.: Fast human detection from joint appearance and foreground feature subset covariances. Computer Vision and Image Understanding 115(10), 1414–1426 (2011)
10. Zaidenberg, S., Boulay, B., Garate, C., Chau, D., Corvee, E., Bremond, F.: Group interaction and group tracking for video-surveillance in underground railway stations. In: Int. Workshop on Behaviour Analysis, ICVS (2011)
11. Zaidenberg, S., Boulay, B., Brémond, F.: A generic framework for video understanding applied to group behavior recognition. In: IEEE Int. Conf. on Advanced Video and Signal-Based Surveillance, AVSS (2012)
12. Descamps, A., Carincotte, C., Gosselin, B.: Person detection for indoor video-surveillance using spatio-temporal integral features. In: Interactive Human Behavior Analysis in Open or Public Spaces Workshop, INTERHUB (2011)
13. Patino, L., Bremond, F., Thonnat, M.: Online learning of activities from video. In: IEEE Int. Conf. on Advanced Video and Signal-Based Surveillance, AVSS (2012)

Author Index